DICTIONARY OF THE
Arts

DICTIONARY OF THE

Arts

Facts On File®

AN INFOBASE HOLDINGS COMPANY

Copyright © 1994 by Helicon Publishing Limited

First published in Great Britain in 1994 by Helicon Publishing
Limited.

Facts On File, Inc.
460 Park Avenue South
New York NY 10016

Library of Congress Cataloging-in-Publication Data

Dictionary of the arts.
       p.   cm.
Includes index.
ISBN 0–8160–3205–X
1. Arts–Dictionaries.   2. Artists–Biography–Dictionaries.
NX80.D53 1994
700'.3–dc20   94–16276
                                              CIP

Printed and bound in Great Britain by
The Bath Press Ltd, Bath, Avon

10 9 8 7 6 5 4 3 2 1

This book is printed on acid-free paper.

INTRODUCTION

None of the arts exists in isolation. For example, architecture, painting, music – and even fashion – have been influenced by, and in turn became a part of, the great movements in cultural history such as the Renaissance and the Enlightenment. In order to address such an intricate web of influences, this dictionary has been specially designed as a broad reader's companion to the arts in as comprehensive a way as possible within the constraints of a concise volume.

To compile the Dictionary, a team of specialist contributors reviewed material in fifteen major areas: architecture, artistic theory, cinema, classical literature, craft and design, dance, fashion, literary terms, literature from around the world, music, mythology, painting, photography, sculpture, and theatre.

The Dictionary places each article in its cultural and historical context. Take, for example, the 20th-century movement 'Post-Modernism'. The entry deals first with architecture. It then relates it to other movements past and present, mentions some exponents of the theory, and finally considers the effects of this movement on literary criticism and music. Each of these links will then, in turn, reveal further associations.

Entries on specific films, paintings, books, poems, and so on, are included only in selected cases.

The Dictionary combines text with chronologies, quotes, tables, and biographies, to form a lively, comprehensive handbook to our cultural heritage.

Arrangement of entries

Entries are ordered alphabetically, as if there were no spaces between words.

Cross-references

These are shown by a ◊ symbol immediately preceding the reference. Cross-referencing is selective; a cross-reference is shown when another entry contains material which is relevant to the subject matter of an entry, in cases where the reader may not otherwise think of looking.

CONTRIBUTORS

General Editor

Chris Murray

Subject Consultants

Christine Avery MA, PhD
Ingrid von Essen
Oliver Harris BA, DPhil (Oxon)
Jacqueline Herald MA
Susan Lahusen BEd, MA
Frances Lass BA
Graham Ley BA, MPhil
Robin Maconie MA
Linda Proud
Tim Pulleine
Emma Shackleton
Mary Shields PhD
Joe Staines
Calum Storrie BArch
Professor Norman Vance PhD
Patricia Warner

EDITORS
Content Editor
Jennifer Speake

Project Editors
Emma Callery
Sheila Dallas

Text Editors
Jane Anson
Frances Lass
Gian Douglas Home
Edith Summerhayes

Production
Tony Ballsdon

Computer Systems Administrator
Lorraine Cotterell

A in music, the first note of the ◊diatonic scale A–G; orchestral ◊concert pitch.

Aalto Alvar (Hugo Alvar Henrik) 1898–1976. Finnish architect and designer, a pioneer of the ◊Modern Movement in his native Finland. Initially working within the confines of the ◊International Style, he later developed a unique architectural style, characterized by asymmetry, curved walls, and contrast of natural materials. He invented a new form of laminated bent-plywood furniture 1932 and won many design awards for household and industrial items.

Aalto's buildings include the Hall of Residence at the Massachusetts Institute of Technology, Cambridge, Massachusetts, 1947–49; Technical High School, Otaniemi, 1962–65; and Finlandia Hall, Helsinki, 1972.

It is the task of the architect to give life a gentler structure.

Alvar Aalto *Connoisseur* June 1987

Aaltonen Wäinö 1894–1966. Finnish sculptor known for his monumental figures and busts portraying citizens of Finland following the country's independence 1917. The bronze monument to the athlete Paavo Nurmi (1897–1973) 1925 (Helsinki Stadium) and the bust of the composer Sibelius 1928 are examples of his work.

Aasen Ivar Andreas 1813–1896. Norwegian philologist, poet, and playwright. Through a study of rural dialects he evolved by 1853 a native 'country language', which he called *Landsmal*, to take the place of literary Dano-Norwegian.

Abba Swedish pop group 1973–81, one of the most successful groups in Europe during the 1970s. Their well-produced songs were characterized by the harmonies of the two female lead singers, Agnetha Fältskog and Anni-Frid (Frida) Lyngstad, and were aimed at a wide audience.

Benny Andersson and Björn Ulvaeus were the lead male performers and songwriters. Abba had a string of international hits beginning with *Waterloo* (winner of the Eurovision Song Contest) 1974 and including *SOS* 1974, *Fernando* 1976, *Dancing Queen* 1976, and *The Winner Takes It All* 1980. There was a revival of interest in their music in the early 1990s.

Abbado Claudio 1933– . Italian conductor, principal director of the Vienna State Opera 1986 and of the Berlin Philharmonic Orchestra from 1989. Associated early in his career with the La Scala Opera, Milan, his wide-ranging repertoire includes a significant number of 20th-century composers, among them Schoenberg, Prokofiev, Janáček, Bartók, and Stockhausen. He has also conducted the European Youth Orchestra from its inception 1977.

Abbate Niccolò dell' *c.* 1512–1571. Italian Mannerist painter. He was active in his hometown of Modena, then in Bologna where his work, mainly frescoes and portraits, reflects the influence of Jacopo da ◊Pontormo. From the early 1550s he worked in France with ◊Primaticcio at Fontainebleau. He contributed significantly to the style of the ◊Fontainebleau School with his slender, sinuous figures, and in his use of mythology prepared the way for the classical landscapes of ◊Poussin and ◊Claude Lorrain.

abbey in the Christian church, a building or group of buildings housing a community of monks or nuns. The word is also applied to a building that was once the church of an abbey, for example, Westminster Abbey, London.

The first abbeys, as established in Syria or Egypt, were mere collections of huts, but during the Middle Ages massive and extensive building complexes were constructed throughout Europe. St Benedict's Abbey at Monte Cassino in Italy and Citeaux and Cluny in France set the pattern. Others include Clairvaux, France; Fountains Abbey, England; and El ◊Escorial, Spain.

Abbey Theatre playhouse in Dublin associated with the Irish literary revival of the early 1900s. The theatre, opened in 1904, staged the works of a number of Irish dramatists, including Lady Gregory, W B Yeats, J M Synge, and Sean O'Casey. Burned down 1951, the Abbey Theatre was rebuilt 1966.

Abbotsford home of Walter ◊Scott from 1811, on the right bank of the Tweed, Borders region, Scotland. Originally a farmhouse, it was rebuilt 1817–25 as a Gothic baronial hall, and is still in the possession of his descendants.

Abbott Berenice 1898–1991. US photographer. She is best known for her portrait studies of artists in the 1920s and for her comprehensive documentation of New York City in the 1930s, culminating in the publication of *Changing New*

York 1939. Her straightforward style was partially influenced by the French photographer Eugène Atget, whose work she rescued from obscurity.

Abbott and Costello stage names of William Abbott (1895–1974) and Louis Cristillo (1906–1959). US comedy duo. They moved to films from vaudeville, and most, including *Buck Privates* 1941 and *Lost in a Harem* 1944, were showcases for their routines. They also appeared on radio and televison.

Abe Kōbō 1924– . Japanese novelist and playwright. He was a leader of the avant-garde, and his familiarity with Western literature, existentialism, Surrealism, and Marxism influences his distinctive treatment of the problems of alienation and loss of identity in postwar Japan. His books include the claustrophobic novel *Suna no onna/Woman of the Dunes* 1962 and minimalist plays such as his trilogy *Boñi natta otoko/The Man Who Turned into a Stick* 1969.

Abercrombie Leslie Patrick 1879–1957. English architect, a pioneer of British town planning. He is known for his work replanning British cities after damage in World War II (such as the Greater London Plan, 1944) and for the new town policy. See also ◊garden city.

Abish Walter 1931– . US writer of Austrian-Jewish origin, who moved to America 1960. Abish uses a tight, flat-styled formalism to investigate modern history and morality in such novels as *Alphabetical Africa* 1974 and *How German Is It?* 1980.

Aboriginal art art of the Australian Aborigines. Traditionally almost entirely religious and ceremonial, it was directed towards portraying stories of the Dreamtime, a creation mythology reflecting the Aboriginal hunter-gatherer lifestyle. Perishable materials were used, as in ◊bark painting and carved trees and logs, and few early works of this type survive. A great deal of rock art remains intact, however, and forms one of the richest continuing traditions in the world. Abstract patterns and stylized figures predominate. Ground and body painting were also practised, chiefly as part of secret initiation rites.

Rock engravings are found throughout the continent. The earliest, such as those in Koonalda Cave, South Australia, and at the Early Man site on Cape York Peninsula, northern Queensland, are characterized by stylized designs of circles, animal tracks, and meandering patterns, and are between 15,000 and 20,000 years old. In the Hawkesbury River region of New South Wales large figures of animals, birds, fish, and spirit beings have been engraved into the sandstone. Cave walls were painted using natural ochres of red and yellow, white pipeclay, and charcoal. Such paintings include the vast galleries in the Laura district of Cape York, which feature the sticklike *Quinkan* spirit figures;

in the Kimberleys, the *Wandjina* figures, towering red and white creatures with halolike headdresses; and in Arnhem Land in Northern Territory, the remarkable 'x-ray' figures – animals and humans with inner organs depicted. Stencils, frequently of hands, are found in all rock-painting areas and were produced by placing an object against the rock wall and then blowing a mouthful of paint over it. Trees and logs carved for ceremonial purposes include the burial poles made by the Tiwi people of Bathurst and Melville Islands, which are painted in complex designs using black, white, red, and yellow, and the carved trees of the Darling Basin region of New South Wales, which were used in initiation ceremonies and burial rites. In central Australia, *churinga*, oval plaques of wood or stone, were incised or painted with highly stylized images of totem figures.

abracadabra magic word first recorded in a Latin poem of the 2nd century AD by the Gnostic poet Serenus Sammonicus. When the letters were written in the form of an inverted pyramid, so that the word could be read both across the top and up the right-hand side, it was used as a health amulet, to ward off illnesses.

abraxas charm found engraved on ancient stones. The Greek letters of the word, when interpreted as numbers, total 365. The word was used by Egyptian Gnostics to describe the supreme being.

abstract art nonrepresentational art. Ornamental art without figurative representation occurs in most cultures. The modern abstract movement in sculpture and painting emerged in Europe and North America between 1910 and 1920. Two approaches produce different abstract styles: images that have been 'abstracted' from nature to the point where they no longer reflect a conventional reality, and nonobjective, or 'pure', art forms, without any reference to reality.

Abstract art began in the avant-garde movements of the late 19th century – Impressionism, Neo-Impressionism, and Post-Impressionism. These styles of painting reduced the importance of the original subject matter and began to emphasize the creative process of painting itself. In the first decade of the 20th century, some painters in Europe began to abandon the established Western conventions of imitating nature and of storytelling and developed a new artistic form and expression. Wassily Kandinsky is generally regarded as the first abstract artist. From 1910 to 1914 he worked on two series, *Improvisations* and *Compositions*, in which he moved gradually towards total abstraction. His highly coloured canvases influenced many younger European artists. In France around 1907, the Cubists Pablo Picasso and Georges Braque also developed a semi-abstract style; their pictures, some partly collage, were composed mainly of fragmented natural images. By 1912 Robert Delaunay had pushed Cubism to complete abstraction. Many variations of abstract art developed in Europe and Russia, as shown in the work of Piet Mondrian, Kasimir Malevich, the Futurists, the Vorticists, and the Dadaists. Sculptors were inspired by the new freedom in form and content, and Constantin Brancusi's versions of *The Kiss* 1907–12 are among the earliest semi-abstract sculptures. Cubist-inspired sculptors such as Raymond Duchamp-Villon (1876–1918) and Jacques Lipchitz moved further towards abstraction, as did the Dadaist Hans Arp. Two exhibitions of European art, one in New York 1913 (the Armory Show), the other in San Francisco 1917, opened the way for abstraction in US art. Many painters, including the young Georgia O'Keeffe, experimented with new styles. Morgan Russell (1886–1953) and Stanton Macdonald-Wright (1890–1973) invented their own abstract style, Synchronism, a rival to Orphism, a similar style developed in France by Delaunay – both emphasized colour over form. Abstract art has dominated Western art from 1920 and has continued to produce many variations. In the 1940s it gained renewed vigour in the works of the Abstract Expressionists. In the 1960s Minimal art provoked outraged reactions from critics and the general public alike.

Abstract Expressionism US movement in abstract art that emphasized the act of painting, the expression inherent in the colour and texture of the paint itself, and the interaction of artist, paint, and canvas. Abstract Expressionism emerged in New York in the early 1940s. Arshile Gorky, Franz Kline, Jackson Pollock, and Mark Rothko are associated with the movement.

Abstract Expressionism may have been inspired by Hans Hofmann and Gorky, who were both working in the USA in the 1940s. Hofmann, who emigrated from Germany in the 1930s, had started to use dribbles and blobs of paint to create expressive abstract patterns, while Gorky, a Turkish Armenian refugee, was developing his highly coloured abstracts using wild organic forms. Abstract Expressionism was not a distinct school but rather a convergence of artistic personalities, each in revolt against the prevailing conventions in US art. The styles of the movement's exponents varied widely: Pollock's huge dripped and splashed work, Willem de Kooning's grotesque figures, Kline's strong calligraphic style, and Robert Motherwell's and Rothko's large, calm canvases. The movement made a strong impression on European painting in the late 1950s.

Absurd, Theatre of the avant-garde drama originating with a group of dramatists in the 1950s, including Samuel Beckett, Eugène Ionesco, Jean Genet, and Harold Pinter. Their work expressed the belief that in a godless universe human existence has no meaning or purpose and therefore all communication breaks down. Logical construction and argument gives way to irrational and illogical speech and to its ultimate conclusion, silence, as in Beckett's play *Breath* 1970.

What I try to do in my plays is to get this recognizable reality of the absurdity of what we do and how we behave and how we speak.

Harold Pinter
On the Theatre of the Absurd

Abul Hasan 1589–1616. Mogul painter who worked at the court of the emperor Jahangir, specializing in portraits but also executing several delicate, closely observed animal studies. A fine example of his work is *Portrait of Jahangir Holding a Portrait of Akbar*, early 17th century (Musée Guimet, Paris). Like many of the Mogul artists of the period, he was influenced by Western art, particularly in his use of colour.

Abú Nuwás Hasan ibn Háni 762– *c*. 815. Arab poet celebrated for the freedom, eroticism, and ironic lightness of touch he brought to traditional forms.

A brook, a bottle, a bench, a way of waiting,/ The body sweetens, the ghost stirs,/ Golden four.

Abú Nuwás *from* **J Kritzeck**
An Anthology of Islamic Literature

Abu Simbel former site of two ancient temples cut into the rock on the banks of the Nile in S Egypt during the reign of Ramses II (1304–1237 BC), commemorating him and his wife Nefertari. The temples were moved, in sections, 1966–67 before the site was flooded by the Aswan High Dam.

Academy Award annual award in many categories, given since 1927 by the American Academy of Motion Picture Arts and Sciences (founded by Louis B Mayer of Metro-Goldwyn-Mayer 1927). Arguably the film community's most prestigious accolade, the award is a gold-plated statuette, which has been nicknamed 'Oscar' since 1931.

Major awards include Best Picture, Best Director, Best Actor and Actress, Best Supporting Actor and Actress, Best Cinematography, Best Visual Effects, Best Screenplay, and Best Music.

Academy Awards: recent winners

1971	Best Picture: *The French Connection*; Best Director: William Friedkin *The French Connection*; Best Actor: Gene Hackman *The French Connection*; Best Actress: Jane Fonda *Klute*
1972	Best Picture: *The Godfather*; Best Director: Bob Fosse *Cabaret*; Best Actor: Marlon Brando *The Godfather*; Best Actress: Liza Minnelli *Cabaret*
1973	Best Picture: *The Sting*; Best Director: George Roy Hill *The Sting*; Best Actor: Jack Lemmon *Save the Tiger*; Best Actress: Glenda Jackson *A Touch of Class*
1974	Best Picture: *The Godfather II*; Best Director: Francis Ford Coppola *The Godfather II*; Best Actor: Art Carney *Harry and Tonto*; Best Actress: Ellen Burstyn *Alice Doesn't Live Here Anymore*
1975	Best Picture: *One Flew Over the Cuckoo's Nest*; Best Director: Milos Forman *One Flew Over the Cuckoo's Nest*; Best Actor: Jack Nicholson *One Flew Over the Cuckoo's Nest*; Best Actress: Louise Fletcher *One Flew Over the Cuckoo's Nest*
1976	Best Picture: *Rocky*; Best Director: John G Avildsen *Rocky*; Best Actor: Peter Finch *Network*; Best Actress: Faye Dunaway *Network*
1977	Best Picture: *Annie Hall*; Best Director: Woody Allen *Annie Hall*; Best Actor: Richard Dreyfuss *The Goodbye Girl*; Best Actress: Diane Keaton *Annie Hall*
1978	Best Picture: *The Deer Hunter*; Best Director: Michael Cimino *The Deer Hunter*; Best Actor: Jon Voight *Coming Home*; Best Actress: Jane Fonda *Coming Home*
1979	Best Picture: *Kramer vs Kramer*; Best Director: Robert Benton *Kramer vs Kramer*; Best Actor: Dustin Hoffman *Kramer vs Kramer*; Best Actress: Sally Field *Norma Rae*
1980	Best Picture: *Ordinary People*; Best Director: Robert Redford *Ordinary People*; Best Actor: Robert De Niro *Raging Bull*; Best Actress: Sissy Spacek *Coal Miner's Daughter*
1981	Best Picture: *Chariots of Fire*; Best Director: Warren Beatty *Reds*; Best Actor: Henry Fonda *On Golden Pond*; Best Actress: Katharine Hepburn *On Golden Pond*
1982	Best Picture: *Gandhi*; Best Director: Richard Attenborough *Gandhi*; Best Actor: Ben Kingsley *Gandhi*; Best Actress: Meryl Streep *Sophie's Choice*
1983	Best Picture: *Terms of Endearment*; Best Director: James L Brooks *Terms of Endearment*; Best Actor: Robert Duvall *Tender Mercies*; Best Actress: Shirley MacLaine *Terms of Endearment*
1984	Best Picture: *Amadeus*; Best Director: Milos Forman *Amadeus*; Best Actor: F Murray Abraham *Amadeus*; Best Actress: Sally Field *Places in the Heart*
1985	Best Picture: *Out of Africa*; Best Director: Sidney Pollack *Out of Africa*; Best Actor: William Hurt *Kiss of the Spiderwoman*; Best Actress: Geraldine Page *The Trip to Bountiful*
1986	Best Picture: *Platoon*; Best Director: Oliver Stone *Platoon*; Best Actor: Paul Newman *The Color of Money*; Best Actress: Marlee Matlin *Children of a Lesser God*
1987	Best Picture: *The Last Emperor*; Best Director: Bernardo Bertolucci *The Last Emperor*; Best Actor: Michael Douglas *Wall Street*; Best Actress: Cher *Moonstruck*
1988	Best Picture: *Rain Man*; Best Director: Barry Levinson *Rain Man*; Best Actor: Dustin Hoffman *Rain Man*; Best Actress: Jodie Foster *The Accused*
1989	Best Picture: *Driving Miss Daisy*; Best Director: Oliver Stone *Born on the 4th of July*; Best Actor: Daniel Day-Lewis *My Left Foot*; Best Actress: Jessica Tandy *Driving Miss Daisy*
1990	Best Picture: *Dances with Wolves*; Best Director: Kevin Costner *Dances with Wolves*; Best Actor: Jeremy Irons *Reversal of Fortune*; Best Actress: Kathy Bates *Misery*
1991	Best Picture: *The Silence of the Lambs*; Best Director: Jonathan Demme *The Silence of the Lambs*; Best Actor: Anthony Hopkins *The Silence of the Lambs*; Best Actress: Jodie Foster *The Silence of the Lambs*
1992	Best Picture: *Unforgiven*; Best Director: Clint Eastwood *Unforgiven*; Best Actor: Al Pacino *Scent of a Woman*; Best Actress: Emma Thompson *Howards End*

a cappella choral music sung without instrumental accompaniment. It is characteristic of ◊gospel music, ◊doo-wop, and the evangelical Christian church movement.

accent in music, the distinctive articulation of individual notes or passages. Accents are dynamic, adding loudness; agogic, enlarging the beat (as in Viennese waltz rhythm); metrical, shifting the beat, as in syncopation; or timbre, as in melody accentuation using a wah-wah note.

accidental in music notation, a sharp, flat, or natural sign preceding a note which changes the pitch of the note by a semitone up (sharp), down (flat), or back to normal (natural). Music written in 'black-note' (sharp and flat) keys may require the rarer double sharp and double flat signs indicating a change in pitch of a full tone.

accompaniment music and players providing a bass line, chord structure, and beat in support of a solo performer.

accordion musical instrument of the free-reed organ family comprising left and right wind chests connected by flexible bellows. The right hand plays melody on a piano-style keyboard of 26–34 keys while the left hand has a system of push buttons for selecting single notes or chord harmonies.

Invented by Cyrill Damien (1772–1847) in Vienna 1829, the accordion spread throughout the world and can be heard in the popular music of Germany, France, China, Russia, and the USA.

Achates character in Virgil's ◊*Aeneid*. Achates was the friend of the hero Aeneas. The name is proverbial for a faithful companion.

Achebe Chinua 1930– . Nigerian novelist. His themes include the social and political impact of European colonialism on African people, and the problems of newly independent African nations. His novels include the seminal *Things Fall Apart* 1958, one of the first African novels to achieve a global reputation, and *Anthills of the Savannah* 1987.

Acheron in Greek mythology, one of the rivers of the underworld. The name was taken from a river in S Epirus that flowed through a deep gorge into the Ionian Sea.

Achilles Greek hero of Homer's ◊*Iliad*. He was the son of Peleus, king of the Myrmidons in Thessaly, and of the sea nymph Thetis, who rendered him invulnerable, except for the heel by which she held him, by dipping him in the river Styx. Achilles killed ◊Hector at the climax of the *Iliad*, and according to subsequent Greek legends was himself killed by ◊Paris, who shot a poisoned arrow into Achilles' heel.

acid house type of ◊house music. The derivation of the term is disputed but may be from 'acid burning', Chicago slang for digital sampling, a recording technique much featured in acid house.

Acmeist movement movement in early 20th-century Russian poetry reacting against ◊Symbolism. Acmeists developed a neo-classical emphasis on clear words about demystified realities. Major figures include Osip ◊Mandelshtam, Anna ◊Akhmatova, and Nikolay Gumilyov (1886–1921), founder of the Acmeist organ *Apollon* (1909–17).

acoustic term describing a musical instrument played without electrical amplification or assistance, for example an acoustic guitar or acoustic piano. It is also a term used by musicians to characterize room response, an important factor in performance. A so-called 'bright' acoustic provides a lively reverberation while a 'dry' or 'muddy' acoustic is lacking in response.

acoustics in music, the science of sound generation and propagation, embracing psycho-acoustics, a branch of communications science; in architecture, the sound-reflecting character of a room.

acronym in music, any coded reference to a name using the letter-names of notes to form a motif. The most widely quoted is B-A-C-H, playing on the German note-names B (B flat) -A-C-H (B natural); Schumann's *Abegg Variations* 1830 is dedicated to his friend Meta Abegg; Berg's *Chamber Concerto* 1923–25 includes motivic references to himself, Schoenberg, and Berg.

acropolis citadel of an ancient Greek town. The Acropolis of Athens contains the ruins of the ◊Parthenon and surrounding complexes, built there during the days of the Athenian empire.

acrylic fibre synthetic fibre often used as a substitute for wool. It was first developed 1947 but not produced in great volumes until the 1950s. Strong and warm, acrylic fibre is often used for sweaters and tracksuits, and as linings for boots and gloves.

acrylic paint any of a range of synthetic substitutes for ◊oil paint, mostly soluble in water. Acrylic paints are used in a variety of painting techniques, from wash to impasto. They dry more quickly than oil paint, but lack the translucency of natural substances.

act in drama, the principal division of a play, usually marking a change of location, time, or mood. Acts are subdivided into scenes. All Shakespeare's plays are printed in five acts. Most modern plays are divided into three acts.

Actaeon in Greek mythology, a hunter who surprised the goddess ◊Artemis while she was bathing. She changed him into a stag and he was torn to pieces by his own hounds.

action painting or *gesture painting* in abstract art, a form of Abstract Expressionism that emphasized the importance of the physical act of painting. Jackson ◊Pollock, the leading exponent, threw, dripped, and dribbled paint on to canvases fastened to the floor. Another principal exponent was Willem de Kooning. The term 'action painting' was coined by the US art critic Harold Rosenberg 1952.

acting performing one or more role(s) in a play or film. In ancient Greece, the speaking actors were distinguished from the ◊chorus, whereas in ancient Indian and in medieval Japanese drama, acting took the form of singing and dancing or stylized movement. Acting skills include body and (in unmasked drama) facial mobility, vocal control, and an ability to portray character and emotional states.

Actors Studio theatre workshop in New York City, established 1947 by Cheryl Crawford and Elia Kazan. Under Lee Strasberg, who became artistic director 1948, it became known for the study of Konstantin Stanislavsky's ◊Method acting.

Adam family of Scottish architects and designers. *William Adam* (1689–1748) was the leading Scottish architect of his day, and his son *Robert Adam* (1728–1792) is considered one of the greatest British architects of the late 18th century, responsible for transforming the prevailing Palladian fashion in architecture into a Neo-Classical style. He designed interiors for many great country houses, including Syon House 1760–69 and Kenwood House 1767–69 (both in London), and earned a considerable reputation as a furniture designer. With his brother *James Adam* (1732–1794), also an architect, he speculatively developed the Adelphi district near Charing Cross, London, largely rebuilt 1936.

Adam Adolphe Charles 1803–1856. French composer of light operas and founder of the Théâtre National, Paris, 1847. His stage works include *Le Postillion de Longjumeau/The Postillion of Longjumeau* 1836 and *Si j'étais Roi/If I Were King* 1852, but he is best remembered for his ballet score for *Giselle* 1841. Some 80 of his works were staged.

Adam de la Halle *c.* 1240– *c.* 1290. French poet and composer. His *Le Jeu de Robin et Marion*, written in Italy about 1282, is a theatrical work with dialogue and songs set to what were apparently popular tunes of the day. It is sometimes called the forerunner of comic opera.

Adamov Arthur 1908–1970. Russian-born French poet and dramatist. A Surrealist, Adamov contributed to the Theatre of the ◊Absurd with his plays *Professeur Taranne* 1953 and *Ping Pong* 1955. His style, influenced by a Brechtian social and political awareness, is best illustrated in *Paolo Paoli* 1957 and *Le Printemps '71/Spring '71* 1961, a history of the Paris Commune of 1871.

Adams Ansel 1902–1984. US photographer best known for his printed images of dramatic landscapes and organic forms of the American West. Light and texture were important elements in his photographs. He was associated with the ◊zone system of exposure estimation and was a founder member of the ◊'f/64' group which advocated precise definition.

In 1916 Adams made his first trip to the Yosemite National Park, California; the Yosemite and the High Sierras remained a major focus of his work throughout his life. Aiming to establish photography as a fine art, he founded the first museum collection of photography, at New York City's Museum of Modern Art 1937.

Adams Henry Brooks 1838–1918. US historian and novelist, a grandson of President John Quincy Adams. He published the acclaimed nine-volume *A History of the United States During the Administrations of Jefferson and Madison* 1889–91, a study of the evolution of democracy in the USA.

His other works include *Mont-Saint-Michel and Chartres* 1904, and a classic autobiography *The Education of Henry Adams* 1907.

> *One friend in a lifetime is much; two are many; three are hardly possible.*
>
> **Henry Adams**
> *The Education of Henry Adams* 1907

Adams John Coolidge 1947– . US composer and conductor, director of the New Music Ensemble 1972–81, and artistic adviser to the San Francisco Symphony Orchestra from 1978. His minimalist techniques are displayed in *Electric Wake* 1968, *Heavy Metal* 1971, *Bridge of Dreams* 1982, and the operas *Nixon in China* 1988 and *The Death of Klinghoffer* 1990.

Adams Richard 1920– . English novelist. He wrote *Watership Down* 1972, a story of rabbits who escape from a doomed warren and work together to establish a new one. As with all Adams' novels, there is an underlying social message. Later novels include *Shardik* 1974, *The Plague Dogs* 1977, and *The Girl on a Swing* 1980.

Adamson Joy 1910–1985. German-born naturalist whose work with wildlife in Kenya, including the lioness Elsa, is described in *Born Free* 1960 which was adapted as a film 1975. She was murdered at her home in Kenya. She worked with her third husband, British game warden *George Adamson* (1906–1989), who was murdered by bandits.

Adamson Robert. Scottish photographer; see ◊Hill and Adamson.

Adcock Fleur 1934– . New Zealand poet, based in England. She has developed a distinctive, unsentimental poetic voice with which she coolly explores contemporary life, love, and personal relationships. Her collections include *The Eye of the Hurricane* 1964, *High Tide in the Garden* 1971, and *The Inner Harbour* 1979. She has also edited *The Oxford Book of Contemporary New Zealand Verse* 1982.

Addison Joseph 1672–1719. English writer. In 1704 he celebrated Marlborough's victory at Blenheim in a poem, *The Campaign*, and subsequently held political appointments, including undersecretary of state and secretary to the Lord-Lieutenant of Ireland 1708. In 1709 he contributed to the *Tatler* magazine, begun by Richard ◊Steele, with whom he was cofounder 1711–12 of the *Spectator*. His essays set a new standard of easy elegance in English prose.

> *'Tis not in mortals to command success/ But we'll do more, Sempronius, we'll deserve it.*
>
> **Joseph Addison** *Cato* 1.2

Adjani Isabelle 1955– . French actress of Algerian-German descent. She played the title role in Truffaut's *L'Histoire d'Adèle H/The Story of Adèle H* 1975 and has since appeared in international productions including *Le Locataire/The Tenant, Nosferatu Phantom der Nacht* 1979, and *Ishtar* 1987.

Adler Larry 1914– . US musician, a virtuoso performer on the harmonica, who commissioned the English composer Vaughan Williams' *Romanza in D flat* 1951.

ad lib(itum) (Latin) 'freely' interpreted, improvised (of a speech, musical performance, and so on), or, in music, can be omitted.

adobe in architecture, a building method employing sun-dried earth bricks; also the individual bricks. The use of earth bricks and the construction of walls by enclosing earth within moulds (*pisé de terre*) are the two principal methods of raw-earth building. The techniques are commonly found in Spain, Latin America, and the southwestern USA.

Jericho is the site of the earliest evidence of building in sun-dried mud bricks, dating from the 8th millennium BC. Firing bricks was not practised until the 3rd millennium BC, and then only occasionally because it was costly in terms of fuel.

The Great Wall of China is largely constructed of earth; whole cities of mud construction exist throughout the Middle East and North Africa, for example Sana in Yemen and Yazd in Iran, and it remains a vigorous vernacular tradition in these areas. A variation of it is found as cob (a mixture of clay and chopped straw) in Devon, England, and in the pueblos of North America.

The Egyptian architect Hassan ◊Fathy was an influential advocate of raw-earth building. Between 1945 and 1948 he built the village of New Gournia in Egypt for 7,000 inhabitants, and demonstrated the value of adobe material in helping to solve the housing problems of the Third World. Recent years have seen a revival of interest in the technique and a number of schemes have been built. Examples are La Luz new town, USA, 1967–73 by Antoine Predock; the Great Mosque of Niono, Mali, 1955–72 by Mason-Lassiné Minta; Wissa Wassef Arts Centre, Harrania, Egypt, 1952 by Ramses Wissa Wassef (1911–1974).

Adonis in Greek mythology, a beautiful youth loved by the goddess ◊Aphrodite. He was killed while boar-hunting but was allowed to return from the underworld for six months every year to rejoin her. The anemone sprang from his blood.

Worshipped as a god of vegetation, he was known as ◊Tammuz in Babylonia, Assyria, and Phoenicia (where it was his sister, ◊Ishtar, who brought him from the underworld). He seems also to have been identified with ◊Osiris, the Egyptian god of the underworld.

Adrastus in Greek mythology, king of Argos, and leader of the expedition of the ◊Seven against Thebes, undertaken to place his son-in-law ◊Polynices on the throne of Thebes.

Aegean art the art of the civilizations that flourished around the Aegean (an area which included mainland Greece, the Cyclades Islands, and Crete) in the Bronze Age, about 2800 BC–1100 BC. Despite cultural interchange by way of trade with the contemporaneous civilizations of Egypt and Mesopotamia, the Aegean cultures developed their own highly distinctive styles.

Cycladic art of the Bronze Age civilization in the Cyclades Islands, about 2500–1400 BC, is exemplified by pottery with incised ornament and marble statuettes, usually highly stylized female nudes representing the Mother Goddess in almost abstract simplicity, her face reduced to an elongated oval with a triangular nose. The Cycladic culture preceded Minoan, ran concurrently with it, and eventually shared its fate, becoming assimilated into the Mycenaean culture.

Minoan art of Bronze Age Crete, about 2300–1100 BC, is of a high aesthetic standard, reflecting the artistic orientation and zest for life of the Minoan people. Its fine pottery, painted in a fresh, spontaneous style with plant and animal motifs curving to suit the form of the vases, comes in various styles but is best represented by 'light-on-dark' and Kamares-style (polychrome on a dark background) ware. Its magnificent palaces, such as Knossos, Phaestos, and Mallia, were decorated with cheerful frescoes depicting scenes from everyday life, plants, birds, leaping fish, and dolphins; fragments remain, such as the lily fresco from Ambisos (Iráklion Museum, Crete). The culture came to an end when, after the eruption of the volcano on Thera (now Santorini) and the destruction of the Minoan centre on that island, the Mycenaeans gained control in the Aegean.

Mycenaean art, about 1580–1100 BC, reflects the warlike preoccupations of the mainland Mycenean society, both in character and in the subjects portrayed. Fortified citadels were developed, such as that of Mycenae itself, which was entered through the Lion Gate, about 1300 BC, so-called because of the massive lion figures, carved from stone, that adorned it. Stylized frescoes decorated its palaces and its pottery, typically dark-on-light, was centred on large bowls, or kraters, depicting scenes of warfare. Perhaps its overriding artistic contribution lies in its metalwork, principally in bronze and gold, for example the royal funeral mask (National Museum, Athens), about 1500 bc. Many of the ideas and art forms of the Mycenean and other early sea-faring civilizations were later adapted by the Greeks (see ◊Greek art).

Aegeus in Greek mythology, king of Athens and father of ◊Theseus who was sent to kill the Cretan ◊Minotaur. On his return, Theseus forgot to substitute white sails for black in a prearranged signal to indicate his success in killing the Minotaur. Believing his son dead, Aegeus leapt into the Aegean Sea.

Aegir in Scandinavian mythology, the god of the sea.

aegis in Greek mythology, originally the shield of Zeus, symbolic of the storm cloud associated with him. In later representations of the goddess ◊Athena, the aegis is commonly shown as a protective animal skin, embellished with the head of the ◊Gorgon Medusa.

Aelfric *c.* 955–1020. Anglo-Saxon writer and abbot, author of two collections of *Catholic Homilies* 990–92, sermons, and the *Lives of the Saints* 996–97, written in Old English prose.

Aeneas in classical mythology, a Trojan prince who became the ancestral hero of the Romans. According to ◊Homer, he was the son of Anchises and the goddess Aphrodite. During the Trojan War he owed his life to the frequent intervention of the gods. The legend on which Virgil's epic poem the Aeneid is based describes his escape from Troy and his eventual settlement in Latium, on the Italian peninsula.

Aeneid Latin narrative poem or epic by ◊Virgil in 12 books, composed in the traditional Homeric metre of hexameters. Written during the last 10 years of the poet's life (30–19 BC), it celebrates Roman imperial values in the role of its Trojan hero, Aeneas, who is destined to found a new city in Italy. After the fall of ◊Troy, Aeneas wanders the Mediterranean with his companions until, landing in North Africa, he falls in love with Dido, Queen of Carthage. He later deserts her and establishes the Trojans in Latium, where the king of the Latini offers him his daughter, Lavinia, in marriage. He is opposed by Turnus, a rival suitor, but eventually kills the latter in singlehanded combat. The poem is indebted to many predecessors (the Greek poet ◊Apollonius of Rhodes, and the Latin writers ◊Ennius and ◊Lucretius) in addition to ◊Homer's *Odyssey* and *Iliad*.

Do not trust the horse, Trojans. Whatever it is, I fear the Greeks even when they bring gifts.

Aeneid **Virgil**

Aeolian harp wind-blown instrument consisting of a shallow soundbox supporting gut strings at low tension and tuned to the same pitch. It produces an eerie harmony that rises and falls with the changing pressure of the wind. It originated in India and China, becoming popular in parts of central Europe during the 19th century.

Aeolus in Greek mythology, the god of the winds, who kept them imprisoned in a cave on the Lipari Islands.

aerial photography or *aerial archaeology* taking photographs from a high level, a technique used in archaeology to detect surface features (such as crop marks, soil marks, shadow marks) that are not clearly visible from ground level and which indicate the presence of ancient features; for example, crops will show differences in growth and colour if they are growing over a buried wall foundation or other stone feature.

Aeschylus *c.* 525– *c.* 456 BC. Athenian dramatist, who developed Greek tragedy by introducing a second actor, thus enabling true dialogue and dramatic action to occur independently of the chorus. Ranked with ◊Euripides and ◊Sophocles as one of the three great tragedians, Aeschylus composed some 90 plays between 500–456 BC, of which seven complete tragedies survive in his name: *Persians* 472 BC, *Seven Against Thebes* 467, *Suppliants* 463, the ◊*Oresteia* trilogy (*Agamemnon*, *Libation-Bearers*, and *Eumenides*) 458, and *Prometheus Bound* (the last, although attributed to him, is of uncertain authorship).

Aeschylus was born at Eleusis in Attica and known to have fought at the battle of Marathon 490 BC. Towards the end of his life, he left Athens for Sicily. His work is characterized by spectacular tragedy, ornate language, and complex and vigorous use of choral song and dance. His *Oresteia* trilogy is the only surviving example from antiquity of three connected plays performed on the same occasion.

Every ruler is harsh whose rule is new.

Aeschylus *Prometheus Bound c.* 478 BC

Aesculapius in Roman mythology, the god of medicine, equivalent to the Greek ◊Asclepius.

Aesir principal gods of Norse mythology – Odin, Thor, Balder, Loki, Freya, and Tyr – whose dwelling place was ◊Asgard.

Aesop by tradition, a writer of Greek fables. According to the historian Herodotus, he lived in the mid-6th century BC and was a slave. The fables, which are ascribed to him, were collected at a later date and are anecdotal stories using animal characters to illustrate moral or satirical points.

Don't count your chickens before they're hatched.

Aesop 'The Milkmaid and the Pail'

---

aestheticism in the arts, the doctrine that art is an end in itself and does not need to have any moral, religious, political or educational purpose. The writer Théophile Gautier popularized the doctrine 'l'art pour l'art' ('art for art's sake') 1832, and it was taken up in mid-19th-century France by the Symbolist poets and painters. It flourished in the English Aesthetic Movement of the late 19th century. An emphasis on form rather than content in art remained influential in the West well into the 20th century.

The idea developed from the 18th-century philosopher Immanuel Kant's view that art can be judged only by its own criteria and not by anything external to it.

Aesthetic Movement English artistic movement of the late 19th century, dedicated to the doctrine of 'art for art's sake' – that is, art as a self-sufficient entity concerned solely with beauty and not with any moral or social purpose. Associated with the movement were the artists Aubrey Beardsley and James McNeill Whistler and the writers Walter Pater and Oscar Wilde.

The idea of art for art's sake, rooted in 18th-century philosophical thinking led by Immanuel Kant, was current in Europe throughout the 19th century, but the English movement in the last two decades tended to advocate extremes of sensibility, which attracted much ridicule. John Ruskin and William Morris were staunch critics of the Aesthetic Movement.

African art art of sub-Saharan Africa, from prehistory onwards, ranging from the art of ancient civilizations to the new styles of post-imperialist African nations. Examples of historic African art are bronze figures from the kingdoms of Benin and Ife (in Nigeria) dating from about AD 1500 and, also on the west coast, in the same period, bronze or brass figures for weighing gold, made by the Ashanti (Ghana).

prehistoric art Rock paintings are found in various regions, notably in the western Sahara, Zimbabwe, South Africa, and, from the end of the period, East Africa. Some of the earliest pictures are of elephants. The images tend to be linear and heavily stylized and sometimes show a geometric style. Terracotta figures from the Nok culture of Nigeria, dating from several centuries BC, are a sophisticated blend of individuality and stylization.

Zimbabwe Ruins of ancient stone buildings from before AD 300 suggest a time of outstanding urban culture in the country's history; sculptures found in the ruins show a high degree of skill.

Benin and Ife The bronze sculptures from the 13th–16th-century kingdoms of Benin and Ife on the west coast of Africa (examples in the British Museum, London) are distinctive in style and demonstrate technical refinement in casting by the lost-wax method. The Ife heads are naturalistic, while those of Benin are more stylized, both showing great artistic confidence. The art of Benin includes high-relief bronze plaques with figurative scenes, and ivory carvings. Some of these appear to have been designed for the Portuguese trade.

Ashanti Metalworkers of the Ashanti people (in present-day Ghana) made weights in highly inventive forms with comically exaggerated figures.

general Over the centuries, much artistic effort was invested in religious and ceremonial objects and masks, with wooden sculpture playing a large role. Many everyday items, such as bowls, stools, drums, and combs, are finely crafted and display a great vitality of artistic invention and expression. Since much pre-19th-century African art has been either lost or ignored, it has occupied a meagre place in Western art-history studies. In the early 20th century, however, West African art had a profound influence on the work of many European painters and sculptors, in particular Picasso, Matisse, Brancusi, Modigliani, and Epstein.

African literature individual African-born writers have made sporadic contributions to European letters since the Renaissance and some African languages, such as Hausa and Swahili, have had Arabic-influenced written forms for several centuries. However, African literature was mainly oral until the 20th century and oral traditions of proverbs, mythological narratives, and poetry (including the ◊praise poem in southern Africa) still persist and influence contemporary writing. The main literary languages are English, French, and Portuguese, although anti-colonial feeling has prompted writing in languages such as Swahili, Ewe, and Kikuyu. On the other hand, African writers such as the poet José Craveirinha (1926–) from Mozambique, writing in Portuguese, have won European literary awards.

Despite Africa's enormous cultural diversity, the development of African writing has been closely associated with a growing sense of African political and cultural identity in the colonial and postcolonial period, and variously linked with Pan-Africanism or, particularly in former French colonies, with the idea of *négritude* (blackness, belonging to a black culture), prominent especially in the 1930s. This owed much to the black American writer W E B Du Bois (*c.* 1868–1963) who became a citizen of Ghana, and the poet and dramatist Aimé Césaire (1913–) from Martinique, as well as to the Senegalese poet and statesman Léopold Senghor.

Among the earlier landmarks of African writing are the South African historical novel of precolonial times *Mhudi* (written 1917, published 1930) by Sol Plaatje (1877–1932) and the plays and poetry of H I E Dhlomo (1905–1945), recreating African landscapes and the achievements of heroes such as the Zulu leader Shaka (died 1828). Later writing, including autobiographies such as that by Es'kia ◊Mphahlele, has paid more attention to the themes of urban deprivation and political oppression and violence, particularly in South Africa. This has energized the poetry of the exiled Dennis Brutus (1924–) and the novels of Alex La Guma (1925–1985) and features in the work of the Kenyan writer ◊Ngugi wa Thiong'o and the Nigerian novelist Cyprian Ekwensi (1921–). The reassertion of precolonial communal life, myth, and tradition, associated with condemnation of the cultural disruptions caused by colonists or Christian missionaries, has been a significant concern of the Ghanaian poet Kofi Awoonor (1935–) and of Nigerian writers such as Chinua ◊Achebe, the Ibo poet Christopher Okigbo (1932–1967), and the novelist Amos Tutuola (1920–), whose mysterious and fantastic narratives draw on Yoruba folk tales. In South Africa, drama has emerged as an important instrument of political protest, particularly in the work of Athol ◊Fugard.

Important women writers include the South Africans Bessie Head (1937–1986) and Miriam Tlali (1933–), the Nigerian Flora Nwapa (1931–), and Mariama Bâ (1929–1981) from Senegal.

African traditional dance tribal and regional African dances with a primarily ritualistic function. These rhythmically complex dances are performed to celebrate the important events in people's lives and are part of the everyday experience. In most cases, the dance focuses on the circle with soloists splitting off and then returning to the main group. Movement is generally directed towards the ground rather than upwards.

Afro-American tradition in dance, the fusion of rhythms and steps from Africa and Europe to form new dance styles such as ◊tap dancing, ◊jazz dance, and ◊jive. Enslaved Africans in North America used dance as a means of preserving their African heritage.

Agamemnon in Greek mythology, a Greek hero of the Trojan wars, son of Atreus, king of Mycenae, and brother of Menelaus. He married Clytemnestra, and their children included Electra, Iphigenia, and Orestes. He sacrificed Iphigenia in order to secure favourable winds for the Greek expedition against Troy, and after a ten years' siege sacked the city, receiving Priam's daughter Cassandra as a prize. On his return home, he and Cassandra were murdered by Clytemnestra and her lover, Aegisthus. His children Orestes and Electra later killed the guilty couple.

Agate James Evershed 1877–1947. British essayist and theatre critic, author of *Ego*, a diary in nine volumes published 1935–49.

I am not interested in what anybody else thinks. My mind is not a bed to be made and remade.

James Agate *Ego* 6

Agee James 1909–1955. US writer. He rose to national prominence as a result of his investigation of the plight of sharecroppers in the South during the Depression published as ◊Let Us Now Praise Famous Men 1941, with photographs by Walker ◊Evans. His screenwriting credits include *The African Queen* 1951 and *The Night of the*

Hunter 1955. His novel *A Death in the Family*, published posthumously, won a Pulitzer Prize 1958.

Agni in Hindu mythology, the god of fire, the guardian of homes, and the protector of humans against evil.

Agnon Shmuel Yosef 1888–1970. Israeli novelist. Born in Buczacz, Galicia (now part of W Ukraine), he made it the setting of his most celebrated work, *A Guest for the Night* 1945. He shared a Nobel prize 1966.

agora in an ancient Greek town, the public meeting place and market, equivalent to the Roman ◊forum. The limits were marked with boundary stones, and trade was regulated. The Agora at Athens contained an altar to the 12 Olympian gods, sanctuaries of Zeus, Apollo, and Hephaestus, the mint, administrative offices of state, fountain houses, shops, and covered arcades (stoas).

Aidoo Ama Ata 1940– . Ghanaian dramatist and writer. *Dilemma of a Ghost* 1965, her best-known play, deals with the difficulties of reconciling a Western education and African values and traditions. She has also written novels such as *Our Sister Killjoy* 1977, and short stories.

Aiken Conrad (Potter) 1899–1973. US poet, novelist, and short-story writer whose *Selected Poems* 1929 won the Pulitzer Prize. His works were influenced by early psychoanalytic theory and the use of the stream-of-consciousness technique. His verse, distinguished by its musicality, includes *A Letter from Li Po* 1955 and *A Seizure of Limericks* 1964. His novels include *Great Circle* 1933, and his collected short stories were published 1960.

Separate we come and separate we go/ And this, be it known, is all that we know.

Conrad Aiken
New York Herald Tribune 1969

Ailey Alvin 1931–1989. US dancer, choreographer, and director. His Alvin Ailey City Center Dance Theater, formed 1958, was the first truly multiracial modern dance company. Its emphasis on dance as entertainment brought dance to a wider audience. Ailey's highly individual choreography blends modern, jazz, and classical dance, and celebrates rural and urban black America in pieces like *Blues Suite* 1958, and the company signature piece *Revelations* 1960.

Aimatov Chingiz 1928– . Kirghiz (central Asia) novelist. His work, drawing on oral epic tradition (the Kirghiz language had no alphabet until 1928), dramatizes the conflict between the tribal customs of the Kirghiz nomads and the

Western values of the Soviet administration, as in *The White Steamship* 1970 and *The Day Lasts Longer than a Century* 1980.

Ainsworth William Harrison 1805–1882. English historical novelist. He wrote more than 40 novels and helped popularize the legends of Dick ◊Turpin in *Rookwood* 1834 and Herne the Hunter in *Windsor Castle* 1843.

air see ◊ayre.

airbrush small fine spray-gun used by artists, graphic designers, and photographic retouchers. Driven by air pressure from a compressor or pressurized can, it can apply a thin, very even layer of ink or paint, allowing for subtle gradations of tone.

aisle in church architecture, usually the areas running parallel to the nave, lying between it and the outer walls. In larger churches, the choir and transepts may be aisled.

Ajanta caves Buddhist cave temples dating from 200 BC to the 7th century AD, near the village of Ajanta in Maharashtra state, India. The Ajanta caves boast some 28 chambers cut from solid granite, which are covered with wall paintings and reliefs of superb artistry, thought to have been executed by monks. See also ◊Indian architecture.

Ajax Greek hero in Homer's *Iliad*. Son of Telamon, king of Salamis, he was second only to Achilles among the Greek heroes in the Trojan War. According to subsequent Greek legends, Ajax went mad with jealousy when ◊Agamemnon awarded the armour of the dead Achilles to ◊Odysseus. He later committed suicide in shame.

Akbar-nama (Deeds of Akbar) book of miniatures (Victoria and Albert Museum, London) painted by ◊Basawan and Chatai about 1595 for Akbar, Mogul emperor of N India. The product of a workshop run by Safavid painters from the court of Shah Tahmasp of Persia, the jewel-like paintings of the exploits of the emperor show not only Persian but also Western influence. See also ◊Indian art and ◊Islamic art.

Akhmatova Anna. Pen name of Anna Andreevna Gorenko 1889–1966. Russian poet. A leading member of the ◊Acmeist movement. Among her works are the cycle *Requiem* 1963 (written in the 1930s), which deals with the Stalinist terror, and *Poem Without a Hero* 1962 (begun 1940).

In the 1920s she published several collections of poetry in the realist style of Osip ◊Mandelshtam, but her lack of sympathy with the post-revolutionary regimes inhibited her writing, and her work was banned 1922–40 and again from 1946. From the mid-1950s her work was gradually rehabilitated in the USSR. In 1989 an Akhmatova Museum was opened in Leningrad (now St Petersburg).

Aksakov Sergei Timofeyevich 1791–1859. Russian writer, born at Ufa, in the Urals. Under the influence of ◊Gogol, he wrote autobiographical novels, including *Chronicles of a Russian Family* 1856 and *Years of Childhood* 1858.

Akutagawa Ryūnosuke 1892–1927. Japanese writer of stories, plays, and poetry. Noted for stylistic virtuosity, he wrote autobiographical fiction and grim satirical fables such as 'Kappa' 1927, but his best works are stories derived from 12th- and 13th-century Japanese tales, retold in the light of modern psychology. Among the best known are 'Jigokuhen' 1918, the story of an obsessively ambitious artist, and 'Rashomon', the basis for a film of the same name by Kurosawa 1951.

alabaster naturally occurring fine-grained white or light-coloured translucent form of gypsum (a common mineral, composed of hydrous calcium sulphate), often streaked or mottled. A soft material, it is easily carved, but seldom used for outdoor sculpture.

Aladdin in the ◊*Arabian Nights,* a poor boy who obtains a magic lamp: when the lamp is rubbed, a jinn (genie, or spirit) appears and fulfils its owner's wishes.

Alaïa Azzedine 1940– . Tunisian-born fashion designer who became popular during the 1980s for his soft leather, stretch fabric, and figure-hugging designs (he is nicknamed the 'King of Cling'). He began making clothes to order 1960 and launched his own label 1965. The 'body' or 'bodysuit', akin to the ◊leotard, is credited to him.

Alain-Fournier pen name of Henri-Alban Fournier 1886–1914. French novelist. His haunting semi-autobiographical fantasy *Le Grand Meaulnes/The Lost Domain* 1913 was a cult novel of the 1920s and 1930s. His life is intimately recorded in his correspondence with his brother-in-law Jacques Rivière. He was killed in action on the Meuse in World War I.

Alarcón Pedro Antonio de 1833–1891. Spanish journalist and writer. The acclaimed *Diario/Diary* was based upon his experiences as a soldier in Morocco. His novel *El Sombrero de tres picos/The Three-Cornered Hat* 1874 was the basis of Manuel de Falla's ballet.

I have a fine sense of the ridiculous, but no sense of humour.

Edward Albee
Who's Afraid of Virginia Woolf? 1962

Albee Edward 1928– . US playwright. His internationally performed plays are associated with the Theatre of the ◊Absurd and include *The Zoo Story* 1959, *The American Dream* 1961, *Who's Afraid of Virginia Woolf?* 1962 (his most successful play; also filmed with Elizabeth Taylor and Richard Burton as the quarrelling, alcoholic, academic couple 1966), and *Tiny Alice* 1965. *A Delicate Balance* 1966 and *Seascape* 1975 both won Pulitzer Prizes.

Albéniz Isaac 1860–1909. Spanish nationalist composer and pianist, born in Catalonia. His works include numerous zarzuelas and operas, the orchestral suites *Española* 1886 and *Catalonia* 1899–1908 (with the assistance of Paul ◊Dukas), and some 250 piano works including the suite *Iberia* 1906–09.

Alberti Leon Battista 1404–1472. Italian Renaissance architect and theorist. He set out the principles of Classical architecture, as well as covering their modification for Renaissance practice, in *De re aedificatoria/On Architecture* 1485. His designs for the churches of San Sebastiano, begun 1460, and San Andrea 1470 (both in Mantua) – the only two extant buildings entirely of his design – are bold in their use of Classical language.

Albinoni Tomaso 1671–1751. Italian Baroque composer of over 40 operas and numerous sonatas and *concerti à cinque* (concertos in five parts) for oboe, trumpet, bassoon, violin, organ, and strings, which helped to establish Baroque orchestral style. His work was studied and adapted by Bach.

The popular *Adagio* often described as being by Albinoni was actually composed from a fragment of original manuscript by his biographer, the Italian musicologist Remo Giazotto (1910–).

Alcaeus *c.* 611–*c.* 580 BC. Greek lyric poet, a friend of ◊Sappho. Born at Mytilene in Lesvos, he was a member of a family opposed to the ruling tyrants, and spent time in exile. The surviving fragments of his poems deal with politics, drinking, and love. The Alcaic stanza is named after him.

alcázar any one of several fortified palaces built by the Moors in Spain.

Alcestis in Greek mythology, the wife of Admetus, king of Thessaly. At their wedding, the god Apollo secured a promise from the ◊Fates that Admetus might postpone his death, when the time came, if he could persuade someone else to die for him. Only his wife proved willing, but she was restored to life by ◊Heracles. Her story was the theme of one of ◊Euripides' earliest plays.

Alcmene in Greek mythology, the wife of Amphitryon. Zeus, the king of the gods, visited Alcmene in the form of her husband, and the child of their union was the Greek hero ◊Heracles.

Alcott Louisa May 1832–1888. US author. Her children's classic ◊*Little Women* 1869 drew on her own home circumstances, the heroine Jo being a partial self-portrait. *Good Wives* 1869 was among its sequels.

Aldington Richard 1892–1962. English poet, novelist, and critic. A leading Imagist (see ◊Imagism), he published the collection *Images* 1915. He wrote biographies of D H Lawrence and T E Lawrence and his novels include *Death of a Hero* 1929 and *All Men are Enemies* 1933. He was married to Hilda ◊Doolittle 1913–37.

Aldiss Brian 1925– . English science-fiction writer, anthologist, and critic. His novels include *Non-Stop* 1958, *The Malacia Tapestry* 1976, and the 'Helliconia' trilogy. *Trillion Year Spree* 1986 is a history of science fiction.

Science fiction is no more written for scientists than ghost stories are written for ghosts.

Brian Aldiss

---

aleatory music method of composition practised by postwar avant-garde composers in which the performer or conductor chooses the order of succession of the composed pieces. Examples of aleatory music include Pierre Boulez's *Piano Sonata No 3* 1956–57, Earle Brown's *Available Forms I* 1961, and Stockhausen's *Momente/Moments* 1961–72. Another term for aleatory music is 'mobile form'.

Aleijadinho (António Francisco Lisboa) *c.* 1738–1814. Brazilian artist, generally considered to be the greatest Brazilian sculptor. Having lost the use of his hands, he sculpted with his tools strapped to them, hence his name, which means 'little cripple'. He worked in a restrained and dignified Rococo style, exemplified in his finest piece *The Twelve Prophets* 1800–05, which stands outside the church of Bom Jesus de Matozinhos, Congonhas do Campo, Brazil.

Aleixandre Vicente 1898–1984. Spanish lyric poet, born in Seville. His verse, such as the surrealist *La destrucción o el amor/The Destruction of Love* 1935, had Republican sympathies, and his work was for a time banned by Franco's government. Nobel Prize for Literature 1977.

Alexandria, School of group of writers and scholars of Alexandria who made the city the chief centre of culture in the Western world from about 331 BC to AD 642. They include the poets Callimachus, Apollonius of Rhodes, and Theocritus; Euclid, pioneer of geometry; Eratosthenes, the geographer; Hipparchus, who developed a system of trigonometry; the astronomer Ptolemy, who gave his name to the

Ptolemaic system of astronomy that endured for over 1,000 years; and the Jewish philosopher Philo. The Gnostics and Neo-Platonists also flourished in Alexandria.

alexandrine a 12-syllable line of verse known to date from the 12th century, and used for almost all French poetry from the 16th century. It has been variously divided into two groups of six syllables (usually in English poetry) or three groups of four syllables (usually in French poetry).

Alexandros in Greek legend, an alternative name for ◊Paris.

Alfieri Vittorio, Count Alfieri 1749–1803. Italian dramatist. The most successful of his 28 plays, most of them tragedies, are *Saul* 1782 and *Mirra* 1786. He is now best remembered for his *Autobiography* 1790, 1803. His works played an important role in the development of Italian nationalism.

Algardi Alessandro *c.* 1598–1654. Italian Baroque sculptor, active in Bologna, Rome, and at the papal court. His major works include the tomb of Pope Leo XI 1634–44 and *Pope Leo driving Attila from Rome* 1646–53, both in St Peter's, Rome.

Although Algardi's work is more restrained than that of his contemporary and rival Bernini, it is wholly Baroque in style, with figures often contorted and full of movement. He was an outstanding portrait sculptor, and it is for these busts, for example *St Philip Neri* 1640 (Sta Maria Vallicella, Rome), that he is now best remembered.

Alger Horatio 1832–1899. US writer of children's books. He wrote over 100 didactic moral tales in which the heroes rise from poverty to riches through hard work, luck, and good deeds, including the series 'Ragged Dick' from 1867 and 'Tattered Tom' from 1871.

It is estimated that his books sold more than 20 million copies. In US usage a 'Horatio Alger tale' has now come to mean any rags-to-riches story, often an implausible one.

Algren Nelson 1909–1981. US novelist. His best-known novel was *The Man with the Golden Arm* 1949 (filmed 1956), a story about gambling and drug addiction, which won the first National Book Award. Other works include two travel books, the prose-poem *Chicago: City on the Make* 1951, and the novel *A Walk on the Wild Side* 1956 (filmed 1962), set in a New Orleans brothel.

Alhambra fortified palace in Granada, Spain, built by Moorish kings, mainly between 1248 and 1354. It stands on a rocky hill and is a fine example of Moorish architecture.

Alice's Adventures in Wonderland children's story by Lewis ◊Carroll, published 1865. Alice dreams she follows the White Rabbit down a rabbit hole and meets fantastic characters such as the Cheshire Cat, the Mad Hatter, and the King and Queen of Hearts.

An Alice-in-Wonderland situation has come to mean an absurd or irrational situation, because of the dreamlike logic of Alice's adventures in the book. With its companion volume *Through the Looking-Glass* 1872, it is one of the most quoted works in the English language.

'If everybody minded their own business,'
said the Duchess in a hoarse growl, 'the
world would go round a deal faster than it
does.'

Lewis Carroll
Alice's Adventures in Wonderland 1865

Alkan pseudonym of Charles-Valentin Morhange 1813–1888. French piano virtuoso and composer whose formidably difficult piano pieces were neglected until the 1970s. Works include *Grande Sonate: Les quatre âges* 1848 and 12 *Etudes* in every minor key 1857.

Alken Henry Thomas 1785–1851. British sporting artist. Fox-hunting and steeplechasing were the subjects that most frequently occupied him, but the whole range of field sports was covered in his volume of 50 prints entitled *National Sports of Great Britain* 1820.

Allan David 1744–1796. Scottish history painter, director of the Academy of Arts in Edinburgh from 1786. He is also known for portraits and for genre paintings such as *Scotch Wedding*, which earned him the title 'the Scottish Hogarth'.

Allan William 1782–1850. Scottish history painter. Born in Edinburgh, he spent several years in Russia and travelled widely in Europe and the Middle East, returning to Edinburgh 1814. He was elected president of the Royal Scottish Academy 1838. His paintings include scenes from Walter Scott's Waverley novels.

allegory in literature, the description or illustration of one thing in terms of another; a work of poetry or prose in the form of an extended metaphor or fable that makes use of symbolic fictional characters.

An example of the use of symbolic fictional character in allegory is the romantic epic *The Faerie Queene* 1590–96 by Edmund Spenser in homage to Queen Elizabeth I. Allegory is often used for moral purposes, as in John Bunyan's *Pilgrim's Progress* 1678. Medieval allegory often used animals as characters; this tradition survives in such works as *Animal Farm* 1945 by George Orwell.

Allegri Gregorio 1582–1652. Italian Baroque composer, maestro di cappella of the Sistine

Chapel, Rome, 1610–29. His output of sacred music includes Magnificats, motets, and the celebrated *Miserere mei* (Psalm 51) for nine voices famously transcribed from memory by Mozart at the age of 14.

allegro in music, a lively or quick passage, movement, or composition.

allemande medium-paced dance in four time, with an upbeat, in two symmetrical sections; the music forms part of a classical ◊suite.

Allen (William) Hervey 1889–1949. US novelist, poet, and biographer. He is best known for his historical novel *Anthony Adverse* 1933, set in the Napoleonic era, and for his biography of Edgar Allen Poe, *Israfel* 1926.

Allen Woody. Adopted name of Allen Stewart Konigsberg 1935– . US film writer, director, and actor, known for his cynical, witty, often self-deprecating parody and offbeat humour. His film *Annie Hall* 1977 won him three Academy Awards.

His other films include *Sleeper* 1973, *Manhattan* 1979, and *Hannah and Her Sisters* 1986, all of which he directed, wrote, and appeared in. From the late 1970s, Allen mixed his output of comedies with straight dramas, such as *Interiors* 1978 and *Another Woman* 1988, while *Crimes and Misdemeanors* 1990 combined humour and straight drama.

Bisexuality immediately doubles your chances of a date on Saturday night.

Woody Allen
New York Herald Tribune 1975

Allende Isabel 1942– . Chilean novelist, one of the leading exponents of ◊magic realism. After the assassination 1973 of her uncle, Chile's socialist president Salvador Allende, exile in Venezuela released memories of family and country which emerged in her first novel *La casa de los espíritos/The House of the Spirits* 1982, now filmed in English. Her later novels *De amor y de sombra/Of Love and Shadows* 1984 and *Eva Luna* 1987 combine fantasy with the 'real' worlds of investigative journalism, filmmaking, and politics. She has also published short stories and children's books.

Allingham Margery (Louise) 1904–1966. English detective novelist, creator of detective Albert Campion, as in *More Work for the Undertaker* 1949. Her detective fiction displays great wit and ingenuity and includes *Tiger in the Smoke* 1952 and *Crime at Black Dudley* 1928.

alliteration in poetry and prose, the use, within a line or phrase, of words beginning with the same sound, as in 'Two tired toads trotting to

Tewkesbury'. It was a common device in Old English poetry, and its use survives in many traditional phrases, such as *dead as a doornail, pretty as a picture.*

Allston Washington 1779–1843. US painter of sea- and landscapes, a pioneer of the Romantic movement in the USA. His handling of light and colour earned him the title 'the American Titian'. He also painted classical, religious, and historical subjects.

He travelled widely in Europe, making contact with the poets Coleridge and Wordsworth. After settling back in the USA, he produced poetic, moody, and visionary scenes, such as *The Moonlight Landscape* 1819 (Museum of Fine Arts, Boston).

The love of gain has never made a painter, but it has marred many.

Washington Allston *Lectures on Art* 1850

Allyson June. Stage name of Ella Geisman 1917– . US film actress, popular in musicals and straight drama in the 1940s and 1950s. Her work includes *Music for Millions* 1945, *The Three Musketeers* 1948, and *The Glenn Miller Story* 1954.

Almagest book compiled by the Greek astronomer Ptolemy during the 2nd century AD, which included the idea of an Earth-centred universe; it was translated into Arabic. Some medieval books on astronomy, astrology, and alchemy were given the same title.

Alma-Tadema Lawrence 1836–1912. Dutch painter who settled in the UK 1870. He painted romantic, idealized scenes from ancient Greek, Roman, and Egyptian life in a distinctive, detailed style.

Alonso Alicia 1921– . Cuban ballerina and director. Purely classical in style, her most famous role was Giselle 1959. She became prima ballerina and director of the National Ballet of Cuba 1959.

alpaca hair fibre of domestic animal similar to the llama, or fabric made from its very soft wool. The chief sources of alpaca wool are Peru and Bolivia.

alphorn wind instrument consisting of a straight wooden tube terminating in a conical endpiece with an upturned bell, sometimes up to 4 m/12 ft in length. It is used to summon cattle and serenade tourists in the highlands of central Europe.

Alston Richard 1948– . English choreographer whose modernist style concentrates on light, speedy, lyrical movements. After studying with Merce ◊Cunningham in New York, he returned to England to become the Ballet Rambert's resident choreographer 1980–86. Among his pieces are *Bell High* 1980, *Sacre du printemps* 1981, and *Midsummer* 1983. He was artistic director of the Rambert Dance Company 1986–92.

Altamira caves decorated with Palaeolithic wall paintings, the first such to be discovered, 1879. The paintings are realistic depictions of bison, deer, and horses in polychrome (several colours). The caves are near the village of Santillana del Mar in Santander province, N Spain; other well-known Palaeolithic cave paintings are in ◊Lascaux, SW France.

altarpiece a painting (more rarely a sculpture) placed on, behind, or above an altar in a Christian church. Altarpieces vary greatly in size, construction, and number of images (◊diptych, ◊triptych, and ◊polyptych). Some are small and portable; some (known as a **retable** or **reredos**, there is no clear distinction) are fixed.

A typical Italian altarpiece has a large central panel, flanked by subsidiary panels, with a **predella**, or strip of scenes, across the bottom. Spanish altarpieces tend to have architecturally elaborate retables. A popular form in northern Europe was the **winged altarpiece**, in which outer wings are hinged so that they can be closed to cover the central panel. Outstanding altarpieces include Duccio's *Maestà* 1308–11 (Cathedral Museum, Siena), Grünewald's *Isenheim Altarpiece* 1515 (Unterlinden Museum, Colmar), and van Eyck's *Adoration of the Mystical Lamb* 1432 (St Bavon, Ghent). Few altarpieces survived the Reformation in Britain.

Altdorfer Albrecht *c.* 1480–1538. German painter and printmaker, active in Regensburg, Bavaria. He is best known for his vast panoramic battle scenes in which his use of light creates movement and drama. On a smaller scale, he also painted some of the first true landscapes (see ◊landscape painting).

With Albrecht Dürer and Lucas Cranach, Altdorfer is regarded as one of the leaders of the German Renaissance. *St George and the Dragon* 1510 (Alte Pinakothek, Munich) is an example of his landscape style; *The Battle of Issus* 1529 (also Munich) is a dramatic panorama.

Altman Robert 1925– . US film director. His antiwar comedy *M.A.S.H.* 1970 was a critical and commercial success; subsequent films include *McCabe and Mrs Miller* 1971, *The Long Goodbye* 1973, *Nashville* 1975, *Popeye* 1980, and *Come Back to the 5 & Dime, Jimmy Dean, Jimmy Dean* 1982. His satire on Hollywood's movers and shakers, *The Player* 1992, marked a return to form.

alto voice or instrument between tenor and soprano, of approximate range G3–D5. The traditional male alto voice of early opera, as revived by English singer James Bowman (1941–), also known as **countertenor**, is trumpetlike and penetrating; the low-register female **contralto**

('contra-alto'), exemplified by Kathleen ◊Ferrier, is rich and mellow in tone. Alto is also the French name for the ◊viola.

Alvárez Quintero Serafin 1871–1938 and Joaquín 1873–1945. Spanish dramatists. The brothers, born near Seville, always worked together and from 1897 produced some 200 comedies, principally dealing with local life in Andalusia. Among them are *Papá Juan: Centenario* 1909 and *Los Mosquitos* 1928.

Alwyn William 1905–1985. British composer. Professor of composition at the Royal Academy of Music 1926–55, he wrote film music (*Desert Victory, The Way Ahead*) and composed symphonies and chamber music.

Amaterasu in Japanese mythology, the sun-goddess, grandmother of Jimmu Tenno, first ruler of Japan, from whom the emperors claim to be descended.

Amati Italian family of violinmakers, who worked in Cremona, about 1550–1700. *Nicolò Amati* (1596–1684) taught Andrea ◊Guarneri and Antonio ◊Stradivari. Nicolò's grandfather Andrea (*c.* 1520–*c.* 1580) brought the violin to its classic form.

Amaya Carmen 1913–1963. Spanish Romany dancer whose inspired, fiery, and passionate style made her popular especially in Argentina. One of a family of dancers, she performed in public from the age of seven and toured the world in the following years.

Amazon in Greek legend, a member of a group of female warriors living near the Black Sea, who cut off their right breasts to use the bow more easily. Their queen, Penthesilea, was killed by Achilles at the siege of Troy. The term Amazon has come to mean a large, strong woman.

The Amazons attacked ◊Theseus and besieged him at Athens, but were defeated, and Theseus took the Amazon Hippolyta captive; she later gave birth to ◊Hippolytus.

Ambler Eric 1909– . English novelist. He excelled in suspense novels involving international intrigue. He used Balkan/Levant settings in the thrillers *The Mask of Dimitrios* 1939 and *Journey into Fear* 1940. His other books include *The Care of Time* 1981.

Amboise Jacques d' 1934– . US dancer who created roles in many of George ◊Balanchine's greatest works as a principal dancer with New York City Ballet. He also appeared in films and TV productions, including *Seven Brides for Seven Brothers* 1954.

ambrosia (Greek 'immortal') in Greek mythology, food of the gods which was supposed to confer eternal life upon all who ate it.

Ambrosian chant in Christian church music, reformed chant introduced by St Ambrose in the

4th century. The number of available modes (scales) was reduced to four; the interval of the fifth was established as the basis of tonal music, having a lower key note, from which the chant rose and to which it returned; and a higher dominant was established at the fifth, around which the chant was elaborated. Ambrosian chant retains many features of Middle Eastern religious chant.

American Ballet Theater (ABT) US company founded 1939 (as Ballet Theater), aiming to present both classical and contemporary American ballet. ABT has a repertoire of exemplary range and quality with celebrity guest appearances. Based in New York, the company tours annually, and is considered one of the top six ballet companies in the world.

Among ABT's first ballerinas were Alicia Markova and Alicia Alonso. In the 1970s ABT opened its doors to the Soviet dancers who defected to the West, such as Rudolf Nureyev, Natalia Makarova, and Mikhail Baryshnikov (artistic director 1980–90).

American literature see ◊United States literature.

Amies (Edwin) Hardy 1909– . English couturier, noted for his tailored clothes for women and menswear designs. He was formerly one of Queen Elizabeth II's dressmakers.

He began working at Lachasse 1934 where he became manager and designer, before opening his own house 1946. During World War II he contributed to the Utility scheme, creating ingenious and elegant clothes that coped with the wartime fabric restrictions. In 1950 he opened a ready-to-wear boutique and was awarded a royal warrant 1955. In 1961 he became linked with Hepworths and is now known mainly as a designer of menswear.

Amis Kingsley 1922– . English novelist and poet, early associated with the ◊Angry Young Men group of writers. A writer of sharply ironic works, which frequently debunk pretentious mediocrity, his first novel, the best-selling ◊Lucky Jim 1954, is a comic portrayal of life in a provincial university. His later novels include The Alteration 1976, which imagines a 20th-century society dominated by the Catholic Church. He is the father of writer Martin Amis.

It was no wonder that people were so horrible when they started life as children.

Kingsley Amis *Lucky Jim* 1954

His other novels, written in a variety of genres, include The Riverside Villas Murder 1937, the spy story The Anti-Death League 1966, and the ghost story The Green Man 1969. His fascination with middle-aged sexuality is demonstrated in such novels as Stanley and the Women 1984 and The

Old Devils 1986 (Booker Prize). His poetry includes A Case of Samples: Poems 1946–56 1956 and Collected Poems 1944–79 1979.

Amis Martin 1949– . English novelist. His works are characterized by their acerbic black humour and include The Rachel Papers 1973, a memoir of adolescence told through flashbacks, Dead Babies 1975, which addresses decadence and sadism, Money 1984, London Fields 1989, and Time's Arrow 1991.

Ammanati Bartolommeo 1511–1592. Italian Mannerist sculptor and architect, influenced by Michelangelo and Andrea Sansovino (c. 1467–1529). His most noted sculpture is the Fountain of Neptune in the Piazza della Signoria, Florence 1560–75. He built the rusticated garden façade of the Palazzo Pitti 1560, Florence, and the graceful bridge of Sta Trinità, Florence, completed 1570 (destroyed 1944 but rebuilt). Ammanati rivalled Vasari as a Mannerist architect.

Ammianus Marcellinus 4th century. Roman soldier and historian. The surviving books of his work, dealing with contemporary affairs in the later Roman Empire, rank him as the last major Roman historian.

Ammon in Egyptian mythology, the king of the gods, the equivalent of Zeus (Roman Jupiter). The name is also spelled Amen/Amun, as in the name of the pharaoh Tutankhamen. In art, he is represented as a ram, as a man with a ram's head, or as a man crowned with feathers. He had temples at Siwa oasis, Libya, and at Thebes, Egypt; his oracle at Siwa was patronised by the classical Greeks.

Amphiaraus in Greek mythology, a visionary from Argos who foresaw his own death in the expedition of the ◊Seven against Thebes. An oracle bearing his name existed in antiquity at Oropos, near Thebes.

Amphion in Greek mythology, one of the two sons of Zeus and ◊Antiope. He built the walls of Thebes by drawing the stones into place with the music from his lyre, a gift from the god ◊Hermes.

amphitheatre (Greek *amphi* 'around') large oval or circular building used by the Romans for gladiatorial contests, fights of wild animals, and other similar events. It is an open structure with a central arena surrounded by rising rows of seats. The ◊Colosseum in Rome, completed AD 80, held 50,000 spectators.

Amphitrite in Greek mythology, one of the daughters of the sea god Nereus and wife of the god ◊Poseidon.

Amphitryon in Greek mythology, a king of Thebes and the husband of ◊Alcmene. Alcmene was seduced by Zeus (who took the form of Amphitryon) and gave birth to ◊Heracles.

Anacreon 6th century BC. Greek lyric poet, who lived in Abdera, Samos, and Athens, where he was favoured both before and after the institution of democracy. His love poetry, of great charm, was later widely imitated in verse known as the *Anacreontics*.

analects or **analecta** any collection of literary fragments taken from one or more sources. More specifically, the *Analects* are a selection of writings by the Chinese philosopher ◊Confucius and his followers, the most important of the four books containing the teachings of Confucianism.

Anchises in classical mythology, a member of the Trojan royal family, loved by the goddess ◊Aphrodite. Their son ◊Aeneas rescued his father on the fall of ◊Troy and carried him from the burning city on his shoulders. The story forms an episode in Virgil's *Aeneid*; in a further episode, Anchises reveals the future greatness of Rome to Aeneas during his son's visit to the underworld.

Ancient Mariner, The Rime of the poem by Samuel Taylor Coleridge, published 1798, describing the curse that falls upon a mariner and his ship when he shoots an albatross.

andante in music, a passage or movement to be performed at a walking pace; that is, at a moderately slow tempo.

Andersen Hans Christian 1805–1875. Danish writer of fairy tales, such as *The Ugly Duckling*, *The Snow Queen*, *The Little Mermaid*, and *The Emperor's New Clothes*. Their inventiveness, sensitivity, and strong sense of wonder have given these stories perennial and universal appeal; they have been translated into many languages. He also wrote adult novels and travel books.

Andersen was born the son of a shoemaker in Odense. His first children's stories were published 1835. Some are based on folklore; others are original. His other works include the novel *The Improvisatore* 1845, romances, and an autobiography *Mit Livs Eventyr* 1855 (translated 1954 as *The Tale of My Life*).

'But the Emperor has nothing on at all!' cried a little child.

Hans Christian Andersen
The Emperor's New Clothes

Anderson Marian 1902– . US contralto whose voice was remarkable for its range and richness. She toured Europe 1930, but in 1939 she was barred from singing at Constitution Hall, Washington, DC, because she was black. In 1955 she sang at the Metropolitan Opera, the first black singer to appear there. In 1958 she was appointed an alternate (deputizing) delegate to the United Nations.

Anderson Maxwell 1888–1959. US dramatist, noted for *What Price Glory?* 1924, a realistic portrayal of the American soldier in action during World War I, co-written with Laurence Stallings. He won a Pulitzer Prize for his comedic prose satire *Both Your Houses* 1933. Most of his plays had moral and social problems as themes.

Anderson wrote numerous other plays, many in the form of verse tragedies, including *Elizabeth the Queen* 1930, *Winterset* 1935, and *Anne of the Thousand Days* 1948.

Anderson Sherwood 1876–1941. US short-story writer and novelist. He is best known for his sensitive, poetic, and experimental naturalism, dealing with the desperation of small-town Midwestern life. His most highly acclaimed work is the story-cycle of *Winesburg, Ohio* 1919; other works include the novel *Dark Laughter* 1925 and the collection of short stories *Death in the Woods* 1933.

I found it impossible to work with security staring me in the face.

Sherwood Anderson to his publisher, on declining a weekly cheque.

Andō Tadao 1941– . Japanese architect whose work employs vernacular materials and styles alongside Modernist techniques. His design for Azuma House in Osaka, Japan 1975, one in a series of private houses, combines an austere, fortresslike façade with a minutely detailed interior. Materials, such as timber and concrete, are sensitively used, continuing the traditions of Japanese domestic architecture.

Andre Carl 1935– . US Minimalist sculptor, best-known for his use of industrial materials. His *Equivalent VIII* 1976 (Tate Gallery, London), in which 120 bricks were stacked in two layers to form a mathematically devised rectangle, caused a public outcry because it seemed to mock the traditional values of creativity and workmanship in art. Andre also pioneered ◊earthworks.

Andrea del Sarto (Andrea d'Agnola di Francesco) 1486–1530. Italian Renaissance painter active in Florence, one of the finest portraitists and religious painters of his time. His frescoes in Florence, such as the *Birth of the Virgin* 1514 (Sta Annunziata), rank among the greatest of the Renaissance. His style is serene and noble, characteristic of High Renaissance art.

Del Sarto trained under Piero de Cosimo and others but was chiefly influenced by ◊Masaccio and ◊Michelangelo. He was the foremost painter in Florence after about 1510, along with Fra Bartolommeo, although he was gradually superseded by the emerging Mannerists during the 1520s. Apart from portraits, such as *A Young Man* (National Gallery, London), he painted many religious works, including the *Madonna of the Harpies* 1517 (Uffizi, Florence), an example of Classical beauty reminiscent of Raphael. His celebrated frescoes are at Sta Annunziata and the Chiostro dello Scalzo, both in Florence.

Andress Ursula 1936– . Swiss actress specializing in glamour leads. Her international career started with *Dr No* 1962. Other films include *She* 1965, *Casino Royale* 1967, *Red Sun* 1971, and *Clash of the Titans* 1981.

Andrews Julie. Stage name of Julia Elizabeth Wells 1935– . British-born US actress and singer. A child performer with her mother and stepfather in British music halls, she first appeared in the USA in the Broadway production *The Boy Friend* 1954. She was the original Eliza Doolittle in the Broadway production of *My Fair Lady* 1956. In 1960 she appeared in Lerner and Loewe's *Camelot* on Broadway. Her films include *Mary Poppins* 1964, *The Sound of Music* 1965, *'10'* 1979, and *Victor/Victoria* 1982.

Andreyev Leonid Nicolaievich 1871–1919. Russian author. Many of his works show an obsession with death and madness, including the symbolic drama *Life of Man* 1907, the melodrama *He Who Gets Slapped* 1915, and the novels *Red Laugh* 1904 and *S.O.S.* 1919 published in Finland, where he fled after the Russian Revolution.

Andrič Ivo 1892–1974. Yugoslav novelist and nationalist. He became a diplomat, and was ambassador to Berlin 1940. *The Bridge on the Drina* 1945 is an epic history of a small Bosnian town. Nobel prize 1961.

He was a member of the Young Bosnia organization (another member of which shot the heir to the Austrian throne 1914), and spent World War I in an internment camp because of his political views.

Androcles traditionally, a Roman slave who fled from a cruel master into the African desert, where he met a crippled lion and pulled a thorn from its paw. The lion later recognized the recaptured slave in the arena and spared his life. The emperor Tiberius was said to have freed them both.

Andromache in Greek legend, the loyal wife of ◊Hector and mother of ◊Astyanax. After the fall of Troy she was awarded to Neoptolemus, Achilles' son; she later married a Trojan seer called Helenus. Andromache is the heroine of Homer's *Iliad* and the subject of a play by ◊Euripides.

Andromache tragedy by ◊Euripides, of uncertain date. Hermione, wife of Neoptolemus, seeks revenge on Andromache, her husband's lover, whom she blames for her own childlessness, but fails in her attempt to kill Andromache and her son. Neoptolemus is murdered by Orestes, a former suitor of Hermione.

Andromeda in Greek mythology, an Ethiopian princess chained to a rock as a sacrifice to a sea monster. She was rescued by ◊Perseus, who married her.

Aneirin 6th century. Welsh poet. He wrote the core of the epic poem *Y Gododdin c.* 600, one of the earliest known poems in Welsh. It describes a battle at Catraeth (Catterick) where the British tribe from Dun Edin (Edinburgh) were heavily defeated by the Northumbrians.

Angelico Fra (Guido di Pietro) *c.* 1400–1455. Italian painter of religious scenes, active in Florence. He was a monk and painted a series of frescoes at the monastery of San Marco, Florence, begun after 1436. He also produced several altarpieces in a style characterized by a delicacy of line and colour.

Fra Angelico joined the Dominican order about 1420. After his novitiate, he resumed a career as a painter of religious images and altarpieces, many of which have small predella scenes beneath them, depicting events in the life of a saint. The central images of the paintings are highly decorated with pure, bright colours and gold-leaf designs, while the predella scenes are often lively and relatively unsophisticated. There is a similar simplicity to his frescoes in the cells at San Marco, which are principally devotional works. Fra Angelico's later fresco sequences, such as *Scenes from the Life of Christ* (Orvieto Cathedral), are more elaborate.

If you have the courage to love, you survive.

Maya Angelou *Observer* Aug 1987

Angelou Maya (born Marguerite Johnson) 1928– . US writer and black activist. She became noted for her powerful autobiographical works, *I Know Why the Caged Bird Sings* 1970 and its four sequels up to *All God's Children Need Travelling Shoes* 1986. Based on her traumatic childhood, they tell of the struggles towards physical and spiritual liberation of a black woman from growing up in the South to emigrating to Ghana.

Lucifer is the patron saint of the visual arts. Colour, form – all these are the work of Lucifer.

Kenneth Anger *The Independent* Jan 1990

Anger Kenneth 1929– . US avant-garde filmmaker, brought up in Hollywood. His films, which dispense with conventional narrative, often use homosexual iconography and a personal form of mysticism. They include *Fireworks* 1947, *Scorpio Rising* 1964, and *Lucifer Rising* 1973. He wrote the exposé *Hollywood Babylon*, the original version of which was published in France 1959.

Anglo-Saxon art English art from the late 5th to the 11th century. Sculpted crosses and ivories, manuscript painting, and gold and enamel jewellery survive, all showing a love of intricate, interwoven designs. The relics of the Sutton Hoo ship burial, 7th century, and the *Lindisfarne Gospels*, about 690 (both British Museum, London) have typical Celtic ornamental patterns. In the manuscripts of southern England, in particular those produced at Winchester and Canterbury, a different style emerged in the 9th century, with delicate, lively pen-and-ink figures and heavily decorative foliage borders.

Anglo-Saxon art was influenced by the Celtic arts of the native Britons, by Roman influences brought by the Christian church, and by Norse arts following the Viking invasions of the 8th century.

Anglo-Saxon Chronicle history of England from the Roman invasion to the 11th century, in the form of a series of chronicles written in Old English by monks, begun in the 9th century (during the reign of King Alfred), and continuing to the 12th century.

The Chronicle, comprising seven different manuscripts, forms a unique record of early English history and of the development of Old English prose up to its final stages in the year 1154, by which date it had been superseded by Middle English.

Anglo-Saxon literature another name for ◊Old English literature.

Angora earlier form of Ankara, ancient city and capital of Turkey, which gave its name to the Angora goat (see ◊mohair), and hence to other species of long-haired animal, such as the Angora rabbit (a native of the island of Madeira) and the Angora cat. Angora 'wool' from these animals has long, smooth fibres, and the demand for the fibre has led to wool farming in Europe, Japan, and the USA.

I was never an Angry Young Man. I am angry only when I hit my thumb with a hammer.

Kingsley Amis on the labelling of authors as 'Angry Young Men' *Eton College Chronicle* 1979

Angry Young Men journalistic term applied to a loose group of British writers of the 1950s and 1960s who expressed dissatisfaction with the prevailing social mores, class distinction, and 'good taste'. It was typified by such works as John Osborne's *Look Back in Anger* 1956, Kingsley Amis' *Lucky Jim* 1954, Colin Wilson's *The*

Outsider 1956, John Braine's *Room at the Top* 1957, and John Wain's *Hurry on Down* 1953. Also linked to the group was theatre critic Kenneth Tynan.

Angst (German 'anxiety') an emotional state of anxiety without a specific cause. In ◊existentialism, the term refers to general human anxiety at having free will, that is, of being responsible for one's actions.

Animal Farm novel 1945 by George ◊Orwell. In this political fable, based on the Russian Revolution, farm animals, led by the pigs Snowball and Napoleon, eject their human exploiters and try to turn their farm into a Utopia. The enterprise fails because of corruption and weakness from within and the leaders end up masquerading as humans. Written in stark, simple prose, it is perhaps the most widely read of Orwell's novels.

Man is the only animal that consumes without producing.

George Orwell *Animal Farm* 1945

Anna Karenina novel by Leo ◊Tolstoy, published 1873–77. It describes a married woman's love affair with Vronski, a young officer, which ends with her suicide.

Annigoni Pietro 1910–1988. Italian painter. He is best known as a portrait painter, his style strongly influenced by Italian Renaissance portraiture. His sitters included John F Kennedy 1961 and Queen Elizabeth II 1955 (National Portrait Gallery, London).

Anouilh Jean 1910–1987. French dramatist. His plays, which are often studies in the contrast between purity and cynical worldliness, include *Antigone* 1944, *L'Invitation au château/Ring Round the Moon* 1947, *Colombe* 1950, and *Becket* 1959, about St Thomas à Becket and Henry II.

Nobody has a more sacred obligation to obey the law than those who make the law.

Jean Anouilh *Antigone* 1944

Ansermet Ernest 1883–1969. Swiss conductor with Diaghilev's Russian Ballet 1915–23. In 1918 he founded the Swiss Romande Orchestra, conducting many first performances of works by Stravinsky.

Antheil George 1900–1959. US composer and pianist, the son of a Polish political exile. He is known for his *Ballet mécanique* 1926, scored for anvils, aeroplane propellers, electric bells, car horns, and pianos.

anthem in music, a short, usually elaborate, religious choral composition, sometimes accompanied by the organ; also a song of loyalty and devotion. Composers of anthems include Byrd, Gibbons, Purcell, Blow, and Handel.

anthology (Greek 'bouquet') collection of verse by various authors, particularly of shorter poems such as epigrams. The earliest known of these is the *Greek Anthology*, which includes a shorter collection by ◊Meleager, known as the *Garland*.

Anthony John 1938– . US fashion designer with his own business from 1971, noted for cardigans, trousers, and evening dresses in satin and sheer wool. He designs for the top end of ready-to-wear fashion, using only natural fabrics. He also designs a menswear collection.

anthropomorphism the attribution of human characteristics to animals, inanimate objects, or deities. It appears in the mythologies of many cultures and as a literary device in fables and allegories.

anti-art in the visual arts, work that is exhibited in a conventional context but makes fun of serious art or challenges the nature of art; it is characteristic of ◊Dada. Marcel Duchamp is credited with introducing the term *c*. 1914, and its spirit is summed up in his attempt to exhibit a urinal (*Fountain* 1917). The term is also used to describe other intentionally provocative art forms.

Antigone in Greek mythology, a daughter of Jocasta, by her son ◊Oedipus. She is the subject of a tragedy by ◊Sophocles.

Antigone tragedy by ◊Sophocles, thought to have been written about 443 BC. Antigone buries her brother Polynices, in defiance of the Theban king Creon, who imprisons her in a cave. Persuaded by the visionary ◊Tiresias to change his mind, Creon finds Antigone has hanged herself. He then learns of the suicide of his son, Haemon, who was to marry Antigone.

None love the messenger who brings bad news.

Sophocles *Antigone c.* 443 BC

Antiope in Greek legend, mother of the twins ◊Amphion and Zethus, whose father was Zeus. She was imprisoned by the tyrant Lycus and his wife Dirce, and freed by her sons, who punished Dirce by tying her to a bull. The scene is represented in a classical marble group, the Farnese Bull, rediscovered in the Renaissance.

antiphon choral music in Greek or Roman liturgy involving the exchange of responses between solo voice and choir, or between choral groups, hence antiphony.

antiphony music exploiting directional and canonic opposition of widely spaced choirs or groups of instruments to create perspectives in sound. It was developed in 17th-century Venice by Giovanni ◊Gabrieli and in Germany by his pupil Heinrich Schütz and Roland de Lassus; an example is the double choir motet *Alma Redemptoris Mater* 1604. The practice was revived in the 20th century by Bartók, Stockhausen, and Berio.

Antipodean Group group of seven Australian figurative artists who maintained Australian themes in their work in preference to international styles of abstract art. Members of the group included Arthur ◊Boyd, his brother David Boyd (1924–), brother-in-law John Perceval (1923–), Robert Dickerson (1924–), Clifton Pugh (1924–), Charles ◊Blackman, and John Brack (1920–). The group held its only exhibition 1959.

antithesis the balancing of two contrasting ideas, usually in the same sentence. For example: 'People with young children often long for peace and quiet; people with peace and quiet often long for children.'

Antoine André 1858–1943. French theatre director. Founder of the Théâtre Libre 1887, he introduced to France the work of international dramatists such as Ibsen (*Ghosts*, performed there 1890) and Strindberg (*Miss Julie*, 1893). He resigned from the company in 1894, but returned to directing 1896–1916.

Antonello da Messina *c.* 1430–1479. Italian painter, born in Messina, Sicily. He was a pioneer in his country of the technique of oil painting, which had been developed by Flemish artists; he probably acquired his knowledge of it in Naples. Flemish influence is reflected in his brushwork, his use of light, and sometimes in his imagery, although his sense of structure is entirely Italian. Surviving works include bust-length portraits and sombre religious paintings.

He visited Venice in the 1470s where his work inspired, among others, the young Giovanni Bellini. His paintings include *St Jerome in His Study* about 1460 (National Gallery, London) and *A Young Man* 1478 (Staatliche Museen, Berlin).

Antonio stage name of Antonio Ruiz Soler 1922– . Spanish dancer, choreographer, and director who toured the world with his partner, Rosario. He established a National Ballet Company 1953, choreographing in a blend of classical ballet and Spanish dance, but is remembered primarily for his mesmerizing personality and dazzling technique as a soloist in pure Spanish dance.

Antonioni Michelangelo 1912– . Italian film director, famous for his subtle presentations of neuroses and personal relationships among the leisured classes. His elliptical approach to narrative is best seen in *L'Avventura* 1960.

Beginning his career making documentaries, Antonioni directed his first feature film, *Cronica di un Amore/Story of a Love Affair* 1950. His other films include *Blow-Up* 1966, *Zabriskie Point* 1970, and *The Passenger* 1975.

Antony and Cleopatra tragedy by William Shakespeare, written and first performed 1607–08. Mark Antony falls in love with the Egyptian queen Cleopatra in Alexandria, but returns to Rome when his wife, Fulvia, dies. He then marries Octavia to heal the rift between her brother Augustus Caesar and himself. Antony returns to Egypt and Cleopatra, but is finally defeated by Augustus. Believing Cleopatra dead, Antony kills himself, and Cleopatra takes her own life rather than surrender to Augustus.

Give me my robe, put on my crown; I have/ Immortal longings in me.

Shakespeare *Antony and Cleopatra* 1607 – 08

Anu Mesopotamian sky god, commonly joined in a trinity with Enlil, the god of storms, and Ea, the god of water.

Anubis in Egyptian mythology, the jackal-headed god of the dead, son of Osiris. Anubis presided over the funeral cult, including embalming, and led the dead to judgement.

Apelles 4th century BC. Greek painter, said to have been the greatest in antiquity. He was court painter to Philip of Macedon and to his son Alexander the Great. None of his work survives, only descriptions of it and Roman copies.

aperture in photography, an opening in the camera that allows light to pass through the lens to strike the film. Controlled by shutter speed and the iris diaphragm, it can be set mechanically or electronically at various diameters.

Aphrodite in Greek mythology, the goddess of love (Roman Venus, Phoenician Astarte, Babylonian Ishtar); said to be either a daughter of Zeus (in Homer) or sprung from the foam of the sea (in Hesiod). She was the unfaithful wife of Hephaestus, the god of fire, and the mother of Eros.

Apollinaire Guillaume. Pen name of Guillaume Apollinaire de Kostrowitsky 1880–1918. French poet of aristocratic Polish descent. He was a leader of the avant-garde in Parisian literary and artistic circles. His novel *Le Poète assassiné/The Poet Assassinated* 1916, followed by the experimental poems *Alcools/Alcohols* 1913 and *Calligrammes/Word Pictures* 1918, show him as a representative of the Cubist and Futurist movements.

Born in Rome and educated in Monaco, Apollinaire went to Paris 1898. His work greatly influenced younger French writers, such as Louis ◊Aragon. He coined the term *Surrealism* to describe his play *Les Mamelles de Tirésias/The Breasts of Tiresias* 1917.

Memories are hunting horns whose sound dies on the wind.

Guillaume Apollinaire *'Cors de Chasse'*

Apollo in Greek and Roman mythology, the god of sun, music, poetry, prophecy, agriculture, and pastoral life, and leader of the Muses. He was the twin child (with ◊Artemis) of Zeus and Leto. Ancient statues show Apollo as the embodiment of the Greek ideal of male beauty. His chief cult centres were his supposed birthplace on the island of Delos, in the Cyclades, and Delphi.

Apollonius of Rhodes lived 3rd century BC. Greek poet, author of the epic *Argonautica* which tells the story of Jason and the Argonauts and their quest for the Golden Fleece. A pupil of ◊Callimachus, he was for a time head of the library at Alexandria.

Appel Karel 1921– . Dutch painter and sculptor, founder of the Expressionist group ◊Cobra 1948. His style employed vivid colours and vigorous brushwork, with often childlike imagery.

Appia Adolphe 1862–1928. Swiss stage designer and theorist. A proponent of 'symbolic design', he advocated reducing the importance of the actor as well as developing the atmospheric use of colour, movement, and lighting. His theories were expressed in *Die Musik und die Inszenierung/Music and Staging 1899*.

'Appleseed', Johnny. US folk hero; see John ◊Chapman.

appliqué embroidery used to create pictures or patterns by 'applying' pieces of material to a background fabric. The pieces are cut into the appropriate shapes and sewn on, providing decoration for wall hangings, furnishing textiles, and clothes.

Apuleius Lucius lived 2nd century AD. Latin writer, the author of *The ◊Golden Ass*, or *Metamorphoses*, a prose fantasy which is the only surviving Latin novel.

aquatint printmaking technique. When combined with ◊etching it produces areas of subtle tone as well as more precisely etched lines. Aquatint became common in the late 18th century.

An etching plate is covered with a fine layer of

resin and then immersed in acid, which bites through the resin, causing tiny pits on the surface of the plate. When printed, a fine, grainy tone is apparent. Lighter tones are created by using acid-resistant varnishes, darker tones by longer exposure to the acid. Gainsborough experimented with aquatint but the first artist to become proficient in the technique was J B Le Prince (1733–1781). Goya, Degas, Pissarro, Picasso, and Rouault are among its finest exponents.

arabesque in ballet, a pose in which the dancer stands on one leg, straight or bent, with the other leg raised behind, fully extended. The arms are held in a harmonious position to give the longest possible line from fingertips to toes. It is one of the fundamental positions in ballet.

arabesque in the visual arts, a linear decoration based on plant forms. It is a feature of ancient Greek and Roman art and is particularly common in Islamic art (hence the term).

Arabian Nights tales in oral circulation among Arab storytellers from the 10th century, probably having their roots in India. They are also known as *The Thousand and One Nights* and include *Ali Baba*, *Aladdin*, *Sinbad the Sailor*, and *The Old Man of the Sea*.

They were supposed to have been told to the sultan by his bride Scheherazade to avoid the fate of her predecessors, who were all executed following the wedding night to prevent their infidelity. She began a new tale each evening, which she would only agree to finish on the following night. Eventually the 'sentence' was rescinded.

The first European translation 1704 was by the French writer Antoine Galland (1646–1715) 1704, although the stories were known earlier. The first English translations were by E W Lane 1838–40 and Richard Burton 1885–88.

Arachne in Greek mythology, a Lydian woman who was so skilful a weaver that she challenged the goddess ◊Athena to a contest. Athena tore Arachne's beautiful tapestries to pieces and Arachne hanged herself. She was transformed into a spider, and her weaving became a cobweb.

The function of genius is to furnish cretins with ideas twenty years later.

Louis Aragon
'Le Porte-Plume' *Traité du Style* 1928

Aragon Louis 1897–1982. French poet and novelist. Beginning as a Dadaist, he became one of the leaders of Surrealism, published volumes of verse, and in 1930 joined the Communist party. Taken prisoner in World War II, he escaped to join the Resistance; his experiences

are reflected in the poetry of *Le Crève-coeur* 1942 and *Les Yeux d'Elsa* 1944.

Arany János 1817–1882. Hungarian writer. His comic epic *The Lost Constitution* 1846 was followed in 1847 by *Toldi*, a product of the popular nationalist school.

In 1864 his epic masterpiece *The Death of King Buda* appeared. During his last years Arany produced the rest of the *Toldi* trilogy, and his most personal lyrics.

Ara Pacis elaborately sculpted altar in Rome, Italy, consecrated 13 BC to mark the return of the first Roman emperor Augustus from the western provinces of Spain and Gaul. Intended as a symbol of the new age of imperial rule, it stood in the Campus Martius, surrounded by a rectangular enclosure. Intricate relief sculpture, among the greatest artistic achievements of the Augustan era, pictured the act of consecration and the imperial family alongside scenes from Roman mythology.

Arbuckle Fatty (Roscoe Conkling) 1887–1933. US silent-film comedian; also a writer and director. His successful career in such films as *The Butcher Boy* 1917 and *The Hayseed* 1919 ended 1921 after a sex-party scandal in which a starlet died.

Arbus Diane 1923–1971. US photographer. Although she practised as a fashion photographer for 20 years, Arbus is best known for her later work which examined the fringes of American society: the misfits, the eccentrics, and the bizarre. Her work has been attacked as cruel and voyeuristic, but it is essentially sympathetic in its unflinching curiosity. *A Box of Ten Photographs*, a limited edition of her work, was published 1970.

Arbuthnot John 1667–1735. Scottish writer and physician, attendant on Queen Anne 1705–14. He was a friend of Alexander Pope, Thomas Gray, and Jonathan Swift and was the chief author of the satiric *Memoirs of Martinus Scriblerus*. He created the English national character of John Bull, a prosperous farmer, in his *History of John Bull* 1712, pamphlets advocating peace with France.

All political parties die at last of swallowing their own lies.

John Arbuthnot

arch in architecture, a curved structure that supports the weight of material over an open space, as in a bridge or doorway. The first arches consisted of several wedge-shaped stones supported by their mutual pressure. The term is also applied to any curved structure that is an arch in form only, such as the Arc de Triomphe, Paris 1806–36.

The Romans are credited with engineering the earliest round keystone arches, used for aqueducts. Other forms of arch include the pointed arch, the corbelled arch of the Maya Indians, the medieval lancet and ogee arches, and the Islamic horseshoe arch.

Archer Jeffrey 1940– . English writer and politician. A Conservative member of Parliament 1969–74, he lost a fortune in a disastrous investment, but recouped it as a best-selling novelist and dramatist. His books, which often concern the rise of insignificant characters to high political office or great business success, include *Not a Penny More, Not a Penny Less* 1975 and *First Among Equals* 1984.

One lesson a man learns in the Harvard Business School is that an executive is only as good as his health.

Jeffrey Archer
Not a Penny More, Not a Penny Less 1975

Archer Thomas 1668–1743. English architect noted for his interpretations of Italian Baroque, which he studied at first hand during a continental Grand Tour 1691–95. He was active 1703–15, after which he took up the post of Controller of Customs at Newcastle. Notable among his designs are the north front of Chatsworth House 1704–05, the church of St John, Smith Square, London 1714–28, and the cathedral of St Philip, Birmingham 1710–15.

archetype typical or perfect specimen of its kind. In the psychology of Jung, it refers to one of the basic roles or situations, received from the collective unconscious, in which people tend to cast themselves – the Hero, the Terrible Mother (stepmother, witch) – and the theme of death and rebirth. Archetypes are recurring motifs in myth, art, and literature.

The figure of the Wanderer condemned to roam the earth until released from a curse appears in the Greek legend of *Odysseus*, in the story of the Wandering Jew (told throughout Europe from the 16th century on), and in the hero of Wagner's opera *The Flying Dutchman*.

Archibald Prize in Australia, an art prize awarded annually since 1921 for an oil or watercolour portrait, generally of a public figure. It has at times been the centre of controversy, the most famous instance being the award of the 1943 prize to William ◊Dobell for his portrait of Joshua Smith. The prize was established under the will of Australian journalist Jules Archibald (1856–1919).

Archigram London-based group of English architects 1960–75 whose designs were experimental and polemical. Central to their philosophy was the belief that architecture should be technological, flexible, and disposable.

The group included Peter Cook (1936–), Dennis Crompton (1935–), David Greene (1937–), Ron Herron (1930–), and Mike Webb (1937–). Cook's concept of 'plug-in, clip-on' architecture was exemplified in Instant City, an idea for an airship that descended from the sky and rejuvenated a sleeping town. Herron designed a mobile 'walking city', 3 km/2 ml long.

Archilochus 7th century BC. Greek poet. Born in the island of Paros, he wrote the earliest Greek personal poetry, concentrating on themes of war and sexuality. He is disarmingly frank on both topics, but also prone to personal invective.

Archipenko Alexander 1887–1964. Ukrainian-born abstract sculptor who lived in France from 1908 and in the USA from 1923. He pioneered Cubist works, experimenting with sculptures in which 'negative form' (holes, voids, and spaces) is as significant as solid form. He also made polychrome reliefs, and later experimented with clear plastic and sculptures incorporating lights.

By experimenting with new materials and by making space, light, and colour important, Archipenko greatly influenced the development of 20th-century sculpture.

architecture art of designing structures. The term covers the design of the visual appearance of structures; their internal arrangements of space; selection of external and internal building materials; design or selection of natural and artificial lighting systems, as well as mechanical, electrical, and plumbing systems; and design or selection of decorations and furnishings. Architectural style may emerge from evolution of techniques and styles particular to a culture in a given time period with or without identifiable individuals as architects, or may be attributed to specific individuals or groups of architects working together on a project.

early architecture Little remains of the earliest forms of architecture, but archaeologists have examined remains of prehistoric sites and documented villages of wooden-post buildings with above-ground construction of organic materials (mud or wattle and daub) from the Upper Palaeolithic, Mesolithic, and Neolithic periods in Asia, the Middle East, Europe, and the Americas. More extensive remains of stone-built structures have given clues to later Neolithic farming communities as well as to the habitations, storehouses, and religious and civic structures of early civilizations. The best documented are those of ancient Egypt, where exhaustive work in the 19th and 20th centuries revealed much about both ordinary buildings and monumental structures, such as the pyramid tombs near modern Cairo and the temple and tomb complexes concentrated at Luxor and Thebes.

Classical The basic forms of Classical architecture evolved in Greece between the 16th and 2nd centuries BC. A hallmark was the post-and-lintel construction of temples and public structures, classified into the Doric, Ionic, and Corinthian ◊orders and defined by simple, scrolled, or acanthus-leaf capitals for support columns. The Romans copied and expanded on Greek Classical forms, notably introducing bricks and concrete and developing the vault, arch, and dome for public buildings and aqueducts.

Byzantine Architecture which developed primarily in the Eastern Roman Empire from the 4th century, with its centre at Byzantium (later named Constantinople, now Istanbul). Its most notable features were churches, some very large, based on the Greek cross plan (Hagia Sophia, Istanbul; St Mark's, Venice), with formalized painted and mosaic decoration.

Islamic Developed from the 8th century, when the Islamic religion spread from its centre in the Middle East west to Spain and east to China and parts of the Philippine Islands. Notable features are the development of the tower with dome and the pointed arch. Islamic architecture, chiefly through Spanish examples such as the Great Mosque at Córdoba and the Alhambra in Granada, profoundly influenced Christian church architecture, for example, the adoption of the pointed arch in Gothic architecture.

Romanesque A style flourishing in Western European Christianity from the 10th to the 12th centuries. It is marked by churches with massive walls for structural integrity, rounded arches, small windows, and resulting dark volumes of interior space. In England the style is generally referred to as Norman architecture (Durham Cathedral). Romanesque enjoyed a renewal of interest in Europe and the USA in the late 19th and early 20th centuries.

Gothic Gothic architecture emerged out of Romanesque. The development of the pointed arch and flying buttress made it possible to change from thick supporting walls to lighter curtain walls with extensive expansion of window areas (and stained-glass artwork) and resulting increases in interior light. Gothic architecture was developed mainly in France from the 12th to 16th centuries. The style is divided into Early Gothic (Sens Cathedral), High Gothic (Chartres Cathedral), and Late or Flamboyant Gothic. In England the corresponding divisions are Early English (Salisbury Cathedral), Decorated (Wells Cathedral), and Perpendicular (King's College Chapel, Cambridge). Gothic was also developed extensively in Germany and neighbouring countries and in Italy.

Renaissance The 15th and 16th centuries in Europe saw the rebirth of Classical form and motifs in the Italian Neo-Classical movement. A major source of inspiration for the great Renaissance architects – Palladio, Alberti, Brunelleschi, Bramante, and Michelangelo – was the work of the 1st-century BC Roman engineer Vitruvius. The Palladian style was later used extensively in England by Inigo Jones; Christopher Wren also worked in the Classical idiom. Classicism, or Neo-Classicism as it is also known, has been popular in the USA from the 18th century, as evidenced in much of the civic and commercial architecture since the time of the early republic (the US Capitol and Supreme Court buildings in Washington; many state capitols).

Baroque European architecture of the 17th and 18th centuries elaborated on Classical models with exuberant and extravagant decoration. In large-scale public buildings, the style is best seen in the innovative works of Giovanni Bernini and Francesco Borromini in Italy and later in those of John Vanbrugh, Nicholas Hawksmoor, and Christopher Wren in England. There were numerous practitioners in France and the German-speaking countries, and notably in Vienna.

Rococo This architecture extends the Baroque style with an even greater extravagance of design motifs, using a new lightness of detail and naturalistic elements, such as shells, flowers, and trees.

Neo-Classical European architecture of the 18th and 19th centuries again focused on the more severe Classical idiom (inspired by archaeological finds), producing, for example, the large-scale rebuilding of London by Robert Adam and John Nash and later of Paris by Georges Haussman.

Neo-Gothic The late 19th century saw a Gothic revival in Europe and the USA, which was evident in churches and public buildings, such as the Houses of Parliament in London, designed by Charles Barry and A W Pugin.

Art Nouveau This architecture, arising at the end of the 19th century, countered Neo-Gothic with sinuous, flowing shapes for buildings, room plans, and interior decoration. The style is characterized by the work of Charles Rennie Mackintosh in Scotland (Glasgow Art School) and Antonio Gaudí in Spain (Church of the Holy Family, Barcelona).

Modernist This style of architecture, referred to as the Modern Movement, began in the 1900s with the Vienna school and the German Bauhaus and was also developed in the US, Scandinavia, and France. With ◊Functionalism as its central precept, its hallmarks are the use of spare line and form, an emphasis on rationalism, and the elimination of ornament. It makes great use of technological advances in materials such as glass, steel, and concrete and of construction techniques that allow flexibility of design. Notable practitioners include Frank Lloyd Wright, Mies van der Rohe, and Le Corbusier. Modern architecture has furthered the notion of the planning of extensive multibuilding projects and of whole towns or communities.

Post-Modernist This style, which emerged in the 1980s in the USA, the UK, and Japan, rejected the Functionalism of the Modern

Western architecture

period/style date	typical building	architect where known
3000 BC – 500 BC ancient		
2700 BC	Pyramid of Khufu/Cheops – Egypt	
2000 BC	Palace of Knossos – Crete	
2000 BC	Ziggurat of Ur – Sumeria	
2000 BC	Stonehenge – England	
1300 BC	Citadel of Tiryns – Greece	
5th century BC – 2nd century AD Classical		
447 – 438 BC	Parthenon, Athens – Greece	Callicrates, Ictinus
c. 14 BC	Aqueduct at Nîmes – France	
AD 70 – 80	Colosseum, Rome – Italy	
118 – c. 128	Pantheon, Rome – Italy	
4th century – 8th century early Christian		
526 – 547	San Vitale, Ravenna – Italy	
9th century Carolingian		
800	Royal Chapel, Aachen – Germany	
10th – 12th century Romanesque		
1078 – 1210	St James' Cathedral, Santiago – Spain	
c. 1110 – 81	Worms Cathedral – Germany	
c. 1131 – 1240	Cefalù Cathedral – Sicily	
12th – 14th century Gothic		
1180 – 1330	Nôtre-Dame Cathedral, Paris – France	
begun 1201	Cloth Hall, Ypres – Belgium	
1220 – 66	Salisbury Cathedral – England	
begun 1221	Burgos Cathedral – Spain	
1248 – 1322	Cologne Cathedral – Germany	
14th century	Doge's Palace – Venice	
15th – early 17th century Renaissance		
1419 – 24	Foundling Hospital, Florence – Italy	Brunelleschi
1420 –38	Dome of Florence Cathedral– Italy	Brunelleschi
begun 1444	Medici-Riccardi Palace, Florence – Italy	Alberti
1502 – 10	Tempietto, Rome – Italy	Bramante
1506 – 64	St Peter's, Rome – Italy	Bramante & Michelangelo
begun c. 1550	Villa Rotonda, Vicenza – Italy	Palladio
begun 1562	Escorial, Madrid – Spain	Herrera the Younger
1616 – 35	Queen's House, Greenwich – England	Inigo Jones
17th – early 18th century Baroque		
1637 – 41	San Carlo alle Quatro Fontane, Rome – Italy	Borromini
1656 – 67	St Peter's Piazza, Rome – Italy	Bernini
begun 1694	Greenwich Hospital – England	Wren
1705 – 24	Blenheim Palace – England	Vanbrugh
18th century Classical Revival		
1722 – 25	Merewith Castle – England	Campbell
1759 – 70	Kedleston Hall – England	Adams
19th century		
1819 – 21	The Schauspielhaus, Berlin – Germany	Schinkel
1824 – 47	British Museum, London – England	Smirke
Gothic Revival		
1840 – 65	Houses of Parliament, London – England	Barry and Pugin
Chicago School		
1890	Wainwright Building, St Louis – USA	Sullivan
20th century Art Nouveau		
1896 – 1910	School of Art, Glasgow – Scotland	Mackintosh
1905 – 10	Casa Milá, Barcelona – Spain	Gaudí
Modern		
1906	Unity Church, Chicago – USA	Wright
1909	AEG Turbine Factory, Berlin – Germany	Behrens
1910	Steiner House, Vienna – Austria	Loos
1919 – 20	Einstein Tower, Potsdam – Germany	Mendelsohn
1947 – 52	Unité d'habitation, Marseilles – France	Le Corbusier
1959 – 73	Sydney Opera House – Australia	Utzon
Post-Modern/High Tech		
1980 – 82	Public Services Building, Portland – USA	Graves
1977 – 82	Staatsgalerie, Stuttgart – Germany	Stirling
1986	Lloyd's Building, London – England	Rogers

Movement in favour of an eclectic mixture of styles and motifs, often Classical. Its use of irony, parody, and illusion is in sharp distinction to the Modernist ideals of truth to materials and form following function.

Architecture comprises two ideas: the mastery of the practical, and the art of the beautiful.

Peter Behrens
on architecture *Architectural Press* 1981

High Tech This building style also developed in the 1980s. It took the ideals of the Modern Movement and expressed them through highly developed structures and technical innovations. Examples include Norman Foster's Hong Kong and Shanghai Bank, Hong Kong, and Richard Rogers' Lloyds Building in the City of London.

Deconstructionism An architectural debate as much as a style, Deconstructionism fragments forms and space by taking the usual building elements of floors, walls, and ceilings and sliding them apart to create a sense of disorientation and movement.

Arcimboldo Giuseppe *c.* 1530–1593. Italian painter and designer, known for his fantastical portraits, human in form but composed of fruit, plant, and animal details. He also designed tapestries and was a successful portrait painter at the court of Rudolf II in Prague. The Surrealists helped to revive interest in his symbolic portraits, which were considered in bad taste at the time of their conception.

arco in music, a direction to play with the bow, or to resume playing with the bow after playing pizzicato (plucked string).

Arden John 1930– . English dramatist. His early plays *Serjeant Musgrave's Dance* 1959 and *The Workhouse Donkey* 1963 contain trenchant social criticism and show the influence of Brecht. Subsequent works, often written in collaboration with his wife, Margaretta D'Arcy, express increasing concern with the political situation in Northern Ireland and dissatisfaction with the professional and subsidized theatre world.

Ares in Greek mythology, the god of war, equivalent to the Roman ◊Mars. The son of Zeus and Hera, he was worshipped chiefly in Thrace.

Arethusa in Greek mythology, a nymph of the fountain and spring of Arethusa in the island of Ortygia near Syracuse, on the south coast of Sicily.

Aretino Pietro 1492–1556. Italian writer. He earned his living, both in Rome and Venice, by publishing satirical pamphlets while under the protection of a highly placed family. His *Letters* 1537–57 are a unique record of the cultural and political events of his time, and illustrate his vivacious, exuberant character. He also wrote poems and comedies.

Born in Arezzo, Aretino began as a protégé of Pope Leo X, but left Rome after the publication of his lewd verses. He settled in Venice, and quickly became known as the 'Scourge of Princes' with his vicious satires on powerful contemporaries; he was also well paid for not taking up his pen.

Anger represents a certain power when a great mind, prevented from executing its own generous desires, is moved by it.

Pietro Aretino
letter to Girolamo Quirini Nov 1537

Argentina, La stage name of Antonia Merce 1890–1936. Argentine Spanish dancer, choreographer, and director. She took her artistic name from the land of her birth. Through the brilliance of her personality and sparkling technique, she became one of the most famous exponents of Spanish dance. She was also known for the sensitive technique of her castanet playing.

Argentine literature the literature of Argentina since independence 1816. The first Latin American territory to revolt against Spain, in 1810, Argentina developed a distinct literary tradition in which Romanticism was energized by imaginative responsiveness to the empty loneliness of the pampas and by liberal resentment of the ruralist dictatorship of Juan Manuel Rosas (died 1852), often equated with barbarism.

Important early writers include the politically disaffected poet Esteban Echeverría (1805–1851) and José Mármol (1817–1871), author of the melodramatic romantic novel *Amalia* 1851. The *gaucho* or nomadic cattleman, resented by progressive critics of Rosas's pastoral vision of Argentina, was transformed by the industrialization that spelled his extinction into a tragically romantic figure, as in *Martín Fierro* 1872–79 by José Hernández (1834–1886). This in turn influenced novels of idealized *gaucho* adventure and coming of age such as *Don Segundo Sombra* 1926 by Ricardo ◊Güiraldes and contributed to the 20th-century literary obsession with Argentinian identity, heroism, and masculinity or machismo in works such as the epic quest-novel *Adán Buenosayres* 1948 by Leopoldo Marechal (1900–1970) and the psychological or philosophical fictions of Ernesto Sábato (1911–) and Eduardo Mallea (1903–).

Poets such as Leopoldo Lugones (1874–1938) registered modernist reactions against romantic and realist convention, influenced by the French avant-garde while retaining distinctively Argentinian settings and national concerns. In politically troubled modern Argentina, cosmopolitan and often apolitical experimental and modernist writing, typified by the influential fictions of Luis Borges (1899–1986). and Julio Cortázar (1916–1984), has provoked neorealist or socialist reactions in the work of Manuel Puig (1932–1990) and the committed Marxist novelist David Viñas (1929–   ).

Argonauts in Greek mythology, the band of heroes who accompanied ◊Jason when he set sail in the *Argo* to find the ◊Golden Fleece.

Argus in Greek mythology, a giant with 100 eyes. When he was killed by Hermes, Hera transplanted his eyes into the tail of her favourite bird, the peacock.

aria (Italian 'air') melodic solo song of reflective character, often with a contrasting middle section, expressing a moment of truth in the action of an opera or oratorio. Pioneered by Giacomo ◊Carissimi, it became a set piece for virtuoso opera singers, for example Handel's aria 'Where'er you walk' from *Semele* 1744 to words by William Congreve. As an instrumental character piece, it is melodious and imitative of a vocal line.

Ariadne in Greek mythology, the daughter of Minos, King of Crete. When ◊Theseus came from Athens as one of the sacrificial victims offered to the ◊Minotaur, she fell in love with him and gave him a ball of thread, which enabled him to find his way out of the labyrinth. When abandoned by Theseus on the island of Naxos, she married ◊Dionysus.

Ariosto Ludovico 1474–1533. Italian poet. He wrote Latin poems and comedies on Classical lines, including the poem ◊*Orlando furioso 1516, published 1532, an epic treatment of the ◊ Roland* story, the perfect poetic expression of the Italian Renaissance.

Ariosto was born in Reggio, and joined the household of Cardinal Ippolito d'Este 1503. He was frequently engaged in ambassadorial missions and diplomacy for the Duke of Ferrara. In 1521 he became governor of a province in the Apennines, and after three years retired to Ferrara, where he died.

Cruelty ever proceeds from a vile mind, and often from a cowardly heart.

Ludovico Ariosto *Orlando Furioso* 1516

Aristophanes *c.* 448–380 BC. Greek comedy dramatist. Of his 11 extant plays (of a total of over 40), the early comedies are remarkable for the violent satire with which he ridiculed the democratic war leaders. He also satirized contemporary issues such as the new learning of Socrates in *The Clouds* 423 BC and the power of women in ◊*Lysistrata* 411 BC. The chorus plays a prominent role, frequently giving the play its title, as in *The Wasps* 422 BC, *The Birds* 414 BC, and *The Frogs* 405 BC.

Aristotle 384–322 BC. Greek philosopher and scientist. Born in Stagira in Thrace, Aristotle studied under ◊Plato, became tutor to Alexander the Great, and in 335 bc opened his own school, the Lyceum, in Athens. His philosophy encompasses ethics, politics, and metaphysics, but many of his most original researches are in the field of natural sciences. His writings on literary theory reflect his interest in psychology; the *Poetics* and the *Rhetoric* were both written after 335 BC.

In the *Poetics*, Aristotle defines tragic drama as an imitation (mimesis) of the actions of human beings, with character subordinated to plot. The audience is affected by pity and fear, but experiences a purgation (catharsis) of these emotions through watching the play. The second book of the *Poetics*, on comedy, is lost. The three books of the *Rhetoric* form the earliest analytical discussion of the techniques of persuasion, and the last presents a theory of the emotions to which a speaker must appeal.

Arjuna Indian prince, one of the two main characters in the Hindu epic ◊*Mahābhārata.*

Arlen Michael. Adopted name of Dikran Kuyumjian 1895–1956. Bulgarian writer of Armenian descent who became a naturalized British subject 1922. His best-selling novel, *The Green Hat* 1924, reflected the stylishly irresponsible spirit of the 1920s.

It is a sorry business to inquire into what men think, when we are every day only too uncomfortably confronted with what they do.

Michael Arlen *The Three-Cornered Moon*

Armani Giorgio 1935– . Italian fashion designer. He launched his first menswear collection 1974 and the following year started designing women's clothing. His work is known for understated styles, precise tailoring, and fine fabrics. He designs for young men and women under the Emporio label.

Armory Show exhibition of modern European art held Feb 1913 in New York. It marked the arrival of abstract art in the USA, and greatly influenced US artists. The exhibition provoked public outrage, and a rioting crowd threatened to destroy Marcel Duchamp's *Nude Descending a Staircase No. 1* 1911 (now in the Museum of Art, Philadelphia).

armour body protection worn in battle. Body armour is depicted in Greek and Roman art. Chain mail was developed in the Middle Ages but the craft of the armourer in Europe reached its height in design in the 15th century, when knights were completely encased in plate armour that still allowed freedom of movement. Medieval Japanese armour was articulated, made of iron, gilded metal, leather, and silk. Contemporary bulletproof vests and riot gear are forms of armour.

Armstrong Louis ('Satchmo') 1901–1971. US jazz cornet and trumpet player and singer. His Chicago recordings in the 1920s with the Hot Five and Hot Seven brought him recognition for his warm and pure trumpet tone, his skill at improvisation, and his quirky, gravelly voice. From the 1930s he also appeared in films.

Armstrong was born in New Orleans. In 1923 he joined the Creole Jazz Band led by the cornet player Joe 'King' ◊Oliver in Chicago, but soon broke away and formed various bands of his own. In 1947 he formed the Louis Armstrong All-Stars. He firmly established the pre-eminence of the virtuoso jazz soloist. He is also credited with the invention of ◊scat singing.

A lot of cats copy the Mona Lisa, but people still line up to see the original.

Louis Armstrong when asked whether he objected to people copying his style

---

Arne Thomas Augustus 1710–1778. English composer of incidental music for theatre who introduced opera in the Italian manner to the London stage with works such as *Artaxerxes* 1762, revised 1777. He is remembered for the songs 'Where the bee sucks' from *The Tempest* 1746, 'Blow, blow thou winter wind' from *As You Like It* 1740, and 'Rule Britannia!' from the masque *Alfred* 1740.

Arnim Ludwig Achim von 1781–1831. German Romantic poet and novelist. Born in Berlin, he wrote short stories, a romance (*Gräfin Dolores/Countess Dolores* 1810), and plays, but left the historical novel *Die Kronenwächter* 1817 unfinished. With Clemens ◊Brentano he collected the German folk songs in *Des Knaben Wunderhorn/The Boy's Magic Horn* 1805–08, several of which were set to music by Gustav Mahler.

Arnold Malcolm (Henry) 1921– . English composer. His work is tonal and includes a large amount of orchestral, chamber, ballet, and vocal music. His overtures *Beckus the Dandipratt* 1948, *A Sussex Overture* 1951, and *Tam O'Shanter* 1955 are well known. His operas include *The Dancing Master* 1951, and he has written music for more than 80 films, including *The Bridge on the River Kwai* 1957, for which he won an Academy Award.

Arnold Matthew 1822–1888. English poet and critic. His poems, characterized by their elegiac mood and pastoral themes, include *The Forsaken Merman* 1849, *Thyrsis* 1867 (commemorating his friend Arthur Hugh Clough), *Dover Beach* 1867, and *The Scholar Gypsy* 1853. Arnold's critical works include *Essays in Criticism* 1865 and 1888, and his highly influential *Culture and Anarchy* 1869, which attacks 19th-century philistinism.

The son of Thomas Arnold, he was educated at public schools and Oxford University. After a short spell as an assistant master at Rugby, Arnold became a school inspector 1851–86. He published two unsuccessful volumes of anonymous poetry, but two further publications under his own name 1853 and 1855 led to his appointment as professor of poetry at Oxford. Arnold first used the word 'philistine' in its present sense in his attack on the cultural values of the middle classes.

And we forget because we must/ And not because we will.

Matthew Arnold 'Absence'

Arp Hans or Jean 1887–1966. French abstract painter and sculptor. He was one of the founders of the ◊Dada movement 1916, and was later associated with the Surrealists. Using chance and ◊automatism, Arp developed an abstract sculpture whose sensuous form suggests organic shapes.

In his early experimental works, such as collages, he collaborated with his wife Sophie Taeuber-Arp (1889–1943).

arpeggio (Italian 'like a harp') in music, the spreading of a chord to sound like a rapid succession of notes, usually from low to high. It is a technique of guitar playing, not of lute playing, where chords are played together on the beat.

arranger in music, a person who adapts or assists in orchestrating the music of another composer at the composer's request. The use of an arranger became established in Hollywood; Rachmaninov, Gershwin, and Leonard Bernstein, amongst others, composed concert works employing such assistance. Composers of unauthorized arrangements include J S Bach (Vivaldi), Mozart (Handel's *Messiah*), and Stravinsky (Tchaikovsky and Pergolesi).

Arrau Claudio 1903–1991. Chilean-born US pianist. A concert performer from the age of five, he specialized in 19th-century music and was known for his magisterial interpretations of Chopin, Beethoven, and Brahms.

Arrian lived 2nd century AD. Greek historian whose *Anabasis/Expedition* is the major literary source of information on the campaigns of Alexander the Great. A governor and commander under the Roman emperor Hadrian, his work was drawn with care from much earlier material.

art in the broadest sense, all the processes and products of human skill, imagination, and invention; the opposite of nature. In contemporary usage, definitions of art usually reflect aesthetic criteria, and the term may encompass literature, music, drama, painting, and sculpture. Popularly, the term is most commonly used to refer to the visual arts. In Western culture, aesthetic criteria introduced by the ancient Greeks still influence our perceptions and judgements of art.

Two currents of thought run through our ideas about art. In one, derived from Aristotle, art is concerned with *mimesis* ('imitation'), the representation of appearances, and gives pleasure through the accuracy and skill with which it depicts the real world. The other view, derived from Plato, holds that the artist is inspired by the Muses (or by God, or by the inner impulses, or by the collective unconscious) to express that which is beyond appearances – inner feelings, eternal truths, or the essence of the age. In the Middle Ages the term 'art' was used, chiefly in the plural, to signify a branch of learning which was regarded as an instrument of knowledge. The seven *liberal arts* consisted of the *trivium*, that is grammar, logic, and rhetoric, and the *quadrivium*, that is arithmetic, music, geometry, and astronomy. In the visual arts of Western civilizations, painting and sculpture have been the dominant forms for many centuries. This has not always been the case in other cultures. Islamic art, for example, is one of ornament, for under the Muslim religion artists are forbidden to usurp the divine right of creation by portraying living creatures. In some cultures masks, tattoos, pottery, and metalwork have been the main forms of visual art. Recent technology has made new art forms possible, such as photography and cinema, and today electronic media have led to entirely new ways of creating and presenting visual images. See also ◊prehistoric art; the arts of ancient civilizations, for examples ◊Egyptian art; indigenous art traditions, for example under ◊Oceanic art; ◊medieval art; the arts of individual countries, such as ◊French art; and individual movements, such as ◊Romanticism, ◊Cubism, and ◊Impressionism; and ◊painting and ◊sculpture.

Artaud Antonin 1896–1948. French actor, writer, and theatre director, influenced by ◊Surrealism. Although his play, *Les Cenci/The Cenci* 1935, was a failure, his concept of the Theatre of ◊Cruelty, intended to release feelings usually repressed in the unconscious, has been an important influence on modern dramatists such as Jean Genet and on directors such as Peter Brook. Declared insane 1936, Artaud was confined in an asylum.

We must wash literature off ourselves. We want to be men first of all, to be human.

Antonin Artaud
Les Oeuvres et les Hommes 1922

Art Deco style in the decorative arts which influenced design and architecture. It emerged in Europe in the 1920s and continued through the 1930s, becoming particularly popular in the USA and France. A self-consciously modern style, originally called 'Jazz Modern', it is characterized by angular, geometrical patterns and bright colours, and by the use of materials such as enamel, chrome, glass, and plastic. The graphic artist Erté was a fashionable exponent.

Artemis in Greek mythology, the goddess of chastity (Roman Diana), the young of all creatures, the Moon, and the hunt. She is the twin sister of ◊Apollo and was worshipped at cult centres throughout the Greek world, one of the largest of which was at Ephesus. Her great temple there, reconstructed several times in antiquity, was one of the ◊Seven Wonders of the World.

art for art's sake artistic theory; see ◊aestheticism.

art history the study of works of art. Johann ◊Winckelmann laid the foundations for a systematic study of art history as early as the mid-18th century, but it did not become an academic discipline until 1844 when a chair was established at Berlin University. Two basic approaches had emerged by the end of the 19th century: the first considered art in relation to its cultural or social context (Jacob ◊Burckhardt, Hippolyte ◊Taine); the second sought to analyse works of art in terms of such 'formal' properties as colour, line, and form (Heinrich ◊Wölfflin). A later approach, rejecting the formalism of Wölfflin, concentrated on ◊iconography, the study of the meaning of works of art (Erwin ◊Panofsky, Emile Mâle).

Arthur 6th century AD. Legendary British king and hero in stories of Camelot (the court of Arthur) and the quest for the ◊Holy Grail. Arthur is said to have been born in Tintagel, Cornwall, and buried in Glastonbury, Somerset. He may have been a Romano-Celtic leader against pagan Saxon invaders.

The legends of Arthur and the knights of the Round Table were developed in the 12th century by ◊Geoffrey of Monmouth, ◊Chrétien de Troyes, and the Norman writer Robert Wace. Later writers on the theme include the anonymous author of *Sir Gawayne and the Greene Knight* 1346, Thomas Malory, Tennyson, T H White, and Mark Twain.

Art Nouveau in the visual arts and architecture, decorative style of about 1890–1910, which makes marked use of sinuous lines reminiscent of unfolding tendrils, stylized flowers and foliage, and flame shapes. In England, it appears in the illustrations of Aubrey Beardsley; in Spain, in the architecture of Antonio Gaudí; in France, in the architecture of Hector Guimard, the art glass of René Lalique, and the posters of Alphonse Mucha; in Belgium, in the houses and shops of Victor Horta; in the USA, in the lamps and metal work of Louis Comfort Tiffany; and in Scotland, in the interior and exterior designs of Charles Rennie Mackintosh. Art Nouveau took its name from a shop in Paris that opened 1895; it was also known as *Jugendstil* in Germany and *Stile Liberty* in Italy, after the fashionable London department store.

Arts and Crafts movement English social and aesthetic movement of the second half of the 19th century. Rejecting mass production, it sought to return to medieval principles of craftsmanship, and was particularly influential in design and architecture. Its leading figure was William ◊Morris; other important members included Charles ◊Ashbee and Norman ◊Shaw, and the movement was supported by the architect A W Pugin and the critic John Ruskin. It strongly influenced the development of ◊Art Nouveau.

Arts Council of Great Britain UK organization, incorporated 1946, which aids music, drama, and visual arts with government funds. It began 1940 as the Council for the Encouragement of Music and the Arts (CEMA) with a grant from the Pilgrim Trust, a UK charity.

Arup Ove 1895–1988. Danish engineer who founded the British-based architectural practice, Arup Associates, noted for the elegant manner in which they employ modern materials, especially concrete, in their designs. Set up 1963, the practice represented Arup's ideal of interdisciplinary cooperation. Examples of their work are at Somerville College, Oxford, 1958–62, and Corpus Christi, Cambridge, 1961–64.

During the 1930s Arup worked with Bertholdt ◊Lubetkin and the Tecton group on a number of projects, including the Penguin Pool, London Zoo 1934–35, which used reinforced concrete in a sculptural fashion (later developed in Arup's own designs).

ASA in photography, a numbering system for rating the speed of films, devised by the American Standards Association. It has now been superseded by ◊ISO, the International Standards Organization.

Ascher Zika (Zigmund) George 1910–1992 and Lida, his wife, died 1983. Czechoslovakian fabric designers. They were known for producing scarves with designs by modern artists including Braque, Picasso, and Matisse, and for designing neon-coloured shaggy mohairs, cheesecloth, lacy fabrics, and dress- and coat-weighted chenilles which were popular from the late 1950s to the early 1970s. Their fabrics were popular with leading couturiers from the 1940s, including Christian Dior, Elsa Schiaparelli, and Mary Quant.

Asclepius in Greek mythology, the god of medicine (Roman Aesculapius) and son of ◊Apollo. His emblem was a staff with a snake coiled around it, since snakes appeared to renew life by shedding their skin. His cult originated in Thessaly in N Greece, but the major sanctuary of the classical period was at Epidaurus. Patients slept in his temple overnight, and treatment was based on the visions they saw in their sleep.

Asgard in Scandinavian mythology, the home of the gods and of the heroes who died in battles. One of its 12 halls was ◊Valhalla. It was reached by a bridge called Bifrost, the rainbow.

Ashbee Charles Robert 1863–1942. British designer, architect, and writer, one of the major figures of the ◊Arts and Crafts movement. He founded a Guild and School of Handicraft in the East End of London 1888, but later modified his views, accepting the importance of machinery and design for industry.

He based his ideas on the social function of art from the writings of William ◊Morris and John ◊Ruskin. His Guild and School of Handicraft (later moved to Chipping Campden, Gloucestershire) aimed to achieve high standards in craftwork and quality of life, which were both threatened by the onset of mass production. At its peak, the guild employed over 100 craftworkers.

Ashbery John 1927– . US poet and art critic. His collections of poetry – including *Self-Portrait in a Convex Mirror* 1975, which won a Pulitzer Prize – are distinguished by their exhuberant artifice and strong visual and musical elements. His most experimental work, *Europe* (in *The Tennis Court Oath* 1962), uses montage and collage methods derived from Cubist painting. Other volumes include *Some Trees* 1956, *Houseboat Days* 1977, *As We Know* 1979, and *A Wave* 1984.

Ashcan School group of US Realist painters active about 1908–14. The school's central figures were Robert Henri, George Luks, William Glackens, Everett Shinn (1876–1953), and John Sloan, all former members of *The Eight* (a group of realist painters who exhibited together 1908 outside of the official circuit). Their subjects were taken from city life, depicting in particular the poor and the outcast. They organized the ◊Armory Show of 1913, which introduced modern European art to the USA.

Ashcroft Peggy 1907–1991. English actress. Her Shakespearean roles included Desdemona in *Othello* (with Paul Robeson) and Juliet in *Romeo and Juliet* 1935 (with Laurence Olivier and John Gielgud), and she appeared in the British TV play *Caught on a Train* 1980 (BAFTA award), the series *The Jewel in the Crown* 1984, and the film *A Passage to India* 1985.

She was born in Croydon, Surrey, where a theatre is named after her.

Ashford Daisy 1881–1972. English author of *The Young Visiters* 1919, a novel of unconscious humour written when she was nine.

Ashkenazy Vladimir 1937– . Russian-born pianist and conductor. In 1962 he was joint winner of the Tchaikovsky Competition with John Ogdon. He settled in England 1963 and moved to Iceland 1968. He was music director of the Royal Philharmonic Orchestra, London, 1987 and of the Berlin Radio Symphony Orchestra from 1989. He excels in Rachmaninov, Prokofiev, and Liszt.

Ashley Laura (born Mountney) 1925–1985. Welsh designer. She established and gave her name to a neo-Victorian country style in clothes and furnishings manufactured by her company from 1953. She founded an international chain of shops.

Ashton Frederick 1904–1988. British choreographer, dancer, and director of the Royal Ballet, London, 1963–70. He studied with Marie Rambert before joining the Sadler's Wells (now Royal) Ballet 1935 as chief choreographer. His choreography is marked by a soft, pliant, classical lyricism. His many works and long association with Margot Fonteyn, for whom he created her most famous roles, contributed to the worldwide reputation of British ballet.

His major works include *Façade* 1931 and *Les Rendezvous* 1933 for Rambert; *Symphonic Variations* 1946, *Cinderella* 1948, *Ondine* 1958, *La Fille mal gardée* 1960, *Marguerite and Armand* – for Margot Fonteyn and Rudolf Nureyev – 1963, and *A Month in the Country* 1976. He contributed much to the popularity of ballet in the mid-20th century.

Ashton Julian Rossi 1851–1942. Australian landscape painter and art teacher born in England. In 1895 he established in Sydney an influential art school, now the Julian Ashton Art School. His work includes a number of watercolours such as *The Milkmaid* 1888 (Art Gallery of New South Wales, Sydney), painted in part in the open air, which captures accurately the hues of crisp winter sunlight. Among his students were Thea Proctor, William Dobell, and Sydney Long.

Asimov Isaac 1920–1992. Russian-born US author and editor of science fiction and non-fiction. He published more than 400 books including his science fiction *I, Robot* 1950 and the *Foundation* trilogy 1951–53, continued in *Foundation's Edge* 1983.

Asimov received a PhD in biochemistry from Columbia University 1948 and joined the faculty of the Boston University Medical School. His non-fiction works include *The Intelligent Man's Guide to Science* 1960.

If my doctor told me I only had six months to live, I wouldn't brood. I'd type a little faster.

Isaac Asimov *Life* 1984

Asplund (Erik) Gunnar 1885–1940. Swedish architect. His early work, for example at the Stockholm South Cemetery 1914, was in the Neo-Classical tradition. Later buildings, such as the Stockholm City Library 1924–27 and the extension of the Gothenburg City Hall 1934–37, developed a refined Modernist-Classical style, culminating in the Stockholm South Cemetery Crematorium 1935–40. His fusion of Classicism and Modernism holds great appeal for many Post-Modern architects and designers.

assemblage in the visual arts, any work of art

constructed of atypical materials, or ◊found objects. The term was first used in the 1950s by French painter Jean ◊Dubuffet to describe his collages and figures created from bits of wood, sponge, paper, and glue. *Junk art* refers to three-dimensional assemblages constructed solely of waste and discarded materials.

Rooted in Cubist collage and the early sculptural assemblages of Picasso and the Italian Futurists, particularly Umberto Boccioni, the technique was later experimented with by the Dadaists and Surrealists for its symbolic and satirical possibilities. The Dada revival of the 1950s and early 1960s reaffirmed it as a technique central to much 20th-century art, typified in the 'combine' paintings of US Pop artist Robert ◊Rauschenberg.

assonance the matching of vowel (or, sometimes, consonant) sounds, generally in poetry. 'Load' and 'moat', 'farther' and 'harder' are examples of assonance, since they match in vowel sounds and syllabic stress pattern, but do not rhyme.

Astaire Fred. Adopted name of Frederick Austerlitz 1899–1987. US dancer, actor, singer, and choreographer. He starred in numerous films, including *Top Hat* 1935, *Easter Parade* 1948, and *Funny Face* 1957, many containing inventive sequences he designed and choreographed himself. He made ten classic films with the most popular of his dancing partners, Ginger Rogers. He later played straight dramatic roles in such films as *On the Beach* 1959. He was the greatest popular dancer of his time.

Astaire was born in Omaha, Nebraska, and taken to New York in 1904. He danced in partnership with his sister **Adele Astaire** (1897–1981) from 1906 until her marriage in 1932, and they became public favourites on Broadway and in London. He entered films 1933. Among his many other films are *Roberta* 1935 and *Follow the Fleet* 1936.

I have no desire to prove anything by dancing ... I just dance.

Fred Astaire

Astor Mary. Stage name of Lucille Langhanke 1906–1987. US film actress, renowned for her poise, whose many films included *Don Juan* 1926, *Dodsworth* 1936, and *The Maltese Falcon* 1941. Her memoirs *My Story* 1959 were remarkable for their frankness.

Asturias Miguel Angel 1899–1974. Guatemalan author and diplomat. He published poetry, Guatemalan legends, and novels, such as *El señor presidente/The President* 1946, *Men of Corn* 1949, and *Strong Wind* 1950, attacking Latin-American dictatorships and 'Yankee imperialism'. Nobel prize 1967.

Astyanax in Greek mythology, the son of ◊Hector and ◊Andromache. After the death of all the sons of ◊Priam in battle at the siege of Troy, the child Astyanax was thrown from the city walls by the victorious Greeks.

Atalanta in Greek mythology, a woman hunter who challenged each of her suitors to a foot race; if they lost they were killed. The goddess ◊Aphrodite gave one of the suitors, Hippomenes, three golden apples to drop so that when Atalanta stopped to pick them up, she lost the race and became his wife.

até in Greek mythology, an infatuation which leads to a failure to distinguish between good and bad courses of action.

Atget Eugène 1857–1927. French photographer. He took up photography at the age of 40, and for 30 years documented urban Paris in some 10,000 images. His photographs were sometimes used by painters and he was admired by the Surrealists. After his death his work was rescued and promoted by the photographer Berenice Abbott.

Athena in Greek mythology, the goddess of war, wisdom, and the arts and crafts (Roman Minerva), who was supposed to have sprung fully grown from the head of Zeus. In Homer's *Odyssey*, she is the protectress of ◊Odysseus and his son Telemachus. Her chief cult centre was Athens, where the ◊Parthenon was dedicated to her.

Atlantis in Greek mythology, an island continent, said to have sunk following an earthquake. The Greek philosopher Plato, who created an imaginary early history for it, described it as a utopia.

Legends about the disappearance of Atlantis may have some connection with the volcanic eruption that devastated Santorini in the Cyclades islands, north of Crete, about 1500 BC. The ensuing earthquakes and tidal waves are believed to have been one cause of the collapse of the empire of Minoan Crete.

Atlas in Greek mythology, one of the ◊Titans who revolted against the gods; as a punishment, he was compelled to support the heavens on his head and shoulders. Growing weary, he asked ◊Perseus to turn him into stone, and he was transformed into Mount Atlas.

atonality music in which the sense of ◊tonality is distorted or obscured; music of no apparent key. Atonality is an effect of expressionist counterpoint, partly aiming to avoid spurious harmonic relationships, in works such as Schoenberg's monodrama *Erwartung/Expectation* 1909. It is used by film and television composers for situations of mystery or horror.

Atreus in Greek mythology, the father of Agamemnon and Menelaus (the Atridae), son of Pelops, and brother of ◊Thyestes, with whom he contested the throne of Mycenae. As part of the feud, Atreus served the flesh of Thyestes' children to their father at a banquet held to confirm the reconciliation of the two brothers.

atrium in architecture, an open inner courtyard. Originally the central court or main room of an ancient Roman house, open to the sky, often with a shallow pool to catch rainwater.

Attenborough Richard 1923– . English director, actor, and producer. He made his screen acting debut in *In Which We Serve* 1942, and later appeared in such films as *Brighton Rock* 1947 and *10 Rillington Place* 1970. He co-produced the socially conscious *The Angry Silence* 1960, and directed *Oh! What a Lovely War* 1969. He subsequently concentrated on directing, including the epic biographies of *Gandhi* (which won eight Academy Awards) 1982, *Cry Freedom* 1987, and *Chaplin* 1992. He is the brother of naturalist David Attenborough.

Attis in classical mythology, a Phrygian god whose death and resurrection symbolized the end of winter and the arrival of spring. Beloved by the goddess ◊Cybele, who drove him mad as a punishment for his infidelity, he castrated himself and bled to death.

Attwell Mabel Lucie 1879–1964. English artist, illustrator of many books for children, including her own stories and verse.

Atwood Margaret (Eleanor) 1939– . Canadian novelist, short-story writer, and poet. Her novels, which often treat feminist themes with wit and irony, include *The Edible Woman* 1969, *Life Before Man* 1979, *Bodily Harm* 1981, *The Handmaid's Tale* 1986, and *Cat's Eye* 1989. Collections of poetry include *Power Politics* 1971, *You are Happy* 1974, and *Interlunar* 1984.

Auber Daniel François Esprit 1782–1871. French operatic composer. He studied under the Italian composer and teacher Luigi Cherubini and wrote about 50 operas, including *La Muette de Portici/The Mute Girl of Portici* 1828 and the comic opera *Fra Diavolo* 1830.

Aubrey John 1626–1697. English biographer and antiquary. His *Lives*, begun 1667, contains gossip, anecdotes, and valuable insights into the celebrities of his time. It was published as *Brief Lives* 1898. *Miscellanies* 1696, a collection of folklore, was the only work to be published during his lifetime.

Auden W(ystan) H(ugh) 1907–1973. English-born US poet. He wrote some of his most original poetry, such as *Look, Stranger!* 1936, in the 1930s when he led the influential left-wing literary group that included Louis MacNeice, Stephen Spender, and Cecil Day Lewis. He moved to the USA 1939, became a US citizen 1946, and adopted a more conservative and Christian viewpoint, for example in *The Age of Anxiety* 1947.

Born in York, Auden was associate professor of English literature at the University of

Michigan from 1939, and professor of poetry at Oxford 1956–61. He also wrote verse dramas with Christopher ◊Isherwood, such as *The Dog Beneath the Skin* and *The Ascent of F6* 1951, and opera librettos, notably for Stravinsky's *The Rake's Progress* 1951.

We must love one another or die.

W H Auden 'September 1, 1939'

Auerbach Frank Helmuth 1931– . British painter, born in Berlin. He is best-known for his portraits and views of London; his style is characterized by thick, heavily worked paint.

Augean stables in Greek mythology, the stables of Augeas, king of Elis in southern Greece. One of the labours of ◊Heracles was to clean out the stables, which contained 3,000 cattle and had never been cleaned before. He was given only one day to do the labour and so diverted the river Alpheus through their yard.

Augier Emile 1820–1889. French dramatist. Reacting against ◊Romanticism, in collaboration with Jules Sandeau he wrote *Le Gendre de M Poirier* 1854, a realistic delineation of bourgeois society.

augmentation in music, notation of a musical figure in larger time values, used in counterpoint in order to combine it with the same figure in smaller time values.

Augustin Eugène 1791–1861. French dramatist, the originator and exponent of 'well-made' plays, which achieved success but were subsequently forgotten. He wrote *Une Nuit de la Garde Nationale* 1815.

'Auld Lang Syne' song written by the Scottish poet Robert Burns about 1789, which is often sung at New Year's Eve gatherings; the title means 'old long since' or 'long ago'.

Aulis in Greek mythology, the point of departure for the Greek expedition against ◊Troy, an anchorage on the eastern coast of Greece.

Auric Georges 1899–1983. French composer. His works include a comic opera, several ballets, and incidental music to films including Jean Cocteau's *Orphée/Orpheus* 1950. He was one of the musical group called ◊*Les Six* who were influenced by Erik ◊Satie.

Aurora in Roman mythology, the goddess of the dawn. Her Greek equivalent is Eos.

Auroras of Autumn, The collection of poems 1950 by US poet Wallace ◊Stevens. The title poem is a dense, meditative lyric on the poet's anxieties about religious belief. It uses the Northern Lights as an image for a world flickering between bright summer and dark winter.

Like a book at evening beautiful but untrue / Like a book on rising beautiful and true.

Wallace Stevens
The Auroras of Autumn 1950

Ausdruckstanz (German 'expressive dance') modern dance form, which reached its peak of creativity during the 1920s. It emphasized intuitive and individual approaches over formal technique and virtuosity. The movement pioneered ◊community dance and the use of improvisation in teaching. Its main exponents were Rudolf von ◊Laban, Mary ◊Wigman, and Kurt ◊Jooss.

Austen Jane 1775–1817. English novelist who described her raw material as 'three or four families in a Country Village'. *Sense and Sensibility* was published 1811, ◊*Pride and Prejudice* 1813, *Mansfield Park* 1814, *Emma* 1816, *Northanger Abbey* and *Persuasion* 1818, all anonymously. She observed speech and manners with wit and precision, revealing her characters' absurdities in relation to high standards of integrity and appropriateness.

She was born at Steventon, Hampshire, where her father was rector, and began writing early; the burlesque *Love and Freindship* (sic), published 1922, was written 1790. In 1801 the family moved to Bath and after the death of her father 1805, to Southampton, finally settling in Chawton, Hampshire, with her brother Edward. Between 1795 and 1798 she worked on three novels. The first to be published (like its successors, anonymously) was *Sense and Sensibility* (drafted in letter form 1797–98). *Pride and Prejudice* (written 1796–97) followed, but *Northanger Abbey*, a skit on the contemporary Gothic novel (written 1798, sold to a London publisher 1803, and bought back 1816), did not appear until 1818. The fragmentary *Watsons* and *Lady Susan*, written about 1803–05, remained unfinished. The success of her published works, however, stimulated Jane Austen to write in rapid succession *Mansfield Park, Emma, Persuasion,* and the final fragment *Sanditon* written 1817. She died in Winchester, and is buried in the cathedral.

There certainly are not so many men of large fortune in the world, as there are pretty women to deserve them.

Jane Austen *Mansfield Park*

Auster Paul 1947– . US novelist. Making experimental use of detective story techniques, he has explored modern urban identity in his acclaimed *New York Trilogy: City of Glass* 1985, *Ghosts* 1986, and *The Locked Room* 1986. Later works in different genres include *In the Country of Last Things* 1987, *Moon Palace* 1989, and *The Music of Chance* 1991.

Austin Alfred 1835–1913. British poet. He published the satirical poem *The Season* 1861, which was followed by plays and volumes of poetry little read today; from 1896 he was poet laureate.

I dare not alter these things, they come to me from above.

Alfred Austin
when accused of writing ungrammatical verse

Australian architecture the architecture of the Australian continent. Traditionally, Aboriginal settlements tended to be based around caves, or a construction of bark huts, arranged in a circular group; there was some variation in different areas.

Architecture of the early settlers includes Vaucluse House and the Sydney home of William Charles Wentworth. Queensland has old-style homes built on stilts for coolness beneath their floors. Outstanding examples of modern architecture are the layout of the town of Canberra, by Walter Burley Griffin (1876–1937); Victoria Arts Centre, Melbourne, by Roy Grounds (1905–1981), who also designed the Academy of Science, Canberra 1958–59; and the Sydney Opera House (1956–73), by Jorn Utzon (1918–). A distinctive Australian tradition of modern architecture has more recently emerged, ranging from the purist work of Harry Seidler (1923–) to the regionalist vernacular of Russell Hall.

Australian art art in Australia dates back some 15,000 to 20,000 years ago to the earliest known examples of Aboriginal art. These are closely linked with religion and mythology and include rock and bark paintings. European-style art developed in the 18th century with landscape painting predominating.

18th century The first European paintings were documentary, depicting the Aborigines, the flora and fauna and topographical scenes of and around Sydney showing the progress of settlement.

19th century Artists such as John Glover (1767–1849) and Conrad Martens endeavoured with European-trained eyes to portray the uniqueness of the Australian landscape. The gold rushes of the 1850s–1880s brought to Australia a number of talented artists. Some, such as Samuel Thomas Gill (1818–1880), recorded the lively

life of the diggings, others like Abram Louis Buvelot (1818–1888) and Eugène von Guérard (1811–1901) used distinctive *plein air* ('open air') styles to capture the light and form of the Australian landscape. This approach was further developed by the painters of the Heidelberg School, notably Tom Roberts, Frederick McCubbin (1885–1917), and Arthur Streeton, who painted in the Impressionist style.

20th century Modernist artists such as Roy de Maistre (1894–1968), Grace Cossington Smith (1892–1985) and Roland Wakelin (1887–1971) encountered opposition, but the acceptance of later modernists, such as Russell Drysdale and William Dobell, reflected a change in public tastes and expectations. Other well-known modern artists include Albert Namatjira and Sidney Nolan, who created a highly individual vision of the Australian landscape and of such folk heroes as Ned Kelly. In the 1940s and 1950s a Sydney-based group of abstract painters, which included John Olsen (1928–), emerged, while in Melbourne the Antipodean Group, which included Arthur Boyd and Charles Blackman, led a reaction against abstract art. Influential contemporary painters include Fred Williams and Brett Whiteley.

Australian literature Australian literature begins with the journals, letters, and memoirs of early settlers and explorers, and reflects the 18th-century interest in science and learning. The first poet of note was Charles Harpur (1813–1868), son of a convict, whose work expresses hope for, and pride in, the new world of the colony. Australian idioms and rhythms were developed by, among others, Henry Kendall (1839–1882) who wrote nature lyrics inspired by coastal scenery, and Adam Lindsay Gordon (1833–1870) whose galloping verses set in the Australian bush were forerunner to the *bush ballads* of A B (Banjo) Paterson (1864–1941) which romanticized and made familiar the outback, droving, and shearing. Henry Lawson (1867–1922) , in verse and prose, depicted the other side of bush life—its harshness, hopelessness, and social injustice—realist themes which were echoed by prose writer Barbara Baynton (1857–1929). Poets of the early 20th century include Bernard O'Dowd (1866–1953), lyricists Mary Gilmore (1865–1962), John Shaw Neilson (1872–1942) and Roderic Quinn (1867–1949), and Christopher Brennan (1870–1932), a classical scholar and contemporary of the bush balladists who was strongly influenced by French symbolist writings. The 1930s and 1940s were dominated by the contrasting strands of nationalism and modernism as demonstrated by the emergence of the *Jindyworobak* and *Angry Penguins* literary movements. Established 20th-century poets include R D FitzGerald (1902–), A D (Alec Derwent) Hope (1907–), Douglas Stewart (1913–1985), Kenneth Slessor (1901–1971) James McAuley (1917–1976), and Judith Wright (1915–). Contemporary poets include

Bruce Beaver (1928–   ), Rodney Hall (1935–   ), and Les Murray (1938–   ).

The first Australian novel in book form was the largely autobiographical *Quintus Servinton*. 1830, by Henry Savery (1791–1842), an account of the transportation system and convict life in Tasmania. English novels set in Australia by visiting writers include *The Recollections of Geoffry Hamlyn* 1859, by Henry Kingsley (1830–1876). The conflict between realism and romance, evident in 19th-century Australian poetry, also appears in novels: *For the Term of His Natural Life* 1874, by Marcus Clarke (1846–1881), and *Robbery Under Arms* 1888, by Rolf Boldrewood (1826–1915), are examples. Elements of both attitudes also appear in the work of later writers such as Joseph Furphy (1843–1912), Henry Handel Richardson (1870–1946), and Miles Franklin (1879–1954). An important influence on Australian poetry and fiction in the early to mid-20th century was the *Bulletin* magazine, which gave encouragement to emerging writers and provided an outlet for their work. Although some 20th-century writers, such as Christina Stead (1902–1983), Martin Boyd (1893–1972), Sumner Locke Elliott (1917–   ), and the dramatist Ray Lawler (1921–   ), became expatriates, most stayed and established their reputations in Australia. The postwar years saw the return from Europe of Patrick White whose modernist approach influenced many emerging poets, novelists, and dramatists, such as Les Murray, Thomas Keneally (1935–   ), and Jack Hibberd (1940–   ). Contemporary writers include Frank Moorhouse (1938–   ), David Ireland (1927–   ), Peter Carey (1943–   ), David Malouf (1934–   ), and Murray Bail (1941–   ) and their work displays a wide range of experimental prose techniques.

Australian National Gallery art gallery in Canberra housing the Australian national collection. The building was opened 1982 and the collection can be viewed in 11 main galleries over three levels. The collection includes Australian Aboriginal and European art, international Western art, and the arts of Oceania, Asia, Africa, and the Americas.

authenticity in music, a trend initiated in Britain 1970 aiming to reproduce the original conditions of early music performance and instrumentation as a means of rediscovering aesthetic terms of reference. It stimulated important practical research in manuscript editing and transcription, instrument-making, dance, architectural acoustics, and vocal techniques and encouraged performance of vocal works in the original language.

Notable exponents include conductors Raymond Leppard, Christopher Hogwood, Andrew Parrott, and Roger Norrington, David Munrow (woodwind), Anthony Rooley (lute), Jaap Schröder (violin), Emma Kirkby (soprano), and Frans Brüggen (flute).

autobiography a person's own biography, or written account of his or her life, distinguished from the journal or diary by being a connected narrative, and from memoirs by dealing less with contemporary events and personalities. *The Boke of Margery Kempe* about 1432–36 is the oldest known autobiography in English.

Forms of autobiography include the confessional, attempting faithful description of moral weakness and the inner life, as in the influential *Confessions* of St Augustine (early 5th century) and Rousseau (1781); the would-be exemplary, seeking to promote a particular cause or outlook espoused by the writer, as in Hitler's *Mein Kampf* (written in the 1920s) or the autobiography of John Stuart Mill (1873); and military and political memoirs, intended as contributions to history.

autochrome in photography, a single-plate additive colour process devised by the ◊Lumière brothers 1903. It was the first commercially available process, in use 1907–35.

Autolycus in Greek mythology, an accomplished thief and trickster, son of the god ◊Hermes, who gave him the power of invisibility.

automatism in the arts, an act of creation which either allows chance to play a major role or which draws on the unconscious mind through free association, states of trance, or dreams. Automatism was fundamental to Surrealism, whose practitioners experimented with automatic writing and automatic drawing, producing streams of words or doodles from the unconscious. It has been taken up other abstract painters, such as the Canadian Automatistes, a group working in Montréal in the 1940s, and the Abstract Expressionist Jackson ◊Pollock.

autos sacramentales (Spanish 'religious plays') Spanish drama form, similar to the ◊mystery plays in England, and well established by the 13th century. These traditional performances were redeveloped in the 17th century by dramatists Lope de Vega and Calderón, whose masterpiece in this form is *El gran teatro del mundo/The Great Theatre of the World* 1641.

Avalon in Celtic legend, the island of the blessed, or paradise; in the legend of King ◊Arthur, the land of heroes, ruled over by ◊Morgan le Fay to which King Arthur is conveyed after his final battle with ◊Mordred. It has been identified since the Middle Ages with Glastonbury in Somerset, SW England.

There enters Avalon a party of twelve men:/Joseph, the flower of Arimathea, is chief of them ...

John of Glastonbury
on Avalon *Chronicles*

avant-garde (French 'advanced guard') in the arts, those artists or works that are in the forefront of new developments in their media. The term was introduced (as was 'reactionary') after the French Revolution, when it was used to describe any socialist political movement.

avant-garde dance experimental dance form that rejects the conventions of classical ballet and modern dance. It is often performed in informal spaces – museums, rooftops, even scaling walls.

In the USA, avant-garde dance has been mainly represented by the work of Merce ◊Cunningham, and by the performances held by artists at the Judson Memorial Church during the 1960s. While retaining technique and rhythm, Cunningham abolished narrative, explicit emotional statements, and any direct connection between dance and music. The Judson collective went further, denying even the necessity for technique and concentrating on the use of everyday movement. They also avoided any attempt at gender stereotyping. Recent developments in the 1980s and 1990s have incorporated some of these characteristics but have also seen a return to skilled movement, such as in the works of Trisha ◊Brown and Mark ◊Morris.

In the UK, leading exponents of avant-garde dance techniques include Michael ◊Clark from the mid-1980s, Rosemary ◊Butcher, and Lloyd ◊Newson. In Germany, Pina ◊Bausch with her Wuppertal Tanztheater (dance theatre), established 1974, has been considered the most compelling influence in European dance since ◊Diaghilev. In Japan, experimental dance is represented by ◊butoh dance companies.

avatar in Hindu mythology, the descent of a deity to Earth in a visible form, for example the ten avatars of ◊Vishnu.

Avedon Richard 1923– . US photographer. A fashion photographer with *Harper's Bazaar* magazine in New York from the mid-1940s, he moved to *Vogue* 1965. He later became the highest-paid fashion and advertising photographer in the world. He became associated with the *New Yorker* 1993. Using large-format cameras, his work consists of intensely realistic images, chiefly portraits.

Avercamp Hendrick 1585–1634. Dutch landscape painter specializing in winter scenes enlivened by colourful, carefully arranged groups of people, skating or talking together. *Winter Scene* about 1609 (National Gallery, London) is typical.

Avery Milton 1893–1965. US painter, whose early work was inspired by Henri ◊Matisse, portraying subjects in thin, flat, richly coloured strokes. His later work, although still figurative, shows the influence of Mark ◊Rothko and other experimental US artists.

Avery Tex (Frederick Bean) 1907–1980. US cartoon-film director who used violent, sometimes surreal humour. At Warner Bros he helped develop Bugs Bunny and Daffy Duck, before moving to MGM 1942 where he created, among others, Droopy the Dog and Screwball Squirrel.

Avianus *c.* AD 400. Roman fable writer. Written in elegiac couplets, his fables number 42 in total, and are dedicated to the emperor Theodosius.

axonometric projection three-dimensional drawing of an object, such as a building, in which the floor plan provides the basis for the visible elevations, thus creating a diagram that is true to scale but incorrect in terms of perspective. Vertical lines are projected up from the plan at the same scale; the usual angle of projection is 45°. An *isometric projection* is a slightly flattened variation.

Ayckbourn Alan 1939– . English dramatist. His prolific output, characterized by comic dialogue and experiments in dramatic structure, includes the trilogy *The Norman Conquests* 1974, *A Woman in Mind* 1986, *Henceforward* 1987, and *Man of the Moment* 1988.

Few women care to be laughed at and men not at all, except for large sums of money.

Alan Ayckbourn *The Norman Conquests*

---

ayre or *air* 16th-century verse song with lute or guitar accompaniment, as in 'It was a lover and his lass' 1600 by Thomas Morley.

Ayrton Michael 1921–1975. English painter, sculptor, illustrator, and writer. From 1961, he concentrated on the ◊Daedalus myth, producing bronzes of Icarus and a fictional autobiography of Daedalus, *The Maze Maker* 1967.

Aytoun or *Ayton* Robert 1570–1638. Scottish poet employed and knighted by James I; he was noted for his love poems. Aytoun is the reputed author of the lines on which Robert Burns based 'Auld Lang Syne'.

Aytoun W(illiam) E(dmonstoune) 1813–1865. Scottish poet, born in Edinburgh, chiefly remembered for his *Lays of the Scottish Cavaliers* 1848 and *Bon Gaultier Ballads* 1855, which he wrote in collaboration with the Scottish nationalist Theodore Martin (1816–1909).

The earth is all the home I have,/ The heavens my wide roof-tree.

W E Aytoun 'The Wandering Jew'

Azorín pen name of José Martínez Ruiz 1873–1967. Spanish writer. His works include volumes of critical essays and short stories, plays and novels, such as the autobiographical *La voluntad/The Choice* 1902 and *Antonio Azorín* 1903. He adopted the name of the hero of the latter as his pen name.

Babbitt satirical novel 1922 by Sinclair ◊Lewis about a Midwestern businessman obsessed with commerce, clubs, and material values. 'Babbittry' came to mean a type of Middle American cultureless innocence.

Babbitt Milton 1916– . US composer and theorist who pioneered the application of information theory to music in the 1950s, introducing set theory to series manipulations and the term 'pitch class' to define every octave identity of a note name. His works include four string quartets, works for orchestra, *Philomel* for soprano and electronic tape 1963–64, and *Ensembles for Synthesizer* 1967, both composed using the 1960 RCA Princeton-Columbia Mark II Synthesizer, which he helped to design.

Babel Hebrew name for the city of Babylon in ancient Mesopotamia, chiefly associated with the *Tower of Babel* which, in the Genesis story in the Old Testament, was erected in the plain of Shinar by the descendants of Noah. It was a ziggurat, or staged temple, seven storeys high (100 m/300 ft) with a shrine of Marduk on the summit. It was built by Nabopolassar, father of Nebuchadnezzar, and was destroyed when Sennacherib sacked the city 689 BC.

Babel Isaak Emmanuilovich 1894–1939/40. Russian writer. Born in Odessa, he was an ardent supporter of the Revolution and fought with Budyenny's cavalry in the Polish campaign of 1921–22, an experience which inspired *Konarmiya/Red Cavalry* 1926. His other works include *Odesskie rasskazy/Stories from Odessa* 1924, which portrays the life of the Odessa Jews.

Babrius lived *c.* 3rd century AD. Roman writer of fables, written in Greek. He probably lived in Syria, where his stories first gained popularity. In 1842 a manuscript of his fables was discovered in a convent on Mount Athos, Greece. There were 123 fables, arranged alphabetically, but stopping at the letter O.

Bacall Lauren. Stage name of Betty Joan Perske 1924– . US actress who became an overnight star when cast by Howard Hawks opposite Humphrey Bogart in *To Have and Have Not* 1944. She and Bogart married 1945, and starred together in *The Big Sleep* 1946. She also appeared in *The Cobweb* 1955 and *Harper* 1966. She returned to Hollywood after an eight-year absence with *Murder on the Orient Express* 1974 and two years later appeared in *The Shootist* 1976.

Bacchae, The tragedy by ◊Euripides, first performed *c.* 405 BC. Pentheus, king of Thebes, rejects the worship of the god Dionysus yet falls under his spell. He is finally torn to pieces in the mountains by Dionysiac worshippers led by his mother, Agave, who emerges from her frenzy to realize what she has done.

Bacchus in Greek and Roman mythology, the god of fertility (see ◊Dionysus) and of wine; his rites (the Bacchanalia) were orgiastic.

A convenient deity invented by the ancients as an excuse for getting drunk.

Ambrose Bierce on Bacchus
The Devil's Dictionary 1911

Bach Carl Philip Emmanuel 1714–1788. German composer, third son of J S Bach. He introduced a new 'homophonic' style, light and easy to follow, which influenced Mozart, Haydn, and Beethoven.

In the service of Frederick the Great 1740–67, he left to become master of church music at Hamburg 1768. He wrote over 200 pieces for keyboard instruments, and published a guide to playing the piano. Through his music and concert performances he helped to establish a leading solo role for the piano in Western music.

Bach Johann Christian 1735–1782. German composer, the 11th son of J S Bach, who became celebrated in Italy as a composer of operas. In 1762 he was invited to London, where he became music master to the royal family. He remained in England until his death, enjoying great popularity both as composer and performer.

Bach Johann Sebastian 1685–1750. German composer. He was a master of ◊counterpoint, and his music epitomizes the Baroque polyphonic style. His orchestral music includes the six *Brandenburg Concertos* 1721, other concertos for keyboard instrument and violin, and four orchestral suites. Bach's keyboard music, for clavier and organ, his fugues, and his choral music are of equal importance. He also wrote chamber music and songs.

Born at Eisenach, Bach came from a distinguished musical family. At 15 he became a chorister at Lüneburg, and at 19 he was organist at Arnstadt. His appointments included positions at the courts of Weimar and Anhalt-Köthen, and from 1723 until his death he was musical director at St Thomas' choir school in Leipzig. He married twice and had over 20 children (although several died in infancy). His second wife, Anna Magdalena Wülkens, was a soprano; she also worked for him when his sight failed in later years.

Bach's sacred music includes 200 church cantatas, the Easter and Christmas oratorios 1732–35 and 1734–35, the two great Passions, of St John and St Matthew, first performed 1723 and 1729, and the Mass in B minor 1724–49. His keyboard music includes a collection of 48 preludes and fugues known as *Das wohltemperierte Clavier/ The Well-Tempered Clavier* 1722–42, the *Goldberg Variations* 1742, and the *Italian Concerto* 1735. Of his organ music the finest examples are the chorale preludes. Two works written in his later years illustrate the principles and potential of his polyphonic art – the *Musikalisches Opfer/ Musical Offering* 1747 and *Die Kunst der Fuge/The Art of Fugue* published posthumously 1751.

Bach Wilhelm Friedemann 1710–1784. German composer, who was also an organist, improviser, and master of ◊counterpoint. He was the eldest son of J S Bach.

background music accompanying music for a stage or film production which serves to establish a mood or stimulate appropriate audience responses. It differs from ◊incidental music in not being part of the action, and in working on the listener subliminally. The use of piped music in shopping malls extends the principle to real life.

Bacon Francis 1561–1626. English politician, philosopher, and essayist. His works include *Essays* 1597, characterized by pith and brevity; *The Advancement of Learning* 1605, a seminal work discussing scientific method; the *Novum Organum* 1620, in which he redefined the task of natural science, seeing it as a means of empirical discovery and a method of increasing human power over nature; and *The New Atlantis* 1626, describing a utopian state in which scientific knowledge is systematically sought and exploited.

The *Baconian Theory*, originated by James Willmot 1785, suggesting that the works of Shakespeare were written by Bacon, is not taken seriously by scholars.

There is nothing makes a man suspect much, more than to know little.

Francis Bacon, 'Of Suspicion'

Bacon Francis 1909–1992. British painter, born in Dublin. Self-taught, he practised abstract art, then developed a stark Expressionist style characterized by distorted, blurred figures enclosed in loosely defined space. One of his best-known works is *Study after Velázquez's Portrait of Pope Innocent X* 1953 (Museum of Modern Art, New York).

Bacon moved to London 1925, began to paint about 1930, and held his first show in London 1949. He destroyed much of his early work. *Three Studies for Figures at the Base of a Crucifixion* about 1944 (Tate Gallery, London) is an early example of his mature style, which is often seen as a powerful expression of the existential anxiety and nihilism of 20th-century life.

Baez Joan 1941– . US folk singer and pacifist activist whose pure soprano in the early 1960s popularized traditional English and American folk songs such as 'Silver Dagger' and 'We Shall Overcome' (an anthem of the civil-rights movement). She helped Bob Dylan at the start of his career, and has recorded many of his songs. She founded the Institute for the Study of Non-Violence in Carmel, California, 1965.

BAFTA acronym for *British Academy of Film and Television Arts*, formed 1959 as a result of the amalgamation of the British Film Academy (founded 1948) and the Guild of Television Producers (founded 1954). For awards, see ◊cinema.

bagatelle (French 'trifle') in music, a short character piece, often for piano.

Bagnold Enid 1889–1981. British author of *National Velvet* 1935, a popular novel about horse racing that was also successful as a film (1944, starring Elizabeth Taylor).

bagpipes any of an ancient family of double-reed folk woodwind instruments employing a bladder or bellows as an air reservoir to a 'chanter' or melody pipe, and optional 'drones' providing a continuous accompanying harmony. Examples include the old French *musette*, Scottish and Irish pipes, smaller Northumbrian pipes, Breton *biniou*, Spanish *gaita*, and numerous variants in Eastern Europe, the Middle East, and North Africa.

The bag has the advantage of being more powerful than the unaided lungs and of being able to sustain notes indefinitely. The Highland bagpipes are the national instrument of Scotland.

Bagritsky Eduard. Pen name of Eduard Dzyubin 1895–1934. Russian poet. One of the Constructivist group, he published the heroic poem *Lay About Opanas* 1926, and collections of verse called *The Victors* 1932 and *The Last Night* 1932.

bailey an open space or court of a stone-built castle.

Bailey David 1938– . British fashion photographer. His work for *Vogue* magazine in the 1960s and his black-and-white portraits of fashionable celebrities did much to define the image of 'swinging London'. He has published several books, including *Box of Pin-ups* 1965 and *Goodbye Baby and Amen* 1969.

Bainbridge Beryl 1934– . English novelist. Acutely observed, peppered with ironic black humour, and often dealing with human self-delusion, her works include *The Dressmaker* 1973, *The Bottle Factory Outing* 1974, *Injury Time* 1977, *An Awfully Big Adventure* 1990, and *The Birthday Boys* 1991.

Among her other works are *Young Adolf* 1978, *The Winter Garden* 1980, and the collected short stories in *Mum and Mr Armitage* 1985.

baion beat slow rhythm of Brazilian origin, used in pop music from the late 1950s onwards; for example, in many recordings produced by Phil Spector. The on beat is followed by a one-beat pause and two half beats.

Baker Chet (Chesney) 1929–1988. US jazz trumpeter. His good looks, occasional vocal performances, and romantic interpretations of ballads helped make him a cult figure. He became known with the Gerry Mulligan Quartet 1952 and formed his own quartet 1953. Recordings include 'My Funny Valentine' and 'The Thrill Is Gone'.

Baker Janet 1933– . English mezzo-soprano. She is noted for the emotional strength and richness of her interpretations of lieder, oratorio, and opera from Purcell to Britten, including a notable Dido in Purcell's *Dido and Aeneas*. She retired from the stage 1981.

Singing lieder is like putting a piece of music under a microscope.

Janet Baker in *Opera News* July 1977

Bakhuyzen Ludolf 1631–1708. Dutch painter of seascapes. *Stormy Sea* 1697 (Rijksmuseum, Amsterdam) is a typically dramatic work.

Bakst Leon; Adopted name of Leon Rosenberg 1866–1924. Russian painter and theatrical designer. He combined intense colours and fantastic images adapted from Oriental and folk art with an Art Nouveau tendency toward graceful surface pattern. His designs for Diaghilev's touring Ballets Russes made a deep impression in Paris 1909–14.

Balakirev Mily Alexeyevich 1837–1910. Russian composer. He wrote orchestral works including the fantasy *Islamey* 1869/1902, piano music, songs, and a symphonic poem *Tamara*, all imbued with the Russian national character and spirit. He was leader of the group known as 'The ◊Mighty Handful' and taught its members, Mussorgsky, Cui, Rimsky-Korsakov, and Borodin.

Balakirev was born at Nizhni Novgorod. At St Petersburg he worked with Mikhail ◊Glinka, established the Free School of Music 1862,

which stressed the national element, and was director of the Imperial Chapel 1883–95.

balalaika Russian musical instrument, resembling a guitar. It has a triangular sound box, frets, and two, three, or four strings played by strumming with the fingers.

Balanchine George 1904–1983. Russian-born US choreographer. After leaving the USSR 1924, he worked with ◊Diaghilev in France. Moving to the USA 1933, he became a major influence on dance, starting the New York City Ballet 1948. He was the most influential 20th-century choreographer of ballet in the USA. He developed an 'American Neo-Classic' dance style and made the New York City Ballet one of the world's great companies. His ballets are usually plotless and are performed in practice clothes to modern music. He also choreographed dances for five Hollywood films.

His many works include *Apollon Musagète* 1928 and *The Prodigal Son* 1929 for Diaghilev, *Serenade* 1934; several works with music by Stravinsky, such as *Agon* 1957 and *Duo Concertante* 1972; and Broadway musicals, such as *On Your Toes* 1936 and *The Boys from Syracuse* 1938.

Balchin Nigel Marlin 1908–1970. British author. During World War II he was engaged on scientific work for the army and wrote *The Small Back Room* 1943, a novel dealing with the psychology of the 'back room boys' of wartime research.

Balcon Michael 1896–1977. English film producer, responsible for the influential Ealing comedies of the 1940s and early 1950s (see ◊Ealing Studios), such as *Kind Hearts and Coronets* 1949, *Whisky Galore!* 1949, and *The Lavender Hill Mob* 1951.

Balder in Norse mythology, the son of Odin and Freya and husband of Nanna, and the best, wisest, and most loved of all the gods. He was killed, at Loki's instigation, by a twig of mistletoe shot by the blind god Hodur.

Baldung Grien Hans 1484/85–1545. German Renaissance painter, engraver, and designer, based in Strasbourg. A prolific artist, he designed tapestries and stained glass, produced many graphic works, and painted religious subjects, portraits, and allegories, notably his several versions of *Death and the Maiden*.

Baldwin James 1924–1987. US writer. He is best known for his depiction of the suffering and despair of black Americans in contemporary society. After his first novel, *Go Tell It On The Mountain* 1953, set in Harlem, and *Giovanni's Room* 1956, about a homosexual relationship in Paris, his writing became more politically indignant with *Another Country* 1962 and *The Fire Next Time* 1963, a collection of essays.

It comes as a great shock to see Gary Cooper killing off the Indians and, although you are rooting for Gary Cooper, that the Indians are you.

James Baldwin speech Feb 1965

Other works include his play *The Amen Corner* 1955, the autobiographical essays *Notes of a Native Son* 1955, and the novel *Just Above My Head* 1979.

Balenciaga Cristobal 1895–1972. Spanish couturier. His influential innovations in women's clothing included drop shoulder lines, nipped-in waists, and rounded hips, followed by three-quarter length sleeves and the pillbox hat. During the 1950s–1960s he moved away from fitted outfits to show loose designs such as a dress known as the 'sack', cut full around the body and gathered or tapered into a narrow hem-band just below the knees, in 1956 and loose full jackets in the 1960s. He retired 1968.

Balfe Michael William 1808–1870. Irish composer and singer. He was a violinist and baritone at Drury Lane, London, when only 16. In 1825 he went to Italy, where he sang in Palermo and at La Scala, and in 1846 he was appointed conductor at Her Majesty's Theatre, London. His operas include *The Bohemian Girl* 1843.

Ball Lucille 1911–1989. US comedy actress. She began her film career as a bit player 1933, and appeared in dozens of movies over the next few years, including *Room Service* 1938 (with the Marx Brothers) and *Fancy Pants* 1950 (with Bob Hope). From 1951 to 1957 she starred with her husband, Cuban bandleader Desi Arnaz, in the television sitcom *I Love Lucy*, the first US television show filmed before an audience. It was followed by *The Lucy Show* 1962–68 and *Here's Lucy* 1968–74.

Balla Giacomo 1871–1958. Italian painter, a leading member of the Futurist group, whose work is concerned with themes of time and movement. Influenced by photographic techniques, he developed a style using multiple images and blurred outlines. His *Dog on a Leash* 1912 (Fine Arts Academy, Buffalo) is one of the best-known Futurist works.

ballad a form of traditional narrative poetry, widespread in Europe and the USA. Ballads are metrically simple, sometimes (as in Russia) unstrophic and unrhymed or (as in Denmark) dependent on assonance. Concerned with some strongly emotional event, the ballad is halfway between the lyric and the epic. Most English ballads date from the 15th century but may describe earlier events. Poets of the Romantic movement both in England and in Germany were greatly influenced by the ballad revival, as seen in, for example, the *Lyrical Ballads* 1798 of ◊Wordsworth and ◊Coleridge. *Des Knaben Wunderhorn/The Boy's Magic Horn* 1805–08, a collection edited by Clemens ◊Brentano and Ludwig von ◊Arnim, was a major influence on 19th-century German poetry. The ballad form was adapted in 'broadsheets' with a satirical or political motive, and in the 'hanging' ballads purporting to come from condemned criminals.

Historically, the ballad was primarily intended for singing at the communal ring-dance, the refrains representing the chorus. Opinion is divided as to whether the authorship of the ballads may be attributed to individual poets or to the community. Later ballads tend to centre on a popular folk hero, such as Robin Hood or Jesse James.

In 19th-century music the refined drawing-room ballad had a vogue, but a more robust tradition survived in the music hall; folk song played its part in the development of pop music, and in this genre slow songs are often called 'ballads' regardless of content.

In the UK collections of ballads were made in the 17th and 18th centuries, for example Bishop Percy's *Reliques of Ancient Poetry* 1765, Scott's *Minstrelsy of the Scottish Border* 1802–03, and Professor F J Child's *English and Scottish Popular Ballads* 1857–59.

ballade in literature, a poetic form developed in France in the later Middle Ages from the ballad, generally consisting of one or more groups of three stanzas of seven or eight lines each, followed by a shorter stanza or envoy, the last line being repeated as a chorus. In music, a ballade is an instrumental piece based on a story; a form used in piano works by ◊Chopin and ◊Liszt.

Ballantyne R(obert) M(ichael) 1825–1894. Scottish writer of children's books. Childhood visits to Canada and six years as a trapper for the Hudson's Bay Company provided material for his adventure stories, which include *The Young Fur Traders* 1856, *Coral Island* 1857, and *Martin Rattler* 1858.

Ballard J(ames) G(raham) 1930– . English novelist. His works include science fiction on the theme of catastrophe and collapse of the urban landscape, such as *The Drowned World* 1962, *Crash!* 1973, and *High-Rise* 1975; the partly autobiographical *Empire of the Sun* 1984, dealing with his internment in China during World War II; and the autobiographical novel *The Kindness of Women* 1991. His fundamentally moral vision is expressed with an untrammelled imagination and pessimistic irony.

ballet (Italian *balletto* 'a little dance') theatrical representation in dance form in which music also plays a major part in telling a story or conveying a mood. Some such form of entertainment existed in ancient Greece, but Western ballet as we know it today first appeared in Italy. From there it was

The ballet repertory

date	ballet	composer	choreographer	place
1670	Le Bourgeois Gentilhomme	Lully	Beauchamp	Chambord
1735	Les Indes Galantes	Rameau	Blondy	Paris
1761	Don Juan	Gluck	Angiolini	Vienna
1778	Les Petits Riens	Mozart	Noverre	Paris
1801	The Creatures of Prometheus	Beethoven	Viganó	Vienna
1828	La Fille mal gardée	Hérold	Aumer	Paris
1832	La Sylphide	Schneitzhoeffer	F Taglioni	Paris
1841	Giselle	Coralli	Perrot	Paris
1842	Napoli	Gade/Helsted/Lumbye/Paulli	Bournonville	Copenhagen
1844	La Esmeralda	Pugni	Perrot	London
1869	Don Quixote	Minkus	M Petipa	Moscow
1870	Coppélia	Delibes	Saint-Léon	Paris
1877	La Bayadère	Minkus	M Petipa	St Petersburg
1877	Swan Lake	Tchaikovsky	Reisinger	Moscow
1890	The Sleeping Beauty	Tchaikovsky	M Petipa	St Petersburg
1892	Nutcracker	Tchaikovsky	M Petipa/Ivanov	St Petersburg
1898	Raymonda	Glazunov	M Petipa	St Petersburg
1907	The Dying Swan	Saint-Saëns	Fokine	St Petersburg
1909	Les Sylphides/Chopiniana	Chopin	Fokine	St Petersburg
1910	The Firebird	Stravinsky	Fokine	Paris
1911	Petrushka	Stravinsky	Fokine	Paris
1911	Le Spectre de la rose	Weber	Fokine	Monte Carlo
1912	L'Après-midi d'un faune	Debussy	Nijinsky	Paris
1913	Le Sacre du printemps/ The Rite of Spring	Stravinsky	Nijinsky	Paris
1917	Parade	Satie	Massine	Paris
1919	The Three-Cornered Hat	Falla	Massine	London
1923	Les Noces	Stravinsky	Nijinska	Paris
1924	Les Biches	Poulenc	Nijinska	Monte Carlo
1927	The Red Poppy	Glière	Lashchilin/Tikhomirov	Moscow
1928	Apollo	Stravinsky	Balanchine	Paris
1929	The Prodigal Son	Prokofiev	Balanchine	Paris
1929	La Valse	Ravel	Nijinska	Monte Carlo
1931	Façade	Walton	Ashton	London
1937	Checkmate	Bliss	de Valois	Paris
1937	Les Patineurs	Meyerbeer/Lambert	Ashton	London
1938	Billy the Kid	Copland	Loring	Chicago
1940	Romeo and Juliet	Prokofiev	Lavrovsky	Leningrad
1942	The Miraculous Mandarin	Bartók	Milloss	Milan
1942	Rodeo	Copland	de Mille	New York
1944	Fancy Free	Bernstein	Robbins	New York
1949	Carmen	Bizet	Petit	London
1951	Pineapple Poll	Sullivan/Mackerras	Cranko	London
1956	Spartacus	Khachaturian	Jacobson	Leningrad
1957	Agon	Stravinsky	Balanchine	New York
1962	Pierrot lunaire	Schoenberg	Tetley	New York
1964	The Dream	Mendelssohn/Lanchbery	Ashton	London
1965	The Song of the Earth	Mahler	MacMillan	Stuttgart
1966	Romeo and Juliet	Prokofiev	MacMillan	London
1968	Enigma Variations	Elgar	Ashton	London
1969	The Taming of the Shrew	Scarlatti/Stolze	Cranko	Stuttgart
1972	Duo Concertante	Stravinsky	Balanchine	New York
1974	Elite Syncopations	Joplin and others	MacMillan	London
1976	A Month in the Country	Chopin/Lanchbery	Ashton	London
1978	Mayerling	Liszt/Lanchbery	MacMillan	London
1978	Symphony of Psalms	Stravinsky	Kylián	Scheveningen, The Netherlands
1980	Gloria	Poulenc	MacMillan	London
1980	Rhapsody	Rachmaninov	Ashton	London
1982	The Golden Age	Shostakovich	Grigorovich	Moscow
1984	Different Drummer	Webern/Schoenberg	MacMillan	London
1986	The Snow Queen	Tovey/Mussorgsky	Bintley	Birmingham
1988	L'allegro, il penseroso ed il moderato	Handel	Morris	Brussels
1989	The Prince of the Pagodas	Britten	MacMillan	London
1991	Winter Dreams	Tchaikovsky	MacMillan	London

brought by Catherine de' Medici to France in the form of a spectacle combining singing, dancing, and declamation. In the 20th century Russian ballet has had a vital influence on the classical tradition in the West, and ballet developed further in the USA through the work of George Balanchine and the American Ballet Theater, and in the UK through the influence of Marie Rambert. ◊Modern dance is a separate development.

history The first important dramatic ballet, the *Ballet comique de la reine*, was produced 1581 by the Italian Balthasar de Beaujoyeux at the French court and was performed by male courtiers, with ladies of the court forming the *corps de ballet*. In 1661 Louis XIV founded L'Académie Royale de Danse, to which all subsequent ballet activities throughout the world can be traced. Long, flowing court dress was worn by the dancers until the 1720s when Marie-Anne Camargo, the first great ballerina, shortened her skirt to reveal her ankles, thus allowing greater movement *à terre* and the development of dancing *en l'air*. It was not until the early 19th century that a Paris costumier, Maillot, invented tights, thus allowing complete muscular freedom. The first of the great ballet masters was Jean-Georges ◊Noverre, and great contemporary dancers were Teresa Vestris (1726–1808), Anna Friedrike Heinel (1753–1808), Jean Dauberval (1742–1806), and Maximilien Gardel (1741–1787). Carlo Blasis is regarded as the founder of classical ballet, since he defined the standard conventional steps and accompanying gestures.

Romantic ballet The great Romantic era of the dancers Marie ◊Taglioni , Fanny Elssler, Carlotta Grisi, Lucile Grahn, and Fanny Cerrito began about 1830 but survives today only in the ballets *Giselle* 1841 and *La Sylphide* 1832. Characteristics of this era were the new calf-length Romantic white dress and the introduction of dancing on the toes, *sur les pointes*. The technique of the female dancer was developed, but the role of the male dancer was reduced to that of her partner.

Russian ballet was introduced to the West by Sergei ◊Diaghilev , who set out for Paris 1909, at about the same time that Isadora ◊Duncan, a fervent opponent of classical ballet, was touring Europe. Associated with Diaghilev were Mikhail Fokine, Vaslav Nijinsky, Anna Pavlova, Léonide Massine, Bronislava Nijinska, George Balanchine, and Serge Lifar. Ballets presented by his company, before its break-up after his death 1929, included *Les Sylphides*, *Schéhérazade*, *Petrushka*, *Le Sacre du printemps/The Rite of Spring*, and *Les Noces*. Diaghilev and Fokine pioneered a new and exciting combination of the perfect technique of imperial Russian dancers and the appealing naturalism favoured by Isadora Duncan. In Russia ballet continues to flourish, the two chief companies being the ◊Kirov and the ◊Bolshoi. Best-known ballerinas are Galina Ulanova and Maya Plisetskaya, and male dancers

include Mikhail Baryshnikov, Irek Mukhamedov, and Alexander Godunov, now dancing in the West.

American ballet was firmly established by the founding of Balanchine's School of American Ballet 1934, and by de Basil's Ballets Russes de Monte Carlo and Massine's Ballet Russe de Monte Carlo, which also carried on the Diaghilev tradition. In 1939 dancer Lucia Chase (1897–1986) and ballet director Richard Pleasant (1906–1961) founded the American Ballet Theater. From 1948 the New York City Ballet, under the guiding influence of Balanchine, developed a genuine American Neo-Classic style.

British ballet Marie Rambert initiated 1926 the company that developed into the Ballet Rambert, and launched the careers of choreographers such as Frederick Ashton and Anthony Tudor. The national company, the Royal Ballet (so named 1956), grew from foundations laid by Ninette de Valois and Frederick Ashton 1928. British dancers include Margot Fonteyn, Alicia Markova, Anton Dolin, Antoinette Sibley, Anthony Dowell, David Wall, Merle Park, and Lesley Collier; choreographers include Kenneth MacMillan.

ballet blanc ballet, such as *Giselle*, in which the female dancers wear calf-length white dresses. The costume was introduced by Marie ◊Taglioni in *La Sylphide* 1832.

ballet d'action ballet with a plot, developed by Jean-Georges ◊Noverre in the 18th century.

Ballet Shoes novel for children by Noel Streatfield (1895–1986), published in the UK 1936, which describes the dancing careers of three adopted children, Pauline, Petrova, and Posy Fossil, brought up in London by a wealthy guardian. This story marked the birth of the career-novel genre, which she continued in *Tennis Shoes* 1937 and *White Boots* 1951.

ballroom dancing collective term for social dances such as the ◊foxtrot, quickstep, ◊tango, and ◊waltz.

Balthus (Balthazar Klossowksi de Rola) 1908– . Polish-born French painter, famed for his enigmatic paintings of interiors featuring languid, prepubescent girls, both clothed and nude, for example *Nude with Cat* about 1954 (National Gallery of Victoria, Melbourne). The studied realism with which his self-absorbed figures are depicted lends his pictures a dreamlike quality.

Balzac Honoré de 1799–1850. French writer, one of the major novelists of the 19th century. His first success was *Les Chouans/The Chouans*, inspired by Walter Scott. This was the beginning of the long series of interrelated novels *La Comédie humaine/The ◊Human Comedy* which includes *Eugénie Grandet* 1833, *Le Père Goriot* 1834, and *Cousine Bette* 1846. He also wrote the Rabelaisian *Contes drolatiques/Ribald Tales* 1833.

Born in Tours, Balzac studied law and worked as a notary's clerk in Paris before turning to literature. His first attempts included tragedies such as *Cromwell* and novels published pseudonymously with no great success. A venture in printing and publishing 1825–28 involved him in a lifelong web of debt. His patroness, Madame de Berny, figures in *Le Lys dans la vallée/The Lily in the Valley* 1836. Balzac intended his major work *La Comédie humaine/The Human Comedy* to comprise 143 volumes, depicting every aspect of society in 19th-century France, of which he completed 80. Titles and characters include *Cousin Pons* 1847, the doctor of *Le Médicin de la campagne/The Country Doctor* 1833, the great businessman of *La Maison de Nucingen/The House of Nucingen* 1838, and the cleric of *Le Curé de village/The Village Parson* 1839. Balzac corresponded constantly with the Polish countess Evelina Hanska after meeting her 1833, and they married four months before his death in Paris. He was buried in the Père Lachaise cemetery, Paris.

Equality may perhaps be a right, but no power on earth can turn it into a fact.

Honoré de Balzac *La Duchesse de Langeais*

Bananarama British pop group formed 1981, a vocal trio until 1992, then a duo comprising founder members Sarah Dallin (1962–) and Keren Woodward (1963–). Initially produced by Stock, Aitken and Waterman, Bananarama were the top-selling female group of the 1980s.

Bancks James Charles 1889–1952. Australian cartoonist, creator of the comic strip *Ginger Meggs* which first appeared in the Sydney *Sun* 1921 and was later syndicated nationally and internationally.

band music group, usually falling into a special category: for example, *military*, comprising woodwind, brass, and percussion; *brass*, solely of brass and percussion; *marching*, a variant of brass; *dance* and *swing*, often like a small orchestra; *jazz*, with no fixed instrumentation; *rock and pop*, generally electric guitar, bass, and drums, variously augmented; and *steel*, from the West Indies, in which percussion instruments made from oildrums sound like marimbas.

Band, the North American rock group 1961–76. They acquired their name when working as Bob Dylan's backing band, and made their solo debut 1968 with *Music from Big Pink*. In their appearance and mysterious lyrics they often reflected a fascination for American history, as in the song 'The Night They Drove Old Dixie Down'. Their unostentatious ensemble playing and strong original material gave rock a new breadth. Albums include *The Band* 1969, *Stage Fright* 1970, and *Northern Lights– Southern Cross* 1975.

banjo resonant stringed musical instrument, with a long fretted neck and circular drum-type sound box covered on the topside only by stretched skin (now usually plastic). It is played with a plectrum. The banjo originated in the American South among black slaves (based on a similar instrument of African origin) and was introduced to Britain 1846.

Bankhead Tallulah 1903–1968. US actress, renowned for her wit and flamboyant lifestyle. Her stage appearances include *Dark Victory* 1934, Lillian Hellman's *The Little Foxes* 1939, and Thornton Wilder's *The Skin of Our Teeth* 1942. Her films include Alfred Hitchcock's *Lifeboat* 1943.

Banks Jeff 1943– . British textile, fashion, and interior designer. He helped establish the Warehouse Utility chain 1974 and combines imaginative designs with inexpensive materials to provide stylish and affordable garments for the younger market.

banshee in Gaelic folklore, a female spirit whose wailing outside a house foretells the death of one of its inhabitants.

bar modular segment of music incorporating a fixed number of beats, as in the phrase 'two/three/four beats to the bar'. It is shown in notation by vertical 'barring' of the musical continuum. The US term is *measure*.

Bara Theda. Stage name of Theodosia Goodman 1890–1955. US silent-film actress. She became known as the 'the vamp', and the first movie sex symbol, after appearing in *A Fool There Was* 1915, based on a poem by Rudyard Kipling, 'The Vampire'. Bara made more than 40 films during her relatively brief film career that extended from 1915 to 1920.

Baraka (Imamu) Amiri. Born LeRoi Jones 1934– . US poet and dramatist. One of the major black voices of his generation, he promoted black poetry and theatre, as well as producing volumes of poetry, novels, plays, and cultural analyses including *Blues People* 1963, a study of jazz. He began his literary career with personal and romantic poetry as in *Preface to a Twenty Volume Suicide Note* 1961, before turning to the theatre as a revolutionary force for black separatism in such plays as *Dutchman* and *The Slave* both 1964.

Barbellion W N P. Pen name of Bruce Frederick Cummings 1889–1919. English diarist, author of *The Journal of a Disappointed Man* 1919, an account of his struggle with the illness multiple sclerosis.

Barber Samuel 1910–1981. US composer of a neo-classical, astringent style. His works include *Adagio for Strings* 1936 and the opera *Vanessa* 1958, which won him one of his two Pulitzer prizes. Another Barber opera, *Antony and*

Cleopatra 1966, was commissioned for the opening of the new Metropolitan Opera House at Lincoln Center, New York City. Barber's music is lyrical and fastidiously worked. His later works include *The Lovers* 1971.

As to what happens when I compose, I really haven't the faintest idea.

Samuel Barber

barbershop in music, a style of unaccompanied close-harmony singing of sentimental ballads, revived in the USA during the 19th century. Traditionally sung by four male voices, since the 1970s it has developed as a style of ◊a cappella choral singing for both male and female voices.

Barbershop originated in 17th-century European barbers' shops, which also offered dental and medical services. Making music was encouraged among waiting customers.

Barbican, the arts and residential complex in the City of London. The Barbican Arts Centre (1982) contains theatres, cinemas, and exhibition and concert halls. The architects were Powell, Chamberlin, and Bon.

Barbirolli John 1899–1970. English conductor noted for his interpretation of Vaughan Williams and Sibelius symphonies. Trained as a cellist, he succeeded Toscanini as conductor of the New York Philharmonic Orchestra 1937–43 and was conductor of the Hallé Orchestra, Manchester, England 1943–70.

Barbizon School French school of landscape painters of the mid-19th century, based at Barbizon in the forest of Fontainebleau. Members included Jean-François Millet, Diaz de la Peña (1807–1876), and Théodore Rousseau. They aimed to paint fresh, realistic scenes, sketching and painting their subjects in the open air.

Barbour John *c.* 1320–1395. Scottish poet. His epic 13,000-line poem, *The Bruce* 1375–78, chronicles the war of Scottish independence and includes a vivid account of Robert Bruce's victory over the English at Bannockburn 1314. It is among the earliest known works of Scottish poetry.

Bardot Brigitte 1934– . French film actress. A celebrated sex symbol of the 1960s, she did much to popularize French cinema internationally. Her films include *Et Dieu créa la femme/And God Created Woman* 1950, *Viva Maria* 1965, and *Shalako* 1968.

Barenboim Daniel 1942– . Israeli pianist and conductor, born in Argentina. Pianist/conductor with the English Chamber Orchestra from 1964, he became conductor of the New York Philharmonic Orchestra 1970 and musical director of the Orchestre de Paris 1975. As a pianist he specialized in the German classic and romantic repertoire; as a conductor he has extended into 19th- and 20th-century French music, including Boulez.

Barham Richard Harris 1788–1845. English writer and clergyman, author of verse tales of the supernatural, and *The Ingoldsby Legends*, published under his pen name Thomas Ingoldsby.

Baring-Gould Sabine 1834–1924. English author, a prolific writer of novels and books of travel, mythology, and folklore. He wrote the words of the hymn 'Onward, Christian Soldiers'.

baritone male voice pitched between bass and tenor, of approximate range G2–F4, well suited to ◊lieder (songs). Famous baritones include Dietrich Fischer-Dieskau and Hermann Prey.

Barker Clive 1952– . English writer whose *Books of Blood* 1984–85 are in the sensationalist tradition of ◊horror fiction.

Barker George 1913–1991. English poet, known for his vivid imagery and passionate lyricism, as in *Calamiterror* 1937, *The True Confessions of George Barker* 1950, *Collected Poems 1930–50*, and the posthumously published *Street Ballads* 1992.

Barker Howard 1946– . English dramatist whose plays, renowned for their uncompromising and poetically dense language, confront the issues of private ambition and the exploitation of power. Among his plays are *Victory* 1982; *The Castle* 1985; *The Last Supper, The Possibilities,* and *The Bite of the Night,* all 1988; and *Seven Lears* 1989. In 1988 he formed The Wrestling School, a theatre company dedicated to the performance of his own work.

bark painting in Australian Aboriginal art, technique of painting on the inner side of a strip of tree bark. Using red, yellow, white, brown, and black pigments, the works were often painted with the fingers as the artist lay inside a low bark-roofed shelter. See ◊Aboriginal art.

Barlach Ernst 1870–1938. German Expressionist sculptor, painter, and poet. Influenced by Russian folk art and by medieval wood sculpture, his simple blocklike figure carvings were intended to express human spiritual longings. His work was condemned as ◊Degenerate Art by the Nazi regime and much of it destroyed. The war memorial in Güstrow cathedral is one of his finest surviving works.

Barlow Joel 1754–1812. US poet and diplomat. A member of the literary circle the 'Connecticut Wits,' he published an epic entitled *The Vision of Columbus* 1787, but is particularly remembered for *Hasty Pudding* 1796, a celebration of an American dessert.

Barnes Djuna 1892–1982. US writer. Her most celebrated novel was *Nightwood* 1936, a dark and idiosyncratic study of decadence. She lived in Paris from the 1920s, and her work was much influenced by European Surrealism. She was also the author of short stories, plays, poems, essays, and portraits.

Barnes William 1800–1886. English poet and cleric who published volumes of poems in the Dorset dialect. His poetry was admired for its charm, linguistic interest, and metrical innovation by Hardy, Tennyson, and Gerard Manley Hopkins. Among his works are *Poems of Rural Life in the Dorset Dialect* 1844, *Hwomely Rhymes* 1859, and *Poems of Rural Life in Common English* 1868.

Barnum P(hineas) T(aylor) 1810–1891. US showman. His American Museum in New York (1843–68) contained a theatre alongside numerous curiosities. In 1871 he established the 'Greatest Show on Earth', a travelling show which included the midget 'Tom Thumb', a circus, a menagerie, and an exhibition of 'freaks', conveyed in 100 railway carriages. He coined the phrase 'there's a sucker born every minute'.

How were the receipts today in Madison Square Garden?

P T Barnum last words 1891

Barocci or **Baroccio** Federico *c.* 1535–1612. Italian artist, born and based in Urbino. He painted religious themes in a highly coloured, sensitive style that falls between Renaissance and Baroque. Many of his pictures such as his *Holy Family* about 1570 show the influence of Raphael (also from Urbino) and Correggio.

Baroja Pio 1872–1956. Spanish novelist of Basque extraction. His works include a trilogy dealing with the Madrid underworld, *La lucha por la vida/The Struggle for Life* 1904–05, and the multivolume *Memorias de un hombre de acción/Memoirs of a Man of Action* 1913–28.

Baroque in art, architecture, and music, a style flourishing in Europe 1600–1750, broadly characterized as expressive, flamboyant, and dynamic. Playing a central role in the crusading work of the Catholic Counter-Reformation, the Baroque used elaborate effects to appeal directly to the emotions. In some of the most characteristic works – such as Bernini's Cornaro Chapel containing his sculpture *The Ecstasy of St Theresa* – painting, sculpture, decoration, and architecture were designed to create a single, dramatic effect. Many masterpieces of the Baroque emerged in churches in Rome, but the style soon spread throughout Europe, changing in character as it did so.

In *painting*, Caravaggio, with his bold use of light and forceful compositions, was an early exponent, but the Carracci family and Guido Reni were more typical of the early Baroque style, producing grandiose visions in ceiling paintings that deployed illusionistic displays of florid architectural decoration. In Catholic Flanders the Baroque is represented by Rubens and van Dyck, and in Spain by Velázquez and Ribera. In Protestant Holland, where patronage had moved from the church to the middle classes, it is represented by Rembrandt, Vermeer, and Frans Hals.

In *sculpture*, the master of Baroque was Bernini, whose *Ecstasy of St Theresa* 1645–52 (Sta Maria della Vittoria, Rome) is a fine example of overt emotionalism. Other Baroque sculptors are Puget and Coysevox, both French.

In *architecture*, straight lines gave way to curved and broken lines; decoration became more important and elaborate; and spaces became more complex, their impact highlighted by the dramatic use of light and shade. Designs were often large-scale, as in Bernini's piazza for St Peter's in Rome. Outstanding Baroque architects included Bernini, Borromini, Cortona, and Longhena in Italy; Le Vau and Hardouin-Mansart in France; and Gibbs, Wren, Hawksmoor, and Vanbrugh in England.

In *music*, the Baroque was characterized by an emphasis on expressing drama and emotion, with extensive use of the ♭ground bass and heavy ornamentation, and a love of spectacular effect. It began with: the Camerata, a society of poets and musicians who revived elements of Greek drama and developed the opera form in Florence; Monteverdi; and Gabrieli, introducing exclamatory and polychoral effects. The sonata, suite, and concerto grosso emerged during the Baroque; the vocal forms of opera, oratorio, and cantata were also developed. Composers of the High Baroque include Corelli and Vivaldi in Italy, J S Bach in Germany, and Handel in England.

The 19th-century Swiss historian Jacob Burckhardt was the first to use the term 'baroque'; he applied it derogatively, meaning 'bizarre, irregular', but the word became respectably absorbed into the language of art history.

Barragán Luis 1902–1988. Mexican architect, known for his use of rough wooden beams, cobbles, lava, and adobe, which he combines in striking and colourful compositions. Mexican vernacular architecture has provided the inspiration for much of his work, although Le Corbusier's influence is also evident in his early designs.

Barrault Jean-Louis 1910–1994. French actor and stage director. He appeared in such films as *La Symphonie fantastique* 1942, *Les Enfants du paradis* 1943–45, and *La Ronde* 1950.

He was producer and director to the

◊Comédie Française 1940–46, and director of the Théâtre de France (formerly Odéon) from 1959 until 1968 when he was dismissed because student protesters were allowed to occupy the theatre.

barre wooden bar running along the walls of a ballet studio at waist height, designed to help dancers keep their balance while going through the initial daily exercises.

barrel organ portable pipe organ, played by turning a handle. The handle works a pump and drives a replaceable cylinder upon which music is embossed as a pattern of ridges controlling the passage of air to the pipes. It is often confused with the barrel or street piano used by buskers, which employed a barrel-and-pin mechanism to control a piano hammer action. The barrel organ was a common entertainment and parish church instrument in England during the 18th and 19th centuries.

Barrett Browning Elizabeth 1806–1861. English poet. In 1844 she published *Poems* (including 'The Cry of the Children'), which led to her friendship with and secret marriage to Robert Browning 1846. The *Sonnets from the Portuguese* 1847 were written during their courtship. Later works include *Casa Guidi Windows* 1851 and the poetic novel *Aurora Leigh* 1857. She was a learned, fiery, and metrically experimental poet.

Barrett Browning was born near Durham. As a child she fell from her pony and injured her spine and was subsequently treated by her father as a confirmed invalid. Freed from her father's oppressive influence, her health improved. She wrote strong verse about social injustice and oppression in Victorian England.

Barrie J(ames) M(atthew) 1860–1937. Scottish dramatist and novelist, author of *The Admirable Crichton* 1902 and the children's fantasy *Peter Pan* 1904.

After early studies of Scottish rural life in plays such as *A Window in Thrums* 1889, his reputation as a dramatist was established with *The Professor's Love Story* 1894 and *The Little Minister* 1897.

Every time a child says 'I don't believe in fairies' there is a little fairy somewhere that falls down dead.

J M Barrie Peter Pan 1904

Barry Charles 1795–1860. English architect of the Neo-Gothic Houses of Parliament at Westminster, London, 1840–60, in collaboration with Augustus ◊Pugin. His early designs for the Travellers' Club, 1829–31, and for the the Reform Club, 1837, both in London, were in Renaissance style.

Barrymore US family of actors, the children of British-born Maurice Barrymore and Georgie Drew, both stage personalities. *Lionel Barrymore* (1878–1954) first appeared on the stage with his grandmother, Mrs John Drew, 1893. He played numerous film roles from 1909, including *A Free Soul* 1931 and *Grand Hotel* 1932, but was perhaps best known for his annual radio portrayal of Scrooge in Dickens' *A Christmas Carol. John Barrymore* (1882–1942) was a flamboyant actor who often appeared on stage and screen with his brother and sister. In his early years he was a Shakespearean actor. From 1923 he acted almost entirely in films, including *Dinner at Eight* 1933, and became a screen idol, nicknamed 'the Profile'. *Ethel Barrymore* (1879–1959) played with the British actor Henry Irving in London 1898 and opened the Ethel Barrymore Theatre in New York 1928; she also appeared in many films from 1914, including *None but the Lonely Heart* 1944.

Barstow Stan 1928– . English novelist. His realist novels describe northern working-class life and include *A Kind of Loving* 1960 (filmed 1962) and *Watchers on the Shore* 1966. His other novels include *A Raging Calm* 1968 and *B Movie* 1987.

Bart Lionel 1930– . English composer, author of both words and music for many musicals including *Fings Ain't Wot They Us'd T'Be* 1959 and *Oliver!* 1960.

Barth John 1930– . US novelist and short-story writer who was influential in the 'academic' experimental movement of the 1960s. His works, typically encyclopedic in scale, are usually interwoven fictions based on language games, his principal concerns being the nature of narrative and the relationship of language to reality. His novels include *The Sot-Weed Factor* 1960, *Giles Goat-Boy* 1966, *Letters* 1979, *Sabbatical: A Romance* 1982, and *The Last Voyage of Somebody the Sailor* 1991.

Barthelme Donald 1931–1989. US writer. His innovative short stories, often first published in the *New Yorker* magazine, display a minimalist economy and a playful sense of the absurd and the irrational, as in the collection *Sixty Stories* 1981. He also wrote the novellas *Snow White* 1967, *The Dead Father* 1975, *Paradise* 1986, and *The King* 1991. Barthelme's works have been seen as model texts for literary criticism based on ◊Deconstruction.

Barthes Roland 1915–1980. French critic and theorist of ◊semiotics, the science of signs and symbols. One of the French 'new critics' and an exponent of ◊structuralism, he attacked traditional literary criticism in his early works, including *Le Degré zéro de l'ecriture/Writing Degree Zero* 1953 and *Sur Racine/On Racine* 1963.

His structuralist approach, which involved exposing and analysing the system of signs, patterns, and laws that a text or sign embodies, is seen at its most playful and inventive in *Mythologies* 1957, a collection of short essays. He also wrote an autobiographical novel, *Roland Barthes sur Roland Barthes* 1975.

What I claim is to live to the full the contradiction of my time, which may well make sarcasm the condition of truth.

Roland Barthes *Mythologies*

Bartholdi Frédéric Auguste 1834–1904. French sculptor, designer of the Statue of Liberty overlooking New York harbour, 1884–86.

Bartholomew Fair comedy by Ben ◊Jonson 1614. In a satirical panorama of one of Jacobean London's great fairs, the representatives of morality, Justice Overdo and Zeal-of-the-Land Busy, are pitted against the tricksters, traders, and puppeteers of the Fair.

Bartók Béla 1881–1945. Hungarian composer. His works combine folk elements with mathematical concepts of tonal and rhythmic proportion. His large output includes six string quartets, a *Divertimento* for string orchestra 1939, concertos for piano, violin, and viola, the *Concerto for Orchestra* 1942–45, a one-act opera *Duke Bluebeard's Castle* 1918, and graded teaching pieces for piano.

A child prodigy, Bartók studied music at the Budapest Conservatory, later working with Zoltán ◊Kodály in recording and transcribing folk music of Hungary and adjoining countries. His ballet *The Miraculous Mandarin* 1919 was banned because of its subject matter (it was set in a brothel). Bartók died in the USA, having fled from Hungary 1940.

Bartolommeo Fra, also called *Baccio della Porta* c. 1472–1517. Italian religious painter of the High Renaissance, active in Florence. He introduced Venetian artists to the Florentine High Renaissance style during a visit to Venice 1508, and on his return introduced Florentine artists to a Venetian use of colour. *The Mystical Marriage of St Catherine* 1511 (Louvre, Paris) is one of his finest works.

Barton John 1928– . English theatre director, associate director of the Royal Shakespeare Company from 1960. He directed and devised numerous productions for the company, including *The Hollow Crown* 1961, *The Wars of the Roses* 1963, Shakespeare's history plays 1964, and *The Greeks* 1980. Television work includes the series of workshops Playing Shakespeare 1982.

Baryshnikov Mikhail 1948– . Latvian-born dancer, now based in the USA. He joined the Kirov Ballet 1967 and, after defecting from the Soviet Union 1974, joined the American Ballet Theater (ABT) as principal dancer. He left to join the New York City Ballet 1978–80, but rejoined ABT as director 1980–90. From 1990 he has danced for various companies including his own modern dance company, White Oak Project. His physical prowess and amazing aerial feats have combined with an impish sense of humour and dash to make him one of the most accessible of dancers.

He has created many roles, for example in Twyla Tharp's *Push Comes to Shove* 1976 and in Jerome Robbins' *Opus 19* 1979 (Prokofiev). He made his film debut in *The Turning Point* 1978 and has since acted in other films, including *White Nights* 1985.

baryton complex bowed stringed instrument producing an intense singing tone. It is based on an 18th-century ◊viol and modified by the addition of sympathetic (freely vibrating) strings.

The baryton was a favourite instrument of Prince Nicholas Esterházy, patron of the Austrian composer Joseph Haydn who, to please him, wrote many trios for violin, baryton, and cello.

Basawan 1556–1605. Mogul painter, one of the finest artists of the period. He contributed paintings to many of the albums of miniatures that were a feature of the Mogul courts, in particular the ◊*Akbar-nama*. Renowned for their subtle characterization, his works also show a novel use of perspective and composition, suggesting that he may have been influenced by Western art.

Bashkirtseff Marie 1860–1884. Russian diarist and painter whose journals, written in French, were cited by Simone de Beauvoir as the archetypal example of 'self-centred female narcissism', but which also revealed the discovery by the female of her independent existence. She died of tuberculosis at 24.

If I had been born a man, I would have conquered Europe. As I was born a woman, I exhausted my energy in tirades against fate, and in eccentricities.

Marie Bashkirtseff *Journal* June 1884

Bashō Pen name of Matsuo Munefusa 1644–1694. Japanese poet. He was a master of the *haiku*, a 17-syllable poetic form with lines of 5, 7, and 5 syllables, which he infused with subtle allusiveness. His *Oku-no-hosomichi/The Narrow Road to the Deep North* 1694, an account of a visit to northern and western Honshū, consists of haiku interspersed with prose passages.

Basie Count (William) 1904–1984. US jazz band leader and pianist who developed the big-band sound and a simplified, swinging style of music. He led impressive groups of musicians in a career spanning more than 50 years. Basie's compositions include 'One O'Clock Jump' and 'Jumpin' at the Woodside'.

His solo piano technique was influenced by the style of Fats Waller. Some consider his the definitive dance band.

basilica Roman public building; a large roofed hall flanked by columns, generally with an aisle on each side, used for judicial or other public business. The earliest known basilica, at Pompeii, dates from the 2nd century BC. This architectural form was adopted by the early Christians for their churches.

Baskerville John 1706–1775. English printer and typographer, who experimented in casting types from 1750 onwards. The Baskerville typeface is named after him. He manufactured fine printing paper and inks, and in 1756 published a quarto edition of the Classical poet Virgil, which was followed by 54 highly crafted books.

basketry ancient craft (Mesolithic–Neolithic) used to make a wide range of objects (from baskets to furniture) by interweaving or braiding rushes, cane, or other equally strong and supple natural fibres. *Wickerwork* is a more rigid type of basketry worked onto a sturdy frame, usually made from strips of willow.

Basketry flourished from the early Middle Ages until the late 19th century (a Basket Maker's Company was formed in London 1569), but cheap imports and alternative packaging led to a decline. In the UK, willow rods (osiers) were specially grown for basketry, and commercial osier beds still survive in Somerset.

bas relief see ◊relief.

bass the lowest male voice, of approximate range C2–D4. The best-known bass singers have been the Russians Fyodor ◊Chaliapin and Boris ◊Christoff. The term also covers the bass instrument of a consort or family, for example bass clarinet, bass tuba, and bassoon, having a similar range. An instrument an octave lower than bass is a contrabass.

basset horn musical ◊woodwind instrument, a wide-bore alto clarinet pitched in F, invented about 1765 and used by Mozart in his *Masonic Funeral Music* 1785, for example, and by Richard Strauss. It was revived 1981 by Stockhausen and features prominently as a solo in the opera cycle *LICHT*. Performers include Alan Hacker and Suzanne Stephens.

bassoon bass double-reed ◊woodwind instrument in B flat, of folded and tapered bore, developed from the Renaissance ◊curtal about 1660 as a continuo instrument to provide bassline support. Further development in the 18th century led to the *double bassoon* or *contrabassoon*, an octave lower. Both instruments demonstrate an agility humorously at variance with their low pitch range and rich, glowing tone, but are also capable of dignified solos at high register, famously in the eerie opening bars of Stravinsky's ballet *Rite of Spring* 1913. The bassoon concert repertoire extends from the early Baroque via Vivaldi, Mozart, and Dukas to Stockhausen.

Bastos Augusto Roa 1917– . Paraguayan writer of short stories and novels, including *Son of Man* 1960 about the Chaco War between Bolivia and Paraguay, in which he fought.

Bates Alan 1934– . English actor, a versatile male lead in over 60 plays and films. His films include *Zorba the Greek* 1965, *Far from the Madding Crowd* 1967, *Women in Love* 1970, *The Go-Between* 1971, *The Shout* 1978, and *Duet for One* 1986.

Bates H(erbert) E(rnest) 1906–1974. English author. Of his many novels and short stories, *The Jacaranda Tree* 1949 and *The Darling Buds of May* 1958 demonstrate the fineness of his natural observation and compassionate portrayal of character. *Fair Stood the Wind for France* 1959 was based on his experience as a Squadron Leader in World War II.

The five chronicles of the Larkin family, begun with *The Darling Buds of May* and *Fair Stood the Wind for France*, and including *When the Green Woods Laugh* 1960, were filmed as a television series in the 1990s.

bathos sudden descent from the sublime to the ridiculous; when at the end of a passage or sequence, it is a form of anticlimax.

batik Javanese technique of dyeing fabrics in which areas to be left undyed in a colour are sealed with wax. Practised throughout Indonesia, the craft was introduced to the West by Dutch traders.

Batoni Pompeo 1708–1787. Italian painter, based in Rome, celebrated for his detailed portraits of princes and British visitors on the Grand Tour.

Baucis and Philemon in classical mythology, a country couple who offered hospitality to the gods Zeus and Hermes, and as a reward were saved from a flood; their cottage was transformed into a temple. The story is told by the Roman poet ◊Ovid in his *Metamorphoses*.

Baudelaire Charles Pierre 1821–1867. French poet whose immensely influential work combined rhythmical and musical perfection with a morbid romanticism and eroticism, finding beauty in decadence and evil. His first and best-known book of verse was *Les Fleurs du mal/ ◊Flowers of Evil* 1857. Later volumes include *Les Paradis artificiels* 1860. He also published studies of Balzac and Flaubert, perceptive art criticism, and an autobiographical novel *La Fantarlo* 1847. He was one of the major figures in the development of ◊Symbolism.

But the real travellers are only those who leave/For the sake of leaving

Charles Baudelaire *The Voyage*

Bauer Ferdinand Lukas 1760–1826. Austrian painter. As the botanical artist on Matthew Flinders' second voyage to Australia 1801, he made more than 1,500 painstakingly detailed drawings of Australian plants and animals. He is commemorated in the name of the Australian plant species *Bauera*.

Bauhaus German school of architecture and design founded 1919 at Weimar in Germany by the architect Walter ◊Gropius in an attempt to fuse art, design, architecture, and crafts into a unified whole. Moved to Dessau under political pressure 1925 (where it was housed in a building designed by Gropius), the school was closed by the Nazis 1933. Among the artists associated with the Bauhaus were the painters Klee and Kandinsky and the architect Mies van der Rohe.

Its ideas were subsequently incorporated in teaching programmes in Europe and the USA, where many of its teachers and students emigrated. Gropius and Marcel ◊Breuer worked together in the USA 1937–40 and the ◊International Style (of which Gropius' Bauhaus building 1925–26 is a hallmark) spread worldwide from there. In 1972 the *Bauhaus Archive* was installed in new premises in Berlin.

Baum L(yman) Frank 1856–1919. US writer, author of the children's fantasy *The Wonderful Wizard of Oz* 1900 and its 13 sequels. The series was continued by another author after his death. The film *The Wizard of Oz* 1939 with Judy Garland became a US classic.

'The road to the City of Emeralds is paved with yellow brick,' said the Witch, 'so you cannot miss it.'

L Frank Baum
The Wonderful Wizard of Oz 1900

Bausch Pina 1940– . German avant-garde dance choreographer and director from 1974 of the Wuppertal Tanztheater (dance theatre). Her works incorporate dialogue, elements of psychoanalysis, comedy, and drama. They include *Le Sacre du printemps* 1975, *Nelken* 1982, and *Arien* 1979. She has been seen as a major figure in challenging the influence of American Post-Modernism on European dance.

Bawa Geoffrey 1919– . Sri Lankan architect, formerly a barrister. His buildings are a contemporary interpretation of vernacular traditions, and include houses, hotels, and gardens. More recently he has designed public buildings such as the new parliamentary complex, near Colombo, 1982, and Ruhuana University, Matara, 1984.

Bax Arnold Edward Trevor 1883–1953. English composer. His works, often based on Celtic legends, include seven symphonies and *The Garden of Fand* 1913–16 and *Tintagel* 1917–19 (both tone poems). He was Master of the King's Musick 1942–53.

Bayeux Tapestry linen hanging made about 1067–70, which gives a vivid pictorial record of the invasion of England by William I (the Conqueror) 1066. It is an embroidery rather than a true tapestry, sewn with woollen threads in blue, green, red, and yellow, 70 m/231 ft long and 50 cm/20 in wide, and containing 72 separate scenes with descriptive wording in Latin. It is exhibited at the museum of Bayeux in Normandy, France.

Baylis Lilian 1874–1937. English theatre manager. She was responsible for re-opening Sadler's Wells Theatre, London, 1931. From 1934 Sadler's Wells specialized in productions of opera and ballet: the resultant companies eventually became the Royal Ballet and the English National Opera.

Bay Psalm Book Puritan rendering of the psalms into metre, printed 1640; it is considered the first work of American literature.

Written by Richard Mather, John Eliot, and 28 other ministers of the Massachusetts Bay Colony, it was published by Stephen Day in Cambridge, Massachusetts, in an edition of 1,700 copies.

Bayreuth town in Bavaria, S Germany, where opera festivals are held every summer. It was the home of composer Richard ◊Wagner, and the Wagner theatre was established 1876 as a performing centre for his operas. It introduced new concepts of opera house design, including provision of an enlarged orchestra pit extending below the stage and projecting the sound outwards and upwards.

Beach Boys, the US pop group formed 1961. They began as exponents of vocal-harmony surf music with Chuck Berry guitar riffs (their hits include 'Surfin' USA' 1963 and 'Help Me, Rhonda' 1965) but the compositions, arrangements, and production by group member Brian Wilson (1942–) became highly complex under the influence of psychedelic rock, as in 'Good Vibrations' 1966. Wilson spent most of the next 20 years in retirement but returned with a solo album 1988.

Beardsley Aubrey (Vincent) 1872–1898. English illustrator and leading member of the ◊Aesthetic Movement. His meticulously executed black-and-white drawings show the influence of Japanese prints and French Rococo, and also display the sinuous line and decorative mannerisms of Art Nouveau. His work was often charged with being grotesque and decadent.

He became known through the *Yellow Book* magazine, for which he was the art editor, and through his drawings for Oscar Wilde's *Salome* 1894.

I have one aim — the grotesque. If I am not grotesque I am nothing.

Aubrey Beardsley

beat in music, a pulsation giving the tempo, for example a conductor's beat, or a unit of tempo, as in four beats to the bar.

beat frequency in musical acoustics, a fluctuation produced when two notes of nearly equal pitch or frequency are heard together. Beats result from the interference between the sound waves of the notes. The frequency of the beats equals the frequency of the notes. Musicians use the effect when tuning their instruments.

Beat Generation or *Beat movement* US literary and social movement of the 1950s and early 1960s that sought personal liberation largely through Eastern mysticism, drugs, and music (particularly jazz). Its writers, rejecting traditional forms, favoured spontaneity and free forms. The most influential writers were Jack ◊Kerouac, Allen ◊Ginsberg, and William ◊Burroughs.

Beatles, the English pop group 1960–70. The members, all born in Liverpool, were John Lennon (1940–80, rhythm guitar, vocals), Paul McCartney (1942– , bass, vocals), George Harrison (1943– , lead guitar, vocals), and Ringo Starr (formerly Richard Starkey, 1940– , drums). Using songs written largely by Lennon and McCartney, they dominated rock music and pop culture in the 1960s.

The Beatles gained early experience in Liverpool and Hamburg, West Germany. They had a top-30 hit with their first record, 'Love Me Do' 1962, followed by 'Please Please Me' which reached number two. Every subsequent single and album released until 1967 reached number one in the UK charts. At the peak of Beatlemania they starred in two films, *A Hard Day's Night* 1964 and *Help!* 1965, and provided songs for the animated film *Yellow Submarine* 1968. Their ballad 'Yesterday' 1965 was covered by 1,186 different performers in the first ten years. The album *Sgt Pepper's Lonely Hearts Club Band* 1967, recorded on two four-track machines, anticipated subsequent technological developments.

The Beatles were the first British group to challenge the US dominance of rock and roll, and continued to influence popular music beyond their break-up 1970. Of the 30 songs most frequently broadcast in the USA 1955–91, 13 were written by members of the Beatles. They pursued separate careers with varying success. George Harrison's biggest hit, 'My Sweet Lord' 1970, fell victim to a plagiarism suit. His album *Cloud Nine* 1987 was particularly well received, and in 1988 he became a member of the Traveling Wilburys, a group that also includes Bob Dylan. Ringo Starr has appeared in a number of films, and his album *Ringo* 1973 came close to being a Beatles reunion. See separate entries for John ◊Lennon and Paul ◊McCartney.

We are more popular than Jesus now. I don't know which will go first — rock and roll or Christianity.

John Lennon on the Beatles
Evening Standard 1966

beat music pop music that evolved in the UK in the early 1960s, known in its purest form as ◊Mersey beat, and as British Invasion in the USA. The beat groups characteristically had a simple, guitar-dominated line-up, vocal harmonies, and catchy tunes. They included the Beatles (1960–70), the Hollies (1962–), and the Zombies (1962–67).

Beaton Cecil 1904–1980. English photographer whose elegant and sophisticated fashion pictures and society portraits often employed exotic props and settings. He adopted a more simple style for his wartime photographs of bomb-damaged London. He also worked as a stage and film designer, notably for the musicals *Gigi* 1959 and *My Fair Lady* 1965.

Beatty Warren. Stage name of Warren Beaty 1937– . US actor, director, and producer. He attracted attention as a young man in such films as *Splendour in the Grass* 1961, then produced and starred as gangster Clyde Barrow in the hugely successful *Bonnie and Clyde* 1967. Later, he directed *Reds* 1981, and *Dick Tracy* 1990, and co-produced *Bugsy* 1992, in which he played the gangster Bugsy Siegel. He is the brother of actress Shirley MacLaine.

Beaumarchais Pierre Augustin Caron de 1732–1799. French dramatist. His great comedies, *Le Barbier de Seville/The Barber of Seville* 1775 and *Le Mariage de Figaro/The Marriage of Figaro* (1778, but prohibited until 1784), form the basis of operas by Rossini and Mozart, with their blend of social criticism and sharp humour.

Beaumont Francis 1584–1616. English dramatist and poet. From about 1608 he collaborated with John ◊Fletcher. Their joint plays include the tragicomedies *Philaster* 1610 and *A King and No King* c. 1611, and *The Maid's Tragedy* c. 1611, *The Woman Hater* c. 1606 and *The Knight of the Burning Pestle* c. 1607, which is a satire on the audience, are ascribed to Beaumont alone.

'Beauty and the Beast' European folk tale. A traveller receives mysterious overnight hospitality in a woodland palace, only meeting the benevolent owner, a hideous creature known as the Beast, the following morning. The Beast, furious at the theft of a rose by the traveller, agrees to forgive him on condition that the traveller's daughter, Beauty, comes willingly to live with him in the palace. Beauty consents and grows to love the Beast for his gentle character, finally breaking the spell of his hideous appearance by agreeing to marry him. The story first appeared in English 1757 in a translation from the French version of Madame de Beaumont.

Beauvoir Simone de 1908–1986. French socialist, feminist, and writer. She taught philosophy at the Sorbonne university in Paris 1931–43. Her book *Le Deuxième Sexe/The Second Sex* 1949 became a seminal work for many feminists. She was the constant companion of Jean-Paul ◊Sartre and explored the implications of ◊existentialism in her writing.

Her novel of postwar Paris, *Les Mandarins/The Mandarins* 1954, has characters resembling the writers Albert Camus, Arthur Koestler, and Sartre. She also published autobiographical volumes and later wrote about ageing.

One is not born a woman. One becomes one.

Simone de Beauvoir *The Second Sex* 1949

Beaux Arts, Ecole des influential art school in Paris, established 1795 to replace the pre-revolutionary Royal Academy; from 1819, architectural training was provided. Through its teaching and its awards and commissions, the school dominated French art and design until its position and principles were undermined by the Impressionists. In architecture, it came to be associated with an ornate, grandiose form of ◊Classicism, termed the 'Beaux Arts style'. Notable examples are the Paris Opéra 1862 by Charles Garnier (1825–1898) and the Gare du Quai d'Orsay 1898–1900 (now the Musée d'Orsay), Paris, by Victor Laloux. The 'Beaux Arts style' was the inspiration for much French 19th-century architecture and also influenced many architects abroad, particularly in the USA.

bebop or *bop* a jazz style, rhythmically complex, virtuosic, and highly improvisational. It was developed in New York in the 1940s and 1950s by Charlie Parker, Dizzy Gillespie, Thelonious Monk, and other black musicians reacting against ◊swing music.

bebung (German 'trembling') musical vibrato achieved on the clavichord by a fluctuation of key pressure impinging on the metal tangent pressing on the string.

Bechet Sidney (Joseph) 1897–1959. US jazz musician, born in New Orleans. He played clarinet and was the first to forge an individual style on soprano saxophone. Bechet was based in Paris in the late 1920s and the 1950s, where he was recognized by classical musicians as a serious artist.

Beckett Samuel 1906–1989. Irish novelist and dramatist who wrote in French and English. His *En attendant Godot* – first performed in Paris 1952, and then in his own translation as *Waiting for Godot* 1955 in London, and New York 1956 – is possibly the best-known example of Theatre of the ◊Absurd, in which life is taken to be meaningless. This genre is taken to further extremes in *Fin de Partie/Endgame* 1957 and *Happy Days* 1961. He was awarded the Nobel Prize for Literature 1969.

Originally a novelist and strongly influenced by James Joyce, Beckett also wrote successfully for radio in plays such as *All That Fall* 1957 and *Embers* 1959.

Vladimir: That passed the time./ Estragon: It would have passed in any case./ Vladimir: Yes, but not so rapidly.

Samuel Beckett *Waiting for Godot* 1952

Beckford William 1760–1844. English author and eccentric. Forced out of England by scandals about his private life, he published *Vathek* 1787 in Paris, a fantastic Arabian Nights tale, and on returning to England 1796 rebuilt his home, Fonthill Abbey in Wiltshire, as a Gothic fantasy.

Beckmann Max 1884–1950. German Expressionist painter and graphic artist. He was influenced both by medieval art and by the ◊*Neue Sachlichkeit* movement, and after World War I his art concentrated on themes of cruelty in human society, as in *Night* 1918–19 (Kunstsammlung Nordrhein-Westfalen, Düsseldorf).

Beckmann was born in Leipzig. He fought in World War I and was discharged following a breakdown, reflected in the agony of his work. Denounced by the Nazi regime (see ◊Degenerate Art), he moved to Amsterdam where he began a series of complex allegorical works. He spent the last three years of his life in the USA.

Beecham Thomas 1879–1961. British conductor and impresario. He established the Royal Philharmonic Orchestra 1946 and fostered the works of composers such as Delius, Sibelius, and Richard Strauss.

The English may not like music, but they absolutely love the noise it makes.

Thomas Beecham
New York Herald Tribune 1961

Beecher Harriet. Unmarried name of Harriet Beecher ◊Stowe, author of *Uncle Tom's Cabin*.

Beelzebub (Hebrew 'lord of the flies') in the New Testament, the leader of the devils, sometimes identified with Satan and sometimes with his chief assistant. In the Old Testament Beelzebub was a fertility god worshipped by the Philistines and other Semitic groups (Baal).

Beerbohm Max 1872–1956. British caricaturist and author. A perfectionist in style, he contributed to *The Yellow Book* 1894; wrote a novel of Oxford undergraduate life *Zuleika Dobson* 1911; and published volumes of caricature, including *Rossetti and His Circle* 1922. He succeeded George Bernard Shaw as critic to the *Saturday Review* 1898.

I have known no man of genius who had not to pay, in some affliction or defect either physical or spiritual, for what the gods had given him.

Max Beerbohm *And Even Now* 1920

Beethoven Ludwig van 1770–1827. German composer and pianist whose mastery of musical expression in every genre made him the dominant influence on 19th-century music. Beethoven's repertoire includes concert overtures; the opera *Fidelio* 1805, revised 1814; five piano concertos and two for violin (one unfinished); 32 piano sonatas, including the *Moonlight* 1801 and *Appassionata* 1804–05; 17 string quartets; the Mass in D (*Missa solemnis*) 1824; and nine symphonies, as well as many youthful works. He usually played his own piano pieces and conducted his orchestral works until he was hampered by deafness 1801; nevertheless he continued to compose.

Born in Bonn, the son and grandson of musicians, Beethoven became deputy organist at the court of the Elector of Cologne at Bonn before he was 12; later he studied under Haydn and possibly Mozart, whose influence dominated his early work. From 1809, he received a small allowance from aristocratic patrons.

Beethoven's career spanned the transition from Classicism to Romanticism. Of his symphonies the best known are the Third (*Eroica*) 1803–04 originally intended to be dedicated to Napoleon, with whom Beethoven became disillusioned), the Fifth 1807–08, the Sixth (*Pastoral*) 1803–08, and Ninth (*Choral*) 1815–24, which includes the passage from Schiller's 'Ode to Joy' chosen as the national anthem of Europe.

Behan Brendan 1923–1964. Irish dramatist. His early experience of prison and knowledge of the workings of the IRA (recounted in his autobiography *Borstal Boy* 1958) provided him with two recurrent themes in his plays. *The Quare Fellow* 1954 was followed by the tragicomedy *The Hostage* 1958, first written in Gaelic.

I'm a Communist by day and a Catholic as soon as it gets dark.

Brendan Behan

---

behemoth (Hebrew 'beasts') in the Old Testament (Job 40), an animal cited by God as evidence of his power; usually thought to refer to the hippopotamus. It is used proverbially to mean any giant and powerful creature.

Behn Aphra 1640–1689. English novelist and playwright, the first woman in England to earn her living as a writer. Her writings were criticized for their explicitness; they frequently present events from a woman's point of view. Her novel *Oroonoko* 1688 is an attack on slavery.

Between 1670 and 1687 fifteen of her plays were produced, including *The Rover*, which attacked forced and mercenary marriages. She had the patronage of James I and was employed as a government spy in Holland 1666.

Behrens Peter 1868–1940. German architect. He pioneered the adaptation of architecture to industry and designed the AEG turbine factory in Berlin 1909, a landmark in industrial architecture. He taught Le Corbusier, Gropius, and Mies van der Rohe.

Beiderbecke Bix (Leon Bismarck) 1903–1931. US jazz cornetist, composer, and pianist. A soloist with the bands of King Oliver, Louis Armstrong, and Paul Whiteman, Beiderbecke was the first acknowledged white jazz innovator. He was influenced by the classical composers Debussy, Ravel, and Stravinsky.

His reputation grew after his early death with the publication of Dorothy Baker's novel *Young Man with a Horn* 1938 based on his life.

Béjart Maurice, adopted name of Maurice Berger, 1927– . French choreographer and ballet director. Believing dance to be 'total theatre', he has staged huge, spectacular productions, for example *Romeo and Juliet* 1966. As director of his Ballet of the 20th Century 1960, based in Brussels until 1987, Béjart's productions included *The Firebird* 1970 and *Kabuki* 1986. Other ballets include *Bolero* 1961 and *Notre Faust* 1975.

[the stage is] the last refuge in our world where a man can discover the exact measure of his own soul.

Maurice Béjart 'Dynamic Tradition' in *Ballet and Modern Dance* 1974

Belasco David 1859–1931. US dramatist and producer. His works include *Madame Butterfly* 1900 and *The Girl of the Golden West* 1905, both of which Puccini used as libretti for operas.

bel canto (Italian 'beautiful song') in music, an 18th-century Italian style of singing with emphasis on perfect technique and beautiful tone. The style reached its peak in the operas of Rossini, Donizetti, and Bellini.

Bel Geddes Norman 1893–1958. US industrial designer, a key member of the small group of US pioneers who helped to establish the profession of industrial design in the interwar years. He was motivated throughout his career by a desire to create a utopian, futuristic environment.

After working in advertising and theatre and film set design, he moved into industrial design 1926. His work in this area included counter scales for the Toledo Scale Company 1929, a range of beds for the Simmons Steel Company 1929, radios for the Radio Corporation of America 1934, and a large number of unrealized futuristic projections of cars, planes, trains, and environments. In 1939 he designed the General Motors stand, Futurama, at the New York World Fair.

Belgian literature there are three literary traditions in the area now called Belgium: Flemish, French, and Walloon. For the Flemish tradition see ◊ Flemish literature. The French includes the 12th-century novella Aucassin et Nicolette, the literature associated with the 15th-century Burgundian court, 19th-century naturalists, aesthetes, and Symbolists (notably Emile Verhaeren (1855–1916)), and internationally known writers as different as the dramatist Maurice ◊ Maeterlinck and the crime novelist Georges ◊ Simenon. Local dialects of Latin and French in the Walloon provinces gave rise to a distinctive vernacular literature, mainly poetic and dramatic, dating back to the 12th century but centred on Liège from the 17th century.

bell musical instrument, made in many sizes, comprising a suspended resonating vessel swung by a handle or from a pivoted frame to make contact with a beater which hangs inside the bell. Church bells are among the most massive structures to be cast in bronze in one piece; from high in a steeple they can be heard for many miles. Their shape, a flared bowl with a thickened rim, is engineered to produce a clangorous mixture of tones. Miniature *handbells* are tuned to resonate harmoniously. Orchestral *tubular bells*, of brass or steel, are tuned to a chromatic scale of pitches and are played by striking with a wooden mallet. A set of steeple bells played from a keyboard is called a *carillon*.

The world's largest bell is the 'Tsar Kolokol' or 'King of Bells', 220 tonnes, cast 1734, which stands on the ground of the Kremlin, Moscow, where it fell when being hung. The 'Peace Bell' at the United Nations headquarters, New York, was cast 1952 from coins presented by 64 countries.

bell in a wind instrument, the flat disc or flare at the opposite end of the tube from the mouthpiece.

Bellamy Edward 1850–1898. US author and social critic. In 1888, deeply concerned with the social problems of the day, he published *Looking Backward: 2000–1887*, a utopian novel. A huge bestseller, it inspired wide public support for Bellamy's political programme of state socialism. He published a second utopian novel, *Equality* 1897.

Bellerophon in Greek mythology, a victim of slander who was sent against the monstrous ◊chimera, which he killed with the help of his winged horse Pegasus. After further trials, he ended his life as a beggar. His story was dramatized by ◊Euripides.

Belli Giuseppe Giocchomo 1791–1863. Italian poet. He wrote more than 2,000 sonnets in the Roman dialect which provide a brilliantly observed satiric account of early 19th-century papal Rome.

Bellini family of Italian Renaissance painters. Jacopo and his sons Gentile and Giovanni were founders of the Venetian school in the 15th and early 16th centuries.
Jacopo (c. 1400–1470) has left little surviving work, but two of his sketchbooks (now in the British Museum and the Louvre) contain his ideas and designs. *Gentile* (c. 1429–1507) assisted in the decoration of the Doge's Palace 1474 and worked in the court of Muhammad II at Constantinople (a portrait of the sultan is in the National Gallery, London). He also painted scenes of contemporary Venetian life, such as *Procession of the Relic of the True Cross* 1496 (Accademia, Venice). *Giovanni* (c.1430–1516), Gentile's younger brother, studied under his father, and painted portraits and various religious subjects. His early works show the influence of his brother-in-law, Mantegna. Generally considered the finest painter of the Bellini family, his style developed from the static manner of mid-15th-century Venetian work towards a High Renaissance harmony and grandeur, as in the altarpiece 1505 in Sta Zaccaria, Venice. He worked in oil rather than tempera, a technique adopted from Antonello da Messina, and introduced a softness of tone, a harmony in composition, and a use of luminous colour that greatly influenced the next generation of painters (including his pupils Giorgione and Titian). He is known for his Madonnas, for example *The Madonna of the Meadows* about 1505 (National Gallery, London).

Bellini Mario 1935– . Italian architect and industrial designer, one of the figures who helped establish Italy as a leading nation in industrial design from the 1960s. He is known for his elegant pieces of office machinery for the ◊Olivetti company (from 1962) and his sophisticated furniture designs for ◊Cassina (from 1964). As a freelance industrial designer, he has worked for a large number of manufacturers, including Brionvega, Poltrona Frau, and Artemide in Italy and Yamaha in Japan, in the areas of furniture and products.

Bellini Vincenzo 1801–1835. Italian opera composer who collaborated with the tenor Giovanni Battista Rubini (1794–1854) to develop a new simplicity of melodic expression in romantic evocations of classic themes, as in *La Sonnambula/The Sleepwalker* and *Norma*, both 1831. In *I Puritani/The Puritans* 1835, his last work, he discovered a new boldness and vigour of orchestral effect.

Bello Andrés 1781–1865. Venezuelan poet and polymath. Regarded as the intellectual father of Latin America, a friend and teacher of the patriot Simón Bolívar, he translated the Romantics Byron and Hugo but defended Neo-Classicism in literature. He celebrated the flora of tropical America in the widely read Virgilian stanzas *Silvas a la agricultura de la zona tórrida/Agriculture in the Tropics* 1826, part of an unfinished epic *América*. He also published an important grammar of the Spanish language 1847 which is still in use.

Belloc (Joseph) Hilaire Pierre 1870–1953. English author, remembered primarily for his nonsense verse for children *The Bad Child's Book of Beasts* 1896 and *Cautionary Tales* 1907. Belloc also wrote travel and religious books (he was a devout Catholic). With G K ◊Chesterton, he advocated a return to the late medieval guild system of commercial association in place of capitalism or socialism.

Bellona in Roman mythology, the goddess of war and wife or sister of ◊Mars, with a temple in the Campus Martius, near the altar of Mars.

Bellow Saul 1915– . Canadian-born US novelist. From his first novel, *Dangling Man* 1944, Bellow has typically set his naturalistic narratives in Chicago and made his central character an anxious, Jewish-American intellectual. In *The Adventures of Augie March* 1953 and *Henderson the Rain King* 1959, he created confident and comic picaresque heroes, before ◊*Herzog* 1964, which pitches a comic but distressed scholar into a world of darkening humanism. Later works, developing Bellow's depiction of an age of urban disorder and indifference, include the near-apocalyptic *Mr Sammler's Planet* 1970, *Humboldt's Gift* 1975, *The Dean's December* 1982, *More Die of Heartbreak* 1987, and the novella *A Theft* 1989. His finely styled works and skilled characterizations won him the Nobel Prize for Literature 1976.

> *Death is the dark backing a mirror needs if we are to see anything.*
>
> **Saul Bellow** *Observer* Dec 1983

Bellows George Wesley 1882–1925. US painter associated with the ◊Ashcan School, known for his vigorous portrayals of the drama of street life and sport. His most famous works, such as *Stag at Sharkey's* 1909, depict the violence and excitement of illegal boxing matches.

bell ringing or *campanology* the art of ringing church bells individually or in sequence by rhythmically drawing on a rope fastened to a wheel rotating the bell, so that it falls back and strikes in time. *Change ringing* is an English art, dating from the 17th century, of ringing a patterned sequence of permutations of 5–12 church bells, using one player to each bell. See also ◊carillon.

belly dancing dance of the Middle East. It is characterized by the use of the hips, spine, shoulders, and stomach muscles rather than the legs. The dance is performed by women and is accompanied by varying rhythms. Traditionally, belly dance was performed only among women as a celebration of birth.

Benchley Robert 1889–1945. US humorist, actor, and drama critic whose books include *Of All Things* 1921 and *Benchley Beside Himself* 1943. His film skit *How to Sleep* illustrates his ability to extract humour from everyday life.

Benda Julien 1867–1956. French writer and philosopher. He was an outspoken opponent of the philosophy of Henri ◊Bergson, and in 1927 published a manifesto on the necessity of devotion to the absolute truth, which he felt his contemporaries had betrayed, *La Trahison des clercs/The Treason of the Intellectuals.*

Benét Stephen Vincent 1898–1943. US poet, novelist, and short-story writer who won a Pulitzer Prize 1929 for his narrative poem of the Civil War, *John Brown's Body* 1928. One of his short stories, 'The Devil and Daniel Webster', became a classic and was made into a play, an opera, and a film (*All That Money Can Buy*). He published more than 17 volumes of verse and prose.

Benjamin Arthur 1893–1960. Australian pianist and composer who taught composition at the Royal College of Music in London from 1925, where Benjamin Britten was one of his pupils. His works include *Jamaican Rumba*, inspired by a visit to the West Indies 1937.

Benjamin George (William John) 1960– . British composer, conductor, and pianist. A pupil of Messiaen, his colourful and sonorous works include *Ringed by the Flat Horizon* 1980, *At First Light* 1982, *Antara* 1987, and *Cascade* 1990.

Benjamin Walter 1892–1940. German Marxist critic and essayist. He wrote on literature, film, art and society, and is now regarded as one of the most important cultural critics of the 20th century. His works include *Einbahnstrasse/One-Way Street* 1928, a montage of aphorisms and essays, and *Illuminationen/Illuminations* 1961, a posthumous collection of some of his most important essays.

His works are a complex and unlikely blend of Marxism and Jewish mysticism. Rejecting more orthodox Marxist views, he was a staunch supporter of modernism, and wrote important essays on Kafka, Brecht, and Baudelaire, and on the relationship between technology, the arts, and society. See also ◊Marxist aesthetic theory.

Benn Gottfried 1886–1956. German lyric poet. Experience as a military physician during World War I encouraged a cynically pessimistic emphasis on human degeneracy and physical decay in his early collections such as *Morgue* and *Fleisch/Flesh*, both 1917. His autobiography *Doppelleben/Double Life* 1950 describes a gradual mellowing into pragmatism. *Primal Vision*, an English translation of selected verse and prose, was published 1961.

Bennett Alan 1934– . English dramatist, screenwriter, and actor. His works (often set in his native north of England) treat subjects such as class, senility, illness, and death with macabre comedy. They include TV films, for example *An Englishman Abroad* 1982; the cinema film *A Private Function* 1984; and plays such as *Forty Years On* 1968, *Getting On* 1971, *Kafka's Dick* 1986, and *The Madness of George III* 1991.

He also wrote the screenplay for *Prick Up Your Ears* 1987, based on the relationship between the dramatist Joe Orton and his lover Kenneth Halliwell. He began his career writing and acting in *Beyond the Fringe* satirical revue in the 1960s.

Life is rather like a tin of sardines – we're all of us looking for the key.

Alan Bennett *Beyond the Fringe* 1960

Bennett Richard Rodney 1936– . English composer of jazz, film music, symphonies, and operas. His film scores for *Far from the Madding Crowd* 1967, *Nicholas and Alexandra* 1971, and *Murder on the Orient Express* 1974 all received Oscar nominations. His operas include *The Mines of Sulphur* 1963 and *Victory* 1970.

Bennett (Enoch) Arnold 1867–1931. English novelist. His major books are set in the industrial Five Towns of the Midlands and are concerned with the manner in which the environment dictates the pattern of his characters' lives. His many novels include *Anna of the Five Towns* 1904, *The Old Wives' Tale* 1908, and the trilogy *Clayhanger,*

Hilda Lessways, and *These Twain* 1910–16.

Benny Jack. Stage name of Benjamin Kubelsky 1894–1974. US comedian notable for his perfect timing and lugubrious manner. Over the years, Benny appeared on the stage, in films, and on radio and television. His radio programme, *The Jack Benny Show* from 1932, made him a national institution. Featuring his wife Mary Livingston, singer Dennis Day, announcer Don Wilson, and valet Eddie 'Rochester' Anderson, it was produced for television in the 1950s. His film appearances, mostly in the 1930s and 1940s, included *To Be or Not to Be* 1942. He also played in *Charley's Aunt* 1941, *It's In the Bag* 1945, and *A Guide for the Married Man* 1967.

Benson E(dward) F(rederic) 1867–1940. English writer. He specialized in novels gently satirizing the foibles of upper-middle-class society, and wrote a series of books featuring the formidable female antagonists Mapp and Lucia, including *Queen Lucia* 1920.

Bentley Edmund Clerihew 1875–1956. English author. He invented the four-line humorous verse form known as the ◊clerihew, used in *Biography for Beginners* 1905 and in *Baseless Biography* 1939. He was also the author of the classic detective story *Trent's Last Case* 1913.

What I like about Clive/ Is that he is no longer alive./ There's a great deal to be said/ For being dead.

Edmund Clerihew Bentley
Biography for Beginners 1905

Bentley John Francis 1839–1902. English architect, a convert to Catholicism, who designed Westminster Cathedral, London (1895–1903). It is outwardly Byzantine but inwardly shaped by shadowy vaults of bare brickwork. The campanile is the tallest church tower in London.

bentwood type of furniture, originally made by steam-heating and then bending rods of wood to form panels. Initially a country style, it was patented in the early 19th century in the USA. 20th-century designers such as Marcel ◊Breuer and Alvar ◊Aalto have developed a different form by bending sheets of plywood.

Beowulf Anglo-Saxon poem (composed *c.* 700), the only complete surviving example of Germanic folk epic. It exists in a single manuscript copied about 1000 in the Cottonian collection of the British Museum.

The hero Beowulf delivers the Danish king Hrothgar from the water-demon Grendel and its monstrous mother, and, returning home, succeeds his cousin Heardred as king of the Geats.

After 50 years of prosperity, he is killed slaying a dragon.

Béranger Pierre Jean de 1780–1857. French poet who wrote light satirical lyrics dealing with love, wine, popular philosophy, and politics.

Berenson Bernard 1865–1959. Lithuanian-born US art historian and connoisseur, once revered as a leading scholar of Italian Renaissance art. He became wealthy through his advisory work for art galleries and for such collectors as Joseph Duveen (1869–1939), although many of his attributions of anonymous Italian paintings were later questioned. His books include *The Drawings of the Florentine Painters* 1903.

beret soft circular woollen or felt cap, without a brim or peak, considered to be of Roman or Greek origin. The two most common beret styles are the *Basque*, which has a narrow band around the base, and the *Modelaine*, which does not have a band.

Berets became fashionable in the 1880s when they were trimmed with flowers, feathers, or ribbons. Since 1900 they have often been worn unadorned.

Berg Alban 1885–1935. Austrian composer. He studied under Arnold ◊Schoenberg and developed a personal twelve-tone idiom of great emotional and stylistic versatility. His relatively small output includes two operas – *Wozzeck* 1925, a grim story of working-class life, and the unfinished *Lulu* 1929–35 – and chamber music incorporating coded references to friends and family.

His music is emotionally expressive, and sometimes anguished, but can also be lyrical, as in the *Violin Concerto* 1935.

Berger John 1926– . English left-wing art critic. In his best-known book, *Ways of Seeing* 1972, he valued art for social rather than aesthetic reasons. He also attacked museums for preserving what is by nature ephemeral. His novels include *A Painter of Our Time* 1958 and *G* 1972 (Booker Prize).

Berger Thomas (Louis) 1924– . US writer. His parodic novels include the picaresque sequence *Crazy in Berlin* 1958, *Reinhart in Love* 1961, *Vital Parts* 1970, and *Reinhart's Women* 1981. Berger also parodied the Western in *Little Big Man* 1964 (filmed 1970), and the detective genre in *Who is Teddy Villanova?* 1977.

Bergman Ingmar 1918– . Swedish stage producer (from the 1930s) and film director (from the 1940s), regarded by many as one of the great masters of modern cinema. His work deals with complex moral, psychological, and metaphysical problems and is often strongly tinged with pessimism. His films include *Wild Strawberries* 1957, *The Seventh Seal* 1957, *Persona* 1966, *Autumn Sonata* 1978 and *Fanny and Alexander* 1982.

Bergman Ingrid 1917–1982. Swedish-born actress. She went to the USA 1939 to appear in David Selznick's *Intermezzo* 1939, and later appeared in *Casablanca* 1942, *For Whom the Bell Tolls* 1943, and *Gaslight* 1944, for which she won an Academy Award.

By leaving her husband to have a child with director Roberto Rossellini, she broke an unofficial moral code of Hollywood star behaviour and was ostracized for many years. During her 'exile', she made films in Europe such as *Stromboli* 1949 (directed by Rossellini). Returning to the USA, she made such films as *Anastasia* 1956, for which she won an Academy Award, and *Murder on the Orient Express* 1974 for which she won her third Academy Award.

Keep it simple. Make a blank face and the music and the story will fill it in.

Ingrid Bergman advice on film acting.

Bergson Henri 1859–1941. French philosopher and writer. In *Creative Evolution* 1907 he expressed his dissatisfaction with Darwin's materialist account of evolution and attempted to prove that all evolution and progress are due to the working of the *élan vital*, or life force. His ideas on time as the duration of experience greatly influenced Marcel ◊Proust. Nobel Prize for Literature 1928.

Berio Luciano 1925– . Italian composer. His work combines serial techniques with commedia dell'arte and antiphonal practices, as in *Alleluiah II* 1958 for five instrumental groups. His prolific output includes nine *Sequenzas/Sequences* 1957–75 for various solo instruments or voice, *Sinfonia* 1969 for voices and orchestra, *Formazioni/Formations* 1987 for orchestra, and the opera *Un re in ascolto/A King Listens* 1984, loosely based on Shakespeare's play *The Tempest*.

Beriosova Svetlana 1932– . British ballerina. Born in Lithuania and brought up partly in the USA, she danced with the Royal Ballet from 1952. Her style had a lyrical dignity and she excelled in *The Lady and the Fool*, *Ondine*, and *Giselle*.

Berkeley Busby. Stage name of William Berkeley Enos 1895–1976. US choreographer and film director. He used ingenious and extravagant sets and teams of female dancers to create large-scale kaleidoscopic patterns through movement and costume when filmed from above, as in *Gold Diggers of 1933* and *Footlight Parade* 1933.

Berkoff Steven 1937– . English dramatist and actor whose abrasive and satirical plays include *East* 1975, *Greek* 1979, and *West* 1983. Berkoff's production of Oscar Wilde's *Salome* was staged 1991.

He formed the London Theatre Group 1968 as a vehicle for his own productions, which have included his adaptations of Kafka's *Metamorphosis* 1969 and *The Trial* 1970, and Poe's *The Fall of the House of Usher* 1974.

In his acting career, he has often been cast as a villainous 'heavy' as in *Beverly Hills Cop* 1984 and *The Krays* 1990. He published his exploration of a leading role in *I Am Hamlet* 1989.

Berlage Hendrikus 1856–1934. Dutch architect, known principally for his design for the Amsterdam Stock Exchange 1897–1903. His individualist style marked a move away from 19th-century revival of historical styles towards Dutch Expressionism.

Berlin Irving. Adopted name of Israel Baline 1888–1989. Russian-born US songwriter. His songs include such hits as 'Alexander's Ragtime Band' 1911, 'Always' 1925, 'God Bless America' 1917 (published 1939), and 'White Christmas' 1942, and the musicals *Top Hat* 1935, *Annie Get Your Gun* 1946, and *Call Me Madam* 1950. He also provided songs for films like *Blue Skies* 1946 and *Easter Parade* 1948.

Berlin grew up in New York and had his first song published 1907. He began providing songs for vaudeville and revues, and went on to own a theatre, the Music Box, where he appeared in his own revues 1921 and 1923. Generally writing both lyrics and music, he was instrumental in the development of the popular song, taking it from jazz and ragtime to swing and romantic ballads.

Berlin Film Festival international film festival held every year in Berlin, Germany; see ◊cinema.

Berlioz (Louis) Hector 1803–1869. French romantic composer, the founder of modern orchestration. Much of his music was inspired by drama and literature and has a theatrical quality. He wrote symphonic works, such as *Symphonie fantastique* 1830–31 and *Roméo et Juliette* 1839; dramatic cantatas including *La Damnation de Faust* 1846 and *L'Enfance du Christ* 1854; sacred music; and three operas: *Benvenuto Cellini* 1838, *Les Troyens* 1856–58, and *Béatrice et Bénédict* 1862.

Time is a great teacher, but unfortunately it kills all its pupils.

Hector Berlioz
Almanach des lettres françaises

Bernanos Georges 1888–1948. French author. He achieved fame 1926 with *Sous le soleil de Satan/The Star of Satan*. His strongly Catholic viewpoint is also expressed in his *Journal d'un curé de campagne/The Diary of a Country Priest* 1936.

Bernhardt Sarah. Stage name of Rosine Bernard 1845–1923. French actress who dominated the stage of her day, frequently performing at the Comédie-Française in Paris. She excelled in tragic roles, including Cordelia in Shakespeare's *King Lear*, the title role in Racine's *Phèdre*, and the male roles of Hamlet and of Napoleon's son in Edmond Rostand's *L'Aiglon*.

Bernini Gianlorenzo (Giovanni Lorenzo) 1598–1680. Italian sculptor, architect, and painter, a leading figure in the development of the Baroque style. His work in Rome includes the colonnaded piazza in front of St Peter's Basilica (1656), fountains (as in the Piazza Navona), and papal monuments. His sculpture includes *The Ecstasy of St Theresa* 1645–52 (Sta Maria della Vittoria, Rome) and numerous portrait busts.

Bernini's sculptural style is full of movement and drama, captured in billowing drapery and facial expressions. His subjects are religious and mythological. A fine example is the marble *Apollo and Daphne* for Cardinal Borghese 1622–25 (Borghese Palace, Rome), with the figures shown in full flight. Inside St Peter's, he created several marble monuments and the elaborate canopy over the high altar. He also produced many fine portrait busts, such as one of Louis XIV of France.

Bernstein Leonard 1918–1990. US composer, conductor, and pianist, one of the most energetic and versatile of US musicians in the 20th century. His works, which established a vogue for realistic, contemporary themes, include symphonies such as *The Age of Anxiety* 1949, ballets such as *Fancy Free* 1944, and scores for musicals, including *Wonderful Town* 1953, *West Side Story* 1957, and *Mass* 1971 in memory of President J F Kennedy.

From 1958 to 1970 he was musical director of the New York Philharmonic. Among his other works are the symphony *Jeremiah* 1944, the ballet *Facsimile* 1946, and the musicals *Candide* 1956 and the *Chichester Psalms* 1965.

Berruguete family of Spanish painters and sculptors. *Pedro Berruguete* (died *c.* 1503) was influenced by Italian Renaissance art and may have worked at the Ducal Palace, Urbino. He was later court painter to Ferdinand and Isabella of Spain and is principally known for his work in Toledo Cathedral 1483–1500. His son *Alonso* (*c.* 1488–1561) was a sculptor and painter and, like his father, also worked in Italy. His altarpieces, in which he combined paintings, carved reliefs, and statuary, introduced the Mannerist style to Spain.

Berry Chuck (Charles Edward) 1926– . US rock-and-roll singer, songwriter, and guitarist. His characteristic guitar riffs became staples of rock music, and his humorous storytelling lyrics were also emulated. He had a string of hits in the 1950s and 1960s beginning with 'Maybellene' 1955.

Born in St Louis, Missouri, Berry began as a blues guitarist in local clubs. Early songs like 'Roll

Over Beethoven' 1956, 'Rock 'n' Roll Music' 1957, 'Sweet Little Sixteen' 1958, and 'Johnny B Goode' 1958 are classics of the genre, and one of them was chosen as a sample of Earth music for the *Voyager* space probes. He was the subject of a film tribute, *Hail! Hail! Rock 'n' Roll* 1987.

Roll over, Beethoven, and tell Tchaikovsky the news.

Chuck Berry 'Roll Over Beethoven' 1956

Berryman John 1914–1972. US poet of emotionally intense, witty, and personal works, often dealing with sexual torments and informed by a sense of suffering. After collections of short poems and sonnets, he wrote *Homage to Mistress Broadstreet* 1956, a romantic narrative featuring the first American poet, Anne Dudley (born 1612), and then introduced his guilt-ridden, antiheroic alter ego, Henry, in *77 Dream Songs* 1964 (Pulitzer Prize) and *His Toy, His Dream, His Rest* 1968.

His poetry has much in common with that of the 'confessional' poets, but his use of humour sets it apart. He also wrote short stories and a biography of Stephen Crane 1950.

berserker legendary Scandinavian warrior whose frenzy in battle transformed him into a wolf or bear howling and foaming at the mouth (hence 'to go berserk'), and rendered him immune to sword and flame.

Bertolucci Bernardo 1940– . Italian film director whose work combines political and historical perspectives with an elegant and lyrical visual appeal. His films include *The Spider's Stratagem* 1970, *Last Tango in Paris* 1972, *1900* 1976, *The Last Emperor* 1987, for which he received an Academy Award, and *The Sheltering Sky* 1990.

Bes in Egyptian mythology, the god of music and dance, usually shown as a grotesque dwarf.

Besant Walter 1836–1901. English writer. He wrote novels in partnership with James Rice (1844–1882), and produced an attack on the social evils of the East End of London, *All Sorts and Conditions of Men* 1882, and an unfinished *Survey of London* 1902–12. He was the brother-in-law of the feminist activist Annie Besant.

bestiary in medieval times, a book with stories and illustrations which depicted real and mythical animals or plants to illustrate a (usually Christian) moral. The stories were initially derived from the Greek *Physiologus*, a collection of 48 such stories, written in Alexandria around the 2nd century AD.

Translations of the *Physiologus* into vernacular languages (French, Italian, and English) date from the 13th century; illustrated versions are known from the 9th century. Much of later and contemporary folklore about animals derives from the bestiary, such as the myth of the phoenix burning itself to be born again.

best seller book that achieves large sales. Listings are based upon sales figures from bookstores and other retail stores.

The Bible has sold more copies than any other book over time, but popular and commercial examples include Charles Monroe Seldon's *In His Steps* 1897, Margaret Mitchell's *Gone With the Wind* 1936, and Dale Carnegie's *How to Win Friends and Influence People* 1937. Current best seller lists appear in newspapers, magazines, and book trade publications. In the UK the paperback with the highest sales in the 1980s was *The Secret Diary of Adrian Mole Aged 13 ³/₄* by Sue Townsend (over three million copies sold).

Betjeman John 1906–1984. English poet and essayist, originator of a peculiarly English light verse, nostalgic, and delighting in Victorian and Edwardian architecture. His *Collected Poems* appeared 1968 and a verse autobiography, *Summoned by Bells*, 1960. He became poet laureate 1972.

One cannot assess in terms of cash or exports and imports an imponderable thing like the turn of a lane or an inn or a church tower or a familiar skyline.

John Betjeman *Observer* 1969

Betrothed, The (Italian *I promessi sposi*) romantic historical novel by Alessandro ◊Manzoni, published 1825–27 and in its final form 1840–42. Set in Lombardy in 1628–31, during a popular insurrection against the Spanish administration, it follows the fortunes of two poor silk weavers whose marriage is prevented until the last chapter by the interference of the tyrannical Don Rodrigo.

Betterton Thomas *c.* 1635–1710. English actor, member of the Duke of York's company after the Restoration. He was greatly admired in many Shakespearean parts, including Hamlet and Othello.

Betti Ugo 1892–1953. Italian dramatist. Some of his most important plays, such as *Frana allo scalo nord/Landslide at the North Station* 1936, concern the legal process (Betti was a judge for many years) and focus on the themes of justice and moral responsibility. Of his many other plays, often austere, even pessimistic, the best known include *La padrone/The Mistress* 1927, *Delitto all'isola delle capre/Crime on Goat Island* 1948 and *La Regina e gli insorte/The Queen and the Rebels* 1949.

Betty William Henry West 1791–1874. English boy actor, called the 'Young Roscius' after the greatest comic actor of ancient Rome. He was famous, particularly in Shakespearean roles, from the age of 11 to 17.

Beuys Joseph 1921–1986. German sculptor and performance artist, one of the leaders of the European avant-garde during the 1970s and 1980s. An exponent of Arte Povera, he made use of so-called 'worthless', unusual materials such as felt and fat. His best-known performance was *How to Explain Pictures to a Dead Hare* 1965. He was also an influential exponent of video art, for example, *Felt TV* 1968.

Beuys saw the artist as a shaman and art as an agent of social and spiritual change.

Bewick Thomas 1753–1828. English wood engraver. He excelled in animal subjects and some of his finest works appear in his illustrated *A General History of Quadrupeds* 1790 and *A History of British Birds* 1797–1804.

BFI abbreviation for the ***British Film Institute***. Founded 1933, the organization was created to promote the cinema as a 'means of entertainment and instruction'. It includes the National Film Archive (1935) and the National Film Theatre (1951), and is involved in publishing books and periodicals, as well as in providing funding for film distribution and exhibition in Britain.

Bhagavad-Gītā (Hindu 'the Song of the Blessed') religious and philosophical Sanskrit poem. Dating from around 300 BC, it forms an episode in the sixth book of the *Mahābhārata*, one of the two great Hindu epics. It is the supreme religious work of Hinduism.

bhangra pop music evolved in the UK in the late 1970s from traditional Punjabi music, combining electronic instruments and ethnic drums. Bhangra bands include Holle Holle, Alaap, and Heera. A 1990s development is ***bhangramuffin***, a reggae-rap-bhangra fusion popularized by Apache Indian (Steve Kapur, 1967–).

Bharat Natyam one of the four main Indian Classical dancing styles (others are ◊Kathak, ◊Kathakali, and ◊Manipuri). It is a female dance solo, over 2,000 years old, performed by Hindu temple dancers, today practised mainly in S India. It is characterized by great strength and austerity and its performances can last up to three hours. The dancer wears a richly decorated brocade blouse and silk sari and is accompanied by cymbals and singing.

It is based on *Bharata Natya Shastra*, a book written *c*. 200 BC–AD 300, on drama for the dance actor.

Biba fashion label best known in the early 1970s for moody, nostalgic clothes and accessories in shades of brown, plum, grey, and pink. It was established 1963 by Barbara Hulanicki and closed in the late 1970s. A major retrospective exhibition was held in Newcastle-upon-Tyne 1993, coinciding with the revival of 1970s fashion.

Biber Heinrich von 1644–1704. Bohemian composer, Kapellmeister at the archbishop of Salzburg's court. A virtuoso violinist, he composed a wide variety of music including 16 *Mystery Sonatas* about 1676 for violin, church music, the opera *Chi la dura la vince* 1687 and various pieces, for example *Serenada/ Nightwatchman Serenade*.

bibliography list of books on a particular subject, or used in the research for a work; or a list of all the books by a particular writer. Bibliography can also mean the study of books.

Biedermeier early to mid-19th-century Germanic style of art and furniture design, derogatorily named after Gottlieb Biedermeier, a humorous pseudonym used by several German poets, embodying bourgeois taste.

Bierce Ambrose (Gwinett) 1842– *c*. 1914. US author. After service in the American Civil War, he established his reputation as a master of the short story, his themes being war and the supernatural, as in *Tales of Soldiers and Civilians* 1891 and *Can Such Things Be?* 1893. He also wrote *The Devil's Dictionary* 1911 (first published as *The Cynic's Word Book* 1906), a collection of ironic definitions showing his sardonic humour. He disappeared in Mexico 1913.

Bierstadt Albert 1830–1902. German-born US landscape painter. His spectacular panoramas of the American wilderness fell out of favour after his death until interest in the ◊Hudson River School was rekindled in the late 20th century. A classic work is *Thunderstorm in the Rocky Mountains* 1859 (Museum of Fine Arts, Boston).

big-band jazz swing music created in the late 1930s and 1940s by bands of 13 or more players, such as those of Duke ◊Ellington and Benny ◊Goodman. Big-band jazz relied on fixed arrangements, where there is more than one instrument to some of the parts, rather than improvisation. Big bands were mainly dance bands, and they ceased to be economically viable in the 1950s.

Big Ben popular name for the bell in the clock tower of the Houses of Parliament in London, cast at the Whitechapel Bell Foundry 1858, and known as 'Big Ben' after Benjamin Hall, First Commissioner of Works at the time. It weighs 13.7 tonnes.

Bihzad Kamal al-Din *c*. 1450–1536. Persian painter of miniatures, known as the 'Persian Raphael'. Although only a few works are firmly attributed to him, he is widely regarded as the finest painter of the Persian miniature. His work shows a novel subtlety in composition and use of colour, as well as enhanced realism.

bikini two-piece version of the women's ◊swimsuit, introduced 1946 in France. Early designs were heavily decorated with frills and artificial flowers. By the 1950s bikinis were popular in France, but they did not become acceptable beachwear until the early 1960s in Britain and around 1965 in the USA. In the 1970s a briefer version of the bikini was introduced; the shapes and designs continue to change with fashion trends.

Bildungsroman German 'education novel' that deals with the psychological and emotional development of its protagonist, tracing his or her life from inexperienced youth to maturity. The first example of the type is generally considered to be C M ◊Wieland's *Agathon* 1765–66, but it was Goethe's *Wilhelm Meisters Lehrjahr/ ◊Wilhelm Meister's Apprenticeship* 1795–96 that established the genre. Although taken up by writers in other languages, it remained chiefly a German form; later examples include Thomas Mann's *Der Zauberberg/The ◊Magic Mountain* 1924 and *Portrait of the Artist as a Young Man* 1916 by James Joyce.

Billy Bunter fat, bespectacled schoolboy who featured in stories by Frank ◊Richards, set at Greyfriars School. His adventures, in which he attempts to raise enough money to fund his passion for eating, appeared in the children's paper *Magnet* between 1908 and 1940, and subsequently in books in the 1940s and on television 1952–62.

binary form in music, a composition in symmetrical halves, the first modulating to the ◊dominant key, the second modulating back to the starting ◊tonic key.

Bingham George Caleb 1811–1879. US painter. The influence of the ◊Hudson River School is evident in such frontier landscapes as *Fur Traders Descending the Missouri* 1845 (Metropolitan Museum of Art, New York).

Binyon Laurence 1869–1943. British poet and art critic. His verse volumes include *Lyric Poems* 1894 and *Odes* 1901, but he is best remembered for his ode 'For the Fallen' 1914, set to music by Elgar. His art criticism includes *Japanese Art* 1909.

They shall grow not old, as we that are left grow old:/ Age shall not weary them, nor the years condemn.

Laurence Binyon 'For the Fallen' 1914

---

biography account of a person's life. When it is written by that person, it is an ◊autobiography.

Biography may consist simply of the factual details of a person's life told in chronological order, but has generally become a matter of interpretation as well as historical accuracy. Unofficial biographies (not sanctioned by the subject) have frequently led to legal disputes over both interpretation and facts.

Among ancient biographers are Xenophon, Plutarch, Tacitus, Suetonius, and the authors of the Gospels of the New Testament. Medieval biography was mostly devoted to religious edification and produced chronicles of saints and martyrs; among secular biographies are *Charlemagne* by Frankish monk Einhard (*c.* 770 –840), *Alfred* by Welsh monk Asser (died *c.* 910), and *Petrarch* by ◊Boccaccio.

In England true biography begins with the early Tudor period and such works as *Sir Thomas More* 1626, written by his son-in-law William Roper (1498–1578). By the 18th century it became a literary form in its own right through Samuel Johnson's *Lives of the Most Eminent English Poets* 1779–81 and James Boswell's biography of Johnson 1791. Nineteenth-century biographers include Robert Southey, Elizabeth Gaskell, G H Lewes, J Morley, and Thomas Carlyle. The general tendency was to provide irrelevant detail and suppress the more personal facts. Lytton Strachey's *Eminent Victorians* 1918 opened the new era of frankness.

Twentieth-century biographers include Richard Ellmann (1918–1987), André Maurois (James Joyce and Oscar Wilde), Michael Holroyd (1935–) (Lytton Strachey and George Bernard Shaw), and Elizabeth Longford (Queen Victoria and Wellington).

The earliest *biographical dictionary* in the accepted sense was that of Pierre Bayle 1696, followed during the 19th century by the development of national biographies in Europe, and the foundation of the *English Dictionary of National Biography* 1882 and the *Dictionary of American Biography* 1928.

Read no history: nothing but biography, for that is life without theory.

Benjamin Disraeli
on biography *Contarini Fleming* 1844

Birtwistle Harrison 1934– . English avant-garde composer. He has specialized in chamber music, for example, his chamber opera *Punch and Judy* 1967 and *Down by the Greenwood Side* 1969.

Birtwistle's early music was influenced by Stravinsky and by the medieval and Renaissance masters, and for many years he worked alongside Peter Maxwell ◊Davies. Orchestral works include *The Triumph of Time* 1972 and *Silbury Air* 1977; he has also written operas including *The Mask of Orpheus* 1986 (with electronic music by Barry Anderson (1935–1987)) and *Gawain* 1991 a reworking of the medieval English poem 'Sir Gawain and the Green Knight'. His tape composition *Chronometer* 1972 (assisted by Peter Zinovieff (1934–)) is based on clock sounds.

bitonality in music, a combination of two parts in different keys, as in Stravinsky's *Duo Concertante* 1931–32 for violin and piano. Music of more than two simultaneous keys is called polytonality.

Bizet Georges (Alexandre César Léopold) 1838–1875. French composer of operas, among them *Les Pêcheurs de perles/The Pearl Fishers* 1863, and *La jolie Fille de Perth/The Fair Maid of Perth* 1866. He also wrote the concert overture *Patrie* and incidental music to Alphonse Daudet's play *L'Arlésienne*. His operatic masterpiece *Carmen* was produced a few months before his death 1875.

Björnson Björnstjerne 1832–1910. Norwegian novelist, playwright, poet, and journalist. His plays include *The Newly Married Couple* 1865 and *Beyond Human Power* 1883, dealing with politics and sexual morality. Among his novels is *In God's Way* 1889. Nobel Prize for Literature 1903.

Black Beauty children's novel by Anna ◊Sewell, published 1877. The book, which describes the experiences of the horse, Black Beauty, under many different owners, revived the genre of 'animal autobiography' popular in the late 18th and early 19th centuries.

Black Boy autobiography of the US writer Richard ◊Wright, published 1945, which gives a vivid and harrowing account of a black boy's experience of growing up in the USA.

black humour humour based on the grotesque, morbid, or macabre. It is often an element of satire. A classic example is Jonathan Swift's 'A Modest Proposal' 1729, in which he argues that eating Irish children would help to alleviate Ireland's poverty. Twentieth-century examples can be found in the works of the Irish writer Samuel Beckett, the routines of the US comic Lenny Bruce (1925–1966), and the drawings of the English caricaturist Gerald Scarfe (1936–). It is also an important element of Theatre of the ◊Absurd.

Blackman Charles Raymond 1928– . Australian artist noted for his figure paintings of children. His work is characterized by simple shapes, often no more than silhouettes, that are boldly coloured and large scale, as in *Suite of Paintings* 1960 (Art Gallery of South Australia, Adelaide).

Blackmore R(ichard) D(oddridge) 1825–1900. English novelist, author of *Lorna Doone* 1869, a romance set on Exmoor, SW England, in the late 17th century.

Black Mountain poets group of experimental US poets of the 1950s who were linked with Black Mountain College, a liberal arts college in North Carolina. They rejected the constraints of rhyme and metre and the politically conservative orthodoxy of T S Eliot's classical, academic poetry. Instead, they pioneered open forms and drew on a wide range of non-Western cultures or hermetic traditions. Leading members included Charles ◊Olson and Robert Creeley (1926–).

Blake Quentin 1932– . English book illustrator and writer. A prolific illustrator of children's books written by other people, he has also written and illustrated his own books for children, including *The Marzipan Pig* 1986.

Blake William 1757–1827. English poet, artist, engraver, and visionary, one of the most important figures of English Romanticism. His lyrics, as in *Songs of Innocence* 1789 and *Songs of Experience* 1794, express spiritual wisdom in radiant imagery and symbolism and are often written with a childlike simplicity. They include 'London' and ' The Tyger!'. In prophetic books like *The Marriage of Heaven and Hell* 1790, *America* 1793, and *Milton* 1804, he created a vast personal mythology. He also created a new composite art form in engraving and hand-colouring his own works.

Blake was born in Soho, London, and apprenticed to an engraver 1771–78. He illustrated the Bible, works by Dante and Shakespeare, and his own poems. His figures are usually long and heavily muscled. In his later years he attracted a group of followers, including Samuel Palmer, who called themselves the Ancients. Henry Fuseli was another admirer. Blake's poem 'Jerusalem' 1820 was set to music by Charles Parry.

A Robin Redbreast in a Cage/Puts all of Heaven in a Rage.

William Blake *Auguries of Innocence* 5

Blakey Art (Muslim name Abdullah Ibn Buhaina) 1919–1990. US jazz drummer and bandleader whose dynamic, innovative style made him one of the jazz greats. He contributed to the development of bebop in the 1940s and subsequently to hard bop, and formed the Jazz Messengers in the mid-1950s, continuing to lead the band for most of his life and discovering many talented musicians.

blank verse in literature, the unrhymed iambic pentameter or ten-syllable line of five stresses. First used by the Italian Gian Giorgio Trissino in his tragedy *Sofonisba* 1514–15, it was introduced to England about 1540 by the Earl of Surrey, who used it in his translation of Virgil's *Aeneid*. It was developed by Christopher Marlowe and Shakespeare, quickly becoming the distinctive verse form of Elizabethan and Jacobean drama. It was later used by Milton in *Paradise Lost* 1667 and by Wordsworth in *The Prelude* 1805.

Blasis Carlo 1797–1878. Italian ballet teacher of French extraction. He was successful as a dancer in Paris and in Milan, where he established a dancing school 1837. His celebrated treatise on the art of dancing, *Traité élémentaire, théoretique et pratique de l'art de la danse/Treatise on the Dance* 1820, forms the basis of classical dance training.

Blaue Reiter, der (German 'the Blue Rider', after a painting by Wassily Kandinsky) loose association of German Expressionist painters (some of whom had previously been members of *die ◊Brücke*) formed 1911 and based in Munich. They were interested in colour values, in folk art, and in the necessity of painting 'the inner, spiritual side of nature', but their individual styles were highly varied. Kandinsky and Franz Marc published a book that outlined their views 1912, and there were two exhibitions 1911, 1912.

Bleasdale Alan 1946– . British dramatist. He gained a national reputation with the series of television dramas *The Boys from the Blackstuff* 1982 which portrayed the pressures and tensions of unemployment on a group of men. It was followed by *GBH* 1991, a psychological study of the leader of a city council in northern England. His stage plays include *Having a Ball* 1981 and *On the Ledge* 1993.

Blessington Marguerite, Countess of Blessington 1789–1849. Irish writer. A doyenne of literary society, she published *Conversations with Lord Byron* 1834, travel sketches, and novels.

Bliss Arthur (Drummond) 1891–1975. English composer and conductor who became Master of the Queen's Musick 1953. Among his works are *A Colour Symphony* 1922; music for ballets *Checkmate* 1937, *Miracle in the Gorbals* 1944, and *Adam Zero* 1946; an opera *The Olympians* 1949; and dramatic film music, including *Things to Come* 1935. He conducted the first performance of Stravinsky's *Ragtime* for 11 instruments 1918.

Blitzstein Marc 1905–1964. US composer. Born in Philadelphia, he was a child prodigy as a pianist at the age of six. He served with the US Army 8th Air Force 1942–45, for which he wrote *The Airborne* 1946, a choral symphony. His operas include *The Cradle Will Rock* 1937.

Blixen Karen, born Karen Christentze Dinesen 1885–1962. Danish writer who wrote mainly in English. She is best known for her short stories, Gothic fantasies with a haunting, often mythic quality, published in such collections as *Seven Gothic Tales* 1934 and *Winter's Tales* 1942 under the name Isak Dinesen. Her autobiography *Out of Africa* 1937 is based on her experience of running a coffee plantation in Kenya.

Bloch Ernest 1880–1959. Swiss-born US composer. Among his works are the lyrical drama *Macbeth* 1910, *Schelomo* for cello and orchestra 1916, five string quartets, and *Suite Hébraïque*, for viola and orchestra 1953. He often used themes based on Jewish liturgical music and folk song.

Blok Alexander Alexandrovich 1880–1921. Russian poet. As a follower of the French Symbolist movement, he used words for their symbolic rather than actual meaning. He backed the 1917 Revolution, as in his poems *The Twelve* 1918, and *The Scythians* 1918, the latter appealing to the West to join in the revolution.

Blomdahl Karl-Birger 1916–1968. Swedish composer of ballets and symphonies in Expressionist style. His opera *Aniara* 1959 incorporates electronic music and is set in a spaceship fleeing Earth after nuclear war.

Bloom Claire 1931– . English actress. She began her film career in Chaplin's *Limelight* 1952 and continued with such films as *Richard III* 1956 and *The Brothers Karamazov* 1958. Her more recent films have included supporting roles in *Sammy and Rosie Get Laid* 1987 and Woody Allen's *Crimes and Misdemeanours* 1989. Her television appearances include *Brideshead Revisited* 1980.

Bloomsbury Group intellectual circle of writers and artists based in Bloomsbury, London, which flourished in the 1920s. It centred on the house of publisher Leonard Woolf (1880–1969) and his wife, novelist Virginia ◊Woolf, and included the artists Duncan ◊Grant and Vanessa Bell (1879–1961), the biographer Lytton ◊Strachey, art critics Roger Fry and Clive Bell (1881–1964), and the economist Maynard Keynes (1883–1946). Typically modernist, their innovatory artistic contributions represented an important section of the English avant-garde. From their emphasis on close interpersonal relationships and their fastidious attitude towards contemporary culture arose many accusations of elitism. They also held sceptical views on social and political conventions and religious practices.

blouse a shirtlike garment worn by women. It can be plain, but tends to be more highly decorated than a man's shirt, with embroidery and differing lapel shapes and sizes. It is made of cotton or any light fabric. The term is also used to refer to the waist-length belted jacket worn by soldiers.

Blow John 1648–1708. British composer. He taught Purcell, and wrote church music, for example the anthem 'I Was Glad when They Said unto Me' 1697. His masque *Venus and Adonis* 1685 is sometimes called the first English opera.

Bloy Léon-Marie 1846–1917. French author. He achieved a considerable reputation with his literary lampoons in the 1880s.

Bluebeard folktale character, popularized by the writer Charles ◊Perrault in France about 1697, and historically identified with Gilles de Rais, a 15th-century French nobleman executed for murdering children. Bluebeard murdered six wives for disobeying his command not to enter a locked room, but was himself killed before he could murder the seventh.

bluegrass US country music of the Appalachian Mountain states, characterized by high harmony singing and virtuoso banjo or mandolin playing. Singer and mandolin player Bill Monroe (1911–) is the founder of the genre with his band the Blue Grass Boys (formed 1938), which 1945–48 included guitarist Lester Flatt (1914–1979) and banjo player Earl Scruggs (1924–). Among other bluegrass musicians are guitarist and singer Jimmy Martin (1927–) and the Dillards duo (formed 1958).

blues type of US folk music that originated in the work songs and Negro spirituals of the rural American South in the late 19th century. It is characterized by a 12-bar construction and melancholy lyrics. The guitar has been the dominant instrument; harmonica and piano are also common. Blues guitar and vocal styles have played a vital part in the development of jazz, rock, and pop music in general.

1920s–1930s The *rural* or *delta blues* was usually performed solo with guitar or harmonica, by such artists as Robert ◊Johnson and Bukka White (1906–1977), but the earliest recorded style, *classic blues*, by such musicians as W C Handy (1873–1958) and Bessie Smith (1894–1937), was sung with a small band.

1940s–1950s The *urban blues*, using electric amplification, emerged in the northern cities, chiefly Chicago. As exemplified by Howlin' Wolf, Muddy Waters, and John Lee Hooker, urban blues became *rhythm and blues*.

1960s The jazz-influenced guitar style of B B King inspired many musicians of the *British blues boom*, including Eric Clapton.

1980s The 'blues *noir*' of Robert Cray (1953–) contrasted with the rock-driven blues playing of Stevie Ray Vaughan (1955–1990).

Blunden Edmund 1896–1974. English poet. He served in World War I and published the prose work *Undertones of War* 1928. His poetry is mainly about rural life. Among his scholarly contributions was the discovery and publication of some poems by the 19th-century poet John ◊Clare.

I am for the woods against the world,/ But are the woods for me?

Edmund Blunden 'The Kiss' 1931

Blunt Wilfrid Scawen 1840–1922. British poet. He married Lady Anne Noel, Byron's granddaughter, and travelled with her in the Middle East, becoming a supporter of Arab nationalism. He also supported Irish Home Rule (he was imprisoned 1887–88), and wrote anti-imperialist books, poetry, and diaries.

blurb on a book jacket or cover, the text extolling the book's merit and giving some idea of what it is about, normally written by the publisher.

Blyton Enid 1897–1968. English writer of children's books. She created the character Noddy and the adventures of the 'Famous Five' and 'Secret Seven', but has been criticized by educationalists for social, racial, and sexual stereotyping.

She dealt with 17 different publishers, and on average wrote some 15 new books per year; she was able to complete a 50,000-word Famous Five adventure in a week.

boater circular straw hat with a flat top and straight brim; the crown is trimmed with a band of ribbon. It forms part of the male uniform, with striped blazers and flannel trousers, for the summer sport of boating, which was particularly popular in the late 19th century.

Boccaccio Giovanni 1313–1375. Italian writer and poet, chiefly known for the collection of tales called the ◊*Decameron* 1348–53. Equally at home with tragic and with comic narrative, he laid the foundations for the Humanism of the Renaissance and raised vernacular literature to the status enjoyed by the ancient classics.

Son of a Florentine merchant, he lived in Naples 1328–41, where he fell in love with the unfaithful 'Fiammetta' who inspired his early poetry. Before returning to Florence 1341 he had written the prose romance Filostrato and the verse narrative *Teseide* (used by Chaucer in his *Troilus and Criseyde* and *The Knight's Tale*). He was much influenced by ◊Petrarch, whom he met 1350.

Boccherini (Ridolfo) Luigi 1743–1805. Italian composer and cellist. He studied in Rome, made his mark in Paris 1768, and was court composer in Prussia and Spain. Boccherini composed some 350 instrumental works, an opera, and oratorios.

Boccioni Umberto 1882–1916. Italian painter, sculptor, and theorist. One of the founders of ◊Futurism, he pioneered a semi-abstract style that sought to depict movement and speed, as in his sculpture *Unique Forms of Continuity in Space* 1913 (Tate Gallery, London).

Böcklin Arnold 1827–1901. Swiss Symbolist painter. His mainly imaginary landscapes have a dreamlike atmosphere, as in his best-known work *Island of the Dead* 1880 (Metropolitan Museum of Art, New York).

He was strongly attracted to Italy and lived for

years in Rome. Many of his paintings are peopled with mythical beings, such as nymphs and naiads.

Bodoni Giambattista 1740–1813. Italian printer who managed the printing press of the duke of Parma and produced high-quality editions of the classics. He designed several typefaces, including one bearing his name, which is in use today.

bodysuit all-in-one garment fitting from neck to ankle like a second skin; often made from stretch fabric. One late 19th-century example was devised by Dr Gustav Jaeger, and made of knitted wool. Associated with fitness and futuristic dress, space-age bodysuits with zip-up front openings were designed for men and women in the 1960s; pioneer designers were Pierre Cardin and Azzedine Alaïa. Bodysuits have since been used for dance and gymnastics, and entered fashion with the craze for body-hugging Lycra garments about 1990; they are now often referred to simply as 'bodies'.

Boehm Theobald 1794–1881. German flautist and composer, inventor of the *Boehm system* of improvements to the flute 1832. Using metal-working skills, he applied a series of levers and keypads to the instrument which improved performance and enabled the pitch holes to be drilled at optimum acoustical positions instead of, as formerly, to suit the player's fingers. His system was later applied to other woodwind instruments.

Bofill Ricardo 1939– . Spanish architect, active largely in France since the late 1970s. He established his reputation with low-cost designs for social housing, notably Walden 7, near Barcelona 1970–75, a geometrically complex scheme. An increasingly grandiose form of ◊Classicism characterizes his later work in France, which includes the housing schemes Les Espaces d'Abraxas at Marne-la-Vallée, near Paris 1978–84, and the Antigone development in Montpellier 1992.

Bogarde Dirk. Stage name of Derek van den Bogaerde 1921– . English actor. He appeared in comedies and adventure films such as *Doctor in the House* 1954 and *Campbell's Kingdom* 1957, before acquiring international recognition for complex roles in Joseph Losey's *The Servant* 1963 and *Accident* 1967, and Luchino Visconti's *Death in Venice* 1971. His other films include *A Bridge Too Far* 1977.

He has also written autobiographical books and novels including *A Postillion Struck by Lightning* 1977 and *Backcloth* 1986.

Bogart Humphrey 1899–1957. US film actor who achieved fame as the gangster in *The Petrified Forest* 1936. He became an international cult figure as the tough, romantic 'loner' in such films as *The Maltese Falcon* 1941 and *Casablanca* 1942. He won an Academy Award for his role in *The African Queen* 1952.

He co-starred in *To Have and Have Not* 1944 and *The Big Sleep* 1946 with Lauren Bacall, who became his fourth wife.

Bogdanovich Peter 1939– . US film director, screenwriter, and producer, formerly a critic. *The Last Picture Show* 1971, a nostalgic look at a small Texas town in the 1950s, was followed by two films that attempted to capture the style of old Hollywood, *What's Up Doc?* 1972 and *Paper Moon* 1973.

Bohan Marc 1926– . French fashion designer who joined the Dior firm 1958, replacing Yves Saint-Laurent, to design couture and ready-to-wear ranges. He was designer to the British couture house Hartnell 1991–92. He is noted for refined, romantic clothes, soft prints, and flattering colours.

Böhm Karl 1894–1981. Austrian conductor known for his stately interpretations of Beethoven, and of Mozart and Strauss operas.

Boiardo Matteo Maria, Count 1434–1494. Italian poet, famed for his *Orlando innamorato/Roland in Love* 1487, a chivalrous epic glorifying military honour, patriotism, and religion. ◊Ariosto's *Orlando furioso* 1516 was conceived as a sequel to this work.

Boileau Nicolas 1636–1711. French poet and critic. After a series of contemporary satires, his *Epîtres/Epistles* 1669–77 led to his joint appointment with Racine as royal historian 1677. Later works include *L'Art poétique/The Art of Poetry* 1674, which in both France and England became the standard guide to the classical principles in literature, and the mock-heroic *Le Lutrin/The Lectern* 1674–83.

Other works include a translation of Longinus, *On the Sublime* 1674. A close friend of Racine, Molière, and La Fontaine, he was elected to the French Academy 1684.

Bol Ferdinand 1610–1680. Dutch painter, a pupil and for many years an imitator of ◊Rembrandt. After the 1660s he developed a more independent style and prospered as a portraitist.

Boldrewood Rolf. Pen name of Thomas Alexander Browne 1826–1915. Australian writer, born in London. He wrote 17 novels, mostly rather stilted romances, but is remembered mainly for *Robbery Under Arms* 1888 and *A Squatter's Life* 1890, which give graphic accounts of life in the outback.

bolero Spanish dance in triple time for a solo dancer or a couple, usually with castanet accompaniment. It was used as the title of a one-act ballet score by Ravel, choreographed by Nijinsky for Ida Rubinstein 1928.

Böll Heinrich 1917–1985. German novelist. A radical Catholic and anti-Nazi, he attacked

Germany's political past and the materialism of its contemporary society. His many publications include poems, short stories, and novels which satirized West German society, for example *Billard um Halbzehn/Billiards at Half-Past Nine* 1959 and *Gruppenbild mit Dame/Group Portrait with Lady* 1971. Nobel Prize for Literature 1972.

Bolshoi Ballet (Russian 'great') Russian ballet company based at the Bolshoi Theatre in Moscow. Founded 1776, it initially recruited its dancers from the Moscow Orphanage where the first classes were conducted 1773. At first overshadowed by the ◊Kirov Ballet, the Bolshoi came into its own in the late 19th century with the first staging of ◊Petipa's *Don Quixote* 1877 and *Swan Lake* 1877. With its mixed repertory of classics and new works, the Bolshoi is noted for its grand-scale productions and the dancers' dramatic and eloquent technique. From 1964 its artistic director has been the choreographer Yuri Grigorovich (1927–) and since the 1960s it has concentrated on highly spectacular and heroic productions of the classics and modern works, such as *Spartacus* 1968 and *The Golden Age* 1982.

Bolt Robert (Oxton) 1924– . English dramatist and screenwriter. He is known for his historical plays, such as *A Man for All Seasons* 1960 (filmed 1966) about Thomas More, and for his screenplays, including *Lawrence of Arabia* 1962 and *Dr Zhivago* 1965 (both Academy Awards).

Among his other screenwriting credits are *Ryan's Daughter* 1970, *The Bounty* 1984, and *The Mission* 1986.

Bomberg David 1890–1957. English painter who applied forms inspired by Cubism and Vorticism to figurative subjects in such early works as *The Mud Bath* 1914 (Tate Gallery, London). Moving away from semi-abstraction in the mid-1920s, his work became more representational and Expressionist.

Bomberg was apprenticed to a lithographer, then studied at the Slade School in London 1911–13, and was a founder member of the ◊London Group. He gained recognition only towards the end of his life.

Bonampak site of a Classic Mayan city, on the river Usumacinta near the Mexico and Guatemala border, with extensive remains of wall paintings depicting battles, torture, and sacrifices. Rediscovered 1948, the paintings shed new light on Mayan society, which to that date had been considered peaceful. See ◊pre-Columbian art.

Bond Edward 1935– . English dramatist. His early work aroused controversy because of the savagery of some of his imagery, for example, the brutal stoning of a baby by bored youths in *Saved* 1965. Other works include *Early Morning* 1968, the last play to be banned in the UK by the Lord Chamberlain; *Lear* 1972, a reworking of Shakespeare's play; *Bingo* 1973, an account of Shakespeare's last days; and *The War Plays* 1985.

We have only one thing to keep us sane, pity; and the man without pity is mad.

Edward Bond *Lear* 1972

bone china or *softpaste* semiporcelain made of 5% bone ash added to 95% kaolin. It was first made in the West in imitation of Chinese porcelain, whose formula was kept secret by the Chinese.

Bonheur Rosa (Marie Rosalie) 1822–1899. French painter best known for her realistic animal painting, including *Horse Fair* 1853 (Metropolitan Museum of Art, New York).

She exhibited at the Paris Salon every year from 1841, and received international awards. In 1894 she became the first woman Officer of the Légion d'Honneur.

Bonington Richard Parkes 1802–1828. English painter who lived in France from 1817. He is noted for his fresh, atmospheric seascapes and landscapes in oil and watercolour, mainly viewed from a high perspective; he also painted historic genre works. He was much admired by Delacroix.

Bonnard Pierre 1867–1947. French painter, designer, and graphic artist. Influenced by Gauguin and Japanese prints, he specialized in intimate domestic scenes and landscapes, his paintings shimmering with colour and light. With other members of *les* ◊*Nabis*, he explored the decorative arts (posters, stained glass, furniture), but is most widely known for his series of nudes, for example, *Nude in the Bath* 1938 (Petit Palais, Paris).

boogie-woogie jazz played on the piano, using a repeated motif for the left hand. It was common in the USA from around 1900 to the 1950s. Boogie-woogie players included Pinetop Smith (1904–1929), Meade 'Lux' Lewis (1905–1964), and Jimmy Yancey (1898–1951). Rock-and-roll pianist Jerry Lee Lewis adapted the style.

bookbinding securing of the pages of a book between protective covers by sewing and/or gluing. Cloth binding was first introduced 1822, but from the mid-20th century synthetic bindings were increasingly employed, and most hardback books are bound by machine.

Bookbinding did not emerge as a distinct craft until printing was introduced to Europe in the 15th century. Until that time scrolls and (from around 1200) codices (see ◊codex) were usual. Gold tooling, the principal ornament of leather bookbinding, was probably introduced to Europe from the East by the Venetian Aldus Manutius (1450–1515).

Booker Prize for Fiction British literary prize of £20,000 awarded annually (from 1969) to a Commonwealth writer by the Booker company (formerly Booker McConnell) for a novel published in the UK during the previous year.

Boorman John 1933– . English film director who, after working in television, directed successful films both in Hollywood (*Point Blank* 1967, *Deliverance* 1972) and in Britain (*Excalibur* 1981, *Hope and Glory* 1987). He is the author of a telling book on film finance, *Money into Light* 1985.

Booth Edwin Thomas 1833–1893. US actor. He was one of America's most acclaimed Shakespearean performers, famous for his portrayal of Hamlet. As lead actor, theatre manager, and producer, he successfully brought to the New York stage numerous Shakespearean tragedies. His career suffered in the wake of the public disgrace of his brother, John Wilkes Booth, who assassinated President Lincoln 1865.

Boothe Claire see ◊Luce, Claire Boothe.

boots footwear covering the feet and ankles, suitable for utilitarian and fashion purposes. Boots vary in height from the ankle to the thigh.
In the 17th century, wide knee-high boots, folded down, were worn by men with tight ◊breeches. In the 19th century women wore low-heeled boots with daywear in the summer and winter, but by the early part of the 20th century boots tended to be used mainly for utilitarian purposes. During the 1960s boots became familiar fashion icons, such as ◊Biba's pink suede knee-high boots. Other materials used by boot designers are leather, plastic, vinyl, and brocaded fabrics.

bop short for ◊*bebop*, a style of jazz.

Borchert Wolfgang 1921–1947. German playwright and prose writer. Borchert was sent home wounded during World War II while serving on the Russian front, where he had been sent for making anti-Nazi comments. *Draussen vor der Tür/The Outsider* 1947 is a surreal play about the chaotic conditions that a German soldier finds when he returns to Germany after walking home from the Russian front.

Boreas in Greek mythology, the north wind which carried off Oreithyia, daughter of a legendary king of Athens. Their children were Calais and Zetes, two of the ◊Argonauts, who freed Phineus (a blind soothsayer, destined to be the future king of Salmydessus in Thrace) from the ◊Harpies.

Borges Jorge Luis 1899–1986. Argentine poet and short-story writer. In 1961 he became director of the National Library, Buenos Aires, and was professor of English literature at the university there. An exponent of ◊magic realism, he is known for his fantastic and paradoxical work *Ficciones/Fictions* 1944.
Borges explored metaphysical themes in early works such as *Ficciones* and *El Aleph/The Aleph, and other Stories* 1949. In a later collection of tales *El informe de Brodie/Dr Brodie's Report* 1972, he adopted a more realistic style, reminiscent of the work of the young Rudyard ◊Kipling, of whom he was a great admirer. *El libro de arena/The Book of Sand* 1975 marked a return to more fantastic themes.

Writing is nothing more than a guided dream.

Jorge Luis Borges *Dr Brodie's Report* 1972

Borglum Gutzon 1867–1941. US sculptor. He created a six-ton marble head of Abraham Lincoln in Washington, DC, and the series of giant heads of presidents Washington, Jefferson, Lincoln, and Theodore Roosevelt, carved on Mount Rushmore, South Dakota (begun 1930).

Borodin Alexander Porfir'yevich 1833–1887. Russian composer. Born in St Petersburg, the illegitimate son of a Russian prince, he became by profession an expert in medical chemistry, but in his spare time devoted himself to writing music. His principal work is the opera *Prince Igor*, left unfinished; it was completed by Rimsky-Korsakov and Glazunov and includes the Polovtsian Dances. His other works include symphonies, songs, and chamber music, using traditional Russian themes.

Borromini Francesco 1599–1667. Italian Baroque architect, one of the two most important (with ◊Bernini, his main rival) in 17th-century Rome. Whereas Bernini designed in a florid, expansive style, his pupil Borromini developed a highly idiosyncratic and austere use of the Classical language of architecture. Bernini's works include the cathedrals of San Carlo alle Quattro Fontane 1637–41 and San Ivo della Sapienza 1643–60, and the Oratory of St Philip Neri 1638–50.

Borrow George Henry 1803–1881. English writer. His books, incorporating his knowledge of languages and Romany lore acquired during his many journeys through Europe and Britain, include *The Bible in Spain* 1843, *Lavengro* 1851, *The Romany Rye* 1857, and *Wild Wales* 1862.

Borrowers, The story for children by Mary Norton (1903–), published in the UK 1952. It describes a family of tiny people who live secretly under the floor in a large country house and subsist by 'borrowing' things from the 'human beans' who live above. Their survival and way of life come under threat in several sequels.

Bosch Hieronymus (Jerome) *c.* 1450–1516. Early Netherlandish painter. His fantastic visions of weird and hellish creatures, as shown in *The Garden of Earthly Delights* about 1505–10 (Prado, Madrid), show astonishing imagination and a complex imagery. His religious subjects focused not on the holy figures but on the mass of ordinary witnesses, placing the religious event in a contemporary Netherlandish context and creating cruel caricatures of human sinfulness.

Bosch is named after his birthplace, s-Hertogenbosch, in North Brabant, the Netherlands. His work, which influenced ◊Brueghel the Elder and foreshadowed Surrealism, was probably inspired by a local religious brotherhood. However, he was an orthodox Catholic and a prosperous painter, not a heretic, as was once believed. After his death, his work was collected by Philip II of Spain.

bossa nova Brazilian dance rhythm of the 1950s, combining samba and cool jazz. It became internationally popular in songs like 'The Girl From Ipanema' 1964.

Boswell James 1740–1795. Scottish biographer and diarist. He was a member of Samuel ◊Johnson's London Literary Club and the two men travelled to Scotland together 1773, as recorded in Boswell's *Journal of the Tour to the Hebrides* 1785. His *Life of Samuel Johnson* was published 1791. Boswell's ability to record Johnson's pithy conversation verbatim makes this a classic of English biography.

Life will not bear to be calmly considered. It appears insipid and ridiculous as a country dance.

James Boswell

Born in Edinburgh, Boswell studied law but centred his ambitions on literature and politics. He first met Johnson 1763, before setting out on a European tour during which he met the French thinkers Rousseau and Voltaire, and the Corsican nationalist general Paoli (1726–1807), whom he commemorated in his popular *Account of Corsica*

1768. In 1766 he became a lawyer, and in 1772 renewed his acquaintance with Johnson in London. Boswell's long-lost personal papers were acquired for publication by Yale University 1949, and the *Journals* are of exceptional interest.

Botero Fernando 1932– . Colombian painter. He studied in Spain and Italy, developing a naive style influenced by South American peasant art, in which, with ironic humour, he depicted fat, doll-like figures, often as parodies of conventional sensuality.

Botta Mario 1943– . Swiss architect, the majority of whose work is in Ticino (the Italian canton of Switzerland). His work shows a strong regionalist interpretation of modern architecture, close attention to topography, and a very formal geometry. These aspects are expressed in a striking series of single-family houses, including Riva San Vitale 1972–73 and Ligometto 1975–76. Other works include a school at Morbio Inferiore 1972–77 and the Staatsbank, Fribourg, 1977–82.

Botticelli Sandro 1445–1510. Florentine painter. He was patronized by the ruling Medici family and deeply influenced by their Neo-Platonic circle. It was for the Medicis that he painted ◊*Primavera* 1478 and *The Birth of Venus* about 1482–84 (both in the Uffizi, Florence). From the 1490s he was influenced by the religious fanatic Savonarola and developed a harshly expressive and emotional style, as seen in his *Mystic Nativity* 1500 (National Gallery, London).

His work for the Medicis was designed to cater to the educated classical tastes of the day. As well as his sentimental and beautiful young Madonnas, he produced a series of inventive compositions, including *tondi* (circular paintings) and illustrations for Dante's ◊*Divine Comedy*. He broke with the Medicis after their execution of Savonarola.

Boucher François 1703–1770. French Rococo painter. Court painter to Louis XV from 1765, he was much patronized for his light-hearted, decorative scenes, which often convey a playful eroticism, as in *Diana Bathing* 1742 (Louvre, Paris).

He also painted portraits and decorative chinoiserie for Parisian palaces, and became director of the Gobelins tapestry works, Paris, 1755.

Boucicault Dion(ysus) Larner 1822–1890. Irish dramatist and actor. His first success was with the social comedy *London Assurance* 1841, and during his long career he wrote or adapted about 200 plays, many of them melodramas, including *The Corsican Brothers* 1852 and *Louis XI* 1855. He moved to the USA 1872.

bouclé textured fancy yarn with a loop pile, used for knitting and weaving clothing.

Boudin Eugène 1824–1898. French artist, a forerunner of the Impressionists, known for his luminous seaside scenes painted in the open air, such as *Harbour of Trouville* (National Gallery, London).

Bouguereau Adolphe William 1825–1905. French academic painter of historical and mythological subjects. He was respected in his day, though not by the Impressionists for whom he was the embodiment of insipid middle-class taste.

Boulanger Lili (Juliette Marie Olga) 1893–1918. French composer, the younger sister of Nadia Boulanger. At the age of 19, she won the Prix de Rome with the cantata *Faust et Hélène* for voices and orchestra.

Boulanger Nadia (Juliette) 1887–1979. French music teacher and conductor. A pupil of Fauré, and admirer of Stravinsky, she included among her composition pupils at the American Conservatory in Fontainebleau, France (from 1921) Aaron Copland, Roy Harris, Walter Piston, and Philip Glass.

Boulez Pierre 1925– . French composer and conductor, founder and director of ◊IRCAM, a music research studio in Paris opened 1977. His music, strictly serial and expressionistic in style, includes the cantatas *Le Visage nuptial* 1946–52 and *Le Marteau sans maître* 1955, both to texts by René Char; *Pli selon pli* 1962 for soprano and orchestra; and *Répons* 1981 for soloists, orchestra, tapes, and computer-generated sounds.

boulle or *buhl* type of ◊marquetry in brass and tortoiseshell. Originally Italian, it has acquired the name of its most skilful exponent, the French artisan André-Charles Boulle (1642–1732).

Boullée Etienne-Louis 1729–1799. French Neo-Classical architect. Although he built very little, he was a major influence on the architecture of his day, and his austere, visionary works have influenced late 20th-century architects such as the Italian Aldo ◊Rossi. Boullée's abstract, geometric style is exemplified in his design for a spherical monument to the scientist Isaac Newton, 150 m/500 ft high.

Boult Adrian (Cedric) 1889–1983. British conductor of the BBC Symphony Orchestra 1930–50 and the London Philharmonic 1950–57. He promoted the work of Holst and Vaughan Williams, and was a celebrated interpreter of Elgar.

Boulting John 1913–1985 and Roy 1913– . British director–producer team that was successful in the years following World War II. Their films include *Brighton Rock* 1947, *Lucky Jim* 1957, and *I'm All Right Jack* 1959. They were twins.

bourdon French musical term for the drone of a hurdy-gurdy or bagpipes, or for a piece of music imitating a drone accompaniment.

Bournonville August 1805–1879. Danish dancer and choreographer. In 1830 he was appointed director of the Royal Danish Ballet, the company for which he both danced and created his ballets. His works, unlike those of the then prevalent Romantic era, are ebullient, warmly good-humoured, and give equal importance to both male and female dancers. His style is marked by swift, fluid footwork accompanied by patterns of arcing leaps. His works, of which only a dozen survive, include a version of *La Sylphide* 1836 and *Napoli* 1842.

bourrée French dance form in fast double two time, accented on the second beat, and starting on the upbeat, the music for which is found in the classical ◊suite.

Bouts Dirk (Dierick) *c.* 1420–1475. Early Netherlandish painter. Born in Haarlem, he settled in Louvain, painting portraits and religious scenes influenced by Rogier van der Weyden and Petrus Christus. *The Last Supper* 1464–68 (St Pierre, Louvain) is one of his finest works.

Bow Clara 1905–1965. US film actress known as a 'Jazz Baby' and the 'It Girl' after her portrayal of a glamorous flapper in the silent film *It* 1927.

Bowdler Thomas 1754–1825. British editor whose prudishly expurgated versions of Shakespeare and other authors gave rise to the verb *bowdlerize*.

Bowen Elizabeth 1899–1973. Irish novelist. She published her first volume of short stories, *Encounters*, in 1923. Her novels include *The Death of the Heart* 1938, *The Heat of the Day* 1949, and *The Little Girls* 1964.

No, it is not only our fate but our business to lose innocence, and once we have lost that, it is futile to attempt a picnic in Eden.

Elizabeth Bowen 'Out of a Book'

Bowie David. Stage name of David Jones 1947– . English pop singer, songwriter, and actor whose career has been a series of image changes. His hits include 'Space Oddity' 1969, 'Jean Genie' 1973, 'Rebel, Rebel' 1974, 'Golden Years' 1975, and 'Underground' 1986. His albums include *The Rise and Fall of Ziggy Stardust and the Spiders from Mars* 1972, *Low* 1977, *Heroes* 1977, *Let's Dance* 1983, and *Black Tie/White Noise* 1993. He has acted in plays and films, including Nicolas Roeg's *The Man Who Fell to Earth* 1976.

Bowles Paul 1910– . US writer and composer. Born in New York City, he studied music composition with Aaron Copland and Virgil Thomson, writing scores for ballets, films, and an opera, *The Wind Remains* 1943, as well as incidental music for plays. He settled in Morocco, the setting of his novels *The Sheltering Sky* 1949 (filmed 1990) and *Let It Come Down* 1952, which chillingly depict the existential breakdown of Westerners unable to survive self-exposure in an alien culture. His autobiography, *Without Stopping*, was published 1972.

Bowles settled permanently in Tangier with his wife, the writer Jane Bowles (1917–1973), after World War II and became greatly influenced by Moroccan storytelling – he later turned to transcribing and translating tales by Mohammed Mrabet and others.

Boyd Arthur Merric Bloomfield 1920– . Australian painter, sculptor, and potter. His work is broadly Expressionist, and often deals with social themes. He established his international reputation with an exhibition held in London 1960. His paintings include *Wimmera Landscape* 1950 and *The Blind Nebuchadnezzar with a Lion* 1967; he is also known for the ceramic sculpture at the Melbourne Olympic Swimming Pool, 1955.

Boyer Charles 1899–1978. French film actor who made his name in Hollywood in the 1930s as the 'great lover' in such films as *The Garden of Allah* 1936 and *Conquest/Maria Walewska* 1937, in which he played Napoleon. Later films include *Love Affair* 1939 and *Gaslight* 1942. He continued as a leading man into the 1950s.

Bo Zhu Yi or *Po Chü-i* 772–846. Chinese poet. President from 841 of the imperial war department, he criticized government policy and wrote poems dealing with the social problems of his age. He is said to have checked his work with an old peasant woman for clarity of expression.

bra or *brassière* undergarment designed to cover and support women's breasts. Created in the early 1900s, the original bra was made in the USA from two handkerchiefs and narrow ribbon. It became popular in the 1920s, helping to achieve the fashionable flat profile by flattening the chest and pushing the breasts downwards.

The bra has undergone many transformations during the 20th century. The shape was most exaggerated during the 1950s when the cups were stiffened and wired. In the late 1980s the bra also became a fashion garment, worn as outer clothing, notably in the designs of Jean-Paul ◊Gaultier for the singer Madonna's 1990 world tour, and of ◊Dolce e Gabbana.

braccio, da (Italian 'on the arm') suffix originally used to distinguish violins, played resting on the arm, from viols played da ◊gamba (on the leg). The term 'viola da braccio' in 17th-century music signifies a violin or viola; today only the viola (German *bratsche*) is so called.

Bracegirdle Anne *c.* 1663–1748. English actress, the mistress of William ◊Congreve, and possibly his wife; she played Millamant in his *The Way of the World*.

Bradbury Malcolm 1932– . British novelist and critic whose writings include comic and satirical portrayals of academic life. He became professor of American studies at the University of East Anglia 1970, and his major work is *The History Man* 1975, set in a provincial English university. Other works include *Rates of Exchange* 1983.

Marriage is the most advanced form of warfare in the modern world.

Malcolm Bradbury *The History Man* 1975

Bradbury Ray (Douglas) 1920– . US author, best known as a writer of science fiction, a genre he helped make 'respectable' to a wider readership. His work shows nostalgia for small-town Midwestern life, and includes *The Martian Chronicles* 1950, *Fahrenheit 451* 1953, *R is for Rocket*, *S is for Space* 1962, and *Something Wicked This Way Comes* 1962.

Some of his short stories are collected in *The Stories of Ray Bradbury* 1980. He also has written several volumes of poetry, television and motion-picture screenplays, radio dramas, and children's stories.

Bradley A(ndrew) C(ecil) 1851–1935. English literary critic and scholar. His study of the plays *Hamlet*, *King Lear*, *Othello*, and *Macbeth* in *Shakespearean Tragedy* 1904 looked at the plays in terms of their major characters. His *Oxford Lectures on Poetry* 1909 were delivered while he was professor of poetry at Oxford 1901–06.

Bradley Scott 1914– . US composer of animation film music. Working for the US film-production company Metro-Goldwyn-Mayer (MGM), with Carl Stalling he developed the ◊click-track which enables a composer to write a music track to any desired tempo for a given length of film. He also introduced classical music to *Tom and Jerry* cartoons, arranging Liszt's *Hungarian Rhapsody No 2* for *Cat Concerto* 1947, and in *The Cat that Hated People* using a twelve-tone row on piccolo to represent Jerry and the same row in reverse played by oboe to represent Tom.

Brady Mathew B *c.* 1823–1896. US photographer. Famed for his skill in photographic portraiture, he published *The Gallery of Illustrious Americans* 1850. With the outbreak of the US Civil War 1861, Brady and his staff became the foremost photographers of battle scenes and military life. Although his war photos were widely reproduced, Brady later suffered a series of financial reverses and died in poverty.

Born in Warren County, New York, Brady served as an apprentice to a portrait painter. Learning the rudiments of photography from Samuel ◊Morse, Brady established his own ◊daguerreotype studio in New York 1844.

Brahma in Hinduism, the creator of the cosmos, who forms with Vishnu and Siva the Trimurti, or three aspects of the absolute spirit.

In the Hindu creation myth, Brahma, the demiurge, is born from the unfolding lotus flower that grows out of Vishnu's navel; after Brahma creates the world, Vishnu wakes and governs it for the duration of the cosmic cycle *kalpa*, the 'day of Brahma', which lasts for 4,200 million earthly years. Unlike Brahman, which is an impersonal principle and of neuter gender, Brahma is a personified god and male.

Brahms Johannes 1833–1897. German composer, pianist, and conductor. Considered one of the greatest composers of symphonic music and of songs, his works include four symphonies; lieder (songs); concertos for piano and for violin; chamber music; sonatas; and the choral *Ein Deutsches Requiem/A German Requiem* 1868. He performed and conducted his own works.

It is not hard to compose, but it is wonderfully hard to let the superfluous notes fall under the table.

Johannes Brahms

In 1853 the violinist Joachim introduced him to Liszt and Schumann, who encouraged him. From 1868 Brahms made his home in Vienna. Although his music belongs to a reflective strain of Romanticism, similar to Wordsworth in poetry, Brahms saw himself as continuing the classical tradition from the point to which Beethoven had brought it. To his contemporaries, he was a strict formalist, in opposition to the romantic sensuality of Wagner. His influence on Mahler and Schoenberg was profound.

Braine John 1922–1986. English novelist. His novel *Room at the Top* 1957 created the character of Joe Lampton, one of the first of the northern working-class anti-heroes. His other novels include *Life at the Top* 1962 and *The Vodi* 1959.

Braithwaite Eustace Adolph 1912– . Guyanese author. His experiences as a teacher in London prompted *To Sir With Love* 1959. His *Reluctant Neighbours* 1972 deals with black/white relations.

Bramah Ernest. Pen name of Ernest Bramah Smith 1868–1948. British short-story writer, creator of Kai Lung, and of Max Carrados, a blind detective.

Bramante Donato *c.* 1444–1514. Italian Renaissance architect and artist. Inspired by Classical designs and by the work of Leonardo da Vinci, he was employed by Pope Julius II in rebuilding part of the Vatican and St Peter's in Rome. The circular Tempietto of San Pietro in Montorio, Rome (commissioned 1502; built about 1510), is possibly his most important completed work. Though small in size, this circular colonnaded building possesses much of the grandeur of ancient Roman buildings.

Branagh Kenneth 1960– . Northern Irish actor, director, and producer. Branagh brought his immense energy to his adaptation of Shakespeare's *Henry V* for the screen 1989. His other directorial and acting credits include *Dead Again* 1991, *Peter's Friends* 1992, and *Much Ado About Nothing* 1993. He is married to actress Emma ◊Thompson with whom he frequently co-stars.

He co-founded, with David Parfitt, the Renaissance Theatre Company 1987, and was a notable Hamlet 1988 and 1992, and Touchstone 1988.

Brancusi Constantin 1876–1957. Romanian sculptor, a seminal figure in 20th-century art. Active in Paris from 1904, he was a pioneer of abstract sculpture, developing increasingly simplified representations of natural or organic forms, for example the *Sleeping Muse* 1910 (Musée National d'Art Moderne, Paris), a sculpted head that gradually comes to resemble an egg.

In 1904 he walked from Romania to Paris, where he worked briefly in Rodin's studio. He began to explore direct carving in marble (producing many versions of Rodin's *The Kiss*), and was one of the first sculptors in the 20th century to carve directly from his material, working with stone, wood, and metal. By the 1930s he had achieved monumental simplicity with structures of simple repeated forms, for example, *Endless Column* and other works commissioned for Tirgu Jiu public park, Romania.

Brand Dollar (Adolf Johannes) former name of South African jazz musician Abdullah ◊Ibrahim.

An actor is a guy who, if you aren't talking about him, isn't listening.

Marlon Brando *Observer* Jan 1956

Brando Marlon 1924– . US actor whose powerful stage presence, mumbling speech, and use of ◊Method acting earned him a place as a distinctive actor. He won best-actor Academy Awards for *On the Waterfront* 1954 and *The Godfather* 1972.

He made his Broadway debut in *I Remember Mama* 1944, and achieved fame in *A Streetcar Named Desire* 1947. His films include *The Men* 1950, *A Streetcar Named Desire* 1951, *Julius Caesar* 1953, *The Wild One* 1954, *Mutiny on the*

Bounty 1962, *Last Tango in Paris* 1973, *Apocalypse Now* 1979, and *The Freshman* 1990.

Brandt Bill 1905–1983. British photographer, born in Germany. During the 1930s he made a series of social records contrasting the lives of the rich and the poor, some of which were presented in his book *The English at Home* 1936. During World War II he documented conditions in London in the Blitz. The strong contrasts in his black-and-white prints often produced a gloomy and threatening atmosphere. His outstanding creative work was his treatment of the nude, published in *Perspective of Nudes* 1961 and *Shadows of Light* 1966.

Brangwyn Frank 1867–1956. British artist; of Welsh extraction, he was born in Bruges, Belgium. He initially worked for William Morris as a textile designer, and subsequently produced furniture, pottery, carpets, schemes for interior decoration and architectural designs, as well as book illustrations, lithographs, and etchings.

Braque Georges 1882–1963. French painter who, with Picasso, founded the Cubist movement around 1907–10. His early work was influenced by Fauvism in its use of pure, bright colour, but from 1907 he developed a geometric style and during the next few years he and Picasso worked very closely developing Cubism. It was during this period that he began to experiment with collage and invented the technique of gluing paper, wood, and other materials to canvas. His later work was more decorative but was more restrained in its use of colour.

Art is meant to disturb, science reassures.

Georges Braque *Pensées sur l'Art*

Brassaï adopted name of Gyula Halesz 1899–1986. French photographer of Hungarian origin who chronicled, mainly by flash, the nightlife of Paris: the prostitutes, street cleaners, and criminals. These pictures were published as *Paris by Night* 1933. Later he turned to more abstract work.

brass instrument any of a class of musical instruments made of brass or other metal, including trumpets, bugles, trombones, and horns. The function of a reed is served by the lips, shaped and tensed by the mouthpiece, acting as a valve releasing periodic pulses of pressurized air into the tube. Orchestral brass instruments are derived from signalling instruments that in their natural or valveless form produce a directionally focused range of tones from the harmonic series by overblowing to as high as the 16th harmonic. They are powerful and efficient generators, and produce tones of great depth and resonance.

In the symphony orchestra the brass instruments are the French horn, trumpet, trombone, and tuba. In the brass band (in descending order of pitch) they comprise the cornet, flugelhorn, tenor horn, B-flat baritone, euphonium, trombone, and bombardon (bass tuba).

Bratby John 1928–1992. English painter, one of the leading exponents of the 'kitchen sink' school of the 1950s whose work concentrated on working-class domestic life.

Brathwaite Edward Kamau 1930– . West Indian historian and poet. Using calypso and work songs as well as more conventional verse forms, he has explored the ways in which the West Indian legacy of slavery has been transcended by the traditions of ritual, music, and dance originating in West Africa, particularly in *Masks* 1968. Other works include *Mother Poem* 1977, *Sun Poem* 1982, and *The Folk Culture of the Slaves of Jamaica* 1970.

Braun AEG German company, manufacturer of sound equipment and domestic appliances, founded 1921 by Max Braun and based in Frankfurt.

The factory was rebuilt 1945 and in 1951 when Max Braun died his son Artur (1925–) began commissioning a number of young and highly innovative German industrial designers associated with the new design school (◊Hochschule für Gestaltung) at Ulm – among them Dieter ◊Rams and Hans Gugelot (1920–1965) – to update the company's product range. Their radically new designs quickly became hallmarks of the stark, geometric design style that developed in Germany at that time.

Brautigan Richard 1935–1984. US novelist, who lived in San Francisco, the setting for many of his playfully inventive and humorous short fictions, often written as dead-pan parodies. He became a cult figure in the late 1960s with such works as *A Confederate General from Big Sur* 1964, his best-seller *Trout Fishing in America* 1967, and *In Watermelon Sugar* 1968. His last novels, before committing suicide, were *The Tokyo–Montana Express* 1980 and *So The Wind Won't Blow It All Away* 1982.

Brave New World novel 1932 by Aldous ◊Huxley. It is set in the future when Humanity is totally controlled on scientific principles by eugenics and drugs. A Savage from outside the boundaries is brought inside and is ultimately maddened by the emotional triviality and meaninglessness of this society's life. The ironic title is taken from Shakespeare's *The Tempest* when Miranda delightedly exclaims 'Oh brave new world that has such people in it.'

Bravo Manuel Alvarez 1902– . Mexican photographer. He was self-taught but received advice from the US photographer Edward Weston. His dark and brooding images convey an essentially tragic vision of his native land.

Brazilian architecture the first substantial buildings in Brazil were Christian churches built by the Jesuits: the church of S Bento in Rio de Janeiro 1652 is in early Baroque style. The second half of the 18th century saw the flowering of a variation of Baroque unique to Brazil; for example, the church of the Bom Jesus at Congonhas do Campo 1777. A number of European styles were imported during the 1800s. From the early 20th century, Brazilian architecture reflects the huge impact of the Modern Movement. The works of Oscar Niemeyer and Lucio Costa (1902–), initially influenced by ◊Le Corbusier, subsequently took on an exuberance of their own, rarely seen in modern architecture. Costa's most renowned work is his plan for Brasilia 1957, the new state capital.

break dance street dance that originated in the USA in the late 1970s. It consists of disjointed, robotic movements or acrobatic spins executed on the back or the head. It is part of the ◊hip-hop culture.

Bream Julian (Alexander) 1933– . British virtuoso of the guitar and lute. He has revived much Elizabethan lute music and encouraged composition by contemporaries for both instruments. Benjamin Britten and Hans Werner Henze have written for him.

Brecht Bertolt 1898–1956. German dramatist and poet, one of the most influential figures in 20th-century theatre. A committed Marxist, he sought to develop an 'epic theatre' which aimed to destroy the 'suspension of disbelief' usual in the theatre and so encourage audiences to develop an active and critical attitude to a play's subject. He adapted John Gay's *The Beggar's Opera* as *Die Dreigroschenoper/The Threepenny Opera* 1928, set to music by Kurt Weill. Later plays include *Mutter Courage/Mother Courage* 1941, set during the Thirty Years' War, and *Der kaukasische Kreidekreis/The ◊Caucasian Chalk Circle* 1949.

As an anti-Nazi, he left Germany 1933 for Scandinavia and the USA. He became an Austrian citizen after World War II; in 1949 he established the Berliner Ensemble theatre group in East Germany. His other works include *Galileo* 1938, *Der gute Mensch von Setzuan/the Good Woman of Setzuan* 1943, and *Der aufhaltsame Aufstieg der Arturo Ui/The Preventable Rise of Arturo Ui* 1958.

Unhappy the land that is in need of heroes.

Bertolt Brecht *Galileo* 1938

---

breeches form of ◊trousers that extend only as far as the knee. Prior to the introduction of trousers in the late 19th century, men wore breeches with stockings as part of their everyday dress. Since the 19th century breeches have been worn mainly for riding or other sports, such as golf, field sports, and walking.

Brel Jacques 1929–1978. Belgian singer and songwriter, active in France from 1953, where his fatalistic ballads made him a star. Of his more than 400 songs, many have in translation been recorded by singers as diverse as Frank Sinatra and David Bowie. *Ne me quitte pas/If You Go Away* 1964 is one of his best-known songs.

Brel worked in the *chansonnier* (singer-songwriter) tradition, often with orchestral arrangements. He also appeared in films. Other Brel songs are *Marieke* 1964, *Les Moribonds/Seasons in the Sun*, *La Colombe*, *Jackie*, and *Amsterdam*. The album *Brel* 1977 was his last work.

Brendel Alfred 1931– . Austrian pianist known for his fastidious and searching interpretations of Beethoven, Schubert, and Liszt. He is the author of *Musical Thoughts and Afterthoughts* 1976 and *Music Sounded Out* 1990.

Brennan Christopher (John) 1870–1932. Australian Symbolist poet, influenced by Baudelaire and Mallarmé. Although one of Australia's greatest poets, he is virtually unknown outside his native country. His complex, idiosyncratic verse includes *Poems* 1914 and *A Chant of Doom and Other Verses* 1918.

Brennan Walter 1894–1974. US film actor. He appeared in many Westerns, including *The Westerner* 1940, *Bad Day at Black Rock* 1955, and *Rio Bravo* 1959.

Brentano Clemens 1778–1842. German Romantic writer. He published a seminal collection of folk tales and songs with Ludwig von ◊Arnim (*Des Knaben Wunderhorn/The Boy's Magic Horn*) 1805–08, and popularized the legend of the Lorelei (a rock in the river Rhine). He also wrote mystic religious verse, as in *Romanzen vom Rosenkranz* 1852.

Brenton Howard 1942– . English dramatist, whose political theatre, deliberately provocative, includes *The Churchill Play* 1974 and *The Romans in Britain* 1980. *Bloody Poetry* 1984 is an examination of the poet Shelley, and he co-wrote *Pravda* 1985 with David Hare and *Moscow Gold* 1990 with activist/writer Tariq Ali.

Breton André 1896–1966. French writer and poet, among the leaders of the ◊Dada movement. *Les Champs magnétiques/Magnetic Fields* 1921, an experiment in automatic writing, was one of the products of the movement. He was also a founder of ◊Surrealism, publishing *Le Manifeste de surréalisme/Surrealist Manifesto* 1924. Other works include *Najda* 1928, the story of his love affair with a medium, and *Poèmes/Poems* 1948.

Breuer Marcel 1902–1981. Hungarian-born architect and designer who studied and taught at the ◊Bauhaus school in Germany during the 1920s. His tubular steel chair 1925 was the first of its kind. He moved to England, then to the USA, where he was in partnership with Walter Gropius 1937–40. His buildings show an affinity with natural materials.

Brian Havergal 1876–1972. English composer of 32 symphonies in visionary Romantic style, including the *Gothic* 1919–27 for large choral and orchestral forces.

Brickhill Paul 1916–1991. Australian writer whose *The Great Escape* 1951 was based on his own experience as a prisoner of war during World War II. It was filmed 1963. He also wrote *The Dambusters* 1951 and *Reach for the Sky* 1954.

brickwork method of construction using bricks made of fired clay or sun-dried earth (see ◊adobe). In wall building, bricks are either laid out as stretchers (long side facing out) or as headers (short side facing out). The two principle patterns of brickwork are **English bond** in which alternate courses, or layers, are made up of stretchers or headers only, and **Flemish bond** in which stretchers and headers alternate within courses.

Some evidence exists of the use of fired bricks in ancient Mesopotamia and Egypt, although the Romans were the first to make extensive use of this technology. In Britain, it was not until the 15th century that brickwork became common, largely through an influx of Flemish refugees. Today's mass production of fired bricks tends to be concentrated in temperate regions where there are plentiful supplies of fuel available.

Brideshead Revisited novel 1945 by Evelyn ◊Waugh. The plot revolves around the deep fascination Charles Ryder feels for the Roman Catholic Flyte family who own the great house, Brideshead. The conclusion contains a melancholy affirmation of spiritual values in spite of human unhappiness. It marked a development beyond Waugh's previous career as a satirist.

bridge in music, a support for the strings of an instrument that determines its length and transmits vibration to the body. In violins, lutes, guitars, and other instruments the bridge is fixed, but in the Indian tambura (long lute) and Japanese koto (zither), bridges are movable to change the tuning.

Bridge Frank 1879–1941. English composer, the teacher of Benjamin Britten. His works include the orchestral suite *The Sea* 1912, and *Oration* 1930 for cello and orchestra.

Bridges Robert (Seymour) 1844–1930. English poet, poet laureate from 1913, author of *The Testament of Beauty* 1929, a long philosophical poem. In 1918 he edited and published posthumously the poems of Gerard Manley ◊Hopkins.

Bridie James. Pen name of Osborne Henry Mavor 1888–1951. Scottish dramatist and professor of medicine, and a founder of the Glasgow Citizens' Theatre. His plays include the comedies *Tobias and the Angel* 1930 and *The Anatomist* 1931.

Brieux Eugène 1858–1932. French dramatist, an exponent of the naturalistic problem play attacking social evils. His most powerful plays are *Les Trois Filles de M Dupont* 1897; *Les Avariés/Damaged Goods* 1901, long banned for its outspoken treatment of syphilis; and *Maternité* 1903.

Brighouse Harold 1882–1958. English dramatist. Born and bred in Lancashire, in his most famous play, *Hobson's Choice* 1916, he dealt with a Salford bootmaker's courtship, using the local idiom.

Brighton Rock novel 1938 by Graham ◊Greene. Seventeen-year-old Pinkie, seeking distinction through crime, commits a squalid murder. He marries Rose, a fellow Roman Catholic, to prevent her giving evidence against him, but he is finally brought to justice through the efforts of Ida, an acquaintance of the murdered man. Although there are detective-story elements, the main interest of the novel lies in its early expression of Greene's lifelong struggle with moral and spiritual questions.

Brill Building centre of US commercial songwriting in the late 1950s and early 1960s. Housed at 1619 Broadway, New York, it was the headquarters of such songwriters as Jerry ◊Leiber and Mike Stoller with Phil ◊Spector.

Other Brill Building songwriters include Doc ◊Pomus and Mort Shuman; Neil Sedaka (1939–) and Howard Greenfield – *Stupid Cupid* 1958, *Oh! Carol* 1959; Ellie Greenwich (1940–) and Jeff Barry (1939–) – *Da Doo Ron Ron* 1963, *Chapel of Love* 1964; Neil Diamond (1941–) – *I'm a Believer* 1966; Gerry Goffin (1939–) and Carole King (1942–) – *Up on the Roof* 1962, *The Loco-Motion* 1962; Cynthia Weil (1942–) and Barry Mann (1939–) – *Uptown* 1962, *We Gotta Get Out of This Place* 1965; Burt Bacharach (1928–) and Hal David (1921–) – *Anyone Who Had a Heart* 1964, *24 Hours from Tulsa* 1964; and Bert Berns (1929–1967) – *Twist and Shout*.

British Academy of Film and Television Arts see ◊BAFTA, ◊cinema.

British Film Institute see ◊BFI.

Brittain Vera 1894–1970. English socialist writer, a nurse to the troops overseas 1915–19, as told in her *Testament of Youth* 1933; *Testament of Friendship* 1950 commemorated Winifred ◊Holtby. She married political scientist Sir George Catlin (1896–1979); their daughter is the Liberal politician Shirley Williams.

Britten (Edward) Benjamin 1913–1976. English composer. He often wrote for the individual voice; for example, the role in the opera *Peter*

Grimes 1945, based on verses by George Crabbe, was created for his life companion Peter ◊Pears. Among his many works are the *Young Person's Guide to the Orchestra* 1946; the chamber opera *The Rape of Lucretia* 1946; *Billy Budd* 1951; *A Midsummer Night's Dream* 1960; and *Death in Venice* 1973.

He studied at the Royal College of Music. From 1939 to 1942 he worked in the USA, then returned to England and devoted himself to composing at his home in Aldeburgh, Suffolk, where he and Pears established an annual music festival. His oratorio *War Requiem* 1962 was written for the rededication of Coventry Cathedral.

I do not easily think in words, because words are not my medium ... I believe so strongly that it is dangerous for artists to talk.

Benjamin Britten 1962

Broadway major avenue in New York running northwest from the tip of Manhattan and crossing Times Square at 42nd Street, at the heart of the theatre district, where Broadway is known as 'the Great White Way'. New York theatres situated outside this area are described as *off-Broadway*; those even smaller and farther away are *off-off-Broadway*, the home of avant-garde and experimental works.

brocade rich woven fabric, produced on a Jacquard loom. It is patterned, normally with more than two colours. Today brocade may be produced from artificial fibres, but it was traditionally made from silk, sometimes with highlights in metal thread.

Broch Hermann 1886–1951. Austrian novelist, who used experimental techniques in *Die Schlafwandler/The Sleepwalkers* 1932, *Der Tod des Vergil/The Death of Virgil* 1945, and *Die Schuldlosen/The Guiltless*, a novel in 11 stories. He moved to the USA 1938 after being persecuted by the Nazis.

broderie anglaise (French 'English embroidery') embroidered fabric, usually white cotton, in which holes are cut in patterns and oversewn, often to decorate lingerie, shirts, and skirts.

Brodsky Joseph 1940– . Russian poet who emigrated to the USA 1972. His work, often dealing with themes of exile, is admired for its wit and economy of language, particularly in its use of understatement. Many of his poems, written in Russian, have been translated into English (*A Part of Speech* 1980). More recently he has also written in English. He was awarded the Nobel Prize for Literature 1987 and became US poet laureate 1991.

broken consort in music, term for a mixed chamber ensemble of Renaissance and early Baroque instruments.

Bromfield Louis 1896–1956. US novelist. Among his books are *The Strange Case of Miss Annie Spragg* 1928, *The Rains Came* 1937, and *Mrs Parkington* 1943, dealing with the golden age of New York society.

Bronson Charles. Stage name of Charles Bunchinsky 1921– . US film actor. He began in a variety of supporting roles from 1952, graduating to larger roles in such films as *The Magnificent Seven* 1960. He worked in Europe in films such as *C'era una Volta il West/Once Upon a Time in the West* 1968 and returned to the USA taking starring roles, often as a hard-bitten loner, such as the vigilante in *Death Wish* 1974 and its sequels. He often appeared with his second wife, actress Jill Ireland, until her death in 1990.

Brontë three English novelists, daughters of a Yorkshire parson. *Charlotte* (1816–1855), notably with *Jane Eyre* 1847 and *Villette* 1853, reshaped autobiographical material into vivid narrative. *Emily* (1818–1848) in *Wuthering Heights* 1847 expressed the intensity and nature mysticism which also pervades her poetry (*Poems* 1846). The more modest talent of *Anne* (1820–1849) produced *Agnes Grey* 1847 and *The Tenant of Wildfell Hall* 1848.

The Brontës were brought up by an aunt at Haworth rectory (now a museum) in Yorkshire. In 1846 the sisters published a volume of poems under the pen names Currer (Charlotte), Ellis (Emily) and Acton (Anne) Bell. In 1847 (using the same names), they published the novels *Jane Eyre*, *Wuthering Heights*, and *Agnes Grey*. During 1848–49 Emily, Anne, and their brother Patrick Branwell all died of tuberculosis, aided in Branwell's case by alcohol and opium addiction; he is remembered for his portrait of the sisters. Charlotte married her father's curate, A B Nicholls, 1854, and died during pregnancy.

Bronzino Agnolo 1503–1572. Italian Mannerist painter active in Florence, court painter to Cosimo I, Duke of Tuscany. He is known for his cool, elegant portraits – *Lucrezia Panciatichi* about 1540 (Uffizi, Florence) is typical – and for the allegory *Venus, Cupid, Folly and Time* about 1545 (National Gallery, London).

Brook Peter 1925– . English director renowned for his innovative productions. His work with the Royal Shakespeare Company (joined 1962) included a production of Shakespeare's *A Midsummer Night's Dream* 1970, set in a white gymnasium and combining elements of circus and commedia dell'arte. In the same year he founded an independent initiative, Le Centre International de Créations Théâtrales/The International Centre for Theatre Research in Paris. Brook's later productions aim to combine elements from different cultures and include *The Conference of the Birds* 1973, based on a Persian story, and *The Mahabarata* 1985–88, a cycle of three plays based on the Hindu epic.

His films include *Lord of the Flies* 1962 and *Meetings with Remarkable Men* 1979.

Brooke Rupert (Chawner) 1887–1915. English poet, symbol of the World War I 'lost generation'. His five war sonnets, the best known of which is 'The Patriot', were published posthumously. Other notable works include 'Grantchester' and 'The Great Lover'.

Born in Rugby, where he was educated, Brooke travelled abroad after a nervous breakdown 1911, but in 1913 won a fellowship at King's College, Cambridge. Later that year he toured America (*Letters from America* 1916), New Zealand, and the South Seas, and in 1914 became an officer in the Royal Naval Division. After fighting at Antwerp, he sailed for the Dardanelles, but died of blood-poisoning on the Greek island of Skyros, where he is buried.

If I should die, think only this of me . . .
That there's some corner of a foreign field/
That is forever England.

Rupert Brooke 'The Soldier' 1915

Brookner Anita 1928– . British novelist whose novels include *Hôtel du Lac* 1984 (Booker Prize), *A Misalliance* 1986, *Latecomers* 1988, and *A Closed Eye* 1991. Her skill is in the subtle portrayal of hopelessness and lack of vitality in her female characters. She also lectures in art history.

Brooks Louise 1906–1985. US actress, known for her dark, enigmatic beauty and for her roles in silent films such as *A Girl in Every Port* 1928, *Die Büchse der Pandora/Pandora's Box*, and *Das Tagebuch einer Verlorenen/Diary of a Lost Girl* both 1929 and both directed by G W ◊Pabst. At 25 she had appeared in 17 films. She retired from the screen 1938.

Brooks Mel. Stage name of Melvin Kaminsky 1926– . US film director and comedian, known for madcap and slapstick verbal humour. He became well known with his record album *The 2,000-Year-Old Man* 1960. His films include *The Producers* 1968, *Blazing Saddles* 1974, *Young Frankenstein* 1975, *History of the World Part I* 1981, and *To Be or Not to Be* 1983.

Brooks Van Wyck 1886–1963. US literary critic and biographer. His five-volume *Makers and Finders: A History of the Writer in America, 1800–1915* 1936–52 was an influential series of critical works on US literature. The first volume *The Flowering of New England* 1936 won a Pulitzer Prize.

An earlier work, *America's Coming-of-Age* 1915, concerned the Puritan heritage and its effects on American literature. His other works include studies of Mark Twain, Henry James, and Ralph Waldo Emerson.

Brothers Karamazov, The novel by Fyodor ◊Dostoevsky, published 1879–80. It describes the reactions and emotions of four brothers after their father is murdered. One of them is falsely convicted of the crime, although his illegitimate brother is guilty.

Brouwer Adriaen 1605–1638. Flemish painter who may have studied with Frans ◊Hals. He worked in Haarlem and Antwerp, and popularized ◊genre paintings of peasant life. His work was admired by Rembrandt and Rubens.

Brown Capability (Lancelot) 1715–1783. English landscape gardener. He acquired his nickname because of his continual enthusiasm for the 'capabilities' of natural landscapes. He advised on gardens of stately homes, including Blenheim, Oxfordshire; Stowe, Buckinghamshire; and Petworth, W Sussex, sometimes also contributing to the architectural designs.

Brown Charles Brockden 1771–1810. US novelist and magazine editor. He introduced the American Indian into fiction and is called the 'father of the American novel'. Inspired by the writings of William Godwin and Mrs Radcliffe, his *Wieland* 1798, *Ormond* 1799, *Edgar Huntly* 1799, and *Arthur Mervyn* (two volumes 1799, 1800) imported the Gothic and fantastic traditions into US fiction.

Brown Earle 1926– . US composer who pioneered ◊graph notation and mobile form during the 1950s, as in *Available Forms II* 1958 for ensemble and two conductors. He was an associate of John ◊Cage.

Brown Ford Madox 1821–1893. English painter associated with the ◊Pre-Raphaelite Brotherhood. His pictures, which include *The Last of England* 1855 (City Art Gallery, Birmingham) and *Work* 1852–65 (City Art Gallery, Manchester), are characterized by their abundance of realistic detail and their use of symbolism.

Brown James 1928– . US rhythm-and-blues and soul singer, a pioneer of funk. Staccato horn arrangements and shouted vocals characterize his hits, which include 'Please, Please, Please' 1956, 'Papa's Got a Brand New Bag' 1965, and 'Say It Loud, I'm Black and I'm Proud' 1968. In that year his TV appearance appealing for calm succeeded in restraining race riots in US cities.

Brown Trisha 1936– . US dancer and choreographer. One of the leading Post-Modernist choreographers, she founded the improvisational Grand Union 1970–76. During the 1960s and early 1970s, Brown devised a series of 'equipment pieces' that utilized harnesses to enable the dancers to perform movements, cantilevered out from the wall. Her later style was more fluid and supple, in contrast to her earlier, deliberately angular movements. Her works include *Roof Piece* 1973, *Accumulation* 1971, and *Glacial Decoy* 1979. Other works include *Son of Gone Fishin'* 1981, *Set and Reset* 1983, and *Lateral Pass* 1985.

Browne Hablot Knight 1815–1882. Real name of English illustrator ◊Phiz.

Browne Thomas 1605–1682. English author and physician. Born in London, he travelled widely in Europe before settling in Norwich 1637. His works display a richness of style as in *Religio Medici/The Religion of a Doctor* 1643, a justification of his profession; *Vulgar Errors* 1646, an examination of popular legend and superstition; *Urn Burial* and *The Garden of Cyrus* 1658; and *Christian Morals*, published posthumously 1717.

We all labour against our own cure; for death is the cure of all diseases.

Thomas Browne *Religio Medici* 1643

Browning Robert 1812–1889. English poet, married to Elizabeth ◊Barrett Browning. His work is characterized by the use of ◊dramatic monologue and an interest in obscure literary and historical figures. It includes the play *Pippa Passes* 1841 and the poems 'The Pied Piper of Hamelin' 1842, 'My Last Duchess' 1842, 'Home Thoughts from Abroad' 1845, and 'Rabbi Ben Ezra' 1864.

Browning, born in Camberwell, London, wrote his first poem 'Pauline' 1833 under the influence of Shelley; it was followed by 'Paracelsus' 1835 and 'Sordello' 1840. The pamphlet series *Bells and Pomegranates* 1841–46 contained *Pippa Passes*, *Dramatic Lyrics* 1842 and *Dramatic Romances* 1845. In 1846 he met Elizabeth Barrett; they married the same year and went to Italy. There he wrote *Men and Women* 1855, which contains some of his finest love poems and dramatic monologues, followed by *Dramatis Personae* 1864 and *The Ring and the Book* 1868–69, based on an Italian murder story. After his wife's death 1861 Browning settled in England and enjoyed an established reputation, although his later works, such as *Red-Cotton Night-Cap Country* 1873, *Dramatic Idylls* 1879–80, and *Asolando* 1889, prompted opposition by their rugged obscurity of style.

Grow old with me!/ The best is yet to be.

Robert Browning 'Rabbi ben Ezra' 1864

Brubeck Dave (David Warren) 1920– . US jazz pianist and composer, leader of the Dave Brubeck Quartet (formed 1951). A student of composers Darius Milhaud and Arnold Schoenberg, Brubeck combines improvisation with classical discipline. Included in his large body of compositions is the internationally popular 'Take Five'.

Bruce Christopher 1945– . English choreographer, dancer, and artistic director of the Rambert Dance Company from 1992. Bruce often mixes modern and classical idioms with overtly political and social themes, as in *Ghost Dances* 1981, which is concerned with political oppression. His other pieces include *Cruel Garden* 1977 and *The Dream is Over* 1987, a tribute to John Lennon.

As a dancer, Bruce's famous roles have been *Pierrot lunaire* 1967 (for the Ballet Rambert), the Faun in *L'Après-midi d'un faune*, and *Petrushka* 1988 (for the London Festival Ballet).

Bruch Max 1838–1920. German composer, professor at the Berlin Academy 1891. He wrote three operas, including *Hermione* 1872. Among the most celebrated of his works are the *Kol Nidrei* for cello and orchestra, violin concertos, and many choral pieces.

Brücke, die (German 'the bridge') German Expressionist art movement 1905–13, formed in Dresden by Ernst Ludwig Kirchner, Schmidt-Rottluff, and others; Emil Nolde was a member 1906–07. Influenced by African art, van Gogh, and Fauvism, they strove for an art which expressed spiritual values, using raw colours and strong, angular lines derived from their highly original work in woodcut. In 1911 the ◊*Blaue Reiter* overtook them as the leading group in German art.

Bruckner (Joseph) Anton 1824–1896. Austrian Romantic composer. He was cathedral organist at Linz 1856–68, and professor at the Vienna Conservatoire from 1968. His works include many choral pieces and 11 symphonies, the last unfinished. His compositions were influenced by Wagner and Beethoven.

Brueghel or *Bruegel* family of Flemish painters. *Pieter Brueghel the Elder* (*c.* 1525–1569) was one of the greatest artists of his time. His pictures of peasant life helped to establish ◊genre painting and he also popularized works illustrating proverbs, such as *The Blind leading the Blind* 1568 (Museo di Capodimonte, Naples). A contemporary taste for the macabre can be seen in *The Triumph of Death* 1562 (Prado, Madrid), which clearly shows the influence of Hieronymus Bosch. One of his best-known works is *Hunters in the Snow* 1565 (Kunsthistorisches Museum, Vienna).

The elder Pieter was nicknamed 'Peasant' Brueghel. Two of his sons were painters. *Pieter Brueghel the Younger* (1564–1638), called 'Hell' Brueghel, specialized in religious subjects, and another son, *Jan Brueghel* (1568–1625), called 'Velvet' Brueghel, painted flowers, landscapes, and seascapes.

Brunelleschi Filippo 1377–1446. Italian Renaissance architect. The first and one of the greatest of the Renaissance architects, he pioneered the scientific use of perspective. He was responsible for the construction of the dome of Florence Cathedral (completed 1436), a feat deemed impossible by many of his contemporaries. His use of simple geometries and a modified Classical language lend his buildings a feeling of tranquillity, to which many other early Renaissance architects aspired. His other works include the Ospedale degli Innocenti 1419 and the Pazzi Chapel 1429, both in Florence.

Brutalism architectural style of the 1950s and 1960s that evolved from the work of Le Corbusier and Mies van der Rohe. Uncompromising in its approach, it stresses functionalism and honesty to materials; steel and concrete are favoured. The term was coined by Alison and Peter ◊Smithson who developed the style in the UK.

The Smithsons' design for Hunstanton School, Norfolk 1949–54, recalls the work of Mies van der Rohe but is more brutally honest, exposing all of the services to view. The Park Hill Housing Estate, Sheffield 1961, by Jack Lynn and Ivor Smith, makes use of the rough concrete (*béton brut*) characteristic of Le Corbusier's later work.

Bryant William Cullen 1794–1878. US poet and literary figure. His most famous poem, 'Thanatopsis', was published 1817. He was co-owner and co-editor of the *New York Evening Post* 1829–78 and was involved in Democratic party politics. However, his resolute opposition to slavery converted him to Republicanism at the inception of the party 1856.

Brynner Yul 1915–1985. Actor, in the USA from 1940, who had a distinctive stage presence and made a shaven head his trademark. He played the king in *The King and I* both on stage 1951 and on film 1956 (Academy Award), and was the leader of *The Magnificent Seven* 1960.

Although his origins were deliberately shrouded in mystery, he is believed to have been born in Sakhalin, an island east of Siberia and north of Japan. He later acknowledged a gypsy background. He made his film debut in a B picture *Port of New York* 1949. His other films include *Taras Bulba* 1962, and *Westworld* 1973.

Bryusov Valery 1873–1924. Russian Symbolist poet, novelist and critic, author of *The Fiery Angel* 1908.

Buchan John, Baron Tweedsmuir 1875–1940. Scottish politician and author. His adventure stories, today criticized for their anti-semitism, include *The Thirty-Nine Steps* 1915, *Greenmantle* 1916, and *The Three Hostages* 1924.

Buchanan Jack 1891–1957. British musical-comedy actor. His songs such as *Good-Night*

Vienna epitomized the period between World Wars I and II.

Büchner Georg 1813–1837. German dramatist. His characters were often individuals pitted against the forces of society. Büchner's plays include *Danton's Death* 1835, which chronicles the power struggle between Danton and Robespierre during the French Revolution; and *Woyzeck* 1836, unfinished at his death, which depicts the despair of a common soldier, crushed by his social superiors. (It was the basis of Alban Berg's opera *Wozzeck* 1925.) Büchner's third play is the comedy *Leonce and Lena* 1836. His plays remained unperformed until well after his death, but have been repeatedly produced in the 20th century.

Buck Pearl S(ydenstricker) 1892–1973. US novelist. Daughter of missionaries to China, she spent much of her life there and wrote novels about Chinese life, such as *East Wind – West Wind* 1930 and *The Good Earth* 1931, for which she received a Pulitzer Prize 1932. She received the Nobel Prize for Literature 1938.

Buckingham Palace London home of the British sovereign, built 1703 for the Duke of Buckingham, but bought by George III 1762 and reconstructed by John ◊Nash 1821–36; a new front was added 1913.

Buckler Ernest (Redmond) 1908– . Canadian novelist. From a Novia Scotia farming background, he has published verse and distinguished short stories including *The Rebellion of Young David and Other Stories* 1975. He is best known for his first novel *The Mountain and the Valley* 1952 which traces the secret growth of artistic vision in a country boy.

Buckley William F(rank) 1925– . US conservative political writer, novelist, and founder-editor of the *National Review* 1955. In such books as *Up from Liberalism* 1959, and in a weekly television debate *Firing Line*, he represented the 'intellectual' right-wing, anti-liberal stance in US political thought.

Budé or *Budaeus* Guillaume 1467–1540. French Renaissance scholar. He persuaded Francis I to found the Collège de France, and also the library that formed the nucleus of the French national library, the Bibliothèque Nationale.

Buffet Bernard 1928– . French figurative painter who created distinctive, thin, spiky forms with bold, dark outlines. He was a precocious talent in the late 1940s.

bugle compact valveless brass instrument with a shorter tube and less flared bell than the trumpet. Constructed of copper plated with brass, it has long been used as a military instrument for giving a range of signals based on the tones of a harmonic series. The bugle is conical whereas the trumpet is cylindrical.

buhl alternative spelling for ◊boulle, a type of marquetry.

Bujones Fernando 1955– . US ballet dancer who joined the American Ballet Theater 1972. A virtuoso performer, he has danced leading roles both in the major classics and in contemporary ballets, including *Swan Lake, La Bayadère*, and *Fancy Free*.

Bukowski Charles 1920– . US writer and poet. He is a prolific author of poems, stories, and novels in which he creates the persona of himself as an ugly lover and angry drunk. His works include *Flower, Fist and Bestial Wail* 1960, *Notes of a Dirty Old Man* 1969, *Post Office* 1971, and *Ham on Rye* 1982. The works were typically printed by small presses or underground magazines.

Bulatović Miodrag 1930–1991. Serbian writer. Self-educated and first noted as a lyric poet drawing on his country's oral tradition, he later disclosed a gift for original, courageous, and grimly satirical narrative. He has published short stories and popular novels of which *The Red Cockerel* 1959 and *Hero on a Donkey* 1964 are the best known.

Bulfinch Charles 1763–1844. US architect. He became one of New England's leading architects after his design for the Massachusetts State House was accepted 1787. His designs include the Hollis Street Church, Harvard's University Hall, the Massachusetts General Hospital, and the Connecticut State House. In 1817 he was appointed architect of the US Capitol by President Monroe.

Bulgakov Mikhail Afanasyevich 1891–1940. Russian novelist and playwright. His novel *The White Guard* 1924, dramatized as *The Days of the Turbins* 1926, deals with the Revolution and the civil war. His satirical approach made him unpopular with the Stalin regime, and he was unpublished from the 1930s. His most important work, *The Master and Margarita*, a fantasy about the devil in Moscow, was not published until 1967.

Bull John *c.* 1562–1628. British composer, organist, and virginalist. Most of his output is for keyboard, and includes ◊'God Save the King'. He also wrote sacred vocal music.

Bull Olaf 1883–1933. Norwegian lyric poet, son of humorist and fiction writer Jacob Breda Bull (1853–1930). He often celebrated his birthplace Christiania (now Oslo) in his poetry.

bullroarer musical instrument used by Australian Aborigines for communication and during religious rites. It consists of a weighted aerofoil (a piece of wood or stone) whirled on a long cord to make a deep whirring noise. It features in a ballet suite *Corroborree* 1946 by the Australian composer John Antill. It is also used in many other parts of the world, including Britain.

Bülow Hans (Guido) Freiherr von 1830–1894. German conductor and pianist. He studied with Richard Wagner and Franz Liszt, and in 1857 married Cosima, daughter of Liszt. From 1864 he served Ludwig II of Bavaria, conducting first performances of Wagner's *Tristan und Isolde* and *Die Meistersinger*. His wife left him and married Wagner 1870.

Bulwer-Lytton Edward George Earle Lytton, 1st Baron Lytton 1803–1873. See ◊Lytton.

Bunin Ivan Alexeyevich 1870–1953. Russian writer. He was the author of *Derevnya/The Village* 1910, a novel which tells of the passing of peasant life; and the short story collection *Gospodin iz San Frantsisko/The Gentleman from San Francisco* 1916, for which he received a Nobel prize 1933. He was also a poet and translated Byron into Russian.

Bunny Rupert Charles Wulsten 1864–1947. Australian-born painter who worked mainly in France. He is known for his Provençal landscapes and for figure compositions such as *The Garden Bench* 1915 (Art Gallery of New South Wales, Sydney).

Bunshaft Gordon 1909–1990. US architect. While working for the architectural practice ◊Skidmore, Owings & Merrill, he produced the first Modernist building to be completely enclosed in curtain walling (walls which hang from a rigid steel frame), the Lever Building 1952 in New York. He also designed the Heinz Company's UK headquarters 1965 at Hayes Park, London.

Buntline Ned. Adopted name of US author Edward Z C ◊Judson.

Buñuel Luis 1900–1983. Spanish Surrealist film director (see ◊Surrealism). He collaborated with Salvador Dali on *Un Chien andalou* 1928 and *L'Age d'or/The Golden Age* 1930, and established his solo career with *Los olvidados/The Young and the Damned* 1950. His works are often anticlerical, with black humour and erotic imagery.

Later films include *Le Charme discret de la bourgeoisie/The Discreet Charm of the Bourgeoisie* 1972 and *Cet Obscur Objet du désir/That Obscure Object of Desire* 1977.

Bunyan John 1628–1688. English author. A Baptist, he was imprisoned in Bedford 1660–72 for unlicensed preaching and wrote *Grace Abounding* 1666, which describes his early spiritual life. During a second jail sentence 1675 he started to write *The ◊Pilgrim's Progress*, the first part of which was published 1678. The fervour and imagination of this allegorical story of Christian's spiritual quest has ensured its continued popularity. Other works include *The Life and Death of Mr Badman* 1680 and *The Holy War* 1682.

Burbage Richard *c.* 1567–1619. English actor, thought to have been Shakespeare's original Hamlet, Othello, and Lear. He also appeared in first productions of works by Ben Jonson, Thomas Kyd, and John Webster. His father *James Burbage* (*c.* 1530–1597) built the first English playhouse, known as 'the Theatre'; his brother *Cuthbert Burbage* (*c.* 1566–1636) built the original ◊Globe Theatre 1599 in London.

Burckhardt Jacob Christoph 1818–1897. Swiss art historian, professor of history at Basel University 1858–93, one of the founders of cultural history as a discipline. His *The Civilization of the Renaissance in Italy* 1860, intended as part of a study of world cultural history, profoundly influenced thought on the Renaissance.

Burges William 1827–1881. English Gothic Revival architect and designer. His style is characterized by sumptuous interiors with carving, painting, and gilding. His chief works are Cork Cathedral 1862–76, and additions to and the remodelling of Cardiff Castle 1868–85 and Castle Coch near Cardiff 1875–91.

Burgess Anthony. Pen name of Anthony John Burgess Wilson 1917–1993. British novelist, critic, and composer. His prolific work includes *A Clockwork Orange* 1962, set in a future London terrorized by teenage gangs, and the panoramic *Earthly Powers* 1980. His vision has been described as bleak and pessimistic, but his work is also comic and satirical, as in his novels featuring the poet Enderby.

A work of fiction should be, for its author, a journey into the unknown, and the prose should convey the difficulties of the journey.

Anthony Burgess *Homage to Qwert Yuiop*

Burgoyne John 1722–1792. British general and dramatist. He served in the American War of Independence and surrendered 1777 to the colonists at Saratoga, New York State, in one of the pivotal battles of the war. He wrote comedies, among them *The Maid of the Oaks* 1775 and *The Heiress* 1786. He figures in George Bernard Shaw's play *The Devil's Disciple* 1896.

Burle Marx Roberto 1909– . Brazilian landscape architect whose work exploits the vivid colours of tropical plants to create spacious painterly landscapes of rhythmic abstract form. Exemplary are Garden-Yacht Club, Pampulha 1943, and Del-Este Park, Caracas 1956. The setting for the new capital of Brasilia, designed by

Lucio Costa (1902–), owes much to his designs.

burlesque in the 17th and 18th centuries, a form of satirical comedy parodying a particular play or dramatic genre. For example, John ◊Gay's *The Beggar's Opera* 1728 is a burlesque of 18th-century opera, and Richard Brinsley ◊Sheridan's *The Critic* 1777 satirizes the sentimentality in contemporary drama. In the USA from the mid-19th century, burlesque referred to a sex-and-comedy show invented by Michael Bennett Leavitt 1866 with acts including acrobats, singers, and comedians. During the 1920s striptease was introduced in order to counteract the growing popularity of the movies; Gypsy Rose Lee was the most famous stripper. Burlesque was frequently banned in the USA.

Burlington Richard Boyle, 3rd Earl of Burlington 1694–1753. Anglo-Irish architectural patron and architect; one of the premier exponents of the Palladian style in Britain. His buildings are characterized by absolute adherence to the Classical rules, for example Chiswick House, London 1725–29, which is based on Palladio's Villa Rotonda, Italy. His major protégé was William ◊Kent.

Burne-Jones Edward Coley 1833–1898. English painter. In 1856 he was apprenticed to the Pre-Raphaelite painter and poet Dante Gabriel ◊Rossetti, who remained a dominant influence. His paintings, inspired by legend and myth, were characterized by elongated forms and subdued tones, as in *King Cophetua and the Beggar Maid* 1880–84 (Tate Gallery, London). He also designed tapestries and stained glass in association with William ◊Morris. His work influenced both Symbolism and Art Nouveau. The best collection of his work is in the Birmingham City Art Gallery.

Burnett Frances (Eliza) Hodgson 1849–1924. English writer who emigrated with her family to the USA 1865. Her novels for children include the sentimental rags-to-riches tale ◊*Little Lord Fauntleroy* 1886 and the less cloying *The ◊Secret Garden* 1911, which has its values anchored in nature mysticism.

Burney Frances (Fanny) 1752–1840. English novelist and diarist, daughter of musician Dr Charles Burney (1726–1814). She achieved success with *Evelina*, a novel published anonymously 1778, became a member of Dr ◊Johnson's circle, received a post at court from Queen Charlotte, and in 1793 married the French émigré General d'Arblay (died 1818). She published three further novels, *Cecilia* 1782, *Camilla* 1796, and *The Wanderer* 1814; her diaries and letters appeared 1842.

Burns John Horne 1916–1953. US novelist. He is known for his acclaimed novel *The Gallery* 1946, a passionate, episodic story set in Naples and North Africa and based on his service in the US army during World War II. He wrote two other novels while an expatriate in Italy, where he died.

Burns Robert 1759–1796. Scottish poet who used the Scots dialect at a time when it was not considered suitably 'elevated' for literature. Burns' first volume, *Poems, Chiefly in the Scottish Dialect*, appeared 1786. In addition to his poetry, Burns wrote or adapted many songs, including 'Auld Lang Syne'.

Burns' fame rests equally on his poems (such as 'Holy Willie's Prayer', 'Tam o' Shanter', 'The Jolly Beggars', and 'To a Mouse') and his songs – sometimes wholly original, sometimes adaptations – of which he contributed some 300 to Johnson's *Scots Musical Museum* 1787–1803 and Thomson's *Scottish Airs with Poetry* 1793–1811. Burns Night is celebrated on 25 January.

Wee, sleekit, cow'rin', tim'rous beastie,/ O what a panic's in thy breastie.

Robert Burns 'To a Mouse' 1786

Burr Raymond 1917–1993. Canadian actor who graduated from playing assorted Hollywood villains to the heroes Perry Mason and Ironside in the long-running television series of the same names. He played the murderer in Alfred Hitchcock's *Rear Window* 1954.

Burra Edward 1905–1976. English painter devoted to themes of city life, its bustle, humour, and grimy squalor. *The Snack Bar* 1930 (Tate Gallery, London) and his watercolour scenes of Harlem, New York, 1933–34, are characteristic. Postwar works include religious paintings and landscapes.

Burroughs Edgar Rice 1875–1950. US novelist. He wrote *Tarzan of the Apes* 1914, the story of an aristocratic child lost in the jungle and reared by apes, and followed it with over 20 more books about the Tarzan character. He also wrote a series of novels about life on Mars.

Burroughs William S(eward) 1914– . US writer. His work is noted for its experimental methods, black humour, explicit homo-eroticism, and apocalyptic vision. In 1944 he met Allen Ginsberg and Jack Kerouac, all three becoming leading members of the ◊Beat Generation. His first novel, *Junkie* 1953, documented his heroin addiction and expatriation to Mexico, where in 1951, he accidentally killed his common-law wife. He settled in Tangier 1954 and wrote his celebrated anti-novel ◊*Naked Lunch* 1959. In Paris, he developed collage-based techniques of writing, resulting in his 'cut-up' science-fiction trilogy, *The Soft Machine* 1961, *The Ticket That Exploded* 1962, and *Nova Express* 1964.

Burton Richard Francis 1821–1890. British explorer, writer, and translator (he knew 35 oriental languages). He travelled mainly in the Middle East and NE Africa, often disguised as a Muslim, and made two attempts to find the source of the Nile, 1855 and 1857–58. He wrote many travel books and his translations include the *Kama Sutra of Vatsyayana* 1883, oriental erotica and the *Arabian Nights* 1885–88, and *The Perfumed Garden* 1886. His wife, who had accompanied him on some journeys, burned his unpublished manuscripts and diaries after his death.

Burton Richard. Stage name of Richard Jenkins 1925–1984. Welsh actor of stage and screen. He had a rich, dramatic voice but his career was dogged by an often poor choice of roles. Films in which he appeared with his wife, Elizabeth ◊Taylor, include *Cleopatra* 1962 and *Who's Afraid of Virginia Woolf?* 1966. Among his later films are *Equus* 1977 and *Nineteen Eighty-Four* 1984.

His other films include *The Spy Who Came in from the Cold* 1966, and *Beckett* 1964. His rendition of Dylan Thomas' *Under Milk Wood* for radio was another of his career highspots.

Burton Robert 1577–1640. English philosopher who wrote an analysis of depression, *Anatomy of Melancholy* 1621, a compendium of information on the medical and religious opinions of the time, much used by later authors.

Bush Alan (Dudley) 1900– . English composer. A student of John ◊Ireland, he later adopted a didactic simplicity in his compositions in line with his Marxist beliefs. He has written a large number of works for orchestra, voice, and chamber groups. His operas include *Wat Tyler* 1952 and *Men of Blackmoor* 1956.

Music was born free, and to win freedom is its destiny.

Ferruccio Busoni

Busoni Ferruccio (Dante Benvenuto) 1866–1924. Italian pianist, composer, and music critic. Much of his music was for the piano, but he also composed several operas including *Doktor Faust*, completed by Philipp Jarnach after his death. An apostle of Futurism, he encouraged the French composer Edgard ◊Varèse.

bustle form of padding, made of materials such as cork, or taking the shape of a metal or whalebone frame, worn under women's skirts in the 1860s–70s. It was attached to the back, below waist level, to act as a base over which the outer fabric would hang. The effect was a much fuller, expanded skirt at the rear.

Butcher Rosemary 1947– . English choreographer and dancer, a leading exponent of

◊avant-garde dance. Her minimalist pieces display a quiet assurance and fluidity and are often performed in unorthodox settings, such as on beaches and in art galleries. They include *Flying Lines* 1985 and *Touch the Earth* 1986.

Butler Reg 1913–1981. English sculptor who taught architecture 1937–39 and was then a blacksmith for many years before becoming known for cast and forged iron works, both abstract and figurative. In 1953 he won an international competition for a monument to *The Unknown Political Prisoner* (a model is in the Tate Gallery, London).

Butler Samuel 1612–1680. English satirist. His poem *Hudibras*, published in three parts 1663, 1664, and 1678, became immediately popular for its biting satire against the Puritans.

Authority intoxicates/ And makes mere sots of magistrates;/ The fumes of it invade the brain,/ And make men giddy, proud, and vain.

Samuel Butler *Miscellaneous Thoughts* 1680

Butler Samuel 1835–1902. English author who made his name 1872 with a satirical attack on contemporary utopianism, *Erewhon* (an anagram of 'nowhere'), but is now remembered for his autobiographical *The ◊Way of All Flesh* written 1872–85 and published 1903.

The Fair Haven 1873 examined the miraculous element in Christianity. *Life and Habit* 1877 and other works were devoted to a criticism of the theory of natural selection. In *The Authoress of the Odyssey* 1897 he maintained that Homer's *Odyssey* was the work of a woman.

It has been said that although God cannot alter the past, historians can.

Samuel Butler *Erewhon* 1872

---

butoh dance Japanese form of ◊avant-garde dance. Developed by Tatsumi Hijikata in the 1960s, it draws on both Japanese traditions and the European avant-garde. It is characterized by a stillness that is contrasted with frantic movements. It emphasizes emotional intensity, represented in a highly stylized manner, rather than physical dexterity. The dancers' faces and bodies are often painted white.

Butor Michel 1926– . French writer, one of the ◊nouveau roman novelists who made radical changes in the traditional form. His works

include *Passage de Milan/Passage from Milan* 1954, *Dégrés/Degrees* 1960, and *L'Emploi du temps/Passing Time* 1963. *Mobile* 1962 is a volume of essays.

Butterfield William 1814–1900. English Gothic Revival architect. His work is characterized by vigorous, aggressive forms and multicoloured striped and patterned brickwork, as in the church of All Saints, Margaret Street, London 1849–59, and Keble College and Chapel, Oxford 1867–83.

His schools, parsonages, and cottages develop an appealing functional secular style that anticipates Philip ◊Webb and other ◊Arts and Crafts architects. At Baldersby, Yorkshire, UK, he designed a whole village of church, rectory, almshouse, school, and cottages 1855–57.

button (French *bouton* 'bud', 'knob') fastener for clothing, originating with Bronze Age fasteners. In medieval Europe buttons were replaced by pins but were reintroduced in the 13th century as a decorative trim and in the 16th century as a functional fastener.

In the 15th and 16th centuries, gold- and silver-plated handmade buttons were popular with the nobility. By the early 19th century, machine-made fabric buttons and ones made of glass and ceramics existed, but they were not strongly featured on garments. By the middle of the 19th century, shell, mother-of-pearl, moulded horn, stamped steel, and brass buttons were popular. In the 1880s there was a revival of the use of enamel buttons developed in the 18th century. The 1920s Art Deco movement increased the popularity of buttons and in the 1930s they were produced in wood, cork, Perspex, and various plastics. By the 1940s a well-dressed man wore approximately 70 buttons, only a few of them functional. After World War II buttons became more functional and less decorative.

buttress in brickwork or masonry, a reinforcement built against a wall to give it strength. A *flying buttress* is an arc transmitting the force of the wall to be supported to an outer buttress, a feature common in Gothic architecture.

Buxtehude Diderik 1637–1707. Danish composer. In 1668 he was appointed organist at the Marienkirche in Lübeck, Germany, where his fame attracted J S Bach and Handel. He is remembered for his organ works and cantatas, written for his evening concerts or *Abendmusiken*; he also wrote numerous trio sonatas for two violins, viola da gamba, and harpsichord.

Byatt A(ntonia) S(usan) 1936– . English novelist and critic. Her fifth novel, *Possession*, won the 1990 Booker Prize. *The Virgin in the Garden* 1978 is a confident, zestfully handled account of a varied group of characters putting on a school play during Coronation year, 1953. It has a sequel, *Still Life* 1980. She also writes literary criticism.

She was born in Sheffield and educated at a Quaker boarding school (with her sister, novelist Margaret Drabble) and at Newnham College, Cambridge.

Bykau Vasil (Russian *Vasily Bykov*) 1924–   . Belorussian writer. In novels such as *The Ordeal* 1970 and *The Mark of Doom* 1982 Bykau seeks to crystallize a specifically Belorussian sense of identity by exploring the severe wartime ordeals of small groups of ordinary people under German occupation.

Byrd William 1543–1623. English composer. His sacred and secular choral music, including over 200 motets and masses for three, four, and five voices, exemplifies the English polyphonic style.

Probably born in Lincoln, he became organist at the cathedral there 1563. He shared with Thomas ◊Tallis the honorary post of organist in Queen Elizabeth's Chapel Royal, and in 1575 he and Tallis were granted a monopoly in the printing and selling of music.

Byrds, the US pioneering folk-rock group 1964–73. Emulated for their 12-string guitar sound, as on the hits 'Mr Tambourine Man' (a 1965 version of Bob Dylan's song) and 'Eight Miles High' 1966, they moved towards country rock in the late 1960s. Their albums include *Fifth Dimension* 1966 and *Sweetheart of the Rodeo* 1968.

The Byrds formed in Los Angeles at the time of the Beatles' greatest influence, and comprised Roger McGuinn (1942–   ), David Crosby (1941–   ), Gene Clark (1941–1991), Chris Hillman (1942–   ), and Michael Clarke (1944–   ), most of whom had a folk-music background. They dissolved 1973 after many changes of line-up that left only the guitarist McGuinn of the original members.

Byron George Gordon, 6th Baron Byron 1788–1824. English poet who became the symbol of Romanticism and political liberalism throughout Europe in the 19th century. His reputation was established with the first two cantos of *Childe Harold* 1812. Later works include *The Prisoner of Chillon* 1816, *Beppo* 1818, *Mazeppa* 1819, and, most notably, the satirical *Don Juan* 1819–24. He left England 1816, spending most of his later life in Italy.

Born in London and educated at Harrow and Cambridge, Byron published his first volume *Hours of Idleness* 1807 and attacked its harsh critics in *English Bards and Scotch Reviewers* 1809. Overnight fame came with the first two cantos of *Childe Harold*, romantically describing his tours in Portugal, Spain, and the Balkans (third canto 1816, fourth 1818). In 1815 he married mathematician Anne Milbanke (1792–1860), with whom he had a daughter, Augusta Ada Byron, separating from her a year later amid much scandal. He then went to Europe, where he became friendly with Percy and Mary ◊Shelley. He engaged in Italian revolutionary politics and sailed for Greece 1823 to further the Greek struggle for independence, but died of fever at Missolonghi. He is remembered for his lyrics, his colloquially easy *Letters*, and as the 'patron saint' of Romantic liberalism.

Byzantine literature literature of the Byzantine Empire, 4th to 15th century. It was written mainly in the Greek *koinē*, a form of Greek accepted as the literary language of the 1st century AD and increasingly archaic and separate from the spoken tongue of the people. Byzantine literature is chiefly concerned with theology, history, and commentaries on the Greek classics. Its chief authors are the theologians St Basil, Gregory of Nyssa, Gregory of Nazianzus, Chrysostom (all 4th century AD) and John of Damascus (8th century); the historians Zosimus (about 500), Procopius (6th century), ◊Psellus (1018–1079), Bryennius and his wife Anna Comnena (about 1100), and Georgius Acropolita (1220–1282). The literary encyclopedia *Suda*, which provides a wealth of information on classical and Byzantine literature, was compiled about 975. Drama was nonexistent, and poetry, save for the hymns of the 6th–8th centuries, scanty and stilted, but there were many popular works about the lives of the saints. The tradition ended with the fall of Constantinople 1453.

Byzantine style style in the visual arts and architecture that originated in the 4th–5th centuries in Byzantium (the capital of the Eastern Roman Empire), and spread to Italy, throughout the Balkans, and to Russia, where it survived for many centuries. It is characterized by heavy stylization, strong linear emphasis, the use of rigid artistic stereotypes, and rich colours such as gold. Byzantine artists excelled in mosaic work, manuscript painting, and religious ◊icon painting. In architecture, the dome supported on pendentives was in widespread use.

Classical examples of Byzantine architecture are the churches of Hagia Sophia Istanbul, 532–37, and St Mark's, Venice, 11th century. Medieval painting styles were influenced by Byzantine art; a more naturalistic style emerged from the 13th century onwards in the West. See also ◊medieval art.

C

cabaletta in music, a short aria with repeats which the singer could freely embellish as a display of virtuosity. In the 19th century the term came to be used for the final section of an elaborate aria.

cabaret theatrical revue traditionally combining satire and song in cafés or bars. Originating in Paris in the late 19th century in venues such as the Moulin Rouge, cabaret was embraced by avant-garde writers and artists. In Germany, Berlin became a centre for an increasingly political cabaret in the 1920s, which was later suppressed by the Nazis. In Britain, satirical revue was revived by the Cambridge Footlights theatre group in *Beyond the Fringe* 1961, before cabaret and alternative comedy combined to provide a new generation of stand-up entertainers during the 1980s, notably from the Comedy Store group in London.

caccia, da (Italian 'hunting') suffix used to describe music or instruments associated with the hunt, for example the oboe da caccia, precursor of the ◊cor anglais, and corno da caccia, or hunting horn.

cacophony clashing, unpleasant sounds; the opposite of euphony.

Cacoyannis Michael 1922– . Greek film director and writer who directed *Zorba the Greek* 1965; other films include *Stella* 1955, *Electra* 1961, and *The Trojan Women* 1971.

cadence in music, the closing progression of a chord sequence, usually of two chords linked by a note in common. A cadence defines the relative completion of a musical sentence in relation to a starting tonality, hence a *perfect cadence* (V–I) corresponding to a full close, a *plagal cadence* (IV–I) corresponding to a weak close, and an *imperfect cadence* (I–V) corresponding to a half close.

cadenza in music, an unaccompanied exhibition passage in the style of an improvisation, inserted by the soloist at the climax of a concerto movement.

The practice of improvising a cadenza largely ceased around 1780, composers thereafter supplying their own in written form. Recently, however, the practice of the interpreter composing a cadenza has re-emerged, with Stockhausen writing new cadenzas for Haydn and Mozart and Nigel Kennedy recording Beethoven's *Violin Concerto* 1805 with a cadenza of his own devising.

Cadmus in Greek mythology, a Phoenician from Tyre, brother of ◊Europa. He founded the city of Thebes in Greece. Obeying the oracle of ◊Athena, Cadmus killed the sacred dragon that guarded the spring of Ares. He sowed the teeth of the dragon, from which sprang a multitude of fierce warriors who fought among themselves; the survivors were considered to be the ancestors of the Theban aristocracy. Cadmus married ◊Harmonia and was credited with the introduction of the (Phoenician) alphabet into Greece.

Caedmon 7th century. Earliest known English poet. According to the Northumbrian historian Bede, when Caedmon was a cowherd at the Christian monastery of Whitby, he was commanded to sing by a stranger in a dream, and on waking produced a hymn on the Creation. The poem is preserved in some manuscripts. Caedmon became a monk and may have composed other religious poems.

Light was first/ Through the Lord's word/ Named day:/ Beauteous, bright creation.

Caedmon *Creation*. The First Day

Cage John 1912–1992. US composer. His interest in Indian classical music led him to the view that the purpose of music was to change the way people listen. From 1948 he experimented with instruments, graphics, and methods of random selection in an effort to generate a music of pure incident. His ideas and collected writings, including *Silence* 1961 and *For the Birds* 1981, have profoundly influenced late 20th-century aesthetics.

Cage studied briefly with Arnold ◊Schoenberg, also with Henry ◊Cowell, and joined others in reacting against the European music tradition in favour of a freer idiom open to non-Western attitudes. Working in films during the 1930s, he assembled and toured a percussion orchestra incorporating ethnic instruments and noisemakers. He invented the prepared piano to tour as accompanist with the dancer Merce Cunningham, a lifelong collaborator. In a later work, *4 Minutes and 33 Seconds* 1952, the pianist sits at the piano reading a score for that length of time but does not play.

Cagney James 1899–1986. US actor whose physical dynamism and staccato vocal delivery made him one of the first stars of talking pictures. Often associated with gangster roles (for example, *The Public Enemy* 1931), he was an actor of great versatility, playing Bottom in *A Midsummer Night's Dream* 1935 and singing and dancing in *Yankee Doodle Dandy* 1942.

Cain James M(allahan) 1892–1977. US novelist who wrote a series of popular novels in the taut, economical idiom of 'hard-boiled' fiction, derived in the main from Ernest Hemingway. His major novels – *The Postman Always Rings Twice* 1934, *Mildred Pierce* 1941, and ◊*Double Indemnity* 1943 – were made into key works of ◊*film noir* during the 1940s.

Caine Michael. Stage name of Maurice Micklewhite 1933– . English actor, an accomplished performer with an enduring Cockney streak. His films include *Alfie* 1966, *Sleuth* 1972, *The Man Who Would Be King* 1975, *Educating Rita* 1983, and *Hannah and Her Sisters* 1986, and many others.

'ça lra' song of the French Revolution, written by a street singer, Ladré, and set to an existing tune by Bécourt, a drummer of the Paris Opéra.

Cajun music music of the French-speaking community of Louisiana, USA, descended from French-Canadians who settled the area in the 18th century. It has a lively rhythm and features steel guitar, fiddle, and accordion.

Calatrava Santiago 1951– . Spanish architect and engineer, noted for his highly expressive and elegant structural solutions. Of these, the Mérida Bridge, Spain (begun 1988), spans the river Guadiana with a 195 m/640 ft arch; the dramatic TGV railway station, Lyon (begun 1989), has a wing roof resembling a bird taking flight; and the East London River Crossing Bridge 1990, 630 m/2,067 ft in length, has a central arch spanning 450 m/1,477 ft contained within its internal structure. More recently, he designed two spectacular suspension bridges in Seville 1992.

Calchas in Greek mythology, a visionary and interpreter of omens for the Greek expedition against ◊Troy, responsible for recommending the sacrifice of ◊Iphigenia by her father ◊Agamemnon, as an atonement for an offence against the goddess ◊Artemis.

Caldecott Randolph 1846–1886. English artist and illustrator of books for children, including *John Gilpin* 1848. He became an illustrator for *Punch* during the 1870s.

Calder Alexander 1898–1976. US abstract sculptor, the inventor of *mobiles*, suspended shapes that move in the lightest current of air. In the 1920s he began making wire sculptures and *stabiles* (static mobiles), coloured abstract shapes attached by lines of wire. Huge versions adorn the Lincoln Center in New York City and UNESCO in Paris.

Calderón de la Barca Pedro 1600–1681. Spanish dramatist and poet. After the death of

Lope de Vega 1635, he was considered to be the leading Spanish dramatist. Most celebrated of his 118 plays is the philosophical *La vida es sueño/Life is a Dream* 1635. His other works include the tragedies *El pintor de su deshonra/The Painter of His Own Dishonour* 1645, *El alcalde de Zalamea/The Mayor of Zalamea* 1640, and *El médico de su honra/The Surgeon of His Honour* 1635; the historical *El príncipe constante/The Constant Prince* 1629; and the dashing intrigue *La dama duende/The Phantom Lady* 1629.

Calderón was born in Madrid. He studied law at Salamanca and served in the army in Milan and the Netherlands (1625–35). By 1636 his first volume of plays was published and he had been made master of the revels at the court of Philip IV. After the death of his mistress he became a Franciscan 1650 and was ordained 1651. As honorary chaplain to the king 1663, he produced outdoor religious plays for the festival of the Holy Eucharist. He died in poverty.

Even in dreams good works are not wasted.

Pedro Calderón de la Barca
La Vida es sueño 1635

Caldwell Erskine (Preston) 1903–1987. US novelist. He achieved great popular success with *Tobacco Road* 1932 and *God's Little Acre* 1933, vivid but somewhat melodramatic depictions of poverty-stricken Southern sharecroppers in the Depression. His literary autobiography, *Call It Experience*, was published 1951.

Callaghan Morley 1903–1990. Canadian novelist and short-story writer whose realistic novels include *Such is My Beloved* 1934, *More Joy in Heaven* 1937, and *Close to the Sun Again* 1977. Deeply influenced both by the Depression and the teaching of the Catholic philosopher Jacques Maritain, he characteristically writes about social misfits and outcasts and the possibilities of personal salvation through the power of love.

His other works include *They Shall Inherit the Earth* 1935, *The Loved and the Lost* 1951, *Stories* 1959, and *A Passion in Rome* 1961.

Callas Maria. Adopted name of Maria Kalogeropoulos 1923–1977. US lyric soprano, born in New York of Greek parents. With a voice of fine range and a gift for dramatic expression, she excelled in operas including *Norma*, *La Sonnambula*, *Madame Butterfly*, *Aïda*, *Tosca*, and *Medea*.

She debuted in Verona, Italy, 1947 and at New York's Metropolitan Opera 1956. Although her technique was not considered perfect, she helped to popularize classical coloratura roles through her expressiveness and charisma.

Callicrates 5th century BC. Athenian architect (with Ictinus) of the ◊Parthenon on the Acropolis.

calligraphy art of handwriting, regarded in China and Japan as the greatest of the visual arts, and playing a key role in Islamic art because the depiction of the human and animal form is forbidden.

The present letter forms have gradually evolved from originals shaped by the tools used to make them—the flat brush on paper, the chisel on stone, the stylus on wax and clay, and the reed and quill on papyrus and skin.

In Europe during the 4th and 5th centuries books were written in square capitals ('majuscules') derived from classical Roman inscriptions (Trajan's Column in Rome is the outstanding example). The *rustic* capitals of the same period were written more freely, the pen being held at a severe angle so that the scribe was less frequently inclined to change the angle for special flourishes. *Uncial* capitals, more rounded, were used from the 4th to the 8th centuries. During this period the *cursive* hand was also developing, and the interplay of this with the formal hands, coupled with the need for speedier writing, led to the small letter forms ('minuscules'). During the 7th century the *half-uncial* was developed with ascending and descending strokes and was adopted by all countries under Roman rule. The cursive forms developed differently in different countries. In Italy the italic script was evolved and became the model for italic typefaces.

Printing and the typewriter reduced the need for calligraphy in the West. In the UK there was a 20th-century revival inspired by Edward Johnston (1872–1944) and Irene Wellington (1904–1984).

Callimachus 310–240 BC. Greek poet and critic known for his epigrams. Born in Cyrene, he taught in Alexandria, Egypt, where he is reputed to have been head of the great library.

Tread where the traffic does not go.

Callimachus

Calliope in Greek mythology, the ◊Muse of epic poetry, and so the most important of all the Muses.

Callisto in Greek mythology, a ◊nymph beloved by Zeus who was changed into a bear by his jealous wife Hera.

Callot Jacques 1592/93–1635. French engraver and painter, influenced by Mannerism. His series of etchings *Great Miseries of War* 1633, prompted by his own experience of the Thirty Years' War, are arrestingly composed and full of horrific detail. One of the greatest etchers, his enormous output includes over 1,400 prints and 1,500 drawings. His love of the grotesque was later to influence Goya.

calotype paper-based photograph using a wax paper negative, the first example of the ◊negative/positive process invented by the English photographer ◊Fox Talbot around 1834.

calypso West Indian satirical ballad with a syncopated beat. Calypso is a traditional song form of Trinidad, a feature of its annual carnival, with roots in W African praise singing. It was first popularized in the USA by Harry Belafonte (1927–) in 1956. Mighty Sparrow (1935–) is Trinidad's best-known calypso singer.

Calypso in Greek mythology, a sea ◊nymph who waylaid the homeward-bound ◊Odysseus for seven years.

Camargo Marie-Anne de Cupis 1710–1770. French ballerina, born in Brussels. She became a ballet star in Paris 1726 and was the first ballerina to attain the 'batterie' (movements involving beating the legs together) previously danced only by men. She shortened her skirt to expose the ankles and her brilliant footwork, gaining more liberty of movement.

Camden Town Group school of British painters 1911–13, based in Camden, London, led by W R ◊Sickert. The work of Spencer Gore (1878–1914) and Harold Gilman (1876–1919) is typical of the group, rendering everyday town scenes in Post-Impressionist style. In 1913 they merged with several smaller groups to form the ◊London Group.

cameo small relief carving of semiprecious stone, shell, or glass, in which a pale-coloured surface layer is carved to reveal a darker ground. Fine cameos were produced in ancient Greece and Rome, during the Renaissance, and in the Victorian era. They were used for decorating goblets and vases, and as jewellery.

camera apparatus used in ◊photography, consisting of a lens system set in a light-proof box inside of which a sensitized film or plate can be placed. The lens collects rays of light reflected from the subject and brings them together as a sharp image on the film; it has marked numbers known as ◊apertures, or f-stops, that reduce or increase the amount of light. Apertures also control depth of field. A shutter controls the amount of time light has to affect the film. There are small-, medium-, and large-format cameras; the format refers to the size of recorded image and the dimensions of the print obtained.

A simple camera has a fixed shutter speed and aperture, chosen so that on a sunny day the correct amount of light is admitted. More complex cameras allow the shutter speed and aperture to be adjusted; most have a built-in exposure meter to help choose the correct combination of shutter speed and aperture for the ambient conditions and subject matter. The most versatile camera is the single lens reflex (◊SLR) which allows the lens to be removed and special lenses attached. A pin-hole camera has a small (pin-sized) hole instead of a lens. It must be left on a firm support during exposures, which are up to ten seconds with slow film, two seconds with fast film and five minutes for paper negatives in daylight. The pin-hole camera gives sharp images from close-up to infinity.

camera obscura darkened box with a tiny hole for projecting the inverted image of the scene outside on to a screen inside. For its development as a device for producing photographs, see ◊photography.

Cameron Charles 1746–1812. Scottish architect. He trained under Isaac Ware (1717–1766) in the Palladian tradition before being summoned to Russia by Catherine The Great 1779. He created the palace complex at Tsarskoe Selo (now Pushkin), planned the town of Sofia, and from 1803, as chief architect of the Admiralty, executed many buildings, including the Naval Hospital and barracks at Kronstadt 1805.

Cameron Julia Margaret 1815–1879. British photographer who made lively and dramatic portraits of the Victorian intelligentsia, often posed as historical or literary figures. Her sitters included her friends Sir John Herschel and the poet Alfred Lord Tennyson, whose *Idylls of the King* she illustrated 1872, and Charles Darwin. She used a large camera, five-minute exposures, and wet plates.

Camilla Volscian woman and warrior, enemy of ◊Aeneas and ally of ◊Turnus in Virgil's *Aeneid*.

camisole woman's undergarment introduced in the 19th century, based on a loose sleeveless bodice. Made of satin, silk, linen, or cotton, it covers the body from the bust to the waist and has thin shoulder straps. It was originally worn as a protective layer between a dress and a corset but became a fashion garment during the 20th century.

Camoëns or *Camões* Luís Vaz de 1524–1580. Portuguese poet and soldier. He went on various military expeditions, and was shipwrecked 1558. His poem *Os Lusiades/The Lusiads* 1572 tells the story of the explorer Vasco da Gama and incorporates much Portuguese history; it has become the country's national epic. His posthumously published lyric poetry is also now valued.

Having wounded an equerry of the king 1552, he was banished to India. He received a small pension, but died in poverty of plague.

camp behaving in an exaggerated and even self-parodying way, particularly in female impersonation and among homosexuals. The British entertainers Kenneth Williams (1926–1987) and Julian Cleary and the Australian Barry ◊Humphries have used camp behaviour to comic effect.

campanile originally a bell tower erected near, or attached to, a church or town hall in Italy. The leaning tower of Pisa is an example; another is the great campanile of Florence, 90 m/275 ft high.

Campbell Colen 1676–1729. Scottish architect, one of the principal figures in British Palladian architecture. His widely influential book *Vitruvius Britannicus* was published 1712. Among his best-known works are Burlington House, London, 1718–19, and Merewith Castle, Kent, 1722–25.

Campbell Mrs Patrick (born Beatrice Stella Tanner) 1865–1940. English actress whose roles included Paula in Pinero's *The Second Mrs Tanqueray* 1893 and Eliza in *Pygmalion*, written for her by G B Shaw, with whom she had an amusing correspondence.

Campbell Roy 1901–1957. South African poet, author of *The Flaming Terrapin* 1924. His poetry displays technical virtuosity, narrative verve, and brilliant metaphor, sometimes applied to satiric ends as in his attack on English literary coteries *The Georgiad* 1931. Among his most successful work are translations from Baudelaire, Lorca, and St John of the Cross.

Born in Durban, he became a professional jouster and bullfighter in Spain and Provence, France. He fought for Franco in the Spanish Civil War and was with the Commonwealth forces in World War II. He recorded his flamboyant life in *Light in a Dark House* 1951.

Campbell Thomas 1777–1844. Scottish poet. After the successful publication of his *Pleasures of Hope* 1799, he travelled in Europe, and there wrote his war poems 'Hohenlinden' and 'Ye Mariners of England'.

Campin Robert, also known as the *Master of Flémalle* c. 1378–1444. Netherlandish painter of the early Renaissance, active in Tournai from 1406, one of the first northern masters to use oil. Several altarpieces are attributed to him.

His outstanding work is the *Mérode Altarpiece* about 1425 (Metropolitan Museum of Art, New York), which shows a characteristic blend of naturalism and elaborate symbolism, together with a new subtlety in modelling and a grasp of pictorial space.

Soul is the Man.

Thomas Campion
'Are You What Your Fair Looks Express?'

Campion Jane 1954– . New Zealand film director. Her first feature film *Sweetie* 1989 was followed by *An Angel at My Table* 1990, based on the autobiographies of Janet Frame. *The Piano* 1993 (her own script) was joint winner of the Palme d'Or at the Cannes Film Festival 1993.

Her work demonstrates versatility and exciting originality.

Campion Thomas 1567–1620. English poet and musician. He was the author of the critical *Art of English Poesie* 1602 and four *Bookes of Ayres*, for which he composed both words and music.

Camus Albert 1913–1960. Algerian-born French writer. A journalist in France, he was active in the Resistance during World War II. His novels, which owe much to ◊existentialism, include *L'Etranger/The Outsider* 1942, *La Peste/The Plague* 1948, and *L'Homme révolté/The Rebel* 1952. He was awarded the Nobel Prize for Literature 1957.

What is a rebel? A man who says no.
Albert Camus *The Rebel* 1952

Canadian art painting and sculpture of Canada after colonization. Until the 19th century French and English influences dominated. Early painters of Canadian life include Cornelius Krieghoff (1815–1872), who recorded Indian and pioneer life, and Paul Kane (1810–1871), painter of the Plains Indians. In the late 19th century, a Canadian style emerged with the landscapes of Tom Thomson (1877–1917) and the 'Group of Seven', formed 1913, which developed an expressive landscape style. Maurice Cullen (1866–1934), an Impressionist, and James Wilson Morrice (1865–1924), a Fauve, introduced new European trends. Before World War II Emily Carr (1871–1945) was one of the most original talents, developing eloquent studies of nature. Canadian artists subsequently joined the international arena. The Automatistes, led by the Surrealist Paul-Emile Borduas (1905–1960), rebelled against the Canadian establishment. Jean-Paul Riopelle (1923–) made a significant contribution to Abstract Expressionism.

Canadian literature Canadian literature in English began early in the 19th century in the Maritime Provinces with the humorous tales of T C Haliburton (1796–1865). Charles Heavysege (1816–1876) published poems combining psychological insight with Puritan values. The late 19th century brought the lyrical output of Charles G D ◊Roberts, Bliss Carman (1861–1929), Archibald Lampman (1861–1899), and Duncan Campbell Scott (1862–1944). Realism in fiction developed with Frederick P ◊Grove, Mazo ◊de la Roche, creator of the 'Jalna' series, and Hugh ◊MacLennan. Humour of worldwide appeal emerged in Stephen ◊Leacock; Brian Moore (1921–), author of *The Luck of Ginger Coffey* 1960; and Mordecai ◊Richler. Also widely read outside Canada was L M Montgomery (1874–1942), whose *Anne of Green Gables* 1908 became a children's classic. US novelist Saul Bellow and the communication theo-

rist Marshall McLuhan were both Canadian-born, as were contemporary novelists Robertson ◊Davies and Margaret ◊Atwood. Recent poetry and fiction, stimulated by journals such as *The Canadian Forum* (founded 1920) and *Canadian Fiction Magazine* (founded 1971) and by a growing number of literary prizes, have become increasingly international in outlook while also drawing attention to contemporary Canadian issues such as racial and linguistic minorities and the environment. See also ◊French Canadian literature.

Canaletto Antonio (Giovanni Antonio Canale) 1697–1768. Italian painter celebrated for his paintings of views (*vedute*) of Venice (his native city) and of London and the river Thames 1746–56.

Much of his work is very detailed and precise, with a warm light and a sparkling of tiny highlights on the green waters of canals and rivers. *The Upper Reaches of the Grand Canal* about 1738 (National Gallery, London) is typical.

Canary Wharf large-scale office development on the Isle of Dogs in London's Docklands, the first phase of which was completed 1992. The complex of offices, surrounding landscaped squares, is best known for its central skyscraper, the tallest in Europe at 244 m/800 ft. Designed by US architect Cesar Pelli (1926–), it sports a pyramid-shaped crown in stainless steel. The site has more recently gained notoriety as a symbol of the recession, much of its office space remaining unlet.

cancan high-kicking stage dance for women (solo or line of dancers) originating in Paris about 1830. The music usually associated with the cancan is the *galop* from Offenbach's *Orpheus in the Underworld*.

Candela Félix 1910– . Spanish-born architect-engineer whose most outstanding work was carried out in Mexico, where he emigrated 1939; since 1970 he has lived in the USA. He has pioneered, and excelled in the design of thin, concrete shell roofs, creating beautiful forms based on the geometry of the hyperbolic paraboloid. His Cosmic Ray Building, University City, Mexico, 1952 has a hyperbolic paraboloid roof 15 mm/$\frac{5}{8}$ in thick to allow cosmic rays to penetrate. In his Church of the Immaculate Virgin, Mexico City, 1953, parabolic vaults create a Gothic feeling of space.

Candide satire by ◊Voltaire, published 1759. The hero experiences extremes of fortune in the company of Dr Pangloss, a personification of the popular belief of the time (partly based on a misunderstanding of the German philosopher Gottfried Leibniz) that 'all is for the best in the best of all possible worlds'. Voltaire exuberantly demonstrates that this idea is absurd and inhumane.

Canetti Elias 1905– . Bulgarian-born writer. He was exiled from Austria as a Jew 1938 and settled in England 1939. His books, written in German, include *Die Blendung/Auto da Fé* 1935. He was awarded the Nobel Prize for Literature 1981.

He was concerned with crowd behaviour and the psychology of power, and wrote the anthropological study *Masse und Machte/Crowds and Power* 1960. His three volumes of memoirs are *Die gerettete Zunge: Geschichte einer Jugend/The Tongue Set Free: Remembrance of a European Childhood* 1977, *Die Fackel im Ohr: Lebensgeschichte 1921–31/The Torch in My Ear* 1980, and *Das Augenspiel/The Play of the Eyes* 1985.

History portrays everything as if it could not have come otherwise. History is on the side of what happened.

Elias Canetti *The Human Province*

Cannes Film Festival international film festival held every year in Cannes, France; see ◊cinema.

Cano Alonso 1601–1667. Spanish sculptor, painter, and architect, an exponent of the Baroque style in Spain. He was active in Seville, Madrid, and Granada and designed the façade of Granada Cathedral 1667. He also created monumental carved screens, such as the reredos (altar screen) in Lebrija, near Seville, and graceful free-standing polychrome carved figures.

From 1637 he was employed by Philip IV to restore the royal collection at the Prado Museum in Madrid. Many of his religious paintings show the influence of the Venetian masters.

canon in music, an echo form for two or more parts employed in classical music, for example by two solo violins in an orchestral movement by Vivaldi or J S Bach, as a means of generating pace and advertising professional skill. Canonic variations may also introduce a difference in starting pitch between the voices, creating ambiguities of tonality; the highest expression is the ◊fugue.

Canova Antonio 1757–1822. Italian. Neo-Classical sculptor, based in Rome from 1781. He received commissions from popes, kings, and emperors for his highly finished marble portrait busts and groups of figures. He made several portraits of Napoleon.

Canova was born near Treviso. His reclining marble *Pauline Borghese as Venus* 1805–07 (Borghese Gallery, Rome) is a fine example of his cool, polished Classicism. He executed the tombs of popes Clement XIII, Pius VII, and Clement XIV. His marble sculptures include *Cupid and Psyche* 1793 (Louvre, Paris) and *The Three Graces* (held in the Victoria and Albert Museum, London, from 1990 while efforts were made to raise the £7.6 million needed to keep it in the UK).

cantata in music, an extended work for voices, from the Italian, meaning 'sung', as opposed to ◊sonata ('sounded') for instruments. A cantata can be sacred or secular, sometimes uses solo voices, and usually has orchestral accompaniment. The first printed collection of sacred cantata texts dates from 1670.

Canterbury Tales, The unfinished collection of stories in prose and verse (*c.* 1387) by Geoffrey ◊Chaucer, told in Middle English by a group of pilgrims on their way to Thomas à Becket's tomb at Canterbury. The tales and preludes are remarkable for their vivid character portrayal and colloquial language.

Each pilgrim has to tell two stories on the way to Canterbury, and two on the way back, but only 24 tales were written.

Cantos, The series of 117 poems written 1925–69 by US poet Ezra ◊Pound. An epic work, its complex collage structure contains a vast body of information drawn from diverse cultures using several languages. It attempted a massive, unifying reappraisal of history, but ended incomplete in fragmentation. It is a key work of modern poetry.

And I am not a demigod, I cannot make it cohere.

Ezra Pound *Canto 116* 1925–69

---

cantus firmus (Latin 'fixed song') in music, any familiar melody employed in counterpart as a reference for the invention of an accompanying melody. In early music, multiple parts were composed one at a time, each referring to the cantus firmus, but not to any other, with sometimes strange harmonic results, for example the final cadence E minor–G major–F major.

canvas plain cloth woven from relatively thick cotton or linen yarn. It is used for baggage, tents, beach shoes, and other utilitarian purposes. In traditional tailoring canvas is used as an interlining for collars and facings. Artist's canvas is stretched taut over a frame (stretcher) and primed before paint is applied to it.

canzona (Italian 'ballad') 16th-century instrumental form modelled on vocal ◊polyphony, adopted by Frescobaldi, J S Bach, Andrea Gabrieli, and Giovanni Gabrieli.

Cao Chan or *Ts'ao Chan* 1719–1763. Chinese novelist. His tragicomic love story *Hung Lou Meng/The Dream of the Red Chamber*, published 1792, involves the downfall of a Manchu family and is semi-autobiographical.

cap brimless soft hat with a stiff peak over the forehead. It is also known as a 'flat cap'. Since the 1960s caps have become popular as fashion accessories, often made out of brightly coloured fabrics, leather, or PVC, sometimes bearing slogans. Baseball caps are a version of the cap, originating in the USA.

Capa Robert. Adopted name of André Friedmann 1913–1954. US photographer, born in Hungary, who specialized in war photography. He covered the Spanish Civil War as a freelance and World War II for *Life* and *Collier's* magazines. His pictures emphasize the human tragedy of war. He was a founder member of the Magnum photographic agency. He died while on an assignment in Vietnam.

cape a shorter version of the ◊cloak, a cape is an outer garment worn over the shoulders and arms, but without slits for the arms. Capes were popular in the late 19th century and again in the 1950s to the mid-1970s.

Čapek Karel 1890–1938. Czech writer whose works often deal with social injustice in an imaginative, satirical way. *R.U.R.* 1921 is a play in which robots (a term he coined) rebel against their controllers; the novel *Válka s Mloky/War with the Newts* 1936 is a science-fiction classic.

Man will never be enslaved by machinery if the man tending the machine be paid enough.

Karel Čapek *News Chronicle* 1938

capital in architecture, a stone placed on the top of a column, pier, or pilaster, and usually wider on the upper surface than the diameter of the supporting shaft. A capital consists of three parts: the top member, called the **abacus**, a block that acts as the supporting surface to the superstructure; the middle portion, known as the bell or **echinus**; and the lower part, called the necking or **astragal**.

Capodimonte porcelain produced in S Italy, usually white, painted with colourful folk figures, landscapes, or flowers. It was first produced under King Charles III of Naples about 1740, and is named after a village north of Naples.

Capote Truman. Pen name of Truman Streckfus Persons 1924–1984. US novelist, journalist, and playwright. After achieving early success as a writer of sparkling prose in the stories of *Other Voices, Other Rooms* 1948 and the novel *Breakfast at Tiffany's* 1958, Capote's career flagged until the sensational 'nonfiction novel', ◊*In Cold Blood* 1965, made him a celebrity.

Later works included *Music for Chameleons* 1980 and the posthumously published *Answered Prayers* 1986, an unfinished novel of scandalous socialite gossip.

Capra Frank 1897–1991. Italian-born US film director. His satirical comedies, which often have the common man pitted against corrupt corporations, were hugely successful in the Depression years of the 1930s. He won Academy Awards for the fairy-tale comedy romance *It Happened One Night* 1934, *Mr Deeds Goes to Town* 1936, and *You Can't Take It With You* 1938. Among his other classic films are *Mr Smith Goes to Washington* 1939, and *It's a Wonderful Life* 1946.

Capra began as a gagman for silent comedies, then directed several films with Harry Langdon (1884–1944). His later films included *A Hole in the Head* 1959 and *A Pocketful of Miracles* 1961.

capriccio in music, an all-purpose name for a lightweight piece, often in the style of a ◊fugue, combining technical virtuosity with entertainment.

Caravaggio Michelangelo Merisi da 1573–1610. Italian early Baroque painter, active in Rome 1592–1606, then in Naples, and finally in Malta. He created a forceful style, using contrasts of light and shade, dramatic foreshortening, and a meticulous attention to detail. His life was as dramatic as his art (he had to leave Rome after killing a man in a brawl).

Born in Caravaggio, near Milan, his early works were ◊genre paintings, incorporating vivid still-life details and sensual portraits of young men. He later turned to religious works, using contemporary settings and non-idealized portraits of men and women from the lower walks of Roman life as saints and Madonnas, as in *Death of the Virgin* 1605–06 (Louvre, Paris). He had a number of direct imitators (Caravaggisti), and several Dutch and Flemish artists who visited Rome, including Honthorst and Terbrugghen, were inspired by him.

carbuncle red precious stone, especially a garnet, cut with a smooth, rounded surface.

Cardiff Jack 1914–   . English director of photography. He is considered one of cinema's finest colour-camera operators for his work on such films as *A Matter of Life and Death* 1946, *The Red Shoes* 1948, and *The African Queen* 1951. He won an Academy Award for *Black Narcissus* 1947. He later directed several films including *Sons and Lovers* 1960.

cardigan knitted overgarment that buttons up in the front. The cardigan was popularized by Coco ◊Chanel in the 1920s and 1930s as part of two- or three- piece outfits.

Originally a long-sleeved military jacket of knitted worsted, trimmed with fur or braid and buttoned down the front, it was named after James Thomas Brudenell, 7th Earl of Cardigan (1797–1868), who led the Charge of the Light Brigade. In the 20th century the style was adapted for casual wear.

Cardin Pierre 1922– . French pioneering fashion designer whose clothes are bold and fantastic. He was the first to launch menswear (1960) and designer ready-to-wear collections (1963) and has given his name to a perfume.

Cardin moved to Paris 1944 and worked in the fashion houses of Madame Paquin, Elsa ◊Schiaparelli, and Christian ◊Dior. He began making theatrical costumes 1949, and launched his first couture collection 1957. He was particularly influential in the 1960s, creating his 'Space Age Collection' of catsuits, tight leather trousers, jumpsuits with bat wings, and close-fitting helmet-style caps 1964, followed 1966 by shift dresses with ring collars from which the fabric was suspended.

Carducci Giosuè 1835–1907. Italian poet. Born in Tuscany, he was appointed professor of Italian literature at Bologna 1860, and won distinction through his lecturing, critical work, and poetry. His revolutionary *Inno a Satana/Hymn to Satan* 1865 was followed by several other volumes of verse, in which his nationalist sympathies are apparent. Nobel prize 1906.

Far better in one's work to forget than to seek to solve the vast riddles of the universe.

Giosuè Carducci *Idillio Maremmano*

Carew Thomas c. 1595– c. 1640. English poet. Often associated with the ◊Cavalier poets, he was a courtier and gentleman of the privy chamber to Charles I, for whom he wrote the spectacular masque *Coelum Britannicum* 1634. *Poems* 1640 reveal his ability to weave metaphysical wit, eroticism, and a jewelled lyricism in his work.

His first important work was an elegy written on the death of the metaphysical poet, John ◊Donne, which was published 1633 in the first edition of Donne's poetry.

Carey Henry 1690–1743. English poet and musician, remembered for the song 'Sally in Our Alley'. 'God Save the King' (both words and music) has also been attributed to him.

Carey Peter 1943– . Australian novelist. His works include *Bliss* 1981, *Illywhacker* (Australian slang for 'con man') 1985, and *Oscar and Lucinda* 1988, which won the Booker Prize. *The Tax Inspector* 1991 is set in modern-day Sydney, and depicts an eccentric Greek family under investigation for tax fraud.

caricature in the arts or literature, an exaggerated portrayal of an individual or type, aiming to ridicule or otherwise expose the subject. Classical and medieval examples of pictorial caricatures survive. Artists of the 18th, 19th, and 20th centuries have often used caricature as a way of satirizing society and politics. Notable exponents include the French artist Honoré Daumier and the German Georg Grosz. In literature, caricatures have appeared since the comedies of Aristophanes in ancient Greece. Shakespeare and Dickens were adept at creating caricatures.

Grotesque drawings have been discovered in Pompeii and Herculaneum, and Pliny refers to a grotesque portrait of the poet Hipponax. Humorous drawings were executed by the ◊Carracci family and their Bolognese followers (the Italian 'eclectic' school of the 16th century). In 1830, Charles Philipon (1800–1862) founded in Paris *La Caricature*, probably the first periodical to specialize in caricature.

British caricaturists include James Gillray, William Hogarth, Thomas Rowlandson, George Cruikshank, Edward Lear, Richard Doyle, George Du Maurier, Max Beerbohm, David Low, 'Vicky' (Victor Weisz, 1913–1966), 'Giles' (Carl Ronald Giles), Ronald Searle, Osbert Lancaster, Mel Calman (1931–), Gerald Scarfe (1936–), Ralph Steadman (1936–), and Peter Fluck and Roger Law (who created the three-dimensional puppets for their satirical television series *Spitting Image*).

carillon a lever-action keyboard struck with the side of the hands and connected by wires to the beaters of up to 70 static bells, on which music in two parts is played. The bells are usually hung in a tower. Carillons are found throughout Europe and the USA; mechanized carillons were the forerunners of musical clocks and boxes.

Carissimi Giacomo 1605–1674. Italian composer of sacred and secular cantatas and motets. As maestro di capella at Sant' Apollinaire, Rome, 1630–74, he pioneered the use of expressive solo aria as a commentary on the Latin biblical text. He wrote five oratorios, including *Jephtha* 1650.

Carlyle Thomas 1795–1881. Scottish essayist and social historian. His works include *Sartor Resartus* 1833–34, describing his loss of Christian belief, *The French Revolution* 1837, the pamphlet *Chartism* 1839, attacking the doctrine of *laissez-faire*, *Past and Present* 1843, the notable *Letters and Speeches of Cromwell* 1845, and the miniature life of his friend, John Sterling 1851. His prose style was idiosyncratic, encompassing grand, thunderous rhetoric and deliberate obscurity.

The history of the world is but the biography of great men.

Thomas Carlyle *On Heroes, Hero-Worship and the Heroic in History* 1841

Carlyle began his *History of Frederick the Great* 1858–65, and after the death of his wife, Jane Baillie Welsh, 1866 edited her letters 1883 and prepared his *Reminiscences* 1881, which shed an unfavourable light on his character and his neglect of her, for which he could not forgive himself. His house in Cheyne Row, Chelsea, London, where they lived from 1834, is a museum. He was also a friend of John Stuart ◊Mill and Ralph Waldo ◊Emerson.

Carmichael Hoagy (Hoagland Howard) 1899–1981. US composer, pianist, singer, and actor. His songs include 'Stardust' 1927, 'Rockin' Chair' 1930, 'Lazy River' 1931, and 'In the Cool, Cool, Cool of the Evening' 1951 (Academy Award).

Carmina Burana medieval Latin verse miscellany compiled from the work of wandering 13th-century scholars and including secular (love songs and drinking songs) as well as religious verse. Carl Orff composed a cantata 1937 based on the material.

Carné Marcel 1909– . French director known for the romantic fatalism of such films as *Drôle de Drame/A Strange Drama* 1936, *Hôtel du Nord/ Northern Hotel* 1938, *Le Quai des brumes/Port of Shadows* 1938, and *Le Jour se lève/Daybreak* 1939. His masterpiece, *Les Enfants du paradis/The Children of Paradise* 1943–45, was made with his longtime collaborator, the poet and screenwriter Jacques Prévert (1900–1977).

Carnegie Dale 1888–1955. US author and teacher who wrote the best-selling self-help book *How to Win Friends and Influence People* 1937. His courses in public speaking, which drew huge audiences, first won him fame, and he was asked to publish them as a book. His other books include *Little Known Facts About Well Known People* 1934 and *How to Stop Worrying and Start Living* 1948.

Carnegie Medal (full name *Library Association Carnegie Medal*) annual award for an outstanding book for children written in English and published in the UK. The medal was first awarded 1937 to Arthur Ransome's *Pigeon Post* (in the ◊*Swallows and Amazons* series). It is named after US industrialist and philanthropist Andrew Carnegie (1835–1919).

Caro Anthony 1924– . English sculptor who has made brightly coloured abstract sculpture from prefabricated metal parts, such as I-beams, angles, and mesh. An example is *Early One Morning* 1962 (Tate Gallery, London).

carol song that in medieval times was associated with a round dance; today carols are associated with festivals such as Easter and Christmas.

Christmas carols were common as early as the 15th century. The custom of singing carols from house to house, collecting gifts, was called wassailing. Many carols, such as 'God Rest You Merry Gentlemen' and 'The First Noel', date from the 16th century or earlier.

Carolingian art the art of the reign of Charlemagne, the first Holy Roman Emperor (800–814), and his descendants until about 900.

In line with his revival of learning and Roman culture, Charlemagne greatly encouraged the arts, which had been in eclipse. Illuminated manuscripts, metalwork, and small-scale sculpture survive from this period. See ◊medieval art.

Carpaccio Vittore 1450/60–1525/26. Italian painter famous for scenes of his native Venice, for example, the series *The Legend of St Ursula* 1490–98 (Accademia, Venice). His paintings are a graceful blend of fantasy and closely observed details from everyday life.

Carpeaux Jean-Baptiste 1827–1875. French sculptor whose lively naturalistic subjects include *La Danse* 1865–69 for the Opéra, Paris (now in the Louvre, Paris) and the *Neapolitan Fisherboy* 1858 (Louvre, Paris).

The Romantic charm of his work belies his admiration for Michelangelo. He studied in Italy 1856–62 and won the Prix de Rome scholarship 1854.

Carpenter Edward 1844–1929. English socialist and writer. Inspired by reading ◊Thoreau, he resigned his post as tutor at Cambridge University 1874 to write poems and books, such as *The Simplification of Life* 1884, *Civilization: Its Cause and Cure* 1889, and *Love's Coming of Age* 1896, a plea for toleration of homosexuality.

Carpenter John 1948– . US director of horror and science-fiction films, notable for such films as *Dark Star* 1974 and *Assault on Precinct 13* 1976.

His subsequent films include the low-budget thriller *Halloween* 1978, *The Fog* 1979, *The Thing* 1982, *Christine* 1983 (adapted from a Stephen King story), *Starman* 1984, and *They Live* 1988. He composes his own film scores, which have sometimes added to the atmosphere of menace that often haunts his movies.

carpet thick textile fabric, generally made of wool, used for covering floors and stairs. There is a long tradition of fine handmade carpets in the Middle East, India, Pakistan, and China. Western carpets are machine-made. Carpets and rugs have also often been made in the home as a pastime, cross and tent stitch on canvas being widely used in the 18th and 19th centuries.

history The earliest known carpets date from c. 500 BC and were excavated at Passypych in SE Siberia, but it was not until the later Middle Ages that carpets reached W Europe from Turkey. Persian carpets (see ◊Islamic art), which reached a still unrivalled peak of artistry in the 15th and 16th centuries, were rare in Britain until the mid-19th century, reaching North America a little later. The subsequent demand led to a revival of organized carpetmaking in Persia. Europe copied oriental technique, but developed Western designs: France produced beautiful work at the Savonnerie and Beauvais establishments under Louis XIV and Louis XV; and Exeter, Axminster, London, and Wilton became British carpetmaking centres in the 18th century, though Kidderminster is the biggest centre today. The first carpet factory in the USA was established in Philadelphia 1791; it is still a large carpet-producing centre.

Carrà Carlo 1881–1966. Italian painter, one of the original members of the Futurist group. His best-known work of the period is *The Funeral of the Anarchist Galli* 1911 (Museum of Modern Art, New York). In 1917 he broke away to form the Metaphysical Painting movement with Giorgio de Chirico, and subsequently developed a frescolike style based on the works of early Renaissance painters such as Masaccio.

Carracci family of Italian painters in Bologna, renowned for painting murals and ceilings. The foremost of them, **Annibale Carracci** (1560–1609), decorated the Farnese Palace, Rome, with a series of mythological paintings united by simulated architectural ornamental surrounds (completed 1604). Rejecting the late Mannerism of his day, he sought to return to the Classicism of the early Renaissance. He is credited with the invention of the modern ◊caricature. **Ludovico Carracci** (1555–1619), with his cousin **Agostino Carracci** (1557–1602), founded Bologna's Academy of Art. Agostino collaborated with his brother Annibale on the Farnese Palace decorative scheme, which paved the way for a host of elaborate murals in Rome's palaces and churches, ever-more inventive illusions of pictorial depth and architectural ornament. Annibale also painted early landscapes such as *Flight into Egypt* 1603 (Doria Gallery, Rome).

Carradine John (Richmond Reed) 1906–1988. US film character actor of gaunt physique. He appeared in many major Hollywood films, such as *Stagecoach* 1939 and *The Grapes of Wrath* 1940, but was later often seen in horror B-movies, including *House of Frankenstein* 1944.

Carreras José 1947– . Spanish operatic tenor whose comprehensive repertoire includes Handel's Samson and whose recordings include *West Side Story* 1984 under Leonard Bernstein. His vocal presence, charmingly insinuating rather than forceful, is favoured for Italian and French romantic roles. Together with Placido Domingo and Luciano Pavarotti, he achieved worldwide fame in a recording of operatic hits released to coincide with the World Cup soccer series in Rome 1990.

Carroll Lewis. Pen name of Charles Lutwidge Dodgson 1832–1898. English author of children's classics *Alice's Adventures in Wonderland* 1865 and its sequel *Through the Looking-Glass* 1872. Among later works was the mock-heroic 'nonsense' poem *The Hunting of the Snark* 1876. He was fascinated by the limits and paradoxes of language and thought, the exploration of which leads to the apparent nonsense of Alice's adventures. An Oxford don, he also published mathematical works.

Dodgson, born in Daresbury, Cheshire, was a mathematics lecturer at Oxford 1855–81. There he first told the fantasy stories to Alice Liddell and her sisters, daughters of the dean of Christ Church. He was a prolific letter writer and inventor of games and puzzles, and was one of the pioneers of portrait photography.

With a name like yours, you might be any shape, almost.

Lewis Carroll
Through the Looking-Glass 1872, ch.6

Carry on films series of low-budget, highly profitable British comedies with an emphasis on the unsubtle double entendre. The first was *Carry on Sergeant* 1958 and the series continued for 20 years with such titles as *Carry on Nurse*, *Carry on Spying*, *Carry on Screaming*, and *Carry on Doctor*.

All were produced by Peter Rogers and directed by Gerald Thomas. Regular stars included Kenneth Williams, Charles Hawtrey, Sid James, and Joan Sims.

Carter Angela 1940–1992. English writer of the ◊magic realist school. Her works are marked by elements of Gothic fantasy, a fascination with the erotic and the violent, tempered by a complex lyricism and a comic touch. Her novels include *The Magic Toyshop* 1967 (filmed 1987) and *Nights at the Circus* 1984. She co-wrote the script for the film *The Company of Wolves* 1984, based on one of her stories. Her last novel was *Wise Children* 1991.

Carter Elliott (Cook) 1908– . US composer. He created intricately structured works in Schoenbergian serial idiom, incorporating 'metrical modulation', an adaptation of standard notation allowing different instruments or groups to remain synchronized while playing at changing speeds. This practice was first employed in his *String Quartet No 1* 1950–51, and to dense effect in *Double Concerto* 1961 for harpsichord and piano. In his eighth decade, his music has shown a new tautness and vitality, as in *Three Occasions for Orchestra* 1986–89.

Carter Family US country- and folk-music group. They were active from the 1920s to 1943 and first recorded 1927. Their material of old ballads and religious songs, and the guitar-picking technique of **Maybelle Carter** (1909–1978), influenced the development of country music, especially ◊bluegrass. Songs they made popular include 'Keep on the Sunny Side', 'Wildwood Flower', and 'Will the Circle Be Unbroken'.

Cartier-Bresson Henri 1908– . French photographer, considered one of the greatest photographic artists. His documentary work was shot in black and white, using a small-format Leica camera. His work is remarkable for its tightly structured composition and his ability to capture the decisive moment. He was a founder member of the Magnum photographic agency.

Cartland Barbara 1904– . English romantic novelist. She published her first book, *Jigsaw* 1921 and since then has produced a prolific stream of stories of chastely romantic love, usually in idealized or exotic settings, for a mainly female audience (such as *Love Climbs In* 1978 and *Moments of Love* 1981).

cartoon humorous or satirical drawing or ◊caricature; a strip cartoon or comic strip; traditionally, the base design for a large fresco, mosaic, or tapestry, transferred to wall or canvas by tracing or pricking out the design on the cartoon and then dabbing with powdered charcoal to create a faint outline. Surviving examples include Leonardo da Vinci's *Virgin and St Anne* (National Gallery, London).

Caruso Enrico 1873–1921. Italian operatic tenor of dark, full-bodied tone and remarkable dynamic range. In 1902 he starred, with Nellie Melba, in Puccini's *La Bohème/Bohemian Girl.* He was among the first opera singers to achieve lasting fame through gramophone recordings.

Carver Raymond 1939–1988. US short-story writer and poet. His writing deals mainly with blue-collar middle America, depicting failed, empty lives in a spare prose. His major works include *Will You Please Be Quiet, Please* 1976, *What We Talk About When We Talk About Love* 1981, *Cathedral* 1983, and *In a Marine Light* 1988, a collection of poetry.

Cary (Arthur) Joyce (Lunel) 1888–1957. English novelist. He used his experiences gained in Nigeria in the Colonial Service (which he entered 1918) as a backdrop to such novels as *Mister Johnson* 1939. Other books include *The Horse's Mouth* 1944, part of a trilogy about the life of an artist, Gulley Jimson.

caryatid building support or pillar in the shape of a female figure, the name deriving from the Karyatides, who were priestesses at the temple of Artemis at Karyai; the male equivalent is a *telamon* or *atlas.*

To make divine things human, and human things divine; such is Bach, the greatest and purest moment in music of all times.

Pablo Casals speech at
Prades Bach Festival 1950

Casals Pablo 1876–1973. Catalan cellist, composer, and conductor. His pioneer recordings of Schubert and Beethoven trios 1905 with violinist Jacques Thibaud and pianist Alfred Corot launched his international career and established the popularity of the cello as a solo instrument, notably the solo suites of J S Bach, recorded 1916. In 1919 he founded the Barcelona orchestra, which he conducted until leaving Spain 1939 to live in Prades, in the French Pyrenees, where he founded an annual music festival. In 1956 he moved to Puerto Rico, where he launched the Casals Festival 1957, and toured extensively in the USA. He wrote instrumental and choral works, including the Christmas oratorio *The Manger.*

Casanova de Seingalt Giovanni Jacopo 1725–1798. Italian adventurer, spy, violinist, librarian, and, according to his *Memoirs,* one of the world's great lovers. From 1774 he was a spy in the Venetian police service. In 1782 a libel got him into trouble, and after more wanderings he was appointed 1785 librarian to Count Waldstein at his castle of Dûx in Bohemia. Here Casanova wrote his *Memoirs* (published 1826–38, although the complete text did not appear until 1960–61).

Cash Johnny 1932– . US country singer, songwriter, and guitarist. His early hits, recorded for Sun Records in Memphis, Tennessee, include the million-selling 'I Walk the Line' 1956. Many of his songs have become classics.

Cash's gruff delivery and storytelling ability distinguish his work. He is widely respected beyond the country-music field for his concern for the underprivileged, expressed in albums like *Bitter Tears* 1964 about American Indians and *Live At Folsom Prison* 1968. He is known as the 'Man in Black' because of his penchant for dressing entirely in that colour.

cashmere natural fibre originating from the wool of the goats of Kashmir, India, used for shawls, scarves, sweaters, and coats. It can also be made artificially.

Cassandra in Greek mythology, the daughter of ◊Priam, king of Troy. Her prophecies (for example, of the fall of Troy) were never believed, because she had rejected the love of the god Apollo. She was murdered with ◊Agamemnon by his wife Clytemnestra, having been awarded as a prize to the Greek hero on his sacking of Troy.

Cassatt Mary 1844–1926. US Impressionist painter and printmaker who settled in Paris 1868. Her popular, colourful pictures of mothers and children show the influence of Japanese prints, for example *The Bath* 1892 (Art Institute, Chicago). She excelled in etching and pastel.

Cassavetes John 1929–1989. US director and actor whose experimental films include *Shadows* 1960 and *The Killing of a Chinese Bookie* 1980. His acting credits include *The Dirty Dozen* 1967 and *Rosemary's Baby* 1968.

Cassina Italian furniture-manufacturing company, established 1923, based in Meda, Italy.

Cassina moved from craft to mass production after 1945 and successfully sold modern design to a sophisticated international niche market, using designers such as Franco Albini (1905–1979), Gio Ponti (1891–1979), and Vico ◊Magistretti. Ponti's 'Superleggera' chair 1957 was among the most successful of Cassina's products.

Cassiopeia in Greek mythology, the mother of the Ethiopian princess ◊Andromeda.

Casson Hugh 1910– . English architect, professor at the Royal College of Art 1953–75, and president of the Royal Academy 1976–84. He was director of architecture for the Festival of Britain on the South Bank in London 1948–51, in which pavilions designed by young architects helped to popularize the ◊Modern Movement. His books include *Victorian Architecture* 1948.

The British love permanence more than they love beauty.

Hugh Casson *The Observer* 1964

Castagno Andrea del *c.* 1421–1457. Italian Renaissance painter, active in Florence. In his frescoes in Sta Apollonia, Florence, he adapted the pictorial space to the architectural framework and followed ◊Masaccio's lead in his use of perspective.

Castagno's work is sculptural and strongly expressive, anticipating the Florentine late 15th-century style, as in his *David* about 1450–57 (National Gallery, Washington, DC).

Castalia spring near Delphi in Greece, sacred to ◊Apollo and the ◊Muses in classical times.

castanets Spanish percussion instrument made of two hollowed wooden shells, held in the palm and drummed together by the fingers to produce a rhythmic accompaniment to dance. Orchestral castanets or 'clappers', mounted on a handle, were employed by silent film effects musicians to imitate the sound of a galloping horse, hence the phrase 'to run like the clappers'.

Castello Branco Camillo Ferreira Botelho, Visconde de Corrêa Botelho 1825–1890. Portuguese novelist. His work fluctuates between mysticism and bohemianism, and includes *Amor de perdição/Love of Perdition* 1862, written during his imprisonment for adultery, and *Novelas do Minho* 1875, stories of the rural north. Other works include *Onde está a felicidade?/Where is Happiness?* 1856 and *A brazileira de Prazins/The Brazilian Girl from Prazins* 1882. He was made a viscount 1885, and committed suicide when overtaken by blindness.

Castiglione Achille 1918– . Italian industrial designer, brother of Livio (1911–1979) and Pier

Giacomo (1913–1968) with whom he worked until their deaths. A key member of the generation of Italian designers who trained as architects before 1939 and became consultant designers for industry after 1945, his work represents modern Italian design at its most innovative and dramatic.

Castiglione has worked for numerous product manufacturers, both in Italy and abroad, but his most notable designs include lights for Flos – among them 'Taraxacum' 1950, a minimal sculptural design – and furniture pieces for Zanotta, including his 'Messandro' stool 1970 which is based on a tractor seat and demonstrates his use of the 'ready-made' in the context of design.

Castiglione Baldassare, Count Castiglione 1478–1529. Italian author and diplomat who described the perfect Renaissance gentleman in *Il Cortegiano/The Courtier* 1528.

Born near Mantua, Castiglione served the Duke of Milan, and in 1506 was engaged by the Duke of Albino on a mission to Henry VII of England. While in Spain 1524 he was made bishop of Avila.

castle fortified building or group of buildings, characteristic of medieval Europe. The castle underwent many changes, its size, design, and construction being largely determined by changes in siege tactics and the development of artillery. Outstanding examples are the 12th-century Krak des Chevaliers, Syria (built by crusaders); 13th-century Caernarvon Castle, Wales; and 15th-century Manzanares el Real, Spain.

Early castles (11th century) consisted of an earthen hill (*motte*) surrounded by wooden palisades enclosing a courtyard (*bailey*). The motte supported a wooden **keep**, a central tower containing store rooms and living quarters. Later developments substituted stone for wood and utilized more elaborate defensive architectural detail such as crenellated **battlements** from which missiles could be discharged, the **portcullis**, a heavy grating which could be let down to close the main gate, and the **drawbridge** crossing the ditch or **moat** surrounding the castle. After the introduction of gunpowder in the 14th century, castles became less defensible, and increases in civil order led to their replacement by unfortified manor houses by the 16th century. Large stone fortifications became popular again in the 18th century, particularly those modelled after the principles of fortification introduced by the French architect Vauban, and were built as late as the first half of the 19th century. In the late 19th century, castle-like buildings were constructed as residences for the wealthy as part of the Romantic revival in Europe and America. See also ◊château.

Castor and Pollux/Polydeuces in Greek mythology, twin sons of Leda (by Zeus), brothers of ◊Helen and ◊Clytemnestra. Protectors of mariners, they were transformed at death into the constellation Gemini.

castrato in music, a high male voice of unusual brilliance and power achieved by castration before puberty, regarded as the ideal timbre for heroic roles in opera by composers from Monteverdi to Wagner. Recordings preserve the voice of Alessandro Moreschi (1858–1922), the last male soprano of the Sistine Chapel.

Catch-22 black-humour novel by Joseph ◊Heller, published 1961, about a US squadron that is ordered to fly an increased number of bombing missions in Italy in World War II; the crazed military justifications involved were described by the novel's phrase 'Catch-22', which has come to represent the dilemma of all false authoritarian logic.

There was only one catch and that was Catch-22, which specified that a concern for one's own safety in the face of dangers that were real and immediate was the process of a rational mind.

Joseph Heller *Catch-22* 1961

Catcher in the Rye, The 1951 novel by US writer J D ◊Salinger about a young man's growing up and his fight to maintain his integrity in a 'phoney' adult world; it has become an international classic.

catharsis emotional purging and purification brought about by the experience of pity and fear, as in tragic drama. Aristotle in his *Poetics* used the term to explain the audience's feelings of relief or pleasure in watching the suffering of characters in a tragedy.

cathedral a bishop's principal church, containing his throne. Because of their importance, cathedrals were for many centuries the main focus of artistic and architectural endeavour. Their artworks include stained glass, frescoes, mosaics, carvings in wood and stone, paintings (such as altarpieces), ironwork, and textiles. Most cathedrals were built during the Middle Ages and reflect the many styles of Romanesque and Gothic architecture.

Romanesque cathedrals include Durham (England), Worms (Germany), and Cefalù (Sicily). Gothic cathedrals include Canterbury, Ely, Winchester, and York (England); Amiens, Chartres, Notre Dame (Paris), and Rouen (France); Cologne, Regensburg, and Ulm (Germany); Florence, Milan, Orvieto, and Siena (Italy); Avila, Burgos, León, Salamanca, and Toledo (Spain); and Uppsala (Sweden). Among the few built since the Middle Ages are Valencia, Spain, 13th–15th century; St Paul's, London, 17th century; SS Peter and Paul in St Petersburg, Russia, both 18th century; Westminster, London, 19th century; Liverpool (Catholic), 20th century.

Cather Willa (Sibert) 1873–1947. US novelist and short-story writer. Her novels frequently explore life in the pioneer West, both in her own time and in past eras; for example, *O Pioneers!* 1913 and *My Antonia* 1918, and *A Lost Lady* 1923. *Death Comes for the Archbishop* 1927 is a celebration of the spiritual pioneering of the Catholic church in New Mexico. She also wrote poetry and essays on fiction.

When kindness has left people, even for a few moments, we become afraid of them as if their reason has left them.

Willa Cather *My Mortal Enemy* 1926

Catherwood Frederick 1799–1854. British topographical artist and archaeological illustrator who accompanied John Lloyd Stephens in his exploration of Central America 1839–40 and the Yucatán 1841–42. His engravings, published 1844, were the first accurate representation of Mayan civilization in the West.

Catlin George 1796–1872. US painter and explorer. From the 1830s he made a series of visits to the Great Plains, painting landscapes and scenes of American Indian life. His style is factual, with close attention to detail.

Catlin produced an exhibition of over 500 paintings with which he toured America and Europe. Many of his pictures are in the Smithsonian Institution, Washington, DC.

Cat on a Hot Tin Roof play 1950 by US writer Tennessee ◊Williams. Family tensions are revealed when a dying wealthy cotton planter, the repressive Big Daddy, makes known the terms of his will, which states that each of his sons must have children. The play ends with the suggestion that the childless son, an alcoholic struggling with homosexual guilt, will be saved by his wife, the 'cat' of the title.

Catullus Gaius Valerius *c.* 84–54 BC. Roman lyric poet, who wrote in a variety of metres and forms, from short narratives and hymns to epigrams. Born in Verona, N Italy, he moved with ease through the literary and political society of late republican Rome. His love affair with the woman he called Lesbia provided the inspiration for many of his poems.

But what a woman says to her lusting lover it is best to write in wind and swift-flowing water.

Catullus *Carmina*

Caucasian Chalk Circle, The play by Bertolt ◊Brecht 1949. The child of a provincial governor in the Caucasus is rescued and brought up by Grusha, a maid, but is finally reclaimed by its natural mother. Forced into assuming the role of judge between the two mothers, a village record-keeper, Azdak, awards the child to Grusha.

Causley Charles (Stanley) 1917– . English poet. He published his first volume *Hands to Dance* 1951. Later volumes include *Johnny Alleluia* 1961, *Underneath the Water* 1968, and *Figgie Hobbin* 1970. His work is rooted in the life and folklore of his native Cornwall and makes use of ballad material and religious themes.

Cavafy Constantinos. Pen name of Konstantínos Pétrou 1863–1933. Greek poet. An Alexandrian, he shed light on Greek history, recreating the classical period with zest. He published only one book of poetry and remained almost unknown until translations of his works appeared 1952.

Cavalcanti Guido *c.* 1255–1300. Italian poet. A Florentine and friend of Dante, he was a leading exponent of the *dolce stil nuovo* (sweet new style). He is remembered for 'Donna mi prega/A Lady Asks Me', a philosophical poem about love, and for his sonnets and *ballate* or ballads. English translators include D G Rossetti and Ezra Pound.

Cavalier poets poets of Charles I's court, including Thomas Carew, Robert Herrick, Richard Lovelace, and John Suckling. They wrote witty, light-hearted love lyrics.

Cavalli (Pietro) Francesco 1602–1676. Italian composer, organist at St Mark's, Venice, and the first to make opera a popular entertainment with such works as *Egisto* 1643 and *Xerxes* 1654, performed in honour of Louis XIV's wedding in Paris. Twenty-seven of his operas survive.

cave temple temple hewn out of rock. The Great and Small Temples at ◊Abu Simbel, Egypt (now relocated) about 1301 BC, were carved out of the mountainside, and in India there are notable Buddhist rock-hewn temples at ◊Ajanta and Karli, and Hindu temples at Badami and Elephanta.

Caxton William *c.* 1422–1491. The first English printer. He learned the art of printing in Cologne, Germany, 1471 and set up a press in Belgium where he produced the first book printed in English, his own version of a French romance, *Recuyell of the Historyes of Troye* 1474. Returning to England 1476, he established himself in London, where he produced the first book printed in England, *Dictes or Sayengis of the Philosophres* 1477.

Caxton, born in Kent, was apprenticed to a London cloth dealer 1438, and set up his own business in Bruges 1441–70; he became governor of the English merchants there, negotiating on their behalf with the dukes of Burgundy. In 1471 he went to Cologne and then set up his own press in Bruges in partnership with Colard Mansion, a calligrapher. The books from Caxton's press in Westminster included editions of the poets Chaucer, John Gower, and John Lydgate (*c.* 1370–1449). He translated many texts from French and Latin and revised some English ones, such as Malory's *Morte d'Arthur*. Altogether he printed about 100 books.

And certaynly our langage now used varyeth ferre from that which was used and spoken when I was borne.

William Caxton 1490

Cecchetti Enrico 1850–1928. Italian ballet master who evolved a system of teaching that greatly improved the technical standards of the dance. His system has been preserved by the Cecchetti Society (founded 1922 and incorporated into the Imperial Society of Teachers of Dancing 1924), and is still widely used. He taught Anna Pavlova and many members of Diaghilev's Ballets Russes.

As a dancer he created the roles of Bluebird and Carabosse in *Sleeping Beauty* 1887. He taught at the Imperial Russian Ballet school 1890–1902 and was the instructor for Diaghilev's Ballets Russes 1910–18. He founded a school in London 1918–25 and then became director of La Scala ballet school in Milan 1925–28.

Cela Camilo José 1916– . Spanish novelist. Among his novels, characterized by their violence and brutal realism, are *La familia de Pascual Duarte/The Family of Pascal Duarte* 1942, and *La colmena/The Hive* 1951. He was awarded the Nobel Prize for Literature 1989.

celesta keyboard glockenspiel producing high-pitched sounds of glistening purity. It was invented by Auguste Mustel 1886 and first used to effect by Tchaikovsky in the *Nutcracker* ballet 1890.

Céline Louis Ferdinand. Pen name of Louis Destouches 1884–1961. French novelist whose writings aroused controversy over their cynicism and anti-semitism. His best-known work is *Voyage au bout de la nuit/Journey to the End of the Night* 1932.

If you aren't rich you should always look useful.

L F Céline
Journey to the End of the Night 1932

Cellini Benvenuto 1500–1571. Italian sculptor and goldsmith working in the Mannerist style;

author of an arrogant but entertaining and informative autobiography (begun 1558). Among his works are a graceful bronze *Perseus* 1545–54 (Loggia dei Lanzi, Florence) and a celebrated gold salt cellar made for Francis I of France 1540–43 (Kunsthistorisches Museum, Vienna).

Cellini was born in Florence and apprenticed to a goldsmith. In 1519 he went to Rome, later worked for the papal mint, and was once imprisoned on a charge of having embezzled pontifical jewels. He worked for a time in France at the court of Francis I, but finally returned to Florence 1545.

The difference between a painting and a sculpture is the difference between a shadow and the thing that casts it.

Benvenuto Cellini
letter to Benedetto Varchi 1547

---

cello common abbreviation for *violoncello*, tenor member of the ◊violin family and fourth member of the string quartet. Its solo potential was recognized by J S Bach, and a concerto repertoire extends from Haydn (who also gave the cello a leading role in his string quartets), and Boccherini to Dvořák, Elgar, Britten, Ligeti, and Lukas Foss. The *Bachianas Brasilieras 1* by Villa-Lobos is scored for eight cellos, and Boulez's *Messagesquisse* 1977 for seven cellos.

Celtic art art of the Celtic peoples of western Europe, emerging about 500 BC, probably on the Rhine. It spread as the Celts moved westwards to Gaul and the British Isles and southwards to Italy and Turkey. Early Celtic art, which reached its high point in 1st-century Britain, excelled in metalwork – in particular weapons and jewellery – decorated with semi-abstract designs based on animal and plant motifs. Metalwork using curving incised lines and inlays of coloured enamel and coral survived at La Tène, a site at Lake Neuchâtel, Switzerland.

In Britain and Ireland, Celtic art flourished with the coming of Christianity, producing sculpture (stone crosses) and, in particular, manuscript illumination, as in *The Book of Kells* about AD 800 (Trinity College, Dublin) and the *Lindisfarne Gospels* (British Museum, London) about AD 690. Celtic art had a profound influence on ◊Anglo-Saxon art.

cembalo short form of *clavicembalo*, an accompanying harpsichord. In classical orchestral music, such as by Handel or Haydn, the cembalo part is taken by the conductor, its music being improvised over a ◊figured bass.

Cennini Cennino born *c.* 1370. Italian painter and writer, remembered for his practical manual on painting *Il Libro dell'arte/The Craftsman's Handbook*, about 1390, a source of fascinating insights into early Italian Renaissance workshop techniques, especially ◊tempera painting. None of his paintings survive.

cenotaph (Greek 'empty tomb') monument to commemorate a person or persons not actually buried at the site, as in the Whitehall Cenotaph, London, designed by Edwin Lutyens to commemorate the dead of both world wars.

censorship, film control of the content and presentation of films. Film censorship dates back almost as far as the cinema. In Britain, censorship was established in 1912, in the USA 1922. In some countries, self-regulation of the industry has not been regarded as sufficient; in the USSR, for example, state censorship forbade the treatment of certain issues.

Censorship in Britain is the responsibility of the British Board of Film Classification (formerly the British Board of Film Censors), run by the film industry, which gives each film a rating. There is a similar body, popularly called the Hays Office (after its first president, 1922–45, Will H Hays), in the USA.

centaur in Greek mythology, a creature half-human and half-horse. Centaurs were supposed to live in Thessaly, and be wild and lawless; the mentor of Heracles, Chiron, was an exception.

The earliest representations of centaurs (about 1800–1000 BC) were excavated near Famagusta, Cyprus, in 1962, and are two-headed. Some female representations also exist.

Centlivre Susannah 1667–1723. English dramatist and actress. Her first play was a tragedy *The Perjured Husband* 1700. Success as a dramatist came with the comedy *The Gamester* 1705, which was followed by *The Busie Body* 1709 and *A Bold Stroke for a Wife* 1718. As an actress, she specialized in male roles as in *The Beau's Duel* 1702.

ceramics objects made from clay, hardened into a permanent form by baking (firing) at very high temperatures in a kiln. Ceramics are used for building construction and decoration (bricks and tiles), for plates and vessels used in the home, and for specialist industrial purposes. Different types of clay and different methods and temperatures of firing create a variety of results. Objects may be hand-built out of slabs of clay, coiled, thrown on a wheel, or cast in a mould. Technically, the main categories are: ◊earthenware, ◊stoneware, and hard- and softpaste porcelain (see under ◊pottery and porcelain).

ceramics: examples through Western history

Roman period potter's wheel; lead glazing, decorative use of slip (watered-down clay).

medieval period sgraffito (scratched) tiles and other products (earthenware decorated with slip of a contrasting colour, which is then scratched through) such as those made in Bologna, Italy. Lead-glazed jugs made in England and France, coloured bright green or yellow-brown with copper or iron oxides. Tin-glazed ware in S Italy and Spain by 13th century, influenced by established Islamic techniques.

14th-century Germany stoneware developed from hard earthenwares; tin glazes developed; colour added by thin slips mixed with high-temperature colours. Later, mottled brown glaze recognized as characteristic of Cologne, and referred to as 'tigerware' in Britain.

15th century Hispano-Moresque painted ware imitated by Italians, developing into majolica by mid-century, using the full range of high-temperature colours; centres of the craft included Tuscany, Faenza, Urbino, and Venice. Some potteries, such as that at Gubbio, additionally used lustre glazes. Typical products are dishes and apothecary jars.

16th century potters from Faenza spread tin-glazed earthenware (majolica) skills to France, Spain, and the Netherlands, where it became known as faience; from Antwerp the technique spread to England. The English in the 17th century named Dutch faience 'Delftware', after the main centre of production.

17th century faience centres developed at Rouen and Moustiers in France, Alcora in Spain, and in Switzerland, Austria, and Germany. Blue underglaze was increasingly used, in imitation of Chinese blue and white designs, reflecting the growth of orientalism.

18th century European developments in porcelain, also in using a rich palette of low-temperature enamel colours. The vitreous enamel process, first developed at Strasbourg about 1750, spread around N Europe.

Cerberus in Greek mythology, the three-headed dog guarding the entrance to ◊Hades, the underworld.

Ceres in Roman mythology, the goddess of agriculture, equivalent to the Greek ◊Demeter.

Cervantes Saavedra, Miguel de 1547–1616. Spanish novelist, playwright, and poet whose masterpiece *Don Quixote* (in full *El ingenioso hidalgo Don Quixote de la Mancha*) was published 1605. In 1613 his *Novelas ejemplares/Exemplary Novels* appeared, followed by *Viaje del Parnaso/The Voyage to Parnassus* 1614. A spurious second part of *Don Quixote* prompted Cervantes to bring out his own second part 1615, often considered superior to the first in construction and characterization.

Born at Alcalá de Henares, he entered the army in Italy, and was wounded in the battle of Lepanto 1571. While on his way back to Spain 1575, he was captured by Barbary pirates and taken to Algiers, where he became a slave until ransomed 1580.

Returning to Spain, he wrote several plays, and in 1585 his pastoral romance *Galatea* was printed. He was employed in Seville 1587 provisioning the Armada. While working as a tax collector, he was imprisoned more than once for deficiencies in his accounts. He sank into poverty, and little is known of him until 1605 when he published *Don Quixote*. The novel was an immediate success and was soon translated into English and French.

There are only two families in the world, as an old grandmother of mine used to say: the Haves and the Have-nots.

Miguel de Cervantes Saavedra
Don Quixote

César adopted name of César Baldaccini 1921– . French sculptor who created imaginary insects and animals using iron and scrap metal and, in the 1960s, crushed car bodies. From the late 1960s he experimented with works in plastic and polyurethane.

Cézanne Paul 1839–1906. French Post-Impressionist painter, a leading figure in the development of modern art. He broke away from the Impressionists' concern with the ever-changing effects of light to develop a style that tried to capture the structure of natural forms, whether in landscapes, still lifes, or portraits. *Cardplayers* about 1890–95 (Louvre, Paris) is typical of his work.

He was born in Aix-en-Provence, where he studied, and was a friend of the novelist Emile Zola. In 1872 Cézanne met Pissarro and lived near him in Pontoise, outside Paris, but soon abandoned Impressionism. His series of paintings of Mont Sainte-Victoire in Provence from the 1880s into the 1900s show an increasing fragmentation of the painting's surface and a movement towards abstraction, with forms being modelled by subtle modulations of colour and square brushstrokes. He was greatly revered by early modern masters, notably Picasso and Braque.

Treat nature in terms of the cylinder, the sphere, the cone, all in perspective ... Nature, for us, lies more in depth than on the surface.

Paul Cézanne

Chabrier (Alexis) Emmanuel 1841–1894. French composer. He wrote *España* 1883, an orchestral rhapsody, and the light opera *Le Roi malgré lui/The Reluctant King* 1887. His colourful orchestration inspired Debussy and Ravel.

Chabrol Claude 1930– . French film director. Originally a critic, he was one of the ◊New Wave directors. His works of murder and suspense, which owe much to Hitchcock, include *Les Cousins/The Cousins* 1959, *Les Biches/The Girlfriends* 1968, *Le Boucher/The Butcher* 1970, and *Cop au Vin* 1984.

chaconne piece of music derived from a dance form, possibly of Spanish origin, in three time, constructed over a ◊ground bass. An example is the aria 'Dido's Lament' from Purcell's opera *Dido and Aeneas* 1689, in which the inevitability of the bass line conveys a sense of Dido's inescapable fate.

Chadwick Lynn 1914– . English abstract sculptor known for his 1940s mobiles (influenced by Alexander Calder) and for welded ironwork from the 1950s, typically spiky, pyramidal 'creatures'.

Chagall Marc 1887–1985. Russian-born French painter and designer; much of his highly coloured, fantastic imagery was inspired by the village life of his boyhood and by Jewish and Russian folk traditions. He designed stained glass, mosaics (for Israel's Knesset in the 1960s), the ceiling of the Paris Opera House 1964, tapestries, and stage sets. He was an original figure, often seen as a precursor of Surrealism, as in *I and the Village* 1911 (Museum of Modern Art, New York).

Chagall lived mainly in France from 1922. Examples of his stained glass can be found in a chapel in Vence, in the south of France, 1950s, and a synagogue near Jerusalem 1961. He also produced illustrated books.

Art is the unceasing effort to compete with the beauty of flowers – and never succeeding.

Marc Chagall 1977

Chaliapin Fyodor Ivanovich 1873–1938. Russian bass singer, born in Kazan (Tatar Republic). He achieved fame in the West through his charismatic recordings, notably as Boris in Mussorgsky's opera *Boris Godunov*. He specialized in Russian, French, and Italian roles.

chalice cup, usually of precious metal, used in celebrating the Eucharist (Holy Communion) in the Christian church.

chalk soft limestone used in stick form as a drawing medium; an ingredient mixed with pigment and a binding agent to make crayons. Chalk drawings exist from prehistoric times; Leonardo da Vinci used chalk extensively in the 15th century. White chalk is used most often on coloured paper to provide highlights. Pavement artists normally work with chalk as it can be easily erased.

chalumeau short thickset double-reed wind instrument, ancestor of the clarinet. It is also the term used to describe the dark lowest register of clarinet tone.

Chamberlin, Powell, and Bon British architectural partnership, established 1952 by Peter Chamberlin (1919–1978), Geoffrey Powell (1920–), and Christoph Bon (1921–). Its commissions include New Hall, Cambridge 1966, Chancellor's Court, Leeds University 1972 (which features aerial walkways at right angles to elongated slabs), and the grandiose Barbican Arts Centre, London, completed 1982.

chamber music music intended for performance in a small room or chamber, rather than in the concert hall, and usually written for instrumental combinations, played with one instrument to a part, as in the string quartet.

Chamber music developed as an instrumental alternative to earlier music for voices such as the madrigal, which allowed accompanying instruments little freedom for technical display. At first a purely instrumental style, it developed through Haydn and Beethoven into a private and often experimental medium making unusual demands on players and audiences alike. During the 20th century, the limitations of recording and radio encouraged many composers to scale down their orchestras to chamber proportions, as in Alban Berg's *Chamber Concerto* and Igor Stravinsky's *Agon*.

Chambers William 1726–1796. Swedish-born English architect. Although he worked in the Neo-Palladian style, he was also a popularizer of Chinese influence (for example, the pagoda in Kew Gardens, London 1762). His best-known work in the Neo-Palladian style is Somerset House, London 1776–86.

Chamisso Adelbert von. Pen name of Louis-Charles-Adélaïde Chamisso de Boncourt 1781–1831. German writer of the story *Peter Schlemihl*, about a man who sold his shadow. He was born into a French family who left France because of the French Revolution; subsequently he went as a botanist on Otto von Kotzebue's trip around the world 1815–18, recounted in *Reise um de Welt* 1821. His verse includes the cycle of lyrics *Frauenliebe und Frauenleben* 1831, set to music by Schumann.

Champaigne Philippe de 1602–1674. French artist, the leading portrait painter of the court of Louis XIII. Of Flemish origin, he went to Paris 1621 and gained the patronage of Cardinal Richelieu. His style is elegant, cool, and restrained. *Ex Voto* 1662 (Louvre, Paris) is his best-known work.

chancel part of a Christian church where the choir and clergy sit, formerly kept separate from the nave. The term originated in the early Middle Ages, when chancels were raised above the level of the nave, from which they were separated by a rood screen, a pierced partition bearing the image of the Crucifixion. The chancel has usually been considered the preserve and responsibility of the clergy, while the upkeep and repair of the nave was left to the parishioners.

Chandler Raymond 1888–1959. US novelist who turned the pulp detective mystery form into a successful genre of literature. He created the quintessential private eye in the tough but chivalric loner, Philip Marlowe, narrator of such books as *The Big Sleep* 1939 (filmed 1946), *Farewell My Lovely* 1940 (filmed 1944), *The Lady in the Lake* 1943 (filmed 1947), and *The Long Goodbye* 1954 (filmed 1975). He also wrote numerous screenplays, notably *Double Indemnity* 1944, *Blue Dahlia* 1946, and *Strangers on a Train* 1951.

Down these mean streets a man must go who is not himself mean, who is neither tarnished nor afraid.

Raymond Chandler
The Simple Art of Murder

Chanel Coco (Gabrielle) 1883–1971. French fashion designer, renowned as a trendsetter. Her designs were inspired by her personal wish for simple, comfortable, and practical clothes. Throughout the 1920s and 1930s her look was widely influential; the basic ingredients were cardigans, woollen jersey dresses, the 'little black dress', bell-bottom trousers, and costume jewellery. Popular colours were grey, navy blue, black, and beige for the day, while for the evening she preferred white, black, and pastel shades.

She closed her workshop 1939 and did not return to fashion until 1954 when she began showing her classic suits again in soft tweed and jersey, often collarless and trimmed with braid and shown with costume jewellery such as artificial pearls or gilt chains. She continued working until her death.

Let us beware of originality; in couture it leads to costume.

Coco Chanel

Chaney Lon (Alonso) 1883–1930. US star of silent films, often in grotesque or monstrous roles such as *The Phantom of the Opera* 1925. A master of make-up, he was nicknamed 'the Man of a Thousand Faces'. He sometimes used extremely painful devices for added effect, as in the title role in *The Hunchback of Notre Dame* 1923, when he carried over 30 kg/70 lb of costume in the form of a heavy hump and harness.

Chaney Lon, Jr (Creighton) 1906–1973. US actor, son of Lon Chaney, who gave an acclaimed performance as Lennie in *Of Mice and Men* 1940. He went on to star in many 1940s horror films, including the title role in *The Wolf Man* 1941. His other work includes *My Favorite Brunette* 1947 and *The Haunted Palace* 1963.

chanson song type common in France and Italy, often based on a folk tune that originated with the ◊troubadours. Josquin ◊Desprez was a chanson composer.

chanson de geste epic poetry of the High Middle Ages in Europe. It probably developed from oral poetry recited in royal or princely courts, and takes as its subject the exploits of heroes, such as those associated with Charlemagne and the crusades. The best known example is the *Chanson de Roland*.

Chanson de Roland early 11th-century epic poem which tells of the real and imaginary deeds of Roland and other knights of Charlemagne, and their last stand against the Basques at Roncesvalles.

chant ritual incantation by an individual or a group, for confidence or mutual support. Chants can be secular (football supporters' chants) or religious. Ambrosian and ◊Gregorian chants are forms of ◊plainsong.

Chantrey Francis Legatt 1781–1841. English sculptor, known for portrait busts and monuments. His unaffected studies of children were much loved in his day, notably *Sleeping Children* 1817 (Lichfield Cathedral).

chapel place of worship used by some Christian denominations; also, a part of a building used for Christian worship. A large church or cathedral may have several chapels.

Chaplin Charlie (Charles Spencer) 1889–1977. English film actor and director. He made his reputation as a tramp with a smudge moustache, bowler hat, and twirling cane in silent comedies from the mid-1910s, including *The Rink* 1916, *The Kid* 1920, and *The Gold Rush* 1925. His work often contrasts buffoonery with pathos, and his later films combine dialogue with mime and music, as in *The Great Dictator* 1940 and *Limelight* 1952. He was one of cinema's most popular stars.

Chaplin was born in south London and first appeared on the music hall stage at the age of five. He joined Mack Sennett's Keystone Company in Los Angeles 1913. Along with Mary Pickford, Douglas Fairbanks, and D W ◊Griffith, Chaplin formed United Artists 1919 as an independent company to distribute their films. His other films include *City Lights* 1931, *Modern Times* 1936, and *Monsieur Verdoux* 1947. *Limelight* 1952 was awarded an Oscar for Chaplin's musical theme. When accused of communist sympathies during the McCarthy witch-hunt, he left the USA 1952 and moved to Switzerland. He received special Oscars 1928 and 1972.

All I need to make a comedy is a park, a policeman and a pretty girl.

Charlie Chaplin *My Autobiography*

Chapman George 1559–1634. English poet and dramatist. His translations of the Greek epics of Homer (completed 1616) were celebrated; his plays include the comedy *Eastward Ho!* (with Jonson and Marston) 1605 and the tragedy *Bussy d'Amboise* 1607.

Chapman John ('Johnny Appleseed') 1774–1845. US pioneer and folk hero, credited with establishing orchards throughout the Midwest by planting seeds as he travelled. Famous as the subject of local legends and folk tales, Chapman was described as a religious visionary with boundless generosity.

chapterhouse in a cathedral, monastery, or other religious establishment, a meeting place. Access is usually via the cloisters. In England, chapterhouses are often polygonal in form.

charcoal black, charred sticks or pieces of wood produced by heating in the absence of air; a porous form of carbon. Charcoal sticks are used by artists for making black line drawings, especially preparatory drawings as charcoal can easily be rubbed out. It can be used to produce a soft effect.

Chardin Jean-Baptiste-Siméon 1699–1779. French painter of naturalistic still lifes and quiet domestic scenes that recall the Dutch tradition. His work is a complete contrast to that of his contemporaries, the Rococo painters. He developed his own technique, using successive layers of paint to achieve depth of tone. He is also generally considered one of the finest exponents of ◊genre painting.

Chareau Pierre 1883–1950. French designer, best known for his Maison de Verre, Paris 1928–31. This predated and influenced development of the 1970s ◊High Tech approach to design in its innovative use of industrial materials, such as studded rubber flooring and glass bricks.

Charles Ray 1930– . US singer, songwriter, and pianist whose first hits were 'I've Got A Woman' 1955, 'What'd I Say' 1959, and 'Georgia on My Mind' 1960. He has recorded gospel, blues, rock, soul, country, and rhythm and blues.

Charleston back-kicking dance of the 1920s that originated in Charleston, South Carolina, and became an American craze following the musical *Runnin' Wild* 1923.

Charon in Greek mythology, the boatman who ferried the dead over the rivers Acheron and Styx to ◊Hades, the underworld. A coin placed on the tongue of the dead paid for their passage.

Charpentier Gustave 1860–1956. French composer who wrote an opera about Paris working-class life, *Louise* 1900. He was a pupil of Massenet.

Charpentier Marc-Antoine 1645–1704. French composer. He wrote incidental music in Italian style to plays by Molière, including *Le Malade imaginaire/The Hypochondriac* 1673. Later in life, as official composer to the Sainte Chapelle, Paris, he composed sacred music in French style, and the opera *Médée* 1693.

Charrière Isabelle van Zuylen de 1740–1805. Dutch writer who settled in Colombier, Switzerland, 1761. Her works include plays, tracts, and novels, among them *Caliste* 1786. She had many early feminist ideas.

Charteris Leslie 1907– . British novelist, a US citizen from 1946. His varied career in many exotic occupations gave authentic background to some 40 novels about Simon Templar, the 'Saint', a gentleman adventurer on the wrong side of the law. The novels have been adapted for films, radio, and television. The first was *The Saint Meets the Tiger* 1928.

Charybdis in Greek mythology, a whirlpool formed by a monster of the same name on one side of the narrow straits of Messina, Sicily, opposite the monster Scylla.

Chase James Hadley. Pen name of René Raymond 1906–1985. British author of the hard-boiled thriller *No Orchids for Miss Blandish* 1939 and other popular novels.

chasing indentation of a design on metal by small chisels and hammers. This method of decoration was familiar in ancient Egypt, Assyria, and Greece; it is used today on fine silverware.

château country house or important residence in France. The term originally applied to a French medieval castle. The château was first used as a domestic building in the late 15th century. By the reign of Louis XIII (1610–43) fortifications such as moats and keeps were no longer used for defensive purposes, but merely as decorative features. The Loire valley contains some fine examples of châteaux.

Chateaubriand François René, vicomte de 1768–1848. French writer, a founder of Romanticism. In exile from the French Revolution 1794–99, he wrote *Atala* 1801 (based on his encounters with North American Indians) and the autobiographical *René*, which formed part of *Le Génie du Christianisme/The Genius of Christianity* 1802. He later wrote *Mémoires d'outre tombe/Memoirs from Beyond the Tomb* 1848–50.

He visited the USA 1791 and, on his return to France, fought for the royalist side which was defeated at Thionville 1792. He lived in exile in England until 1800. When he returned to France, he held diplomatic appointments under Louis XVIII.

The original writer is not he who refrains from imitating others, but he who can be imitated by none.

François René Chateaubriand
Le Génie du Christianisme

Chatterji Bankim Chandra 1838–1894. Indian novelist. Born in Bengal, where he established his reputation with his first book, *Durges-Nandini* 1864, he became a favourite of the nationalists. His book *Ananda Math* 1882 contains the Indian national song 'Bande-Mataram'.

Chatterton Thomas 1752–1770. English poet whose medieval-style poems and brief life were to inspire English Romanticism. Born in Bristol, he studied ancient documents he found in the Church of St Mary Redcliffe and composed poems he ascribed to a 15th-century monk, 'Thomas Rowley', which were accepted as genuine. He committed suicide in London, after becoming destitute.

Chatwin Bruce 1940–1989. English writer. His works include *The Songlines* 1987, written after living with Aborigines; the novel *Utz* 1988, about a manic porcelain collector in Prague; and travel pieces and journalism collected in *What Am I Doing Here?* 1989.

Chaucer Geoffrey *c.* 1340–1400. English poet. *The ◊Canterbury Tales*, a collection of stories told by a group of pilgrims on their way to Canterbury, reveals his knowledge of human nature and his stylistic variety, from urbane and ironic to simple and bawdy. Early allegorical poems, including *The Book of the Duchess*, were influenced by French poems like the *Roman de la Rose*. His *Troilus and Criseyde* is a substantial narrative poem about the tragic betrayal of an idealized courtly love.

Chaucer was born in London. Taken prisoner in the French wars, he had to be ransomed by Edward III 1360. He married Philippa Roet 1366, becoming in later life the brother-in-law of the politician John of Gaunt. He achieved various appointments and was sent on missions to Italy (where he may have met ◊Boccaccio and ◊Petrarch), France, and Flanders. His early work

showed formal French influence, as in his adaptation of the French allegorical poem on courtly love, *Romaunt of the Rose*; more mature works reflected the influence of Italian realism, as in his long narrative poem *Troilus and Criseyde*, adapted from Boccaccio. In *The Canterbury Tales* he showed his own genius for metre and characterization. He was the most influential English poet of the Middle Ages.

He was a verray, parfit gentil Knyght.

Geoffrey Chaucer
The Canterbury Tales Prologue

Chaudhuri Nirad Chandra 1897– . Indian writer and broadcaster. He attracted attention with his *Autobiography of an Unknown Indian* 1950 which illuminates the clash of British and Indian civilizations. A first visit to England, previously known to him only through its literature, produced the quirky *A Passage to England* 1959. Later works include *The Continent of Circe* 1965, an erudite critique of Indian culture, and *Thy Hand Great Anarch* 1987, critical of the impact of British culture on India.

Chávez Carlos 1899–1978. Mexican composer and pianist whose music incorporates national and pre-Columbian folk elements, for example *Chapultepec: Republican Overture* 1935. He composed a number of ballets, seven symphonies, and concertos for both violin and piano. He was founder-director of the Mexico Symphony Orchestra 1928–48.

Chayefsky (Sidney) Paddy 1923–1981. US screenwriter and dramatist of great passion and insight. He established his reputation with naturalistic television plays, at least two of which were adapted for cinema: *Marty* 1955 (for which he won an Oscar for the film screenplay) and *Bachelor Party* 1957. He also won Oscars for the bitterly satirical *The Hospital* 1971 and *Network* 1976.

His stage plays include *The Tenth Man* 1959 and *Gideon* 1961. He wrote the screenplay for Ken Russell's *Altered States* 1980, which was very loosely based on Chayefsky's novel of the same name.

cheesecloth fine muslin or cotton fabric of very loose weave, originally used to press curds during the cheesemaking process. It was popular for clothing in the 1970s.

Cheever John 1912–1982. US writer whose stories and novels focus on the ironies of upper-middle-class life in suburban America. His short stories were frequently published in *The New Yorker* magazine. His first novel was *The Wapshot Chronicle* 1957, for which he won the

National Book Award. Others include *Falconer* 1977. His *Stories of John Cheever* 1978 won the Pulitzer Prize.

Chekhov Anton (Pavlovich) 1860–1904. Russian dramatist and writer of short stories. His plays concentrate on the creation of atmosphere and delineation of internal development, rather than external action. His first play, *Ivanov* 1887, was a failure, as was *The Seagull* 1896 until revived by Stanislavsky 1898 at the Moscow Art Theatre, for which Chekhov went on to write his finest plays: ◊*Uncle Vanya* 1899, The ◊*Three Sisters* 1901, and The ◊*Cherry Orchard* 1904.

Chekhov was born in Taganrog, S Russia. He qualified as a doctor 1884, but devoted himself to writing short stories rather than practising medicine. The collection *Particoloured Stories* 1886 consolidated his reputation and gave him leisure to develop his style, as seen in *My Life* 1895, *The Lady with the Dog* 1898, and *In the Ravine* 1900.

People don't notice whether it's winter or summer when they're happy. If I lived in Moscow I don't think I'd care what the weather was like.

Anton Chekhov *The Three Sisters* 1901

Chelsea porcelain factory porcelain factory thought to be the first in England. Based in SW London, it dated from the 1740s, when it was known as the Chelsea Porcelain Works. It produced softpaste porcelain in imitation of Chinese high-fired porcelain. Later items are distinguished by the anchor mark on the base. Chelsea porcelain includes plates and other items decorated with botanical, bird, and insect paintings.

The factory was taken over by William Duesbury of Derby 1769 (after which the so-called 'Chelsea-Derby' was produced), and pulled down 1784.

chemise woman's undergarment usually made from two pieces of fabric sewn together at the shoulders and sides. It can be collarless and sleeveless. Often worn between the body and the corset, the chemise was made of linen, lawn, or silk. During the 19th century it was modified to become a blouse.

Chénier André de 1762–1794. French poet, born in Constantinople. His lyrical poetry was later to inspire the Romantic movement, but he was known in his own time for his uncompromising support of the constitutional royalists after the Revolution. In 1793 he went into hiding, but finally he was arrested and, on 25 July 1794, guillotined. While in prison he wrote *Jeune Captive/Captive Girl* and the political *Iambes*, published after his death.

Little griefs make us tender; great ones make us hard.

André de Chénier

---

chenille (French 'caterpillar') fancy special-effect yarn of soft, hairy texture. In the past it was made from silk, but is now usually made from cotton.

Chéret Jules 1836–1932. French lithographer and poster artist. His early posters, such as those in the 1860s for the Circus Rancy, pioneered the medium. Later works show the influence of the Impressionists and Toulouse-Lautrec.

Cherry Orchard, The play by Anton ◊Chekhov, first produced in Moscow 1904. Its theme is the demise of the way of life of a landowning family, symbolized by the felling of a cherry orchard after it has been sold to a developer.

Cherubini Luigi (Carlo Zanobi Salvadore Maria) 1760–1842. Italian composer. His first opera *Quinto Fabio* 1779 was produced at Alessandria. Following appointment as court composer to King George III of England 1784–88, he settled in Paris, where he produced a number of dramatic works including *Médée* 1797, *Les Deux Journées* 1800, and the ballet *Anacréon* 1803. After 1809 he devoted himself largely to church music.

I recommend you to take care of the minutes: for hours will take care of themselves.

Earl of Chesterfield letter to his son, Nov 1747

Chesterfield Philip Dormer Stanhope, 4th Earl of Chesterfield 1694–1773. English politician and writer, author of *Letters to his Son* 1774, which gave voluminous instruction on aristocratic manners and morals. A member of the literary circle of Swift, Pope, and Bolingbroke, he incurred the wrath of Dr Samuel ◊Johnson by failing to carry out an offer of patronage.

One bears great things from the valley, only small things from the peak.

G K Chesterton *The Hammer of God*

Chesterton G(ilbert) K(eith) 1874–1936. English novelist, essayist, and poet, author of numerous short stories featuring a Catholic priest, Father Brown, who solves crimes by drawing on his knowledge of human nature. Other novels include the fantastic *The Napoleon of*

Notting Hill 1904 and *The Man Who Was Thursday* 1908, an allegory on the problem of evil.

Born in London, he studied art but quickly turned to journalism. Like Hilaire Belloc, he was initially a socialist sympathizer.

Chevalier Maurice 1888–1972. French singer and actor. He began as dancing partner to the revue artiste ◊Mistinguett at the ◊Folies-Bergère, and made numerous films including *Innocents of Paris* 1929 (which revived his song 'Louise'), *The Merry Widow* 1934, and *Gigi* 1958.

chiaroscuro (Italian 'light-dark') in painting and graphic art, the balanced use of light and shade, particularly where contrasting luminous and opaque materials are represented, for example, glinting metal and dark velvet. Masters of chiaroscuro include Leonardo da Vinci, Rembrandt, and Caravaggio. The term is also used to describe a monochromatic painting employing light and dark shades only.

Chicago School in architecture, a 19th-century North American movement, centred in Chicago, which heralded the arrival of the ◊skyscraper with its emphasis on verticality. The practice of Daniel H Burnham (1846–1912) and John Welbourn Root (1850–1891) produced two noted exemplars: the 16-storey Monadnock building 1889–91 and the Reliance building 1890–94, both in Chicago. The latter comprised a steel frame with glass infill – an obvious precursor of many 20th-century skyscrapers. The school's greatest exponent, however, was Louis ◊Sullivan.

Developing in the wake of the Chicago fire 1871, which demonstrated the need for alternatives to the traditional exposed cast-iron frame, the school found an early proponent in William Le Baron Jenney (1832–1907), whose Home Insurance building, Chicago 1883–85, had a metal frame sheathed in brick, which allowed for multi-storey construction.

Chicano theatre Mexican-American community theatre movement, notably the Teatro Campesino founded 1965 in California by Luis Valdez (1940–), which was responsible for the first festival of Chicano theatre 1970; the Teatro de los Barrios, founded 1969 in Texas; and Teatro de la Esperanza, founded 1971 by Jorge Huerta (1942–) in California.

chiffon lightweight plain-weave fabric, typically of silk or a synthetic filament with slightly crinkled texture. It is used for women's scarves, blouses, and dresses.

Chikamatzu Monzaemon 1653–1725. Japanese dramatist who wrote over 150 plays for the puppet and ◊kabuki theatres in Osaka. His plays for puppets were usually either domestic tragedies such as *The Love Suicides at Sonezaki* 1703, or heroic historical dramas as in *The Battles of Coxinga* 1715. The plays are written in prose.

children's literature works specifically written for children. The earliest known illustrated children's book in English is ◊*Goody Two-Shoes* 1765, possibly written by Oliver Goldsmith. *Fairy tales* were originally part of a vast range of oral literature, credited only to the writer who first recorded them, such as Charles Perrault. During the 19th century several writers, including Hans Christian Andersen, wrote original stories in the fairy tale genre; others, such as the Grimm brothers, collected (and sometimes adapted) existing stories.

Early children's stories were written with a moral purpose; this was particularly true in the 19th century, apart from the unique case of Lewis Carroll's ◊*Alice* books. The late 19th century was the great era of children's literature in the UK, with Lewis Carroll, Beatrix Potter, Charles Kingsley, and J M Barrie. It was also the golden age of illustrated children's books, with such artists as Kate Greenaway and Randolph Caldecott. In the USA, Louise May Alcott's ◊*Little Women* 1869 and its sequels found a wide audience. Among the most popular 20th-century children's writers in English have been Kenneth Grahame (*The* ◊*Wind in the Willows* 1908) and A A Milne (◊*Winnie-the-Pooh* 1926) in the UK; and, in the USA, Laura Ingalls Wilder (*Little House on the Prairie* 1935), E B White (*Stuart Little* 1945, *Charlotte's Web* 1952), and Dr Seuss (*Cat in the Hat* 1957). Canadian Lucy Maud Montgomery's series that began with *Anne of Green Gables* 1908 was widely popular. *Adventure stories* have often appealed to children even when these were written for adults; examples include ◊*Robinson Crusoe* by Daniel Defoe; the satirical ◊*Gulliver's Travels* by Jonathan Swift, and ◊*Tom Sawyer* 1876 and *Huckleberry Finn* 1884 by Mark Twain. Many recent children's writers have been influenced by J R R Tolkien whose *The* ◊*Hobbit* 1937 and its sequel, the three-volume *Lord of the Rings* 1954–55, are set in the comprehensively imagined world of 'Middle-earth'. His friend C S Lewis produced the allegorical chronicles of Narnia, beginning with *The Lion, the Witch and the Wardrobe* 1950. Rosemary Sutcliff's *The Eagle of the Ninth* 1954, Philippa Pearce's *Tom's Midnight Garden* 1958, and Penelope Lively's *The Wild Hunt of Hagworthy* 1971 are other outstanding books by children's authors who have exploited a perennial fascination with time travel. Writers for younger children combining stories and illustrations of equally high quality include Maurice Sendak (*Where the Wild Things Are* 1963) and Quentin Blake (*Mister Magnolia* 1980). Roald Dahl's *James and the Giant Peach* 1961 is the first of his popular children's books which summon up primitive emotions and have an imperious morality. More realistic stories for teenagers are written by US authors such as Judy Blume and S E Hinton.

chimera or *chimaera* in Greek mythology, a fire-breathing animal with a lion's head, a goat's body, and a tail in the form of a snake; hence any apparent hybrid of two or more creatures. The chimera was killed by the hero ◊Bellerophon on the winged horse Pegasus.

chimurenga (Shona 'struggle') Zimbabwean pop music developed in the 1970s, particularly by Thomas Mapfumo (1945–), transposing to electric guitar the sound of the *mbira*, or thumb piano, an instrument of the region. Mapfumo used traditional rhythms and melodies in new ways combined with a political message.

Chinese architecture style of building in China. Traditionally of timber construction, few existing buildings predate the Ming dynasty (1368–1644), but records such as the *Ying Tsao Fa Shih/Method of Architecture* 1103 show that Chinese architecture changed little throughout the ages, either for the peasants or for the well-to-do. Curved roofs are a characteristic feature; also typical is the pagoda with a number of curved tiled roofs, one above the other. The Great Wall of China was built about 228–210 BC as a northern frontier defence, and Beijing's fine city walls, of which only a small section remains, date from the Ming period.

Chinese buildings usually face south, a convention which can be traced back to the 'Hall of Brightness', a building from the Zhou dynasty (1050–221 BC), and is still retained in the functionally Western-style Chinese architecture of the present day. Although some sections of Beijing have been destroyed by modernization it still contains fine examples of buildings from the Ming dynasty, such as the Altar of Heaven, the ancestral temple of the Ming tombs, and the Five Pagoda Temple. The introduction of Buddhism from India exerted considerable influence on Chinese architecture.

Chinese art the painting and sculpture of China. From the Bronze Age to the Cultural Revolution, Chinese art shows a stylistic unity unparalleled in any other culture. From about the 1st century AD Buddhism inspired much sculpture and painting. The **Han dynasty** (206 BC–AD 220) produced outstanding metalwork, ceramics, and sculpture. The **Song dynasty** (960–1278) established standards of idyllic landscape and nature painting in a delicate calligraphic style.

Neolithic art Accomplished pottery dates back to about 2500 BC, already showing a distinctive Chinese approach to form.

Bronze Age art Rich burial goods, with bronzes and jade carvings, survive from the second millennium BC, decorated with hieroglyphs and simple stylized animal forms. Astonishing life-size terracotta figures from the Qin period (about 221–206 BC) guard the tomb of Emperor Shi Huangdi in the old capital of Xian. Bronze horses, naturalistic but displaying the soft curving lines of the Chinese style, are a feature of the Han dynasty.

early Buddhist art Once Buddhism was established in China it inspired a monumental art, with huge rock-cut Buddhas and graceful linear relief sculptures at the monasteries of Yungang, about 460–535, and Longmen. Bronze images show the same curving lines and rounded forms.

Tang dynasty (618–907) Increasing sophistication is evident in idealized images and naturalistic portraits, such as the carved figures of Buddhist monks (Luohan). This period also produced brilliant metalwork and delicate ceramics, particularly of robed figures and animals. It is known that the aims and, broadly speaking, the style of Chinese painting were already well established, but few paintings survive, with the exception of some Tang scrolls and silk paintings.

Song dynasty (960–1278) The golden age of painting was during the Song dynasty. The imperial court created its own workshop, fostering a fine calligraphic art, mainly devoted to natural subjects – landscape, mountains, trees, flowers, birds, and horses – though genre scenes of court beauties were also popular. Scrolls, albums, and fans of silk or paper were painted with watercolours and ink, using soft brushes that produced many different effects. Painting was associated with literature, and painters added poems or quotations to their work to intensify the effect. Ma Yuan and Xia Gui (active *c.* 1180–1230) are among the painters; Mu-Chi was a monk known for exquisite brushwork. The Song dynasty also produced the first true porcelain, achieving a classic simplicity and delicacy in colouring and form.

Ming dynasty (1368–1644) Painters continued the landscape tradition, setting new standards in idealized visions. The painter Dong Qichang wrote a history and theory of Chinese painting. The Song style of porcelain gradually gave way to increasingly elaborate decoration in rich, polychrome enamels and the famous Ming blue-and-white patterned ware.

Qing dynasty (1644–1911) The so-called Individualist Spirits emerged, painters who developed bolder, personal styles of brushwork.

20th century The strong spirit that supported traditional art began to fade in the 19th and 20th centuries, but attempts to incorporate modernist ideas have been frowned on by the authorities. Not directly concerned with the representation of political events, Chinese art took some years before responding to the political upheavals of this century. Subsequently, response to official directives produced a period of Soviet-style Realism followed by a reversion to a peasant school of painting, which was the officially favoured direction for art during the Cultural Revolution.

influence Chinese art had a great impact on surrounding countries. The art of Korea was almost wholly inspired by Chinese example for many centuries. Along with Buddhism, Chinese styles of art were established in Japan in the 6th–7th centuries BC and continued to exert a profound influence, though Japanese culture soon developed an independent style.

Chinese literature the earliest written records in Chinese date from about 1500 BC; the earliest extant literary works date from about 800 BC.

poetry Chinese poems, often only four lines long, and written in the ancient literary language understood throughout China, consist of rhymed lines of a fixed number of syllables, ornamented by parallel phrasing and tonal pattern. The oldest poems are contained in the *Book of Songs* (800–600 BC). Some of the most celebrated Chinese poets are the nature poet T'ao Ch'ien (372–427), the master of technique Li Po, the autobiographical Bo Zhu Yi, and the wide-ranging Su Tung-p'o (1036–1101); and among the moderns using the colloquial language under European influence and experimenting in free verse are Hsu Chih-mo (1895–1931), and Pien Chih-lin (1910–   ).

prose Histories are not so much literary works as collections of edited documents with moral comment, whereas the essay has long been cultivated under strict rules of form and style. An example of the latter genre is *Upon the Original Way* by Han Yü (768–824), recalling the nation to Confucianism. Until the 16th century the short story was confined to the anecdote, startling by its strangeness and written in the literary language – for example, the stories of the poetic Tuan Ch'eng-shih (died 863); but after that time the more novelistic type of short story, written in the colloquial tongue, developed by its side. The Chinese novel evolved from the street storyteller's art and has consequently always used the popular language. The early romances *Three Kingdoms*, *All Men are Brothers*, and *Golden Lotus* are anonymous, the earliest known author of this genre being Wu Che'ng-en (*c.* 1505–1580); the most realistic of the great novelists is Ts'ao Chan (died 1763).

Twentieth-century Chinese novels have largely adopted European form, and have been influenced by Russia, as have the realistic stories of Lu Hsün. In typical Chinese drama, the stage presentation far surpasses the text in importance (the dialogue was not even preserved in early plays), but there have been experiments in the European manner. Some recent writing such as the stories of Bai Hua (1930–   ) has been energized by the tension between humanist individualism and the collectivist ideology of the communist state. Personal and family experience of China's social and political upheavals in the 20th century has been recorded in some distinguished autobiographical works such as *Wild Swans. Three Daughters of China* 1991 by Jung Ching (1952–   ).

chinoiserie in the decorative arts and architecture, the use of Chinese styles and motifs in Western art, especially in the late 17th to early 19th centuries. Chinese lacquerwork and porcelain were imported into Europe in the 17th century and became popular with Rococo designers.

chintz printed fabric, usually glazed, popular for furnishings. In England in the late 16th and 17th centuries the term was used for Indian painted and printed cotton fabrics (calicos) and later for European printed fabrics.

Such textiles were made in India from very early times. In England chintz became so popular by the early 18th century that in 1722 Parliament legislated against the importation and manufacture of chintz, to protect the British silk and wool industries. The legislation against manufacture was repealed 1744. In the mid-19th century chintz was superseded by a stronger fabric, ◊cretonne, but it has become popular again for soft furnishings.

Chippendale Thomas *c.* 1718–1779. English furniture designer. He set up his workshop in St Martin's Lane, London, 1753. His book *The Gentleman and Cabinet Maker's Director* 1754 was a significant contribution to furniture design. Although many of his most characteristic designs are Rococo, he also employed Louis XVI, Chinese, Gothic, and Neo-Classical styles. He worked mainly in mahogany.

Chirico Giorgio de 1888–1978. Greek-born Italian painter whose style presaged Surrealism in its use of enigmatic imagery and dreamlike settings, for example, *Nostalgia of the Infinite* 1911 (Museum of Modern Art, New York).

In 1917, with Carlo Carrà, he founded the school of ◊Metaphysical Painting, which aimed to convey a sense of mystery and hallucination. This was achieved by distorted perspective, dramatic lighting, and the use of dummies and statues in place of human figures. In the 1930s he repudiated the modern movement in art, and began reworking the styles of the old masters.

Chiron in Greek mythology, the son of Kronos by a sea nymph. A ◊centaur, he was the wise tutor of ◊Jason and ◊Achilles, among others.

chitarrone type of long-necked bass lute (archlute) incorporating freely vibrating bass strings which are twice the length (sounding an octave lower) of up to seven double courses of manually stopped strings, used in Renaissance and early Baroque ensembles to provide a firm and resonant bass line.

Chodowiecki Daniel Nikolaus 1726–1801. German painter and engraver, known for his intimate pictures of German middle-class life. His works include engravings of scenes from the

Seven Years' War and the life of Christ, and the portrait *The Parting of Jean Calas from his Family* 1767 (Berlin-Dahlem Museum).

choir body of singers, usually of sacred music, of more than one voice to a part, whose members are able to sight read music and hold a melody. A traditional cathedral choir of male voices is required to sing responses, hymns, and psalms appropriate to the church calendar.

The choir was the principal medium for the development of Renaissance polyphony, with instruments initially reading from vocal parts and only subsequently evolving distinct instrumental styles. The Venetian antiphonal style of Monteverdi and Gabrieli treats voices and instruments as opposing choirs. During the 19th century choir festivals became a popular feature of musical life, promoting mixed-voice choral singing by amateur groups.

choir in a cathedral, the area used by the choir, usually part of the chancel.

Cholmondeleys British all-female dance company founded 1984 by Lea Anderson, its chief choreographer and dancer. The group specializes in short, dry-humoured pieces characterized by a sharp and quirky movement style. *Baby, Baby, Baby* 1985, a pastiche of 1960s pop girl groups, illustrates their deadpan approach. Other more serious pieces include *No Joy*, an exploration of human behaviour that uses sign language.

The all-male counterpart, also founded by Lea Anderson 1988, is called the *Featherstonehaughs* (pronounced 'fan-shaws').

Chopin Frédéric (François) 1810–1849. Polish composer and pianist. He made his debut as a pianist at the age of eight. As a performer, Chopin revolutionized the technique of pianoforte-playing, turning the hands outwards and favouring a light, responsive touch. His compositions for piano, which include two concertos and other works with orchestra, are characterized by great volatility of mood, and rhythmic fluidity.

From 1831 he lived in Paris, where he became known in the fashionable salons, although he rarely performed in public. In 1836 the composer Liszt introduced him to Madame Dudevant (George ◊Sand), with whom he had a close relationship 1838–46. During this time she nursed him in Majorca for tuberculosis, while he composed intensively and for a time regained his health. His music was made the basis of the ballet *Les Sylphides* by Fokine 1909 and orchestrated by Alexander Gretchaninov (1864–1956), a pupil of Rimsky-Korsakov.

Nothing is more odious than music without hidden meaning.

Frédéric Chopin

Chopin Kate 1851–1904. US novelist and short-story writer. Her novel *The Awakening* 1899, the story of a married New Orleans woman's awakening to her sexuality, caused a sensation of hostile criticism, which effectively ended her career. It is now regarded as a classic of feminist sensibility. She was also the author of poignant tales of Creole and Cajun life in *Bayou Folk* 1894.

chorale traditional hymn tune of the German Protestant church, usually harmonized in four parts for singing by a congregation.

chord in music, a group of three or more notes sounded together. The resulting combination of tones may be either harmonious or dissonant.

choreography art of creating and arranging ballet and dance for performance; originally, in the 18th century, the art of dance notation.

chorus body of usually untrained male and female singers of secular unison songs, or providing the refrain element of solo verse song. A stage chorus in opera or musicals is normally a trained body of singers providing a dispersed accompaniment in four or more parts to principal soloists.

chorus in classical Greek drama, the group of actors who jointly comment on the main action or advise the main characters.

The action in Greek plays took place offstage; the chorus provided a link in the drama when the principals were offstage. The chorus did not always speak in unison; it was common for members of the chorus to show some individuality. The device of a chorus has also been used by later dramatists.

Chrétien de Troyes lived second half of the 12th century. French poet, born in Champagne. His epics, which introduced the concept of the ◊Holy Grail, include *Lancelot, ou le chevalier de la charrette*; *Perceval, ou le conte du Graal*, written for Philip, Count of Flanders; *Erec*; *Yvain, ou le chevalier au Lion*; and other Arthurian romances.

Christie Agatha (born Miller) 1890–1976. English detective novelist who created the characters Hercule ◊Poirot and Miss Jane ◊Marple. She wrote more than 70 novels, including *The Murder of Roger Ackroyd* 1926 and *Ten Little Indians* 1939. Her play *The Mousetrap*, which opened in London 1952, is the longest continuously running show in the world.

She was born in Torquay, married Col Archibald Christie 1914, and served during World War I as a nurse. Her first crime novel, *The Mysterious Affair at Styles* 1920, introduced Hercule Poirot. She often broke 'purist' rules, as in *The Murder of Roger Ackroyd* in which the narrator is the murderer. She caused a nationwide sensation 1926 by disappearing for ten days, possibly because of amnesia, when her husband fell in love with another woman.

Christie Julie 1940– . English film actress who became a star following her award-winning performance in *Darling* 1965. She also appeared in *Doctor Zhivago* 1965, *The Go-Between* and *McCabe and Mrs Miller*, both 1971, *Don't Look Now* 1973, *Heat and Dust* 1982, and *Power* 1986.

Christine de Pisan 1364–1430. French poet and historian. Her works include love lyrics, philosophical poems, a poem in praise of Joan of Arc, a history of Charles V, and various defences of women, including *La Cité des dames/The City of Ladies* 1405.

Born in Venice, she was brought to France as a child when her father entered the service of Charles V. In 1389, after the death of her husband, the Picardian nobleman Etienne Castel, she began writing to support herself and her family.

Just as women's bodies are softer than men's, so their understanding is sharper.

Christine de Pisan
The City of Ladies 1405

Christo adopted name of Christo Javacheff 1935– . US sculptor, born in Bulgaria, active in Paris in the 1950s and in New York from 1964. He is known for his 'packages': structures, such as bridges and buildings, and even areas of coastline, temporarily wrapped in synthetic fabric tied down with rope. The *Running Fence* 1976 installed across several miles of open country in California was a typically ephemeral work. In 1991 he mounted a simultaneous project, *The Umbrellas*, in which a series of enormous umbrellas were erected across valleys in both the USA and Japan.

Christoff Boris 1918– . Bulgarian bass singer of soulful, massive tone whose operatic debut 1946 marked him out for darker roles, including Mussorgsky's Boris Godunov, Ivan the Terrible in Rimsky-Korsakov's *The Maid of Pskov* 1868–72, and Boito's Mephistopheles. His greater range is revealed in recordings of the complete songs of Mussorgsky.

Christus Petrus active 1440s, died 1472/3. Flemish painter, a master at Bruges from 1444 and follower of Jan van ◊Eyck (some of whose paintings he may have completed after the master's death). His *The Madonna with Two Saints* 1457 (Städel, Frankfurt) is an early example of the use of perspective in N European art.

chromaticism in music, the use of enriched harmonies for added expression, practised by 19th-century composers mainly of French and Russian schools, for example Rimsky-Korsakov, Scriabin, Debussy, Ravel, Messiaen, Honegger, and Dutilleux. Chromatic harmonies are ambiguous consonances rather than expressionist dissonances, influenced by the sounds of music imported from Indonesia and Japan and heard, for example, at the Paris Exposition 1889, which influenced Debussy.

chromatic scale musical scale proceeding by semitones. In theory the inclusion of all 12 notes makes it a neutral scale without the focus provided by the seven-tone diatonic major or minor scale; in practice however, owing to small deviations from equal temperament, it is possible for a trained ear to identify the starting point of a randomly chosen chromatic scale.

Chukovsky Kornei Ivanovitch 1882–1969. Russian critic and poet. The leading authority on the 19th-century Russian poet Nekrasov, he was also an expert on the Russian language, as in, for example, *Zhivoi kak zhizn/Alive as Life* 1963. He was also beloved as 'Grandpa' Kornei Chukovsky for his nonsense poems, which owe much to English nursery rhymes and nonsense verse.

church building designed as a Christian place of worship. Churches were first built in the 3rd century, when persecution ceased under the Holy Roman emperor Constantine. The original church design was based on the Roman ◊basilica, with a central nave, aisles either side, and an apse at one end.

Church Frederic Edwin 1826–1900. US painter, a student of Thomas Cole and follower of the ◊Hudson River School's tradition of grand landscape. During the 1850s he visited South America and the Arctic and became known for his meticulous and dramatic depictions of exotic landscapes.

Churchill Caryl 1938– . English dramatist. Her plays include the innovative and feminist *Cloud Nine* 1979 and *Top Girls* 1982, a study of the hazards encountered by 'career' women throughout history; *Serious Money* 1987, which satirized the world of London's brash young financial brokers; and *Mad Forest* 1990, set in Romania during the overthrow of the Ceausescu regime.

Churchill Charles 1731–1764. British satirical poet. At one time a priest in the Church of England, he wrote coarse personal satires dealing with political issues. His poems include *The Rosciad* 1761, a satire on the London stage; *The Prophecy of Famine* 1763, the first of his political satires; and *Epistle to Hogarth* 1763, which he wrote after a quarrel with the artist, William Hogarth.

Churrigueresque style of late-Baroque architecture characterized by lavish sculptural decoration, originating in Spain in the late 17th century. The term is also used to describe other forms of Spanish late-Baroque architecture, especially in Mexico and South America.

The style was named after the Churriguera family of architects and sculptors; *José Benito de Churriguera* (1665–1725), the best-known member of the family, was responsible for the layout of the town of Nuevo Baztan, Spain 1709. Its lavishness was taken to extremes by its two leading exponents, **Narciso Tomé** (active 1715–1742) and **Pedro de Ribera** (1683–1742); the latter was responsible for the wildly extravagant doorway to the Hospicio San Fernando, Madrid 1738.

Chu Ta (Pa Ta Shan Jen) *c.* 1625–*c.* 1705. Chinese painter; a member of the Ming imperial family, he became a Buddhist priest and led a solitary life. He painted many landscapes but is better known for his often whimsical portrayals of birds, animals, and plants. His style is remarkable for its simplicity and spontaneity, a bird or leaf being depicted with just a few bold strokes.

CIAM (abbreviation for *Congrès Internationaux d'Architecture Moderne*) loose association of architects responsible from 1928 for the formulation and dissemination of a Modernist orthodoxy (see ◊Modern Movement). CIAM's predominantly Functionalist ethic, which included strict delination of housing, industrial, and commercial zones by green belts and an emphasis on high-rise mass housing, was to dominate architecture and town planning until the 1950s.

Cibachrome in photography, a process of printing directly from transparencies. It can be home-processed and the rich, saturated colours are highly resistant to fading. It was introduced 1963.

Cicero Marcus Tullius 106–43 BC. Roman orator, writer, and politician. His speeches and philosophical and rhetorical works have often been regarded as models of Latin prose, and his letters provide a picture of contemporary Roman life. As consul 63 BC he exposed the Roman politician Catiline's conspiracy in four major orations.

Born in Arpinium, Cicero became an advocate in Rome, spent three years in Greece studying oratory, and after the dictator Sulla's death distinguished himself in Rome with the prosecution of the corrupt Roman governor, Varres. When the First Triumvirate was formed 59 BC, Cicero was briefly exiled and devoted himself to literature. He sided with Pompey during the civil war (49–48) but was pardoned by Julius Caesar and returned to Rome. After Caesar's assassination 44 BC he supported Octavian (the future emperor Augustus) and violently attacked Antony in speeches known as the *Philippics*. On the reconciliation of Antony and Octavian he was executed by Antony's agents.

There is nothing so absurd but some philosopher has said it.

Cicero *De Divinatione*

Cid, **El cantar** or **poema de mio** anonymous Spanish epic poem dating from *c.* 1140, the greatest and earliest surviving literary epic of Castile. The Cid (Arabic *sayyid*, 'master') was an historical figure, Rodrigo Díaz de Vivar (*c.* 1040–1099), a knight of Castile. The poem, interspersed with lyrical passages and lively dialogue, celebrates his real and legendary exploits against the Moors and the adventures of his daughters.

Cid, The (French 'Le Cid') tragicomedy by Pierre ◊Corneille 1637. The lovers Rodrigue and Chimène are separated by a quarrel between their fathers. Rodrigue kills Chimène's father in a duel, but then defends Seville heroically against an attack by the Moors, winning the name of Cid (Arabic *sayyid* 'master'). After Rodrigue defeats Chimène's champion in a second duel, the lovers are reconciled by the king of Castile.

Cimabue Giovanni (Cenni di Peppi) *c.* 1240–1302. Italian painter, active in Florence, traditionally styled the 'father of Italian painting'. His paintings retain the golden background of Byzantine art but the figures have a new naturalism. Among the works attributed to him are *Maestà* about 1280 (Uffizi, Florence), a huge Gothic image of the Virgin, with a novel softness and solidity that points forwards to Giotto. His *Crucifix* in Sta Croce, Florence, was damaged by the flood of 1966.

Cimarosa Domenico 1749–1801. Italian composer of operas including *Il Matrimonio segreto/The Secret Marriage* 1792, also of orchestral and keyboard music.

cimbalom in music, a Hungarian pedestal ◊dulcimer modernized during the 19th century from a gipsy instrument, and consisting of a box-shaped resonator over which strings are stretched laterally, the performer playing front to back rather than across, using light beaters. The sound is brittle, not unlike a ◊fortepiano.

Cimino Michael 1943– . US film director whose reputation was made by *The Deer Hunter* 1978, a moral epic set against the Vietnam War (five Academy Awards). A later film, the Western *Heaven's Gate* 1980, lost its backers, United Artists, some $40 million, and subsequently became a byword for commercial disaster in the industry. He also made *The Year of the Dragon* 1986, and *Desperate Hours* 1990.

A film lives, becomes alive, because of its shadows, its spaces.

Michael Cimino in *Variety* July 1980

'Cinderella' traditional European fairy tale, of which about 700 versions exist, including one by

Charles ◊Perrault. Cinderella is an ill-treated youngest daughter who is enabled by a fairy godmother to attend the royal ball. She captivates Prince Charming but must flee at midnight, losing a tiny glass slipper by which the prince later identifies her.

cine camera camera that takes a rapid sequence of still photographs – 24 frames (pictures) each second. When the pictures are projected one after the other at the same speed on to a screen, they appear to show movement, because our eyes hold on to the image of one picture before the next one appears.

The cine camera differs from an ordinary still camera in having a motor that winds the film on. The film is held still by a claw mechanism while each frame is exposed. When the film is moved between frames, a semicircular disc slides between the lens and the film and prevents exposure.

cinema 20th-century form of art and entertainment consisting of 'moving pictures' in either black and white or colour, projected on to a screen. Cinema borrows from the other arts, such as music, drama, and literature, but is entirely dependent for its origins on technological developments, including the technology of action photography, projection, sound reproduction, and film processing and printing (see ◊photography).

film history The first moving pictures were shown in the 1890s. Thomas A Edison persuaded James J Corbett (1866–1933), the world boxing champion 1892–97, to act a boxing match for a film. The Lumière brothers in France, Latham in the USA, R W Paul (1869–1943) in England, and others were making moving pictures of actual events (for example, *The Derby* 1896, shown in London on the evening of the race), and of simple scenes such as a train coming into a station. In 1902 Georges Méliès of France made the fantasy story film *A Trip to the Moon*, and in 1903 Edwin Porter directed *The Great Train Robbery* for Edison. This was a story in a dramatic setting, and cost about $100 to make. The film was shown all over the world, and earned more than $20,000.

film technique For a number of years, films of indoor happenings were shot out of doors by daylight in Hollywood, USA. The fairly constant sunny climate was the basis of its success as a centre of film production. The first film studio was Edison's at Fort Lee, New Jersey, but the Astoria Studios in New York City turned out many popular silents and early 'talkies', since it was near Broadway and could therefore make use of the theatre stars on its doorstep. In England, the pioneer company of Cricks and Martin set up a studio at Mitcham. D W Griffith, the US director, revolutionized film technique, introducing the close-up, the flashback, the fade-out, and the fade-in. His first epic was *The Birth of a Nation* 1915, and his second, *Intolerance*, with spectacular scenes

in the Babylonian section, followed 1916.

film personalities At first, players' names were of no importance, although one who appeared nameless in *The Great Train Robbery*, G M Anderson (1882–1971), afterwards became famous as 'Bronco Billy' in a series of cowboy films, the first Westerns. The first movie performer to become a name was Mary Pickford; cinemagoers found her so attractive that they insisted on knowing who she was. World War I virtually stopped film production in Europe, but Hollywood continued to flourish in the 1920s, creating such stars as Rudolph Valentino, Douglas Fairbanks Sr, Lillian Gish, Gloria Swanson, Richard Barthelmess (1895–1963), and Greta Garbo (dramatic actors); and Charlie Chaplin, Buster Keaton, and Harold Lloyd (comedians). The introduction of sound from the late 1920s ended the careers of silent stars with unsuitable voices, and changed the style of acting to one more natural than mimetic. British stage stars who made the transition to film include Edith Evans, Alec Guinness, Laurence Olivier, and Ralph Richardson. US stars of the golden Hollywood era include Clark Gable, the Marx Brothers, Judy Garland, Greta Garbo, and Joan Crawford. Although many Hollywood stars were 'made' by the studios, American stage actors such as Humphrey Bogart, Henry Fonda, Spencer Tracy, Katharine Hepburn, and Bette Davis also became stars in 1930s Hollywood and continued to act in films for many years.

artistic development Concern for artistry began with Griffith, but also developed in Europe, particularly in the USSR and Germany, where directors exploited film's artistic possibilities during both the silent and the sound eras. Silent films were never completely silent; there was usually a musical background, integral to the film, whether played by a solo pianist in a suburban cinema or a 100-piece orchestra in a big city theatre. (In Japan there was always a narrator.) The arrival of sound films (John Barrymore as *Don Juan* 1926 and Al Jolson as *The Jazz Singer* 1927), seen at first as having only novelty value, soon brought about a wider perspective and greater artistic possibilities through the combination of sight and sound. Successful directors of early sound films included Jean Renoir in France, Fritz Lang and F W Murnau in Germany, Mauritz Stiller in Sweden, Alfred Hitchcock in Britain, John Ford, and Frank Capra in the USA. After World War II, Japanese films were first seen in the West (although the industry dates back to the silent days), and India developed a thriving cinema industry. Apart from story films, the industry produced newsreels of current events and documentaries depicting factual life, of which the pioneers were US filmmaker Robert Flaherty (*Nanook of the North* 1922, *Man of Aran* 1934) and the Scot John Grierson (*Drifters* 1929, *Night Mail* 1936); animated cartoon films, which achieved their first success with Patrick Sullivan's (1887–1933) *Felix the Cat* 1917, were later surpassed in popularity by Walt Disney's Mickey

cinema: chronology

1826–34	Various machines invented to show moving images: the stroboscope, zoetrope, and thaumatrope.
1872	Eadweard Muybridge demonstrated movement of horses' legs by using 24 cameras.
1877	Invention of Praxinoscope; developed as a projector of successive images on screen 1879 in France.
1878–95	Marey, a French physiologist, developed various types of camera for recording human and animal movements.
1887	Augustin le Prince produced the first series of images on a perforated film; Thomas A Edison, having developed the phonograph, took the first steps in developing a motion-picture recording and reproducing device to accompany recorded sound.
1888	William Friese-Greene (1855–1921) showed the first celluloid film and patented a movie camera.
1889	Edison invented 35-mm film.
1890–94	Edison, using perforated film, developed his Kinetograph camera and Kinetoscope individual viewer; developed commercially in New York, London, and Paris.
1895	The Lumière brothers projected, to a paying audience, a film of an oncoming train arriving at a station. Some of the audience fled in terror.
1896	Charles Pathé introduced the Berliner gramophone, using discs in synchronization with film. Lack of amplification, however, made the performances ineffective.
1899	Edison tried to improve amplification by using banks of phonographs.
1900	Attempts to synchronize film and disc were made by Leon Gaumont (1863–1946) in France and Goldschmidt in Germany, leading later to the Vitaphone system of the USA.
1902	Georges Méliès made *Le Voyage dans la lune/A Trip to the Moon*.
1903	The first Western was made in the USA: *The Great Train Robbery* by Edwin Porter.
1906	The earliest colour film (Kinemacolor) was patented in Britain by George Albert Smith (1864–1959).
1907–11	The first films shot in the Los Angeles area called Hollywood. In France, Emile Cohl (1857–1938) experimented with film animation.
1910	With the influence of US studios and fan magazines, film actors and actresses began to be recognized as international stars.
1911	The first Hollywood studio, Horsley's Centaur Film Company, was established, followed in 1915 by Carl Laemmle's Universal City and Thomas Ince's studio.
1912	In Britain, Eugene Lauste designed experimental 'sound on film' systems.
1914–18	Full newsreel coverage of World War I.
1915	*The Birth of a Nation*, D W Griffith's epic on the American Civil War, was released in the USA.
1917	35 mm was officially adopted as the standard format for motion picture film by the Society of Motion Picture Engineers of America.
1918–19	A sound system called Tri-Ergon was developed in Germany, which led to sound being recorded on film photographically. Photography with sound was also developed in the USA by Lee De Forest in his Phonofilm system.
1923	First sound film (as Phonofilm) demonstrated.
1926	*Don Juan*, a silent film with a synchronized music score, was released.
1927	Release of the first major sound film, *The Jazz Singer*, consisting of some songs and a few moments of dialogue, by Warner Brothers, New York City. The first Academy Awards (Oscars) were presented.
1928	Walt Disney released his first Mickey Mouse cartoon, *Steamboat Willie*. The first all-talking film, *Lights of New York*, was released.
1930	*The Big Trail*, a Western filmed and shown in 70-mm rather than the standard 35-mm format, was released. 70 mm is still used, mainly for big-budget epics such as *Lawrence of Arabia*.
1932	Technicolor (three-colour) process introduced and used for a Walt Disney cartoon film.
1935	*Becky Sharp*, the first film in three- colour Technicolor was released.
1937	Walt Disney released the first feature-length (82 minutes) cartoon, *Snow White and the Seven Dwarfs*.
1939	*Gone With the Wind*, regarded as one of Hollywood's greatest achievements, was released.
1952	Cinerama, a wide-screen presentation using three cameras and three projectors, was introduced in New York.
1953	Commercial 3-D (three-dimensional) cinema and wide-screen CinemaScope were launched in the USA. CinemaScope used a single camera and projector to produce a wide-screen effect with an anamorphic lens. The 3-D cameras were clumsy and the audiences disliked wearing the obligatory glasses. The new wide-screen cinema was accompanied by the introduction of Stereographic sound, which eventually became standard.
1959	The first film in Smell-O-Vision, *The Scent of Mystery*, was released. The process did not catch on.
1980	Most major films were released in Dolby stereo.
1981	Designated 'the Year of Color Film' by director Martin Scorsese in a campaign to draw attention to, and arrest, the deterioration of colour film shot since 1950.
1982	One of the first and most effective attempts at feature-length, computer-generated animation was *Tron*, Walt Disney's $20-million bid to break into the booming fantasy market. 3-D made a brief comeback; some of the films released that used the process, such as *Jaws 3-D* and *Friday the 13th Part 3*, were commercial successes, but the revival was short-lived.
1987	US House Judiciary Committee petitioned by leading Hollywood filmmakers to protect their work from electronic 'colorization', the new process by which black-and-white films were tinted for television transmission.
1988	Robert Zemeckis' (1952–) *Who Framed Roger Rabbit* set new technical standards in combining live action with cartoon animation.

Awards for Best Film from Four Top Festivals

Cannes Film Festival

Palme d'Or for Best Film

1985　*When Father Was Away on Business* (Yugoslavia)
1986　*The Mission* (UK)
1987　*Under the Sun of Satan* (France)
1988　*Pelle the Conqueror* (Denmark)
1989　*sex, lies and videotape* (USA)
1990　*Wild at Heart* (USA)
1991　*Barton Fink* (USA)
1992　*The Best Intentions* (Sweden)
1993　*The Piano* (NZ/Australia); *Farewell My Concubine* (Hong Kong/China)

Venice Film Festival

Golden Lion for Best Film

1985　*Sans Toit ni loi* aka *Vagabonde* (France)
1986　*Le Rayon vert* (France)
1987　*Au Revoir les Enfants* (France)
1988　*La Leggenda del Santo Bevitore/The Legend of the Holy Drinker* (Italy)
1989　*Beiqing Chengshi/City of Sadness* (Taiwan)
1990　*Rosencrantz and Guildenstern are Dead* (UK)
1991　*Urga* (Russia)
1992　*Story of Qiu Ju* (China)
1993　*Short Cuts* (USA); *Three Colours-Blue* (Poland)

Berlin Film Festival

Golden Bear for Best Film

1985　*Wetherby* (UK); *Die Frau und der Fremde* (FRG)
1986　*Stammheim* (FRG)
1987　*The Theme* (USSR)
1988　*Red Sorghum* (China)
1989　*Rain Man* (USA)
1990　*Skylarks on a String* (Czechoslovakia); *Music Box* (USA)
1991　*La Casa del Sorriso/House of Smiles* (Italy)
1992　*Grand Canyon* (USA)
1993　*Woman from the Lake of Centred Souls* (China); *Wedding Banquet* (Taiwan)

British Academy of Film and Television Arts (BAFTA)

Best Film Awards

1985　*The Killing Fields* (UK)
1986　*The Purple Rose of Cairo* (USA)
1987　*A Room with a View* (UK)
1988　*Jean de Florette* (France)
1989　*The Last Emperor* (USA)
1990　*Dead Poets Society* (USA)
1991　*Goodfellas* (USA)
1992　*The Commitments* (UK)
1993　*Howards End* (UK)

Mouse character, who first appeared in *Steamboat Willie* 1928, and the feature-length *Snow White and the Seven Dwarfs* 1937 and others. During the 1930s classic dramas and screwball comedies were made; during the 1940s war films predominated; and during the 1950s *film noir* and Technicolor musicals competed with early television.

the influence of television By the 1950s, increasing competition from television, perceived at the time as a threat to the studio system of film production and distribution, led the film industry to concentrate on special effects (CinemaScope, Cinerama, Todd AO) and wide-screen spectaculars dealing with historical and biblical themes, for example, *Cleopatra* 1963. Also exploited were the horror genre and areas of sexuality and violence considered unsuitable for family television viewing. Other popular genres were the Chinese Western or kung-fu film, which had a vogue in the 1970s, and science fiction, such as *Star Wars* 1977, *Close Encounters of the Third Kind* 1977, and *ET* 1982, with expensive special effects.

Throughout the 1980s cinema production was affected by the growth during the preceding decade of the video industry, which made films available for viewing on home television screens.

CinemaScope trade name for a wide-screen process using anamorphic lenses, in which images are compressed during filming and then extended during projection over a wide curved screen. The first film to be made in CinemaScope was *The Robe* 1953.

cinéma vérité (French 'cinema truth') school of documentary filmmaking that aims to capture real events and situations as they occur without major directorial, editorial, or technical control. It first came into vogue around 1960 with the advent of lightweight cameras and sound equipment.

The American school of cinema vérité, called 'Direct Cinema', used the camera as a passive observer of events. Its main practitioners were Richard Leacock (1921–), D A Pennebaker (1930–), and Albert and David Maysles (1926– , 1932–).

Cinerama wide-screen process devised 1937 by Fred Waller of Paramount's special-effects department. Originally three 35-mm cameras and three projectors were used to record and project a single image. Three aspects of the image were recorded and then projected on a large curved screen with the result that the images blended together to produce an illusion of vastness. The first Cinerama film was the travelogue *This Is Cinerama* 1952, but the first story feature was *How the West Was Won* 1962. The process was subsequently abandoned in favour of a single-lens 70-mm process.

Circe in Greek mythology, an enchantress living on the island of Aeaea. In Homer's *Odyssey*, she turned the followers of ◊Odysseus into pigs. Odysseus, bearing the herb moly provided by Hermes to protect him from the same fate, forced her to release his men.

circumlocution roundabout, verbose way of speaking or writing when someone tries to appear impressive or is being deliberately unclear, perhaps to disguise the truth.

Charles Dickens in the novel *Little Dorrit* invented the Circumlocution Office as a satirical representation of a typical government department.

circus (Latin 'circle') entertainment, often held in a large tent ('big top'), involving performing animals, acrobats, and clowns. In 1871 P T ◊Barnum created the 'Greatest Show on Earth' in the USA. The popularity of animal acts decreased in the 1980s. Originally, in Roman times, a circus was an arena for chariot races and gladiatorial combats.

cire perdue or ***lost-wax technique*** bronze-casting method. A model is made of wax and enclosed in an envelope of clay and plaster, with a small hole in the bottom. When heat is applied, the wax melts and runs away through the hole, and the clay and plaster becomes a hard mould. Molten bronze is poured in and allowed to cool; then the clay envelope is cut away.

The result is a bronze cast that exactly reproduces the original and is formed in a single piece. The bronze will be hollow if the original wax model was made around a core of burnt clay. The earliest examples of the technique date from about 3000 BC, found both in Ancient Egypt and Ur.

cithara ancient musical instrument, resembling a lyre but with a flat back. It was strung with wire and plucked with a plectrum or (after the 16th century) with the fingers. The bandurria and laud, still popular in Spain, are instruments of the same type.

cittern plucked stringed instrument, usually of almond shape, with a flat back. It originated about 1500, is easy to play, and was a popular alternative to the lute. Larger forms include the pandora and the orpharion. It was superseded in the 19th century by the guitar.

cladding thin layer of external covering on a building; for example, tiles, wood, stone, concrete.

Clair René. Adopted name of René-Lucien Chomette 1898–1981. French filmmaker, originally a poet, novelist, and journalist. His early comedy *Sous les Toits de Paris/Under the Roofs of Paris* 1930 made great use of the new innovation

of sound. His other films include *Entr'acte* 1924, *Le Million*, and *A nous la Liberté* both 1931.

Clapton Eric 1945– . English blues and rock guitarist, singer, and songwriter. Originally a blues purist, then one of the pioneers of heavy rock with Cream 1966–68, he returned to the blues after making the landmark album *Layla and Other Assorted Love Songs* 1970 by Derek and the Dominos. Solo albums include *Journeyman* 1989 and the acoustic *Unplugged* 1992.

Clapton, born in Surrey, was a member of the Yardbirds 1963–65 but left when the group turned from rhythm and blues to experimental rock. During his year with John Mayall's Bluesbreakers 1965–66, 'Clapton is God' graffiti began to appear on British walls. After the groundbreaking rock of Cream, he formed the short-lived supergroup Blind Faith 1969. He sought a lower profile 1970–72, playing with US duo Delaney and Bonnie, and adopted a more laid-back style with his solo album *461 Ocean Boulevard* 1974. Other albums include *Money and Cigarettes* 1983 and *August* 1986.

Clare John 1793–1864. English poet. His work includes *Poems Descriptive of Rural Life and Scenery* 1820, *The Village Minstrel* 1821, and *The Shepherd's Calendar* 1827. The dignified simplicity and truth of his descriptions of both landscape and emotions have been rediscovered and appreciated in the 20th century.

Born at Helpstone, near Peterborough, the son of a farm labourer, Clare spent most of his life in poverty. He was given an annuity from the Duke of Exeter and other patrons, but had to turn to work on the land. He spent his last 20 years in Northampton asylum. His early life is described in his autobiography, first published 1931.

He could not die when trees were green,/ For he loved the time too well.

John Clare 'The Dying Child'

---

clarinet any of a family of single-reed ◊woodwind instruments of cylindrical bore, developed from the double-reed chalumeau by German instrument-maker J C Denner about 1700 and used in the Baroque orchestra as an instrument of trumpetlike tone. In their concertos for clarinet, Mozart and Weber exploited its range of tone from the dark chalumeau low register rising to brilliance, and its capacity for sustained dynamic control.

A broad range of clarinets remain in current use, including piccolo E flat and D, soprano B flat and A (standard orchestral clarinets), alto F (military band), B flat bass, and sinuous contra-basses in E flat and B flat, the latter virtually inaudible on its own.

Clarissa novel 1747–48 by Samuel ◊Richardson in the form of letters between the characters. The heroine is pursued by the attractive but unprincipled Lovelace. He rapes her and the consequent loss of autonomy and identity leads to her tragic decline and eventual death. The book's length (originally eight volumes) helps to explain its current lack of popularity, but Richardson's psychological subtlety and inexhaustible sympathy for his women characters ensure a place for the book in the development of the novel form.

Clark Kenneth, Lord Clark 1903–1983. English art historian, director of the National Gallery, London, 1934–45. His books include *Leonardo da Vinci* 1939, *Landscape into Art* 1949, and *The Nude* 1956, which he considered his best book. He popularized the history of art through his television series *Civilization*, broadcast in the UK 1969.

All great civilizations, in their early stages, are based on success in war.

Kenneth Clark *Civilization* 1969

Clark Michael 1962– . Scottish avant-garde dancer whose bare-bottomed costumes and outlandish stage props have earned him as much celebrity as his innovative dance technique. A graduate of the Royal Ballet school, he formed his own company, the Michael Clark Dance Company, in the mid-1980s and became a leading figure in the British ◊avant-garde dance scene. In 1991 he played Caliban in Peter Greenaway's film *Prospero's Books*. He premiered his *Mmm... Modern Masterpiece* 1992.

Clarke Arthur C(harles) 1917– . English science-fiction and non-fiction writer. His works include *Childhood's End* 1953 and *2001: A Space Odyssey* 1968 (which was made into a film by Stanley Kubrick), and *2010: Odyssey Two* 1982.

Any sufficiently advanced technology is indistinguishable from magic.

Arthur C Clarke *The Lost Worlds of 2001*

Clarke Jeremiah 1659–1707. English composer. Organist at St Paul's, he composed 'The Prince of Denmark's March', a harpsichord piece that was arranged by Henry ◊Wood as a 'Trumpet Voluntary' and wrongly attributed to Purcell.

Clarke Marcus Andrew Hislop 1846–1881. Australian writer. Born in London, he went to Australia when he was 18 and worked as a journalist in Victoria. He wrote *For the Term of his Natural Life* 1874, a novel dealing with life in the early Australian prison settlements.

Clash, the English rock band 1976–85, a driving force in the British ◊punk movement. Reggae and rockabilly were important elements in their sound. Their albums include *The Clash* 1977, *London Calling* 1979, and *Combat Rock* 1982.

The Clash's left-wing political commitment was reflected in their lyrics; the main songwriters were founder members Joe Strummer (John Mellors, 1952–) and Mick Jones (1955–).

Classicism in art, music, and literature, a style that emphasizes the qualities traditionally considered characteristic of ancient Greek and Roman art, that is, reason, balance, objectivity, restraint, and strict adherence to form. The term Classicism (also ◊Neo-Classicism) is often used to characterize the culture of 18th-century Europe, and contrasted with 19th-century Romanticism.

Claudel Paul 1868–1955. French poet and dramatist. A fervent Catholic, he was influenced by the Symbolists and achieved an effect of mystic allegory in such plays as *L'Annonce faite à Marie/ Tidings Brought to Mary* 1912 and *Le Soulier de satin/The Satin Slipper* 1929, set in 16th-century Spain. His verse includes *Cinq Grandes Odes/Five Great Odes* 1910.

Claude Lorrain (Claude Gelée) 1600–1682. French landscape painter, active in Rome from 1627. His distinctive, luminous, Classical style had a great impact on late 17th- and 18th-century taste. In his paintings, insignificant figures (mostly mythological or historical) are typically lost in great expanses of poetic scenery, as in *The Enchanted Castle* 1664 (National Gallery, London).

Born in Lorraine, he established himself in Rome, where his many patrons included Pope Urban VIII. His *Liber Veritatis* (begun 1644), which contains some 200 drawings after his finished works, was made to prevent forgeries of his work by contemporaries.

Claudet Antoine François Jean 1797–1867. French-born pioneer of photography who worked in London. He made ◊daguerreotype portraiture commercially viable when he discovered that chlorine and iodine vapour increased the sensitivity of the plate and greatly reduced exposure time. His other innovations include the earliest light meter and the introduction of painted backgrounds into studio portraits.

Claudian (Claudius Claudianus) *c.* 370–404. Last of the great Latin poets of the Roman Empire, probably born in Alexandria, Egypt. He wrote official panegyrics, epigrams, and the mythological epic *The Rape of Proserpine*.

claves musical percussion instrument of Latin American origin, consisting of small hardwood batons struck together.

clavichord small domestic keyboard instrument of delicate tone developed in the 16th century on the principle of the ◊monochord. The first clavichords had few strings, using a keyboard-based array of metal tangents combining the function of plectrum and bridge to define and produce a range of pitches. Later instruments increased the number of strings. The sound is clear and precise, and a form of vibrato (◊bebung) is possible by varying finger pressure on the key. It was superseded in the 18th century by the fortepiano.

clavier in music, general term for an early ◊keyboard instrument.

Clay Frederic 1838–1889. British composer, born in Paris. Clay wrote light operas and the cantata *Lalla Rookh* 1877, based on a poem by Thomas Moore.

Clayton Jack 1921– . English film director, originally a producer. His first feature, *Room at the Top* 1958, heralded a new maturity in British cinema. Other works include *The Innocents* 1961, *The Great Gatsby* 1974, and *The Lonely Passion of Judith Hearne* 1987.

Cleese John 1939– . English actor and comedian who has written for and appeared in both television programmes and films. On British television, he is particularly associated with the comedy series *Monty Python's Flying Circus* and *Fawlty Towers*. His films include *Monty Python and the Holy Grail* 1974, *The Life of Brian* 1979, and *A Fish Called Wanda* 1988.

clef in music, a symbol prefixed to a five-line stave indicating the pitch range to which the written notes apply. Introduced as a visual aid in plainchant notation, it is based on the letter G (treble clef), F (bass clef), or C (soprano, alto, tenor clefs), establishing middle C (C4) as a prime reference pitch, G4 a fifth higher for higher voices, and F3 a fifth lower for lower voices.

The C clef is now comparatively rare, except for viola, cello, and bassoon; for most other instruments the G and F clefs are standard.

Cleland John 1709–1789. English author, best known for his bawdy novel *Fanny Hill, the Memoirs of a Woman of Pleasure* 1748–49 which he wrote to free himself from his creditors. The book was considered immoral. Cleland was called before the Privy Council, but was granted a pension to prevent further misdemeanours.

Clemens Samuel Langhorne. Real name of the US writer Mark ◊Twain.

Clemente Francesco 1952– . Italian painter, at the forefront of ◊Neo-Expressionism in the 1970s. His use of hand-drawn imagery, rendered in an expressive, naive, and colourful style, was a reaction to the high-tech approach of ◊Photorealism. The erotic, gesturing figures that characterize his work are frequently mutilated and often images of himself, as in *Midnight Sun*

No. VI 1982 (private collection). Roman art and Indian mystical and folkloric references have provided the inspiration for much of his work.

Clementi Muzio 1752–1832. Italian pianist and composer. He settled in London 1782 as a teacher and then as proprietor of a successful piano and music business. He was the founder of the present-day technique of piano playing, and his series of studies, *Gradus ad Parnassum* 1817, is still in use.

Clements John 1910–1988. British actor and director whose productions included revivals of Restoration comedies and the plays of George Bernard Shaw.

clerihew humorous verse form invented by Edmund Clerihew ◊Bentley, characterized by a first line consisting of a person's name. The four lines rhyme AABB, but the metre is often distorted for comic effect. An example, from Bentley's *Biography for Beginners* 1905, is: 'Sir Christopher Wren/Said, I am going to dine with some men./If anybody calls/Say I am designing St Paul's.'

click-track in film music, a technique to aid the coordination of music and film action invented by composers Carl Stalling and Scott ◊Bradley. Holes punched in the soundtrack of a composer's working print click at a desired tempo measured in frames, allowing the composer to construct a musical phrase to climax at a precise moment in the film action.

A feature of cartoon films from 1937, the click-track was also employed by the composer Max ◊Steiner for feature romance films, in which context it is called 'Mickey-Mousing'.

Cliff Clarice 1899–1972. English pottery designer. Her Bizarre ware, characterized by brightly coloured floral and geometric decoration on often geometrically shaped china, became very popular in the 1930s and increasingly collectable in the 1970s and 1980s.

Born in the Potteries, she started as a factory apprentice at the age of 13, trained at evening classes, and worked for many years at the Wilkinson factory. In 1963 she became art director of the factory, which was part of the Royal Staffordshire Pottery in Burslem.

Clift (Edward) Montgomery 1920–1966. US film and theatre actor. A star of the late 1940s and 1950s in films such as *Red River* 1948, *A Place in the Sun* 1951, and *From Here to Eternity* 1953, he was disfigured in a car accident 1957 but continued to make films. He played the title role in *Freud* 1962.

Clio in Greek mythology, the ◊Muse of history.

cloak a one-piece enveloping garment worn on the shoulders, tied or clasped at the neck or chest, and reaching the knees or ankles. A cloak is generally longer than a cape, which is usually elbow-or hip-length. It often has slits cut into the front of the fabric for arms. Cloaks were popular during the late 19th century and again in the 1960s.

cloisonné ornamental craft technique in which thin metal strips are soldered in a pattern on to a metal surface, and the resulting compartments (*cloisons*) filled with coloured ◊enamels and fired. The technique was probably developed in the Byzantine Middle East and traded to Asia and Europe. Cloisonné vases and brooches were made in medieval Europe, but the technique was perfected in Japan and China during the 17th, 18th, and 19th centuries.

cloister in a convent or monastery, a covered walkway, usually surrounding and opening on to a courtyard. The church would be linked to other areas of the convent or monastery via the cloisters.

Close Glenn 1948– . US actress who received Academy Award nominations for her roles as the embittered 'other woman' in *Fatal Attraction* 1987 and as the scheming antiheroine of *Dangerous Liaisons* 1988. She played Gertrude in Franco Zeffirelli's film of *Hamlet* 1990 and appeared as an opera star in *Meeting Venus* 1991.

Her first film was *The World According to Garp* 1982; other screen appearances include *The Big Chill* 1983 and *Jagged Edge* 1985. More recently, she has had roles on Broadway in Tom Stoppard's *The Real Thing* and Michael Frayn's *Benefactors*.

Clouet François *c.* 1515–1572. French portrait painter who succeeded his father Jean Clouet as court painter. He worked in the Italian Mannerist style. His half-nude portrait *The Lady in Her Bath* about 1570 (National Gallery, Washington) is traditionally thought to be of Diane de Poitiers, but may be a likeness of Marie Touchet, mistress of Charles IX.

Clouet Jean (known as *Janet*) *c.* 1486–1541. French artist, court painter to Francis I. His portraits and drawings, often compared to Holbein's, show an outstanding naturalism.

Clough Arthur Hugh 1819–1861. English poet. Many of his lyrics are marked by a melancholy scepticism that reflects his struggle with his religious doubt.

---

*Thou shalt not kill; but need'st not strive/
Officiously to keep alive.*

Arthur Hugh Clough
The Last Decalogue 1861

Clurman Harold 1901–1980. US theatre director and critic. He helped found the independent Group Theatre 1931 (other members were Lee Strasberg and Elia Kazan), and directed plays by Clifford Odets (*Awake and Sing* 1935) and William Saroyan. He wrote theatre criticism for the *New Republic* 1948–52 and *The Nation* from 1953.

cluster in music, the effect of playing simultaneously and without emphasis all the notes within a chosen interval. It was introduced by US composer Henry ◊Cowell in the piano piece *The Banshee* 1925, for which using a ruler on the keys is recommended. Its use in film and radio incidental music symbolizes a hallucinatory or dreaming state, presumably because it resembles an internalized disturbance of normal hearing.

Clytemnestra in Greek mythology, the wife of ◊Agamemnon. With the help of her lover Aegisthus, she murdered her husband and his paramour Cassandra on his return from the Trojan War, and was in turn killed by her son Orestes.

Coade stone artificial cast stone widely used in the UK in the late 18th century and early 19th century for architectural ornamentation, keystones, decorative panels, and rustication.

Coades Artificial Stone Manufactory was opened 1769 in Lambeth, S London, by Eleanor Coade (1709–1796), a modeller in clay. She allied mass production to the Neo-Classical taste of the time with great success.

coat outdoor garment with sleeves, collar, and sometimes a hood, which covers the body from the shoulders to the waist, hips, knees, or ankles. Designed to protect the body from the weather, coats are both fashion and utilitarian garments. See also ◊jacket and ◊mackintosh.

Coates Nigel 1949– . English architect. While teaching at the Architectural Association in London in the early 1980s, Coates and a group of students founded NATO (**N**arrative **A**rchitecture **To**day) and produced an influential series of manifestos and drawings on the theme of the imaginative regeneration of derelict areas of London. Coates promoted an eclectic and narrative form of architecture that went against the contemporary grain.

Give me, Lord, neither poverty nor riches.

William Cobbett

Cobbett William 1763–1835. British Radical politician and journalist, who published the weekly *Political Register* 1802–35. He spent much time in North America. His crusading essays on the conditions of the rural poor were collected as *Rural Rides* 1830.

Born in Surrey, the self-taught son of a farmer, Cobbett enlisted in the army 1784 and served in Canada. He subsequently lived in the USA as a teacher of English, and became a vigorous pamphleteer, at this time supporting the Tories. In

1800 he returned to England. With increasing knowledge of the sufferings of the farm labourers, he became a Radical and leader of the working-class movement. He was imprisoned 1809–11 for criticizing the flogging of British troops by German mercenaries. He visited the USA again 1817–19. He became a strong advocate of parliamentary reform, and represented Oldham in the Reformed Parliament after 1832.

Cobden-Sanderson Thomas James 1840–1922. British bookbinder and painter. Influenced by the designer William ◊Morris and the Pre-Raphaelite painter ◊Burne- Jones, he opened his own work-shop in Maiden Lane, London, 1884; he founded the Doves Press 1900–16.

Cobra group of European Expressionist painters formed by the Dutch artist Karel Appel 1948. Other leading members were the Dane Asgar Jorn (1914–1973) and the Belgian-born painters Corneille (1922–) and Pierre Alechinsky (1927–). Stongly influenced by the art of both children and the insane, the group developed an expressive and dynamic form of abstract paint-ing, using thick, heavily worked paint and strong colours.

Coburn Alvin Langdon 1882–1966. American-born photographer who settled in Britain. He produced several books of atmospheric photogravures, including *New York* 1910 and a portrait album *Men of Mark* 1913. His work tended towards abstraction and in 1917 he exhibited with the Vorticists (an English avant-garde group of artists) a number of frag-mented, abstract images which he called 'Vortographs'.

Coburn James 1928– . US film actor, popular in the 1960s and 1970s. Rough-hewn and tall, he was ideal for starring roles in action films such as *The Magnificent Seven* 1960, *Pat Garrett and Billy the Kid* 1973, and *Cross of Iron* 1977.

Cochran C(harles) B(lake) 1872–1951. British impresario who promoted entertainment ranging from wrestling and roller-skating to Diaghilev's Ballets Russes.

I am interested in everything so long as it is well done. I would rather see a good jug-gler than a bad Hamlet.

C B Cochran *Secrets of a Showman*

Cochran Eddie 1938–1960. US rock-and-roll singer, songwriter, and guitarist who created clas-sic rock songs like 'Summertime Blues' 1958 and 'C'mon Everybody' 1959 as well as slower romantic numbers ('Dark, Lonely Street' 1958, 'Three Steps to Heaven' 1960).

Cochran was born in Oklahoma but began his career in Los Angeles as a session musician. His first record was 'Skinny Jim' 1956, and he appeared in the 1956 film *The Girl Can't Help It* singing 'Twenty Flight Rock'. He was killed in a car crash while touring the UK with fellow rocker Gene Vincent (1935–1971).

Cockaigne, Land of in medieval English folk-lore, a mythical country of leisure and idleness, where fine food and drink were plentiful and to be had for the asking.

Cockerell Charles 1788–1863. English architect who built mainly in a Neo-Classical style derived from antiquity and from the work of Christopher Wren. His buildings include the Cambridge University Library (now the Cambridge Law Library) 1837–42 and the Ashmolean Museum and Taylorian Institute in Oxford 1841–45.

Cocteau Jean 1889–1963. French poet, drama-tist, and film director. A leading figure in European Modernism, he worked with Picasso, Diaghilev, and Stravinsky. He produced many volumes of poetry, ballets such as *Le Boeuf sur le toit/The Ox on the Roof* 1920, plays, for example, *Orphée/Orpheus* 1926, and a mature novel of bourgeois French life, *Les Enfants terribles/Children of the Game* 1929, which he made into a film 1950.

Victor Hugo ... a madman who thought he was Victor Hugo.

Jean Cocteau *Opium*

---

coda in music, a concluding section of a move-ment added to emphasize the destination key.

codex (plural *codices*) a book from before the invention of printing: in ancient times wax-coated wooden tablets; later, folded sheets of parchment were attached to the boards, then bound together. The name 'codex' was used for all large works, collections of history, philosophy, and poetry, and during the Roman Empire designated collections of laws. During the 2nd century AD codices began to replace the earlier rolls. They were widely used by the medieval Christian church to keep records, from about 1200 onwards.

codpiece fabric bag covering the male genitals, worn over men's breeches during the 15th and 16th centuries as a part of everyday dress.

Coetzee J(ohn) M 1940– . South African author whose novel *In the Heart of the Country* 1975 dealt with the rape of a white woman by a black man. In 1983 he won Britain's Booker Prize for *The Life and Times of Michael K*. Other works include *Waiting for the Barbarians* 1982 and *Foe* 1987.

Cohan George M(ichael) 1878–1942. US com-poser. His Broadway hit musical *Little Johnny*

Jones 1904 included his songs 'Give My Regards to Broadway' and 'Yankee Doodle Boy'. 'You're a Grand Old Flag' 1906 further associated him with popular patriotism, as did his World War I song 'Over There' 1917.

Cohan Robert Paul 1925– . US choreographer and founding artistic director of the ◊London Contemporary Dance Theatre (LCDT) 1969–89; artistic adviser of LCDT 1992– . A student of Martha ◊Graham and co-director of her company 1966–69, his choreography is a development of her style. Blending elements of American jazz dance and Graham's modern dance, Cohan's work is marked by a thematic vagueness and a willingness to utilize modern technology as in *Video-Life* 1987. His works include *Cell* 1969, a study on the loss of individuality; *Waterless Method of Swimming Instruction* 1974; and the television ballet *A Mass for Man* 1985.

Colbert Claudette. Stage name of Claudette Lily Cauchoin 1905– . French-born film actress who lived in Hollywood from childhood. She was ideally cast in sophisticated, romantic roles, but had a natural instinct for comedy and appeared in several of Hollywood's finest, including *It Happened One Night* 1934 and *The Palm Beach Story* 1942.

Cole Thomas 1801–1848. US painter, founder of the ◊Hudson River School of landscape artists. Apart from panoramic views such as *The Oxbow* 1836 (Metropolitan Museum of Art, New York), he painted a dramatic historical series, *The Course of Empire* 1836 (New York Historical Society), influenced by the European artists Claude Lorrain, Turner, and John Martin. Cole wrote *An Essay on American Scenery* 1835.

Coleman Ornette 1930– . US alto saxophonist and jazz composer. In the late 1950s he rejected the established structural principles of jazz for free avant-garde improvisation. He has worked with small and large groups, ethnic musicians of different traditions, and symphony orchestras. His albums include *The Shape of Jazz to Come* 1959, *Chappaqua Suite* 1965, and *Skies of America* 1972.

Cole, Old King legendary British king, supposed to be the father of St Helena, who married the Roman emperor Constantius, father of Constantine; he is also supposed to have founded Colchester. The historical Cole was possibly a north British chieftain named Coel, of the 5th century, who successfully defended his land against the Picts and Scots. The nursery rhyme is recorded only from 1709.

Coleridge Samuel Taylor 1772–1834. English poet, one of the founders of the Romantic movement. A friend of Southey and Wordsworth, he collaborated with the latter on *Lyrical Ballads* 1798, a collection which had a profound influence on the development of the English Romantic movement. His poems include 'The Rime of the Ancient Mariner', 'Christabel', and 'Kubla Khan'; critical works include *Biographia Literaria* 1817.

While at Cambridge University, Coleridge was driven by debt to enlist in the Dragoons, and then in 1795, as part of an abortive plan to found a communist colony in the USA with Robert Southey, married Sarah Fricker, from whom he afterwards separated. He became addicted to opium and from 1816 lived in Highgate, London, under medical care. As a philosopher, he argued that even in registering sense-perceptions the mind was performing acts of creative imagination, rather than being a passive arena in which ideas interact mechanistically. A brilliant talker and lecturer, he was expected to produce some great work of philosophy or criticism. His *Biographia Literaria* 1817, much of it based on German ideas, is full of insight but its formlessness and the limited extent of his poetic output indicates a partial failure of promise.

No man was ever yet a great poet, without being at the same time a profound philosopher.

Samuel Taylor Coleridge
Biographia Literaria 1817

Coleridge Sara 1802–1852. English woman of letters, editor of the work of her father Samuel Taylor Coleridge. She was also a writer and translator.

Colette Sidonie-Gabrielle 1873–1954. French writer. At 20 she married Henri Gauthier-Villars, a journalist known as 'Willy', under whose name and direction her four 'Claudine' novels, based on her own early life, were written. Divorced 1906, she worked as a striptease and mime artist for a while, but continued to write. Works from this later period include *Chéri* 1920, *La Fin de Chéri/The End of Chéri* 1926, and *Gigi* 1944.

collage (French 'gluing' or 'pasting') technique of pasting paper and other materials to a surface to create a picture. Picasso and Braque were the first to use collage, and the technique was frequently exploited by the Dadaists and Surrealists. Exponents include Hans Arp, Max Ernst, and Kurt Schwitters.

Many artists also experimented with *photomontage*, creating compositions from pieces of photographs rearranged with often disturbing effects. John Heartfield was an outstanding early photomontagist.

Collier Lesley 1947– . British ballerina, a principal dancer of the Royal Ballet from 1972. She created roles in Kenneth MacMillan's *Anastasia*

1971 and *Four Seasons* 1975, Hans van Manen's *Four Schumann Pieces* 1975, Frederick Ashton's *Rhapsody*, and Glen Tetley's *Dance of Albiar* both 1980.

Collins (William) Wilkie 1824–1889. English author of mystery and suspense novels. He wrote *The Woman in White* 1860 (with its fat villain Count Fosco), often called the first English detective novel, and *The Moonstone* 1868 (with Sergeant Cuff, one of the first detectives in English literature).

Collins Phil(lip David Charles) 1951– . English pop singer, drummer, and actor. A member of the group Genesis from 1970, he has also pursued a successful middle-of-the-road solo career since 1981, with hits (often new versions of old songs) including 'In the Air Tonight' 1981 and 'Groovy Kind of Love' 1988. He starred as the train robber Buster Edwards in the film *Buster* 1988.

Collins William 1721–1759. British poet. His *Persian Eclogues* 1742 were followed in 1746 by his series 'Odes', including the poem 'To Evening'.

Collodi Carlo. Pen name of Carlo Lorenzini 1826–1890. Italian journalist and writer who in 1881–83 wrote *Le avventure di Pinocchio/The Adventures of Pinocchio*, a children's story of a wooden puppet that became a human boy.

How it happened that Mr Cherry, the carpenter, found a piece of wood that laughed and cried like a child.

Carlo Collodi
The Adventures of Pinocchio 1883

Colman Ronald 1891–1958. English actor, in Hollywood from 1920, who played suave and dashing roles in *Beau Geste* 1924, *The Prisoner of Zenda* 1937, *Lost Horizon* 1937, and *A Double Life* 1947, for which he received an Academy Award.

Colombo Joe 1930–1971. Italian industrial designer, a member of the postwar generation of designers who created a sophisticated, sculptural style for banal industrial goods. He is best known for his plastic chairs designed for Kartell, notable among them his 'Chair 4860' 1965 which brought a new respectability to the material.

Colombo moved from a background in fine art into design 1955. Based in Milan, he designed many other furniture pieces and domestic appliances with the same rigorous style, among them his 'Poker' card table 1968 and his air conditioner for Candy 1970, for a wide range of manufacturers.

Colonna Vittoria *c.* 1492–1547. Italian poet. Many of her Petrarchan sonnets idealize her husband, who was killed at the battle of Pavia 1525. She was a friend of Michelangelo, who addressed sonnets to her.

colonnade row of columns supporting arches or an entablature.

colophon decorative device on the title page or spine of a book, the trademark of the individual publisher. Originally a colophon was an inscription on the last page of a book giving the writer or printer's name and the place and year of publication.

coloratura in music, a rapid ornamental vocal passage with runs and trills. A *coloratura soprano* is a light, high voice suited to such music.

Colosseum amphitheatre in ancient Rome, begun by the emperor Vespasian to replace the one destroyed by fire during the reign of Nero, and completed by his son Titus AD 80. It was 187 m/615 ft long and 49 m/160 ft high, and seated 50,000 people. Early Christians were martyred there by lions and gladiators. Caged animals were brought to the arena from stone cells below by a series of lifts and pulleys, and an awning could be raised above it to shelter spectators from the sunlight. It could also be flooded for mock sea battles.

Colossus of Rhodes bronze statue of Apollo erected at the entrance to the harbour at Rhodes 292–280 BC. Said to have been about 30 m/100 ft high, it was counted as one of the Seven Wonders of the World, but in 224 BC fell as a result of an earthquake.

Coltrane John (William) 1926–1967. US jazz saxophonist who first came to prominence 1955 with the Miles ◊Davis quintet, later playing with Thelonious Monk 1957. He was a powerful and individual artist, whose performances featured much experimentation. His 1960s quartet was highly regarded for its innovations in melody and harmony.

Like Charlie Parker, Coltrane marked a watershed in jazz. The free-jazz movement of the 1960s owed much to his extended exploratory solos, for example on *Giant Steps* 1959, the year he traded tenor saxophone for soprano. A highly original musician, he has been much imitated, but the deeply emotional tone of his playing, for example on *A Love Supreme* 1964, is impossible to copy.

Colum Padraic 1881–1972. Irish poet and dramatist. He was associated with the foundation of the Abbey Theatre, Dublin, where his plays *Land* 1905 and *Thomas Muskerry* 1910 were performed. His *Collected Poems* 1932 show his gift for lyrical expression.

Columbia Pictures US film production and distribution company founded 1924. It grew out of a smaller company founded 1920 by Harry and Jack Cohn and Joe Brandt. Under Harry Cohn's guidance, Columbia became a major studio by the 1940s, producing such commercial hits as *Gilda* 1946. After Cohn's death 1958 the studio remained successful, producing such international films as *Lawrence of Arabia* 1962.

column in architecture, a structure, round or polygonal in plan, erected vertically as a support for some part of a building. Cretan paintings reveal the existence of wooden columns in Aegean architecture about 1500 BC. The Hittites, Assyrians, and Egyptians also used wooden columns, and they are a feature of the monumental architecture of China and Japan. In Classical architecture there are five principal types of column; see ◊order.

Colville Alex 1920– . Canadian painter, a prominent Realist artist, whose style has affinities with that of Andrew ◊Wyeth. His somewhat melancholic paintings depict smooth, broad-bodied nudes and figures of working men as remote from the Canadian landscape they inhabit. He is also an accomplished animal painter, for example *Hound in Field* 1958 (National Gallery of Canada, Ottawa).

Comédie Française French national theatre (for both comedy and tragedy) in Paris, founded 1680 by Louis XIV. Its base is the Salle Richelieu on the right bank of the river Seine, and the Théâtre de l'Odéon, on the left bank, is a testing ground for avant-garde ideas.

comedy drama that aims to make its audience laugh, usually with a happy or amusing ending, as opposed to ◊tragedy. The comic tradition has enjoyed many changes since its Greek roots; the earliest comedy developed in ancient Greece, in the topical and fantastic satires of Aristophanes. Great comic dramatists include Shakespeare, Molière, Carlo Goldoni, Pierre de Marivaux, George Bernard Shaw, and Oscar Wilde. Genres of comedy include pantomime, satire, farce, black comedy, and ◊commedia dell'arte.

Comedy is the last refuge of the noncōn-formist mind.

Gilbert Seldes on comedy
New Republic Dec 1954

The comic tradition was established by the Greek dramatists Aristophanes and Menander, and the Roman writers Terence and Plautus. In medieval times, the Vices and Devil of the Morality plays developed into the stock comic characters of the Renaissance *comedy of humours* with such notable villains as Ben Jonson's Mosca in *Volpone*. The timeless comedies

of Shakespeare and Molière were followed in England during the 17th century by the witty *comedy of manners* of Restoration writers such as George Etherege, William Wycherley, and William Congreve. Their often coarse but always vital comedies were toned down in the later Restoration dramas of Richard Sheridan and Oliver Goldsmith. Sentimental comedy dominated most of the 19th century, though little is remembered in the late 20th century, which prefers the realistic tradition of Shaw and the elegant social comedies of Wilde. The polished comedies of Nöel Coward and Terence Rattigan from the 1920s to 1940s were eclipsed during the late 1950s and the 1960s by a trend towards satire and cynicism as seen in the works of Joe Orton and Peter Nichols, alongside absurdist comedies by Samuel Beckett, Jean Genet, and Tom Stoppard. From the 1970s the 'black comedies' of Alan Ayckbourn have dominated the English stage, with the political satires of Dario ◊Fo affecting the radical theatre.

Comme des Garçons trade name of Rei ◊Kawakubo, Japanese fashion designer. Her asymmetrical, seemingly shapeless designs, often sombre in colour and sometimes torn and crumpled, combine Eastern and Western ideas of clothing.

commedia dell'arte popular form of Italian improvised comic drama in the 16th and 17th centuries, performed by trained troupes of actors and involving stock characters and situations. It exerted considerable influence on writers such as Molière and Carlo Goldoni, and on the genres of ◊pantomime, harlequinade, and the ◊Punch and Judy show. It laid the foundation for a tradition of mime, strong in France, that has continued with the modern mime of Jean-Louis Barrault and Marcel Marceau.

community architecture movement enabling people to work directly with architects in the design and building of their own homes and neighbourhoods. Projects include housing at Byker, Newcastle, UK, by Ralph ◊Erskine, and the work of the Lewisham Self-Build Housing Association, London, 1977–80, pioneered by Walter ◊Segal; the revitalization of the town of Bologna, Italy; and the University of Louvain, Belgium, by Lucien Kroll (1927–).

community dance movement to encourage the practice and appreciation of dance in the community. Community dance projects, funded by arts bodies and local authorities, have existed in Britain since the 1960s.

Composite in classical architecture, one of the five types of ◊column. See ◊order.

Composition in Red, Yellow and Blue oil painting by Piet ◊Mondrian 1920 (Stedelijk, Amsterdam) in which primary colours and grey and black are composed in squares and rectangles banded by black borders. Representing Mondrian's search for ultimate simplicity in geometric composition, it has become a key work of the 20th century, greatly influencing modern design and architecture.

Compton-Burnett Ivy 1892–1969. English novelist. She used dialogue to show reactions of small groups of characters dominated by the tyranny of family relationships. Her novels, set at the turn of the century, include *Pastors and Masters* 1925, *More Women Than Men* 1933, and *Mother and Son* 1955.

computer art art produced with the help of a computer. Since the 1950s the aesthetic use of computers has been increasingly evident in most artistic disciplines, including film animation, architecture, and music. Computer graphics has been the most developed area, with the 'paintbox' computer liberating artists from the confines of the canvas. It is now also possible to programme computers in advance to generate graphics, music, and sculpture, according to 'instructions' which may include a preprogrammed element of unpredictability. The first major exhibition of computer art was 'Cybernetic Serendipity' 1968, at the Institute of Contemporary Arts, London.

Conceptual art or *Concept art* or *Conceptualism*, a style of art, originating in the 1960s in the USA, which aims to express ideas rather than create visual images. Its materials include, among others, photographs, written information, diagrams, sound, and video tapes. Continuing the tradition of ◊Dada and ◊anti-art, Conceptual art aims to raise questions about the nature of art by flouting artistic conventions. As well as its theorist Sol LeWitt (1928–), its practitioners include Joseph Kosuth (1945–), Allan Krapow, and Bruce Nauman (1941–).

Conceptual art overlaps with ◊performance art where it uses the human body as a medium for expression; some artists, such as Joseph ◊Beuys, are practitioners of both.

concertante term in music descriptive of an orchestral concerto in which a number of instruments perform solo, as in the sinfonia concertante works of Haydn and Mozart.

concertina portable reed organ related to the ◊accordion but smaller in size and hexagonal in shape, with buttons for keys. It was invented in England in the 19th century.

concert master in music, the leader of an orchestra, usually the principal violinist.

concerto composition, usually in three movements, for solo instrument (or instruments) and orchestra. It developed during the 18th century from the *concerto grosso* form for string orchestra, in which a group of solo instruments (concerto) is contrasted with a full orchestra (ripieno).

Corelli and Torelli were early concerto composers, followed by Vivaldi, Handel, and Bach (*Brandenburg Concertos*). Mozart wrote about 40 concertos, mostly for piano. Recent concertos by Ligeti (*Double Concerto* 1972 for flute and oboe), Berio (*Concerto for Two Pianos* 1972–73), and Carter (*Violin Concerto* 1990) have developed the concerto relationship along new lines.

concerto grosso musical term for orchestra (Italian 'grand consort') transferred to the musical form predating the 18th-century symphony. The concerto grosso was a composition for a relatively small ensemble featuring a solo instrumental group or concertino in opposition to an accompanying group or ripieno.

concert pitch standard pitch to which concert ensembles tune up. In a symphony orchestra it is normally the pitch A4, which is common to instruments of the string orchestra. It is given by the oboe, otherwise by the concert master (principal violin) or deputy, or by the piano or organ if featured, as their tuning is fixed in advance.

Conchobar in Celtic mythology, king of Ulster whose intended bride, Deirdre, eloped with Noísi. She died of sorrow when Conchobar killed her husband and his brothers.

concrete building material composed of cement, stone, sand, and water. It has been used since Egyptian and Roman times. Since the late 19th century, it has been increasingly employed as an economical alternative to materials such as brick and wood, and has been combined with steel to increase its tension capacity. See ◊reinforced concrete and ◊prestressed concrete.

history
c. 5600 BC Earliest discovered use of concrete at Lepenski Vir, Yugoslavia (hut floors in Stone Age village).

2500 BC Concrete used in Great Pyramid at Giza by Egyptians.

2nd century BC Romans accidentally discovered the use of lime and silicon/alumina to produce 'pozzolanic' cement.

AD 127 Lightweight concrete (using crushed pumice as aggregate) used for walls of Pantheon, Rome.

Medieval times Concrete used for castles (infill in walls) and cathedrals (largely foundation work).

1756 John Smeaton produced the first high-quality cement since Roman times (for rebuilding of Eddystone lighthouse, England).

1824 Joseph Aspdin patented Portland cement in Britain.

1854 William Wilkinson patented reinforced concrete in Britain – first successful use in a building.

1880s First continuous-process rotary cement kiln installed (reducing costs of manufacturing cement).

1898 François Hennébique produced first multi-storey reinforced concrete building in Britain (factory in Swansea).

1926 Eugène Freysinnet began experiments on prestressed concrete in France.

1930s USA substituted concrete for limestone during federal building projects of the Great Depression; also used extensively for pavements, roadbeds, bridge approaches, dams, and sports facilities (stadiums, swimming pools, tennis courts, playgrounds).

1940s–1950s Much use of poured concrete to rebuild war-torn cities of Europe and the Middle East.

1960s–1990s Widespread use of concrete in industrialized countries as an economical house and office building material instead of traditional materials.

concrete music (French *musique concrète*) music created by reworking natural sounds recorded on disc or tape, developed 1948 by Pierre Schaeffer and Pierre Henry in the drama studios of Paris Radio. *Concrete sound* is pre-recorded natural sound used in electronic music, as distinct from purely synthesized tones or noises.

Conder Charles 1868–1909. Australian artist, born in London, who painted in watercolour and oil. In 1888 Conder joined Tom ◊Roberts in Melbourne forming the Australian Impressionist group which became known as the ◊Heidelberg School.

Although his early work, such as *The Departure of the SS Orient – Circular Quay* 1888 (Art Gallery of New South Wales, Sydney), is distinctly Impressionist in style, he later became known for his delicate watercolours painted on silk and for series of lithograph prints, such as *Carnival* 1905 (executed following his return to Europe 1890).

conductor in music, the director of an orchestra who beats time, cues entries, and controls the overall expression and balance of a performance.

Conductors of ballet and opera are normally resident, on a full-time contract, available for the ongoing preparation of new repertoire. Conductors of symphony orchestras are more often freelance, star performers in their own right, under temporary contract for concert or recording purposes and thus more reliant on the expertise of orchestras.

Confucius (Latinized form of **Kong Zi**, 'Kong the master') 551–479 BC. Chinese sage whose name is given to the ethical system of Confucianism, placing emphasis on moral order and the observance of the established patriarchal family and social relationships of authority, obedience, and mutual respect. He devoted his life to relieving suffering among the poor through governmental and administrative reform. *The Analects of Confucius*, a compilation of his teach-ings, was published after his death and within 300 years of his death, his teaching was adopted by the Chinese state.

Study the past, if you would divine the future.

Confucius

conga Latin American dance, originally from Cuba, in which the participants form a winding line, take three steps forwards or backwards, and then kick.

Congreve William 1670–1729. English drama-tist and poet. His first success was the comedy *The Old Bachelor* 1693, followed by *The Double Dealer* 1694, *Love for Love* 1695, the tragedy *The Mourning Bride* 1697, and *The Way of the World* 1700. His plays, which satirize the social affecta-tions of the time, are characterized by elegant wit and wordplay, and complex plots.

conjunto (Spanish 'band') rural Mexican music featuring accordion and percussion, an influence on Texas country music and ◊Tex-Mex. Cuban salsa bands are also often called *conjuntos*.

Connery Sean 1930– . Scottish film actor, the first interpreter of James Bond in several films based on the novels of Ian Fleming. His films include *Dr No* 1962, *From Russia with Love* 1963, *Marnie* 1964, *Goldfinger* 1964, *Diamonds Are Forever* 1971, *A Bridge Too Far* 1977, *The Name of the Rose* 1986, and *The Untouchables* 1987 (Academy Award).

Connolly Cyril 1903–1974. English critic and author. As founder and editor of the literary mag-azine *Horizon* 1930–50, he had considerable critical influence. His works include *The Rock Pool* 1935, a novel of artists on the Riviera, and *The Unquiet Grave* 1944, a series of reflections published under the pseudonym of Palinurus.

Imprisoned in every fat man a thin one is wildly signalling to be let out.

Cyril Connolly 1937

Conrad Joseph. Pen name of Teodor Jozef Conrad Korzeniowski 1857–1924. English novel-ist, born in the Ukraine of Polish parents. He joined the French merchant navy at the age of 17 and first learned English at 21. His greatest works include the novels ◊*Lord Jim* 1900, *Nostromo* 1904, *The Secret Agent* 1907, and *Under Western Eyes* 1911, the short novel ◊*Heart of Darkness* 1902 and the short story 'The Shadow Line' 1917. These combine a vivid sensuous evocation of various lands and seas with a rigorous, humane scrutiny of moral dilemmas, pitfalls, and desperation.

Conrad is regarded as one of the greatest of modern novelists. His prose style, varying from eloquently sensuous to bare and astringent, keeps the reader in constant touch with a mature, truth-seeking, creative mind.

The terrorist and the policeman come from the same basket.

Joseph Conrad *The Secret Agent*

Conran Jasper 1959– . English fashion designer known for using quality fabrics to create comfortable garments. He launched his first collection 1978 and has rarely altered the simple, successful style he then adopted. He has also designed costumes for the stage.

Conran Terence 1931– . British designer and retailer of furnishings, fashion, and household goods. He was founder of the Storehouse group of companies, including Habitat and Conran Design, with retail outlets in the UK, the USA, and elsewhere.

In 1964 he started the Habitat company, then developed Mothercare. The Storehouse group gained control of British Home Stores 1986.

conservation, architectural attempts to maintain the character of buildings and historical areas. In England this is subject to a growing body of legislation that has designated more ◊listed buildings. There are now over 6,000 conservation areas throughout England alone.

consonance in music, a combination of two or more tones that is pleasing to the ear. It is the opposite of a dissonance, and is judged consonant by the absence of a ◊beat frequency.

consort in music, term for a chamber ensemble of Renaissance or Baroque instruments of uniform sonority, for example recorders or viols. A non-uniform ensemble, comprising mixed instruments, is called a *broken consort*.

Constable John 1776–1837. English artist, one of the greatest landscape painters of the 19th century. He painted scenes of his native Suffolk, including *The ◊Haywain* 1821 (National Gallery, London), as well as castles, cathedrals, landscapes, and coastal scenes in other parts of Britain. Constable inherited the Dutch tradition of sombre Realism, in particular the style of Jacob ◊Ruisdael. He aimed to capture the momentary changes of the weather as well as to create monumental images of British scenery, as in *The White Horse* 1819 (Frick Collection, New York) and *Salisbury Cathedral from the Bishop's Grounds* 1827 (Victoria and Albert Museum, London).

Constable's paintings are remarkable for their atmospheric effects and were admired by many French painters including Eugène Delacroix. Notable are *The Leaping Horse* 1825 (Royal Academy of Arts, London), *The Cornfield* 1826 (National Gallery, London), and *Dedham Vale* 1828 (National Gallery of Scotland, Edinburgh). His many oil sketches are often considered among his best work.

Constable first worked in his father's mills in East Bergholt, Suffolk, but in 1795 was sent to study art in London. He was finally elected to the Royal Academy 1829. His many imitators included his son **Lionel**. In Nov 1990 *The Lock* 1824 was sold at Sotheby's, London, to a private collector for the record price of £10.78 million.

Constant de Rebecque (Henri) Benjamin 1767–1830. French writer and politician. An advocate of the Revolution, he opposed Napoleon and in 1803 went into exile. Returning to Paris after the fall of Napoleon 1814 he proposed a constitutional monarchy. He published the autobiographical novel *Adolphe* 1816, which reflects his affair with Madame de ◊Staël, and later wrote the monumental study *De la Religion* 1825–31.

Constructivism revolutionary movement in Russian art and architecture, founded in Moscow 1917 by Vladimir Tatlin, which drew its inspiration and materials from modern industry and technology. Initially confined to sculpture, its ideas were later adopted and expanded upon in architecture. Associated with the movement was the artist and architect El Lissitzky, the artists Naum Gabo and Antoine Pevsner, and the architects Vladimir Melnikov and Alexander (1883–1959), Leonid (1880–1933), and Viktor (1882–1950) Vesnin. By 1932 official Soviet disapproval had brought the movement effectively to a close, but its ideas had already spread to Europe, influencing the ◊Bauhaus and De ◊Stijl schools of architecture and design. Today, ◊Deconstructionism and much ◊High Tech architecture reflect its influence.

Inspired by Cubism and Futurism, Constructivist artists sought to produce abstract forms from industrial materials. Tatlin's early abstract pieces, made of wood, metal, and clear plastic, were hung on walls or suspended from ceilings. In architecture, the movement produced technologically advanced, machinelike buildings, as in the Vesnin brothers' design for the Pravda building, Leningrad (now St Petersburg) 1923. However, it was Tatlin's unrealized design for a monument to the Third International (his sole venture into engineering) which produced Constructivism's most potent architectural image: a huge, tilting, spiral, with revolving glass chambers – a cube, a cylinder, and a pyramid – suspended within its central core.

contact improvisation in dance, improvised movement sequences often in avant-garde dance. The sequences are the result of intuitive communication between two or more dancers, which is used to explore the changes in the dynamics of movement between them. It was instigated by US dancer/teacher Steve Paxton (1939–) 1972. Contact improvisation is used both as a choreographic tool and as a form of therapy through movement.

Conti Tom 1945– . British stage and film actor specializing in character roles. His films include *The Duellists* 1977, *Merry Christmas Mr Lawrence* 1982, *Reuben, Reuben* 1983, *Beyond Therapy* 1987, and *Shirley Valentine* 1989.

continuity in cinema, the coordination of shots and sequences in the production of a film.

continuo abbreviation for *basso continuo*; in music, the bass line on which a keyboard player, often accompanied by a bass stringed instrument, built up a harmonic accompaniment in 17th-century Baroque music.

contrabassoon larger version of the ◊bassoon, sounding an octave lower.

contralto in music, a low-register female voice, also called an ◊*alto*.

contrapposto in the visual arts, a pose in which one part of the body twists away from another part, the weight of the body being balanced on one leg rather than two. First achieved in Greek sculpture of the 6th century BC, contrapposto was revived in the free-standing statues of the Renaissance, notably Donatello's *David* 1430s (Bargello, Florence) and Michelangelo's *David* 1504 (Accademia, Florence).

Allowing for greater expressiveness and a use of sinuous line, it was subsequently employed and much elaborated upon by Mannerist painters and sculptors.

contrapuntal in music, a work employing ◊counterpoint, multiple parts of imitative melody.

Cooder Ry(land Peter) 1947– . US guitarist, singer, and composer whose explorations of various forms of American music (Tex-Mex, jazz, Hawaiian, and so on) and bottleneck slide playing have gained him much session work and a cult following. His records include *Into the Purple Valley* 1972, *Borderline* 1980, and *Get Rhythm* 1987; he has written music for many films, including *Paris, Texas* 1984.

Cook Peter 1937– . English comic actor and musician. With his partner Dudley Moore, he appeared in revue (*Beyond the Fringe* 1959–64) and opened London's first satirical nightclub, the Establishment, 1960. His films include *The Wrong Box* 1966, *Bedazzled* 1968, *The Bed Sitting Room* 1969, a parody of *The Hound of the Baskervilles* 1977, and *Supergirl* 1984.

Cooke Alistair 1908– . British-born US journalist. He was *Guardian* correspondent in the USA 1948–72, and broadcasts a weekly *Letter from America* on BBC radio.

Cooke Sam 1931–1964. US soul singer and songwriter who began his career as a gospel singer and turned to pop music 1956. His hits include 'You Send Me' 1957 and 'Wonderful World' 1960 (re-released 1986). His smooth tenor voice gilded some indifferent material, but his own song 'A Change Is Gonna Come' 1965 is a moving civil-rights anthem.

Cooney Ray(mond) 1932– . British actor, director, and dramatist, known for his farces *Two into One* 1981 and *Run for Your Wife* 1983.

Cooper Gary 1901–1962. US film actor. He epitomized the lean, true-hearted Yankee, slow of speech but capable of outdoing the 'bad guys'. His films include *Lives of a Bengal Lancer* 1935, *Mr Deeds Goes to Town* 1936, *Sergeant York* 1940 (Academy Award), and *High Noon* 1952 (Academy Award). In 1960 he received a special Academy Award for his lifetime contribution to cinema.

Cooper James Fenimore 1789–1851. US writer of 50 novels, becoming popular with *The Spy* 1821. He wrote volumes of *Leatherstocking Tales* about the frontier hero Leatherstocking and American Indians before and after the American Revolution, including *The Last of the Mohicans* 1826. Still popular as adventures, his novels have been reappraised for their treatment of social and moral issues in the settling of the American Frontier.

Cooper Samuel 1609–1672. English portrait miniaturist. His subjects included Milton, members of Charles II's court, the diarist Samuel Pepys' wife, and Oliver Cromwell.

Cooper Susie. Married name Susan Vera Barker 1902– . English pottery designer. Her style has varied from colourful Art Deco to softer, pastel decoration on more classical shapes. She started her own company 1929, which later became part of the Wedgwood factory, where she was senior designer from 1966.

Coop Himmelbau Viennese-based architectural practice, founded 1968 by Wolf Prix (1942–) and Helmut Swiczonsky (1944–), that promotes a radical skeletal architecture, essentially Constructivist in character. Projects to date include Red Angel Bar, 1980–81, and Atelier Baumann, 1984–85 (both in Vienna).

Coover Robert (Lowell) 1932– . US novelist who writes stylized, satirical fantasies using American myths to reinterpret history such as *The Origin of the Brunists* 1965, an investigation of mystical sects. Later novels include *Gerald's Party* 1986, which parodies the murder mystery, and *Pinocchio in Venice* 1991, a scatological reworking of the classic fable.

He also wrote *The Public Burning* 1977, which dramatizes Vice President Nixon's meeting Uncle Sam shortly before the execution of the Rosenberg spies.

Copeau Jacques 1879–1949. French theatre director who advocated a simplification of stage setting. He founded a company at the Vieux-Colombier Theatre 1913, where he directed plays by Molière and Shakespeare, notably *The Winter's Tale* 1921. In 1924 he established a school for young performers in Burgundy. He was a director of the Comédie Française 1936–41.

Coper Hans 1920–1981. German potter, originally an engineer. His work resembles Cycladic Greek pots in its monumental quality.

Coperario John. Assumed name of John Cooper *c.* 1570–1626. English composer of songs with lute or viol accompaniment. His works include several masques, such as *The Masque of Flowers* 1614, and sets of fantasies for organ and solo viol.

Copland Aaron 1900–1990. US composer. His early works, such as his piano concerto 1926, were in the jazz idiom but he gradually developed a gentler style with a regional flavour drawn from American folk music. Among his works are the ballets *Billy the Kid* 1939, *Rodeo* 1942, *Appalachian Spring* 1944 (based on a poem by Hart Crane), and *Inscape for Orchestra* 1967.

Born in New York, Copland studied in France with Nadia Boulanger, and taught from 1940 at the Berkshire Music Center, now the Tanglewood Music Center, near Lenox, Massachusetts. He took avant-garde European styles and gave them a distinctive American accent. His eight film scores, including *The Heiress* 1949, set new standards for Hollywood.

Copley John Singleton 1738–1815. US painter. He was the leading portraitist of the colonial period, but from 1775 lived mainly in London, where he painted lively historical scenes such as *The Death of Major Pierson* 1783 (Tate Gallery, London).

Some of his historical paintings are unusual in that they portray dramatic events of his time, such as *Brook Watson and the Shark* 1778 (National Gallery, Washington, DC).

Coppola Francis Ford 1939– . US film director and screenwriter. He directed *The Godfather* 1972, which became one of the biggest money-making films of all time, and its sequels *The Godfather Part II* 1974, which won seven Academy Awards, and *The Godfather Part III* 1990. His other films include *Apocalypse Now* 1979, *One from the Heart* 1982, *Rumblefish* 1983, *The Outsiders* 1983, and *Dracula* 1992.

After working on horror B-films, his first successes were *Finian's Rainbow* 1968 and *Patton* 1969, for which his screenplay won an Academy Award. Among his other films are *The Conversation* 1972, *The Cotton Club* 1984, *Tucker: The Man and His Dream* 1988, and *Gardens of Stone* 1987.

Coptic art the art of the indigenous Christian community of 5th–8th century Egypt. Flat and colourful in style, with strong outlines and stylized forms, it shows the influence of Byzantine, late Roman, and ancient Egyptian art. Wall paintings, textiles, stone and ivory carvings, and manuscript illuminations remain, the most noted examples of which are in the Coptic Museum, Cairo. The influence of Coptic art was widespread in the Christian world, and Coptic interlacing patterns may have been the source for the designs of Irish and Northumbrian illuminated gospels. For the later period of Fatimid art, 10th–11th centuries, see ◊Islamic art.

Coralli Jean 1779–1854. French dancer and choreographer who made his debut as a dancer 1802. He choreographed *Le Diable boîteux* 1836 for the Austrian ballerina Fanny Elssler (1810–1884), *Giselle* 1841, and *La Péri* 1843 for the Italian ballerina Carlotta Grisi (1819–1899).

cor anglais or *English horn* alto ◊oboe in E flat with a distinctive tulip-shaped bell and warm nasal tone, heard to pastoral effect in Rossini's overture to *William Tell* 1829, and portraying a plaintive Sasha the duck in Prokofiev's *Peter and the Wolf* 1936.

Corbière Tristan 1845–1875. French poet. His volume of poems *Les Amours jaunes/Yellow Loves* 1873 went unrecognized until Paul Verlaine called attention to it 1884. Many of his poems, such as 'La Rhapsodie foraine/ Wandering Rhapsody', deal with life in his native Brittany.

Corbusier, Le French architect; see ◊Le Corbusier.

corduroy durable cotton or rayon velvet cut-pile fabric which can have differing widths of ribs or cords. Until the 19th century it was mainly used for the clothing of livery and agricultural workers but later it became a common fabric for breeches and jackets worn in field sports. During the 20th century it became popular in casual fashion garments.

Corelli Arcangelo 1653–1713. Italian composer and violinist. He was one of the first virtuoso exponents of the Baroque violin and his music, marked by graceful melody, includes a set of *concerti grossi* and five sets of chamber sonatas.

Born near Milan, he studied in Bologna and in about 1685 settled in Rome, under the patronage of Cardinal Pietro Ottoboni, where he published his first violin sonatas.

Corelli Marie. Pseudonym of Mary Mackay 1855–1924. English romantic novelist. Trained for a musical career, she turned instead to writing (she was said to be Queen Victoria's favourite novelist) and published *The Romance of Two Worlds* 1886. Her works were later ridiculed for their pretentious style.

Corinna lived 6th century BC. Greek lyric poet, from Tanagra in Boeotia, who may have been a contemporary of ◊Pindar. Only fragments of her poetry survive.

Corinthian in Classical architecture, one of the five types of column; see ◊order.

Corman Roger 1926– . US film director and prolific producer of low-budget, highly profitable films, mainly in the youth and science-fiction genres. One of the most consistently commercial film directors working outside the Hollywood studio system, Corman has over 200 films to his credit since 1954. Among his directed work was a series of Edgar Allan Poe adaptations, beginning with *The House of Usher* 1960.

Corman also fostered some of the leading names in cinema such as Francis Ford Coppola, Martin Scorsese, and Jack Nicholson, who benefited from Corman's independent company New World Pictures, and later Concorde/New Horizons.

cornamuse Renaissance capped double-reed woodwind musical instrument of straight bore and with a clear, reedy tone.

Corneille Pierre 1606–1684. French dramatist. His tragedies, such as *Horace* 1640, *Cinna* 1641, and *Oedipe* 1659, glorify the strength of will governed by reason, and established the French classical dramatic tradition. His first comedy, *Mélite*, was performed 1629, followed by others that gained him a brief period of favour with Cardinal Richelieu. His early masterpiece, *Le Cid* 1636, was attacked by the Academicians, although it received public acclaim, and was produced in the same year as *L'Illusion comique/The Comic Illusion*.

Although Corneille enjoyed public popularity, periodic disfavour with Richelieu marred his career, and it was not until 1639 that Corneille (again in favour) produced plays such as *Polyeucte* 1643, *Le Menteur* 1643, and *Rodogune* 1645, leading to his election to the Académie 1647. His later plays were approved by Louis XIV.

When there is no peril in the fight, there is no glory in the triumph.

Pierre Corneille *Le Cid* 1636

Cornell Joseph 1903–1972. US sculptor, the first American Surrealist artist, known for his poetic series of 'boxes' containing oddly juxtaposed objects, for example *Bubble Set* 1936 (Wadsworth Atheneum, Hartford, Connecticut). Cornell was influenced by the European Surrealists and first exhibited with them in a New York gallery in the 1930s. His constructions display such varied items as birds' eggs, photographs, wine glasses, and dolls' heads, creating a highly personal 'theatre' of memory and nostalgia, with references to literature, art history, music, and dance.

Cornell Katherine 1898–1974. German-born US actress. Her first major success came with an appearance on Broadway in *Nice People* 1921. This debut was followed by a long string of New York stage successes, several of which were directed by her husband, Guthrie McClintic. From 1930 she began to produce her own plays; the most famous of them, *The Barretts of Wimpole Street* 1931, was later taken on tour and produced for television 1956.

Born in Berlin of American parents, Cornell was attracted to the stage at an early age, appearing with the Washington Square Players 1916.

cornet three-valved brass band instrument, soprano member in B flat of a group of valved horns developed in Austria and Germany about 1820–50 for military band use. Of cylindrical bore, its compact shape and deeper conical bell allow greater speed and agility of intonation than the trumpet, at the expense of less tonal precision and brilliance.

The cornet is typically played with vibrato, and has its own repertoire of virtuoso pieces, heard in brass band concerts and contests, and consisting of voice-like airs, character pieces, Victorian dance forms, and sets of variations in antique ◊divisions style.

cornett woodwind precursor of the orchestral brass ◊cornet, of narrow conical bore and with a cup mouthpiece. Members include the straight soprano **mute cornett**, a curved alto **cornetto**, S-shaped tenor **lysarden**, and double S-shaped **serpent**. Its clear trumpetlike tone made it a favoured instrument of Renaissance broken consorts and Baroque orchestras.

cornucopia (Latin 'horn of plenty') in Greek mythology, one of the horns of the goat Amaltheia, which was caused by Zeus to refill itself indefinitely with food and drink. In paintings, the cornucopia is depicted as a horn-shaped container spilling over with fruit and flowers.

Corot Jean-Baptiste Camille 1796–1875. French painter, creator of a distinctive landscape style using a soft focus and a low-key palette of browns, ochres, and greens. His early work, including Italian scenes of the 1820s, influenced the ◊Barbizon School of painters. Like them, Corot worked outdoors, but he also continued a conventional academic tradition with his romanticized paintings of women.

Born in Paris, Corot lived in Rome 1825–28, where he learnt the tradition of classical landscape painting, centred around a historical or mythological incident.

corps de ballet dancers in a ballet company who usually dance in groups, in support of the soloists. At the Paris Opéra this is the name given to the whole company.

Correggio Antonio Allegri da *c.* 1494–1534. Italian painter of the High Renaissance whose style followed the Classical grandeur of Leonardo and Titian but anticipated the Baroque in its emphasis on movement, softer forms, and contrasts of light and shade.

Based in Parma, he painted splendid illusionistic visions in the cathedral there, including the remarkable *Assumption of the Virgin* 1526–30. His religious paintings, for example, the night scene *Adoration of the Shepherds* about 1527–30 (Gemäldegalerie, Dresden), and mythological scenes, such as *Jupiter and Io* about 1532 (Wallace Collection, London), were much admired in the 18th century.

I, too, am a painter.

Correggio on seeing Raphael's *St Cecilia* in Bologna, *c.* 1525

---

corroboree Australian Aboriginal ceremonial dance. Some corroborees record events in everyday life and are non-sacred, public entertainments; others have a religious significance and are of great ritual importance, relating to initiation, death, fertility, disease, war, and so on. The dancers' movements are prescribed by tribal custom and their bodies and faces are usually painted in clay in traditional designs. The dance is accompanied by song and music is provided by clapping sticks and the ◊didjeridu. All these elements, as well as the dance itself, form the corroboree.

corset undergarment originally worn over a chemise. It was contructed with whalebone, which was used to give the garment shape, and laced tightly at the front or back to give women a slim and shapely profile. Despite protests against the physical damage caused by corsets, they were widely used in the 19th century to achieve the then-fashionable small waist. In the early 20th century the boned corset was replaced by woven elastic, and later by girdles, as fashion moved away from the slim-waisted profile to a more natural look.

A redesigned form of the corset appeared briefly 1947 to create Christian ◊Dior's 'New Look' – a tucked-in waist and flared skirt. In the early 1990s corsets became fashionable again as outer garments, popularized by the singer Madonna when she wore Jean-Paul ◊Gaultier's corset-based designs for her 1990 world tour.

Cortázar Julio 1914–1984. Argentine writer whose novels include *The Winners* 1960, *Hopscotch* 1963, and *Sixty-two: A Model Kit* 1968. One of his several volumes of short stories includes *Blow-up*, adapted for a film by the Italian director Michelangelo Antonioni.

Cortona Pietro da. Italian Baroque painter; see ◊Pietro da Cortona.

Corvo Baron 1860–1913. Assumed name of British writer Frederick ◊Rolfe.

Costello Elvis. Stage name of Declan McManus 1954– . English rock singer, songwriter, and guitarist who emerged as part of the ◊New Wave. His intricate yet impassioned lyrics have made him one of Britain's foremost songwriters.

The great stylistic range of his work was evident from his 1977 debut *My Aim Is True* and was further extended 1993 when he collaborated with the classical Brodsky Quartet on the song cycle *The Juliet Letters*. His albums include *Goodbye Cruel World* 1984 and *Mighty Like a Rose* 1991. His hits range from the political rocker 'Oliver's Army' 1979 to the country weepy 'Good Year for the Roses' 1981 and the punning pop of 'Everyday I Write the Book' 1983.

Costner Kevin 1955– . US film actor who emerged as a star in the late 1980s, with his role as detective Elliot Ness in *The Untouchables* 1987. Increasingly identified with the embodiment of idealism and high principle, Costner went on to direct and star in *Dances With Wolves* 1990, a Western sympathetic to the native American Indian, which won several Academy Awards. Subsequent films include *Robin Hood – Prince of Thieves* 1991, *JFK* 1991, and *The Bodyguard* 1992.

Cosway Richard 1742–1821. English artist. Elected to the Royal Academy 1771, he was an accomplished miniaturist and painted members of the Prince Regent's court.

Cotman John Sell 1782–1842. English landscape painter, with John Crome a founder of the ◊Norwich School. His early watercolours were bold designs in simple flat washes of colour, for example *Greta Bridge, Yorkshire* about 1805 (British Museum, London).

Cotten Joseph 1905–1994. US actor, intelligent and low-keyed, who was brought into films by Orson Welles. Cotten gave outstanding performances in *Citizen Kane* 1941, *The Magnificent Ambersons* 1942, and *The Third Man* 1949. He appeared uncredited as the drunken coroner in Welles' *Touch of Evil* 1958.

counterpoint in music, the art of combining different forms of an original melody with apparent freedom while preserving a harmonious effect. Giovanni Palestrina and J S Bach were masters of counterpoint.

It originated in ◊plainsong, with two independent vocal lines sung simultaneously (Latin *punctus contra punctum* 'note against note').

countertenor highest natural male voice, also called an ◊**alto**. It was favoured by the Elizabethans for heroic brilliance of tone and was revived in the UK by Alfred Deller (1912–1979).

country and western or *country music* popular music of the white US South and West; it evolved from the folk music of the English, Irish, and Scottish settlers and has a strong blues influence. Characteristic instruments are slide guitar, mandolin, and fiddle. Lyrics typically extol family values and traditional sex roles, and often have a strong narrative element. Country music encompasses a variety of regional styles, and ranges from mournful ballads to fast and intricate dance music.

history 1920s Jimmie Rodgers wrote a series of 'Blue Yodel' songs that made him the first country-music recording star. *1930s* Nashville, Tennessee, became a centre for the country-music industry, with the Grand Ole Opry a showcase for performers. The Carter Family arranged and recorded hundreds of traditional songs. Hollywood invented the singing cowboy.

1940s Hank Williams emerged as the most significant singer and songwriter; *western swing* spread from Texas.

1950s The *honky-tonk* sound; Kentucky *bluegrass*; ballad singers included Jim Reeves (1923–1964) and Patsy Cline (1932–1963).

1960s Songs of the Bakersfield, California, school, dominated by Buck Owens (1929–) and Merle Haggard, contrasted with lush Nashville productions of such singers as George Jones and Tammy Wynette (1942–).

1970s Dolly Parton and Emmylou Harris (1947–); the Austin, Texas, *outlaws* Willie Nelson and Waylon Jennings (1937–); *country rock* pioneered by Gram Parsons (1946–1973).

1980s Neo-traditionalist *new country* represented by Randy Travis (1963–), Dwight Yoakam (1957–), and k d lang.

1990s US pop charts invaded by cowboy-hat-wearing singers like Garth Brooks (1961–).

Couperin François *le Grand* 1668–1733. French composer, well-known member of a French musical family which included his uncle Louis (1626–1661), composer for organ and harpsichord. A favoured composer of Louis XIV, François Couperin composed numerous chamber concertos and harpsichord suites, and published a standard keyboard tutor *L'Art de toucher le clavecin/The Art of Playing the Harpsichord* 1716 in which he laid down guidelines for fingering, phrasing, and ornamentation.

couplet in literature, a pair of lines of verse, usually of the same length and rhymed. The *heroic couplet*, consisting of two rhymed lines in iambic pentameter, was widely adopted for epic poetry, and was a convention of both serious and mock-heroic 18th-century English poetry, as in the work of Alexander ◊Pope. An example, from Pope's *An Essay on Criticism*, is: 'A little learning is a dang'rous thing;/Drink deep, or taste not the Pierian spring.'

courante (French 'running') 17th-century French court dance. Initially fast in tempo, with an emphasis on mime, it later became codified in a much slower and graver form. It was a favourite dance of Louis XIV. The music for the dance, in three time and with regular offbeat syncopations, is used in the instrumental ◊suite.

Courbet Gustave 1819–1877. French artist, a portrait, genre, and landscape painter. Reacting against academic trends, both Classicist and Romantic, he became the major exponent of ◊Realism, depicting contemporary life with an unflattering frankness. His *Burial at Ornans* 1850 (Musée d'Orsay, Paris), showing ordinary working people gathered round a village grave, shocked the public and the critics with its 'vulgarity'. His spirit of Realism was continued by Edouard ◊Manet.

I deny that art can be taught.

Gustave Courbet letter to prospective students 1861

Courrèges André 1923– . French fashion designer who is credited with inventing the miniskirt 1964. His 'space-age' designs – square-shaped short skirts and trousers – were copied worldwide in the 1960s.

Courrèges worked for Cristóbal ◊Balenciaga 1950–61, and founded his own label 1961. From 1966 he produced both couture and ready-to-wear lines of well-tailored designs, often in pastel shades.

course group of strings of a musical instrument which are tuned to the same pitch and played as one string. Lutes, guitars, and mandolins have double courses, harpsichords have triple courses, and pianos range from heavy single courses in the bass to quadruple courses in the extreme treble. The 12-string guitar is a modern example of a double-course instrument, each pair tuned to the octave rather than to the unison.

courtly love medieval European code of amorous conduct between noblemen and noblewomen. Originating in 11th-century Provence, France, it was popularized by ◊troubadours under the patronage of Eleanor of Aquitaine, and codified by André le Chapelain. Essentially, it was concerned with the (usually) unconsummated love between a young bachelor knight and his lord's lady. The affair between ◊Lancelot of the Lake and ◊Guinevere is a classic example.

The theme was usually treated in an idealized form, but the relationship did reflect the social realities of noble households, in which the lady of the household might be the only noblewoman among several young unmarried knights. It inspired a great deal of medieval and 16th-century art and literature, including the 14th-century ◊*Roman de la Rose* and Chaucer's *Troilus and Criseyde*.

Courtneidge Cicely 1893–1980. British comic actress and singer who appeared both on stage and in films. She married comedian Jack Hulbert (1892–1978), with whom she formed a successful variety partnership.

Coveri Enrico 1952–1990. Italian fashion designer who set up his own business 1979. A bold designer of young, fun-loving clothes, he was best known for knitted tops and trousers in strong colours, and for incorporating comic characters and Pop art in his designs.

Coveri was born in Florence and studied at its Accademia delle Belle Arti. He started working freelance for several companies, creating knitwear and sportswear under the Touche label, 1973, and five years later moved to Paris to work at the Espace Cardin. By the time of his death, his own business had achieved a turnover of £100 million.

Coward Noël 1899–1973. English dramatist, actor, revue-writer, director, and composer, who epitomized the witty and sophisticated man of the theatre. From his first success with *The Young Idea* 1923, he wrote and appeared in plays and comedies on both sides of the Atlantic such as *Hay Fever* 1925, *Private Lives* 1930 with Gertrude Lawrence, *Design for Living* 1933, *Blithe Spirit* 1941, and *A Song at Twilight* 1966. His revues and musicals included *On With the Dance* 1925 and *Bitter Sweet* 1929.

Coward also wrote for and acted in films, including the patriotic *In Which We Serve* 1942 and the sentimental *Brief Encounter* 1945. After World War II he became a nightclub and cabaret entertainer, performing songs like *Mad Dogs and Englishmen*.

Cowell Henry 1897–1965. US composer and theorist whose pioneering *New Musical Resources* published 1930 sought to establish a rationale for modern music. He worked with Percy Grainger 1941 and alongside John Cage. Although remembered as a discoverer of piano effects such as strumming the strings in *Aeolian Harp* 1923, and clusters in *The Banshee* 1925, he was also an astute observer and writer of new music developments. Cowell also wrote chamber and orchestral music and was active as a critic and publisher of 20th-century music.

Cowley Abraham 1618–1667. English metaphysical poet. He introduced the Pindaric ode (based on the work of the Greek poet Pindar) to English poetry, and published metaphysical verse with elaborate imagery, as well as essays. His best-known collection is *The Mistress* 1647.

I believe a composer must forge his own forms out of the many influences that play upon him and never close his ears to any part of the world of sound …

Henry Cowell

Cowper William 1731–1800. English poet. He trained as a lawyer, but suffered a mental breakdown 1763 and entered an asylum, where he underwent an evangelical conversion. He later wrote hymns (including 'God Moves in a Mysterious Way'). His verse includes the six books of *The Task* 1785.

Cox David 1783–1859. English artist. He studied under John ◊Varley and made a living as a drawing master. His watercolour landscapes, many of scenes in N Wales, show attractive cloud effects, and are characterized by broad colour washes on rough, tinted paper.

Coysevox Antoine 1640–1720. French Baroque sculptor at the court of Louis XIV. He was employed at the palace of Versailles, contributing a stucco relief of a triumphant Louis XIV to the Salon de la Guerre.

He also produced portrait busts, for example a terracotta of the artist Le Brun 1676 (Wallace Collection, London), and more sombre monuments, such as the *Tomb of Cardinal Mazarin* 1689–93 (Louvre, Paris).

Cozens John Robert 1752–1797. English landscape painter, a watercolourist, whose Romantic views of Europe, painted on tours in the 1770s and 1780s, influenced both Thomas Girtin and Turner.

His father, *Alexander Cozens* (about 1717–1786), also a landscape painter, taught drawing at Eton public school and produced books on landscape drawing.

Crabbe George 1754–1832. English poet. Originally a doctor, he became a cleric 1781, and wrote grimly realistic verse on the poor of his own time: *The Village* 1783, *The Parish Register* 1807, *The Borough* 1810 (which includes the story used in Benjamin Britten's opera *Peter Grimes*), and *Tales of the Hall* 1819.

Crabtree William 1905–1991. English architect who designed the Peter Jones department store in Sloane Square, London 1935–39, regarded as one of the finest Modern Movement buildings in England. The building was technically innovative in its early application of the curtain wall, which flows in a gentle curve from the King's Road into the square.

Craig Edward Gordon 1872–1966. British director and stage designer. His innovations and theories on stage design and lighting effects, expounded in *On the Art of the Theatre* 1911, had a profound influence on stage production in Europe and the USA. He was the son of actress Ellen Terry.

Craik Dinah Maria (born Mulock) 1826–1887. British novelist, author of *John Halifax, Gentleman* 1857, the story of the social betterment of a poor orphan through his own efforts.

Cranach Lucas 1472–1553. German painter, etcher, and woodcut artist, a leading figure in the German Renaissance. He painted many full-length nudes and precise and polished portraits, such as *Martin Luther* 1521 (Uffizi, Florence).

Born at Kronach in Bavaria, he settled at Wittenberg 1504 to work for the elector of Saxony. He is associated with the artists Albrecht Dürer and Albrecht Altdorfer and was a close friend of Martin Luther, whose portrait he painted several times. *The Flight into Egypt* 1504 (Staatliche Museum, Berlin) is typical. His religious paintings feature splendid landscapes. His second son, **Lucas Cranach the Younger** (1515–1586), had a similar style and succeeded his father as director of the Cranach workshop.

Crane (Harold) Hart 1899–1932. US poet. His long mystical poem *The Bridge* 1930 uses the Brooklyn Bridge as a symbolic key to the harmonizing myth of modern America, seeking to link humanity's present with its past in an epic continuum. His work, which was influenced by T S Eliot, is notable for its exotic diction and dramatic rhetoric. He committed suicide by jumping overboard from a steamer bringing him back to the USA after a visit to Mexico.

Crane Stephen 1871–1900. US writer who introduced grim realism into the US novel. His book, *The Red Badge of Courage* 1895, deals vividly with the US Civil War in a prose of impressionist, visionary naturalism.

Born in Newark, New Jersey, he moved to the tenements of New York City to work as a journalist. There he wrote his naturalistic fables of urban misery, the self-published *Maggie: A Girl of the Streets: A Story of New York* 1893, which was rejected by many editors because of its shocking subject matter. He was a war correspondent in Mexico, Greece, and Cuba, the latter assignment inspiring one of his most acclaimed stories, *The Open Boat* 1897, an account of a shipwreck that dramatizes man's exposure to indifferent nature. He also published two volumes of poetry: *The Black Riders* 1895 and *War is Kind* 1899.

Crane Walter 1845–1915. English artist, designer, and book illustrator. He was influenced by William ◊Morris and became an active socialist in the 1880s.

While apprenticed to W J Linton (1812–1898), a wood engraver, he came under the influence of the Pre-Raphaelites. His book illustrations, both for children's and for adult books, included an edition of Spenser's *Faerie Queene* 1894–96.

Cranko John 1927–1973. British choreographer, born in South Africa, a pivotal figure in the ballet boom of the 1960s. He joined Sadler's Wells, London, 1946 as a dancer, becoming their resident choreographer 1950. In 1961 he became director of the Stuttgart Ballet, where he achieved the 'Stuttgart Ballet Miracle', turning it into a world-class company with a vital and exhilarating repertory. He excelled in the creation of full-length narrative ballets, such as *Romeo and Juliet* 1958 and *Onegin* 1965. He is also known for his one-act ballets, peopled with comic characters, as in *Pineapple Poll* 1951 and *Jeu de Cartes* 1965.

craquelure network of fine cracks on a painting's surface due to age. In tempera paintings the cracks are barely visible, whereas in oil paintings they can be very distinctive. Craquelure is an authentic sign of age and, where artificially induced in forged works of art, is usually detectable.

Crashaw Richard 1613–1649. English religious poet of the metaphysical school. He published a book of Latin sacred epigrams 1634, then went to Paris, where he joined the Roman Catholic Church; his collection of poems *Steps to the Temple* appeared 1646.

cravat scarf worn mainly by men around the neck instead of a tie, often with a shirt. During the 17th century cravats formed part of everyday dress; they were made of muslin or linen and tied around the neck, sometimes in a bow.

Crawford Joan. Stage name of Lucille Le Seur 1908–1977. US film actress who became a star with her performance as a flapper (liberated young woman) in *Our Dancing Daughters* 1928. Later she appeared as a sultry, often suffering, mature woman. Her films include *Mildred Pierce* 1945 (for which she won an Academy Award), *Sudden Fear* 1952, and *Whatever Happened to Baby Jane?* 1962.

crayon drawing stick made of a mineral substance (chalk, lamp black, charcoal, or red ochre) that is fixed in an oil or wax medium.

creation myth legend of the origin of the world. All cultures have ancient stories of the creation of the Earth or its inhabitants. Often these involve the violent death of a primordial being from whose body everything then arises; the giant Ymir in Scandinavian mythology is an example. Marriage between heaven and earth is another common explanation, as in Greek mythology (Uranus and Gaia).

Creation of Adam, The fresco (Sistine Chapel ceiling, Vatican) by ◊Michelangelo 1511, showing God reaching out to the earthbound Adam who, though painted as the ultimate in male beauty and form, is lifeless, lacking divine energy. The composition represented not only the culmination of Michelangelo's artistic achievement but also the flowering of all that had been learnt in art, especially as regards anatomy, during the early Renaissance period. The recent restoration of the ceiling has been the subject of some controversy.

Creon in Greek mythology, brother of ◊Jocasta, father of Haemon, and king of Thebes in Sophocles' *Antigone*.

crepe fabric woven from yarns spun with an extra-high twist, giving it a crinkled texture. The effect can be imitated by various chemical finishes applied selectively, causing fibres to shrink in some areas.

cretonne strong unglazed cotton cloth, printed with a design and used for wall hangings and upholstery. It originally referred to a fabric with an unusual weave of hempen warp and linen weft, made in France. Cretonne was manufactured in the UK from about 1865.

Crime and Punishment novel by Russian writer Fyodor ◊Dostoevsky, published 1866. It analyses the motives of a murderer and his reactions to the crime he has committed.

crime fiction variant of ◊detective fiction distinguished by emphasis on character and atmosphere rather than the solving of a mystery. Examples are the works of Dashiell Hammett and Raymond Chandler during the 1930s and, in the second half of the 20th century, Patricia Highsmith and Ruth Rendell.

The English writer William Godwin's *Caleb Williams* 1794 is a forerunner that points to the continuing tendency in crime fiction for serious psychological exploration to be linked with political radicalism.

crinoline stiff fabric, originally made of horsehair, widely used in 19th-century women's clothing. It was used to create skirts of great width in the 1850s when the cage-frame crinoline, made with steel hoops, was introduced. Promoted by the Empress Eugénie in France, the style became popular throughout Europe. The frame was modified around 1865 when the skirts were flattened at the front, leaving a fuller skirt at the back. By the late 1860s many crinolines were discarded altogether in favour of a far narrower profile.

Criterion, The English quarterly literary review 1922–39 edited by T S Eliot. His poem *The Waste Land* was published in its first issue. It also published W H Auden, Ezra Pound, James Joyce, and D H Lawrence, and introduced the French writers Marcel Proust and Paul Valéry to English-language readers.

Crivelli Carlo 1435–1495. Italian painter in the early Renaissance style, active in Venice. He painted extremely detailed, decorated religious works, sometimes festooned with garlands of fruit. His figurative style is strongly Italian, reflecting the influence of Mantegna and Tura. His *Annunciation* 1486 (National Gallery, London) is his best-known work.

crochet craft technique similar to both knitting and lacemaking, in which one hooked needle is used to produce a loosely looped network of wool or cotton.

Remains of crocheted clothing have been discovered in 4th-century Egyptian tombs. In 19th-century Europe the craft was popular among Victorian ladies, and the availability of fine machine-made thread made it possible to create fine laces. Both garments and trims are still produced by crocheting.

Crome John 1768–1821. English landscape painter, founder of the ◊Norwich School with John Sell Cotman 1803. His works include *The Poringland Oak* 1818 (Tate Gallery, London), showing Dutch influence.

Crompton Richmal. Pen name of Richmal Crompton Lamburn 1890–1969. British writer. She is remembered for her stories about the mischievous schoolboy ◊William.

Crosby Bing (Harry Lillis) 1904–1977. US film actor and singer who achieved world success with his distinctive style of crooning in such songs as 'Pennies from Heaven' 1936 (featured in a film of the same name) and 'White Christmas' 1942. He won an acting Oscar for *Going My Way* 1944, and made a series of 'road' film comedies with Dorothy Lamour and Bob Hope, the last being *Road to Hong Kong* 1962.

Crossley Paul 1944– . British pianist, joint artistic director of the London Sinfonietta from 1988. A specialist in the works of such composers as Maurice Ravel, Olivier Messiaen, and Michael Tippett, he studied with Messiaen and French pianist Yvonne Loriod (1924–).

crossover in music, having mainstream appeal though originating in a more confined genre. A rhythm-and-blues or country record, for example, that enters the pop chart is a crossover hit.

Crowley John 1942– . US writer of science fiction and fantasy, notably *Little, Big* 1980 and *Aegypt* 1987, which contain esoteric knowledge and theoretical puzzles.

Crows over Wheatfield oil painting by Vincent van Gogh 1890 (Van Gogh Museum, Amsterdam). The dark stormy sky and violent use of impasto has often been said to express the torment of van Gogh's mind in the last year of his life, spent in an asylum for the insane at St-Rémy in S France.

Crucible, The drama by Arthur ◊Miller 1953. Inspired by the contemporary McCarthy persecutions of artists and writers, Miller dramatized the story of the Salem witch-hunt in Puritan New England, 1692. John Proctor attempts to take a stand against a rising tide of superstitious violence but is undermined by the guilt he feels about his affair with the young girl, Abigail. Although admitting to his lechery, Proctor ultimately refuses to confess to being in league with the Devil and is hanged.

Cruelty, Theatre of theory advanced by Antonin ◊Artaud in his book *Le Théâtre et son double/Theatre and its Double* 1938 and adopted by a number of writers and directors. It aims to substitute gesture and sound for spoken dialogue, and to shock the audience into awareness through the release of feelings usually repressed by conventional behaviour. In the UK, Artaud's ideas particularly influenced the producer and director Peter ◊Brook.

Cruikshank George 1792–1878. English painter and illustrator, remembered for his political cartoons and illustrations for Charles Dickens' *Oliver Twist* and Daniel Defoe's *Robinson Crusoe*.

Crumb George Henry 1929– . US composer of imagist works. He employed unusual graphics and imaginative sonorities, such as the ◊musical saw in *Ancient Voices of Children* 1970, settings of poems by Lorca.

crumhorn ('curved horn') any of a capped double-reed Renaissance woodwind family of musical instruments, with soprano, alto, tenor, and bass members. Of narrow cylindrical bore and curved upwards like a walking stick, it dates from the 15th century and emits a buzzing tone.

Crystal Palace glass and iron building designed by Joseph ◊Paxton, housing the Great Exhibition of 1851 in Hyde Park, London; later rebuilt in modified form at Sydenham Hill 1854 (burned down 1936).

Cubism revolutionary movement in early 20th-century art, particularly painting, pioneering abstract forms. Its founders, Georges Braque and Pablo Picasso, were admirers of Paul Cézanne and were inspired by his attempt to create a highly structured visual language. In *analytical Cubism* (1907–12) three-dimensional objects were split into facets and analysed before being 'reassembled' as complex two-dimensional images. In *synthetic Cubism* (after 1912) the images became simpler, the colours brighter, and ◊collage was introduced. The movement attracted such painters as Juan Gris, Fernand Léger, and Robert Delaunay, and the sculptor Jacques Lipchitz. Its message was that a work of art exists in its own right rather than as a representation of the real world.

Cubitt Thomas 1788–1855. English builder and property developer. One of the earliest speculators, Cubitt, together with his brother Lewis Cubitt (1799–1883), rebuilt much of Belgravia, London, an area of Brighton, and the east front of Buckingham Palace.

Cuchulain Celtic hero, the chief figure in a cycle of Irish legends. He is associated with his uncle Conchobar, king of Ulster; his most famous exploits are described in *Taín Bó Cuailnge/The Cattle Raid of Cuchulain*.

Cui César Antonovich 1853–1918. Russian composer and writer, of French parentage. An army engineer by profession, he became a member of 'The ◊Mighty Handful' group of composers and an enthusiastic proponent of Russian nationalist music in the press. Despite this, his own musical tastes tended towards the France of Auber and Meyerbeer in operas *Angelo* 1876 based on Victor Hugo and *Le Flibustier/The Buccaneer* 1889 on a play by Jean Richepin.

Cukor George 1899–1983. US film director of sophisticated dramas and light comedies. He moved to the cinema from the theatre, and was praised for his skilled handling of such stars as Greta Garbo (in *Camille* 1937) and Katharine Hepburn (in *The Philadelphia Story* 1940). He won an Academy Award for the direction of *My Fair Lady* 1964.

cummings e(dward) e(stlin) 1894–1962. US poet. His work is marked by idiosyncratic punctuation and typography (for example, his own name is always written in lower case), and a subtle, lyric celebration of life. Before his first collection *Tulips and Chimneys* 1923, cummings published an avant-garde novel, *The Enormous Room* 1922, based on his internment in a French concentration camp during World War I. His typographical experiments were antecedents of the concrete and sound poetry of the 1960s.

listen: there's a hell/ of a good universe next door: let's go.

e e cummings
'Pity this busy monster, manunkind'

Cunha Euclydes da 1866–1909. Brazilian writer. His novel *Os Sertões/Rebellion in the Backlands* 1902 describes the Brazilian *sertão* (backlands), and how a small group of rebels resisted government troops.

Cunningham Imogen 1883–1976. US photographer. Her early photographs were romantic but she gradually rejected pictorialism, producing clear and detailed plant studies 1922–29. With Ansel Adams and Edward Weston, she was a founder member of the ◊'f/64' group which advocated precise definition. From the mid-1930s she concentrated on portraiture.

Cunningham Merce 1919– . US choreographer and dancer, the father of Post-Modernist, or experimental, dance. He liberated dance from its relationship with music, allowing it to obey its own dynamics. Along with his friend and collaborator, composer John ◊Cage, he introduced chance into the creative process, such as tossing coins to determine options. Influenced by Martha ◊Graham, with whose company he was soloist 1939–45, he formed his own avant-garde dance company and school in New York 1953.

His works include *The Seasons* 1947, *Antic Meet* 1958, *Squaregame* 1976, and *Arcade* 1985.

Cunningham worked closely with composers, such as Cage, and artists, such as Robert Rauschenberg, when staging his works; among them *Septet* 1953, *Suite for Five* 1956, *Crises* 1960, *Winterbranch* 1964, *Scramble* 1967, *Signals* 1970, and *Sounddance* 1974.

Cupid in Roman mythology, the god of love, identified with the Greek ◊Eros.

Cure, the English rock band formed 1976, part of the ◊goth pop scene and enduringly popular with fans. Albums include *Three Imaginary Boys* 1979, *The Head on the Door* 1985, and *Wish* 1992. Their singer, songwriter, and guitarist is Robert Smith (1957–).

Curnow Allen 1911– . New Zealand poet, dramatist, anthologist, and critic. As a poet and critic he has explored the possibilities of cultural identity in New Zealand, stressing both the isolation of the poet (particularly in *Island and Time* 1941) and the need for poets and the people to speak the same language. Language itself is the focus of more recent work such as *Trees, Effigies, Moving Objects* 1972 and *An Incorrigible Music* 1979.

curtain wall in a building, external, lightweight, non-loadbearing wall (either glazing or cladding) that is hung from a metal frame rather than built up from the ground like a brick wall; the framework it shields is usually of concrete or steel. Curtain walls are typically used in high-rise blocks, one of the earliest examples being the Reliance Building in Chicago 1890–94 by Daniel Burnham (1846–1912) and John Wellborn Root (1850–1891). In medieval architecture, the term refers to the outer wall of a castle.

In the early 20th century, the curtain wall was developed in two buildings by Walter ◊Gropius: the Model Factory, Deutsche Werkbund Exhibition, Cologne 1914, and the Bauhaus, Dessau 1925–26. Since World War II its use has spread dramatically, initially in the USA with iconic buildings such as the Lever House, New York 1952, by ◊Skidmore, Owings and Merrill, and the Seagram Building, New York, 1956–59, by ◊Mies van der Rohe.

curtal capped double-reed Renaissance woodwind instrument, ancestor of the ◊bassoon, of folded conical bore and mild reedy tone, also known as the *dulcian*.

Curtis Tony. Stage name of Bernard Schwartz 1925– . US film actor whose best work was characterized by a nervous energy, as the press agent in *Sweet Smell of Success* 1957 and the drag-disguised musician on the run from the mob in *Some Like It Hot* 1959. He also starred in *The Vikings* 1958 and *The Boston Strangler* 1968.

Curtiz Michael. Adopted name of Mihaly Kertész 1888–1962. Hungarian-born film director. He worked in Austria, Germany, and France before moving to the USA in 1926, where he made several films with Errol Flynn (*Captain Blood* 1935). He directed *Mildred Pierce* 1945, which revitalized Joan Crawford's career, and *Casablanca* 1942 (Academy Award).

His wide range of films include *The Private Lives of Elizabeth and Essex* 1939, *The Adventures of Robin Hood* 1938, *Yankee Doodle Dandy* 1942, and *White Christmas* 1954.

Curwen John 1816–1880. English cleric and educator. In about 1840 he established the **tonic sol-fa** system of music notation (originated in the 11th century by Guido d'Arezzo) in which the notes of the diatonic major scale are named by syllables (doh, ray, me, fah, soh, lah, te) to simplify singing at sight.

Cusack Cyril 1910– . Irish actor who joined the Abbey Theatre, Dublin 1932 and appeared in many of its productions, including Synge's *The Playboy of the Western World*. In Paris he won an award for his solo performance in Beckett's *Krapp's Last Tape*. In the UK he has played many roles as a member of the Royal Shakespeare Company and the National Theatre Company.

Cushing Peter 1913– . British actor who specialized in horror roles in films made at Hammer studios 1957–73, including *Dracula* 1958, *The Mummy* 1959, and *Frankenstein Must Be Destroyed* 1969. Other films include *Doctor Who and the Daleks* 1966, *Star Wars* 1977, and *Top Secret* 1984.

Cuyp Aelbert 1620–1691. Dutch painter of countryside scenes, seascapes, and portraits. His idyllically peaceful landscapes are bathed in a golden light, reflecting the influence of Claude Lorrain, for example, *A Herdsman with Cows by a River* about 1650 (National Gallery, London). His father, *Jacob Gerritsz Cuyp* (1594–1652), was also a landscape and portrait painter.

Cybele in Phrygian mythology, an earth goddess, identified by the Greeks with ◊Rhea and honoured in Rome.

Cyclops in Greek mythology, one of a race of Sicilian giants, who had one eye in the middle of the forehead and lived as shepherds. ◊Odysseus blinded the Cyclops ◊Polyphemus in Homer's *Odyssey*.

cymbal ancient percussion instrument of indefinite pitch, consisting of a shallow circular brass dish suspended at the centre; either used in pairs clashed together or singly, struck with a beater. Smaller finger cymbals or *crotala*, used by Debussy and Stockhausen, are precise in pitch. Turkish or 'buzz' cymbals incorporate loose rivets to extend the sound.

Cymbeline play by ◊Shakespeare, first acted about 1610 and printed 1623. It combines various sources to tell the story of Imogen (derived from Ginevra in Boccaccio's *Decameron*), the daughter of the legendary British king Cymbeline, who proves her virtue and constancy after several ordeals.

Cynewulf early 8th century. Anglo-Saxon poet. He is thought to have been a Northumbrian monk and is the undoubted author of 'Juliana' and part of the 'Christ' in the Exeter Book (a collection of poems now in Exeter Cathedral), and of the 'Fates of the Apostles' and 'Elene' in the Vercelli Book (a collection of Old English manuscripts housed in Vercelli, Italy), in all of which he inserted his name by using runic acrostics.

Cyrano de Bergerac Savinien 1619–1655. French writer. He joined a corps of guards at 19 and performed heroic feats which brought him fame. He is the hero of a classic play by Edmond ◊Rostand, in which his excessively long nose is used as a counterpoint to his chivalrous character.

Czechoslovak literature Czech writing first flourished in the 14th century and was stimulated by Hussite protestantism and the early Renaissance, but the Catholic Habsburgs effectively drove the indigenous literary tradition into exile, where the polymath Amos Komensky (Comenius) (1592–1670) wrote his prose masterpiece *Labyrint svě ta a ráj srdce/Labyrinth of the World and Paradise of the Heart* 1631. The tradition revived with the romantic poetry of Karel Hynek ◊Mácha and the *Máj* group he inspired, which included the poet Vitězslaw Hálek (1835–1874). After the establishment of the independent state of Czechoslovakia 1918, literature flourished with the plays of Karel ◊Čapek and František Langer (1888–1965), the poetry of Jaroslav ◊Seifert, and the later fiction of Jaroslav ◊Hašek. After the communist takeover 1948 literature stagnated until the 1960s when writers such as Milan ◊Kundera and Miroslav ◊Holub became prominent.

Slovakian emerged as a literary language only in the 18th century. It served as a medium for literary patriots such as L'udovít Štur (1815–1856), and came of age in the 20th century in fine lyric poetry such as that of Ivan Krasko (1876–1958), a symbolist, and Vojtech Mihálik (1926–).

Czerny Carl 1791–1857. Austrian composer and pianist. He wrote an enormous quantity of religious and concert music, but is chiefly remembered for his books of graded studies and technical exercises used in piano teaching, including the *Complete Theoretical and Practical Pianoforte School* 1839 which is still in widespread use.

da capo (Italian 'from the top') term in written music instructing a player that the music at that point starts from the beginning. It is abbreviated to 'D.C.'. A companion instruction is dal segno ('from the sign').

Dada or **Dadaism** artistic and literary movement founded 1915 in Zürich, Switzerland, by the Romanian poet Tristan Tzara (1896–1963) and others in a spirit of rebellion and disillusionment during World War I. Other Dadaist groups were soon formed by the artists Marcel ◊Duchamp and ◊Man Ray in New York, Francis ◊Picabia in Barcelona, and Kurt ◊Schwitters in Germany. The Dadaists produced deliberately anti-aesthetic images, often using photomontages with worded messages to express their political views, and directly scorned established art, as in Duchamp's *Mona Lisa* 1919, where a moustache and beard were added to Leonardo's classic portrait.

With the German writers Hugo Ball and Richard Huelsenbeck, Tzara founded the Cabaret Voltaire in Zürich 1916, where works by Hans Arp and the pioneer Surrealist Max Ernst, and others were exhibited. In New York in the same period the artist Man Ray met Duchamp and Picabia and began to apply Dadaist ideas to photography. The first international Dada exhibition was in Paris 1922. Dada had a considerable impact on early 20th-century art, questioning established artistic conventions and values. In the 1920s it evolved into Surrealism.

Dadd Richard 1817–1886. English painter. In 1843 he murdered his father and was committed to an asylum, but continued to paint minutely detailed pictures of fantasies and fairy tales, such as *The Fairy Feller's Master-Stroke* 1855–64 (Tate Gallery, London).

Daedalus in Greek mythology, an Athenian artisan supposed to have constructed for King Minos of Crete the labyrinth in which the ◊Minotaur was imprisoned. When Minos became displeased with him, Daedalus fled from Crete with his son

◊Icarus using wings made by them from feathers fastened with wax.

Daglish Eric Fitch 1892–1966. British artist and author. He wrote a number of natural history books, and illustrated both these and classics by Izaak Walton, Henry Thoreau, Gilbert White, and W H Hudson with exquisite wood engravings.

Daguerre Louis Jacques Mande 1789–1851. French pioneer of photography. Together with Joseph Niépce, he is credited with the invention of photography (though others were reaching the same point simultaneously). In 1838 he invented the daguerreotype, a single-image process superseded ten years later by ◊Fox Talbot's negative/positive process.

daguerreotype in photography, a single-image process using mercury vapour and an iodine-sensitized silvered plate; it was invented by Louis Daguerre 1838.

Dahl Johann Christian 1788–1857. Norwegian landscape painter in the Romantic style. He trained in Copenhagen but was active chiefly in Dresden from 1818. The first great painter of the Norwegian landscape, his style recalls that of the Dutch artist Jacob van ◊Ruisdael.

Dahl Roald 1916–1990. British writer, celebrated for short stories with a twist, for example, *Tales of the Unexpected* 1979, and for children's books, including *Charlie and the Chocolate Factory* 1964. He also wrote the screenplay for the James Bond film *You Only Live Twice* 1967.

His autobiography *Going Solo* 1986 recounted his experiences as a fighter pilot in the RAF.

Do you know what breakfast cereal is made of? It's made of all those little curly wooden shavings you find in pencil sharpeners!

Roald Dahl
Charlie and the Chocolate Factory 1964

Dalcroze Emile Jaques – see ◊Jaques-Dalcroze, Emile.

Dali Salvador 1904–1989. Spanish painter and designer. In 1929 he joined the Surrealists and became notorious for his flamboyant eccentricity. Influenced by the psychoanalytic theories of the Austrian physician Sigmund Freud, he developed a repertoire of striking, hallucinatory images — distorted human figures, limp pocket watches, and burning giraffes — in superbly draughted works, which he termed 'hand-painted dream photographs'. *The Persistence of Memory* 1931 (Museum of Modern Art, New York) is typical. By the late 1930s he had developed a more conventional style — this, and his apparent Fascist sympathies, led to his expulsion from the Surrealist movement 1938.

It was in this more traditional, though still highly inventive and idiosyncratic style that he painted such celebrated religious works as *The Crucifixion* 1951 (Glasgow Art School). He also painted portraits of his wife Gala.

Dali, born near Barcelona, initially came under the influence of the Italian Futurists. He is credited as co-creator of Luis Buñuel's Surrealist film *Un Chien andalou* 1928, but his role is thought to have been subordinate; he abandoned filmmaking after collaborating on the script for Buñuel's *L'Age d'or* 1930. He also designed ballet costumes, scenery, jewellery, and furniture. The books *The Secret Life of Salvador Dali* 1942 and *Diary of a Genius* 1966 are autobiographical. He was buried beneath a crystal dome in the museum of his work at Figueras on the Costa Brava, Spain.

There is only one difference between a madman and me. I am not mad.

Salvador Dali *The American* July 1956

Dallapiccola Luigi 1904–1975. Italian composer. Initially a Neo-Classicist, he adopted a lyrical twelve-tone style after 1945. His works include the operas *Il prigioniero/The Prisoner* 1949 and *Ulisse/Ulysses* 1968, as well as many vocal and instrumental compositions.

dal segno (Italian 'from the sign') term in written music instructing a player that the music at that point recommences from a place other than the beginning, indicated in the score by a crossed 'S' sign. The abbreviated form is 'D.S.'. To start from the beginning the instruction is da capo ('from the top').

Daly Augustin 1838–1899. US theatre manager. He began as a drama critic and dramatist before building his own theatre in New York 1879 and another, Daly's, in Leicester Square, London 1893.

Damon and Pythias in Greek mythology, devoted friends. When Pythias was condemned to death by the Sicilian tyrant Dionysius, Damon offered his own life as security to allow Pythias the freedom to go and arrange his affairs. When Pythias returned, they were both pardoned.

Dana Richard Henry, Jr 1815–1882. US author and lawyer who went to sea and worked for his passage around Cape Horn to California and back, then wrote an account of the journey *Two Years before the Mast* 1840. He also published *The Seaman's Friend* 1841, a guide to maritime law.

Danaë in Greek mythology, daughter of Acrisius, king of Argos. He shut her up in a bronze tower because of a prophecy that her son would kill his grandfather. Zeus became enamoured of her and descended in a shower of gold; she gave birth to ◊Perseus.

dance rhythmic movement of the body, usually performed in time to music. Its primary purpose may be religious, magical, martial, social, or artistic – the last two being characteristic of nontraditional societies. The pre-Christian era had a strong tradition of ritual dance, and ancient Greek dance still exerts an influence on dance movement today. Although Western folk and social dances have a long history, the Eastern dance tradition long predates the Western. The European classical tradition dates from the 15th century in Italy, the first printed dance text from 16th-century France, and the first dance school in Paris from the 17th century. The 18th century saw the development of European classical ballet as we know it today, and the 19th century saw the rise of Romantic ballet. In the 20th century ◊modern dance firmly established itself as a separate dance idiom, not based on classical ballet, and many divergent styles and ideas have grown from a willingness to explore a variety of techniques and amalgamate different traditions.

history European dance is relatively young in comparison to that of the rest of the world. The first Indian book on dancing, the *Natya Sastra*, existed a thousand years before its European counterpart. The *bugaku* dances of Japan, with orchestra accompaniment, date from the 7th century and are still performed at court. When the Peking (Beijing) Opera dancers first astonished Western audiences during the 1950s, they were representatives of a tradition stretching back to 740, the year in which Emperor Ming Huang established the Pear Garden Academy. The first comparable European institution, L'Académie Royale de Danse, was founded by Louis XIV 1661. In the European tradition social dances have always tended to rise upwards through the social scale; for example, the medieval court dances derived from peasant country dances. One form of dance tends to typify a whole period, thus the galliard represents the 16th century, the minuet the 18th, the waltz the 19th, and the quickstep represents ballroom dancing in the first half of the 20th century. The nine dances of the modern world championships in ◊ballroom dancing are the standard four (◊waltz, ◊foxtrot, ◊tango, and quickstep), the Latin American styles (samba, rumba, cha-cha-cha, and paso doble), and the Viennese waltz. A British development since the 1930s, which has spread to some extent abroad, is 'formation' dancing in which each team (usually eight couples) performs a series of ballroom steps in strict coordination. Popular dance crazes have included the Charleston in the 1920s, jitterbug in the 1930s and 1940s, ◊jive in the 1950s, the twist in the 1960s, disco and jazz dancing in the 1970s, and break dancing in the 1980s. In general, since the 1960s popular dance in the West has moved away from any prescribed sequence of movements and physical contact between participants, the dancers performing as individuals with no distinction between the male and the female

dance: chronology

1000 BC	King David danced 'with all his might' before the ark of the Covenant in Jerusalem – one of the earliest known instances of ritual dance.
405	*Bacchants* by Euripides was staged in Athens. The play demanded a considerable amount of dancing.
142	Consul Scipio Aemilianus Africanus closed the burgeoning dance schools of Rome in a drive against hedonism.
AD 774	Pope Zacharias forbade dancing.
1050	The *Ruodlieb*, a poem written by a monk at Tegernsee, Bavaria, contained the first European reference to dancing in couples.
1313	Rabbi Hacén ben Salomo of Zaragoza, in Aragon, like many other Jews in medieval times, was the local dancing master.
1489	A rudimentary allegorical ballet was performed in honour of the marriage of the Duke of Milan, at Tortona, Italy.
1581	In Paris, the first modern-style unified ballet, the *Ballet comique de la reine*, was staged at the court of Catherine de' Medici.
1588	Dance and ballet's first basic text, *L'Orchésographie*, by the priest Jehan Tabouret, was printed in Langres, near Dijon.
1651	In London, John Playford published *The English Dancing Master*. The 18th edition (1728) described 900 country dances.
1661	Louis XIV founded L'Académie Royale de Danse in Paris.
1670	The first classic ballet, *Le Bourgeois Gentilhomme*, was produced in Chambord, France.
1681	La Fontaine, the first professional female ballet dancer, made her debut in *Le Triomphe de l'amour* at the Paris Opéra.
1734	The dancer Marie Sallé adopted the gauze tunic, precursor to the Romantic tutu, and Marie Camargo shortened her skirts.
1738	The Kirov Ballet was established in St Petersburg, Russia.
1760	The great dancer and choreographer Jean-Georges Noverre published in Lyons *Lettres sur la Danse et sur les Ballets*, one of the most influential of all ballet books.
1776	The Bolshoi Ballet was established in Moscow.
1778	Noverre and Mozart collaborated on *Les Petits Riens* in Paris. The cast included the celebrated Auguste Vestris.
late 1700s	The waltz originated in Austria and Germany from a popular folk dance, the *Ländler*.
1820	Carlo Blasis, teacher and choreographer, published his *Traité élémentaire théoretique et pratique de l'art de la danse* in Milan which, together with his later works of dance theory, codified techniques for future generations of dancers.
1821	The first known picture of a ballerina *sur les pointes*, the French Fanny Bias by F Waldeck, dates from this year.
1832	The first performance of *La Sylphide* at the Paris Opéra opened the Romantic era of ballet and established the central significance of the ballerina. Marie Taglioni, the producer's daughter, who created the title role, wore the new-style Romantic tutu.
1841	Ballet's Romantic masterpiece *Giselle* with Carlotta Grisi in the leading role, was produced in Paris.
1845	Four great rival ballerinas of the Romantic era – Taglioni, Grisi, Fanny Cerrito, and Lucille Grahn – appeared together in Perrot's *Pas de Quatre* in London.
1866	*The Black Crook*, the ballet extravaganza from which US vaudeville and musical comedy developed, began its run of 474 performances in New York.
1870	*Coppélia*, 19th-century ballet's comic masterpiece, was presented in Paris.
1877	*La Bayadère* and *Swan Lake* were premiered in Moscow, but the latter failed through poor production and choreography. The Petipa-Ivanov version, in which Pierina Legnani performed 32 *fouettés*, established the work 1895.
1897	Anna Pavlova made her debut in St Petersburg with the Imperial Russian Ballet.
1905	Isadora Duncan appeared in Russia, making an immense impression with her 'anti-ballet' innovations derived from Greek dance.
1906	Vaslav Nijinsky made his debut in St Petersburg.
1909	The first Paris season given by Diaghilev's troupe of Russian dancers, later to become known as the Ballets Russes, marked the beginning of one of the most exciting periods in Western ballet.
1913	The premiere of Stravinsky's *The Rite of Spring* provoked a scandal in Paris.
1914	The foxtrot developed from the two-step in the USA.
1915	The Denishawn School of Dancing and Related Arts was founded in Los Angeles.
1926	Martha Graham, one of the most innovative figures in Modern dance, gave her first recital in New York. In England, students from the Rambert School of Ballet, opened by Marie Rambert 1920, gave their first public performance in *A Tragedy of Fashion*, the first ballet to be choreographed by Frederick Ashton.
1928	The first performance of George Balanchine's *Apollon Musagète* in Paris, by the Ballets Russes, marked the birth of Neo-Classicism in ballet.
1931	Ninette de Valois' Vic-Wells Ballet gave its first performance in London. In 1956 the company became the Royal Ballet.
1933	The Hollywood musical achieved artistic independence through Busby Berkeley's kaleidoscopic choreography in *42nd Street* and Dave Gould's airborne finale in *Flying Down to Rio*, in which Fred Astaire and Ginger Rogers appeared together for the first time.
1939	The American Ballet Theater was founded in New York.
1940	The Dance Notation Bureau was established in New York for recording ballets and dances.
1948	The New York City Ballet was founded with George Balanchine as artistic director and principal choreographer. The film *The Red Shoes* appeared, choreographed by Massine and Robert Helpmann, starring Moira Shearer.
1950	The Festival Ballet, later to become the London Festival Ballet, was created by Alicia Markova and Anton Dolin, who had first danced together with the Ballets Russes de Monte Carlo 1929.

(cont.)

dance: chronology (*cont.*)	
1952	Gene Kelly starred and danced in the film *Singin' in the Rain*.
1953	The US experimental choreographer Merce Cunningham, who often worked with the composer John Cage, formed his own troupe.
1956	The Bolshoi Ballet opened its first season in the West at Covent Garden in London, with Galina Ulanova dancing in *Romeo and Juliet*.
1957	Jerome Robbins conceived and choreographed the musical *West Side Story*, demonstrating his outstanding ability to work in both popular and classical forms.
1960	The progressive French choreographer Maurice Béjart became director of the Brussels-based Ballet du XXième Siècle company.
1961	Rudolf Nureyev defected from the USSR while dancing with the Kirov Ballet in Paris. He was to have a profound influence on male dancing in the West. The South African choreographer John Cranko became director and chief choreographer of the Stuttgart Ballet, transforming it into a major company.
1962	Glen Tetley's ballet *Pierrot lunaire*, in which he was one of the three dancers, was premiered in New York. In the same year he joined the Nederlands Dans Theater.
1965	US choreographer Twyla Tharp produced her first works.
1966–67	The School of Contemporary Dance was founded in London, from which Robin Howard and the choreographer Robert Cohan created the London Contemporary Dance Theatre, later to become an internationally renowned company. The choreographer Norman Morrice rejoined the Ballet Rambert as director and the company began to concentrate on contemporary works.
1968	Arthur Mitchell, the first black principal dancer to join the New York City Ballet, founded the Dance Theatre of Harlem.
1974	Mikhail Baryshnikov defected from the USSR while dancing with the Kirov Ballet in Toronto, and made his US debut with the American Ballet Theater.
1977	The release of Robert Stigwood's film *Saturday Night Fever* popularized disco dancing worldwide.
1980	Natalia Makarova, who had defected from the USSR 1979, staged the first full-length revival of Petipa's *La Bayadère* in the West with the American Ballet Theater in New York.
1981	Wayne Sleep, previously principal dancer with the Royal Ballet, starred as lead dancer in Andrew Lloyd-Webber's musical *Cats*, choreographed by Gillian Lynne.
1983	Peter Martins, principal dancer with the New York City Ballet, became choreographer and codirector with Jerome Robbins on the death of Balanchine. Break dancing became widely popular in Western inner cities.
1984	The avant-garde group Michael Clark and Company made its debut in London.
1990	*Maple Leaf Rag*, Martha Graham's final work, was premiered in New York City.. Classical dancer Peter Schaufuss became artistic director of the Berlin Ballet.
1991	The Royal Ballet moved to Birmingham, England, adopting the new name of the Birmingham Royal Ballet.

role. Dances requiring skilled athletic performance, such as the hustle and the New Yorker, have been developed. In classical dance, the second half of the 20th century has seen a great cross-fertilization from dances of other cultures. Troupes visited the West, not only from the USSR and Eastern Europe, but from such places as Indonesia, Japan, South Korea, Nigeria, and Senegal. In the 1970s jazz dance, pioneered in the USA by Matt Mattox, became popular; it includes elements of ballet, modern, tap, Indian Classical, Latin American, and Afro-American dance. Freestyle dance is loosely based on ballet with elements of jazz, ethnic, and modern dance.

Dance is the only art of which we ourselves are the stuff of which it is made.

Ted Shawn on dance *Time* July 1955

Dance Charles 1946– . English film and television actor who became known when he played the sympathetic Guy Perron in *The Jewel in the Crown* 1984. He has also appeared in *Plenty* 1986, *Good Morning Babylon*, *The Golden Child* both 1987, and *White Mischief* 1988.

Dance George, *the Younger* 1741–1825. English architect, best remembered for his unorthodox designs for Newgate Prison 1770–80, London (demolished 1902). An exponent of the Neo-Classical tradition, which he absorbed on a visit to Italy as a young man, he retained a highly individual and innovative in style. He was to exert a lasting influence on his pupil, John ◊Soane. Indeed, his design for All Hallows Church, London Wall, 1765–67, can be seen as a precursor of Soane's refined Classicism. His father *George Dance, the Elder* was the architect of the Mansion House 1739–42, London.

dance of death (German *Totentanz*, French *danse macabre*) popular theme in painting of the late medieval period, depicting an allegorical representation of death (usually a skeleton) leading the famous and the not-so-famous to the grave. One of the best-known representations is a series of woodcuts (1523–26) by Hans Holbein the Younger. It has also been exploited as a theme in music, for example the *Danse macabre* of Saint-Saëns 1874, an orchestral composition in which the xylophone was introduced to represent dancing skeletons.

Dance Umbrella annual British dance festival, held in London, established 1978. Its aim is to develop contemporary dance in Britain at all levels. Its artistic director and founder is Val Bourne (1938–   ).

dandy male figure conspicuous for tasteful fastidiousness, particularly in dress. The famous Regency dandy George ('Beau') Brummell (1778–1840) helped to give literary currency to the figure of the dandy, particularly in England and France, providing a model and symbol of the triumph of style for the Francophile Oscar ◊Wilde and for 19th-century French writers such as Charles ◊Baudelaire, J K ◊Huysmans, and the extravagantly romantic novelist and critic Jules-Amédée Barbey d'Aurevilly (1808–1889), biographer of Brummell.

Daniel Samuel 1562–1619. English poet, author of the sonnet collection *Delia* 1592. From 1603 he was master of the revels at court, for which he wrote masques.

Custom that is before all law, Nature that is above all art.

Samuel Daniel *A Defence of Rhyme* 1603

Daniels Sarah 1957–   . British dramatist. Her plays explore contemporary feminist issues, and include *Ripen Our Darkness* 1981, *Masterpieces* 1983, *Byrthrite* 1987, *Neaptide* 1984, *Beside Herself* 1990, and *Head-Rot Holiday* 1992, concerning women condemned to mental institutions.

Daninos Pierre 1913–   . French author. Originally a journalist, he was liaison agent with the British Army at Dunkirk in 1940, and created in *Les Carnets du Major Thompson/The Notebooks of Major Thompson* 1954 a humorous Englishman who caught the French imagination.

Danish literature Danish writers of international fame emerged in the 19th century: Hans Christian Andersen, the philosopher Søren Kierkegaard, and the critic Georg Brandes (1842–1927), all of whom played a major part in the Scandinavian literary awakening, encouraging Ibsen and others. The novelists Henrik Pontoppidan (1857–1943), Karl Gjellerup (1857–1919), and Johannes Jensen (1873–1950) were all Nobel prizewinners.

Dankworth John 1927–   . British jazz musician, composer, and bandleader, a leading figure in the development of British jazz from about 1950. His film scores include *Saturday Night and Sunday Morning* 1960 and *The Servant* 1963.

D'Annunzio Gabriele 1863–1938. Italian poet, novelist, and playwright. Marking a departure from 19th-century Italian literary traditions, his use of language and style of writing earned him much criticism in his own time. His novels, often combining elements of corruption, snobbery, and scandal, include *L'innocente* 1891 and *Il triomfo della morte/The Triumph of Death* 1894.

His first volume of poetry, *Primo vere/In Early Spring* 1879, was followed by further collections of verse, short stories, novels, and plays (he wrote the play *La Gioconda* for the actress Eleonora ◊Duse1898). After serving in World War I, he led an expedition of volunteers 1919 to capture Fiume, which he held until 1921, becoming a national hero. Influenced by Nietzsche's writings, he later became an ardent exponent of Fascism.

Dante Alighieri 1265–1321. Italian poet. His masterpiece *La divina commedia/The Divine Comedy* 1307–21 is an epic account in three parts of his journey through Hell, Purgatory, and Paradise, during which he is guided part of the way by the poet Virgil; on a metaphorical level the journey is also one of Dante's own spiritual development. Other works include the philosophical prose treatise *Convivio/The Banquet* 1306–08, the first major work of its kind to be written in Italian rather than Latin; *Monarchia/On World Government* 1310–13, expounding his political theories; *De vulgari eloquentia/Concerning the Vulgar Tongue* 1304–06, an original Latin work on Italian, its dialects, and kindred languages; and *Canzoniere/Lyrics*, containing his scattered lyrics.

Dante was born in Florence, where in 1274 he first met and fell in love with Beatrice Portinari (described in *La vita nuova/New Life* 1283–92). His love for her survived her marriage to another and her death 1290 at the age of 24. He married Gemma Donati 1291.

In 1289 Dante fought in the battle of Campaldino, won by Florence against Arezzo, and from 1295 took an active part in Florentine politics. In 1300 he was one of the six Priors of the Republic, favouring the moderate 'White' Guelph party rather than the extreme papal 'Black' Ghibelline faction; when the Ghibellines seized power 1302, he was convicted in his absence of misapplication of public money, and sentenced first to a fine and then to death. He escaped from Florence and spent the remainder of his life in exile, in central and N Italy.

There is no greater sorrow than to recall a time of happiness in misery.

Dante Alighieri
The Divine Comedy 1307–21: Inferno, V

---

danzon Cuban folk dance in two/four rhythm.

Daphne in Greek mythology, a ◊nymph who was changed into a laurel tree to escape from ◊Apollo's amorous pursuit.

Da Ponte Lorenzo (Conegliano Emmanuele) 1749–1838. Librettist renowned for his collaboration with Mozart in *The Marriage of Figaro* 1786, *Don Giovanni* 1787, and *Così fan tutte* 1790. His adaptations of contemporary plays are deepened by a rich life experience and understanding of human nature.

d'Arblay, Madame married name of British writer Fanny ◊Burney.

Darío Rubén. Pen name of Félix Rubén García Sarmiento 1867–1916. Nicaraguan poet. His first major work *Azul/Azure* 1888, a collection of prose and verse influenced by French Symbolism, created a sensation. He went on to establish **modernismo**, the Spanish-American modernist literary movement, distinguished by an idiosyncratic and deliberately frivolous style that broke away from the prevailing Spanish provincialism and adapted French poetic models. His vitality and eclecticism influenced every poet writing in Spanish after him, both in the New World and in Spain.

Dart Thurston 1921–1971. English harpsichordist and musicologist whose pioneer reinterpretations of Baroque classics such as Bach's *Brandenburg Concertos* helped to launch the trend towards authenticity in early music.

Das Kapital three-volume work presenting the theories of German philosopher and social theorist Karl Marx on economic production, published 1867–95. It focuses on the exploitation of the worker and appeals for a classless society where the production process and its rewards are shared equally.

Daudet Alphonse 1840–1897. French novelist. He wrote about his native Provence in *Lettres de mon moulin/Letters from my Mill* 1866, and created the character Tartarin, a hero epitomizing southern temperament, in *Tartarin de Tarascon* 1872 and two sequels.

Other works include the play *L'Arlésienne/The Woman from Arles* 1872, for which Bizet composed the music; and *Souvenirs d'un homme de lettres/Recollections of a Literary Man* 1889.

Daudet Léon 1867–1942. French writer and journalist, who founded the militant right-wing royalist periodical *Action Française* 1899 after the Dreyfus case. During World War II he was a collaborator with the Germans. He was the son of Alphonse Daudet.

Daumier Honoré 1808–1879. French artist. His sharply dramatic and satirical cartoons dissected Parisian society. He produced over 4,000 lithographs and, mainly after 1860, powerful, sardonic oil paintings that were little appreciated in his lifetime.

Daumier drew for *La Caricature, Charivari*, and other periodicals. He created several fictitious stereotypes of contemporary figures and was once imprisoned for an attack on King Louis Philippe. His paintings show a fluent technique and a mainly monochrome palette. He also produced

sculptures of his caricatures, such as the bronze statuette of *Ratapoil* about 1850 (Louvre, Paris).

Davenant William 1606–1668. English poet and dramatist, poet laureate from 1638. His *Siege of Rhodes* 1656 is sometimes considered the first English opera. His plays include *The Wits* and *Love and Honour*, both 1634.

David statue in marble by ◊Michelangelo 1501–04 (Accademia, Florence). The subject of David, biblical boy hero who killed the giant Goliath, was a popular symbol of the small republic of Florence; that Michelangelo portrayed him as a giant was seen as a grand statement of civic confidence. The sculpture's size (about 5.5 m/18 ft) combined with the mastery of its execution has made it a symbol of the Renaissance itself.

David Félicien César 1810–1876. French composer. His symphonic fantasy *The Desert* 1844 was inspired by travels in Palestine. He was one of the first Western composers to introduce oriental scales and melodies into his music.

David Gerard c. 1450–1523. Netherlandish painter active chiefly in Bruges from about 1484. His style follows that of Rogier van der ◊Weyden, but he was also influenced by the taste in Antwerp for Italianate ornament. *The Marriage at Cana* about 1503 (Louvre, Paris) is an example of his work.

David Jacques-Louis 1748–1825. French Neo-Classical painter. He was an active supporter of, and unofficial painter to, the republic during the French Revolution, and was imprisoned 1794–95. In his *Death of Marat* 1793 (Musées Royaux, Brussels), he turned political murder into Classical tragedy. Later he devoted himself to the newly created Empire in paintings such as the vast, pompous *Coronation of Napoleon* 1805–07 (Louvre, Paris).

David won the Prix de Rome 1774 and studied in Rome 1776–80. Back in Paris, his strongly Classical themes and polished style soon earned him success; an important picture from this period is *The Oath of the Horatii* 1784 (Louvre, Paris). During the Revolution he was elected to the Convention, became a member of the Committee of Public Safety, and narrowly escaped the guillotine. He was later appointed court painter to the emperor Napoleon, for whom he created such grand images as *Napoleon Crossing the Alps* 1800 (Louvre, Paris). After Napoleon's fall, David was banished by the Bourbons and settled in Brussels. Among his finest works are *The Rape of the Sabine Women* 1799 (Louvre, Paris) and *Mme Récamier* 1800 (Louvre, Paris).

David Copperfield novel by Charles ◊Dickens, published 1849–50. The story follows the orphan David Copperfield from his school days and early poverty to eventual fame as an author. Among the characters he encounters are Mr Micawber, Mr Peggotty, and Uriah Heep.

Davidson John 1857–1909. Scottish poet whose modern, realistic idiom, as in 'Thirty Bob a Week', influenced T S ◊Eliot.

Davies Henry Walford 1869–1941. English composer and broadcaster. From 1934 he was Master of the King's Musick, and he contributed to the musical education of Britain through regular radio talks. His compositions include the cantata *Everyman* 1904, the 'Solemn Melody' 1908 for organ and strings, chamber music, and part songs.

Davies Peter Maxwell 1934– . English composer and conductor. His music combines medieval and serial codes of practice with a heightened Expressionism as in his opera *Taverner* 1962–68. Other works include the opera *The Lighthouse* 1980. He was appointed conductor of the BBC Scottish Symphony Orchestra 1985.

Davies Robertson 1913– . Canadian novelist. He published the first novel of his Deptford trilogy *Fifth Business* 1970, a panoramic work blending philosophy, humour, the occult, and ordinary life. Other works include *A Mixture of Frailties* 1958, *The Rebel Angels* 1981, and *What's Bred in the Bone* 1986.

Davies Siobhan 1950– . English choreographer and dancer. She was a founding member of the London Contemporary Dance Theatre (LCDT) 1967 and became its resident choreographer 1983–87. She is the founder and director of Siobhan Davies and Dancers 1981. Her Siobhan Davies Company was premiered during the 10th Dance Umbrella festival 1988. Her works, such as *Bridge the Distance* (for the LCDT) 1985, display a quiet, cool intensity. Other works include *Celebration* 1978 and *Embarque* 1988 (both for the Rambert Dance Company).

Davies W(illiam) H(enry) 1871–1940. Welsh poet, born in Monmouth. He went to the USA where he lived the life of a vagrant and lost his right foot stealing a ride under a freight car. His first volume of poems was *Soul's Destroyer* 1906. He published his *Autobiography of a Super-Tramp* 1908.

Davin Dan(iel) 1913–1990. New Zealand novelist and short-story writer, based in Oxford since 1945. His Irish Catholic upbringing and his wartime experience with the New Zealand Division provided the background for his acclaimed early novels *Cliffs of Fall* 1945 and *For the Rest of Our Lives* 1947.

His social and psychological concerns are reflected in *Selected Stories* 1981, in critical studies, and in an autobiography *Closing Times* 1975.

da Vinci see ◊Leonardo da Vinci, Italian Renaissance artist.

Davis Bette 1908–1989. US actress. She entered films 1930, and established a reputation as a forceful dramatic actress with *Of Human Bondage* 1934. Later films included *Dangerous* 1935 and *Jezebel* 1938, both winning her Academy Awards, *All About Eve* 1950, and *Whatever Happened to Baby Jane?* 1962. She continued to make films throughout the 1980s such as *The Whales of August* 1987, in which she co-starred with Lillian Gish.

Her screen trademarks were a clipped, precise diction and a flamboyant use of cigarettes. Her appeal to female audiences came from her portrayal of wilful, fiercely independent women who survived despite the adversities thrown at them.

Davis Colin 1927– . English conductor. He was musical director at Sadler's Wells 1961–65, chief conductor of the BBC Symphony Orchestra 1967–71, musical director of the Royal Opera, Covent Garden, 1971–86, and chief conductor of the Bavarian Radio Symphony Orchestra from 1986. He is particularly associated with the music of Berlioz, Mozart, and Tippett.

Davis Miles (Dewey, Jr) 1926–1991. US jazz trumpeter, composer, and bandleader, one of the most influential and innovative figures in jazz. He pioneered bebop with Charlie Parker 1945, cool jazz in the 1950s, and jazz-rock fusion from the late 1960s. His albums include *Birth of the Cool* 1957 (recorded 1949 and 1950), *Sketches of Spain* 1959, *Bitches Brew* 1970, and *Tutu* 1985.

Davis, born in Illinois, joined Charlie Parker's group 1946–48. In 1948 he began an association with composer and arranger Gil Evans (1912–1988) that was to last throughout his career. His quintet in 1955 featured the saxophone player John Coltrane, who recorded with Davis until 1961; for example, *Kind of Blue* 1959. In 1968 Davis introduced electric instruments, later adding electronic devices to his trumpet and more percussion to his band. He went on to use disco backings, record pop songs, and collaborate with rock musicians, remaining changeable to the end.

Davis Sammy, Jr 1925–1990. US entertainer. His starring role in the Broadway show *Mr Wonderful* 1956, his television work, and his roles in films with Frank Sinatra's 'Rat Pack' – among them, *Ocean's Eleven* 1960 and *Robin and the Seven Hoods* 1964 – made him a celebrity. He also appeared in the film version of the opera *Porgy and Bess* 1959. He published two memoirs, *Yes I Can* 1965 and *Why Me?* 1989.

Born in New York City, Davis appeared on stage at age four and became a member of the Will Mastin Trio 1932. Recognized as one of the best tap dancers in the country, he served as an army entertainer during World War II and became a nightclub headliner in the 1950s.

Davis Stuart 1894–1964. US abstract painter. Much of his work shows the influence of both jazz tempos and Cubism in its use of hard-edged geometric shapes in primary colours and

◊collage. In the 1920s he produced paintings of commercial packaging, such as *Lucky Strike* 1921 (Museum of Modern Art, New York), that foreshadowed Pop art.

Davy Jones personification of a malevolent spirit of the sea. The phrase 'gone to Davy Jones' locker' is used by sailors referring to those drowned at sea.

Dawe (Donald) Bruce 1930– . Australian poet. His most successful poems are distinguished by wittily inventive use of everyday language and imagery, addressing serious subjects with unsentimental yet gentle dignity. Collections include *No Fixed Address* 1962, *Condolences of the Season* 1971, and *Just a Dugong at Twilight* 1975. His collected poems were published as *Sometimes Gladness* 1978.

Dawson Peter 1882–1961. Australian bass-baritone, remembered for his elegant recordings of marching songs and ballads from World War I.

Day Doris. Stage name of Doris von Kappelhoff 1924– . US film actress and singing star of the 1950s and early 1960s, mostly in musicals and, often with Rock Hudson, coy sex comedies. Her films include *Tea for Two* 1950, *Calamity Jane* 1953, *Love Me or Leave Me* 1955, and Hitchcock's *The Man Who Knew Too Much* 1956. With *Pillow Talk* 1959, *Lover Come Back* 1962, and other 1960s light sex comedies, she played a self-confident but coy woman who caused some of the biggest male stars to capitulate.

Day Lewis Cecil 1904–1972. Irish poet, British poet laureate 1968–72. With W H Auden and Stephen Spender, he was one of the influential left-wing poets of the 1930s. He also wrote detective novels under the pseudonym **Nicholas Blake**.

Born at Ballintubber, Ireland, he was educated at Oxford and then taught at Cheltenham College 1930–35. His work, which includes *From Feathers to Iron* 1931 and *Overtures to Death* 1938, is marked by accomplished lyrics and sustained narrative power. Professor of poetry at Oxford 1951–56, he published critical works and translations from Latin of Virgil's *Georgics* and the *Aeneid*.

In 1968 he succeeded John Masefield as poet laureate. His autobiography, *The Buried Day* 1960, was followed by a biography written by his eldest son, Sean, 1980.

There's a kind of release/And a kind of torment in every/Goodbye for every man.

Cecil Day Lewis 'Departure in the Dark'
Short is the Time 1943

Dazai Osamu. Pen name of Shuji Tsushima 1909–1948. Japanese novelist and short-story writer. The title of his novel *The Setting Sun* 1947

became identified in Japan with the dead of World War II.

D.C. in music, abbreviation for *da capo* (Italian 'from the beginning').

Dean Basil 1888–1978. British founder and director-general of Entertainments National Service Association (◊ENSA) 1939, which provided entertainment for the Allied forces in World War II.

Dean James (Byron) 1931–1955. US actor. Killed in a car accident after the public showing of his first film, *East of Eden* 1955, he posthumously became a cult hero with *Rebel Without a Cause* 1955 and *Giant* 1956. His image has endured as the classic icon of teenage rebellion throughout the decades since his death.

Death of a Salesman play 1949 by Arthur ◊Miller, the story of the defeated sales representative Willy Loman, which captured the limitations and deceptions of the American dream of success.

Debussy (Achille-) Claude 1862–1918. French composer. He broke with German Romanticism and introduced new qualities of melody and harmony based on the whole-tone scale, evoking oriental music. His work includes *Prélude à l'après-midi d'un faune/Prelude to the Afternoon of a Faun* 1894, illustrating a poem by Mallarmé, and the opera *Pelléas et Mélisande* 1902.

Among his other works are numerous piano pieces, songs, orchestral pieces such as *La Mer* 1903–05, and the ballet *Jeux* 1910–13. Debussy also published witty and humorous critical writing about the music of his day, featuring the fictional character Monsieur Croche 'antidilettante' (professional debunker), a figure based on Erik ◊Satie.

Music is the arithmetic of sounds as optics is the geometry of light.

Claude Debussy

---

decadence in literary and artistic criticism, the decline that follows a time of great cultural achievement. It is typified by world-weariness, self-consciousness, and the search for new stimulation through artistic refinement and degenerate behaviour. The term is used especially in connection with the *fin-de-siècle* styles of the late 19th century (Symbolism, the Aesthetic Movement, and Art Nouveau). It has been applied to such artists and writers as Rimbaud, Oscar Wilde, and Aubrey Beardsley.

Decameron, The collection of tales by the Italian writer Giovanni Boccaccio, brought together 1348–53. Ten young people, fleeing plague-stricken Florence, amuse their fellow travellers by each telling a story every day of the ten days they spend together. The work had a great influence on English literature, particularly on Chaucer's *Canterbury Tales*.

De Carlo Giancarlo 1919– . Italian architect, whose series of buildings in the Renaissance hill town of Urbino (begun 1952) are notable in their sensitivity towards context and urban continuity. The Faculty of Education, Urbino 1968–76, respects the fabric of the town while opening out towards the Umbrian countryside with a glazed cascade of lecture theatres.

De Carlo worked under the patronship of Carlo Bo, rector of Urbino University, and in 1959 helped to found **Team 10**, following the collapse of ◊CIAM. His other works include the student residences, Urbino 1962–66 and 1973–83, and the Mazzorbo housing scheme, Venice 1979–85.

Decline and Fall of the Roman Empire historical work by Edward ◊Gibbon, published in England 1776–88.

Deconstruction in literary theory, a radical form of ◊structuralism, pioneered by the French philosopher Jacques Derrida (1930–), which views text as a 'decentred' play of structures, lacking any ultimately determinable meaning.

Through analysis of the internal structure of a text, particularly its contradictions, Deconstructionists demonstrate the existence of subtext meanings — often not those that the author intended — and hence illustrate the impossibility of attributing fixed meaning to a work. Roland ◊Barthes laid the foundations of Deconstruction in his book *Mythologies* 1957 in which he studied the inherent instability between sign and referent in a range of cultural phenomena, including not only literary works but also such things as advertising, cookery, wrestling, and so on.

Deconstructionism in architecture, a style that fragments forms and space by taking the usual building elements of floors, walls, and ceilings and sliding them apart to create a sense of disorientation and movement. Its proponents include Zaha Hadid in the UK, Frank Gehry and Peter Eisenman in the USA, and Coop Himmelbau in Austria. Essentially Modernist, it draws inspiration from the optimism of the Soviet avant-garde of the 1920s.

Decorated in architecture, the second period of English Gothic, covering the latter part of the 13th century and the 14th century. Chief characteristics include ornate window tracery, the window being divided into several lights by vertical bars called mullions; sharp spires ornamented with crockets and pinnacles; complex church vaulting; and slender arcade piers. The reconstruction of Exeter Cathedral (begun about 1270) is a notable example.

de Falla Manuel. Spanish composer; see ◊Falla, Manuel de.

de Filippo Eduardo 1900–1984. Italian actor and dramatist. He founded his own company in Naples 1932, which was strongly influenced by the ◊commedia dell'arte, and for which he wrote many plays. These include his finest comedies, *Filumena Marturano* 1946, *Napoli milionaria!* 1945, *Questi fantasmi!/These Ghosts!* 1946, *Grande magia/Grand Magic* 1951, and *Saturday, Sunday, Monday* 1959.

Defoe Daniel 1660–1731. English writer. His ◊*Robinson Crusoe* 1719, though purporting to be a factual account of shipwreck and solitary survival, was influential in the development of the novel. The fictional *Moll Flanders* 1722 and the partly factual *A Journal of the Plague Year* 1724 are still read for their realism. A prolific journalist and pamphleteer, he was imprisoned 1702–04 for the ironic *The Shortest Way with Dissenters* 1702.

Defoe first achieved fame with the satire *The True-Born Englishman* 1701. His version of the contemporary short story 'True Relation of the Apparition of One Mrs Veal' 1706 first revealed a gift for realistic narrative.

Necessity makes an honest man a knave.

Daniel Defoe *Serious Reflections of Robinson Crusoe* 1720

Degas (Hilaire Germain) Edgar 1834–1917. French Impressionist painter and sculptor. He devoted himself to lively, informal studies (often using pastels) of ballet, horse racing, and young women working. From the 1890s he turned increasingly to sculpture, modelling figures in wax in a fluent, naturalistic style.

Degas studied under a pupil of Ingres and worked in Italy in the 1850s, painting Classical themes. In 1861 he met Manet, and exhibited regularly with the Impressionists 1874–86. His characteristic style soon emerged, showing the influence of Japanese prints and of photography in inventive compositions and unusual viewpoints, as in *Woman with Chrysanthemums* 1865 (Metropolitan Museum of Art, New York). An example of his sculpture is *The Little Dancer* 1881 (Tate Gallery, London).

Degenerate Art (German *Entartete Kunst*) art condemned by the Nazi regime, the name taken from a travelling exhibition mounted by the Nazi Party 1937 to show modern art as 'sick' and 'decadent' – a view that fitted with Nazi racial theories. The exhibition was paralleled by the official Great German Art Exhibition to display officially approved artists. However, five times as many people (more than 3 million) saw the former as the latter. Artists condemned included Beckmann, Nolde, Kandinsky, Matisse, Barlach, and Picasso.

De Havilland Olivia 1916– . US actress, a star in Hollywood from the age of 19, when she appeared in *A Midsummer Night's Dream* 1935. She later successfully played challenging dramatic roles in *Gone With the Wind* 1939, *To Each His Own* (Academy Award) and *Dark Mirror* 1946, and *The Snake Pit* 1948. She won her second Academy Award for *The Heiress* 1949, and played in *Lady in a Cage* and *Hush, Hush, Sweet Charlotte*, both 1964. She is the sister of actress Joan Fontaine.

Deianira in Greek mythology, wife of ◊Heracles, who won her in combat, and mother of his sons, considered ancestors of the Dorian Greeks. She killed Heracles by mistake, giving him poison instead of an aphrodisiac, and in her grief committed suicide. Her story is dramatized in Sophocles' *Women of Trachis*.

Deighton Len 1929– . British author of spy fiction, including *The Ipcress File* 1963 and the trilogy *Berlin Game, Mexico Set,* and *London Match* 1983–85, featuring the spy Bernard Samson. Samson was also the main character in Deighton's trilogy *Spy Hook* 1988, *Spy Line* 1989, and *Spy Sinker* 1990.

Deirdre in Celtic mythology, the beautiful intended bride of ◊Conchobar. She eloped with Noísi, and died of sorrow when Conchobar killed him and his brothers.

Dekker Thomas *c.* 1572–*c.* 1632. English dramatist and pamphleteer who wrote mainly in collaboration with others. His play *The Shoemaker's Holiday* 1599 was followed by collaborations with Thomas Middleton, John Webster, Philip Massinger, and others. His pamphlets include *The Gull's Hornbook* 1609, a lively satire on the fashions of the day.

de Kooning Willem 1904– . Dutch-born US painter who emigrated to the USA 1926 and worked as a commercial artist. After World War II he became, together with Jackson Pollock, one of the leaders of the Abstract Expressionist movement, although he retained figural images, painted with quick, violent brushstrokes. His *Women* series, exhibited 1953, was criticized for its grotesque depictions of women.

Delacroix Eugène 1798–1863. French Romantic painter. His prolific output included religious and historical subjects and portraits of friends, among them the musicians Paganini and Chopin. Antagonistic to the French academic tradition, he evolved a highly coloured, fluid style, as in *The Death of Sardanapalus* 1829 (Louvre, Paris).

The *Massacre at Chios* 1824 (Louvre, Paris) shows Greeks enslaved by wild Turkish horsemen, a contemporary atrocity (his use of a contemporary theme recalls Géricault's example). His style was influenced by the English landscape painter Constable. Delacroix also produced illustrations

for works by Shakespeare, Dante, and Byron. His *Journal* is a fascinating record of his times.

Delafield E M. Pen name of Edmée Elizabeth Monica de la Pasture 1890–1931. British writer, remembered for her amusing *Diary of a Provincial Lady* 1931, skilfully exploiting the foibles of middle-class life.

Delalande Michel-Richard 1657–1726. French organist and composer for the court of Louis XIV. His works include grand motets and numerous orchestral suites.

de la Mare Walter 1873–1956. English poet, known for his verse for children, such as *Songs of Childhood* 1902, and the novels *The Three Royal Monkeys* 1910 for children and, for adults, *The Memoirs of a Midget* 1921. He excelled at creating a sense of eeriness and sypernatural mystery.

His first book, *Songs of Childhood*, appeared under the pseudonym Walter Ramal. Later works include poetry for adults (*The Listeners* 1912 and *Collected Poems* 1942), anthologies (*Come Hither* 1923 and *Behold this Dreamer* 1939), and short stories.

de la Ramée Louise. British novelist who wrote under the name of ◊Ouida.

de la Renta Oscar 1932– . US fashion designer with his own luxury ready-to-wear label from 1965, later diversifying into perfumes, swimwear, and jewellery. In 1993 he began designing the couture collections for the couture house Balmain. He is noted for the use of opulent fabrics in evening clothes.

de la Roche Mazo 1885–1961. Canadian novelist. Experience of life in an area of southern Ontario dominated by large estates centred on big houses gave her the idea for the immensely popular 15-novel saga of the Whiteoaks of Jalna 1927–60. It is characterized by primitive passions seen against a background of nature and animal life and given unity by the brooding presence of the Anglo-Irish matriarch Adeline Whiteoak and her descendants.

Delaroche Paul 1797–1856. French historical artist. His melodramatic, often sentimental, historical paintings achieved great contemporary popularity; an example is *Lady Jane Grey* 1833 (National Gallery, London).

Delaunay Robert 1885–1941. French painter, a pioneer of abstract art. With his wife Sonia Delaunay-Terk, he developed a style known as ◊Orphism, an early variation of Cubism, focusing on the effects of pure colour contrasts.

Working from the colour theories of the French chemist Michel Chevreul, Delaunay and his wife explored the simultaneous effects of light on disc-like planes of radiant, contrasting colour, their aim being to produce a visual equivalent to music. In 1912 Delaunay painted several series, notably *Circular Forms* (almost purely abstract) and *Simultaneous Windows* (inspired by Parisian cityscapes).

Delaunay-Terk Sonia 1885–1979. French painter and textile designer born in Russia, active in Paris from 1905. With her husband Robert Delaunay, she was a pioneer of abstract art.

De Laurentiis Dino 1919– . Italian film producer. His early films, including Fellini's *La strada/The Street* 1954, brought more acclaim than later epics such as *Waterloo* 1970. He then produced a series of Hollywood films: *Death Wish* 1974, *King Kong* (remake) 1976, and *Dune* 1984.

Delibes (Clément Philibert) Léo 1836–1891. French composer. His lightweight, perfectly judged works include the ballet *Coppélia* 1870, *Sylvia* 1876, and the opera *Lakmé* 1883.

DeLillo Don 1936– . US novelist. His dark and highly complex novels examine images of American culture, power, conspiracy, and obsession. They include: the news media as a network of controls in *Americana* 1971; sport as a cult in *End Zone* 1972; mathematics and myth in *Ratner's Star* 1976; the Kennedy assassination in ◊*Libra* 1988; and celebrity, terrorism, and disaster in *Mao II* 1991.

Delius Frederick (Theodore Albert) 1862–1934. English composer of haunting, richly harmonious works including the opera *A Village Romeo and Juliet* 1901; the choral pieces *Appalachia* 1903, *Sea Drift* 1904, *A Mass of Life* 1905; orchestral works such as *In a Summer Garden* 1908, *A Song of the High Hills* 1911; chamber music; and songs.
  Born in Bradford, he tried orange-growing in Florida, before studying music in Leipzig 1888, where he met Grieg. From 1890 Delius lived mainly in France and in 1903 married the artist Jelka Rosen. Although blind and paralysed for the last ten years of his life, he continued to compose.

della Robbia Italian family of artists; see ◊Robbia, della.

Deller Alfred 1912–1979. English singer who revived the ◊countertenor voice and repertoire of 16th- to 18th-century music. He founded the Deller Consort 1950 and made notable recordings of Dowland, Blow, and Purcell.

Delon Alain 1935– . French film actor of smooth good looks who graduated from youthful charmer to character roles. He appeared in *Purple Noon* 1960, *Rocco e i suoi fratelli/Rocco and His Brothers* 1960, *Il gattopardo/The Leopard* 1963, *Texas Across the River* 1966, *Scorpio* 1972, and *Swann in Love* 1983.

Delorme Philibert c. 1512–1570. French Renaissance architect, remembered principally as author of two important architectural treatises *Nouvelles Intentions* 1561 and *Architecture* 1567. His building work includes the tomb of Francis I in St Denis, begun 1547, and extensions to the château of Chenonceaux 1557, including the first storey of the picturesque covered bridge; little else remains intact.

Delphi city of ancient Greece, situated in a rocky valley north of the gulf of Corinth, on the southern slopes of Mount Parnassus, site of a famous ◊oracle in the temple of Apollo. The site was supposed to be the centre of the Earth and was marked by a conical stone, the *omphelos*. The oracle was interpreted by priests from the inspired utterances of the Pythian priestess until it was closed down by the Roman emperor Theodosius I AD 390.

Delsarte François 1811–1871. French music teacher and theoretician. He devised a system of of body movements, designed to develop coordination, grace, and expressiveness, which greatly inspired the pioneers of modern dance, such as Emile ◊Jaques-Dalcroze and Ted Shawn (see ◊Denishawn).

del Sarto Andrea 1486–1531. Italian Renaissance painter; see ◊Andrea del Sarto.

Delvaux Paul 1897– . Belgian Surrealist painter, renowned for his unearthly canvases portraying female nudes in settings of ruined, classical architecture. He was initially influenced by Dali, Chirico, and Magritte, but later developed his own unique style, reflecting a preoccupation with time, eroticism, and death. His nudes are typically somnabulant and frequently accompanied by stilled locomotives, skeletons, half-moons, and mirrors, as in *Sleeping Venus* 1944 (Tate Gallery, London).

Demachy Robert 1859–1936. French photographer. By a complex manipulation of the printing process, using oils and gums, he produced hazy and impressionistic images, largely of young women in landscape or 'backstage' settings. He wrote several books about his printing techniques.

Demeter in Greek mythology, the goddess of agriculture (Roman Ceres), daughter of Kronos and Rhea, and mother of Persephone by Zeus. Demeter and Persephone were worshipped in a sanctuary at Eleusis, where one of the foremost mystery religions (open only to the initiated) of Greece was celebrated. She was later identified with the Egyptian goddess ◊Isis.

De Mille Agnes 1909–1989. US dancer and choreographer. She introduced popular dance idioms into ballet with such works as *Rodeo* 1942. One of the most significant contributors to the American Ballet Theater with dramatic ballets like *Fall River Legend* 1948, based on the Lizzie Borden murder case, she also led the change on Broadway to new-style musicals with her choreography of *Oklahoma!* 1943, *Carousel* 1945, and others.
  De Mille studied ballet with Marie Rambert in the UK, dancing in ballets and musicals in

Europe before making her debut as a choreographer in the USA. She was the niece of film director Cecil B DeMille.

De Mille Cecil B(lount) 1881–1959. US film director and producer. He entered films 1913 with Jesse L Lasky (with whom he later established Paramount Pictures), and was one of the founders of Hollywood. He specialized in biblical epics, such as *The Sign of the Cross* 1932 and *The Ten Commandments* 1923; remade 1956. He also made the 1952 Academy-Award-winning *The Greatest Show on Earth*.

Remember you are a star. Never go across the alley even to dump garbage unless you are dressed to the teeth.

Cecil B De Mille advice to a film actress

---

de Morgan William Frend 1839–1917. English pottery designer. He set up his own factory 1888 in Fulham, London, producing tiles and pottery painted with flora and fauna in a style typical of the Arts and Crafts movement.

Inspired by William ◊Morris and Edward ◊Burne-Jones, he started designing tiles and glass for Morris' Merton Abbey factory. His work was influenced by Persian and Italian styles – he spent many months in Italy in later years – and he also developed lustre techniques (a way of covering pottery with an iridescent metallic surface).

Demosthenes *c.* 384–322 BC. Athenian politician famed for his oratory. From 351 BC he led the party that advocated resistance to the growing power of Philip of Macedon, and in his *Philippics*, a series of speeches, incited the Athenians to war.

Dench Judi (Judith Olivia) 1934– . English actress who made her professional debut as Ophelia in *Hamlet* 1957 with the Old Vic Company. Her Shakespearean roles include Viola in *Twelfth Night* 1969, Lady Macbeth 1976, and Cleopatra 1987. She is also a versatile comedy actress and has directed *Much Ado about Nothing* 1988 and John Osborne's *Look Back in Anger* 1989 for the Renaissance Theatre Company.

Her films include *Wetherby* 1985, *A Room with a View* 1986, and *A Handful of Dust* 1988.

Deneuve Catherine 1943– . French actress acclaimed for her poise and her performance in Roman Polanski's film *Repulsion* 1965. She also appeared in *Les Parapluies de Cherbourg/Umbrellas of Cherbourg* 1964 (with her sister Françoise Dorléac (1942–1967)), *Belle de jour* 1967, *Hustle* 1975, *Le Dernier Métro/The Last Metro* 1980, *The Hunger* 1983, and *Indochine* 1993.

denier unit used in measuring the fineness of yarns, equal to the mass in grams of 9,000 metres of yarn. Thus 9,000 metres of 15 denier nylon,

used in nylon stockings, weighs 15 g/0.5 oz, and in this case the thickness of thread would be 0.00425 mm/0.0017 in. The term is derived from the French silk industry; the *denier* was an old French silver coin.

denim cotton twill fabric with coloured warp (lengthwise yarns) and undyed weft, originating in France (hence the name 'de Nîmes'). In its most classic form, indigo blue and heavyweight, it is used for jeans and dungarees. It became fashionable in the early 1970s, and many variations followed, including lighter-weight dress fabrics and stone-washed, overdyed, and brushed finishes in many colours.

De Niro Robert 1943– . US actor of great magnetism and physical presence. He won Academy Awards for his performances in *The Godfather Part II* 1974 and *Raging Bull* 1980, for which role he put on weight in the interests of authenticity as the boxer gone to seed, Jake LaMotta. His other films include *Mean Streets* 1973, *Taxi Driver* 1976, *The Deer Hunter* 1978, *The Untouchables* 1987, *Midnight Run* 1988, and *Cape Fear* 1992. He showed his versatility in *The King of Comedy* 1982 and other Martin Scorsese films.

Denis Maurice 1870–1943. French painter, illustrator, and art theorist, chiefly important as a founder-member and spokesman for *les* ◊*Nabis*. His friendship with Gauguin and admiration for Italian Renaissance art are reflected in his flat, decorative paintings of figures and landscapes, for example *The Muses or Sacred Wood* 1893 (Musée National d'Art Moderne, Paris).

Denis was the author of several influential articles and books on art theory, including *Théories, 1890–1910*, republished 1920. He also illustrated numerous books and executed large murals on religious themes, notably that in Sainte-Marguerite du Vésinet 1901–03.

Denishawn School of Dancing and Related Arts US modern dance company and school founded 1915 by dancers Ruth St Denis (1879–1968) and Ted Shawn (1891–1972) in Los Angeles. It was designed to improve body, mind, and soul, and provided the training ground for numerous exponents of modern dance including Martha Graham, Doris Humphrey, and Charles Weidman (1901–1975). The company toured extensively until 1931.

The school reflected the exotic influences of its two founders. Ruth St Denis' seductive interpretations of dances from India, Egypt, and Asia — such as *Cobras*, *Incense*, and *Radha*, all 1906 — were hugely popular in both America and Europe. She choreographed the Babylonian dances in D W Griffith's film, *Intolerance* 1916, making use of sinuous body movements and draperies. Shawn drew on native American and aboriginal folklore for inspiration for his dances, which he toured with Ted Shawn and his Men Dancers through the 1930s. His efforts to raise the masculine role in dance from its secondary status paved the way for male stars, such as Nureyev, to emerge.

denouement the unravelling of the plot of a work of fiction. In a typical structure, the denouement would come just before the end, following the climax. The detective story is a genre where the complication of plot usually needs a lengthy denouement, where all is explained to the reader.

De Palma Brian 1941– . US film director, especially of thrillers. His technical mastery and enthusiasm for spilling blood are shown in films such as *Sisters* 1973, *Carrie* 1976, and *The Untouchables* 1987. His *Bonfire of the Vanities* 1990 was a critical and commercial failure.

Depardieu Gérard 1948– . French actor renowned for his imposing physique and screen presence. His films include *Deux Hommes dans la ville* 1973, *Le Camion* 1977, *Mon Oncle d'Amérique* 1980, *The Moon in the Gutter* 1983, *Jean de Florette* 1985, and *Cyrano de Bergerac* 1990. His English-speaking films include the US romantic comedy *Green Card* 1990 and *1492 – Conquest of Paradise* 1992.

At 20 you have many desires that hide the truth, but beyond 40 there are only real and fragile truths — your abilities and your failings.

Gérard Depardieu *Observer* March 1991

---

deposition in Christian art, a depiction of the body of Christ being taken down from the cross. Notable examples include van der Weyden's *Deposition* about 1430 (Prado, Madrid) and Ruben's *Descent from the Cross* 1612–14 (Notre-Dame Cathedral, Antwerp).

De Quincey Thomas 1785–1859. English author whose works include *Confessions of an English Opium-Eater* 1821 and the essays 'On the Knocking at the Gate in Macbeth' 1823 and 'On Murder Considered as One of the Fine Arts' 1827. His work had a powerful influence on Charles Baudelaire and Edgar Allan Poe, among others. He was a friend of the poets Wordsworth and Coleridge.

Derain André 1880–1954. French painter. He experimented with the strong, almost primary colours associated with ◊Fauvism but later developed a more sombre landscape and figurative style. *Pool of London* 1906 (Tate Gallery, London) is a typical work. He also produced costumes and scenery for Diaghilev's Ballets Russes.

dervish dance religious dance of Islam. Part of the mystical Sufi tradition, its aim is to reach spiritual awareness with a trance-like state created by continual whirling. This spinning symbolizes the Earth's orbit of the Sun.

Deschamps Eustache 1346–1406. French poet, born in Champagne. He was the author of more than 1,000 ballades, and the *Miroir de mariage/The Mirror of Marriage*, an attack on women.

Friends – those relatives that one makes for one's self.

Eustache Deschamps *L'Ami*

De Sica Vittorio 1901–1974. Italian film director and actor. His *Bicycle Thieves* 1948 is a landmark of Italian neorealism. Later films included *Umberto D* 1952, *Two Women* 1960, and *The Garden of the Finzi-Continis* 1971. His considerable acting credits include *Madame de ...* 1953 and *The Millionaires* 1960. He won four Academy Awards for best foreign film with *Shoeshine* 1946, *Bicycle Thieves*, *Yesterday Today and Tomorrow* 1964, and *The Garden of the Finzi-Continis*.

Design Museum museum in London's Docklands dedicated to mass-produced goods with an emphasis on design. Opened 1989 and supported by the designer-entrepreneur Terence Conran, it sets out to promote 'awareness of the importance of design in education, industry, commerce and culture'.

The museum is unique in exhibiting design outside the traditional contexts of fine art or technology. It houses a permanent study collection, a 'review' section for contemporary products, and temporary exhibits.

Desprez Josquin. Franco-Flemish composer; see ◊Josquin Desprez.

Dessau Paul 1894–1979. German composer. His work includes incidental music to Bertolt Brecht's theatre pieces; an opera, *Der Verurteilung des Lukullus* 1949, also to a libretto by Brecht; and numerous choral works and songs.

He studied in Berlin, becoming a theatre conductor until moving to Paris 1933, where he studied Schoenberg's serial method with René Leibowitz. He collaborated with Brecht from 1942, when they met as political exiles in the USA, returning with him to East Berlin 1948.

detective fiction novel or short story in which a mystery is solved mainly by the action of a professional or amateur detective. Where the mystery to be solved concerns a crime, the work may be called **crime fiction**. The earliest work of detective fiction as understood today was 'The Murders in the Rue Morgue' 1841 by Edgar Allan Poe, and his detective Dupin became the model for those who solved crimes by deduction from a series of clues. A popular deductive sleuth was Sherlock Holmes in the stories by Arthur Conan Doyle.

The 'golden age' of the genre was the period from the 1920s to the 1940s, when the leading writers were women – Agatha Christie, Margery Allingham, and Dorothy L Sayers. Types of detective fiction include the *police procedural*, where the mystery is solved by detailed police work, as in the work of Swedish writers Maj Sjowall and Per Wahloo; the *inverted novel*, where the identity of the criminal is known from the beginning and only the method or the motive remains to be discovered, as in *Malice Aforethought* by Francis Iles; and the *hard-boiled school* of private investigators begun by Raymond Chandler and Dashiell Hammett, which became known for its social realism and explicit violence. More recently, the form and traditions of the genre have been used as a framework within which to explore other concerns, as in *Innocent Blood* and *A Taste for Death* by P D James, *The Name of the Rose* by Umberto Eco, and the works of many women writers who explore feminist ideas, as in *Murder in the Collective* by Barbara Wilson.

Like most genres, crime fiction has produced its oddities. *Murder in Pastiche* by Marion Mainwaring is written in the styles of nine famous writers. Agatha Christie, Georgette Heyer, and Ellis Peters have all written detective novels with historical settings. *Murder Off Miami* by Dennis Wheatley was a dossier containing real clues such as photographs, ticket stubs, and hairpins for the reader to use in solving the mystery; the solution was in a closed envelope at the back of the book.

Deucalion in Greek mythology, the son of ◊Prometheus, and an equivalent of Noah in the Old Testament. Warned by his father of a coming flood, Deucalion and his wife Pyrrha built an ark. After the waters had subsided, the stones they were instructed by a god to throw over their shoulders became men and women.

deus ex machina (Latin 'a god from the machine') far-fetched or unlikely event that resolves an intractable difficulty. The phrase was originally used in classical Greek and Roman tragedy to indicate a god lowered from 'heaven' on to the stage by machinery to resolve the plot.

Deutscher Werkbund German design reform organization set up 1907 to promote high standards of design within manufacturing industry. Membership covered a wide spectrum of people involved in design in different capacities, among them a number of key architect-designers such as Peter ◊Behrens and Henry Van de Velde (1863–1957). The emphasis was upon the need for a rational, standardized, democratic, modern design movement which could align itself with industrial production. It provided a model which was emulated widely in many other countries.

de Valois Ninette. Stage name of Edris Stannus 1898– . Irish-born English choreographer, dancer, and teacher. In setting up the Vic-Wells Ballet 1931 (later the Royal Ballet and Royal Ballet School) she was, along with choreographer Frederick ◊Ashton, one of the architects of British ballet. Among her works are *Job* 1931 and *Checkmate* 1937. She worked with Sergei Diaghilev in Paris (1923–25) before opening a dance academy in London 1926.

developing in photography, the process that produces a visible image on exposed photographic ◊film, involving the treatment of the exposed film with a chemical developer.

The developing liquid consists of a reducing agent that changes the light-altered silver salts in the film into darker metallic silver. The developed image is made permanent with a fixer, which dissolves away any silver salts which were not affected by light. The developed image is a negative, or reverse image: darkest where the strongest light hit the film, lightest where the least light fell. To produce a positive image, the negative is itself photographed, and the development process reverses the shading, producing the final print. Colour and black-and-white film can be obtained as direct reversal, slide, or transparency material. Slides and transparencies are used for projection or printing with a positive-to-positive process such as Cibachrome.

Devine George 1910–1965. English actor and theatre director. A director of the Young Vic training school from 1946, he was appointed artistic director of the English Stage Company at the Royal Court Theatre, London 1956, which became the home of the new wave of British dramatists, including John Osborne, Arnold Wesker, and John Arden.

Dewey Melvil 1851–1931. US librarian. In 1876, he devised the Dewey decimal system of classification for accessing, storing, and retrieving books, widely used in libraries. The system uses the numbers 000 to 999 to designate the major fields of knowledge, then breaks these down into more specific subjects by the use of decimals.

de Wint Peter 1784–1849. English landscape painter, of Dutch descent. He was a notable watercolourist, painting landscapes of the Lincolnshire area in particular.

dhola deep-toned Indian drum, barrel-shaped and played at both ends. It is played with the hands and produces a flexible tone that rises from bass to the tenor register.

diablo cojuelo, El (*The Lame Devil*) Spanish satirical novel in the ◊picaresque tradition by Luis Velez de Guevara (1579–1644), derived from Jewish legend. It was first published 1641 and later adapted by Alain-René ◊Le Sage as *Le Diable boiteux* 1707. The lame devil exposes hypocrisy and social evils to his companion Cleofás as they fly over the rooftops.

Diaghilev Sergei Pavlovich 1872–1929. Russian ballet impresario who in 1909 founded the Ballets Russes/Russian Ballet (headquarters in Monaco), which he directed for 20 years. Through this company he brought Russian ballet to the West, introducing and encouraging a dazzling array of dancers, choreographers, composers, and artists, such as Anna Pavlova, Vaslav Nijinsky, Bronislava Nijinksa, Mikhail Fokine, Léonide Massine, George Balanchine, Igor Stravinsky, Sergey Prokofiev, Pablo Picasso, and Henri Matisse.

Dial, The US magazine of transcendentalism 1840–44, founded in Boston by several of the transcendentalist group, including Margaret Fuller (1810–1850) and Ralph Waldo Emerson, its first and second editors respectively. Publishing Henry Thoreau and other major essayists and poets, it had great intellectual influence. Several later magazines used the same title. *The Dial* of the 1920s published modern poetry and criticism under Marianne Moore's editorship.

dialogue conversation between two or more people. Dialogue is direct speech, so it is represented in writing as a series of quotations, using quotation marks or, in dramatic dialogue, the characters' names followed by their speeches.

Diana in Roman mythology, the goddess of chastity, hunting, and the Moon, daughter of Jupiter and twin of Apollo. Her Greek equivalent is the goddess ◊Artemis.

diary informal record of day-to-day events, observations, or reflections, usually not intended for a general readership. One of the earliest diaries extant is that of a Japanese noblewoman, the *Kagero Nikki* 954–974, and the earliest known diary in English is that of Edward VI (ruled 1547–53). Notable diaries include those of Samuel Pepys and Anne Frank. The writer John Evelyn, the Quaker George Fox, and in the 20th century the writers André Gide and Katherine Mansfield were also diarists.

diatonic scale in music, a scale consisting of the seven notes of any major or minor key.

Dick Philip K(endred) 1928–1982. US science-fiction writer whose works often deal with religion and the subjectivity of reality. His protagonists are often alienated individuals struggling to retain their integrity in a technologically dominated world. His novels include *The Man in the High Castle* 1962, *Simulcra* 1964, and *Do Androids Dream of Electric Sheep?* 1968 (filmed as *Blade Runner* 1982).

Dickens Charles 1812–1870. English novelist, popular for his memorable characters and his portrayal of the social evils of Victorian England. In 1836 he published the first number of the *Pickwick Papers*, followed by *Oliver Twist* 1838, the first of his 'reforming' novels; *Nicholas Nickleby* 1839; *Barnaby Rudge* 1841; *The Old Curiosity Shop* 1841; and *David Copperfield* 1849. Among his later books are *A Tale of Two Cities* 1859 and *Great Expectations* 1861.

Born in Portsea, Hampshire, the son of a clerk, Dickens received little formal education, although a short period spent working in a blacking factory in S London, while his father was imprisoned for debt in the Marshalsea prison during 1824, was followed by three years in a private school. In 1827 he became a lawyer's clerk, and then after four years a reporter for the *Morning Chronicle*, to which he contributed the *Sketches by Boz*. In 1836 he married Catherine Hogarth, three days after the publication of the first number of the *Pickwick Papers*. Originally intended merely as an accompaniment to a series of sporting illustrations, the adventures of Pickwick outgrew their setting and established Dickens' reputation. In 1842 he visited the USA, where his attack on the pirating of English books

Dickens: major works

title	date	well-known characters
The Pickwick Papers	1836	Mr Pickwick, Sam Weller, Mr Snodgrass, Mr Jingle, Mr and Mrs Bardell
Oliver Twist	1838	Oliver Twist, Fagin, Mr Bumble, The Artful Dodger
Nicholas Nickleby	1839	Nicholas Nickleby, Wackford Squeers, Madame Mantalini, Smike, Vincent Crummles
The Old Curiosity Shop	1841	Little Nell, Dick Swiveller, Daniel Quilp
Barnaby Rudge	1841	Simon Tappertit (Sim), Miss Miggs, Gashford
A Christmas Carol	1843	Ebenezer Scrooge, Bob Cratchit, Marley's Ghost, Tiny Tim
Martin Chuzzlewit	1843	Martin Chuzzlewit (Junior), Mr Pecksniff, Mrs Gamp, Tom Pinch
Dombey and Son	1848	Dombey, Paul and Florence Dombey, Edith Granger, James Carker, Major Bagstock
David Copperfield	1849	David Copperfield, Mr Micawber, Mr Dick, Uriah Heep, Little Em'ly, Betsey Trotwood
Bleak House	1853	John Jarndyce, Esther Summerson, Harold Skimpole, Lady Dedlock, Mrs Jellyby
Hard Times	1854	Gradgrind, Tom and Louisa Gradgrind, Josiah Bounderby, Bitzer, Cissy Jupe
Little Dorrit	1857	Amy Dorrit, Flora Finching, Mr Merille
A Tale of Two Cities	1859	Dr Manette, Charles Darnay, Sydney Carton, Jerry Cruncher, Madame Defarge
Great Expectations	1861	Pip, Estella, Miss Havisham, Joe Gargery, Wemmick, Magwitch
Our Mutual Friend	1865	Noddy Boffin, Silas Wegg, Mr Podsnap, Betty Higden, Bradley Headstone, Reginald Wilfer
The Mystery of Edwin Drood (unfinished)	1870	Rosa Bud, John Jasper

by American publishers chilled his welcome; his experiences are reflected in *American Notes* and *Martin Chuzzlewit* 1843. In 1843 he published the first of his Christmas books, *A Christmas Carol*, followed 1844 by *The Chimes*, written in Genoa during his first long sojourn abroad, and in 1845 by the even more successful *Cricket on the Hearth*. A venture as editor of the Liberal *Daily News* 1846 was short-lived, and *Dombey and Son* 1848 was largely written abroad. *David Copperfield*, his most popular novel, appeared 1849 and contains many autobiographical incidents and characters. Returning to journalism, Dickens inaugurated the weekly magazine *Household Words* 1850, reorganizing it 1859 as *All the Year Round*; many of his later stories were published serially in these periodicals. In 1857 Dickens met the actress Ellen Ternan and in 1858 agreed with his wife on a separation; his sister-in-law remained with him to care for his children. In 1858 he began giving public readings from his novels, which proved such a success that he was invited to make a second US tour 1867. Among his later novels are *Bleak House* 1853, *Hard Times* 1854, *Little Dorrit* 1857, and *Our Mutual Friend* 1865. *Edwin Drood*, a mystery story influenced by the style of his friend Wilkie ◊Collins, was left incomplete on his death.

Now what I want is, Facts … Facts alone are wanted in life.

Charles Dickens *Hard Times* 1854

Dickens Monica (Enid) 1915–1992. British writer. Her first books were humorous accounts of her experiences in various jobs, beginning as a cook (*One Pair of Hands* 1939); she went on to become a novelist. She was a great-granddaughter of Charles Dickens.

Dickey James (Lafayette) 1923– . US poet, critic, and novelist. His fiction deals mainly with guilt arising from acts of individual or collective cruelty and the struggle for survival. His powerful best seller *Deliverance* 1970 (filmed 1972) is a menacing thriller about four men canoeing down a dangerous river. His poetry, initially traditional, turned to more open forms as in *The Central Motion: Poems 1968–1978* 1979.

Dickinson Emily (Elizabeth) 1830–1886. US poet. She wrote most of her poetry between 1850 and the late 1860s and was particularly prolific during the Civil War years. She experimented with poetic rhythms, rhymes, and forms, as well as language and syntax. Her work is characterized by a wit and boldness that seem to contrast sharply with the reclusive life she led in Amherst, Massachusetts. Very few of her many short, mystical poems were published during her lifetime, and her work became well known only in the 20th

century. The first collection of her poetry, *Poems by Emily Dickinson*, was published 1890.

Because I could not stop for Death -/He kindly stopped for me -/The Carriage held but just Ourselves -/And Immortality.

Emily Dickinson

Diddley Bo. Stage name of Ellas Bates McDaniel 1928– . US rhythm-and-blues guitarist, singer, and songwriter whose distinctive syncopated beat ('Shave and a haircut, two bits') became a rock staple; it can be heard in many of his classic songs, including *Bo Diddley* 1955, *Who Do You Love?* 1955, and *Mona* 1956.

Bo Diddley, born in Mississippi, recorded for the Chess label in Chicago 1955–74. ◊Muddy Waters had a hit with his song *Mannish Boy* (also known as *I'm a Man*) 1955. Relying more on distortion than technique, Bo Diddley's guitar style has influenced generations of garage bands.

Diderot Denis 1713–1784. French philosopher. He is closely associated with the ◊Enlightenment, the European intellectual movement for social and scientific progress, and was editor of the hugely influential ◊*Encyclopédie* 1751–80. An expanded and politicized version of the English encyclopedia 1728 of Ephraim Chambers (*c.* 1680–1740), this work exerted an enormous influence on contemporary social thinking with its materialism and anticlericalism. Its compilers were known as *Encyclopédistes*.

Diderot's materialism, most articulately expressed in *D'Alembert's Dream*, published after his death, sees the natural world as nothing more than matter and motion. His account of the origin and development of life is purely mechanical.

Didion Joan 1934– . US novelist and journalist. Her sharp, culturally evocative writing includes the novel *A Book of Common Prayer* 1970 and the essays of *The White Album* 1979.

didjeridu or *didgeridoo* musical lip-reed wind instrument, made from a hollow eucalyptus branch 1.5 m/4 ft long and blown to produce rhythmic, booming notes of relatively constant pitch. It was first developed and played by Australian Aborigines.

Dido Phoenician princess, legendary founder of Carthage, N Africa, who committed suicide to avoid marrying a local prince. In the Latin epic *Aeneid*, Virgil represents her death as the result of her desertion by the Trojan hero ◊Aeneas.

Dietrich Marlene (Maria Magdalene) 1904–1992. German-born US actress and singer who appeared with Emil Jannings in both the German and American versions of the film *The Blue Angel* 1930, directed by Josef von Sternberg.

She stayed in Hollywood, becoming a US citizen 1937. Her husky, sultry singing voice added to her appeal. Her other films include *Blonde Venus* 1932, *Destry Rides Again* 1939, and *Just a Gigolo* 1978. She was the subject of Maximilian Schell's documentary *Marlene* 1983.

The average man is more interested in a woman who is interested in him than he is in a woman – any woman – with beautiful legs.

Marlene Dietrich

---

diffusion in fashion, a phenomenon which arose in the 1980s whereby designer clothes are made available in a less expensive range. Cheaper fabrics combined with the basic elements of the designer's style make the clothes more affordable than the main ready-to-wear collection. The range usually remains associated with the designer's name, but is differentiated by the label. Diffusion ranges are often made under licence, and aimed at a younger market or a more casual style.

Dike ancient Greek concept of Justice, at times personified, typically as one of the ◊Horae (goddesses of the seasons) with Peace (Irene) and Good Order (Eunomia), daughters of Themis and Zeus.

dime novel melodramatic paperback novel of a series started in the USA in the 1850s, published by Beadle and Adams of New York, which frequently dealt with Deadwood Dick and his frontier adventures. Authors included Edward L Wheeler, E Z C Judson, Prentiss Ingraham, and J R Coryell. The 'Nick Carter' Library added detective stories to the genre. Like British 'penny dreadfuls', dime novels attained massive sales and were popular with troops during the American Civil War and World War I.

Today's mass-market paperbacks continue to serve readers of Westerns, mystery, science fiction, romance, and detective fiction that grew out of the dime-novel concept.

diminution in music, a reduction of interval size, of chord, loudness level, or note values of a theme.

Dine Jim 1935– . US pop artist. He experimented with combinations of paintings and objects, such as a bathroom sink attached to a canvas. Dine was a pioneer of ◊happenings in the 1960s and of ◊environment art.

Dinesen Isak 1885–1962. Pen name of Danish writer Karen ◊Blixen, born Karen Christentze Dinesen.

Ding Ling 1904–1986. Chinese novelist. Her works include *Wei Hu* 1930 and *The Sun Shines over the Sanggan River* 1951.

She was imprisoned by the Guomindang (Chiang Kai-shek's nationalists) in the 1930s, wrongly labelled as rightist and expelled from the Communist Party 1957, imprisoned in the 1960s and intellectually ostracized for not keeping to Maoist literary rules; she was rehabilitated 1979. Her husband was the writer Hu Yapin, executed by Chiang Kai-shek's police 1931.

Diomedes in Greek mythology, the son of Tydeus, and a prominent Greek leader in Homer's *Iliad*.

Dionysus in Greek mythology, the god of wine (son of Semele and Zeus), and also of orgiastic excess. He was attended by women called maenads, who were believed to be capable of tearing animals to pieces with their bare hands when under his influence. He was identified with the Roman ◊Bacchus, whose rites were less savage.

Dior Christian 1905–1957. French couturier. He established his own Paris salon 1947 and made an impact with the 'New Look' – long, cinch-waisted, and full-skirted — after wartime austerity.

He worked with Robert Piquet as design assistant 1938 and for Lucien Lelong 1941–46. His first collection 1947 was an instant success and he continued to be popular during the 1950s when he created elegant and sophisticated looks with slim skirts and large box-shaped jackets. His last collection 1957 was based on a waistless shift-style dress with the skirt narrowing towards the hem.

My dream is to save [women] from nature.

Christian Dior quoted in *Collier's* 1955

Dioscuri in classical mythology, title of ◊Castor and Pollux, meaning 'sons of Zeus'.

diptych painting or sculpture (usually in ivory) consisting of two panels hinged together, most often employed as a portable altar or ◊altarpiece. *The Wilton Diptych* about 1395 (National Gallery, London) is an example.

Directoire style French decorative arts style of the period from about 1792 to 1799, following the Revolution. The style, which took its name from the Directory, the government of the day, introduces revolutionary art motifs, such as the pike of freedom, into ◊Neo-Classicism. A noted furniture designer working in the style was Georges Jacob (1739–1814).

director in the theatre, film or television, a person who conducts rehearsals for actors and co-ordinates other aspects of production. In early periods of theatre, rehearsals were conducted by the dramatist, the leading actor, or a prompter.

From the late 19th century the role of the director in co-ordinating performance with scenic design, and in providing a stylistic discipline for the actors, became paramount. The director is also expected to provide an interpretation of the theatrical script, and in the cinema may be regarded as the 'author' of the film.

Dire Straits UK rock group formed 1977 by guitarist, singer, and songwriter Mark Knopfler (1949–). Their tasteful musicianship was tailor-made for the new compact-disc audience, and their 1985 LP *Brothers in Arms* went on to sell 20 million copies. Other albums include *On Every Street* 1991. Knopfler is also much in demand as a producer.

dirge song of lamentation for the dead. A poem of mourning is usually called an ◊elegy.

Dis in Roman mythology, the god of the underworld, also known as Orcus; he is equivalent to the Greek god ◊Pluto, ruler of Hades. Dis is also a synonym for the underworld itself.

disassociation of sensibility divorce between intellect and emotion. T S ◊Eliot coined this phrase 1921 in an essay on the metaphysical poets of the 17th century. He suggested that Donne, Marvell, and their contemporaries 'feel their thought as immediately as the odour of a rose' whereas later poets disengage intellect from emotion.

Disch Thomas M(ichael) 1940– . US writer and poet, author of such science-fiction novels as *Camp Concentration* 1968 and *334* 1972.

disco music international style of dance music of the 1970s with a heavily emphasized beat, derived from ◊funk. It was designed to be played in discotheques rather than performed live; hence the production was often more important than the performer, and drum machines came to dominate.

Self-produced US disco group KC and the Sunshine Band (formed 1973) had five number-one hits, including 'Shake Your Booty' 1976. German producer Giorgio Moroder (1941–) created numerous disco hits, many of them with US singer Donna Summer (1948–), including 'Love to Love You, Baby' 1975 and 'I Feel Love' 1977. US producer Nile Rodgers (1952–) is a member of disco group Chic (1977–83), whose hits include 'Everybody Dance' 1978 and 'Good Times' 1979. Disco music was celebrated in the 1977 film *Saturday Night Fever*.

discotheque club for dancing to pop music on records (discs), originating in the 1960s.

Disney Walt(er Elias) 1901–1966. US filmmaker and animator, a pioneer of family entertainment. He established his own studio in Hollywood 1923, and his first Mickey Mouse cartoons (*Plane Crazy*, which was silent, and *Steamboat Willie*, which had sound) appeared 1928. In addition to short cartoons, the studio later made feature-length animated films, including *Snow White and the Seven Dwarfs* 1938, *Pinocchio* 1940, and *Dumbo* 1941. Disney's cartoon figures, for example Donald Duck, also appeared in comic books worldwide. In 1955, Disney opened the first theme park, Disneyland, in California.

Using the new medium of sound film, Disney developed the 'Silly Symphony', a type of cartoon based on the close association of music with visual images. He produced these in colour from 1932, culminating in the feature-length *Fantasia* 1940. The Disney studio also made nature-study films such as *The Living Desert* 1953, which have been criticized for their fictionalization of nature: wild animals were placed in unnatural situations to create 'drama'. Feature films with human casts were made from 1946, such as *The Swiss Family Robinson* 1960 and *Mary Poppins* 1964. Disney also produced the first television series in colour 1961.

I love Mickey Mouse more than any woman I've ever known.

Walt Disney

Dispatches book 1977 by US writer Michael ◊Herr. A vivid novel of war reportage, it reveals the reality of fear and death behind the images of patriotism and heroism in America's involvement in the Vietnam War. It was the first powerful treatment of the subject.

D'Israeli Isaac 1766–1848. British scholar, father of Benjamin Disraeli and author of *Curiosities of Literature* 1791–93 and 1823.

dissonance in music, a combination of two or more tones displeasing to the ear. It is the opposite of a consonance, and is judged dissonant by the presence of a ◊beat frequency.

dithyramb song sacred to the Greek god ◊Dionysus, performed alongside tragedies and comedies at religious ceremonies in ancient Athens from the 7th century BC. Later examples were dedicated to other gods. Dithyrambs were performed by a choir, probably accompanied by flute music.

divertissement (French 'entertainment') dance, or suite of dances, within a ballet or opera, where the plot comes to a halt for a display of technical virtuosity, such as the character dances in the last act of *Coppélia* by Delibes, or the last acts of *Sleeping Beauty* and *A Midsummer Night's Dream*.

Divine Comedy, The epic poem by ◊Dante Alighieri 1307–21, describing a journey through Hell, Purgatory, and Paradise. The poet Virgil is Dante's guide through Hell and Purgatory; to each of the three realms, or circles, Dante assigns historical and contemporary personages according to their moral (and also political) worth. In Paradise Dante finds his lifelong love Beatrice. The poem makes great use of symbolism and allegory, and influenced many English writers including Milton, Byron, Shelley, and T S Eliot.

Abandon hope, all ye who enter here!

Dante *Divine Comedy*: 1307–21:
Inferno III

---

divisions in music, an old method of improvising ◊variations by dividing the basic note values of a theme into smaller fractions representing higher tempi in proportion to the original time values (see ◊diminution).

Dix Otto 1891–1969. German painter, a major exponent of the harsh Realism current in Germany in the 1920s and closely associated with the ◊*Neue Sachlichkeit* group. He is known chiefly for his unsettling 1920s paintings of prostitutes and sex murders and for his powerful series of works depicting the hell of trench warfare, for example *Flanders: After Henri Barbusse 'Le Feu'* 1934–36 (Nationalgalerie, Berlin).

Dix was a considerable portraitist, as exemplified in *Dr Heinrich Stadelmann* 1920 (Art Gallery of Ontario, Toronto), and he also painted allegorical works in a style reminiscent of 16th-century Flemish and Italian masters.

He trained at the art academies of Dresden and Düsseldorf, and his early work shows the influence of ◊Kokoschka and Italian ◊Futurism. In 1933 he was dismissed from his teaching post at the Dresden Art Academy by the Nazis, and branded a decadent. His experiences as a serving soldier in World War I and as a prisoner-of-war 1945–46 instilled in him a profound horror of armed conflict.

Dixieland jazz jazz style that originated in New Orleans, USA, in the early 20th century, dominated by cornet, trombone, and clarinet. The trumpeter Louis Armstrong emerged from this style. The **trad jazz** movement in the UK in the 1940s–1950s was a Dixieland revival.

The Party line is that there is no Party line.

Milovan Djilas
Disputed Barricade

Djilas Milovan 1911– . Yugoslav political writer and dissident. He was ousted from a senior position in Yugoslavia's postwar communist government because of his advocacy of greater political pluralism. His writings, including the

books *The New Class* 1957 and *The Undivided Society* 1969, were banned until May 1989.

DMus abbreviation for *Doctor of Music*.

Dobell William 1899–1970. Australian portraitist and genre painter. He is best known for his portraits, which include *Mrs South Kensington* 1937 (Art Gallery of New South Wales, Sydney) and *The Billy Boy* 1943 (Australian War Memorial, Canberra). His *Portrait of the Artist* (Joshua Smith) which won the 1943 Archibald Prize was the subject of an unsuccessful court case when challenged as caricature by two fellow entrants.

Döblin Alfred 1878–1957. German novelist. His *Berlin-Alexanderplatz* 1929 owes much to James Joyce in its minutely detailed depiction of the inner lives of a city's inhabitants, and is considered by many to be the finest 20th-century German novel. Other works include *November 1918: Eine deutsche Revolution/A German Revolution* 1939–50 (published in four parts) about the formation of the Weimar Republic.

Born in Stettin (modern Szczecin, Poland) to a Yiddish-speaking family, he grew up in Berlin where he practised as a doctor until 1933 when his books were banned and he was exiled; he moved first to France and from 1941 lived in the USA.

Doctor Faustus, The Tragical History of drama by Christopher ◊Marlowe, published (in two versions) 1604 and 1616, first performed in England 1594. The play, based on a medieval legend, tells how Faustus surrenders his soul to the devil in return for 24 years of life and the services of Mephistopheles, who will grant his every wish.

I've always wanted my work to be accessible. Literature, after all, is for people, not for some secret society.

E L Doctorow

Doctorow E(dgar) L(awrence) 1931– . US novelist. He achieved critical and commercial success with his third novel, *The Book of Daniel* 1971, the story of the Rosenberg spy case told by their fictional son, which established Doctorow as an imaginative and experimental revisionist of American history. It was followed by his bestseller, *Ragtime* 1975, which dramatized the Jazz Age.

His other novels include *Loon Lake* 1980, a montage narrative set in 1936, *World's Fair* 1985, about a Jewish boyhood in 1930s New York, and *Billy Bathgate* 1989, the story of a child apprenticed to the gangster Dutch Schultz.

Dodds Johnny 1892–1940. US jazz clarinettist, generally ranked among the top New Orleans jazz clarinettists. He played with Louis Armstrong,

Jelly Roll Morton, and the New Orleans Wanderers, as well as his own trio and orchestra, and was acclaimed for his warmth of tone and improvisation.

dodecaphony music composed according to the ◊twelve-tone system of composition.

Dodgson Charles Lutwidge. Real name of writer Lewis ◊Carroll.

Dohnányi Ernst von (Ernö) 1877–1960. Hungarian pianist, conductor, composer, and teacher whose compositions include *Variations on a Nursery Song* 1914 and *Second Symphony for Orchestra* 1948.

Born in Bratislava, he studied in Budapest, then established his name as a concert pianist in the UK and the USA. He became conductor of the Budapest Philharmonic 1919, musical director of Hungarian Broadcasting 1931, and director of the Budapest conservatory 1934. Rumoured to have been friendly with the Nazis during the 1930s and 1940s, he left Hungary 1948 and subsequently settled in the USA.

Doisneau Robert 1912– . French photographer known for his sensitive and often witty depictions of ordinary people and everyday situations within the environs of Paris. His most famous image, *Baiser de l'Hôtel de Ville/The Kiss at the Hôtel de Ville*, was produced for *Life* magazine 1950.

Dolce e Gabbana Domenico Dolce 1958– and Stefano Gabbana 1963– . Italian fashion designers, established 1982, who showed their first women's collection 1985 and became well known for their sexy designs based on bra tops, corset-style dresses, and stretch leggings. They launched a menswear collection 1990 and in 1991 began designing the mainstream label Complice for the Milanese manufacturing company Girombelli. Their 1992 collection reached a new level of maturity, appealing to a wider range of women.

Dolci Carlo 1616–1686. Italian painter of the late Baroque period, active in Florence. He created intensely emotional versions of religious subjects, such as *The Martyrdom of St Andrew* 1646 (Pitti, Florence).

Dolci was the foremost painter in Florence of his day and continued to be much admired in the 18th century. He was also a portraitist, and was sent to Austria 1675 to paint the Medici wife of the emperor Leopold I.

Dolin Anton. Stage name of Sydney Healey-Kay 1904–1983. British dancer and choreographer, the first British male dancer to win an international reputation. As a dancer, his reputation rested on his commanding presence, theatricality, and gymnastic ability. His most famous partnership was with Alicia Markova. After studying under Vaslav Nijinsky, he was a leading member of Sergei Diaghilev's company 1924–29.

He formed the Markova–Dolin Ballet Company with Markova 1935–38, and was a guest soloist with the American Ballet Theater 1940–46.

He created roles in Bronislava Nijinska's *Le Train bleu* 1924 and George Balanchine's *The Prodigal Son* 1929 while with the Ballets Russes; and Satan in Ninette de Valois' *Job* 1931.

Doll's House, The (Norwegian *Et dukkehjem*) play by Henrik ◊Ibsen, first produced in Norway 1879. It describes the blackmail of Nora, the sheltered wife of a successful lawyer, the revelation of her guilty secret to her husband, and the subsequent marital breakdown.

Dolmetsch Arnold 1858–1940. Swiss-born English musician and instrument-maker who worked in Boston and Paris as a restorer and maker of early musical instruments before establishing a workshop in Haslemere, England, 1917. Together with his family, including his son Carl (1911–), he revived interest in the practical performance of solo and consort music for lute, recorders, and viols, and established the Baroque soprano (descant) recorder as an inexpensive musical instrument for schools.

dome in architecture, roof form which is usually hemispherical and constructed over a circular, square, or octagonal space in a building. A feature of Islamic and Roman architecture, the dome was revived during the Renaissance.

The dome first appears in Assyrian architecture, later becoming a feature of Islamic mosques (after the notable example in the Byzantine church of ◊Hagia Sophia, Istanbul AD 532–37) and Roman ceremonial buildings: the Pantheon in Rome, about AD 118, is 43.5 m/143 ft in diameter. Rediscovered during the Renaissance, the dome features prominently in Brunelleschi's Florence cathedral 1420–38, Bramante's Tempietto at San Pietro in Montorio, Rome, 1502–10, and St Peter's, Rome, 1588–90, by Giacomo della Porta (about 1537–1602). Other notable examples are St Paul's, London, 1675–1710, by Christopher Wren, and the Panthéon, Paris, 1757–90, by Jacques Soufflot 1713–80. In the 20th century Buckminster Fuller has developed the ◊geodesic dome (a type of space-frame).

Domenichino real name Domenico Zampieri 1581–1641. Italian Baroque painter and architect, active in Bologna, Naples, and Rome. He began as an assistant to the ◊Carracci family of painters and continued the early Baroque style in, for example, frescoes 1624–28 in the choir of S Andrea della Valle, Rome. He is considered a pioneer of landscape painting in the Baroque period.

When the early, Classical form of Baroque was superseded by High Baroque, Domenichino retreated to Naples.

Domenico Veneziano *c.* 1400–1461. Italian painter, active in Florence. His few surviving frescoes and altarpieces show a remarkably subtle use of colour and light (which recurs in the work of Piero della Francesca, who worked with him).

He worked in Sta Egidio, Florence, on frescoes now lost. Remaining works include the *Carnesecchi Madonna and two Saints* (National Gallery, London) and the *St Lucy Altarpiece*, now divided between Florence (Uffizi), Berlin (Staatliche Museen), Cambridge (Fitzwilliam), and Washington, DC (National Gallery).

dominant in music, the fifth note of the diatonic scale, for example, G in the key of C.

Domingo Placido 1937– . Spanish lyric tenor specializing in Italian and French 19th-century operatic roles to which he brings a finely tuned dramatic temperament. As a youth in Mexico, he sang baritone roles in zarzuela (musical theatre), moving up to tenor as a member of the Israel National Opera 1961–64. Since his New York debut 1965 he has established a world reputation as a sympathetic leading tenor, and has made many films including the 1988 version of Puccini's *Tosca* set in Rome, and the 1990 Zeffirelli production of Leoncavallo's *I Pagliacci/The Strolling Players*.

I think it's a duty for a singer while he is at his best to let everyone around the world hear him.

Placido Domingo

Domino 'Fats' (Antoine) 1928– . US rock-and-roll pianist, singer, and songwriter, exponent of the New Orleans style. His hits include 'Ain't That a Shame' 1955 and 'Blueberry Hill' 1956.

Donat Robert 1905–1958. English actor of Anglo-Polish parentage. He started out in the theatre and made one film in Hollywood (*The Count of Monte Cristo* 1934). His other films include Alfred Hitchcock's *The Thirty-Nine Steps* 1935, *Goodbye, Mr Chips* 1939 for which he won an Academy Award, and *The Winslow Boy* 1948.

Donatello (Donato di Niccolo) *c.* 1386–1466. Italian sculptor of the early Renaissance, born in Florence. He was instrumental in reviving the Classical style, as in his graceful bronze statue of the youthful *David* about 1433 (Bargello, Florence) and his equestrian statue of the general *Gattamelata* 1447–50 (Piazza del Santo, Padua). The course of Florentine art in the 15th century was strongly influenced by his work.

Donatello introduced true perspective in his relief sculptures, such as the panel of *St George Slaying the Dragon* about 1415–17 (San Michele, Florence). He absorbed Classical influences during a stay in Rome 1430–32, and *David* is said to be the first life-size, free-standing nude since antiquity. In his later work, such as his wood-

carving of the aged *Mary Magdalene* about 1456 (Baptistry, Florence), he sought dramatic expression through a distorted, emaciated figural style.

Donellan Declan 1953– . British theatre director, co-founder of the **Cheek by Jowl** theatre company 1981, and associate director of the National Theatre from 1989. His irreverent and audacious productions include many classics, such as Racine's *Andromaque* 1985, Corneille's *Le Cid* 1987, and Ibsen's *Peer Gynt* 1990.

Donen Stanley 1924– . US film director, formerly a dancer, who co-directed two of Gene Kelly's best musicals, *On the Town* 1949 and *Singin' in the Rain* 1952. His other films include *Seven Brides For Seven Brothers* 1954, *Charade* 1963 and *Two for the Road* 1968.

Donizetti Gaetano 1797–1848. Italian composer who created more than 60 operas, including *Lucrezia Borgia* 1833, *Lucia di Lammermoor* 1835, *La Fille du régiment* 1840, *La Favorite* 1840, and *Don Pasquale* 1843. They show the influence of Rossini and Bellini, and are characterized by a flow of expressive melodies.

Don Juan character of Spanish legend, Don Juan Tenorio, supposed to have lived in the 14th century and notorious for his debauchery. Tirso de Molina, Molière, Mozart, Byron, and George Bernard Shaw have featured the legend in their works.

For God's sake hold your tongue, and let me love.

John Donne 'The Canonization'

Donne John 1571–1631. English metaphysical poet. His work consists of love poems, religious poems, verse satires, and sermons, most of which were first published after his death. His religious poems show the same passion and ingenuity as his love poetry. A Roman Catholic in his youth, he converted to the Church of England and finally became dean of St Paul's Cathedral, where he is buried.

Donne was brought up in the Roman Catholic faith and matriculated early at Oxford to avoid taking the oath of supremacy. Before becoming a law student 1592 he travelled in Europe. During his four years at the law courts he was notorious for his wit and reckless living. In 1596 he sailed as a volunteer in an expedition against Spain with the Earl of Essex and Walter Raleigh, and on his return became private secretary to Sir Thomas Egerton, Keeper of the Seal. This appointment was ended by his secret marriage to Ann More (died 1617), niece of Egerton's wife, and they endured many years of poverty. The more passionate and tender of his love poems were probably written to her. From 1621 to his death

Donne was dean of St Paul's. His sermons rank him with the century's greatest orators, and his fervent poems of love and hate, violent, tender, or abusive, give him a unique position among English poets. His verse was not published in collected form until after his death, and was long out of favour, but he is now recognized as one of the greatest English poets.

Don Quixote de la Mancha satirical romance by the Spanish novelist Miguel de Cervantes, published in two parts 1605 and 1615. Don Quixote, a self-styled knight, embarks on a series of chivalric adventures accompanied by his servant Sancho Panza. Quixote's imagination leads him to see harmless objects as enemies to be fought, as in his tilting at windmills. English translators include Tobias Smollett 1775.

Doolittle Hilda. Pen name **HD** 1886–1961. US poet who went to Europe 1911, and was associated with Ezra Pound and the British writer Richard ◊Aldington (to whom she was married 1913–37) in founding the Imagist school of poetry (see ◊Imagism), advocating simplicity, precision, and brevity. Her work includes the *Sea Garden* 1916 and *Helen in Egypt* 1961, as well as *End to Torment* 1958, a memoir of Ezra Pound.

Doors, the US psychedelic rock group formed 1965 in Los Angeles by Jim Morrison (1943–1971, vocals), Ray Manzarek (1935– , keyboards), Robby Krieger (1946– , guitar), and John Densmore (1944– , drums). Their first hit was 'Light My Fire' from their debut album *The Doors* 1967. They were noted for Morrison's poetic lyrics and flamboyant performance.

Morrison's extended, melodramatic recitations set against repetitive guitar and organ patterns gave the Doors a sinister, sexual quality. The standard of their albums was uneven, with *Morrison Hotel* 1970 probably the best of their later output.

doo-wop US pop-music form of the 1950s, a style of harmony singing without instrumental accompaniment or nearly so, almost exclusively by male groups. The name derives from the practice of having the lead vocalist singing the lyrics against a backing of nonsense syllables from the other members of the group.

Doo-wop had roots in the 1930s with rhythm-and-blues groups like the Ink Spots and in gospel music. It was practised by street-corner groups in the inner cities, some of whom went on to make hit records; for example, 'Earth Angel' by the Penguins 1954 and 'Why Do Fools Fall in Love' by Frankie Lymon and the Teenagers 1956. The first doo-wop record to be a number-one US pop hit was 'The Great Pretender' by the Platters 1955.

doppelgänger (German 'double-goer') apparition of a living person, a person's double, or a guardian spirit. The German composer and writer E T A Hoffman wrote a short story called *Die Doppelgänger* in 1821. English novelist Charles Williams used the idea to great effect in his novel *Descent into Hell* 1937.

Dorati Antál 1906–1988. US conductor, born in Hungary. He toured with ballet companies 1933–45 and went on to conduct orchestras in the USA and Europe in a career spanning more than half a century. Dorati gave many first performances of Bartók's music and recorded all Haydn's symphonies with the Philharmonia Hungarica.

Doré Gustave 1832–1883. French artist, chiefly known as a prolific illustrator, and also active as a painter, etcher, and sculptor. He produced closely worked engravings of scenes from, for example, Rabelais, Dante, Cervantes, the Bible, Milton, and Edgar Allan Poe.

Doré was born in Strasbourg. His views of Victorian London 1869–71, concentrating on desperate poverty and overcrowding in the swollen city, were admired by van Gogh.

Doric in Classical architecture, one of the five types of column; see ◊order.

Dorsey Tommy 1905–1956 and Jimmy 1904–1957. US bandleaders, musicians, and composers during the ◊swing era. They worked together in the Dorsey Brothers Orchestra 1934–35 and 1953–56, but led separate bands in the intervening period. The Jimmy Dorsey band was primarily a dance band; the Tommy Dorsey band was more jazz-oriented and featured the singer Frank Sinatra 1940–42. Both Dorsey bands featured in a number of films in the 1940s, and the brothers appeared together in *The Fabulous Dorseys* 1947.

Dos Passos John (Roderigo) 1896–1970. US author. He made his reputation with the war novels *One Man's Initiation* 1919 and *Three Soldiers* 1921. His major work is the trilogy *U.S.A.* 1930–36. An epic, panoramic view of US life through three decades, and inspired by a communist and anarchist historical approach, it used such innovative structural devices as the 'Newsreel', a collage of documentary information, and the 'Camera Eye', the novelist's own stream-of-consciousness. His other works include *Manhattan Transfer* 1925, an expressionist montage novel of the modern city.

Dostoevsky Fyodor Mihailovich 1821–1881. Russian novelist. Remarkable for their profound psychological insight, Dostoevsky's novels have greatly influenced Russian writers, and since the beginning of the 20th century have been increasingly influential abroad. In 1849 he was sentenced to four years' hard labour in Siberia, followed by army service, for printing socialist propaganda. *The House of the Dead* 1861 recalls his prison experiences, followed by his major works *Crime and Punishment* 1866, *The Idiot*

1868–69, and *The Brothers Karamazov* 1879–80.

Born in Moscow, the son of a physician, Dostoevsky was for a short time an army officer. His first novel, *Poor Folk*, appeared in 1846. In 1849, during a period of intense tsarist censorship, he was arrested as a member of a free-thinking literary circle and sentenced to death. After a last-minute reprieve he was sent to the penal settlement at Omsk for four years, where the terrible conditions increased his epileptic tendency. Finally pardoned 1859, he published the humorous *Village of Stepanchikovo*, *The House of the Dead*, and *The Insulted and the Injured* 1862. Meanwhile he had launched two unsuccessful liberal periodicals, in the second of which his *Letters from the Underworld* 1864 appeared. Compelled to work by pressure of debt, he quickly produced *Crime and Punishment* 1866 and *The Gambler* 1867, before fleeing the country to escape from his creditors. He then wrote *The Idiot* (in which the hero is an epileptic like himself), *The Eternal Husband* 1870, and *The Possessed* 1871–72.

Returning to Russia 1871, he again entered journalism and issued the personal miscellany *Journal of an Author*, in which he discussed contemporary problems. In 1875 he published *A Raw Youth*, but the great work of his last years is *The ◊Brothers Karamazov* 1879–80.

Dou Gerrit (Gerard) 1613–1675. Dutch genre painter, a pupil of Rembrandt, known for small domestic interiors, minutely observed. His teacher's influence can be clearly seen in *Tobit* 1632–33 (National Gallery, London).

Dou was born in Leiden, where he founded a painters' guild with Jan Steen. He had many pupils, including Gabriel Metsu.

double bass large bowed four-stringed (sometimes five-stringed) musical instrument, the bass of the ◊violin family. It is descended from the bass viol or violone. Until 1950, after which it was increasingly superseded by the electric bass, it also provided bass support (plucked) for jazz and dance bands. Performers include Domenico ◊Dragonetti, composer of eight concertos, the Russian-born US conductor Serge Koussevitsky (1874–1951), and the US virtuoso Gary Karr. The double bass features in the well-loved 'Elephants' solo, No 5 of Saint-Saëns' *Carnival of the Animals* 1897.

Double Indemnity novel 1945 by US writer James M ◊Cain. Narrated by insurance salesman, Walter Neff, the plot concerns a *femme fatale* Phyllis Nerdlinger, who entraps him into murdering her husband. The subsequent elaborate insurance fraud opens up a Pandora's box of self-destructive sexual desire, guilt, and suspicion. In 1944 it was turned into a key work of ◊film noir by director Billy Wilder, who co-authored the screenplay with Raymond Chandler.

doublet close-fitting jacket, with or without sleeves, worn by men. Derived from the gipon, which was a tight-fitting jacket with long sleeves and buttons down the front, the doublet formed part of everyday dress from the mid-15th century. In the 16th century, as fashions changed, the doublet was worn long to the knees, but with a parting at the front to reveal the ◊codpiece. During the 18th century the length of the doublet shrank and it eventually evolved into the ◊waistcoat.

Doughty Charles Montagu 1843–1926. English travel writer, author of *Travels in Arabia Deserta* 1888, written after two years in the Middle East searching for Biblical relics. He influenced T E ◊Lawrence ('Lawrence of Arabia').

Douglas Alfred (Bruce) 1870–1945. British poet who became closely associated in London with the Irish writer Oscar ◊Wilde. Their relationship led to Wilde's conviction for homosexual activity, imprisonment, and early death, through the enmity of Douglas' father, the 9th Marquess of Queensberry. Douglas wrote the self-justifactory *Oscar Wilde and Myself* 1914 and *Oscar Wilde, A Summing-Up* 1940.

Douglas Gavin (or Gawain) 1475–1522. Scottish poet whose translation into Scots of Virgil's *Aeneid* 1515 was the first translation from the classics into a vernacular of the British Isles.

Douglas Kirk. Stage name of Issur Danielovitch Demsky 1916– . US film actor. Usually cast as a dynamic though often ill-fated hero, as in *Spartacus* 1960, he was a major star of the 1950s and 1960s in such films as *Ace in the Hole* 1951, *The Bad and the Beautiful* 1953, *Lust for Life* 1956, *The Vikings* 1958, *Seven Days in May* 1964, and *The War Wagon* 1967. He continues to act and produce. He is the father of actor Michael Douglas.

Douglas Michael 1944– . US film actor and producer. His acting range includes both romantic and heroic leads in films such as *Romancing the Stone* 1984 and *Jewel of the Nile* 1985, both of which he produced. He won an Academy Award for his portrayal of a ruthless businessman in *Wall Street* 1987. Among his other films are *Fatal Attraction* 1987 and *Basic Instinct* 1991.

Douglas first achieved recognition in the television series *The Streets of San Francisco* 1972–76. He is the son of actor Kirk Douglas.

Douglas Norman 1868–1952. British diplomat and travel writer (*Siren Land* 1911 and *Old Calabria* 1915, dealing with Italy); his novel *South Wind* 1917 is set in his adopted island of Capri.

You can tell the ideals of a nation by its advertisements.

Norman Douglas *South Wind* 1917

Douglas-Home William 1912–1992. Scottish dramatist. His plays include *The Chiltern Hundreds* 1947, *The Secretary Bird* 1968, and *Lloyd George Knew My Father* 1972.

Doulton Henry 1820–1897. English ceramicist. He developed special wares for the chemical, electrical, and building industries, and established the world's first stoneware-drainpipe factory 1846. From 1870 he created art pottery and domestic tablewares in Lambeth, S London, and Burslem, near Stoke-on-Trent.

Dove Cottage small house at Grasmere in the English Lake District where William Wordsworth settled with his sister Dorothy 1799, and later with his wife Mary Hutchinson 1802. He wrote much of his best work here, including 'Ode. Intimations of Immortality', 'Michael' and 'Resolution and Independence', before reluctantly moving to a larger house 1808. It is now a museum with manuscripts, portraits, and other memorabilia.

Dowell Anthony 1943– . British classical ballet dancer of refined, polished style. He was principal dancer with the Royal Ballet 1966–86, and director 1986– .

Dowell joined the Royal Ballet 1961. The choreographer Frederick Ashton chose him to create the role of Oberon in *The Dream* 1964 opposite Antoinette Sibley, the start of an outstanding partnership. His other noted performances include those in Anthony Tudor's *Shadowplay* 1967, Ashton's *Monotones* 1965, and van Manen's *Four Schumann Pieces* 1975.

Dowland John 1563–1626. English composer of lute songs. He introduced daring expressive refinements of harmony and ornamentation to English Renaissance style in the service of an elevated aesthetic of melancholy, as in the masterly *Lachrymae* 1605.

downbeat in music, the downward movement of a conductor's hand or baton, signifying the starting point or strong beat of a musical bar.

Dowson Ernest 1867–1900. British poet, one of the 'decadent' poets of the 1890s. He wrote the lyric with the refrain 'I have been faithful to thee, Cynara! in my fashion'.

Doxiadis Constantinos 1913–1975. Greek architect and town planner; designer of Islamabad, the capital of Pakistan.

Doyle Arthur Conan 1859–1930. British writer, creator of the detective Sherlock Holmes and his assistant Dr Watson, who first appeared in *A Study in Scarlet* 1887 and featured in a number of subsequent stories, including *The Hound of the Baskervilles* 1902. Conan Doyle also wrote historical romances (*Micah Clarke* 1889 and *The White Company* 1891) and the scientific romance *The Lost World* 1912.

Born in Edinburgh, qualified as a doctor, and during the second South African War (or Boer War) was senior physician of a field hospital. His Sherlock Holmes character featured in several books, including *The Sign of Four* 1889 and *The Valley of Fear* 1915, as well as in volumes of short stories, first published in the *Strand Magazine*. In his later years Conan Doyle became a spiritualist.

Doyle Richard 1824–1883. English caricaturist and book illustrator. In 1849 he designed the original cover for the humorous magazine *Punch*.

D'Oyly Carte Richard 1844–1901. British producer of the Gilbert and Sullivan operas at the Savoy Theatre, London, which he built. The D'Oyly Carte Opera Company founded 1876 was disbanded 1982 following the ending of its copyright monopoly on the Gilbert and Sullivan operas. The present company, founded 1988, moved to the Alexandra Theatre, Birmingham, 1991.

Drabble Margaret 1939– . British writer. Her novels include *The Millstone* 1965, *The Middle Ground* 1980, *The Radiant Way* 1987, *A Natural Curiosity* 1989, and *The Gates of Ivory* 1991. She portrays contemporary life with toughness and sensitivity, often through the eyes of intelligent modern women. She edited the 1985 edition of the *Oxford Companion to English Literature*.

Dracula in the novel *Dracula* 1897 by Bram ♢Stoker, the caped count who, as a ♢vampire, drinks the blood of beautiful women. The original of Dracula is thought to have been Vlad Tepes, or Vlad the Impaler, a 15th-century ruler of the principality of Wallachia in Eastern Europe, who used to impale his victims and then mock them.

dragon mythical reptilian beast, often portrayed as winged and breathing fire. An occasional feature of classical legend (♢Andromeda), dragons later held a central place as opponents of gods and heroes in Vedic, Teutonic (♢Siegfried), Anglo-Saxon, and Christian (St George) mythologies, possibly accounting for their heraldic role on medieval banners and weaponry.

In Christian art the dragon is linked with the devil; in traditional Chinese belief it is a symbol of divinity and royalty, associated with storms and rain.

Dragonetti Domenico 1763–1846. Italian-born virtuoso double-bass player and composer. He established the instrument's solo credentials in tours of Britain and Europe, performing a repertoire including a transcription for bass of Beethoven's *Cello Sonata in D* 1811. His own compositions include eight concertos and numerous string quartets.

drama in theatre, any play composed to be performed by actors for an audience. The term is also used collectively to group plays into historical or stylistic periods — for example, Greek drama, Restoration drama – as well as referring to the whole body of work written by a dramatist for performance. Drama is distinct from literature in that it is a performing art open to infinite interpretation, the product not merely of the dramatist but also of the collaboration of director, designer, actors, and technical staff. See also ◊comedy, ◊tragedy, ◊mime, and ◊pantomime.

dramatic monologue poem consisting of a speech by a single character, in which his or her thoughts, character, and situation are revealed to the reader. It developed from the soliloquy, a monologue spoken in a play. It was a particularly popular form in the 19th century. Examples include Robert Browning's 'My Lost Duchess' and T S Eliot's 'Love Song of J Alfred Prufrock'.

Drayton Michael 1563–1631. English poet. His volume of poems *The Harmony of the Church* 1591 was destroyed by order of the archbishop of Canterbury. His greatest poetical work was the topographical survey of England, *Poly-Olbion* 1612–22, in 30 books.

Dreiser Theodore (Herman Albert) 1871–1945. US writer who wrote the naturalist novels *Sister Carrie* 1900 and *An American Tragedy* 1925, based on the real-life crime of a young man, who in his drive to 'make good', drowns a shop assistant he has made pregnant. It was filmed as *A Place in the Sun* 1951.

Born in Terre Haute, Indiana, Dreiser was a journalist 1889–90 in Chicago and was editor of several magazines. His other novels include *The Financier* 1912, *The Titan* 1914, and *The Genius* 1915. *An American Tragedy* finally won him great popularity after years of publishing works that had been largely ignored. His other works range from autobiographical pieces to poems and short stories. Although his work is criticized for being technically unpolished, it is praised for its powerful realism and sincerity. In the 1930s he devoted much of his energy to the radical reform movement.

dress versatile one-piece garment for women, incorporating a bodice and skirt which may be combined in a wide variety of styles. A dress may have long or short sleeves or no sleeves at all; the length can vary from very long to very short; it can be made of any fabric; and designs can be adapted to suit all occasions and all seasons. 'Dress' is also a general term for clothing, sometimes indicating formality.

Dreyer Carl Theodor 1889–1968. Danish film director. His wide range of films include the austere silent classic *La Passion de Jeanne d'Arc/The Passion of Joan of Arc* 1928 and the Expressionist horror film *Vampyr* 1932, after the failure of which Dreyer made no full-length films until *Vredens Dag/Day of Wrath* 1943. His two late masterpieces are *Ordet/The Word* 1955 and *Gertrud* 1964.

Dreyfuss Henry 1904–1972. US industrial designer, a major pioneer of design in the interwar years. He moved through stage and store design before setting up an independent office 1929. Notable designs include his black bakelite telephone 'Bell 33' 1933 for Bell Telephone and the streamlined train 'Twentieth Century Limited' 1941 for the New York Central Railroad.

After World War II he worked on a system of anthropometrics (the study of the size and proportions of the human body), disseminated through his two influential books *Designing for People* 1955 and *The Measure of Man* 1960.

Drinkwater John 1882–1937. British poet and dramatist. He was a prolific writer of lyrical and reflective verse, and also wrote many historical plays, including *Abraham Lincoln* 1918.

Those book-learned fools who miss the world.

John Drinkwater
From Generation to Generation

---

drone in music, an accompanying constant tone or harmony, usually octave or fifth. It is a feature of many classical and folk traditions, and is produced by many instruments of folk music, including the Indian vina, bagpipes, and hurdy-gurdy. Drone effects in written music include the organ ◊pedal point and the ◊musette dance form.

drum any of a class of percussion instruments including **slit drums** made of wood, **steel drums** fabricated from oil drums, and a majority group of **skin drums** consisting of a shell or vessel of wood, metal, or earthenware across one or both ends of which is stretched a membrane of hide or plastic. Drums are struck with the hands or with a stick or pair of sticks; they are among the oldest instruments known.

Orchestral drums consist of timpani, ◊tambourine, ◊snare, side, and bass drums, the latter either single-headed (with a single skin) and producing a ringing tone, called a gong drum, or double-headed (with two skins) and producing a dense booming noise of indeterminate pitch. Military bands of foot soldiers employ the snare and side drums, and among cavalry regiments a pair of kettledrums mounted on horseback are played on ceremonial occasions.

Dance band drums have evolved from the 'traps' of Dixieland jazz into a battery of percussion employing a range of stick types. In addition to snare and foot-controlled bass drums, many feature a scale of pitched bongos and tom-toms, as well as suspended cymbals, hi-hat (foot-controlled double cymbals), cowbells, and temple blocks. Recent innovations include the rotary tunable rototoms, electronic drums, and the drum machine, a percussion synthesizer.

Drummond William 1585–1649, also known as Drummond of Hawthornden. Scottish poet. He was one of the first Scottish poets to use southern English, and his *Poems* 1614 also show the strong influence of continental models.

Drummond de Andrade Carlos 1902–1987. Brazilian writer, generally considered the greatest modern Brazilian poet, and a prominent member of the Modernist school. His verse, often seemingly casual, continually confounds the reader's expectations of the 'poetical'.

Drury Lane Theatre theatre first opened 1663 on the site of earlier London playhouses. It was twice burned; the present building dates from 1812.

Dr Who hero of a British science-fiction television series of the same name, created 1963 by Sidney Newman and Donald Wilson; his space vehicle is the *Tardis* (acronym from *T*ime *a*nd *r*elative *d*imensions *i*n *s*pace). The actors who have played Dr Who are William Hartnell (1908–1975), Jon Pertwee (1919–), Patrick Troughton (1920–), Tom Baker (1936–), Peter Davison (1951–), and Colin Baker (1943–).

dryad in Greek mythology, a forest ◊nymph or tree spirit.

Dryden John 1631–1700. English poet and dramatist, noted for his satirical verse and for his use of the heroic couplet. His poetry includes the verse satire *Absalom and Achitophel* 1681, *Annus Mirabilis* 1667, and 'St Cecilia's Day' 1687. Plays include the heroic drama *The Conquest of Granada* 1670–71, the comedy *Marriage à la Mode* 1672, and *All for Love* 1678, a reworking of Shakespeare's *Antony and Cleopatra*.

On occasion, Dryden trimmed his politics and his religion to the prevailing wind, and, as a Roman Catholic convert under James II, lost the post of poet laureate (to which he had been appointed 1668) at the Revolution of 1688. Critical works include *Essay on Dramatic Poesy* 1668. Later ventures to support himself include a translation of Virgil 1697.

Errors, like straws, upon the surface flow/ He who would search for pearls must dive below.

John Dryden *All for Love* Prologue 1678

---

dry point in printmaking, a technique of engraving on copper, using a hard, sharp tool. The resulting lines tend to be fine and angular, with a strong furry edge created by the metal shavings. Dürer, Rembrandt, and Max Beckmann were outstanding exponents.

Drysdale (George) Russell 1912–1981. Australian artist, born in England into a family with Australian connections. In 1944 he produced a series of wash drawings for the *Sydney Morning Herald* recording the effects of a severe drought in W New South Wales. The bleakness of life in the Australian outback is a recurring theme in his work, which typically depicts the dried-out, scorched landscape with gaunt figures reflecting fortitude in desolation and poverty. Children appear frequently, as in *The Gatekeeper's Wife* 1965 (National Library, Canberra).

Dr Zhivago novel by the Russian writer Boris ◊Pasternak, published (in Italy) 1957. The novel describes how Zhivago, a doctor and poet, becomes disillusioned with the Russian revolution. It was banned in the USSR as a 'hostile act' and only published there in magazine form 1988.

D.S. in music, abbreviation for *dal segno* (Italian 'from the sign').

dub in pop music, a ◊remix, usually instrumental, of a reggae recording, stripped down to the rhythm track. Dub originated in Jamaica with the disc jockeys of mobile sound systems, who would use their playback controls to cut parts of tracks; later it became common practice to produce a studio dub version as the B-side of a single.

Du Bellay Joaquim *c.* 1522–1560. French poet and prose writer who published the great manifesto of the new school of French poetry, the Pléiade: *Défense et illustration de la langue française* 1549. He also wrote sonnets inspired by Petrarch and his meditations on the vanished glories of Rome, *Antiquités de Rome* 1558, influenced English writers such as Edmund Spenser who translated some of his work.

Dubuffet Jean 1901–1985. French artist who originated *Art Brut*, 'raw or brutal art', in the 1940s. Inspired by graffiti and children's drawings, he used such varied materials as plaster, steel wool, and straw in his paintings and sculptures to produce highly textured surfaces.

Art Brut emerged 1945 with an exhibition of Dubuffet's own work and of paintings by psychiatric patients and naive, or untrained, artists. His own paintings and sculptural works have a similar quality, primitive and expressive.

Duccio di Buoninsegna *c.* 1255–1319. Italian painter, a major figure in the Sienese school whose influence on the development of painting was profound. His greatest work is his altarpiece for Siena Cathedral, the *Maestà* 1308–11 (Cathedral Museum, Siena). The figure of the Virgin is essentially Byzantine in style, with much gold detail, but depicted with warmth and tenderness. His skill in narrative is displayed on the back of the main panel of the *Maestà* in scenes from the Passion of Christ.

Duchamp Marcel 1887–1968. French-born US artist. He achieved notoriety with his *Nude Descending a Staircase No 2* 1912 (Philadelphia

Museum of Art), influenced by Cubism and Futurism. An active exponent of ◊Dada, he invented ◊ready-mades, everyday items (for example, a bicycle wheel mounted on a kitchen stool) which he displayed as works of art.

A major early work that focuses on mechanical objects endowed with mysterious significance is *La Mariée mise à nu par ses célibataires, même/The Bride Stripped Bare by Her Bachelors, Even* 1915–23 (Philadelphia Museum of Art). Duchamp continued to experiment with ◊collage, mechanical imagery, and sculptural ◊assemblages throughout his career. He lived mostly in New York and became a US citizen 1954.

Dudintsev Vladimir Dmitriyevich 1918– . Soviet novelist, author of the remarkably frank *Not by Bread Alone* 1956, a depiction of Soviet bureaucracy and inefficiency.

duet or *duo* music or ensemble of two voices or instruments. A piano duet is normally two players sharing a single instrument (also called 'piano four- hands'); a piano duo is two players on two pianos.

Dufay Guillaume 1400–1474. Flemish composer of secular songs and sacred music, including 84 songs and eight masses. His work marks a transition from the style of the Middle Ages to the expressive melodies and rich harmonies of the Renaissance.

Dufy Raoul 1877–1953. French painter and designer. Inspired by ◊Fauvism he developed a fluent, brightly coloured style in watercolour and oils, painting scenes of gaiety and leisure, such as horse racing, yachting, and life on the beach. He also designed tapestries, textiles, and ceramics.

Duiker Johannes 1890–1935. Dutch architect of the 1920s and 1930s avant-garde. A member of the De ◊Stijl group, his works demonstrate great structural vigour. They include the Zonnestraal Sanatorium, Hilversum, 1926–28, co-designed with Bernard Bijvoet (1889–), and the Open Air School 1929–30 and Handelsblad-Cineac News Cinema 1934, both in Amsterdam.

Dukas Paul (Abraham) 1865–1935. French composer and teacher whose scrupulous orchestration and chromatically enriched harmonies were admired by Debussy. His small output includes the opera *Ariane et Barbe-Bleue/Ariane and Bluebeard* 1907 and the animated orchestral scherzo *L'Apprenti sorcier/The Sorcerer's Apprentice* 1897.

dulcimer musical instrument, a form of ◊zither, consisting of a shallow open trapezoidal soundbox across which strings are stretched laterally; they are horizontally struck by lightweight hammers or beaters. It produces clearly differentiated pitches of consistent quality and is more agile and wide-ranging in pitch than the harp or lyre. In Hungary the dulcimer, or cimbalom, is in current use.

Dumas Alexandre 1802–1870. French author, known as Dumas *père* (the father). He is remembered for his historical romances, the reworked output of a 'fiction-factory' of collaborators. They include *Les Trois Mousquetaires/The Three Musketeers* 1844 and its sequels. His play *Henri III et sa cour/Henry III and His Court* 1829 established French romantic historical drama. Dumas *fils* was his son.

All for one and one for all.

Alexandre Dumas (père) *The Three Musketeers* 1844

Dumas Alexandre 1824–1895. French author, known as Dumas *fils* (the son of Dumas *père*) and remembered for the play *La Dame aux camélias/The Lady of the Camellias* 1852, based on his own novel and the source of Verdi's opera *La Traviata*.

Du Maurier Daphne 1907–1989. British novelist whose romantic fiction includes *Jamaica Inn* 1936, *Rebecca* 1938, and *My Cousin Rachel* 1951, and is set in Cornwall. Her work, though lacking in depth and original insights, is made compelling by her fine story-telling gift. *Jamaica Inn*, *Rebecca*, and her short story 'The Birds' were made into films by the English director Alfred Hitchcock. She was the granddaughter of George Du Maurier.

Du Maurier George (Louis Palmella Busson) 1834–1896. French-born British cartoonist and author of the novel *Trilby* 1894, the story of a natural singer able to perform only under the hypnosis of Svengali, her tutor.

Dunaway Faye 1941– . US film actress whose first starring role was in *Bonnie and Clyde* 1967. Her subsequent films, including *Network* 1976 (for which she won an Academy Award) and *Mommie Dearest* 1981, received a varying critical reception. She also starred in Roman Polanski's *Chinatown* 1974 and *The Handmaid's Tale* 1990.

Dunbar William c. 1460–c. 1520. Scottish poet at the court of James IV. His poems include a political allegory, 'The Thrissil and the Rois' 1503, and the lament with the refrain ' Timor mortis conturbat me' about 1508.

Duncan Isadora 1877–1927. US dancer. A pioneer of modern dance, she adopted an emotionally expressive free form, dancing barefoot and wearing a loose tunic, inspired by the ideal of Hellenic beauty. She danced solos accompanied to music by Beethoven and other great composers, believing that the music should fit the grandeur of the dance. Having made her base in Paris 1908, she toured extensively, often returning to Russia after her initial success there 1904.

She died in an accident when her long scarf caught in the wheel of the sportscar in which she was travelling. She was equally notorious for her private life as for her work, which was considered scandalous at the time. Her frequent alliances with artists and industrialists, her marriage to the Russian poet Sergei Esenin, and the tragedy of her two children who were drowned in a freak car accident, were documented in her autobiography *My Life* 1927.

People do not live nowadays – they get about ten per cent out of life.

Isadora Duncan
This Quarter Autumn 'Memoirs'

Duncan Robert (Edward) 1919– . US poet. A key figure in the San Francisco Renaissance of the 1950s (other poets include Kenneth Rexroth (1905–1982), Gary ◊Snyder, and Philip Lamantia (1927–)), he was also, after meeting the poet Charles Olson, an important member of the ◊Black Mountain poets. His first major collection, *The Opening of the Field* 1960, was influenced by Walt Whitman, Ezra Pound, William Carlos Williams, and Olson. Other collections include *Roots and Branches* 1964, *Bending the Bow* 1968, and *Ground Work: Before the War* 1984.

dungarees (Hindi *dungri* 'coarse calico material') garment consisting of trousers and a bib panel with shoulder straps, used by workmen in the early 20th century and by women during World War II. In the 1940s–60s dungarees became a fashion garment and appeared with extra pockets and flaps, made in denim and other lightweight fabrics.

Dunham Katherine 1912– . US dancer and choreographer. She was noted for a free, strongly emotional method, and employed her extensive knowledge of anthropology as a basis for her dance techniques and choreography. Her interests lay in the fusion of modern and Afro-Caribbean dance. In 1940 Dunham established an all-black dance company, which toured extensively. She also choreographed for and appeared in Hollywood films.

Dunne Irene 1904–1990. US actress. From 1930 to 1952, she appeared in a wide variety of films, including musicals and comedies, but was perhaps most closely associated with the genre of romantic melodrama, for example, *Back Street* 1932.

Dunsany Edward John Moreton Drax Plunkett, 18th Baron Dunsany 1878–1957. Irish writer, author of the 'Jorkens' stories, beginning with *The Travel Tales of Mr Joseph Jorkens*, which employed the convention of a narrator (Jorkens) sitting in a club or bar. He also wrote short ironic heroic fantasies, collected in *The Gods of Pegana* 1905 and other books. His first play, *The Glittering Gate*, was performed at the Abbey Theatre, Dublin 1909.

Dunstable John *c.* 1385–1453. English composer of songs and anthems, considered one of the founders of Renaissance harmony.

Duparc (Marie Eugène) Henri Fouques 1848–1933. French composer. He studied under César ◊Franck. His songs, though only 15 in number, are memorable for their lyric sensibility.

Du Pré Jacqueline 1945–1987. English cellist. She was celebrated for her proficient technique and powerful interpretations of the classical cello repertory, particularly of Elgar. She had an international concert career while still in her teens and made many recordings.

She married the Israeli pianist and conductor Daniel ◊Barenboim 1967 and worked with him in concerts, as a duo, and in a conductor-soloist relationship until her playing career was ended by multiple sclerosis. Although confined to a wheelchair for the last 14 years of her life, she continued to work as a teacher and to campaign on behalf of other sufferers from the disease.

Durand Asher Brown 1796–1886. US painter and engraver. His paintings express communion with nature, as in *Kindred Spirits* 1849, a tribute to Thomas Cole, William Cullen Bryant, and the Catskill Mountains. The founding of the ◊Hudson River School of landscape art is ascribed to Cole and Durand.

Duras Marguerite 1914– . French author. Her work includes short stories (*Des Journées entières dans les arbres* 1954, stage adaption *Days in the Trees* 1965), plays (*La Musica* 1967), and film scripts (*Hiroshima mon amour* 1960). She also wrote novels including *Le Vice-Consul* 1966, evoking an existentialist world from the setting of Calcutta, *L'Amant* 1984 (Prix Goncourt), and *Emily L.* 1989. *La Vie materielle* 1987 appeared in England as *Practicalities* 1990. Her autobiographical novel, *La Douleur* 1986, is set in Paris in 1945.

Dürer Albrecht 1471–1528. German artist, the leading figure of the northern Renaissance. He was born in Nuremberg and travelled widely in Europe. Highly skilled in drawing and a keen student of nature, he perfected the technique of woodcut and engraving, producing woodcut series such as the *Apocalypse* 1498 and copperplate engravings such as *The Knight, Death, and the Devil* 1513 and *Melancholia* 1514. His paintings include altarpieces and meticulously observed portraits, including many self-portraits.

He was apprenticed first to his father, a goldsmith, then in 1486 to Michael Wolgemut (1434–1519), a painter, woodcut artist, and master of a large workshop in Nuremberg. At the age of 13 he drew a portrait of himself from the mirror, the first known self-portrait in the history of European art. From 1490 he travelled widely, studying Netherlandish and Italian art, then visited Colmar, Basel, and Strasbourg and returned to Nuremberg 1495. Other notable journeys were to Venice 1505–07, where he met the painter Giovanni Bellini, and to Antwerp 1520, where he was made court painter to Charles V of Spain and the Netherlands (recorded in detail in his diary).

If a man devotes himself to art, much evil is avoided that happens otherwise if one is idle.

Albrecht Dürer *Outline of a General Treatise on Painting c.* 1510

Durrell Gerald (Malcolm) 1925– . British naturalist, director of Jersey Zoological Park from 1959. He is the author of travel and natural history books, and the humorous memoir *My Family and Other Animals* 1956. He is the brother of Lawrence Durrell.

Durrell Lawrence (George) 1912–1990. British novelist and poet. Born in India, he joined the foreign service and lived mainly in the E Mediterranean, the setting of his novels, including the Alexandria Quartet: *Justine, Balthazar, Mountolive,* and *Clea* 1957–60; he also wrote travel books. His heady prose and bizarre characters reflect his exotic sources of inspiration. He was the brother of the naturalist Gerald Durrell.

Shyness has laws: you can only give yourself, tragically, to those who least understand.

Lawrence Durrell *Justine* 1957

Dürrenmatt Friedrich 1921–1991. Swiss dramatist and writer, author of experimental and satirical tragicomedies, for example *The Visit* 1956 and *The Physicists* 1962. His fascination with the absurd and with black humour can also be seen in his novels, such as *Das Versprechen/The Pledge* 1958.

Duse Eleonora 1859–1924. Italian actress. She was the mistress of the poet Gabriele ◊D'Annunzio from 1897, as recorded in his novel *Il fuoco/The Flame of Life.*

Dutch art painting and sculpture of the Netherlands. The rise of the Dutch nation in the second half of the 16th century saw the full emergence of Dutch art with Frans Hals; Pieter Lastman (1585–1633), the teacher of Rembrandt; and Gerard van Honthorst.

17th century Among the many masters of this period were Rembrandt and his pupil Gerard Douw (1613–1675); Adriaen van Ostade, who painted Flemish peasant scenes; Gerard Ter Borch the Younger (1617–1681), the first painter of characteristic Dutch interiors; Albert Cuyp; Jan Steen; Jakob van Ruisdael, renowned for his landscapes; Pieter de Hooch; Jan Vermeer; Willem van de Velde, sea painter to Charles II of England; Jan van der Heyden (1637–1712); and Meindert Hobbema.

18th and 19th centuries There was a marked decline in Dutch art, except for the genre painters Cornelis Troost (1697–1750) and Jozef Israels, and the outstanding genius of Vincent van Gogh.

Dutch literature literature of the Netherlands. The earliest known poet to use the Dutch dialect was Henric van Veldeke in the 12th century, but the finest example of early Gothic literature is *Van Den Vos Reinaarde/About Reynard the Fox* by a poet known as 'Willem-who-made-the-Madoc'. To the golden age of the Renaissance belong Pieter C Hooft (1581–1647), lyricist, playwright, and historian; Constantijn Huygens (1596–1687); Gerbrand A Bredero (1585–1618); the lyricist, satirist, and dramatic poet Joost van den Vondel (1587–1679); and the poet Father Jacob Cats (1577–1660).

As in art, the 18th century was a period of decline for Dutch literature, although the epic poet Willem Bilderdijk (1756–1831) ranks highly. The Romantic movement found its fullest expression in the nationalist periodical *De Gids/The Guide* founded 1837. Other writers of the period were Nicolas Beets (1814–1903) and Eduard Douwes Dekker (1820–1887), who wrote novels under the pen name 'Multatuli'. Among writers of the late 19th-century revival were Herman Gorter (1864–1927), Albert Verwey (1865–1937), Frederick van Eeden (1860–1932), Louis Couperus (1863–1923), and Arthur van Schendel (1874–1946).

After World War I Hendrik Marsman (1899–1940), a rhetorical 'vitalist' influenced by German Expressionism, led a school counterbalanced by the more sober Forum group of critic Menno Ter Braak (1902–1940). The Forum tradition has been challenged by younger writers associated with the journal *Merlyn* 1962–66. The mid-20th century was dominated by the often tragic fiction of Simon Vestdijk (1898–1971), the anti-realist poetry of Gerrit Achterberg (1905–1962), and the *novelle* of Nenco (J H F Gronloh, 1882–1961). More recent writers include the sombrely satirical poet and novelist Willem Frederik Herman (1921–) and the experimentalist poet L J Swaanswijk (1924–). See also ◊Flemish literature.

Dutilleux Henri 1916– . French composer of instrumental music in elegant Neo-Romantic style. His works include *Métaboles* 1962–65 for orchestra and *Ainsi la Nuit/Thus the Night* 1975–76 for string quartet.

Duvivier Julien 1896–1967. French film director whose work includes *La Belle Equipe* 1936, *Un*

Carnet de bal 1937, *La Fin du jour* 1938, as well as several Hollywood films including *Tales of Manhattan* 1942.

Dvořák Antonin (Leopold) 1841–1904. Czech composer. International recognition came with two sets of *Slavonic Dances* 1878, 1886, and he was director of the National Conservatory, New York, 1892–95. Works such as his *New World Symphony* 1893 reflect his interest in American folk themes, including black and native American. He wrote nine symphonies; tone poems; operas, including *Rusalka* 1900; large-scale choral works; the *Carnival* 1891–92 and other overtures; violin and cello concertos; chamber music; piano pieces; and songs. His Romantic music extends the classical tradition of Beethoven and Brahms and displays the influence of Czech folk music.

Dyck Anthony van 1599–1641. Flemish painter. Born in Antwerp, van Dyck was an assistant to Rubens 1618–20, then briefly worked in England at the court of James I, and moved to Italy 1622. In 1626 he returned to Antwerp, where he continued to paint religious works and portraits. From 1632 he lived in England and produced numerous portraits of royalty and aristocrats, such as *Charles I on Horseback* about 1638 (National Gallery, London).

dye-transfer print in photography, a print made by a relatively permanent colour process that uses red, yellow, and blue separation negatives printed together.

Dylan Bob. Adopted name of Robert Allen Zimmerman 1941– . US singer and songwriter whose lyrics provided catchphrases for a generation and influenced innumerable songwriters. He began in the folk-music tradition. His early songs, as on his albums *Freewheelin'* 1963 and *The Times They Are A- Changin'* 1964, were associated with the US civil-rights movement and anti-war protest. From 1965 he worked in an individualistic rock style, as on the albums *Highway 61 Revisited* 1965 and *Blonde on Blonde* 1966.

Dylan's early songs range from the simple, catchy 'Blowin' in the Wind' 1962 to brooding indictments of social injustice like 'The Ballad of Hollis Brown' 1963. When he first used an electric rock band 1965, he was criticized by purists, but the albums that immediately followed are often cited as his best work, with songs of spite ('Like a Rolling Stone') and surrealistic imagery ('Visions of Johanna') delivered in his characteristic nasal whine. The film *Don't Look Back* 1967 documents the 1965 British tour.

Of Dylan's 1970s albums, *Blood on the Tracks* 1975 was the strongest. *Slow Train Coming* 1979 was his first album as a born-again Christian, a phase that lasted several years and alienated all but the die-hard fans. *Oh, Mercy* 1989 was seen as a partial return to form, but *Under the Red Sky* 1990 did not bear this out. However, *The Bootleg Years* 1991, a collection of 58 previously unreleased items from past years, reasserted his standing. In 1992 he released *Good As I Been To You*, which consisted of traditional tunes and was his first completely solo acoustic album since *Another Side of Bob Dylan* 1964.

Come mothers and fathers/ Throughout the land/ And don't criticize/ What you can't understand.

Bob Dylan 'The Times They Are A-Changin'' 1963

---

dynamics in music, symbols indicating relative loudness, changes in loudness such as *crescendo* and *dimuendo*, or loudness in accentuation such as *rinforzando*.

dystopia imaginary society whose evil qualities are meant to serve as a moral or political warning. The term was coined in the 19th century by the English philosopher John Stuart Mill, and is the opposite of a ◊Utopia. George Orwell's *1984* 1949 and Aldous Huxley's *Brave New World* 1932 are examples of novels about dystopias. Dystopias are common in science fiction.

Aborigines, some of which he later developed into oil paintings, such as *A Bivouac of Travellers in an Australian Cabbage Tree Forest, Daybreak 1838* (Rex Nan Kivell Collection, National Library, Canberra). Portraits done in New South Wales include the full-length standing figure of *Captain John Piper* 1826.

Early English in architecture, the first of the three periods of the English Gothic style, late 12th century to late 13th century. It is characterized by tall, elongated windows (lancets) without mullions (horizontal bars), often grouped in threes, fives, or sevens; the pointed arch; pillars of stone centres surrounded by shafts of black Purbeck marble; and dog-tooth (zig-zag) ornament. Salisbury Cathedral (begun 1220) is almost entirely Early English.

Early English in language, general name for the range of dialects spoken by Germanic settlers in England between the 5th and 11th centuries AD. The literature of the period includes ◊*Beowulf*, an epic in West Saxon dialect, shorter poems of melancholic dignity such as *The Wanderer* and *The Seafarer*, and prose chronicles, Bible translations, spells, and charms.

earthenware pottery made of porous clay and fired at relatively low temperatures of up to 1,200°C/2,200°F. It does not vitrify but remains porous, unless glazed. Earthenware may be unglazed (flowerpots, wine-coolers) or glazed (most tableware); the glaze and body characteristically form quite separate layers.

The most ancient pottery was fired earthenware (terracotta), which is known to date back to the Mesolithic period in N Europe and E Africa. Today, pots fired in the traditional method for local use in parts of South America, Indonesia, Africa, and the Indian subcontinent are sometimes burnished to a smooth finish, which strengthens them. They often have an attractively uneven distribution of shades due to different rates of oxidization in the low temperature of an open fire (about 600°C/1,000°F); kiln-fired pots (fired at 1,000–1,200°C/1,832–2,200°F) are more evenly coloured and matt.

earthwork an artwork which involves the manipulation of the natural environment and/or the use of natural materials, such as earth, stones, or wood, largely a phenomenon of the late 1960s and the 1970s. Although some were exhibited in galleries, most earthworks were vast and usually constructed on remote, deserted sites and hence only known of through photographs and plans. Robert ◊Smithson and Michael Heizer (1944–), two leading exponents, engaged in physically overpowering works, for example, Heizer's *Complex One, Central Eastern Nevada* (1972, unfinished), an elongated, pyramidal hill of rammed earth supported by steel and concrete.

The Earthworks or Land art movement drew its inspiration from ◊Conceptual art, seeking to

---

Eagling Wayne 1950– . Canadian dancer who joined the Royal Ballet in London 1969, becoming a soloist 1972 and a principal dancer 1975. He appeared in *Gloria* 1980 and other productions. In Sept 1991 he became artistic director of the Dutch National Ballet.

Eakins Thomas 1844–1916. US painter. A trained observer of human anatomy and a devotee of photography, Eakins attempted to achieve a powerful visual Realism. His most memorable subjects are medical and sporting scenes, characterized by strong contrasts between light and shade, as in *The Gross Clinic* 1875 (Jefferson Medical College, Philadelphia), a group portrait of a surgeon, his assistants, and students.

The big artist ... keeps a sharp eye on Nature and steals her tools.

Thomas Eakins

Ealing Studios British film-producing company headed by Michael ◊Balcon 1937–58. The studio is best remembered for a series of comedies, which had an understated, self-deprecating humour such as *Passport to Pimlico*, *Kind Hearts and Coronets*, *Whisky Galore!* all 1949, *The Man in the White Suit* 1951, and *The Ladykillers* 1955.

The studios also made movies in other genres such as the crime thriller *The Blue Lamp* 1950 and the war story *The Cruel Sea* 1952.

Eames Charles 1907–1978 and Ray 1916–1988. US designers, a husband-and-wife team who worked together in California 1941–78. They created some of the most highly acclaimed furniture designs of the 20th century: a moulded plywood chair 1945–46; the Lounge Chair, a black leather-upholstered chair 1956; and a fibreglass armchair 1950–53.

Earle Augustus 1793–1838. British artist. He spent three years in Australia where he produced a series of drawings of landscapes and expand the concept of art, and of sculpture in particular, and to redefine attitude both to technology and to the natural environment.

Eastman George 1854–1932. US entrepreneur and inventor who founded the Eastman Kodak photographic company 1892. From 1888 he marketed his patented daylight-loading flexible roll films (to replace the glass plates used previously) and portable cameras. By 1900 his company was selling a pocket camera for as little as one dollar.

My work is done. Why wait?

George Eastman suicide note

Eastwood Clint 1930– . US film actor and director. As the 'Man with No Name' in *A Fistful of Dollars* 1964 and *The Good, the Bad, and the Ugly* 1966, he started the vogue for 'spaghetti Westerns' (made in Italy or Spain). Later Westerns which he both starred in and directed include *High Plains Drifter* 1973, *Outlaw Josey Wales* 1976, and *Unforgiven* 1992 (two Academy Awards). Other films include *In the Line of Fire* 1993.

Eastwood starred in the TV series *Rawhide* and in the 'Dirty Harry' series of films, and directed *Bird* 1988. He was elected mayor of Carmel, California 1986.

Echegaray José 1832–1916. Spanish dramatist. His social dramas include *O locura o santidad/Madman or Saint* 1877, and *El gran Galeoto/The World and his Wife* 1881. Nobel prize 1904.

Echo in Greek mythology, a ◊nymph who pined away until only her voice remained, after being rejected by Narcissus.

eclecticism in artistic theory, the use of motifs and elements from various styles, periods, and geographical areas. This selection and recombination of features from different sources is a characteristic of Victorian architecture, for example, J F Bentley's design for Westminster Cathedral, London, 1895–1903, in Byzantine style.

Eco Umberto 1932– . Italian writer, semiologist, and literary critic. His works include *The Role of the Reader* 1979, the 'philosophical thriller' *The ◊Name of the Rose* 1983, and *Foucault's Pendulum* 1988.

Edda two collections of early Icelandic literature that together constitute our chief source for Old Norse mythology. The term strictly applies to the *Younger* or *Prose Edda*, compiled by Snorri Sturluson, a priest, about AD 1230.

The *Elder* or *Poetic Edda* is the collection of poems discovered around 1643 by Brynjólfr

Sveinsson, written by unknown Norwegian poets of the 9th to 12th centuries.

Edgar David 1948– . English dramatist. After early work as a journalist, Edgar turned to documentary and political theatre. *Destiny*, about the extreme right-wing in Britain, was produced by the Royal Shakespeare Company 1976. Other plays include *The Jail Diary of Albie Sachs* 1978; his adaptation from Dickens for the RSC, *The Life and Adventures of Nicholas Nickleby* 1980; and *The Shape of the Table* 1990, on the collapse of the Eastern bloc in Europe.

Edgeworth Maria 1767–1849. Irish novelist. Her first novel, *Castle Rackrent* 1800, dealt with Anglo-Irish country society and was followed by the similar *The Absentee* 1812 and *Ormond* 1817. As a writer of socially concerned and historical novels, she influenced Walter Scott. She was a fervent proponent of women's education and has been re-evaluated by 20th-century feminists.

Edson J(ohn) T(homas) 1928– . English writer of Western novels. His books, numbering 129 by 1990 and with 25 million copies sold, have such titles as *The Fastest Gun in Texas* and feature a recurring hero, Rapido Clint.

Edwards Blake. Adopted name of William Blake McEdwards 1922– . US film director and writer, formerly an actor. Specializing in comedies, he directed the series of *Pink Panther* films 1963–78, starring Peter Sellers. His other work includes *Breakfast at Tiffany's* 1961 and *Blind Date* 1986.

Eggleston William 1937– . US photographer whose banal scenes of life in the Deep South are transformed by his use of the dye transfer technique into intense, superreal images of richly saturated colour. In 1984 he documented Elvis Presley's home at Graceland.

Egyptian architecture, ancient the dynastic period spanning the years 4000–30 BC saw the emergence of a distinctive Egyptian architecture, best represented in its tombs and temples. Monumental in style, these were built exclusively for the higher echelons of society, particularly pharaohs and priests. Of the tombs, the ◊pyramids are the most striking. These evolved from mastaba – simple tomb structures with sloping sides – through stepped pyramids, such as that at Sakkara about 2650 BC, to the familiar regular pyramids at El Gîza, about 2600–2480 BC. Temple architecture of the period is characterized by huge, sloping or 'battered' walls and pylons, pyramidal towers flanking the entrances. Famous examples are at Karnak, about 1570–1085, and at Luxor, about 1570–1200.

Egyptian art, ancient the art of ancient Egypt, which falls into three main periods – the Old, Middle, and New Kingdoms – beginning about 3000 BC and spanning 2,000 years overall. During this time, despite some stylistic development, there is remarkable continuity, representing a deeply religious and traditionalist society. Sculpture and painting are highly stylized, following strict conventions and using symbols of a religion centred on the afterlife and idealization of the dead, their servants, families, and possessions. Depictions of the human form show the face and legs in profile, the upper torso facing forwards, the hips three quarters turned, and the eye enlarged and enhanced.

During Egypt's slow decline in power, the style of art remained conservative and subservient to religion, but the level of technical expertise continued to be high, with an almost constant and prolific production of artefacts. Major collections of Egyptian art are to be found in the National Museum, Cairo, and in the British Museum, London.

the early dynastic period and the Old Kingdom (2920–2134 BC) is exemplified by the monumental statue of the Great Sphinx at El Gîza, about 2530 BC. A gigantic lion figure with a human head, the sphinx is carved from an outcrop of natural rock, 56.4 m/185 ft long and 19.2 m/63 ft high, and guards the path to the pyramid of Khafre. A rich collection of grave goods survive from the period, including clothes, ornaments, jewellery, and weapons, as well as statues in stone and precious metals. The stylistic conventions of painting – such as showing the human figure with head, legs, and feet in profile, the eyes and shoulders frontally – are established. Vivid wall paintings, such as *Geese of Medum* (National Museum, Cairo), about 2530, show a variety of scenes from the life of the time.

Middle Kingdom (2040–1640 BC), a period when Egypt was reunited under one ruler, is typified by tombs hewn from rock, attempts at realism in frescoes, and deepened perception in portrait sculpture, for example the head of Sesostris III (National Museum, Cairo). Typical of the period are sculptures of figures wrapped in mantles, with only head, hands, and feet showing.

New Kingdom (1550–1070 BC) is represented by a softer and more refined style of painting and a new sophistication in jewellery and furnishings. The golden age of the 18th dynasty, 1550–1070 BC, saw the the building of the temples of Karnak and Luxor and the maze of tombs in the Valley of the Kings. The pharaohs of the period, Ikhnaton and Tutankhamen, inspired a most extravagant style, as exemplified in the carved images of these godlike creatures, the statues of Ikhnaton, the golden coffins of Tutankhamen's mummified body (National Museum, Cairo), about 1361–1352 BC, and the head of Ikhnaton's queen, Nefertiti (Museo Archaeologico, Florence), about 1360 BC. The monumental statues of Ramses II in Abu Simbel date from the 13th century BC.

Ehrenburg Ilya Grigorievich 1891–1967. Soviet writer, born in Kiev, Ukraine. His controversial work *The Thaw* 1954 depicts artistic circles in the USSR and contributed to the growing literary freedom of the 1950s.

Eichendorff Joseph Freiherr von 1788–1857. German Romantic poet and novelist, born in Upper Silesia. His work was set to music by Schumann, Mendelssohn, and Wolf.

Eiffel (Alexandre) Gustave 1832–1923. French engineer who constructed the *Eiffel Tower* for the 1889 Paris Exhibition. The tower, made of iron, is 320 m/1,050 ft high, and stands in the Champ de Mars, Paris.

Eiffel set up his own business in Paris and quickly established his reputation with the construction of a series of ambitious railway bridges, of which the 160 m/525 ft span across the Douro at Oporto, Portugal, was the longest. In 1881 he provided the iron skeleton for the Statue of Liberty which stands in New York harbour.

Eisenman Peter 1932– . US architect who came to prominence as a member of the ◊New York Five group, along with Richard Meier and Michael Graves. His work draws on mathematics and philosophy, especially ◊Deconstructionism. Early experiments in complexity, such as House X 1978, have led to increasingly scrambled designs, such as Fin d'Ou T Hou S 1983.

A more recent commission, the Wexner Centre for the Visual Arts, Ohio, 1985–90, has let him explore his interest in grids and the concept of 'non-building' in a large public project.

Eisenstein Sergei Mikhailovich 1898–1948. Soviet film director who pioneered film theory and introduced the use of montage (the juxtaposition of shots to create a particular effect) as a means of propaganda, as in *The Battleship Potemkin* 1925.

The Soviet dictator Stalin banned the second (and last) part of Eisenstein's projected three-film epic *Ivan the Terrible* 1944–46. His other films include *Strike* 1925, *October* 1928, *Que Viva Mexico!* 1931–32, and *Alexander Nevsky* 1938.

eisteddfod (Welsh 'sitting') traditional Welsh gathering lasting up to a week and dedicated to the encouragement of the bardic arts of music, poetry, and literature. Dating from pre-Christian times, eisteddfods are held annually.

Eldem Sedad Hakki 1908– . Turkish architect whose work is inspired by the spatial harmony and regular rhythms of the traditional Turkish house. These qualities are reinterpreted in modern forms with great sensitivity to context, as in the Social Security Agency Complex, Zeyrek, Istanbul, 1962–64, and the Atatürk Library, Istanbul, 1973.

Elder Mark 1947– . English conductor, music director of the English National Opera (ENO) from 1979 and of the Rochester Philharmonic Orchestra, USA, from 1989.

Elder worked at Glyndebourne from 1970, conducted with the Australian Opera from 1972, and joined the ENO 1974. As principal conductor of the ENO, he specializes in 19th- and 20th-century repertoire.

El Dorado fabled city of gold believed by the 16th-century Spanish and other Europeans to exist somewhere in the area of the Orinoco and Amazon rivers.

Electra in Greek mythology, daughter of ◊Agamemnon and ◊Clytemnestra, and sister of ◊Orestes and ◊Iphigenia. Her hatred of her mother for murdering her father and her desire for revenge, fulfilled on the return of her brother Orestes, made her the subject of tragedies by the Greek dramatists Aeschylus, Sophocles, and Euripides. In Euripides' tragedy she joins with Orestes in killing Clytemnestra.

Electra title of two separate tragedies by ◊Sophocles and ◊Euripides, produced in Greece about 410 BC and 417 BC, respectively. In both plays Electra is devastated by the murder of her father Agamemnon at the hands of her mother Clytemnestra. With the help of her brother, Orestes, she takes her revenge, killing Clytemnestra and her lover, Aegisthus.

electronic music term first applied 1954 to edited tape music composed primarily of electronically generated and modified tones, serially organized to objective scales of differentiation, to distinguish it from the more intuitive method ology of ◊concrete music. The term was subsequently extended to include prerecorded vocal and instrumental sounds organized in a similar way. Stockhausen, Berio, Babbitt, and Maderna are pioneers of electronic music.

elegy ancient Greek verse form, originally combining a ◊hexameter with a shorter line in a couplet. It was used by the Greeks for ◊epigrams, short narratives, and discursive poems, and adopted by the Roman poets (◊Ovid, ◊Propertius), particularly for erotic verse.

In contemporary usage, the term refers to a nostalgic poem or a lament, often a funeral poem. Thomas Gray's 'Elegy Written in a Country Churchyard' 1751 is one of the best-known elegies in English. An elegy is likely to be a personal and private expression of grief.

Elgar Edward (William) 1857–1934. English composer. His *Enigma Variations* appeared 1899, and although his celebrated choral work, the oratorio setting of John Henry Newman's *The Dream of Gerontius*, was initially unpopular in Britain, it was well received at Düsseldorf 1902, leading to a surge of interest in his earlier works, including the *Pomp and Circumstance* marches.

Among his later works are oratorios, two symphonies, a violin concerto, a cello concerto, chamber music, songs, and the tone-poem *Falstaff* 1913.

Things take shape without my knowing it. I am only the lead pencil and cannot foresee.

Edward Elgar

Elgin marbles collection of ancient Greek sculptures, including the famous frieze and other sculptures from the Parthenon at Athens, assembled by the 7th Earl of Elgin. Sent to England 1812, and bought for the nation 1816 for £5,000, they are now in the British Museum. Greece has repeatedly asked for them to be returned to Athens.

Eliot George. Pen name of Mary Ann Evans 1819–1880. English novelist whose works include the pastoral *Adam Bede* 1859, *The ◊Mill on the Floss* 1860, with its autobiographical elements, *Silas Marner* 1861, which contains elements of the folktale, *Felix Holt* 1866, and *Daniel Deronda* 1876. ◊*Middlemarch*, published serially 1871–72, is considered her greatest novel for its confident handling of numerous characters and central social and moral issues. Her work is pervaded by a penetrating and compassionate intelligence.

Born at Chilvers Coton, Warwickshire, George Eliot had a strict evangelical upbringing. In 1841 she was converted to free thought, a post-Reformation movement opposed to Christian dogma. As assistant editor of the *Westminster Review* under John Chapman 1851–53, she made the acquaintance of Thomas Carlyle, Harriet Martineau, Herbert Spencer, and the philosopher and critic George Henry Lewes (1817–1878). Lewes was married but separated from his wife, and from 1854 he and Eliot lived together in a relationship that she regarded as a true marriage and that continued until his death. In 1880 she married John Cross (1840–1924).

Nothing is so good as it seems beforehand.

George Eliot *Silas Marner* 1861

Eliot T(homas) S(tearns) 1888–1965. US poet, playwright, and critic who lived in London from 1915. His first volume of poetry, *Prufrock and Other Observations* 1917, introduced new verse forms and rhythms; further collections include *The ◊Waste Land* 1922, *The Hollow Men* 1925, and *Old Possum's Book of Practical Cats* 1939. His plays include *Murder in the Cathedral* 1935 and *The Cocktail Party* 1949. His critical works include *The Sacred Wood* 1920. He was awarded the Nobel Prize for Literature 1948.

Eliot was born in St Louis, Missouri, and was

educated at Harvard, the Sorbonne, and Oxford. He settled in London 1915 and became a British subject 1927. He was for a time a bank clerk, later lecturing and entering publishing at Faber & Faber. As editor of *The Criterion* 1922–39, he influenced the thought of his generation.

Prufrock and Other Observations expressed the disillusionment of the generation affected by World War I and caused a sensation with its experimental form and rhythms. His reputation was established by the desolate modernity of *The Waste Land*. *The Hollow Men* continued on the same note, but *Ash Wednesday* 1930 revealed the change in religious attitude that led him to become a Catholic. Among his other works are *Four Quartets* 1943, a religious sequence in which he seeks the eternal reality, and the poetic dramas *Murder in the Cathedral* (about Thomas à Becket); *The Cocktail Party*; *The Confidential Clerk* 1953; and *The Elder Statesman* 1958. His collection *Old Possum's Book of Practical Cats* was used for the popular British composer Andrew Lloyd Webber's musical *Cats* 1981. His critical works include *Notes toward the Definition of Culture* 1949.

Poetry is not a turning loose of emotion, but an escape from emotion; it is not the expression of personality, but an escape from personality.

T S Eliot
'Tradition and the Individual Talent'

Elizabethan literature literature produced during the reign of Elizabeth I of England (1558–1603). This period saw a remarkable florescence of the arts in England, and the literature of the time is characterized by a new energy, richness, and confidence. Renaissance humanism, Protestant zeal, and geographical discovery all contributed to this upsurge of creative power. Drama was the dominant form of the age, and ◊Shakespeare and ◊Marlowe were popular with all levels of society. Other writers of the period include Edmund Spenser, Sir Philip Sidney, Francis Bacon, Thomas Lodge, Robert Greene, and John Lyly.

During the Elizabethan period, the resources of English were increased by the free adoption of words from Latin. This was accompanied by a growing belief that English was capable of all the requirements of great literature. There was a balance between the university and courtly elements and the coarse gusto of popular culture. Music was closely related to literature, and competence in singing and musical composition was seen as a normal social skill. Successive editions of the Bible were produced during these years, written with dignity, vividness, and the deliberate intention of reaching a universal audience.

Ellington Duke (Edward Kennedy) 1899–1974. US pianist who had an outstanding career as a composer and arranger of jazz. He wrote numerous pieces for his own jazz orchestra, accentuating the strengths of individual virtuoso instrumentalists, and became one of the leading figures in jazz over a 55-year period. Some of his most popular compositions include 'Mood Indigo', 'Sophisticated Lady', 'Solitude', and 'Black and Tan Fantasy'. He was one of the founders of big-band jazz.

There are only two kinds of music: good and bad.

Duke Ellington

Ellis (Henry) Havelock 1859–1939. English psychologist and writer of many works on the psychology of sex, including *Studies in the Psychology of Sex* (seven volumes) 1898–1928.

Every artist writes his own autobiography.

Havelock Ellis *The New Spirit*

Ellis Bret Easton 1964– . US novelist. He is the author of *Less Than Zero* 1985, a novel dealing with the alienation of affluent youth; *The Rules of Attraction* 1987, about sex on a college campus; and the controversial *American Psycho* 1991, about a Wall Street psychopath, which vividly depicts the urban violence of contemporary American life.

Ellison Ralph (Waldo) 1914– . US novelist. His *Invisible Man* 1952 portrays with humour and energy the plight of a black man whom postwar American society cannot acknowledge; it is regarded as one of the most impressive novels published in the USA in the 1950s. He also wrote essays collected in *Shadow and Act* 1964.

Elsheimer Adam 1578–1610. German painter and etcher, active in Rome from 1600. His small paintings, nearly all on copper, depict landscapes darkened by storm or night, with figures picked out by beams of light, as in *The Rest on the Flight into Egypt* 1609 (Alte Pinakothek, Munich).

Eluard Paul. Pen name of Eugène Grindel 1895–1952. French poet, born in Paris. He expressed the suffering of poverty in his verse, and was a leader of the Surrealists. He fought in World War I, which inspired his *Poèmes pour la paix/Poems for Peace* 1918, and was a member of the Resistance in World War II. His books include *Poésie et vérité/Poetry and Truth* 1942 and *Au Rendezvous allemand/To the German Rendezvous* 1944.

Elysée Palace (French *Palais de l'Elysée*) building in Paris erected 1718 for Louis d'Auvergne, Count of Evreux. It was later the home of Mme de Pompadour, Napoleon I, and Napoleon III, and became the official residence of the presidents of France 1870.

Elysium in Greek mythology, originally another name for the ◊Islands of the Blessed, to which favoured heroes were sent by the gods to enjoy a life after death. It was later a region in ◊Hades.

Elytis Odysseus. Pen name of Odysseus Alepoudelis 1911– . Greek poet, born in Crete. His verse celebrates the importance of the people's attempts to shape an individual existence in freedom. His major work *To Axion Esti/Worthy It Is* 1959 is a lyric cycle, parts of which have been set to music by Theodorakis. He was awarded the Nobel Prize for Literature 1979.

Elzevir Louis 1540–1617. Founder of the Dutch printing house Elzevir in the 17th century. Among the firm's publications were editions of Latin, Greek, and Hebrew works, as well as French and Italian classics.

Born at Louvain, Elzevir was obliged to leave Belgium in 1580 because of his Protestant and political views. He settled at Leyden as a bookseller and printer.

Emanuel, David 1952– and Elizabeth 1953– . British fashion designers who opened their own salon 1977. They specialized in off-the-shoulder, ornate and opulent evening wear. In 1981 Lady Diana Spencer, now Princess of Wales, commissioned the Emanuels to design her wedding dress. In 1990 Elizabeth Emanuel established her own label in London, continuing to design outfits for singers, actresses, and members of the British royal family.

emblem any visible symbol; a moral maxim expressed pictorially with an explanatory epigram. Books of emblems were popular in Renaissance Europe. The first emblem book was by Andrea Alciati of Milan; first printed in Augsburg 1531, it had some 175 editions in several languages. In England *Emblems* 1635, a religious work, was compiled by Francis Quarles (1592–1644).

embossing relief decoration on metals, which can be cast, chased, or repoussé, and executed by hand or machine. In the 16th century the term was also used for carved decorations on wood.

Embossed bindings for books were developed from the early 19th century; the leather is embossed before binding.

embroidery the art of decorating cloth with a needle and thread. It includes ◊broderie anglaise, ◊gros point, and ◊petit point, all of which have been used for the adornment of costumes, gloves, book covers, furnishings, and ecclesiastical vestments.

The earliest embroidery that survives in England is the stole and maniple (a decorative strip of silk worn over the arm), found in the tomb of St Cuthbert in Durham and dating from 905. The ◊Bayeux Tapestry is an embroidery dating from 1067–70. In Britain embroidery on canvas and linen for household purposes, together with ◊appliqué, was popular early in the 20th century. Since the 1950s there has been a revival of creative embroidery in many countries.

Emerson Peter Henry 1856–1936. English landscape photographer whose aim was to produce uncontrived naturalistic images of the countryside. He believed in differential focusing, the idea that only part of the picture should be sharply focused. His first book, *Life and Landscape on the Norfolk Broads*, was produced in collaboration with the painter T F Goodall 1886. Emerson's theories were set out in *Naturalistic Photography* 1889 but a year later he recanted and largely gave up photography 1900.

Emerson Ralph Waldo 1803–1882. US philosopher, essayist, and poet. He settled in Concord, Massachusetts, which he made a centre of transcendentalism, and wrote *Nature* 1836, which states the movement's main principles emphasizing the value of self-reliance and the godlike nature of human souls. His two volumes of *Essays* (1841, 1844) made his reputation: 'Self-Reliance' and 'Compensation' are among the best known. His poems include 'The Rhodora', 'Threnody', and 'Brahma'. His later works include *Representative Men* 1850 and *The Conduct of Life* 1870.

The truth, the hope of any time, must always be sought in minorities.

Ralph Waldo Emerson

---

empathy the ability to understand or imaginatively enter into another person's situation or feelings; the projection of one's feelings on to objects, such as works of art.

Empire style French decorative arts style prevalent during the rule of the emperor Napoleon Bonaparte (1804–14). A late form of ◊Neo-Classicism, it featured motifs drawn from ancient Egyptian as well as Greek and Roman art. Dark woods and draperies were also frequently used. The influence of the style extended through Europe and North America.

Empson William 1906–1984. English poet and critic, born in Yorkshire. He was professor of English literature at Tokyo and Beijing (Peking), and from 1953 to 1971 at Sheffield University. His critical work examined the potential variety of meaning in poetry, as in *Seven Types of Ambiguity* 1930 and *The Structure of Complex Words* 1951. His *Collected Poems* were published 1955.

enamel vitrified (glasslike) coating of various colours used for decorative purposes on a metallic or porcelain surface. In ◊*cloisonné* the various sections of the design are separated by thin metal wires or strips. In *champlevé* the enamel is poured into engraved cavities in the metal surface.

The ancient art of enamelling is believed to be of Near Eastern origin. The Egyptians, Greeks, and Romans enamelled their jewellery, and Byzantium was famed for enamels from about the 9th to 11th centuries. The enamelled altarpiece at St Mark's, Venice, which was brought from Constantinople, still survives. Byzantine work was emulated in Europe, particularly in Saxony, Brunswick, and in the Rhine valley. German enamellers were later employed in France, and during the 13th and 14th centuries the art was introduced into Italy and China. The chief centres of enamelling during the 15th and 16th centuries were the cities of Lorraine and Limoges, France.

encaustic painting technique of painting, commonly used by the Egyptians, Greeks, and Romans, in which coloured pigments are mixed with molten wax and painted on panels. In the 20th century the technique has been used by the US artist Jasper Johns.

encore (French 'again') in music, the repetition of a piece that has already been played, or, more usually, an unprogrammed extra item, usually short and well known, played at the end of a concert to please an enthusiastic audience.

Encyclopédie encyclopedia in 35 volumes written 1751–77 by a group of French scholars (*Encyclopédistes*) including D'Alembert and Diderot, inspired by the English encyclopedia produced by Ephraim Chambers 1728. Religious scepticism and ◊Enlightenment social and political views were a feature of the work.

The first 28 volumes 1751–72 were edited by Diderot. A further five volumes were produced by other editors 1776–77 and the two-volume index was completed 1780.

Endo Shusako 1923– . Japanese novelist. A convert to Catholic Christianity, he studied modern French religious writing in Lyons 1950. This encouraged his fictional explorations of cultural conflict and moral and spiritual perplexity in sympathetically treated unheroic lives, disclosing a 'mudswamp' of moral inertia in contemporary Japanese life. Among his best-known works, much translated, are the historical novel *Chinmoky/ Silence* 1967 and *Kuchibue o fuku toki/When I Whistle* 1979.

Endymion in Greek mythology, a beautiful young man loved by Selene, the Moon goddess. He was granted eternal sleep in order to remain forever young. Keats' poem *Endymion* 1818 is an allegory of searching for perfection.

Engel Carl Ludwig 1778–1840. German architect, who from 1815 worked in Finland. His great Neo-Classical achievement is the Senate Square in Helsinki, which includes his Senate House 1818–22 and University Building 1828–32, and the domed Lutheran cathedral 1830–40.

Engleheart George 1752–1829. English miniature painter. Born in Kew, London, he studied under Joshua Reynolds and in over 40 years painted nearly 5,000 miniatures, including copies of many of Reynolds' portraits.

English architecture the main styles in English architecture are: Anglo-Saxon, Norman, Early English (of which Westminster Abbey is an example), Decorated, Perpendicular (15th century), Tudor (a name chiefly applied to domestic buildings of about 1485–1558), Jacobean, Stuart (including the Renaissance and Queen Anne styles), Georgian, the Gothic revival of the 19th century, Modern, and Post-Modern. Notable architects include Christopher Wren, Inigo Jones, John Vanbrugh, Nicholas Hawksmoor, Charles Barry, Edwin Landseer Lutyens, Hugh Casson, Basil Spence, Frederick Gibberd, Denys Lasdun, Richard Rogers, Norman Foster, James Stirling, Terry Farrell, Quinlan Terry, and Zahia Hadid.

Anglo-Saxon (5th–11th century) Much of the architecture of this period, being of timber, has disappeared. The stone church towers that remain, such as at Earls Barton, appear to imitate timber techniques with their 'long and short work' and triangular arches. Brixworth Church, Northamptonshire, is another example of Anglo-Saxon architecture, dating from *c.* 670.

Norman (11th–12th century) William the Conqueror inaugurated an enormous building programme. He introduced the *Romanesque style* of round arches, massive cylindrical columns, and thick walls. At Durham Cathedral 1093–*c.* 1130, the rib vaults were an invention of European importance in the development of the Gothic style.

Gothic architecture The *Early English* (late 12th–late 13th century) began with the French east end of Canterbury Cathedral, designed 1175 by William of Sens (died *c.* 1180), and attained its English flowering in the cathedrals of Wells, Lincoln, and Salisbury. A simple elegant style of lancet windows, deeply carved mouldings, and slender, contrasting shafts of Purbeck marble. *Decorated* (late 13th–14th century) is characterized by a growing richness in carving and a fascination with line. The double curves of the ogee arch, elaborate window tracery, and vault ribs woven into star patterns may be seen in such buildings as the Lady Chapel at Ely and the Angel Choir at Lincoln. Exeter Cathedral is another example of the Decorated style. The gridded and panelled cages of light of the *Perpendicular* (late 14th–mid 16th century) style are a dramatic contrast to the Decorated period. Although they lack the richness and invention of the 14th century, they often convey an impressive sense of unity, space, and power. The chancel of Gloucester Cathedral is early Perpendicular whereas King's College Chapel, Cambridge, is late Perpendicular.

Tudor and Elizabethan (1485–1603) This period saw the Perpendicular style interwoven with growing Renaissance influence. Buildings develop a conscious symmetry elaborated with continental Patternbrook details. Hybrid and exotic works result such as Burghley House, Cambridgeshire, 1552–87, and Hardwick Hall, Derbyshire, 1590–97. Smythson's Longleat House 1568–75 in Wiltshire is another building of the period.

Jacobean (1603–25) A transition period, with the Renaissance influence becoming more pronounced. Hatfield House 1607–12 in Hertfordshire is Jacobean, so also is Blickling Hall in Norfolk, redesigned around a medieval moated house and completed 1628. Both were designed by the architect Robert Lyminge.

English Renaissance (17th–early 18th century) The provincial scene was revolutionized by Inigo Jones with the Queen's House, Greenwich, 1616–35, and the Banqueting House, Whitehall, 1619–22. Strict Palladianism appeared among the half-timber and turrets of Jacobean London. With Christopher Wren a restrained Baroque evolved showing French Renaissance influence, for example St Paul's Cathedral, London, 1675–1710. Under Nicholas Hawksmoor and John Vanbrugh a theatrical Baroque style emerged, exemplifed in their design for Blenheim Palace, Oxfordshire, 1705–20.

Georgian architecture (18th–early 19th century) Lord Burlington, reacting against the Baroque, inspired a revival of the pure Palladian style of Inigo Jones, as in Chiswick House 1725–29, London. William Kent, also a Palladian, invented the picturesque garden, as at Rousham, Oxfordshire. Alongside the great country houses, an urban architecture evolved of plain, well-proportioned houses, defining elegant streets and squares; John Wood the Younger's Royal Crescent, Bath, was built 1767–75. The second half of the century mingled Antiquarian and Neo-Classical influences, exquisitely balanced in the work of Robert Adam at Kedleston Hall 1759–70. John Nash carried Neo-Classicism into the new century; his designs include Regent Street, London, begun 1811 and the Royal Pavilion, Brighton, 1815–21. By the dawn of the Victorian era Neo-Classicism had become a rather bookish Greek Revival, for example the British Museum 1823–47.

19th century Throughout the century Classic and Gothic engaged with Victorian earnestness in the 'Battle of the Styles': Gothic for the Houses of Parliament 1840–60 (designed by Barra and Pugin), Renaissance for the Foreign Office 1860–75. Meanwhile, the great developments in engineering and the needs of new types of build-

ings, such as railway stations, transformed the debate. Joseph Paxton's prefabricated Crystal Palace 1850–51 was the most remarkable building of the era. The Arts and Crafts architects Philip Webb and Norman Shaw brought renewal and simplicity inspired by William Morris.

20th century The early work of Edwin Landseer Lutyens and the white rendered houses of Charles Voysey such as Broadleys, Windermere 1898–99, maintained the Arts and Crafts spirit of natural materials and simplicity. Norman Shaw, however, developed an Imperial Baroque style. After World War I classicism again dominated, grandly in Lutyens' New Delhi government buildings 1912–31. There was often a clean Scandinavian influence as in the RIBA building, London, 1932–34, which shows growing Modernist tendencies. The Modern Movement arrived fully with continental refugees such as Bertholdt Lubetkin, the founder of the Tecton architectural team that designed London Zoo 1934–38.

The strong social dimension of English 20th-century architecture is best seen in the new town movement. Welwyn Garden City was begun 1919 and developed after World War II. The latest of the new towns, Milton Keynes, was designated 1967. Recently English architects have again achieved international recognition, for example Norman Foster and Richard Rogers for their High-Tech innovative Lloyds Building, London, 1979–84. James Stirling's work maintained a Modernist technique and planning while absorbing historical and contextual concerns. Recent Post-Modern architecture includes the Sainsbury Wing of the National Gallery, London, designed by Robert Venturi 1991.

English art painting and sculpture in England from the 11th century. For English art before the 11th century see ◊Anglo-Saxon art.

medieval (11th–15th century) The painting and sculpture of this period were entirely religious: illuminated manuscripts, carvings in wood and stone for churches and cathedrals, wall painting (now mostly lost), and carvings in ivory. The *Wilton Diptych* late 14th century (National Gallery, London), showing Richard II presented to the Virgin and Child, is a rare example of panel painting.

Tudor and Elizabethan (15th–16th century) The German artist Hans Holbein painted portraits of Henry VIII's court, and Nicholas Hilliard, perfecting the art of the miniature, painted portraits of Elizabeth I's court. Portraiture was to become one of English art's most enduring achievements.

17th century English art was revitalized by foreign artists. The Flemish painters Peter Paul Rubens and Anthony van Dyck painted portraits of the court; the Flemish sculptor John Michael Rysbrack carved portraits and monuments. Grinling Gibbons, a Dutch sculptor, became renowned for his woodcarvings, such as panels for St Paul's Cathedral. In 1711 the German artist Godfrey Keller opened the first English academy of art.

18th century Joshua Reynolds, Thomas Gainsborough, George Romney, and Thomas Lawrence produced a distinctive style of English portraiture. William Hogarth and Thomas Rowlandson developed a satirical art in styles suggesting political cartoons, and George Stubbs the sporting picture. John Flaxman's sculptures were in the Neo-Classical style, while the highly individual paintings and drawings of Henry Fuseli and William Blake were an early expression of Romanticism.

19th century Landscape painting flourished, with works by John Constable, J M W Turner, Samuel Palmer, Thomas Girtin, and John Sell Cotman. The Pre-Raphaelite movement was established in the 1840s, its members – such as Holman Hunt, Dante Gabriel Rossetti, and John Everett Millais – concentrating on religious, literary, and genre subjects. Realism was represented by William Frith, an idealized view of classical Greece and Rome by Lord Leighton. Animal painting was continued by Edwin Landseer. French Impressionism influenced the work of Philip Wilson Steer and Walter Sickert.

20th century A wide variety of styles and movements have flourished, from the Post-Impressionism of the Camden Town School to Pop art and Conceptualism. Painters include Stanley Spencer, Matthew Smith, Graham Sutherland, L S Lowry, Edward Burra, Ben Nicholson, Paul Nash, David Bomberg, Duncan Grant, Gwen John, Lucian Freud, Francis Bacon, Richard Hamilton, and David Hockney. Sculptors include Jacob Epstein, Barbara Hepworth, Henry Moore, Elisabeth Frink, Reg Butler, Anthony Caro, and Richard Long.

English horn alternative name for ◊cor anglais, a musical instrument of the oboe family.

English literature for the earliest surviving English literature see ◊Old English literature.

12th–15th century: Middle English period With the arrival of a Norman ruling class at the end of the 11th century, the ascendancy of Norman-French in cultural life began, and it was not until the 13th century that the native literature regained its strength. Prose was concerned chiefly with popular devotional use, but verse emerged typically in the metrical chronicles, such as Layamon's *Brut*, and the numerous romances based on the stories of Charlemagne, the Arthurian legends, and the classical episodes of Troy. First of the great English poets was Geoffrey Chaucer, whose early work reflected the predominant French influence, but later that of Renaissance Italy. Of purely native inspiration was *The Vision of Piers Plowman* of William Langland in the old alliterative verse, and the anonymous *Pearl*, *Patience*, and *Gawayne and the*

Grene Knight. Chaucer's mastery of versification was not shared by his successors, the most original of whom was John Skelton. More successful were the anonymous authors of songs and carols, and of the ballads, which (for example those concerned with Robin Hood) often formed a complete cycle. Drama flowered in the form of ◊miracle and ◊morality plays, and prose, although still awkwardly handled by John Wycliffe (*c.* 1320–1384) in his translation of the Bible, rose to a great height with Thomas Malory in the 15th century.

16th century: Elizabethan The Renaissance, which had first touched the English language through Chaucer, came to delayed fruition in the 16th century. Thomas Wyatt and Henry Surrey used the sonnet and blank verse in typically Elizabethan forms and prepared the way for Edmund Spenser, Philip Sidney, Samuel Daniel, Thomas Campion, and others. With Thomas Kyd and Christopher Marlowe, drama emerged into theatrical form; it reached the highest level in Shakespeare and Ben Jonson. Elizabethan prose is represented by Richard Hooker, Thomas North, Roger Ascham, Raphael Holinshed, John Lyly, and others.

17th century English prose achieved full richness in the 17th century, with the Authorized Version of the Bible 1611, Francis Bacon, John Milton, John Bunyan, Jeremy Taylor, Thomas Browne, Izaak Walton, and Samuel Pepys. Most renowned of the 17th-century poets were Milton and John Donne; others include the religious writers George Herbert, Richard Crashaw, Henry Vaughan, and Thomas Traherne, and the Cavalier poets Robert Herrick, Thomas Carew, John Suckling, and Richard Lovelace. In the **Restoration period** (from 1660) Samuel Butler and John Dryden stand out as poets. Dramatists include Thomas Otway and Nathaniel Lee in tragedy. Comedy flourished with William Congreve, John Vanbrugh, and George Farquhar.

18th century: the Augustan Age Alexander Pope developed the poetic technique of Dryden; in prose Richard Steele and Joseph Addison evolved the polite essay, Jonathan Swift used satire, and Daniel Defoe exploited his journalistic ability. This century saw the development of the ◊novel, through the epistolary style of Samuel Richardson to the robust narrative of Henry Fielding and Tobias Smollett, the comic genius of Laurence Sterne, and the Gothic 'horror' of Horace Walpole. The Neo-Classical standards established by the Augustans were maintained by Samuel Johnson and his circle – Oliver Goldsmith, Edmund Burke, Joshua Reynolds, Richard Sheridan, and others – but the romantic element present in the work of poets James Thomson, Thomas Gray, Edward Young, and William Collins was soon to overturn them.

19th century The *Lyrical Ballads* 1798 of William Wordsworth and Samuel Taylor Coleridge were the manifesto of the new Romantic age. Lord Byron, Percy Bysshe Shelley, and John Keats form a second generation of Romantic poets. In fiction Walter Scott took over the Gothic tradition from Mrs Radcliffe, to create the ◊historical novel, and Jane Austen established the novel of the comedy of manners. Criticism gained new prominence with Coleridge, Charles Lamb, William Hazlitt, and Thomas De Quincey. During the 19th century the novel was further developed by Charles Dickens, William Makepeace Thackeray, the Brontës, George Eliot, Anthony Trollope, and others. The principal poets of the reign of Victoria were Alfred Tennyson, Robert and Elizabeth Browning, Matthew Arnold, the Rossettis, William Morris, and Algernon Swinburne. Among the prose writers of the era are Thomas Macaulay, John Newman, John Stuart Mill, Thomas Carlyle, John Ruskin, and Walter Pater. The transition period at the end of the century saw the poetry and novels of George Meredith and Thomas Hardy; the work of Samuel Butler and George Gissing; and the plays of Arthur Pinero and Oscar Wilde. Although a Victorian, Gerald Manley Hopkins anticipated the 20th century with the experimentation of his verse forms.

20th century Poets of World War I include Siegfried Sassoon, Rupert Brooke, Wilfred Owen, and Robert Graves. A middle-class realism developed in the novels of H G Wells, Arnold Bennett, E M Forster, and John Galsworthy while the novel's break with traditional narrative and exposition came through the Modernists James Joyce, D H Lawrence, Virginia Woolf, Somerset Maugham, Aldous Huxley, Christopher Isherwood, Evelyn Waugh, and Graham Greene. Writers for the stage include George Bernard Shaw, Galsworthy, J B Priestley, Noël Coward, and Terence Rattigan, and the writers of poetic drama, such as T S Eliot, Christopher Fry, W H Auden, Christopher Isherwood, and Dylan Thomas. The 1950s and 1960s produced the 'kitchen sink' dramatists, including John Osborne and Arnold Wesker. The following decade saw the rise of Harold Pinter, John Arden, Tom Stoppard, Peter Shaffer, Joe Orton, and Alan Ayckbourn. Poets since 1945 include Thom Gunn, Roy Fuller, Philip Larkin, Ted Hughes, and John Betjeman; novelists include William Golding, Iris Murdoch, Angus Wilson, Muriel Spark, Margaret Drabble, Kingsley Amis, Anthony Powell, Alan Sillitoe, Anthony Burgess, John Fowles, Ian McEwan, Martin Amis, Angela Carter, and Doris Lessing.

engraving art of creating a design by means of inscribing blocks of metal, wood, or some other hard material with a point. With *intaglio printing* the design is cut into the surface of a plate, usually metal. It is these cuts, often very fine, which hold the ink. In *relief printing*, by contrast, it is the areas left when the rest has been cut away which are inked for printing. See ◊printmaking.

enharmonic in music, term describing a harmony capable of alternative interpretations, used as a link between passages of normally unrelated key. For example, an enharmonic modulation from C sharp to F major plays on the equivalence, in keyboard terms, of the notes E sharp and F.

Enlightenment European intellectual movement that reached its high point in the 18th century. Enlightenment thinkers were believers in social progress and in the liberating possibilities of rational and scientific knowledge. They were often critical of existing society and were hostile to religion, which they saw as keeping the human mind chained down by superstition.

The American and French revolutions were justified by Enlightenment principles of human natural rights. Leading representatives of the Enlightenment were ◊Voltaire, ◊Lessing, and ◊Diderot.

Ennius Quintus 239–169 BC. Early Roman poet who wrote tragedies based on the Greek pattern. His epic poem *Annales* deals with Roman history.

The Roman state survives by its ancient customs and its manhood.

Quintus Ennius *Annales*

ENSA (*Entertainments National Service Association*) organization formed 1938–39 to provide entertainment for British and Allied forces during World War II. Directed by Basil ◊Dean from headquarters in the Drury Lane Theatre, it provided a variety of entertainment throughout the UK and also in all war zones.

Ensor James 1860–1949. Belgian painter and printmaker. In a bold style employing vivid colours, he created a surreal and macabre world inhabited by masked figures and skeletons. Such works as his famous *Entry of Christ into Brussels* 1888 (Musée Royale des Beaux-Arts, Brussels) anticipated Expressionism.

entablature in classical architecture, the upper part of an ◊order, situated above the column and principally composed of the architrave, frieze, and cornice.

entrechat (French 'cross-caper') in ballet, crisscrossing of the legs while the dancer is in the air. There are two movements for each beat. Wayne ◊Sleep broke ◊Nijinsky's record of an *entrechat dix* (five beats) with an *entrechat douze* (six beats) 1973.

environment art large sculptural or spatial works that create environments which the spectator may enter and become absorbed in. Environments frequently incorporate sensory stimuli, such as sound or movement, to capture the observer's attention. The US artists Jim ◊Dine and Claes ◊Oldenburg were early exponents in the 1960s.

Eos in Greek mythology, the goddess of the dawn (Roman Aurora).

epic narrative poem or cycle of poems dealing with some great deed – often the founding of a nation or the forging of national unity – and often using religious or cosmological themes. The two major epic poems in the Western tradition are the *Iliad* and the *Odyssey*, attributed to Homer, and which were probably intended to be chanted in sections at feasts.

Greek and later criticism, which considered the Homeric epic the highest form of poetry, produced the genre of *secondary epic* – such as the *Aeneid* of Virgil, Tasso's *Jerusalem Delivered*, and Milton's *Paradise Lost* – which attempted to emulate Homer, often for a patron or a political cause. The term is also applied to narrative poems of other traditions: the Anglo-Saxon *Beowulf* and the Finnish *Kalevala*; in India the *Rāmayana* and *Mahābhārata;* and the Babylonian *Gilgamesh*. All of these evolved in different societies to suit similar social needs and used similar literary techniques.

epigram short, witty, and pithy saying or short poem. The poem form was common among writers of ancient Rome, including Catullus and Martial. In English, the epigram has been employed by Ben Jonson, George Herrick, Alexander Pope, Jonathan Swift, W B Yeats, and Ogden Nash. An epigram was originally a religious inscription.

The writers Oscar Wilde and Dorothy Parker produced many epigrams in conversation as well as writing. Epigrams are often satirical; for example, Wilde's observation: 'Speech was given us to conceal our thoughts.'

epigraphy (Greek *epigráphein* 'to write on') art of writing with a sharp instrument on hard, durable materials such as stone; also the scientific study of epigraphical writings or inscriptions.

epilogue postscript to a book; a short speech or poem at the end of a play, addressed directly to the audience.

Epimetheus in Greek mythology, the brother of ◊Prometheus and husband of ◊Pandora. He opened Pandora's box, releasing all the evils that it contained.

epistle in the New Testament, any of the 21 letters to individuals or to the members of various churches written by Christian leaders, including the 13 written by St Paul. The term also describes a letter with a suggestion of pomposity

and literary affectation, and a letter addressed to someone in the form of a poem, as in the epistles of ◊Horace and Alexander ◊Pope.

The *epistolary novel*, a story told as a series of (fictitious) letters, was popularized by Samuel ◊Richardson in the 18th century.

epitaph inscription on a tomb, or a short tribute to a dead person.

epithet word or phrase that characterizes a person, place, or thing, especially when used instead of the name or in addition to it; for example, Richard the *Lion-Heart*.

Epstein Jacob 1880–1959. English sculptor, born in New York. Initially influenced by Rodin, he turned to primitive forms after Brancusi and is chiefly known for his controversial muscular nude figures such as *Genesis* 1931 (Whitworth Art Gallery, Manchester). He was better appreciated as a portraitist (bust of Einstein, 1933), and in later years executed several monumental figures, notably the expressive bronze of *St Michael and the Devil* 1959 (Coventry Cathedral).

In 1904 he moved to England, where most of his major work was done. An early example showing the strong influence of ancient sculptural styles is the angel over the tomb of Oscar Wilde 1912 (Père Lachaise cemetery, Paris), while *Rock Drill* 1913–14 (Tate Gallery, London) is Modernist and semi-abstract. These and his nude figures outraged public sensibilities.

They are a form of statuary which no careful father would wish his daughter, or no discerning young man his fiancée, to see.

Review of **Jacob Epstein's** work in the *Evening Standard and St James Gazette* 1912

Equity common name for the *British Actors' Equity Association*, the UK trade union for professional actors in theatre, film, and television, founded 1929. In the USA its full name is the *American Actors' Equity Association* and it deals only with performers in the theatre.

Erasmus Desiderius 1466–1536. Dutch scholar and leading humanist of the Renaissance era. He taught and studied throughout Europe and was a prolific writer. His pioneer edition of the Greek New Testament with parallel Latin translation 1516 exposed the Vulgate as a second-hand document. He also edited the writings of St Jerome and the early Christian authorities and published *Encomium Moriae/The Praise of Folly* 1509 (a satire on church and society that quickly became an international bestseller) and *Colloquia* (dialogues on contemporary subjects) 1519.

Erasmus was born in Rotterdam, and as a youth he was a monk in an Augustinian monastery near Gouda. After becoming a priest, he went to study in Paris 1495. He paid the first of a number of visits to England 1499, where he met the physician Thomas Linacre, the politician Thomas More, and the Bible interpreter John Colet, and for a time was professor of divinity and Greek at Cambridge University. He published the first edition of *Adagia/Adages*, a popular collection of Greek and Latin sayings with commentaries, 1500. In 1521 he went to Basel, Switzerland, where he edited the writings of the early Christian leaders.

Erato in Greek mythology, the ◊Muse of love poetry.

Erebus in Greek mythology, the god of darkness; also the intermediate region between upper Earth and ◊Hades.

Erinyes in Greek mythology, another name for the ◊Furies.

Eris in Greek mythology, the personification of Strife, companion of the war-god ◊Ares and a daughter of Night.

Erl-King in Germanic folklore, the king of the elves. He inhabited the Black Forest and lured children to their deaths. The Romantic writer J W Goethe's poem 'Erlkönig' was set to music by Schubert 1816.

Ernst Max 1891–1976. German Surrealist who worked in France 1922–38 and in the USA from 1941. He was an active Dadaist, experimenting with collage, photomontage, and surreal images, and helped found the Surrealist movement 1924.

Ernst first exhibited in Berlin 1916. He produced a 'collage novel', *La Femme cent têtes* 1929, worked on films with Salvador Dali and Luis Buñuel, and designed sets and costumes for Sergei Diaghilev's Ballets Russes. His pictures range from precise Surrealist images to highly textured, imaginary landscapes, employing *frottage* (rubbing colour or graphite on to paper laid over a textured surface).

The virtue of pride, which was once the beauty of mankind, has given place to the fount of all ugliness, Christian humility.

Max Ernst

Eros in Greek mythology, boy-god of love, traditionally armed with bow and arrows. He was the son of ◊Aphrodite, and fell in love with ◊Psyche. He is identified with the Roman Cupid.

Erskine Ralph 1914– . English-born architect who settled in Sweden 1939. He specialized in ◊community architecture before it was named as such. A deep social consciousness and a concern to mould building form in response to climate determine his architecture. His Byker Estate in Newcastle-upon-Tyne 1969–80, where a sheltering wall of dwellings embraces the development, involved a lengthy process of consultation with the residents.

A later project is the 'Ark', an office building in Hammersmith, London 1989–91. Its ship-like form shelters the internal activities from an adjoining motorway.

Erté adopted name of Romain de Tirtoff 1892–1990. Russian designer and illustrator, active in France and the USA. An exponent of ◊Art Deco, he designed sets and costumes for opera, theatre, and ballet, and his drawings were highly stylized and expressive, featuring elegant, curvilinear women.

Erté (the name was derived from the French pronunciation of his initials) went to Paris 1911 to work as a theatre and ballet set designer. From 1916 to 1926 he produced covers for US fashion magazine *Harper's Bazaar*, and went to Hollywood 1925 to work as a designer on several films. He continued to design sets and costumes in Europe and the USA for many decades. His illustrations were influenced by 16th-century Persian and Indian miniatures.

Escher M(aurits) C(ornelis) 1898-1972. Dutch graphic artist. His prints are often based on mathematical concepts and contain paradoxes and illusions. The lithograph *Ascending and Descending* 1960, with interlocking staircases creating a perspective puzzle, is a typical work.

Escorial, El abbey and palace in the Guadarrama Mountains, 42 km/26 mi NW of Madrid, Spain. El Escorial was built 1563–84 for Philip II. Designed by Juan Bautista de Toledo and Juan de Herrera in an austere Renaissance style, it houses a famous art collection and a fine library.

Esenin or *Yesenin*, Sergey 1895–1925. Soviet poet, born in Konstantinovo (renamed Esenino in his honour). He went to Petrograd 1915, attached himself to the Symbolists, welcomed the Russian Revolution, revived peasant traditions and folklore, and initiated the Imaginist group of poets 1919. A selection of his poetry was translated in *Confessions of a Hooligan* 1973. He was married briefly to US dancer Isadora Duncan 1922–23.

Espronceda José de 1808–1842. Spanish poet. Originally one of the Queen's guards, he lost his commission because of his political activities, and was involved in the Republican uprisings of 1835 and 1836. His lyric poetry and lifestyle both owed much to Lord Byron.

Esquivel Adolfo 1932– . Argentinian sculptor and architect. As leader of the Servicio de Paz y Justicia (Peace and Justice Service), a

Catholic–Protestant human-rights organization, he was awarded the 1980 Nobel Peace Prize.

essay short piece of non-fiction, often dealing from a personal point of view with some particular subject. The essay became a recognized genre with French writer Montaigne's *Essais* 1580 and in English with Francis Bacon's *Essays* 1597. Today the essay is a part of journalism: articles in the broadsheet newspapers are in the essay tradition.

Abraham Cowley, whose essays appeared 1668, brought a greater ease and freedom to the genre than it had possessed before in England, but it was with the development of periodical literature in the 18th century that the essay became a widely used form. The great names are Joseph Addison and Richard Steele, with their *Tatler* and *Spectator* papers, and later Samuel Johnson and Oliver Goldsmith. In North America the politician and scientist Benjamin Franklin was noted for his style.

A new era was inaugurated by Charles Lamb's *Essays of Elia* 1820; to the same period belong Leigh Hunt, William Hazlitt, and Thomas De Quincey in England, C A Sainte-Beuve in France, and Ralph Waldo Emerson and Henry Thoreau in the USA. From the 19th century the essay was increasingly used in Europe and the USA as a vehicle for literary criticism. Hazlitt may be regarded as the originator of the critical essay, and his successors include Matthew Arnold and Edmund Gosse. Thomas Macaulay, whose essays began to appear shortly after those of Lamb, presents a strong contrast to Lamb with his vigorous but less personal tone.

There was a revival of the form during the closing years of the 19th and beginning of the 20th centuries, in the work of R L Stevenson, Oliver Wendell Holmes, Anatole France, Théophile Gautier, and Max Beerbohm. The literary journalistic tradition of the essay was continued by James Thurber, Mark Twain, H L Mencken, Edmund Wilson, Desmond MacCarthy, and others, and the critical essay by George Orwell, Cyril Connolly, F R Leavis, T S Eliot, Norman Mailer, John Updike, and others.

Esterházy, Schloss palace of the princes Esterházy in the city of Eisenstadt, Austria. Originally a medieval stronghold, it was rebuilt in the Baroque style 1663–72. Under the patronage of the Esterházys, the composer Josef Haydn was Kappelmeister here for 30 years.

Estonian literature a rich oral tradition of folk poetry from the 14th to the 17th century gave rise to a strongly poetic written literature in the 19th century. Estonian legend supplied F R Kreutzwald (1803–1882) with the basis for his synthetic epic *Kalevipoeg* 1857–61, which in turn inspired the new romantic nationalist movement in which the poets Lydia Koidula (1843–1886) and Anna Haava (1864–1957) were prominent.

Realist writing in the later 19th century, typified by the novels of Eduard Vilde (1865–1933) and Juhan Liiv (1864–1913), was superseded by the Neo-Romanticism of 'Young Estonia', led by the scholar-poet Gustav Suits (1883–1956). This was followed from 1917 by the less formalist lyricism of the 'Siuru' group, particularly Marie Under (1883–), in its turn yielding to the intellectual aestheticism of the 'Arbujal' group in the 1930s, including Betti Alver (1906–).

From 1945 until the 1960s Stalinist discipline caused Estonian writing to be dominated by exiles, often based in Stockholm, but there has since been a resurgence of writing in Estonia, presided over by the widely translated historical novelist Jaan Kross (1920–).

etching printmaking technique in which a metal plate (usually copper or zinc) is covered with a waxy overlayer (ground) and then drawn on with an etching needle. The exposed areas are then 'etched', or bitten into, by a corrosive agent (acid), so that they will hold ink for printing.

The method was developed in Germany about 1500, the earliest dated etched print being of 1513. Among the earliest etchers were Dürer, van Dyck, Hollar, and Rembrandt. Some artists combine etching with ◊aquatint.

Eteocles in Greek mythology, son of the incestuous union of ◊Oedipus and ◊Jocasta and brother of ◊Polynices. He denied his brother a share in the kingship of Thebes, thus provoking the expedition of the ◊Seven against Thebes, in which he and his brother died by each other's hands.

Etherege George *c.* 1635–1691. English Restoration dramatist whose play *Love in a Tub* 1664 was the first attempt at the comedy of manners (a genre further developed by Congreve and Sheridan). Later plays include *She Would If She Could* 1668 and *The Man of Mode, or Sir Fopling Flutter* 1676.

When love grows diseas'd, the best thing we can do is put it to a violent death; I cannot endure the torture of a lingring and consumptive passion.

George Etherege
The Man of Mode

Etruscan art the art of the inhabitants of Etruria, central Italy, a civilization which flourished 8th–2nd century BC. The Etruscans produced sculpture, painting, pottery, metalwork, and jewellery. Etruscan terracotta coffins (*sarcophagi*), carved with reliefs and topped with portraits of the dead reclining on one elbow, were to influence the later Romans and early Christians.

Most examples of Etruscan painting come

from excavated tombs, whose frescoes depict scenes of everyday life, mythology, and mortuary rites, typically in bright colours and a vigorous, animated style. Scenes of feasting, dancing, swimming, fishing, and playing evoke a confident people who enjoyed life to the full, and who even in death depicted themselves in a joyous and festive manner. The decline of their civilization, in the shadow of Rome's expansion, is reflected in their later art, which loses its original *joie de vivre* and becomes sombre.

Influences from archaic Greece and the Middle East are evident, as are those from the preceding Iron Age Villanovan culture, but the full flowering of Etruscan art represents a unique synthesis of existing traditions and artistic innovation, which was to have a profound influence on the development of Western art.

Etty William 1787–1849. English painter who specialized in nudes. He also painted mythological or historical subjects such as *Telemachus Rescuing Antiope* 1811. Many of his paintings are in the York City Art Gallery, England.

étude musical exercise designed to develop technique.

Eugene Onegin novel in verse by Aleksandr ◊Pushkin, published 1823–31. Eugene Onegin, bored with life but sensitive, rejects the love of Tatanya, a humble country girl; she later rises in society and in turn rejects him. Onegin was the model for a number of Russian literary heroes.

Eumenides (Greek 'kindly ones') in Greek mythology, appeasing name for the ◊Furies.

euphonium tenor valved brass band instrument of the bugle type, often mistaken for a tuba, and called a *baryton* in Germany.

euphony any pleasing combination of sounds; the opposite is cacophony.

euphuism affected style of writing full of high-flown language and far-fetched metaphors, especially in imitation of English playwright John ◊Lyly's *Euphues: The Anatomy of Wit* 1578 and *Euphues and his England* 1580.

eurhythmics practice of coordinated bodily movement as an aid to musical development. It was founded about 1900 by the Swiss musician Emile ◊Jaques-Dalcroze, professor of harmony at the Geneva conservatoire. He devised a series of 'gesture' songs, to be sung simultaneously with certain bodily actions.

Euripides *c.* 485–*c.* 406 BC. Athenian tragic dramatist, ranked with ◊Aeschylus and ◊Sophocles as one of the three major Greek tragedians. He wrote about 90 plays, of which 18 and some long fragments survive. These include *Alcestis* 438 BC, ◊*Medea* 431, *Hippolytus* 428, the satyr-drama *Cyclops* about 424–423, ◊*Electra* 417, *Trojan Women* 415, *Iphigenia in Tauris* 413, *Iphigenia in Aulis* about 414–412, and *The*

Bacchae about 405 (the last two were produced shortly after his death).

Euripides' questioning of contemporary mores and shrewd psychological analyses made him unpopular, if not notorious, during his lifetime, and he was cruelly mocked by the contemporary comic playwright ◊Aristophanes, but he had more influence on the development of later drama than either Aeschylus or Sophocles. He transformed tragedy with unheroic themes, sympathetic and disturbing portrayals of women's anger, and plots of incident and reunion. Towards the end of his life he left Athens for Macedon.

My tongue swore, but my mind's unsworn.

Euripides *Hippolytus* 428 BC

Europa in Greek mythology, the daughter of the king of Tyre, carried off by Zeus (in the form of a bull); she personifies the continent of Europe.

Eurydice in Greek mythology, the wife of ◊Orpheus. She was a dryad, or forest nymph, and died from a snake bite. Orpheus attempted unsuccessfully to fetch her back from the realm of the dead.

Euston Road School group of British artists based at an art school in Euston Road, London, 1937–39. William Coldstream (1908–1987) and Victor Pasmore were teachers there. Despite its brief existence, the school influenced many British painters with its emphasis on careful, subdued naturalism.

Euterpe in Greek mythology, the ◊Muse of lyric poetry.

Evans Edith 1888–1976. English character actress who performed on the London stage and on Broadway. Her many imposing performances include the Nurse in *Romeo and Juliet* (first performed 1926); her film roles include Lady Bracknell in Oscar Wilde's comedy *The Importance of Being Earnest* 1952 and Betsy in the television version of *David Copperfield* 1969. Among her other films are *Tom Jones* 1963 and *Crooks and Coronets* 1969.

I may never have been very pretty but I was jolly larky and that's what counts in the theatre.

Edith Evans

Evans Walker 1903–1975. US photographer best known for his documentary photographs of people in the rural American South during the Great Depression. Many of his photographs appeared in James Agee's book ◊*Let Us Now Praise Famous Men* 1941.

Evelyn John 1620–1706. English diarist and author. He was a friend of Samuel Pepys, and like him remained in London during the Plague and the Great Fire. He wrote some 300 books, including his diary, first published 1818, which covers the period 1640–1706.

Born in Surrey, he enlisted for three years in the Royalist army 1624, but withdrew on finding his estate exposed to the enemy and lived mostly away from England until 1652. He declined all office under the Commonwealth, but after the Restoration enjoyed great favour, received court appointments, and was one of the founders of the Royal Society.

I saw Hamlet Prince of Denmark played, but now the old plays began to disgust this refined age.

John Evelyn 26 Nov 1661

Everage Dame Edna. Character of an Australian 'housewife-superstar', from Moonie Ponds, Victoria, created by Barry ◊Humphries.

Everly Brothers, the US pop duo whose close bluegrass harmonies suited both sentimental ballads ('Ebony Eyes' 1961) and upbeat rock songs ('Bird Dog' 1958). Their string of significant hits began with 'Bye Bye Love 1957 and ended with 'The Price of Love' 1965.

Don Everly (1937–) and his brother Phil (1939–) came from a Kentucky family of country musicians and first recorded in 1956. They wrote some of their own biggest hits ('('Til) I Kissed You' 1959, 'Cathy's Clown' 1960) but much of their material was written by Felice Bryant (born Scaduto, 1925–) and Boudleaux Bryant (1920–1987), including 'Wake Up, Little Susie' 1957 and 'All I Have to Do Is Dream' 1958. The Everly Brothers broke up 1973 and reunited ten years later.

exemplum in Western medieval and Renaissance literature, a short narrative text that contains a moral. Examples include works by the French essayist ◊Montaigne, the philosopher Blaise Pascal, and the Italian political theorist ◊Machiavelli.

exeunt (Latin 'they go out') a stage direction to indicate that two or more actors leave the stage. *Exeunt omnes* indicates that all the actors leave the stage.

existentialism branch of philosophy based on the concept of an absurd universe where humans have free will. Existentialists argue that philosophy must begin from the concrete situation of the individual in such a world, and that humans are responsible for and the sole judge of their actions as they affect others, though no one else's existence is real to the individual. The origin of existentialism is usually traced back to the Danish philosopher ◊Kierkegaard; among its proponents were Martin Heidegger in Germany and Jean-Paul ◊Sartre in France.

Man is nothing else but what he makes of himself. Such is the first principle of existentialism.

Jean-Paul Sartre on existentialism

---

exposition in music, the opening statement of a classical sonata, concerto, or symphony first movement, in which the principal themes are clearly outlined.

exposure meter instrument used in photography for indicating the correct exposure – the length of time the camera shutter should be open under given light conditions. Meters use substances such as cadmium sulphide and selenium as light sensors. These materials change electrically when light strikes them, the change being proportional to the intensity of the incident light. Many cameras have a built-in exposure meter that sets the camera controls automatically as the light conditions change.

expression in music, signs or words providing a dramatic context for the interpretation of neutral performance indicators for tempo, dynamics, phrasing, and so on.

expressionism in music, use of melodic or harmonic distortion for expressive effect, associated with Schoenberg, Hindemith, Krenek, and others.

Expressionism style of painting, sculpture, and literature that expresses inner emotions; in particular, a movement in early 20th-century art in northern and central Europe. Expressionists tended to distort or exaggerate natural appearance in order to create a reflection of an inner world; the Norwegian painter Edvard Munch's *Skriket/The Scream* 1893 (National Gallery, Oslo) is perhaps the most celebrated example. Expressionist writers include August Strindberg and Frank Wedekind.

Other leading Expressionist artists were James Ensor, Oskar Kokoschka, and Chaïm Soutine. The *die* ◊*Brücke* and *der* ◊*Blaue Reiter* groups were associated with this movement, and the Expressionist trend in German art emerged even more strongly after World War I in the work of Max Beckmann and Georg Grosz.

Eyck Aldo van 1918– . Dutch architect with a strong commitment to social architecture. His works include an orphans' home, the Children's

---

some musical expressions

accelerando	gradually faster	*presto, prestissimo*	at speed, at high speed
adagio, adagietto	easy-going	*quasi*	sort of, rather
agitato	agitated	*ripieno*	the accompanying ensemble
alla breve	four beat as two to the bar	*ritardando*	gradually coming to a stop
allargando	spreading out in tempo	*ritenuto*	pulling back
allegro, allegretto	with lightness of action	*ritornello*	refrain
andante, andantino	with movement	*rubato*	borrowed (time)
brio, con	with spirit	*secco*	with a dry tone
calando	winding down, slower and softer	*segno*	cue sign
cantabile	singing	*segue*	follow on
capo (da)	from the top (beginning)	*sempre*	always
concerto	the solo (group): cf ripieno	*sforzato, sforzando*	with a forced tone
crescendo	gradually louder	*smorzando*	smothering, stifling the tone
deciso	firmly	*sotto voce*	in an undertone
diminuendo	gradually softer	*spiccato*	bounced (of the bow off the string)
divisi a 2, 3, etc.	divided in 2, 3, etc. parts	*staccato, -issimo*	short, very short
dolce, dolcissimo	soft and sweetly	*subito*	sudden, suddenly
doloroso	mournfully	*Takt*	(German) beat, metre, bar (measure)
espressivo	with expression	*tema*	theme
flatterzung	(German) fluttertongue	*tenuto*	holding back
fuoco, con	with fire	*tessitura*	range of instrument or voice
giocoso	with fun	*tranquillo*	calmly
grave	with gravity	*tanto*	so much
largo, larghetto	expansively	*troppo*	too much
legato	smoothly	*via*	remove (eg mute)
lento	slowly	*veloce*	at speed
l'istesso (tempo)	the same (tempo)	*vivo, vivace*	with life
loco	in (its usual) place	*voce, voci*	voice, voices
lungo, lunga	long	*volante*	as though flying
misterioso	mysteriously	*wieder*	(German) again
molto	much, very	*Zeitmass*	(German) tempo
pesante	weightily	*zingaresca*	gipsy
poco, pochissimo	a little, very little	*zu 2*	(German) 1. for 2 players; 2. in 2 parts
portamento	lifting (note to note)		

Home 1957–60, and a refuge for single mothers, Mothers' House 1978 (both in Amsterdam).

Eyck Jan van *c.* 1390–1441. Flemish painter of the early northern Renaissance, one of the first to work in oils. His paintings are technically brilliant and sumptuously rich in detail and colour. In his *Giovanni Arnolfini and his Wife* 1434 (National Gallery, London), the bride and groom appear in a domestic interior crammed with disguised symbols, a kind of pictorial marriage certificate.

Little is known of his brother **Hubert van Eyck** (died 1426), who is supposed to have begun the massive and complex altarpiece in St Bavo's cathedral, Ghent, *The Adoration of the Mystical Lamb*, completed by Jan 1432.

Jan van Eyck is known to have worked in The Hague 1422–24 for John of Bavaria, Count of Holland. He served as court painter to Philip the Good, Duke of Burgundy, from 1425, and worked in Bruges from 1430. Philip the Good valued him not only as a painter but also as a diplomatic representative, sending him to Spain and Portugal 1427 and 1428, and he remained in the duke's employ after he settled in Bruges.

Oil painting allowed for subtler effects of tone and colour and greater command of detail than the egg-tempera technique then in common use, and van Eyck took full advantage of this.

Eyre Richard (Charles Hastings) 1943– . English stage and film director who succeeded Peter Hall as artistic director of the National Theatre, London, 1988. His stage productions include *Guys and Dolls* 1982, *Bartholomew Fair* 1988, *Richard III* 1990, which he set in 1930s Britain; and *Night of the Iguana* 1992. His films include *The Ploughman's Lunch* 1983, *Laughterhouse* (US *Singleton's Pluck*) 1984, and *Tumbledown* 1988 for television.

If you call something the National Theatre it is inviting people to throw bricks at it.

Richard Eyre *Observer* Aug 1986

Fairbanks Douglas, Sr. Stage name of Douglas Elton Ulman 1883–1939. US actor. He played acrobatic swashbuckling heroes in silent films such as *The Mark of Zorro* 1920, *The Three Musketeers* 1921, *Robin Hood* 1922, *The Thief of Bagdad* 1924, and *Don Quixote* 1925. He was married to film star Mary Pickford ('America's Sweetheart') 1920–35. In 1919 he founded United Artists with Charlie Chaplin and D W Griffith.

The man that's out to do something has to keep in high gear all the time.

Douglas Fairbanks Sr on success

'f/64' group group of US photographers, including Edward ◊Weston, Ansel ◊Adams, and Imogen ◊Cunningham, formed 1932. The sharp focus and clarity of their black-and-white pictures was achieved by setting the lens aperture to f/64.

Fabergé Peter Carl 1846–1920. Russian goldsmith and jeweller. Among his masterpieces was a series of jewelled Easter eggs, the first of which was commissioned by Alexander III for the tsarina 1884.

His workshops in St Petersburg and Moscow were celebrated for the exquisite delicacy of their products, especially the use of gold in various shades. Fabergé died in exile in Switzerland.

fable story, in either verse or prose, in which animals or inanimate objects are given the mentality and speech of human beings to point out a moral. Fables are common in folklore and children's literature, and range from the short fables of the ancient Greek writer Aesop to the modern novel ◊*Animal Farm* by George Orwell.

Fabulists include the Roman Phaedrus, French poet La Fontaine and, in English, Geoffrey Chaucer and Jonathan Swift.

Fabritius Carel 1622–1654. Dutch painter, a pupil of Rembrandt. His own style, lighter and with more precise detail than his master's, is evident for example in *The Goldfinch* 1654 (Mauritshuis, The Hague). He painted religious scenes and portraits.

façade in architecture, the front or principal face of a building.

Faerie Queene, The poem by Edmund ◊Spenser, published 1590–96, dedicated to Elizabeth I. Drawing on the traditions of chivalry and courtly love, the poem was planned as an epic in 12 books, following the adventures of 12 knights, each representing a different chivalric virtue, beginning with the Red Cross Knight of holiness. Only six books were completed. Spenser used a new stanza form, later adopted by Keats, Shelley, and Byron.

Fairbanks Douglas, Jr 1909– . US actor of suave, dashing appearance, who often appeared in the same type of swashbuckling film roles as his father, Douglas Fairbanks; for example, in *Catherine the Great* 1934 and *The Prisoner of Zenda* 1937.

Fairburn Arthur Rex Dugard 1904–1957. New Zealand poet and publicist. His critical view of New Zealand life, art, and letters, stimulated by absence in England in the early 1930s, issued in a stream of pamphlets, satirical verse, and colourfully imaginative poetic works. His numerous publications include *Three Poems: Dominion, The Voyage, To a Friend in the Wilderness* 1952 and the satirical volumes *The Rakehelly Man* 1946 and *The Disadvantages of Being Dead* (published posthumously 1958).

Fairweather Ian 1891–1974. Australian artist, born in Scotland. He travelled extensively in Asia before settling in Australia and the influence of contact with Chinese, Indonesian, and Australian Aboriginal cultures is evident in works such as *Monastery* 1960 (Australian National Gallery, Canberra). His paintings are abstract in style, and use the natural colours of the earth.

fairy tale magical story, usually a folk tale in origin. Typically in European fairy tales, a poor, brave, and resourceful hero or heroine goes through testing adventures to eventual good fortune.

The Germanic tales collected by the ◊Grimm brothers have been retold in many variants. Charles ◊Perrault retellings include 'Cinderella' and 'The Sleeping Beauty'. The form may also be adapted for more individual moral and literary purposes, as was done by Danish writer Hans Christian ◊Andersen.

Falconet Etienne-Maurice 1716–1791. French sculptor whose works range from Baroque to gentle Rococo in style. He directed sculptural modelling at the Sèvres porcelain factory 1757–66. His bronze equestrian statue *Peter the Great* in St Petersburg was commissioned 1766 by Catherine II.

Falla Manuel de (full name Manuel Maria de Falla y Matheu) 1876–1946. Spanish composer. His opera *La vida breve/Brief Life* 1905 (performed 1913) was followed by the ballets *El amor brujo/Love the Magician* 1915 and *El sombrero de tres picos/The Three-Cornered Hat* 1919, and his most ambitious concert work, *Noches en los jardines de España/Nights in the Gardens of Spain* 1916. The folk idiom of southern Spain is an integral part of his compositions. He also wrote songs and pieces for piano and guitar.

Born in Cádiz, he lived in France, where he was influenced by the Impressionist composers Debussy and Ravel. In 1939 he moved to Argentina.

Fall of Man, the myth that explains the existence of evil as the result of some primeval wrongdoing by humanity. It occurs independently in many cultures. The biblical version, recorded in the Old Testament (Genesis 3), provided the inspiration for the epic poem *Paradise Lost* 1667 by John ◊Milton.

The Fall of Man (as narrated in the Bible) occurred in the Garden of Eden when the Serpent tempted Eve to eat the fruit of the Tree of Knowledge. Disobeying God's will, she ate the fruit and gave some to Adam. This caused their expulsion from the Garden and, in Milton's words, 'brought death into the world and all our woe'.

falsetto in music, a male voice singing in the female (soprano or alto) register.

Famous Five series of 21 stories for children by Enid ◊Blyton, published in the UK 1942–63, which describe the adventures of the 'Five' (four children and a dog) who spend their holidays together. The same author's *Secret Seven* series 1949–63 has a similar theme.

fan fashion accessory, opening from the folded state into a semicircular shape which is held in the hand and gently moved backwards and forwards to create a circulation of air, cooling the holder of the fan.

Fans were introduced into Europe through trade routes from the East in the late 15th–early 16th centuries. Made of materials such as sandalwood, ivory, mother-of-pearl, tortoiseshell, feathers, silk, paper, and lace, and sometimes decorated with hand-painted designs, fans reached the height of popularity in the 18th century.

For the black man there is only one destiny. And it is white.

Franz Fanon, *Black Skin White Masks*

Fanon Frantz 1925–1961. French political writer. His experiences in Algeria during the war for liberation in the 1950s led to the writing of *Les Damnés de la terre/The Wretched of the Earth* 1964, which calls for violent revolution by the peasants of the Third World.

fantasia or *fantasy*, *phantasy*, or *fancy* in music, a free-form instrumental composition for keyboard or chamber ensemble, originating in the late Renaissance, and much favoured by English composers Dowland, Gibbons, and Byrd. It implies the free manipulation of musical figures without regard to models of form. Later composers include Telemann, Bach, and Mozart.

fantasy fiction nonrealistic fiction. Much of the world's fictional literature could be classified under this term but, as a commercial and literary genre, fantasy started to thrive after the success of J R R Tolkien's *The Lord of the Rings* 1954–55. Earlier works by such writers as Lord Dunsany, Hope Mirrlees, E R Eddison, and Mervyn Peake, which are not classifiable in fantasy subgenres such as ◊science fiction, ◊horror, or ghost story, could be labelled fantasy.

Much fantasy is pseudomedieval in subject matter and tone. Recent works include Ursula K Le Guin's *Earthsea* series 1968–91, Stephen Donaldson's *Chronicles of Thomas Covenant* 1978–83, and, in the more urban tradition, John Crowley's *Little, Big* 1980, Michael Moorcock's *Gloriana* 1978, and Gene Wolfe's *Free, Live Free* 1985. Such books largely overlap in content with the ◊magic realism of writers such as Gabriel García Márquez, Angela Carter, and Isabel Allende.

Well-known US fantasy authors include Thomas Pynchon (as, for example, in *V*), and Ray Bradbury, whose works are often in the science fiction genre.

Fantin-Latour (Ignace) Henri (Joseph Théodore) 1836–1904. French painter excelling in delicate still lifes, flower paintings, and portraits. *Homage à Delacroix* 1864 (Musée d'Orsay, Paris) is a portrait group featuring several poets, authors, and painters, including Charles Baudelaire and James McNeill Whistler.

farandole old French dance in six-eight time, originating in Provence. The dancers join hands in a chain and follow the leader to the accompaniment of tambourine and pipe. There is a farandole in Act II of Tchaikovsky's ballet *The Sleeping Beauty*.

farce form of popular comedy involving stereotyped characters in complex, often improbable situations frequently revolving around extramarital relationships (hence the term 'bedroom farce').

Originating in the physical knockabout comedy of Greek satyr plays and the broad humour of medieval religious drama, the farce was developed and perfected during the 19th century by Eugène Labiche (1815–1888) and Georges Feydeau (1862–1921) in France and Arthur Pinero in England.

Two successful English series in this century have been Ben ◊Travers' Aldwych farces in the 1920s and 1930s and the Whitehall farces produced by Brian Rix during the 1950s and 1960s.

Farhi Nicole. French fashion designer who works in the UK producing understated easy-to-wear styles in natural earth-tone fabrics and knitwear. She began designing for the mainstream fashion label French Connection and for Stephen Marks 1973 (the label Stephen Marks was changed to Nicole Farhi 1983). In 1989 she launched a menswear collection, with soft unstructured jackets and casual separates.

Farmer Frances 1913–1970. US actress who starred in such films as *Come and Get It* 1936, *The Toast of New York* 1937, and *Son of Fury* 1942, before her career was ended by alcoholism and mental illness.

Farnaby Giles 1563–1640. English composer of madrigals, psalms for the *Whole Booke of Psalms* 1621, edited by Thomas Ravenscroft (1582–1633), and music for virginals (an early keyboard instrument), over 50 pieces being represented in the 17th-century manuscript collection the ◊*Fitzwilliam Virginal Book*.

Farquhar George 1677–1707. Irish dramatist. His plays *The Recruiting Officer* 1706 and *The Beaux' Stratagem* 1707 are in the tradition of the Restoration comedy of manners, although less robust.

Charming women can true converts make,/ We love the precepts for the teacher's sake.

George Farquhar
The Constant Couple 1699

Farrell J(ames) G(ordon) 1935–1979. English historical novelist, born in Liverpool, author of *Troubles* 1970, set in Ireland, and *The Siege of Krishnapur* 1973.

Farrell James T(homas) 1904–1979. US novelist and short-story writer. His naturalistic documentary of the Depression, the *Studs Lonigan* trilogy 1932–35 comprising *Young Lonigan, The Young Manhood of Studs Lonigan,* and *Judgment Day*, describes the development of a young Catholic man in Chicago after World War I, and was written from his own experience. *The Face of Time* 1953 is one of his finest works.

Farrell Terry 1938– . British architect working in a Post-Modern idiom, largely for corporate clients seeking an alternative to the rigours of Modernist or High-Tech office blocks. His Embankment Place scheme 1991 sits theatrically on top of Charing Cross station in Westminster, London, and has been likened to a giant jukebox. He has also designed Alban Gate in the City of London 1992.

Farrell's style is robust and eclectic, and he is not afraid to make jokes in architecture, such as the gaily painted giant egg cups that adorn the parapet of his TV AM building in Camden, London, 1981–82.

Farrow Mia 1945– . US film and television actress. Popular since the late 1960s, she was associated with the director Woody Allen, both on and off screen 1982–92. She starred in his films *Zelig* 1983, *Hannah and Her Sisters* 1986, and *Crimes and Misdemeanors* 1990, as well as in Roman Polanski's *Rosemary's Baby* 1968.

fashion style of clothing currently in vogue. Throughout history, in addition to its primarily functional purpose, clothing has been a strong social status symbol, conveying information about the class, rank, and wealth of the wearer. Fashions were formerly set by the court and ruling classes. In the 19th century the role of the individualistic fashion designer emerged, creating clothes exclusively for wealthy clients. Mass production and ◊diffusion ranges in the 20th century have made the latest designs accessible to a much wider public.

In recent times fashion has also become a vehicle for political statement, usually rebellious, and a means of reflecting the mood of the times.

Fassbinder Rainer Werner 1946–1982. West German film director who began as a fringe actor and founded his own 'anti-theatre' before moving into films. His works are mainly stylized indictments of contemporary German society. He made more than 40 films, including *Die bitteren Tränen der Petra von Kant/The Bitter Tears of Petra von Kant* 1972, *Angst essen Seele auf/Fear Eats the Soul* 1974, and *Die Ehe von Maria Braun/The Marriage of Maria Braun* 1979.

Fassett Kaffe 1940– . US knitwear and textile designer, in the UK from 1964. He co-owns a knitwear company and his textiles appear in important art collections around the world.

Fassett took up knitting when he encountered Shetland yarns on a trip to Scotland, and now designs and produces for Missoni, Bill Gibb, and others.

fata morgana (Italian 'Morgan the Fairy') a mirage, often seen in the Strait of Messina and traditionally attributed to the sorcery of ◊Morgan le Fay. She was believed to reside in Calabria, a region of S Italy.

Fates in Greek mythology, the three female figures who determined the destiny of human lives. They were envisaged as spinners: Clotho spun the thread of life, Lachesis twisted the thread, and Atropos cut it off. They are analogous to the Roman Parcae and Norse ◊Norns.

Fathers and Sons novel by Ivan Turgenev, published in Russia 1862. Its hero, Bazarov, rejects the traditional values of his landowning family in

fashion: chronology

late BC–early centuries AD	Tunics and togas were worn around the Mediterranean and Europe, woven to shape.
8th century–	The spread of Islam and Western contact during the Crusades (11th–12th century) influenced fashion; Near and Middle Eastern traditions of cutting garments to shape adopted by the West.
1515	Early record of styles conveyed by means of fashion dolls; François I asked Isabella d'Este in Mantua, Italy, to send one dressed in miniature version of her latest fashion, including hairstyle and undergarments, to be copied and presented to women in France.
1678	*Le Nouveau Mercure galante* published in Paris, first fashion journal in modern sense (lasted only one year).
1759–	*The Lady's Magazine* was the first English women's journal to feature fashion plates and articles; fashion coverage gained momentum through the 18th century, coinciding with the Industrial Revolution and growth of consumerism.
1789	French Revolution, after which it was politically incorrect to dress extravagantly; French embroidery and lavish decoration abandoned in favour of simple clothes modelled on English tailored country clothing.
1851	US social reformer Amelia Bloomer visited Britain, promoting her costume of shortened dress and Turkish-style trousers ('bloomers'); dress reform movement grew, aimed at physically liberating women.
1858	British-born Charles Worth established his fashion house in Paris; the birth of haute couture.
1860	Crinolines, introduced in 1850s, became exceedingly wide (up to 1.8 m/6 ft in diameter).
1876	Plimsolls (flat rubber-soled canvas sports shoes) were patented, opening up more active sports for both men and women.
1870s–	Some women's magazines included paper patterns for home dressmaking.
c. 1880	Aesthetic dress of subdued colours and understated decoration worn by sophisticated artistic and reforming women in reaction against fussy high Victorian fashion.
1884	International Health Exhibition held in London: exhibitions of 'hygienic' and 'rational' reform dress.
1890s	Leg-of-mutton sleeves entered general fashion, now influenced by avant-garde dress reformers, allowing women more arm movement.
1900–10	Known as 'La Belle Epoque' in France; S-bend profile, lace trimmings and light silks and muslins represented the epitome of feminine elegance.
1910	*Schéhérazade* ballet produced by Diaghilev in Paris sparked off a wave of Orientalism in Western fashion. Women liberated from tight corseting and narrow waists, but restricted around the knees instead by 'hobble skirts'.
1912	Paul Poiret launched the first designer perfume range.
1920–	Coco Chanel designed and popularized the 'little black dress' and casual two- and three-piece classics made from jersey fabric.
1920s	Lucien Lelong, Jean Patou, Jeanne Lanvin, and other Parisian couturiers established ready-to-wear ranges sold through boutiques. The 'garçonne' look: boyish straight-lined dresses, Eton crop or shingled hair, suntan, and cosmetics; bright 'jazz' colours and abstract patterns reflected syncopated Afro-American musical rhythms. Electrification of factories and standardization of garment sizes, pioneered by US assembly-line system of production, made fashion cheaper and more available.
1925	Skirts were worn shorter than ever before.
1928	Italian-born Elsa Schiaparelli launched her fashion career in Paris with trompe l'oeil knitted jumpers.
1929	Men's Dress Reform Party founded in Britain, advocating shorts and coloured loose-fitting open-necked shirts; other Western countries followed suit.
1930s	Bias-cut long-line dresses became fashionable; Madeleine Vionnet was already known for her designs.
1939	Nylon stockings exhibited at New York World Fair.
1941	Clothes rationing introduced in Britain (June).
1945–	American GI vest worn as outerwear, to become known as the T-shirt.
1947	Christian Dior showed his first collection, dubbed the 'New Look'.
1950s	Brigitte Bardot married Sasha Distel; her gingham and broderie anglaise wedding dress was much copied.
1953	Teddy boys emerged, wearing long draped jackets, 'slim Jim' ties, and drainpipe trousers.
1955	Bazaar, Mary Quant's first boutique, opened in the Kings Road, Chelsea, London.
c. 1956	Youth movements were by now influencing fashion; Elvis Presley and James Dean were image idols; beatnik style (Beat Generation).
1960–	The Mods were wearing 'sharp' (clean-cut, close-fitting, neat) Italian suits.
1961	The film *Jules et Jim* set fashion trends; Jeanne Moreau looked up-to-the minute wearing 1920s dresses designed by Pierre Cardin.
1965	Miniskirts and trouser suits became acceptable.
1968	See-through and plastic mini-dresses by Courrèges; Space Age concept in fashion.
1971	Malcolm McLaren and Vivienne Westwood opened their Let It Rock shop in the Kings Road, London, selling secondhand Fifties clothes (shop later renamed Sex, selling 'bondage' gear).
early 1970s	Hippie fashions and the 'ethnic look' entered general fashion, incorporating Indian block-printed cottons, cheesecloth, embroidery, velvet, and so on. Nostalgia reflected in floral-print 'granny' dresses by Laura Ashley. Gloria Vanderbilt jeans launched, anticipating 1980s obsession with the designer label.
1970s	Commercialization of pop videos; performers' image and related products (printed T-shirts, and so on) almost more important than the music, and very influential.
1974–5	Giorgio Armani set up his business and developed lightweight, unstructured jacket, revolutionizing menswear.
1976	Punk spiky hair-dos, black leather, safety pins, and chains widely featured in the British press; punk group the Sex Pistols dressed by Malcolm McLaren and Vivienne Westwood.
late 1970s	Power dressing; wide shoulders and pin stripes for professional women. *(cont.)*

fashion: chronology (cont.)

1980	New Romantic look; 'genderbending', mixing and playing with masculine and feminine in dress, exemplified by British singer Boy George and his group Culture Club.
1980s	Japanese designers' loose-fitting monochrome clothes (mostly grey and black); understated, no decoration, often sculptural use of cut and cloth. Best-known designers were Yohji Yamomoto, Issey Miyake, and Rei Kawakubo of Comme des Garçons. French designer Jean-Paul Gaultier, inspired by British punk, featured underwear (especially corsets) as outerwear.
1989	Launch of the first 'ecocollections' (fashion claiming to be environment-friendly) and T-shirts printed with 'Save the Rainforest' slogans in Western Europe and USA.
1992	'Grunge' style, a designed misfitting and dishevelled look, mixing new and secondhand clothes (a feature of British street style for the past two decades), represented conscious anti-fashion and environmental awareness in a period of world recession.

favour of nihilistic revolutionary ideas, but his love for a noblewoman destroys his beliefs.

Fathy Hassan 1900–1989. Egyptian architect. In his work at the village of New Gournia in Upper Egypt 1945–48, he demonstrated the value of indigenous building technology and natural materials in solving contemporary housing problems. This, together with his book *The Architecture of the Poor* 1973, influenced the growth of ◊community architecture enabling people to work directly with architects in building their homes.

Compare the square to the vertical skyscraper – which is right for humanity and culture?

Hassan Fathy in *The Architect* Nov 1986

Faulkner William (Harrison) 1897–1962. US novelist. His works are noted for their difficult narrative styles and epic mapping of a quasi-imaginary Southern region, Yoknapatawpha County. His third and most celebrated novel, *The ◊Sound and the Fury* 1929, deals with the decline of a Southern family, told in four voices, beginning with an especially complex stream-of-consciousness narrative. He was recognized as one of America's greatest writers only after World War II, and awarded the Nobel Prize for Literature 1949.

Faulkner served in World War I and his first novel, *Soldier's Pay* 1929, is about a war veteran. After the war he returned to Oxford, Mississippi, on which he was to model the town of Jefferson in the county of Yoknapatawpha, the setting of his major novels. Later works using highly complex structures include *As I Lay Dying* 1930, *Light in August* 1932, and *Absalom, Absalom!* 1936. These were followed by his less experimental trilogy, *The Hamlet* 1940, *The Town* 1957, and *The Mansion* 1959, covering the rise of the materialistic Snopses family. Other works include *The Unvanquished* 1938, stories of the Civil War; and *The Wild Palms* 1939.

A writer needs three things, experience, observation, and imagination, any two of which, at times any one of which, can supply the lack of the others.

William Faulkner 1958

Faunus in Roman mythology, the god of fertility and prophecy, with goat's ears, horns, tail and hind legs, identified with the Greek ◊Pan.

Fauré Gabriel (Urbain) 1845–1924. French composer of songs, chamber music, and a choral *Requiem* 1888. He was a pupil of Saint-Saëns, became professor of composition at the Paris Conservatoire 1896 and was director from 1905 to 1920.

Faust legendary magician who sold his soul to the Devil. The historical Georg Faust appears to have been a wandering scholar and conjurer in Germany at the start of the 16th century. Goethe, Heine, Thomas Mann, and Paul Valéry all used the legend, and it inspired musical works by Schumann, Berlioz, Gounod, Boito, and Busoni.

Earlier figures such as Simon Magus (1st century AD, Middle Eastern practitioner of magic arts) contributed to the Faust legend. In 1587 the first of a series of Faust books appeared. Marlowe's tragedy, *Dr Faustus*, was acted 1594. In the 18th century the story was a subject for pantomime in England and puppet plays in Germany, and was developed by Goethe into his masterpiece.

Faust play by Johann Wolfgang von ◊Goethe, completed in two parts 1808 and 1832. Mephistopheles attempts to win over the soul of the world-weary Faust but ultimately fails after helping Faust in the pursuit of good.

Fauvism (French *fauve* 'wild beast') style of painting characterized by a bold use of vivid colours inspired by the work of van Gogh, Cézanne, and Gaugin. A short-lived but influential art movement, Fauvism originated in Paris 1905 with an exhibition at the Salon d'Automne by Henri ◊Matisse and others. The critic Louis

Vauxcelles described the exhibitors as *'les fauves'*. Rouault, Dufy, Marquet, Derain, and Signac were early Fauves.

Fear and Loathing in Las Vegas reportage novel 1971 by US journalist Hunter S ◊Thompson, illustrated by British artist Ralph Steadman. Subtitled 'A Savage Journey to the Heart of the American Dream', it is the outrageous narrative of Doctor Gonzo's nightmare drive through Nixon-era America, fuelled by drugs, alcohol, and the compulsive desire to keep moving.

Federalist Papers, the in US politics, a series of 85 letters published 1788 in the newly independent USA, attempting to define the relation of the states to the nation, and making the case for a federal government. The papers were signed 'Publius', the joint pseudonym of three leading political figures: Alexander Hamilton, John Jay, and James Madison.

Federal Theater Project US arts employment scheme 1935–39 founded as part of Roosevelt's New Deal by the Works Progress Administration; it provided affordable theatre throughout the USA and had long-term influence on modern US drama.

Federal Writers' Project US arts project founded 1934 by the Works Progress Administration to encourage and employ writers during the Depression, generate compilations of regional records and folklore, and develop a series of guides to states and regions.

Federman Raymond 1928– . US writer. His playful Post-Modernist texts draw on his French-Jewish boyhood, his family's death in Auschwitz, and his postwar emigration to America. He coined the term 'surfiction' to describe a form of writing, including that of his own, Steve Katz (1935–), Gilbert Sorrentino (1929–), and Ronald Sukenick, which lays bare narrative conventions, resists interpretation, and engages with historical reality. His works include *Double or Nothing* 1971, *The Voice in the Closet* 1979, and *The Twofold Vibration* 1982.

fedora soft felt hat from the Tyrol, Austria, with a tapered crown and a centre crease. Fedoras were popular for men and women towards the end of the 19th century for sporting activities.

feedback in music, a continuous tone, usually a high-pitched squeal, caused by the overloading of circuits between electric guitar and amplifier as the sound of the speakers is fed back through the guitar pickup. Deliberate feedback is much used in rock music.

The electric-guitar innovator Les Paul used feedback in recording ('How High the Moon' 1954) but it was generally regarded by producers as an unwanted noise until the Beatles introduced it on 'I Feel Fine' 1964. Both live and in recording, feedback was employed especially by The Who, Jimi Hendrix, and the Velvet Underground in the 1960s, and by noise and grunge bands in the 1980s and 1990s.

Feininger Lionel 1871–1956. US abstract artist, an early Cubist. He worked at the ◊Bauhaus school of design and architecture in Germany 1919–33, and later helped to found the Bauhaus in Chicago. Inspired by Cubism and *der ◊Blaue Reiter*, he developed a style based on translucent geometric planes arranged in subtle harmonic patterns.

Feininger was born in New York, the son of German immigrants. While in Germany, he and Alexei von Jawlensky, Wassily Kandinsky, and Paul Klee exhibited together. He returned to the USA after the rise of the Nazis.

Feldman Morton 1926–1988. US composer. An associate of John Cage and Earle Brown in the 1950s, he devised an indeterminate notation based on high, middle, and low instrumental registers and time cells of fixed duration for his *Projection* series for various ensembles 1950–51, later exploiting the freedoms of classical notation in a succession of reflective studies in vertical tone mixtures including *Madame Press Died Last Week at 90* 1970.

Fellini Federico 1920–1993. Italian film director and screenwriter whose work has been a major influence on modern cinema. His films combine dream and fantasy sequences with satire and autobiographical detail. They include *I vitelloni/The Young and the Passionate* 1953, *La strada/The Street* 1954 (Academy Award), *Le notti di Cabiria/Nights of Cabiria* 1956 (Academy Award), *La dolce vita* 1960,*Otto e mezzo/8 1/2* 1963 (Academy Award), *Satyricon* 1969, *Roma* 1972, *Amarcord* 1974 (Academy Award), *La città delle donne/City of women* 1980, and *Ginger e Fred/Ginger and Fred* 1986. He was presented with a Special Academy Award for his life's work 1993.

Distinctively 'Felliniesque', his work is intensely personal and vividly original. Peopled with circus, carnival, and music-hall characters and the high society of Roma, his films created iconic images such as that of actress Anita Ekberg in the Trevi Fountain, Rome, in *La dolce vita*. Marcello Mastroianni repeatedly acted as Fellini's alter ego and Giulietta Masina, his wife from 1943, also appeared in several of his films.

Going to the cinema is like returning to the womb; you sit there, still and meditative in the darkness, waiting for life to appear on the screen.

Federico Fellini

---

felt matted fabric of hair fibres and/or wool, made by joining them together using pressure, heat, or chemical action. The origin of felt is in the steppes of Central Asia where shoes, hats, blankets, and other items were made by nomadic herding peoples.

femme fatale (French 'fatal woman') woman

who brings about the ruin of her lovers; contrasted with the *femme fragile*, the typical Pre-Raphaelite pale, unearthly woman. The *femme fatale* was common in Romantic literature; for example, the heroine of the play *Salomé* by Oscar Wilde and the character of Lulu in *Pandora's Box* by Frank Wedekind.

Fender (Clarence) Leo 1909–1991. US inventor of the solid-body electric guitar, the Fender Broadcaster 1948 (renamed the Telecaster 1950), and the first electric bass guitar, the Fender Precision, 1951. The Fender Stratocaster guitar dates from 1954. In 1965 he sold the Fender name to CBS, which continues to make the instruments.

Fender began making amplifiers and Hawaiian-style guitars 1945, and built solid-body guitars for several country musicians. Although the guitarist and producer Les ◊Paul was also working independently on a solid-body electric guitar, Fender was the first to get his model on the market. The design was totally new, with a one-piece neck bolted on to a wooden body, and could easily be mass-produced.

Fénelon François de Salignac de la Mothe 1651–1715. French writer and ecclesiastic. He entered the priesthood 1675 and in 1689 was appointed tutor to the duke of Burgundy, grandson of Louis XIV. For him he wrote his *Fables* and *Dialogues des morts/Dialogues of the Dead* 1690, *Télémaque/Telemachus* 1699, and *Plans de gouvernement/Plans of Government*.

Télémaque, with its picture of an ideal commonwealth, had the effect of a political manifesto, and Louis banished Fénelon to Cambrai, where he had been consecrated archbishop 1695. Fénelon's mystical *Maximes des saints/Sayings of the Saints* 1697 had also led to condemnation by Pope Innocent XII and a quarrel with the Jansenists, who believed that only those chosen by God beforehand received salvation.

To love nothing is not to live; to love but feebly is to languish rather than live.

François Fénelon
A un Homme du monde 1699

Fenton Roger 1819–1869. English photographer best known for his comprehensive documentation of the Crimean War 1855. He was a founder member of the Photographic Society (later the Royal Photographic Society) in London 1853 but completely gave up photography 1860.

Ferber Edna 1887–1968. US novelist and dramatist. Her novel *Show Boat* 1926 was adapted as an operetta 1927 by Jerome Kern and Oscar Hammerstein II, and her plays, in which she collaborated with George S Kaufmann, include *The Royal Family* 1927, about the Barrymore theatrical family, *Dinner at Eight* 1932, and *Stage Door* 1936.

Her novels include *The Girls* 1921, *So Big* 1924 (Pulitzer Prize), *Cimarron* 1930, *Giant* 1952 (filmed 1956), about Texas, and *Ice Palace* 1959, about Alaska.

Fergus mac Roigh in Celtic mythology, a king of Ulster, a great warrior. He was the tutor of ◊Cuchulain.

Fermor Patrick (Michael) Leigh 1915– . English travel writer who joined the Irish Guards 1939 after four years' travel in central Europe and the Balkans. His books include *The Traveller's Tree* 1950, *A Time to Keep Silence* 1953, *Mani* 1958, *Roumeli* 1966, *A Time of Gifts* 1977, and *Between the Woods and the Water* 1986.

Ferneyhough Brian 1943– . English composer. His uncompromising, detailed compositions include *Carceri d'Invenzione*, a cycle of seven works inspired by the engravings of Piranesi, *Time and Motion Studies* 1974–77, and string quartets.

Ferragamo Salvatore 1898–1960. Italian shoemaker who created elegant and sophisticated shoes and was known for his innovative designs. He experimented with cork, lace, needlework, raffia, and snail shells, among other materials, and is credited with creating the wedge heel 1938, followed by the platform shoe, and the 'invisible' shoe 1947 which consisted of clear nylon uppers and a suede heel. During his lifetime he created over 20,000 shoes and registered 350 patents.

Ferrier Kathleen (Mary) 1912–1953. English contralto who brought warmth and depth of conviction to English oratorio roles during wartime and subsequently to opera and lieder (songs), including Gluck's *Orfeo*, Mahler's *Das Lied von der Erde/The Song of the Earth*, and the role of Lucretia in Benjamin Britten's *The Rape of Lucretia* 1946.

Ferrier Susan Edmundstone 1782–1854. Scottish novelist, born in Edinburgh. Her anonymously published books include *Marriage* 1818, *Inheritance* 1824, and *Destiny* 1831, all of which give a lively picture of Scottish manners and society.

Feydeau Georges 1862–1921. French comic dramatist. He is the author of over 60 farces and light comedies, which have been repeatedly revived in France at the Comédie Française and abroad. These include *La Dame de chez Maxim/The Girl from Maxim's* 1899, *Une Puce à l'oreille/A Flea in her Ear* 1907, *Feu la mère de Madame/My Late Mother-in-Law*, and *Occupe-toi d'Amélie/Look after Lulu*, both 1908.

fiction in literature, any work in which the content is completely or largely invented. The term describes imaginative works of narrative prose (such as the novel or the short story), and is distinguished from *non-fiction* (such as history, biography, or works on practical subjects), and *poetry*.

This usage reflects the dominance in contemporary Western literature of the novel as a vehicle for imaginative literature: strictly speaking, poems can also be fictional (as opposed to factual). Genres such as the historical novel often combine a fictional plot with real events; biography may also be 'fictionalized' through the use of imagined conversations or events.

fiddle any instrument from a widespread family of bowed lutes consisting of one or more strings stretched the full length of a fingerboard terminating in a soundbox. The timbre of a fiddle depends on the resonance of the soundbox. Larger instruments produce a fuller tone, while smaller soundboxes give a pinched, nasal tone.

Most fiddles are flat-backed; the 13th-century **rebec**, however, is tear-shaped and has a convex back like a lute. Many fiddles incorporate 'sympathetic strings' which vibrate when the string next to them is sounded, enriching the overall effect. In folk fiddle traditions, from the gypsy music of Eastern Europe to US country and western, the violin was widely adopted as the successor to the fiddle.

Fiedler Arthur 1894–1979. US orchestra conductor. Concerned to promote the appreciation of music among the public, he founded the Boston Sinfonetta chamber-music group 1924. He reached an even wider audience with the Esplanade concerts along the Charles River from 1929. Fiedler's greatest fame was as founder and conductor of the Boston Pops Orchestra 1930, dedicated to popularizing light classical music through live and televised concert appearances.

Field Sally 1946– . US film and television actress. She won an Academy Award for *Norma Rae* 1979 and again for *Places in the Heart* 1984. Her other films include *Hooper* 1978, *Absence of Malice* 1981, and *Murphy's Romance* 1985.

Fielding Henry 1707–1754. English novelist. His greatest work, *The History of Tom Jones, a Foundling* 1749 (which he described as 'a comic epic in prose'), realized for the first time in English the novel's potential for memorable characterization, coherent plotting, and perceptive analysis. In youth a prolific dramatist, he began writing novels with *An Apology for the Life of Mrs Shamela Andrews* 1741, a merciless parody of Samuel ◊Richardson's *Pamela*.

He was appointed Justice of the Peace for Middlesex and Westminster in 1748. In failing health, he went to recuperate in Lisbon in 1754, writing on the way *A Journal of a Voyage to Lisbon*.

His designs were strictly honourable, as the phrase is; that is, to rob a lady of her fortune by marrying her.

Henry Fielding *Tom Jones* 1749

Fields Gracie. Stage name of Grace Stansfield 1898–1979. English comedian and singer, much loved by the public. Her humorously sentimental films include *Sally in Our Alley* 1931 and *Sing as We Go* 1934.

Fields W C. Stage name of William Claude Dukenfield 1879–1946. US actor and screenwriter. His distinctive speech and professed attitudes such as hatred of children and dogs gained him enormous popularity in such films as *David Copperfield* 1935, *My Little Chickadee* (co-written with Mae West) and *The Bank Dick* both 1940, and *Never Give a Sucker an Even Break* 1941.

Originally a vaudeville performer, he incorporated his former stage routines, such as juggling and pool playing, into his films. He was also a popular radio performer.

Anyone who hates small dogs and children can't be all bad.

W C Fields

fife (German *Pfeife*) small transverse ◊flute of similar range to the piccolo. Of Swiss origin, the fife is a popular military band instrument, played with the side drums and associated with historic parades.

figured bass in 18th-century music, notation of a leading harpsichord or organ part indicating the bass line in standard notation, and the remaining music by numerical chord indications, allowing the player to fill in as necessary. It arose because the keyboard player often doubled as conductor, and is still practised by session musicians.

film, art of see ◊cinema.

film noir (French 'dark film') a term originally used by French critics to describe films characterized by pessimism, cynicism, and a dark, sombre tone. It has been used to describe black-and-white Hollywood melodramas of the 1940s and 1950s that portrayed the seedy side of life.

Typically, the *film noir* is shot with lighting that emphasizes shadow and stark contrasts, abounds in night scenes, and contains a cynical antihero – for example, Philip Marlowe as played by Humphrey Bogart in *The Big Sleep* 1946.

film, photographic strip of transparent material (usually cellulose acetate) coated with a light-sensitive emulsion, used in cameras to take pictures. The emulsion contains a mixture of light-sensitive silver halide salts (for example, bromide or iodide) in gelatin. When the emulsion is exposed to light, the silver salts are invisibly altered, giving a latent image, which is then made visible by the process of ◊developing. Films differ in their sensitivities to light, this being indicated by their speeds. Colour film consists of several layers of emulsion, each of which records a different colour in the light falling on it.

In *colour film* the front emulsion records blue light, then comes a yellow filter, followed by layers that record green and red light respectively. In the developing process the various images in the layers are dyed yellow, magenta (red), and cyan (blue), respectively. When they are viewed, either as a transparency or as a colour print, the colours merge to produce the true colour of the original scene photographed.

film score originally a symphonic poem composed as a loosely aligned accompaniment to a major silent film, or background music improvised or assembled by pit musicians with the aid of a Kinothek theme catalogue. With the arrival of optical sound on film came the fully synchronized Hollywood film score. Composers in the European Romantic tradition, including Erich Korngold, Max Steiner, and Franz Waxman, initially tried to adapt the symphonic style to the faster-moving screen action; a more successful transition was made by animated film music specialists, such as Scott ◊Bradley. After 1950 a younger generation including Alec North and Elmer Bernstein adopted simpler, jazz-orientated idioms.

Composers for silent films include Saint-Saëns, Honegger, and Edmund Meisel, whose music for Eisenstein's *Battleship Potemkin* 1925 was banned by the authorities. Composers for sound film include Auric, Copland, Prokofiev, Walton, Bernard Herrmann, and Ennio Morricone.

finale in music, a normally fast final movement of a classical four-movement work, or an elaborate conclusion of an opera incorporating a variety of ensembles.

Finch Peter 1916–1977. Australian-born English cinema actor who began his career in Australia before moving to London 1949 to start on an international career with such roles as those in *A Town Like Alice* 1956, *The Trials of Oscar Wilde* 1960, *Sunday, Bloody Sunday* 1971, and *Network* 1976, for which he won an Academy Award.

fin de siècle (French 'end of century') the art and literature of the 1890s; decadent.

fine arts (or *beaux arts*) art that exists primarily to create beauty, as opposed to the decorative or applied arts, which exist primarily for day-to-day use. They include painting, sculpture, some graphic art, and, despite its function, architecture. Music and poetry are sometimes called fine arts.

fingerboard upper surface and continuation of the neck of a string instrument against which the fingers press to alter the pitch. Violins have smooth fingerboards, allowing the player scope to alter the pitch continuously; other instruments such as the guitar and lute, have ◊frets attached or inlaid to regulate intonation.

Finney Albert 1936– . English stage and film actor. He created the title roles in Keith Waterhouse's stage play *Billy Liar* 1960 and John Osborne's *Luther* 1961, and was associate artistic director of the Royal Court Theatre 1972–75. Later roles for the National Theatre include Tamburlaine in Marlowe's tragedy 1976 and *Macbeth* 1978. His films include *Saturday Night and Sunday Morning*

1960, *Tom Jones* 1963, *Murder on the Orient Express* 1974, and *The Dresser* 1984.

Finnish architecture the earliest Finnish architecture was wooden and hence little survives although some ecclesiastical buildings (Turku Cathedral, Lohja Church) date from the 15th century. Following a Classical movement in the 18th century and a Neo-Classical period (typified by Helsinki's centre, designed by Carl Ludvig Engel 1820), Finland developed a strongly individualistic style of architecture. The 1890s saw a fusion of Art Nouveau concepts and vernacular style, followed by a thriving Modernist stage (led by Alvar Aalto) and visionary town planning (for example, Tapiola garden suburb by Aarne Ervi (1910–1977)). The 1980s have seen the evolution of Post-Modernism or 'organic' Finnish architecture (such as Tampere City Library by Raimo Pietila).

The fusion of Art Nouveau and local Finnish style and motifs by architects such as Lars Sonck (1870–1956) and the Saarinen-Gesellius-Lindgren practice in the 1890s placed Finnish architecture in a wider world context. Eliel Saarinen went on to gain international reputation in the USA. Later Modernist and Post-Modernist developments, such as the Yhtyneet Kuvalahdet (United Magazines) building in Helsinki by Ilmo Valjakka, have been internationally acclaimed.

Finn Mac Cumhaill legendary Irish hero, identified with a general who organized an Irish regular army in the 3rd century. James Macpherson featured him (as Fingal) and his followers in the verse of his popular epics 1761–63, which were supposedly written by a 3rd-century bard, ◊Ossian. Although challenged by the critic Dr Johnson, the poems were influential in the Romantic movement.

Finnish literature some fragments of Finnish literature survive from the 12th century; the first book was a primer published 1544. A complete Bible in Finnish was issued in Stockholm 1642. But the predominance of the Swedes and Swedish in Finland inhibited the growth of literature in Finnish until the 19th century, when it was launched with the publication 1835 of Elias Lönnrot's epic folk verse compilation *Kalevala*. The earliest Finnish writer was Aleksis Kivi, whose classic comedy *Seitsemän veljestä/Seven Brothers* was published 1870. The turn of the century saw the emergence of a crop of broadly realist writers, including Suhani Aho (1861–1921), Ilmari Kianto (1874–1970), and Joel Lehtonen (1881–1943) and the lyric poet Eino Leino (1878–1926). Mika Waltari (1908–1979) attracted attention abroad with his *Sinuhe egyptilä/Sinuhe the Egyptian* 1945. Frans Emil Sillanpää (1888–1964) received a Nobel Prize 1939. Vä inö Linna's *Tuntematon sotilas/The Unknown Soldier* is the definitive account of the winter war of 1939. Modern writers include the poets Pentti Saarikoski (1937–1983) and Paavo Haaviko (1931–) and the novelists Veijo Meri (1928–), Antti Tuuri (1944–), and Leena Krohn (1947–).

Fiorucci Elio 1935– . Italian designer and retailer who established the Fiorucci label in the 1960s, but who became best known in the 1970s for bright, casual clothing including slimfit jeans, sold internationally through Fiorucci boutiques.

fipple flute term describing a whistle, such as the Baroque recorder, that has a plug or 'fipple' inserted into the mouthpiece to direct the flow of air precisely at the aerofoil.

Firbank Ronald 1886–1926. English novelist. His work, set in the Edwardian decadent period, has a malicious humour and includes *Caprice* 1916, *Valmouth* 1918, and the posthumous *Concerning the Eccentricities of Cardinal Pirelli* 1926.

Firdausi Abdul Qasim Mansur *c.* 935–1020. Persian poet, whose epic *Shahnama/The Book of Kings* relates the history of Persia in 60,000 verses.

Fischer-Dieskau Dietrich 1925– . German baritone singer whose intelligently focused and subtly understated interpretations of opera and lieder (songs) introduced a new depth and intimacy to a wide-ranging repertoire extending in opera from Gluck to Berg's Wozzeck, Henze, and Britten, and from Bach arias to lieder of Schubert, Wolf, and Schoenberg. Since 1973 he has also conducted.

Fischl Eric 1948– . US Realist painter, the most prominent artist of his generation, known for his narrative, frequently disturbing paintings of suburban Americans at play. His figures are shown on the beach or indoors, often engaged in such intimate activities as dressing or making love. His straightforward handling of sexual themes has been considered shocking, as in *Bad Boy* 1981 (Saatchi Collection, London).

Fitzgerald Edward 1809–1883. English poet and translator whose poetic version of the *Rubaiyat of Omar Khayyám* 1859, with its resonant and melancholy tone, is generally considered more an original creation than a true translation.

Fitzgerald Ella 1918– . US jazz singer, recognized as one of the finest, most lyrical voices in jazz, both in solo work and with big bands. She is celebrated for her smooth interpretations of songs by George and Ira Gershwin, and Cole Porter.

Fitzgerald's first hit was 'A-Tisket, A-Tasket' 1938. She excelled at ◊scat singing and was widely imitated in the 1950s and 1960s. She is among the best-selling recording artists in the history of jazz. Her albums include *Ella Fitzgerald Sings the Rodgers and Hart Songbook*, *Duke Ellington Songbook*, and other single-composer sets in the 1950s, and *Ella and Louis* 1956 with trumpeter Louis Armstrong.

Fitzgerald F(rancis) Scott (Key) 1896–1940. US novelist and short-story writer. His early autobiographical novel *This Side of Paradise* 1920 made him known in the postwar society of the East Coast, and *The ◊Great Gatsby* 1925 epitomizes the Jazz Age.

A big man has no time really to do anything but just sit and be big.

F Scott Fitzgerald
This Side of Paradise 1920

Fitzgerald was born in Minnesota. His first book, *This Side of Paradise*, reflected his experiences at Princeton University. In *The Great Gatsby* 1925 the narrator resembles his author, and Gatsby, the self-made millionaire, is lost in the soulless society he enters. Fitzgerald's wife Zelda Sayre (1900–1948), a schizophrenic, entered an asylum 1930, after which he declined into alcoholism. Her descent into mental illness forms the subject of *Tender is the Night* 1934. His other works include numerous short stories and the novels *The Beautiful and the Damned* 1922 and *The Last Tycoon*, which was unfinished at his death.

Fitzwilliam Virginal Book manuscript collection of 297 mainly English 17th-century compositions for keyboard instruments copied by Francis Tregian and acquired by Richard Fitzwilliam (1745–1816) who bequeathed it to Cambridge University. Among composers represented are William Byrd, John Bull, and Giles Farnaby.

Flagellation of Christ tempera painting on panel of the 1450s by ◊Piero della Francesca (Galleria delle Marche, Palazzo Ducale, Urbino). Although small in scale (about 62 × 81 cm/24 × 32 in) when compared to Piero's great fresco cycles, it is one of his masterpieces in its faultless use of perspective. The meaning of the painting, particularly the prominence and identity of the three figures in the foreground, has excited much speculation.

flageolet whistle flute of tapered bore popular in France and England as a town band instrument during the 17th–19th centuries.

Flagg James Montgomery 1877–1960. US illustrator. His World War I recruiting poster 'I Want You', features a haggard image of Uncle Sam modelled on Flagg himself.

Flagstad Kirsten (Malfrid) 1895–1962. Norwegian soprano whose Bayreuth debut 1933 established her as a Wagnerian leading soprano of majestic presence, notably as Fricka in *Das Rheingold/The Rhinegold* and Brünnhilde in *Götterdämmerung/Twilight of the Gods*. In 1950 she gave the premiere of Richard Strauss' *Four Last Songs* 1948.

Flaherty Robert 1884–1951. US film director, one of the fathers of documentary filmmaking. He exerted great influence through his pioneer documentary of Inuit life, *Nanook of the North* 1922, a critical and commercial success.

Later films include *Moana* 1926, a South Seas documentary; *Man of Aran* 1934, *Elephant Boy* 1936, and the Standard Oil-sponsored *Louisiana Story* 1948. Critics subsequently raised questions about the truthfulness of his documentary method.

Flamboyant in French architecture, the Late Gothic style contemporary with the ◊Perpendicular style in England. It is characterized by flamelike decorative work in windows, balustrades, and other projecting features.

flamenco music and dance of the Andalusian gypsies of S Spain, evolved from Andalusian and Arabic folk music. The *cante* (song) is sometimes performed as a solo but more often accompanied by guitar music and passionate improvised dance. Hand clapping, finger clicking (castanets are a more recent addition), and enthusiastic shouts are all features. Male flamenco dancers excel in powerful, rhythmic footwork while the female dancers place emphasis on the graceful and erotic movements of their hands and bodies.

Flanagan Bud. Stage name of Robert Winthrop 1896–1968. British comedian, leader of the 'Crazy Gang' from 1931 to 1962. He played in variety theatre all over the world and, with his partner Chesney Allen, popularized such songs as 'Underneath the Arches'.

flannel woven woollen fabric with a napped (raised) surface, which gives it a warm, smooth appearance and obscures its underlying plain or twill cloth construction. It is used for suiting materials. The term is also used for a washing cloth of cotton towelling.

flat in music, a note or a key that is played lower in pitch than the written value, indicated by a flat sign or key signature. It can also refer to inaccurate intonation by a player.

Flaubert Gustave 1821–1880. French writer. One of the major novelists of the 19th century, he was the author of ◊*Madame Bovary* 1857, *Salammbô* 1862, *L'Education sentimentale/ Sentimental Education* 1869, and *La Tentation de Saint Antoine/The Temptation of St Anthony* 1874. Flaubert also wrote the short stories *Trois Contes/Three Tales* 1877. His dedication to art resulted in a meticulous prose style, realistic detail, and psychological depth, which is often revealed through interior monologue.

Poetry is as exact a science as geometry.

Gustave Flaubert

Flavin Dan 1933– . US sculptor and environmental artist, specializing in the use of light technology. His simple installations using standard coloured or white neon tubes alter the viewer's perceptions of the surrounding space, as in the coloured-neon arrangement *Untitled (to Agrati)* 1964 (Saatchi Collection, London).

Flaxman John 1755–1826. English Neo-Classical sculptor and illustrator. From 1775 he worked for the Wedgwood pottery as a designer. His public works include the monuments of Nelson 1808–10 in St Paul's Cathedral, London, and of Burns and Kemble in Westminster Abbey.

Flaxman was born in York and studied at the Royal Academy in London. From 1787 to 1794 he was in Rome directing the Wedgwood studio there. Apart from designs for Wedgwood ware, he modelled friezes on classical subjects and produced relief portraits. In 1810 he became the first professor of sculpture at the Royal Academy.

Flecker James Elroy 1884–1915. British poet. During a career in the consular service, he wrote several volumes of verse, including *The Bridge of Fire* 1907, *The Golden Journey to Samarkand* 1913, and *The Old Ships* 1915.

Fleming Ian 1908–1964. English author of suspense novels featuring the ruthless, laconic James Bond, British Secret Service agent 007. The first novel in the series was *Casino Royale* 1953. Most of the novels were made into successful films.

Flemish art painting and sculpture of Flanders (now divided between Belgium, the Netherlands, and France). A distinctive Flemish style emerged in the early 15th century based on manuscript illumination and the art of the Burgundian court. It is distinguished by keen observation, minute attention to detail, bright colours, and superb technique – oil painting was a Flemish invention. Apart from portraits, Flemish art is chiefly religious and often set in contemporary landscapes, townscapes, and interiors. Flemish sculpture shows German and French influence.

15th century Jan van Eyck made Bruges the first centre of Flemish art; other schools arose in Tournai, Ghent, and Louvain. The great names of the early period were Rogier van der Weyden, Dierick Bouts, Hugo van der Goes, Hans Memling, and Gerard David.

16th century Italian influences were strongly felt, and the centre shifted to Antwerp, where Quentin Matsys worked. Hieronymus Bosch painted creatures from his own wild imagination, but the pictures of Pieter Brueghel the Elder are realistic reflections of Flemish life.

17th century Rubens and his school created a new powerful style, which was continued by van Dyck and others. Teniers and many minor artists continued the tradition of genre painting.

Flemish art declined after the 17th century, although contemporary Belgian artists of importance include Ensor and Magritte.

Flemish literature in Belgium, Flemish literature in its written form was the same as Dutch and was stimulated by the declaration, following the revolution of 1830–39, that French was the only official language in Belgium (it remained so until 1898). J F Willems (1793–1846) brought out a magazine that revived medieval Flemish works. Modern writers in Flemish took their tone from the romantic poetry of Karel Lodewijk

Ledeganck (1805–1847) and the historical and social novels of Hendrik Conscience (1812–1883). In *Vlaemsche Dichtoefeningen/Flemish Exercises in Poetry* 1858 Guido Gezelle (1830–1899) moved away from Romanticism towards Impressionism. His nephew Stijn Streuwels (1871–1969), the most popular prose writer of his generation, wrote novels about the country life of Flanders. New literary perspectives were heralded in the journal *Van Nu en Straks/Of Now and Later* 1893–1903 conducted by August Vermeylen (1872–1945). In the earlier 20th century Cyriel Buysse (1859–1932) and Willem Elschott (1882–1960) were leading novelists. Contemporary writers include the popular novelist, dramatist, and poet Hugo Claus (1929–   ).

Fletcher John 1579–1625. English dramatist. He is remarkable for his range, which included tragicomedy and pastoral dramas, in addition to comedy and tragedy. He collaborated with ◊Beaumont, producing, most notably, *Philaster* 1609 and *The Maid's Tragedy* 1610–11. He is alleged to have collaborated with Shakespeare on *The Two Noble Kinsmen* and *Henry VIII* 1612.

Among plays credited to Fletcher alone are the pastoral drama *The Faithful Shepherdess* 1610, the tragedy *Bonduca* c. 1611–14, and the comedy *The Wild Goose Chase* 1621.

But what is past my help, is past my care.

John Fletcher The Double Marriage

Flett John 1963–1991. British fashion designer who achieved international recognition while still training at St Martin's School of Art, London. In the late 1980s his collections were bought by top fashion houses, but an attempt to set up his own business ran into financial difficulties. In 1989 he moved to Paris to join Claude Montana, and from there went to Enrico Coveri's Italian house. He was in Florence to sign a rainwear and knitwear contract with manufacturer Zuccoli when he died suddenly of a heart attack.

Flint William Russell 1880–1970. Scottish artist, president of the Royal Society of Painters in Water-Colour 1936–56, known for his watercolours of mildly erotic nudes.

Flora in Roman mythology, the goddess of flowers, youth, and spring.

Florio Giovanni *c.* 1553–1625. English translator, born in London, the son of Italian refugees. He translated Michel ◊Montaigne's essays in 1603.

Though manners make, yet apparel shapes.

Giovanni Florio *Second Frutes*

Flotow Friedrich (Adolf Ferdinand), Freiherr von 1812–1883. German composer who wrote 18 operas, including *Martha* 1847.

flower power youth movement of the 1960s; see ◊hippie.

Flowers of Evil (French *Les Fleurs du mal*) a collection of poems by Charles Baudelaire, published in France 1857, which deal with the conflict between good and evil. The work was condemned by the censor as endangering public morals, but paved the way for Rimbaud, Verlaine, and the Symbolist school.

flugelhorn alto valved brass band instrument of the bugle type. In B flat, it has a similar range to the cornet but is of mellower tone.

flute or *transverse flute* side-blown soprano woodwind instrument of considerable antiquity. The flute is difficult to master but capable of intricate melodies and expressive tonal shading. The player blows across an end hole, the air current being split by the opposite edge which causes pressure waves to form within the tube. The fingers are placed over holes in the tube to create the notes. The flute has an extensive concert repertoire, including familiar pieces by J S Bach, Mozart, and the pastoral refrain of Debussy's *L'Après-midi d'un faune/Afternoon of a Faun* 1894. Vivaldi wrote a number of concertos for piccolo, and Maderna has composed for alto and bass flutes. Performers include James ◊Galway and the Italian Severino Gazzelloni (1919–   ).

Flynn Errol. Stage name of Leslie Thompson 1909–1959. Australian-born US film actor. He is renowned for his portrayal of swashbuckling heroes in such films as *Captain Blood* 1935, *Robin Hood* 1938, *The Charge of the Light Brigade* 1938, *The Private Lives of Elizabeth and Essex* 1939, *The Sea Hawk* 1940, and *The Master of Ballantrae* 1953.

In *The Sun Also Rises* 1957 he portrayed a middle-aged Hemingway roué, and in *Too Much Too Soon* 1958 he portrayed actor John Barrymore. Flynn wrote an autobiography, *My Wicked, Wicked Ways* 1959. He became a US citizen 1942.

f-number or **f-stop** measure of the relative aperture of a telescope or camera lens; it indicates the light-gathering power of the lens. In photography, each successive f-number represents a halving of exposure speed.

Fo Dario 1926–   . Italian dramatist. His plays are predominantly political satires combining black humour with slapstick. They include *Morte accidentale di un anarchico/Accidental Death of an Anarchist* 1970, and *Non si paga non si paga/Can't Pay? Won't Pay!* 1975/1981.

He has also written a one-man show, *Mistero buffo* 1969, based on the medieval mystery plays; and a handbook on the skills of the comic performer, *Tricks of the Trade* 1991.

Focillon Henri 1881–1943. French art historian who taught both in Europe and the USA. An authority on the Middle Ages, for example *Art d'Occident/Art of the West* 1938, his writings explore two themes in particular: the role of technique in artistic creation and the extent to which art reflects the worldview of a period.

In *Vie des formes/The Life of Forms in Art* 1934, he analyses the evolution of style in terms of three interrelated stages: the experimental, the classical, and the baroque.

focus in photography, the distance that a lens must be moved in order to focus a sharp image on the light-sensitive film at the back of the camera. The lens is moved away from the film to focus the image of closer objects. The focusing distance is often marked on a scale around the lens; however, some cameras now have an automatic focusing (autofocus) mechanism that uses an electric motor to move the lens.

Fokine Mikhail 1880–1942. Russian choreographer and dancer, born in St Petersburg. He was chief choreographer to the Ballets Russes 1909–14, and with ◊Diaghilev revitalized and reformed the art of ballet, promoting the idea of artistic unity among dramatic, musical, and stylistic elements.

His creations for Diaghilev include some of the most famous works in the ballet repertory, such as *Les Sylphides* 1909, *Schéhérazade* 1910, *The Firebird* 1910, *Le Spectre de la rose* 1911, and *Petrushka* 1911. He also created *The Dying Swan* for Anna Pavlova 1907. As a dancer, he was first soloist with the Maryinsky Theatre (later the Kirov) 1904.

Folies-Bergère music hall in Paris, France, built 1869, named after its original proprietor. In the 20th century, it featured lavish productions and striptease acts.

folk dance dance characteristic of a particular people, nation, or region. Many European folk dances are derived from the dances accompanying the customs and ceremonies of pre-Christian times. Some later became ballroom dances (for example, the minuet and waltz). Once an important part of many rituals, folk dance has tended to die out in industrialized countries. Examples of folk dance are Morris dance, farandole, and jota. The preservation of folk dance in England was promoted by the work of Cecil ◊Sharp.

folk music body of traditional music, originally transmitted orally. Many folk songs originated as a rhythmic accompaniment to manual work or to mark a specific ritual. Folk song is usually melodic, not harmonic, and the modes used are distinctive of the country of origin; see ◊world music.

A burgeoning interest in ballad poetry in the later 18th century led to the discovery of a rich body of folk song in Europe. The multi-ethnic background of the USA has conserved a wealth of material derived from European, African, and Latin American sources. A revival of interest in folk music began in the USA in the 1950s led by researcher Alan Lomax (1915–) and the singers Henry Belafonte (1927–), Odetta (1930–), Pete Seeger, Woody Guthrie, and Joan Baez, and Bob Dylan who wrote new material in folk-song style, dealing with contemporary topics such as nuclear weapons and racial prejudice.

In England the late 19th century saw a development in the transcribing and preserving of folk tunes by such people as the Rev Sabine Baring-Gould and Cecil ◊Sharp. The Folk Song Society was founded 1898 and became the English Folk Dance and Song Society 1911; they censored much of their material. The folk revival of the 1980s was furthered by rock guitarist Richard ◊Thompson and groups such as the Pogues (formed 1983), and there was growing interest in roots, or world, music, encompassing traditional as well as modern music from many cultures.

Fonda Henry 1905–1982. US actor whose engaging style made him ideal in the role of the American pioneer and honourable man. His many films include *The Grapes of Wrath* 1940, *My Darling Clementine* 1946, *12 Angry Men* 1957, and *On Golden Pond* 1981, for which he won the Academy Award for best actor. He was the father of actress Jane Fonda and actor and director Peter Fonda (1939–).

Fonda Jane 1937– . US actress. Her varied films roles include *Cat Ballou* 1965, *Barefoot in the Park* 1967, *Barbarella* 1968, *They Shoot Horses, Don't They?* 1969, *Julia* 1977, *The China Syndrome* 1979, *On Golden Pond* 1981, in which she appeared with her father, Henry Fonda. She won Academy Awards for *Klute* 1971 and *Coming Home* 1978. She is active in left-wing politics and in promoting physical fitness.

You spend your life doing something they put people in asylums for.

Jane Fonda on acting

Fontainebleau School French school of Mannerist painting and sculpture. It was established at the court of François I, who brought Italian artists to Fontainebleau, near Paris, to decorate his hunting lodge: Rosso Fiorentino arrived 1530, Francesco Primaticcio came 1532. They evolved a distinctive decorative style using a combination of stucco relief and painting.

Their work, with its exuberant ornamental and figurative style, had a lasting impact on French art in the 16th century. Others associated with the school include Benvenuto Cellini and Niccolò dell'Abbate.

Fontana Domenico 1543–1607. Italian architect. He was appointed architect to Pope Sixtus V and undertook various important commissions in

Rome, notably the Lateran Palace 1586–88 and the Vatican library 1587–90. He also assisted in the completion of the dome of St Peter's 1588–90. After 1592 he settled in Naples, where he designed the Royal Palace 1600–02.

Fontana Lucio 1899–1968. Italian painter and sculptor. He developed a unique abstract style, presenting bare canvases with straight parallel slashes. His *White Manifesto* 1946 argued for the blending of scientific ideas with new art forms.

Fontane Theodor 1819–1898. German novelist. Born in Brandenburg, the vividly rendered setting of his novels, he worked as a journalist and wrote stirring popular ballads and topographical books before turning to realist fiction. His best work, such as the historical novel *Vor dem Sturm/Before the Storm* 1878, a critical but sympathetic account of Prussian aristocratic life, and *Effi Briest* 1898, is marked by superb characterization and a concern with the position of women.

Fontanne Lynn 1887–1983. US actress, one-half of the husband-and-wife acting partnership known as the 'Lunts' with her husband Alfred ◊Lunt.

Fonteyn Margot. Stage name of Peggy (Margaret) Hookham 1919–1991. English ballet dancer. She made her debut with the Sadler's Wells Ballet in *Nutcracker* 1934 and first appeared as Giselle 1937, eventually becoming prima ballerina of the Royal Ballet, London. Renowned for her perfect physique, clear line, musicality, and interpretive powers, she created many roles in Frederick ◊Ashton's ballets and formed a legendary partnership with Rudolf ◊Nureyev. She did not retire from dancing until 1979.

Fonteyn's first major role was in Ashton's *Le Baiser de la fée* 1935; other Ashton ballets include *Symphonic Variations* 1946, *Ondine* 1958 (filmed 1959), and *Marguerite and Armand* 1963 (filmed 1972). She also appeared in Macmillan's *Romeo and Juliet* 1965 (filmed 1966) with Nureyev.

foot unit of metrical pattern in poetry; see metre. The five most common types of foot in English poetry are iamb (v –), trochee (– v), dactyl (– vv), spondee (—), and anapaest (vv –) (the symbol v stands for an unstressed syllable and – for a stressed one).

Forbes Bryan (John Clarke) 1926– . British film producer, director, and screenwriter. After acting in such films as *An Inspector Calls* 1954, he made his directorial debut with *Whistle Down the Wind* 1961; among his other films are *The L-Shaped Room* 1962, *The Wrong Box* 1966, and *The Raging Moon* 1971.

Ford Ford Madox. Adopted name of Ford Hermann Hueffer 1873–1939. English author of more than 82 books, the best known of which is the novel *The Good Soldier* 1915. He founded and edited the *English Review* 1909, to which Thomas Hardy, D H Lawrence, and Joseph Conrad contributed. He excelled at a comic mixture of invention and reportage. He also founded *The Transatlantic Review* 1924. He was a grandson of the painter Ford Madox Brown.

Ford Glenn (Gwyllym Samuel Newton) 1916– . Canadian-born US actor, active in Hollywood from the 1940s to the 1960s. Usually cast as the tough but good-natured hero, he was equally at home in Westerns, thrillers, and comedies. His films include *Gilda* 1946, *The Big Heat* 1953, and *Dear Heart* 1965.

Ford Harrison 1942– . US film actor who often plays the unintentional hero. He became internationally known as Han Solo in George Lucas' trilogy *Star Wars* 1977, *The Empire Strikes Back* 1980, and *Return of the Jedi* 1983, and created the role of Indiana Jones in Steven Spielberg's *Raiders of the Lost Ark* 1981, *Indiana Jones and the Temple of Doom* 1984, and *Indiana Jones and the Last Crusade* 1989. Other films include *Blade Runner* 1982, *The Mosquito Coast* 1987, *Presumed Innocent* 1990, and *The Fugitive* 1993.

Ford John 1586–c. 1640. English poet and dramatist. His play *'Tis Pity She's a Whore* (performed about 1626, printed 1633) is a study of incest between brother and sister. His other plays include *The Lover's Melancholy* 1629, *The Broken Heart* 1633, *Love's Sacrifice* 1633, and *The Chronicle History of Perkin Warbeck* 1634. Dwelling on themes of pathos and frustration, they reflect the transition from a general to an aristocratic audience for drama.

Ford John. Adopted name of Sean O'Feeney 1895–1973. US film director. Active from the silent film era, he was one of the key creators of the 'Western', directing *The Iron Horse* 1924; *Stagecoach* 1939 became his masterpiece. He won Academy Awards for *The Informer* 1935, *The Grapes of Wrath* 1940, *How Green Was My Valley* 1941, and *The Quiet Man* 1952.

Other films include *They Were Expendable* 1945, *Rio Grande* 1950, *Mr Roberts* 1955, *The Last Hurrah* 1958, and *The Man Who Shot Liberty Valance* 1962.

Forester C(ecil) S(cott) 1899–1966. English novelist, born in Egypt. He wrote a series of historical novels set in the Napoleonic era that, beginning with *The Happy Return* 1937, cover the career – from midshipman to admiral – of Horatio Hornblower.

He also wrote *Payment Deferred* 1926, a subtle crime novel, and *The African Queen* 1938, later filmed with Humphrey Bogart.

formalism in artistic, literary, and musical theory, an emphasis on form and formal structures at the expense of content. Formalism also refers more narrowly to a Russian school of literary theory in the 1920s, which defined literature by its formal, aesthetic qualities, and did not recognize its social content.

Formalism fell into disrepute as an aesthetic self-indulgence and was the focus of the cultural purges of 1948 under Stalin. It was superseded by ◊Socialist Realism.

Formby George 1904–1961. English comedian. He established a stage and screen reputation as an apparently simple Lancashire working lad, and sang such songs as 'Mr Wu' and 'Cleaning Windows', accompanying himself on the ukulele. His father was a music-hall star of the same name.

Forster E(dward) M(organ) 1879–1970. English novelist, concerned with the interplay of personality and the conflict between convention and instinct. His novels include *A Room with a View* 1908, *Howards End* 1910, and *A Passage to India* 1924. He also wrote short stories, for example ' The Eternal Omnibus' 1914; criticism, including *Aspects of the Novel* 1927; and essays, including *Abinger Harvest* 1936.

Forster published his first novel, *Where Angels Fear to Tread*, in 1905. He enhances the superficial situations of his plots with unexpected insights in *The Longest Journey* 1907, *A Room with a View*, and *Howards End*. His many years spent in India and his experience as secretary to the Maharajah of Dewas 1921 provided him with the material for *A Passage to India*, which explores the relationship between the English and the Indians. *Maurice*, published 1971, has a homosexual theme.

Faith, to my mind, is a stiffening process, a sort of mental starch, which should be applied as sparingly as possible.

E M Forster *What I Believe*

Forsyth Frederick 1938– . English thriller writer. His books include *The Day of the Jackal* 1970, *The Dogs of War* 1974, *The Fourth Protocol* 1984, and *The Negotiator* 1990.

He was a Reuters correspondent and BBC radio and television reporter before making his name with *The Day of the Jackal*, dealing with an attempted assassination of President de Gaulle of France. Later novels were *The Odessa File* 1972, and *The Devil's Alternative* 1979.

fortepiano early 18th-century piano invented by Italian maker Bartolommeo Christofori about 1709, having small, leather-bound hammers and harpsichord-style strings. Present-day performers include Trevor Pinnock, Gustav Leonhardt, and Jörg Demus.

Fortuna in Roman mythology, the goddess of chance and good fortune, identified with the Greek ◊Tyche.

forum (Latin 'market') in an ancient Roman town, the meeting place and market, like the Greek ◊agora. At Rome the Forum Romanum contained the Senate House, the public speaking platform, covered halls for trading, temples of Saturn, Concord, and the Divine Augustus, and memorial arches. Later constructions included the Forum of Caesar (temple of Venus), the Forum of Augustus (temple of Mars), and the colonnaded Forum of Trajan, containing Trajan's Column.

Foscolo Ugo 1777–1827. Italian author. An intensely patriotic Venetian, he fought with the French against the invading Austrians. Disillusionment with Napoleon inspired his very popular novel *Ultime lettere di Jacopo Ortis/Last Letters of Jacopo Ortis* 1802. His blank-verse patriotic poem 'Dei sepolchri'/'Of the Sepulchres' 1807 made his name and was followed by the tragedies *Aiace/Ajax* 1811 and *Ricciarda* 1812. His last years were spent in exile in England as a literary journalist and Italian teacher.

Foss Lukas 1922– . US composer and conductor whose stylistically varied works, including the cantata *The Prairie* 1942 and *Time Cycle* for soprano and orchestra 1960, express an ironic view of tradition.

Born in Germany, he studied in Europe before settling in the USA 1937. A student of Hindemith, his vocal music is composed in Neo-Classical style; in the mid-1950s he began increasingly to employ improvisation. Foss has also written chamber and orchestral music in which the players imitate tape-recorded effects.

Fosse Bob (Robert) 1927–1987. US film director who entered films as a dancer and choreographer from Broadway, making his directorial debut with *Sweet Charity* 1968. He received an Academy Award for his second film as director, *Cabaret* 1972. Other films include *All That Jazz* 1979.

Foster Jodie. Stage name of Alicia Christian Foster 1962– . US film actress and director who began as a child in a great variety of roles. She starred in *Taxi Driver* and *Bugsy Malone* both 1976, when only 14. Subsequent films include *The Accused* 1988 and *The Silence of the Lambs* 1991 (she won Academy Awards for both), and *Sommersby* 1993. She made her directorial debut with *Little Man Tate* 1991.

Foster Norman 1935– . English architect of the High Tech school. His buildings include the Willis Faber & Dumas insurance offices, Ipswich, 1975, the Sainsbury Centre for the Visual Arts, Norwich, 1977, the headquarters of the Hong Kong and Shanghai Bank, Hong Kong, 1986, and Stansted Airport, Essex, 1991.

He has won numerous international awards for his industrial architecture and design, including RIBA awards for the Stansted project and the Sackler Galleries extension at the Royal Academy of Art, London, 1992, which is a sensitive, yet overtly modern, addition to an existing historic building.

Foster Stephen Collins 1826–1864. US song-writer. He wrote sentimental popular songs including 'My Old Kentucky Home' 1853 and 'Beautiful Dreamer' 1864, and rhythmic minstrel songs such as 'Oh! Susanna' 1848 and 'Camptown Races' 1850.

fouetté in ballet, a type of ◊pirouette in which one leg is extended to the side and then into the knee in a whiplike action, while the dancer spins on the supporting leg. Odile performs 32 *fouettés* in Act III of *Swan Lake*.

found object (French *objet trouvé*) in the visual arts, an object that has no intrinsic aesthetic value, such as a piece of wood or rusty machinery, but which is 'found' by an artist and displayed as a work of art or ◊anti-art. Its use was popular among the Surrealists. See also ◊ready-made.

Fountains Abbey Cistercian abbey in North Yorkshire, England. It was founded about 1132, and closed 1539 at the Dissolution of the Monasteries. The ruins were incorporated into a Romantic landscaped garden 1720–40 with lake, formal water garden, temples, and a deer park.

Fouquet or *Foucquet* Jean *c.* 1420–*c.* 1481. French painter. He became court painter to Charles VIII 1448 and to Louis XI 1475. His *Melun Diptych* about 1450 (Musées Royaux, Antwerp, and Staatliche Museen, Berlin) shows Italian Renaissance influence.

Fowles John 1926– . English writer whose novels, often concerned with illusion and reality and with the creative process, include *The Collector* 1963, *The Magus* 1965, *The French Lieutenant's Woman* 1969 (filmed 1981), *Daniel Martin* 1977, *Mantissa* 1982, and *A Maggot* 1985.

Fox James 1939– . English film actor, usually cast in upper-class, refined roles but celebrated for his portrayal of a psychotic gangster in Nicolas Roeg's *Performance* 1970, which was followed by an eight-year break from acting. Fox appeared in *The Servant* 1963 and *Isadora* 1968. He returned to acting in *No Longer Alone* 1978. His other films include *Runners* 1984, *A Passage to India* 1984, and *The Russia House* 1990.

Fox Talbot William Henry 1800–1877. English pioneer of photography. He invented the paper-based ◊calotype process, the first negative/positive method. Fox Talbot made ◊photograms several years before Louis ◊Daguerre's invention was announced.

In 1851 he made instantaneous photographs and in 1852 photo engravings. *The Pencil of Nature* 1844–46 by Fox Talbot was the first book of photographs published.

foxtrot ballroom dance originating in the USA about 1914. It has alternating long and short steps, supposedly like the movements of the fox.

Fragonard Jean-Honoré 1732–1806. French painter, the leading exponent of the Rococo style

(along with his master Boucher). His light-hearted subjects, often erotic, include *The Swing* about 1766 (Wallace Collection, London). Mme de Pompadour was one of his patrons.

Frame Janet 1924– . New Zealand novelist. After being wrongly diagnosed as schizophrenic, she reflected her experiences 1945–54 in the novel *Faces in the Water* 1961 and the autobiographical *An Angel at My Table* 1984.

'For your own good' is a persuasive argument that will eventually make man agree to his own destruction.

Janet Frame *Faces in the Water* 1961

Frampton George James 1860–1928. English sculptor. His work includes the statue of *Peter Pan* 1911 in Kensington Gardens and the Edith Cavell memorial near St Martin-in-the-Fields, London, 1920.

France Anatole. Pen name of François Anatole Thibault 1844–1924. French writer renowned for the wit, urbanity, and style of his works. His earliest novel was *Le Crime de Sylvestre Bonnard/The Crime of Sylvester Bonnard* 1881; later books include the autobiographical series beginning with *Le Livre de mon ami/My Friend's Book* 1885, the satiric *L'île des pingouins/Penguin Island* 1908, and *Les Dieux ont soif/The Gods Are Athirst* 1912. He was awarded the Nobel Prize for Literature 1921.

They [the poor] have to labour in the face of the majestic equality of the law, which forbids the rich as well as the poor to sleep under bridges, to beg in the streets, and to steal bread.

Anatole France *Le Lys rouge* 1894

Francesca Piero della. See ◊Piero della Francesca, Italian painter.

Francis Sam 1923– . US painter and printmaker, a leading second-generation Abstract Expressionist, whose buoyant paintings fused American and European abstract styles. He is known for his large, splashed and splattered, floating forms, executed in a high-keyed palette against a white ground, for example *Middle Blue* £5 1960 (University Art Museum, Berkeley, California).

Franck César Auguste 1822–1890. Belgian composer. His music, mainly religious and Romantic in style, includes the Symphony in D minor 1866–68, *Symphonic Variations* 1885 for piano and orchestra, the *Violin Sonata* 1886, the oratorio *Les Béatitudes/The Beatitudes* 1879, and many organ pieces.

Frank Anne 1929–1945. German diarist who fled to the Netherlands with her family 1933 to escape Nazi anti-Semitism. After two years in hiding in Amsterdam 1942–44, they were betrayed and she died in Belsen concentration camp. Her diary of her time in hiding was published 1947.

The Diary of Anne Frank has sold 20 million copies in more than 50 languages and has been made into a play and a film publicizing the fate of millions. Previously suppressed portions of the diary were published 1989.

Frank Robert 1924– . US photographer born in Switzerland, best known for his informal and unromanticized pictures of American life. These were published, with a foreword by the US novelist Jack Kerouac, as *The Americans* 1959. Since then he has concentrated mainly on filmmaking.

Frankel Benjamin 1906–1973. English composer and teacher. He studied the piano in Germany and continued his studies in London while playing jazz violin in nightclubs. His output includes chamber music and numerous film scores, notably *The Man in the White Suit* 1951 and *A Kid for Two Farthings* 1955.

Frankenstein or ***The Modern Prometheus*** Gothic horror story by Mary ◊Shelley, published in England 1818. Frankenstein, a scientist, discovers how to bring inanimate matter to life, and creates a man-monster. When Frankenstein fails to provide a mate to satisfy the creature's human emotions, it seeks revenge by killing Frankenstein's brother and bride. Frankenstein dies in an attempt to destroy his creation.

Frankenthaler Helen 1928– . US Abstract Expressionist painter, inventor of the colour-staining technique whereby the unprimed, absorbent canvas is stained or soaked with thinned-out paint, creating deep, soft veils of translucent colour.

Franklin Aretha 1942– . US soul singer whose gospel background infuses her four-octave voice with a passionate conviction and authority. Her hits include 'Respect' 1967, 'Chain of Fools' 1968, and the albums *Lady Soul* 1968, *Amazing Grace* 1972, and *Who's Zoomin' Who?* 1985.

Franklin (Stella Maria Sarah) Miles 1879–1954. Australian novelist. Her first novel, *My Brilliant Career* 1901, autobiographical and feminist, drew on her experiences of rural Australian life. *My Career Goes Bung*, written as a sequel, was not published until 1946. A literary award bearing her name is made annually for novels.

Fraser Antonia 1932– . English author of biographies, including *Mary Queen of Scots* 1969; historical works, such as *The Weaker Vessel* 1984;

and a series of detective novels featuring investigator Jemima Shore. She is married to the dramatist Harold Pinter, and is the daughter of Lord Longford.

Freeman (Lawrence) Bud 1906–1991. US jazz saxophonist who took part in developing the Chicago style in the 1920s. His playing was soft and elegant, and he worked and recorded with a number of bands, as well as cofounding the World's Greatest Jazz Band in the 1970s.

free-reed instrument musical wind instrument such as the mouth organ, accordion, or harmonium, that employs tuned metal tongues vibrating at a predetermined frequency as valves controlling the escape of air under pressure. Free reeds do not ◊overblow, but the mouth organ can be made to 'bend' the pitch by varying the air pressure.

free verse poetry without metrical form. At the beginning of the 20th century, many poets believed that the 19th century had accomplished most of what could be done with regular metre, and rejected it, in much the same spirit as John Milton in the 17th century had rejected rhyme, preferring irregular metres that made it possible to express thought clearly and without distortion.

This was true of T S ◊Eliot and the Imagists; it was also true of poets who, like the Russians Esenin and Mayakovsky, placed emphasis on public performance. The shift to free verse began under the very different influences of US poet Walt Whitman and French poet Stéphane Mallarmé.

Poets including Robert Graves and W H Auden have criticized free verse on the ground that it lacks the difficulty of true accomplishment, but their own metrics would have been considered loose by earlier critics. The freeness of free verse is largely relative.

French Daniel Chester 1850–1931. US sculptor, principally of public monuments, whose most famous works include *The Minute Man* 1875 in Concord, Massachusetts, *John Harvard* 1884 at Harvard College, *Alma Mater* at Columbia University, and the imposing seated *Abraham Lincoln* 1922 in the Lincoln Memorial, Washington, DC.

French Leonard William 1928– . Australian artist, noted for his abstract portrayal of religious themes. He received the Blake Prize for his *Campion* 1962 series, which deals with the life and death of Edmund Campion, the 16th-century Jesuit priest and martyr. French is also known for his stained-glass work which includes 16 windows in the National Library, Canberra.

French architecture the architecture of France. *early Christian* The influence of France's rich collection of Roman buildings (ranging from amphitheatres to temples and aqueducts) can be seen in early Christian church building, which began even before the Romans retreated. The baptistery of St Jean at Poitiers and the crypt of Jouarre near Meaux, both 5th century, use Roman architectural effects to their own ends.

Romanesque Such early Roman-influenced buildings gave way to the first distinctive Romanesque architecture, which reached its zenith in the abbey at Cluny (begun 1088). The style developed and took on regional characteristics, such as tunnel and other types of vaulting, for example, St Philibert at Tournus 11th century.

Gothic The abbey church of St Denis, near Paris, 1130–44, marks the beginning of the Gothic style, characterized by the use of pointed arches and rib vaulting. The cathedral of Notre Dame, Paris, begun 1160, is an example of **Early Gothic** 1130–90. The cathedrals at Chartres, begun 1194, Reims, begun 1211, and Bourges, begun 1209 are examples of **lancet Gothic** 1190–1240. French **Late Gothic**, or the **Flamboyant style** 1350–1520, characterized by flowing tracery, is best represented at Caudebec-en-Caux in Normandy, about 1426, and Moulins in Burgundy.

Renaissance Arriving in France from Italy late in the 15th century, the Renaissance made its greatest impact on the building of châteaux, especially in the Loire valley, for example, Blois 1515–24 and Chambord 1519–47.

Baroque After a long period of religious warfare, architecture was again given priority. Henry IV's interest in town planning manifested itself in such works as the Place des Vosges, Paris (begun 1605). The Baroque style found expression in Le Vau's work on the château of Vaux-le-Vicomte 1657–61, the gardens of which were designed by Le Nôtre; the two later worked extensively at Versailles. Under Louis XIV, Hardouin-Mansart enlarged Versailles 1678 and built Les Invalides, Paris 1680–91.

Neo-Classicism In the 18th century there was a definite move towards Classicism, culminating in the severe works of Boullée and Ledoux. The Classical influence continued in the 19th century, perpetuated to some extent by the revolution of 1789, with works such as the Madeleine, Paris 1804–49, by P A Vignon (1762–1828). By the middle of the century, the grandiose Beaux Arts style was established, most spectacularly in the Opéra, Paris, 1861–74, by Charles Garnier (1825–1898). It was challenged by both the Rationalist approach of Labrouste who was responsible for the Library of Ste Geneviève, Paris, 1843–50, and by the Gothic Revival as detailed in the writings of Viollet-le-Duc.

Art Nouveau Art Nouveau developed towards the end of the 19th century, with centres in Nancy and Paris. Hector Guimard's Paris Métro station entrances, with their flamboyant metal arches, are famous examples of the style.

The Modern Movement In the 1920s the Swiss-born Le Corbusier emerged as the leading exponent of the Modern Movement in France. His masterpieces range from the cubist Villa Savoye at Poissy 1929–31 to the vast, gridlike Unité d'habitation at Marseilles 1947–52. Since the 1950s technological preoccupations have been evident in much modern architecture in France, beginning with the work of Jean Prouvé, for instance his Refreshment Room at Evian 1957, and continuing in more recent projects, such as the Pompidou Centre, Paris, by Renzo Piano and Richard Rogers 1971–77, and the Institut du Monde Arabe, Paris, 1981–87, by Jean Nouvel.

In the 1980s, Paris became the site for a number of *Grands Projets* initiated by President Mitterrand, including I M Pei's glass pyramid for the Louvre 1989, the conversion by Gui Aulenti of the Gare d'Orsay into the Musée d'Orsay 1986, La Villette by Bernard Tschumi (partially opened 1985), La Défense by Johan Otto von Spreckelsen 1989.

French art painting and sculpture of France. A number of styles have emerged in France over the centuries, from Gothic in the Middle Ages, through Impressionism in the late 19th century, to Cubism, Surrealism, and others in the 20th century.

11th–14th centuries The main forms of artistic expression were manuscript painting, architecture, and sculpture. France played the leading role in creating the Gothic style.

15th century The miniatures of Jean Fouquet and the *Très Riches Heures* (illuminated prayer books) of the Limbourg brothers show remarkable naturalism and flair for ornamentation.

16th century Artists were influenced by Italian Mannerism – the school of Fontainebleau flourishing – but the miniature tradition was sustained by the court painters such as Jean Clouet.

17th century Landscape painting became increasingly popular. Two exceptional exponents of the genre were the Classicists Poussin and Claude Lorrain.

18th century French painting and sculpture became dominant throughout Europe. Popular Rococo painters were Watteau, Fragonard, and Boucher. Chardin's naturalistic still lifes and genre scenes show Dutch influence. The Neo-Classical French school was founded by David.

early 19th century Ingres was the most widely admired painter. Delacroix was the leader of the Romantic movement. Géricault excelled as a history and animal painter.

mid-19th century Courbet and Manet were the great rebels in art, breaking with age-old conventions. The Barbizon School of landscape painting was followed by the Impressionists: Monet, Renoir, Degas, and others.

late 19th century The Pointillist Seurat took the

Impressionists' ideas further. The individual Post-Impressionist styles of Cézanne and Gauguin helped prepare the way for Modernism. Rodin's powerful, realistic works in bronze and stone dominated sculpture.

1900–40 The period of the School of Paris, with several major movements flourishing in the city. Fauvism, showing the influence of Gauguin with his emphasis on pure colour, was introduced by Matisse and others. Cubism, deriving from Cézanne, was invented by Picasso and Braque. Surrealism evolved in the 1920s, with André Breton as a central figure. During the 1930s the abstraction–création movement developed a form of abstract art constructed from non-figurative, usually geometrical elements.

1945–90 After World War II the centre of the art world shifted from France to the USA. Leading artists of the period include Yves Klein and Jean Dubuffet.

French Canadian literature F-X Garneau's *Histoire du Canada* 1845–48 inspired a school of patriotic verse led by Octave Crémazie (1827–1879) and continued by Louis Fréchette (1838–1908). A new movement began after 1900 with such poets as André Lozeau (1878–1924), Paul Morin (1889–1963), Robert Choquette (1862–1941), Alain Grandbois (1900–1975), Hector St Denys Garneau (1912–1943), Eloi de Grandmont (1921–1970), and Pierre Trottier (1925–). Fiction reached a high point with Louis Hémon (1880–1914) whose *Maria Chapdelaine* inspired many genre works. Outstanding later novelists are Germaine Guèvremont (1893–1968), Gabrielle Roy (1909–1983), 'Ringuet' (Philippe Panneton) (1895–1960), Robert Elie (1915–1973), Roger Lemelin (1919–), and Yves Thériault (1915–1983). Antonine Maillet (1929–), an Acadian novelist from New Brunswick, was awarded the Prix Goncourt 1979.

French horn musical ◊brass instrument, a descendant of the natural hunting horn, valved and curved into a circular loop, with a funnel-shaped mouthpiece and wide bell.

French literature the literature of France.

The Middle Ages The *Chanson de Roland* (c. 1080) is one of the early *chansons de geste* (epic poems about deeds of chivalry), which were superseded by the Arthurian romances (seen at their finest in the work of Chrétien de Troyes in the 12th century), and by the classical themes of Alexander, Troy, and Thebes. Other aspects of French medieval literature are represented by the anonymous *Aucassin et Nicolette* of the early 13th century; the allegorical *Roman de la Rose/Romance of the Rose*, the first part of which was written by Guillaume de Lorris (c. 1230) and the second by Jean de Meung (c. 1275); and the satirical *Roman de Renart/Story of Renard* of the late 12th century. The period also produced the historians

Villehardouin, Joinville, Froissart, and Comines, and the first great French poet, François Villon.

16th century: the Renaissance One of the most celebrated poets of the Renaissance was Ronsard, leader of La ◊*Pléiade* (a group of seven writers); others included ◊Marot at the beginning of the 16th century and Mathurin Régnier (1573–1613) at its close. In prose the period produced the broad genius of Rabelais and the essayist Montaigne.

17th century The triumph of form with the great Classical dramatists Corneille, Racine, and Molière, the graceful brilliance of La Fontaine, and the poet and critic Boileau. Masters of prose in the same period include the philosophers Pascal and Descartes; the preacher Bossuet; the critics La Bruyère, Fénelon, and Malebranche; and La Rochefoucauld, Cardinal de Retz, Mme de Sévigné, and Le Sage.

18th century The age of the ◊Enlightenment and an era of prose, with Montesquieu, Voltaire, and Rousseau; the scientist Buffon; the encyclopedist Diderot; the ethical writer Vauvenargues; the novelists Prévost and Marivaux; and the memoir writer Saint-Simon.

19th century Poetry came to the fore again with the Romantics Lamartine, Hugo, Vigny, Musset, Leconte de Lisle, and Gautier; novelists of the same school were George Sand, Stendhal, and Dumas *père*, while criticism is represented by Sainte-Beuve, and history by Thiers, Michelet, and Taine. The realist novelist Balzac was followed by the school of Naturalism, whose representatives were Flaubert, Zola, the Goncourt brothers, Alphonse Daudet, Maupassant, and Huysmans. Nineteenth-century dramatists include Hugo, Musset, and Dumas *fils*. Symbolism, a movement of experimentation and revolt against Classical verse and materialist attitudes, with the philosopher Bergson as one of its main exponents, found its first expression in the work of Gérard de Nerval, followed by Baudelaire, Verlaine, Mallarmé, Rimbaud, Corbière, and the prose writer Villiers de l'Isle Adam; later writers in the same tradition were Henri de Régnier and Laforgue.

20th century Drama and poetry revived with Valéry, Claudel, and Paul Fort, who advocated 'pure poetry'; other writers were the novelists Gide and Proust, and the critics Thibaudet (1874–1936) and later St John Perse, also a poet. The Surrealist movement, which developed from 'pure poetry' through the work of Eluard and Apollinaire, influenced writers as diverse as Giraudoux, Louis Aragon, and Cocteau. The literary reaction against the Symbolists was seen in the work of Charles Péguy, Rostand, de Noailles, and Romain Rolland. Twentieth-century novelists in the Naturalist tradition were Henri Barbusse, Jules Romains, Julian Green, François Mauriac, Francis Carco, and Georges Duhamel. Other prose writers were Maurois, Malraux,

Montherlant, Anatole France, Saint-Exupéry, Alain-Fournier, Pierre Hamp, and J R Bloch, while the theatre flourished with plays by J J Bernard, Anouilh, Beckett, and Ionesco. World War II had a profound effect on French writing, and distinguished postwar writers include the existentialists Sartre and Camus, 'Vercors' (pen name of Jean Bruller), Simone de Beauvoir, Alain Robbe-Grillet, Romain Gary, Nathalie Sarraute, and Marguerite Duras.

Freneau Philip Morin 1752–1832. US poet whose *A Political Litany* 1775 was a mock prayer for deliverance from British tyranny. His other works include *The British Prison-Ship* 1781, about his experiences as a British prisoner. He was a professional journalist, the first in the USA.

fresco mural painting technique using water-based paint on wet plaster. Some of the earliest frescoes (about 1750–1400 BC) were found in Knossos, Crete (now preserved in the Heraklion Museum). Fresco reached its finest expression in Italy from the 13th to the 17th centuries. Giotto, Masaccio, Michelangelo, and many other artists worked in the medium. In the 20th century the Mexican muralists Orozco and Rivera used fresco.

In *fresco secco* ('dry fresco') paint is applied to dry plaster.

Frescobaldi Girolamo 1583–1643. Italian composer and virtuoso keyboard player, organist at St Peter's, Rome 1608–28. His fame rests on numerous keyboard toccatas, fugues, ricercares, and capriccios in which he advanced keyboard technique and exploited ingenious and daring modulations of key.

fret inlaid ridge of ivory or metal, or circlet of nylon, on the fingerboard of a plucked or bowed string instrument, against which a string is pressed to change pitch.

Freud Lucian 1922– . German-born British painter, one of the greatest contemporary figurative artists. He combines meticulous accuracy with a disquieting intensity, emphasizing the physicality of his subjects, whether nudes, still lifes, or interiors. His portrait of *Francis Bacon* 1952 (Tate Gallery, London) is one of his best-known works. He is a grandson of the Austrian psychiatrist Sigmund Freud.

Freya in Scandinavian mythology, the goddess of married love and the hearth, wife of Odin and mother of Thor. Friday is named after her.

Freysinnet Eugène 1879–1962. French engineer who revealed the full structural potential of ◊reinforced concrete with his technically innovative designs, and later pioneered the use of ◊prestressed concrete. His huge airship hangars in reinforced concrete at Orly 1916–24 (destroyed 1944) were purely functional structures and yet the elegance of their slender, arched forms made them architectural landmarks.

Friedrich Caspar David 1774–1840. German Romantic landscape painter, active mainly in Dresden. He imbued his subjects – mountain scenes and moonlit seas – with poetic melancholy and was later admired by Symbolist painters. *The Cross in the Mountains* 1808 (Gemäldegalerie, Dresden) and *Moonrise over the Sea* 1822 (Nationalgalerie, Berlin) are among his best-known works.

Friel Brian 1929– . Northern Irish dramatist. His first success was with *Philadelphia, Here I Come!* 1964, which dealt with the theme of exile. In 1980 he founded the Field Day Theatre Company, which produced *Translations* 1981, a study of British cultural colonialism in 19th-century Ireland. Other plays include *The Freedom of the City* 1973, about victims of the Ulster conflict, *Faith Healer* 1980, and the critically acclaimed *Dancing at Lughnasa* 1990.

fringe theatre productions that are anti-establishment or experimental, and performed in converted or informal venues (warehouses, pubs), in contrast to subsidized or mainstream commercial theatre. In the UK, the term originated in the 1960s from the activities held on the 'fringe' of the Edinburgh Festival. The US equivalent is off-off-Broadway (off-Broadway is mainstream theatre that is not on Broadway).

Frink Elisabeth 1930–1993. British sculptor of rugged, naturalistic bronzes, mainly based on human and animal forms, for example the *Alcock Brown Memorial* for Manchester airport 1962, *In Memoriam* (heads), and *Running Man* 1980.

Frisch Max 1911– . Swiss dramatist. Inspired by ◊Brecht, his early plays such as *Als der Krieg zu Ende war/When the War Is Over* 1949 are more romantic in tone than his later symbolic dramas, such as *Andorra* 1962, dealing with questions of identity. He wrote *Biedermann und die Brandstifter/The Fire Raisers* 1958.

Frith William Powell 1819–1909. English painter of large contemporary scenes featuring numerous figures and incidental detail. *Ramsgate Sands* 1854 (Royal Collection, London), bought by Queen Victoria, is a fine example, as is *Derby Day* 1856–58 (Tate Gallery, London).

Fröding Gustaf 1860–1911. Swedish lyric poet. Inspired by the European Romantics, radical in politics, engaged in the revolt against Naturalism, he charted new possibilities for Swedish verse by uniting colloquial language with musical form. His themes are often melancholy and despairing, reflecting his history of mental instability. His collections include *Guitarr och dragharmonika/Guitar and Concertina* 1891 and *Stank och flikar/Splashes and Rags* 1896.

frontier literature writing reflecting the US experience of frontier and pioneer life, long central to US literature. The category includes James

Fenimore Cooper's *Leatherstocking Tales*; the frontier humour writing of Artemus Ward, Bret Harte, and Mark Twain; dime novels; Westerns; the travel records of Francis Parkman; and the pioneer romances of Willa Cather. Much modern American writing has been influenced by the frontier theme.

Frost Robert (Lee) 1874–1963. US poet. His accessible, colloquial blank verse, often flavoured with New England speech patterns, is written with an individual voice and penetrating vision. His poems include 'Mending Wall' ('Something there is that does not love a wall'), 'The Road Not Taken', and 'Stopping by Woods on a Snowy Evening' and are collected in *A Boy's Will* 1913, *North of Boston* 1914, *New Hampshire* 1924 (Pulitzer Prize), *Collected Poems* 1930 (Pulitzer Prize), *A Further Range* 1936 (Pulitzer Prize), and *A Witness Tree* 1942 (Pulitzer Prize).

I never dared to be radical when young/
For fear it would make me conservative
when old.

Robert Frost 'Precaution' 1936

Fry Christopher 1907– . English dramatist. He was a leader of the revival of verse drama after World War II with *The Lady's Not for Burning* 1948, *Venus Observed* 1950, and *A Sleep of Prisoners* 1951. He has also written screenplays and made successful translations of Anouilh and Giraudoux.

Indulgences, not fulfilment, is what the
world/Permits us.

Christopher Fry
A Phoenix Too Frequent 1950

Fry Edwin Maxwell 1899–1987. British architect, a pioneer of the ◊Modern Movement in Britain. Representative is his Sun House, Hampstead, London, 1935, with its horizontally banded windows and white stucco finish. Fry worked in partnership with Walter ◊Gropius 1934–36, and with Denys ◊Lasdun (among others) 1951–58. He was ◊Le Corbusier's senior architect at Chandigarh, India 1951–54.

Fry Roger Eliot 1866–1934. English artist and art critic, a champion of Post-Impressionism and an admirer of Cézanne. He was a member of the Bloomsbury Group and founded the ◊Omega Workshops to improve design and to encourage young artists. His critical essays, which were influential in the 1920s and 1930s, are contained in *Vision and Design* 1920.

Frye (Herman) Northrop 1912– . Canadian literary critic, concerned especially with the role and practice of criticism and the relationship between literature and society. His *Anatomy of Criticism* 1957 was very influential.

f-stop in photography, another name for ◊f-number.

Fuentes Carlos 1928– . Mexican novelist, lawyer, and diplomat whose first novel *La región más transparente/Where the Air Is Clear* 1958 encompasses the history of the country from the Aztecs to the present day.

More than other Mexican novelists he presents the frustrated social philosophy of the failed Mexican revolution. He received international attention for *The Death of Artemio Cruz* 1962, *Terra nostra* 1975, and *El gringo viejo/The Old Gringo* 1985. *The gampaign* 1991 is set during the revolutionary wars leading to independence in Latin America.

Fugard Athol 1932– . South African dramatist, director, and actor whose plays often deal with the effects of apartheid. His first successful play was *The Blood Knot* 1961, which was produced in London and New York. This was followed by *Hello and Goodbye* 1965 and *Boesman and Lena* 1969. Other plays include *Statements After an Arrest under the Immorality Act* 1973, *A Lesson from Aloes* 1980, *Master Harold and the Boys* 1982, *A Place With the Pigs* 1987, and *My Children! My Africa!* 1989. His film roles include General Smuts in *Gandhi 1982*.

fugue (Latin 'flight') in music, a contrapuntal form with two or more subjects (principal melodies) for a number of parts, which enter in succession in direct imitation or transposed to a higher or lower key, and may be combined in augmented form (larger note values). It represents the highest form of contrapuntal ingenuity in works such as J S Bach's *Das musikalische Opfer/The Musical Offering* 1747, on a theme of Frederick II of Prussia, and Beethoven's *Grosse Fuge/Great Fugue* for string quartet 1825–26.

Fuller (Richard) Buckminster 1895–1983. US architect, engineer, and social philosopher who embarked on an unorthodox career in an attempt to maximize energy resources through improved technology. In 1947 he invented the lightweight ◊geodesic dome; within 30 years over 50,000 had been built.

He also invented a Dymaxion (a combination of the words 'dynamics' and 'maximum') house 1928 and car 1933 that were inexpensive and utilized his concept of using the least amount of energy output to gain maximum interior space and efficiency, respectively. Among his books are *Ideas and Integrities* 1963, *Utopia or Oblivion* 1969, and *Critical Path* 1981.

Fuller Peter 1947–1990. English art critic who from the mid-1970s attacked the complacency of the art establishment and emphasized tradition over fashion. From 1988 these views, and an increased interest in the spiritual power of art, were voiced in his own magazine *Modern Painters*.

Fuller Roy 1912– . English poet and novelist. His collections of poetry include *Poems* 1939, *Epitaphs and Occasions* 1951, *Brutus's Orchard* 1957, *Collected Poems* 1962, and *The Reign of Sparrows* 1980. Novels include *My Child, My Sister* 1965 and *The Carnal Island* 1970.

Fuller Thomas 1608–1661. English writer. He was chaplain to the Royalist army during the Civil War and, at the Restoration, became the king's chaplain. He wrote a *History of the Holy War* 1639, *Good Thoughts in Bad Times* 1645, its sequel *Good Thoughts in Worse Times* 1647, and the biographical *Worthies of England* 1662.

Security is the mother of danger and the grandmother of destruction.

Thomas Fuller
The Holy State and the Profane State 1642

---

full score in music, a complete transcript of a composition showing all parts individually, as opposed to a **short score** or **piano score** that is condensed into fewer lines of music.

Functionalism in architecture and design, the principle of excluding everything that serves no practical purpose. Central to 20th-century ◊Modernism, the Functionalist ethic developed as a reaction against the 19th-century practice of imitating and combining earlier styles. Its finest achievements are in the realms of ◊Industrial architecture and office furnishings.

Leading exponents of Functionalism were the German ◊Bauhaus school, the Dutch group De ◊Stijl, and the Scandinavians, especially the Swedish and Finnish designers. Prominent architects in the field were ◊Le Corbusier and Walter ◊Gropius.

fundamental in musical acoustics, the lowest ◊harmonic of a musical tone, corresponding to the audible pitch.

funk dance music of black US origin, relying on heavy percussion. Leading exponents include James Brown and George Clinton (1940–).

Initially used for a hard-bop jazz style and as a loose term of approbation in rhythm and blues, funk became a defined category in the 1970s as ◊disco music geared to a black audience, less slick and mechanical than mainstream disco.

Furies in Greek mythology, the Erinyes, appeasingly called the Eumenides ('kindly ones'). They were the daughters of Earth or of Night, represented as winged maidens with serpents twisted in their hair. They punished such crimes as filial disobedience, murder, inhospitality, and oath-breaking, but were also associated with fertility.

Furness Frank 1839–1912. US architect whose eclectic yet highly original work has had considerable influence on the development of his country's architecture. His best-known building is the Pennsylvania Academy of Fine Arts, Philadelphia, 1871–76, which reflects the influence of ◊Viollet-le-Duc while anticipating ◊Post-Modernism, in particular the work of Michael ◊Graves, in its dramatic manipulation of space and idiosyncratic decoration.

furniture movable functional items such as tables, chairs, and beds needed to make a room or a home more comfortable and easier to live and work in. Furniture may be made from a wide variety of materials, including wood, stone, metal, plastic, papier-mâché, glass, cane, and textiles. Styles vary from plain utilitarian to richly ornate, and decoration may be added in the form of carving, inlay, veneer, paint, gilding, or upholstery.

Furniture reflects evolving technology and fashion, and has often been valued as a status symbol. The quantity and variety of furniture, as well as its comfort, have increased in the West, especially in the last 300 years.

history:

The ancient Mediterranean Wood is the most commonly used material for making furniture, but because it decays quite quickly, very little ancient furniture survives. The ancient Egyptians had wooden beds, chairs, tables, and stools, decorated with carving, gilding, or veneer. Egyptian woodworkers are thought to have invented the mortice and tenon joint, which strengthened and stabilized frames of seats and items such as chests. In Classical Greece and Rome only the wealthiest people owned furniture; much of this was made of bronze and stone, some of it carved to look like wood. The feet of chairs and tables in the ancient world were often shaped like animals' paws or hoofs. Couches were an important feature of wealthy Greek and Roman households, since people both reclined on them during meals and slept on them at night. Tables were usually low enough to be stored under couches when not in use. A common style of chair in ancient Greece was the *klismos*, which had curved legs. The Romans adopted many Greek furniture designs, adapting them to suit their own tastes; they liked upholstered chairs and stools, and introduced large tables made from a single slab of marble, supported at either end by carved upright slabs.

Oriental furniture In ancient times furniture was a sign of social rank, and only the very wealthy owned the expertly crafted furniture that was first produced in China during the 3rd century BC. Styles in China later divided into the simple forms found in people's homes, and the ornate items made for emperors and their officials. All furniture, however, was skilfully made, with precisely cut joints which eliminated the need for nails or dowels. Japanese furniture was made of wood, often lacquered and inlaid with shells. It was both sparse and lightweight, consisting mainly of storage cabinets and low tables, since people traditionally both sat and slept on mats on the floor. Furniture in ancient India was more luxurious; a wealthy home might have canopied beds and divans, tables, storage chests for clothes, benches, and chairs, all lavishly draped and upholstered with spreads, curtains, and pillows.

medieval Europe Most of the furniture made before 1300 in Europe was crudely built of painted or gilded wood. Landowners and important clergy travelled a great deal, frequently taking their entire households and furniture along with them. Thus, although furniture was heavy and solid, much of it could be dismantled for carrying from place to place. Folding X-frame chairs with fabric seats were popular, and chests were important pieces of furniture, since they were portable, and could be used for seating as well as storage. Hinges were often made of leather, which was cheap and easily obtained; more valuable chests had decorative iron hinges and locks.

the Renaissance From about 1300, fashionable Italian furnituremakers produced work for their wealthy clients that showed the influence of ancient Greece and Rome, and their ideas soon spread to the rest of Europe. They used finer wood than their predecessors, and decorated their work with intricate carvings, gilding, and paintings. Chests were still important, but were more grandly decorated than anything earlier. The addition of legs to chests led to the development of cupboards and cabinets containing small drawers. Cabinets were built in two parts, with a top section resting on a larger base. Elaborately carved four-poster beds were hung with expensive curtains, often embroidered with flowers, birds, or scenes from Classical mythology.

17th-century Europe Classical designs were still very much in evidence, but with far more decoration added than before. World exploration brought new and exotic materials to European furnituremakers, who inlaid furniture with tropical woods, semi-precious stones, and shells. Walnut replaced oak as the fashionable wood to use, and rich upholstery became a desirable status symbol. Chests of drawers on legs, tall cupboards, and long sideboards developed from Renaissance cabinets and cupboards. Furniture became more and more luxurious, especially under the influence of the French king Louis XIV, whose new furniture for his palace at Versailles featured the new technique of veneering, as well as carving, lacquer, and precious metals, especially silver.

early 18th-century Europe After the grand and heavy Louis XIV style, fashions entered the Rococo period, becoming lighter and more frivo-

lous. Following Louis XIV's death, power passed to a regent, the Duke of Orléans, who preferred more graceful designs known as the Régence style. Under the next king, Louis XV, gentle curves replaced straight lines; legs of furniture were carved into S-curves, the fronts of cupboards and chests of drawers were curved and had decorative, assymetrical bronze and ormolu mounts swirling across them in the form of plants and animals. A low chest of drawers on legs, the commode, was popular in most of Europe. The Chinese-inspired style known as chinoiserie produced such features as wooden furniture carved to look like bamboo and then lacquered. British furniture design was more subdued: the Palladian style continued to use Classical elements and the Queen Anne style was very simple and restrained.

Neo-Classicism In the second half of the 18th century European furniture design turned away from flowing Rococo curves and back to straight lines, symmetry, and Classical motifs; this became known as the Neo-Classical period. In Britain this style was typefied by the elegant designs of Robert Adam, which were decorated with urns, columns, and mouldings based on those of ancient Rome. Mahogany was the fashionable wood of the period. Pale colours were popular, some furniture was painted white and decorated with gilding.

North America Around the end of the 18th century the North American colonies, which until now had followed English fashions, began to develop styles of their own. One notable style was Shaker furniture. Based on traditional English wooden furniture, it is elegant and functional, without any decoration.

early 19th century The Neo-Classical period in France gave way to the Empire style, developed under Napoleonic rule. It was drawn from ancient Roman, Greek, and Egyptian architecture, and was heavy and imposing. Curved legs on furniture were fashionable, as well as elaborately carved sphinxes and characters from Classical mythology. Beds were draped with silk or velvet hung from above to give the impression of a tent. Following Napoleon's exile, the grand Empire style which had been associated with him gradually lost its appeal. In Britain and the USA another variation on the Neo-Classical style was the Regency style. This was similar to the French Empire style, but was lighter and more graceful, and instead of carved decoration, brass inlay became the fashion, along with Oriental-style lacquer.

mid-19th century Much of this period was taken up with revivals of earlier styles. Gothic details were added to Regency furniture; Rococo and Renaissance revivals followed, with decoration and upholstery applied liberally. Mahogany remained popular, but now it was used to make heavy, ornate furniture, often with mirrored doors. In contrast with earlier periods, rooms now tended to be crowded with furniture, resulting in a jumbled profusion of styles, decoration, and ornament.

late 19th century The Arts and Crafts movement was a reaction against mass-produced furniture and textiles. It tried to promote high standards of design in hand-made furniture, producing simpler, solidly made items with subtler decoration that depended more on the workmanship involved than on ostentation. In keeping with the movement's aims, furniture was more likely to be made of oak than the earlier mahogany. At the same time, and to some extent overlapping with Arts and Crafts, Art Nouveau developed, also as a reaction to the heavy revival styles. The fashion now was for flowing, natural shapes, with an extreme tendency towards asymmetry. Both the furniture itself and its decoration featured curving plant shapes, curving water patterns, and wispy, curving female forms with flowing hair. Metalwork and carved wood lent themselves well to Art Nouveau designs. Both the Arts and Crafts movement and Art Nouveau fell from fashion after World War I.

20th century This century has produced a number of furniture styles. This is due not only to the variety of new materials that have become available, such as plastic, plywood, steel, aluminium, and fibreglass, but also to the fact that furniture is almost exclusively mass-produced, making it easier for styles to change more rapidly. There has been a demand for lightweight, inexpensive furniture that is easy to maintain. The ◊Bauhaus school, founded 1919, pioneered the use of tubular steel frames for furniture. Art Deco, between the two World Wars, developed out of the non-naturalistic elements of Art Nouveau, using designs that could be mass-produced. It was unusual among modern styles in that it used non-functional ornament, such as zigzags, circles, triangles, and suns, to decorate furniture. Smaller houses have meant that, as well as simplifying the design of individual pieces of furniture, designers have tended to simplify the look of a room by reducing the amount of furniture in it, moving away from the cluttered 19th-century look and coming closer to the Classical or Japanese style.

Furtwängler (Gustav Heinrich Ernst Martin) Wilhelm 1886–1954. German conductor who ascended rapidly from theatre to opera orchestras in Mannheim 1915–20 and Vienna 1919–24, then to major appointments in Leipzig and with Vienna, and the Berlin Philharmonic Orchestra 1924–54. His interpretations of Wagner, Bruckner, and Beethoven were valued expressions of monumental national grandeur, but he also gave first performances of Bartók, Schoenberg's *Variations for Orchestra* 1928, and Hindemith's opera *Mathis der Maler/Mathis the Painter* 1934, a work implicitly critical of the Nazi regime.

Fuseli Henry (Johann Heinrich Füssli) 1741–1825. British Romantic artist, born in Switzerland. He painted macabre and dreamlike images, such as *The Nightmare* 1781 (Institute of Arts, Detroit), which come close in feelings of horror and the unnatural to the English 'Gothic' novels of his day. His subjects include scenes from Milton and Shakespeare.

He was a perceptive critic and translated ◊Winckelmann's highly influential *Reflections on the Painting and Sculpture of the Greeks.*

fusion in music, a combination of styles; the term usually refers to jazz-rock fusion. Jazz trumpeter Miles Davis began to draw on rock music in the late 1960s, and jazz-rock fusion flourished in the 1970s with bands like Weather Report (formed 1970 in the USA) and musicians like English guitarist John McLaughlin (1942–   ).

Mixing different styles is common in pop music and the spread of world music has accelerated the invention of different fusions.

Futurism literary and artistic movement 1909–14, originating in Paris. The Italian poet ◊Marinetti published the *Futurist Manifesto* 1909 urging Italian artists to join him in Futurism. In their works the Futurists eulogized the modern world and the 'beauty of speed and energy'. Combining the shifting geometric planes of Cubism with vibrant colours, they aimed to capture the dynamism of a speeding car or train by the simultaneous repetition of forms. As a movement Futurism died out during World War I, but the Futurists' exultation in war and violence was seen as an early manifestation of fascism.

Gino Severini painted a topsy-turvy landscape as if seen from the window of a moving train, in *Suburban Train Arriving in Paris* 1915 (Tate Gallery, London), and Giacomo Balla attempted to represent speed in such pictures as *Abstract Speed-wake of a Speeding Car* 1919 (Tate Gallery, London). Umberto Boccioni, a sculptor, froze his figures as if they were several frames of a film moving at once.

The work of many Futurist painters, such as Carlo Carrà and Luigi Russolo (1885–1947), is characterized by forms fragmented by penetrating shafts of light. These, together with their use of colour, infuse a feeling of dynamic motion into their work. ◊Vorticism was a similar movement in Britain 1912–15, glorifying modern technology, energy, and violence.

Fyffe Will 1885–1947. Scottish music-hall comedian remembered for his vivid character sketches and for his song *I Belong to Glasgow.*

But when I get a couple of drinks on a Saturday, /Glasgow belongs to me.

Will Fyffe 'I Belong to Glasgow'

scale. His first novel, *The Recognitions* 1955, explores the idea of forgery in social and sexual relations and in art. It was followed by the encyclopedic *JR* 1975, written entirely in dialogue, which deals with money and power, and *Carpenter's Gothic* 1985.

Gaia or *Ge* in Greek mythology, the goddess of the Earth. She sprang from primordial Chaos and herself produced Uranus, by whom she was the mother of the ◊Cyclopes and ◊Titans.

Gaillard Slim (Bulee) 1916–1991. US jazz singer, songwriter, actor, and musician. A light, humorous performer, he claimed to have invented his own language, Vout (nonsense syllables as in scat singing). His first hit was 'Flat Foot Floogie' 1938.

Gable (William) Clark 1901–1960. US actor. A star for more than 30 years in 90 films, he played romantic roles such as Rhett Butler in *Gone With the Wind* 1939. His other films include *The Painted Desert* 1931 (his first), *It Happened One Night* 1934 (Academy Award), *Mutiny on the Bounty* 1935, and *The Misfits* 1960. He was nicknamed the 'King' of Hollywood.

Gabo Naum. Adopted name of Naum Neemia Pevsner 1890–1977. US abstract sculptor, born in Russia. One of the leading exponents of ◊Constructivism, he left the USSR for Germany 1922 and taught at the ◊Bauhaus in Berlin, a key centre of design. He lived in Paris and England in the 1930s, then settled in the USA 1946. He was one of the first artists to make ◊kinetic sculpture and often used transparent coloured plastics. Many of his drawings and sculptures are in the Tate Gallery, London.

Gabrieli Giovanni *c.* 1555–1612. Italian composer who succeeded his uncle Andrea Gabrieli (*c.* 1533–1585) as organist of St Mark's basilica, Venice. His sacred and secular works include numerous madrigals, motets, and the antiphonal *Sacrae Symphoniae* 1597, sacred canzonas and sonatas for brass choirs, strings, and organ, in spatial counterpoint.

Gaddi family of Italian painters in Florence. *Gaddo Gaddi* (*c.* 1250–*c.* 1330) was a painter and mosaicist. His son *Taddeo* (*c.* 1300–*c.* 1366) was the most important artist of the family. Giotto's pupil and assistant for 24 years, he developed a style which combined his master's monumentality of form with a delicate sense of colour. An example of his work is the fresco cycle *Life of the Virgin* (completed 1338) in Santa Croce, Florence. Taddeo's son *Agnolo* (active 1369–96) also painted frescoes in Santa Croce, *The Story of the Cross* 1380s, and produced panel paintings in characteristic pale pastel colours.

Gaddis William 1922– . US novelist. He is a distinctive and satirical stylist of non-psychological work, often written on a vast, perplexing

Gainsborough Thomas 1727–1788. English landscape and portrait painter. In 1760 he settled in Bath and painted society portraits. In 1774 he went to London and became one of the original members of the Royal Academy. He was one of the first British artists to follow the Dutch example in painting realistic landscapes rather than imaginative Italianate scenery.

Born in Sudbury, Suffolk, Gainsborough began to paint while still at school. In London he learned etching and painting, but remained largely self-taught. His sitters included Sir Charles Holte, the actor David Garrick, the royal family, the Welsh actress Mrs Siddons, the writer Dr Johnson, the politician Edmund Burke, and the dramatist Richard Sheridan.

Galahad in Arthurian legend, one of the knights of the Round Table. Galahad succeeded in the quest for the ◊Holy Grail because of his virtue. He was the son of ◊Lancelot of the Lake.

Galatea in Greek mythology, a sea ◊nymph who loved a Sicilian shepherd by the name of Acis. When he was killed by his rival, the Cyclops Polyphemus, Galatea transformed her lover's blood into the river Acis. Pygmalion, a king of Cyprus, made a statue (later named Galatea) that he married after it was brought to life by the goddess Aphrodite.

Gallant Mavis (née Young) 1922– . Canadian short-story writer and novelist, based in Paris. A regular contributor to the *New Yorker* magazine, she has published two novels and increasingly acclaimed collections of short fiction, notably *The Pegnitz Junction* 1973, and *From the Fifteenth District* 1979, set in various European countries.

Her work, which is distinguished by adroitly shifting points of view, perhaps influenced by cinema technique, often deals with the themes of cultural isolation and displacement.

Gallé Emile 1846–1904. French Art Nouveau glassmaker. He produced glass in sinuous forms or rounded, solid-looking shapes almost as heavy as stone, typically decorated with flowers or leaves in colour on colour.

After training in Europe, he worked at his father's glass factory and eventually took it over. He was a founder of the Ecole de Nancy, a group of French Art Nouveau artists who drew inspiration from his 1890s work and adopted his style of decoration and techniques.

Gallegos Rómulo 1884–1969. Venezuelan politician and writer. He was Venezuela's first democratically elected president 1948 before being overthrown by a military coup the same year. He was also a professor of philosophy and literature. His novels include *La trepadora/The Climber* 1925 and *Doña Bárbara* 1929.

Galliano John 1960– . British fashion designer whose elegant and innovative designs are often inspired by historical motifs (for example, 'Dickensian' clothing), the elements of which he redesigns to create progressive collections. In 1990 he designed the costumes for a production of Ashley Page's ballet *Corrulao*, performed by the Ballet Rambert. In the same year he began showing his collections in Paris.

galliard spirited 16th-century court dance in triple time, with an upbeat, originating from Lombardy, Italy. It was a very athletic dance, full of complicated steps, mainly performed by couples and popular in the court of Elizabeth I of England. It became increasingly lascivious in the 17th century. The music for the galliard is often paired with that for a ◊pavane; it is based on the same melody.

Gallico Paul (William) 1897–1976. US author. Originally a sports columnist, he began writing fiction in 1936. His many books include *The Snow Goose* 1941.

Galsworthy John 1867–1933. English novelist and dramatist whose work examines the social issues of the Victorian period. He wrote *The Forsyte Saga* 1922 and its sequel *A Modern Comedy* 1929. His other novels include *The Country House* 1907 and *Fraternity* 1909; plays include *The Silver Box* 1906.

Galsworthy first achieved recognition with *The Man of Property* 1906, the first instalment of the *Forsyte* series, which includes *In Chancery* and *To Let*. Soames Forsyte, the central character, is the embodiment of Victorian values and feeling for property, and the wife whom he also 'owns' – Irene — was based on Galsworthy's wife. Later additions to the series are *A Modern Comedy* 1929, which contained *The White Monkey*, *The Silver Spoon*, and *Swan Song*, and the short stories *On Forsyte Change* 1930. He was awarded the Nobel Prize for Literature 1932.

Galt John 1779–1839. Scottish novelist, author of *Annals of the Parish* 1821, in which he portrays the life of a Lowlands village, using the local dialect.

Born in Ayrshire, he moved to London 1804 and lived in Canada 1826–29. He founded the Canadian town of Guelph, and Galt, on the Grand River, Ontario, was named after him.

Galway James 1939– . Irish flautist, born in Belfast. He palyed with the London Symphony Orchestra 1966, Royal Philharmonic Orchestra 1967–69, and was principal flautist with the Berlin Philharmonic Orchestra 1969–75, before taking up a solo career.

gamba, da (Italian 'on the leg') in music, suffix used to distinguish a viol played resting on the leg from a member of the violin family played under the chin, or 'on the arm' (viola da braccia).

gamelan Indonesian orchestra employing tuned gongs, xylophones, metallophones (with bars of metal), cymbals, drums, flutes, and fiddles, the music of which has inspired such Western composers as Debussy, Colin McPhee, John Cage, Benjamin Britten, and Philip Glass.

Originally court music with Hindustan influences, it withdrew under Dutch colonial administration to rural communities, and was played as an accompaniment to ceremonial occasions, dancing, and puppet theatre. The music is improvised and based on interlocking tonal and rhythmic patterns. Javanese gamelan music uses a seven-tone *pelog* scale, Balinese preferring a five-tone *slendro* scale. The scales of gongs vary in precise pitch, but incorporate matched pairs that deviate slightly in pitch.

Gance Abel 1889–1981. French film director of grandiose melodramas, whose *Napoléon* 1927 was one of the most ambitious silent epic films. It features colour tinting and triple-screen sequences, as well as multiple-exposure shots, and purported to suggest that Napoleon was the fulfilment of the French Revolution.

Ganesh Hindu god, son of Siva and Parvati; he is represented as elephant-headed and is worshipped as a remover of obstacles.

gangsta rap hardcore ◊rap-music style reflecting the violent street life of the US ghettos. Ice Cube (1968–) put gangsta rap in the pop charts with such albums as *Amerikkka's Most Wanted* 1990 and *The Predator* 1992, and Ice-T with *Original Gangsta* 1991.

Ganymede in Greek mythology, a youth so beautiful he was chosen as cupbearer to Zeus.

garage band rock group that uses limited musical means (basic line-up, few chords) for a rough, aggressive, or subversive effect. Closely related to ◊punk and ◊noise, it is not a clearly defined genre; the term came into use in the 1960s. The Stooges (see Iggy ◊Pop) have been cited as the ultimate garage band, and the recording '96 Tears' 1966 by ? and the Mysterians (sic) is considered a classic garage record.

Garbo Greta. Stage name of Greta Lovisa Gustafsson 1905–1990. Swedish-born US film actress. She went to the USA 1925, and her captivating beauty and leading role in *Flesh and the Devil* 1927 made her one of Hollywood's most popular stars. Her later films include *Mata Hari* 1931, *Grand Hotel* 1932, *Queen Christina* 1933, *Anna Karenina* 1935, *Camille* 1936, and *Ninotchka* 1939. Her ethereal qualities and romantic mystery on the screen intermingled with her seclusion in private life. She retired 1941.

García Lorca Federico, Spanish poet. See ◊Lorca, Federico García.

García Márquez Gabriel 1928– . Colombian novelist. His sweeping novel *Cien años de soledad/One Hundred Years of Solitude* 1967 (which tells the story of a family over a period of six generations) is an example of magic realism, a technique used to heighten the intensity of realistic portrayal of social and political issues by introducing grotesque or fanciful material. Nobel Prize for Literature 1982.

His other books include *El amor en los tiempos del cólera/Love in the Time of Cholera* 1985 and *The General in His Labyrinth* 1991, which describes the last four months of Simón Bolívar's life.

Garcilaso de la Vega 1503–1536. Spanish poet. A soldier, he was a member of Charles V's expedition 1535 to Tunis; he was killed in battle at Nice. His verse, some of the greatest of the Spanish Renaissance, includes sonnets, songs, and elegies, often on the model of Petrarch.

garden city in the UK, a town built in a rural area and designed to combine town and country advantages, with its own industries, controlled developments, private and public gardens, and cultural centre. The idea was proposed by Ebenezer ◊Howard, who in 1899 founded the Garden City Association, which established the first garden city: Letchworth in Hertfordshire.

A second, Welwyn, 35 km/22 mi from London, was started 1919. Similar schemes in Europe and in the USA have not generally kept the economic structure or the industrial self-sufficiency of the rural belt which formed an integral part of Howard's original idea. The New Towns Act 1946 provided the machinery for developing new towns on some of the principles advocated by Howard (for example Stevenage, begun 1947).

Gardner Ava 1922–1990. US film actress, a sensuous star in such films as *The Killers* 1946, *Pandora and the Flying Dutchman* 1951, and *The Barefoot Contessa* 1954, a tragically slanted Cinderella tale of a Romany girl who becomes an international celebrity. Her later roles include that of Lillie Langtry in *The Life and Times of Judge Roy Bean* 1972. She remained active in films until the 1980s, when she retired to London.

Gardner Erle Stanley 1889–1970. US author of best-selling crime fiction. He created the charac-

ter of the lawyer-detective Perry Mason, who was later featured in films and on television. Originally a lawyer, Gardner gave up his practice with the success of the first Perry Mason stories.

Gardner Helen 1908–1986. British scholar and critic. She edited the poetry and prose of Donne and other metaphysical poets and the *New Oxford Book of English Verse* 1972. She was Merton Professor of English Literature at Oxford 1966–75. She wrote a study of T S Eliot's *Four Quartets* published 1978.

Gardner Isabella Stewart 1840–1924. US art collector and founder of the Isabella Stewart Gardner Museum in Boston, USA. As an art collector, she specialized in the works of the Renaissance and of the Dutch masters. Her private art gallery in Boston was opened as a public museum 1903.

Gardner John 1917– . English composer. Professor at the Royal Academy of Music from 1956, he has produced a symphony 1951; the opera *The Moon and Sixpence* 1957, based on a Somerset Maugham novel; and other works, including film music.

gargoyle spout projecting from the roof gutter of a building, often a church or cathedral, with the purpose of directing water away from the wall. The term is usually applied to the ornamental forms found in Gothic architecture; these were carved in stone in the form of fantastic animals, angels, or human heads.

Garland Judy. Stage name of Frances Gumm 1922–1969. US singer and actress whose performances are marked by a compelling intensity. Her films include *The Wizard of Oz* 1939 (which featured the tune that was to become her theme song, 'Over the Rainbow'), *Babes in Arms* 1939, *Strike Up the Band* 1940, *Meet Me in St Louis* 1944, *Easter Parade* 1948, *A Star is Born* 1954, and *Judgment at Nuremberg* 1961.

She began her acting career 1935 in the Andy Hardy series. She was the mother of actress and singer Liza Minnelli.

Garner Helen 1942– . Australian novelist, journalist, and short-story writer. Her early experience as a secondary school teacher has helped her to engage realistically with the inner-city life of Melbourne. She won the National Book Council's Award for her novel *Monkey Grip* 1977, which was filmed 1981. Her other books include *Honour and Other People's Children* 1980 and *The Children's Bach* 1984.

Garret Almeida 1799–1854. Portuguese poet, novelist, and dramatist. As a liberal, in 1823 he was forced into 14 years of exile. His works, which he saw as a singlehanded attempt to create a national literature, include the prose *Viagens na Minha Terra/Travels in My Homeland* 1843–46 and the tragedy *Frei Luis de Sousa* 1843.

Garrick David 1717–1779. English actor and theatre manager. From 1747 he became joint licensee of the Drury Lane Theatre with his own company, and instituted a number of significant theatrical conventions including concealed stage lighting and banishing spectators from the stage. He played Shakespearean characters such as Richard III, King Lear, Hamlet, and Benedick, and collaborated with George Colman (1732–1794) in writing the play *The Clandestine Marriage* 1766. He retired from the stage 1766, but continued as a manager.

Garshin Vsevolod 1855–1888. Russian short-story writer. He served in the Russo-Turkish War and was invalided home 1878. His stories, fewer than 20, include allegories, fairy tales, and war stories, among them 'The Red Flower' 1883 and 'Four Days' 1877, set during the war.

Gaskell 'Mrs' (Elizabeth Cleghorn, born Stevenson) 1810–1865. English novelist. Her most popular book, *Cranford* 1853, is the study of small, close-knit circle in a small town, modelled on Knutsford, Cheshire. Her other books, which often deal with social concerns, include include *Mary Barton* 1848, *North and South* 1855, *Sylvia's Lovers* 1863–64, and the unfinished *Wives and Daughters* 1866. Also of note is her frank and sympathetic biography of her friend Charlotte ◊Brontë 1857.

Gass William (Howard) 1924– . US experimental writer and theoretician. His novels, which parody genres and use typography and layout variations to emphasize the physical reality of the book, include *Omensetter's Luck* 1966 and *Willie Master's Lonesome Wife* 1968. Other works include the short-story collection *In the Heart of the Heart of the Country* 1968, and two volumes of criticism *Fiction and the Figures of Life* 1970, and *The World Within the Word* 1978.

Gaudí Antonio 1852–1926. Spanish architect distinguished for his flamboyant ◊Art Nouveau style. Gaudí worked almost exclusively in Barcelona, designing both domestic and industrial buildings. He introduced colour, unusual materials, and audacious technical innovations. His spectacular Church of the Holy Family, Barcelona, begun 1883, is still under construction.

His design for Casa Milá, a blocks of flats in Barcelona (begun 1905), is wildly imaginative, with an undulating façade, vertically thrusting wrought-iron balconies, and a series of sculpted shapes that protrude from the roof. The central feature of his Parque Güell in Barcelona is a snakelike seat faced with a mosaic of broken tiles and cutlery.

Gaudier-Brzeska Henri (Henri Gaudier) 1891–1915. French artist, active in London from 1911; he is regarded as one of the outstanding sculptors of his generation. He studied art in Bristol, Nuremberg, and Munich, and became a member of the English Vorticist movement, which sought to reflect the energy of the industrial age through an angular, semi-abstract style. From 1913 his sculptures showed the influence of Brancusi, Jacob Epstein, and primitive art. He was killed in action during World War I.

Gauguin Paul 1848–1903. French Post-Impressionist painter. Going beyond the Impressionists' notion of reality, he sought a more direct experience of life in the rich colours of the South Sea islands and the magical rites of its people. His work, often heavily symbolic and decorative, is characterized by his sensuous use of pure colours. Among his paintings is *Le Christe jaune/The Yellow Christ* 1889 (Albright-Knox Art Gallery, Buffalo, New York State).

Influenced by Symbolism, he chose subjects reflecting his interest in the beliefs of other cultures. He made brief visits to Martinique and Panama 1887–88, and in 1888 spent two troubled months with van Gogh in Arles. He lived in Tahiti 1891–93 and 1895–1901 and from 1901 in the Marquesas Islands, where he died. It was while in Tahiti that he painted one of his best-known works *Where Do We Come From? What Are We? Where Are We Going?* 1897 (Museum of Fine Art, Boston).

Gaultier Jean-Paul 1952– . French fashion designer who, after working for Pierre Cardin, launched his first collection 1978, designing clothes that went against fashion trends, inspired by London's street style. Humorous and showy, his clothes are among the most influential in the French ready-to-wear market. He designed the costumes for Peter Greenaway's film *The Cook, the Thief, His Wife and Her Lover* 1989 and the singer Madonna's outfits for her world tour 1990.

Gautier Théophile 1811–1872. French Romantic poet whose later works emphasized the perfection of form and the polished beauty of language and imagery (for example, *Emaux et camées/Enamels and Cameos* 1852). He was also a novelist (*Mlle de Maupin* 1835) and later turned to journalism.

gauze diaphanous woven fabric of silk, cotton, fine worsted yarn, or other fibre. Paired warp threads are twisted between each insert of weft, to achieve an open structure.

gavotte light-hearted dance in four/four time, originating from the Pays de Gap, France, whose inhabitants were called Gavots. Originally a folk dance, it was adopted by Marie Antoinette's court. It continued to develop ever more complicated steps until it could be performed only by professional dancers. The music for or derived from the gavotte, which starts on the upbeat, is found in the classical ◊suite.

Gawain in Arthurian legend, one of the knights of the Round Table who participated in the quest for the ◊Holy Grail. He is the hero of the 14th-century epic poem *Sir Gawayne and the Greene Knight*.

Gay John 1685–1732. British poet and dramatist. He wrote *Trivia* 1716, a verse picture of 18th-century London. His *The Beggar's Opera* 1728, a 'Newgate pastoral' using traditional songs and telling of the love of Polly for highwayman Captain Macheath, was an extraordinarily popular success. Its satirical political touches led to the banning of *Polly*, a sequel.

He was a friend of the writers Alexander ◊Pope and John Arbuthnot.

An open foe may prove a curse,/ But a pretended friend is worse.

John Gay *The Shepherd's Dog and the Wolf*

Gaye Marvin 1939–1984. US soul singer and songwriter whose hits, including 'Stubborn Kinda Fellow' 1962, 'I Heard It Through the Grapevine' 1968, and 'What's Goin' On' 1971, exemplified the Detroit ◊Motown sound.

Ge in Greek mythology, an alternative name for ◊Gaia, goddess of the Earth.

Geddes Patrick 1854–1932. Scottish town planner who established the importance of surveys, research work, and properly planned 'diagnoses before treatment'. His major work is *City Development* 1904. His protégé was Lewis ◊Mumford.

Geertgen tot Sint Jans *c.* 1460–1490. Dutch painter, of whom little is known; his name means 'Little Gerard of (the Order of) St John'. Of the few works firmly attributed to him, two best exhibit his characteristic charm and delicacy: *The Nativity* (National Gallery, London), a night scene lit solely by the radiance of the infant Jesus, and *St John in the Wilderness* (Staatliche Museum, Berlin), which shows a subtle mastery of landscape (both dated around the 1480s).

Gehry Frank 1929– . US architect, based in Los Angeles. His architecture approaches abstract art in its use of collage and montage techniques. His own experimental house in Santa Monica 1977, Edgemar Shopping Center and Museum, Santa Monica 1988, and the Vitra Furniture Museum, Weil am Rhein, Switzerland 1989 – his first building in Europe – demonstrate his vitality.

Geisel Theodor Seuss; better known as *Dr Seuss*. 1904–1991. US author of children's books including *And to Think That I Saw It on Mulberry Street* 1937 and the classic *Horton Hatches the Egg* 1940. After winning Academy Awards for documentary films 1946 and 1947, he returned to writing children's books, including *Horton Hears a Who* 1954 and *The Cat in the Hat* 1957.

Born in Springfield, Massachusetts, USA, and educated at Dartmouth, Geisel began his career as a cartoonist and illustrator. He later wrote books for adults, including *Oh, the Places You'll Go!* 1989.

Geldof Bob 1954– . Irish rock singer, leader of the group the Boomtown Rats 1975–86. In the mid-1980s he instigated the charity Band Aid, which raised about £60 million for famine relief, primarily for Ethiopia.

In partnership with musician Midge Ure (1953–), Geldof gathered together many pop celebrities of the day to record Geldof's song 'Do They Know It's Christmas?' 1984, donating all proceeds to charity (it sold 7 million copies). He followed it up with two simultaneous celebrity concerts 1985 under the name Live Aid, one in London and one in Philadelphia, which were broadcast live worldwide.

But Prime Minister, I don't think that the possible death of 120 million people is a matter for charity. It is a matter of moral imperative.

Bob Geldof to Margaret Thatcher on the threatened famine in Africa 1985

Genée Adeline. Stage name of Anina Jensen 1878–1970. Danish-born British dancer, president of the Royal Academy of Dancing 1920–54. Her most famous role was Swanilda in *Coppélia*, which she danced with infectious vivacity and charm.

Born in Aarhus, she settled in England 1897. Her work was commemorated by the *Adeline Genée Theatre* 1967–89, East Grinstead, Sussex.

Genet Jean 1910–1986. French dramatist, novelist, and poet. His turbulent life and early years spent in prison are reflected in his drama, characterized by ritual, role-play, and illusion, in which his characters come to act out their bizarre and violent fantasies. His plays include *Les Bonnes/The Maids* 1947, *Le Balcon/The Balcony* 1957, and two plays dealing with the Algerian situation: *Les Nègres/The Blacks* 1959 and *Les Paravents/The Screens* 1961. His best-known novels include *Notre Dame des fleurs/Our Lady of the Flowers* 1944 and *Miracle de la rose/Miracle of the Rose* 1946.

God is white.

Jean Genet *The Blacks*

---

genre a particular kind of work within an art form, differentiated by its structure, content, or style. For instance, the novel is a literary genre and the historical novel is a genre of the novel. The Western is a genre of film, and the symphonic poem is a musical genre.

genre painting the depiction of scenes (often domestic) from everyday life. Genre paintings were enormously popular in the Netherlands and Flanders in the 17th century; Vermeer, de Hooch, and Brouwer were leading exponents.

Gentile da Fabriano *c.* 1370–1427. Italian painter of frescoes and altarpieces, one of the most important exponents of the International Gothic style. Gentile was active in Venice, Florence, Siena, Orvieto, and Rome and collaborated with the artists Pisanello and Jacopo Bellini. His *Adoration of the Magi* 1423 (Uffizi, Florence) is typically rich in detail and colour.

Gentileschi Artemisia 1593–*c.* 1652. Italian painter, born in Rome. She trained under her father Orazio Gentileschi, but her work is more melodramatic than his. Active in England, Florence, and Rome, she settled in Naples from about 1630 and focused on macabre and grisly subjects popular during her day, such as *Judith Decapitating Holofernes* about 1620 (Uffizi, Florence).

Gentileschi Orazio 1563–1639. Italian painter, born in Pisa. He was a follower and friend of Caravaggio, whose influence can be seen in the dramatic treatment of light and shade in *The Annunciation* 1623 (Galleria Sabauda, Turin). From 1626 he lived in London, painting for King Charles I.

He painted a series of ceilings for the Queen's House at Greenwich, now in Marlborough House, London.

Gentlemen Prefer Blondes witty 1925 novel by US writer Anita ◊Loos that tells the story of the classic female gold-digger Lorelei Lee, filmed 1953 with Marilyn Monroe and Jane Russell. The novel's 1928 sequel was called *But Gentlemen Marry Brunettes*.

geodesic dome hemispherical dome, a type of ◊space-frame, whose surface is formed out of short rods arranged in triangles. The rods lie on geodesics (the shortest lines joining two points on a curved surface). This type of dome allows large spaces to be enclosed using the minimum of materials, and was patented by US architect and engineer Buckminster ◊Fuller 1954.

Geoffrey of Monmouth *c.* 1100–1154. Welsh writer and chronicler. While a canon at Oxford, he wrote *Historia Regum Britanniae/History of the Kings of Britain* about 1139, which included accounts of the semi-legendary kings Lear, Cymbeline, and Arthur, and *Vita Merlini*, a life of the legendary wizard.

George Stefan 1868–1933. German poet. His early poetry was inspired by French ◊Symbolism, but his concept of himself as regenerating the

German spirit first appears in *Das Teppich des Lebens/The Tapestry of Life* 1899, and later in *Der siebente Ring/The Seventh Ring* 1907. *Das neue Reich/The New Empire* 1928 shows his realization that World War I had not had the right purifying effect on German culture. He rejected Nazi overtures and emigrated to Switzerland 1933.

georgette thin woven silk fabric, often of crepe yarn or construction.

Georgian period of English architecture, furniture-making, and decorative art between 1714 and 1830. The architecture is mainly Classical in style, although external details and interiors were often rich in Rococo carving. Furniture was frequently made of mahogany and satinwood, and mass production became increasingly common; designers included Thomas Chippendale, George Hepplewhite, and Thomas Sheraton. The silver of this period is particularly fine, and ranges from the earlier, simple forms to the ornate, and from the Neo-Classical style of Robert Adam to the later, more decorated pre-Victorian taste. See also ◊English architecture.

Gerhard Roberto 1896–1970. Spanish-born British composer. He studied with Enrique Granados and Arnold Schoenberg and settled in England 1939, where he composed twelve-tone works in Spanish style. He composed the *Symphony No 1* 1952–55, followed by three more symphonies and chamber music incorporating advanced techniques. His opera *The Duenna* 1947 received its British premiere 1992 (it was premiered in Wiesbaden, Germany, 1957).

Gerhardie William (born Gerhardi) 1895–1977. British novelist, born in Russia. His novels include *Futility: A Novel on Russian Themes* 1922 and *The Polyglots* 1925, both of which draw on his Russian upbringing.

Géricault Théodore (Jean Louis André) 1791–1824. French Romantic painter and graphic artist. *The Raft of the Medusa* 1819 (Louvre, Paris) was notorious in its day for exposing a relatively recent scandal in which shipwrecked sailors had been cut adrift and left to drown. His other works include *The Derby at Epsom* 1821 (Louvre, Paris) and pictures of cavalry. He also painted portraits, including remarkable studies of the insane, such as *A Kleptomaniac* 1822–23 (Musée des Beaux Arts, Ghent).

With the brush we merely tint, while the imagination alone produces colour.

Théodore Géricault letter *c.* 1821

German Edward 1862–1936. English composer. He is remembered for his operettas *Merrie England* 1902 and *Tom Jones* 1907, and he wrote many other instrumental, orchestral, and vocal works.

German architecture the architecture of Germany which, in its early history and development, takes in that of Austria and the former Czechoslovakia. Little evidence remains of Roman occupation. The earliest buildings of note date from the reign of Charlemagne (742–814), for example, the chapel at Aachen 805.

Romanesque The abbey church of St Riquier at Centual 799 provided a model from which the German Romanesque style developed, reaching its peak in the cathedrals of Mainz 1081 and Worms about 1175, and in the many Romanesque churches (with distinctive trefoil-shaped east ends) that existed in Cologne prior to the city's devastation in World War II.

Gothic The German Gothic style was derived from northern French Gothic, but evolved its own distinctive character, incorporating elements of the hall churches of Westphalia and Bavaria, which had side aisles equal in height to the nave, as well as elements of the brick town halls of NE Germany, such as the late-14th-century example at Torun (now in Poland). Examples range from St Elizabeth at Marburg 1237, a hall church with trefoil-shaped east end and northern French Gothic features, to the pure High Gothic east end of Cologne Cathedral 1248.

Renaissance The Renaissance was influential only spasmodically in Germany, its flow being interrupted by the Thirty Years' War 1618–48. However, the works of Elias Holl (1573–1646), especially his town hall in Augsburg 1615–20, are significant.

Baroque and Rococo Around 1700 Italian Baroque made itself felt in southern Germany, culminating in the works of Fischer von Erlach and Hildebrandt in Vienna and in the Zwinger pavilion in Dresden 1709 by Matthaeus Pöppelmann (1662–1736). In church building the brothers Cosmas (1686–1739) and Eqid (1692–1750) Asam created a masterpiece of German Baroque in the tiny St John Nepomuk in Munich 1733–46. Balthasar Neumann outstepped his Baroque predecessors, creating such Rococo masterpieces as the palace at Würzburg 1720–44.

Neo-Classicism In northern Germany Neo-Classicism developed in reaction to the excesses of the Rococo style, manifesting itself first in the designs of Friedrich Gilly (1772–1800), and later in the work of Karl Friedrich Schinkel, active mostly in Berlin, and Leo von Klenze (1784–1864) in Munich. Klenze's Alte Pinakothek 1826–36 is one of the seminal works of museum building. Klenze also worked in styles other than the Neo-Classical and his architecture marks the beginning of an eclectic approach in German building that was to last until the end of the century.

20th-century trends At the start of the 20th century many of the ideas at the heart of modern architecture found expression in Germany. The machine aesthetic of Peter Behrens gave rise to the Bauhaus school and the early works of Walter Gropius and Mies van der Rohe, later classed as hallmarks of the International Style. Expressionism in architecture was also influenced by Behrens and developed by Erich Mendelsohn and Hans Pöelzig (1869–1936). Most of these architects were to flee Germany in the years immediately preceding World War II, leaving the way clear for the totalitarian Neo-Classicism of the Nazi architect, Albert Speer.

In the years of reconstruction following the war many towns and cities were rebuilt in an orthodox Modernist style, the historic centre of Dresden being one exception. Distinctive voices did emerge, however, among them that of the Expressionist Hans Scharoun. The Berlin Philharmonic 1956–83 is his masterpiece. Through the 1970s and 1980s the works of Oswald Mathias Ungers (1929–) and Joseph Paul Kleihues (1933–) have been notable for creating a form of lyrical Rationalism. The German Architecture Museum, Frankfurt 1979–84, by Ungers is a good example.

German art painting and sculpture in the Germanic north of Europe from the early Middle Ages.

Middle Ages A revival of the arts was fostered by the emperor Charlemagne in the early 9th century. In the late 10th and early 11th centuries new styles emerged under the Ottoman emperors. German artists produced remarkable work in Romanesque and, later, Gothic styles. Wood carving played a major religious role in art.

15th century The painter Stefan Lochner, active in Cologne, excelled in the International Gothic style. Sculptors included Hans Mültscher (c. 1400–57) and the wood carvers Veit Stoss and Tilman Riemenschneider, active in Nuremberg and Poland.

16th century The outstanding figure of the Renaissance in Germany was Albrecht Dürer; other painters included Hans Baldung Grien, Lucas Cranach, Albrecht Altdorfer, Mathias Grünewald, and Hans Holbein.

17th and 18th centuries Huge wall and ceiling paintings in both Baroque and Rococo style decorated new churches and princely palaces. Neo-Classicism was introduced by Anton Mengs.

19th century Caspar David Friedrich was a pioneer of Romantic landscape painting in the early 19th century. At the turn of the century came the Jugendstil style (corresponding to French Art Nouveau) and the artists' colony at Worpswede.

20th century The movement known as *die Brücke* (the Bridge) launched German Expressionism, its exponents using the vivid colours of the French Fauves. It was followed by the Munich Expressionist group *der Blaue Reiter* (Blue Rider). After World War I, Otto Dix, George Grosz, and Max Beckmann developed satirical styles, based on Expressionism and *Neue*

Sachlichkeit. The Bauhaus school of design, emphasizing the dependence of form on function, had enormous impact abroad. The painter Max Ernst moved to Paris and became a founding member of Surrealism. From the 1930s avant-garde movements were denounced as degenerate (see ◊Degenerate Art). Artists of international note since 1945 include Joseph Beuys and Anselm Kiefer.

German literature the literature of Germany.

Old High German The most substantial extant work of the period is the fragmentary alliterative poem the *Hildebrandslied* (about 800).

Middle High German There was a flowering of the vernacular, which had been forced into subservience to Latin after the early attempts at encouragement by Charlemagne. The court epics of Hartmann von Aue (*c.* 1170–1215), Gottfried von Strassburg (flourished 1200), and Wolfram von Eschenbach (flourished early 13th century) were modelled on French style and material, but the folk-epic, the *Nibelungenlied*, revived the spirit of the old heroic Germanic sagas. Adopted from France and Provence, the *Minnesang* reached its height in the lyric poetry of Walther von der Vogelweide (*c.* 1170–*c.* 1230).

Early Modern This period begins in the 16th century with the standard of language set by Martin Luther's Bible. Also in this century came the climax of popular drama in the *Fastnachtsspiel* as handled by the songwriter Hans Sachs. In the later 16th and early 17th centuries French influence was renewed and English influence, by troupes of players, was introduced. Martin Opitz's *Buch von der deutschen Poeterey* 1624, in which he advocates the imitation of foreign models, epitomizes the German Renaissance, which was followed by the Thirty Years' War, vividly described in H J C Grimmelshausen's *Simplicissimus* 1669.

18th century French Classicism predominated, but Romanticism was anticipated by the Germanic *Messias* 1748–73 of Klopstock. Both the playwright G E Lessing and the critic J G Herder were admirers of Shakespeare, and Herder's enthusiasm inaugurated the *Sturm und Drang* phase which emphasized individual inspiration. His collection of folk songs was symptomatic of the feeling that inspired the ballad *Lenore* 1773 by Gottfried Bürger (1747–1794). The greatest representatives of the Classical period at the end of the century were Wolfgang von Goethe and Friedrich Schiller.

19th century In the early years of the century the Romantic school flourished, its theories based on the work of J L Teck and the brothers August and Friedrich von Schlegel. Major Romantics included Novalis, Achim von Arnim, Clemens Brentano, J F von Eichendorff, Adelbert von Chamisso, J L Uhland, and E T A Hoffmann. With the playwrights Heinrich von Kleist and Franz Grillparzer, stress on the poetic element in

drama ended, and the psychological aspect soon received greater emphasis. Emerging around 1830 was the 'Young German' movement, with Heinrich Heine among its leaders, which the authorities tried to suppress. Other 19th-century writers include Jeremias Gotthelf (1797–1854), who recounted stories of peasant life; the psychological novelist Friedrich Spielhagen (1829–1911); poets and novella writers Gottfried Keller and Theodor Storm (1817–1888); and the realist novelists Wilhelm Raabe (1831–1910) and Theodor Fontane (1818–1883). Influential in literature, as in politics and economics, were Karl Marx and Friedrich Nietzsche.

20th century Outstanding writers included the lyric poets Stefan George and Rainer Maria Rilke; the poet and dramatist Hugo von Hofmannsthal (1874–1929); and the novelists Thomas and Heinrich Mann, E M Remarque, and Hermann Hesse. Just before World War I Expressionism emerged in the poetry of Georg Trakl (1887–1914). It dominated the novels of Franz Kafka and the plays of Ernst Toller (1893–1939), Franz Werfel, and Georg Kaiser, and was later to influence Bertolt Brecht. Under Nazism many good writers left the country, while others were silenced or ignored. After World War II came the Swiss dramatists Max Frisch and Friedrich Dürrenmatt, the German novelists Heinrich Böll, Christa Wolf (1929–), and Siegfried Lenz (1926–), the poet Paul Celan (1920–1970), and the poet and novelist Günter Grass.

Gershwin George 1898–1937. US composer of concert works including the tone poems *Rhapsody in Blue* 1924 and *An American in Paris* 1928, and popular musicals and songs, many with lyrics by his brother *Ira Gershwin* (1896–1983), including 'I Got Rhythm', ''S Wonderful', and 'Embraceable You'. His opera *Porgy and Bess* 1935 incorporated jazz rhythms and popular song styles in an operatic format.

Gertler Mark 1891–1939. English painter. He was a pacifist and a noncombatant during World War I, and his best-known work, *Merry-Go-Round* 1916 (Tate Gallery, London), is often seen as an expressive symbol of anti-militarism. He suffered from depression and committed suicide.

Gesamtkunstwerk (German 'total work of art') work of art that combines different art forms – for example, music, poetry, dance, painting – integrating them so that none dominates the others. The term was used by the composer Richard Wagner and remains particularly associated with his music-dramas. See also ◊mixed media.

gesso (Italian 'gypsum') in painting and gilding, an absorbent white ground made of a gluey mixture of plaster and size. Traditionally, gesso was used as a preparatory base for panels and canvases, especially in ◊tempera painting.

Getty J(ean) Paul 1892–1976. US oil billionaire, president of the Getty Oil Company from 1947, and founder of the Getty Museum (housing the world's highest-funded art collections) in Malibu, California.

In 1985 his son *John Paul Getty Jr* (1932–) established an endowment fund of £50 million for the National Gallery, London.

Getz Stan(ley) 1927–1991. US saxophonist, one of the foremost tenor-sax players of his generation. In the 1950s he was a leading exponent of the cool jazz school, as on the album *West Coast Jazz* 1955. In the 1960s he turned to the Latin American bossa nova sound, which gave him a hit single, 'The Girl from Ipanema' 1964. Later he experimented with jazz-rock fusion.

Ghiberti Lorenzo 1378–1455. Italian sculptor and goldsmith. In 1402 he won the commission for a pair of gilded bronze doors for Florence's Baptistry. He produced a second pair (1425–52), the *Gates of Paradise*, one of the masterpieces of the early Italian Renaissance. They show a sophisticated use of composition and perspective, and the influence of Classical models.

He also wrote *Commentarii/Commentaries* about 1450, a mixture of art history, manual, and autobiography.

Ghirlandaio Domenico *c.* 1449–1494. Italian fresco painter, head of a large and prosperous workshop in Florence. His fresco cycle 1486–90 in Sta Maria Novella, Florence, includes portraits of many Florentines and much contemporary domestic detail. He also worked in Pisa, Rome, and San Gimignano, and painted many portraits.

Ghosts (Norwegian *Gengangere*) play by Norwegian dramatist Henrik ◊Ibsen, first produced in Chicago, USA, 1882. Mrs Alving hides the profligacy of her late husband. The past catches up with her when her son inherits his father's syphilis and unwittingly plans to marry his half-sister.

Giacometti Alberto 1901–1966. Swiss sculptor and painter who trained in Italy and Paris. In the 1930s, in his Surrealist period, he began to develop his characteristic spindly constructions. His mature style of emaciated, rough-textured, single figures emerged in the 1940s. *Man Pointing* 1947 is one of many examples in the Tate Gallery, London.

Giambologna (Giovanni da Bologna or Jean de Boulogne) 1529–1608. Flemish-born sculptor active mainly in Florence and Bologna. In 1583 he completed his public commission for the Loggia dei Lanzi in Florence, *The Rape of the Sabine Women*, a dynamic group of muscular, contorted figures and a prime example of Mannerist sculpture. He also produced the *Neptune Fountain* 1563–67 in Bologna and the equestrian statues of the Medici grand dukes Cosimo and Ferdinando.

giant in many mythologies and folklore, a person of extraordinary size, often characterized as stu-

pid and aggressive. In Greek mythology the giants grew from the spilled blood of Uranus and rebelled against the gods. During the Middle Ages, wicker effigies of giants were carried in midsummer processions in many parts of Europe and sometimes burned.

Gibberd Frederick 1908–1984. English architect and town planner, a pioneer of the ◊Modern Movement in England. His works include the new towns of Harlow, England, and Santa Teresa, Venezuela; the Catholic Cathedral, Liverpool, 1960; and the Central London Mosque, Regent's Park, 1969.

Gibbon Edward 1737–1794. British historian. He wrote one major work, arranged in three parts, *The History of the Decline and Fall of the Roman Empire* 1776–88, a continuous narrative from the 2nd century AD to the fall of Constantinople 1453. He began work on it while in Rome 1764. Although immediately successful, he was compelled to reply to attacks on his account of the early development of Christianity by a *Vindication* 1779. His *Autobiography*, pieced together from fragments left by Gibbon, appeared 1796.

All that is human must retrograde if it does not advance.

Edward Gibbon *The History of the Decline and Fall of the Roman Empire*

Gibbon Lewis Grassic. Pen name of James Leslie Mitchell 1901–1935. Scottish novelist, author of the trilogy *A Scots Quair: Sunset Song, Cloud Howe,* and *Grey Granite* 1932–34, set in the Mearns, south of Aberdeen, where he was born and brought up. Under his real name he wrote *Stained Radiance* 1930 and *Spartacus* 1933.

Gibbons Grinling 1648–1721. Dutch woodcarver who settled in England *c.* 1667. He produced carved wooden panels (largely of birds, flowers, and fruit) for St Paul's Cathedral, London, and for many large English country houses including Petworth House, Sussex, and Hampton Court, Surrey. He was carpenter to English monarchs from Charles II to George I.

Features of his style include acanthus whorls in oak, and trophies of musical instruments in oak and limewood.

Gibbons Orlando 1583–1625. English composer of sacred anthems, instrumental fantasias, and madrigals including *The Silver Swan* for five voices 1612. From a family of musicians, he became organist at Westminster Abbey, London, 1623.

Gibbons Stella (Dorothea) 1902–1989. English journalist. She is remembered for her *Cold Comfort Farm* 1932, a classic satire on the regional novel, in particular the works of Mary ◊Webb.

Gibbs James 1682–1754. Scottish Neo-Classical architect. He studied under the late Baroque architect Carlo Fontana (1638–1714) in Rome and was a close friend and follower of Christopher ◊Wren. His buildings include St Mary-le-Strand, London 1714–17, St Martin-in-the-Fields, London 1722–26, and the circular Radcliffe Camera, Oxford 1737–49, which shows the influence of Italian Mannerism.

Gibran Khalil 1883–1931. Lebanese-American essayist, artist, and mystic poet. Brought to Boston 1895, he studied in Beirut and Paris before settling in New York 1912. A Maronite Christian influenced by the Bible, Blake, and Nietzsche, he wrote in both Arabic and English, exploring the themes of love, nature, longing for homeland, and romantic rebellion, including, controversially, the rebellion of women against arranged marriages. He is best known in the West for *The Prophet* 1923.

Gibson Charles Dana 1867–1944. US illustrator. He portrayed an idealized type of American young woman, known as the 'Gibson Girl'.

Gibson Mel 1956– . Australian actor who became an international star following lead roles in *Mad Max* 1979 and *Mad Max II* 1982 which was released in the USA as *Road Warrior*. His other films include *The Year of Living Dangerously* 1982, *Mutiny on the Bounty* 1984 as Fletcher Christian, and the *Lethal Weapon* series, in which Danny Glover co-starred.

Gibson William 1948– . US writer whose debut novel *Neuromancer* 1984 established the 'cyberpunk' genre of computer-talk fantasy adventure and won both the Hugo and Nebula awards for science fiction. It was followed by *Count Zero* 1986 and *Mona Lisa Overdrive* 1988. Other works include *The Difference Engine* 1990, co-written with Bruce Sterling, about Babbage's original 19th-century computer.

Gide André 1869–1951. French novelist, playwright, and critic. His work is largely autobiographical and concerned with the conflict between desire and conventional morality. It includes *L'Immoraliste/The Immoralist* 1902, *La Porte étroite/Strait Is the Gate* 1909, *Les Caves du Vatican/The Vatican Cellars* 1914, and *Les Faux-monnayeurs/The Counterfeiters* 1926. He was a cofounder of the influential literary periodical *Nouvelle Revue Française* and kept an almost life-long *Journal*. Nobel Prize for Literature 1947.

Sadness is almost never anything but a form of fatigue.

André Gide *Journal*

Gielgud John 1904– . English actor and director, renowned as one of the greatest Shakespearean actors of his time. He made his debut at the Old Vic 1921, and his numerous stage appearances ranged from roles in works by Chekhov and Sheridan to those of Alan Bennett, Harold Pinter, and David Storey. Gielgud's films include *Becket* 1964, *Oh! What a Lovely War* 1969, *Providence* 1977, *Chariots of Fire* 1980, and *Prospero's Books* 1991. He won an Academy Award for his role as a butler in *Arthur* 1981.

Gigli Beniamino 1890–1957. Italian lyric tenor whose radiant tone and affectionate characterizations brought a natural realism to roles in Puccini, Gounod, and Massenet.

Gigli Romeo 1950– . Italian fashion designer who founded his own label 1984 and achieved acclaim for his sombre colours, long languid dresses, clear lines, and exaggerated shapes. He also designs for the label Callaghan and in 1993 launched a collection of carpets.

gigue lively dance in 6/8 or 12/8 time, popular in France during the early 1700s, possibly derived from the jig. Music for or derived from the gigue, which starts on the beat, is featured in the classical ◊suite.

Gilbert Alfred 1854–1934. English sculptor, influenced by Art Nouveau, whose statue *Eros* 1887–93 in Piccadilly Circus, London, was erected as a memorial to the 7th Earl of Shaftesbury.

Gilbert Cass 1859–1934. US architect, a major developer of the ◊skyscraper. He designed the Woolworth Building, New York, 1913, the highest building in America (868 ft/265 m) when built and famous for its use of Gothic decorative detail.

Gilbert W(illiam) S(chwenk) 1836–1911. British humorist and dramatist who collaborated with composer Arthur ◊Sullivan, providing the libretti for their series of light comic operas from 1871; they include *HMS Pinafore* 1878, *The Pirates of Penzance* 1879, and *The Mikado* 1885.

Born in London, he became a lawyer 1863, but in 1869 published a collection of his humorous verse and drawings, *Bab Ballads*, which was followed by a second volume 1873.

A wandering minstrel I – A thing of shreds and patches.

W S Gilbert *The Mikado* 1885

Gilbert and George Gilbert Proesch (1943–) and George Passmore (1942–). English painters and performance artists. They became known in the 1960s for their presentations of themselves as works of art, or 'living sculptures'. They also produce large emblematic photoworks. Their use of both erotic and ambiguous political material has made them controversial.

Gil Blas de Santillane influential novel by Alain-René ◊Le Sage published in four volumes 1715–35. It is a picaresque romance set in Spain in which the easy-going, adaptable hero experiences poverty and wealth, the favour of the great, and disgrace and imprisonment, before finally retiring to enjoy country life. There was an English translation by Tobias Smollett 1749.

Gilchrist Ellen 1935– . US short-story writer and novelist, noted for sharp and stylish social tragi-comedy. Her collections include *In the Land of Dreamy Dreams* 1981, *Victory Over Japan* 1985, and *Light Can Be Both Wave and Particle* 1990. Her novels include *Net of Jewels* 1992.

gilding application of gilt (gold or a substance that looks like it) to a surface. From the 19th century, gilt was often applied to ceramics and to the relief surfaces of woodwork or plasterwork to highlight a design.

The gold layer can be created in a number of ways. From 1853 until the late 1860s, brown gold – a mixture of gold chloride, bismuth oxide, and borax – could be painted on ceramics to produce a dull golden surface when fired. It could then be polished. With design transfers, more intricate patterns could be used. The transfers were printed in ink containing asphalt, oil, and gold size (a gluey mixture) over gold leaf. This was applied on a coating of isinglass painted over glaze. Liquid gold, which was seldom used before 1850, allowed brilliant decoration, but it depended on the ability of oils containing sulphur to dissolve gold and hold it in suspension, so often the results were short-lived. Fire gilding, developed in the late 18th century and still in use, employs an amalgam of powdered gold painted over glaze. Acid gilding, used in the UK at the Minton china factory from 1863, allows areas of matt and brilliantly polished surfaces. Acid applied to the surface of ceramics leaves the rest of the surface slightly raised, so when the whole is gilded and burnished, the acid-etched areas remain unpolished.

In Japan, a technique of applying gold leaf cut into fine strips (*kirikane*) was developed, reaching its peak in the 12th century. It gives a different quality of line from painting with powdered gold, and was much used to decorate Buddhist sculptures and other works of art.

Gilgamesh hero of Sumerian, Hittite, Akkadian, and Assyrian legend, and lord of the Sumerian city of Uruk. The 12 verse books of the *Epic of Gilgamesh* were recorded in a standard version on 12 cuneiform tablets by the Assyrian king Ashurbanipal's scholars in the 7th century BC, and the epic itself is older than Homer's *Iliad* by at least 1,500 years.

The *Epic*'s incident of the Flood is similar to the Old Testament account, since Abraham had been a citizen of the nearby city of Ur in Sumer.

Gill Eric 1882–1940. English sculptor, engraver, and writer. He designed the typefaces Perpetua 1925 and Gill Sans (without serifs) 1927, and created monumental stone sculptures with clean, simplified outlines, such as *Prospero and Ariel* 1929–31 (on Broadcasting House, London).

He studied lettering at the Central School of Art in London under Edward Johnston (1872–1944), and began his career carving inscriptions for tombstones. Gill was a leader in the revival of interest in the craft of lettering and book design. His views on art combine Catholicism, socialism, and the Arts and Crafts tradition.

Gillespie Dizzy (John Birks) 1917–1993. US jazz trumpeter who, with Charlie ◊Parker, was the chief creator and exponent of the ◊bebop style (*Groovin' High* is a CD reissue of their seminal 78-rpm recordings). Gillespie influenced many modern jazz trumpeters, including Miles Davis.

Although associated mainly with small combos, Gillespie formed his first big band 1945 and toured with a big band in the late 1980s, as well as in the intervening decades; a big band can be heard on *Dizzy Gillespie at Newport* 1957.

Gillray James 1757–1815. English caricaturist. His 1,500 cartoons, 1779–1811, satirized the French, George III, politicians, and social follies of his day.

Gilpin William 1724–1804. English artist. He is remembered for his essays on the 'picturesque', which set out precise rules for the production of this effect.

Ginner Charles 1878–1952. English painter of street scenes and landscapes, strongly influenced by Post-Impressionism. He settled in London 1910, and was one of the ◊London Group.

Ginsberg (Irwin) Allen 1926– . US poet and political activist. His reputation as a visionary, overtly political poet was established by ◊*Howl* 1956, which expressed and shaped the spirit of the ◊Beat Generation. His poetry draws heavily on Oriental philosophies and utilizes mantric breath meditations.

His other major poem, 'Kaddish' 1961, deals with the breakdown and death of his schizophrenic mother. His *Collected Poems 1947–1980* was published 1985.

What if someone gave a war & Nobody came?/ Life would ring the bells of Ecstasy and Forever be Itself again.

Allen Ginsberg *The Fall of America* 1973

Giono Jean 1895–1970. French novelist whose books are chiefly set in Provence. *Que ma Joie demeure/Joy of Man's Desiring* 1935 is an attack on life in towns and a plea for a return to country life.

In 1956 he published a defence of Gaston

Dominici, who allegedly murdered an English family on holiday, maintaining that the old farmer exemplified the misunderstandings between town and country people.

Giordano Luca 1634–1705. Italian Baroque painter, born in Naples, active in Florence in the 1680s. In 1692 he was summoned to Spain by Charles II and painted ceilings in the Escorial palace for the next ten years.

In Florence Giordano painted a ceiling in the Palazzo Medici-Riccardi 1682–83. He also produced altarpieces and frescoes for churches. His work shows a variety of influences, including Paolo ◊Veronese, and tends to be livelier than that of earlier Baroque painters.

Giorgione da Castelfranco (Giorgio Barbarelli) c. 1475–1510. Italian Renaissance painter, active in Venice, probably trained by Giovanni Bellini. His work greatly influenced Titian and other Venetian painters. His subjects are imbued with a sense of mystery and treated with a soft technique, reminiscent of Leonardo da Vinci's later works, as in *The Tempest* 1504 (Accademia, Venice).

Giorgione created the Renaissance poetic landscape, with rich colours and a sense of intimacy; an example is the *Sleeping Venus* about 1510 (Gemäldegalerie, Dresden), a work which may have been completed by Titian.

Giotto di Bondone 1267–1337. Italian painter and architect whose influence on the development of painting in Europe was profound. He broke away from the conventions of ◊International Gothic and introduced a naturalistic style, painting saints as real people, lifelike and expressive; an enhanced sense of volume and space also characterizes his work. He painted cycles of frescoes in churches at Assisi, Florence, and Padua.

Giotto was born in Vespignano, north of Florence. The interior of the Arena Chapel, Padua, was covered by him in a fresco cycle (completed by 1306) illustrating the life of Mary and the life of Jesus. Giotto's figures occupy a definite pictorial space, and there is an unusual emotional intensity and dignity in the presentation of the story. In one of the frescoes he made the Star of Bethlehem appear as a comet; Halley's comet had appeared 1303, just two years before.

From 1334 he was official architect to the city of Florence and from 1335 overseer of works at the cathedral; he designed the campanile, which was completed after his death by Andrea Pisano.

Girardon François 1628–1715. French academic sculptor. His *Apollo Tended by Nymphs*, commissioned 1666, is one of several marble groups sculpted for the gardens of Louis XIV's palace at Versailles.

Giraudoux (Hippolyte) Jean 1882–1944. French playwright and novelist who wrote the plays *Amphitryon 38* 1929 and *La Folle de Chaillot/The Madwoman of Chaillot* 1945. His novels include *Suzanne et la Pacifique/Suzanne and the Pacific* 1921, *Eglantine* 1927, and *Les Aventures de Jérôme Bardini* 1930. His other plays include *La Guerre de Troie n'aura pas lieu/Tiger at the Gates* 1935.

The law is the most powerful of schools for the imagination. No poet ever interpreted nature as freely as a lawyer interprets the truth.

Jean Giraudoux
La Guerre de Troie n'aura pas lieu

---

girdle boneless, lightweight, elastic form of ◊corset which became popular as an undergarment for women in the 1920s. Covering the stomach and hips, it often had elastic side panels to hold up stockings. Gradually replaced by lighter underwear in the second half of the 20th century, the girdle has become virtually obsolete since the 1970s.

Girtin Thomas 1775–1802. English painter of watercolour landscapes, a friend of J M W Turner. His work is characterized by broad washes of strong colour and bold compositions, for example *The White House at Chelsea* 1800 (Tate Gallery, London).

Gish Lillian. Stage name of Lillian de Guiche 1896–1993. US film and stage actress who worked with the director D W Griffith, playing virtuous heroines in *Way Down East* and *Orphans of the Storm* both 1920. She made a notable Hester in Victor Sjöström's *The Scarlet Letter* (based on the novel by Nathaniel Hawthorne). Her career continued well into the 1980s with movies such as *The Whales of August* 1987. She was the sister of the actress **Dorothy Gish** (1898–1968).

Gissing George (Robert) 1857–1903. English writer, dealing with social issues. Among his books are *New Grub Street* 1891 and the autobiographical *Private Papers of Henry Ryecroft* 1903.

Giugiaro Giorgio 1938– . Italian industrial designer who established himself internationally as an independent automotive designer with his Volkswagen Golf 1973, the very popular successor to the Beetle. He went on to create other memorable automotive designs as well as a large number of diverse products, including cameras for Nikon in the late 1970s. His design for a pasta shape 1983, dubbed 'Marielle', confirmed his role as a universal 'form-giver'.

Giulini Carlo Maria 1914– . Italian conductor, joint musical director of the Los Angeles Philharmonic Orchestra 1978–84. At Milan Radio 1946–51 he revived rare operas by Scarlatti, Malapiero, and Bartók; his 1951 radio production of Haydn's opera *Il mondo della luna/The World on the Moon* 1777 attracted Toscanini who recommended his appointment at La Scala 1953–55, where he worked with Maria Callas, Zeffirelli, and Visconti. He is noted for interpretations of Verdi, Bach, Mozart, and Beethoven, blending Italian lyricism with the austere monumentality of the German tradition.

Giulio Romano *c.* 1499–1546. Italian painter and architect. An assistant to Raphael, he developed a Mannerist style, creating effects of exaggerated movement and using rich colours, for example the frescoes in the Palazzo del Tè, Mantua, begun 1526.

Givenchy Hubert de 1927– . French fashion designer whose simple, reasonably priced mix-and-match blouses, skirts, and slacks earned him instant acclaim when he opened his couture house in Paris 1952. He was noted for his embroidered and printed fabrics and his imaginative use of accessories. In the 1960s he designed both screen and personal wardrobes for Audrey Hepburn.

Glackens William James 1870–1938. US painter. He was a member of the Ashcan School and one of 'the Eight', a group of Realists who exhibited at New York's Macbeth Gallery 1908. Glackens' painting eventually evolved into a Realism that was strongly influenced by Impressionism. He painted subjects from everyday urban life, as well as those from fashionable society.

glam rock or *glitter rock* pop music in a conventional rock style performed by elaborately made-up and overdressed musicians. English singers Marc Bolan (1947–1977) and David ◊Bowie and the band Roxy Music (1970–83) pioneered glam rock in the early 1970s.

Glasgow Ellen 1873–1945. US novelist. Her books, set mainly in her native Virginia, often deal with the survival of tough heroines in a world of adversity and include *Barren Ground* 1925, *The Sheltered Life* 1932, *Vein of Iron* 1935, and *In This Our Life* 1941 (Pulitzer Prize).

Glasgow School name given to two distinct groups of Scottish artists. The earlier of the two groups, also known as the **Glasgow Boys**, was a loose association of late-19th-century artists influenced by the ◊Barbizon School and ◊Impressionism. Leading members included James Guthrie and John ◊Lavery. The later, more important group was part of the ◊Art Nouveau movement, its most important member being Charles Rennie ◊Mackintosh.

Glass Philip 1937– . US composer. As a student of Nadia Boulanger, he was strongly influenced by Indian music; his work is characterized by repeated rhythmic figures that are continually expanded and modified. His compositions include the operas *Einstein on the Beach* 1976, *Akhnaten* 1984, and *The Making of*

the *Representative for Planet 8* 1988, and the *'Low' Symphony* 1992 on themes from David Bowie's *Low* album.

glaze transparent vitreous coating for pottery and porcelain, applied by dipping a formed ceramic body into it or by painting it onto the surface. It is fixed by firing in a kiln. It gives the object a shiny protective finish.

Gleizes Albert 1881–1953. French Cubist painter and theorist, chiefly remembered for his pioneering book *De Cubisme* 1912, written with Jean Metzinger (1883–1956). Influenced initially by Picasso and Braque and later by Robert Delaunay, Gleizes painted in an exuberant manner, filling the entire canvas with tilting, interpenetrating planes, as in *Harvest Threshing* 1912 (Solomon R Guggenheim Museum, New York). He helped found the *Section d'Or* in Paris 1912–14, an exhibition society for disseminating the work of Cubist painters.

gliding tone musical tone, continuously rising or falling in pitch between preset notes, produced by a synthesizer.

Glinka Mikhail Ivanovich 1804–1857. Russian composer. He broke away from the prevailing Italian influence and turned to Russian folk music as the inspiration for his opera *A Life for the Tsar* (originally *Ivan Susanin*) 1836. His later works include the opera *Ruslan and Lyudmila* 1842 and the instrumental fantasia *Kamarinskaya* 1848.

glissando in music, a rapid uninterrupted scale produced by sliding the finger across a keyboard or harp strings, or along the fingerboard of a violin or guitar. In wind instruments, it corresponds to a gliding tone, a famous example being the clarinet glissando at the start of Gershwin's *Rhapsody in Blue* 1924.

glitter rock another name for ◊glam rock, a 1970s pop fashion.

Globe Theatre 17th-century London theatre, octagonal and open to the sky, near Bankside, Southwark, where many of Shakespeare's plays were performed by Richard Burbage and his company. Built 1599 by Cuthbert Burbage, it was burned down 1613 after a cannon, fired during a performance of *Henry VIII*, set light to the thatch. It was rebuilt 1614 but pulled down 1644. The site was rediscovered Oct 1989 near the remains of the contemporaneous Rose Theatre.

In 1987 planning permission was granted to the US film producer Sam Wanamaker (1919–1993) to build a working replica of the theatre on its original site.

glockenspiel percussion instrument of light metal keys mounted on a carrying frame for use in military bands or on a standing frame for use in an orchestra (in which form it resembles a small xylophone or celesta).

Glover Denis 1912–1980. New Zealand poet. A member of the influential Phoenix group in the 1930s, he was first noted for satirical works such as *Six Easy Ways of Dodging Debt Collectors* 1936 and *The Arraignment of Paris* 1937, lampooning some women poets. His poems show a sympathy with ordinary lives, such as the unsuccessful gold prospector in his popular sequence *Arawata Bill* 1952.

Gluck Christoph Willibald von 1714–1787. German composer who settled in Vienna as kapellmeister to Maria Theresa 1754. In 1762 his *Orfeo ed Euridice/Orpheus and Eurydice* revolutionized the 18th-century conception of opera by giving free scope to dramatic effect. *Orfeo* was followed by *Alceste/Alcestis* 1767 and *Paride ed Elena/Paris and Helen* 1770.

Born in Erasbach, Bavaria, he studied music at Prague, Vienna, and Milan, went to London 1745 to compose operas for the Haymarket, but returned to Vienna 1746 where he was knighted by the pope. In 1762 his *Iphigénie en Aulide/Iphigenia in Aulis* 1774, produced in Paris, brought to a head the fierce debate over the future of opera in which Gluck's French style had the support of Marie Antoinette while his Italian rival Nicolò Piccinni (1728–1800) had the support of Madame Du Barry. With *Armide* 1777 and *Iphigénie en Tauride/Iphigenia in Tauris* 1779 Gluck won a complete victory over Piccinni.

The greatest beauties of melody and harmony become faults and imperfections when they are not in their proper place.

Christoph Willibald von Gluck

Glyndebourne site of an opera house in East Sussex, England, established 1934 by John Christie (1882–1962). Operas are staged at an annual summer festival and a touring company is also based there. It closed 1992 for extensive rebuilding work.

gnome in fairy tales, a small, mischievous spirit of the earth. The males are bearded, wear tunics and hoods, and often guard an underground treasure.

The *garden gnome*, an ornamental representation of these spirits, was first brought from Germany to England 1850 by Charles Isham for his mansion Lamport Hall, Northamptonshire.

Gobbi Tito 1913–1984. Italian baritone singer of vibrant bel canto allied to a resourceful talent for verismo characterization in Italian opera, notably Verdi and Puccini, and as Figaro in *Le Nozze di Figaro/The Marriage of Figaro*.

Gobelins French tapestry factory, originally founded as a dyeworks in Paris by Gilles and Jean Gobelin about 1450. The firm began to produce tapestries in the 16th century, and in 1662 the establishment was bought for Louis XIV by his minister Colbert. With the support of the French government, it continues to make tapestries.

Godard Jean-Luc 1930– . French film director, one of the leaders of ◊New Wave cinema. His works are often characterized by experimental editing techniques and an unconventional dramatic form. His films include *A bout de Souffle/Breathless* 1959, *Vivre sa Vie/It's My Life* 1962, *Weekend* 1968, *Sauve qui peut (la vie)/Slow Motion* 1980, and *Je vous salue, Marie/Hail Mary* 1985.

Photography is truth. The cinema is truth 24 times per second.

Jean-Luc Godard *Le Petit Soldat*

Goddard Paulette. Stage name of Marion Levy 1911–1990. US film actress. She starred with comedian Charlie Chaplin (to whom she was married 1936–42) in *Modern Times* 1936 and *The Great Dictator* 1940, and her other films include the British-made version of Oscar Wilde's play *An Ideal Husband* 1948.

'God Save the King/Queen' British national anthem. The melody resembles a composition by John Bull and similar words are found from the 16th century. In its present form it dates from the 1745 Rebellion, when it was used as an anti-Jacobite Party song.

In the USA the song 'America', with the first line 'My country, 'tis of thee', is sung to the same tune. Variations on the theme 'America' were composed by Charles Ives 1891.

Godwin Edward William 1833–1886. English architect whose reputation was established by his competition-winning Gothic Revival design for Northampton Town Hall 1861. However, his style was at its most original in his domestic buildings. His White House in Tite Street, Chelsea, 1877–79, designed for the painter James Whistler (now demolished), suggested Japanese influence with its varied façade and startlingly simple interior of bare, plain-coloured walls.

Godwin William 1756–1836. English philosopher, novelist, and father of Mary Shelley. His *Enquiry concerning Political Justice* 1793 advocated an anarchic society based on a faith in people's essential rationality. At first a Nonconformist minister, he later became an atheist. His first wife was Mary Wollstonecraft.

Goehr (Peter) Alexander 1932– . British composer, born in Berlin, professor of music at Cambridge from 1976. A lyrical but often hard-edged serialist, he nevertheless usually remained within the forms of the symphony and traditional chamber works, and more recently turned to tonal and even Neo-Baroque models. Works include the opera *Arden muss sterben/Arden Must Die* 1966, the music theatre piece *Naboth's Vineyard* 1968, and *Metamorphosis/Dance* 1974.

Goes Hugo van der, died 1482. Flemish painter, chiefly active in Ghent. His *Portinari Altarpiece* about 1475 (Uffizi, Florence) is a huge oil painting of the Nativity, full of symbolism and naturalistic detail, while his *Death of the Virgin* about 1480 (Musée Communale des Beaux Arts, Bruges) is remarkable for the varied expressions on the faces of the apostles.

Goethe Johann Wolfgang von 1749–1832. German poet, novelist, and dramatist, generally considered the founder of modern German literature, and leader of the Romantic ◊*Sturm und Drang* movement. His works include the autobiographical *Die Leiden des Jungen Werthers/The Sorrows of the Young Werther* 1774 and ◊*Faust* 1808, his masterpiece. A visit to Italy 1786–88 inspired the classical dramas *Iphigenie auf Tauris/Iphigenia in Tauris* 1787 and *Torquato Tasso* 1790.

Goethe was born in Frankfurt-am-Main, and studied law. Inspired by Shakespeare, to whose work he was introduced by ◊Herder, he wrote the play *Götz von Berlichingen* 1773. *The Sorrows of the Young Werther* and the poetic play *Faust* made him known throughout Europe. Other works include the ◊*Wilhelm Meister* novels 1795–1829. Between 1775 and 1785 he served as prime minister at the court of Weimar.

He who seizes the right moment,/ Is the right man.

Johann Wolfgang von Goethe *Faust*
1808

Goff Bruce Alonzo 1904–1982. US architect whose work is frequently described as 'organic' in form. Initially influenced by Frank Lloyd ◊Wright, he later developed a highly individual approach, characterized by unlikely combinations of materials and styles. His most striking project is the Bavinger House, Oklahoma, 1949, composed of a spiralling wall of stone with a steel mast at its centre; 'living bowls' and a staircase are suspended from the mast. Although poetic in his expression of free-flowing space, the quality of his executed designs has been criticized.

Gogh Vincent van 1853–1890. Dutch Post-Impressionist painter. He tried various careers, including preaching, and began painting in the 1880s, his early works often being sombre depictions of peasant life, such as *The Potato Eaters* 1885 (Van Gogh Museum, Amsterdam). Influenced by both the Impressionists and Japanese prints, he developed a freer style characterized by intense colour and expressive brushwork, as seen in his *Sunflowers* series 1888.

Born in Zundert, van Gogh worked for a time as a schoolmaster in England before he took up painting. He studied under Antoine Mauve in The Hague, and briefly in Antwerp, before moving to Paris 1886 where his brother Theo worked as an art dealer. He met Paul ◊Gauguin in Paris and when he settled in Arles, Provence, 1888, Gauguin joined him there. After a quarrel, van Gogh cut off part of his own earlobe, and in 1889 he entered an asylum; the following year he committed suicide.

His numerous works (over 800 paintings and 700 drawings) include still lifes, portraits (many of himself), and landscapes, including *The Starry Night* 1889 (Museum of Modern Art, New York) and *Crows over Wheatfield* 1890 (Van Gogh Museum, Amsterdam). The Arles paintings vividly testify to his intense emotional involvement in his art. *Irises* 1889 was sold for the record price of $53.9 million at Sotherby's, New York, 1987.

Gogol Nicolai Vasilyevich 1809–1852. Russian writer. His first success was a collection of stories, *Evenings on a Farm near Dikanka* 1831–32, followed by *Mirgorod* 1835. Later works include *Arabesques* 1835, the comedy play *The Inspector General* 1836, and the picaresque novel *Dead Souls* 1842, which satirizes Russian provincial society.

Gogol was born near Poltava. He tried several careers before entering the St Petersburg civil service. From 1835 he travelled in Europe, and it was in Rome that he completed the earlier part of *Dead Souls* 1842. Other works include the short stories 'The Overcoat' and 'The Nose'.

Gambling is the great leveller. All men are equal – at cards.

Nicolai Vasilyevich Gogol *Gamblers*

Golden Ass, The or *Metamorphoses* ◊picaresque adventure by the Roman writer Lucius Apuleius, written in Latin about AD 160, sometimes described as the world's first novel. Lucius, transformed into an ass, describes his exploits with a band of robbers, weaving into the narrative several ancient legends, including that of Cupid and Psyche.

Golden Fleece in Greek mythology, the fleece of the winged ram Chrysomallus, which hung on an oak tree at Colchis and was guarded by a dragon. It was stolen by ◊Jason and the Argonauts.

golden section visually satisfying ratio, widely used in art and architecture. In a line divided by the golden section, the shorter length is to the larger as the larger is to the sum of the two, very roughly a ratio of 3 to 5. A ***golden rectangle*** is one that, within a larger rectangle, has its length and breadth in this ratio. In van Gogh's picture

Mother and Child, for example, the Madonna's face fits perfectly into a golden rectangle.

'Goldilocks and the Three Bears' children's story about a little girl who finds a cottage in the woods with no one at home. She makes use of the chairs, dishes, and beds, all in triplicate, but flees when the returning owners prove to be three bears. In the first printed version by Robert Southey 1837, the trespasser was an old woman, but successive retellings transformed her into a golden-haired child.

Golding William 1911–1993. English novelist. His work is often principally concerned with the fundamental corruption and evil inherent in human nature. His first book, *Lord of the Flies* 1954, concerns the degeneration into savagery of a group of English schoolboys marooned on a Pacific island. *Pincher Martin* 1956 is a study of greed and self-delusion. Later novels include *The Spire* 1964 and *Darkness Visible* 1979. He was awarded the Nobel Prize for Literature 1983.

The Sea Trilogy, *Rites of Passage* 1980 (Booker Prize), *Close Quarters* 1987, and *Fire Down Below* 1989, tells the story of a voyage to Australia through the eyes of a callow young aristocrat.

Goldoni Carlo 1707–1793. Italian dramatist, born in Venice. He wrote popular comedies for the Sant'Angelo theatre, which drew on the traditions of the ◊commedia dell'arte, *Il servitore di due padroni/The Servant of Two Masters* 1743, *Il bugiardo/The Liar* 1750, and *La locandiera/Mine Hostess* 1753. In 1761 he moved to Paris, where he directed the Italian theatre and wrote more plays, including *L'Eventail/The Fan* 1763.

Goldsmith Jerry (Jerrald) 1930– . US composer of film music who originally worked in radio and television. His prolific output includes *Planet of the Apes* 1968, *The Wind and the Lion* 1975, *The Omen* 1976 (Academy Award), and *Gremlins* 1984.

Goldsmith Oliver 1728–1774. Irish writer whose works include the novel *The Vicar of Wakefield* 1766; the poem 'The Deserted Village' 1770; and the play *She Stoops to Conquer* 1773. In 1761 Goldsmith met Samuel Johnson, and became a member of his 'club'. *The Vicar of Wakefield* was sold (according to Johnson's account) to save him from imprisonment for debt.

Goldsmith was the son of a cleric. He was educated at Trinity College, Dublin, and Edinburgh, where he studied medicine 1752. After travelling extensively in Europe, he returned to England and became a hack writer, producing many works, including *History of England* 1764 and *Animated Nature* 1774. One of his early works was *The Citizen of the World* 1762, a series of letters by an imaginary Chinese traveller. In 1764 he published the poem 'The Traveller', and followed it with collected essays 1765.

Goldwyn Samuel. Adopted name of Samuel Goldfish 1882–1974. US film producer. Born in Poland, he emigrated to the USA 1896. He founded the Goldwyn Pictures Corporation 1917, which eventually merged into Metro-Goldwyn-Mayer (MGM) 1924, although he was not part of the deal. He remained an independent producer for many years, making classics such as *Wuthering Heights* 1939, *The Little Foxes* 1941, *The Best Years of Our Lives* 1946, and *Guys and Dolls* 1955.

He was famed for his illogical aphorisms known as 'goldwynisms', for example, ' Include me out'.

An oral contract is not worth the paper it's written on.

Samuel Goldwyn

Gollancz Victor 1893–1967. British left-wing writer and publisher, founder in 1936 of the Left Book Club. His own firm published plays by R C Sherriff and novels by Daphne Du Maurier, Elizabeth Bowen, and Dorothy L Sayers, among others.

Gombrich Ernst 1909– . Austrian-born British art historian. His work on art history and theory is noted for its depth of analysis and the connections it makes with other fields, such as psychology. His best-known work is *The Story of Art* 1950, written for a popular audience.

He came to Britain 1936 to work at the University of London Warburg Institute, where he was director 1959–76.

Gombrowicz Witold 1904–1969. Polish dramatist and novelist. His technique of grotesque and fantastic allegory was expressed in *Iowna, Princess of Burgundy* 1957, *Marriage* 1963, and *Operetta* 1969. He was an exile from 1939.

Gonçalves Nuño active 1450–1471. Portuguese artist, court painter to Alfonso V. His finest surviving work is the St Vincent ◊polyptych about 1465–67 (National Museum of Art, Lisbon). Covering six panels, it depicts Portuguese society in the form of a crowded gallery, with figures ranging from Alfonso and Henry the Navigator to clerics and fishermen. His work owes much to contemporary Flemish painting in its striking realism and bold use of colour.

Goncharov Ivan Alexandrovitch 1812–1891. Russian novelist. His first novel, *A Common Story* 1847, was followed in 1858 by his humorous masterpiece *Oblomov*, which satirized the indolent Russian landed gentry.

Goncourt, de the brothers Edmond 1822–1896 and Jules 1830–1870. French writers. They collaborated in producing a compendium, *L'Art du XVIIIième siècle/18th-Century Art* 1859–75, historical studies, and a *Journal* published 1887–96 that depicts French literary life of their day.

Edmond de Goncourt founded the Académie Goncourt, opened 1903, which awards an annual prize, the ◊Prix Goncourt, to the author of the best French novel of the year. Equivalent to the Commonwealth Booker Prize in prestige, it has a monetary value of only 50 francs.

Genius is the talent of a man who is dead.

Edmond and **Jules de Goncourt** *Journal*

González Julio 1876–1942. Spanish sculptor and painter, notable for establishing the use of wrought and welded iron as an expressive sculptural medium. Influenced by Cubism, Russian Constructivism, and Surrealism, his early sculptures are open, linear designs using rods and bands of iron, for example *Woman with a Mirror* about 1936–37 (IVAM, Centro Julio González, Valencia). From the mid-1930s, he produced moulded, fragmented torsos from sheet iron and his naturalistic, commemorative sculptures of Spanish peasant women in revolt, for example *Montserrat* 1936–37 (Stedelijk Museum, Amsterdam).

Goodman Benny (Benjamin David) 1909–1986. US clarinetist, nicknamed the 'King of Swing' for the new jazz idiom he introduced with arranger Fletcher Henderson (1897–1952). In 1934 he founded his own 12-piece band, which combined the expressive improvisatory style of black jazz with disciplined precision ensemble playing. He is associated with such numbers as 'Blue Skies' and 'Let's Dance'.

In 1938 he embarked on a parallel classical career, recording the Mozart *Clarinet Quintet* with the Budapest String Quartet, and comissioning new works from Bartók (*Contrasts* 1939), Copland, Hindemith, and others. He also recorded jazz with a sextet 1939–41 that included the guitarist Charlie Christian (1916–1942).

Goodman Paul 1911– . US writer and social critic whose many works (novels, plays, essays) express his anarchist, anti-authoritarian ideas. He studied young offenders in *Growing up Absurd* 1960.

Good Soldier Svejk, The (Czech *Osudy dobrého vójaka Svejka*) humorous Czech novel by Jaroslav ◊Hašek, serially published 1921–23 but unfinished when the author died. An earthy picaresque narrative with vivid dialogue, drawing on the author's experiences with the Austrian army 1915, it depicts a shrewd, sardonic, wayward survivor with an endearing disrespect for political and military authority.

'Goody Two-Shoes' children's story of unknown authorship but possibly by Oliver Goldsmith, published 1765 by John Newbery (1713–1767). The heroine, Margery, is an orphan who is distraught when her brother goes to sea, but quickly recovers when she receives a gift of new shoes. She educates herself, dispenses goodness, and is eventually reunited with her brother.

Gordian knot in Greek mythology, the knot tied by King Gordius of Phrygia that – so an oracle revealed – could be unravelled only by the future conqueror of Asia. According to tradition, Alexander the Great, unable to untie it, cut it with his sword in 334 BC.

Gordimer Nadine 1923– . South African novelist, an opponent of apartheid and censorship. Her finest writing is characterized by beautiful evocations of the rural Transvaal, effective renderings of sexuality, and interacting characters from different racial backgrounds. Her first novel, *The Lying Days*, appeared 1953; her other works include *The Conservationist* 1974, the volume of short stories *A Soldier's Embrace* 1980, and *July's People* 1981. She was awarded the Nobel Prize for Literature 1991.

Literature is one of the few areas left where black and white feel some identity of purpose; we all struggle under censorship.

Nadine Gordimer *Writers at Work* 1984

Gordon Richard. Pen name of Gordon Ostlere 1921– . British author of a series of light-hearted novels on the career of a young doctor, beginning with *Doctor in the House* 1952. Many of them were filmed.

Górecki Henryk Mikolaj 1933– . Polish composer whose study with Messiaen and exposure to avant-garde influences after 1956 led him to abandon a politically correct Neo-Classical style and seek out new sonorities. He later adopted a slow-moving tonal idiom appealing to revived religious tradition, often on tragic themes from Polish history, as in *Old Polish Music* for orchestra 1969, and his *Symphony No 3* 1976, which propelled him to fame in the West 1992.

Gorgon in Greek mythology, any of three sisters, Stheno, Euryale, and Medusa, who had wings, claws, enormous teeth, and snakes for hair. Medusa, the only one who was mortal, was killed by ◊Perseus, but even in death her head was still so frightful that it turned the onlooker to stone.

Gorky Arshile 1904–1948. Armenian-born US painter. He painted in several Modernist styles before developing a semi-abstract surreal style, using organic shapes and vigorous brushwork. His works, such as *The Liver Is the Cock's Comb* 1944 (Albright-Knox Art Gallery, Buffalo), are noted for their sense of fantasy.

Among Gorky's major influences were Picasso, Kandinsky, Miró, and Cézanne, and he in turn influenced the emerging Abstract Expressionists. He lived in the USA from 1920.

Gorky Maxim. Pen name of Alexei Peshkov 1868–1936. Russian writer. Born in Nizhni Novgorod (named Gorky 1932–90 in his honour), he was exiled 1906–13 for his revolutionary principles. He learned to write only what was officially approved and his works, which include the play *The Lower Depths* 1902 and the memoir *My Childhood* 1913–14, combine realism with optimistic faith in the potential of the industrial proletariat.

gospel music vocal music developed in the 1920s in the black Baptist churches of the US South from ◊spirituals. Outstanding among the early gospel singers was Mahalia Jackson, but from the 1930s to the mid-1950s male harmony groups predominated, among them the Dixie Hummingbirds, the Swan Silvertones, and the Five Blind Boys of Mississippi.

Many of those classic gospel groups continued to perform into the 1990s, though with altered line-ups. The Edwin Hawkins Singers (formed 1967) had a pop hit 1969 with the hymn 'Oh Happy Day'.

The founder of gospel music is Thomas A Dorsey (1899–   ) from Georgia, who from 1932 wrote hundreds of gospel compositions, including 'Peace in the Valley' 1937 and 'Take My Hand, Precious Lord'. White gospel, or *country gospel*, includes religious ballads popular in ◊bluegrass; many country singers have also recorded Dorsey's material.

Gossaert Jan, Flemish painter, known as ◊Mabuse.

Gosse Edmund William 1849–1928. English writer and critic whose strict Victorian upbringing is reflected in his masterly autobiographical work *Father and Son* (published anonymously 1907). His father was a member of the Plymouth Brethren, a Christian fundamentalist sect that rejected the evolutionary ideas of Darwin. As a literary critic and biographer, he was responsible for introducing the Norwegian dramatist Ibsen to England.

goth member of a youth movement characterized in fashion by black, dramatic clothing and black-and-white make-up, and in music by portentous, swirling synthesizer riffs and angst-ridden lyrics. Goth began in the north of England in the late 1970s. Goth bands include the ◊Cure and Siouxsie and the Banshees (formed 1976).

Gothic architecture style of architecture that flourished in Europe from the mid-12th century to the end of the 15th century. It is characterized by the vertical lines of tall pillars and spires, greater height in interior spaces, the pointed arch, rib vaulting, and the flying buttress.

Gothic architecture originated in Normandy and Burgundy, France, in the 12th century. The term Gothic was at first used disparagingly of medieval art by Renaissance architects, perhaps deriving from the 16th-century critic Vasari's attribution of medieval artistic styles to the Goths who destroyed 'Classicism'. The style prevailed in W Europe until the 16th century when Classic architecture was revived.

In *France*, Gothic architecture may be divided into four periods. *Early Gothic* (1130–90) saw the introduction of ogival (pointed) vaults, for example Notre Dame, Paris (begun 1160). In *lancet Gothic* (1190–1240) pointed arches were tall and narrow, as in Chartres Cathedral (begun 1194), and Bourges Cathedral (begun 1209). *Rayonnant Gothic* (1240–1350) takes its name from the series of chapels that radiate from the cathedral apse, as in Sainte Chapelle, Paris, 1226–30. *Late Gothic* or the *Flamboyant style* (1350–1520) is exemplified in St Gervais, Paris.

In *Italy* Gothic had a classical basis. A notable example of Italian Gothic is Milan Cathedral.

In *Germany*, the Gothic style until the end of the 13th century was at first heavily influenced by that of France; for example Cologne Cathedral, the largest in N Europe, was built after the model of Amiens.

In *England* the Gothic style is divided into *Early English* (1200–75), for example, Salisbury Cathedral; *Decorated* (1300–75), for example, York Minster; and *Perpendicular* (1400–1575), for example, Winchester Cathedral.

Gothic art style of painting and sculpture that dominated European art from the late 12th century until the early Renaissance. Manuscripts were lavishly decorated, and the façades of the great Gothic churches held hundreds of sculpted figures and profuse ornamentation. Stained glass replaced mural painting to some extent in N European churches. See also ◊medieval art, ◊International Gothic.

Gothic novel literary genre established by Horace Walpole's *The Castle of Otranto* 1765 and marked by mystery, violence, and horror; other exponents were the English writers Anne Radcliffe, Matthew 'Monk' Lewis, Mary Shelley, the Irish writer Bram Stoker, and Edgar Allan Poe in the USA.

Gothic Revival the resurgence of interest in Gothic architecture, as displayed in the late 18th and 19th centuries, notably in Britain and the USA. Gothic Revival buildings include Barry and Pugin's Houses of Parliament, London, 1836–65, and St Pancras Station Hotel 1868–74 by Gilbert Scott; the Town Hall, Vienna 1872–83, by Friedrich von Schmidt (1825–1891); and Trinity Church, New York, 1846, by Richard Upjohn (1802–1878).

The growth of Romanticism led some writers, artists, and antiquaries to embrace a fascination with Gothic forms that emphasized the supposedly bizarre and grotesque aspects of the Middle Ages. During the Victorian period, however, a far better understanding of Gothic forms was achieved, and this resulted in some impressive Neo-Gothic architecture, as well as some desecration of genuine Gothic churches in the name of 'restoration'.

Götterdämmerung (German 'twilight of the gods') in Germanic mythology, a great battle in which the ancient gods (the ◊Aesir) were destroyed by the forces of evil, allowing a new order to come into existence. (See also ◊Ragnarök.) It was the basis of Wagner's opera *Götterdämmerung* 1874.

Gottschalk Louis Moreau 1829–1869. US composer and pianist whose adoption of Creole and American folk music, Latin American rhythms and dance forms, and striking coloristic effects won the admiration of Berlioz, Liszt, Offenbach, and others. His compositions include *Souvenir d'Andalousie/Souvenir of Andalusia* 1851 for piano and orchestra and numerous piano pieces, among which are *La Gallina: danse cubaine/La Gallina: Cuban dance* of about 1868 and *Le Banjo – esquisse américaine/Banjo – American Sketch* 1854–55.

gouache or *body colour* painting medium in which watercolour is mixed with white pigment. Applied in the same way as watercolour, gouache gives a chalky finish similar to that of ◊tempera painting. It has long been popular in continental Europe, where Dürer and Boucher were both masters of the technique. Poster paints are usually a form of gouache.

Goujon Jean *c.* 1510–1565. French Renaissance sculptor whose Mannerist style, developed under the influence of ◊Primaticcio and ◊Cellini at Fontainebleau, is tempered with a graceful Classicism. Characteristic of his work are the slender nymphs in bas relief on his *Fountain of the Innocents* 1549 (Louvre, Paris).

Gould Elliott. Stage name of Elliot Goldstein 1938– . US film actor. A successful child actor, his film debut *The Night They Raided Minsky's* 1968 led rapidly to starring roles in such films as *M.A.S.H.* 1970, *The Long Goodbye* 1972, and *Capricorn One* 1978.

Gounod Charles François 1818–1893. French composer and organist whose operas, notably *Faust* 1859 and *Roméo et Juliette* 1867, and church music including *Messe solennelle/Solemn Mass* 1849 combine graceful melody and elegant harmonization. His *Méditation sur le prélude de Bach/Meditation on Bach's 'Prelude'* 1889 for soprano and instruments, based on Prelude No 1 of Bach's *Well-Tempered Clavier*, achieved popularity as 'Gounod's *Ave Maria*'.

Gourmont Remy de 1858–1915. French critic and novelist. A prolific essayist, he influentially disseminated the aesthetic doctrines of French ◊Symbolism, committed to the relativity of truth

and the necessarily aesthetic basis of all literary judgement. His rather čerebral novels include *Sixtine: Roman de la vie cérébrale/Very Woman* 1890.

goût grec (French 'Greek taste') French anti-Rococo style of the second half of the 18th century, inspired by Classical art and architecture. Furnishings decorated with urns, heavy festoons, and meander scroll patterns were fashionable.

Gower John *c.* 1330–1408. English poet. He is remembered for his tales of love *Confessio Amantis* 1390, written in English, and other poems in French and Latin. He was a friend and contemporary of Geoffrey Chaucer.

gown outer garment, often an elegant or formal dress for women. Introduced in the late 14th century, it fitted the upper part of the body but fell loosely from the waist, and had a high upright collar. In England, during the reign of Henry VIII the gown was adapted to feature a low-cut neck and bell-shaped sleeves. Today the term is often used to refer to a formal evening dress.

In other contexts, a gown can also be the protective outer clothing worn by surgeons and support staff during operations or the formal outer garment worn by academics, judges, or peers, also known as a robe.

Goya Francisco José de Goya y Lucientes 1746–1828. Spanish painter and engraver. He painted portraits of four successive kings of Spain; his series of etchings include the famous *Los Caprichos* 1797–98 and *The Disasters of War* 1810–14, both depicting the horrors of the French invasion of Spain. Among his later works are the 'Black Paintings' (Prado, Madrid), with such horrific images as *Saturn Devouring One of His Sons* about 1822.

Goya was born in Aragon and was for a time a bullfighter, the subject of some of his etchings. After studying in Italy, he returned to Spain and was employed on a number of paintings for the royal tapestry factory as well as numerous portraits. In 1789 he was appointed court painter to Charles IV. The eroticism of his *Naked Maja* and *Clothed Maja* about 1800–05 (Prado, Madrid) caused such outrage that he was questioned by the Inquisition. *The ◊Shootings of May 3rd 1808* 1814 (Prado, Madrid), painted for Ferdinand VII, is passionate in its condemnation of the inhumanity of war.

Goyen Jan van 1596–1656. Dutch landscape painter, active in Leiden, Haarlem, and from 1631 in The Hague. A pioneer of the Realist style of landscape with ◊Ruisdael, he sketched from nature and studied clouds and light effects.

Gozzoli Benozzo *c.* 1421–1497. Florentine painter, a late exponent of the ◊International Gothic style. He is known for his fresco *The Procession of the Magi* 1459–61 in the chapel of the Palazzo Medici-Riccardi, Florence, where the walls are crowded with figures, many of them portraits of the Medici family.

G.P. in music, abbreviation for 'general pause', a moment where all players are silent.

Grable Betty (Elizabeth Ruth) 1916–1973. US actress, singer, and dancer, who starred in *Moon over Miami* 1941, *I Wake Up Screaming* 1941, and *How to Marry a Millionaire* 1953. As a publicity stunt, her legs were insured for a million dollars. Her popularity peaked during World War II when US soldiers voted her their number-one pin-up girl.

Graces in Greek mythology, three goddesses (Aglaia, Euphrosyne, and Thalia), daughters of Zeus and Hera, personifications of pleasure, charm, and beauty; the inspirers of the arts and the sciences.

graffiti (Italian 'scratched drawings') inscriptions or drawings carved, scratched, or drawn on public surfaces, such as walls, fences, or public-transport vehicles. *Tagging* is the act of writing an individual logo on surfaces with spray paint or large felt-tip pens. The term 'graffiti' is derived from a traditional technique in Italian art (*sgraffito*) of scratching a design in the thin white plaster on a wall.

Graham Martha 1893–1991. US dancer, choreographer, teacher, and director. The greatest exponent of modern dance in the USA, she developed a distinctive vocabulary of movement, the *Graham Technique*, now taught worldwide. Her pioneering technique, designed to express inner emotion and intention through dance forms, represented the first real alternative to classical ballet.

Graham founded her own dance school 1927 and started a company with students from the school 1929. She created over 170 works, including *Appalachian Spring* 1944 (score by Aaron Copland), *Clytemnestra* 1958, the first full-length modern dance work, and *Lucifer* 1975. She danced in most of the pieces she choreographed until her retirement from performance in the 1960s. Graham had a major influence on such choreographers in the contemporary dance movement as Robert Cohan, Glen Tetley, Merce Cunningham, Norman Morrice, Paul Taylor, and Robert North.

Believe me, my young friend, there is nothing – absolutely nothing – half so much worth doing as simply messing about in boats.

Kenneth Grahame
The Wind in the Willows 1908

Grahame Kenneth 1859–1932. Scottish author. The early volumes of sketches of childhood, *The*

Golden Age 1895 and *Dream Days* 1898, were followed by his masterpiece *The Wind in the Willows* 1908, an animal fantasy created for his young son, which was dramatized by A A Milne as *Toad of Toad Hall* 1929.

Grainger Percy Aldridge 1882–1961. Australian-born experimental composer and pianist remembered for piano transcriptions, songs, and instrumental pieces drawing on folk idioms, including *Country Gardens* 1925, and for his settings of folk songs, such as *Molly on the Shore* 1921.

He studied in Frankfurt, moved to London, then settled in the USA 1914. Grainger shared his friend Ferruccio ◊Busoni's vision of a free music, devising a synthesizer and composing machine far ahead of its time.

Grammy award any of several prizes given annually by the US National Academy of Recording Arts and Sciences since 1958. The categories include Album of the Year, Record of the Year (single), Best New Artist of the Year, and Best Performance subdivided by sex and genre.

The recipients of the Grammy awards are chosen by the US record industry; in 1993, English guitarist Eric Clapton received six for his *Unplugged* album.

Granados Enrique 1867–1916. Spanish composer and pianist. His piano-work *Goyescas* 1911, inspired by the art of ◊Goya, was converted to an opera 1916.

Grand Guignol genre of short horror play originally produced at the Grand Guignol theatre in Montmartre, Paris (named after the bloodthirsty character Guignol in late 18th-century marionette plays).

grand opera type of opera without any spoken dialogue (unlike the *opéra-comique*), as performed at the Paris Opéra 1820s–80s. Grand operas were extremely long (five acts), and included incidental music and a ballet. Composers of grand opera include D F E Auber, Giacomo Meyerbeer, and Ludovic Halévy; examples include Verdi's *Don Carlos* 1867 and Meyerbeer's *Les Huguenots* 1836.

Grange Kenneth 1929– . English industrial designer, a member of the London-based Pentagram group of graphic and industrial designers since 1972. He was among the first British designers to work as a consultant to industry and, from the late 1950s, has created a vast number of lasting designs for a range of manufacturers both at home and abroad.

Notable examples include the Kodak 'Brownie 44A' camera 1959 and the 'Chef' food mixer for Kenwood 1964. They demonstrate a simple elegance and a pragmatism which characterize British industrial design.

Granger (James) Stewart 1913–1993. British film actor. After several leading roles in British romantic films during World War II, he moved to

Hollywood 1950 and subsequently appeared in such fanciful films as *Scaramouche* 1952, *The Prisoner of Zenda* 1952, and *Moonfleet* 1955.

Grant Cary. Stage name of Archibald Leach 1904–1986. British-born actor who became a US citizen 1942. His witty, debonair personality made him a screen favourite for more than three decades. He was directed by Alfred ◊Hitchcock in *Suspicion* 1941, *Notorious* 1946, *To Catch a Thief* 1955, and *North by Northwest* 1959. He received a 1970 Academy Award for general excellence.

His other films include *She Done Him Wrong* 1933, *Bringing Up Baby* 1937, and *The Philadelphia Story* 1940.

Grant Duncan 1885–1978. Scottish painter and designer, a member of the ◊Bloomsbury Group and a pioneer of Post-Impressionism in the UK. He lived with the painter Vanessa Bell (1879–1961) from about 1914 and worked with her on decorative projects, such as those at the ◊Omega Workshops. Later works, such as *Snow Scene* 1921, show great fluency and a subtle use of colour.

Granville-Barker Harley 1877–1946. British theatre director and author. He was director and manager with J E Vedrenne at the Royal Court Theatre, London, 1904–18, producing plays by Shaw, Yeats, Ibsen, Galsworthy, and Masefield. His works include the plays *Waste* 1907, *The Voysey Inheritance* 1905, and *The Madras House* 1910. His series of *Prefaces to Shakespeare* 1927–47 influenced the staging of Shakespeare for many years.

Rightly thought of there is poetry in peaches... even when they are canned.

Harley Granville-Barker
The Madras House 1910

---

graph notation in music, an invented sign language representing unorthodox sounds objectively in pitch and time, or alternatively representing sounds of orthodox music in a visually unorthodox manner. A form of graph notation for speech patterns used in phonetics was adopted by Stockhausen in *Carré/Squared* 1959–60.

Graphic representation of sounds has been stimulated in modern times by both art and technology. Artists have experimented with visual images representing sounds; in 1940 Villa-Lobos composed *New York Skyline* based on the outline of a photograph projected on to graph paper and thence to music manuscript. Léon Scott's *phonautograph* 1856 for recording visual traces of speech sounds was the forerunner of much more sophisticated technology. The sound spectrograph developed 1944 by engineers at Bell Telephone Laboratories introduced a much

improved projection of audio events in pitch and time, providing a model for Stockhausen's iconic score *Elektronische Studie II/Electronic Study II* 1953–54. Cage's graphic scores of the 1950s revive memories of film experiments in the 1930s, as may be said of many European composers of graphic scores from the period 1959–70.

Grappelli Stephane 1908– . French jazz violinist who played in the Quintette du Hot Club de France 1934–39, in partnership with the guitarist Django ◊Reinhardt. Romantic improvisation is a hallmark of his style.

Grappelli spent World War II in the UK and returned several times to record there, including a number of jazz albums with the classical violinist Yehudi Menuhin in the 1970s. Of his other collaborations, an LP with the mandolinist David Grisman (1945–) reached the US pop chart 1981.

Grass Günter 1927– . German writer. The grotesque humour and socialist feeling of his novels *Die Blechtrommel/The Tin Drum* 1959 and *Der Butt/The Flounder* 1977 are also characteristic of many of his poems.

Born in Danzig (now Gdánsk), he studied at the art academies of Düsseldorf and Berlin, worked as a writer and sculptor (first in Paris and later in Berlin), and in 1958 won the coveted 'Group 47' prize.

Grateful Dead, the US psychedelic rock group formed 1965. Their shows feature long improvisations and subtle ensemble playing, seldom fully captured in recording; albums include *Live Dead* 1969, *Workingman's Dead* 1970, and *Built to Last* 1989.

Formed at the heart of the San Francisco ◊hippie scene, the Dead still represent an alternative life style to a core of fans (Deadheads) who follow the constantly touring band around the world. Remaining founder members are Jerry Garcia (1942–), guitar; Phil Lesh (1940–), bass; Bob Weir (1947–), guitar; and Bill Kreutzmann (1946–), drums. Out of their vast repertoire of original and nonoriginal material, they are especially identified with the song 'Truckin'' (from *American Beauty* 1970).

Graves Michael 1934– . US architect whose work, in the Post-Modernist idiom, is distinctive for the refined, elegant manner in which it blends classical and vernacular elements. Originally a member of the ◊New York Five group, with Peter Eisenman and Richard Meier, Graves went on to develop a highly idiosyncratic, colourful style, as represented in the Public Services building, Portland, Oregon, 1980–82, and Humana Tower, Louisville, Kentucky, 1986.

Graves Robert (Ranke) 1895–1985. English poet and author. He was severely wounded on the Somme in World War I, and his frank autobiography *Goodbye to All That* 1929 is one of the outstanding war books. Other works include the poems *Over the Brazier* 1916; two historical novels of imperial Rome, *I Claudius* and *Claudius the God*, both 1934; and books on myth – for example, *The White Goddess* 1948.

In love as in sport, the amateur status must be strictly maintained.

Robert Graves *Occupation: Writer*

Gravity's Rainbow novel 1973 by US writer Thomas ◊Pynchon. It is an epic narrative of conspiracy, paranoia, science, and history set during World War II. Taking the trajectory of the German V2 rocket as its main image, the novel is a quest for meaning in a world of impending chaos. It is a major work of ◊Post-Modernism.

Gray Eileen 1879–1976. Irish-born architect and furniture designer. Her Art Deco furniture explored the use of tubular metal, glass, and new materials such as aluminium.

After training as a painter at the Slade School of Art, London, she worked for a Japanese lacquer painter in Paris. She set up her own workshop and gradually concentrated on the design of furniture, woven textiles, and interiors.

Gray Thomas 1716–1771. English poet whose 'Elegy Written in a Country Churchyard' 1751 is one of the most quoted poems in English. Other poems include 'Ode on a Distant Prospect of Eton College', 'The Progress of Poesy', and 'The Bard'; these poems are now seen as the precursors of Romanticism.

Far from the madding crowd's ignoble strife

Thomas Gray *Elegy Written in a Country Churchyard* 1751

Great Expectations novel by Charles ◊Dickens, published 1861. Philip Pirrip ('Pip'), brought up by his sister and her husband, the blacksmith Joe Gargery, rejects his humble background and pursues wealth, which he believes comes from the elderly, eccentric Miss Havisham. Ultimately, through adversity, he recognizes the value of his origins.

I had cherished a profound conviction that her bringing me up by hand, gave her no right to bring me up by jerks.

Charles Dickens *Great Expectations*

Great Gatsby, The novel 1925 by US writer F Scott ◊Fitzgerald. It is the tale of the dazzling, enigmatic Gatsby who becomes a millionaire in order to win back his first love but whose dream ends in death and his own murder. The novel, set in the 1920s Jazz Age, depicts the corruption of the American enchantment with wealth.

Greco, El (Doménikos Theotokopoulos) 1541–1614. Spanish painter called 'the Greek' because he was born in Crete. He studied in Italy, worked in Rome from about 1570, and by 1577 had settled in Toledo. He painted elegant portraits and intensely emotional religious scenes with increasingly distorted figures and flickering light; for example, *The Burial of Count Orgaz* 1586 (church of San Tomé, Toledo).

Greek architecture the architecture of ancient Greece is the base for virtually all architectural developments in Europe. The Greeks invented the ◊entablature, which allowed roofs to be hipped (inverted V-shape), and perfected the design of arcades with support columns. There were three styles, or orders, of columns: Doric (with no base), Ionic (with scrolled capitals), and Corinthian (with acanthus-leafed capitals).

Of the Greek orders, the **Doric** is the oldest; it is said to have evolved from a former timber prototype. The finest example of a Doric temple is the Parthenon in Athens (447–438 BC). The origin of the **Ionic** is uncertain. The earliest building in which the Ionic capital appears is the temple of Artemis (Diana) at Ephesus (530 BC). The gateway to the Acropolis in Athens (known as the Propylaea) has internal columns of the Ionic order. The finest example is the Erechtheum (421–406 BC) in Athens. The **Corinthian** order belongs to a later period of Greek art. A leading example is the temple of Zeus (Jupiter) Olympius in Athens (174 BC), completed under Roman influence AD 129. The monumental and sumptously ornamental Mausoleum in Halicarnassus (353 BC) was one of the ◊Seven Wonders of the World.

Greek art the sculpture, mosaic, and crafts of ancient Greece (no large-scale painting survives). It is usually divided into three periods: *Archaic* (late 8th century–480 BC), showing Egyptian influence; *Classical* (480–323 BC), characterized by dignified and eloquent realism; and *Hellenistic* (323–27 BC), more exuberant or dramatic. Sculptures of human figures dominate all periods, and vase painting was a focus for artistic development for many centuries.

Archaic period Statues of naked standing men (*kouroi*) and draped females (*korai*) show an Egyptian influence in their rigid frontality. By about 500 BC the figure was allowed to relax its weight on to one leg. Subjects were usually depicted smiling.

Classical period Expressions assumed a dignified serenity. Further movement was introduced in new poses, such as in Myron's bronze *Diskobolus/The Discus Thrower* 460–50 BC, and in the rhythmic Parthenon reliefs of riders and horses supervised by Phidias. Polykleitos' sculpture *Doryphoros/The Spear Carrier* 450–440 BC was of such harmony and poise that it set a standard for beautiful proportions. Praxiteles introduced the female nude into the sculptural repertory with the graceful *Aphrodite of Cnidus* about 350 BC. It was easier to express movement in bronze, hollow-cast by the lost-wax method, but relatively few bronze sculptures survive, and many are known only through Roman copies in marble.

Hellenistic period Sculptures such as the *Winged Victory of Samothrace* with its dramatic drapery, and the tortured *Laocoön* explored the effects of movement and deeply felt emotion.

vase painting Artists worked as both potters and painters until the 5th century BC, and the works they signed were exported throughout the empire. Made in several standard shapes and sizes, the pots served as functional containers for wine, water, and oil. The first decoration took the form of simple lines and circles, out of which the *Geometric style* emerged near Athens in the 10th century BC. It consisted of precisely drawn patterns, such as the key meander. Gradually the bands of decoration multiplied and the human figure, geometrically stylized, was added. About 700 BC the potters of Corinth invented the *Black Figure* technique in which unglazed red clay was painted in black with mythological scenes and battles in a narrative frieze. About 530 BC Athenian potters reversed the process and developed the more sophisticated *Red Figure* pottery, which allowed for more detailed and elaborate painting of the figures in red against a black background. Their style grew increasingly naturalistic, showing lively scenes from daily life. The finest examples date from the mid-6th to the mid-5th century BC in Athens. Later painters tried to follow major art trends and represent spatial depth, dissipating the unique quality of their fine linear technique.

crafts The ancient Greeks excelled in carving gems and cameos and in metalwork. They also invented the pictorial mosaic, and from the 5th century BC onwards floors were paved with coloured pebbles depicting mythological subjects. Later, specially cut cubes of stone and glass called *tesserae* were used, and Greek artisans working for the Romans reproduced paintings, such as *Alexander at the Battle of Issus* from Pompeii, the originals of which are lost.

Greek literature literature of Greece, ancient and modern.

ancient The two pre-eminent figures in early Greek literature were Homer, reputed author of the epic narrative poems the *Iliad* and *Odyssey*, and Hesiod, whose *Works and Days* deals with morals as they pertain to agricultural life. Lyric poets included Sappho and Pindar, while prose was developed by the historians Herodotus and Thucydides. During the 5th century BC Athens was the home of the tragedians Aeschylus, Sophocles, and Euripides, and the comic dramatist Aristophanes. Following the defeat of Athens by Sparta 404 came a period dominated by prose, with the historian Xenophon, the idealist philosopher Plato, the orators Isocrates and Demosthenes, and the scientific teacher Aristotle.

After 323 BC and the death of Alexander the Great, Athens lost its political importance, but was still a university town with such teachers as Epicurus, Zeno, and Theophrastus, and the comic dramatist Menander. Early on in this Hellenistic period, Alexandria became a centre of Greek culture with the establishment of its library at the court of the Ptolemies, which was graced by scientists such as Euclid, and the poets Callimachus, Apollonius, and Theocritus.

During the 2nd century BC Rome became a new centre for Greek thought and literature, and Polybius, an historian, spent most of his life there; in the 1st century BC Rome also sheltered the geographer Strabo, the critic and teacher Dionysius of Halicarnassus, and a number of Greek poets such as Archias, Antipater, and Philodemus, some of whose epigrams were collected by Meleager in the first *Greek Anthology*.

The 1st century AD saw the work of the Jewish writers Philo Judaeus and Josephus, the New Testament writers, and the biographer and essayist Plutarch; these were followed in the 2nd century by the satirist Lucian and the anecdotal writer Athenaeus.

To the 3rd century belong the historians Cassius Dio and Herodian, the Christian fathers Clement and Origen, and the neo-Platonists, led by Plotinus; the earliest Greek novels date from approximately the same period (*Theagenes and Chariclea* by Heliodorus). A feature of the 4th and 5th centuries was the revival of derivative epic. For medieval Greek literature, see ◊Byzantine literature.

modern After the fall of Constantinople, the Byzantine tradition was perpetuated in the Classical Greek writing of, for example, the 15th-century chronicles of Cyprus, various historical works in the 16th and 17th centuries, and educational and theological works in the 18th century. The 17th and 18th centuries saw much controversy over whether to write in the Greek vernacular (*Demotic*), the classical language (*Katharevousa*), or the language of the Eastern Orthodox Church. Adamantios Korais (1748–1833), the first great modern writer, produced a compromise language; he was followed by the prose and drama writer and poet Aleksandros Rhangavis ('Rangabe') (1810–1892), and many others.

The 10th-century epic of *Digenis Akritas* is usually considered to mark the beginnings of modern Greek vernacular literature, and the Demotic was kept alive in the flourishing Cretan literature of the 16th and 17th centuries, in numerous popular songs, and in the Klephtic ballads of the 18th century. With independence in the 19th century the popular movement became prominent with the Ionian poet Dionysios Solomos (1798–1857), Andreas Kalvos (1796–1869), and others, and later with Iannis Psichari (1854–1929), short-story writer and dramatist, and the prose writer Alexandros Papadiamandis (1851–1911), who influenced many younger writers, for example Konstantinos Hatzopoulos (1868–1921), poet and essayist. After the 1920s, the novel began to emerge with Stratis Myrivilis (1892–1969) and Nikos Kazantzakis (1885–1957), author of *Zorba the Greek* 1946 and also a poet. There were also the Nobel-prize-winning poets George ◊Seferis and Odysseus ◊Elytis.

Greek Revival architectural style that arose in the late 18th century with the opening up of Greece and its ancient architectural heritage to the West; until then Roman architecture had been considered the only true Classical style. A number of British architects became associated with the Greek Revival, notably John Soane, John Nash, C R Cockerell, Sir Robert Smirke, and William Henry Playfair. In Germany, Leopold von Klenze (1784–1864) and Karl Friedrich Schinkel were exponents of the style.

Two events – the publication 1762 and 1789 of two volumes of *Antiquities of Athens* by Nicholas Revett (1725–1804) and James Stuart, and the arrival in London of the Parthenon sculptures (the ◊Elgin marbles) – acted as catalysts of the movement.

Green Henry. Pen name of Henry Vincent Yorke 1905–1974. British novelist whose works (for example *Loving* 1945, and *Nothing* 1950) are characterized by an experimental colloquial prose style and extensive use of dialogue.

Greenaway Kate 1846–1901. English illustrator, known for her drawings of children. In 1877 she first exhibited at the Royal Academy, London, and began her collaboration with the colour-printer Edmund Evans, with whom she produced a number of children's books, including *Mother Goose*.

Greenaway Peter 1942– . British director of highly stylized, often controversial, cerebral but richly visual films. His feeling for perspective and lighting reveal his early training as a painter. His films, such as *A Zed & Two Noughts* 1985, are hallmarked by puzzle motifs and numerical games. Greenaway's other films include *The Draughtsman's Contract* 1982, *Belly of an Architect* 1986, *Drowning by Numbers* 1988, *The Cook, the Thief, his Wife and her Lover* 1989, *Prospero's Books* 1991, and *The Baby of Macon* 1993.

Greenaway Medal (full name *Library Association Kate Greenaway Medal*) annual award for an outstanding illustrated book for children published in the UK, first awarded 1955.

green belt area surrounding a large city, officially designated not to be built on but preserved where possible as open space (for agricultural and recreational use). In the UK the first green belts were established from 1938 around conurbations such as London in order to prevent urban sprawl. New towns were set up to take the overspill population.

Greene (Henry) Graham 1904–1991. English writer whose novels of guilt, despair, and penitence are set in a world of urban seediness or political corruption in many parts of the world. They include ◊*Brighton Rock* 1938, *The Power and the Glory* 1940, *The Heart of the Matter* 1948, *The Third Man* 1950, *The Honorary Consul* 1973, and *Monsignor Quixote* 1982.

Catholics and Communists have committed great crimes, but at least they have not stood aside, like an established society, and been indifferent. I would rather have blood on my hands than water like Pilate.

Graham Greene *The Comedians*

Green Man or *Jack-in-the-Green* in English folklore, figure dressed and covered in foliage, associated with festivities celebrating the arrival of spring. His face is represented in a variety of English church carvings, in wood or stone, often with a protruding tongue. Similar figures also occur in French and German folklore, the earliest related carvings being at Trèves, France, now Trier, Germany, on the river Mosel (about AD 200).

Greenstreet Sydney 1879–1954. British character actor. He made an impressive film debut in *The Maltese Falcon* 1941 and became one of the cinema's best-known villains. His other films include *Casablanca* 1942 and *The Mask of Dimitrios* 1944.

Greenwich Village in New York City, a section of lower Manhattan (from 14th Street south to Houston Street and from Broadway west to the Hudson River), which from the late 19th century became the bohemian and artistic quarter of the city and, despite expensive rentals, remains so.

More generally, its name suggests the spirit of avant-gardism and political radicalism in US culture; it is variously associated with left-wing causes, sexual liberation, experimental art and theatre, and new magazines and movements. This attitude caused the adjoining section of the Lower East Side, east of Broadway, now far more outrageous than 'the Village', to be called the **East Village**.

Greenwood Walter 1903–1974. English novelist of the Depression, born in Salford. His own lack of a job gave authenticity to *Love on the Dole* 1933, later dramatized and filmed.

Gregorian chant any of a body of plainsong choral chants associated with Pope Gregory the

Great (540–604), which became standard in the Roman Catholic Church.

Gregory Isabella Augusta (borne Persse) 1852–1932. Irish dramatist, associated with W B Yeats in creating the ◊Abbey Theatre, Dublin, 1904. Her plays include the comedy *Spreading the News* 1904 and the tragedy *Gaol Gate* 1906. Her journals 1916–30 were published 1946.

Grendel in the Old English epic poem *Beowulf*, the male monster that the hero has to kill.

Greuze Jean Baptiste 1725–1805. French painter of sentimental narrative works, such as *The Bible Reading* 1755 (Louvre, Paris). Many of his works were reproduced in engravings.

Greville Charles (Cavendish Fulke) 1794–1865. British diarist. He was Clerk of the Council in Ordinary 1821–59, an office which brought him into close contact with all the personalities of the court and of both political parties. They provided him with much of the material for his *Memoirs* 1817–60.

Greville Fulke, 1st Baron Brooke 1554–1628. English poet and courtier, friend and biographer of Philip Sidney. Greville's works, none of them published during his lifetime, include *Caelica*, a sequence of poems in different metres; *The Tragedy of Mustapha* and *The Tragedy of Alaham*, tragedies modelled on the Latin Seneca; and the *Life of Sir Philip Sidney* 1652. He has been commended for his plain style and tough political thought.

Grey (Pearl) Zane 1872–1939. US author of Westerns, such as *Riders of the Purple Sage* 1912. He wrote more than 80 books and was primarily responsible for the creation of the Western as a literary genre.

Grey Beryl 1927– . British dancer. Prima ballerina with the Sadler's Wells Company 1942–57, she then danced internationally, and was artistic director of the London Festival Ballet 1968–79. Her roles included the Black Queen in *Checkmate*, and Odette-Odile in *Swan Lake*.

Grieg Edvard Hagerup 1843–1907. Norwegian nationalist composer. Much of his music is small-scale, particularly his songs, dances, sonatas, and piano works, strongly identifying with Norwegian folk music. Among his orchestral works are the *Piano Concerto in A Minor* 1869 and the incidental music for Henrik Ibsen's *Peer Gynt* 1876, which was commissioned by Ibsen and the Norwegian government.

Grieg studied at the Leipzig Conservatoire and in Copenhagen. He was a director of the Christiania (Oslo) Philharmonic Society 1866 and was involved in the formation of the Norwegian Academy of Music.

Grierson John 1898–1972. Scottish film producer, director, and theoretician. He was a sociologist who pioneered the documentary film in Britain, describing it as 'the creative treatment of actuality'. He directed *Drifters* 1929 and produced 1930–35 *Industrial Britain, Song of Ceylon*, and *Night Mail*. During World War II he created the National Film Board of Canada. Some of his writings were gathered in *Grierson on Documentary* 1946.

griffin mythical monster, the supposed guardian of hidden treasure, with the body, tail, and hind legs of a lion, and the head, forelegs, and wings of an eagle. It is often found in heraldry, for example the armorial crest of the City of London, and two griffins on the Thames Embankment guard its western boundary.

Griffith D(avid) W(ark) 1875–1948. US film director, an influential figure in the development of cinema as an art. He made hundreds of 'one-reelers' 1908–13, in which he pioneered the techniques of masking, fade-out, flashback, crosscut, close-up, and long shot. After much experimentation with photography and new techniques he directed *The Birth of a Nation* 1915, about the aftermath of the Civil War, later criticized as degrading to blacks.

His other films include the epic *Intolerance* 1916, *Broken Blossoms* 1919, *Way Down East* 1920, *Orphans of the Storm* 1921, and *The Struggle* 1931. He was a cofounder of United Artists 1919. He made two unsuccessful sound films and subsequently lived forgotten in Hollywood until his death.

Grillparzer Franz 1791–1872. Austrian poet and dramatist. His plays include the tragedy *Die Ahnfrau/The Ancestress* 1817, the classical *Sappho* 1818, and the trilogy *Das goldene Vliess/The Golden Fleece* 1821.

Born in Vienna, Grillparzer worked for the Austrian government service 1813–56. His historical tragedies *König Ottokars Glück und Ende/King Ottocar, His Rise and Fall* 1825 and *Ein treuer Diener seines Herrn/A True Servant of His Master* 1826 both involved him with the censor. There followed his two greatest dramas, *Des Meeres und der Liebe Wellen/The Waves of Sea and Love* 1831, returning to the Hellenic world, and *Der Traum, ein Leben/A Dream Is Life* 1834. He wrote a bitter cycle of poems *Tristia ex Ponto* 1835 after an unhappy love affair.

Grimaldi Joseph 1779–1837. British clown, born in London, the son of an Italian actor. He appeared on the stage at two years old. He gave his name 'Joey' to all later clowns, and excelled as 'Mother Goose' performed at Covent Garden 1806.

Grimm brothers Jakob Ludwig Karl 1785–1863 and Wilhelm 1786–1859, philologists and collectors of German fairy tales such as 'Hansel and Gretel' and 'Rumpelstiltskin'. Joint compilers of an exhaustive dictionary of German, they saw the study of language and the collecting of folk tales as strands in a single enterprise.

Encouraged by a spirit of Romantic nationalism the brothers collected stories from friends, relatives, and villagers. *Kinder und Hausmärchen/ Nursery and Household Tales* were published as successive volumes 1812, 1815, and 1822. Jakob was professor of philology at Göttingen. His *Deutsche Grammatick/German Grammar* 1819 was the first historical treatment of the Germanic languages.

Grimmelshausen Hans Jacob Christofel von 1625–1676. German picaresque novelist whose *Der Abenteuerliche Simplicissimus/The Adventurous Simplicissimus* 1669 reflects his experiences in the Thirty Years' War.

Grimshaw Nicholas 1939– . British architect whose work has developed along ◊High-Tech lines, diverging sharply from that of his former partner, Terry ◊Farrell. His *Financial Times* printing works, London, 1988, is an uncompromising industrial building, exposing machinery to view through a glass outer wall. The British Pavilion for Expo '92 in Seville, created in similar vein, addressed problems of climatic control, incorporating a huge wall of water in its façade and sail-like mechanisms on the roof.

Gris Juan 1887–1927. Spanish painter, one of the earliest Cubists. He developed a distinctive geometrical style, often strongly coloured. He experimented with paper collage and made designs for Diaghilev's Ballets Russes 1922–23.

grisaille monochrome painting in shades of grey, either used as a ground for an oil painting, or as a work in its own right simulating the effect of bas ◊relief. The latter technique was used by the Italian Renaissance painter and engraver ◊Mantegna.

Gropius Walter Adolf 1883–1969. German architect who lived in the USA from 1937. He was an early exponent of the ◊International Style defined by glass curtain walls, cubic blocks, and unsupported corners, for example, the model factory and office building at the 1914 Cologne Werkbund exhibition, designed with Adolph Meyer. A founder-director of the ◊Bauhaus school in Weimar 1919–28, he advocated teamwork in design and artistic standards in industrial production. He was responsible for the new Bauhaus premises at Dessau 1925–26, a hallmark of the International Style.

From 1937 he was professor of architecture at Harvard. His other works include the Fagus Works (a shoe factory in Prussia) 1911 and the Harvard Graduate Centre 1949–50.

The human mind is like an umbrella – it functions best when open.

Walter Gropius in the *Observer* 1965

gros point embroidery that uses wool to fill netting (see ◊petit point). It is normally used in colourful designs on widely spaced canvas.

Grossmith George 1847–1912. British actor and singer. Turning from journalism to the stage, in 1877 he began a long association with the Gilbert and Sullivan operas, in which he created a number of parts. He collaborated with his brother **Weedon Grossmith** (1853–1919) on the comic novel *Diary of a Nobody* 1894.

Grosz Georg 1893–1959. German Expressionist painter and graphic artist, a founder of the Berlin Dada group 1918. Grosz excelled in savage satirical drawings criticizing the government and the military establishment. After numerous prosecutions he fled his native Berlin 1932 and went to the USA where he became a naturalized American 1938.

Grotowski Jerzy 1933– . Polish theatre director. His ascetic theory of performance in *Towards a Poor Theatre* 1968 has had a great influence on experimental theatre in the USA and Europe. His most famous productions were *Akropolis* 1962, *The Constant Prince* 1965, and *Apocalypsis cum Figuris* 1969, which he toured widely.

He directed in Opole (from 1959) and then in Wroclaw (from 1965); his company, originally the Theatre of the Thirteen Rows, was renamed the Laboratory Theatre 1962.

ground bass in music, a bass line that repeats cyclically, over which an evolving harmonic-melodic structure is laid. Examples are the ◊chaconne and ◊passacaglia.

Grove Frederick Philip 1879–1948. Canadian novelist and essayist. His experiences as an itinerant farmhand and schoolteacher on the prairies gave substance to his evocative sketches *Over Prairie Trails* 1922 and his realist tragedies *Settlers of the Marsh* 1925 and *Fruits of the Earth* 1933, exploring the emotional and spiritual costs of pioneer life, material success, and family conflict in rural Manitoba.

Grundy, Mrs symbol of rigid moral propriety, first introduced as a character in Thomas Morton's play *Speed the Plough* 1798.

Grünewald (Mathias or Mathis Neithardt or Gothardt) *c.* 1475–1528. German painter, active in Mainz, Frankfurt, and Halle. He was court painter, architect, and engineer to the archbishop of Mainz 1508–14. His few surviving paintings show an intense involvement with religious subjects. His *Isenheim Altarpiece* 1515 (Unterlinden Museum, Colmar, France), with its tortured figure of Jesus, recalls medieval traditions.

grunge rock-music style of the early 1990s, characterized by a thick, abrasive, distorted sound. Grunge evolved from ◊punk in the Seattle, Washington, area of the USA and came to prominence with the chart success of the band ◊Nirvana 1991.

The Melvins (formed in Seattle early 1980s) pioneered grunge; Pearl Jam (formed in Seattle 1990) have been the most commercially successful grunge-inspired group in the wake of Nirvana.

Guardi Francesco 1712–1793. Italian painter. He produced souvenir views of his native Venice that were commercially less successful than Canaletto's but are now considered more atmospheric, with subtler use of reflected light.

Guare John 1938– . US dramatist best known for his screenplay of Louis Malle's *Atlantic City* 1980. His stage plays include *House of Blue Leaves* 1971 and *Six Degrees of Separation* 1990.

Guareschi Giovanni 1909–1968. Italian author of short stories featuring the friendly feud between parish priest Don Camillo and the communist village mayor.

Guarini Giovanni 1924–1983. Italian architect whose intricate carved Baroque designs were produced without formal architectural training. Guarini was a secular priest of the Theatine Order, and many of his buildings are religious; for example, the Chapel of the Holy Shroud, Turin 1667–90. His greatest secular work is the undulating Palazzo Carignano, Turin, 1679.

Guarneri family of stringed-instrument makers of Cremona, Italy. Giuseppe 'del Gesù' Guarneri (1698–1744) produced the finest models.

Gucci Italian–US company manufacturing and retailing leather luggage and accessories from the 1960s, and designing clothes for men and women from 1969. The Gucci family firm was founded in Italy in the 15th century.

In 1905 Guccio Gucci moved from millinery to saddlery, and the business was expanded by his three sons, principally Aldo Gucci (1905–1990), who was responsible for the company's growth in the USA. The Gucci label became an international status symbol in the 1970s. In the early 1990s interest in Gucci grew again, following the introduction of a range of relaxed sportswear-orientated outfits, and the reworking of Gucci loafers in brightly coloured suede.

Guercino, Il (Giovanni Francesco Barbieri) 1591–1666. Italian Baroque painter, active chiefly in Rome. In his ceiling painting of *Aurora* 1621–23 (Villa Ludovisi, Rome), the chariot-borne figure of Dawn rides across the heavens; the architectural framework is imitated in the painting, giving the illusion that the ceiling opens into the sky.

Guercino's use of dramatic lighting recalls ◊Caravaggio, but his brighter colours reflect a contrasting mood. His later works, produced when he had retired to Bologna, are calmer, the colours less striking.

Guernica large oil painting (3.5 m × 7.8 m/ 11 ft 5 in × 25 ft 6 in) by Picasso as a mural for the Spanish pavilion at the Paris Exposition Universelle 1937 (now in the Prado, Madrid), inspired by the bombing of Guernica, the seat of the Basque parliament during the Spanish Civil War. The painting, executed entirely in black, white, and grey, was the culmination of years of experimentation. It has since become a symbol of the senseless destruction of war.

Guido Reni. Italian painter, see ◊Reni.

Guimard Hector 1867–1942. French architect and leading exponent of the ◊Art Nouveau style in France. His flamboyant designs of glazed canopies for a number of Paris Métro station exteriors are one of Art Nouveau's most enduring images.

In another of his projects, the Castel Béranger apartment block, Paris, 1894–98, he emphasized the importance of detail by designing each apartment to a different plan. Within the building, the Art Nouveau style is apparent on everything from stonework to door handles.

Guinevere Welsh *Gwenhwyfar* in British legend, the wife of King ◊Arthur. Her adulterous love affair with the knight ◊Lancelot of the Lake led ultimately to Arthur's death.

Guinness Alec 1914– . English actor of stage and screen. His films include *Great Expectations* 1946, *Kind Hearts and Coronets* 1949 (in which he played eight parts), *The Bridge on the River Kwai* 1957 (Academy Award), and *Star Wars* 1977.

Guinness joined the Old Vic 1936. A subtle character actor, he played the enigmatic spymaster in TV adaptations of John Le Carré's *Tinker, Tailor, Soldier, Spy* 1979 and *Smiley's People* 1981.

An actor is totally vulnerable ... from head to toe, his total personality is exposed to critical judgement – his intellect, his bearing, his diction, his appearance. In short, his ego.

Alec Guinness *New York Times Magazine* May 1964

Güiraldes Ricardo 1886–1927. Argentine novelist and poet. Contact with French avant-garde writing in Paris 1910 influenced the controversially innovative poetry and prose of his collection *El cencerro de cristal/The Crystal Bell* 1915. Deep feeling for his native land characterizes his stories *Cuentos de muerte y de sangre/ Tales of Death and Blood* 1915 and his novel *Don Segundo Sombra* 1926, a poetic idealization of Argentinian *gaucho* (nomadic cattleman) life, his best-known work.

guitar six-stringed, or twelve-stringed, flat-bodied musical instrument, plucked or strummed with the fingers. The *Hawaiian guitar*, laid across the lap, uses a metal bar to produce a distinctive gliding tone; the solid-bodied *electric guitar*, developed in the 1950s, mixes and amplifies vibrations from microphone contacts at different points to produce a range of tone qualities.

Derived from a Moorish original, the guitar spread throughout Europe in medieval times, becoming firmly established in Italy, Spain, and the Spanish American colonies. Its 20th-century revival owes much to Andrés ◊Segovia, Julian ◊Bream, and John ◊Williams. The guitar's prominence in popular music can be traced from the traditions of the US mid-West; it played a supporting harmony role in jazz and dance bands during the 1920s and adapted quickly to electric amplification.

Gulliver's Travels satirical novel by the Irish writer Jonathan ◊Swift published 1726. The four countries visited by the narrator Gulliver ridicule different aspects of human nature, customs, and politics.

Gulliver's travels take him to *Lilliput*, whose inhabitants are only 15 cm/6 in tall; *Brobdignag*, where they are gigantic; *Laputa*, run by mad scientists; and the land of the *Houyhnhnms*, horses who embody reason and virtue, while the human *Yahoos* have only the worst human qualities.

He [the emperor] is taller by almost the breadth of my nail than any of his court, which alone is enough to strike an awe into the beholders.

Jonathan Swift *Gulliver's Travels* 1726

Guston Philip 1913–1980. Canadian-born US painter. Initially inspired by the Mexican muralists, he developed a fluid, abstract style in the 1950s. He later returned to a harsh, dynamic figuration, satirizing contemporary life with cartoonlike drawings in livid pinks, greys, white, and black, as in *Painting, Smoking, Eating* 1973 (Stedelijk Museum, Amsterdam).

Largely self-taught, Guston began his career executing murals for the Federal Arts Project 1935–42. The Impressionist style of abstraction he adopted in the 1950s placed him squarely within the New York School of Abstract Expressionism.

Guthrie Tyrone 1900–1971. British theatre director, notable for his innovative approach. Administrator of the ◊Old Vic and Sadler's Wells theatres 1939–45, he helped found the Ontario (Stratford) Shakespeare Festival 1953 and the Minneapolis theatre now named after him. He pioneered the modern concept of open-stage productions for medieval and Renaissance plays.

Guthrie Woody (Woodrow Wilson) 1912–1967. US folk singer and songwriter whose left-wing protest songs, 'dustbowl ballads', and 'talking blues' influenced, among others, Bob Dylan; they include 'Deportees', 'Hard Travelin'', and 'This Land Is Your Land'. His son *Arlo Guthrie* (1947–), also a folk singer, is best known for the Vietnam-draft epic 'Alice's Restaurant' 1967.

Guttuso Renato 1912–1987. Italian painter, a leading exponent of Social Realism during and after World War II and a committed anti-Fascist. Social and political comment remained an essential part of his work, as in *Occupation of Uncultivated Land in Sicily* 1949–50 (Gemaldgalerie Neue Meister, Dresden).

His varied subject matter includes street scenes, land and seascapes, still lifes, interiors, nudes, and large allegories of contemporary life based on well-known works by old and modern masters.

Guys Constantin 1805–1892. Dutch-born French illustrator, remembered for his witty drawings of Paris life during the Second Empire. He was with the English poet ◊Byron at Missolonghi, Greece, and made sketches of the Crimean War for the *Illustrated London News*. Baudelaire praised his 'modernity'.

Gwyn (or *Gwynn*) Nell (Eleanor) 1651–1687. English comedy actress from 1665, formerly an orange-seller at Drury Lane Theatre, London. The poet Dryden wrote parts for her, and from 1669 she was the mistress of Charles II.

Let not poor Nellie starve.

Charles II last words

Gyokudo Uragami 1745–1820. Japanese painter, known for the vibrant quality of his brushwork. He painted mainly landscapes, executed in a Chinese style but with a sense of the personal and intimate typical of Japanese art.

habanera or *havanaise* slow dance in 2/4 time, originating in Havana, Cuba, which was introduced into Spain during the 19th century. There is a celebrated example of this dance in Bizet's opera *Carmen*.

Hackman Gene 1931– . US actor. He became a star as 'Popeye' Doyle in *The French Connection* 1971 and continued to play a variety of often combative roles in such films as *The Conversation* 1974, *The French Connection II* 1975, *Mississippi Burning* 1988, and *Unforgiven* 1992.

Hades in Greek mythology, the underworld where spirits went after death, usually depicted as a cavern or pit underneath the Earth, the entrance of which was guarded by the three-headed dog Cerberus. It was presided over by the god Pluto or Hades (Roman Dis). Pluto was the brother of Zeus and married ◊Persephone, daughter of Demeter and Zeus. *Tartarus* was where the wicked were punished, for example, Tantalus.

Hadid Zahia 1950– . British architect, an exponent of ◊Deconstructionism, influential through her drawings rather than buildings. Her unbuilt competition-winning entry for Hong Kong's Peak Club 1983 established her reputation, and in 1993 she completed her first major building, a fire station for the Vitra Furniture Factory at Weil-am-Rhein, Germany.

Hâfiz Shams al-Din Muhammad *c.* 1326–1390. Persian lyric poet who was born in Shiraz and taught in a Dervish college there. His *Diwan*, a collection of short odes, extols the pleasures of life and satirizes his fellow Dervishes.

There is an ambush everywhere from the army of accidents; therefore the rider of life runs with loosened reins.

Hâfiz *Diwan* 14th century

Haggard H(enry) Rider 1856–1925. English novelist. He used his experience in the South African colonial service in his romantic adventure tales, including *King Solomon's Mines* 1885 and *She* 1887.

Haggard Merle 1937– . US country singer, songwriter, and musician (guitar and fiddle) whose songs deal with working-class tribulations and extol patriotism. He had hits with, among others, 'I Am a Lonesome Fugitive' 1966, 'Sing Me Back Home' 1967, 'Mama Tried' 1968, and 'Okie from Muskogee' 1969. He has made tribute albums to several of his influences, among them Jimmie Rodgers 1969, Bob Wills 1970, 1974, and Elvis Presley 1977, and recorded many duet albums, for example with George Jones 1982 and Willie Nelson 1983, 1987.

Hagia Sophia or *Santa Sophia* (Greek 'holy wisdom') Byzantine building in Istanbul, Turkey, built 532–37 as an Eastern Orthodox cathedral, replacing earlier churches. From 1204 to 1261 it was a Catholic cathedral; from 1453 to 1934 an Islamic mosque; and in 1934 it became a museum. Lavishly decorated with marble and mosaics, and having a huge central dome pierced by 40 windows, it is one of the greatest masterpieces of Byzantine architecture.

ha-ha in landscape gardening, a sunken boundary wall permitting an unobstructed view beyond a garden; a device much used by Capability ◊Brown.

haiku seventeen-syllable Japanese verse form, usually divided into three lines of five, seven, and five syllables. ◊Bashō popularized the form in the 17th century. It evolved from the 31-syllable *tanka* form dominant from the 8th century.

Traditionally haiku contain a word or expression relating the poem to a particular season; for example, 'the moon' refers to autumn, 'the hazy moon' to spring. Within each season, haiku are subclassified by topic: weather, fields and mountains; temples and shrines; human affairs; birds and other animals; trees and flowers. The stress on simplicity and intuitive perception came to haiku from Zen Buddhism. The two greatest haiku poets after Bashō were Yosa Buson (1716–1783) and Kobayashi Issa (1763–1827).

Haitink Bernard 1929– . Dutch conductor. He has been associated with the Concertgebouw Orchestra, Amsterdam, from 1958, and the London Philharmonic Orchestra from 1967; musical director at Glyndebourne 1977–87 and at the Royal Opera House, Covent Garden, London, from 1987. A noted interpreter of Mahler and Shostakovich, he also conducted Mozart's music for the film *Amadeus*, after the play by Peter Schaffer.

Hakluyt Richard 1553–1616. English geographer whose chief work is *The Principal Navigations, Voyages and Discoveries of the English Nation* 1598–1600. He was assisted by Sir Walter Raleigh.

He lectured on cartography at Oxford, became geographical adviser to the East India Company, and was an original member of the Virginia Company. The *Hakluyt Society*, established 1846, published later accounts of exploration.

Hale Sarah Josepha Buell 1788–1879. US poet, author of 'Mary had a Little Lamb' 1830.

Halévy Ludovic 1834–1908. French novelist and librettist. He collaborated with Hector Crémieux in the libretto for Offenbach's *Orpheus in the Underworld*; and with Henri Meilhac on librettos for Offenbach's *La Belle Hélène* and *La Vie parisienne*, as well as for Bizet's *Carmen*.

Haley Bill 1927–1981. US pioneer of rock and roll who was originally a western-swing musician. His songs 'Rock Around the Clock' 1954 (recorded with his group the Comets and featured in the 1955 film *Blackboard Jungle*) and 'Shake, Rattle and Roll' 1955 were big hits of the early rock-and-roll era.

Hall (Marguerite) Radclyffe 1883–1943. English novelist. *The Well of Loneliness* 1928 brought her notoriety because of its lesbian theme. Its review in the *Sunday Express* newspaper stated: 'I had rather give a healthy boy or girl a phial of prussic acid than this novel'. Her other works include the novel *Adam's Bread* 1926 and four volumes of poetry.

Hall Peter (Reginald Frederick) 1930– . English theatre, opera, and film director. He was director of the Royal Shakespeare Theatre in Stratford-on-Avon 1960–68 and developed the Royal Shakespeare Company 1968–73 until appointed director of the National Theatre 1973–88, succeeding Laurence Olivier. He founded the Peter Hall Company 1988.

Hall's stage productions include Beckett's *Waiting for Godot* 1955, *The Wars of the Roses* 1963, Pinter's *The Homecoming* stage 1967 and film 1973, *The Oresteia* 1981, and *Orpheus Descending* 1988. He has directed operas at Covent Garden, Bayreuth, and New York, and in 1984 was appointed artistic director of opera at Glyndebourne, with productions of *Carmen* 1985 and *Albert Herring* 1985–86.

We do not necessarily improve with age: for better or worse we become more like ourselves.

Peter Hall in the *Observer* Jan 1988

Hals Frans *c.* 1581–1666. Flemish-born painter of lively portraits, such as the *Laughing Cavalier* 1624 (Wallace Collection, London), and large groups of military companies, governors of charities, and others (many examples in the Frans Hals Museum, Haarlem, the Netherlands). In the 1620s he experimented with genre scenes.

Halston trade name of Roy Halston Frowick 1932–1990. US fashion designer who showed his first collection 1969 and created a vogue for easy-to-wear clothes that emphasized the body but left it free to move. In 1973 he diversified into loungewear, luggage, and cosmetics.

hamam in Islamic architecture, a bath house, either public or private.

Hamilton Edith 1867–1963. German-born US educator and classical scholar, best remembered as a collector and translator of ancient myths. Her anthologies *Mythology* 1942 and *The Great Age of Greek Literature* 1943 became standard textbooks. Other important works include *The Greek Way* 1930 and *The Roman Way* 1932.

Hamilton Iain Ellis 1922– . Scottish composer. His intensely emotional and harmonically rich works include striking viola and cello sonatas; the ballet *Clerk Saunders* 1951; the operas *Pharsalia* 1968 and *The Royal Hunt of the Sun* 1967–69, which renounced melody for inventive chordal formations; and symphonies.

Hamilton Richard 1922– . English artist, a pioneer of Pop art. His collage *Just What Is It That Makes Today's Homes So Different, So Appealing?* 1956 (Kunsthalle, Tübingen, Germany) is often cited as the first Pop art work: its 1950s interior, inhabited by the bodybuilder Charles Atlas and a pin-up, is typically humorous, concerned with popular culture and contemporary kitsch.

His series *Swingeing London 67* 1967 comments on the prosecution for drugs of his art dealer Robert Fraser and the singer Mick Jagger.

Hamlet tragedy by William ◊Shakespeare, first performed 1601–02. Hamlet, after much hesitation, avenges the murder of his father, the king of Denmark, by the king's brother Claudius, who has married Hamlet's mother. The play ends with the death of all three.

He is haunted by his father's ghost demanding revenge, is torn between love and loathing for his mother, and becomes responsible for the deaths of his lover Ophelia, her father and brother, and his student companions Rosencrantz and Guildenstern. In the monologue beginning 'To be, or not to be' he contemplates suicide.

Hammershøi Vilhelm 1864–1916. Danish painter, known for his evocative domestic interiors rendered with monumental simplicity in a muted palette of greys, greens, and soft blacks. His quiet, Neo-Classical rooms often feature a young woman, alone and with her back turned, as in *Interior with a Seated Woman* 1908 (Aarhus Kunstmuseum, Aarhus).

His work, exemplifying the inner strength and mysticism of the Nordic spirit, occupies a central place in Scandinavian art.

Hammerstein Oscar, II 1895–1960. Lyricist and librettist who collaborated with Richard

◊Rodgers over a period of 16 years on some of the best-known American musicals, including *Oklahoma!* 1943 (Pulitzer Prize), *Carousel* 1945, *South Pacific* 1949 (Pulitzer Prize), *The King and I* 1951, and *The Sound of Music* 1959.

Show Boat 1927, with music by Jerome Kern, represented a major step forward in integration of plot and character.

Hammett (Samuel) Dashiell 1894–1961. US crime novelist. He introduced the 'hard-boiled' detective character into fiction and attracted a host of imitators, with works including *The Maltese Falcon* 1930 (filmed 1941), *The Glass Key* 1931 (filmed 1942), and his most successful novel, the light-hearted *The Thin Man* 1932 (filmed 1934). His Marxist politics were best expressed in *Red Harvest* 1929, which depicts the corruption of capitalism in 'Poisonville'.

Hammond Joan 1912– . Australian soprano, born in New Zealand. She made her debut in *The Messiah* 1938 and in opera the following year. Her principal repertoire is Wagner and Italian opera to Puccini.

Hammond organ electric organ invented in the USA by Laurens Hammond 1934 and widely used in gospel music. Hammond applied valve technology to miniaturize Thaddeus Cahill's original 'tone-wheel' concept, introduced draw-slide registration to vary timbre, and incorporated a distinctive tremulant using rotating speakers. The Hammond organ was a precursor of the synthesizer.

Hamnett Katharine 1948– . British fashion designer, particularly popular in the UK and Italy. Her oversized T-shirts promoting peace and environmental campaigns attracted attention 1983–84. She produces well-cut, inexpensive designs for men and women, predominantly in natural fabrics. In 1989 she began showing her collections in Paris, and in 1993 launched hand-knitwear and leather collections.

Hampton Lionel 1909– . US jazz musician, a top bandleader of the 1940s and 1950s. Originally a drummer, Hampton introduced the vibraphone, an electronically vibrated percussion instrument, to jazz music. With the Benny ◊Goodman band from 1936, he fronted his own big band 1941–65 and subsequently led small groups.

Hamsun Knut 1859–1952. Norwegian novelist whose first novel *Sult/Hunger* 1890 was largely autobiographical. Other works include *Pan* 1894 and *The Growth of the Soil* 1917, which won him a Nobel prize 1920. His hatred of capitalism made him sympathize with Nazism, and he was fined 1946 for collaboration.

Hancock Tony (Anthony John) 1924–1968. British lugubrious comedian on radio and television. *Hancock's Half Hour* from 1954 showed him famously at odds with everyday life. He also appeared in films, including *The Rebel* 1960 and *The Wrong Box* 1966.

Handel Georg Friedrich 1685–1759. German composer who became a British subject 1726. His first opera, *Almira*, was performed in Hamburg 1705. In 1710 he was appointed Kapellmeister to the elector of Hanover (the future George I of England). In 1712 he settled in England, where he established his popularity with such works as the *Water Music* 1717 (written for George I). His great choral works include the *Messiah* 1742 and the later oratorios *Samson* 1743, *Belshazzar* 1745, *Judas Maccabaeus* 1747, and *Jephtha* 1752.

Born in Halle, he abandoned the study of law 1703 to become a violinist at Keiser's Opera House in Hamburg. Visits to Italy 1706–10 inspired a number of operas and oratorios, and in 1711 his opera *Rinaldo* was performed in London. *Saul* and *Israel in Egypt* (both 1739) were unsuccessful, but his masterpiece the *Messiah* was acclaimed on its first performance in Dublin 1742. Other works include the pastoral *Acis and Galatea* 1718 and a set of variations for harpsichord that were later nicknamed 'The Harmonious Blacksmith'. In 1751 he became totally blind.

Handke Peter 1942– . Austrian novelist and playwright whose first play *Insulting the Audience* 1966 was an example of 'anti-theatre writing'. His novels include *Die Hornissen/The Hornets* 1966 and *Die Angst des Tormanns beim Elfmeter/The Goalie's Anxiety at the Penalty Kick* 1970. He wrote and directed the film *Linkshändige Frau/The Left-handed Woman* 1977.

Handley Tommy 1896–1949. English radio comedian. His popular programme *ITMA* (*It's That Man Again*) ran from 1939 until his death.

Hanging Gardens of Babylon in antiquity, gardens at Babylon, the capital of Mesopotamia, considered one of the ◊Seven Wonders of the World. According to legend, King Nebuchadnezzar constructed the gardens in the 6th century BC for one of his wives, who was homesick for her birthplace in the Iranian mountains. Archaeological excavations at the site of Babylon, 88 km/55 mi S of Baghdad in modern Iraq, have uncovered a huge substructure that may have supported irrigated gardens on terraces.

'Hansel and Gretel' folk tale of a brother and sister abandoned by their destitute parents and taken in by a witch who lives in a gingerbread cottage. She plans to fatten Hansel up for eating, but is tricked by Gretel, and the children return home with the witch's treasure. The story was collected by the ◊Grimm brothers and made into a children's opera by Engelbert Humperdinck, first performed 1893.

Hansom Joseph Aloysius 1803–1882. English architect and inventor. His works include the Birmingham town hall 1831, but he is remembered as the designer of the *hansom cab* 1834, a two-wheel carriage with a seat for the driver on the outside.

Hanuman in the Sanskrit epic ◊*Rāmāyana*, the Hindu monkey god and king of Hindustan (N India). He helped Rama (an incarnation of the god Vishnu) to retrieve his wife Sita, abducted by Ravana of Lanka (now Sri Lanka).

happening an event which combines the visual arts and improvised theatre. Happenings became popular in the USA in the 1960s, influenced by the composer John Cage's theories concerning the role of chance in art, and are closely related to both ◊performance art and ◊environment art. Happenings were associated particularly with the US painter Allen Kaprow (1927–), who first used the term 1959, as well as with the pop artists Jim Dine, Roy Lichtenstein, Claes Oldenburg, and Robert Rauschenberg.

Artists such as Yves Klein in France and Joseph Beuys in Germany have developed the political potential of happenings.

hardcore in pop music, of any style, extreme and generally less commercial: hardcore ◊techno is a minimalist electronic dance music; hardcore ◊rap is aggressive or offensive; hardcore punk rejects form and melody for speed and ◊noise.

There are several main tendencies within hardcore punk. The very similar styles known as thrash, speed metal, and grindcore, are played on guitars and drums as fast as possible with loud, angry shouting; exponents include Napalm Death (formed in England 1982). The most influential US hardcore band has been Black Flag (formed 1977).

The term 'artcore' is sometimes used for bands like Sonic Youth that employ noise with a more nuanced effect.

hard-edge painting style of ◊abstract art characterized by sharply defined areas of flat colour. It originated in the late 1950s in reaction to ◊Abstract Expressionism, stressing a calculated, detached approach rather than one characterized by spontaneity and emotion. Leading exponents

include US artists Ad Reinhardt (1913–1967) and Kenneth ◊Noland.

Hardouin-Mansart Jules 1646–1708. French architect to Louis XIV from 1675. He designed the lavish Baroque extensions to the palace of Versailles (from 1678) and Grand Trianon. Other works include the Invalides Chapel (1680–91), the Place de Vendôme (from 1698), and the Place des Victoires, all in Paris.

Hardy Oliver 1892–1957. US film comedian, member of the duo ◊Laurel and Hardy.

Hardy Thomas 1840–1928. English novelist and poet. His novels, set in rural 'Wessex' (his native West Country), portray intense human relationships played out in a harshly indifferent natural world. They include *Far From the Madding Crowd* 1874, *The Return of the Native* 1878, *The Mayor of Casterbridge* 1886, *The Woodlanders* 1887, *Tess of the d'Urbervilles* 1891, and *Jude the Obscure* 1895. His poetry includes the *Wessex Poems* 1898, the blank-verse epic of the Napoleonic Wars *The Dynasts* 1904–08, and several volumes of lyrics.

Born in Dorset, Hardy was trained as an architect. His first success was *Far From the Madding Crowd*. *Tess of the d'Urbervilles*, subtitled 'A Pure Woman', outraged public opinion by portraying as its heroine a woman who had been seduced. The even greater outcry that followed *Jude the Obscure* 1895 reinforced Hardy's decision to confine himself to verse.

My argument is that War makes rattling good history; but Peace is poor reading.

Thomas Hardy *The Dynasts* 1904–08

Hare David 1947– . British dramatist, director and screenwriter, whose plays include *Slag* 1970, *Teeth 'n' Smiles* 1975, *Plenty* 1978, *Pravda* 1985 (with Howard ◊Brenton), *Wrecked Eggs* 1986, and *Racing Demon* 1990. His films include

---

Hardy: major works

title	date	well-known characters
Under the Greenwood Tree	1872	Joseph Bowman, Fancy Day Dick Dewy, Reuben Dewy, William Dewy, Arthur Maybold, Farmer Fred Shiner.
Far From the Madding Crowd	1874	William Boldwood, Bathsheba Everdene, Gabriel Oak, Joseph Poorgrass, Fanny Robin, Lyddy Smallbury, Sergeant Francis Troy.
The Return of the Native	1878	Christian Cantle, Grandfer Cantle, Diggory Venn, Eustacia Vye, Clym Yeobright, Mrs Yeobright, Thomasin Yeobright, Damon Wildeve.
The Trumpet Major	1880	Festus Derriman, Anne Garland, Mrs Garland, Bob Loveday, John Loveday.
The Mayor of Casterbridge	1886	Suke Damson, Donald Farfrae, Elizabeth Jane Henchard, Mrs Henchard, Michael Henchard, Richard Newson, Lucetta Templeman/Le Sueur.
The Woodlanders	1887	Felice Charmond, Robert Creedle, Edred Fitzpiers, Grace Melbury, Marty South, Giles Winterbourne.
Tess of the d'Urbervilles	1891	Mercy Chant, Angel Clare, Rev James Clare, Dairyman Crick, Car Darch, Izz Huett, Marian, Retty Priddle, Alec d'Urberville, Tess Durbeyfield, John and Joan Durbeyfield.
Jude the Obscure	1895	Sue Bridehead, Arabella Donn, Jude Fawley, Little Father Time, Richard Phillotson.

Wetherby and *Plenty* both 1985, and *Paris by Night* 1988. He has also published an autobiography *Writing Left-Handed* 1991.

Harington John 1561–1612. English translator of Ariosto's *Orlando furioso* and author of *The Metamorphosis of Ajax*, a ribald history of the privy ('jakes'). Elizabeth I of England referred to him as 'that saucy poet, my godson', and banished him from court on several occasions but also installed the water closet he invented.

Harlem Renaissance movement in US literature in the 1920s that used Afro-American life and black culture as its subject matter; it was an early manifestation of black pride in the USA. The centre of the movement was the Harlem section of New York City.

Harlem was the place where aspects of Afro-American culture, including jazz, flourished from the early 20th century, and attracted a new white audience. The magazine *Crisis*, edited by W E B DuBois (1868–1963), was a forum for the new black consciousness; writers associated with the movement include Langston Hughes, Zora Neale Hurston, James Weldon Johnson, and Countee Cullen (1903–1946).

Harlow Jean. Stage name of Harlean Carpenter 1911–1937. US film actress, the first 'platinum blonde' and the wisecracking sex symbol of the 1930s. Her films include *Hell's Angels* 1930, *Red Dust* 1932, *Platinum Blonde* 1932, *Dinner at Eight* 1933, *China Seas* 1935, and *Saratoga* 1937, during the filming of which she died (her part was completed by a double).

Harmonia in Greek mythology, the daughter of Ares and Aphrodite, wife of ◊Cadmus of Thebes, and mother of Io, Semele (the mother of ◊Dionysus), and Agave (the mother of ◊Pentheus).

harmonica or ◊*mouth organ* pocket-sized reed organ blown directly from the mouth, invented by Charles Wheatstone 1829.

The *glass harmonica* (or *armonica*) is based on the principle of playing a wine glass with a wet finger. Devised by Benjamin Franklin, it consists of a graded series of glass bowls nested on a spindle and resting in a trough part-filled with water. Rotated by a foot pedal, it emits pure tones of unchanging intensity when touched. Mozart, Beethoven, and Schubert all wrote pieces for it.

harmonics in music, a series of partial vibrations that combine to form a musical tone. The number and relative prominence of harmonics produced determines an instrument's tone colour (timbre). An oboe is rich in harmonics, the flute has few. Harmonics conform to successive divisions of the sounding air column or string: their pitches are harmonious.

harmonium keyboard reed organ of the 19th century, powered by foot-operated bellows and incorporating lever-action knee swells to influence dynamics. It was patented by Debain of Paris 1848. Widely adopted in the USA as a home and church instrument, in France and Germany the harmonium flourished as a concert solo and orchestral instrument, being written for by Karg-Elert, Schoenberg (*Herzgewächse/Heart's Bloom* 1907), and Stockhausen (*Der Jahreslauf/The Course of the Years* 1977).

harmony in music, any simultaneous combination of sounds, as opposed to melody, which is a succession of sounds. Although the term suggests a pleasant or agreeable sound, it is applied to any combination of notes, whether consonant or dissonant. The theory of harmony deals with the formation of chords and their interrelation and logical progression.

The founder of harmonic theory was Jean-Philippe ◊Rameau. In his *Traité de l'harmonie/Treatise on Harmony* 1722, he established a system of chord classification on which subsequent methods of harmony have been based.

harp plucked musical string instrument, with the strings stretched vertically within a wood and brass soundbox of triangular shape. The orchestral harp is the largest instrument of its type. It has up to 47 diatonically tuned strings, in the range B0–C7 (seven octaves), and seven double-action pedals to alter pitch. Composers for the harp include Mozart, Ravel, Salzedo, and Holliger.

Recorded from biblical times, the harp existed in the West as early as the 9th century, and it was common among medieval minstrels. At that time it was quite small, and was normally placed on the knees. It evolved in size because of a need for increased volume following its introduction into the orchestra in the 19th century. The harp has also been used in folk music, as both a solo and accompanying instrument, and is associated with Wales and Ireland.

harpsichord the largest and grandest of 18th-century keyboard string instruments, used in orchestras and as a solo instrument. The strings are plucked by 'jacks' made of leather or quill, and multiple keyboards offering variation in tone are common. The revival of the harpsichord repertoire in the 20th century owes much to Wanda Landowska and Ralph Kirkpatrick (1911–1984).

Harpy (plural *Harpies*) in early Greek mythology, a wind spirit; in later legend the Harpies have horrific women's faces and the bodies of vultures.

Harris Frank 1856–1931. Irish journalist, later in the USA, who wrote colourful biographies of Oscar Wilde and George Bernard Shaw, and an autobiography, *My Life and Loves* 1926, originally banned in the UK and the USA for its sexual content.

Harris Joel Chandler 1848–1908. US author, born in Georgia. He wrote tales narrated by the former slave 'Uncle Remus', based on black folklore, and involving the characters Brer Rabbit and the Tar Baby.

Harris Richard 1932– . Irish film actor known for playing dominating characters in such films as *This Sporting Life* 1963. His other films include *Camelot* 1967, *A Man Called Horse* 1970, *Robin and Marian* 1976, *Tarzan the Ape Man* 1981, *The Field* 1990, and *Unforgiven* 1992. He won the 1990 Evening Standard Award for best actor in Pirandello's *Henry IV*.

Harris Roy 1898–1979. US composer, born in Oklahoma, who used American folk tunes. Among his works are the 10th Symphony 1965 (known as 'Abraham Lincoln') and the orchestral *When Johnny Comes Marching Home* 1935.

Harrison Rex (Reginald Carey) 1908–1990. English film and theatre actor. He appeared in over 40 films and numerous plays, often portraying sophisticated and somewhat eccentric characters, such as the waspish Professor Higgins in *My Fair Lady* 1964 (Academy Award), the musical version of *Pygmalion*. His other films include *Blithe Spirit* 1945, *The Ghost and Mrs Muir* 1947, and *Dr Doolittle* 1967.

Harrison Tony 1937– . British poet, translator, and dramatist who caused controversy with his poem *V* 1987, dealing with the desecration of his parents' grave by Liverpool football supporters, and the play *The Blasphemers' Banquet* 1989, which attacked (in the name of Molière, Voltaire, Byron, and Omar Khayyam) the death sentence on Salman Rushdie. He has also translated and adapted Molière.

Hart Moss 1904–1961. US dramatist. He collaborated with such major figures as Irving Berlin, Cole Porter, Kurt Weill, and Ira Gershwin. Among Hart's most famous works are *The Man Who Came to Dinner* 1939 and the films *Gentlemen's Agreement* 1947 and *A Star is Born* 1954. Late in his career he became one of Broadway's most successful directors. His autobiography, *Act One*, appeared 1959.

Harte (Francis) Bret 1836–1902. US writer. He became a goldminer at 18 before founding the *Overland Monthly* 1868 in which he wrote short stories of the pioneer West, for example *The Luck of Roaring Camp* and poems such as *The Heathen Chinee*. From 1885 he settled in England after five years as US consul in Glasgow.

Hartley L(eslie) P(oles) 1895–1972. English novelist, noted for his exploration of the sinister. His books include the trilogy *The Shrimp and the Anemone* 1944, *The Sixth Heaven* 1946, and *Eustace and Hilda* 1947, on the intertwined lives of a brother and sister. Later works include *The Boat* 1949, *The Go-Between* 1953 (also a film), and *The Hireling* 1957.

> *The past is a foreign country: they do things differently there.*
>
> **L P Hartley** *The Go-Between* 1953

Hartly Marsden 1877–1943. US avant-garde painter. His works range from brightly coloured Expressionist representations of German soldiers and German military symbols, such as *Portrait of a German Officer* 1914 (Metropolitan Museum of Art, New York), to New England landscapes, such as *Log Jam, Penobscot Bay* 1940–41 (Detroit Institute of Art), painted in his later 'primitive' style.

Born in Lewiston, Maine, USA, he travelled in Europe to study art. He exhibited 1913 with the *Blaue Reiter* group and returned to the USA to exhibit with the Armory Show 1913.

Hartnell Sir Norman 1901–1979. British fashion designer, known for his ornate evening gowns and tailored suits and coats. He worked briefly for the designer Lucille (1863–1935) before founding his own studio 1923. Appointed dressmaker to the British royal family 1938, he created Queen Elizabeth II's wedding dress, when she was Princess Elizabeth, 1947, and her coronation gown 1953. The Hartnell fashion house closed 1992.

Harunobu Suzuki 1725–1770. Japanese artist, a leading exponent of ◊ukiyo-e and one of the first printmakers to use colour effectively. His work displays a sure sense of composition and line and features domestic scenes, courtesans, and actors among its subjects.

Harvey Jonathan Dean 1939– . English composer whose use of avant-garde and computer synthesis techniques is allied to a tradition of visionary Romanticism in works such as *Inner Light II* 1977 for voices, instruments, and ◊tape music and *Mortuos plango, vivos voco/I Mourn the Dead, I Call the Living* 1980 for computer-manipulated concrete sounds, realized at ◊IRCAM.

Harvey Laurence. Adopted name of Lauruska Mischa Skikne 1928–1973. British film actor of Lithuanian descent who worked both in England (*Room at the Top* 1958) and in Hollywood (*The Alamo* 1960, *The Manchurian Candidate* 1962).

Hašek Jaroslav 1883–1923. Czech writer. His masterpiece is an anti-authoritarian comic satire on military life under Austro-Hungarian rule, *The ◊Good Soldier Svejk* 1921–23. During World War I he deserted to Russia, and eventually joined the Bolsheviks.

Hassam Childe 1859–1935. US Impressionist painter and printmaker. He studied in Paris 1886–89 and later became one of the members of 'the Ten', a group of American Impressionists who exhibited together until World War I. His *Flag Day* 1919 (County Museum, Los Angeles) is typical.

hat head covering, with a shaped crown and sometimes with a brim, worn by both men and women for practical and decorative purposes. There are many styles of hats, for example the ◊trilby, ◊homburg, ◊boater, ◊beret, ◊cap, and ◊fedora.

Hathaway Anne 1556–1623. Englishwoman, daughter of a yeoman farmer, who married William ◊Shakespeare 1582. She was born at Shottery, near Stratford, where her cottage can still be seen.

Hathor in ancient Egyptian mythology, the sky goddess, later identified with ◊Isis.

Hauptmann Gerhart 1862–1946. German dramatist. A strong proponent of an uncompromising naturalism in the theatre, Hauptmann's work has been widely produced. *Die Weber/The Weavers* 1892, his finest play, is an account of a revolt of Silesian weavers in 1844. His other plays include *Vor Sonnenaufgang/Before Dawn* 1889, the comedy *Der Biberpelz/The Beaver Coat* 1893, and a tragicomedy of the Berlin underworld *Die Ratten/The Rats* 1910.

Haussmann Georges Eugène, Baron Haussmann 1809–1891. French administrator who replanned medieval Paris 1853–70 to achieve the current city plan, with long wide boulevards and parks. The cost of his scheme and his authoritarianism caused opposition, and he was made to resign from his post.

haute couture (French 'high dressmaking') term derived from 'couture', which means sewing or needlework, denoting high-quality made-to-measure clothing designed by a couturier (a fashion designer who produces couture clothing). It is an expensive line of clothing which relies heavily upon the work of specialists to execute a couturier's design. Many couture houses have closed since the mass production of inexpensive ready-to-wear clothing was introduced in the 1950s.

Havel Václav 1936– . Czech dramatist and politician, president of Czechoslovakia 1989–92 and president of the Czech Republic from 1993. His plays include *The Garden Party* 1963 and *Largo Desolato* 1985, about a dissident intellectual. His plays were banned after the Soviet clampdown on Czechoslovakia 1968.

Hawkes John (Clendennin Burne Jr) 1925– . US novelist. His writing is characterized by a Gothic, macabre violence, nightmarish landscapes, and oblique plotting. His novels include *The Cannibal* 1949, dealing with the horror of authoritarian power in Nazi Germany; *The Lime Twig* 1961, a thriller set in postwar London; and *Second Skin* 1964, a first-person recollection set on a tropical island. His later novels became

more accessible and include *Travesty* 1976, *The Passion Artist* 1979, and *Whistlejacket* 1988.

Hawkins Coleman (Randolph) 1904–1969. US virtuoso tenor saxophonist. He was, until 1934, a soloist in the swing band led by Fletcher Henderson (1898–1952), and was an influential figure in bringing the jazz saxophone to prominence as a solo instrument.

Hawkins Jack 1910–1973. British film actor often cast in authoritarian roles. His films include *The Cruel Sea* 1953, *Bridge on the River Kwai* 1957, *The League of Gentlemen* 1959, *Zulu* 1963, and *Waterloo* 1970. After an operation for throat cancer that removed his vocal chords 1966 his voice had to be dubbed.

Hawks Howard 1896–1977. US director, screenwriter, and producer of a wide range of classic films in virtually every American genre. Swift-moving and immensely accomplished, his films include the gangster movie *Scarface* 1932, the comedy *Bringing Up Baby* 1938, the ◊film noir *The Big Sleep* 1946, and *Gentlemen Prefer Blondes* 1953.

Hawksmoor Nicholas 1661–1736. English architect, assistant to Christopher ◊Wren in designing various London churches and St Paul's Cathedral and joint architect with John ◊Vanbrugh of Castle Howard and Blenheim Palace. His genius is displayed in a quirky and uncompromising style incorporating elements from both Gothic and Classical sources.

The original west towers of Westminster Abbey, long attributed to Wren, were designed by Hawksmoor 1734–36, completed after his death 1745. After 1712 Hawksmoor completed six of the 50 new churches planned for London under the provisions made by the Fifty New Churches Act 1711.

Haworth Parsonage home of the English novelists Charlotte, Emily, and Anne ◊Brontë. Their father, Patrick Brontë, was vicar of Haworth, a hillside village on the edge of the Yorkshire moors, from 1820 until his death 1861. *Wuthering Heights*, *Jane Eyre*, and *Agnes Grey* were written here 1847. The house was given to the Brontë Society 1928 and is now a Brontë museum.

Hawthorne Nathaniel 1804–1864. US writer, author of American literature's first great classic novel, *The Scarlet Letter* 1850. Set in 17th-century Puritan Boston, it tells the powerful allegorical story of a 'fallen woman' and her daughter who are judged guilty according to man's, not nature's laws. He wrote three other novels, including *The House of the Seven Gables* 1851, and many short stories, a form he was instrumental in developing, including *Tanglewood Tales* 1853, classic Greek legends retold for children.

Hay Will 1888–1949. British comedy actor. Originally a music-hall comedian, he made many films from the 1930s in which he was usually cast as an incompetent in a position of authority, including *Good Morning Boys* 1937, *Oh Mr Porter* 1938, *Ask a Policeman* 1939, and *My Learned Friend* 1944.

Hayden Sterling. Stage name of John Hamilton 1916–1986. US film actor who played leading Hollywood roles in the 1940s and early 1950s. Although later seen in some impressive character roles, his career as a whole failed to do justice to his talent. His work includes *The Asphalt Jungle* 1950, *Johnny Guitar* 1954, *Dr Strangelove* 1964, and *The Godfather* 1972.

Haydn Franz Joseph 1732–1809. Austrian composer. A teacher of Mozart and Beethoven, he was a major exponent of the classical sonata form in his numerous chamber and orchestral works (he wrote more than 100 symphonies). He also composed choral music, including the oratorios *The Creation* 1798 and *The Seasons* 1801. He was the first great master of the string quartet.

Born in Lower Austria, he was kapellmeister 1761–90 to Prince Esterházy. His work also includes operas, church music, and songs, and the 'Emperor's Hymn', adopted as the Austrian, and later the German, national anthem.

Melody is the main thing; harmony is useful only to charm the ear.

Franz Joseph Haydn

Haydon Benjamin Robert 1786–1846. English painter. His attempts at the 'grand style' include many gigantic canvasses such as *Christ's Entry into Jerusalem* 1820 (Philadelphia, USA) but he is better known for his genre pictures such as *The Mock Election* and *Chairing the Member*. He also painted portraits of Wordsworth and Keats. He published *Autobiography and Memoirs* 1853, a lively account of the contemporary art scene and his own tragicomic life.

Hays Office film regulation body in the USA 1922–45. Officially known as the Motion Picture Producers and Distributors of America, it was created by the major film companies to improve the industry's image and provide internal regulation, including a strict moral code.

The office was headed by Will H Hays (1879–1954). A Production Code, listing all the subjects forbidden to films, was begun 1930 and lasted until 1966, when it was replaced by a ratings system.

Haywain, The oil painting by John ◊Constable 1821 (National Gallery, London), in which the artist broke with academic tradition to work directly from nature. It shows a landscape of Suffolk watermeadows with a shallow river in the foreground being forded by two farmers in a wagon. It won a gold medal at the Paris Salon of 1824 and influenced painters of the Romantic movement and, later, the Impressionists.

Hayworth Rita. Stage name of Margarita Carmen Cansino 1918–1987. US dancer and film actress who gave vivacious performances in 1940s musicals and steamy, erotic roles in *Gilda* 1946 and *Affair in Trinidad* 1952. She was known as Hollywood's 'goddess' during the height of her career. She was married to Orson Welles 1943–48 and appeared in his film *The Lady from Shanghai* 1948. She gave assured performances in *Pal Joey* 1957 and *Separate Tables* 1958.

Hazlitt William 1778–1830. English essayist and critic whose work is characterized by invective, scathing irony, and a gift for epigram. His critical essays include *Characters of Shakespeare's Plays* 1817–18, *Lectures on the English Poets* 1818–19, *English Comic Writers* 1819, and *Dramatic Literature of the Age of Elizabeth* 1820. Other works are *Table Talk* 1821–22, *The Spirit of the Age* 1825, and *Liber Amoris* 1823.

Without the aid of prejudice and custom, I should not be able to find my way across the room.

William Hazlitt

Head Bessie 1937–1986. South African writer who lived in exile in Botswana. Her work is concerned with questions of private and national identity, incorporating an unidealized sense of social and communal history. Her novels include *When Rain Clouds Gather* 1969, *Maru* 1971, and *A Question of Power* 1973.

Head Edith 1900–1981. US costume designer for Hollywood films who won eight Academy Awards for her designs, in such films as *The Heiress* 1949, *All About Eve* 1950, and *The Sting* 1973.

Heal Ambrose 1872–1959. English cabinet-maker who took over the Heal's shop from his father and developed it into a large London store. He initially designed furniture in the Arts and Crafts style, often in oak, but in the 1930s he started using materials such as tubular steel. Heal was a founder member of the Design and Industries Association, which aimed to improve the quality of mass-produced items.

Heaney Seamus (Justin) 1939– . Irish poet, born in County Derry, who has written powerful verse about the political situation in Northern Ireland. Collections include *North* 1975, *Field Work* 1979, and *Station Island* 1984. In 1989, he was elected professor of poetry at Oxford University.

Hearn (Patrick) Lafcadio 1850–1904. Greek-born US writer and translator who lived in Japan from 1890 and became a Japanese citizen. His many books on Japanese life and customs introduced the country to many Western readers, for example, *Glimpses of Unfamiliar Japan* 1893 and *In Ghostly Japan* 1904.

A journalist, Hearn was sent to Japan to write an article for a US magazine and never left. His sympathetic understanding of the country and its culture made him accepted and appreciated by the Japanese, and his writings are still widely read. From 1896 he taught English literature at Tokyo University.

Heartfield John (Helmut Hertzfelde) 1891–1968. German painter and graphic artist, one of the greatest exponents of photomontage. Influenced by the aims and techniques of both Dada and the *Neue Sachlichkeit* group, he developed a highly original style, employing incongruous images of contemporary German life to satirize capitalism and Nazism.

Heart of Darkness short novel by Joseph ◊Conrad, published 1902. Marlow, the narrator, tells of his journey by boat into the African interior to meet a company agent, Kurtz, who has adopted local customs and uses barbaric methods to exercise power over the indigenous people.

Heart of Midlothian, The novel 1818 by Walter ◊Scott. It centres around Effie Deans, imprisoned for alleged infanticide, and her half-sister, Jeanie Deans, who travels to London and obtains for her a pardon from Queen Caroline. The supposedly murdered child is revealed to have been kidnapped and brutalized; in ignorance, he kills the father who is searching for him. With its convincing and compassionate character studies and substantial social background it is probably the most accessible and lasting of all Scott's novels.

heavy metal style of rock music characterized by a heavy bass beat, histrionic guitar solos, and a macho swagger. Heavy metal developed out of the hard rock of the late 1960s and early 1970s, was performed by such groups as Led Zeppelin and Deep Purple, and enjoyed a resurgence in the late 1980s. Bands include Van Halen (formed 1974), Def Leppard (formed 1977), and Guns n' Roses (formed 1987).

Hebe in Greek mythology, the goddess of youth, daughter of Zeus and Hera.

Hecataeus 6th–5th century BC. Greek historian and geographer from Miletus. An intellectual successor to the early Ionian philosophers, Hecataeus wrote what was probably the first historical work of a genealogical kind. He was a major influence on the historian ◊Herodotus.

Hecate in Greek mythology, the goddess of witchcraft and magic, sometimes identified with ◊Artemis and the Moon.

Hecht Ben 1893–1964. US dramatist, screenwriter and film director, formerly a journalist. His

play *The Front Page* 1928 was adapted several times for the cinema by other writers. His own screenplays included *Twentieth Century* 1934, *Gunga Din* and *Wuthering Heights*, both 1939, *Spellbound* 1945, and *Actors and Sin* 1952. His directorial credits include *Crime Without Passion* 1934. His autobiography, *Child of the Century*, was published 1954.

The rule in the art world is: you cater to the masses or you kowtow to the elite; you can't have both.

Ben Hecht

Heckel Erich 1883–1970. German painter, lithographer, and illustrator. Trained as an architect, he turned to painting 1905, founding the German Expressionist group *die* ◊*Brücke* 1905 with fellow students Ernst Ludwig ◊Kirchner and Karl ◊Schmidt-Rottluff. *Two Men at a Table* 1912 (Kunsthaus, Hamburg) exemplifies his severe, angular, heavily contoured style. His subject matter ranges from starved figures, interiors, and landscapes to primitive nudes in bucolic settings.

heckelphone musical instrument, a wide-bore baritone ◊oboe in B flat. It was introduced by the German maker Wilhelm Heckel (1856–1909) and adopted by Richard Strauss in the opera *Salome* 1905.

Hector in Greek mythology, a Trojan prince, son of King Priam and husband of Andromache, who, in the siege of ◊Troy, was the foremost warrior on the Trojan side until he was killed by ◊Achilles.

Hecuba in Greek mythology, the wife of King Priam of Troy, and mother of Hector and ◊Paris. She was captured by the Greeks after the fall of Troy.

Hedda Gabler play by Henrik ◊Ibsen, first produced 1891. Trapped in small-town society, Hedda Gabler takes out her spiritual and sexual frustrations on everyone from her ineffectual academic husband to the reformed alcoholic writer Lövborg. When her mean-spirited revenge backfires, she commits suicide.

Heidelberg School group of Australian Impressionist artists (including Tom Roberts, Arthur Streeton, and Charles Conder) working near the village of Heidelberg in Melbourne in the 1880s–90s. The school had its most famous exhibition 1889, called the '9 by 5', from the size of the cigar-box lids used.

Heidi novel for children by the Swiss writer Johanna Spyri (1827–1901), published 1881 in Germany. Heidi, an orphan girl, shares a simple life with her grandfather high on a mountain. Three years spent in Frankfurt as companion to a crippled girl, Clara, convince Heidi that city life is not for her and she returns to her mountain home.

Heifetz Jascha 1901–1987. Russian-born US violinist, one of the great virtuosos of the 20th century. He first performed at the age of five, and before he was 17 had played in most European capitals, and in the USA, where he settled 1917. He popularized a clear, unemotional delivery suited to radio and recording.

Heike monogatari Japanese chronicle, written down in the 14th century but based on oral legend describing events that took place 200 years earlier, recounting the struggle for control of the country between the rival Genji (Minamoto) and Heike (Taira) clans. The conflict ended the Heian period and resulted in the introduction of the first shogunate (military dictatorship). Many Japanese dramas are based on material from the chronicle.

Heine Heinrich 1797–1856. German Romantic poet and journalist who wrote *Reisebilder/Pictures of Travel* 1826–31, blending travel writing and satire, and *Buch der Lieder/Book of Songs* 1827. From 1831 he lived mainly in Paris, working as a correspondent for German newspapers and publishing *Neue Gedichte/New Poems* 1844. He excelled in both the Romantic lyric and satire. Schubert and Schumann set many of his lyrics to music.

In 1835 he headed a list of writers forbidden to publish in Germany. He contracted a spinal disease 1845 that confined him to his bed from 1848 until his death.

Heinlein Robert A(nson) 1907– . US science-fiction writer, associated with the pulp magazines of the 1940s, who wrote the militaristic novel *Starship Troopers* 1959 and the utopian cult novel *Stranger in a Strange Land* 1961. His work helped to increase the legitimacy of science fiction as a literary genre.

Hel or *Hela* in Norse mythology, the goddess of the underworld.

Helen in Greek mythology, the daughter of Zeus and Leda, and the most beautiful of women. She married ◊Menelaus, King of Sparta, but during his absence, was abducted by Paris, Prince of Troy. This precipitated the Trojan War. Afterwards she returned to Sparta with her husband.

Helicon mountain in central Greece, on which was situated a spring and a sanctuary sacred to the ◊Muses.

Heliodorus ?3rd century BC. Ancient Greek novelist. His *Aethiopica*, a romance set in Delphi and Egypt, is generally considered the best of the ancient novels; it describes in poetic prose the loves of Theagenes and Chariclea. It was translated in the 16th century.

Helios in Greek mythology, the sun god – thought to make his daily journey across the sky in a chariot – and father of ◊Phaethon.

Helle in Greek mythology, the daughter of Athamas, King of Thessaly, and sister of Phryxes.

With her brother she ran away from Ino, their cruel stepmother, on a ram with a ◊Golden Fleece. Helle fell into the sea and drowned, thus giving her name to the *Hellespont* ('sea of Helle').

Hellenistic period period in Greek civilization from the death of Alexander 323 bc until the accession of the Roman emperor Augustus 27 BC. Alexandria in Egypt was the centre of culture and commerce during this period, and Greek culture spread throughout the Mediterranean region and the near East.

Heller Joseph 1923– . US novelist. He drew on his experiences in the US air force in World War II to write his best-selling ◊*Catch-22* 1961, satirizing war and its bureaucracy. A film based on the book appeared 1970.

His other works include the novels *Something Happened* 1974 and *Good As Gold* 1979; and the plays *We Bombed in New Haven* 1968 and *Clevinger's Trial* 1974.

Hellman Lillian 1907–1984. US dramatist whose work is concerned with contemporary political and social issues, as in *The Children's Hour* 1934, *The Little Foxes* 1939, and *Toys in the Attic* 1960. In the 1950s she was summoned to appear before the House Committee on Un-American Activities.

She lived 31 years with the writer Dashiell Hammett, and in her will set up a fund to promote Marxist doctrine. Since her death there has been dispute over the accuracy of her memoirs, for example *Pentimento* 1973.

I cannot and will not cut my conscience to fit this year's fashions.

Lillian Hellman letter to the House Un-American Activities Committee May 1952

Helmholtz resonator spherical vessel of metal or glass with an opening and an earpiece on opposite sides, from a harmonic series of 19 such vessels constructed for German physicist Hermann Helmholtz (1821–1894) as an instrument of acoustic analysis. Placed in the ear, it acts as an acoustic filter, allowing only sounds of a particular pitch to be heard. Helmholtz also used resonators in series with tuning forks as sound sources in pioneering experiments in synthesizing instrumental timbres.

Helpmann Robert 1909–1986. Australian dancer, choreographer, and actor. The leading male dancer with the Sadler's Wells Ballet, London, 1933–50, he partnered Margot ◊Fonteyn in the 1940s.

His forte was characterization rather than virtuosity, best displayed in his role as the comic Ugly Sister in Ashton's *Cinderella*. His other comic roles include Doctor Coppelius in *Coppélia* and the bridegroom in Ashton's *A Wedding Bouquet*, but he was equally at home in dramatic roles, such as the Red King in Ninette de Valois' *Checkmate*. His film appearances include *The Red Shoes* 1948, *The Tales of Hoffman* 1951, *Chitty Chitty Bang Bang* 1968, and the title role in Nureyev's *Don Quixote* 1973.

Hemingway Ernest (Miller) 1899–1961. US writer. War, bullfighting, and fishing are used symbolically in his work to represent honour, dignity, and primitivism – prominent themes in his short stories and novels, which include *A Farewell to Arms* 1929, *For Whom the Bell Tolls* 1941, and *The Old Man and the Sea* 1952 (Pulitzer Prize). His deceptively simple writing style attracted many imitators. He received the Nobel Prize for Literature 1954.

He was born in Oak Park, Illinois, and in his youth developed a passion for hunting and adventure. He became a journalist and was wounded while serving on a volunteer ambulance crew in Italy in World War I. His style was influenced by Gertrude ◊Stein, who also introduced him to bullfighting, a theme in his first novel, *'Fiesta' (The Sun Also Rises)* 1927, and the memoir *Death in the Afternoon* 1932. *A Farewell to Arms* deals with wartime experiences on the Italian front, and *For Whom the Bell Tolls* has a Spanish Civil War setting. He served as war correspondent both in that conflict and in Europe during World War II. After a full life, physical weakness, age, and depression contributed to his suicide.

A man can be destroyed but not defeated.

Ernest Hemingway *The Old Man and the Sea* 1952

Hendrix Jimi (James Marshall) 1942–1970. US rock guitarist, songwriter, and singer, legendary for his virtuoso guitar technique and flamboyance. In 1966 he formed a trio, the Jimi Hendrix Experience, and recorded 'Hey Joe' and 'Purple Haze', both 1967. His experimental guitar technique influenced both rock and jazz. *Are You Experienced?* 1967 was his first album. His performance at the 1969 Woodstock festival included a memorable version of 'The Star-Spangled Banner' and is recorded in the film *Woodstock*.

Once you're dead, you're made for life.

Jimi Hendrix (attrib.)

Henri Robert. Adopted name of Robert Henry Cozad 1865–1929. US painter, a leading figure in the transition between 19th-century conventions and Modern art in America. He was a principal member of the ◊Ashcan School.

Henry, O pen name of William Sydney Porter 1862–1910. US short-story writer whose collections include *Cabbages and Kings* 1904 and *The Four Million* 1906. His stories are written in a colloquial style and employ skilled construction with surprise endings.

Henryson Robert 1430–1505. Scottish poet. His works include versions of Aesop and the *Testament of Cresseid*, a work once attributed to Chaucer, which continues Chaucer's story of *Troilus and Criseyde* by depicting the betrayal and wretched afterlife of Troilus.

Henslowe Philip died 1616. English theatre manager who owned the Fortune, Hope, and ◊Rose theatres in London. He wrote a diary, in which he kept his accounts of transactions for his theatres, and of loans and payments to actors and dramatists. The diary provides invaluable material evidence for the study of the English theatre in the age of Shakespeare.

Henty G(eorge) A(lfred) 1832–1902. British war correspondent, author of numerous historical novels for children, including *With the Allies to Peking* 1904.

Henze Hans Werner 1926– . German composer whose immense and stylistically restless output is marked by a keen literary sensibility and seductive use of orchestral coloration, as in the opera *Elegy for Young Lovers* 1959–61 and the cantata *Being Beauteous* 1963.

Following the student unrest of 1968 he suddenly renounced the wealthy musical establishment in favour of a militantly socialist stance in works such as the abrasive *El Cimarrón* 1969–70 and *Voices* 1973, austere settings of 22 revolutionary texts in often magical sonorities. Among recent works are the opera *Das Verratene Meer/The Sea Betrayed* 1992.

Hepburn Audrey (Audrey Hepburn-Rushton) 1929–1993. British actress of Anglo-Dutch descent who often played innocent, childlike characters. Slender and doe-eyed, she set a different style from the more ample women stars of the 1950s. After playing minor parts in British films in the early 1950s, she became a Hollywood star in *Roman Holiday* 1951, such films as *Funny Face* 1957, *My Fair Lady* 1964, and *Wait Until Dark* 1968. Among her later films were *Robin and Marian* 1976.

Hepburn Katharine 1909– . US actress who made feisty self-assurance her trademark. She appeared in such films as *Morning Glory* 1933 (Academy Award), *Little Women* 1933, *Bringing Up Baby* 1938, *The Philadelphia Story* 1940, *Woman of the Year* 1942, *The African Queen* 1951, *Pat and Mike* 1952 (with her frequent partner Spencer Tracy), *Guess Who's Coming to Dinner* 1967 (Academy Award), *Lion in Winter* 1968 (Academy Award), and *On Golden Pond* 1981

(Academy Award). She also had a distinguished stage career.

Hephaestus in Greek mythology, the god of fire and metalcraft (Roman Vulcan), son of Zeus and Hera, and husband of Aphrodite. He was lame.

Hepplewhite George died 1786. English furnituremaker whose name is associated with Neo-Classicism. His reputation rests upon his book of designs *The Cabinetmaker and Upholsterer's Guide*, published posthumously 1788, which contains over 300 designs, characterized by simple elegance and utility. No piece of furniture has been identified as being made by him.

Hepworth Barbara 1903–1975. English sculptor. She developed a distinctive abstract style, creating hollowed forms of stone or wood with spaces bridged by wires or strings; many later works are in bronze.

She worked in concrete, bronze, wood, and aluminium, but her preferred medium was stone. She married first the sculptor John Skeaping and second the painter Ben ◊Nicholson. Under Nicholson's influence she became more interested in abstract form. In 1939 she moved to St Ives, Cornwall (where her studio is now a museum).

I rarely draw what I see. I draw what I feel in my body.

Barbara Hepworth

Hera in Greek mythology, the goddess of women and marriage (Roman Juno), sister-consort of Zeus, mother of Hephaestus, Hebe, and Ares.

Heracles in Greek mythology, a hero (Roman Hercules), son of Zeus and Alcmene, famed for strength. While serving Eurystheus, King of Argos, he performed 12 labours, including the cleansing of the ◊Augean stables. Driven mad by the goddess Hera, he murdered his first wife Megara and their children, and was himself poisoned by mistake by his second wife ◊Deianira.

Herbert Frank (Patrick) 1920–1986. US science-fiction writer, author of the *Dune* series from 1965 (filmed by David Lynch 1984), large-scale adventure stories containing serious ideas about ecology and religion.

Herbert George 1593–1633. English metaphysical poet. His volume of religious poems, *The Temple*, appeared 1633, shortly before his death. His intense though quiet poems embody his religious struggles ('The Temper', 'The Collar') or poignantly contrast mortality and eternal truth ('Vertue', 'Life') in a deceptively simple language.

Be calm in arguing; for fierceness makes Error a fault and truth discourtesy.

George Herbert 'The Church Porch'

Herbert Victor 1859–1924. Irish-born US conductor and composer. In 1893 he became conductor of the 22nd Regiment Band, also composing light operettas for the New York stage. He was conductor of the Pittsburgh Philharmonic 1898–1904, returning to New York to help found the American Society of Composers, Authors, and Publishers (ASCAP) 1914.

Herbert Zbigniew 1924– . Polish poet. His poetry, avant-garde, ironic, and formally accomplished, achieves classical precision and control. He published few poems in the communist-inspired epoch of Socialist Realism 1949–54 but his collection *Struna swiatla/Chord of Light* 1956 was soon followed by *Hermes, pies i gwiazda/Hermes, a Dog and a Star* 1957 and *Studium przedmiotu/A Study of the Object* 1961. He has also written radio plays.

Hercules Roman form of ◊Heracles.

Herder Johann Gottfried von 1744–1803. German poet, critic, and philosopher. Herder's critical writings indicated his intuitive rather than reasoning trend of thought. He collected folk songs of all nations 1778, and in the *Ideen zur Philosophie der Geschichte der Menschheit/Outlines of a Philosophy of the History of Man* 1784–91 he outlined the stages of human cultural development.

Born in East Prussia, Herder studied at Königsberg where he was influenced by Kant, became pastor at Riga, and in 1776 was called to Weimar as court preacher. He gave considerable impetus to the ◊Sturm und Drang Romantic movement in German literature.

Herling-Grudziński Gustaw 1919– . Polish novelist and essayist. An anti-Nazi journalist in 1939, he was deported to a Russian labour camp during the war, an experience reflected in his autobiographical novel *Inny swiat/A World Apart* 1953. He later fought with the Allies and eventually settled in Italy. Some of his stories were collected and translated as *The Island* 1967. His work was officially suppressed in Poland until 1988.

Herman Woody (Woodrow) 1913–1987. US bandleader and clarinettist. A child prodigy, he was leader of his own orchestra at 23, and after 1945 formed his Thundering Herd band. Soloists in this or later versions of the band included Lester ◊Young and Stan ◊Getz.

Hermaphroditus in Greek mythology, the son of Hermes and Aphrodite. He was loved by a ◊nymph who prayed for eternal union with him, so that they became one body with dual sexual characteristics, hence the term hermaphrodite.

Hermes in Greek mythology, a god, son of Zeus and ◊Maia; messenger of the gods. He wore winged sandals, a wide-brimmed hat, and carried a staff around which serpents coiled. Identified with the Roman Mercury and ancient Egyptian Thoth, he protected thieves, travellers, and merchants.

Hermione in Greek mythology, the daughter of Menelaus and Helen, and wife to ◊Neoptolemos and subsequently ◊Orestes.

Hero and Leander in Greek mythology, a pair of lovers. Hero was a priestess of Aphrodite at Sestos on the Hellespont, in love with Leander on the opposite shore at Abydos. When he was drowned while swimming across during a storm, she threw herself into the sea.

Herodotus *c.* 484–424 BC. Greek historian. After four years in Athens, he travelled widely in Egypt, Asia, and the Black Sea region of eastern Europe, before settling at Thurii in S Italy 443 BC. He wrote a nine-book history of the Greek–Persian struggle that culminated in the defeat of the Persian invasion attempts 490 and 480 BC. Herodotus was the first historian to apply critical evaluation to his material, while also recording divergent opinions.

heroic couplet alternative name for the iambic pentameter couplet (two lines of five unstressed/stressed feet; see ◊foot, ◊metre), because of its frequent use in epic or heroic poetry.

Herondas 3rd century BC. Greek author of mimes. Eight short works survive, revealing a realistic eye for seedy transactions and human motives. It is not clear whether they were intended for performance or for reading, but they reflect the theatrical qualities of the Greek mime, a form based on the caricature of types and bizarre situations.

Hero of Our Time, A novel by the Russian writer Mikhail Lermontov, published 1840. It consists of five stories about a bitter, cynical nobleman and officer, whose attitude is contrasted with that of an older, dutiful officer.

Herr Michael 1940– . US writer. ◊*Dispatches* 1977, his book of Vietnam reportage, became an international best seller, praised for its bold and savage depiction of war. Co-author of several screenplays, including *Apocalypse Now* 1979 and *Full Metal Jacket* 1987, he also wrote *Walter Winchell* 1990, a hybrid screenplay/novel vividly dramatizing the life of the famous 1940s gossip columnist.

Herrera Francisco, *the Elder* 1576–1656. Spanish painter, active in Seville. He painted genre and religious scenes, with bold effects of light and shade.

Herrera Francisco, *the Younger* 1622–1685. Spanish still-life painter. He studied in Rome and worked in Seville and Madrid, where he was court painter and architect. His paintings reflect Murillo's influence.

Herrick Robert 1591–1674. English poet and cleric, born in Cheapside, London. He published *Hesperides* 1648, a collection of sacred and pastoral poetry admired for its lyric quality, including 'Gather ye rosebuds' and 'Cherry ripe'.

To work a wonder, God would have her shown, / At once, a bud, and yet a rose full-blown.

Robert Herrick 'The Virgin Mary'

Herriot James. Pen name of James Alfred Wight 1916– . English writer. A practising veterinary surgeon from 1940, he wrote of his experiences in a series of books including *If Only They Could Talk* 1970, *All Creatures Great and Small* 1972, and *The Lord God Made Them All* 1981.

Herrmann Bernard 1911–1975. US film composer whose long career began with *Citizen Kane* 1940 and included collaborations with Alfred Hitchcock (*North by Northwest* 1959 and *Psycho* 1960) and François Truffaut (*Fahrenheit 451* 1966). He wrote his best scores for thriller and mystery movies, and was a major influence in the establishment of a distinctively American musical imagery.

Herschel John Frederick William 1792–1871. English scientist and astronomer, son of William Herschel. A friend of the photography pioneer ◊Fox Talbot, Herschel coined the terms 'photography', 'negative', and 'positive', discovered sodium thiosulphite as a fixer of silver halides, and invented the cyanotype process. During the early days of photography he gave lectures on the subject and exhibited his own images.

Hertzberger Herman 1932– . Dutch architect working in the tradition of ◊Brutalism. In similar style to Aldo van Eyck, his designs create a spatial framework that invites the user to occupy and complete the building. Notable examples of his work are the Central Beheer office building, Apeldoorn, 1970–72, and the Music Centre, Utrecht, 1976–78.

Herzog novel 1964 by US writer Saul ◊Bellow. It is the story of a twice-divorced Jewish college professor who suffers intense, but comically treated, emotional and intellectual crises. After failing to shoot his second wife's lover, Herzog makes relative peace with himself and abandons his faith in intellectual salvation.

Herzog Werner 1942– . German film director who often takes his camera to exotic and impractical locations. His original and visually splendid films include *Aguirre der Zorn Gottes/Aguirre Wrath of God* 1972, *Nosferatu Phantom der Nacht/Nosferatu Phantom of the Night* 1979, and *Fitzcarraldo* 1982.

I make films to rid myself of them, like ridding myself of a nightmare.

Werner Herzog

Heseltine Philip (Arnold). Real name of the English composer Peter ◊Warlock.

Hesiod Greek poet, supposed to have lived a little later than Homer, and, according to his own account, born in Boeotia. He is the author of *Works and Days*, a moralizing and didactic poem of rural life, and the *Theogony*, an account of the origin of the world and of the gods. Both poems include the myth of ◊Pandora.

Hesperides in Greek mythology, the Greek maidens who guarded a tree bearing golden apples in the Islands of the Blessed (also known as the Hesperides). The apples were taken by the hero ◊Heracles, in one of his labours.

Hesse Hermann 1877–1962. German writer who became a Swiss citizen 1923. A conscientious objector in World War I and a pacifist opponent of Hitler, he published short stories, poetry, and novels, including *Peter Camenzind* 1904, *Siddhartha* 1922, and ◊*Steppenwolf* 1927. Later works, such as *Das Glasperlenspiel/The Glass Bead Game* 1943, show the influence of Indian mysticism and Jungian psychoanalysis. He was awarded the Nobel Prize for Literature 1946.

If you hate a person, you hate something in him that is part of yourself. What isn't part of ourselves doesn't disturb us.

Hermann Hesse *Demian*

Hestia in Greek mythology, the goddess of the hearth (Roman Vesta), daughter of ◊Kronos and Rhea.

Heston Charlton. Stage name of Charles Carter 1924– . US film actor who often starred in biblical and historical epics, for example, as Moses in *The Ten Commandments* 1956, and in the title role in *Ben-Hur* 1959 (Academy Award). His other film appearances include *Major Dundee* 1965 and *Earthquake* 1974.

heterophony form of group musicmaking found in folk music worldwide, in which the same melody line is presented simultaneously in plain and individually embellished forms.

hexameter (Greek 'six measures') verse line of six metrical feet. The hexameter was the metre of the Greek epic poet ◊Homer, and became the standard verse form for all ancient epic writers. It was also used in other kinds of poetry, notably the elegy. A line of iambic hexameter is called an ◊alexandrine.

Heywood Thomas *c.* 1570–*c.* 1650. English actor and dramatist. He wrote or adapted over 220 plays, including the domestic tragedy *A Woman Kilde with Kindnesse* 1602–03. He also wrote an *Apology for Actors* 1612, in answer to attacks on the morality of the theatre.

Hiawatha, The Song of poem written by H W Longfellow 1855. It is an Indian legend told in the lilting metre of the Finnish national epic *Kalevala*. It was based on data collected by Henry R Schoolcraft (1793–1864).

Hickey William 1749–1830. English writer, whose entertaining *Memoirs* were first published 1913–1925.

Higgins George V 1939– . US novelist who wrote many detective and underworld novels, often set in Boston, including *The Friends of Eddie Coyle* 1972, *The Impostors* 1986, and *Trust* 1989.

Higgins Jack. Pseudonym of English novelist Harry ◊Patterson.

highlife West African popular music that comes in two main styles: guitar-band highlife, which focuses on storytelling songs; and highlife dance music, played by larger bands that include brass instruments. Highlife has been popular throughout English-speaking W Africa since the 1920s.

Highlife originated with the importation of guitars in the early 20th century and subsequently combined diverse traditional forms with external influences (jazz, calypso, reggae, disco, soca). The rhythm of the first big highlife hit, *Yaa Amponsah* by Ghanaian Kwame Asare 1927, was repeatedly reworked in later decades. Ghanaian E T Mensah (1919–) introduced Afro-Cuban rhythms and electric guitars with his Tempos Band from 1948. Prince Nico Mbarga (1950–) revitalized Nigerian highlife with Zairean guitar style in the 1970s.

Highsmith Patricia 1921– . US crime novelist. Her first book, *Strangers on a Train* 1950, was filmed by Alfred Hitchcock. She wrote a series dealing with the amoral Tom Ripley, including *The Talented Mr Ripley* 1956, *Ripley Under Ground* 1971, and *Ripley's Game* 1974. She excels in tension and psychological exploration of character.

High Tech (abbreviation for *high technology*) in architecture, an approach to design, originating in the UK in the 1970s, which concentrates on technical innovation, often using exposed structure and services as a means of creating exciting forms and spaces. The Hong Kong and

Shanghai Bank, Hong Kong 1986, designed by Norman ◊Foster, is a masterpiece of High Tech architecture.

Other outstanding examples are the Lloyds Building in the City of London, 1986, by Richard ◊Rogers, which dramatically exhibits the service requirements of a large building, and Nicholas ◊Grimshaw's *Financial Times* printing works, London, 1988.

Hikmet Nazim 1902–1963. Turkish poet. Acclaimed since his death as a revolutionary hero, he was educated at Moscow University and was imprisoned in Turkey for his activities as a communist propagandist. His much-translated poems, which were banned in Turkey during his lifetime, include *Memleketimden insan manzar-alari/Portraits of People from My Land* and *Seyh Bedreddin destani/The Epic of Shayk Bedreddin* 1936, about a religious revolutionary in 15th-century Anatolia.

Hildebrandt Johann Lucas von 1668–1745. Italian-born Austrian architect, who trained under Carlo Fontana (1638–1714), the leading Baroque architect in late 17th-century Rome, and was successor to Viennese court architect Johann Fischer von Erlach (1656–1723). His Baroque masterpiece is the Belvedere, Vienna, 1693–1724, which comprises the Upper and Lower Palaces, divided by magnificent gardens.

Hill and Adamson David Octavius Hill 1802–1870 and Robert R Adamson 1821–1848. Scottish photographers who worked together 1843–48, making extensive use of the ◊calotype process in their portraits of leading members of the Free Church of Scotland and their views of Edinburgh and the Scottish fishing village of Newhaven. They produced around 2,500 calotypes. Their work was rediscovered around 1900.

Hiller Wendy 1912– . English actress. Her many roles include Catherine Sloper in *The Heiress* 1947 and Eliza in the film version of Shaw's *Pygmalion* 1938. Her other films include *The Elephant Man* 1980.

Hilliard Nicholas *c.* 1547–1619. English miniaturist and goldsmith, court artist to Elizabeth I and James I. His sitters included the explorers Francis Drake and Walter Raleigh. A fine collection of his brilliant, highly detailed portraits, set in gold cases, including *An Unknown Young Man Amid Roses* about 1590, is in the Victoria and Albert Museum, London. Between 1597 and 1603 he wrote a treatise on miniature painting called *The Arte of Limning*.

Hilton James 1900–1954. English novelist. He settled in Hollywood as one of its most successful scriptwriters, for example, *Mrs Miniver*. His books include *Lost Horizon* 1933, envisaging Shangri-la, a remote district of Tibet where time stands still; *Goodbye, Mr Chips* 1934, a portrait of an old schoolmaster; and *Random Harvest* 1941.

Hilton Walter *c.* 1340–1396. English mystic, author of *The Ladder of Perfection*, a devotional treatise on ascetism and contemplation. It prescribes for the restoration of God's image in the soul by enduring the 'dark night' of detachment from worldly things. Hilton spent most of his life as an Augustinian canon.

Himes Chester (Bomar) 1909–1984. US novelist. After serving seven years in prison for armed robbery, he published his first novel *If He Hollers Let Him Go* 1945, a powerful depiction of racist victimization set in a Californian shipyard. He later wrote in the crime thriller genre, most notably in *The Real Cool Killers* 1958, *Rage in Harlem* 1965, and *Cotton Comes to Harlem* 1965. He also published two volumes of autobiography, *The Quality of Hurt* 1972 and *My Life of Absurdity* 1976.

Hindemith Paul 1895–1963. German composer and teacher. His operas *Cardillac* 1926, revised 1952, and *Mathis der Maler/Mathis the Painter* 1933–35, are theatrically astute and politically aware; as a teacher in Berlin 1927–33 he encouraged the development of a functional modern repertoire ('Gebrauchsmusik'/'utility music') for home and school.

In 1939 he emigrated to the USA, where he was influential in promoting a measured Neo-Classical idiom of self-evident contrapuntal mastery but matter-of-fact tone, exemplified in *Ludus Tonalis* for piano 1942 and the *Symphonic Metamorphoses on Themes of Carl Maria von Weber* 1944. In later life he revised many of his earlier compositions to conform with a personal theory of tonality.

Hine Lewis 1874–1940. US sociologist and photographer. His dramatic photographs of child labour conditions in US factories at the beginning of the 20th century led to changes in state and local labour laws.

hip-hop popular music originating in New York in the early 1980s, created with scratching (a percussive effect obtained by manually rotating a vinyl record) and heavily accented electronic drums behind a ◊rap vocal. Within a decade, digital sampling had largely superseded scratching. The term 'hip-hop' also comprises break dancing and graffiti.

hippie member of a youth movement of the late 1960s, also known as *flower power*, which originated in San Francisco, California, and was characterized by nonviolent anarchy, concern for the environment, and rejection of Western materialism. The colourful psychedelic style of the hippies, inspired by drugs such as LSD, emerged in fabric design, graphic art, and music by bands such as Love (1965–71), the ◊Grateful Dead, Jefferson Airplane (1965–74), and ◊Pink Floyd.

Hippolytus in Greek mythology, the son of Theseus. When he rejected the love of his stepmother, Phaedra, she falsely accused him of making advances to her and turned Theseus against him. Killed by Poseidon at Theseus' request, he was in some accounts of the legend restored to life when his innocence was proven.

Hiroshige Andō 1797–1858. Japanese artist, one of the leading exponents of ◊ukiyo-e prints, an art form whose flat, decorative style and choice of everyday subjects greatly influenced the development of Western art. His landscape prints, often employing snow or rain to create atmosphere, include *53 Stations on the Tokaido Highway* 1833. Whistler and van Gogh were among Western painters influenced by him.

Hiroshige was born in Edo (now Tokyo), and his last series, *100 Famous Views of Edo* 1856–58, was incomplete at his death. He is thought to have made over 5,000 different prints.

historical novel fictional prose narrative set in the past. Literature set in the historic rather than the immediate past has always abounded, but in the West Walter Scott began the modern tradition by setting imaginative romances of love, impersonation, and betrayal in a past based on known fact; his use of historical detail, and subsequent imitations of this technique by European writers, gave rise to the genre.

Some historical novels of the 19th century were overtly nationalistic, but most were merely novels set in the past to heighten melodrama while providing an informative framework; the genre was used by Alessandro Manzoni, Victor Hugo, Charles Dickens, and James Fenimore Cooper, among many others. In the 20th century the historical novel also became concerned with exploring psychological states and the question of differences in outlook and mentality in past periods. Examples of this are Robert Graves' novels about the Roman emperor *I, Claudius* and *Claudius the God*, and Margaret Yourcenar's *Memoirs of Hadrian*.

The less serious possibilities of the historical novel were exploited by writers in the early 20th century in the form of the *historical romance*, which was revived with some success in the late 1960s. The historical novel acquired subgenres – the stylized *Regency novel* of Georgette Heyer (1902–1974) and her imitators, and the Napoleonic War sea story of C S Forester. These forms have developed their own conventions, particularly when imitating a hugely popular predecessor – this has happened in large degree to the *Western*, many of which use gestures from Owen Wister's classic *The Virginian*, and to the novel of the US South in the period of the Civil War, in the wake of Margaret Mitchell's *Gone With the Wind*. In the late 20th century sequences of novels about families, often industrialists of the early 19th century, became popular.

historicism in architecture and the visual arts, the copying of styles from the past, for example the Gothic and Classical revivals of the 19th century. It implies a detailed imitation, rather than

the ironic reference that is common in ◊Post-Modernism or the selection of existing styles to combine with an artist's own work as in ◊eclecticism.

history painting painting genre depicting scenes taken from classical sources, mythology, the Bible, and literary classics, such as Dante's *Divine Comedy*. From the early Renaissance, when ◊Alberti first documented the style, until the decline of the academic tradition in the 19th century, history painting was regarded as the highest form of painting, its purpose being to express noble themes and sentiments. Examples include David's *The Oath of the Horatii* 1784 (Louvre, Paris), and Benjamin ◊West's *The Death of General Wolfe* 1770 (National Gallery of Canada, Ottawa), one of the first to depict a scene from contemporary history.

Hitchcock Alfred 1899–1980. British film director who became a US citizen 1955. A master of the suspense thriller, he was noted for his meticulously drawn storyboards that determined his camera angles and for his cameo 'walk-ons' in his own films. His *Blackmail* 1929 was the first successful British talking film; *The Thirty-Nine Steps* 1935 and *The Lady Vanishes* 1939 are British suspense classics. He went to Hollywood 1940, where he made *Rebecca* 1940, *Notorious* 1946, *Strangers on a Train* 1951, *Rear Window* 1954, *Vertigo* 1958, *Psycho* 1960, and *The Birds* 1963. His last film was the comedy thriller *Family Plot* 1976.

There is no terror in a bang, only in the suspense.

Alfred Hitchcock

Hitchens Ivon 1893–1979. English painter. His semi-abstract landscapes were painted initially in natural tones, later in more vibrant colours. He also painted murals, for example *Day's Rest, Day's Work* 1963 (Sussex University). From the 1940s Hitchens lived in a forest near Midhurst in Sussex which provided the setting for many of his paintings.

Hoban James C 1762–1831. Irish-born architect who emigrated to the USA. He designed the White House, Washington, DC; he also worked on the Capitol and other public buildings.

Hobbema Meindert 1638–1709. Dutch landscape painter. A pupil of Ruisdael, his early work is derivative, but later works are characteristically realistic and unsentimental. His best-known work is *The Avenue, Middelharnis* 1689 (National Gallery, London). He was popular with English collectors in the 18th and 19th centuries, and influenced English landscape painting.

Hobbit, The or *There and Back Again* a fantasy for children by J R R ◊Tolkien, published in the

UK 1937. It describes the adventures of Bilbo Baggins, a 'hobbit' (small humanoid) in an ancient world, Middle-Earth, populated by dragons, dwarves, elves, and other mythical creatures, including the wizard Gandalf. *The Hobbit*, together with Tolkien's later trilogy *The Lord of the Rings* 1954–55, achieved cult status in the 1960s. By 1991, 35 million copies had been sold worldwide, more than any other work of fiction.

Hochhuth Rolf 1931– . Swiss dramatist whose controversial play *Soldaten/Soldiers* 1968 implied that the British politician Churchill was involved in a plot to assassinate the Polish general Sikorski. *Der Stellvertieter/The Representative* 1963 dealt with the Nazi holocaust of the Jews.

Hochschule für Gestaltung German educational institution for design 1951–68, established in Ulm to carry on the work of the prewar ◊Bauhaus which had been closed by the Nazis. The school was notable for its rigorous commitment to a systematic design methodology and for the severe minimalism of the designs which emerged from it. The majority of Germany's most influential industrial designers of the postwar years, Hans Gugelot (1920–1965) among them, graduated from the Hochschule.

Hockney David 1937– . English painter, printmaker, and designer, resident in California. He exhibited at the Young Contemporaries Show of 1961 and contributed to the Pop art movement. He developed an individual figurative style, as in his portrait *Mr and Mrs Clark and Percy* 1971 (Tate Gallery, London) and has experimented prolifically with technique. His views of swimming pools reflect a preoccupation with surface pattern and effects of light. He has also produced drawings, etchings (*Six Fairy Tales from the Brothers Grimm*, 1970), photo collages, and sets for opera at La Scala, Milan, and the Metropolitan Opera House, New York.

Hockney, born in Yorkshire, studied at Bradford School of Art and the Royal College of Art, London. He was the subject of Jack Hazan's semidocumentary 1974 film *A Bigger Splash*.

We live in an age where the artist is forgotten. He is a researcher. I see myself that way.

David Hockney 1991

Hodler Ferdinand 1853–1918. Swiss painter. His dramatic Art Nouveau paintings of allegorical, historical, and mythological subjects include large murals with dreamy Symbolist female figures, such as *Day* about 1900 (Kunsthaus, Zürich). His work prefigured Expressionism.

Hoffman Dustin 1937– . US actor who became popular in the 1960s with his unconven-

tional looks, short stature, and versatility. He won Academy Awards for his performances in *Kramer vs Kramer* 1979 and *Rain Man* 1988. His other films include *The Graduate* 1967, *Midnight Cowboy* 1969, *Little Big Man* 1970, *All the President's Men* 1976, *Tootsie* 1982, and *Hook* 1991. He appeared on Broadway in the 1984 revival of *Death of a Salesman*, which was also filmed for television 1985.

Hoffmann E(rnst) T(heodor) A(madeus) 1776–1822. German composer and writer. He composed the opera *Undine* 1816, but is chiefly renowned as an author and librettist of fairy stories, including *Nussknacker/Nutcracker* 1816. His stories inspired ◊Offenbach's *Tales of Hoffmann*.

Hoffmann Josef 1870–1956. Austrian architect and designer. Influenced by Art Nouveau, he was one of the founders of the Wiener Werkstätte/Vienna Workshops (a modern design cooperative of early 20th-century Vienna), and a pupil of Otto ◊Wagner. One of his best-known works is the Purkersdorf Sanatorium 1903–05.

Hofmann Hans 1880–1966. German-born painter, active in Paris and Munich from 1915 until 1932, when he moved to the USA. In addition to bold brushwork (he experimented with dribbling and dripping painting techniques in the 1940s), he used strong expressive colours, his works strongly influencing the development of Abstract Expressionism. In the 1960s he moved towards a hard-edged abstract style.

Hogan Paul 1940– . Australian TV comic, film actor, and producer. The box-office hit *Crocodile Dundee* (considered the most profitable film in Australian history) 1986 and *Crocodile Dundee II* 1988 (of which he was also co-writer and producer) brought him international fame.

Hogarth William 1697–1764. English painter and engraver who produced portraits and moralizing genre scenes, such as the series of prints *A Rake's Progress* 1735. His portraits are remarkably direct and full of character, for example *Heads of Six of Hogarth's Servants* about 1750–55 (Tate Gallery, London).

Hogarth was born in London and apprenticed to an engraver. He published *A Harlot's Progress*, a series of six engravings, 1732. Other series followed, including *Marriage à la Mode* 1745, *Industry and Idleness* 1749, and *The Four Stages of Cruelty* 1751. In his book *The Analysis of Beauty* 1753 he attacked uncritical appreciation of the arts and proposed a double curved line as a key to visual beauty.

Hogg James 1770–1835. Scottish novelist and poet, known as the 'Ettrick Shepherd'. Born in Ettrick Forest, Selkirkshire, he worked as a shepherd at Yarrow 1790–99. Until the age of 30, he was illiterate. His novel *Confessions of a Justified Sinner* 1824 is a masterly portrayal of personified evil.

Hokusai Katsushika 1760–1849. Japanese artist, the leading printmaker of his time and a major exponent of ◊ukiyo-e. He published *36 Views of Mount Fuji* about 1823–29, and produced outstanding pictures of almost every kind of subject–birds, flowers, courtesans, and scenes from legend and everyday life. *Under the Wave at Kanagawa* (British Museum, London) is typical.

Hokusai was born in Edo (now Tokyo) and studied wood engraving and book illustration. He was interested in Western painting and perspective and introduced landscape as a woodblock-print genre. His *Manga*, a book crammed with inventive sketches, was published in 13 volumes from 1814.

Holbein Hans, *the Elder* c. 1464–1524. German painter, active in Augsburg. His works include altarpieces, such as that of *St Sebastian* 1516 (Alte Pinakothek, Munich). He also painted portraits and designed stained glass.

Holbein Hans, *the Younger* 1497/98–1543. German painter and woodcut artist; the son and pupil of Hans Holbein the Elder. Holbein was born in Augsburg. In 1515 he went to Basel, where he became friendly with the scholar and humanist Erasmus and illustrated his *Praise of Folly*; he painted three portraits of him 1523. He travelled widely in Europe and while in England as painter to Henry VIII he created a remarkable evocation of the English court in a series of graphic, perceptive portraits, the best known being those of Henry VIII and Thomas More. During his time at the English court, he also painted miniature portraits, inspiring Nicholas Hilliard. One of the finest graphic artists of his age, he executed a woodcut series *Dance of Death* about 1525, and designed title pages for Luther's New Testament and More's *Utopia*. Pronounced Renaissance influence emerged in the *Meyer Madonna* 1526, a fine altarpiece in Darmstadt.

Holborne Anthony 1584–1602. English composer in the service of Queen Elizabeth I whose collection *The Cittharn Schoole* 1597 contains pieces for cittern and bass viol. A further collection *Pavans, Galliards, Almains and Other Short Aeirs* was published 1599.

Holden Charles 1875–1960. English Modernist architect known for his massive, austere, stone-faced buildings such as the headquarters of London Transport, over St James's Station, London, 1927–29, and the Senate House, University of London, 1932. Following World War II, he was responsible, with William ◊Holford, for the town-planning report for the City of London 1946–47.

Holden Edith 1871–1920. British artist and naturalist. Daughter of a Birmingham manufacturer, she made most of her observations near her native city, and her journal, illustrated with her own watercolours, was published 1977 as *The Country Diary of an Edwardian Lady*.

Holden William. Stage name of William Franklin Beedle 1918–1981. US film actor, a star in the late 1940s and 1950s. He played a wide variety of leading roles in such films as *Sunset Boulevard* 1950, *Stalag 17* 1953, *The Wild Bunch* 1969, and *Network* 1976.

Hölderlin Friedrich 1770–1843. German lyric poet. His poetry attempted to reconcile Christianity and the religious spirit of ancient Greece and to naturalize the forms of Greek verse in German. His work includes *Hyperion* 1797–99, an epistolary novel, translations of Sophocles 1804, and visionary poems such as the elegy 'Menons Klagen um Diotima'/'Menon's Lament for Diotima' and the brilliantly apocalyptic 'Patmos', written just before the onset of madness 1806.

Holford William, Baron Holford 1907–1975. British architect, born in Johannesburg. A leading architect/planner of his generation, he was responsible for much post-war redevelopment, including the plan for the City of London (with Charles ◊Holden) and the precinct for St Paul's Cathedral, London, 1955–56.

Holiday Billie. Stage name of Eleanora Gough McKay 1915–1959. US jazz singer, also known as 'Lady Day'. She made her debut in Harlem clubs and became known for her emotionally charged delivery and idiosyncratic phrasing; she brought a blues feel to performances with swing bands. Songs she made her own include 'Stormy Weather', 'Strange Fruit', and 'I Cover the Waterfront'.

Hollar Wenceslaus 1607–1677. Bohemian engraver, active in England from 1637. He was the first landscape engraver to work in England and recorded views of London before the Great Fire of 1666.

Holliger Heinz 1939– . Swiss oboist and composer of avant-garde works in lyric expressionist style, including *Siebengesang/Sevensong* 1967 for amplified oboe, voices, and orchestra. He has given first performances of Berio, Krenek, Henze, and Stockhausen.

Holly Buddy. Stage name of Charles Hardin Holley 1936–1959. US rock-and-roll singer, guitarist, and songwriter, born in Lubbock, Texas. Holly had a distinctive, hiccuping vocal style and was an early experimenter with recording techniques. Many of his hits with his band, the Crickets, such as 'That'll Be the Day' 1957, 'Peggy Sue' 1957, and 'Maybe Baby' 1958, have become classics. He died in a plane crash.

Hollywood district in the city of Los Angeles, California; the centre of the US film industry from 1911. It is the home of film studios such as 20th Century Fox, MGM, Paramount, Columbia Pictures, United Artists, Disney, and Warner Brothers. Many film stars' homes are situated nearby in Beverly Hills and other communities adjacent to Hollywood.

Hollywood is a place where they pay you a thousand dollars for a kiss and fifty cents for your soul.

Marilyn Monroe on Hollywood

Holmes, Sherlock fictitious private detective, created by the English writer Arthur Conan ◊Doyle in *A Study in Scarlet* 1887 and recurring in novels and stories until 1914. Holmes' ability to make inferences from slight clues always astonishes the narrator, Dr Watson.

The criminal mastermind against whom Holmes repeatedly pits his wits is Professor James Moriarty. Holmes is regularly portrayed at his home, 221b Baker Street, London, where he plays the violin and has bouts of determined action interspersed by lethargy and drug-taking. His characteristic pipe and deerstalker hat were the addition of an illustrator.

Holmes Oliver Wendell 1809–1894. US writer and physician. In 1857 he founded *The Atlantic Monthly* with J R Lowell, in which were published the essays and verse collected in 1858 as *The Autocrat of the Breakfast-Table*, a record of the imaginary conversation of boarding-house guests.

Holst Gustav(us Theodore von) 1874–1934. English composer of distant Swedish descent. He wrote operas, including *Sávîtri* 1908 and *At the Boar's Head* 1924; ballets; choral works, including *Hymns from the Rig Veda* 1908–12 and *The Hymn of Jesus* 1917; orchestral suites, including *The Planets* 1914–16; and songs. He was a lifelong friend of Ralph ◊Vaughan Williams, with whom he shared an enthusiasm for English folk music. His musical style, although tonal and drawing on folk song, tends to be severe. He was the father of Imogen Holst (1907–   ), musicologist and his biographer.

Never compose anything unless the not composing of it becomes a positive nuisance to you.

Gustav Holst letter to William Gillies Whittaker 1921

Holtby Winifred 1898–1935. English novelist, poet, and journalist. She was an ardent advocate of women's freedom and racial equality, and wrote the novel *South Riding* 1936, set in her native Yorkshire. Her other works include an analysis of women's position in contemporary society *Women and a Changing Civilization* 1934.

Holub Miroslav 1933–   . Czech poet. A doctor specializing in immunology, amidst the discouragements of communist rule he has in terse and allusive poems testified courageously to humanistic values. His collections include *Kam tece krev/Where the Blood Flows* 1963, *Udalosti/Events* 1971, and *Naopal/On the Contrary* 1982. *Notes of a Clay Pigeon*, a volume of poems in English translation, appeared 1977.

Holy Grail in medieval Christian legend, the dish or cup used by Jesus at the Last Supper, supposed to have supernatural powers. Together with the spear with which he was wounded at the Crucifixion, it was an object of quest by King Arthur's knights in certain stories incorporated in the Arthurian legend.

According to one story, the blood of Jesus was collected in the Holy Grail by Joseph of Arimathaea at the Crucifixion, and he brought it to Britain where he allegedly built the first church, at Glastonbury. At least three churches in Europe possess vessels claimed to be the Holy Grail.

Holyrood House royal residence in Edinburgh, Scotland. The palace was built 1498–1503 on the site of a 12th-century abbey by James IV. It has associations with Mary, Queen of Scots, and Charles Edward, the Young Pretender.

homburg felt hat, made in Homburg, Germany, in the early 19th century. Like the ◊fedora, it has a high crown with a crease in the middle. A dark band of fabric is sewn around the base of the crown. The homburg was made fashionable by Edward VII of England.

Homer according to ancient tradition, the author of the Greek narrative epics, the ◊*Iliad* and the ◊*Odyssey* (both derived from oral tradition). Little is known about the man, but modern research suggests that both poems should be assigned to the 8th century BC, with the *Odyssey* the later of the two. The predominant dialect in the poems indicates that Homer may have come from an Ionian Greek settlement, such as Smyrna or Chios, as was traditionally believed.

The epics, dealing with military values, social hierarchy, and the emotions and objectives of a heroic class of warriors, supported or opposed by the gods, had an immediate and profound effect on Greek society and culture and were a major influence on the Roman poet ◊Virgil in the composition of his *Aeneid*. In the Renaissance a revival of the study of Greek brought translations from Alexander Pope and George Chapman. Modern writers influenced by Homer include James Joyce and Nikos Kazantzakis.

As the generation of leaves, so is that of men.

Homer *Iliad*

Homer Winslow 1836–1910. US painter and lithographer, known for his vivid seascapes, in both oil and watercolour, which date from the 1880s and 1890s.

Born in Boston, Homer made his reputation as a Realist painter with *Prisoners from the Front* 1866 (Metropolitan Museum of Art, New York), recording the miseries of the American Civil War. After a visit to Paris he turned to lighter subjects, such as studies of country life, which reflect early Impressionist influence.

homily sermon or lecture giving advice on a moral or contentious issue.

homophony music comprising a melody lead and accompanying harmony, in contrast to *heterophony* and *polyphony* in which different melody lines of equal importance are combined.

Hon'ami Kōbetsu Japanese designer, calligrapher, and potter. As the central figure of a community dedicated to reviving the traditional arts and crafts of Kyoto, Kōbetsu influenced all aspects of Japanese design. Famed for his calligraphy and ceramics for tea ceremonies, he also produced lacquer pieces, one of the finest of which is the *Boat Bridge Writing Box* early 17th century (National Museum, Tokyo).

Hondecoeter Melchior d' 1636–1695. Dutch artist who painted large pictures of birds (both domestic fowl and exotic species) in grandiose settings.

Honegger Arthur 1892–1955. Swiss composer, one of ◊*Les Six*. His work was varied in form, for example, the opera *Antigone* 1927, the ballet *Skating Rink* 1922, the oratorio *Le Roi David/King David* 1921, programme music (*Pacific 231* 1923), and the *Symphonie liturgique/Liturgical Symphony* 1946. He also composed incidental music for Abel Gance's silent movie classics *La Roue/The Wheel* 1923 and *Napoléon* 1927.

There is no doubt that the first requirement for a composer is to be dead.

Arthur Honegger *Je suis compositeur?*

Honthorst Gerrit van 1590–1656. Dutch painter who used extremes of light and shade, influenced by ◊Caravaggio. He painted biblical, mythological, and genre paintings.

Around 1610–12 he was in Rome, studying Caravaggio. Later he visited England, painting *Charles I* 1628 (National Portrait Gallery, London), and later became court painter in The Hague.

Hooch Pieter de 1629–1684. Dutch painter, active in Delft and, later, Amsterdam. The harmonious domestic interiors and courtyards of his Delft period were influenced by Vermeer. *The Courtyard of a House in Delft* 1658 (National Gallery, London) is a typical work.

Hood Raymond Mathewson 1881–1934. US architect of several New York skyscrapers of the 1920s and 1930s, and a member of the team responsible for the Rockefeller Center, New York, 1929. Two of his skyscrapers, the *Daily News* building, 1930, and McGraw-Hill building, 1931, with its distinctive green-tile cladding, are seminal works of the ◊Art Deco style.

With S Gordon Jeeves he built the National Radiator building in London 1928, faced with black tiles and coloured Egyptian-style decoration.

Hood Thomas 1799–1845. English poet and humorist. Born in London, he entered journalism, and edited periodicals, for example, *Hood's Monthly Magazine* 1844. Although remembered primarily for his comic verse, for example, 'Miss Kilmansegg', he also wrote serious poems such as 'Song of the Shirt' 1843, a protest against poorly paid labour, and 'Bridge of Sighs' 1843, about the suicide of a prostitute.

Hooker John Lee 1917– . US blues guitarist, singer, and songwriter, one of the foremost blues musicians. His first record, 'Boogie Chillen' 1948, was a blues hit and his percussive guitar style made him popular with a rock audience from the 1950s. His albums include *Urban Blues* 1968 and *Boom Boom* 1992 (also the title of his 1962 song).

Hooker was born in Mississippi and learned from the delta folk-blues players before moving north and taking up the urban, electric style on early recordings like 'Hobo Blues' and 'Crawlin' King Snake' (both 1949).

Hope Anthony. Pen name of Anthony Hope Hawkins 1863–1933. English novelist whose romance *The Prisoner of Zenda* 1894, and its sequel *Rupert of Hentzau* 1898, introduced the imaginary Balkan state of Ruritania.

Hope Bob. Stage name of Leslie Townes Hope 1903– . British-born US comedian, best remembered for seven films he made with Bing ◊Crosby and Dorothy Lamour between 1940 and 1953, whose titles all began *The Road to* (*Singapore, Zanzibar, Morocco, Utopia, Rio, Bali,* and *Hong Kong*). Other films include *The Cat and the Canary* 1939 and *The Facts of Life* 1960.

He was taken to the USA 1907, and became a Broadway and radio star in the 1930s. He has received several special Academy Awards.

A bank is a place that will lend you money if you can prove that you don't need it.

Bob Hope

Hopkins Anthony 1937– . Welsh actor. Among his stage appearances are *Equus, Macbeth,*

Pravda, and the title role in *King Lear*. His films include *The Lion in Winter* 1968, *A Bridge Too Far* 1977, *The Elephant Man* 1980, *84 Charing Cross Road* 1986, *The Silence of the Lambs* (Academy *Remains of the Day* 1993, and *Shadowlands* 1994.

Hopkins Gerard Manley 1844–1889. English poet and Jesuit priest. His work, which is marked by its originality of diction and rhythm and includes 'The Wreck of the Deutschland' and ' The Windhover', was published posthumously 1918 by Robert Bridges. His poetry is profoundly religious and records his struggle to gain faith and peace, but also shows freshness of feeling and delight in nature. His employment of 'sprung rhythm' (combination of traditional regularity of stresses with varying numbers of syllables in each line) greatly influenced later 20th-century poetry.

Hopkins converted to Roman Catholicism 1866 and in 1868 began training as a Jesuit. He was ordained 1877 and taught Greek and Latin at University College, Dublin, 1884–89.

Hopper Dennis 1936– . US film actor and director who caused a sensation with the anti-establishment *Easy Rider* 1969, but whose *The Last Movie* 1971 was poorly received by the critics. He made a comeback in the 1980s directing such films as *Colors* 1988. His work as an actor includes *Rebel Without a Cause* 1955, *The American Friend/Der amerikanische Freund* 1977, *Apocalypse Now* 1979, and *Blue Velvet* 1986.

Hopper Edward 1882–1967. US painter and etcher, one of the foremost American Realists. His views of life in New England and New York in the 1930s and 1940s, painted in rich, dark colours, convey a brooding sense of emptiness and solitude, as in *Nighthawks* 1942 (Art Institute, Chicago). Hopper's teacher Robert ◊Henri, associated with the ◊Ashcan School, was a formative influence.

If you could say it in words there would be no reason to paint it.

Edward Hopper

Hopper Hedda 1890–1966. US actress and celebrity reporter. From 1915 she appeared in many silent films and after a brief retirement was hired as a radio gossip reporter 1936. From 1938 Hopper wrote a syndicated newspaper column about the private lives of the Hollywood stars. She carried on a widely publicized feud with rival columnist Louella Parsons.

Hoppner John 1758–1810. English portrait painter, a follower of Joshua Reynolds and rival to Thomas Lawrence. He became portrait painter to the Prince of Wales (later George IV) 1789 and a Royal Academician 1795. Among his paintings are portraits of the royal princesses, William Pitt, and Admiral Nelson.

Horace 65–8 BC. Roman lyric poet and satirist. He became a leading poet under the patronage of Emperor Augustus. His works include *Satires* 35–30 BC; the four books of *Odes*, about 25–24 BC; *Epistles*, a series of verse letters; and an influential critical work, *Ars poetica*. They are distinguished by their style, wit, discretion, and patriotism.

Born at Venusia, S Italy, the son of a freedman, Horace fought under Brutus at Philippi, lost his estate, and was reduced to poverty. In about 38 Virgil introduced him to Maecenas, who gave him a farm in the Sabine hills and recommended him to the patronage of Augustus.

Seize the day, and put as little trust as you can in tomorrow.

Horace *Odes* 25–24 BC

Horae in Greek mythology, the goddesses of the seasons, daughters of Zeus and ◊Themis, three or four in number, sometimes personified (see ◊Dike).

Hordern Michael 1911– . English character actor who has appeared in stage roles such as Shakespeare's Lear and Prospero, and in plays by Tom Stoppard and Harold Pinter. His films include *The Man Who Never Was* 1956, *The Spy Who Came in From the Cold* 1965, *The Bed Sitting Room* 1969, and *Joseph Andrews* 1976.

horn member of a family of lip-reed instruments used for signalling and ritual, and sharing features of a generally conical bore (although the orchestral horn is of part conical and part straight bore) and curved shape, producing a pitch of rising or variable inflection.

The modern valve horn is a 19th-century hybrid B flat/F instrument; the name **French horn** strictly applies to the earlier *cor à pistons* which uses lever-action rotary valves and produces a lighter tone. The **Wagner tuba** is a horn variant in tenor and bass versions devised by Wagner to provide a fuller horn tone in the lower range. Composers for horn include Mozart, Haydn, Richard Strauss (*Till Eulenspiegel* 1895), Ravel, and Benjamin Britten (*Serenade for Tenor, Horn and Strings* 1943).

Horniman Annie Elizabeth Frederika 1860–1937. English pioneer of repertory theatre who subsidized the ◊Abbey Theatre, Dublin (built 1904), and founded the Manchester company at the Gaiety Theatre 1908.

Hornung E(rnest) W(illiam) 1866–1921. English novelist who, at the prompting of Arthur Conan ◊Doyle, created 'A J Raffles', the gentleman-burglar, and his assistant Bunny Manders in *The Amateur Cracksman* 1899.

Horowitz Vladimir 1904–1989. Russian-born US pianist. He made his US debut 1928 with the New York Philharmonic Orchestra. A leading interpreter of Liszt, Schumann, and Rachmaninov, he toured worldwide until the early 1950s when he retired to devote more time to recording. His rare concert appearances 1965–86 displayed undiminished brilliance.

horror genre of fiction and film, devoted primarily to scaring the reader or audience, but often also aiming to be cathartic through their exaggeration of the bizarre and grotesque. Dominant figures in the horror tradition are Mary Shelley (◊*Frankenstein* 1818), Edgar Allan Poe, Bram Stoker, H P Lovecraft and, among contemporary writers, Stephen King and Clive Barker.

Horror is derived from the Gothic novel, which dealt in shock effects, as well as from folk tales and ghost stories throughout the ages. Horror writing tends to use motifs such as vampirism, the eruption of ancient evil, and monstrous transformation, which often derive from folk traditions, as well as more recent concerns such as psychopathology.

Horsley John Calcott 1817–1903. English artist. A skilled painter of domestic scenes, he was also responsible for frescoes in the Houses of Parliament and is credited with designing the first Christmas card.

Horst-Wessel-Lied song introduced by the Nazis as a second German national anthem. The text was written to a traditional tune by Horst Wessel (1907–1930), a Nazi 'martyr'.

Horta Victor 1861–1947. Belgian Art Nouveau architect. He was responsible for a series of apartment buildings in Brussels, the first of which, Hôtel Tassel 1892, is striking in its use of sinuous forms and decorative ironwork in the interior, particularly the staircase. His sumptuous Hôtel Solvay 1895–1900 and Maison du Peuple 1896–1899 are more complete, interior and exterior being unified in a stylistic whole.

Horus in ancient Egyptian mythology, the hawkheaded sun god, son of Isis and Osiris, of whom the pharaohs were declared to be the incarnation.

Hosking Eric (John) 1909–1990. English wildlife photographer known for his documentation of British birds, especially owls. Beginning at the age of eight and still photographing in Africa at 80, he covered all aspects of birdlife and illustrated a large number of books, published between 1940 and 1990.

Hoskins Bob 1942– . British character actor who progressed to fame from a series of supporting roles. Films include *The Long Good Friday* 1980, *The Cotton Club* 1984, *Mona Lisa* 1985, *A Prayer for the Dying* 1987, and *Who Framed Roger Rabbit?* 1988.

Hotteterre Jacques-Martin 1674–1763. French flautist, bassoonist, and instrument maker. He came from a family of woodwind instrument makers and composers responsible for developing the orchestral Baroque flute and bassoon from folk antecedents. A respected performer and teacher, he wrote a tutor for the transverse flute and composed trio sonatas and suites for flute and bassoon.

Houdini Harry. Stage name of Erich Weiss 1874–1926. US escapologist and conjurer. He was renowned for his escapes from ropes and handcuffs, from trunks under water, from straitjackets and prison cells. He also campaigned against fraudulent mindreaders and mediums.

Houdon Jean-Antoine 1741–1828. French sculptor, a portraitist who made characterful studies of Voltaire and a Neo-Classical statue of George Washington, commissioned 1785.

His other subjects included the philosophers Diderot and Rousseau, the composer Gluck, the emperor Napoleon, and the American politician Benjamin Franklin. Houdon also produced popular mythological figures, such as *Diana* and *Minerva*.

Hours, Book of in medieval Europe, a collection of liturgical prayers for the use of the faithful. Books of Hours appeared in England in the 13th century, and contained short prayers and illustrations, each prayer being suitable for a different hour of the day, in honour of the Virgin Mary. The enormous demand for Books of Hours was a stimulus for the development of Gothic illumination. A notable example is *Les Très Riches Heures du Duc de Berry*, illustrated in the early 15th century by the ◊Limbourg brothers.

Household Geoffrey 1900–1988. British espionage and adventure novelist. His *Rogue Male* 1939 concerned an Englishman's attempt to kill Hitler, and the enemy hunt for him after his failure. Household served with British intelligence in World War II.

Houseman John 1902–1988. US theatre, film, and television producer and character actor, born in Romania. He co-founded the Mercury Theater with Orson Welles, and collaborated with directors such as Max Ophuls, Vicente Minelli, and Nicholas Ray. He won an Academy Award for his acting debut in *The Paper Chase* 1973, and recreated his role in the subsequent TV series. Among the films he produced are *The Bad and the Beautiful* 1952 and *Lust for Life* 1956.

house music dance music of the 1980s originating in the inner-city clubs of Chicago, USA, combining funk with European high-tech pop. *Acid house* has minimal vocals and melody, instead surrounding the mechanically emphasized 4/4 beat with stripped-down synthesizer riffs and a wandering bass line. Other variants include *hip house*, with rap elements, and *acid jazz*.

If a line of poetry strays into my memory, my skin bristles so that the razor ceases to act.

Alfred Edward Housman lecture: *The Name and Nature of Poetry* Cambridge, 9 May 1933

Housman A(lfred) E(dward) 1859–1936. English poet and classical scholar. His *A Shropshire Lad* 1896, a series of deceptively simple, nostalgic, balladlike poems, was popular during World War I. This was followed by *Last Poems* 1922 and *More Poems* 1936.

Houston Whitney 1963– . US soul ballad singer who has had a string of consecutive number-one hits in the USA and Britain. They include 'Saving All My Love for You' 1985, 'I Wanna Dance With Somebody' ('Who Loves Me') 1987, 'Where Do Broken Hearts Go' 1988, and 'I Will Always Love You' 1992. She made her acting debut in the film *The Bodyguard* 1992.

Howard Alan 1937– . British actor whose appearances with the Royal Shakespeare Company include the title roles in *Henry V*, *Henry VI*, *Coriolanus*, and *Richard III*.

Howard Constance 1919– . English embroiderer who helped to revive creative craftwork after World War II. Her work included framed pictures with fabrics outlined in bold black threads, wall hangings, and geometric studies in strong colour.

Howard Ebenezer 1850–1928. English town planner and pioneer of the ideal of the ◊garden city, through his book *Tomorrow* 1898 (republished as *Garden Cities of Tomorrow* 1902).

Howard Leslie. Stage name of Leslie Stainer 1893–1943. English actor whose films include *The Scarlet Pimpernel* 1935, *The Petrified Forest* 1936, *Pygmalion* 1938, and *Gone With the Wind* 1939.

Howard Trevor (Wallace) 1916–1989. English actor whose films include *Brief Encounter* 1945, *Sons and Lovers* 1960, *Mutiny on the Bounty* 1962, *Ryan's Daughter* 1970, and *Conduct Unbecoming* 1975.

Howe James Wong. Adopted name of Wong Tung Jim 1899–1976. Chinese-born director of film photography, who lived in the USA from childhood. One of Hollywood's best cinematographers, he is credited with introducing the use of hand-held cameras. His work ranges from *The Alaskan* 1924 to *Funny Lady* 1975 and notably includes *Sweet Smell of Success* 1957.

Howells William Dean 1837–1920. US novelist and editor. The 'dean' of US letters in the post-Civil War era, and editor of *The Atlantic Monthly*, he championed the realist movement in fiction and encouraged many younger authors. He wrote 35 novels, 35 plays, and many books of poetry, essays, and commentary.

His novels, filled with vivid social detail, include *A Modern Instance* 1882 and *The Rise of Silas Lapham* 1885, about the social fall and moral rise of a New England paint manufacturer, a central fable of the 'Gilded Age'.

'Howl' poem 1956 by US poet Allen ◊Ginsberg. Written in long, chanting cadences, the poem protests against modern American materialism and conformism. It caused an immediate sensation on its first public reading in San Francisco 1955 and became a powerful call to the emerging ◊Beat Generation.

I saw the best minds of my generation destroyed by madness, starving hysterical naked . . .

Allen Ginsberg 'Howl' 1956

Howlin' Wolf Stage name of Chester Arthur Burnett 1910–1976. US blues singer, songwriter, harmonica player, and guitarist, characterized by a harsh, compelling vocal style. His most influential recordings, made in Chicago, feature the electric guitarist Hubert Sumlin (1931–) and include 'Smokestack Lightnin' 1956, 'Little Red Rooster' 1961, and 'Killin' Floor' 1965. Howlin' Wolf got his nickname from a habitual falsetto vocal call. He had a large, charismatic presence and his music is rough-edged and uncompromising.

Hrabal Bohumil 1914– . Czechoslovak writer, who began writing after 1962. His novels depict ordinary people caught up in events they do not control or comprehend, including *Ostře sledované vlaky/Closely Observed Trains* 1965, filmed 1967.

Hsia Kuei active 1190–1230. Chinese landscape painter, known for the brilliance and range of his brushwork, particularly his vigorous 'axe cut' strokes. Like ◊Ma Yuan, he worked in the refined and lyrical tradition of the southern Song court. One of his finest works is the long handscroll *Ten Thousand Li of the Yangtze* (National Palace Museum, Taipei).

hubris in Greek thought, an act of transgression or overweening pride. In ancient Greek tragedy, hubris was believed to offend the gods, and to lead to retribution.

Hudson Rock. Stage name of Roy Scherer Jr 1925–1985. US film actor, a star from the mid-1950s to the mid-1960s, who appeared in several melodramas directed by Douglas Sirk and in three comedies co-starring Doris Day (including *Pillow Talk* 1959). He went on to have a successful TV career in the 1970s.

Hudson W(illiam) H(enry) 1841–1922. British author, born of US parents in Argentina. He was inspired by recollections of early days in Argentina to write the romances *The Purple Land* 1885 and *Green Mansions* 1904, and his autobiographical *Far Away and Long Ago* 1918. He wrote several books on birds, and on the English countryside, for example, *Nature in Down-Land* 1900 and *A Shepherd's Life* 1910.

Hudson River School group of US landscape painters of the early 19th century. They were inspired by the dramatic scenery of the Hudson River Valley and the Catskill Mountains in New York State, and also by the Romantic landscapes of Turner and John Martin. The first artist to depict the region was Thomas ◊Cole. The group also included Asher B ◊Durand and Frederic Edwin ◊Church.

Hughes Howard R 1905–1976. US tycoon. Inheriting wealth from his father, who had patented a successful oil-drilling bit, he created a legendary financial empire. A skilled pilot, he manufactured and designed aircraft. He formed a film company in Hollywood and made the classic film *Hell's Angels* 1930, about aviators of World War I; later successes included *Scarface* 1932 and *The Outlaw* 1944. From his middle years he was a recluse.

Hughes Langston 1902–1967. US poet and novelist. Known as 'the Poet Laureate of Harlem' he became one of the foremost black American literary figures, writing such collections of poems as *The Weary Blues* 1926. In addition to his poetry he wrote a series of novels, short stories, and essays. His autobiography *The Big Sea* appeared 1940.

Hughes Richard (Arthur Warren) 1900–1976. English writer. His study of childhood, *A High Wind in Jamaica*, was published 1929, and the trilogy *The Human Predicament* 1961–73.

Hughes Ted 1930– . English poet, poet laureate from 1984. His work includes *The Hawk in the Rain* 1957, *Lupercal* 1960, *Wodwo* 1967, and *River* 1983, and is characterized by its harsh portrayal of the crueller aspects of nature. In 1956 he married the poet Sylvia Plath.

It took the whole of Creation / To produce my foot, my each feather:/ Now I hold Creation in my foot.

Ted Hughes 'Hawk Roosting'

Hughes Thomas 1822–1896. English writer, author of the children's book *Tom Brown's School Days* 1857, a story of Rugby school under headmaster Thomas Arnold. It had a sequel, *Tom Brown at Oxford* 1861.

Hugo Victor (Marie) 1802–1885. French poet, novelist, and dramatist. The *Odes et poésies diverses* appeared 1822, and his verse play *Hernani* 1830 established him as the leader of French Romanticism. More volumes of verse followed between his series of dramatic novels, which included *Notre-Dame de Paris* 1831, later filmed as *The ◊Hunchback of Notre Dame* 1924, 1939, and *Les ◊Misérables* 1862, adapted as a musical 1980.

Born at Besançon, Hugo was the son of one of Napoleon's generals. Originally a monarchist, his support of republican ideals in the 1840s led to his banishment 1851 for opposing Louis Napoleon's coup d'état. He lived in exile in Guernsey until the fall of the empire 1870, later becoming a senator under the Third Republic. He died a national hero and is buried in the Panthéon, Paris.

The word is the verb and the verb is God.

Victor Hugo *Contemplations* 1856

Hulme Keri 1947– . New Zealand poet and novelist. She won the Commonwealth Booker Prize with her first novel *The Bone People* 1985, which lyrically incorporates the more mystical aspects of Maori experience. Other works include the novella *Lost Possessions* 1985, *The Windeater/Te Kaihau* 1986, a collection of short stories, and *Strands* 1990, a book of poetry.

Hulme T(homas) E(rnest) 1881–1917. British philosopher, critic, and poet, killed on active service in World War I. His *Speculations* 1924 influenced T S ◊Eliot and his few poems inspired the Imagist movement (see ◊Imagism).

Human Comedy, The (French *La Comédie humaine*) series of novels by Honoré de ◊Balzac, published 1842–46, which aimed to depict every aspect of 19th-century French life. Of the 143 planned, 80 were completed. These include studies of human folly and vice, as in *Le Recherche de l'absolu/The Search for the Absolute*, and analyses of professions or ranks, as in *L'Illustre Gaudissart/The Famous Gaudissart* and *Le Curé de village/The Village Parson*.

humanism belief in the potential of human nature rather than in religious or transcendental values. Humanism culminated as a cultural and literary force in 16th-century Renaissance Europe in line with the period's enthusiasm for classical literature and art, growing individualism, and the ideal of the all-round man who should be statesman and poet, scholar and warrior. ◊Erasmus is a great exemplar of Renaissance humanism.

Renaissance humanism originated in the literary studies undertaken in the 13th and 14th centuries by such men as ◊Petrarch. It gained momentum with the scholarly study of literary texts and, as a result, the rediscovery of the great body of ancient Greek literature for the West.

Humperdinck Engelbert 1854–1921. German composer. He studied in Cologne and Munich and assisted Richard Wagner in the preparation of *Parsifal* 1879 at Bayreuth. He wrote the musical fairy operas *Hänsel und Gretel* 1893, and *Königskinder/King's Children* 1910.

Humphrey Doris 1895–1958. US choreographer, dancer, and teacher, one of the pioneers of modern dance. Her movement technique was based on the shifting imbalance of weight, either falling towards or recovering from two absolute positions – the upright or horizontal. Her works includes *The Shakers* 1930, *With My Red Fires* 1936, and *Day on Earth* 1947. Her book *The Art of Making Dances* 1959 is still a highly regarded study on choreography.

A graduate of the ◊Denishawn School, Humphrey taught at Bennington College, Vermont, USA, from 1934 and at the Juilliard from 1952. As a teacher and theorist, she was responsible for codifying the radical ideas of the 1920s and 1930s into a usable vocabulary of movement and has influenced two generations of modern dance exponents.

Humphries (John) Barry 1934– . Australian actor and author who is best known for his satirical one-person shows and especially for the creation of the character of Mrs (later Dame) Edna Everage. His comic strip 'The Adventures of Barry Mackenzie', published in the British weekly *Private Eye* 1963–74, was the basis for two films, *The Adventures of Barry Mackenzie* 1972 and *Barry Mackenzie Holds His Own* 1974, in which Humphries also acted.

Hunchback of Notre Dame, The historical novel by Victor ◊Hugo published 1831. Set in 15th-century Paris, it describes the corrupt and obsessive love of the archdeacon of the cathedral of Notre Dame for a gipsy dancer who is served with devotion by the hunchbacked bellringer. Colourful and violent, it has many vivid scenes, including a dramatic midnight attack on the cathedral.

Hungarian literature written literature has been traced back to 1200 but it was a rich surviving oral literature that influenced Bálint Balassi (1554–1594) and the development of a secular poetic tradition in the 16th century.

Hapsburg Hungary welcomed the Baroque, reflected in major poets such as Miklós Zrínyi (1620–1664). The Enlightenment stimulated writers such as the lyric poet Mihály Csokonai Vitéz (1773–1805) but the national epics of János ◊Arany and the revolutionary fervour of his friend Sándor ◊Petöfi reached a much wider public.

The Hungarian novel, influenced by European Realism, was developed by the arch-romantic Mór Jókai (1825–1904) and his biographer Kálmán Mikszáth (1847–1910). In the early 20th century the leftist literary magazine *Nyugat* involved distinguished writers including the symbolist poet Endre Ady (1877–1919). Socialist writing, such as the work of Tibor Déry (1894–1977), flourished between the wars. Although the suppression of the 1956 uprising discouraged writers who had benefited from a post-Stalinist thaw, influentially courageous and troubled poets such as Ferenc Juhász (1928–) and László Nagy (1925–1978) have continued to confront the intractable problems of life, death, and Hungary.

Hunt (James Henry) Leigh 1784–1859. English poet and essayist. The appearance in his Liberal newspaper *The Examiner* of an unfavourable article that he had written about the Prince Regent caused him to be convicted for libel and imprisoned 1813. The friend and later enemy of Byron, he also knew Keats and Shelley.

His verse is little appreciated today, but he influenced the Romantics, and his book on London *The Town* 1848 and his *Autobiography* 1850 survive. The character of Harold Skimpole in Dickens' *Bleak House* was allegedly based on him.

Stolen kisses are always sweeter.

Leigh Hunt in *The Indicator*

Hunt William Holman 1827–1910. English painter, one of the founders of the ◊Pre-Raphaelite Brotherhood 1848. Obsessed with realistic detail, he travelled from 1854 onwards to Syria and Palestine to paint biblical subjects. His works include *The Awakening Conscience* 1853 (Tate Gallery, London) and *The Light of the World* 1854 (Keble College, Oxford).

Huppert Isabelle 1955– . French actress with an international reputation for her versatility in such films as *La Dentellière/The Lacemaker* 1977, *Violette Nozière* 1978, *Heaven's Gate* 1980, and *Madame Bovary* 1990.

hurdy-gurdy musical stringed instrument resembling a violin in tone but using a form of keyboard to play a melody and drone strings to provide a continuous harmony. An inbuilt wheel, turned by a handle, acts as a bow.

Hurok Solomon 'Sol' 1888–1974. Russian-born US theatrical producer. From 1914 he produced musical and theatrical events and over the years arranged US appearances for the most prominent figures in European music and dance. His autobiographical *Impresario* and *S Hurok Presents* appeared 1946 and 1953 respectively.

Hurston Zora Neale 1901–1960. US writer, associated with the ◊Harlem Renaissance. She collected traditional Afro-American folk tales in *Mules and Men* 1935 and *Tell My Horse* 1938. Among her many other works are the novel *Their Eyes Were Watching God* 1937 and her autobiography *Dust Tracks on a Road* 1942.

Although her conservative philosophy of her later years alienated many of her contemporaries, she was a key figure for following generations of black women writers, including Alice Walker, who edited a collection of her writings, *I Love Myself When I Am Laughing* 1979.

Hurt William 1950– . US actor whose films include *Altered States* 1980, *The Big Chill* 1983, *Kiss of the Spider Woman* 1985 (Academy Award), *Broadcast News* 1987, and *The Accidental Tourist* 1988.

Huston John 1906–1987. US film director, screenwriter, and actor. An impulsive and individualistic filmmaker, he often dealt with the themes of greed, treachery in human relationships, and the loner. His works as a director include *The Maltese Falcon* 1941 (his debut), *The Treasure of the Sierra Madre* 1948 (in which his father Walter Huston starred and for which both won Academy Awards), *The African Queen* 1951, and his last, *The Dead* 1987.

His other films include *Key Largo* 1948, *Moby Dick* 1956, *The Misfits* 1961, *Fat City* 1972, and *Prizzi's Honor* 1984. He was the father of actress Anjelica Huston.

There's nothing duller than a respectable actor. Actors should be rogues, mountebanks and strolling players.

John Huston 1967

Huston Walter 1884–1950. Canadian-born US actor. His career alternated between stage acting and appearances in feature films. He received critical acclaim for his Broadway performance in *Desire Under the Elms* 1924. In 1948 he won the Academy Award for the best supporting actor for his role in *The Treasure of Sierra Madre*.

Born in Toronto, Canada, Huston trained and worked as an engineer before choosing a theatrical career. He was the father of director John Huston who wrote and directed *The Treasure of Sierra Madre*.

Huxley Aldous (Leonard) 1894–1963. English writer of novels, essays, and verse. From the disillusionment and satirical eloquence of *Crome Yellow* 1921, *Antic Hay* 1923, and *Point Counter Point* 1928, Huxley developed towards the Utopianism exemplified by *Island* 1962. The science-fiction novel ◊*Brave New World* 1932 shows human beings mass produced in laboratories and rendered incapable of freedom by indoctrination and drugs.

Huxley's later devotion to mysticism led to his experiments with the hallucinogenic drug mescalin, recorded in *The Doors of Perception* 1954. He also wrote the novel *Eyeless in Gaza* 1936, and two historical studies, *Grey Eminence* 1941 and *The Devils of Loudun* 1952. He was the grandson of Thomas Henry Huxley and brother of Julian Huxley.

Huxley Thomas Henry 1825–1895. English scientist and humanist. Following the publication of Charles Darwin's *On the Origin of Species* 1859, he became known as 'Darwin's bulldog', and for many years was a prominent champion of evolution. In 1869, he coined the word 'agnostic' to express his own religious attitude.

He wrote *Man's Place in Nature* 1863, textbooks on physiology, and innumerable scientific papers. His later books, such as *Lay Sermons* 1870, *Science and Culture* 1881, and *Evolution and Ethics* 1893 were expositions of scientific humanism. His grandsons include Aldous, Andrew, and Julian Huxley.

It is the customary fate of new truths to begin as heresies and to end as superstitions.

Thomas Henry Huxley 'The coming of age of the Origin of the Species' 1880

Huysmans J(oris) K(arl) 1848–1907. French novelist of Dutch ancestry. His novel *Marthe* 1876, the story of a courtesan, was followed by other novels, all of which feature solitary protagonists. His best-known work is *A rebours/Against Nature* 1884, a novel of self-absorbed aestheticism that symbolized the 'decadent' movement. He ended his life in a religious order.

Hyacinth in Greek mythology, the son of Amyclas, a Spartan king. He was loved by Apollo and Zephyrus, who killed him in jealousy. His blood became a flower.

Hyde Douglas 1860–1949. Irish scholar and politician. Founder president of the Gaelic League 1893–1915 (aiming to promote a cultural, rather than political, nationalism), he was president of Eire 1938–45. He was the first person to write a book in modern Irish and to collect Irish folklore, as well as being the author of the first literary history of Ireland. His works include *Love Songs of Connacht* 1894.

Hyde-White Wilfred 1903–1991. English actor, best known for character roles in British and occasionally US films, especially the role of Colonel Pickering in the screen version of *My Fair Lady* 1964. He tended to be cast as an eccentric or a pillar of the establishment, and sometimes as a mixture of the two.

Hydra in Greek mythology, a huge monster with nine heads. If one were cut off, two would grow in its place. One of the 12 labours of ◊Heracles was to kill it.

Hygieia in Greek mythology, the goddess of health (Roman Salus), daughter of Asclepius.

Hymen in Greek mythology, a god of the marriage ceremony. In painting, he is represented as a youth carrying a bridal torch.

hypo in photography, a term for sodium thiosulphate, discovered 1819 by John ◊Herschel, and used as a fixative for photographic images since 1837.

Hypsipyle in Greek mythology, a princess, later queen of Lemnos in the Aegean Sea, host and partner of ◊Jason. Captured by pirates and taken to the mainland, she gave assistance to the ◊Seven against Thebes, and was rescued from slavery by her sons.

I

and American theatre in the 20th century has been profound.

The strongest man in the world is the man who stands most alone.

Henrik Ibsen *An Enemy of the People* 1882

Ibáñez Vicente Blasco 1867–1928. Spanish novelist and politician, born in Valencia. His novels include *La barraca/The Cabin* 1898, the best of his regional works; *Sangre y arena/Blood and Sand* 1908, the story of a famous bullfighter; and *Los cuatro jinetes del Apocalipsis/The Four Horsemen of the Apocalypse* 1916, a product of the effects of World War I. He was actively involved in revolutionary politics.

IBM (International Business Machines) US company, manufacturer of business machines. Founded 1924, it became an important patron of modern design in the post-1945 years.

In 1947, Thomas J Watson Jr, son of the founder of the company, hired Eliot ◊Noyes as chief design consultant. Previously an employee of Norman ◊Bel Geddes, Noyes ensured that IBM worked with the best architects – among them ◊Mies van der Rohe and Marcel ◊Breuer – and designed many of the company's machines, including the 'Selectric' electric typewriter 1961.

Ibrahim Abdullah. Adopted name of 'Dollar' Brand 1934–1990. South African pianist and composer who first performed in the USA 1965 and has had a great influence on the fusion of African rhythms with American jazz. His compositions range from songs to large works for orchestra.

Ibsen Henrik (Johan) 1828–1906. Norwegian dramatist and poet, whose realistic and often controversial plays revolutionized European theatre. Driven into exile 1864–91 by opposition to the satirical *Love's Comedy* 1862, he wrote the verse dramas *Brand* 1866 and *Peer Gynt* 1867, followed by realistic plays dealing with social issues, including *Pillars of Society* 1877, *The* ◊*Doll's House* 1879, ◊*Ghosts* 1881, *An Enemy of the People* 1882, and ◊*Hedda Gabler* 1891. By the time he returned to Norway, he was recognized as the country's greatest living writer.

His later plays, which are more symbolic, include *The Master Builder* 1892, *Little Eyolf* 1894, *John Gabriel Borkman* 1896, and *When We Dead Awaken* 1899. His influence on European

Icarus in Greek mythology, the son of ◊Daedalus, who with his father escaped from the labyrinth in Crete by making wings of feathers fastened with wax. Icarus plunged to his death when he flew too near the Sun and the wax melted.

icon in the Greek or Eastern Orthodox Church, a representation of Jesus, Mary, an angel, or a saint, in painting, low relief, or mosaic. The painted icons were traditionally done on wood. After the 17th century and mainly in Russia, a *riza*, or gold and silver covering that leaves only the face and hands visible (and may be adorned with jewels presented by the faithful in thanksgiving), was often added as protection.

Icons were regarded as holy objects, based on the doctrine that God became visible through Christ. Icon painting originated in the Byzantine Empire, but many examples were destroyed by the iconoclasts, who called for the destruction of religious images, in the 8th and 9th centuries. The Byzantine style of painting predominated in the Mediterranean region and in Russia until the 12th century, when Russian, Greek, and other schools developed. Notable among them was the Russian ◊Novgorod School, inspired by the work of the Byzantine refugee ◊Theophanes the Greek. Andrei ◊Rublev is the outstanding Russian icon painter.

iconography in art history, significance attached to symbols that can help to identify subject matter (for example, a saint holding keys usually represents St Peter) and place a work of art in its historical context. The pioneer of this approach was the German art historian Erwin ◊Panofsky.

ikat textile produced by resist-printing the warp or weft before ◊weaving. The term is Indonesian, but ikat fabrics are also produced in parts of Africa.

ikebana (Japanese 'living flower') Japanese art of flower arrangement. It dates from the 6th–7th century when arrangements of flowers were placed as offerings in Buddhist temples, a practice learned from China. In the 15th century, ikebana became a favourite pastime of the nobility. The oldest of the Japanese ikebana schools is Ikenobo at Kyoto (7th century).

Iliad Greek epic poem, product of an oral tradition; it was possibly written down by 700 BC and is attributed to ◊Homer. Its title is derived from Ilion, the Greek name for Troy. Its subject is the wrath of the Greek hero Achilles at the loss of his concubine Briseis, and at the death of his friend Patroclus, during the Greek siege of Troy. The poems ends with the death of the Trojan hero Hector at the hands of Achilles.

Ilium in classical legend, an alternative name for the city of ◊Troy, taken from its founder Ilus.

Imagism movement in Anglo-American poetry that flourished 1912–14 and affected much US and British poetry and critical thinking thereafter. A central figure was Ezra Pound, who asserted the principles of free verse, complex imagery, and poetic impersonality.

Pound encouraged Hilda Doolittle to sign her verse H D Imagiste and in 1914 edited the *Des Imagistes* anthology. Poets subsequently influenced by this movement include T S Eliot, William Carlos Williams, Wallace Stevens, and Marianne Moore. Imagism established modernism in English-language verse.

Imber Naphtali Herz 1856–1909. Itinerant Hebrew poet. A Zionist and champion of the restoration of Hebrew as a modern spoken language, he wrote *Hatikva/The Hope* 1878, which became the Zionist anthem 1897 and the Israeli national anthem 1948. He wrote in Hebrew and Yiddish.

Born in Austria-Hungary, Imber travelled to Palestine and worked as secretary to the wife of British General Oliphant, then went to England and the USA.

impasto (Italian 'mixture' or 'thick colour') in painting, surface texture achieved by a combination of thickly applied paint (usually oil) and bold work with a brush or palette knife. Van ◊Gogh was a master of impasto.

Importance of Being Earnest, The romantic stage comedy by Oscar ◊Wilde, first performed 1895. The courtships of two couples are comically complicated by confusions of identity and by the overpowering Lady Bracknell.

The Impressionists ... look and perceive harmoniously, but without aim. O

Paul Gauguin *The Intimate Journals of Paul Gauguin*

---

impressionism in music, a style of composition emphasizing instrumental colour and texture. The term was first applied to the music of ◊Debussy.

Impressionism movement in painting that originated in France in the 1860s and dominated European and North American painting in the late 19th century. The Impressionists wanted to depict real life, to paint straight from nature, and to capture the changing effects of light. The term was first used abusively to describe Monet's painting *Impression, Sunrise* 1872 (Musée Marmottan, Paris). Other Impressionists were Renoir and Sisley, and the style was adopted for periods by Cézanne, Manet, Degas, and others.

The starting point of Impressionism was the 'Salon des Refusés', an exhibition 1873 of work rejected by the official Salon. This was followed by the Impressionists' own exhibitions 1874–86, where their work aroused fierce opposition. Their styles were diverse, but all experimented with effects of light and movement created with distinct brushstrokes and fragments of colour juxtaposed on the canvas rather than mixed on the palette. By the 1880s, the movement's central impulse had dispersed, and a number of new styles emerged, later described as Post-Impressionism.

impromptu in music, a 19th-century character piece in the style of an improvisation. Composers of piano impromptus include Schubert and Chopin.

improvisation creating a play, a poem, a piece of music, or any other imaginative work, using available resources but without preparation; creating while performing. In music, improvisation is often based upon an established model; a fresh and personal interpretation of the model is created at each performance.

Incan art see ◊pre-Columbian art.

Inchbald Elizabeth 1753–1821. English author and actress. She wrote *A Simple Story* 1791 and *Nature and Art* 1796, both romances in which gifted, high-spirited heroines struggle against society's restraints on women. She also wrote plays including *I'll Tell You What* 1786 and *Lovers Vows* 1798 (freely translated from Kotzebue's *Das Kind der Liebe*).

incidental music accompanying music to stage or film drama that, in addition to setting a mood (see ◊background music), is also part of the action, as in Thomas ◊Arne's music (including songs) for the stage, music for ◊masques, and so on.

In Cold Blood nonfiction novel 1965 by US writer Truman ◊Capote. Subtitled 'A True Account of a Multiple Murder and its Consequences', it was based on interviews and tells of the murder of a Kansas farming family 1959 by two psychopaths and their subsequent trial and execution. The book was hailed for its vivid treatment of social issues and launched the genre of creative reportage, promoted as the New Journalism.

incubus in the popular belief of the Middle Ages, male demon who had sexual intercourse with women in their sleep. Supposedly the women then gave birth to witches and demons. *Succubus* is the female equivalent.

indeterminacy in music, the absence of specific instruction concerning a significant element of a composition. A ◊mobile piece is unspecific in terms of the order of sections; a graphic score is indeterminate in notation or timing. Composers of indeterminate music include ◊Berio, ◊Stockhausen, and the Polish composer Roman Haubenstock-Ramati (1919–). All music is indeterminate to some degree, since no two live performances can be totally alike.

Indian architecture the architecture of the Indian subcontinent. In function, design, and decoration, Indian architecture was for many centuries essentially religious. The Mogul invasions beginning in AD 1000 brought Islamic styles to India, and the British presence introduced European influences.

Buddhist The classical architecture of India emerged during the Buddhist dynasties, which began in the 4th century BC. Cave temples appeared in the 3rd century BC, imitating the structure and decoration of the wooden architecture of the period (now entirely lost). From small rock-cut shrines and sanctuaries, they evolved into large complex temples and monasteries, their walls richly decorated with reliefs, statues, or paintings. They include the temple at Karli (1st century AD) and the ◊Ajanta caves. The earliest surviving ◊stupas, reliquary mounds, date from the 2nd century BC. They too became larger and more complex, culminating in such monuments as the Great Stupa of Sanchi (3rd century BC–1st century AD), a huge dome surrounded by railings and elaborately carved gateways. Secular buildings from the Buddhist period include the palace of Emperor Asoka (264–228 BC) at Patna, modelled on a palace in Persepolis, Persia.

Hindu Although examples of Hindu architecture can be dated to the last centuries BC, a characteristic style began to flourish in the 6th century AD with the growth of Hindu dynasties. Hindu temples initially drew heavily on Buddhist styles, though their plans were based on mandalas, schematic diagrams of the creation of the universe. The Temple of Vishnu at Deogarh (6th century) is the earliest extant stone-built temple. The Elephanta cave temples, richly decorated with carvings, date from the 8th–9th centuries. Many Hindu temples were sculpted out of rock (rather than cut into rock, as cave temples were), as at Ellora 8th century AD, where the Temple of Kailasa, which is the world's largest monolithic temple, imitates a stone-built temple. The five rock-cut temples at Mahabalipuram, dating from the 7th century AD, illustrate the various styles in use (they may have been used as architectural models). Whether rock-cut or stone built, Hindu temples became highly ornate, and characterized by a high tower covering the main shrine. The Visvanatha Temple, Khajurãho, is typical. In the north, Hindu architecture began to decline following the Mogul invasions which began AD 1000. In the south, where it continued to develop, vast compounds grew up around temples, the gates of the perimeter walls becoming large, highly carved pyramids.

Muslim This can be divided into two periods. During the early period a Persian style was imported directly. The Great Mosque in Delhi, the Qutb-ul-Islam 1193, is the most representative example. During the second period, beginning 1526 with the founding of the Mogul dynasty, the evolution of Indian architecture was influenced by local architects and craftsmen. This era gave rise to such monuments as the Tomb of Humayum, Delhi, 1569, the now-abandoned city of Fatehpur Sikri 1568–75, and the Taj Mahal, Agra, one of the most familiar architectural images of India.

Western The architecture of the colonial period and independence has carried on in the complex tradition ranging from Sir Edwin Lutyens and Sir Herbert Baker's plan for New Delhi onwards to Le Corbusier's plan and buildings for Chandigarh 1951–56.

Indian art the arts of the Indian subcontinent (present-day India, Pakistan, and Bangladesh). Indian art dates back to the ancient Indus Valley civilization, about 3000–1500 BC, centred on the cities of Harappa and Mohenjo Daro. Surviving artefacts reflect the influence of ◊Mesopotamian art. Beginning about 1800 BC, the Aryan invasions gave rise to the Hindu religion and arts celebrating its gods, heroes, and scenes from the two great epics, the *Mahābhārata* and the *Rāmāyana*. From the 6th century BC, Buddhist art developed, following the life and enlightenment of the Buddha Sakyamuni. A third strand was added in the 16th–17th centuries when the Mogul Empire introduced ◊Islamic art to the subcontinent.

Buddhist art Early Buddhist art developed in relation to the architecture of the stupa (temple shrines to the Buddha and his disciples), typically using symbols to represent the Buddha. The first appearance of the Buddha in human form was in the sculptures of the Mathura tradition (2nd century BC) and those of Gandhara (2nd–6th centuries BC) – possibly the greatest school of Buddhist sculpture. The Gandhara sculptures show Greek influence and, along with the Buddhist religion, were exported to China, Korea, and Japan. The profound depth of relief of the Mathura work was followed by the gentler sculptures of the Gupta period (4th–6th centuries AD). The ◊Ajanta caves near Bombay, first begun about 200 BC, contain the finest example of Gupta art – mural paintings from the 5th–7th centuries which, though religious in intent, reflect a sophisticated, courtly society.

Hindu art From the 4th century AD, influenced by Buddhist art, Hindu artists created huge temple complexes; for example, at Orissa, Konarak, and ◊Khajurãho. They also built cave sanctuaries, the most famous being at Elephanta, near

Bombay, with a monumental depiction of the three forces of creation, preservation, and destruction, portrayed as Shiva with three heads. The caves at Ellora feature an ensemble of religious art (Buddhist, Hindu, and Jain) dating from the 6th and 7th centuries. At Khajurāho, celestial dancing girls, the Asparas, adorn the temple façades. Later Hindu art includes the jewel-like depictions from the lives of Krishna and Rama in palm-leaf manuscripts, known as Rajput paintings.

Mogul art From the 11th century, Muslim invaders destroyed Buddhist and Hindu temple art and introduced the mosque and, with it, Islamic art styles. By the 16th century, the Moguls had established an extensive empire. Persian painters were imported and Hindu artists trained in their workshops, a fusion that formed part of the liberal emperor Akbar's cultural plan and resulted in the exquisite miniature paintings of the courts of Jahangir and Shah Jahan. The subjects of miniature painting ranged from portraiture and histories to birds, animals, and flowers.

Indian literature literature of the Indian sub-continent, written in Sanskrit, in the Dravidian languages such as Tamil, in the vernacular languages derived from Sanskrit, such as Urdu and Hindi, and, largely in this century, English.

Sanskrit The oldest surviving examples of Indian literature are the sacred Hindu texts from the Vedic period of about 1500–200 BC. These include the ◊*Veda*s and the later *Upanishads* 800–200 BC, which are philosophical reflections upon the *Vedas*. Of the same period are the *Sutras* 500–200 BC, collections of aphorisms and doctrinal summaries, including the *Kamasutra* on erotic love. During the epic period (400 BC–AD 400) two major epics were written down: the ◊*Mahābhārata* (which contains the ◊*Bhagavad-Gītā*) and the shorter ◊*Rāmāyana*, both about 300 BC. By the classical period (from AD 400), lyric poetry, romances, and drama had developed, the leading poet and dramatist of the period being ◊Kālidāsa. The *Panchatantra*, a collection of Hindu myths, were written down in the 4th century AD.

Dravidian The Dravidian languages of the south, which are unrelated to Sanskrit, had their own strong and ancient literary traditions, though gradually they were influenced by the literatures of the north. The two major works of Tamil are the verse anthologies the *Pattuppattu* and the *Ettutogaiad*, both 1st century AD.

vernacular By AD 1000 extensive vernacular literatures had developed – largely through popularizations of Sanskrit classics – in those languages derived from Sanskrit, such as Urdu, Hindi, and Gujarati. From the 17th century, Urdu poetry flourished at the Mogul court, where it was strongly influenced by classical Persian literature.

The poets Asadullah Ghalib (1797–1869) and Muhammad Iqbāl wrote in Urdu and Persian. Bengali literature in particular was encouraged by the wide use of printing presses in the 19th century. Bengali writers include Bankim Chandra Chatterji, Romesh Chunder Dutt (1848–1909), and Rabindranath Tagore who was awarded the Nobel Prize for Literature 1913. The spiritual and political leader Mohandas Gandhi (1869–1948) wrote in Gujarati.

indie (short for *independent*) in music, a record label that is neither owned nor distributed by one of the large companies ('majors') that dominate the industry. The independent labels are often quicker to respond to new trends and more idealistic in their aims. *Indie music* therefore tends to be experimental and unpolished.

Independent labels have existed as long as the recording industry, but the term became current in the UK with the small labels created to disseminate punk rock in the 1970s. In the 1980s they provided a home for the hardcore bands, for uncategorizable bands with cult followings, like the Fall, and the Smiths. Towards 1990 the burgeoning dance-music scene and a new wave of guitar groups dominated the indies. The British music papers publish separate charts of independent record sales.

Indra Hindu god of the sky, shown as a four-armed man on a white elephant, carrying a thunderbolt. The intoxicating drink soma is associated with him.

industrial architecture any type of building that has emerged as a direct result of the Industrial Revolution, for example factories, warehouses, stations, office buildings, department stores, and certain types of bridge. Typically, industrial structures employ standardized, mass-produced components, commonly associated with engineering. More importantly, they are unadorned, even anti-decorative. Although principally utilitarian, this style of building has influenced the development of the ◊Modern Movement and many parallels can be drawn between Industrial architecture and the ◊High Tech approach.

Landmark structures in the UK include the iron lattice-work bridge at Coalbrookdale 1777–79; King's Cross Station, London, 1851–52, by Lewis Cubitt (1799–1883); and the Boatstore, Sheerness Royal Naval Dockyard 1858–60. In the USA the development of Industrial architecture is closely linked to the ◊Chicago School, while in continental Europe it is associated with a tradition of engineering, as in the AEG turbine factory, Berlin 1909, by Peter ◊Behrens, and the airship hangars at Orly, France 1916–24, by Eugène ◊Freysinnet. Other more recent examples feature in the work of Pier Luigi ◊Nervi and Santiago ◊Calatrava, notably his spectacular suspension bridges in Seville, Spain.

industrial design: chronology

1907	The Deutscher Werkbund was formed in Germany. The German architect Peter Behrens designed the first corporate identity for the AEG company. Bakelite, the first fully synthetic plastic, was invented.
1908	Adolf Loos' influential book *Ornament and Crime* was published.
1913	The first mass-produced 'Model T' car came off Henry Ford's assembly line in his Highland Park factory.
1914	Debate between Herman Muthesius (1861–1934) and Henri Van de Velde (1863–1957) over the importance of standardization in design.
1919	The Bauhaus design school opened in Weimar, Germany.
1925	The Exhibition of Decorative Arts, which gave its name to the term 'Art Deco', was held in Paris.
1926	Henry Ford closed down his car production factory for six months to tool up for a new model. Norman Bel Geddes left shop window design and opened a New York office as an industrial designer.
1927	*Domus* magazine was founded in Italy.
1929	Raymond Loewy (1893–1956) was employed by Gestetner to redesign the duplicating machine.
1932	The redesigned Gestetner duplicating machine was launched.
1933	The Bauhaus school was closed by the Nazis. Bel Geddes published his book *Horizons*.
1938	The Olivetti company employed Marcello Nizzoli as consultant designer.
1939	The New York World's Fair was held with exhibits designed by all the leading US industrial designers.
1940	Walter Dorwin Teague published his book *Design This Day*.
1944	The Council of Industrial Design was formed in England.
1945	Ettore Sottsass and Vico Magistretti set up their design offices in Milan.
1946	The *Britain Can Make It* exhibition was held at the Victoria and Albert Museum in London.
1947	IBM took on Eliot Noyes as chief design consultant.
1948	Nizzoli designed the 'Lexicon 80' typewriter for Olivetti.
1949	*Design* magazine was founded in London.
1951	The Hochschule für Gestaltung was formed in Ulm, Germany. The Festival of Britain was held in London. The Milan Triennale showed work from many countries. Raymond Loewy published his book *Never Leave Well Enough Alone*. The Braun company was taken over by the sons of its founder.
1955	The Braun company employed Dieter Rams. Henry Dreyfuss published *Designing for People*.
1957	Gio Ponti's 'Superleggera' chair was launched by Cassina.
1958	Olivetti employed Ettore Sottsass as the consultant designer for its computer section.
1962	Mario Bellini started working as the consultant designer for Olivetti's typewriter section.
1968	The Milan Triennale was closed prematurely as a result of student action. The Hochschule at Ulm was closed by the local authorities.
1969	'frogdesign', a design consultancy which was to become known for its work on high-technology products, among them Apple Computers, was formed in Germany. Sottsass designed the 'Valentine' typewriter for Olivetti.
1972	The exhibition *The New Domestic Landscape* was held in New York.
1973	Victor Papanek's *Design for the Real World* was published.
1980	The Boilerhouse Design Gallery opened in London.
1981	The first Memphis group show was held in Milan.
1983	Richard Sapper's 'Bollitore' kettle was launched by Alessi in Italy.
1987	The last Memphis group show was held.
1989	The Design Museum opened in London's Docklands.

industrial design a branch of artistic activity that came into being as a result of the need to design machine-made products, introduced by the Industrial Revolution in the 18th century. The purpose of industrial design is to ensure that goods satisfy the demands of fashion, style, function, materials, and cost.

Industrial design became a fully fledged professional activity in the early 20th century through the efforts of the pioneering US industrial designers who worked with the large-scale manufacturers of the new mass-produced technological goods – Eastman Kodak, Gestetner, General Electric, and others. From the USA the profession moved across the Atlantic in the years after 1945. Germany and Italy made special contributions to its evolution after that date and by the 1980s all the main industrialized countries had their own industrial design professions,

complete with design education systems and programmes of support, whether through governmental or privately sponsored bodies.

industrial music avant-garde music that uses electronic distortion, metal percussion, and industrial tools to achieve deafening, discordant effects, often combined with imagery intended to shock or disgust. Throbbing Gristle (formed 1976 in the UK), Einstürzende Neubauten (formed 1980 in Germany), and Non (formed early 1980s in the USA) are leading industrial bands.

The music is distributed chiefly on independent (◊indie) labels and through alternative networks.

Indy (Paul Marie Théodore) Vincent d' 1851–1931. French composer. He studied under César ◊Franck, and was one of the founders of the *Schola Cantorum*. His works include operas

(*Fervaal* 1897), symphonies, tone poems (*Istar* 1896), and chamber music.

Rhythm, the primitive and predominating element of all art.

Vincent d'Indy
Cours de composition musicale

Ingres Jean-Auguste-Dominique 1780–1867. French painter, a student of David and leading exponent of the Neo-Classical style. He studied and worked in Rome about 1807–20, where he began the *Odalisque* series of sensuous female nudes, then went to Florence, and returned to France 1824. His portraits painted in the 1840s–50s are meticulously detailed and highly polished.

Ingres' style developed in opposition to Romanticism. Early works include portraits of Napoleon. Later he painted huge ceilings for the Louvre and for Autun Cathedral. His portraits include *Madame Moitessier* 1856 (National Gallery, London).

Drawing is the true test of art.

Jean-Auguste-Dominique Ingres

ink coloured liquid used for writing, drawing, and printing. Traditional ink (blue, but later a permanent black) was produced from gallic acid and tannic acid, but inks are now based on synthetic dyes.

inlay decorative technique used on furniture until replaced by ◊marquetry in the 17th century. A pattern composed of differently coloured woods or other materials such as horn or ivory is inset into the solid wood of the piece of furniture.

Inness George 1825–1894. US landscape painter influenced by the ◊Hudson River School. His early works, such as *The Delaware Valley* 1865 (Metropolitan Museum of Art, New York), are on a grand scale and show a concern for the natural effects of light. Later he moved towards Impressionism.

Subject is nothing, treatment makes the picture.

George Inness

Inoue Yasushi 1907–1991. Japanese writer (fiction, travel essays, art history) whose interest in China and central Asia is evident in many stories and historical novels. The novels feature isolated protagonists at dramatic moments of Asian history. Examples are *Tempyō no iraka* 1957/*The Roof Tile of Tempyo* 1976, *Koshi*, based on the life of Confucius, and *Shirobama*, describing a childhood in old Japan.

intaglio design cut into the surface of gems or seals by etching or engraving; an ◊engraving technique.

interior design design, decoration, and furnishing of the inside of a building. In recent times the trend has been towards a less ornate and more functional style, fostered by the interaction of architects and designers working in teams, whether to remodel existing interiors, for example Misha Black and Hugh Casson, or in new buildings, for example Gio Ponti's Pirelli building in Milan, Oscar ◊Niemeyer's capital city of Brasília, and the many works of ◊Le Corbusier, Eero ◊Saarinen, and ◊Skidmore, Owings & Merrill. International-style furniture – light, geometric, simple, and functional – was designed, often by architects, to complement modern architecture.

Some indication of ancient interior design is given by Egyptian tomb artefacts, Greek vase paintings, and in the elaborate wall paintings and floor mosaics found in the preserved Roman cities of Pompeii and Herculaneum. In medieval Europe, furniture was simple and wall tapestries came to be used for decoration and insulation. The Renaissance saw more elaborate decoration in palaces and villas with painted ceilings, wall paintings, and intricate mouldings. The later Baroque and Rococo styles developed very elaborate ornamentation and carving.

The first English architects to design a building as an integrated whole were the ◊Adam brothers, for example Syon House, Middlesex. Other early names associated with interior design in England include Inigo ◊Jones and Grinling ◊Gibbons. In Victorian times William ◊Morris designed carpets, wallpaper, and furniture, as did Charles Rennie ◊Mackintosh and Adolph ◊Loos.

intermezzo a one-act comic opera, such as Pergolesi's *La Serva Padrona*/*The Maid as Mistress* 1732; also a short orchestral interlude played between the acts of an opera to denote the passage of time; by extension, a short piece for an instrument to be played between other more substantial works, such as Brahms' *Three Intermezzos for Piano* 1892.

'Internationale' international revolutionary socialist anthem; composed 1870 and first sung 1888. The words by Eugène Pottier (1816–1887) were written shortly after Napoleon III's surrender to Prussia; the music is by Pierre Degeyter. It was the Soviet national anthem 1917–44.

International Gothic late Gothic style of painting prevalent in Europe in the 14th and 15th centuries. It is characterized by strong decorative qualities and greater realism. Exponents include Simone ◊Martini and the Franco-Flemish ◊Limbourg brothers.

International Style or *International Modern* architectural style, an early and influential phase of the ◊Modern Movement, originating in Western Europe in the 1920s, but finding its fullest expression in the 1930s, notably in the USA. Although sometimes used to refer to the Modern Movement as a whole, it here describes an architectural output, centred around the 1920s and 1930s, with distinct stylistic qualities: a dominance of geometrical, especially rectilinear, forms; emphasis on asymmetrical composition; large expanses of glazing; and white rendered walls. Important buildings in what could be termed the 'classic' period of the style are Walter ◊Gropius' Bauhaus building, Dessau, Germany, 1925–26, ◊Le Corbusier's Villa Savoye, Poissy, France, 1927–31, Alvar ◊Aalto's Viipuri Library, Finland (now in Russia) 1927–35, and ◊Mies van der Rohe's Barcelona Pavilion 1929.

Philip ◊Johnson and Alfred Barr coined the term 'International Style' 1932 to describe the work of Le Corbusier, Gropius, and Mies van der Rohe (among others) during the preceding decade.

interval in music, the pitch difference between two notes, expressed in terms of the diatonic scale, for example a fifth, or as a harmonic ratio, 3:2.

intonation in music, the means by which a performer maintains correct tuning. Pitch accuracy requires continuous slight adjustments of pitch in those instruments for which it is feasible. This may be achieved by finger positioning on string instruments, a combination of finger and breath technique on wind instruments, using the tuning slide on a trumpet, or inserting the left hand into the bell of a horn.

Invalides, Hôtel des building in Paris, south of the Seine, founded 1670 as a home for disabled soldiers. The church Dôme des Invalides contains the tomb of Napoleon I.

inversion in music, the mirror-image of a melody used in counterpoint; alternatively a chord in which the natural order of notes is rearranged.

Invisible Man novel 1952 by US writer Ralph ◊Ellison about an unnamed hero who discovers that because of his blackness he lacks all social identity in postwar US society.

Io in Greek mythology, a princess loved by Zeus, who transformed her into a heifer to hide her from the jealousy of his wife Hera.

Ion in Greek mythology, son of ◊Apollo, ancestor of the Ionian or eastern Greeks, and subject of a play by ◊Euripides.

Ionesco Eugène 1912– . Romanian-born French dramatist, a leading exponent of the Theatre of the ◊Absurd. Most of his plays are in one act and concern the futility of language as a means of communication. These include *La Cantatrice chauve/The Bald Prima Donna* 1950 and *La Leçon/The Lesson* 1951. Later full-length plays include *Rhinocéros* 1958 and *Le Roi se meurt/Exit the King* 1961. He has also written memoirs and a novel, *Le Solitaire/The Hermit* 1973.

To look at life from the viewpoint of someone already dead, if that were possible, is absolutely enchanting.

Eugène Ionesco *The Hermit* 1973

Ionic in Classical architecture, one of the five types of column; see ◊order.

Iphigenia in Greek mythology, a daughter of Agamemnon and Clytemnestra. She was sacrificed by her father at Aulis to secure favourable winds for the Greek fleet in the expedition against Troy, on instructions from the prophet ◊Calchas. According to some accounts, she was saved by the goddess ◊Artemis, and made her priestess.

Ipoustéguy Jean Robert 1920– . French sculptor, painter, and draughtsman, known for his innovative combination of figurative and abstract traditions in sculpture. Typically, his work symbolizes the trials of modern man, generally in the form of an upright male figure both supported and entrapped by rigid armatures, as in *Val de Grâce* 1977 (Galerie Claude Bernard, Paris).

Iqbāl Muhammad 1875–1938. Islamic poet and thinker. His literary works, in Urdu and Persian, were mostly verse in the classical style, suitable for public recitation. He sought through his writings to arouse Muslims to take their place in the modern world.

His most celebrated work, the Persian *Asrā-e khūdī/Secrets of the Self* 1915, put forward a theory of the self that was opposite to the traditional abnegation found in Islam. He was an influence on the movement that led to the creation of Pakistan.

IRCAM acronym for *Institut de Recherche et de Coordination Acoustique-Musique* (Institute for Musico-Acoustic Research and Coordination), an organization founded 1977 in Paris for research into electronic music, using computers, synthesizers, and so on. Its director is Pierre ◊Boulez. There is a remarkable live recording studio with programmable acoustic and movable floor and ceiling panels. The principal computing facility is the 4X series synthesizer developed by Pepino di Giugno and capable of transforming instrumental sound in real time.

Other features are exceptional voice synthesis software and timbre interpolation software. IRCAM is housed beneath the Pompidou Arts Centre.

Ireland John (Nicholson) 1879–1962. English composer. His works include the mystic orchestral prelude *The Forgotten Rite* 1917 and the piano solo *Sarnia* 1941. Benjamin ◊Britten was his pupil.

Irene in Greek mythology, the goddess of peace (Roman Pax). She was sometimes regarded as one of the Horae, who presided over the seasons and the order of nature, and were the daughters of Zeus and Themis.

Irish literature early Irish literature, in Gaelic, consists of the sagas, which are mainly in prose, and a considerable body of verse. The chief cycles are that of Ulster, which deals with the mythological ◊Conchobar and his followers, and the Ossianic, which has influenced European literature through James ◊Macpherson's version.

Early Irish poetry has a unique lyric quality and consists mainly of religious verse and nature poetry, for example, St Patrick's hymn and Ultán's hymn to St Brigit. Much pseudo-historical verse is also extant, ascribed to such poets as Mael Mura (9th century), Mac Liac (10th century), and Flann Mainistrech (11th century). Religious literature in prose includes sermons, saints' lives (for example, those in the *Book of Lismore* and in the writings of Michael O'Clery), and visions. History is represented by annals and by isolated texts like the *Cogad Gaedel re Gallaib*, an account of the Viking invasions by an eye-witness. The 'official' or 'court' verse of the 13th to 17th centuries was produced by a succession of professional poets, notably Tadhg Dall O'Huiginn (died *c.* 1617), Donnchadh Mór O'Dálaigh (died 1244), and Geoffrey Keating (died 1646), who wrote in both verse and prose. The bardic schools ceased to exist by the end of the 17th century. Metre became accentual, rather than syllabic. The greatest exponents of the new school were Egan O'Rahilly (early 18th century) and the religious poet Tadhg Gaelach O'Súilleabhá in. The late 19th century onwards saw a resurgence of Irish literature written in English. Oscar ◊Wilde, G B ◊Shaw, and James ◊Joyce represent those who chose to live outside Ireland. More culturally nationalistic were the writers including W B ◊Yeats who supported the Gaelic League (aiming to revivify the Irish language) and founded the Abbey Theatre Company in Dublin: this provided a milieu for the realism and fantasy of J M ◊Synge and the intensity and compassion of Sean ◊O'Casey. Since World War II, Ireland has produced the Nobel prize-winning dramatist Samuel ◊Beckett, novelists of the calibre of Brian ◊Moore and Edna O'Brien (1936–), and poet Seamus ◊Heaney.

Irons Jeremy 1948– . English stage, television and film actor. His stage performances include *Godspell* 1971, *Wild Oats* 1976–77, *Richard III* 1986. He became widely known through the tele-vision series *Brideshead Revisited* and the film *The French Lieutenant's Woman* both 1981. Other films include *Betrayal* 1982, *Swann in Love* 1983, *The Mission* 1985, *Dead Ringers* 1988, *Reversal of Fortune* 1990 (Academy Award), *Waterland* 1992, and *Damage* 1993.

irony literary technique that achieves the effect of 'saying one thing and meaning another' through the use of humour or mild sarcasm. It can be traced through all periods of literature, from classical Greek and Roman epics and dramas to the good-humoured and subtle irony of ◊Chaucer to the 20th-century writer's method for dealing with nihilism and despair, as in Samuel Beckett's *Waiting for Godot*.

The Greek philosopher Plato used irony in his dialogues, in which Socrates elicits truth through a pretence of naivety. Sophocles' use of dramatic irony also has a high seriousness, as in *Oedipus Rex*, where Oedipus prays for the discovery and punishment of the city's polluter, little knowing that it is himself. Eighteenth-century scepticism provided a natural environment for irony, with Jonathan ◊Swift using the device as a powerful weapon in *Gulliver's Travels* and elsewhere.

Irving Henry. Stage name of John Brodribb 1838–1905. English actor. He established his reputation from 1871, chiefly at the Lyceum Theatre in London, where he became manager 1878. He staged a series of successful Shakespearean productions, including *Romeo and Juliet* 1882, with himself and Ellen ◊Terry playing the leading roles. He was the first actor to be knighted, 1895.

Irving John 1942– . US novelist. His bizarre and funny novels include his best-seller, *The World According to Garp* 1978, a vivid comic tale about a novelist killed by a disappointed reader; and *A Prayer for Owen Meany* 1988, about the events that follow the killing by a young boy of his best friend's mother in a baseball accident.

Irving Washington 1783–1859. US essayist and short-story writer. He published a mock-heroic *History of New York* 1809, supposedly written by the Dutchman 'Diedrich Knickerbocker'. In 1815 he went to England where he published *The Sketch Book of Geoffrey Crayon, Gent.* 1820, which contained such stories as 'Rip Van Winkle' and 'The Legend of Sleepy Hollow'.

His other works include *The Alhambra* 1832, sketches about Spanish subjects, and *Tour of the Prairies* 1835, about the American West. His essays and tales remain popular.

Whenever a man's friends begin to compliment him about looking young, he may be sure that they think he is growing old.

Washington Irving *Bracebridge Hall*
'Batchelors' 1822

Isaacs Jorge 1837–1895. Columbian writer. Son of an English Jew, he settled in Bogotá 1864 and began to publish poetry and fiction. Despite a career in public life, he is chiefly remembered for the famous romantic novel *María* 1867, an idyllic picture of life in his native Cauca Valley.

Isherwood Christopher (William Bradshaw) 1904–1986. English novelist. He lived in Germany 1929–33 just before Hitler's rise to power, a period that inspired *Mr Norris Changes Trains* 1935 and *Goodbye to Berlin* 1939, creating the character of Sally Bowles (the basis of the musical *Cabaret* 1968). Returning to England, he collaborated with W H ◊Auden in three verse plays.

Ishiguro Kazuo 1954– . Japanese-born English novelist. His novel *An Artist of the Floating World* won the 1986 Whitbread Prize, and *The Remains of the Day* won the 1989 Booker Prize. His work is characterized by a sensitive style and subtle structure.

Ishiguro's first novel, *A Pale View of Hills*, takes place mainly in his native Nagasaki, dealing obliquely with the aftermath of the atom bomb. *An Artist of the Floating World* is set entirely in Japan but thematically linked to *The Remains of the Day* (filmed 1993), which is about an English butler coming to realize the extent of his self-sacrifice and self-deception. All three have in common a melancholy reassessment of the past.

Ishtar Mesopotamian goddess of love and war, worshipped by the Babylonians and Assyrians, and personified as the legendary queen Semiramis.

Isis the principal goddess of ancient Egypt. She was the daughter of Geb and Nut (Earth and Sky), and as the sister-wife of Osiris searched for his body after his death at the hands of his brother, Set. Her son Horus then defeated and captured Set, but cut off his mother's head because she would not allow Set to be killed. She was later identified with ◊Hathor. The cult of Isis ultimately spread to Greece and Rome.

Iskander Fazil 1929– . Georgian satirical writer. He attracted attention with 'Sozvezdie kozlotura/The Goatibex Constellation' 1966, an effective satire on the bureaucratic control of agriculture. *Sandro iz Chegema/Uncle Sandro of Chegem* 1973 sardonically explores Stalinist politics and the cultural contrast between the distinctive traditions of his native region of Abkhazia and Soviet importations.

Islamic architecture the architecture of the Muslim world, highly diverse but unified by climate, culture, and a love of geometric and arabesque ornament, as well as by the mobility of ideas, artisans, and architects throughout the region. The central public buildings are ◊mosques, often with a dome and ◊minaret; domestic houses face an inner courtyard and are grouped together, with vaulted streets linking the blocks.

The *mosque* is the centre of religious life throughout the Islamic world, the *masjid* or 'place of prostration'. The major mosque in a city is the *masjid al-jum'a*, the Friday mosque. The mosque form originated in Muhammad's house in Medina (where he fled from Mecca 622). It was a mud-walled courtyard enclosure with a shaded perimeter. The elements of the mosque are essentially functional rather than symbolic. There is no division between the sacred and secular. A *mihrab* niche indicates the orientation to Mecca. To the right of the *mihrab* stands the *minbar*, the pulpit. A minaret signifies the presence of the mosque and provides a platform from which the muezzin calls the faithful to prayer. A courtyard *sahn* is a place of gathering for the community.

The Arab-type mosque plan of columned halls surrounding a courtyard is found throughout N Africa, Arabia, Syria, and Mesopotamia; an example is the mosque of Ahmad ibn Tulun, Cairo, Egypt, 876–79. The other great mosque type is the four-*eyvan* mosque originating in Iran. Here the courtyard has a high *eyvan*, or arched recess, in the centre of each side. This plan comes from the Persian house and is seen at its noblest in the Masjid-i- Jum'a in Isfahan, Iran, 8th–18th centuries. A very flexible plan form, it is found from Cairo to central Asia in mosques, theological colleges, caravanserais, and hospitals.

In the Ottoman Empire, the stimulus of ◊Hagia Sophia (532–37), Istanbul, the great church of Justinian, inspired the development of the imperial Turkish mosque in which the open courtyard of the Arab and Iranian mosques is translated into a great space enclosed by a large central dome; an example is the Suleymaniye, Istanbul, 1550–57, by Sinan.

The *minaret* was originally square, following the towers of Christian churches. Spiral minarets are found but most commonly they take the form of a tapering cylindrical tower.

The *Islamic city* is a highly organic entity. The basic cellular unit is the courtyard house, representing the desire for privacy and familial obligations of Muslim life. The houses are grouped into quarters, often of a tribal or ethnic character. Each quarter has its own mosques and facilities. At the centre of the city stands the focus of the community, the congregational mosque, the *masjid al-jum'a*. The arteries of this intricate organism are the vaulted streets of the souk, or bazaar, which thread outwards from the *masjid al-jum'a* towards the great gates of the enclosing fortified walls. The key monuments and facilities of the city are found along the souk—the religious colleges, baths, hospitals, and fountains. Examples of these are found in Fez, Morocco; Aleppo, Syria; and Isfahan, Iran.

Islamic private houses are invariably inward-looking courtyard houses. A bent corridor (for privacy) leads from the gated entry from the public lane into a courtyard paved with tiles, often planted with shade trees and with a pool at the centre. Surrounding the courtyard are the principal rooms of the house. Different sides of the courtyard may provide separate accommodation for sections of the extended family.

decoration and colour In Islam there is a general dislike of figurative representation. As a consequence, architectural decoration relies on calligraphic script and abstract ornament, often combined with a passion for colour, intensified by the desert environment. The domes and courts of such buildings as the 17th-century Masjid-i-Sháh, Isfahan, Iran, are entirely clothed in faience tiles. Arabic script is used extensively in the earliest surviving Islamic building, the Dome of the Rock, Jerusalem, AD 691, and thereafter the word of God plays a significant role in architectural decoration.

Islamic gardens In a largely arid region, the Islamic garden represents an image of paradise. The basic plan is a rectangular enclosure walled against the dust of the desert and divided into at least four sections by water channels. Pavilions are placed at focal points within the gardens. An example is Chehel Sutun, Isfahan, 17th century.

Islamic art art and design of the Muslim world, dating from the foundation of the Islamic faith in the 7th century AD. The traditions laid down by Islam created devout, painstaking craftsmen whose creative purpose was the glory of God. Elements and motifs were borrowed from ◊Byzantine, ◊Coptic, and ◊Persian Sassanian traditions and fused into a distinctive decorative style, based on Arabic calligraphy. Sculpture was prohibited and carvers turned instead to exquisite inlay and fretwork, notably on doors and screens, in Islamic monuments such as the Alhambra Palace, Granada, Spain, and the Taj Mahal, India. Today, Islamic art is to be found predominantly in Egypt, Iran, Iraq, Turkey, the Indian subcontinent, and the Central Asian Republics.

calligraphy Regarded as the highest of all arts due to its role in transcribing the Koran, calligraphy was used to decorate pottery, textiles, metalwork, and architecture. Scripts ranged in style from the cursive Naskh with its extended flourishes to the angular Kufic. Interlacing patterns based on geometry and stylized plant motifs (including the swirling ◊arabesque) typically framed and enhanced the lettering.

ceramics Drawing on Chinese techniques and styles, Muslim potters developed their own distinctive, often coloured, lustres and glazes, which were later influential in the development of European ceramics. In the 11th–12th centuries Turkish Seljuk pottery was noted for its lively designs. In the 16th century, Iznik in Turkey became an important centre, producing beautiful wares, typically blue plant forms against a white ground, and glazed and coloured tilework for mosque decoration.

miniature painting A court tradition of miniature painting developed, which was primarily representational, featuring both humans and animals. Derived from the ivory carvings of Fatimid Egypt (AD 969–1171), it flourished in Persia during the Timurid (15th century) and Safavid (1507–1736) dynasties. The Tabriz school was transplanted to India by the Mogul emperor Akbar (see ◊Indian art).

textiles Islamic weavers, notably those of the Fatimid period, produced silk brocades and carpets of an unprecedented fineness and beauty. Turkish *ushak* medallion carpets were exported to the West in the 16th century and featured in many Renaissance paintings, adorning floors, walls, and desks.

Islands of the Blessed or *Hesperides* in Greek mythology, lands, situated at the western end of the Earth, near the river Oceanus, where heroes and other mortals favoured by the gods were sent to enjoy a life after death.

ISO in photography, a numbering system for rating the speed of films, devised by the International Standards Organization.

Isocrates 436–338 BC. Athenian orator who may have been a friend of the philosopher Socrates when a young man. He was a professional speechwriter and teacher of rhetoric, and a persistent advocate of Greek unity and supremacy.

Isolde or *Iseult* in Celtic and medieval legend, the wife of King Mark of Cornwall who was brought from Ireland by his nephew ◊Tristan. She and Tristan accidentally drank the aphrodisiac given to her by her mother for her marriage, were separated as lovers, and finally died together.

isorhythm in music, a form in which a given rhythm cyclically repeats, although the corresponding melody notes may change. It was used in European medieval music, and is still practised in classical Indian music. The composers Berg, Cage, and Messiaen used isorhythmic procedures.

Isozaki Arata 1931– . Japanese architect. One of Kenzo ◊Tange's team 1954–63, he has tried to blend Western Post-Modernism with elements of traditional Japanese architecture. His works include Ochanomizu Square, Tokyo (retaining the existing façades), the Museum of Contemporary Art, Los Angeles (begun 1984), and buildings for the 1992 Barcelona Olympics.

Architecture is a machine for the production of meaning.

Arata Isozaki
in *Contemporary Architects* 1980

Israels Jozef 1824–1911. Dutch painter. In 1870 he settled in The Hague and became a leader of the **Hague School** of landscape painters, who shared some of the ideals of the ◊Barbizon School in France. His low-keyed and sentimental scenes of peasant life recall the work of ◊Millet.

Italian architecture architecture of the Italian peninsula after the fall of the Roman Empire. In the earliest styles – Byzantine, Romanesque, and Gothic – the surviving buildings are mostly churches. From the Renaissance and Baroque periods there are also palaces, town halls, and so on.

Byzantine (5th–11th centuries) Italy is rich in examples of this style of architecture, which is a mixture of Oriental and classical elements; examples are the monuments of Justinian in Ravenna and the basilica of San Marco, Venice, about 1063.

Romanesque (10th–13th centuries) In N Italy buildings in this style are often striped in dark and light marble; Sicily has Romanesque churches.

Gothic (13th–15th centuries) Italian Gothic differs a great deal from that of N Europe. Façades were elaborately decorated: mosaics and coloured marble were used, and sculpture placed around windows and doors. The enormous cathedral of Milan, 15th century, was built in the N European style.

Renaissance (15th–16th centuries) The style was developed by the Florentine Brunelleschi and Alberti, inspired by Classical models. The sculptor Michelangelo is associated with the basilica of St Peter's, Rome. In Venice the villas of Palladio continued the purity of the High Renaissance. Other outstanding architects of the Renaissance include Bramante, Giulio Romano, Sangallo, Vignola, and Sansovino.

Baroque (17th century) The Baroque style flourished with the oval spaces of Bernini (for example, the church of S Andrea al Quirinale, Rome) and Borromini, Cortona, and the fantasies of Guarini in Turin (such as the church of S Lorenzo).

Neo-Classicism (18th–19th centuries) In the 18th century Italian architecture was less significant, and a dry Classical revival prevailed. In the 19th century Neo-Classicism was the norm, as in much of Europe.

20th century The Futurist visions of Sant'Elia opened the century. Between World Wars I and II pure Modernism was explored (under the influence of Fascism) together with a stripped Classicism, as in the Rationalism of Terragni. Nervi's work showed the expressive potential of reinforced concrete. Terragni and Gio Ponti pioneered the Modern Movement. Since the 1970s, Neo-Rationalism and a related concern with the study of the traditional types of European cities have exerted great influence, led by the work and writings of Aldo Rossi. High Tech architecture is represented by Renzo Piano.

Italian art painting and sculpture of Italy from the early Middle Ages to the present. Schools of painting arose in many of the city-states, including Florence and Siena and, by the 15th century, Venice. Florence was a major centre of the Renaissance, along with Venice, and Rome was the focus of the High Renaissance and Baroque styles.

13th century (Italian *Duecento*) The painter Cimabue was said by the poet Dante to be the greatest painter of his day. Already there was a strong tradition of fresco painting and monumental painted altarpieces, often reflecting Byzantine art. A type of Gothic Classicism was developed by the sculptors Nicola and Giovanni Pisano.

14th century (*Trecento*) The Florentine painter Giotto broke with prevailing styles. Sienese painting remained decoratively stylized but became less sombre, as exemplified by the work of Simone Martini and the Lorenzetti brothers.

15th (*Quattrocento*) *and 16th* (*Cinquecento*) *centuries* The Renaissance style was seen as a 'rebirth' of the Classical spirit. The earliest artists of the Renaissance were based in Florence. The sculptor Ghiberti worked on the Baptistery doors of Florence Cathedral; Donatello set new standards in naturalistic and Classically inspired sculpture. Masaccio and Uccello made advances in employing scientific perspective in painting. In the middle and later part of the century many sculptors and painters were at work in Florence: Verrocchio, Pollaiuolo, Botticelli, Fra Angelico, Fra Filippo Lippi, and Filippino Lippi, among others. In Venice the Bellini family of painters influenced their successors Giorgione and Titian. Tintoretto was Titian's most notable pupil. The High Renaissance was dominated by the many-sided genius of Leonardo da Vinci, the forceful sculptures and frescoes of Michelangelo, and the harmonious paintings of Raphael.

17th century (*Seicento*) The dramatic Baroque style was developed by, among others, the sculptor and architect Bernini, and by the painter Caravaggio, who made effective use of light and shade to create high drama.

18th (*Settecento*) *and early 19th* (*Ottocento*) *centuries* Neo-Classicism was inspired by the rediscovery of Classical Roman works. The sculptor Canova was an exponent. Piranesi produced engravings. The foremost artists in Venice in the 18th century were Canaletto and Tiepolo.

20th century (*Novecento*) The Futurist movement, founded 1910 and dominated by Boccioni, tried to portray phenomena such as speed and electricity in their paintings and sculptures. The first dreamlike Metaphysical paintings of de

Chirico date from the same period. The paintings of Modigliani and the sculptures of Marini are among the finest Italian work of the period.

Italian literature the literature of Italy originated in the 13th century with the Sicilian school, which imitated Provençal poetry, amd Italian began to replace Latin as the literary language.

medieval The works of St Francis of Assisi and Jacopone da Todi reflect the religious faith of that time. Guido Guinicelli (1230–c. 1275) and Guido Cavalcanti developed the spiritual conception of love and influenced Dante Alighieri, whose *Divina commedia/Divine Comedy* 1307–21 is generally recognized as the greatest work of Italian literature. Petrarch was a humanist and a poet, celebrated for his sonnets, while Boccaccio is principally known for his tales.

Renaissance The *Divina commedia* marked the beginning of the Renaissance. Boiardo dealt with the Carolingian epics in his *Orlando innamorate/Roland in Love* 1487, which was completed and transformed by Lodovico Ariosto as *Orlando furioso/The Frenzy of Roland* 1516. Their contemporaries Niccolò Machiavelli and Francesco Guicciardini (1483–1540) are historians of note. Torquato Tasso wrote his epic *Gerusalemme liberata/ Jerusalem Delivered* 1574 in the spirit of the Counter-Reformation.

17th century This period was characterized by the exaggeration of the poets Giovanni Battista Marini (1569–1625) and Gabriello Chiabrera (1552–1638). In 1690 the 'Academy of Arcadia' was formed, including among its members Innocenzo Frugoni (1692–1768) and Metastasio. Other writers include Salvator Rosa, the satirist.

18th century Giuseppe Parini (1729–1799) ridiculed the abuses of his day, while Vittorio Alfieri attacked tyranny in his dramas. Carlo Goldoni wrote comedies.

19th century Ugo Foscolo is chiefly remembered for his patriotic verse. Giacomo Leopardi is not only the greatest lyrical poet since Dante but also a master of Italian prose. The Romantic Alessandro Manzoni is best known as a novelist, and influenced among others the novelist Antonio Fogazzaro. A later outstanding literary figure, Giosuè Carducci, was followed by the verbose Gabriele d'Annunzio, writing of sensuality and violence, and Benedetto Croce, historian and philosopher, who between them dominated Italian literature at the turn of the century.

20th century Writers include the realist novelists Giovanni Verga and Grazia Deledda, winner of the Nobel prize 1926, the dramatist Luigi Pirandello, and the novelists Ignazio Silone and Italo Svevo. Poets of the period include Dino Campana and Giuseppe Ungaretti; and among the modern school are Nobel Prizewinners Eugenio Montale and Salvatore Quasimodo. Novelists of the post-Fascist period include Alberto Moravia, Carlo Levi, Cesare Pavese, Vasco Pratolini (1913–), Elsa Morante (1916–), Natalia Ginsburg (1916–), Giuseppe Tomasi, Prince of Lampedusa, and the writers Italo Calvino, Leonardo Sciascia, and Primo Levi.

italic style of printing in which the letters slope to the right *like this*, introduced by the printer Aldus Manutius of Venice 1501. It is usually used side by side with the erect Roman type to distinguish titles of books, films, and so on, and for purposes of emphasis and (mainly in the USA) citation. The term 'italic' is also used for the handwriting style developed for popular use 1522 by Vatican chancery scribe Ludovico degli Arrighi, which became the basis for modern italic script.

Ithaca (Greek *Itháki*) Greek island in the Ionian Sea, area 93 sq km/36 sq mi. Important in preclassical Greece, Ithaca was (in Homer's poem) the birthplace of ◊Odysseus, though this is sometimes identified with the island of Leukas (some archaeologists have equated ancient Ithaca with Leukas rather than modern Ithaca).

Ives Charles (Edward) 1874–1954. US composer who experimented with ◊atonality, quarter tones, clashing time signatures, and quotations from popular music of the time. He wrote five symphonies, including *Holidays Symphony* 1904–13, chamber music, including the *Concord Sonata*, and the orchestral *Three Places in New England* 1903–14 and *The Unanswered Question* 1908.

Strauss remembers; Beethoven dreams.

Charles Ives *Essays before a Sonata*

Ivory James 1928– . US film director who established his reputation with the Indian-made *Shakespeare Wallah* 1965, which began collaborations with Ishmail ◊Merchant and writer Ruth Prawer ◊Jhabvala. Ivory subsequently directed films in various genres in India, the USA, and Europe, but became associated with adaptations of classic literature, including *The Bostonians* 1984, *A Room with a View* 1987, and *Maurice* 1987, *Howards End* 1992. He directed *The Remains of the Day* 1993.

Ixion in Greek mythology, a king whom Zeus punished for his crimes by binding him to a fiery wheel rolling endlessly through the underworld.

J

'Jack and the Beanstalk' English fairy tale in which Jack is the lazy son of a poor widow. When he exchanges their cow for some magic beans, the beans grow into a beanstalk up which Jack climbs to a realm above the clouds. There he tricks a giant out of various magical treasures before finally cutting down the beanstalk and so causing the giant to fall to his death.

jacket short ◊coat, usually coming to the waist or hip, worn by both men and women. Jackets are worn in combination with skirts and trousers to form ◊suits, or separately, both indoors and outdoors. They are both fashion and utilitarian garments.

Jackson Alexander Young 1882–1974. Canadian landscape painter, a leading member of the *Group of Seven*, who aimed to create a specifically Canadian school of landscape art.

Jackson Betty 1940– . British fashion designer who produced her first collection 1981 and achieved an international reputation as a designer of young, up-to-the-minute clothes. She rescales separates into larger proportions and makes them in boldly coloured fabrics. In 1991 she launched her own accessories range.

Jackson Charles (Reginald) 1903–1968. US novelist. He wrote the acclaimed *The Lost Weekend* 1944, a powerful study of alcoholism, which was made into an Academy Award-winning film 1945. His other novels include *The Fall of Valor* 1946, dealing with homosexuality, and *The Outer Edges* 1948.

Jackson Glenda 1936– . English actress and politician, Labour member of Parliament from 1992. She has made many stage appearances for the Royal Shakespeare Company, including *Marat/Sade* 1966, Hedda in *Hedda Gabler* 1975, and Cleopatra in *Antony and Cleopatra* 1978. Her films include the Oscar-winning *Women in Love* 1969, *Sunday Bloody Sunday* 1971, and *A Touch of Class* 1973. On television she played Queen Elizabeth I in *Elizabeth R* 1971.

Jackson Mahalia 1911–1972. US gospel singer. She made her first recording 1934, and her version of the gospel song 'Move on Up a Little Higher' was a commercial success 1945. Jackson became a well-known radio and television performer in the 1950s and was invited to sing at the presidential inauguration of John F Kennedy.

Born in New Orleans and brought up in a religious home, she began singing religious music in the choir of her local church. In 1927 she left home for Chicago and became a member of the Greater Salem Baptist Church choir, where she distinguished herself as an outstanding soloist.

Jackson Michael 1958– . US rock singer and songwriter whose videos and live performances are meticulously choreographed. His first solo hit was 'Got to Be There' 1971; his worldwide popularity peaked with the albums *Thriller* 1982 and *Bad* 1987. The follow-up was *Dangerous* 1991.

He turned professional 1969 as the youngest member of **the Jackson Five**, who had several hits on Motown Records, beginning with their first single, 'I Want You Back'. The group left Motown 1975 and changed its name to **the Jacksons**. Michael was the lead singer, but soon surpassed his brothers in popularity as a solo performer. From *Off the Wall* 1979 to *Bad*, his albums were produced by Quincy ◊Jones. *Thriller* sold 41 million copies, a world record, and yielded an unprecedented number of hit singles, among them 'Billie Jean' 1983.

Jacob Joseph 1854–1916. Australian-born US folklorist and collector of fairy tales. He published collections of vividly re-told fairy stories such as *English Fairy Tales* 1890, *Celtic Fairy Tales* 1892 and 1894, and *Indian Fairy Tales* 1892.

Jacobean style in the arts, particularly in architecture and furniture, during the reign of James I (1603–25) in England. Following the general lines of Elizabethan design, but using classical features more widely, it adopted many motifs from Italian ◊Renaissance design.

Jacobs W(illiam) W(ymark) 1863–1943. British author who used his childhood knowledge of London's docklands in amusing short stories such as 'Many Cargoes' 1896. He excelled in the macabre, for example 'The Monkey's Paw' 1902.

Jade Emperor in Chinese religion, the supreme god, Yu Huang, of pantheistic Taoism, who watches over human actions and is the ruler of life and death.

Jaeger natural fibre clothing design company started up 1883 by London businessman Lewis Tomalin, inspired by the philosophy of Dr Gustav Jaeger, a German professor of zoology and physiology who campaigned for the benefit of wearing wool next to the skin. In 1884 Tomalin began manufacturing 100% woollen underwear. In the 1900s he expanded to manufacture cardigans, dressing gowns, and knitted skirts and tops. Since the 1920s Jaeger has become synonymous with quality ready-to-wear clothing in wool and natural fibres, though it now also uses synthetics and blends.

James Elmore. Adopted name of Elmore Brooks 1918–1963. US blues guitarist, singer, and songwriter, whose electric slide-guitar style had great impact on rock music. He is particularly associated with the song 'Dust My Broom' (written by Robert ◊Johnson, his main influence) 1952, as well as 'It Hurts Me Too' 1952, 'The Sky Is Crying' 1960, and 'Shake Your Money Maker' 1961. James was born in Mississippi but was active mainly in Chicago from 1952.

It is art that makes life, makes interest, makes importance ... and I know of no substitute whatever for the force and beauty of its process.

Henry James
letter to H G Wells July 1915

James Henry 1843–1916. US novelist, who lived in Europe from 1875 and became a naturalized British subject 1915. His novels deal with the social, moral, and aesthetic issues arising from the complex relationship of European to American culture. Initially a master of psychological realism, noted for the complex subtlety of his prose style, James became increasingly experimental, writing some of the essential works of early Modernism. His major novels include *The Portrait of a Lady* 1881, *The Bostonians* 1886, *What Maisie Knew* 1887, *The Ambassadors* 1903, and *The Golden Bowl* 1904. He also wrote more than a hundred shorter works of fiction, notably the novella *The Aspern Papers* 1888 and the supernatural/psychological riddle *The Turn of the Screw* 1898.

Other major works include *Roderick Hudson* 1876, *The American* 1877, *Washington Square* 1881, *The Tragic Muse* 1890, *The Spoils of Poynton* 1897, *The Awkward Age* 1899, and *The Wings of the Dove* 1902.

James M(ontague) R(hodes) 1862–1936. British writer, theologian, linguist, and medievalist. He wrote *Ghost Stories of an Antiquary* 1904 and other supernatural tales.

James P(hyllis) D(orothy) 1920– . British detective novelist, creator of the characters Superintendent Adam Dalgliesh and private investigator Cordelia Gray. She was a tax official, hospital administrator, and civil servant before turning to writing. Her books include *Death of an Expert Witness* 1977, *The Skull Beneath the Skin* 1982, and *A Taste for Death* 1986. She was made a baroness 1991.

Janáček Leoš 1854–1928. Czech composer. He became director of the Conservatoire at Brno 1919 and professor at the Prague Conservatoire 1920. His music, highly original and influenced by Moravian folk music, includes arrangements of folk songs, operas (*Jenůfa* 1904, *The Cunning Little Vixen* 1924), and the choral *Glagolitic Mass* 1926.

Each folk song contains an entire man; his body, his soul, his surroundings, everything, everything. He who grows up among folk songs, grows into a complete man.

Leoš Janáček

Jane Eyre novel 1847 by Charlotte ◊Brontë. The orphan Jane becomes governess to the ward of Mr Rochester. Employer and governess fight a mutual fascination until Jane agrees to marriage. The revelation that Mr Rochester already has a wife, the mad Bertha, who is imprisoned in his attic, causes Jane's flight. She returns to marry Rochester after Bertha has killed herself by setting the house on fire. In this ever popular book, romantic themes derive distinction from Brontë's powerful intellect and imagination.

Janequin Clément *c.* 1472– *c.* 1560. French composer of chansons and psalms, choirmaster of Angers Cathedral 1534–37, based in Paris from 1549. His songs of the 1520s–30s are witty and richly textured in imitative effects, for example 'Le Chant des oiseaux'/'Birdsong', 'La Chasse'/'The Hunt', 'Les Cris de Paris'/'Street Cries of Paris', and 'La Bataille de Marignan'/'The Battle of Marignan' 1515 which incorporates battle sounds such as the clashing of swords and the cries of warriors.

Jannings Emil. Stage name of Theodor Friedrich Emil Jarenz 1882–1950. German actor in films from 1914. In *Der Blaue Engel/The Blue Angel* 1930 he played a schoolteacher who becomes disastrously infatuated with Marlene Dietrich. His other films include *Der Letzte Mann/The Last Laugh* 1924, *Faust* 1926, and *The Last Command* 1928.

Janus in Roman mythology, the god of doorways and passageways, patron of the beginning of the day, month, and year, after whom January is named; he is represented as having two faces, one looking forwards and one back. In Roman ritual, the doors of Janus in the Forum were closed when peace was established.

Japanese architecture the buildings of Japan, notably domestic housing, temples and shrines, castles, and modern high-rises. Traditional Japanese buildings were made of wood with sliding doors, screens, and paper windows; they had projecting eaves and harmonious proportions. Temples and town planning derived from 6th-century Chinese sources. Western styles were introduced from the mid-19th century.

traditional Farmhouses with a thatched roof, an earthen floor and a raised wooden living area date back more than 1,500 years and can still be found. In the towns, from the 14th century, the front room, which could be closed off from the street by a lattice screen, might be a shop or workshop, with living quarters at the back and on the second floor. Wood, the most abundant building material, was to some extent earthquake-resistant but fires were frequent. The Japanese had introduced prefabricated components by the 14th century so that a small family home could be erected in a couple of days. The best-known module is the tatami straw mat, the universal floor covering from the 17th century, which is also used to measure room size; however, the size of a tatami mat, around 1×2 m/3 $\times$ 6 ft, varies somewhat in different parts of the country. Sliding room dividers (*fusuma*) make the interior space adaptable, and wall panels and paper windows (*shōji*) can be slid back in hot weather. A narrow veranda encircles the house under the eaves; the steep roofs are thatched, tiled, or covered with cypress bark. The emphasis is on simple, geometrical design, uncluttered space, and functional use of natural materials. A town house would have a small enclosed garden; a house with grounds would be oriented to the maximum appreciation of the surrounding nature. The imperial Katsura Palace 1620–58 epitomizes the restrained elegance of the traditional style, in this period also called tea-house style.

shrines Shintō shrines are built in the style of prehistoric storehouses, raised off the ground on piers, and are characterized by crossed ridge-pole weights (*katsuogi*) projecting at the top of the gables, and a thatched roof. They are made of untreated wood which is allowed to weather, and rebuilt when necessary. The most important shrines are Izumo Taisha in Shimane prefecture on SW Honshū and Ise Jingū in Mie prefecture, on the Ise peninsula. The latter is demolished every 20 or 30 years and a new, identical building erected, a replica of a 7th-century one. The entrance to the grounds of a shrine is marked by a red-painted *torii* gate shaped like an H with a projecting beam across the top.

temples Buddhism was brought to Japan in the 6th century from China, and Chinese influence is especially evident in the many-storeyed ◊pagodas and the hipped and gabled, tiled roofs. Although generally single-storey, the most important buildings have double roofs.

The design is based on pillars spaced at fixed intervals; the walls are not load-bearing. A feature of many temples is the exposed timber beams and complex brackets (no nails were used). The oldest surviving temple, and the world's oldest wooden building, is the Hyōryū-ji in Nara, about AD 690. An early temple complex would contain a hall where the Buddha image was housed (*kondō*), a lecture hall (*kodō*), and a pagoda; later ones may have additional halls, sutra repositories, and a refectory. The central gate (*chūmon*) has a heavy roof similar to the buildings, and contains sculptures of guardian deities. The outstanding temple of the Heian period (794–1195) is the 11th-century Hōō-dō of the Byōdōin, in Uji near Kyoto, originally built as a nobleman's villa. Its shape is said to suggest a phoenix, and it is mirrored in the lake on which it stands.

castles The civil wars of the 15th and 16th centuries caused the erection of a number of castles, nearly all of which have been destroyed, though some were rebuilt after World War II. Walled and moated, they were complex stone and wood structures of many roofs and towers, combining solidity with an impression of floating. Himeji near Osaka, which still stands, has a six-storey keep and two smaller towers; Osaka Castle is said to have had 48 large and 76 small towers. Soon after 1600 the country was at peace and castle building declined.

town planning The early capitals, such as Nara and Kyoto, were laid out on a Chinese symmetrical grid, with the emperor's palace in the north and a broad avenue leading down the middle from the palace gate to the main gate of the city; each section held a temple and a market square. The modern city of Sapporo is also designed on a rectangular grid, but modelled on US cities. Other modern Japanese cities have grown more haphazardly, and houses are not numbered consecutively along the street but in the order they were built. The enormous devastation of Japan by bombing in World War II left few houses standing, so that modern buildings predominate.

modern architecture The Japanese emulation of foreign models after the country's isolation ended in the mid-19th century included the erection of Western-style buildings, some designed by foreign architects, such as the American Frank Lloyd ◊Wright's Imperial Hotel, Tokyo, 1916, others by Japanese, such as the huge Versailles-style Akasaka Palace, Tokyo, 1909, by Tōkuma Katayama (1853–1917) and the Bank of Tokyo 1890–96 by Kingo Tatsuno (1854–1919). Notable Japanese architects of the late 20th century are Kenzō ◊Tange, Arata ◊Isozaki, and Tadao ◊Andō. Traditional aesthetics and sensitive adaptation to the site still characterize the best Japanese architecture.

Japanese art the painting, sculpture, printmaking, and design of Japan. Early Japanese art was influenced by China. Painting later developed a distinct Japanese character, bolder and more angular, with the spread of Zen Buddhism in the 12th century. Ink painting and calligraphy flourished, followed by book illustration and decorative screens. Japanese prints developed in the 17th century, with multicolour prints invented around 1765. Buddhist sculpture proliferated from 580, and Japanese sculptors excelled at portraits. Japanese pottery stresses simplicity.

Jōmon **period** (10,000–300 BC) This was characterized by cord-marked pottery.

Yayoi **period** (300 BC–AD 300) Elegant pottery with geometric designs and *dōtaku*, bronze bells decorated with engravings, were produced.

Kofun **period** (300–552) Burial mounds held *haniwa*, clay figures, some of which show Chinese influence.

Asuka **period** (552–646) Buddhist art, introduced from Korea 552, flourished in sculpture, metalwork, and embroidered silk banners. Painters' guilds were formed.

Nara **period** (646–794) Religious and portrait sculptures were made of bronze, clay, or lacquer. A few painted scrolls, screens, and murals survive. Textiles were decorated with batik, tie-dye, stencils, embroidery, and brocade.

Heian **period** (794–1185) Buddhist statues became formalized and were usually made of wood. Shinto images emerged. A native style of secular painting, yamato-e, developed, especially in scroll painting, with a strong emphasis on surface design. Lacquerware was also decoratively stylized.

Kamakura **period** (1185–1392) Sculpture and painting became vigorously realistic. Portraits were important, as were landscapes and religious, narrative, and humorous picture scrolls.

Ashikaga or *Muromachi* **period** (1392–1568) The rapid ink sketch in line and wash introduced by Zen priests from China became popular and the Kanō School of painting was established. Pottery gained in importance from the spread of the tea ceremony. Masks and costumes were made for Nō theatre.

Momoyama **period** (1568–1615) Artists produced beautiful screens to decorate palaces and castles. The arrival of Korean potters inspired new styles.

Tokugawa or *Edo* **period** (1615–1867) The ukiyo-e print, depicting everyday life, originated in genre paintings of 16th- and 17th-century kabuki actors and teahouse women. It developed into the woodcut and after 1740 the true colour print, while its range of subject matter expanded. *Ukiyo-e* artists include Utamaro and Hokusai. Lacquer and textiles became more sumptuous. Tiny carved figures (*netsuke*) were mostly made from ivory or wood.

Meiji **period** (1868–1912) Painting was influenced by styles of Western art, for example Impressionism.

Shōwa **period** (1926–89) Attempts were made to revive the traditional Japanese painting style and to combine traditional and foreign styles.

Japanese literature earliest surviving works include the 8th-century *Man'yōshū/Collection of a Myriad Leaves*, with poems by Hitomaro and Akahito (the principal form being the tanka, a five-line stanza of 5, 7, 5, 7, 7 syllables), and the prose *Kojiki/Record of Ancient Matters*. The late 10th and early 11th centuries produced such writers as Sei Shōnagon and ◊Murasaki Shikibu, whose *The Tale of Genji* is one of the finest works of Japanese literature. During the 14th century the ◊Nō drama developed from ceremonial religious dances, combined with monologues and dialogues. *◊Heike monogatari* was written in the 14th century. In the early 15th century ◊Zeami wrote manuals on drama.

The 17th century brought such scholars of Chinese studies as Fujiwara Seika (1561–1619) and Arai Hakuseki (1657–1725). This period also saw the beginnings of ◊kabuki, the popular drama of Japan, of which Chikamatsu Monzaemon (1653–1724) is the chief exponent; of ◊haiku (the stanza of three lines of 5, 7, and 5 syllables), popularized by Bashō; and of the modern novel, as represented by Ihara Saikaku (1642–1693). Among those reacting against Chinese influence was the poet and historian Motoori Norinaga (1730–1801). The late 19th and early 20th centuries saw the replacement of the obsolete Tokugawa style as a literary medium with the modern colloquial language; the influence of Western and Russian literature (usually encountered through English translations) produced writers such as the Realist Tsubouchi Shōyo (1859–1935), author of an important study of the novel 1885–86, followed by the Naturalist and 'Idealistic' novelists, whose romantic preoccupation with self-expression gave rise to the still popular 'I-novels' of, for example, ◊Dazai Osamu.

A reaction against the autobiographical school came from Natsume Sōseki, Nagai Kafū (1879–1959), and ◊Tanizaki Junichirō, who found inspiration in past traditions or in self-sublimation; later novelists include Kawabata Yasunari (Nobel Prize 1968) and Mishima Yukio. Shimazaki Tōson (1872–1943) introduced Western-style poetic trends, including Symbolism, but the traditional forms of haiku and tanka are still widely used. Western-style modern drama, inspired by Ibsen and Strindberg, has been growing since the turn of the century (as seen in the work of Shingeki, for example). After World War II, under democratic rule, the experience of cultural dislocation and problems of identity were addressed by a new generation of often leftist writers such as Abe Kōbō, Ōe Kenzáburō, and Murakami Haruki, using narrative and dramatic techniques developed from Western Modernism.

Jaques-Dalcroze Emile 1865–1950. Swiss composer and teacher. He is remembered for his system of physical training by rhythmical movement to music (◊eurhythmics), and founded the Institut Jaques-Dalcroze in Geneva 1915.

Jarman, Derek 1942–1994. English avant-garde film director. Jarman made several low-budget, highly innovative features, often with homoerotic associations. His films include *Sebastiane* 1976, with dialogue spoken in Latin; *Caravaggio* 1986; *Edward II* 1991, a free adaptation of Christopher Marlowe's play; and his biography of the philosopher *Wittgenstein* 1993.

Jarnach Philipp 1892–1982. German composer of Catalan/French descent. After studies in Paris he met Busoni in Zurich 1915 and remained to complete the latter's opera *Doktor Faust* 1925 after Busoni's death. His own works, in Italianate Neo-Classical style, include orchestral and chamber music.

Järnefelt (Edvard) Armas 1869–1958. Finnish composer who is chiefly known for his 'Praeludium' and the lyrical 'Berceuse' 1909 for small orchestra, from music for the drama *The Promised Land*.

Jarrett Keith 1945– . US jazz pianist and composer, an eccentric innovator who performs both alone and with small groups. Jarrett was a member of the rock-influenced Charles Lloyd Quartet 1966–67, and played with Miles Davis 1970–71. *The Köln Concert* 1975 is a characteristic solo live recording.

Jarry Alfred 1873–1907. French satiric dramatist whose grossly farcical *Ubu Roi* 1896 foreshadowed the Theatre of the ◊Absurd and the French Surrealist movement in its freedom of staging and subversive humour.

Jason in Greek mythology, the leader of the Argonauts who sailed in the Argo to Colchis in search of the ◊Golden Fleece. He eloped with ◊Medea, daughter of the king of Colchis, who had helped him achieve his goal, but later deserted her.

Jawlensky Alexei von 1864–1941. Russian painter, a major figure in the German revolutionary art movements of the early 1900s. Like his close friend Kandinsky, he was influenced by both Fauvism and Russian folk art. He reached his most abstract style 1908–10 with paintings

such as *Murnau* 1910 (National Gallery of Art, Washington, DC), but is best known for his Expressionist portraits of women, for example *Helene with Red Turban* 1910 (Solomon R Guggenheim Museum, New York).

jazz polyphonic, syncopated music characterized by solo virtuosic improvisation, which developed in the USA at the turn of the 20th century. Initially music for dancing, often with a vocalist, it had its roots in black American and other popular music. As jazz grew increasingly complex and experimental, various distinct forms evolved. Seminal musicians include Louis Armstrong, Charlie Parker, and John Coltrane.

jazz chronology

1880–1900 Originated chiefly in New Orleans from ragtime.

1920s During Prohibition, the centre of jazz moved to Chicago (Louis Armstrong, Bix Beiderbecke) and St Louis. By the end of the decade the focus had shifted to New York City (Art Tatum, Fletcher Henderson), to radio and recordings.

1930s The *swing* bands used call-and-response arrangements with improvised solos of voice and instruments (Paul Whiteman, Benny Goodman).

1940s Swing grew into the *big-band* era with jazz composed as well as arranged (Glenn Miller, Duke Ellington); rise of *West Coast* jazz (Stan Kenton) and rhythmically complex, highly improvised *bebop* (Charlie Parker, Dizzy Gillespie, Thelonius Monk).

1950s Jazz had ceased to be dance music; *cool jazz* (Stan Getz, Miles Davis, Lionel Hampton, Modern Jazz Quartet) developed in reaction to the insistent, 'hot' bebop and *hard bop*.

1960s *Free-form* or *free jazz* (Ornette Coleman, John Coltrane).

1970s *Jazz rock* (US group Weather Report, formed 1970; British guitarist John McLaughlin, 1942–); jazz funk (US saxophonist Grover Washington Jr, 1943–); more eclectic free jazz (US pianist Keith Jarrett).

1980s Resurgence of tradition (US trumpeter Wynton Marsalis; British saxophonist Courtney Pine, 1965–) and avant-garde (US chamber-music Kronos Quartet, formed 1978; anarchic British group Loose Tubes, 1983–89).

Jazz Age the hectic and exciting 1920s in the USA, when 'hot jazz' became fashionable as part of the general rage for spontaneity and social freedom. The phrase is attributed to the novelist F Scott Fitzgerald.

jazz dance dance based on African techniques and rhythms, developed by black Americans around 1917. It entered mainstream dance in the 1920s, mainly in show business, and from the 1960s the teachers and choreographers Matt

◊Mattox and Luigi (1925–) expanded its vocabulary. Contemporary choreographers as diverse as Jerome ◊Robbins and Alvin ◊Ailey used it in their work.

jeans denim trousers, traditionally blue, originally cut from jean cloth ('jene fustian'), a heavy canvas made in Genoa, Italy. In the 1850s Levi Strauss (1830–1902), a Bavarian immigrant to the USA, made sturdy trousers for goldminers in San Francisco out of jean material intended for wagon covers. Hence they became known as 'Levis'. Later a French fabric, *serge de Nîmes* (corrupted to 'denim'), was used. Denim jeans became fashionable casual wear in the 1950s in the USA and have since been produced in a wide variety of styles by many designers.

Jefferies (John) Richard 1848–1887. British naturalist and writer, whose books on the countryside included *Gamekeeper at Home* 1878, *Wood Magic* 1881, and *Story of My Heart* 1883.

Jeffers (John) Robinson 1887–1962. US poet. He wrote free verse and demonstrated an antagonism to human society. His collected volumes include *Tamar and Other Poems* 1924, *The Double Axe* 1948, and *Hungerfield and Other Poems* 1954.

Jeffrey Francis, Lord 1773–1850. Scottish lawyer and literary critic. Born in Edinburgh, he was a founder and editor of the *Edinburgh Review* 1802–29. In 1830 he was made Lord Advocate, and in 1834 a Scottish law lord. He was hostile to the Romantic poets, and wrote of Wordsworth's *Excursion*: 'This will never do.'

Jekyll Gertrude 1843–1932. English landscape gardener and writer. She created over 200 gardens, many in collaboration with the architect Edwin Landseer ◊Lutyens. In her books, she advocated natural gardens of the cottage type, with plentiful herbaceous borders.

Originally a painter and embroiderer, she took up gardening at the age of 48 because of worsening eyesight. Her home at Munstead Wood, Surrey, was designed for her by Lutyens.

Jekyll and Hyde two conflicting sides of a personality, as in the novel by the Scottish writer R L Stevenson, *The Strange Case of Dr Jekyll and Mr Hyde* 1886, where the good Jekyll by means of a potion periodically transforms himself into the evil Hyde.

Jellicoe Geoffrey 1900– . English architect, landscape architect, and historian. His contribution to 20th-century thinking on landscapes and gardens has been mainly through his writings, notably *Landscape of Man* 1975. However, he has also made an impact as a designer, working in a contemplative and poetic vein and frequently incorporating water and sculptures. Representative of his work are the Kennedy Memorial at Runnymede, Berkshire, 1965 and the gardens at Sutton Place, Sussex, 1980–84.

Jencks Charles 1939– . US architectural theorist who lives in Britain. He coined the term 'Post-Modern architecture' and wrote *The Language of Post-Modern Architecture* 1984.

Jenner Henry (Gwas Myhal) 1849–1934. English poet. He attempted to revive Cornish as a literary language, and in 1904 published a handbook of the Cornish language.

Jennings Humphrey 1907–1950. British documentary filmmaker who introduced a poetic tone and subjectivity to factually based material. He was active in the General Post Office Film Unit from 1934 and his wartime films vividly portrayed London in the Blitz: *London Can Take It* 1940, *This Is England* 1941, and *Fires Were Started* 1943.

Jerome Jerome K(lapka) 1859–1927. English journalist and writer. His works include the humorous essays *Idle Thoughts of an Idle Fellow* 1889, the novel *Three Men in a Boat* 1889, and the play *The Passing of the Third Floor Back* 1907.

jeté in dance, a jump from one foot to the other. A *grand jeté* is a big jump in which the dancer pushes off on one foot, holds a brief pose in midair, and lands lightly on the other foot.

jewellery objects worn for ornament, such as rings, brooches, necklaces, pendants, earrings, and bracelets. Jewellery has been made from a wide variety of materials, including precious metals, gemstones, amber, teeth, bone, glass, and plastics.

history of Western jewellery

3rd millenium BC Babylonian styles and metalworking techniques reached the Aegean. The Minoans in Crete used the filigree technique, and made large ornaments of embossed gold, silver, and electrum, featuring mythical subjects.

Hellenistic period (from c. 330 BC) Widespread use of coloured stones and glass, and dipped enamel earrings (metal core dipped into molten glass and then shaped with regular glassworking techniques); also animal or human-headed gold earrings.

western Roman Empire The Romans were passionate collectors and wearers of gold jewellery and finely engraved gemstone cameos; they were the first to use rings as a sign of betrothal. Hooped earrings threaded with beads and other forms developed, also gold hairpins and bronze fibulae (brooches) based on Celtic forms.

medieval period Most jewellery was restricted to court and ecclesiastical circles. Byzantine influence led to much enamelling. Crowns, buckles, clasps, and brooches used to fasten cloaks were decorated with enamelled heraldic motifs. Jewelled embroidery was used for ecclesiastical vestments and ceremonial gloves.

late-14th-century Europe Jewellery became more luxurious and was worn for its decorative value and as a display of wealth, rather than as a functional accessory to dress.

Renaissance Many more techniques of gemcutting were developed to increase sparkle; many devotional rings were worn, and more necklaces and bracelets appeared as women's sleeves were cut wider and necklines became lower. Pendants adorned necklaces, hair, and headdresses—some opened up to reveal religious scenes in miniature. Rosaries were worn as necklaces. Auspicious objects such as jewelled Renaissance pomanders were believed to protect against plague.

17th century First appearance of memorial jewellery incorporating woven or plaited hair. Fashionable women wore strings of pearls.

18th century Matching sets of jewellery (*parure*) worn by fashionable women, comprising earrings, brooch, necklace, and bracelet or stomacher. Daytime jewellery consisted of paste and non-precious gemstones; foil-backed enamels were made into buckles and miniature receptacles attached to belts; the best of these were made in France, but copies were made elsewhere in Europe.

19th century Etiquette proscribed dress jewels from daytime wear; tortoiseshell, jet, coral, and ivory were worn instead. From the 1860s novel jewellery was increasingly worn – insects, locomotives, and household objects and tools. Arts and Crafts and Art Nouveau jewellery was much simpler in design, emphasizing organic forms. Around 1900 more conventional but superbly crafted jewellery appeared, designed by Tiffany and Cartier.

late 19th century–20th century Synthetic gemstones developed along with the chemical industry and polymer science. As the 20th century progressed, costume jewellery was increasingly worn for effect, and from the 1930s onwards everyday, inexpensive materials such as steel, Bakelite, and other kinds of plastic were used. Silver jewellery in simple modern forms designed by Georg Jensen was influential. In the 1970s a new generation of jewellers, trained in art schools rather than through apprenticeship in the trade, placed emphasis on new design ideas rather than value of materials; much contemporary jewellery is affordable and fun.

Jewish-American writing US writing in English shaped by the Jewish experience. It was produced by the children of Eastern European immigrants who came to the USA at the end of the 19th century, and by the 1940s second- and third-generation Jewish-American writers had become central to US literary and intellectual life. Nobel prize-winning authors include Saul Bellow 1976 and Isaac Bashevis Singer 1978.

The first significant Jewish-American novel was Abraham Cahan's *The Rise of David Levinsky* 1917. During the 1920s many writers, including Ludwig Lewisohn and Mary Antin, signalled the Jewish presence in US culture. In the 1930s Mike Gold's *Jews Without Money* and Henry Roth's *Call It Sleep* showed in fiction the immigrant Jewish struggle to adapt to the US experience. Novelists Bernard Malamud, Philip Roth, and Norman Mailer, poets Karl Shapiro, Delmore Schwartz (1913–1966), and Muriel Rukeyser (1913–1980), dramatists and screenwriters Arthur Miller, S N Behrman (1893–1973), Neil Simon, and Woody Allen, and critics Lionel Trilling and Irving Howe (1920–) made Jewish experience fundamental to US writing. In the 1950s the Jewish-American novel, shaped by awareness of the Holocaust, expressed themes of human responsibility. Many subsequent writers, including Stanley Elkin (1930–), Joseph Heller, Chaim Potok, Denise Levertov (1923–), Grace Paley, and Cynthia Ozick, have extended the tradition.

Jew's harp musical instrument consisting of a two-pronged metal frame inserted between the teeth, and a springlike tongue plucked with the finger. The resulting drone excites resonances in the mouth that can be varied in pitch to produce a melody.

Jhabvala Ruth Prawer 1927– . Adoptively Indian novelist and film script writer. Born in Cologne of Polish parents and educated in England, she went to live in India when she married 1951. Her novels explore the idiosyncratic blend of East and West in the Indian middle class, as in *Esmond in India* 1957. She has also written terse short stories about urban India and successful film scripts for Merchant Ivory, including a treatment of her own novel *Heat and Dust*, awarded the Booker Prize 1975. Her film scripts for *A Room with a View* 1987 and *Howards End* 1992 both received Academy awards.

Jiménez Juan Ramón 1881–1958. Spanish lyric poet. Born in Andalusia, he left Spain during the civil war to live in exile in Puerto Rico. Nobel prize 1956.

Jindyworobaks (Aboriginal 'takeover') Australian literary group 1938–53. Founded by Reginald Ingamells (1931–1955), it encouraged an individual Australian character in the country's literature.

Jingdezhen or *Chingtechen* or *Fou-liang* town in Jiangxi, China. Ming blue-and-white china was produced here, the name of the clay (kaolin) coming from Kaoling, a hill east of Jingdezhen; some of the best Chinese porcelain is still made here.

jinn in Muslim mythology, class of spirits able to assume human or animal shape.

Jiricna Eva 1939– . Czech architect who has worked in the UK since 1968. Her fashion shops, bars, and cafés for the ◊Joseph chain are built in a highly refined Modernist style.

jit or *jit jive* Zimbabwean pop music developed in the 1980s: a bouncy, cheerful dance music with a bright guitar sound inspired by the *mbira*, or thumb piano, a traditional instrument in southern Africa.

jive energetic American dance that evolved from the jitterbug, popular in the 1940s and 1950s; a forerunner of rock and roll.

Joachim Joseph 1831–1907. Austro-Hungarian violinist and composer. He studied under Mendelssohn and founded the Joachim Quartet (1869–1907). Joachim played and conducted the music of his friend Brahms. His own compositions include pieces for violin and orchestra, chamber, and orchestral works.

Joan mythical Englishwoman supposed to have become pope in 855, as John VIII, and to have given birth to a child during a papal procession. The myth was exposed in the 17th century.

Jocasta in Greek mythology, wife of Laius, sister of Creon, and mother and wife of ◊Oedipus, by whom she was mother to ◊Antigone, ◊Eteocles, ◊Polynices, and Ismene. She married Oedipus in ignorance, as his reward for killing the ◊Sphinx. In Sophocles' version of the story, she committed suicide on discovering his true identity, although Euripides and Statius give the death of her sons as the reason for her suicide.

John Augustus (Edwin) 1878–1961. Welsh painter, known for his portraits, including *The Smiling Woman* 1910 (Tate Gallery, London) of his second wife, Dorelia McNeill. His sitters included such literary and society figures as Thomas Hardy, Dylan Thomas, W B Yeats, and Cecil Beaton. He led a bohemian and nomadic life and was the brother of the artist Gwen ◊John.

John Elton. Stage name of Reginald Kenneth Dwight 1947– . English pop singer, pianist, and composer, noted for his melodies and elaborate costumes and glasses. His best-known LP, *Goodbye Yellow Brick Road* 1973, includes the hit 'Bennie and the Jets'. Other successful songs include 'Nikita' 1985 and 'Sacrifice' 1989, from the album *Sleeping with the Past*. His output is prolific and his hits have continued intermittently into the 1990s.

From his second album, *Elton John* 1970, to *Blue Moves* 1976 he enjoyed his greatest popularity, especially in the USA, and worked exclusively with the lyricist Bernie Taupin (1950–).

John Gwen 1876–1939. Welsh painter who lived in France for most of her life. Many of her paintings depict young women or nuns (she converted to Catholicism 1913), but she also painted calm, muted interiors. Her style was characterized by a sensitive use of colour and tone.

John Bull imaginary figure who is a personification of England, similar to the American Uncle Sam. He is represented in cartoons and caricatures as a prosperous farmer of the 18th century.

The name was popularized by Dr John ◊Arbuthnot's *History of John Bull* 1712, advocating the Tory policy of peace with France.

Johns 'Captain' W(illiam) E(arl) 1893–1968. British author, from 1932, of popular novels of World War I flying ace 'Biggles', now sometimes criticized for chauvinism, racism, and sexism. Johns was a flying officer in the RAF (there is no rank of captain) until his retirement 1930.

I teach a boy to be a man ... I teach the spirit of teamwork, loyalty to the crown, the Empire, and lawful authority.

W E Johns interviewed 1948

Johns Jasper 1930– . US painter, sculptor, and printmaker, one of the foremost exponents of ◊Pop art. He rejected abstract art, favouring such mundane subjects as flags, maps, and numbers as a means of exploring the relationship between image and reality. His work employs pigments mixed with wax (encaustic) to create a rich surface with unexpected delicacies of colour. He has also created collages and lithographs. One of his best-known works is the bronze *Ale Cans* 1960 (Kunstmuseum, Basel).

Johnson Celia 1908–1982. British actress, perceived as quintessentially English, who starred with Trevor Howard in the romantic film *Brief Encounter* 1946. Her later films include *The Captain's Paradise* 1953 and *The Prime of Miss Jean Brodie* 1968.

Johnson Eastman 1824–1906. US painter born in Germany, trained in Düsseldorf, The Hague, and Paris. Painting in the open air, he developed a fresh and luminous landscape style.

Johnson James Weldon 1871–1938. US writer, lawyer, diplomat, and social critic. He was editor of *New York Age* 1912–22 and was active in the National Association for the Advancement of Colored People (NAACP). As poet and anthropologist, he became one of the chief figures of the ◊Harlem Renaissance of the 1920s. His autobiography *Along This Way* was published 1933.

Johnson Pamela Hansford 1912–1981. British novelist, who in 1950 married C P ◊Snow; her novels include *Too Dear for My Possessing* 1940 and *The Honours Board* 1970.

Johnson Philip (Cortelyou) 1906– . US architect who coined the term 'International Style' 1932. Originally designing in the style of ◊Mies van der Rohe, he later became an exponent of ◊Post-Modernism. He designed the giant

AT&T building in New York 1978, a pink skyscraper with a Chippendale-style cabinet top.

Early this morning,/ When you knocked upon my door,/ I said 'Hello, Satan,/ I believe it's time to go.'

Robert Johnson 'Me and the Devil Blues'

Johnson Robert *c.* 1912–1938. US blues guitarist, songwriter, and singer. He was an exponent of the acoustic delta blues, though his style, with distinctive bottleneck slide playing, foreshadowed the development of urban blues. His work has been studied by countless guitar players and his songs include 'Love in Vain', 'Terraplane Blues', 'Crossroads', and 'Hellhound on My Trail' (all 1936–37). All his 29 recordings were made in Texas 1936 and 1937; he was murdered 1938.

A man, Sir, should keep his friendship in constant repair.

Samuel Johnson

Johnson Samuel, known as 'Dr Johnson', 1709–1784. English lexicographer, author, and critic, also a brilliant conversationalist and the dominant figure in 18th-century London literary society. His *Dictionary*, published 1755, remained authoritative for over a century, and is still remarkable for the vigour of its definitions. In 1764 he founded the Literary Club, whose members included the painter Joshua Reynolds, the political philosopher Edmund Burke, the dramatist Oliver Goldsmith, the actor David Garrick, and James ◊Boswell, Johnson's biographer.

Born in Lichfield, Staffordshire, Johnson became first an usher and then a literary hack. In 1735 he married Elizabeth Porter and opened a private school. When this proved unsuccessful he went to London with his pupil David Garrick, becoming a regular contributor to the *Gentleman's Magazine* and publishing the poem *London* 1738. Other works include the satire imitating Juvenal, *Vanity of Human Wishes* 1749, the philosophical romance *Rasselas* 1759, an edition of Shakespeare 1765, and the classic *Lives of the Most Eminent English Poets* 1779–81. His first meeting with Boswell was 1763. A visit with Boswell to Scotland and the Hebrides 1773 was recorded in *Journey to the Western Isles of Scotland* 1775. He was buried in Westminster Abbey and his house, in Gough Square, London, is preserved as a museum; his wit and humanity are documented in Boswell's classic biography *Life of Samuel Johnson* 1791.

Johnson Uwe 1934– . German novelist who left East Germany for West Berlin 1959, and wrote of the division of Germany in, for example, *Anniversaries* 1977.

Jolson Al. Stage name of Asa Yoelson 1886–1950. Russian-born US singer and entertainer. Popular in Broadway theatre and vaudeville, he was chosen to star in the first talking picture, *The Jazz Singer* 1927.

Jones Allen 1937– . English painter, sculptor, and printmaker, a leading Pop artist. Executed in the style of commercial advertising, his colourful paintings unabashedly celebrate the female form, for example, *Perfect Match* 1966–67 (Wallraf-Richartz Museum, Cologne).

His witty, abbreviated imagery of women clad in bustiers, garter-belts, stocking tops, and stiletto-heeled shoes is intended as a comment on male fantasies and sexual fetishes.

Jones Charles Martin (Chuck) 1912– . US film animator and cartoon director who worked at Warner Bros with characters such as Bugs Bunny, Daffy Duck, Wile E Coyote, and Elmer Fudd.

Jones George 1931– . US country singer. His expressive vocal technique is usually employed on sentimental ballads (*Good Year for the Roses* 1970, *The Grand Tour* 1974) or honky-tonk (dance-hall) numbers (*The Race Is On* 1964), often in duets.

Jones was born in Texas and first recorded in 1954. During and after his marriage to singer Tammy Wynette (1942–) they made many records together, including the hits *We're Gonna Hold On* 1973 and *Golden Ring* 1976.

Jones Gwyneth 1936– . Welsh soprano who has performed as Sieglinde in *Die Walküre* and Desdemona in *Otello*.

Jones Henry Arthur 1851–1929. British dramatist. Among some 60 of his melodramas, *Mrs Dane's Defence* 1900 is most notable as an early realist problem play.

Jones Inigo 1573–*c.* 1652. English Classical architect who introduced the Palladian style to England. Born in London, he studied in Italy where he encountered the works of Palladio. He was employed by James I to design scenery for Ben Jonson's masques and appointed Surveyor of the King's Works 1615–42. He designed the Queen's House, Greenwich, 1616–35, and his English Renaissance masterpiece, the Banqueting House in Whitehall, London, 1619–22. His work was to provide the inspiration for the Palladian Revival a century later.

Jones John Luther 'Casey' 1864–1900. US railroad engineer and folk hero. His death on the 'Cannonball Express', while on an overnight run 1900, is the subject of popular legend. Colliding with a stalled freight train, he ordered his fireman to jump to safety and rode the 'Cannonball' to his death. The folk song 'Casey Jones' is an account of the event.

Jones Quincy (Delight) 1933– . US musician, producer, composer, and arranger who has worked in jazz, rock, and pop. By 1991 he had won 19 Grammy awards and composed scores for 37 films. Among his production credits is Michael Jackson's *Thriller* 1982; his own albums include *Walking in Space* 1969 and *Back on the Block* 1990.

Jong Erica (Mann) 1942– . US novelist and poet. She won a reputation as a feminist poet with her first collection *Fruits & Vegetables* 1971. Her novel *Fear of Flying* 1973 depicted a liberated woman's intense sexual adventures and became an instant best-seller. It was followed by two sequels *How To Save Your Own Life* 1977 and *Parachutes and Kisses* 1984. Other works include her non-fictional *Witches* 1981, and a portrait of Henry Miller *The Devil at Large* 1993.

Jongkind Johan Barthold 1819–1891. Dutch painter active mainly in France. His studies of the Normandy coast show a keen observation of the natural effects of light. He influenced the Impressionist painter ◊Monet.

Jonson Ben(jamin) 1572–1637. English dramatist, poet, and critic. *Every Man in his Humour* 1598 established the English 'comedy of humours', in which each character embodies a 'humour', or vice, such as greed, lust, or avarice. This was followed by *Cynthia's Revels* 1600 and *Poetaster* 1601. His first extant tragedy is *Sejanus* 1603, with Burbage and Shakespeare as members of the original cast. The great comedies of his middle years include *Volpone, or The Fox* 1606, *The Alchemist* 1610, and ◊*Bartholomew Fair* 1614. He wrote extensively for court entertainment with the ◊masques he produced with the scenic designer Inigo ◊Jones.

Jonson was born in Westminster, London, and entered the theatre as actor and dramatist 1597. In 1598 he narrowly escaped the gallows for killing a fellow player in a duel. He collaborated with Marston and Chapman in *Eastward Ho!* 1605, and shared their imprisonment when official exception was taken to the satirization of James I's Scottish policy.

Fortune, that favours fools.

Ben Jonson *The Alchemist* 1610

Jooss Kurt 1901–1979. German choreographer and teacher who attempted to synthesize ballet with modern dance. His socially conscious works, such as the acclaimed antiwar *The Green Table* 1932, strove to express his ideal of dance as a voice for the common man.

He founded the Folkwang School and company 1927 in Essen, Germany. Forced out by the Nazis, Jooss established a base at Dartington Hall, Devon, England, 1934. In 1949 he returned to his Essen school, where he worked until he retired 1968.

Joplin Janis 1943–1970. US blues and rock singer, born in Texas. She was lead singer with the San Francisco group Big Brother and the Holding Company 1966–68. Her biggest hit, Kris Kristofferson's 'Me and Bobby McGee', was released on the posthumous *Pearl* LP 1971.

Joplin Scott 1868–1917. US ◊ragtime pianist and composer, active in Chicago. His 'Maple Leaf Rag' 1899 was the first instrumental sheet music to sell a million copies, and 'The Entertainer', as the theme tune of the film *The Sting* 1973, revived his popularity. He was an influence on Jelly Roll Morton and other early jazz musicians.

Jordaens Jacob 1593–1678. Flemish painter, born in Antwerp. His style follows Rubens, whom he assisted in various commissions. Much of his work is exuberant and on a large scale, including scenes of peasant life and mythological subjects, as well as altarpieces and portraits.

Jordan Dorothea 1762–1816. Irish actress. She made her debut 1777, and retired 1815. She was a mistress of the Duke of Clarence (later William IV); they had ten children with the name FitzClarence.

Joseph trade name of Joseph Ettedgui (date of birth unknown). French Moroccan retailer and fashion designer who is known for popularizing the collections of designers such as Katherine ◊Hamnett, ◊Kenzo, Azzedine ◊Alaïa and John ◊Richmond in the UK. He founded the Joseph Tricot label 1979, which is characterized by soft oversized knitwear and jerseys. In 1985 he launched Joseph Bis, a ◊diffusion line, and Le Joseph, which specializes in jeans wear.

Josephs Wilfred 1927– . British composer. As well as film and television music, he has written nine symphonies, concertos, and chamber music. His works include the *Jewish Requiem* 1969 and the opera *Rebecca* 1983.

Josquin Desprez or *des Prés* 1440–1521. French-Flemish composer whose synthesis of Flemish structural counterpoint and Italian harmonic expression, acquired in the service of the Rome papal chapel 1484–1503, marks a peak in Renaissance vocal music. In addition to masses on secular as well as sacred themes, including the *Missa 'L'Homme armé'/Mass on 'The Armed Man'* 1504, he also wrote secular chansons such as 'El Grillo'/'The Cricket' employing imitative vocal effects.

jota traditional northern Spanish dance in lively triple time for one or more couples who play the castanets, accompanied by guitar and singing. There is a *jota* in Manuel de ◊Falla's *The Three-Cornered Hat*.

Joyce Eileen 1912–1991. Australian concert pianist whose playing combined subtlety with temperamental fire. Her immense repertoire included over 70 works for piano and orchestra. She made her UK debut 1930 and retired in the early 1960s.

Joyce James (Augustine Aloysius) 1882–1941. Irish writer, born in Dublin, who revolutionized the form of the English novel with his 'stream of consciousness' technique. His works include *Dubliners* 1914 (short stories), *Portrait of the Artist as a Young Man* 1916, *Ulysses* 1922, and *Finnegans Wake* 1939.

Ulysses, which records the events of a single Dublin day, experiments with language and combines direct narrative with the unspoken and unconscious reactions of the characters. Banned at first for obscenity in the USA and the UK, it enjoyed great impact. It was first published in Paris, where Joyce settled after World War I. *Finnegans Wake* continued Joyce's experiments with language.

Judith in the Old Testament, a Jewish widow who saved her community from a Babylonian siege by pretending to seduce and then beheading the enemy general Holofernes. Her story is much represented in Western art.

Judson Edward Zane Carroll, better known by his pen name 'Ned Buntline' 1823–1886. US author. Specializing in short adventure stories, he developed a stereotyped frontier hero in the pages of his own periodicals *Ned Buntline's Magazine* and *Buntline's Own*. In his dime novels in the 1870s, he immortalized Buffalo Bill Cody.

Jugendstil German term for ◊Art Nouveau

Julian of Norwich *c.* 1342–1413. English mystic. She lived as a recluse, and recorded her visions in *Revelations of Divine Love c.* 1391, which shows the influence of neo-Platonism.

longer jumpers became popular. Today jumpers of all shapes and sizes are mass produced, often in bright colours and with bold designs.

Jungle Book, The collection of short stories for children by Rudyard ◊Kipling, published in two volumes 1894 and 1895. Set in India, the stories feature a boy, Mowgli, reared by wolves and the animals he encounters in the jungle. The stories inspired the formation by Baden Powell of the Wolf Cub division of the Boy Scout movement.

Junius, Letters of series of letters published in the English *Public Advertiser* 1769–72, under the pseudonym Junius. Written in a pungent, epigrammatic style, they attacked the 'king's friends' in the interests of the opposition Whigs. They are generally believed to have been written by Sir Philip Francis (1740–1818).

Junk art in the visual arts, a form of ◊assemblage.

Juno in Roman mythology, the principal goddess, identified with the Greek ◊Hera. The wife of Jupiter and queen of heaven, she was concerned with all aspects of women's lives.

Jupiter or *Jove* in Roman mythology, the chief god, identified with the Greek ◊Zeus. He was god of the sky, associated with lightning and thunderbolts; protector in battle; and bestower of victory. The son of Saturn, he married his sister Juno, and reigned on Mount Olympus as lord of heaven. His most famous temple was on the Capitoline Hill in Rome.

Jurgens Curt (Curd Jürgens) 1912–1982. German film and stage actor who was well established in his native country before moving into French and then Hollywood films in the 1960s. His films include *Operette/Operetta* 1940, *Et Dieu créa la femme/And God Created Woman* 1956, *Lord Jim* 1965, and *The Spy Who Loved Me* 1977.

Just So Stories collection of stories for small children by Rudyard ◊Kipling, published 1902. Many of the stories offer amusing explanations of how certain animals acquired their characteristic appearance, such as 'How the Leopard got his Spots', and 'How the Camel got his Hump'. They originated in stories that the author told his children.

I saw not sin: for I believe it has no manner of substance nor no part of being, nor could it be known but by the pain it is cause of.

Julian of Norwich
Revelations of Divine Love c. 1391

This is the first of punishments, that no guilty man is acquitted if judged by himself.

Juvenal *Satires*

---

jumper long-sleeved woollen top reaching to the waist or below. During the 1940s short waist-length designs were popular, often worn as part of two-or three-piece outfits. In the 1950s looser and

Juvenal *c.* AD 60–140. Roman satirical poet. His 16 surviving satires give an explicit and sometimes brutal picture of the corrupt Roman society of his time. He may have lived in exile under the emperor Domitian, and remained very poor.

kabuki (Japanese 'music, dance, skill') drama originating in late 16th-century Japan, drawing on ◊Nō, puppet plays, and folk dance. Its colourful, lively spectacle became popular in the 17th and 18th centuries. Many kabuki actors specialize in particular types of character, female impersonators (*onnagata*) being the biggest stars.

Kabuki was first popularized in Kyoto 1603 by the dancer Izumo Okuni who gave performances with a chiefly female troupe; from 1629 only men were allowed to act, in the interests of propriety. Unlike Nō actors, kabuki actors do not wear masks. The art was modernized and its following revived in the 1980s by Ennosuke III (1940–).

Kafka Franz 1883–1924. Czech novelist, born in Prague, who wrote in German. His three unfinished allegorical novels *Der Prozess/The ◊Trial* 1925, *Der Schloss/The Castle* 1926, and *Amerika/America* 1927 were posthumously published despite his instructions that they should be destroyed. His short stories include 'Die Verwandlung'/'The Metamorphosis' 1915, in which a man turns into a huge insect. His vision of lonely individuals trapped in bureaucratic or legal labyrinths can be seen as a powerful metaphor for modern experience.

kaftan loosely cut ankle-length garment which opens at the front and has long wide sleeves; it is often tied with a sash of silk or cotton. Kaftans can be made from almost any fabric, although satin and heavily embroidered fabrics have frequently been used.

They were popularized by Christian Dior in the 1950s when he showed versions of the kaftan worn open over evening dresses. Yves Saint-Laurent also produced kaftan-inspired designs in the 1960s. During the 1970s kaftans became popular as evening and casual wear. The kaftan is believed to have originated in ancient Mesopotamia.

Kahlo Frida 1907–1954. Mexican painter. Combining the folk arts of South America with Classical and Modern styles, she concentrated on surreal self-portraits in which she explored both her own physical disabilities (she was crippled in an accident when 15) and broader political and social issues. Her work became popular during the 1980s.

Kahn Louis 1901–1974. US architect, born in Estonia. A follower of ◊Mies van de Rohe, he developed a classically romantic style, in which functional 'servant' areas such as stairwells and air ducts feature prominently, often as towerlike structures surrounding the main living and working, or 'served', areas. His projects are characterized by an imaginative use of concrete and brick and include the Richards Medical Research Building, University of Pennsylvania, 1958–60, and the British Art Centre at Yale University 1969–77.

Kairos in Greek mythology, the personification of Opportunity. He is portrayed in Greek art as bald at the back, but with long hair at the front.

Kaiser Georg 1878–1945. German playwright, the principal exponent of German ◊Expressionism. His large output includes *Die Bürger von Calais/The Burghers of Calais* 1914 and *Gas* 1918–20.

kakiemon Japanese white-body porcelain made in W Kyushu, fashionable in the West from the 1620s and again in the 1990s. It is made at the Nangawara kiln in Arita by a line of potters established by Sakaida Kakiemon I (1599–1666).

Kakiemon ware has decorations in red, green, blue, and black, usually birds or flowers, modelled on Chinese porcelain of the 17th century. It is one of several types of porcelain from the Arita area, near Nagasaki. High-quality copies are now made by the 13th-generation Kakiemon, and lesser copies are made by industrial companies throughout the region.

Kalevala Finnish national epic poem compiled from legends and ballads by Elias Lönnrot 1835–49; its hero is Väinämöinen, god of music and poetry.

Kalf Willem 1619–1693. Dutch painter, active in Amsterdam from 1653. He specialized in still lifes set against a dark background. These feature arrangements of glassware, polished metalwork, decorated porcelain, and fine carpets, with the occasional half-peeled lemon (a Dutch still-life motif).

Kali in Hindu mythology, the goddess of destruction and death. She is the wife of ◊Siva.

Kālidāsa lived 5th century AD. Indian epic poet and dramatist. His works, in Sanskrit, include the classic drama ◊*Sakuntalā*, the love story of King Dushyanta and the nymph Sakuntalā.

Kandinsky Wassily 1866–1944. Russian painter, a pioneer of abstract art. Born in

Moscow, he travelled widely, settling in Munich 1896. Between 1910 and 1914 he produced the series *Improvisations* and *Compositions*, the first known examples of purely abstract work in 20th-century art. He was an originator of the ◊*Blaue Reiter* movement 1911–12. From 1921 he taught at the ◊Bauhaus school of design. He moved to Paris 1933, becoming a French citizen 1939.

Kandinsky originally experimented with Post-Impressionist styles and Fauvism. His highly coloured works had few imitators, but his theories on composition, published in *Concerning the Spiritual in Art* 1912, were taken up by the abstractionists.

Kane Sheik Hamidou 1928– . Senegalese novelist, writing in French. His first novel, *L'Aventure ambiguë/Ambiguous Adventure* 1961, is an autobiographical account of a young African alienated from the simple faith of his childhood and initiated into an alien Islamic mysticism, before being immersed in materialist French culture.

Kanō School Japanese school of painting founded by Kanō Masanobu (*c.* 1434–1530); it was responsible for much palace and temple decoration of the period, characterized by broad, sweeping designs painted in rich colours on a gold background. Its two outstanding exponents were the prolific Kanō Eitoku (1543–1590) and his pupil Kanō Sanraku (*c.* 1560–1635), whose style was more restrained than that of his master's. Typical of the school are Sanraku's paintings on the sliding doors of the Daikaku-ji Temple in Kyoto.

Kantor Tadeusz 1915–1990. Polish theatre director and scene designer. He founded his experimental theatre Cricot 2 in 1955, and produced such plays as *Dead Class* 1975, with which he became internationally known. Later productions include *Wielopole, Wielopole* 1980, *Let the Artists Die* 1985, and *I Shall Never Return* 1988.

kapellmeister (German 'chapel master') chief conductor and chorus master, also resident composer for a private chapel, responsible for musical administration.

Karadzić Vuk 1787–1864. Serbian linguist, collector of folk songs and popular stories, compiler of a Serbian grammar 1815 and dictionary 1818 and 1852, and translator of the New Testament 1847.

karagoz Turkish shadow-puppet plays, which take their name from the leading character Karagoz. He is an unpretentious 'everyman' who is contrasted with the hypocritical Hacivat. The element of caricature was taken from popular or street theatre, and relies heavily on comic dialogue.

Karajan Herbert von 1908–1989. Charismatic Austrian conductor who dominated European classical music performance after 1947, principal conductor of the Berlin Philharmonic Orchestra 1955–89, artistic director of the Vienna State Opera 1957–64, and of the Salzburg Festival 1956–60. A perfectionist, he cultivated an orchestral sound of notable smoothness and transparency; he also staged operas and directed his own video recordings. He recorded the complete Beethoven symphonies three times, and had a special affinity with Mozart and Bruckner, although his repertoire extended from Bach to Schoenberg.

Karan Donna 1948– . US fashion designer with her own label since 1984. As well as trendy, wearable sportswear in bright colours, and tight, clingy clothes such as the bodysuit, she produces executive workwear. In 1989 she launched a ready-to-wear line, DKNY. In 1992–93 she moved away from the structured look of the 1980s to produce lighter, casual, and more fluid outfits.

karaoke (Japanese 'empty orchestra') amateur singing in public to prerecorded backing tapes. Karaoke originated in Japan and spread to other parts of the world in the 1980s. Karaoke machines are jukeboxes of backing tracks to well-known popular songs, usually with a microphone attached and lyrics displayed on a video screen.

In Japan, where karaoke machines have been installed not only in bars but also in taxis, karaoke had become a £1.1-billion industry by 1991. Karaoke machines can hold up to 4,000 songs with on-screen lyrics.

Karg-Elert Sigfrid 1877–1933. German composer. After studying at Leipzig he devoted himself to the European harmonium. His numerous concert pieces and graded studies including *66 Choral Improvisations* 1908–10 exploit a range of impressionistic effects such as the 'endless chord'.

Karloff Boris. Stage name of William Henry Pratt 1887–1969. English-born US actor best known for his work in the USA. He achieved Hollywood stardom with his role as the monster in the film *Frankenstein* 1931. Several popular sequels followed as well as starring appearances in other horror films including *Scarface* 1932, *The Lost Patrol* 1934, and *The Body Snatcher* 1945.

Karsh Yousuf 1908– . Canadian portrait photographer, born in Armenia. He is known for his formal and dramatically lit studies of the famous. His most notable picture is the defiant portrait of Winston Churchill which appeared on the cover of *Life* magazine 1941.

Kathak one of the four main Indian dance styles (others are ◊Bharat Natyam, Kathakali, and ◊Manipuri). It is primarily concerned with music and rhythm, with the story subsumed to secondary importance, and is danced on the floor (not on a raised stage) amid a seated audience. The feet of the dancers, adorned by ankle bells, are used as percussion instruments.

Kathakali one of the four main Indian dance styles (others are ◊Bharat Natyam, Kathak, and

◊Manipuri). It is an integration of drama, singing, and instrumental music, characterized by a range of highly stylized gestures. It originated in the extreme south of India and reached its artistic peak during the 17th century. The stories are derived from Hindu mythology and each individual character is represented by a different coloured mask or make-up. It is performed in a temple or public square after dusk, with performances sometimes lasting the entire night.

Kauffmann Angelica 1741–1807. Swiss Neo-Classical painter who worked extensively in England, with the keen support of Joshua Reynolds. She was in great demand as a portraitist, but also painted mythological scenes for large country houses.

Born in Grisons, she lived in Italy until 1765 and in England 1765–81.

Kaufman George S(imon) 1889–1961. US dramatist. He is the author (often in collaboration with others) of many Broadway hits, including *Of Thee I Sing* 1931, a Pulitzer Prize-winning satire on US politics; *You Can't Take It with You* 1936; *The Man Who Came to Dinner* 1939; and *The Solid Gold Cadillac* 1952. Many of his plays became classic Hollywood films.

Kawabata Yasunari 1899–1972. Japanese novelist, translator of Lady Murasaki, and author of *Snow Country* 1947 and *A Thousand Cranes* 1952. His novels are characterized by melancholy and loneliness. He was the first Japanese to win the Nobel Prize for Literature, in 1968.

Kawakubo Rei 1942– . Japanese fashion designer who established Comme des Garçons. She graduated 1964 in fine art from Keio University, Tokyo, and in 1967 began working as a freelance stylist. In 1973 she established Comme des Garçons, and her first women's collection was shown in Tokyo 1975. She launched her Homme line 1978 and Homme Plus 1984.

She has always scorned conventional fashion, trying to produce timeless clothes such as womenswear in plain colours and graded tones in simple shapes which defy Western ideas of showing off the body, taking on a life of their own. She has been highly influential, especially in the 1980s.

Kaye Danny. Stage name of David Daniel Kaminski 1913–1987. US actor, comedian, and singer. He appeared in many films, including *Wonder Man* 1944, *The Secret Life of Walter Mitty* 1946, and *Hans Christian Andersen* 1952.

He achieved success on Broadway in *Lady in the Dark* 1940. He also starred on television, had his own show 1963–67, toured for UNICEF, and guest-conducted major symphony orchestras in later years.

Kazan Elia 1909– . US stage and film director, a founder of the ◊Actors Studio 1947. Plays he directed include *The Skin of Our Teeth* 1942, *A*

Streetcar Named Desire 1947 (filmed 1951), *Death of a Salesman* 1949, and *Cat on a Hot Tin Roof* 1955; films include *Gentleman's Agreement* 1947 (Academy Award), *On the Waterfront* 1954, *East of Eden* 1955, and *The Visitors* 1972.

Kazantzakis Nikos 1885–1957. Greek writer whose works include the poem *I Odysseia/The Odyssey* 1938 (which continues Homer's *Odyssey*), and the novels *Zorba the Greek* 1946, *The Greek Passion*, and *The Last Temptation of Christ*, both 1951. *Zorba the Greek* was filmed 1964 and *The Last Temptation of Christ* (controversially) 1988.

kazoo simple wind instrument adding a buzzing quality to the singing voice on the principle of 'comb and paper' music.

Kean Edmund 1787–1833. British tragic actor, noted for his portrayal of villainy in the Shakespearean roles of Shylock, Richard III, and Iago. He died on stage, playing Othello opposite his son as Iago. His life story was turned into a romantic myth and dramatized by both the elder Dumas and Jean-Paul Sartre.

Keane Molly (Mary Nesta) 1905– . Irish novelist whose comic novels of Anglo-Irish life include *Good Behaviour* 1981, *Time After Time* 1983, and *Loving and Giving* 1988. She also writes under the name M J Farrell.

Keaton Buster (Joseph Frank) 1896–1966. US comedian, actor, and film director. After being a star in vaudeville, he became one of the great comedians of the silent-film era, with an inimitable deadpan expression (the 'Great Stone Face') masking a sophisticated acting ability. His films include *One Week* 1920, *The Navigator* 1924, *The General* 1927, and *The Cameraman* 1928.

Keats John 1795–1821. English Romantic poet who produced work of the highest quality and promise before dying at the age of 25. *Poems* 1817, *Endymion* 1818, the great odes (particularly 'Ode to a Nightingale' and 'Ode on a Grecian Urn' written 1819, published 1820), and the narratives 'Lamia', 'Isabella', and 'The Eve of St Agnes' 1820, show his lyrical richness and talent for drawing on both classical mythology and medieval lore.

Born in London, Keats studied at Guy's Hospital 1815–17, but then abandoned medicine for poetry. *Endymion* was harshly reviewed by the Tory *Blackwood's Magazine* and *Quarterly Review*, largely because of Keats' friendship with the radical writer Leigh Hunt (1800–1865). In 1819 he fell in love with Fanny Brawne (1802–1865). Suffering from tuberculosis, he sailed to Italy 1820 in an attempt to regain his health, but died in Rome. Valuable insight into Keats' poetic development is provided by his *Letters*, published 1848.

keep or *dungeon* or *donjon* the main tower of a castle, containing enough accommodation to serve as living quarters under siege conditions.

Keillor Garrison 1942– . US writer and humorist. His hometown Anoka, Minnesota, in the American Midwest, inspired his popular, richly comic stories about Lake Wobegon, including *Lake Wobegon Days* 1985 and *Leaving Home* 1987, which often started as radio monologues about 'the town that time forgot, that the decades cannot improve'. Later works include *We Are Still Married* 1989 and *Radio Romance* 1991.

Keïta Salif 1949– . Malian singer and song-writer whose combination of traditional rhythms and vocals with electronic instruments made him popular in the West in the 1980s; in Mali he worked 1973–83 with the band Les Ambassadeurs and became a star throughout W Africa, moving to France 1984. His albums include *Soro* 1987 and *Amen* 1991.

kelim oriental carpet or rug that is flat, pileless, and reversible. Kelims are made by a tapestry-weave technique. Weft thread of one colour is worked to and fro in one area of the pattern; the next colour continues the pattern from the adjacent warp thread, so that no weft thread runs across the full width of the carpet.

Keller Gottfried 1819–1890. Swiss poet and novelist whose books include *Der Grüne Heinrich/Green Henry* 1854–55. He also wrote short stories, of which the collection *Die Leute von Seldwyla/The People of Seldwyla* 1856–74 describes small-town life.

Keller Helen Adams 1880–1968. US author and campaigner for the blind. She became blind and deaf after an illness when she was only 19 months old, but the teaching of Anne Sullivan, her lifelong companion, enabled her to learn the names of objects and eventually to speak. Keller graduated with honours from Radcliffe College 1904; published several books, including *The Story of My Life* 1902; and toured the world, lecturing to raise money for the blind. She was born in Alabama.

Kelly Emmett 1898–1979. US clown and circus performer who created his 'Weary Willie' clown character while with the Hagenbeck-Wallace circus 1931. Joining the Ringling Brothers and Barnum and Bailey Circus 1942, he made 'Weary Willie' into one of the most famous clowns in the world.

Kelly Gene (Eugene Curran) 1912– . US film actor, dancer, choreographer, and director. He was a major star of the 1940s and 1950s in a series of MGM musicals, including *On the Town* 1949, *Singin' in the Rain* 1952 (both of which he codirected), and *An American in Paris* 1951. He also directed *Hello Dolly* 1969.

Kelly Grace (Patricia) 1928–1982. US film actress who retired from acting after marrying Prince Rainier III of Monaco 1956. She starred in *High Noon* 1952, *The Country Girl* 1954, for which she received an Academy Award, and *High Society* 1955. She also starred in three Hitchcock films – *Dial M for Murder* 1954, *Rear Window* 1954, and *To Catch a Thief* 1955.

Kelman James 1946– . Scottish novelist and short-story writer. His works, which make effective use of the trenchant speech patterns of his native Glasgow, include the novels *The Busconductor Hines* 1984 and *A Disaffection* 1989; the short-story collections *Greyhound for Breakfast* 1987 and *The Burn* 1991; and the play *The Busker* 1985.

Kemble Fanny (Frances Anne) 1809–1893. English actress, daughter of Charles Kemble (1775–1854). She first appeared as Shakespeare's Juliet 1829. In 1834, on a US tour, she married a Southern plantation owner and remained in the USA until 1847. Her *Journal of a Residence on a Georgian Plantation* 1835 is a valuable document in the history of slavery.

Kemble (John) Philip 1757–1823. English actor and theatre manager. He excelled in tragedy, including the Shakespearean roles of Hamlet and Coriolanus. As manager of Drury Lane 1788–1803 and Covent Garden 1803–17 in London, he introduced many innovations in theatrical management, costume, and scenery.

He was the son of the strolling player Roger Kemble (1721–1802), whose children included the actors Charles Kemble (1775–1854) and Mrs ◊Siddons.

Kemp, Will died 1603. English clown. A member of several Elizabethan theatre companies, he joined the Chamberlain's Men 1594, acting in the roles of Dogberry in Shakespeare's *Much Ado About Nothing* and Peter in *Romeo and Juliet*. He published *Kempe's Nine Days' Wonder* 1600, an account of his nine-day dance to Norwich from London.

Kempe Margery c. 1373–c. 1439. English Christian mystic. She converted to religious life after a period of mental derangement, and travelled widely as a pilgrim. Her *Boke of Margery Kempe* about 1420 describes her life and experiences, both religious and worldly. It has been called the first autobiography in English.

Kempe Rudolf 1910–1976. German conductor. Renowned for the clarity and fidelity of his interpretations of the works of Richard Strauss and ◊Wagner's *Ring* cycle, he conducted Britain's Royal Philharmonic Orchestra 1961–75 and was musical director of the Munich Philharmonic from 1967.

Kempff Wilhelm (Walter Friedrich) 1895–1991. German pianist and composer who excelled at the 19th-century classical repertory of Beethoven, Brahms, Chopin, and Liszt. He resigned as director of the Stuttgart Conservatory when only 35 to concentrate on performing; he later played with Pablo Casals, Yehudi Menuhin, and Pierre Fournier.

Keneally Thomas (Michael) 1935– . Australian novelist who won the Booker Prize with *Schindler's Ark* 1982, a novel based on the true account of Polish Jews saved from the gas chambers in World War II by a German industrialist. Other works include *Woman of the Inner Sea* 1992.

Keneally has also written *The Chant of Jimmie Blacksmith* 1972, filmed 1978 and based on the life of the Aboriginal bushranger Jimmy Governor, *Confederates* 1980, *A Family Madness* 1986, *The Playmaker* 1987, and *To Asmara* 1989.

Kennedy Nigel 1956– . British violinist, credited with expanding the audience for classical music. His 1986 recording of Vivaldi's *Four Seasons* sold more than 1 million copies. He retired from the classical concert platform 1992.

Kennedy was educated at the Yehudi Menuhin School, Surrey, England, and the Juilliard School of Music, New York. He has allied Menuhin's ethic of openness and populism to modern marketing techniques. By cultivating a media image that challenges conventional standards of dress and decorum, he has succeeded in attracting young audiences to carefully understated performances of J S Bach, Max Bruch, and Alban Berg. His repertoire of recordings also includes jazz.

Kennedy William 1928– . US novelist, author of the *Albany Trilogy* consisting of *Legs* 1976, about the gangster 'Legs' Diamond; *Billy Phelan's Greatest Game* 1983, about a pool player; and *Ironweed* 1984 (Pulitzer Prize), about a baseball player's return to the city of Albany, New York State. He also wrote *Quinn's Book* 1988.

Kent William 1686–1748. English architect, landscape gardener, and interior designer. Working closely with ◊Burlington, he was foremost in introducing the Palladian style to Britain from Italy, excelling in richly carved, sumptuous interiors and furnishings, as at Holkham Hall, Norfolk (begun 1734). Immensely versatile, he also worked in a Neo-Gothic style, and was a pioneer in Romantic landscape gardening, for example, the grounds of Stowe House in Buckinghamshire. Horace Walpole called him 'the father of modern gardening'.

Kenton Stan 1912–1979. US exponent of progressive jazz, who broke into West Coast jazz 1941 with his 'wall of brass' sound. He helped introduce Afro-Cuban rhythms to US jazz, and combined jazz and classical music in compositions like 'Artistry in Rhythm' 1943.

Kenzo trade name of Kenzo Takada 1940– . Japanese fashion designer, active in France from 1964. He opened his shop Jungle JAP 1970, and by 1972 he was well established, known initially for unconventional designs based on traditional Japanese clothing. He also produces innovative designs in knitted fabrics.

Kern Jerome (David) 1885–1945. US composer. Many of Kern's songs have become classics, notably 'Smoke Gets in Your Eyes' from his musical *Roberta* 1933. He wrote the operetta *Show Boat* 1927, which includes the song 'Ol' Man River'.

Based on Edna Ferber's novel, *Show Boat* was the first example of serious musical theatre in the USA.

Kern wrote dozens of hit songs and musicals from 1904 and Hollywood movies from the beginning of the sound era 1927. He worked mainly with lyricist Otto Harbach but also with Ira Gershwin, Oscar Hammerstein II, Dorothy Fields, and Johnny Mercer.

I had nothing to offer anybody except my own confusion.

Jack Kerouac *On the Road* 1957

Kerouac Jack (Jean Louis) 1923–1969. US novelist who named and epitomized the ◊Beat Generation of the 1950s. The first of his autobiographical books, *The Town and the City* 1950, was followed by the rhapsodic ◊*On the Road* 1957. Other works written with similar free-wheeling energy and inspired by his interests in jazz and Buddhism include *The Dharma Bums* 1958, *Doctor Sax* 1959, *Desolation Angels* 1965, and *Mexico City Blues* 1959 (verse).

Kerr Deborah 1921– . British actress who often played genteel, ladylike roles. Her performance in British films such as *Major Barbara* 1940 and *Black Narcissus* 1946 led to starring parts in Hollywood: *Quo Vadis* 1951, *From Here to Eternity* 1953, and *The King and I* 1956. She retired 1969, but made a comeback with *The Assam Garden* 1985.

Kertész André 1894–1986. Hungarian-born US photographer whose spontaneity had a great impact on photojournalism. A master of the 35-mm-format camera, he recorded his immediate environment (Paris, New York) with wit and style.

Kesey Ken 1935– . US writer. He used his experience of working in a mental hospital as the basis for his best-selling first novel ◊*One Flew Over the Cuckoo's Nest* 1962 (filmed 1975). In the mid-1960s he gave up writing and became one of the leaders of the hippie movement. He returned to writing with *Kesey's Garage Sale* 1973 and *Demon Box* 1988. Kesey's life as a hippie was described by Tom ◊Wolfe in his *Electric Kool-Aid Acid Test*.

kettledrum see ◊timpani.

key in music, the ◊diatonic scale around which a piece of music is written; for example, a passage in the key of C major will mainly use the notes of the C major scale. The term is also used for the lever activated by a ◊keyboard player, such as a piano key, or the finger control on a woodwind instrument.

Key Francis Scott 1779–1843. US lawyer and poet who wrote the song 'The Star-Spangled Banner' while Fort McHenry, Baltimore, was besieged by British troops 1814; since 1931 it has been the national anthem of the USA.

keyboard set of 'keys' (levers worked by the fingers or feet) arranged in order, forming part of various *keyboard instruments* and enabling the performer to play a much larger number of strings or reeds than could otherwise be controlled. The keyboard is a major innovation of Western music, introduced to medieval instruments of the organ type (including the portative organ and the reed organ), and subsequently transferred to Renaissance stringed instruments such as the clavichord and hurdy-gurdy. Keyboard instruments were designed to enable precise and objective reproduction of musical intervals, without the intervention of musical expression.

Khachaturian Aram Il'yich 1903–1978. Armenian composer. His use of folk themes is shown in the ballets *Gayaneh* 1942, which includes the 'Sabre Dance', and *Spartacus* 1956.

Khajurāho town in Madhya Pradesh, central India, former capital of the Candella monarchs, and site of 35 sandstone temples – Jain, Buddhist, and Hindu – built in the 10th and 11th centuries. The temples are covered inside and out with erotic relief sculptures symbolizing mystic union with the deity. The Parshvanatha Temple about 950–70 has the finest array, providing outstanding examples of medieval Hindu art as well as some of the world's most sensual images.

Kiefer Anselm 1945– . German Neo-Expressionist painter. He studied under Joseph ◊Beuys and his works include monumental landscapes on varied surfaces, often with the paint built up into heavily textured impasto with other substances. Much of his work deals with recent German history.

Kierkegaard Søren (Aabye) 1813–1855. Danish philosopher and writer, considered to be the founder of ◊existentialism. He argued that no system of thought could explain the unique experience of the individual. He defended Christianity, suggesting that God cannot be known through reason but only through a 'leap of faith'. Kierkegaard was a prolific author, but his chief works are *Enten-Eller/Either–Or* 1843, *Begrebet Angest/Concept of Dread* 1844, and

Efterskrift/Postscript 1846, which summed up much of his earlier writings.

'Killers, The' short story, published in *Men Without Women* 1928, by US writer Ernest ◊Hemingway. When two killers arrive in a lunchroom to murder 'the Swede', young Nick Adams runs to warn him, and is stunned to find the former prizefighter passively waiting for death. A work of intense power and economy, it deals with Hemingway's major themes of virility and death.

Kilmer Joyce 1886–1918. US poet. His first collection of poems *Summer of Love* was published 1911. He later gained an international reputation with the title work of *Trees and Other Poems* 1914.

Kilvert Francis 1840–1879. English cleric who wrote a diary recording social life on the Welsh border 1870–79, published 1938–39. He delineated landscape and human experience with great sensitivity and vividness.

kimono traditional Japanese costume. Already worn in the Heian period (more than 1,000 years ago), it is still used by women for formal wear and informally by men.

For the finest kimonos a rectangular piece of silk (about 11 m/36 ft × 0.5 m/1.5 ft) is cut into seven pieces for tailoring. The design (which must match perfectly over the seams and for which flowers are the usual motif) is then painted by hand, using various processes, and may be enhanced by embroidery or gilding. The accompanying *obi*, or sash, about 4 m/13 ft × 10 cm/4 in for men and wider for women, is also embroidered.

kinetic art in the visual arts, a work of art (usually sculpture) incorporating real or apparent movement. The term, coined by Naum ◊Gabo and Antoine ◊Pevsner in the 1920s, encompasses Alexander ◊Calder's celebrated 1930s mobiles as well as the mechanical kinetic works of Swiss sculptor Jean Tinguely (1925–), which were programmed to destroy themselves (thus also pertaining to ◊performance art).

King Albert. Adopted name of Albert Nelson 1923–1992. US blues guitarist and singer whose ringing style influenced numerous rock guitarists. His recordings for the Stax label, such as *Born Under a Bad Sign* and *Crosscut Saw* (both 1967), became classics and made him popular beyond the blues circuit. His playing also shows psychedelic and funk influences.

King B B (Riley) 1925– . US blues guitarist, singer, and songwriter, one of the most influential electric-guitar players, who became an international star in the 1960s. His albums include *Blues Is King* 1967, *Lucille Talks Back* 1975, and *Blues 'n' Jazz* 1983.

King Stephen 1946– . US writer of best-selling horror novels with small-town or rural settings. Many of his works have been filmed, including *Carrie* 1974, *The Shining* 1978, and *Christine* 1983.

King Lear tragedy by William ◊Shakespeare, first performed 1605–06. Lear, king of Britain, favours his grasping daughters, Goneril and Regan, with shares of his kingdom but refuses his third, honest daughter, Cordelia, a share because she will not falsely flatter him. Rejected by Goneril and Regan, the old and unbalanced Lear is reunited with Cordelia but dies of grief when she is murdered.

Kingsley Ben (Krishna Banji) 1944– . British film actor who usually plays character parts. He played the title role of *Gandhi* 1982, for which he won an Academy Award, and appeared in *Betrayal* 1982, *Testimony* 1987, and *Pascali's Island* 1988.

Kingsley Charles 1819–1875. English author. A rector, he was known as the 'Chartist clergyman' because of such social novels as *Alton Locke* 1850. His historical novels include *Westward Ho!* 1855. He also wrote *The ◊Water Babies* 1863.

Kingsley Mary Henrietta 1862–1900. British ethnologist. She made extensive expeditions in W Africa, and published lively accounts of her findings, for example *Travels in West Africa* 1897. She died while nursing Boer prisoners during the South African War. She was the niece of the writer Charles Kingsley.

Kingston Maxine Hong 1940– . US writer. A major voice of Chinese-American culture, her semi-fictional *The Woman Warrior: Memoirs of a Girlhood Among Ghosts* 1976 was followed by *China Men* 1980, which continued her imaginative chronicling of family history and cultural folklore.

Kinski Klaus 1926–1991. German actor of skeletal appearance who featured in Werner Herzog's films *Aguirre Wrath of God* 1972, *Nosferatu/Phantom of the Night* 1979, and *Fitzcarraldo* 1982. His other films include *For a Few Dollars More* 1965, *Dr Zhivago* 1965, and *Venom* 1982. He was the father of the actress Nastassja Kinski (1961–).

Kipling (Joseph) Rudyard 1865–1936. English writer, born in India. *Plain Tales from the Hills* 1888, about Anglo-Indian society, contains the earliest of his masterly short stories. His books for children, including *The ◊Jungle Book* 1894–95, *◊Just So Stories* 1902, *Puck of Pook's Hill* 1906, and the novel *Kim* 1901, reveal his imaginative identification with the exotic. Poems such as 'Danny Deever', 'Gunga Din', and 'If–' express an empathy with common experience, which contributed to his great popularity, together with a vivid sense of 'Englishness' (sometimes denigrated as a kind of jingoist imperialism). His work is increasingly valued for its complex characterization and subtle moral viewpoints. Nobel prize 1907.

Kirchner Ernst Ludwig 1880–1938. German Expressionist artist, a leading member of the *die ◊Brücke* group in Dresden from 1905 and in Berlin from 1911. His Dresden work, which includes paintings and woodcuts, shows the influence of African and medieval art. In Berlin he turned to city scenes and portraits, using lurid colours and bold diagonal paint strokes recalling woodcut technique. He suffered a breakdown during World War I and settled in Switzerland, where he committed suicide.

Kirchman Jacob 1710–1792. German-born organist and composer who settled in London about 1730 and founded a family firm of harpsichordmakers which dominated the British market during the late 18th century and moved into piano manufacture 1809.

Kirkland Gelsey 1952– . US ballerina of effortless technique and innate musicality. She joined the New York City Ballet 1968, where George Balanchine staged a new *Firebird* for her 1970 and Jerome Robbins chose her for his *Goldberg Variations* 1971 and other ballets. In 1974 Mikhail Baryshnikov sought her out and she joined the American Ballet Theater 1975, where they danced in partnership, for example in *Giselle*.

Kirov Ballet Russian ballet company based in St Petersburg, founded 1738. Originally called the Imperial Ballet, it was renamed 1935 (after an assassinated Communist Party leader). The Kirov dancers are renowned for their cool purity of line, lyrical mobility, and gravity-defying jumps; the corps de ballet is famed for its precision and musicality. The classical ballets of Marius ◊Petipa make up the backbone of the company's repertory and many of the world's most acclaimed classical dancers, such as Anna Pavlova, Rudolf Nureyev, and Mikhail Baryshnikov, are graduates of the company. Oleg Vinogradov (1937–) has been its artistic director since 1972.

Kitaj Ron B 1932– . US painter and graphic artist, active in Britain. His work is mainly figurative, and employs a wide range of allusions to art, history, and literature. *The Autumn of Central Paris (After Walter Benjamin)* 1972–74 is a typical work. His distinctive use of colour was in part inspired by studies of the Impressionist painter Degas. Much of Kitaj's work is outside the predominant avant-garde trend and inspired by diverse historical styles. Some compositions are in triptych form.

kitchen-sink painters loose-knit group of British painters, active in the late 1940s and early 1950s. They depicted drab, everyday scenes with an aggressive technique and often brilliant, 'crude' colour. The best known were John ◊Bratby, Derrick Greaves (1927–), Edward Middleditch (1923–1987), and Jack Smith (1928–). The group disbanded after a few years but interest in them revived in the 1990s.

kitsch (German 'trash') in the arts, anything claiming to have an aesthetic purpose but which is tawdry and tasteless. It usually applies to cheap sentimental works produced for the mass market, such as those found in souvenir shops and chain stores, but it is also used for any art that is considered in bad taste.

In the 1960s Pop art began to explore the potential of kitsch, and since the 1970s pop culture and various strands of Post-Modernism have drawn heavily on it. The US artist Jeff Koons (1955–   ) employs kitsch extensively.

Klee Paul 1879–1940. Swiss artist, one of the most original of the 20th century. He settled in Munich 1906, joined the ◊Blaue Reiter group 1912, and worked at the ◊Bauhaus school of design 1920–31, returning to Switzerland 1933. Endlessly inventive and playful, his many works are an exploration of the potential of line, plane, and colour. Suggesting a childlike innocence, they are based on the belief in a reality beyond appearances. *Twittering Machine* 1922 (Museum of Modern Art, New York) is typical.

Klee travelled with the painter August Macke to Tunisia 1914, a trip that transformed his sense of colour. His influential views on art were presented in *Pedagogical Sketchbook* 1925. Other publications include *On Modern Art* 1948. The Klee Foundation, Berne, has a large collection of his work.

Klein Calvin (Richard) 1942–   . US fashion designer whose collections are characterized by the smooth and understated, often in natural fabrics such as mohair, wool, and suede in subtle colours. He set up his own business 1968 specializing in designing coats and suits, and expanded into sportswear in the mid-1970s. His designer jeans became a status symbol during the same period.

Klein Roland 1938–   . French fashion designer, active in the UK from 1965. He opened his own-label shop 1979 and from 1991 designed menswear for the Japanese market.

Klein Yves 1928–1962. French painter and leading exponent of the Neo-Dada movement. He painted bold abstracts and devised provocative experimental works, including imprints of nude bodies.

Kleist (Bernd) Heinrich (Wilhelm) von 1777–1811. German dramatist whose comedy *Der zerbrochene Krug/The Broken Pitcher* 1808 (published 1812) and drama *Prinz Friedrich von Homburg/The Prince of Homburg* 1810 (published 1821) achieved success only after his suicide. His dominant themes are corruption, duty, and obsessional feelings.

Kleist entered the Prussian army at the age of 14, remaining for five years. His novella *Michael Kohlhaus* 1808 describes a righteous schoolmaster led to carry out robbery and murder for political ends. His tragedy *Penthesilea* 1808 has the love of the Amazon queen for the Greek warrior Achilles as its subject.

Klemperer Otto 1885–1973. German conductor who is celebrated for his interpretation of contemporary and Classical music (especially Beethoven and Brahms). He conducted the Los Angeles Orchestra 1933–39 and the Philharmonia Orchestra, London, from 1959.

Kliegl John H 1869–1959 and Anton T 1872–1927. German-born US brothers who in 1911 invented the brilliant carbon-arc (*klieg*) lights used in television and films. They also created scenic effects for theatre and film.

Klimt Gustav 1862–1918. Austrian painter, influenced by Jugendstil (Art Nouveau) and Symbolism; a founding member of the Vienna ◊Sezession group 1897. His paintings have a jewelled effect similar to mosaics, for example *The Kiss* 1909 (Musée des Beaux-Arts, Strasbourg). His many portraits include *Judith I* 1901 (Österreichische Galerie, Vienna).

Kline Franz 1910–1962. US Abstract Expressionist painter. He created large, graphic compositions in black and white using angular forms, like magnified calligraphic brushstrokes. He did not introduce colour into his work until the late 1950s.

God and I both knew what it meant once; now God alone knows.

Friedrich Klopstock

Klopstock Friedrich Gottlieb 1724–1803. German poet whose religious epic *Der Messias/The Messiah* 1748–73 and *Oden/Odes* 1771 anticipated Romanticism.

Kneller Godfrey 1646–1723. German-born portrait painter who lived in England from 1674. He was court painter to Charles II, James II, William III, and George I. Among his paintings are the series *Hampton Court Beauties* (Hampton Court, Richmond, Surrey, a sequel to Peter Lely's *Windsor Beauties*), and 48 portraits of the members of the Whig Kit Cat Club 1702–17 (National Portrait Gallery, London).

Knickerbocker School group of US writers working in New York State in the early 19th century, which included Washington Irving, James Kirke Paulding (1778–1860), and Fitz-Greene Halleck (1790–1867). The group took its name from Irving's comic *History of New York by Diedrich Knickerbocker* 1809.

Knight Laura 1877–1970. English painter. She focused on detailed, narrative scenes of Romany, fairground, and circus life, and the ballet.

Knipper Lev Konstantinovich 1898–1974. Soviet composer. His early work shows the influence of Stravinsky, but after 1932 he wrote in a more popular idiom, as in the symphony *Poem of Komsomol Fighters* 1933–34 with its mass battle songs. He is known in the West for his song 'Cavalry of the Steppes'.

knitting method of making fabric by looping and knotting yarn with two needles. Knitting may have developed from ◊**crochet**, which uses a single hooked needle, or from *netting*, using a shuttle.

A mechanized process for making stockings was developed in the 16th century, but it was not until the mid-20th century that machine knitting was revolutionized with the introduction of synthetic yarns, coloured dyes, and methods of texturing and elasticizing.

knot intertwinement of parts of one or more ropes, cords, or strings, to bind them together or to other objects. It is constructed so that the strain on the knot will draw it tighter. Bends or hitches are knots used to fasten ropes together or to other objects; when two ropes are joined end to end, they are spliced. The craft of ◊macramé uses knots to form decorative pieces and fringes.

Kodály Zoltán 1882–1967. Hungarian composer and educationist. With Béla Bartók, he recorded and transcribed Magyar folk music, the scales and rhythm of which he incorporated in a deliberately nationalist style. His works include the cantata *Psalmus Hungaricus* 1923, a comic opera *Háry János* 1925–27, and orchestral dances and variations. His 'Kodály method' of school music education is widely practised.

Koestler Arthur 1905–1983. Hungarian-born English author. Imprisoned by the Nazis in France 1940, he escaped to England. His novel *Darkness at Noon* 1940, regarded as his masterpiece, is a fictional account of the Stalinist purges, and draws on his experiences as a prisoner under sentence of death during the Spanish Civil War.

Koestler's other novels include *Thieves in the Night* 1946, *The Lotus and the Robot* 1960, and *The Call Girls* 1972. His nonfiction – he wrote extensively about creativity, parapsychology, science, and culture – includes *The Yogi and the Commissar* 1945, *The Sleepwalkers* 1959, *The Act of Creation* 1964, *The Ghost in the Machine* 1967, *The Roots of Coincidence* 1972, *The Heel of Achilles* 1974, and *The Thirteenth Tribe* 1976. Autobiographical works include *Arrow in the Blue* 1952 and *The Invisible Writing* 1954.

One may not regard the world as a sort of metaphysical brothel for emotions.

Arthur Koestler *Darkness at Noon* 1940

Koetsu Hanami 1558–1637. Japanese designer, calligrapher, and potter. As the central figure of a community dedicated to reviving the traditional arts and crafts of Kyoto, Koetsu influenced all aspects of Japanese design. Famed for his callig-

raphy and ceramics for tea ceremonies, he also produced lacquer pieces, one of the finest of which is the *Boat Bridge Writing Box* early 17th century (National Museum, Tokyo).

Kokoschka Oskar 1886–1980. Austrian Expressionist painter and writer who lived in England from 1938. Initially influenced by the Vienna ◊Sezession painters, he painted vivid seascapes and highly charged portraits. His writings include several plays.

After World War I Kokoschka worked in Dresden, then in Prague, and fled from the Nazis to England, taking British citizenship 1947. To portraiture he added panoramic landscapes and townscapes in the 1920s and 1930s, and political allegories in the 1950s.

Kollwitz Käthe 1867–1945. German sculptor and printmaker. Her early series of etchings depicting workers and their environment are bold, realistic, and harshly expressive. Later themes include war, death, and maternal love.

kora 21-string instrument of W African origin made from gourds, with a harplike sound. Traditionally played by griots (hereditary troubadours) of the old Mali empire to accompany praise songs and historical ballads, it was first incorporated into an electronically amplified band by Guinean Mory Kante (1950–   ).

Korda Alexander 1893–1956. Hungarian-born British film producer and director, a dominant figure in the British film industry during the 1930s and 1940s. His films include *The Private Life of Henry VIII* 1933, *The Third Man* 1950, and *Richard III* 1956.

Korin Ogata *c.* 1660–1716. Japanese painter and kimono designer whose style is highly decorative, typically combining brightly coloured, naturalistic and stylized elements against a gold background. His *Iris Screen* early 18th century (Nezu Art Museum, Tokyo) is one of his best-known works.

Korngold Erich Wolfgang 1897–1957. Austrian-born US composer. He began composing while still in his teens and achieved early recognition when his opera *Die tote Stadt/Dead City* was premiered simultaneously in Hamburg and Cologne 1920. In 1934 he moved to Hollywood to become a composer for Warner Brothers. His film scores, in richly orchestrated and romantic style, include *The Adventures of Robin Hood* 1938 and *Of Human Bondage* 1946.

The creative man in a police state has always been trapped in a cage where he can fly as long as he doesn't touch the wires.

Jerzy Kosiński

Kosiński Jerzy 1933–1991. Polish-born US author, in the USA from 1957. His childhood experiences as a Jew in Poland during World War II are recounted in *The Painted Bird* 1965, a popular success. The novel that established his cult status, the comic media satire *Being There* 1971 (filmed 1979), was followed by increasingly violent works such as *The Devil Tree* 1974, *Pinball* 1982, and *The Hermit of 69th Street* 1987.

Kosztolányi Deszö 1885–1936. Hungarian poet, novelist, and critic. He was associated with the literary magazine *Nyugat/The West*, founded 1908, but unlike others in that circle he was more interested in aesthetic than social questions. His sympathetic observation of human weakness is apparent in his poem cycle *A szegeny kisgyermek panaszai/The Complaints of a Poor Little Child* 1910 and his novel *Edes Anna/Wonder Maid* 1926, a tale of a servant girl.

koto Japanese musical instrument; a long zither of ancient Chinese origin, having 13 silk strings supported by movable bridges. It rests on the floor and the strings are plucked with ivory plectra, producing a brittle sound.

Koudelka Josef 1939– . Czech photographer best known for his photographs of East European gypsies whose vanishing way of life he has recorded. He also photographed the Russian invasion of Czechoslovakia 1968 and the inauguration of Václav Havel as president of Czechoslovakia 1989.

Koussevitsky Serge 1874–1951. Russian musician and conductor, well known for his work in the USA. He established his own orchestra in Moscow 1909, introducing works by Prokofiev, Rachmaninov, and Stravinsky. Although named director of the State Symphony after the Bolshevik Revolution 1917, Koussevitsky left the USSR for the USA, becoming director of the Boston Symphony Orchestra 1924.

Krasiński Zygmunt 1812–1859. Polish dramatist and romantic poet who lived and wrote in exile but whose messianic vision of Polish sacrifice and resurrection in poems such as 'Przedświt/The Moment Before Dawn' 1843 inspired his countrymen.

Kreisler Fritz 1875–1962. Austrian violinist and composer, a US citizen from 1943. His prolific output of recordings in the early 20th century introduced a wider public to classical music from old masters such as J S Bach and Couperin to moderns such as de Falla and Rachmaninov. He also composed and recorded romantic pieces in the style of the classics, often under a pseudonym.

kremlin citadel or fortress of Russian cities. The Moscow kremlin dates from the 12th century, and the name 'the Kremlin' was once synonymous with the Soviet government.

Krenek Ernst 1900–1991. Austrian-born US composer and theorist. Following early popular success with jazz-influenced operas *Jonny spielt auf/Johnny Strikes Up* 1926 and *Leben des Orest/Life of Orestes* 1930, he supported himself as a critic while working on the ambitious twelve-tone opera *Karl V/Charles V* 1938. He moved to teaching posts in the USA 1939 but remained in contact with postwar developments in extended serialism and aleatoric music with *Quaestio Temporis/In Search of Time* 1957, and with electronic music in *Spiritus intelligentiae sanctus* 1956.

Kreutzer Rodolphe 1766–1831. French violinist and composer of German descent to whom Beethoven dedicated his violin sonata Opus 47, known as the *Kreutzer Sonata*.

Krier Leon 1946– . Luxembourg architect who lives and works in Britain. He has built little but his anti-Modernist arguments have helped to revive vernacular traditions and 19th-century Neo-Classicism. Prince Charles commissioned him 1988 to design a model village, Poundbury, adjoining Dorchester, Dorset.

Krishna incarnation of the Hindu god ◊Vishnu. Many stories are told of Krishna's mischievous youth, and he is the charioteer of Arjuna in the *Bhagavad-Gītā*.

Kronos or *Cronus* in Greek mythology, the ruler of the world and one of the ◊Titans. He was the father of Zeus, who overthrew him.

Kryukov Fyodor 1870–1920. Russian writer, alleged by Alexander ◊Solzhenitsyn to be the real author of *And Quiet Flows the Don* by Mikhail ◊Sholokhov.

Kubelik Jan 1880–1940. Czech violinist and composer. He performed in Prague at the age of eight, and became one of the world's greatest virtuosos; he also wrote six violin concertos.

Kubelik Rafael 1914– . Czech conductor and composer, son of violinist Jan Kubelik. His works include symphonies and operas, such as *Veronika* 1947. He was musical director of the Royal Opera House, Covent Garden, London, 1955–58.

Kubrick Stanley 1928– . US film director, producer, and screenwriter. His films include *Paths of Glory* 1957, *Dr Strangelove* 1964, *2001: A Space Odyssey* 1968, *A Clockwork Orange* 1971, and *The Shining* 1979.

More than any of his American contemporaries, Kubrick achieved complete artistic control over his films, which have been eclectic in subject matter and ambitious in both scale and technique. His other films include *Lolita* 1962 and *Full Metal Jacket* 1987.

The great nations have always acted like gangsters, and the small nations like prostitutes.

Stanley Kubrick 1963

Kundera Milan 1929– . Czech writer, born in Brno. His first novel, *The Joke* 1967, brought him into official disfavour in Prague, and, unable to publish further works, he moved to France. Other novels include *The Book of Laughter and Forgetting* 1979 and *The Unbearable Lightness of Being* 1984 (filmed 1988).

In the world of eternal return the weight of unbearable responsibility lies heavy on every move we make.

Milan Kundera *The Unbearable Lightness of Being* 1984

Kuniyoshi Utagawa 1797–1861. Japanese printmaker. His series *108 Heroes of the Suikoden* depicts heroes of the Chinese classic novel *The Water Margin*. Kuniyoshi's dramatic, innovative style lent itself to warriors and fantasy, but his subjects also include landscapes and cats.

Kupka Frank (František) 1871–1957. Czech painter and illustrator, a pioneer of non-representational art. He studied in Prague, Vienna, and Paris, where he lived from 1895. His *Amorpha, Fugue in Two Colours: Red and Blue* 1912 (Národni Galerie, Prague) is thought to be the earliest example of an entirely abstract painting.

Kureishi Hanif 1954– . British dramatist and novelist, whose work concentrates on the lives of Asians living in Britain. His early plays *Outskirts* 1981 and *Birds of Passage* 1983 were followed by the screenplays for the films *My Beautiful Laundrette* 1984 and *Sammy and Rosie Get Laid* 1987, both directed by Stephen Frears.

Kurosawa Akira 1929– . Japanese director whose film *Rashōmon* 1950 introduced Western audiences to Japanese cinema. Epics such as *Shichinin no samurai/Seven Samurai* 1954 combine spectacle with intimate human drama.

Kurosawa's films with a contemporary setting include *Drunken Angel* 1948 and *Ikiru/Living*

1952, both using illness as metaphor. *Yōjimbō* 1961, *Kagemusha* 1981, and *Ran* 1985 (loosely based on Shakespeare's *King Lear*) are historical films with an increasingly bleak outlook.

To be an artist means never to look away.

Akira Kurosawa in the *Guardian* 1980

Kuti Fela Anikulapo 1938– . Nigerian singer, songwriter, and musician, a strong proponent of African nationalism and ethnic identity. His albums of big-band African funk include *Coffin for Head of State* 1978, *Teacher Don't Teach Me Nonsense* 1987, and *Underground System* 1993.

Kuti had his first local hit 1971 and soon became a W African star. His political protest songs (in English) caused the Nigerian army to attack his commune 1974 and again 1977, and he has been a political prisoner. Unsparing in his attacks on neocolonialism and corruption, he holds up Idi Amin as a role model.

Kuznetsov Anatoly 1930–1979. Russian writer. His novels *Babi Yar* 1966, describing the wartime execution of Jews at Babi Yar, near Kiev, and *The Fire* 1969, about workers in a large metallurgical factory, were seen as anti-Soviet. He lived in Britain from 1969.

Kyd Thomas *c.* 1557–1595. English dramatist, author in about 1588 of a bloody revenge tragedy, *The Spanish Tragedy*, which anticipated elements present in Shakespeare's *Hamlet*.

Thus must we toil in other men's extremes,/ That know not how to remedy our own.

Thomas Kyd *The Spanish Tragedy c.* 1588

Laban Rudolf von 1879–1958. Hungarian dance theoretician, known as the leader of modern dance theory. He invented ◊Labanotation, an accurate, detailed system of recording steps and movements. He also tried to order the principles of human motion into specific systems, such as *choreutics* (the relationship of the body to the space it occupies) and *eukinetics* (formulation of all possible types and directions of body movements). He researched the connection between psychology and motion in his theoretical work.

Labanotation comprehensive system of accurate dance notation (*Kinetographie Laban*) devised 1928 by Rudolf von ◊Laban. It uses a set of graphic symbols arranged on a vertical staff that represents the human body. The varying length of the symbols indicates the timing of the movements. It is commonly used as a means of copyright protection for choreographers.

Labèque Katia (1950–) and Marielle (1952–). French duo-pianists, sisters, whose career began 1961. Their repertoire has encompassed works by classical composers (Bach, Mozart, Brahms) as well as modern pieces (Stravinsky, Messiaen, Boulez). They also play ragtime.

Labrouste Pierre-François-Henri 1801–1875. French architect, a pioneer in his use of such materials as iron. His Library of Ste Geneviève, Paris 1843–50, has a slender and elegant ironwork frame supporting a vaulted ceiling. The severity of its flat stone façade, punctuated by round-headed windows, is in stark contrast to the decorative ◊Beaux Arts style, which was dominant at the time.

Party loyalty lowers the greatest of men to the petty level of the masses.

Jean de La Bruyère The Characters

La Bruyère Jean de 1645–1696. French essayist. He was born in Paris, studied law, took a post in the revenue office, and in 1684 entered the service of the French commander the Prince of Condé. His *Caractères* 1688, satirical portraits of his contemporaries, made him many enemies.

Labyrinth in Greek mythology, the maze designed by the Athenian artisan Daedalus at Knossos in Crete for King Minos, as a home for the Minotaur – a monster, half man and half bull. After killing the Minotaur, Theseus, the prince of Athens, was guided out of the Labyrinth by a thread given to him by the king's daughter, Ariadne.

lace delicate, decorative, openwork textile fabric. Lace is a European craft with centres in Belgium, Italy, France, Germany, and England.

Needlepoint or *point* lace (a development of embroidery) originated in Italy in the late 15th or early 16th centuries. Lace was first made from linen thread and sometimes also with gold, silver, or silk; cotton, wool, and synthetic fibres have been used more recently.

Bobbin or *pillow* ('true') lace is made by twisting threads together in pairs or groups, according to a pattern marked out by pins set in a cushion. It is said to have been invented by Barbara Uttmann (born 1514) of Saxony; elaborate patterns may require over a thousand bobbins.

machine lace From 1589 attempts were made at producing machine-made lace, and in 1809 this was achieved by John Heathcote using a bobbin net machine; the principles of this system are kept today in machines making plain net. The earliest machine for making true lace, reproducing the movements of the workers' fingers, was invented in England by John Leavers 1813. It had a wooden frame with mostly wooden moving parts, but worked on the same principle as the modern machines in Nottingham, England, the centre of machine-made lace.

Laclos Pierre Choderlos de 1741–1803. French author. An army officer, he wrote a single novel in letter form, *Les Liaisons dangereuses/Dangerous Liaisons* 1782, an analysis of moral corruption. It was adapted as a play 1985 by Christopher Hampton (1945–) and as a film 1988, directed by Stephen Frears (1941–).

Lacoste fashion label identified with a short-sleeved tennis shirt with a collar, button-down neck, and small crocodile emblem on the chest. It was launched 1933 by a French tennis star, René Lacoste (1905–), who was nicknamed *'le Crocodile'* because of his aggressive nature on the court.

lacquer waterproof resinous varnish obtained from Oriental trees *Toxicodendron verniciflua*, and used for decorating furniture and art objects. It can be applied to wood, fabric, leather, or other materials, with or without added colours. The technique of making and carving small lacquerwork objects was developed in China, probably as early as the 4th century BC, and was later adopted in Japan.

Lacroix Christian 1951– . French fashion designer who opened his couture and ready-to-wear business 1987, after working with Jean ◊Patou 1981–87. He made headlines with his fantasy creations, including the short puffball skirt, rose prints, and low décolleté necklines.

Ladd Alan 1913–1964. US actor whose first leading role, as the professional killer in *This Gun for Hire* 1942, made him a star. His most famous role was as the gunslinging stranger in *Shane* 1953, but his career declined after the mid-1950s. However, his last role in *The Carpetbaggers* 1964 is considered one of his best. His other films include *The Blue Dahlia* 1946.

La Farge John 1835–1910. US painter and ecclesiastical designer. He is credited with the revival of stained glass in America and also created woodcuts, watercolours, and murals. Lafarge visited Europe 1856 and the Far East 1886. In the 1870s he turned from landscape painting (inspired by the French painter ◊Corot) to religious and still-life painting. Decorating the newly built Trinity Church in Boston, Massachusetts, he worked alongside the sculptor Saint-Gaudens.

Lafayette Marie-Madeleine, Comtesse de Lafayette 1634–1693. French author. Her *Mémoires* of the French court are keenly observed, and her *La Princesse de Clèves* 1678 is the first French psychological novel and *roman à clef* ('novel with a key'), in that real-life characters (including the writer François de ◊La Rochefoucauld, who was for many years her lover) are presented under fictitious names.

La Fontaine Jean de 1621–1695. French poet. He was born at Château-Thierry, and from 1656 lived largely in Paris, the friend of the playwrights Molière and Racine, and the poet Boileau. His works include *Fables* 1668–94 and *Contes* 1665–74, a series of witty and bawdy tales in verse.

Better a living beggar than a dead emperor.

Jean de La Fontaine
La Matrone d'Ephèse

Laforgue Jules 1860–1887. French poet who pioneered ◊free verse and who inspired later French and English writers.

Lagerfeld Karl (Otto) 1939– . German-born fashion designer, a leading figure on the fashion scene from the early 1970s. As design director at Chanel for both the couture and ready-to-wear collections from 1983, he updated the Chanel look. He showed his first collection under his own label 1984.

Lagerfeld joined Chloé in the early 1960s, where he became known for high-quality ready-to-wear clothing. As fashion consultant to Fendi from 1967, he made many innovative jackets and coats.

Lagerkvist Pär 1891–1974. Swedish author of lyric poetry, dramas (including *The Hangman* 1935), and novels, such as *Barabbas* 1950. He was awarded the 1951 Nobel Prize for Literature.

Lagerlöf Selma 1858–1940. Swedish novelist. Her first work was the romantic historical novel *Gösta Berling's Saga* 1891. The children's fantasy *Nils Holgerssons underbara resa/The Wonderful Voyage of Nils Holgersson* 1906–07 grew from her background as a schoolteacher. She was the first woman to receive a Nobel prize, in 1909.

Lake Veronica. Stage name of Constance Frances Marie Ockelman 1919–1973. US film actress who was almost as celebrated for her much imitated 'peekaboo' hairstyle as for her acting. She co-starred with Alan Ladd in several films during the 1940s, including *This Gun for Hire* and *The Glass Key* both 1942, and *The Blue Dahlia* 1946. She also appeared in *Sullivan's Travels* 1942 and *I Married a Witch* 1942.

Lalique René 1860–1945. French designer and manufacturer of ◊Art Nouveau glass, jewellery, and house interiors. The Lalique factory continues in production at Wingen-sur-Moder, Alsace, under his son Marc and granddaughter Marie-Claude.

Lalo (Victor Antoine) Edouard 1823–1892. French composer. His Spanish ancestry and violin training are evident in the *Symphonie Espagnole* 1873 for violin and orchestra, and *Concerto for Cello and Orchestra* 1877. He also wrote an opera, *Le Roi d'Ys* 1887.

Lam Wifredo (Wilfredo) 1902–1982. Cuban painter. Influenced by Surrealism in the 1930s (he lived in Paris 1937–41), he created a semi-abstract style using mysterious and sometimes menacing images and symbols, mainly taken from Caribbean traditions. His *Jungle* series, for example, contains voodoo elements. He visited Haiti and Martinique in the 1940s, Paris 1952, and also made frequent trips to Italy.

Lamanova Nadezhda. Russian fashion designer who before the revolution made French-style clothes for fashionable society. After 1917 she became involved in teaching and designing mass-produced clothing for the proletariat. In an attempt to break away from imitations of Paris-led style, she wrote extensively on the social role of dress, on the most efficient ways of designing and producing, and on Soviet identity in dress.

Lamartine Alphonse de 1790–1869. French poet. He wrote romantic poems, including *Méditations poétiques* 1820, followed by *Nouvelles méditations/New Meditations* 1823, and *Harmonies* 1830. His *Histoire des Girondins/History of the*

Girondins 1847 helped to inspire the revolution of 1848.

Lamb Charles 1775–1834. English essayist and critic. He collaborated with his sister *Mary Lamb* (1764–1847) on *Tales from Shakespeare* 1807, and his *Specimens of English Dramatic Poets* 1808 helped to revive interest in Elizabethan plays. As 'Elia' he contributed essays to the *London Magazine* from 1820 (collected 1823 and 1833).

Born in London, Lamb was educated at Christ's Hospital. He was a contemporary of ◊Coleridge, with whom he published some poetry 1796. He was a clerk at India House 1792–1825, when he retired to Enfield. His sister Mary stabbed their mother to death in a fit of insanity 1796, and Charles cared for her between her periodic returns to an asylum.

The human species, according to the best theory I can form of it, is composed of two distinct races: the men who borrow, and the men who lend.

Charles Lamb *The Two Races of Men*

---

lambada Brazilian dance music that became internationally popular 1989. It combines elements of calypso, zouk, and reggae. The record 'Lambada' by Kaoma was the best-selling single of 1989 in Europe.

Lambert George Washington Thomas 1873–1930. Australian painter and sculptor, born in Russia of American parents. In Sydney he studied with Julian ◊Ashton. In 1917 he was appointed official war artist with the Australian Light Horse in Palestine, resulting in a series of paintings, drawings and sculptures, many of which are in the Australian War Memorial, Canberra. He is also known for his landscapes and portraits.

Lamburn Richmal Crompton. Full name of British writer Richmal ◊Crompton.

Lamming George 1927– . Barbadian novelist and poet, author of the autobiographical *In the Castle of my Skin* 1953, describing his upbringing in the small village where he was born. His imaginative explorations of Caribbean history and society sustain a political vision of a future resting with the common people and depending on the creative union of the minds of the artist and the politician.

Lampedusa Giuseppe Tomasi di 1896–1957. Italian aristocrat, author of *Il gattopardo/The Leopard* 1958, a novel set in his native Sicily during the period following its annexation by Garibaldi 1860. It chronicles the reactions of an aristocratic family to social and political upheavals.

lampoon satirical attack (see ◊satire) on a person in verse or prose, most commonly in the form of a vicious character sketch.

Lancaster Burt (Burton Stephen) 1913– . US film actor, formerly an acrobat. A star from his first film, *The Killers* 1946, he proved himself adept both at action roles and more complex character parts as in such films as *From Here to Eternity* 1953, *Elmer Gantry* 1960 (Academy Award), *The Leopard/Il gattopardo* 1963, *The Swimmer* 1968, and *Atlantic City* 1980.

Lancelot of the Lake in British legend, one of King Arthur's knights, the lover of Queen Guinevere. Originally a folk hero, he first appeared in the Arthurian cycle of tales in the 12th century.

Lancret Nicolas 1690–1743. French painter. His graceful *fêtes galantes* (festive groups of courtly figures in fancy dress) followed a theme made popular by Watteau. He also illustrated amorous scenes from the *Fables* of La Fontaine.

Land Edwin Herbert 1909–1991. US inventor of the ◊Polaroid Land camera 1947, which developed the film in one minute inside the camera and produced an 'instant' photograph.

ländler Austrian country dance in 3/4 or 3/8 time, in which couples spin and clap. It was very popular in the late 18th century and composers, such as Mozart, Beethoven, and Schubert, wrote music in the rhythm of the dance.

Landor Walter Savage 1775–1864. English poet and essayist. He lived much of his life abroad, dying in Florence, where he had fled after a libel suit 1858. His works include the epic *Gebir* 1798 and *Imaginary Conversations of Literary Men and Statesmen* 1824–29.

Landowska Wanda 1877–1959. Polish harpsichordist and scholar. She founded a school near Paris for the study of early music, and was for many years one of the few artists regularly performing on the harpsichord. In 1941 she moved to the USA.

landscape architecture designing artificial landscapes, composed of both natural and man-made elements. Frederick Law Olmsted (1822–1903), who was responsible for the layout of Central Park, New York, 1857, is considered one of its earliest exponents. Today, the work of landscape architects frequently involves the creation of national parks, the reclamation of industrial sites, and, in the UK, the creation of 'new towns'. Following World War II, landscape architecture played a signficant role in the reconstruction of many European cities and towns.

landscape painting painting genre depicting natural scenery. In China, landscape painting was well established by the 8th century. In the West, it did not emerge as a distinct genre until the early 16th century, although backdrops of natural scenery were used from Roman times. It flourished in 17th-century Holland (Hobbema, Ruisdael) and France (Poussin, Claude Lorrain), in 18th-century Italy (Canaletto, Guardi), and in 19th-century England (Constable, Turner, Cotman). Examples include Hobbema's *The Avenue, Middelharnis* 1689 (National Gallery, London), Constable's *The ◊Haywain* 1821 (National Gallery, London), and Cézanne's *Aix: Rocky Landscape* 1885–87 (Tate Gallery, London).

Altdorfer's *Landscape with a Footbridge* about 1520 (National Gallery, London) is the first true landscape in Western art, although enhancement of the natural setting is evident in earlier works by ◊Giorgione and ◊Patinir.

Landseer Edwin Henry 1802–1873. English painter, sculptor, and engraver of animal studies. Much of his work reflects the Victorian taste for sentimental and moralistic pictures, for example *Dignity and Impudence* 1839 (Tate Gallery, London). The *Monarch of the Glen* 1850 (John Dewar and Sons Ltd), depicting a highland stag, was painted for the House of Lords. His sculptures include the lions at the base of Nelson's Column in Trafalgar Square, London, 1857–67.

If people only knew as much about painting as I do, they would never buy my pictures.

Edwin Landseer
quoted in C Lennie Landseer *The Victorian*

Lane Edward William 1801–1876. English traveller and translator, one of the earliest English travellers to Egypt to learn Arabic; his pseudo-scholarly writings, including *Manners and Customs of the Modern Egyptians* 1836 and an annotated translation of the *Arabian Nights* 1838–40, propagated a stereotyped image of the Arab world.

Lang Andrew 1844–1912. Scottish historian and folklore scholar. His writings include historical works; anthropological essays, such as *Myth, Ritual and Religion* 1887 and *The Making of Religion* 1898, which involved him in controversy with the anthropologist James G Frazer; novels; and a series of children's books, beginning with *The Blue Fairy Tale Book* 1889.

Lang Fritz 1890–1976. Austrian film director whose films are characterized by a strong sense of fatalism and alienation. His German films include *Metropolis* 1927, the sensational *M* 1931, in which Peter Lorre starred as a child-killer, and the series of Dr Mabuse films, after which he fled from the Nazis to Hollywood 1935. His US films include *Fury* 1936, *You Only Live Once* 1937, *Scarlet Street*

1945, *Rancho Notorious* 1952, and *The Big Heat* 1953. He returned to Germany and directed a third picture in the Dr Mabuse series 1960.

lang k d 1961– . Canadian singer whose mellifluous voice and androgynous image gained her a wide following beyond the country-music field where she first established herself. Her albums are *Angel With a Lariat* 1987, *Shadowland* 1988, *Absolute Torch and Twang* 1989, the mainstream *Ingénue* 1992 and *Even Cowgirls get the Blues*, 1993.

As a vocalist, she has been particularly influenced by US country singer Patsy Cline, whose material she often covers. She made her debut as an actress 1992 starring in the film *Salmonberries* by Percy Adlon.

Lange Dorothea 1895–1965. US photographer who was hired 1935 by the federal Farm Security Administration to document the westward migration of farm families from the Dust Bowl of the southern central USA. Her photographs, characterized by a gritty realism, were widely exhibited and subsequently published as *An American Exodus: A Record of Human Erosion* 1939.

Langland William c. 1332–c. 1400. English poet. His alliterative *Vision Concerning Piers Plowman* appeared in three versions between about 1367 and 1386, but some critics believe he was responsible for only the first of these. The poem forms a series of allegorical visions, in which Piers develops from the typical poor peasant to a symbol of Jesus, and condemns the social and moral evils of 14th-century England.

In a somer season, when soft was the sonne.

William Langland
Vision Concerning Piers Plowman. Prologue

Langtry Lillie. Stage name of Emilie Charlotte le Breton 1853–1929. English actress, mistress of the future Edward VII. She was known as the 'Jersey Lily' from her birthplace in the Channel Islands and considered to be one of the most beautiful women of her time.

She was the daughter of a rector, and married Edward Langtry (died 1897) in 1874. She first appeared professionally in London 1881, and had her greatest success as Rosalind in Shakespeare's *As You Like It*. In 1899 she married Sir Hugo de Bathe.

Lanier Sidney 1842–1881. US flautist and poet. His *Poems* 1877 contain interesting metrical experiments, in accordance with the theories expounded in his *Science of English Verse* 1880, on the relation of verse to music.

Lanvin Jeanne 1867–1946. French fashion designer known for her mother-and-daughter ensembles, which she began making in the early 1900s. The influence of Oriental patterns 1910 led her to create Eastern-style evening wear in velvet and satin, and she became well known for her chemise-style designs just before World War I. Her work was characterized by fine craftsmanship and embroidery and her label became a prosperous couture business.

Laocoön in classical mythology, a Trojan priest of Apollo and a visionary, brother of Anchises. He and his sons were killed by serpents when he foresaw disaster for Troy in the ◊Trojan horse left by the Greeks. The scene of their death is the subject of a classical marble group, rediscovered in the Renaissance, and forms an episode in Virgil's *Aeneid*.

Lapiths in Greek mythology, a people of Thessaly in northern Greece, often represented in Greek art in a battle with their neighbours the ◊centaurs (half man and half horse) at the wedding of their king, Pirithous.

Lardner Ring(old Wilmer) 1885–1933. US short-story writer. A sports reporter, he based his characters on the people he met professionally. His collected volumes of short stories include *You Know Me, Al* 1916, *Round Up* 1929, and *Ring Lardner's Best Short Stories* 1938, all written in colloquial language.

lares and penates in Roman mythology, spirits of the farm and of the store cupboard, often identified with the family ancestors, whose shrine was the centre of worship in Roman homes.

Larionov Mikhail Fedorovich 1881–1964. Russian painter, active in Paris from 1919. With his wife Natalia Goncharova, he pioneered a semi-abstract style known as **Rayonnism** in which subjects appear to be deconstructed by rays of light from various sources. He is best remembered for his childlike *Soldier* series 1908–11, which was heavily influenced by Russian folk art. Larionov also produced stage sets for Diaghilev's Ballets Russes from 1915. In Paris he continued to work as a theatrical designer and book illustrator.

Larkin Philip 1922–1985. English poet. His perfectionist, pessimistic verse includes *The North Ship* 1945, *The Whitsun Weddings* 1964, and *High Windows* 1974. He edited *The Oxford Book of 20th-Century English Verse* 1973.

Born in Coventry, Larkin was educated at Oxford, and from 1955 was librarian at Hull University. He also wrote two novels.

Deprivation is for me what daffodils were for Wordsworth.

Philip Larkin in the *Observer* 1979

La Rochefoucauld François, duc de La Rochefoucauld 1613–1680. French writer. His *Réflexions, ou sentences et maximes morales/ Reflections, or Moral Maxims* 1665 is a collection of brief, epigrammatic, and cynical observations on life and society, with the epigraph 'Our virtues are mostly our vices in disguise'. He was a lover of Mme de ◊Lafayette.

Born in Paris, he became a soldier, and took part in the Fronde revolts against the administration of chief minister Mazarin during Louis XIV's minority. His later years were divided between the court and literary society.

One is never so happy or so unhappy as one thinks.

La Rochefoucauld *Maxims*

Larsson Carl 1853–1919. Swedish painter, engraver, and illustrator. His watercolours of domestic life, subtly coloured and full of detail, were painted for his book *Ett Hem/A Home* 1899.

Lartigue Jacques-Henri 1894–1986. French photographer. He began taking photographs of his family at the age of seven, and went on to make ◊autochrome colour prints of women. During his lifetime he took over 40,000 photographs, documenting everyday people and situations.

Lascaux cave system in SW France with prehistoric wall paintings. It is richly decorated with realistic and symbolic paintings of buffaloes, horses, and red deer of the Upper Palaeolithic period, about 18,000 BC. The caves, near Montignac in the Dordogne, were discovered 1940. Similar paintings are found in ◊Altamira, Spain. The opening of the Lascaux caves to tourists led to deterioration of the paintings; the caves were closed 1963 and a facsimile opened 1983.

Lascaux is the Parthenon of prehistory.

Cyril Connolly
on Lascaux *Ideas and Places* 1953

Lasdun Denys 1914– . English Modernist architect. Many of his designs emphasize the horizontal layering of a building, creating the effect of geological strata extending into the surrounding city or landscape. This effect can be seen in his designs for the University of East Anglia, Norwich, 1962–68, and the National Theatre on London's South Bank 1976–77. Other works of note include Keeling House council flats, Bethnal Green, London, 1952–55 and the Royal College of Physicians in Regent's Park, London, 1960–64.

Lassus Roland de, also known as *Orlando di Lasso c.* 1532–1594. Franco-Flemish composer. His works include polyphonic sacred music, songs, and madrigals, including settings of poems by his friend ◊Ronsard, *'Bonjour mon coeur'/'Good day my heart'* 1564 being one of them.

Latin literature literature written in the Latin language.

early literature Only a few hymns and inscriptions survive from the earliest period of Latin literature before the 3rd century BC. Greek influence began with the work of Livius Andronicus (*c.* 284–204 BC), who translated the *Odyssey* and Greek plays into Latin. Naevius and Ennius both attempted epics on patriotic themes; the former used the native 'Saturnian' metre, but the latter introduced the Greek hexameter. Plautus and Terence successfully adapted Greek comedy to the Latin stage. Lucilius (190–103 BC) founded Latin verse satire, while the writings of Cato the Elder were the first important works in Latin prose.

Golden Age (70 BC–AD 18) In the *De Rerum natura* of Lucretius, and the passionate lyrics of Catullus, Latin verse reached maturity. Cicero set a standard for Latin prose, in his orations, philosophical essays, and letters. To the same period of the Roman republic belong the commentaries of Caesar on his own campaigns.

Augustan Age (43 BC–AD 18) Within the Golden Age, this is usually regarded as the finest period of Latin literature. There is strong patriotic feeling in the work of the poets Virgil and Horace and the historian Livy, who belonged to the emperor Augustus' court circle. Virgil produced the one great Latin epic, the *Aeneid*, while Horace brought charm and polish to both lyric and satire. Younger poets of the period were Ovid, who wrote ironically about love and mythology, and the elegiac and erotic poets Tibullus and Propertius.

Silver Age (18–c. 130) The second major period of imperial literature begins with the writers of Nero's reign: the Stoic philosopher Seneca; Lucan, author of the epic *Pharsalia*; the satirist Persius; and the novelist Petronius. Around the end of the 1st century and at the beginning of the 2nd came the historian and annalist Tacitus and the satirical poet Juvenal; other writers of this period were the epigrammatist Martial, the scientific encyclopedist Pliny the Elder, the letter-writer Pliny the Younger, the critic Quintilian, the historian Suetonius, and the epic poet Statius.

2nd–5th century Only one pagan writer of importance appeared, the romancer Apuleius, but there were some able Christian writers, such as Tertullian and Cyprian, who were followed by Arnobius (died 327) and Lactantius (died 325). In the 4th century there was a poetic revival, with Ausonius, Claudian, and the Christian poets Prudentius and St Ambrose. The Classical period ends, and the Middle Ages begin, with St Augustine's *City of God* and St Jerome's translation of the Bible in the 5th century.

Middle Ages Throughout the Middle Ages, Latin remained the language of the church and was normally employed for theology, philosophy, histories, and other learned works. Latin verse, adapted to rhyme and non-classical metres, was used both for hymns and for the secular songs of scholars, as in the ◊Carmina Burana. Medieval Latin vernacular gradually evolved into the regional and national Romance languages, including French, Italian, and Spanish. Even after the Reformation, Latin retained its prestige as the international language of scholars and was used as such by the English writers Thomas More, Francis Bacon, John Milton, and many others.

La Tour Georges de 1593–1652. French painter, active in Lorraine. He was patronized by the duke of Lorraine, Richelieu, and perhaps also by Louis XIII. Many of his pictures are illuminated by a single source of light, with deep contrasts of light and shade, as in *Joseph the Carpenter* about 1645 (Louvre, Paris). They range from religious paintings to domestic genre scenes.

Latvian literature religious works were composed in the 16th century or earlier but an ancient heritage of oral folk song survived to be a major influence on the literature of the mid-19th-century national awakening, such as the lyric poetry of Juris Alunāns (1832–1864) and the epic *Lāčplēsis/Bearslayer* 1888 by Andrejs Pumpurs (1841–1902). Despite realist and symbolist interludes, the folk tradition has been a major influence on 20th-century verse and prose, stimulated by the movement for independence from Germany and Russia. Though many poets and novelists are scattered in exile, the national literature is sustained by writers such as the dramatist Martins Zīverts (1903–) and the lyric poet Veronika Strēlerte (1912–).

Lauder Harry. Stage name of Hugh MacLennan 1870–1950. Scottish music-hall comedian and singer who began his career as an 'Irish' comedian.

Laughton Charles 1899–1962. English actor who became a US citizen 1950. Initially a classical stage actor, he joined the Old Vic 1933. His films include such roles as the king in *The Private Life of Henry VIII* 1933 (Academy Award), Captain Bligh in *Mutiny on the Bounty* 1935, and Quasimodo in *The Hunchback of Notre Dame* 1939. In 1955 he directed *Night of the Hunter* and in 1962 appeared in *Advise and Consent*.

Method actors give you a photograph.
Real actors give you an oil painting.

Charles Laughton in *Playboy* 1962

Laurel and Hardy Stan Laurel (stage name of Arthur Stanley Jefferson) (1890–1965) and Oliver Hardy (1892–1957). US film comedians who were one of the most successful comedy teams in film history (Stan was slim, Oliver rotund). Their partnership began 1927, survived the transition from silent films to sound, and resulted in more than 200 short and feature-length films. Among these are *Pack Up Your Troubles* 1932, *Our Relations* 1936, and *A Chump at Oxford* 1940.

Laurel, a British-born former music-hall comedian, produced several of their feature films notably *Way Out West* 1937.

Lauren Ralph 1939– . US fashion designer, producing menswear under the Polo label from 1968, women's wear from 1971, children's wear, and home furnishings from 1983. He also designed costumes for the films *The Great Gatsby* 1973 and *Annie Hall* 1977.

Laurence Margaret 1926–1987. Canadian writer whose novels include *The Stone Angel* 1964 and *A Jest of God* 1966, both set in the Canadian prairies, and *The Diviners* 1974. She also wrote short stories set in Africa, where she lived for a time. She is particularly adept at demonstrating the interactions of character and environment and tracing the mental processes of suspicion and defensive deviousness.

Lavery John 1856–1941. Irish portrait-painter of Edwardian society, who studied in Glasgow, London, and Paris. He was influenced by the Impressionists and Whistler.

Lawes Henry 1596–1662. British composer whose works include music for Milton's masque *Comus* 1634. His brother **William Lawes** (1602–1645) was also a composer, notably for viol consort.

Lawler Ray(mond Evenor) 1921– . Australian actor and dramatist whose work includes *The Summer of the Seventeenth Doll* 1955, a play about sugar-cane cutters, in which he played the lead role in the first production in Melbourne.

Lawrence D(avid) H(erbert) 1885–1930. English writer whose work expresses his belief in emotion and the sexual impulse as creative and true to human nature. The son of a Nottinghamshire miner, Lawrence studied at University College, Nottingham, and became a teacher. His writing first received attention after the publication of the semi-autobiographical *Sons and Lovers* 1913, which includes a portrayal of his mother (died 1911). Other novels include *The Rainbow* 1915, *Women in Love* 1921, and *Lady Chatterley's Lover* 1928. Lawrence also wrote short stories (for example 'The Woman Who Rode Away') and poetry.

In 1914 he married Frieda von Richthofen, ex-wife of his university professor, with whom he had run away 1912. Frieda was the model for Ursula Brangwen in *The Rainbow*, which was suppressed for obscenity, and its sequel, *Women in Love*. Lawrence's travels in search of health (he suffered from tuberculosis, from which he eventually died near Nice) prompted books such as *Mornings in Mexico* 1927. *Lady Chatterley's Lover* was banned as obscene in the UK until 1960.

I like to write when I feel spiteful: it's like having a good sneeze.

D H Lawrence
letter to Lady Cynthia Asquith Nov 1913

Lawrence Gertrude 1898–1952. English actress who began as a dancer in the 1920s and later took leading roles in musical comedies. Her greatest successes were in the play *Private Lives* 1930–31, written especially for her by Noël Coward, with whom she co-starred, and *The King and I* 1951.

Lawrence T(homas) E(dward), known as *Lawrence of Arabia* 1888–1935. English scholar, translator, and soldier. Appointed to the military intelligence department in Cairo, Egypt, during World War I, he took part in negotiations for an Arab revolt against the Ottoman Turks, and in 1916 attached himself to the emir Faisal. He became a guerrilla leader of genius, combining raids on Turkish communications with the organization of a joint Arab revolt, described in *The Seven Pillars of Wisdom* 1926.

Lawrence Thomas 1769–1830. English painter, the leading portraitist of his day. He became painter to George III 1792 and president of the Royal Academy 1820–30. *Queen Charlotte* 1789 (National Gallery, London) is one of his finest portraits.

In addition to British royalty, he painted a series of European sovereigns and dignitaries, including Pope Pius VIII (Waterloo Chamber, Windsor Castle, Berkshire) commissioned after the Allied victory at Waterloo.

Lawson Henry 1867–1922. Australian short-story writer. First noted for verse about bush life and social and political protest, he is now remembered chiefly for his stories. Direct experience of travelling in the outback in a severe drought 1892 reinforced the grim realism of his vision of Australian rural life. His best work, represented by the collections *While the Billy Boils* 1896 and *Joe Wilson and his Mates* 1901, is sharply detailed, colloquial, and ironically understated.

Laxness Halldor 1902– . Icelandic novelist who wrote about Icelandic life in the style of the early sagas. His novel *Salka Valka* 1931–32 is a vivid, realistic portrayal of a small fishing community and centres on a strong female character. He was awarded a Nobel prize 1955.

Layamon lived about 1200. English poet, author of the *Brut*, a chronicle of about 30,000 alliterative lines on the history of Britain from the legendary Brutus onwards, which gives the earliest version of the Arthurian legend in English.

Lazarus Emma 1849–1887. US poet, author of the poem on the base of the Statue of Liberty that begins: 'Give me your tired, your poor/Your huddled masses yearning to breathe free.'

Leach Bernard 1887–1979. British potter. His simple designs, inspired by a period of study in Japan, pioneered a revival of the art. He established the Leach Pottery at St Ives, Cornwall, 1920.

Leacock Stephen Butler 1869–1944. Canadian economist and humorist. His humour has survived his often rather conservative political writings. His butts include the urban plutocracy and (in the parodies of *Frenzied Fictions* 1918) popular fiction, as well as human folly generally. His other humorous works include *Literary Lapses* 1910 and the controversial because recognizable *Sunshine Sketches of a Little Town* 1912.

Leadbelly stage name of Huddie Ledbetter *c.* 1889–1949. US blues and folk singer, songwriter, and guitarist who was a source of inspiration for the urban folk movement of the 1950s. He was 'discovered' in prison by folklorists John Lomax (1875–1948) and Alan Lomax (1915–), who helped him begin a professional concert and recording career 1934. His songs include 'Rock Island Line' and 'Good Night, Irene'.

leading note in music, the seventh note of an ascending ◊diatonic scale, so-called because it 'leads' inevitably to the upper tonic or key note. It is tuned ◊sharp in minor keys to maintain its leading character.

Lean David 1908–1991. English film director. His films, noted for their painstaking craftsmanship, include early work codirected with playwright Noël Coward. *Brief Encounter* 1946 established Lean as a leading talent. Among his later films are such accomplished epics as *The Bridge on the River Kwai* 1957 (Academy Award), *Lawrence of Arabia* 1962 (Academy Award), and *Dr Zhivago* 1965. The unfavourable reaction to *Ryan's Daughter* 1970 caused him to withdraw from filmmaking for over a decade, but *A Passage to India* 1984 represented a return to form.

---

*And hand in hand, on the edge of the sand/
They danced by the light of the moon.*

Edward Lear
'The Owl and the Pussy-Cat' 1871

Lear Edward 1812–1888. English artist and humorist. His *Book of Nonsense* 1846 popularized the limerick (a five-line humorous verse). He first attracted attention by his paintings of birds, and

later turned to landscapes. He travelled to Italy, Greece, Egypt, and India, publishing books on his travels with his own illustrations, and spent most of his later life in Italy.

Leatherstocking Tales, The five novels by James Fenimore ◊Cooper, describing the ideal US frontiersman, Natty Bumppo, also known as Leatherstocking or the Deerslayer: *The Pioneers* 1823, *The Last of the Mohicans* 1826, *The Prairie* 1827, *The Pathfinder* 1840, and *The Deerslayer* 1841.

Leaves of Grass collection of poems by US writer Walt ◊Whitman, published anonymously 1855 and augmented through many editions up to 1892. With its long lines, 'barbaric yawp' metre, and all-embracing, mythic ambition, the book exercised a major influence on US verse. See also ◊'Song of Myself'.

Leavis F(rank) R(aymond) 1895–1978. English literary critic. With his wife Q D Leavis (1906–1981) he cofounded and edited the review *Scrutiny* 1932–53. He championed the work of D H Lawrence and James Joyce and in 1962 attacked C P Snow's theory of 'The Two Cultures' (the natural alienation of the arts and sciences in intellectual life). His other works include *New Bearings in English Poetry* 1932 and *The Great Tradition* 1948. He was a lecturer at Cambridge University.

Poetry can communicate the actual quality of experience with a subtlety and precision unapproachable by any other means.

F R Leavis
New Bearings in English Poetry 1932

Le Brun Charles 1619–1690. French artist, court painter to Louis XIV from 1662. In 1663 he became director of the French Academy and of the Gobelins factory, which produced art, tapestries, and furnishings for the new palace of Versailles.

In the 1640s he studied under the painter Poussin in Rome, returning to Paris 1646. He worked on large decorative schemes including the *Galerie des Glaces* (Hall of Mirrors) at Versailles 1679–84. He also painted portraits.

A committee is an animal with four back legs.

John Le Carré
Tinker, Tailor, Soldier, Spy 1974

Le Carré John. Pen name of David John Cornwell 1931– . English writer of thrillers. His low-key realistic accounts of espionage include *The Spy Who Came in from the Cold* 1963, *Tinker, Tailor, Soldier, Spy* 1974, *Smiley's People* 1980, and *The Russia House* 1989. He was a member of the Foreign Service 1960–64.

Leclair Jean-Marie 1697–1764. French violinist and composer. Originally a dancer and ballet-master, he composed ballet music, an opera, *Scilla et Glaucus*, and violin concertos.

Leconte de Lisle Charles Marie René 1818–1894. French poet. He was born on the Indian Ocean Island of Réunion, settled in Paris 1846, and headed the anti-Romantic group *Les ◊Parnassiens* 1866–76. His work drew inspiration from the ancient world, as in *Poèmes antiques/ Antique Poems* 1852, *Poèmes barbares/Barbaric Poems* 1862, and *Poèmes tragiques/Tragic Poems* 1884.

Le Corbusier adopted name of Charles-Edouard Jeanneret 1887–1965. Swiss-born French architect, an early and influential exponent of the ◊Modern Movement and one of the most innovative of 20th-century architects. His distinct brand of Functionalism first appears in his town-planning proposals of the early 1920s, which advocate 'vertical garden cities' (multi-storey villas, zoning of living and working areas, and traffic separation) as solutions to urban growth and chaos. From the 1940s several of his designs for multi-storey villas were realized, notably his Unité d'habitation, Marseilles, 1947–52 (now demolished), using his modulor system of standard-sized units mathematically calculated according to the proportions of the human figure.

His white-stuccoed, Cubist-style villas of the 1920s were designed as 'machines for living in', maximizing on space and light through open-plan interiors, use of *pilotis* (stilts carrying the building), and roof gardens. He moved on to a more expressive mode (anticipating ◊Brutalism) with rough, unfinished exteriors, as in the Ministry of Education, Rio de Janeiro, 1936–45, designed with Lucio Costa (1902–) and Oscar ◊Niemeyer. In the post-war reconstruction period, his urbanization theories were highly influential, disseminated through the work of the urban planning body ◊CIAM, although only in the grid-like layout of the new city of Chandigarh, India, 1951–56, was he able to see his visions of urban zoning fully realized. His sculptural design for the church of Notre-Dame du Haut du Ronchamp 1950–54, worked out in the minutest detail, is a supreme example of aesthetic Functionalism.

Le Corbusier was originally a painter and engraver, but turned his attention to the problems of contemporary industrial society. His books *Vers une Architecture/Towards a New Architecture* 1923 and *Le Modulor* 1948 have had worldwide significance for town planning and building design.

> *A house is a machine for living in.*
> **Le Corbusier**
> *Vers une Architecture/Towards a New Architecture* 1923

Lecouvreur Adrienne 1692–1730. French actress. She performed at the Comédie Française national theatre, where she first appeared 1717. Her many admirers included the philosopher Voltaire and the army officer Maurice de Saxe; a rival mistress of the latter, the Duchesse de Bouillon, is thought to have poisoned her.

Leda in Greek mythology, the wife of Tyndareus and mother of ◊Clytemnestra. Zeus, who came to her as a swan, was the father of her other children: ◊Helen of Troy and the twins ◊Castor and Pollux.

Ledoux Claude-Nicolas 1736–1806. French Neo-Classical architect, stylistically comparable to E L ◊Boullée in his use of austere, geometric forms, exemplified in his series of 44 toll houses surrounding Paris (of which only four remain), notably the Barrière de la Villette in the Place de Stalingrad, Paris, 1785–89.

Led Zeppelin UK rock group 1969–80, founders of ◊heavy metal. Their overblown style, with long solos, was based on rhythm and blues; songs like 'Stairway to Heaven' have become classics.

Jimmy Page (1944–), a former member of the Yardbirds, had been an important 1960s session guitarist; the drumming of John Bonham (1948–1980) is said to have been digitally sampled more often than any other. The vocalist was Robert Plant (1948–).

Lee Bruce. Stage name of Lee Yuen Kam 1941–1973. US 'Chinese Western' film actor, an expert in kung fu, who popularized the Oriental martial arts in the West with pictures such as *Fists of Fury* 1972 (made in Hong Kong) and *Enter the Dragon* 1973, his last film.

Lee Christopher 1922– . English film actor whose gaunt figure was memorable in the title role of *Dracula* 1958 and several of its sequels. He has not lost his sinister image in subsequent Hollywood productions. His other films include *Hamlet* 1948, *The Mummy* 1959, *Julius Caesar* 1970, and *The Man with the Golden Gun* 1974.

Lee Gypsy Rose 1914–1970. US entertainer. An 'elegant lady' in striptease routines, she was popular in literary circles. Also a published author, she wrote two mystery novels *The G-String Murders* 1941 and *Mother Finds a Body* 1942. Her autobiography *Gypsy: A Memoir* 1957 was adapted for stage 1959 and film 1962.

Lee Laurie 1914– . English writer, born near Stroud, Gloucestershire. His works include the autobiographical novel *Cider with Rosie* 1959, a classic evocation of a rural childhood; nature poetry such as *The Bloom of Candles* 1947; and travel writing including *A Rose for Winter* 1955.

Lee Nathaniel 1653–1692. English dramatist. From 1675 on, he wrote a number of extravagant tragedies, such as *The Rival Queens* 1677, about the two wives of Alexander the Great.

Lee Spike (Shelton Jackson) 1957– . US film director, actor and writer. His work presents the bitter realities of contemporary African-American life in an aggressive, often controversial manner. His films, in which he sometimes appears, include *She's Gotta Have It* 1986, *Do The Right Thing* 1989, *Jungle Fever* 1991, and *Malcolm X* 1992.

Leech John 1817–1864. English caricaturist. He illustrated many books, including Dickens' *A Christmas Carol*, and during 1841–64 contributed about 3,000 humorous drawings and political cartoons to *Punch* magazine.

Le Fanu (Joseph) Sheridan 1814–1873. Irish writer, born in Dublin. He wrote mystery novels and short stories, such as *The House by the Churchyard* 1863, *Uncle Silas* 1864, and *In a Glass Darkly* 1872.

Left Book Club book club formed in Britain 1936 to circulate to its members political books intended to counter the upsurge of fascism. Its founder was the publisher Victor ◊Gollancz. It produced mainly non-fiction, of which an example is George Orwell's *The Road to Wigan Pier* 1937. It was disbanded 1948.

legato (Italian 'tied') term used to describe music that is phrased smoothly and continuously.

legend (Latin *legendum* 'to be read') traditional or undocumented story about famous people. The term was originally applied to the books of readings designed for use in Christian religious service, and was extended to the stories of saints read in monasteries. A collection of such stories was the 13th-century *Legenda Aurea/The Golden Legend* by Jacobus de Voragine.

Léger Fernand 1881–1955. French painter and designer, associated with ◊Cubism. From around 1909 he evolved a characteristic style of simplified forms, clear block outlines, and bold colours. Mechanical forms are constant themes in his work, which includes designs for the Swedish Ballet 1921–22, murals, and the abstract film *Ballet mécanique/Mechanical Ballet* 1924.

leggings knitted protective leg-covering, reaching from knee to ankle, worn by dancers; also, a waist-to-ankle figure-hugging fashion garment of the 1980s and 1990s encasing the legs in a stretch fabric, typically lycra. Worn mainly by women, leggings evolved from the sportswear of the 1970s fitness cult.

Le Gray Gustave 1820–1882. French photographer who in 1850 invented the waxed paper negative, a more efficient version of the ◊calotype where the paper is waxed before being coated with silver iodide. He also experimented with printing images using more than one negative, notably in his detailed seascapes which use a separate negative for sea and sky.

Le Guin Ursula K(roeber) 1929– . US writer of science fiction and fantasy. Her novels include *The Left Hand of Darkness* 1969, which questions sex roles; the *Earthsea* series 1968–91; *The Dispossessed* 1974, which compares an anarchist and a capitalist society; *Orsinian Tales* 1976; and *Always Coming Home* 1985.

legwarmers long, knitted, footless socks worn from thigh to ankle, originally used by dancers to keep muscles warm. In the early 1970s, as keep-fit and disco dancing became fashionable, legwarmers were worn with bodysuits and leotards, and sometimes for everyday wear over tight-fitting jeans.

Lehár Franz 1870–1948. Hungarian composer. He wrote many operettas, among them *The Merry Widow* 1905, *The Count of Luxembourg* 1909, *Gypsy Love* 1910, and *The Land of Smiles* 1929. He also composed songs, marches, and a violin concerto.

Lehmann Lotte 1888–1976. German soprano. She excelled in Wagnerian operas and was an outstanding Marschallin in Richard ◊Strauss' *Der Rosenkavalier*.

Lehmann Rosamond (Nina) 1901–1990. English novelist whose books include *Dusty Answer* 1927, *The Weather in the Streets* 1936, *The Echoing Grove* 1953, and, following a long silence, *A Sea-Grape Tree* 1976. Once neglected as too romantic, her novels have regained popularity in the 1980s because of their sensitive portrayal of female adolescence.

One can present people with opportunities.
One cannot make them equal to them.

Rosamond Lehmann
The Ballad and the Source 1944

Lehmbruck Wilhelm 1881–1919. German sculptor, painter, and printmaker, a leading Expressionist of the early 1900s, whose elongated, sorrowing figures carry great emotional power. His principal works are a distillation of archaic and classical forms, their pathos derived from the artist's innate melancholy and his impressions of the chaos of war. *The Fallen* 1915–16 (Lehmbruck Estate, Duisburg) is a late masterpiece in cast stone.

Leiber and Stoller Jerry Leiber 1933– and Mike Stoller 1933– . US songwriters and record producers who wrote a number of classic pop and rock songs of the 1950s and early 1960s, including hits for vocal group the Coasters ('Riot in Cell Block Number Nine' 1953, 'Searchin'' 1957, 'Poison Ivy' 1959) and songs for early Elvis Presley films such as 'Jailhouse Rock' 1957. Storytelling and tongue-in-cheek humour characterize their work, ranging from 'Love Potion Number Nine' (a 1959 hit for vocal group the Clovers) to 'Is That All There Is?' (a 1969 hit for jazz singer Peggy Lee 1920–). They worked as producers with pop/soul vocal group the Drifters in the 1960s.

Leiber and Stoller met in California 1949 and began collaborating on rhythm-and-blues material, Leiber writing the lyrics and Stoller the music.

Leibovitz Annie 1950– . US photographer whose elaborately staged portraits of American celebrities appeared first in *Rolling Stone* magazine and later in *Vanity Fair*. The odd poses in which her sitters allow themselves to be placed suggest an element of self-mockery.

Leigh Mike 1943– . English dramatist and filmmaker, noted for his sharp, carefully improvised social satires. He directs his own plays, which evolve through improvisation before they are scripted. His work for television includes *Nuts in May* 1976 and *Abigail's Party* 1977; his films include *High Hopes* 1989, *Life Is Sweet* 1991, and *Naked* 1993.

Leigh Vivien. Stage name of Vivien Mary Hartley 1913–1967. Indian-born English actress who appeared on the stage in London and New York, and won Academy Awards for her performances as Scarlett O'Hara in *Gone With the Wind* 1939 and as Blanche du Bois in *A Streetcar Named Desire* 1951.

She was married to Laurence Olivier 1940–60 and starred with him in the play *Antony and Cleopatra* 1951. Her films include *Lady Hamilton* 1941, *Anna Karenina* 1948, and *Ship of Fools* 1965.

Leighton Frederic, Baron Leighton 1830–1896. English painter and sculptor. He specialized in Classical Greek subjects such as *Captive Andromache* 1888 (Manchester City Art Gallery). He became president of the Royal Academy 1878. His house and studio near Holland Park, London, is now a museum.

leitmotif (German 'leading motif') in music, a recurring theme or motif used to illustrate a character or idea. Wagner frequently used this technique in his operas, and it was later adopted in music for film.

Lelong Lucien 1889–1958. French couturier who opened a fashion house 1923. He created models for his wife, the society beauty Princess Natalie Paley, who publicized his style. In the 1920s he became one of the first couturiers to establish a boutique (Lelong Editions) selling ready-to-wear clothes; they cost £10–20, whereas model (haute couture) dresses were between 50 and 100 guineas. During World War II he was head of the Chambre Syndicale de la Haute Couture.

Lely Peter. Adopted name of Pieter van der Faes 1618–1680. Dutch painter, active in England from 1641, who painted fashionable portraits in the style of van Dyck. His subjects included Charles I, Cromwell, and Charles II. He painted a series of admirals, *Flagmen* (National Maritime Museum, London), and one of *The Windsor Beauties* (Hampton Court, Richmond), fashionable women of Charles II's court.

Lemmon Jack (John Uhler III) 1925– . US character actor, often cast as the lead in comedy films, such as *Some Like It Hot* 1959 but equally skilled in serious roles, as in *The China Syndrome* 1979, *Save the Tiger* 1973 (Academy Award), and *Missing* 1982.

Le Nain family of French painters, the brothers *Antoine* (c. 1588–1648), *Louis* (c. 1593–1648), and *Mathieu* (c. 1607–1677). They were born in Laon, settled in Paris, and were among the original members of the French Academy in 1648. Attribution of works among them is uncertain. They chiefly painted sombre and dignified scenes of peasant life.

L'Enfant Pierre Charles 1754–1825. French-born US architect and engineer, remembered for his survey and plan for the city of Washington 1791–92. Although he was dismissed from the project before he was able to design any major buildings, the constructed layout is much as he conceived it, clearly reflecting the plan of his native Versailles.

Lennon John (Ono) 1940–1980. UK rock singer, songwriter, and guitarist, in the USA from 1971; a founder member of the ◊Beatles. Both before the band's break-up 1970 and in his solo career, he collaborated intermittently with his wife Yoko Ono (1933–). 'Give Peace a Chance', a hit 1969, became an anthem of the peace movement. His solo work alternated between the confessional and the political, as on the album *Imagine* 1971. He was shot dead by a fan.

His first solo album, *John Lennon/Plastic Ono Band* 1970, contained deeply personal songs like 'Mother' and 'Working Class Hero'; subsequent work, though uneven, included big hits like 'Whatever Gets You Through the Night' 1974. He often worked with producer Phil ◊Spector. On *Rock 'n' Roll* 1975 Lennon covered nonoriginal songs that the Beatles had played in the early 1960s. *Double Fantasy* 1980, made in collaboration with Ono, reached number one in the album charts after his death.

At the height of Beatlemania, Lennon published two small books of his drawings and nonsense writings, *In His Own Write* 1964 and *A Spaniard in the Works* 1965.

Lennox Charlotte 1720–1804. American-born English novelist. Her popular novel *The Female Quixote* 1752 describes how the beautiful and intelligent Arabella creates comic misunderstandings through interpreting real life as if it were a French romance. Lennox died penniless in spite of producing *Shakespear Illustrated* 1753–54 (an anthology of Shakespearean sources), and the novels *Henrietta* 1753, *Sophia* 1761, and *Euphemia* 1790.

Leno Dan 1861–1904. British comedian. A former acrobat, he became the idol of the music halls, and was considered the greatest of ◊pantomime 'dames'.

Le Nôtre André 1613–1700. French landscape gardener, creator of the gardens at Versailles 1662–90 and les Tuileries, Paris. His grandiose scheme for Versailles complemented Le Vau's original design for the palace façade, extending its formal symmetry into the surrounding countryside with vast *parterres* (gardens having beds and paths arranged to form a pattern), radiating avenues, and unbroken vistas.

His earlier work at Vaux-le-Viscomte, outside Paris 1657–61, anticipates the Versailles plan, but on a smaller scale.

Lenya Lotte. Adopted name of Karoline Blamauer 1905–1981. Austrian actress and singer. She was married five times, twice to the composer Kurt ◊Weill, first in 1926, with whom she emigrated to the USA 1935. She appeared in several of the Brecht–Weill operas, notably *Die Dreigroschenoper/The Threepenny Opera* 1928. Her plain looks and untrained singing voice brought added realism to her stage roles.

Leonard Elmore (John, Jr) 1925– . US author of Westerns and thrillers, marked by vivid dialogue, as in *City Primeval* 1980, *La Brava* 1983, *Stick* 1983, *Glitz* 1985, *Freaky Deaky* 1988, and *Get Shorty* 1990.

Leonardo da Vinci 1452–1519. Italian painter, sculptor, architect, engineer, and scientist. One of the greatest figures of the Italian Renaissance, he was active in Florence, Milan, and, from 1516, France. As state engineer and court painter to the duke of Milan, he painted the *Last Supper* mural about 1495 (Sta Maria delle Grazie, Milan), and on his return to Florence painted the *Mona Lisa* (Louvre, Paris) about 1503–06. His notebooks and drawings show an immensely inventive and enquiring mind, studying aspects of the natural world from anatomy to aerodynamics.

Leonardo was born at Vinci in Tuscany and studied under ◊Verrocchio in Florence in the 1470s. His earliest dated work is a sketch of the Tuscan countryside 1473 (Uffizi, Florence); other early works include drawings, portraits, and religious scenes, such as the unfinished *Adoration of the Magi* (Uffizi), which was commissioned 1481. About 1482 he went to the court of Lodovico Sforza in Milan. In 1500 he returned to Florence (where he was architect and engineer to Cesare Borgia 1502), and then to Milan 1506. He went to France 1516 and died at Château de Cloux, near Amboise, on the river Loire. Apart from portraits, religious themes, and historical paintings, Leonardo's greatest legacies were his notebooks and drawings. He influenced many of his contemporary artists, including Michelangelo, Raphael, Giorgione, and Bramante. He also revolutionized painting style. Instead of a white background, he used a dark one to allow the overlying colour a more three-dimensional existence. He developed the use of 'aerial perspective' whereby the misty atmosphere changes the colours of the landscape as it dissolves into the distance, and also *sfumato*, the blurring of outlines through the use of subtle gradations of tone – both give his pictures their characteristic air of mysteriousness. His principle of grouping figures within an imaginary pyramid, linked by their gestures and facial expressions, became a High Renaissance compositional rule. His two versions of the Madonna and child with St Anne, *Madonna of the Rocks* (Louvre, Paris, and National Gallery, London) exemplify all these ideas. Other chief works include the ◊*Mona Lisa* (wife of Francesco del Giocondo, hence also known as *La Gioconda*) and the *Battle of Anghiari* 1504–05, formerly in the Palazzo Vecchio, Florence.

The poet ranks far below the painter in the representation of visible things – and far below the musician in that of invisible things.

Leonardo da Vinci from the *Notebooks*

Leoncavallo Ruggiero 1857–1919. Italian operatic composer, born in Naples. He played in restaurants, composing in his spare time, until the success of *I Pagliacci/The Strolling Players* 1892. His other operas include *La Bohème/The Bohemian Girl* 1897 (contemporary with Puccini's version) and *Zaza* 1900.

Leone Sergio 1928–1989. Italian film director, responsible for popularizing 'spaghetti' Westerns (Westerns made in Italy and Spain, usually with a US leading actor and a European supporting cast and crew) and making a world star of Clint ◊Eastwood. His films include *Per un pugno di dollari/A Fistful of Dollars* 1964, *C'era una volta il West/Once Upon a Time in the West* 1968, and *C'era una volta il America/Once Upon a Time in America* 1984.

Leonov Leonid 1899– . Russian novelist and playwright, author of the novels *The Badgers* 1925 and *The Thief* 1927, and the drama *The Orchards of Polovchansk* 1938.

Leopardi Giacomo, Count Leopardi 1798–1837. Italian romantic poet. The first collection of his uniquely pessimistic poems, *I Versi/Verses*, appeared 1824, and was followed by his philosophical *Operette morali/Minor Moral Works* 1827, in prose, and *I Canti/Lyrics* 1831.

Born at Recanati of a noble family, Leopardi wrote many of his finest poems, including his patriotic odes, before he was 21. Throughout his life he was tormented by ill health, by the consciousness of his deformity (he was hunchbacked), by loneliness and a succession of unhappy love affairs, and by his 'cosmic pessimism' and failure to find consolation in any philosophy.

leotard one-piece stretch garment, with or without sleeves, covering the body from the shoulders to the thighs, originally worn by acrobats and dancers and then for other sporting activities. The leotard became popular as fashion wear in the 1970s and 1980s. It derives its name from the French trapeze artist Jules Léotard (died 1870). The 'body' or 'bodysuit' introduced by Azzedine ◊Alaïa and worn under skirts, shorts, or trousers to achieve a smooth waistline, derives from the leotard.

Leppard Raymond 1927– . English conductor and musicologist whose imaginative reconstructions of Monteverdi and Cavalli operas did much to generate popular interest in early opera and to stimulate academic investigation of the performance implications of early music manuscript scores.

leprechaun (Old Irish 'small body') in Irish folklore, a fairy in the shape of an old man, sometimes conceived as a cobbler, with a hidden store of gold.

Lermontov Mikhail Yurevich 1814–1841. Russian Romantic poet and novelist. In 1837 he was sent into active military service in the Caucasus for writing a revolutionary poem on the death of Pushkin, which criticized court values, and for participating in a duel. Among his works are the psychological novel *A ◊Hero of Our Time* 1840 and a volume of poems *October* 1840.

Lerner Alan Jay 1918–1986. US lyricist, collaborator with Frederick Loewe on musicals including *Brigadoon* 1947, *Paint Your Wagon* 1951, *My Fair Lady* 1956, *Gigi* 1958, and *Camelot* 1960.

Le Sage Alain-René 1668–1747. French novelist and dramatist. Born in Brittany, he abandoned law for literature. His novels include *Le Diable boîteux/The Devil upon Two Sticks* 1707 and his picaresque masterpiece ◊*Gil Blas de Santillane* 1715–35, which is much indebted to Spanish originals.

Lessing Doris (May) (née Taylor) 1919– . British novelist, born in Iran. Concerned with social and political themes, particularly the place of women in society, her work includes *The Grass is Singing* 1950, the five-novel series *Children of Violence* 1952–69, *The Golden Notebook* 1962, *The Good Terrorist* 1985, and *The Fifth Child* 1988. She has also written an 'inner space fiction' series *Canopus in Argus: Archives* 1979–83, and under the pen name 'Jane Somers', *The Diary of a Good Neighbour* 1981.

Lessing Gotthold Ephraim 1729–1781. German dramatist and critic. His plays include *Miss Sara Sampson* 1755, *Minna von Barnhelm* 1767, *Emilia Galotti* 1772, and the verse play *Nathan der Weise* 1779. His works of criticism *Laokoon* 1766 and *Hamburgische Dramaturgie* 1767–68 influenced German literature. He also produced many theological and philosophical writings.

Laokoon analysed the functions of poetry and the plastic arts; *Hamburgische Dramaturgie* reinterpreted Aristotle and attacked the restrictive form of French classical drama in favour of the freer approach of Shakespeare.

A man who does not lose his reason over certain things has none to lose.

Gotthold Ephraim Lessing *Emilia Galotti*

Les Six (French 'The Six') a group of French composers: Georges Auric, Louis Durey (1888–1979), Arthur Honegger, Darius Milhaud, Francis Poulenc, and Germaine Tailleferre (1892–1983). Formed 1917, the group had Jean ◊Cocteau as its spokesman and adopted Erik ◊Satie as its guru; it was dedicated to producing works free from foreign influences and reflecting contemporary attitudes. The group split up in the early 1920s.

Lethaby William Richard 1857–1931. English architect. An assistant to Norman ◊Shaw, he embraced the principles of William Morris and Philip Webb in the ◊Arts and Crafts movement, and was cofounder and first director of the Central School of Arts and Crafts from 1894. He wrote a collection of essays entitled *Form in Civilization* 1922.

Lethe in Greek mythology, a river of the underworld whose waters, when drunk, brought forgetfulness of the past.

Leto in Greek mythology, a goddess, mother by Zeus of ◊Artemis and ◊Apollo, to whom she gave birth on the Aegean island of Delos, which became their sanctuary.

letter written or printed message, chiefly a personal communication. Letters are valuable as reflections of social conditions and of literary and political life. Legally, ownership of a letter (as a document) passes to the recipient, but the copyright remains with the writer.

Outstanding examples include:

ancient Cicero, Pliny the Younger, and St Paul;

medieval Abelard and Héloïse (12th-century France), the Paston family (15th-century England);

16th century Erasmus (the Netherlands), Luther, Melanchthon (Germany), Spenser, Sidney (England);

17th century Donne, Milton, Cromwell, Dorothy Osborne, Wotton (England); Pascal, Mme de Sévigné (France);

18th century Pope, Walpole, Swift, Mary Wortley Montagu, Chesterfield, Cowper, Gray (England); Bossuet, Voltaire, Rousseau (France);

19th century Emerson, J R Lowell (USA); Byron, Lamb, Keats, Fitzgerald, Stevenson (England); George Sand, Saint-Beuve, Goncourt brothers (France); Schiller, Goethe (Germany); Gottfried Keller (Switzerland);

20th century T E Lawrence, G B Shaw, Ellen Terry, Katherine Mansfield (England); Rilke (Germany).

The best letters seem to me the most delightful of all written things – and those that are not the best the most negligible.

Henry James on letters 1899

Let Us Now Praise Famous Men book 1941 (begun 1936) by US writer James ◊Agee and US photographer Walker ◊Evans. Agee's impressionistic prose and Evans' stark pictures record the dignified poverty of three Southern white cotton farmers during the Depression. It is a unique work of social documentary.

Le Vau Louis 1612–1670. French architect, a leading exponent of the Baroque style. His design for the château of Vaux-le-Vicomte outside Paris (begun 1657) provided the inspiration for the remodelling of Versailles, on which he worked from 1669. Many of Le Vau's additions to the palace, notably the elegantly symmetrical garden façade, were altered by later enlargements under ◊Hardouin-Mansart. Le Vau also contributed to the east front of the Louvre 1667 and designed les Tuileries, Paris.

Lever Charles James 1806–1872. Irish novelist. He wrote novels of Irish and army life, such as *Harry Lorrequer* 1837, *Charles O'Malley* 1840, and *Tom Burke of Ours* 1844.

Levertov Denise 1923– . English-born US poet. She published her first volume of poetry *The Double Image* 1946, after which she moved to America. In the 1950s she was associated with the ◊Black Mountain poets, and in the 1960s campaigned for civil rights. Poetry collections include *Here and Now* 1957 and *Candles in Babylon* 1982; her essays on political, feminist, and creative issues appeared in *O Taste and See* 1964 and *The Poet in the World* 1973.

Levi Primo 1919–1987. Italian novelist. He joined the anti-Fascist resistance during World War II, was captured, and sent to the concentration camp at Auschwitz. He wrote of these experiences in *Se questo è un uomo/If This Is a Man* 1947. His other books, all based on his experience of the war, include *Periodic Tables* 1975 and *Moments of Reprieve* 1981.

leviathan in the Old Testament, a sea monster (thought to be the whale), later associated in Christian literature with Satan. The term was also used to describe the monstrous qualities of wealth or power invested in one person, as in the political treatise *Leviathan* by the English philosopher Thomas Hobbes.

Levinson Barry 1932– . US film director and screenwriter. Working in Hollywood's mainstream, he has been responsible for some of the best adult comedy films of the 1980s and 1990s. Winning cult status for the offbeat realism of *Diner* 1982, Levinson went on to make such large-budget movies as *Good Morning Vietnam* 1987, *Tin Men* 1987, *Rain Man* 1988 (Academy Awards for best picture and best director), *Bugsy* 1991, and *Toys* 1992.

Levinson began his career as a scriptwriter for television comedy programmes such as *The Carol Burnett Show*. Later, he turned to writing feature films such as *High Anxiety* 1977 (with Mel Brooks), *And Justice For All* 1979, and *Unfaithfully Yours* 1983.

Lewis Cecil Day. Irish poet; see ◊Day Lewis.

Lewis C(live) S(taples) 1898–1963. British academic and writer, born in Belfast. His books include the medieval study, *The Allegory of Love* 1936, and the space fiction, *Out of the Silent Planet* 1938. He was a committed Christian and wrote essays in popular theology such as *The Screwtape Letters* 1942 and *Mere Christianity* 1952; the autobiography *Surprised by Joy* 1955; and a series of books of Christian allegory for children, set in the magic land of Narnia, including *The Lion, the Witch, and the Wardrobe* 1950.

Lewis Jerry. Stage name of Joseph Levitch 1926– . US comic actor and director. Formerly in partnership with Dean Martin 1946–56, their film debut was in *My Friend Irma* 1949. He was revered as a solo performer by French critics ('Le Roi du Crazy'), but films that he directed such as *The Nutty Professor* 1963 were less well received in the USA. He appeared in a straight role opposite Robert De Niro in *The King of Comedy* 1982.

Lewis Jerry Lee 1935– . US rock-and-roll and country singer and pianist. His trademark was the boogie-woogie-derived 'pumping piano' style in hits such as 'Whole Lotta Shakin' Going On' and 'Great Balls of Fire' 1957; later recordings include 'What Made Milwaukee Famous' 1968.

Lewis Matthew Gregory 1775–1818. British writer, known as 'Monk' Lewis from his gothic horror romance *The Monk* 1795.

Lewis (Harry) Sinclair 1885–1951. US novelist. He made a reputation with satirical, but sentimental, social documentary novels, principally *Main Street* 1920, depicting American small-town life; and *Babbitt* 1922, the story of a real-estate dealer of the Midwest caught in the conventions of his milieu. These were followed by *Arrowsmith* 1925, a study of the pettiness in medical science; *Elmer Gantry* 1927, a satiric portrayal of evangelical religion; and *Dodsworth* 1929, about a US industrialist. He was the first American to be awarded the Nobel Prize for Literature, in 1930.

Lewis (Percy) Wyndham 1886–1957. English writer and artist. He pioneered ◊Vorticism, which with its feeling of movement sought to reflect the age of industry, and edited *Blast*, a journal proclaiming its principles. He had a hard and aggressive style in both his writing and his painting. His literary works include the novels *Tarr* 1918 and *The Childermass* 1928, the essay *Time and Western Man* 1927, and autobiographies. Of his paintings, his portraits are memorable, such as those of the writers Edith Sitwell and T S Eliot.

Lewton Val. Stage name of Vladimir Ivan Leventon 1904–1951. Russian-born US film producer, responsible for a series of atmospheric B horror films made for RKO in the 1940s, including *Cat People* 1942 and *The Body Snatcher* 1946. He co-wrote several of his films under the adopted name of Carlos Keith.

Leyden Lucas van. See ◊Lucas van Leyden, Dutch painter.

Lhôte André 1885–1962. French painter, art teacher, and critic. He opened the Académie Montparnasse 1922. He also wrote treatises on landscape painting and figure painting. Inspired by Cubism, his own paintings are complex compositions of geometrical forms painted in pure colours, for example *Rugby* 1917 (Museum of Modern Art, Paris).

Liberace Wladziu Valentino 1919–1987. US pianist who performed popular classics in a flamboyant style (for example, Beethoven's *Moonlight Sonata* reduced to four minutes). His playing was overshadowed by his extravagant outfits and the candelabra always adorning his piano. *The Liberace Show* had a regular slot on US television in the 1950s.

liberal arts or *the arts* collective term for the visual arts, music, and literature together with certain subjects of study, such as philosophy, history, languages, and sociology. The concept dates back to the classical idea of the pursuits worthy of a free man (which were seen as intellectual rather than manual).

Liberty Arthur Lasenby 1843–1917. English shopkeeper and founder of a shop of the same name in London 1875. Originally importing Oriental goods, it gradually started selling British Arts and Crafts and Art Nouveau furniture, tableware, and fabrics. Art Nouveau is sometimes still called *stile Liberty* in Italy.

Libra novel 1988 by US writer Don ◊DeLillo. Using a complex structure, it tells the story of the assassination of President John F Kennedy seen through the life of Lee Harvey Oswald, and deals with the wider plots and conspiracies of the event. The novel is a bold treatment of a vital event in American modern history.

libretto (Italian 'little book') the text of an opera or other dramatic vocal work, or the scenario of a ballet.

licensing practice by which fashion designers allow manufacturers to use their names on cosmetics, perfume bottles, jewellery, and other fashion and household accessories. It was pioneered by Pierre ◊Cardin whose name has become widely known as a brand of perfume as well as for his fashion design work.

Lichtenstein Roy 1923– . US Pop artist. He uses advertising imagery and comic-strip techniques, often focusing on popular ideals of romance and heroism, as in *Whaam!* 1963 (Tate Gallery, London). He has also produced sculptures in brass, plastic, and enamelled metal.

lied (German 'song', plural **lieder**) musical dramatization of a poem, usually for solo voice and piano; referring to Romantic songs of Schubert, Schumann, Brahms, and Hugo Wolf.

Lifar Serge 1905–1986. Ukrainian dancer and choreographer. Born in Kiev, he studied under ◊Nijinsky, joined the Diaghilev company 1923, and was artistic director and principal dancer of the Paris Opéra 1929–44 and 1947–59. He completely revitalized the company and in so doing, reversed the diminished fortunes of French ballet.

A great experimenter, he produced his first ballet without music, *Icare* 1935. He developed the role of the male dancer in his *Prometheus* 1929 and *Romeo and Juliet* (music by Prokofiev) 1955.

Life US weekly magazine of photo journalism, which recorded US and world events pictorially 1936–72 and again from 1978. It was founded by Henry Luce, owner of Time Inc., who bought the title of an older magazine. It ceased publication 1972, although a few 'Special Report' issues occasionally appeared after that date. In 1978 the magazine was revived, issued monthly, focusing more on personalities than on current news.

Ligeti György (Sándor) 1923– . Hungarian-born Austrian composer who developed a dense, highly chromatic, polyphonic style in which melody and rhythm are sometimes lost in shifting blocks of sound. He achieved international prominence with *Atmosphères* 1961 and *Requiem* 1965, which achieved widespread fame as background music for Stanley Kubrick's film epic *2001: A Space Odyssey* 1968. Other works include an opera *Le Grand Macabre* 1978, and *Poème symphonique* 1962, for 100 metronomes.

It is precisely a dread of deep significance and ideology that makes any kind of engaged art out of the question for me.

György Ligeti

---

limbo West Indian dance in which the performer leans backwards from the knees to pass under a pole, which is lowered closer to the ground with each attempt.

Limbourg brothers Franco-Flemish painters, Paul (Pol), Herman, and Jan (Hennequin, Janneken), active in the late 14th and early 15th centuries, first in Paris, then at the ducal court of Burgundy. They produced richly detailed manuscript illuminations, including two Books of ◊Hours.
Patronized by Jean de Berry, duke of Burgundy, from about 1404, they illustrated two Books of Hours that are masterpieces of the ◊International Gothic style, the *Belles Heures* about 1408 (Metropolitan Museum of Art, New York), and *Les Très Riches Heures du Duc de Berry* about 1413–15 (Musée Condé, Chantilly). Their miniature paintings include a series of scenes representing the months, presenting an almost fairytale world of pinnacled castles with lords and ladies, full of detail and brilliant decorative effects. All three brothers were dead by 1416.

limerick five-line humorous verse, often non-sensical, which first appeared in England about 1820 and was popularized by Edward ◊Lear. An example is:
'There was a young lady of Riga,
Who rode with a smile on a tiger;
They returned from the ride
With the lady inside,
And the smile on the face of the tiger'.

Lind Jenny 1820–1887. Swedish soprano of remarkable range, nicknamed the 'Swedish nightingale'. She toured the USA 1850–52 under the management of P T ◊Barnum.

Lindsay Jack 1900–1990. Australian writer based in London. His enduring leftist sympathies pervade an enormous and varied literary output; he published over 100 books, including poems and classical translations, notably his *Catullus* 1929, political studies, historical novels with settings ranging from ancient Pompeii to 19th-century England, and biographies of Helen of Troy, Blake, Turner, and William Morris.

Lindsay (Nicholas) Vachel 1879–1931. US poet. He wandered the country, living by reciting his ballad-like verse, collected in volumes including *General William Booth Enters into Heaven* 1913, *The Congo* 1914, and *Johnny Appleseed* 1928.

lingerie (French *linge* 'linen') general term for women's underwear and night attire.

Lipatti Dinu 1917–1950. Romanian pianist who perfected a small repertoire, notably of the works of Chopin. He died of leukaemia at 33.

Lipchitz Jacques 1891–1973. Lithuanian-born sculptor, active in Paris from 1909; he emigrated to the USA 1941. He was one of the first Cubist sculptors, his best-known piece being *Man with a Guitar* 1916 (Museum of Modern Art, New York). In the 1920s he experimented with small open forms he called 'transparents'. His later works, often political allegories, were characterized by heavy, contorted forms.

Li Po 705–762. Chinese poet. He used traditional literary forms, but his exuberance, the boldness of his imagination, and the intensity of his feeling have won him recognition as perhaps the greatest of all Chinese poets. Although he was mostly concerned with higher themes, he is also remembered for his celebratory verses on drinking.

Lippi Filippino *c.* 1457–1504. Italian painter of the Florentine school, trained by Botticelli. He produced altarpieces and several fresco cycles, full of detail and drama, elegantly and finely drawn. His frescoes, typical of late 15th-century Florentine work, can be found in Sta Maria sopra Minerva, Rome, in Sta Maria Novella, Florence, and elsewhere. His best-known painting is *The Vision of St Bernard* 1486. He was the son of Filippo Lippi.

Lippi Fra Filippo *c.* 1406–1469. Italian painter whose works include frescoes depicting the lives of St Stephen and St John the Baptist in Prato Cathedral 1452–66. He also painted many altarpieces of Madonnas and groups of saints.
Lippi was born in Florence and patronized by the Medici family. The painter and biographer Giorgio ◊Vasari gave a colourful account of his life including how, as a monk, he was tried in the 1450s for abducting a nun (the mother of his son Filippino).

Lippmann Gabriel 1845–1921. French doctor who invented the direct colour process in photography. He was awarded the Nobel Prize for Physics 1908.

Lippmann Walter 1889–1974. US liberal political commentator. From 1921 Lippmann was the chief editorial writer for the *New York World* and from 1931 wrote the daily column 'Today and Tomorrow', which was widely syndicated through the *New York Herald Tribune*. Among his books are *A Preface to Morals* 1929, *The Good Society* 1937, and *The Public Philosophy* 1955.

Lisboa António Francisco. Brazilian sculptor; see ◊Aleijadinho.

Lispector Clarice 1925–1977. Brazilian writer, born in the Ukraine. She was particularly concerned with the themes of adolescence, femininity, alienation, and self-awareness. Her first novel *Perto do Coração Selvagem/Near to the Savage Heart* 1944, published when she was 19, was followed by other novels and distinguished short stories, including *A Legião Estrangeira/The Foreign Legion* 1964.

Lissitzky El (Eliezer Markowich) 1890–1947. Russian painter, designer, printmaker, typographer, and illustrator, a pioneer of non-objective art. A trained architect-engineer, Lissitzky taught with Chagall and Malevich at the art school in Vitebsk 1919 and, inspired by the latter's use of pure geometrical form, swiftly turned to abstract art. Travelling between Russia, Germany, and Switzerland, he spread the ideas of the Russian avant-garde through his art, lectures, and radical designs for typography and exhibition displays. His theories influenced De ◊Stijl and ◊Bauhaus teaching, and were later transmitted to the USA.

listed building in Britain, a building officially recognized as having historical or architectural interest and therefore legally protected from alteration or demolition. In England the listing is drawn up by the Secretary of State for the Environment under the advice of the English Heritage organization, which provides various resources for architectural conservation.

There are about 500,000 listed buildings in England and around 1 million in Britain as a whole. Over the last 25 years the number of listed buildings has increased fivefold. In England they are divided into categories I, II, and II and in Scotland A, B, and C. Grade I buildings, which are defined as being of 'exceptional interest', constitute less than 2% of entries on the list. Grade II buildings constitute about 4% of entries. The listing system incorporates all pre-1700 buildings that have not been substantially altered, and almost all those built between 1700 and 1840.

Liszt Franz 1811–1886. Hungarian pianist and composer. An outstanding virtuoso of the piano, he was an established concert artist by the age of 12. His expressive, romantic, and frequently chromatic works include piano music (*Transcendental Studies* 1851), masses and oratorios, songs, an opera, a symphony, piano concertos, and organ music. Much of his music is programmatic; he also originated the symphonic poem.

Liszt was taught by his father, then by Carl Czerny (1791–1857). He travelled widely in Europe, producing an opera *Don Sanche* in Paris at the age of 14. As musical director and conductor at Weimar 1848–59, he championed the music of Berlioz and Wagner.

Retiring to Rome, he turned again to his early love of religion, and in 1865 became a secular priest (adopting the title Abbé), while continuing to teach and give concert tours for which he also made virtuoso piano arrangements of orchestral works by Beethoven, Schubert, and Wagner. He died at Bayreuth in Germany.

To us musicians the work of Beethoven parallels the pillars of smoke and fire which led the Israelites through the desert.

Franz Liszt
letter to Wilhelm von Lenz 1852

---

literary criticism establishment of principles governing literary composition, and the assessment and interpretation of literary works. Contemporary criticism offers analyses of literary works from structuralist, semiological, feminist, Marxist, and psychoanalytical perspectives, whereas earlier criticism tended to deal with moral or political ideas, or with a literary work as a formal object independent of its creator.

The earliest systematic literary criticism was the *Poetics* of Aristotle; a later Greek critic was the author of the treatise *On the Sublime*, usually attributed to Longinus. Horace and Quintilian were influential Latin critics. The Italian Renaissance introduced humanist criticism, and the revival of classical scholarship exalted the authority of Aristotle and Horace. Like literature itself, European criticism then applied Neo-Classical, Romantic, and modern approaches.

literary prizes awards for literature, usually annual and for a specific category (poetry, nonfiction, children's, and so on). The ◊Nobel Prize for Literature is international; other prizes are usually for books first published in a particular language or country, such as the ◊Booker Prize (Commonwealth), the ◊Prix Goncourt (France), the ◊Pulitzer Prize (USA), the Miles ◊Franklin Award (Australia), and the Akutagawa Prize (Japan).

literature words set apart in some way from ordinary everyday communication. In the ancient oral traditions, before stories and poems were written down, literature had a mainly public function – mythic and religious. As literary works came to be preserved in writing, and, eventually, printed, their role became more private, serving as a vehicle for the exploration and expression of emotion and the human situation.

In the development of literature, aesthetic

criteria have come increasingly to the fore, although these have been challenged on ideological grounds by some recent cultural critics. The English poet and critic Coleridge defined *prose* as words in their best order, and *poetry* as the 'best' words in the best order. The distinction between poetry and prose is not always clear-cut, but in practice poetry tends to be metrically formal (making it easier to memorize), whereas prose corresponds more closely to the patterns of ordinary speech. Poetry therefore had an early advantage over prose in the days before printing, which it did not relinquish until comparatively recently. Over the centuries poetry has taken on a wide range of forms, from the lengthy narrative such as the ◊epic, to the lyric, expressing personal emotion in songlike form; from the ◊ballad, and the 14-line ◊sonnet, to the extreme conciseness of the 17-syllable Japanese ◊haiku. Prose came into its own in the West as a vehicle for imaginative literature with the rise of the novel in the 18th century, and ◊fiction has since been divided into various genres such as the historical novel, detective fiction, fantasy, and science fiction. See also the literature of particular countries, under ◊United States literature, ◊English literature, ◊French literature, and so on.

lithography printmaking technique invented 1798 by Aloys Senefelder, based on the mutual repulsion of grease and water. A drawing is made with greasy crayon on an absorbent stone, which is then wetted. The wet stone repels ink (which is greasy) applied to the surface and the crayon absorbs it, so that the drawing can be printed. Lithographic printing is used in book production, posters, and prints, and this basic principle has developed into complex processes.

Lithuanian literature vernacular writing dates from the 16th century but the secular literary tradition begins with the nature poetry of Kristijonas Donelaitis (1714–1780) and folksong collections in the 18th century. Nineteenth-century romantic nationalism and oppression created a wider audience for patriotic verse and short stories. The banned journal *Aušra/Dawn* 1883–86 gave its name to a generation of patriotic writers, including the lyric and dramatic poet Jonas Mačiulis (Maironis) (1862–1932). Though Soviet occupation drove many writers into exile, the novelist and dramatist Vincas Krėvė (1882–1954) and the poet Vincas Mykolaitis-Putinas (1893–1967) have emerged as major national writers.

Little Lord Fauntleroy novel for children by Frances Hodgson ◊Burnett, published 1886. Cedric, a seven-year-old, golden-haired boy, lives in New York but discovers that his grandfather is an English earl who disinherited Cedric's father for marrying an American. The father dies, Cedric becomes Lord Fauntleroy and goes to live with his grandfather, where he lives a life of luxury, dressed in black velvet, although his mother is ostracized. Under the boy's influence the grandfather mellows, improving the lot of his tenants and accepting Cedric's mother.

Little Review, The US literary magazine 1914–29, founded in Chicago by Margaret Anderson. It published many experimental writers including W B Yeats, Ezra Pound, T S Eliot, and William Carlos Williams, and was banned for publishing part of James Joyce's *Ulysses*. The *Little Review* was variously published in New York, Paris, and elsewhere.

Little Richard stage name of Richard Penniman 1932– . US rock singer and pianist. He was one of the creators of rock and roll with his wildly uninhibited renditions of 'Tutti Frutti' 1956, 'Long Tall Sally' 1956, and 'Good Golly Miss Molly' 1957. His subsequent career in soul and rhythm and blues was interrupted by periods as a Seventh-Day Adventist cleric.

Little Women novel for children by Louisa M ◊Alcott published 1868, one of the most popular children's books ever written. It describes the daily life of a New England family in reduced circumstances, and the tensions and harmony between the four teenage daughters, Meg, Jo, Beth, and Amy. It was followed by a sequel *Good Wives* 1869.

Littlewood Joan 1914– . English theatre director. She established the Theatre Workshop 1945 and was responsible for many vigorous productions at the Theatre Royal, Stratford, London, 1953–75, such as *A Taste of Honey* 1959, Brendan Behan's *The Hostage* 1959–60, and *Oh, What a Lovely War* 1963.

Living Theater experimental US theatre group, 1947–70, founded by Judith Malina (1926–) and Julian Beck (1925–1985). Committed anarchists, Beck and Malina promoted avant-garde plays and radical dramatic techniques in opposition to the prevailing naturalism and ◊Method acting. They produced works by Gertrude Stein, Paul Goodman, Brecht, and Lorca and won international recognition for such plays as *The Connection* 1959 by Jack Gelber (1932–). In 1964 they took up 'voluntary exile' in Europe. The group production *Paradise Now* 1968, subverting all dramatic categories, was considered to have expressed the anarchic spirit of the 1960s. In 1970 the the company split into several groups and dispersed.

Livy Titus Livius 59 BC–AD 17. Roman historian, author of a *History of Rome* from the city's foundation to 9 BC, based partly on legend. It was composed of 142 books, of which 35 survive, covering the periods from the arrival of Aeneas in Italy to 293 BC and from 218 to 167 BC.

Llewellyn Richard. Pen name of Richard Vivian Llewellyn Lloyd 1907–1983. Welsh writer. *How Green Was My Valley* 1939, a novel about a S Wales mining family, was made into a play and a film.

Lloyd Harold 1893–1971. US film comedian, noted for his 'trademark' of thick horn-rimmed glasses and straw hat, and for the daring stunts of his cliff-hangers. He appeared from 1913 in silent and talking films. His silent films include *Grandma's Boy* 1922, *Safety Last* 1923, and *The Freshman* 1925. His first talkie was *Movie Crazy* 1932. He produced films after 1938, including the anthologies *Harold Lloyd's World of Comedy* 1962 and *Funny Side of Life* 1964.

Lloyd Marie. Stage name of Matilda Alice Victoria Wood 1870–1922. English music-hall artist whose Cockney songs embodied the music-hall traditions of 1890s comedy.

Lloyd Webber Andrew 1948– . English composer. His early musicals, with lyrics by Tim Rice, include *Joseph and the Amazing Technicolor Dreamcoat* 1968; *Jesus Christ Superstar* 1970, and *Evita* 1978, based on the life of the Argentine leader Eva Perón. He also wrote *Cats* 1981, based on T S Eliot's *Old Possum's Book of Practical Cats*, *Starlight Express* 1984, *The Phantom of the Opera* 1986, and *Aspects of Love* 1989.

Other works include *Variations for Cello* 1978, written for his brother *Julian Lloyd Webber* (1951–) who is a solo cellist, and a *Requiem Mass* 1985.

Lochner Stephan died 1451. German painter, active in Cologne from 1442, a master of the ◊International Gothic style. Most of his work is still in Cologne, notably the *Virgin in the Rose Garden* about 1440 (Wallraf-Richartz Museum) and *Adoration of the Magi* 1448 (Cologne Cathedral). His work combines the delicacy of the International Gothic style with the naturalism of Flemish painting.

Lockwood Margaret. Stage name of Margaret Mary Lockwood 1919–1990. English actress. Between 1937 and 1949 she acted exclusively in the cinema, appearing in Alfred Hitchcock's *The Lady Vanishes* 1938 and in *The Wicked Lady* 1945. After 1955 she made only one film, *The Slipper and the Rose* 1976, although she periodically appeared on stage and on television until her retirement 1980.

Lodge David (John) 1935– . English novelist, short-story writer, dramatist, and critic. Much of his fiction concerns the role of Catholicism in mid-20th-century England, exploring the situation both through broad comedy and parody, as in *The British Museum is Falling Down* 1967, and realistically, as in *How Far Can You Go?* 1980. *Nice Work* 1988 was short-listed for the Booker Prize. His other works include *Changing Places* 1975 and its sequel *Small World* 1984, both satirical 'campus' novels; the play, *The Writing Game* 1990; and *Paradise News* 1991.

Literature is mostly about having sex and not much about having children; life is the other way round.

David Lodge
The British Museum is Falling Down 1967

Lodge Thomas *c.* 1558–1625. English author whose romance *Rosalynde* 1590 was the basis of Shakespeare's play *As You Like It*.

Loewe Frederick 1901–1988. US composer of musicals. In 1942 he joined forces with the lyricist Alan Jay Lerner, and their joint successes include *Brigadoon* 1947, *Paint Your Wagon* 1951, *My Fair Lady* 1956, *Gigi* 1958, and *Camelot* 1960.

Born in Berlin, the son of an operatic tenor, he studied under Busoni, and in 1924 went with his father to the USA.

Lofting Hugh 1886–1947. English writer and illustrator of children's books, including the 'Dr Dolittle' series, in which the hero can talk to animals. Born in Maidenhead, Berkshire, Lofting was originally a civil engineer. He went to the USA 1912.

Lohengrin in late 13th-century Germanic legend, a hero, son of ◊Parsifal. Lohengrin married Princess Elsa, who broke his condition that she never ask his origin, and he returned to the temple of the ◊Holy Grail. Wagner based his German opera *Lohengrin* 1848 on the story.

Loki in Norse mythology, one of the ◊Aesir (the principal gods), but the cause of dissension among the gods, and the slayer of ◊Balder. His children are the Midgard serpent Jörmungander, which girdles the Earth, the wolf Fenris, and Hela, goddess of death.

Lolita novel 1955 by US writer Vladimir ◊Nabokov. It is the narrative of Humbert Humbert, a middle-aged European academic, whose infatuation with an adolescent girl who becomes his step-daughter and his mistress leads to murder. A darkly comic work about erotic obsession and artistic desire, whose subject matter caused great controversy, it is regarded as a modern masterpiece.

I am sufficiently proud of my knowing something to be modest about my not knowing all.

Vladimir Nabokov *Lolita*

Lombard Carole. Stage name of Jane Alice Peters 1908–1942. US comedy film actress. A warm and witty actress, she starred in several celebrated comedies of the 1930s and early 1940s: *Twentieth Century* 1934, *My Man Godfrey* 1936, and *To Be or Not to Be* 1942. She was married to Clark Gable 1939 until her death in a plane crash.

London Jack (John Griffith) 1876–1916. US writer and adventurer, a prolific author of naturalistic novels, adventure stories, and socialist reportage. His works, which are often based on his own life, typically concern the human struggle for survival against extreme natural forces, as dramatized in such novels as *The Call of the Wild* 1903, *The Sea Wolf* 1904, and *White Fang* 1906. By 1906 he was the most widely read writer in the USA and had been translated into 68 languages.

London Contemporary Dance Theatre British modern dance company formed by entrepreneur Robin Howard 1967. Its aim was to introduce modern dance based on the principles of Martha ◊Graham to Britain. Its first artistic director was Robert Cohan who, after leaving 1989, returned to the company as artistic adviser 1992. Several important choreographers have emerged from the company and its school, such as Richard ◊Alston and Siobhan ◊Davies.

Howard established the London Contemporary Dance School 1966, the only European institution authorized to teach the Graham method.

London Group art society formed 1915 in London when the ◊Camden Town Group, the Vorticists, and several smaller groups came together to provide an opportunity for young avant-garde artists to exhibit. Its members have included Walter ◊Sickert, Vanessa Bell, and Paul ◊Nash. The group still exists.

London, Museum of museum of London's history. It was formed by the amalgamation of the former Guildhall (Roman and medieval) and London (Tudor and later) Museums, housed from 1976 in a building at the junction of London Wall and Aldersgate, near the Barbican.

Long Richard 1945– . English Conceptual artist, in the vanguard of 1960s young artists wishing to break away from studio-created art. Working both outdoors and on-the-spot in galleries, he used natural materials such as stone, slate, wood, and mud to represent the ritualized traces of early peoples, notably in *River Avon Driftwood* 1977 (Museum of Contemporary Art, Ghent). He created his celebrated stone circles and rivers of sticks during walks in remote areas of Ireland, the Himalayas, Africa, and Iceland. Only photographic records remain of much of his work.

Long Day's Journey Into Night, A drama by Eugene ◊O'Neill 1956. The tight-fisted actor, James Tyrone, proves helpless in the face of his wife's morphine addiction, while the two sons, Jamie and Edmund, a consumptive, are dragged down into depression and drink by their mother's nervous collapse. The play was acknowledged by O'Neill to be explicitly autobiographical.

Longfellow Henry Wadsworth 1807–1882. US poet, remembered for ballads ('Excelsior', 'The Village Blacksmith', 'The Wreck of the Hesperus') and the mythic narrative epics *Evangeline* 1847, *The Song of ◊Hiawatha* 1855, and *The Courtship of Miles Standish* 1858.

Born in Portland, Maine, Longfellow graduated from Bowdoin College and taught modern languages there and at Harvard University 1835–54, after which he travelled widely. The most popular US poet of the 19th century, Longfellow was also an adept translator. His other works include six sonnets on Dante, a translation of Dante's *Divine Comedy*, and *Tales of a Wayside Inn* 1863, which includes the popular poem 'Paul Revere's Ride.'

Let us, then, be up and doing, With a heart for any fate.

Henry Wadsworth Longfellow
'A Psalm of Life'

Longhena Baldassare 1598–1682. Venetian Baroque architect, responsible for the striking church of Sta Maria della Salute at the entrance to the Grand Canal, Venice, 1630–87. This Baroque masterpiece is of octagonal plan, with a massive dome anchored to its base by giant scrolls. His other Venetian works include the Palazzo Rezzonico (begun 1667) and the Palazzo Pesaro (begun 1676).

Longinus Cassius AD 213–273. Greek philosopher, who taught in Athens for many years. He was formerly thought to be the author of the famous literary critical treatise *On the Sublime*, which influenced the English poets John Dryden and Alexander Pope.

Loos Adolf 1870–1933. Austrian architect and author of the article *Ornament and Crime* 1908, in which he rejected the ornamentation and curved lines of the Viennese *Jugendstil* movement (see ◊Art Nouveau). His buildings include private houses on Lake Geneva 1904 and the Steiner House in Vienna 1910.

Loos Anita 1893–1981. US writer, author of the humorous fictitious diary *◊Gentlemen Prefer Blondes* 1925. She became a screenwriter 1912 and worked on more than 60 films, including D W ◊Griffith's *Intolerance* 1916.

Lope de Vega (Carpio) Felix. Spanish poet and dramatist; see ◊Vega, Lope de.

Lorca Federico García 1898–1936. Spanish poet and playwright, born in Granada. His plays include *Bodas de sangre/Blood Wedding* 1933 and *La casa de Bernarda Alba/The House of Bernarda Alba* 1936. His poems include 'Lament', written for the bullfighter Mejías. Lorca was shot by the Falangists during the Spanish Civil War.

Romancero gitano/Gipsy Ballad-book 1928 shows the influence of the Andalusian songs of the area. In 1929–30 Lorca visited New York, and his experiences are reflected in *Poeta en Nuevo York/Poet in New York* 1940. Returning to Spain, he founded a touring theatrical company and began to write plays.

Lord Jim novel 1900 by Joseph ◊Conrad. Jim is a young merchant seaman who betrays his ideals by succumbing to a moment of panic, deserting his ship's passengers in a crisis. He spends the rest of his life trying to make up for this lapse, becoming an influence for peace and good order in a remote Malayan community. Conrad characteristically combines an adventure story with a compelling enquiry into the nature of moral choice.

Lorelei in Germanic folklore, a river ◊nymph of the Rhine who lures sailors onto the rock where she sits combing her hair. She features in several poems, including 'Die Lorelei' by the German Romantic writer Heine.

Loren Sophia. Stage name of Sofia Scicolone 1934– . Italian film actress whose boldly sensual appeal was promoted by her husband, producer Carlo Ponti. Her work includes *Aida* 1953, *The Key* 1958, *La Ciociara/Two Women* 1960, *Judith* 1965, and *Firepower* 1979.

Lorenzetti Ambrogio active 1319–1348. Italian painter who worked in Siena and Florence. His allegorical frescoes *Good and Bad Government* 1337–39 (Town Hall, Siena) include a detailed panoramic landscape and a view of the city of Siena which shows an unusual mastery of spatial effects.

Lorenzetti Pietro active 1320–1348. Italian painter of the Sienese school who worked in Assisi. His frescoes in the Franciscan basilica, Assisi, reflect the Florentine painter Giotto's concern with mass and weight, as in his *Birth of the Virgin* 1342 (Cathedral Museum, Siena). He was the brother of Ambrogio Lorenzetti.

Lorimer Robert Stoddart 1864–1929. Scottish architect, the most prolific architect representative of the Scottish Arts and Crafts Movement. Lorimer drew particularly from Scottish vernacular buildings of the 16th and 17th centuries to create a series of mansions and houses, practically planned with picturesque, turreted exteriors. Examples of his work include Ardkinglas House, Argyll, 1906, and Ruwallan House, Ayrshire, 1902.

Lorrain Claude. French painter; see ◊Claude Lorrain.

Lorre Peter. Stage name of Lazlo Löwenstein 1904–1964. Hungarian character actor with bulging eyes, high voice, and melancholy mien.

He made several films in Germany before moving to Hollywood 1935. He appeared in *M* 1931, *Mad Love* 1935, *The Maltese Falcon* 1941, *Casablanca* 1942, *Beat the Devil* 1953, and *The Raven* 1963. He directed one film *Der Verlorene/The Lost One* 1953.

Los Angeles Victoria de 1923– . Spanish soprano. She is renowned for her elegantly refined interpretations of Spanish songs and for the roles of Manon and Madame Butterfly in Puccini's operas.

Losey Joseph 1909–1984. US film director influenced by Italian neorealism and German expressionism. Blacklisted as a former communist in the anticommunist McCarthy era, he settled in England, where his films included *The Servant* 1963, *Accident* 1967, and *The Go-Between* 1971.

Lost Generation, the disillusioned US literary generation of the 1920s, members of which went to live in Paris. The phrase is attributed to the writer Gertrude Stein in Ernest Hemingway's early novel of 1920s Paris, *'Fiesta' (The Sun Also Rises)* 1927.

lost-wax technique method of making sculptures; see ◊*cire perdue.*

Loti Pierre, pseudonym of Julien Viaud 1850–1930. French novelist. He depicted the lives of Breton sailors in novels such as *Pêcheur d'Islande/The Iceland Fisherman* 1886. His extensive experience of the East as a naval officer was transmuted into very popular exotic fictions such as *Aziyadé* 1879 and *Madame Chrysanthème* 1887 and sometimes melancholy travel books and reminiscences such as *Un Jeune Officier pauvre/A Poor Young Officer* 1923.

Lotto Lorenzo *c.* 1480–1556. Italian painter, born in Venice, active in Bergamo, Treviso, Venice, Ancona, and Rome. His early works were influenced by Giovanni Bellini; his mature style belongs to the High Renaissance. He painted religious works but is best-known for his portraits, such as *Andrea Odoni* (Hampton Court, London), which often convey a sense of unease or an air of melancholy.

Lotus-Eaters in Homer's *Odyssey*, a mythical people living on the lotus plant, which induced travellers to forget their journey home.

Louis Morris 1912–1962. US abstract painter. From Abstract Expressionism he turned to the colour-staining technique developed by Helen ◊Frankenthaler, using thinned-out acrylic paints poured on rough canvas to create the illusion of vaporous layers of colour. The series *Veils* 1959–60 and *Unfurleds* 1960–61 are examples.

Louis XIV style French decorative arts style prevalent during the reign of the 'Sun King' (1643–1715), characterized by both ornate Baroque features and classical themes. It was used especially for the sumptuous formal furniture made for the royal palaces. The interior designer Charles Lebrun (1619–1690) designed all the furniture, tapestries, and carpets for Versailles and the Louvre in Louis XIV style.

The Louis XV style (1715–74) was the French Rococo, a lighter style than Louis XIV, characterized by the use of chinoiserie, asymmetry, and the scroll motif. The Louis XVI style (1774–92) represented early ◊Neo- Classicism.

Louvre French art gallery, former palace of the French kings, in Paris. It was converted to an art gallery 1793 to house the royal collections. Two of its best-known exhibits are the sculpture *Venus de Milo* and Leonardo da Vinci's painting the *Mona Lisa*.

Today the gallery comprises seven sections: ancient, Oriental, Egyptian, painting, sculpture, applied arts, and drawing.

Lovecraft H(oward) P(hillips) 1890–1937. US writer of horror fiction whose stories of hostile, supernatural forces have lent names and material to many other writers in the genre. Much of his work on this theme was collected in *The Outsider and Others* 1939.

Lovelace Richard 1618–1658. English poet. Imprisoned 1642 for petitioning for the restoration of royal rule, he wrote 'To Althea from Prison', and in a second term in jail 1648 revised his collection *Lucasta* 1649.

Lowell Amy (Lawrence) 1874–1925. US poet who began her career by publishing the conventional *A Dome of Many-Colored Glass* 1912 but eventually succeeded Ezra Pound as leader of the Imagists (see ◊Imagism). Her works, in free verse, include *Sword Blades and Poppy Seed* 1916.

Lowell J(ames) R(ussell) 1819–1891. US poet whose works range from the didactic *The Vision of Sir Launfal* 1848 to such satirical poems as *The Biglow Papers* 1848. As a critic, he developed a deep awareness of the US literary tradition. He was also a diplomat and served as minister to Spain 1877–80 and England 1880–85.

His early poetry, complex and tightly structured, focused on spiritual crises. His later poetry (from the 1850s) was looser and drew freely on his personal relationships, his involvement in left-wing politics, and his periods of mental instability.

No man is born into the world whose work/ Is not born with him; there is always work,/ And tools to work withal, for those who will.

J R Lowell 'A Glance Behind the Curtain' 1843

Lowell Robert (Traill Spence, Jr) 1917–1977. US poet whose works include *Lord Weary's Castle* 1946 (Pulitzer Prize), *Life Studies* 1959, and *For the Union Dead* 1964.

During World War II he was imprisoned for five months for conscientious objection and during the 1960s he campaigned against the war in Vietnam. Among his best-known poems are 'Memories of West Street and Lepke' and 'Skunk Hour'.

---

light of the oncoming train.

Robert Lowell 'Day by Day'

Lowry L(aurence) S(tephen) 1887–1976. English painter. Born in Manchester, he lived mainly in nearby Salford and painted northern industrial townscapes. In the 1920s he developed a naive style characterized by matchstick figures and an almost monochrome palette.

Loy Myrna. Stage name of Myrna Williams 1905– . US film actress who played Nora Charles in the *Thin Man* series (1934–47) costarring William Powell. Her other films include *The Mask of Fu Manchu* 1932 and *The Rains Came* 1939.

Lubetkin Bertholdt 1901–1990. Russian-born architect who settled in the UK 1930 and formed, with six young architects, a group called Tecton. His pioneering designs include Highpoint I, a block of flats in Highgate, London, 1933–35, and the curved lines of the Penguin Pool 1933 at London Zoo, which employ ◊reinforced concrete to sculptural effect.

During the 1930s, Tecton was responsible for many buildings erected in England in the ◊International Style then flourishing elsewhere in Europe, including the Gorilla House 1937 at London Zoo and a health centre for the London borough of Finsbury 1938. The group was also a training ground for the avant-garde architects of the next generation, such as Denys Lasdun.

Lubitsch Ernst 1892–1947. German film director known for his stylish comedies, who worked in the USA from 1921. His sound films include *Trouble in Paradise* 1932, *Design for Living* 1933, *Ninotchka* 1939, and *To Be or Not to Be* 1942.

Starting as an actor in silent films in Berlin, he turned to writing and directing, including *Die Augen der Mummie Ma/The Eyes of the Mummy* 1918 and *Die Austernprinzessin/The Oyster Princess* 1919. In the USA he directed the silent films *The Marriage Circle* 1924 and *The Student Prince* 1927.

Lubovitch Lar 1943– . US modern-dance choreographer and director of the Lar Lubovitch Dance Company, founded 1976. He was the first to use Minimalist music, for which he created a new style of movement in works such as *Marimba* 1977 and *North Star* 1978.

Lucan (Marcus Annaeus Lucanus) AD 39–65. Latin poet, born in Córdoba, Spain. He was a nephew of the writer Seneca and favourite of Nero until the emperor became jealous of his verse. Lucan then joined a republican conspiracy and committed suicide on its failure. His epic poem *Pharsalia* deals with the civil wars of Caesar and Pompey, and was influential in the Middle Ages and Renaissance.

Lucas George 1944– . US director and producer. He wrote and directed *Star Wars* 1977, wrote and produced *The Empire Strikes Back* 1980, and *Return of the Jedi* 1983. His other films as director include *THX 1138* 1971 and *American Graffiti* 1973. Later works as a producer include *Raiders of the Lost Ark* 1981, *Indiana Jones and the Temple of Doom* 1984, *Willow* 1988, and *Indiana Jones and the Last Crusade* 1989.

Lucas van Leyden 1494–1533. Dutch painter and engraver, active in Leiden and Antwerp. He was a pioneer of Netherlandish genre scenes, for example *The Chess Players* (Staatliche Museen, Berlin). His woodcuts and engravings were inspired by Albrecht Dürer, whom he met in Antwerp 1521.

Luce Clare Boothe 1903–1987. US journalist, playwright, and politician. She was managing editor of *Vanity Fair* magazine 1933–34, and wrote several successful plays, including *The Women* 1936 and *Margin for Error* 1940, both of which were made into films.

Lucian c. 125– c. 190. Greek writer of satirical dialogues, in which he pours scorn on religions and mocks human pretensions. He was born at Samosata in Syria and for a time was an advocate at Antioch, but later travelled before settling in Athens about 165. He occupied an official post in Egypt, where he died.

All that belongs to mortals is mortal; all things pass us by, or if not, we pass them by.

Lucian *Greek Anthology*

Lucky Jim first novel 1954 by Kingsley ◊Amis. The anti-hero Jim Dixon, a young history lecturer in a provincial university, is comically at odds with what he sees as the falsity of the life around him. Jim escapes from academia to a job offered by the rich uncle of his desirable conquest, the amenable Christine. Although much of the humour now seems puerile, the linguistic agility and vigour were evidence of an original new talent.

Lucretius (Titus Lucretius Carus) c. 99–55 BC. Roman poet and philosopher whose *De Rerum natura/On the Nature of the Universe* envis-

aged the whole universe as a combination of atoms, and had some concept of evolutionary theory.

What is food to one man is bitter poison to others.

Lucretius *On the Nature of the Universe*

Luening Otto 1900– . US composer. He studied in Zurich with Philipp Jarnach, and privately with Feruccio Busoni. He was appointed to Columbia University 1949, and in 1951 began a series of pioneering compositions for instruments and tape, some in partnership with Vladimir Ussachevsky (1911–) *(Incantation* 1952, *Poem in Cycles and Bells* 1954). In 1959 he became co-director, with Milton Babbitt and Ussachevsky, of the Columbia-Princeton Electronic Music Center.

Lugosi Bela. Stage name of Bela Ferenc Blasko 1882–1956. Hungarian-born US film actor. Acclaimed for his performance in *Dracula* on Broadway 1927, Lugosi began acting in feature films 1930. His appearance in the film version of *Dracula* 1931 marked the start of Lugosi's long career in horror films – among them, *Murders in the Rue Morgue* 1932, *The Raven* 1935, and *The Wolf Man* 1941.

Lu Hsün alternative transliteration of Chinese writer ◊Lu Xun.

Lukács Georg 1885–1971. Hungarian philosopher who made important contributions to ◊Marxist aesthetics and literary theory. He believed, as a cultural relativist, that the highest art was that which reflected the historical movement of the time: for the 20th century, this meant ◊Socialist Realism. Lukács joined the Hungarian Communist Party 1918 and was deputy minister of education during the short-lived Hungarian Soviet Republic, 1919. One of his best-known works is *The Theory of the Novel* 1916.

Luks George 1867–1933. US painter and graphic artist, a member of the ◊Ashcan School. His paintings capture the excitement and colour of life in New York City's slums.

Lully Jean-Baptiste. Adopted name of Giovanni Battista Lulli 1632–1687. French composer of Italian origin who was court composer to Louis XIV. He composed music for the ballet, for Molière's plays, and established French opera with such works as *Alceste* 1674 and *Armide et Renaud* 1686. He was also a ballet dancer.

Lumet Sidney 1924– . US film director with a prolific and eclectic body of work covering such powerful, intimate dramas as *12 Angry Men* 1957, or intense, urban dramas such as *Serpico* 1973, and *Dog Day Afternoon* 1975. Among his other films are **Fail Safe** 1964 and **Equus** 1977.

Lumière Auguste Marie 1862–1954 and Louis Jean 1864–1948. French brothers who pioneered cinematography. In 1895 they patented their cinematograph, a combined camera and projector operating at 16 frames per second, and opened the world's first cinema in Paris to show their films.

The Lumières' first films were short static shots of everyday events such as **La Sorties des Usines Lumière** 1895 about workers leaving a factory and **L'Arroseur arrosé** 1895, the world's first fiction film. Production was abandoned 1900.

luminism method of painting, associated with the ◊Hudson River School in the 19th century, that emphasized the effects of light on water.

Luna in Roman mythology, the goddess of the moon.

Lunt Alfred 1893–1977. US actor. He went straight from school into the theatre, and in 1922 married the actress Lynn Fontanne with whom he subsequently co-starred in more than 30 plays. They formed a sophisticated comedy duo, and the New York Lunt–Fontanne Theatre was named after them. Their shows included **Design for Living** by Noël Coward 1933, **There Shall Be No Nigh**t 1940–41, and **The Visit** 1960.

Luo Guan Zhong or Luo Kuan-chung lived 14th century. Chinese novelist who reworked popular tales into **The Romance of the Three Kingdoms** and **The Water Margin**.

Luo Kuan-chung alternative transliteration of Chinese writer ◊Luo Guan Zhong.

Lurçat Jean 1892–1966. French artist who revived tapestry design, as in **Le Chant du Monde** 1957–63. Inspired by Cubism and later Surrealism, his work is characterized by strong colours and bold stylization.

Lurex trademark for a shiny, often coloured, plastic-coated aluminium thread.

Lurie Alison 1926– . US novelist and critic. Her subtly written and satirical novels include **Imaginary Friends** 1967; **The War Between the Tates** 1974; **Foreign Affairs** 1985, a tale of transatlantic relations that won the Pulitzer Prize; and **The Truth About Lorin Jones** 1988.

lute any of a family of stringed musical instruments of the 14th–18th century, including the mandore, theorbo, and chitarrone. Lutes are pear-shaped with up to seven ◊courses (single or double strings) and are plucked with the fingers; their music is written in ◊tablature and chords are played simultaneously, not arpeggiated as for guitar. Members of the lute family were used both as solo instruments and for vocal accompaniment, and were often played in addition to, or instead

of, keyboard instruments in larger ensembles and in opera. Modern lutenists include Julian ◊Bream and Anthony Rooley (1944–   ).

Lutosławski Witold 1913–   . Polish composer and conductor, born in Warsaw. His early major compositions, such as **Variations on a Theme of Paganini** 1941 for two pianos and **First Symphony** 1947, drew some criticism from the government. After 1956, under a more liberal regime, he adopted avant-garde techniques, including improvisatory and aleatoric forms, in **Venetian Games** 1961. His fastidious output includes three symphonies, **Paroles tissées/ Teased Words** 1965 for tenor and chamber orchestra, dedicated to Peter Pears, and **Chain I** for orchestra 1981.

Lutyens (Agnes) Elisabeth 1906–1983. English composer. Her works, using the twelve-tone system, are expressive and tightly organized, and include chamber music, stage, and orchestral works. Her choral and vocal works include a setting of the Austrian philosopher Ludwig Wittgenstein's **Tractatus** and a cantata **The Tears of Night**. She also composed much film and incidental music. She was the youngest daughter of architect Sir Edwin Landseer Lutyens.

Lutyens Edwin Landseer 1869–1944. English architect. His designs ranged from the picturesque, such as Castle Drogo, Devon, 1910– 30, to Renaissance-style country houses, and ultimately evolved into a Classical style as in the Cenotaph, London, 1919, and the Viceroy's House, New Delhi, 1912–31. His complex use of space, interest in tradition, and distorted Classical language have proved of great interest to a number of Post-Modern architects, especially Robert Venturi.

Luxembourg, Palais du palace in Paris, France, in which the Senate sits. It was built 1615 for the Queen Marie de' Medici by Salomon de Brosse (about 1571–1626).

Lu Xun pen name of Chon Shu-jêu 1881–1936. Chinese short-story writer. His three volumes of satirically realistic stories, **Call to Arms**, **Wandering,** and **Old Tales Retold**, reveal the influence of the Russian writer Nicolai Gogol. He was also an important polemical essayist and literary critic.

lycanthropy in folk belief, the transformation of a human being into a wolf; or, in psychology, a delusion involving this belief.

Lyceum London theatre situated in Wellington Street, near the Strand. It was opened 1809 (rebuilt 1834) and in 1878–1902, under the management of Henry ◊Irving, saw many of the actress Ellen Terry's triumphs.

lycra synthetic fibre composed mainly of elastomer and other stretch fibres. It was introduced as a fabric for underwear, such as girdles, bras, and support stockings, but it became a popular material for sports and casual wear such as stretch leggings in the 1980s–90s.

Lydgate John *c.* 1370– *c.* 1450. English poet. He was a Benedictine monk and later prior. His numerous works were often translations or adaptations, such as *Troy Book* and *Falls of Princes*.

Lydgate was probably born at Lydgate, Suffolk; he entered the Benedictine abbey of Bury St Edmunds, was ordained 1397, and was prior of Hatfield Broadoak 1423–34. He was a friend of the poet Geoffrey Chaucer.

Lyly John *c.* 1553–1606. English dramatist and author of the romance *Euphues, or the Anatomy of Wit* 1578. Its elaborate stylistic devices gave rise to the word 'euphuism' for an affected rhetorical style.

Lynch David 1946– . US film director. His dark, original work is peopled with grotesque and criminal characters, often acting out their stories in small town settings. Films include *Eraserhead* 1976, *The Elephant Man* 1980, *Dune* 1984, *Blue Velvet* 1986, and *Wild at Heart* 1990. He created the cult television series *Twin Peaks* 1989–90 which he followed with the feature film prequel *Twin Peaks: Fire Walk with Me* 1992.

Lynn Vera 1917– . British singer, known as the 'Forces' Sweetheart' of World War II. She became famous with such songs as 'We'll Meet Again', 'White Cliffs of Dover', and in 1952 'Auf Wiederseh'n, Sweetheart'.

lyre stringed instrument of great antiquity. It consists of a soundbox with two curved arms extended upwards to a crosspiece to which four to ten strings are attached. It is played with a plectrum or the fingers. It originated in Asia, and was widespread in ancient Greece and Egypt. Tuned to a given ◊mode, it provided a pitch guide for vocal melody and embellishment.

lyricism the expressive or sensual qualities of a work. For instance, lyric poetry expresses the writer's thoughts and feelings. In painting, lyrical abstraction (*abstraction lyrique*) refers to a French style of abstract art of the 1940s and 1950s that was more spontaneous and expressive than geometrical abstraction (see ◊Tachisme).

Lysippus or *Lysippos* 4th century BC. Greek sculptor. He made a series of portraits of Alexander the Great (Roman copies survive, including examples in the British Museum and the Louvre) and also sculpted the *Apoxyomenos*, an athlete (copy in the Vatican), and a colossal *Hercules* (lost).

Lysistrata Greek comedy by Aristophanes, produced 411 BC. The women of Athens and Greece, tired of war, refuse to make love to their husbands and occupy the Acropolis to force a peace between the Athenians and the Spartans.

Lytton Edward George Earle Bulwer-Lytton, 1st Baron Lytton of Knebworth 1803–1873. English writer. His novels successfully followed every turn of the public taste of his day and include the Byronic *Pelham* 1828, *The Last Days of Pompeii* 1834, and *Rienzi* 1835. His plays include *Richelieu* 1838.

His other works include an essay on Milton 1825 published in the *Edinburgh Review* and a volume of verse, *Lays of Ancient Rome* 1842.

Macbeth tragedy by William ◊Shakespeare, first performed 1605–06. Acting on a prophecy by three witches that he will be king of Scotland, Macbeth, egged on by Lady Macbeth, murders King Duncan and becomes king but is eventually killed by Macduff. The play was based on the 16th-century historian Holinshed's *Chronicles*.

Macbeth George 1932–1992. Scottish poet and novelist. His early poetry, such as *A Form of Words* 1954, often focused on violent or macabre events. *The Colour of Blood* 1967 and *Collected Poems 1958–1970* 1971 show mastery of both experimental and traditional styles and a playful wit. There are strong erotic elements in his eight novels, which include *The Seven Witches* 1978 and *Dizzy's Woman* 1986.

McCabe John 1939– . English pianist and composer whose works include three symphonies, two violin concertos, an opera *The Play of Mother Courage* 1974, and orchestral works including *The Chagall Windows* 1974 and *Concerto for Orchestra* 1982. He was director of the London College of Music 1983–90.

McCarthy Mary (Therese) 1912–1989. US novelist and critic. Much of her work looks probingly at US society, for example, the novel *The Groves of Academe* 1952, which describes the anti-Communist witch-hunts of the time, and *The Group* 1963 (filmed 1966), which follows the post-college careers of eight women.

McCartney Paul 1942– . UK rock singer, songwriter, and bass guitarist; former member of the ◊Beatles, and leader of the pop group Wings 1971–81. His subsequent solo hits have included collaborations with Michael Jackson and Elvis Costello. Together with composer Carl Davis, McCartney wrote the *Liverpool Oratorio* 1991, his first work of classical music.

MacCormac Richard 1938– . British architect whose work shows a clear geometrical basis. The residential building at Worcester College, Oxford, 1983 epitomizes his approach: the student rooms are intricately related in a complex geometrical plan and stepped section.

He became president of the Royal Institute of British Architects 1991. His other works include Coffee Hall flat, Milton Keynes, 1974 and Fitzwilliam College, Cambridge, 1986. His work remains human with a concern for the well-made object reminiscent of the Arts and Crafts tradition.

McCowen Alec 1925– . British actor. His Shakespearean roles include Richard II and the Fool in *King Lear*; he is also known for his dramatic one-man shows.

Maazel Lorin (Varencove) 1930– . US conductor and violinist, musical director of the Pittsburgh Symphony Orchestra from 1986. A wide-ranging repertoire includes opera, from posts held at Berlin, Vienna, Bayreuth, and Milan, in addition to the symphonic repertoire, in particular Sibelius and Tchaikovsky. His orchestral preparation is noted for its inner precision and dynamic range.

He recorded the *Requiem Mass* 1985 and *Variations for Cello and Six-Piece Rock Band* 1978, orchestrated 1986 (after Paganini) by Andrew Lloyd Webber.

Mabinogion, The (Welsh *mabinogi* 'instruction for young poets') collection of medieval Welsh myths and folk tales put together in the mid-19th century and drawn from two manuscripts: *The White Book of Rhydderch* 1300–25 and *The Red Book of Hergest* 1375–1425.

The Mabinogion proper consists of four tales, three of which concern a hero named Pryderi. Other stories in the medieval source manuscripts touch on the legendary court of King ◊Arthur.

Mabuse Jan. Adopted name of Jan Gossaert c. 1478–c. 1533. Flemish painter, active chiefly in Antwerp. His common name derives from his birthplace, Maubeuge. His visit to Italy 1508 with Philip of Burgundy started a new vogue in Flanders for Italianate ornament and Classical detail in painting, including sculptural nude figures, as in his *Neptune and Amphitrite* about 1516 (Staatliche Museen, Berlin). His other works include *The Adoration of the Magi* (National Gallery, London).

Macaulay Rose 1881–1958. English novelist. The serious vein of her early novels changed to light satire in *Potterism* 1920 and *Keeping up Appearances* 1928. Her later books include *The Towers of Trebizond* 1956.

Macaulay Thomas Babington, Baron Macaulay 1800–1859. English historian, essayist, poet, and politician, secretary of war 1839–41. His *History of England* in five volumes 1849–61 celebrates the

McCrea Joel 1905–1991. US film actor who rapidly graduated to romantic leads in the 1930s and played in several major 1930s and 1940s productions, such as *Dead End* 1937 and *Sullivan's Travels* 1941. In later decades he was associated almost exclusively with the Western genre, notably *Ride the High Country* 1962, now recognized as a classic Western film.

McCullers Carson (Smith) 1917–1967. US novelist. Most of her writing, including the novels *The Heart is a Lonely Hunter* 1940 and *Reflections in a Golden Eye* 1941, is set in her native South. Her work, like that of Flannery ◊O'Connor, has been characterized as 'Southern Gothic' for its images of the grotesque, using physical abnormalities to project the spiritual and psychological distortions of Southern experience. Her other works include her novel, *The Member of the Wedding* 1946, which was also a stage success, and the novella *The Ballad of the Sad Café* 1951.

McCullin Don(ald) 1935– . British war photographer who started out as a freelance photojournalist for the Sunday newspapers. His coverage of hostilities in the Congo 1967, Vietnam 1968, Biafra 1968 and 1970, and Cambodia 1970 are notable for their pessimistic vision. He has published several books of his work, among them *Destruction Business*.

MacDermot Galt 1928– . US composer. He wrote the rock musical *Hair* 1967, with lyrics by Gerome Ragni and James Rado. It challenged conventional attitudes about sex, drugs, and the war in Vietnam.

In the UK, the musical opened in London 1968, on the same day stage censorship ended.

McDiarmid Hugh. Pen name of Christopher Murray Grieve 1892–1978. Scottish nationalist and Marxist poet. His works include *A Drunk Man looks at the Thistle* 1926 and two *Hymns to Lenin* 1930 and 1935.

Macdonald George 1824–1905. Scottish novelist and children's writer. *David Elginbrod* 1863 and *Robert Falconer* 1868 are characteristic novels but his children's stories, including *At the Back of the North Wind* 1871 and *The Princess and the Goblin* 1872, are today more often read. Mystical imagination pervades all his books and this inspired later writers including G K Chesterton, C S Lewis, and J R R Tolkien.

MacDowell Edward Alexander 1860–1908. US Romantic composer, influenced by ◊Liszt. His works include the *Indian Suite* 1896 and piano concertos and sonatas. He was at his best with short, lyrical piano pieces, such as 'To a Wild Rose' from *Woodland Sketches* 1896.

McDowell Malcolm 1943– . English actor who played the rebellious hero in Lindsay Anderson's film *If...* 1969 and confirmed his acting abilities in Stanley Kubrick's *A Clockwork Orange* 1971.

Other films include *O Lucky Man* 1973, *Caligula* 1979, and *Blue Thunder* 1983.

McEvoy Ambrose 1878–1927. English artist who painted delicate watercolour portraits of society women.

McEwan Ian 1948– . English novelist and short-story writer. His works often have sinister or macabre undertones and contain elements of violence and bizarre sexuality, as in the short stories in *First Love, Last Rites* 1975. His novels include *The Comfort of Strangers* 1981 and *The Child in Time* 1987. *Black Dogs* 1992 was shortlisted for the Booker Prize.

McGinley Phyllis 1905–1978. Canadian-born US writer of light verse. She was a contributor to the *New Yorker* magazine and published many collections of social satire. Her works include *One More Manhattan* 1937 and *The Love Letters of Phyllis McGinley* 1954.

McGonagall William 1830–1902. Scottish poet, noted for the unintentionally humorous effect of his extremely bad serious verse: for example, his poem on the Tay Bridge disaster of 1879.

Mácha Karel Hynek 1810–1836. Czech romantic poet chiefly remembered for his patriotic and influential lyrical epic *Máj/May* 1836.

Machado Antonio 1875–1939. Spanish poet and dramatist. Born in Seville, he was inspired by the Castilian countryside in his lyric verse, contained in *Campos de Castilla/Countryside of Castile* 1912.

Machado de Assis Joaquim Maria 1839–1908. Brazilian writer and poet, regarded as the greatest Brazilian novelist. His sceptical, ironic wit is well displayed in his 30 volumes of novels and short stories, including *Epitaph for a Small Winner* 1880 and *Dom Casmurro* 1900.

Machaut Guillame de 1300–1377. French poet and composer. Born in Champagne, he was in the service of John of Bohemia for 30 years and, later, of King John the Good of France. He gave the *ballade* and *rondo* forms a new individuality and ensured their lasting popularity. His *Messe de Nostre Dame/Notre Dame Mass,* first performed in Reims Cathedral 1364, is an early masterpiece of *ars nova,* 'new (musical) art', exploiting unusual rhythmic complexities.

Machen Arthur (Llewellyn) 1863–1947. Welsh author whose stories of horror and the occult include *The Great God Pan* 1894 and *House of Souls* 1906. *The Hill of Dreams* 1907 is partly autobiographical.

Machiavelli Niccolò 1469–1527. Italian politician and author whose name is synonymous with cunning and cynical statecraft. In his most celebrated political writings, *Il principe/The Prince* 1513 and *Discorsi/Discourses* 1531, he discussed ways in which rulers can advance the interests of their states (and themselves) through an often amoral and opportunistic manipulation of other people.

Machiavelli was born in Florence and was second chancellor to the republic 1498–1512. When the Medici came to power 1512, he was arrested and imprisoned on a charge of conspiracy, but in 1513 was released to exile in the country. *The Prince*, based on his observations of the politician and military leader Cesare Borgia, is a guide for the future prince of a unified Italian state (which did not occur until the Risorgimento in the 19th century). In *L'Arte della guerra/The Art of War* 1520 Machiavelli outlined the provision of an army for a prince, and in *Historie fiorentine/History of Florence* he analysed the historical development of Florence until 1492. Among his later works are the comedies *Clizia* 1515 and *La Mandragola/The Mandrake* 1524.

One of the most powerful safeguards a prince can have against conspiracies is to avoid being hated by the populace.

Niccolò Machiavelli *The Prince* 1513

MacInnes Colin 1914–1976. English novelist, son of the novelist Angela Thirkell. His work is characterized by sharp depictions of London youth and subcultures of the 1950s, as in *City of Spades* 1957 and *Absolute Beginners* 1959.

Macke August 1887–1914. German Expressionist painter, a founding member of the ◊*Blaue Reiter* group in Munich. With Franz ◊Marc he developed a semi-abstract style derived from Fauvism and Orphism. He was killed in World War I.

He first met Marc and Kandinsky 1909, and in 1912 he and Marc went to Paris, where they encountered the abstract style of Robert Delaunay. In 1914 Macke visited Tunis with Paul ◊Klee, and was inspired to paint a series of brightly coloured watercolours largely composed of geometrical shapes but still representational.

McKellen Ian (Murray) 1939– . English actor acclaimed as the leading Shakespearean player of his generation. His stage roles include Richard II 1968, Macbeth 1977, Max in Martin Sherman's *Bent* 1979, Platonov in Chekhov's *Wild Honey* 1986, Iago in *Othello* 1989, and Richard III 1990. His films include *Priest of Love* 1982 and *Plenty* 1985.

Mackendrick Alexander 1912–1993. US-born Scottish film director and teacher responsible for some of ◊Ealing Studios' finest comedies, including *Whisky Galore!* 1949 and *The Man in the White Suit* 1951. After *Mandy* 1952 he left for Hollywood, where he made the acerbic *Sweet Smell of Success* 1957.

Mackenzie Compton 1883–1972. Scottish author. He published his first novel *The*

Passionate Elopement 1911. Later works were *Carnival* 1912, *Sinister Street* 1913–14 (an autobiographical novel), and the comic *Whisky Galore* 1947. He published his autobiography in ten 'octaves' (volumes) 1963–71.

McKern (Reginald) Leo 1920– . Australian character actor, active in the UK. He is probably best known for his portrayal of the barrister Rumpole in the television series *Rumpole of the Bailey*. His films include *Moll Flanders* 1965, *A Man for All Seasons* 1966, and *Ryan's Daughter* 1970.

Mackerras Charles 1925– . Australian conductor who has helped to make the music of the Czech composer ◊Janáček better known. He was conductor of the English National Opera 1970–78.

mackintosh waterproof coat created in the 19th century, made from a waterproof woollen fabric, patented 1823 by Charles Macintosh, and Charles Goodyear's vulcanized rubber, created 1839. The first mackintoshes of the late 19th century were neck-to-ankle garments. In the 20th century the mackintosh was redesigned to create styles such as the trenchcoat, a belted calf-length coat based on military coats, and the raincoat, a lightweight version of the mackintosh. Fabric inventions have since enabled manufacturers to create waterproof coats from synthetic blends.

Mackintosh Charles Rennie 1868–1928. Scottish architect, designer, and painter, initially working in the ◊Art Nouveau idiom but later developing a unique style, both rational and expressive. His chief works include the Glasgow School of Art 1896, various Glasgow tea rooms 1897 to about 1911, and Hill House, Helensburgh, 1902–03.

Influenced by the Arts and Crafts movement, he designed furniture and fittings, cutlery, and lighting to go with his interiors. Although initially influential, particularly on Austrian architects such as J M Olbrich and Josef Hoffman, Mackintosh was not successful in his lifetime and has only recently come to be regarded as a pioneer of modern design.

Mackmurdo Arthur H 1851–1942. English designer and architect. He founded the Century Guild 1882, a group of architects, artists, and designers inspired by William ◊Morris and John ◊Ruskin. His textile designs are forerunners of ◊Art Nouveau.

MacLaine Shirley. Stage name of Shirley MacLean Beatty 1934– . Versatile US actress whose films include Alfred Hitchcock's *The Trouble with Harry* 1955 (her debut), *The Apartment* 1960, and *Terms of Endearment* 1983, for which she won an Academy Award.

MacLaine trained as a dancer and has played in musicals, comedy, and dramatic roles. Her many offscreen interests (politics, writing) have limited her film appearances. She is the sister of Warren Beatty.

Maclean Alistair 1922–1987. Scottish adventure novelist whose first novel, *HMS Ulysses* 1955, was based on wartime experience. It was followed by *The Guns of Navarone* 1957 and other adventure novels. Many of his books were made into films.

Maclean Fitzroy Hew 1911– . Scottish writer and diplomat whose travels in the USSR and Central Asia inspired his *Eastern Approaches* 1949 and *A Person from England* 1958. His other books include *To the Back of Beyond* 1974, *Holy Russia* 1979, and *Bonnie Prince Charlie* 1988.

MacLeish Archibald 1892–1982. US poet. He made his name with the long narrative poem 'Conquistador' 1932, which describes Cortés' march to the Aztec capital, but his later plays in verse, *Panic* 1935 and *Air Raid* 1938, deal with contemporary problems.

He was born in Illinois, was assistant secretary of state 1944–45, and helped to draft the constitution of UNESCO. From 1949 to 1962 he was Boylston Professor of Rhetoric at Harvard, and his essays in *Poetry and Opinion* 1950 reflect his feeling that a poet should be 'committed', expressing his outlook in his verse.

A faith cannot be a faith against but for.
Archibald MacLeish
Survey Graphic Feb 1941

MacLennan (John) Hugh 1907–1990. Canadian novelist and essayist. He has explored the theme of an emerging Canadian identity in realist novels such as *Barometer Rising* 1941 and *Two Solitudes* 1945, which confronts the problems of cooperation between French- and English-speaking Canadians. Later works include *The Watch that Ends the Night* 1959 and *Voices in Time* 1981, bleakly imagining Montréal after a nuclear holocaust.

Maclise Daniel 1806–1870. Irish artist, active in London from 1827. He drew caricatures of literary contemporaries, such as Dickens, and his historical paintings include *The Meeting of Wellington and Blücher on the Field of Waterloo* and *The Death of Nelson*, both 1860s murals in the House of Lords, London.

MacMillan Kenneth 1929–1992. Scottish choreographer. After studying at the Sadler's Wells Ballet School, he was director of the Royal Ballet 1970–77 and then principal choreographer 1977–92. He was also director of Berlin's German Opera ballet company 1966–69. A daring stylist, he often took risks with his choreography, expanding the ballet's vocabulary with his frequent use of historical sources, reli-

gious music, and occasional use of dialogue. His works include *Romeo and Juliet* 1965 (filmed 1966) for Margot Fonteyn and Rudolf Nureyev. He is also renowned for his work with the Canadian dancer Lynn Seymour, such as *Le Baiser de la fée* 1960 and *The Invitation* 1960.

McMurtry Larry (Jeff) 1936– . US writer. Many of his works were made into films, including *Terms of Endearment* 1975, the film of which won the 1983 Academy Award for Best Picture. He also wrote *The Desert Rose* 1983, *Lonesome Dove* 1986 (Pulitzer Prize), *Texasville* 1987, and *Buffalo Girls* 1990.

Born in Wichita Falls, Texas, USA, McMurtry mostly wrote about the Southwest and about his home state of Texas in particular. Among his many other titles are *Horseman, Pass By* 1961 (film *Hud* 1963), *Leaving Cheyenne* 1963 (film *Lovin' Molly* 1963), and *The Last Picture Show* 1966 (film 1971).

MacNeice Louis 1907–1963. British poet, born in Belfast. He made his debut with *Blind Fireworks* 1929 and developed a polished ease of expression, reflecting his classical training, as in *Autumn Journal* 1939. He is noted for his low-key, socially committed but politically uncommitted verse.

Later works include the play *The Dark Tower* 1947, written for radio, for which medium he also wrote features 1941–49; a verse translation of Goethe's *Faust*; and the radio play *The Administrator* 1961. He also translated Aeschylus' *Agamemnon* 1936.

McPartland Jimmy (James Duigald) 1907–1991. US cornet player, one of the founders of the Chicago school of jazz in the 1920s. He was influenced by Louis Armstrong and Bix Beiderbecke, whom he replaced in a group called the Wolverines 1924. He also recorded with guitarist Eddie Condon, and from the late 1940s often worked with his wife, British pianist *Marian McPartland* (1920–).

McPhee Colin 1900–1964. US composer whose studies of Balinese music 1934–36 produced two works, *Tabuh-tabuhan* for two pianos and orchestra 1936 and *Balinese Ceremonial Music* for two pianos 1940, which influenced Benjamin Britten, also John Cage and later generations of US composers.

Macpherson James 1736–1796. Scottish writer and literary forger, author of *Fragments of Ancient Poetry collected in the Highlands of Scotland* 1760, followed by the epics *Fingal* 1761 and *Temora* 1763, which he claimed as the work of the 3rd-century bard ◊Ossian. After his death they were shown to be forgeries.

When challenged by Dr Samuel Johnson, Macpherson failed to produce his originals, and a committee decided 1797 that he had combined fragmentary materials with oral tradition. Nevertheless, the works of 'Ossian' influenced the development of the Romantic movement in Britain and in Europe.

McQueen Steve (Terrence Steven) 1930–1980. US actor, a film star of the 1960s and 1970s, admired for his portrayals of the strong, silent loner, and noted for performing his own stunt work. After television success in the 1950s, he became a film star with *The Magnificent Seven* 1960. His films include *The Great Escape* 1963, *Bullitt* 1968, *Papillon* 1973, and *The Hunter* 1980.

macramé art of making decorative fringes and lacework with knotted threads. The name comes from the Arabic word for 'striped cloth', which is often decorated in this way.

Macready William Charles 1793–1873. English actor. He made his debut at Covent Garden, London, 1816. Noted for his roles as Shakespeare's tragic heroes (Macbeth, Lear, and Hamlet), he was partly responsible for persuading the theatre to return to the original texts of Shakespeare and abandon the earlier, bowdlerized versions. He was manager of Drury Lane Theatre, London, 1841–43.

MacWhirter John 1839–1911. British landscape painter whose works include *June in the Austrian Tyrol, Spindrift* and various watercolours.

Madame Bovary novel by Gustave ◊Flaubert, published in France 1857. It aroused controversy by its portrayal of a country doctor's wife driven to suicide by a series of unhappy love affairs.

maddrassah in Islamic architecture, theological school comprising a prayer hall, classrooms, and lodgings, often arranged around a central courtyard.

Maderna Bruno 1920–1973. Italian composer and conductor. He collaborated with Luciano Berio in setting up an electronic studio in Milan. His compositions combine aleatoric and graphic techniques (see ◊aleatory music, ◊graph notation) with an elegance of sound. They include a pioneering work for live and prerecorded flute, *Musica su due dimensioni* 1952, numerous concertos, and *Hyperion* 1965, a 'mobile opera', consisting of a number of composed scenes that may be combined in several ways.

Madoc, Prince legendary prince of Gwynedd, Wales, supposed to have discovered the Americas and to have been an ancestor of a group of light-skinned, Welsh-speaking Indians in the American West.

Madonna stage name of Madonna Louise Veronica Ciccone 1958– . US pop singer and actress who presents herself on stage and in videos with an exaggerated sexuality. Her first hit was 'Like a Virgin' 1984; others include 'Material Girl' 1985 and 'Like a Prayer' 1989. Her films include *Desperately Seeking Susan* 1985, *Dick Tracy* 1990, the documentary *In Bed with Madonna* 1991, and *A League of Their Own* 1992.

In the early years of her career she frequently employed Catholic trappings in her dress and stage show. Her book *Sex*, a collection of erotic photographs interspersed with explicit short stories, was published 1992, coinciding with the release of the dance album *Erotica*.

Without you, I'm nothing ... without Elvis, you're nothing.

Madonna to her stage cast and crew 1990

---

madrigal form of secular song in four or five parts, usually sung without instrumental accompaniment. It originated in 14th-century Italy. Madrigal composers include Andrea ◊Gabrieli, ◊Monteverdi, Thomas ◊Morley, and Orlando ◊Gibbons.

maenad in Greek mythology, one of the women participants in the orgiastic rites of ◊Dionysus; maenads were also known as *Bacchae*.

maestà (Italian 'in majesty') in Christian art, a depiction of the enthroned Madonna and Child surrounded by angels and saints. Examples include Duccio's *Maestà Altarpiece* 1309–11 (Cathedral Museum, Siena) and Giotto's *Madonna Enthroned* about 1310 (Uffizi, Florence).

During the Renaissance, images of the Madonna and Child gradually became more intimate and earthbound, the attendant angels being replaced by saints and the donors who had commissioned the work.

maestro di capella (Italian 'chapel master') Italian equivalent of Kapellmeister.

Maeterlinck Maurice, Count Maeterlinck 1862–1949. Belgian poet and dramatist. His plays include *Pelléas et Mélisande* 1892, *L'Oiseau bleu/The Blue Bird* 1908, and *Le Bourgmestre de Stilmonde/The Burgomaster of Stilemonde* 1918. The latter work celebrates Belgian resistance in World War I, a subject that led to his exile in the USA 1940. Nobel prize 1911.

We possess only the happiness we are able to understand.

Count Maurice Maeterlinck
Wisdom and Destiny

Magic Mountain, The (German *Der Zauberberg*) novel by Thomas ◊Mann, published in Germany 1924. An ironic portrayal of the lives of a group of patients in a Swiss sanatorium, it shows the beauty and futility of their sheltered existence.

magic realism in 20th-century literature, a fantastic situation realistically treated, as in the works of many Latin American writers such as

Isabel ◊Allende, Jorge Luis ◊Borges, and Gabriel ◊García Márquez.

The technique of magic realism was pioneered in Europe by E T A Hoffman and Hermann Hesse. The term was coined in the 1920s to describe German paintings. In the UK it has been practised by, among others, Angela ◊Carter.

Magistretti Vico 1920– . Italian architect and furniture designer, active in Milan from 1945. A member of the generation which created the postwar modern Italian design movement, he has worked closely with the Arflex and ◊Cassina companies, among others, to create many lasting furniture designs in the modern style.

magnum opus (Latin) a great work of art or literature.

Magnum Photos Inc cooperative photographic agency founded 1947 by Robert ◊Capa, Henri ◊Cartier-Bresson, David Seymour ('Chim'), and George Rodger.

Magritte René 1898–1967. Belgian Surrealist painter whose paintings focus on visual paradoxes and everyday objects taken out of context. Recurring motifs include bowler hats, apples, and windows, for example *Golconda* 1953 (private collection), in which men in bowler hats are falling from the sky to a street below.

Magritte joined the other Surrealists in Paris 1927, returning to Brussels 1930. His most influential works are those that question the relationship between image and reality, as in *The Treason of Images* 1928–29 (Los Angeles County Museum of Art), in which a picture of a smoker's pipe appears with the words 'Ceci n'est pas une pipe' (This is not a pipe).

Mahābhārata (Sanskrit 'great poem of the Bharatas') Sanskrit Hindu epic consisting of 18 books and 90,000 stanzas, probably composed in its present form about 300 BC. It forms with the ◊Rāmāyana the two great epics of the Hindus. It contains the ◊Bhagavad-Gītā, or *Song of the Blessed*, an episode in the sixth book.

The poem, set on the plain of the Upper Ganges, deals with the fortunes of the rival families of the Kauravas and the Pandavas and reveals the ethical values of ancient Indian society and individual responsibility in particular.

Mahfouz Naguib 1911– . Egyptian novelist and playwright. His novels, which deal with the urban working class, include the semi-autobiographical *Khan al-Kasrain/The Cairo Trilogy* 1956–57. His *Children of Gebelawi* 1959 was banned in Egypt because of its treatment of religious themes. Nobel Prize for Literature 1988.

Mahler Alma (born Schindler) 1879–1964. Austrian pianist and composer of lieder (songs). She was the daughter of the artist Anton Schindler and abandoned composing when she married the composer Gustav Mahler 1902.

After Mahler's death she lived with the architect Walter Gropius; their daughter Manon's death inspired Berg's Violin Concerto. She later married the writer Franz Werfel.

Mahler Gustav 1860–1911. Austrian composer and conductor of epic symphonies expressing a world-weary Romanticism in visionary tableaux incorporating folk music and pastoral imagery. He composed 14 symphonies (three unnumbered), many with voices, including *Symphony No 2 'Resurrection'* 1884–86, revised 1893–96, also orchestral lieder (songs) including *Das Lied von der Erde/The Song of the Earth* 1909 and *Kindertotenlieder/Dead Children's Songs* 1901–04.

Mahler was born in Bohemia (now the Czech Republic); he studied at the Vienna Conservatoire, and conducted in Prague, Leipzig, Budapest, and Hamburg 1891–97. He was director of the Vienna Court Opera from 1897 and conducted the New York Philharmonic from 1910.

To write a symphony is, for me, to construct a world.

Gustav Mahler

Maia in Greek mythology, daughter of ◊Atlas and mother of ◊Hermes.

Maids of Honour, the (Spanish *Las Meninas*) oil painting by Diego ◊Velázquez 1656 (Prado, Madrid). The composition is of the Infanta who, together with her companions, is watching the painter at work on a portrait of her parents. The point of view is that of the King and Queen themselves (shown reflected in a mirror on the back wall) – a daring pictorial experiment. Picasso painted 44 variations on its theme 1957.

Once a newspaper touches a story, the facts are lost forever, even to the protagonists.

Norman Mailer *The Presidential Papers*

Mailer Norman 1923– . US writer and journalist. One of the most prominent figures of postwar American literature, he gained wide attention with his first, best-selling book *The ◊Naked and the Dead* 1948, a naturalistic war novel. His later works, which use sexual and scatological material, show his personal engagement with history, politics, and psychology. Always a pugnacious and controversial writer, his polemics on the theory and practice of violence-as-sex brought him into direct conflict with feminist Kate Millet in a series of celebrated debates during the 1970s.

His other books include *An American Dream* 1965, *The Armies of the Night* 1968 (Pulitzer Prize), *The Executioner's Song* 1979 (Pulitzer Prize), and two massive novels, *Ancient Evenings* 1983, and *Harlot's Ghost* 1991.

Maillol Aristide Joseph Bonaventure 1861–1944. French artist who turned to sculpture in the 1890s. His work, which is mainly devoted to the female nude, shows the influence of classical Greek art but tends towards simplified rounded forms.

Maillol was influenced by *les ◊Nabis*. A typical example of his work is *Fame* for the Cézanne monument in Aix-en-Provence.

Main Street classic satirical novel by Sinclair ◊Lewis, published 1920, which made the American small-town Main Street the exemplification of enduring if simplistic social values.

majolica or ***maiolica*** tin-glazed ◊earthenware and the richly decorated enamel pottery produced in Italy in the 15th to 18th centuries. The name derives from the Italian form of Majorca, the island from where Moorish lustreware made in Spain was shipped to Italy. During the 19th century the word was used to describe moulded earthenware with relief patterns decorated in coloured glazes.

Makarova Natalia 1940– . Russian ballerina. She danced with the Kirov Ballet 1959–70, then sought political asylum in the West, becoming one of the greatest international dancers of the ballet·boom of the 1960s and 1970s. A dancer of exceptional musicality and heightened dramatic sense, her roles include the title role in *Giselle* and Aurora in *The Sleeping Beauty*. She has also danced modern works including Jerome Robbins' *Other Dances* 1976, which he created for her.

She has also produced ballets, such as *La Bayadère* 1974, for the American Ballet Theater, and *Swan Lake* 1988, for the London Festival Ballet.

Makeba Miriam (Zenzile) 1932– . South African singer, in political exile 1960–90. She was one of the first world-music performers to make a name in the West, and is particularly associated with 'The Click Song', which features the glottal clicking sound of her Xhosa language. She was a vocal opponent of apartheid, and South Africa banned her records.

Makeba sang with a group called the Skylarks 1956–59. Introduced to US audiences 1960 when folk music was popular, she performed many traditional songs as well as South African pop songs, such as 'Pata Pata' and 'Mbube', with jazz stylings.

Making of Americans, The novel 1925 by US writer Gertrude ◊Stein. A massive and difficult work, it chronicles three generations of a German-American family. She applied a Cubist style of constant repetition and variation of the same phrases to create a new aesthetic sensibility appropriate to the emergence of America as a world power.

Malamud Bernard 1914–1986. US novelist and short-story writer. He first attracted attention with *The Natural* 1952, a mythical story about a baseball hero. It established Malamud's central concern of moral redemption and transcendence, which was more typically dealt with in books set in Jewish immigrant communities. These drew on the magical elements and mores of the European Yiddish tradition and include such novels as *The Assistant* 1957, *The Fixer* 1966, *Dubin's Lives* 1979, and *God's Grace* 1982.

Short-story collections include *The Magic Barrel* 1958, *Rembrandt's Hat* 1973, and *The Stories of Bernard Malamud* 1983.

The past exudes legend: one can't make pure clay of time's mud.

Bernard Malamud *Dubin's Lives* 1979

Malevich Kasimir 1878–1935. Russian abstract painter. In 1912 he visited Paris where he was influenced by Cubism, and in 1913 launched his own abstract style, ◊***Suprematism***. He reached his most abstract in *White on White* about 1918 (Museum of Modern Art, New York), a white square painted on a white background, but later returned to figurative themes treated in a semi-abstract style.

Malherbe François de 1555–1628. French poet and grammarian, born in Caen. He became court poet about 1605 under Henry IV and Louis XIII. He advocated reform of language and versification, and established the 12-syllable alexandrine as the standard form of French verse.

Malipiero Gian Francesco 1882–1973. Italian composer and editor of Monteverdi and Vivaldi. His own works include operas in a Neo-Classical style, based on Shakespeare's *Julius Caesar* 1934–35 and *Antony and Cleopatra* 1936–37.

Mallarmé Stéphane 1842–1898. French poet who founded the Symbolist school with Paul Verlaine. His belief that poetry should be evocative and suggestive was reflected in *L'Après-midi d'un faune/Afternoon of a Faun* 1876, which inspired the composer Debussy.

Later works are *Poésies complètes/Complete Poems* 1887, *Vers et prose/Verse and Prose* 1893, and the prose *Divagations/Digressions* 1897.

Malle Louis 1932– . French film director. After a period as assistant to director Robert Bresson, he directed *Les Amants/The Lovers* 1958, audacious for its time in its explicitness. His subsequent films, made in France and the USA,

include *Zazie dans le métro* 1961, *Viva Maria* 1965, *Pretty Baby* 1978, *Atlantic City* 1980, *Au Revoir les Enfants* 1988, *Milou en mai* 1989, and *Damage* 1993.

Malory Thomas 15th century. English author of the prose romance *Le Morte d'Arthur* about 1470. It is a translation from the French, modified by material from other sources, and it deals with the exploits of King Arthur's knights of the Round Table and the quest for the ◊Holy Grail.

Malouf David 1934– . Australian poet, novelist, and short-story writer of Lebanese and English extraction. His poetry collections include *Neighbours in a Thicket* 1974, which won several awards, *Wild Lemons* 1980, and *First Things Last* 1980. Malouf's first novel *Johnno* 1975 deals with his boyhood in Brisbane. It was followed by *An Imaginary Life* 1978 and other novels, including *Fly Away Peter* 1982, *The Great World* 1990, and *Remembering Babylon* 1993.

Malraux André 1901–1976. French writer. An active antifascist, he gained international renown for his novel *La Condition humaine/Man's Estate* 1933, set during the Nationalist/Communist Revolution in China in the 1920s. *L'Espoir/Days of Hope* 1937 is set in Civil War Spain, where he was a bomber pilot in the International Brigade. In World War II he supported the Gaullist resistance, and was minister of cultural affairs 1960–69.

Mamet David 1947– . US dramatist, film screenwriter, and director. His *American Buffalo* 1975, about a gang of hopeless robbers, was his first major success. It was followed by *Sexual Perversity in Chicago* 1978 and *Glengarry Glen Ross* 1983, a dark depiction of American business ethics, the film version of which he directed 1992. His other film work has included screenplays for *The Postman Always Rings Twice* 1981, *The Verdict* 1982, and *The Untouchables* 1987. He made his directorial debut with *House of Games* 1987.

Mammon evil personification of wealth and greed; originally a Syrian god of riches, cited in the New Testament as opposed to the Christian god.

Mamoulian Rouben 1898–1987. Armenian stage and film director who lived in the USA from 1923. After several years on Broadway he turned to films, making the first sound version of *Dr Jekyll and Mr Hyde* 1932 and *Queen Christina* 1933. His later work includes *The Mark of Zorro* 1940 and *Silk Stockings* 1957.

mandala symmetrical design in Hindu and Buddhist art, representing the universe; it is used in some forms of meditation.

Mandelshtam Osip Emilevich 1891–1938. Russian poet, a leader of the ◊Acmeist movement. Son of a Jewish merchant, he was sent to a concentration camp by the communist authorities in the 1930s and died there. His posthumously published work, with its classic brevity, established his reputation as one of the greatest 20th-century Russian poets.

His wife Nadezhda's memoirs of her life with her husband, *Hope Against Hope*, were published in the West 1970, but not until 1988 in the USSR.

Mandeville John. Supposed author of a 14th-century travel manual for pilgrims to the Holy Land, originally written in French and probably the work of Jean d'Outremeuse of Liège. As well as references to real marvels, such as the pyramids, there are tales of headless people with eyes in their shoulders and other such fantastic inventions.

mandolin plucked string instrument with four to six pairs of strings (◊courses), tuned like a violin, which flourished 1600–1800, and for which Vivaldi composed two concertos about 1736. The *Neapolitan mandolin* is a different instrument which appeared about 1750. Composers include Beethoven, Hummel, Schoenberg, and Stravinsky in *Agon* 1955–57. It takes its name from its almond-shaped body (Italian *mandorla* 'almond').

Manes in ancient Rome, the spirits of the dead, worshipped as divine and sometimes identified with the gods of the underworld (Dis and Proserpine).

Manet Edouard 1832–1883. French painter, active in Paris, one of the foremost French artists of the 19th century. Rebelling against the academic tradition, he developed a clear and unaffected realist style. His subjects were mainly contemporary, such as *A Bar at the Folies-Bergère* 1882 (Courtauld Art Gallery, London).

Manet, born in Paris, trained under a history painter and was inspired by Goya and Velázquez and also by Courbet. His *Déjeuner sur l'herbe/Picnic on the Grass* 1863 and *Olympia* 1865 (both Musée d'Orsay, Paris) offended conservative tastes in their matter-of-fact treatment of the nude body. He never exhibited with the Impressionists, although he was associated with them from the 1870s.

Manipuri one of the four main Indian dance styles (others are ◊Bharat Natyam, ◊Kathak, and ◊Kathakali). Originating in the northeast of India, it has its roots in folklore sources. Danced with a light, lyrical grace and uncomplicated technique by many dancers, its dramas are supported by dialogue and song.

Mann Anthony. Stage name of Emil Anton Bundmann 1906–1967. US film director who made a series of violent but intelligent 1950s Westerns starring James Stewart, such as *Winchester '73* 1950. He also directed the epic *El Cid* 1961. His other films include *The Glenn Miller Story* 1954 and *A Dandy in Aspic* 1968.

Mann Heinrich 1871–1950. German novelist who fled to the USA 1937 with his brother Thomas Mann. His books include *Im Schlaraffenland/In the Land of Cockaigne* 1901; *Professor Unrat/The Blue Angel* 1904, depicting the sensual downfall of a schoolmaster; a scathing trilogy dealing with the Kaiser's Germany *Das Kaiserreich/The Empire* 1918–25; and two volumes on the career of Henry IV of France 1935–38.

Mann Thomas 1875–1955. German novelist and critic, concerned with the theme of the artist's relation to society. His first novel was *Buddenbrooks* 1901, which, followed by *Der Zauberberg/The ◊Magic Mountain* 1924, led to a Nobel prize 1929. Notable among his works of short fiction is *Der Tod in Venedig/Death in Venice* 1913.

Mann worked in an insurance office in Munich and on the staff of the periodical *Simplicissimus*. His opposition to the Nazi regime forced him to leave Germany and in 1940 he became a US citizen. Among his other works are a biblical tetralogy on the theme of Joseph and his brothers 1933–44, *Dr Faustus* 1947, *Die Bekenntnisse des Hochstaplers Felix Krull/Confessions of Felix Krull* 1954, and a number of short stories, including 'Tonio Kröger' 1903.

If you are possessed by an idea, you find it expressed everywhere, you even smell it.

Thomas Mann *Death in Venice* 1913

Mannerism in painting, sculpture, and architecture, a style characterized by a subtle but conscious breaking of the 'rules' of classical composition – for example, displaying the human body in an off-centre, distorted pose, and using harsh, non-blending colours. The aim was to unsettle the viewer. The term was coined by Giorgio ◊Vasari and used to describe the 16th-century reaction to the peak of Renaissance Classicism. Strictly speaking, it refers to a style developed by painters and architects working in Italy (primarily Rome and Florence) during the years 1520s–90s, beginning with, and largely derived from, the later works of Michelangelo in painting and architecture. It includes the works of the painters Giovanni ◊Rosso and ◊Parmigianino, the architect ◊Giulio Romano, and the sculptor ◊Giambologna.

The term has been extended to cover similar styles in other arts and in other countries, for example, the works of the Spanish painter El Greco and the French Fontainebleau School.

Manning Olivia 1911–1980. British novelist. Among her books are the semi-autobiographical series set during World War II. These include *The Great Fortune* 1960, *The Spoilt City* 1962, and *Friends and Heroes* 1965, forming the 'Balkan trilogy', and a later 'Levant trilogy'.

Man Ray adopted name of Emmanuel Rudnitsky 1890–1977. US photographer, painter, and sculptor, active mainly in France; associated with the Dada movement. His pictures often showed Surrealist images, for example, the photograph *Le Violon d'Ingres* 1924.

Man Ray was born in Philadelphia, but lived mostly in Paris from 1921. He began as a painter and took up photography 1915, the year he met the Dada artist Duchamp in New York. In 1922 he invented the **rayograph**, a black-and-white image obtained without a camera by placing objects on sensitized photographic paper and exposing them to light; he also used the technique of **solarization** (partly reversing the tones on a photograph). His photographs include portraits of many artists and writers.

Mansart Jules Hardouin-. See ◊Hardouin-Mansart, Jules.

Mansfield Jayne. Stage name of Vera Jayne Palmer 1933–1967. US actress who had a short career as a kind of living parody of Marilyn Monroe in films including *The Girl Can't Help It* 1956 and *Will Success Spoil Rock Hunter?* 1957.

Mansfield Katherine. Pen name of Kathleen Beauchamp 1888–1923. New Zealand writer who lived most of her life in England. Her delicate artistry emerges not only in her volumes of short stories – such as *In a German Pension* 1911, *Bliss* 1920, and *The Garden Party* 1923 – but also in her *Letters* and *Journal*.

Born near Wellington, New Zealand, she was educated in London, to which she returned after a two-year visit home, where she published her earliest stories. She married the critic John Middleton Murry 1913.

Whenever I prepare for a journey I prepare as though for death. Should I never return, all is in order. This is what life has taught me.

Katherine Mansfield *Journal* Jan 1922

Mansur active late 16th century/early 17th century. Mogul painter. He started work at the court of the emperor Akbar, contributing several miniatures to the ◊Akbar-nama, and later painted court scenes and portraits at the court of Jahangir. He is best known for his animal paintings, which combine close observation and highly decorative stylization.

Mantegna Andrea *c.* 1431–1506. Italian Renaissance painter and engraver, active chiefly in Padua and Mantua, where some of his frescoes remain. Paintings such as *The Agony in the Garden* of about 1455 (National Gallery, London) reveal a dramatic linear style, mastery of perspective, and strongly Classical architectural detail.

Mantegna was born in Vicenza. Early works include frescoes for the Eremitani Church in Padua painted during the 1440s (badly damaged during World War II). From 1460 he worked for Ludovico Gonzaga in Mantua, producing an outstanding fresco series in the Ducal Palace in the 1470s and later *The Triumphs of Caesar* (Hampton Court, near London). He was influenced by the sculptor Donatello and in turn influenced the Venetian painter Giovanni Bellini (his brother-in-law) and the German artist Albrecht Dürer.

Manu in Hindu mythology, the founder of the human race, who was saved by ◊Brahma from a deluge.

Manzoni Alessandro, Count Manzoni 1785–1873. Italian poet and novelist, author of the historical romance *I promessi sposi/The ◊Betrothed* 1825–27, set in Spanish-occupied Milan during the 17th century. He is regarded as the greatest Italian novelist although later writers have often avoided his extreme romanticism. Verdi's *Requiem* commemorates him.

Manzù Giacomo 1908–1991. Italian sculptor who, from the 1930s, worked mostly in bronze. Although a left-wing agnostic, he received many religious commissions, including the *Door of Death* 1964 for St Peter's basilica, Rome, and a portrait bust of Pope John XXIII 1963. His figures reveal a belief in the innate dignity of the human form.

Mapplethorpe Robert 1946–1989. US art photographer known for his use of racial and homo-erotic imagery in chiefly fine platinum prints. He developed a style of polished elegance in his gallery art works, whose often culturally forbidden subject matter caused controversy.

marble metamorphosed limestone that takes and retains a good polish; it is used in building and sculpture. In its pure form it is white; mineral impurities give it various colours and patterns. Carrara, Italy, is known for white marble.

Marble Arch triumphal arch in London designed by John ◊Nash to commemorate Nelson's victories. Intended as a ceremonial entry to Buckingham Palace, in 1851 it was moved to Hyde Park at the end of Oxford Street.

Marc Franz 1880–1916. German Expressionist painter, associated with Wassily Kandinsky in founding the ◊*Blaue Reiter* movement. Animals played an essential part in his view of the world, and bold semi-abstracts of red and blue animals, particularly horses, are characteristic of his work.

Marceau Marcel 1923– . French mime artist. He is the creator of the clown-harlequin Bip and mime sequences such as 'Youth, Maturity, Old Age, and Death'.

Marduk in Babylonian mythology, the sun god, creator of Earth and humans.

Margiela Martin. Belgian fashion designer whose 'deconstruction' designs have questioned conventions of dress since he launched his first collection 1988. Taking used fabrics and secondhand clothes, he reworks the pieces, often making familiar garments into new outfits. His 1993 collection continued literally to unpick conventional clothes design as he produced dresses made out of a couple of secondhand garments, jeans where the seams had been unpicked and worked into a skirt, and a fencing jacket that fastened with velcro.

Marie de France *c.* 1150–1215. French poet, thought to have been the half-sister of Henry II of England, and abbess of Shaftesbury 1181–1215. She wrote *Lais* (verse tales that dealt with Celtic and Arthurian themes) and *Ysopet*, a collection of fables.

marimba bass ◊xylophone of Latin American origin with wooden rather than metal tubular resonators.

Marin John 1870–1953. US painter of seascapes in watercolour and oil, influenced by Impressionism. He visited Europe 1905–11 and began his paintings of the Maine coast 1914.

We can admire nothing else today but the formidable symphonies of bursting shells and the crazy sculptures modelled by our inspired artillery among the enemy hordes!

Filippo Tommaso Marinetti
reporting Italy's invasion of Libya in
L'Intransigent 1911

Marinetti Filippo Tommaso 1876–1944. Italian author who in 1909 published the first manifesto of ◊Futurism, which called for a break with tradition in art, poetry, and the novel, and glorified the machine age.

Marinetti illustrated his theories in *Mafarka le futuriste: Roman africain/Mafarka the Futurist: African Novel* 1909. His best-known work is *Manifesto tecnico della letteratura futuristica/Technical Manifesto of Futurist Literature* 1912 (translated 1971). He also wrote plays, a volume on theatrical practice 1916, and a volume of poems *Guerra sola igiene del mondo/War the Only Hygiene of the World* 1915.

Marini Marino 1901–1980. Italian sculptor. Inspired by ancient art, he developed a distinctive horse-and-rider theme, reducing the forms to an elemental simplicity. He also produced fine portraits in bronze.

marionette type of ◊puppet, a jointed figure controlled from above by wires or strings. Intricately crafted marionettes were used in

Burma (now Myanmar) and Ceylon (now Sri Lanka) and later at the courts of Italian princes in the 16th–18th centuries.

Marivaux Pierre Carlet de Chamblain de 1688–1763. French novelist and dramatist. His sophisticated comedies include *Le Jeu de l'amour et du hasard/The Game of Love and Chance* 1730 and *Les Fausses Confidences/False Confidences* 1737; his novel *La Vie de Marianne/The Life of Marianne* 1731–41 has autobiographical elements. Marivaux gave the word *'marivaudage'* (oversubtle lovers' conversation) to the French language.

He was born and lived for most of his life in Paris, writing for both of the major Paris theatre companies: the ◊Comédie Française and the Comédie Italienne, which specialized in ◊commedia dell'arte.

Mark in Celtic legend, king of Cornwall, uncle of ◊Tristan, and suitor and husband of ◊Isolde.

Markevich Igor 1912–1983. Russian-born conductor and composer whose austere ballet *L'Envol d'Icare/The Flight of Icarus* 1932 influenced Bartók. After World War II he concentrated on conducting, specializing in Russian and French composers 1880–1950.

Markova Alicia. Adopted name of Lillian Alicia Marks 1910– . British ballet dancer. She danced with ◊Diaghilev's company 1925–29, was the first resident ballerina of the Vic-Wells Ballet 1933–35, partnered Anton ◊Dolin in their own Markova–Dolin Ballet Company 1935–38, and danced with the Ballets Russes de Monte Carlo 1938–41, Ballet Theater, USA, 1941–46, and the London Festival Ballet 1950–52. A dancer of delicacy and lightness, she is associated with the great classical ballets, such as *Giselle*. She created a number of roles in Frederick ◊Ashton's early ballets, such as *Façade* 1931.

Marlborough House mansion in Pall Mall, London. Designed by Christopher ◊Wren, it was the 1st Duke of Marlborough's London home; later users include Edward VII (as Prince of Wales), Queen Mary (consort of George V), and, from 1962, gatherings of Commonwealth members.

Marley Bob (Robert Nesta) 1945–1981. Jamaican reggae singer and songwriter, a Rastafarian whose songs, many of which were topical and political, popularized reggae worldwide in the 1970s. They include 'Get Up, Stand Up' 1973 and 'No Woman No Cry' 1974; his albums include *Natty Dread* 1975 and *Exodus* 1977.

The core of Marley's band the Wailers was formed around 1960, and they began making local hits combining rock steady (a form of ◊ska), soul, and rock influences. *Catch a Fire* 1972 was a seminal reggae album, but the international breakthrough came with *Burnin'* 1973, containing the song 'I Shot the Sheriff'. Marley toured Africa 1978 and began to incorporate African elements in his music. His last album was *Uprising* 1980.

Marlowe Christopher 1564–1593. English poet and dramatist. His work includes the blank-verse plays *Tamburlaine the Great c.* 1587, *The Jew of Malta c.* 1589, *Edward II* and *Dr Faustus*, both *c.* 1592, the poem *Hero and Leander* 1598, and a translation of Ovid's *Amores*.

Marlowe was born in Canterbury and educated at Cambridge University, where he is thought to have become a government agent. His life was turbulent, with a brief imprisonment in connection with a man's death in a brawl (of which he was cleared), and a charge of atheism (following statements by the dramatist Thomas ◊Kyd under torture). He was murdered in a Deptford tavern, allegedly in a dispute over the bill, but it may have been a political killing.

Excess of wealth is cause of covetousness.

Christopher Marlowe
The Jew of Malta c. 1589

Marmontel Jean François 1723–1799. French novelist and dramatist. He wrote tragedies and libretti, and contributed to the ◊*Encyclopédie*. In 1758 he obtained control of the journal *Le Mercure/The Mercury*, in which his *Contes moraux/Moral Studies* 1761 appeared. Other works include *Bélisaire/Belisarius* 1767 and *Les Incas/The Incas* 1777.

Marot Clément 1496–1544. French poet, known for his translation of the *Psalms* 1539–43. His graceful, witty style became a model for later writers of light verse.

Marple, Miss fictional amateur detective (a prim and gentle spinster) who appears in 13 of Agatha ◊Christie's novels, beginning with *The Murder at the Vicarage* 1930 and ending with *Sleeping Murder* 1976. Miss Marple's avid interest in human behaviour and undervalued but acute mind produces solutions to highly intricate mysteries that baffle the police.

Marquand J(ohn) P(hillips) 1893–1960. US writer. Author of a series of stories featuring the Japanese detective Mr Moto, he later made his reputation with gently satirical novels of Boston society, including *The Late George Apley* 1937 (Pulitzer Prize) and *H M Pulham, Esq* 1941.

Marquet Pierre Albert 1875–1947. French painter of landscapes and Parisian scenes, chiefly the river Seine and its bridges. He was associated with ◊Fauvism but soon developed a more conventional, naturalistic style.

marquetry inlaying of various woods, bone, or ivory, usually on furniture, to create ornate patterns and pictures. *Parquetry* is the term used for geometrical inlaid patterns. The method is thought to have originated in Germany or Holland.

Márquez Gabriel García. See ◊García Márquez, Colombian novelist.

Marquis Don(ald Robert Perry) 1878–1937. US author. He is chiefly known for his humorous writing, including *Old Soak* 1921, which portrays a hard-drinking comic, and *archy and mehitabel* 1927, verse adventures typewritten by a literary cockroach.

Marriott Steve 1947–1991. UK pop singer and guitarist, successful in the mid-1960s as lead singer with the Small Faces, a mod group, but less successful with Humble Pie 1969–1975. The Small Faces had a number-one hit in 1966 with 'All or Nothing'.

Marriott was briefly in a band called the Moments before forming the Small Faces 1965 with Ronnie Lane, Ian McLagen, and Kenny Jones. They were popular on the London mod scene and soon had a hit with 'Whatcha Gonna Do About It?' 1965, followed by 'Sha La La La Lee', and 'My Mind's Eye'.

Marryat Frederick (Captain) 1792–1848. English naval officer and writer. His adventure stories include *Peter Simple* 1834 and *Mr Midshipman Easy* 1836; he also wrote a series of children's books, including *Children of the New Forest* 1847.

Mars in Roman mythology, the god of war, depicted as a fearless warrior. The month of March is named after him. He is equivalent to the Greek Ares.

Marsalis Branford 1960– . US saxophonist. Born in New Orleans, he was taught by his father Ellis Marsalis, and played alto in Art Blakey's Jazz Messengers 1981, alongside his brother Wynton Marsalis. He was tenor/soprano lead saxophonist on Wynton's 1982 world tour, and has since recorded with Miles Davis, Tina Turner, and Dizzy Gillespie. His first solo recording was *Scenes in the City* 1983.

Marsalis Wynton 1961– . US trumpet player who has recorded both classical and jazz music. He was a member of Art Blakey's Jazz Messengers 1980–82 and also played with Miles Davis before forming his own quintet. At one time this included his brother Branford Marsalis on saxophone.

'Marseillaise, La' French national anthem; the words and music were composed 1792 as a revolutionary song by the army officer Claude Joseph Rouget de Lisle (1760–1836).

Marsh Ngaio 1899–1982. New Zealand writer of detective fiction. Her first detective novel *A Man Lay Dead* 1934 introduced her protagonist Chief Inspector Roderick Alleyn.

Marston John 1576–1634. English satirist and dramatist. His early plays *Antonio and Mellida* and the tragic *Antonio's Revenge* 1599 were followed by the comedies *The Malcontent* 1604 and *The Dutch Courtesan* 1605.

Marston also collaborated with dramatists George Chapman and Ben Jonson in *Eastward Ho!* 1605, which satirized the Scottish followers of James I, and for which the authors were imprisoned.

Marsyas in Greek mythology, a ◊satyr who took up the pipes thrown down by the goddess Athena and challenged the god Apollo to a musical contest. On losing, he was flayed alive.

Martens Conrad 1801–1878. Australian landscape painter, born in London. In 1832–34 he was topographer on the *Beagle* with Charles Darwin. He settled in Sydney 1835 and there produced a large number of drawings, watercolours, and oil paintings, including many views of the harbour, such as *Sydney from Vaucluse* 1864 (Dixson Galleries, Sydney).

Martí José 1853–1895. Cuban poet, cited by Fidel Castro 1959 as the 'intellectual author' of the revolution which led to Cuban independence. His verse, written in a modernist idiom, includes the collection *Versos sencillos/Plain Verses* 1891.

Martial (Marcus Valerius Martialis) AD 41–104. Latin poet and epigrammatist. Born in Bilbilis, Spain, Martial settled in Rome AD 64, where he lived a life of poverty and dependence. His poetry, often obscene, is keenly observant of all classes in contemporary Rome.

My poems are licentious, but my life is pure.

Martial *Epigrams* AD 86

Martin John 1789–1854. English Romantic painter of grandiose landscapes and ambitious religious subjects, such as *Belshazzar's Feast* (several versions). Other examples of his work are *The Plains of Heaven* 1851–53 and the apocalyptic *The Last Judgement* 1853 (both Tate Gallery, London). Martin often made mezzotint engravings from his own work; he also illustrated Milton's *Paradise Lost*.

Martin Leslie 1908– . English architect. He was co-editor (with Naum ◊Gabo and Ben ◊Nicholson) of the review *Circle*, which helped to introduce the Modern Movement to England. With Peter Moro (1911–) and Robert Matthew (1905–1975), he designed the Royal Festival Hall, London, 1951. In 1991 he received a RIBA award for his series of buildings for the Gulbenkian Foundation, Lisbon (completed 1984), which span a period of 30 years.

Martin Violet Florence 1862–1915. Irish novelist who wrote under the pen name Martin Ross. She collaborated with her cousin Edith Somerville on tales of Anglo-Irish provincial life – for example, *Some Experiences of an Irish RM* 1899.

Martin du Gard Roger 1881–1958. French novelist who realistically recorded the way of life of the bourgeoisie in the eight-volume *Les Thibault/The World of the Thibaults* 1922–40. Nobel prize 1937.

Martineau Harriet 1802–1876. English journalist, economist, and novelist who wrote popular works on economics, children's stories, and articles in favour of the abolition of slavery.

Martinez Maria Montoya 1890–1980. Pueblo Indian potter who revived the traditional silvery black-on-black ware (made without the wheel) at San Ildefonso Pueblo, New Mexico, USA.

Martínez Ruiz José. Real name of ◊Azorín, Spanish author.

Martín Fierro influential Argentinian epic poem written 1872–79 by José Hernández (1834–1886). Romantic and occasionally satirical, it describes the life of the *gaucho* or nomadic cattleman on the pampas just as his way of life was becoming extinct.

Martini Simone. Sienese painter; see ◊Simone Martini.

Martins Peter 1946– . Danish-born US dancer, choreographer, and ballet director. He was principal dancer with the New York City Ballet (NYCB) from 1969, its joint ballet master (with Jerome Robbins) from 1983, and its director from 1990. He is especially noted for his partnership with Suzanne Farrell, with whom he danced Balanchine's *Jewels* 1967.

He created roles in, among others, Robbins' *Goldberg Variations* 1971 and Balanchine's *Stravinsky Violin Concerto* and *Duo Concertante* both 1972, and has choreographed many ballets, for example, *Calcium Night Light* 1978.

Martinu Bohuslav (Jan) 1890–1959. Czech composer who settled in New York after the Nazi occupation of Czechoslovakia 1939. His music is voluble, richly expressive, and has great vitality. His works include the operas *Julietta* 1937 and *The Greek Passion* 1959, symphonies, and chamber music.

Marvell Andrew 1621–1678. English metaphysical poet and satirist. His poems include 'To His Coy Mistress' and 'Horatian Ode upon Cromwell's Return from Ireland'. He was committed to the parliamentary cause, and was member of Parliament for Hull from 1659. He devoted his last years mainly to verse satire and prose works attacking repressive aspects of government.

Marvin Lee 1924–1987. US film actor who began his career playing violent, often psychotic villains and progressed to playing violent, occasionally psychotic heroes. His work includes *The Big Heat* 1953, *The Killers* 1964, and *Cat Ballou* 1965.

Marx Brothers team of US film comedians: Leonard *Chico* (from the 'chicks' – women – he chased) 1887–1961; Adolph, the silent *Harpo* (from the harp he played) 1888–1964; Julius *Groucho* (from his temper) 1890–1977; Milton *Gummo* (from his gumshoes, or galoshes) 1897–1977, who left the team before they began making films; and Herbert *Zeppo* (born at the time of the first zeppelins) 1901–1979, part of the team until 1935. They made a total of 13 zany films 1929–49 including *Animal Crackers* 1930, *Monkey Business* 1931, *Duck Soup* 1933, *A Day at the Races* 1937, *A Night at the Opera* 1935, and *Go West* 1940.

Marxist aesthetic theory the thought relating to the arts in Marxist countries. Early Marxists saw art as a means of communicating socialist ideals to the masses, covering subjects relevant to their everyday lives ('proletarian art'). In the Soviet Union, ◊Socialist Realism became dominant 1932, ousting Formalism, which emphasized form over content. Modernism, with its emphasis on abstraction and the individual artist's personal feelings, was dismissed as decadent by socialist critics such as Georg ◊Lukács.

The term also refers, albeit differently, to Marxist theorists working in western Europe. Critics who championed Modernism, such as Herbert Marcuse (1898–1979) and Max Horkheimer (1898–1979), believed in the autonomy and creativity of art as an antidote to repressive ideology. Walter ◊Benjamin was interested in the way that technological developments made art accessible to the masses, challenging the elitist nature of art. Other Western Marxist theorists include Lucien Goldmann (1913–1970) and Louis Althusser (1918–1990).

Mary Poppins collection of children's stories by P(amela) L(yndon) Travers (1906–), published in the UK 1934. They feature the eccentric Mary Poppins who looks after the children of the Banks family and entertains her charges by using her magical powers. Sequels include *Mary Poppins Comes Back* 1935.

Masaccio (Tommaso di Giovanni di Simone Guidi) 1401–1428. Florentine painter, a leader of the early Italian Renaissance. His frescoes in Sta Maria del Carmine, Florence, 1425–28, which he painted with Masolino da Panicale, show a decisive break with Gothic conventions. He was the first painter to apply the scientific laws of perspective, newly discovered by the architect Brunelleschi, and achieved a remarkable sense of space and volume.

Masaccio's frescoes in the Brancacci Chapel of Sta Maria del Carmine (late 1420s) include scenes from the life of St Peter, notably *The Tribute Money*, and *Adam and Eve's Expulsion from Paradise*. They have a monumental grandeur, without trace of Gothic decorative detail, unlike the work of his colleague and teacher Masolino. Masaccio's figures have solidity and weight and are clearly set in three-dimensional space. Other works by

Masaccio are the *Trinity* about 1428 (Sta Maria Novella, Florence) and the polyptych for the Carmelite church in Pisa 1426 (National Gallery, London/Staatliche Museen, Berlin/Museo di Capodimonte, Naples). Although his career marks a turning point in Italian art, he attracted few imitators.

Mascagni Pietro 1863–1945. Italian composer of the one-act opera *Cavalleria rusticana/Rustic Chivalry*, first produced in Rome 1890, in the new ◊verismo or realistic style.

Masefield John 1878–1967. English poet and novelist. His early years in the navy inspired *Salt Water Ballads* 1902 and several adventure novels; he also wrote children's books, such as *The Box of Delights* 1935, and plays. He was poet laureate from 1930.

I must go down to the sea again, for the call of the running tide / Is a wild call and a clear call that may not be denied.

John Masefield 'Sea Fever' 1902

Masekela Hugh 1939– . South African trumpet player, exiled from his homeland 1960–90, who has recorded jazz, rock, and mbaqanga (township jive). His albums include *Techno-Bush* 1984. An opponent of apartheid, he left South Africa with his wife, singer Miriam ◊Makeba.

mask artificial covering for part or all of the face, or for the whole head, associated with ritual or theatrical performances in many cultures. Theatrical traditions using masks include ancient Greek drama (full head masks), Japanese Nō (facial masks), and the Italian commedia dell'arte (caricatured half-masks). In the 20th century masked performance has been re-explored in experimental and mainstream theatrical productions.

Masolino (Tommaso da Panicale) *c.* 1383– *c.* 1447. Florentine painter who worked with ◊Masaccio on the fresco cycle in the Brancacci Chapel of Sta Maria del Carmine, Florence, about 1425. He shared Masaccio's enthusiasm for the newly discovered technique of perspective but reverted, after the younger man's death, to his own preferred decorative style, in the tradition of ◊International Gothic.

Mason A(lfred) E(dward) W(oodley) 1865–1948. British novelist, author of a tale of cowardice redeemed in the Sudan, *The Four Feathers* 1902, and a series featuring the detective Hanaud of the Sûreté, including *At the Villa Rose* 1910.

Mason Bobbie Ann 1940– . US writer. Her novel *In Country* 1985 was acclaimed for its portrayal of the impact of the Vietnam War on remote rural lives. It was followed by *Spence + Lila* 1988 and a collection of stories *Love Life* 1989.

Mason James 1909–1984. English actor who portrayed romantic villains in British films of the 1940s. After *Odd Man Out* 1947 he worked in the USA, often playing intelligent but troubled, vulnerable men, notably in *A Star Is Born* 1954. He returned to Europe 1960, where he made *Lolita* 1962, *Georgy Girl* 1966, and *Cross of Iron* 1977. His final role was in *The Shooting Party* 1984.

Mason Ronald Alison Kells 1905–1971. New Zealand poet and dramatist. Classical studies influenced his characteristic stripped language, tense rhythms, and strict verse forms. These features, in combination with a sombre, sometimes macabre intensity of feeling, were all apparent even in his precocious early collection *The Beggar* 1924, followed by *No New Thing* 1934. A more buoyant vision emerged in *This Dark Will Lighten* 1941.

masonry the craft of constructing stonework walls. The various styles of masonry include ***random rubblework***, irregular stones arranged according to fit; ***coursed rubblework***, irregular stones placed in broad horizontal bands, or courses; ***ashlar masonry***, smooth, square-cut stones arranged in courses; ***Cyclopean masonry***, large polygonal stones cut to fit each other; and ***rustification***, large stones separated by deep joints and chiselled or hammered into a variety of styles. Rustification is usually employed at the base of buildings, on top of an ashlar base, to give an appearance of added strength.

masque spectacular and essentially aristocratic entertainment with a fantastic or mythological theme in which music, dance, and extravagant costumes and scenic design figured larger than plot. Originating in Italy, it reached its height of popularity at the English court between 1600 and 1640, with the collaboration of Ben ◊Jonson as writer and Inigo ◊Jones as stage designer. ◊Milton also wrote masque verses. Composers include Henry ◊Lawes, ◊Byrd, and ◊Purcell.

The masque had great influence on the development of ballet and opera, and the elaborate frame in which it was performed developed into the proscenium arch.

Mass in music, the setting of the invariable parts of the Christian Mass, that is, the *Kyrie*, *Gloria*, *Credo*, *Sanctus* with *Benedictus*, and *Agnus Dei*. A notable example is J S Bach's *Mass in B Minor*.

Massenet Jules Emile Frédéric 1842–1912. French composer of opera, notably *Manon* 1884, *Le Cid* 1885, and *Thaïs* 1894; among other works is the orchestral suite *Scènes pittoresques* 1874.

Masses, The US left-wing magazine that published many prominent radical writers 1911–17, including John Reed and Max Eastman. It was superseded by *The Liberator* 1918–25 and then by *New Masses*, which advanced the cause of proletarian writing during the Depression years of the 1930s.

Massine Léonide 1895–1979. Russian choreographer and dancer with the Ballets Russes. He was a creator of comedy in ballet and also symphonic ballet using concert music. His works include the first Cubist-inspired ballet, *Parade* 1917, *La Boutique fantasque* 1919, and *The Three-Cornered Hat* 1919.

He succeeded Mikhail ◊Fokine at the Ballets Russes and continued with the company after Sergei ◊Diaghilev's death, later working in both the USA and Europe.

Massinger Philip 1583–1640. English dramatist, author of *A New Way to Pay Old Debts* c. 1625. He collaborated with John ◊Fletcher and Thomas ◊Dekker, and has been credited with a share in writing Shakespeare's *Two Noble Kinsmen* and *Henry VIII*.

Ambition, in a private man a vice,/Is, in a prince, the virtue.

Philip Massinger *The Bashful Lover*

Masson André 1896–1987. French artist and writer, a leader of Surrealism until 1929 when he quarrelled with the writer André Breton. His interest in the unconscious mind led him to experiment with automatic drawing – simple pen-and-ink work – and later textured accretions of pigment, glue, and sand. His automatic drawings influenced Gorky and the Expressionists. During World War II he moved to the USA, then returned to France and painted landscapes.

Master of the King's/Queen's Musick honorary appointment to the British royal household, the holder composing appropriate music for state occasions. The first was Nicholas Lanier, appointed by Charles I 1626; later appointments have included Elgar and Bliss. The present holder, Malcolm ◊Williamson, was appointed 1975.

Masters Edgar Lee 1869–1950. US poet. In his book *Spoon River Anthology* 1915, a collection of free-verse epitaphs, the people of a small town tell of their frustrated lives.

Masters John 1914–1983. British novelist, born in Calcutta, who served in the Indian army 1934–47. He wrote a series of books dealing with the Savage family throughout the period of the Raj – for example, *Nightrunners of Bengal* 1951, *The Deceivers* 1952, and *Bhowani Junction* 1954.

Mastroianni Marcello 1924– . Italian film actor, most popular for his carefully understated roles as an unhappy romantic lover in such films as Antonioni's *La notte/The Night* 1961. He starred in several films with Sophia Loren, including *Una giornata speciale/A Special Day* 1977, and worked with Fellini in *La dolce vita* 1960, *8½* 1963, and *Ginger and Fred* 1986.

Masur Kurt 1928– . German conductor, music director of the New York Philharmonic from 1990. His speciality is late Romantic and early 20th-century repertoire, in particular Mendelssohn, Liszt, Bruch, and Prokofiev. He was conductor of the Dresden Philharmonic Orchestra 1955–58 and 1967–72, before making his London debut 1973 with the New Philharmonia.

He was prominent in the political campaigning that took place prior to German unification.

Mather Cotton 1663–1728. American theologian and writer. He was a Puritan minister in Boston, and wrote over 400 works of history, science, annals, and theology, including *Magnalia Christi Americana/The Great Works of Christ in America* 1702, a vast compendium of early New England history and experience. Mather appears to have supported the Salem witch-hunts.

There is nothing more difficult for a truly creative painter than to paint a rose, because before he can do so he has first to forget all the roses that were ever painted.

Henri Matisse

Matisse Henri 1869–1954. French painter, sculptor, illustrator, and designer; one of the most original creative forces in early 20th-century art. Influenced by Impressionism, Post-Impressionism, and later Cubism, he developed a style characterized by surface pattern, strong, sinuous line, and brilliant colour. Among his favoured subjects were odalisques (women of the harem), bathers, and dancers; for example, *The Dance* 1910 (The Hermitage, St Petersburg). Later works include pure abstracts, as in his collages of coloured paper shapes (*gouaches découpées*) and the designs 1949–51 for the decoration of a chapel for the Dominican convent in Vence, near Nice. He also designed sets and costumes for Diaghilev's Ballets Russes.

In 1904 Matisse worked with Signac in the south of France in a Neo-Impressionist style. The following year he was the most important of the Fauve painters exhibiting at the Salon d'Automne, painting with bold brushstrokes, thick paint, and strong colours. He soon abandoned conventional perspective in his continued experiments with colour and expressive line, and in 1910 an exhibition of Islamic art further influenced him towards the decorative. He settled in the south of France 1914. In the 1920s his colours became brighter, his lines more graceful: *Odalisque in Red Trousers* 1922 (Musée National d'Art Moderne, Paris) is typical. Noted among his sculptures is *The Back I–IV* 1909 to about 1929 (Tate Gallery, London), a series of four sculptures in ◊relief, presenting increasingly abstract images of a woman's back.

Matsys (also **Massys** or **Metsys**) Quentin *c.* 1465–1530. Flemish painter, born in Louvain, active in Antwerp. He painted religious subjects such as the *Lamentation over Christ* 1511 (Musées Royaux, Antwerp) and portraits set against landscapes or realistic interiors. Other works include the *St Anne Altarpiece* 1509 (Musées Royaux, Brussels) and a portrait of *Erasmus* 1517 (Museo Nazionale, Rome).

Matta (Roberto Sebastien Antonio Matta Eschaurren) 1911– . Chilean-born French painter, a leading figure, along with André ◊Masson, of Surrealist-inspired automatic painting, in which images are allowed to flow from the unconscious through the hand directly on to paper or canvas. His expressed intention in much of his work is an attempt to define the anxieties of the age through the force and motion of forms, as in *Years of Fear* 1942 (Solomon R Guggenheim Museum, New York).

Matthau Walter. Stage name of Walter Matuschanskavasky 1922– . US character actor, impressive in both comedy and dramatic roles. He gained film stardom in the 1960s after his stage success in *The Odd Couple* 1965. His many films include *Kotch* 1971, *Charley Varrick* 1973, and *The Sunshine Boys* 1975.

Mattox Matt 1921– . US jazz dancer and teacher. He pioneered jazz dance in the USA and appeared in many films; for example, *Seven Brides for Seven Brothers* 1954. From 1970 he taught at the Dance Centre, London, and later in Paris.

Matura Mustapha 1939– . Trinidad-born British dramatist. Cofounder of the Black Theatre Cooperative 1978, his plays deal with problems of ethnic diversity and integration. These include *As Time Goes By* 1971, *Play Mas* 1974, and *Meetings* 1981. Other works include *Playboy of the West Indies* 1984 and *Trinidad Sisters* 1988 (adaptations of plays by Synge and Chekhov respectively) and *The Coup* 1991.

Mature Victor 1915– . US actor, film star of the 1940s and early 1950s. He gave strong performances in, among others, *My Darling Clementine* 1946, *Kiss of Death* 1947, and *Samson and Delilah* 1949.

Maufe Edward 1883–1974. British architect. His works include the Runnymede Memorial and Guildford Cathedral.

Maugham (William) Somerset 1874–1965. English writer. His work includes the novels *Of Human Bondage* 1915, *The Moon and Sixpence* 1919, and *Cakes and Ale* 1930; the short-story collections *The Trembling of a Leaf* 1921 and *Ashenden* 1928; and the plays *Lady Frederick* 1907 and *Our Betters* 1923.

No married man's ever made up his mind till he's heard what his wife has got to say about it.

Somerset Maugham *Lady Frederick*

Maupassant Guy de 1850–1893. French author who established a reputation with the short story 'Boule de suif'/'Ball of Fat' 1880 and wrote some 300 short stories in all. His novels include *Une Vie/A Woman's Life* 1883 and *Bel-Ami* 1885. He was encouraged as a writer by Gustave ◊Flaubert.

Mauriac François 1885–1970. French novelist. His novel *Le Baiser au lépreux/A Kiss for the Leper* 1922 describes the conflict of an unhappy marriage. The irreconcilability of Christian practice and human nature is examined in *Fleuve de feu/River of Fire* 1923, *Le Désert de l'amour/The Desert of Love* 1925, and *Thérèse Desqueyroux* 1927. Nobel Prize for Literature 1952.

Let us be wary of ready-made ideas about courage and cowardice: the same burden weighs infinitely more heavily on some shoulders than on others.

François Mauriac *Second Thoughts*

Maurois André. Pen name of Emile Herzog 1885–1967. French novelist and writer whose works include the semi- autobiographical *Bernard Quesnay* 1926 and fictionalized biographies, such as *Ariel* 1923, a life of Shelley.

In World War I he was attached to the British Army, and the essays in *Les Silences du Colonel Bramble* 1918 offer humorously sympathetic observations on the British character.

mausoleum large, free-standing, sumptuous tomb. The term derives from the magnificent sepulchral monument built for King Mausolus of Caria (died 353 BC) by his wife Artemisia at Halicarnassus in Asia Minor (modern-day Bodrum in Anatolia, Turkey); it was considered one of the ◊Seven Wonders of the World. Today, little remains at the site of the original monument, although some fragmentary sculptures from it are kept in the British Museum, London.

Later examples of mausolea include the Mausoleum of Galla Placidia (5th century AD) at

Ravenna, Italy, the ◊Taj Mahal, and the sepulchral chapel built by Queen Victoria for Prince Albert at Frogmore, England.

Mavor O H. Real name of the Scottish dramatist James ◊Bridie.

Mayakovsky Vladimir 1893–1930. Russian Futurist poet who combined revolutionary propaganda with efforts to revolutionize poetic technique in his poems '150,000,000' 1920 and 'V I Lenin' 1924. His satirical play *The Bedbug* 1928 was taken in the West as an attack on philistinism in the USSR.

Art is not a mirror to reflect the world, but a hammer with which to shape it.

Vladimir Mayakovsky

Mayan art see ◊pre-Columbian art.

Mayer Louis B(urt). Adopted name of Eliezer Mayer 1885–1957. Russian-born US film producer. He began producing films 1917 and in 1924 he founded ◊Metro-Goldwyn-Mayer (MGM) with Samuel ◊Goldwyn. It was Mayer who was largely responsible for MGM's lavish style. He retired 1951.

Mayer Robert 1879–1985. German-born British philanthropist who founded the Robert Mayer Concerts for Children and the Transatlantic Foundation Anglo-American Scholarships.

Ma Yuan *c.* 1190–1224. Chinese landscape painter who worked in the lyrical tradition of the southern Song court. His paintings show a subtle use of tone and gentler brushwork than those of his contemporary ◊Hsia Kuei.

maze labyrinthine arrangement of passages or paths. One of the earliest was the Cretan maze constructed by Daedalus, within which the mythical Minotaur was said to live.

The maze at Hampton Court, near London, dates from 1689. Longleat has Britain's longest maze.

mazurka lively national dance of Poland from the 16th century. In triple time, it is characterized by foot-stamping and heel-clicking, together with a turning movement.

mbalax pop music of W Africa with polyrhythmic percussion and dramatic vocal harmonies. Evolving from the traditional rhythms of the Mandinka people, and absorbing a Cuban influence, it incorporated electric guitars and other Western instruments in the 1970s. The singer Youssou ◊N'Dour made mbalax known outside Africa.

mbaqanga or *township jive* South African pop music, an urban style that evolved in the 1960s,

with high-pitched, choppy guitar and a powerful bass line: it draws on funk, reggae, and (vocally) on South African choral music. Mahlathini (1937–) and the Mahotella Queens are long-established exponents.

McGahern John 1934– . Irish novelist. He won early acclaim for *The Barracks* 1963, a study of the mind of a dying woman. His books explore Irish settings and issues as in *Amongst Women* 1991, about an ageing member of the IRA. His other works include *The Dark* 1965, *Nightlines* 1970, *The Leavetaking*, and *The High Ground* 1985.

McGrath John 1935– . Scottish dramatist and director. He founded the socialist 7:84 Theatre Companies in England 1971 and Scotland 1973, and is the author of such plays as *Events Guarding the Bofors Gun* 1966; *The Cheviot, the Stag, and the Black, Black Oil* 1973, a musical account of the economic exploitation of the Scottish highlands; and *The Garden of England* 1985.

McInerney Jay 1955– . US novelist. His first novel, *Bright Lights, Big City* 1984, was a richly comic portrait of a bright young man in Manhattan society. It was followed by *Ransom* 1985 and *Story of My Life* 1988.

McKim, Mead & White US firm of architects, established 1879 by Charles Follen McKim (1847–1909), William Rutherford Mead (1846–1928), Stanford White (1853–1906), and Joseph Merrill Wells (died 1890). Their early work was inspired by Italian High Renaissance architecture rather than the flamboyant Baroque style popular in the USA at the time, as evident in their design for the Boston Public Library 1887, which owes much to ◊Labrouste's Library of Ste Geneviève.

Other notable buildings by the firm include Columbia University 1893 and Pennsylvania railway station 1904–10 (now demolished).

Medea in Greek mythology, the sorceress daughter of the king of Colchis. When ◊Jason reached Colchis, she fell in love with him, helped him acquire the ◊Golden Fleece, and they fled together. When Jason later married Creusa, daughter of the king of Corinth, Medea killed his bride with the gift of a poisoned garment, and then killed her own two children by Jason.

Medea Greek tragedy by ◊Euripides, produced 431 BC. It deals with the later part of the legend of Medea: her murder of Jason's bride and of her own children by Jason after his desertion of her.

medieval art painting and sculpture in Europe and parts of the Middle East, dating roughly from the 3rd century to the emergence of the Renaissance in Italy in the 1400s. This includes early Christian, Byzantine, Celtic, Anglo-Saxon, and Carolingian art. The Romanesque style was the first truly international style of medieval times, superseded by Gothic in the late 12th century. Religious sculpture, frescoes, and manuscript illumination proliferated; panel painting was introduced only towards the end of the Middle Ages.

early Christian art (3rd–5th centuries AD) This dates from when Christianity was made one of the official religions of the Roman state. Churches were built and artistic traditions adapted to the portrayal of the new Christian saints and symbols. Roman burial chests (sarcophagi) were adopted by the Christians and the imagery of pagan myths was gradually transformed into biblical themes.

Byzantine art (4th–15th centuries) This developed in the Eastern Empire, centred on Byzantium (modern Istanbul). The use of mosaic associated with the ◊Byzantine style also appears in church decoration in the West. In Ravenna, for example, churches of the 5th and 6th centuries present powerful religious images on walls and vaults in brilliant, glittering colour and a bold, linear style. The Byzantine style continued for many centuries in icon painting in Greece and Russia.

Celtic and Anglo-Saxon art (4th–9th centuries) Stemming from the period when S Europe was overrun by Germanic tribes from the north, this early medieval art consists mainly of portable objects, such as articles for personal use or adornment. Among the invading tribes, the Anglo-Saxons, particularly those who settled in the British Isles, excelled in metalwork and jewellery, often in gold with garnet or enamel inlays, ornamented with highly stylized, plant-based interlace patterns with animal motifs. This type of ornament was translated into manuscript illumination produced in Christian monasteries, such as the decorated pages of the Northumbrian 7th-century *Lindisfarne Gospels* (British Museum, London) or the Celtic 8th-century *Book of Kells* (Trinity College, Dublin, Ireland).

Carolingian art (9th–10th centuries) Carolingian art centred around manuscript illumination, which flourished in Charlemagne's empire, drawing its inspiration from the late Classical artistic traditions of the early Christian, Byzantine, and Anglo-Saxon styles. Several monasteries produced richly illustrated prayer books and biblical texts. Carved ivories and delicate metalwork, especially for bookcovers, and small-scale sculptures were also produced.

Romanesque or *Norman art* (10th–12th centuries) This is chiefly evident in church architecture and church sculpture, on capitals and portals, and in manuscript illumination. Romanesque art was typified by the rounded arch, and combined naturalistic elements with the fantastic, poetical, and pattern-loving Celtic and Germanic traditions. Imaginary beasts and medieval warriors mingle with biblical themes. Fine examples remain throughout Europe, from N Spain and Italy to France, the Germanic lands

of the Holy Roman Empire, England, and Scandinavia. *Gothic art* (late 12th–15th centuries) Gothic art developed as large cathedrals were built in Europe. Sculptural decoration in stone became more monumental, and stained glass filled the tall windows, as at Chartres Cathedral, France. Figures were also carved in wood. Court patronage produced exquisite small ivories, goldsmiths' work, devotional books illustrated with miniatures, and tapestries depicting romantic tales. Panel painting, initially on a gold background, evolved in N Europe into the highly decorative but more realistic ◊*International Gothic* style.

medium in the arts, the physical means used to convey information or create a work of art, or the category of work resulting from these means – for instance, oil on canvas, the written word, television, and computer graphics. In painting, a medium is the liquid forming a suspension of the pigment.

Medusa in Greek mythology, a mortal woman who was transformed into a ◊Gorgon. Medusa was slain by ◊Perseus; the winged horse ◊Pegasus was supposed to have sprung from her blood. Her head was so hideous – even in death – that any beholder was turned to stone.

Meegeren Hans van 1889–1947. Dutch forger, mainly of Vermeer's paintings. His 'Vermeer' *Christ at Emmaus* was bought for Rotterdam's Boymans Museum 1937. He was discovered when a 'Vermeer' sold to the Nazi leader Goering was traced back to him after World War II. Sentenced to a year's imprisonment, he died two months later.

Mehta Ved 1934– . Indian journalist. He was educated at blind schools in Bombay and the USA, and later at Oxford and Harvard. A staff writer for the *New Yorker* since 1960 (he took US citizenship 1975), he has written family and personal chronicles such as as *Daddyji* 1971 and *The Ledge between the Streams* 1984 and essays on philosophical, theological, and historical issues collected in volumes such as *Fly and the Fly-Bottle* 1963.

Mehta Zubin 1936– . Indian-born US conductor, music director of the New York Philharmonic from 1978. He specializes in robust, polished interpretations of 19th- and 20th-century repertoire, including contemporary US composers.

Meier Richard 1934– . US architect whose white designs spring from the poetic Modernism of the ◊Le Corbusier villas of the 1920s. Originally one of the ◊New York Five, Meier has remained closest to its purist ideals. His abstract style is at its most mature in the Museum für Kunsthandwerk (Museum of Arts and Crafts), Frankfurt, Germany, which was completed 1984.

Earlier schemes are the Bronx Developmental Centre, New York, 1970–76, and the Athenaeum–New Harmony, Indiana, 1974. He is the architect for the Getty Museum, Los Angeles, due to open 1996.

Architecture does not transcend the function of the building, it embodies it.

Richard Meier

Meiningen Theatre German court theatre of the late 19th century whose innovations in staging, scene design, lighting, and period research had an influence on directors such as André Antoine and Stanislavsky. The company was led by actress Ellen Franz (1839–1923) and directed by her husband Duke Georg of Saxe-Meiningen (1826–1914) and toured its productions 1874–90.

Meiselas Susan 1948– . US freelance war photographer who has covered conflicts in Nicaragua and El Salvador. Her brilliant ◊Cibachrome prints seem antiheroic in their intention.

Meissen ware or *Dresden china* a delicate, hardpaste porcelain made in Meissen, near Dresden, Germany. Meissen ware was the first hardpaste porcelain made in Europe following the discovery of the process 1710. Its quality and fine decoration, particularly in Rococo and Chinese styles, made it the most popular and influential porcelain of the first half of the 18th century.

Meistersinger (German 'master singer') one of a group of German lyric poets, singers, and musicians of the 14th–16th centuries, who formed guilds for the revival of minstrelsy. Hans ◊Sachs was a Meistersinger, and Wagner's opera *Die Meistersinger von Nürnberg* 1868 depicts the tradition.

Melba Nellie. Adopted name of Helen Porter Mitchell 1861–1931. Australian soprano whose recordings of Italian and French romantic opera, including a notable *Lucia di Lammermoor*, are distinguished by a radiant purity and technical finesse. She studied in Paris under Marchesi 1886, and made her opera debut 1887.

Peach melba (half a peach plus vanilla ice cream and melba sauce, made from sweetened, fresh raspberries) and *melba toast* (crisp, thin toast) are named after her.

Meleager about 140–170 BC. Greek philosopher and epigrammatist, compiler of an ◊anthology of epigrams, known as the *Garland*, for which he wrote an introduction, comparing each poet to an appropriate flower. His own epigrams are mostly erotic, and successfully combine sophistication with feeling.

Méliès Georges 1861–1938. French film pioneer. From 1896 to 1912 he made over 1,000 films, mostly fantasies (*Le Voyage dans la lune/A Trip to the Moon* 1902). He developed trick effects, slow motion, double exposure, and dissolves, and in 1897 built Europe's first film studio at Montreuil.

Beginning his career as a stage magician, Méliès' interest in cinema was sparked by the Lumière brothers' cinematograph, premiered 1895. He constructed a camera and founded a production company, Star Film. Méliès failed to develop as a filmmaker and he went bankrupt 1913.

Mellon Andrew William 1855–1937. US financier who donated his art collection to found the National Gallery of Art, Washington, DC, 1937. His son, *Paul Mellon* (1907–), was its president 1963–79. He funded Yale University's Center for British Art, New Haven, Connecticut, and donated major works of art to both collections.

Melnikov Konstantin Stepanovich 1890–1974. Soviet architect, noted for his imaginative interpretations of the Constructivist ethic. His design for the Rusakov Workers Club, Moscow, 1927–28, leans towards Expressionism, with its interior dominated by cantilevered segments from the highest of three auditoria that extend over the open ground-floor plan. The Club was later to influence James ◊Stirling in his Leicester University Engineering Building 1959–63.

melodrama play or film with romantic and sensational plot elements, often concerned with crime, vice, or catastrophe. Originally it meant a play accompanied by music. The early melo dramas used extravagant theatrical effects to heighten violent emotions and actions artificially. By the end of the 19th century, melodrama had become a popular genre of stage play.

Beginning with the early work of ◊Goethe and ◊Schiller, melodrama was popularized in France by Pixérécourt (1773–1844), whose *L'Enfant de mystère* was first introduced to England in an unauthorized translation by Thomas Holcroft as *A Tale of Mystery* 1802. Melodramas were frequently played against a Gothic background of mountains or ruined castles.

melody (Greek *melos* 'song') in music, a distinctive sequence of notes sounded consecutively within an orderly pitch structure such as a scale or a mode. A melody may be a tune in its own right, or it may form a theme running through a longer piece of music.

Melpomene in Greek mythology, the ◊Muse of tragedy.

Melville Herman 1819–1891. US writer whose ◊*Moby-Dick* 1851 was inspired by his whaling experiences in the South Seas and is considered to be one of the masterpieces of American literature. These experiences were also the basis for earlier fiction, such as the adventure narratives of *Typee* 1846 and *Omoo* 1847. *Billy Budd, Sailor* was completed just before his death and published 1924. Although most of his works were unappreciated during his lifetime, today he is one of the most highly regarded of US authors.

Melville was born in Albany, New York, and went to sea as a cabin boy 1839. His love for the sea was inspired by this and later voyages. He published several volumes of verse, as well as short stories (*The Piazza Tales* 1856). Melville worked in the New York customs office 1866–85, writing no prose from 1857 until *Billy Budd*. This work was the basis of an opera by Benjamin Britten 1951, and was made into a film 1962.

Old age is always wakeful; as if, the longer linked with life, the less man has to do with aught that looks like death.

Herman Melville *Moby-Dick*

Memling (or *Memlinc*) Hans *c.* 1430–1494. Flemish painter, born near Frankfurt-am-Main, Germany, but active in Bruges. He painted religious subjects and portraits. *The Donne Triptych* about 1480 (National Gallery, London) is one of his best-known works.

Memling is said to have been a pupil of van der Weyden, but his style is calmer and softer. His portraits include *Tommaso Portinari and His Wife* about 1480 (Metropolitan Museum of Art, New York), and he decorated the *Shrine of St Ursula* 1489 in the Hospital of St John, Bruges, which is now the Memling Museum.

Memphis informal group of Italian designers established 1981, headed by Ettore ◊Sottsass and including Michele de Lucchi (1951–), George Sowden, and Nathalie du Pasquier, based in Milan. It put together a series of annual exhibitions 1981–87 challenging the conventional language of 'good design'.

Whom the gods love dies young.

Menander *The Double Deceiver*

Menander *c.* 342–291 BC. Greek comic dramatist, born in Athens. Previously only known by reputation and some short fragments, Menander's comedy *Bad-tempered Man* 316 BC, was discovered 1957 on Egyptian papyrus. Substantial parts of *The Samian Woman, The Arbitration, The Unkindest Cut,* and *The Shield* are also extant. His comedies, with their wit and

ingenuity of plot, often concerning domestic intrigue, were adapted by the Roman comic dramatists ◊Plautus and ◊Terence.

Mencken H(enry) L(ouis) 1880–1956. US essayist and critic, known as 'the sage of Baltimore'. His unconventionally phrased, satirical contributions to the periodicals *The Smart Set* and *American Mercury* (both of which he edited) aroused controversy.

Injustice is relatively easy to bear; what stings is justice.

H L Mencken *Prejudices*

Mendelsohn Erich 1887–1953. German Expressionist architect who caused a sensation with his sculptural curved design for the Einstein Tower, Potsdam, 1919–20. His later work fused Modernist and Expressionist styles; in Britain he built the de la Warr Pavilion 1935–36 in Bexhill-on-Sea, East Sussex. In 1941 he settled in the USA, where he designed the Maimonides Hospital, San Francisco, 1946–50.

Mendelssohn (-Bartholdy) (Jakob Ludwig) Felix 1809–1847. German composer, also a pianist and conductor. His music has a lightness and charm of Classical music, applied to Romantic and descriptive subjects. Among his best-known works are *A Midsummer Night's Dream* 1827; the *Fingal's Cave* overture 1832; and five symphonies, which include the 'Reformation' 1830, the 'Italian' 1833, and the 'Scottish' 1842. He was instrumental in promoting the revival of interest in J S Bach's music.

Menelaus in Greek mythology, king of Sparta, son of Atreus, brother of ◊Agamemnon, and husband of ◊Helen. With his brother he was joint leader of the Greek expedition against ◊Troy.

Mengs Anton Raffael 1728–1779. German Neo-Classical painter, born in Bohemia. He was court painter in Dresden 1745 and in Madrid 1761; he then worked alternately in Rome and Spain. The ceiling painting *Parnassus* 1761 (Villa Albani, Rome) is an example of his work.

Mengs' father was a painter of miniatures at the Dresden court and encouraged his son to specialize in portraiture. In 1755 he met the art connoisseur Johann Winckelmann, a founder of Neo-Classicism; Mengs adopted his artistic ideals and wrote a treatise *Beauty in Painting*.

Meninas, Las painting by Velázquez; see ◊*Maids of Honour, The.*

Menotti Gian Carlo 1911– . Italian-born US composer of small-scale realist operas in tonal idiom, including *The Medium* 1946, *The Telephone* 1947, *The Consul* 1950, *Amahl and the Night Visitors* 1951 (the first opera to be written for television), and *The Saint of Bleecker Street* 1954. He has also written orchestral and chamber music. He was co-librettist with Samuel ◊Barber for the latter's *Vanessa* and *A Hand of Bridge*.

Melody is a form of remembrance. It must have a quality of meritability in our ears.

Gian Carlo Menotti *Time* May 1950

Mentor in Homer's *Odyssey*, an old man, adviser to ◊Telemachus in the absence of his father ◊Odysseus. His form is often taken by the goddess Athena.

Menuhin Yehudi 1916– . US-born violinist and conductor. His solo repertoire extends from Vivaldi to Enescu. He recorded the Elgar *Violin Concerto* 1932 with the composer conducting, and commissioned the *Sonata* for violin solo 1944 from an ailing Bartók. He has appeared in concert with sitar virtuoso Ravi Shankar, and with jazz violinist Stephane Grappelli.

He made his debut with an orchestra at the age of 11 in New York. A child prodigy, he achieved great depth of interpretation, and was often accompanied on the piano by his sister **Hephzibah** (1921–1981). In 1959 he moved to London and became a British subject 1985. He founded the Yehudi Menuhin School of Music in Stoke d'Abernon, Surrey, 1963.

Menzies William Cameron 1896–1957. US art director of films, later a director and producer, who was one of Hollywood's most imaginative and talented designers. He was responsible for the sets of such classics as *Gone With the Wind* (Academy Award for best art direction) 1939 and *Foreign Correspondent* 1940. His films as director include *Things to Come* 1936 and *Invaders from Mars* 1953.

Mephistopheles or *Mephisto* another name for the devil, or an agent of the devil, associated with the ◊Faust legend.

Mercer David 1928–1980. British dramatist. He first became known for his television plays, including *A Suitable Case for Treatment* 1962, filmed as *Morgan, A Suitable Case for Treatment* 1966; stage plays include *After Haggerty* 1970.

Merchant Ismail 1936– . Indian film producer, known for his stylish collaborations with James ◊Ivory on films including *Shakespeare Wallah* 1965, *The Europeans* 1979, *Heat and Dust* 1983, *A Room with a View* 1987, *Maurice* 1987, *Howards End* 1992, and *The Remains of the Day* 1993.

Merchant of Venice, The comedy by William ◊Shakespeare, first performed 1596–97. Antonio, a rich merchant, borrows money from Shylock, a Jewish moneylender, promising a pound of flesh if the sum is not repaid; when Shylock presses his claim, the heroine, Portia, disguised as a lawyer, saves Antonio's life.

Mercury in Roman mythology, a god, identified with the Greek ◊Hermes, and like him represented with winged sandals and a winged staff entwined with snakes. He was the messenger of the gods, and was associated particularly with commerce.

Meredith George 1828–1909. English novelist and poet. His realistic psychological novel, *The Ordeal of Richard Feverel* 1859, engendered both scandal and critical praise. His best-known novel *The Egoist* 1879, is superbly plotted and dissects the hero's self-centredness with merciless glee. The sonnet sequence *Modern Love* 1862 reflects the failure of his own marriage to the daughter of Thomas Love Peacock.

His other works include *Evan Harrington* 1861, *Diana of the Crossways* 1885, and *The Amazing Marriage* 1895. His verse includes *Poems and Lyrics of the Joy of Earth* 1883.

Speech is the small change of silence.

George Meredith
The Ordeal of Richard Feverel 1859

---

merengue Latin American dance music with a lively 2/4 beat. Accordion and saxophone are prominent instruments, with ethnic percussion. It originated in the Dominican Republic and became popular in New York in the 1980s.

Mérimée Prosper 1803–1870. French author. Among his works are the short novels *Colomba* 1841, *Carmen* 1846 (the basis for Bizet's opera), and the *Lettres à une inconnue/Letters to an Unknown Girl* 1873.

Born in Paris, he entered the public service and under Napoleon III was employed on unofficial diplomatic missions.

Merlin legendary magician and counsellor to King ◊Arthur. Welsh bardic literature has a cycle of poems attributed to him, and he may have been a real person. He is said to have been buried in a cave in the park of Dynevor Castle, Dyfed.

mermaid mythical sea creature (the male is a *merman*), having a human head and torso and a fish's tail. The dugong and seal are among suggested origins for the idea.

Merrie England book published 1893 by socialist journalist Robert Blatchford (1851–1943), calling nostalgically for an end to industrialism and a return to the rural way of life.

Mersey beat pop music of the mid-1960s that originated in the northwest of England. It was also known as the Liverpool sound or ◊beat music in the UK. It was almost exclusively performed by all-male groups, the most popular being the Beatles.

Mesopotamian art the art of the ancient civilizations which grew up in the area around the Tigris and Euphrates rivers, now in Iraq. Mesopotamian art, which was largely used to glorify powerful dynasties, achieved great richness and variety.

Sumerian (3500–2300 BC) The first of the powerful Mesopotamian civilizations, Sumer was concentrated in the cities of Ur, Eridu, and Uruk in southern Mesopotamia. The Sumerians built temples on top of vast ziggurats (stepped towers) and also vast, elaborately decorated palaces. Sculptures include erect, stylized figures carved in marble and characterized by clasped hands and huge eyes: those found at the Abu Temple, Tell Asmar, date from 2700 BC. Earlier sculptures in alabaster, such as the *Female Head* 3000 BC (Iraq Museum, Baghdad), show a greater naturalism and sensitivity. Inlay work is seen in the *Standard of Ur* 2500 BC, a box decorated with pictures in lapis lazuli, shell, and red sandstone. The Sumerians, who invented writing about 3000 BC, produced many small, finely carved cylindrical seals made of marble, alabaster, carnelian, lapis lazuli, and stone.

Akkadian (2300–2150 BC) The Akkadian invaders quickly assimilated Sumerian styles. The stele (decorated upright slab) *Victory of Naram-Sin* 2200 BC (Louvre, Paris), carved in relief, depicts a military campaign of the warlike Akkadians. The technical and artistic sophistication of bronze sculpture is illustrated by the *Head of an Akkadian King* 2200 BC (Iraq Museum, Baghdad).

Assyrian (1400–600 BC) The characteristic Assyrian art form was narrative relief sculpture, which was used to decorate palaces, for example, the Palace of Ashurbanipal (7th century BC). Its dramatic and finely carved reliefs, including dramatic scenes of a lion hunt, are in the British Museum, London. Winged bulls with human faces, carved partially in the round, stood as sentinels at the royal gateways (Louvre, Paris).

Babylonian (625–538 BC) Babylon, although it had ancient traditions, came to artistic prominence in the 6th century BC, when it flourished under King Nebuchadnezzar II. He built the ◊Hanging Gardens of Babylon, a series of terraced gardens. The Babylonians practised all the Mesopotamian arts and excelled in brightly coloured glazed tiles, used to create relief sculptures. An example is the Ishtar Gate (about 575 BC) from the Temple of Bel, the biblical Tower of Babel (Pergamon Museum, Berlin, and Metropolitan Museum of Art, New York).

Messager André Charles Prosper 1853–1929. French composer and conductor. He studied under Saint-Saëns. Messager composed light operas, such as *La Béarnaise* 1885 and *Véronique* 1898.

Messiaen Olivier 1908–1992. French composer, organist, and teacher. His music is mystical in character, vividly coloured, and incorporates transcriptions of birdsong. Among his works are the *Quartet for the End of Time* 1941, the large-scale *Turangalîla Symphony* 1949, and solo organ and piano pieces. As a teacher at the Paris Conservatoire from 1942, he influenced three generations of composers.

His theories of melody, harmony, and rhythm, drawing on medieval and Oriental music, have inspired contemporary composers such as ◊Boulez and ◊Stockhausen.

I doubt that one can find in any music, however inspired, melodies and rhythms that have the sovereign freedom of bird song.

Olivier Messiaen

Meštrović Ivan 1883–1962. Yugoslav sculptor, a US citizen from 1954. His works include portrait busts of the sculptor Rodin (with whom he is often compared), President Hoover, Pope Pius XI, and many public monuments.

Metalious Grace (born Repentigny) 1924–1964. US novelist. She wrote many short stories but made headlines with *Peyton Place* 1956, an exposé of life in a small New England town, which was made into a film 1957 and a long-running television series.

Metaphysical Painting (Italian *pittura metafisica*) Italian painting style, conceived 1917 by Giorgio de ◊Chirico and Carlo ◊Carrà, which sought to convey a sense of mystery through the use of dreamlike imagery. Reacting against both Cubism and Futurism, it anticipated Surrealism in the techniques it employed, notably the incongruous juxtaposition of familiar objects. Though short-lived – it had disbanded by the early 1920s – its influence was considerable.

metaphysical poets group of early 17th-century English poets whose work is characterized by ingenious, highly intricate wordplay and unlikely or paradoxical imagery. Among the leading metaphysical poets are John Donne, George Herbert, Andrew Marvell, Richard Crashaw, and Henry Vaughan.

Metastasio pen name of Pietro Trapassi 1698–1782. Italian poet and the leading librettist of his day, creating 18th-century Italian *opera seria* (serious opera).

Method US adaptation of ◊Stanislavsky's teachings on acting and direction, in which importance is attached to the psychological building of a role rather than the technical side of its presentation. Emphasis is placed on improvisation, aiming for a spontaneous and realistic style of acting. One of the principal exponents of the Method was the US actor and director Lee Strasberg, who taught at the ◊Actors Studio in New York.

metre in poetry, the recurring pattern of stressed and unstressed syllables in a line of ◊verse. The unit of metre is a foot. Metre is classified by the number of feet to a line: a minimum of two and a maximum of eight. A line of two feet is a dimeter. They are then named, in order, trimeter, tetrameter, pentameter, hexameter, heptameter, and octameter.

metre in music, the timescale represented by the beat. Metre is regular, rhythm irregular. Metre can be *simple* as in 2/4, 3/4, 4/8, and so on, where each beat divides into two sub-beats; *compound metre* as in 6/8, 9/8, 12/16, and so on, consists of sub-beats 'compounded' or aggregated in units of three. The numerical sign for metre is a *time signature*, of which the upper number represents the number of beats in the bar, the lower number the type of beat, expressed as a fraction of a unit (*semibreve*). Hence 3/4 is three crotchet (quarter-note) beats to the bar and 6/8 is two beats each of three quavers (eighth notes).

Metro-Goldwyn-Mayer (MGM) US film-production company 1924–1970s. MGM was formed by the amalgamation of the Metro Picture Corporation, the Goldwyn Picture Corporation, and Louis B Mayer Pictures. One of the most powerful Hollywood studios of the 1930s–1950s, it produced such prestige films as *David Copperfield* 1935 and *The Wizard of Oz* 1939. Among its stars were Greta Garbo, Clark Gable, and Elizabeth Taylor.

metronome clockwork device, invented by Johann Maelzel 1814, using a sliding weight to regulate the speed of a pendulum to assist in setting tempo, particularly in music. It is now largely superseded by silent digital display devices.

Metropolitan Museum of Art, New York leading US art museum. Founded 1870 and opened 1880, it possesses vast collections covering many periods and styles.

Metropolitan Opera Company foremost opera company in the USA, founded 1883 in New York City. The Metropolitan Opera House (opened 1883) was demolished 1966, and the company moved to the new Metropolitan Opera House at the Lincoln Center.

Metsu Gabriel 1629–1667. Dutch painter, born in Leiden, active in Amsterdam from 1657. His main subjects were ◊genre scenes, usually with a few well-dressed figures. He was skilled in depicting rich glossy fabrics.

Meyerbeer Giacomo. Adopted name of Jakob Liebmann Beer 1791–1864. German composer of spectacular operas, including *Robert le diable* 1831 and *Les Huguenots* 1836. From 1826 he lived mainly in Paris, returning to Berlin after 1842 as musical director of the Royal Opera.

Let me tell you that I – who am but a humble worm – am sometimes ill for a whole month after a first night.

Giacomo Meyerbeer

Meyerhold Vsevolod 1874–1940. Russian actor and director. Before the revolution of 1917 he developed a strong interest in ◊commedia dell'arte and stylized acting. He developed a system of actor-training known as *bio-mechanics*, which combined insights drawn from sport, the circus, and modern studies of time and motion. He produced the Russian poet Mayakovsky's futurist *Mystery-Bouffe* 1918 and 1921, and later his *The Bed Bug* 1929.

A member of the Moscow Art Theatre, he was briefly director of its Studio Theatre under Stanislavsky 1905. He received state support from 1920, but was arrested 1938 and shot under the Stalinist regime.

Meynell Alice (born Thompson) 1847–1922. English poet. She published *Preludes* 1875 and her collected poems appeared 1923. She married the author and journalist Wilfrid Meynell (1852–1948).

mezzanine (Italian *mezzano* 'middle') architectural term for a storey with a lower ceiling placed between two main storeys, usually between the ground and first floors of a building.

mezzo- or *mezza-* (Italian 'half') term used in music of medium range or intensity, as in mezzosoprano, mezzoforte (mf), and so on. The short form 'mezzo' stands for mezzo-soprano.

mezzo-soprano (sometimes shortened to *mezzo*) female singing voice with an approximate range A4–F5, between contralto and soprano. Janet ◊Baker is a well-known exponent.

mezzotint (Italian 'half tint') print produced by a method of etching in density of tone rather than line, popular in the 18th and 19th centuries. A copper or steel plate is worked with a tool that raises an even, overall burr (rough edge), which will hold ink. Areas of burr are then scraped and smoothed away to produce a range of lighter tones.

Michelangelo Buonarroti 1475–1564. Italian sculptor, painter, architect, and poet, active in his native Florence and in Rome. His giant talent dominated the High Renaissance. The marble *David* 1501–04 (Accademia, Florence) set a new standard in nude sculpture. His massive figure style was translated into fresco in the Sistine Chapel 1508–12 and 1536–41 (Vatican). Other works in Rome include the dome of St Peter's basilica. His influence, particularly on the development of ◊Mannerism, was profound.

Born near Florence, he was a student of Ghirlandaio and trained under the patronage of Lorenzo de' Medici. His patrons later included several popes and Medici princes. In 1498–99 he completed the *Pietà* (St Peter's, Rome), a technically brilliant marble sculpture that established his reputation. Also in Rome he began the great tomb of Pope Julius II: *The Slaves* about 1513 (Louvre, Paris) and *Moses* about 1515 (San Pietro in Vincoli, Rome) were sculpted for this unfinished project. His grandiose scheme for the ceiling of the Sistine Chapel tells the Old Testament story from Genesis to the Deluge, and on the altar wall he later added a vast and dramatic *Last Judgement* 1536–41. From 1516 to 1534 he was again in Florence, where his chief work was the design of the Medici sepulchral chapel in San Lorenzo. Returning to Rome he became chief architect of St Peter's 1547. His friendship with Vittoria Colonna, a noblewoman, inspired many of his sonnets and madrigals. There are collections of his drawings in the Uffizi, Florence, and the Louvre, Paris.

Trifles make perfection, and perfection is no trifle.

Michelangelo

Michelozzo di Bartolomeo 1396–1472. Italian sculptor and architect who worked with Ghiberti and Donatello. Although overshadowed by such contemporaries as ◊Brunelleschi and ◊Alberti, he was the chosen architect of Cosimo de' Medici and was commissioned by him to design the Palazzo de' Medici (now Palazzo Medici-Riccardi, Florence), begun in the 1440s, and the library of the monastery of San Marco, about 1436.

Michelucci Giovanni 1891–1990. Italian architect, a leading exponent of ◊Rationalism in the 1930s. He produced numerous urban projects characterized by a restrained Modernism, for example, the Sta Maria Novella Station in Florence 1934–37. He departed from his Rationalist principles in his design for the church of San Giovanni 1961 by the Autostrada del Sole near Florence, a fluid, sculptural composition in poured concrete.

Mickiewicz Adam 1798–1855. Polish revolutionary poet whose *Pan Tadeusz* 1832–34 is Poland's national epic. He died in Constantinople while raising a Polish corps to fight against Russia in the Crimean War.

microtone in music, any precisely determined division of the octave smaller than a semitone.

Midas in Greek mythology, a king of Phrygia who was granted the gift of converting all he touched to gold, and who, for preferring the music of Pan to that of Apollo, was given ass's ears by the latter.

middle C white note, C4, at the centre of the piano keyboard, indicating the division between left- and right-hand regions and between the treble and bass staves of printed music. Middle C is also the pitch indicated by a C clef, for example, for viola.

Middlemarch: A Study of Provincial Life novel by George ◊Eliot, published in England 1871–72. Set in the fictitious provincial town of Middlemarch, the novel has several interwoven plots played out against a background of social and political upheaval.

Middleton Thomas *c.* 1570–1627. English dramatist. He produced numerous romantic plays, tragedies, and realistic comedies, both alone and in collaboration, including *A Fair Quarrel* and *The Changeling* 1622 with William Rowley; *The Roaring Girl* with Thomas Dekker; and *Women Beware Women* 1621.

The devil has a care of his footmen.

Thomas Middleton
A Trick to Catch the Old One 1608

MIDI acronym for *musical instrument digital interface*, a manufacturer's standard allowing different pieces of digital music equipment used in composing and recording to be freely connected.

The information-sending device (any electronic instrument) is called a controller, and the reading device (such as a computer) the sequencer. Pitch, dynamics, decay rate, and stereo position can all be transmitted via the interface.

A computer with a MIDI interface can input and store the sounds produced by the connected instruments, and can then manipulate these sounds in many different ways, including in printed score form.

Midsummer Night's Dream, A comedy by William ◊Shakespeare, first performed 1595–96. Hermia, Lysander, Demetrius, and Helena in their various romantic endeavours are subjected to the playful manipulations of the fairies Puck and Oberon in a wood near Athens. Titania, queen of the fairies, is similarly bewitched and falls in love with Bottom, a stupid weaver, whose head has been replaced with that of an ass.

Mies van der Rohe Ludwig 1886–1969. German architect, a leading exponent of the ◊International Style, who practised in the USA from 1937. He succeeded Walter ◊Gropius as director of the ◊Bauhaus 1929–33. He designed the bronze-and-glass Seagram building in New York City 1956–59 and numerous apartment buildings.

He became professor at the Illinois Technical Institute 1938–58, for which he designed a new campus on characteristically functional lines from 1941. He also designed the National Gallery, Berlin, 1963--68.

Architecture is the will of an epoch translated into space.

Ludwig Mies van der Rohe

Mifune Toshiro 1920– . Japanese actor who appeared in many films directed by Akira ◊Kurosawa, including *Rashōmon* 1950, *Shichinin no samurai/Seven Samurai* 1954, and *Throne of Blood* 1957. He has occasionally appeared in European and American films: *Grand Prix* 1966 and *Hell in the Pacific* 1969.

Mighty Handful, The (Russian *Moguchaya kuchka*) also known as *The Five* or *The Mighty Five* term applied by art critic Vladimir Stasov to the St Petersburg group of five composers – César Cui, Mily Balakirev, Alexander Borodin, Modest Mussorgsky, and Nicolai Rimsky-Korsakov – whose establishment of a distinctively Russian nationalist idiom he promoted.

mihrab in Islamic architecture, niche in the wall of a mosque indicating the direction of Mecca to those taking part in prayers.

Miles Bernard (Baron Miles) 1907–1991. English actor and producer. He appeared on stage as Briggs in *Thunder Rock* 1940 and Iago in *Othello* 1942, and his films include *Great Expectations* 1947. He founded a trust that in 1959 built the City of London's first new theatre for 300 years, the Mermaid, which presents a mixed classical and modern repertoire.

Milhaud Darius 1892–1974. French composer, a member of the group of composers known as ◊*Les Six*. Among his prolific works are the operas *Christophe Colombe/Christopher Columbus* 1928 and *Bolívar* 1943, and the jazz ballet *La Création du monde/The Creation* 1923.

From travels in Brazil 1919–23 he acquired a taste for Latin American rhythms and percussion. Much of his music is polytonal, ingenious, and structurally inventive.

Mill John Stuart 1806–1873. English philosopher and economist who wrote *On Liberty* 1859, the classic philosophical defence of liberalism, and *Utilitarianism* 1863, a version of the 'greatest happiness for the greatest number' principle in ethics. His progressive views inspired *On the Subjection of Women* 1869.

He was born in London, the son of James Mill. In 1822 he entered the East India Company, where he remained until retiring 1858. In 1826, as described in his *Autobiography* 1873, he passed through a mental crisis; he found his father's bleakly intellectual Utilitarianism emotionally unsatisfying and abandoned it for a more human philosophy influenced by Coleridge and Wordsworth. His philosophical and political writings include *A System of Logic* 1843 and *Considerations on Representative Government* 1861.

Men do not desire to be rich, but to be richer than other men.

John Stuart Mill
'Essay on Social Freedom'

Millais John Everett 1829–1896. English painter, a founder member of the ◊Pre-Raphaelite Brotherhood (PRB) 1848. By the late 1850s he had left the PRB, and his style became more fluent and less detailed.

One of his PRB works, *Christ in the House of His Parents* 1850 (Tate Gallery, London), caused an outcry on its first showing, since its realistic detail was considered unfitting to a sacred subject. Later works include sentimental child-studies, such as *The Boyhood of Raleigh* 1870 (Tate Gallery, London) and *Bubbles* 1886 (a poster for Pears soap), and portraits. He was elected president of the Royal Academy 1896.

Millay Edna St Vincent 1892–1950. US poet who wrote romantic, emotional verse, including *Renascence and Other Poems* 1917 and *The Harp-Weaver and Other Poems* 1923 (Pulitzer Prize 1924).

millefiore (Italian 'a thousand flowers') ornamental glassmaking technique. Coloured glass rods are arranged in bundles so that the cross-section forms a pattern. When the bundle is heated and drawn out thinly, the design becomes reduced in scale. Slices of this are used in glass-bead manufacture and can be set side by side and fused into metalware.

The technique is of ancient origin and was used in Anglo-Saxon jewellery and metalwork. It was revived in 16th-century Venice, then in 19th-century France and Britain for paperweights, doorknobs, and ornamental glass.

A good newspaper, I suppose, is a nation talking to itself.

Arthur Miller *Observer* 1961

Miller Arthur 1915– . US dramatist. His plays deal with family relationships and contemporary American values, and include ◊*Death of a Salesman* 1949 and *The* ◊*Crucible* 1953. He was married 1956–61 to the film star Marilyn

Monroe, for whom he wrote the film *The Misfits* 1960.

Among other plays are *All My Sons* 1947, *A View from the Bridge* 1955, *After the Fall* 1964, based on his relationship with Monroe, and *The Price* 1968. He also wrote the television film *Playing for Time* 1980.

Miller Glenn 1904–1944. US trombonist and, as bandleader, exponent of the big-band swing sound from 1938. He composed his signature tune 'Moonlight Serenade' (a hit 1939). Miller became leader of the US Army Air Force Band in Europe 1942, made broadcasts to troops throughout the world during World War II, and disappeared without trace on a flight between England and France.

Miller Henry 1891–1980. US writer. From 1930 to 1940 he lived a bohemian life in Paris, where he wrote his fictionalized, sexually explicit, autobiographical trilogy *Tropic of Cancer* 1934, *Black Spring* 1936, and *Tropic of Capricorn* 1938. They were banned in the USA and England until the 1960s.

Born in New York City, Miller settled in Big Sur, California, 1944 and wrote the autobiographical *The Rosy Crucifixion* trilogy, consisting of *Sexus* 1949, *Plexus* 1949, and *Nexus* 1957 (published as a whole in the USA 1965). Inspired by Surrealism, Miller was a writer of exuberant and comic prose fuelled by anarchist passion, and was later adopted as a guru by the followers of the ◊Beat Generation. His other works include *The Colossus of Maroussi* 1941, *The Air-Conditioned Nightmare* 1945, and *The Time of the Assassins* 1956.

Millet Jean François 1814–1875. French artist, a leading member of the ◊Barbizon School, who painted scenes of peasant life and landscapes. *The Angelus* 1859 (Musée d'Orsay, Paris) was widely reproduced in his day.

Millin Sarah Gertrude (born Liebson) 1889–1968. South African novelist, an opponent of racial discrimination, as seen in, for example, *God's Step-Children* 1924.

Mill on the Floss, The novel 1860 by George ◊Eliot. The central character is Maggie Tulliver, clever and lively daughter of the miller of Dorlcote Mill on the river Floss. Her entanglement with the deformed Philip Wakem, son of her father's enemy, and Stephen Guest, her cousin's betrothed, leads to the tragic conclusion in which Maggie and her brother Tom are drowned by the flooding river.

Mills John 1908– . English actor of considerable versatility who appeared in films such as *In Which We Serve* 1942, *The Rocking Horse Winner* 1949, *The Wrong Box* 1966, and *Oh! What a Lovely War* 1969. He received an Academy Award for *Ryan's Daughter* 1970. He is the father of the actresses Hayley Mills and Juliet Mills.

Mills Brothers US vocal group who specialized in close-harmony vocal imitations of instruments, comprising Herbert Mills (1912–), Harry Mills (1913–1982), John Mills (1889–1935), and Donald Mills (1915–). Formed 1922, the group first broadcast on radio 1925, and continued to perform until the 1950s. Their 70 hits include 'Lazy River' 1948 and 'You Always Hurt the One You Love' 1944.

Milne A(lan) A(lexander) 1882–1956. English writer. His books for children were based on the teddy bear and other toys of his son Christopher Robin (*Winnie-the-Pooh* 1926 and *The House at Pooh Corner* 1928). He also wrote children's verse (*When We Were Very Young* 1924 and *Now We Are Six* 1927) and plays, including an adaptation of Kenneth Grahame's *The Wind in the Willows* as *Toad of Toad Hall* 1929.

Milosz Czeslaw 1911– . Polish writer, born in Lithuania. He became a diplomat before defecting and becoming a US citizen. His poetry in English translation, classical in style, includes *Selected Poems* 1973 and *Bells in Winter* 1978.

His collection of essays *The Captive Mind* 1953 concerns the impact of communism on Polish intellectuals. Among his novels are *The Seizure of Power* 1955, *The Issa Valley* 1981, and *The Land of Ulro* 1984. Nobel Prize for Literature 1980.

Milton John 1608–1674. English poet whose epic ◊*Paradise Lost* 1667 is one of the landmarks of English literature. Early poems including *Comus* (a masque performed 1634) and *Lycidas* (an elegy 1638) showed Milton's superlative lyric gift. Latin secretary to Oliver Cromwell during the Commonwealth period, he also wrote many pamphlets and prose works, including *Areopagitica* 1644, which opposed press censorship.

Born in London and educated at Christ's College, Cambridge, Milton was a scholarly poet, ambitious to match the classical epics, and with strong theological views. Of polemical temperament, he published prose works on republicanism and church government. His middle years were devoted to the Puritan cause and pamphleteering, including one on divorce (*The Doctrine and Discipline of Divorce* 1643, which was based on his own experience of marital unhappiness) and another (*Areopagitica*) advocating freedom of the press. From 1649 he was (Latin) secretary to the Council of State. His assistants (as his sight failed) included Andrew Marvell. He married Mary Powell 1643, and their three daughters were later his somewhat unwilling scribes. After Mary's death 1652, the year of his total blindness, he married twice more, his second wife Catherine Woodcock dying in childbirth, while Elizabeth Minshull survived him for over half a century. *Paradise Lost* 1667 and the less successful sequel *Paradise Regained* 1671 were written when he was blind and in some political danger (after the restoration of Charles II), as was *Samson Agonistes* 1671, a powerful if untheatrical play. He is buried in St Giles', Cripplegate, London.

Ask for this great Deliverer now, and find him / Eyeless in Gaza, at the Mill with slaves.

John Milton *Samson Agonistes* 1671

---

mime type of acting in which gestures, movements, and facial expressions replace speech. It has developed as a form of theatre, particularly in France, where Marcel ◊Marceau and Jean-Louis ◊Barrault have continued the traditions established in the 19th century by Deburau and the practices of the ◊commedia dell'arte in Italy. In ancient Greece, mime was a crude, realistic comedy with dialogue and exaggerated gesture.

minaret slender turret or tower attached to a Muslim mosque or to buildings designed in that style. It has one or more balconies, from which the *muezzin* calls the people to prayer five times a day. See also ◊Islamic architecture.

minbar or *mimbar* in Islamic architecture, a high platform in a mosque from which Friday prayers are read, lying adjacent to the ◊mihrab.

Minerva in Roman mythology, the goddess of intelligence, and of handicrafts and the arts, equivalent to the Greek ◊Athena. From the earliest days of ancient Rome, there was a temple to her on the Capitoline Hill, near the Temple of Jupiter.

Mingus Charles 1922–1979. US jazz bassist and composer. He played with Louis Armstrong, Duke Ellington, and Charlie Parker. His experimentation with ◊atonality and dissonant effects opened the way for the new style of free collective jazz improvisation of the 1960s.

Based on the West Coast until 1951, Mingus took part in the development of cool jazz. Subsequently based in New York, he worked with a number of important musicians and expanded the scope of the bass as a lead instrument. Recordings include *Pithecanthropus Erectus* 1956 and *Mingus at Monterey* 1964.

miniature painting painting on a very small scale, notably early manuscript paintings, and later miniature portraits, sometimes set in jewelled cases. The art of manuscript painting was developed in Classical times in the West and revived in the Middle Ages. Several Islamic countries, for example Persia and India, developed strong traditions of manuscript art. Miniature portrait painting enjoyed a vogue in France and England in the 16th–19th centuries.

Jean Clouet and Holbein the Younger both practised the art for royal patrons. Later in the 16th century Nicholas Hilliard painted miniatures exclusively and set out the rules of this portrait style in his treatise *The Arte of Limning* (written 1597–1603).

Minimalism movement in abstract art (mostly sculpture) and music towards severely simplified composition. Minimal art developed in the USA in the 1950s in reaction to ◊Abstract Expressionism, shunning its emotive approach in favour of impersonality and elemental, usually geometrical, shapes. It has found its fullest expression in sculpture, notably in the work of Carl ◊Andre, who employs industrial materials in modular compositions. In music, from the 1960s, it has manifested itself in large-scale statements based on layers of imperceptibly shifting repetitive patterns; major Minimalist composers are Steve ◊Reich and Philip ◊Glass.

Minnelli Liza 1946– . US actress and singer, daughter of Judy ◊Garland and the director Vincente Minnelli. She achieved stardom in the Broadway musical *Flora, the Red Menace* 1965 and in the film *Cabaret* 1972. Her subsequent films include *New York, New York* 1977 and *Arthur* 1981.

Minnelli Vincente 1910–1986. US film director who specialized in musicals and occasional melodramas. His best films, such as *Meet Me in St Louis* 1944 and *Lust for Life* 1956, display great visual flair.

Minnesinger any of a group of German lyric poets of the 12th and 13th centuries who, in their songs, dealt mainly with the theme of courtly love without revealing the identity of the object of their affections. Minnesingers included Dietmar von Aist, Friedrich von Hausen, Heinrich von Morungen, Reinmar, and Walther von der Vogelweide.

Minos in Greek mythology, a king of Crete (son of Zeus and Europa), who demanded a yearly tribute of young men and girls from Athens for the ◊Minotaur. After his death, he became a judge in ◊Hades.

Minotaur in Greek mythology, a monster, half man and half bull, offspring of Pasiphaë, wife of King Minos of Crete, and a bull. It lived in the Labyrinth at Knossos, and its victims were seven girls and seven youths, sent in annual tribute by Athens, until ◊Theseus killed it, with the aid of Ariadne, the daughter of Minos.

minster in the UK, a church formerly attached to a monastery: for example, York Minster. Originally the term meant a monastery, and in this sense it is often preserved in place names, such as Westminster.

minstrel medieval musician who travelled from place to place singing and reciting the poetry of the ◊troubadours.

minstrel show an entertainment in which performers, some with blackened faces, sing, dance, and tell jokes. They were popular in the USA about 1850–1930 and later in the UK.

Minstrel shows date from the 18th century in America as amateur entertainments; the first professional touring company was the Virginia Minstrels (formed 1843). Songs made popular by minstrel shows include 'Turkey in the Straw' 1834 and 'Buffalo Gals, Won't You Come Out Tonight?' 1844. Minstrel shows were gradually superseded by ◊vaudeville.

Minton Thomas 1765–1836. English potter. He first worked under the potter Josiah Spode, but in 1789 established himself at Stoke-on-Trent as an engraver of designs (he originated the 'willow pattern') and in the 1790s founded a pottery there, producing high-quality bone china, including tableware.

minuet French country dance in three time adapted as a European courtly dance of the 17th century. The music was later used as the third movement of a classical four-movement symphony where its gentle rhythm provides a foil to the slow second movement and fast final movement.

miracle play another name for ◊mystery play.

Miranda Carmen. Stage name of Maria de Carmo Miranda da Cunha 1909–1955. Portuguese dancer and singer who lived in Brazil from childhood. Her Hollywood musicals include *Down Argentine Way* 1940 and *The Gang's All Here* 1943. Her hallmarks were extravagant costumes and headgear adorned with tropical fruits, a staccato singing voice, and fiery temperament.

Miró Joan 1893–1983. Spanish Surrealist painter, born in Barcelona. In the mid-1920s he developed an abstract style, lyrical and often witty, with amoeba shapes, some linear, some highly coloured, generally floating on a plain background.

During the 1930s his style became more sober and after World War II he produced larger abstracts. He experimented with sculpture and printmaking and produced ceramic murals (including two in the UNESCO building, Paris, 1958). He also designed stained glass and sets for the ballet impresario Sergei Diaghilev.

Mirren Helen 1946– . British actress whose stage roles include both modern and classical. Her Shakespearean roles include Lady Macbeth and Isabella in *Measure for Measure*. Her films include *The Long Good Friday* 1981 and *Cal* 1984; and *Prime Suspect* 1990 for television.

Misanthrope, Le comedy by ◊Molière, first produced in France 1666. The play contrasts the noble ideals of Alceste with the worldliness of his lover Célimène.

mise en scène (French 'stage setting') in cinema, the composition and content of the frame in terms of background scenery, actors, costumes, props, camera movement, and lighting.

Misérables, Les novel by Victor ◊Hugo, published in France 1862. On release from prison, Jean Valjean attempts to hide his past by assuming a series of false identities. He cares for a young girl, Cosette, who believes Valjean to be her father. When she marries he reveals the truth but dies a broken man.

The novel was adapted as a musical by Alain Boublil and Claude-Michel Schönberg in Paris 1980 and went on to enjoy huge international success. It was adapted for the London stage by Trevor Nunn and John Caird, presented by Cameron Mackintosh, and first performed at the Barbican 1985.

misericord or *miserere* in church architecture, a projection on the underside of a hinged seat of the choir stalls, used as a rest for a priest when standing during long services. Misericords are often decorated with carvings.

Mishima Yukio 1925–1970. Japanese novelist whose work often deals with sexual desire and perversion, as in *Confessions of a Mask* 1949 and *The Temple of the Golden Pavilion* 1956. He committed hara-kiri (ritual suicide) as a protest against what he saw as the corruption of the nation and the loss of the samurai warrior tradition.

The period of childhood is a stage on which time and space become entangled.

Yukio Mishima
Confessions of a Mask 1949

Missoni knitwear fashion label established in the UK 1953 by Italian designers Rosita and Ottavio Missoni. Producing individual knitwear, characterized by bold colours and geometrical patterns, Missoni has become an international business and has raised the profile of knitwear on the fashion scene.

Mistinguett stage name of Jeanne Bourgeois 1873–1956. French actress and dancer. A leading music-hall artist in Paris from 1899, she appeared in revues at the Folies-Bergère, Casino de Paris, and Moulin Rouge. She was known for the song 'Mon Homme' and her partnership with Maurice Chevalier.

Mistral Gabriela. Pen name of Lucila Godoy de Alcayaga 1889–1957. Chilean poet who wrote *Sonnets of Death* 1915. She was awarded the Nobel Prize for Literature 1945.

She was consul of Chile in Spain, and represented her country at the League of Nations and the United Nations.

Mitchell Arthur 1934–1990. US dancer, director of the Dance Theater of Harlem, which he founded with Karel Shook (1920–) 1968. Mitchell was a principal dancer with the New York City Ballet 1956–68, creating many roles in Balanchine's ballets, such as *Agon* 1967.

Mitchell Joni. Adopted name of Roberta Joan Anderson 1943– . Canadian singer, songwriter, and guitarist. She began in the 1960s folk style and subsequently incorporated elements of rock and jazz with confessional, sophisticated lyrics. Her albums include *Blue* 1971 and *Hejira* 1976.

Mitchell Margaret 1900–1949. US novelist, born in Atlanta, Georgia, which is the setting for her one book, the bestseller *Gone With the Wind* 1936 (Pulitzer Prize), a story of the US Civil War. It was filmed starring Vivien Leigh and Clark Gable 1939.

After all, tomorrow is another day.

Margaret Mitchell closing words of *Gone With the Wind*

Mitchum Robert 1917– . US film actor, a star for more than 30 years, equally at home as the relaxed modern hero or psychopathic villain. His films include *Out of the Past* 1947, *The Night of the Hunter* 1955, and *The Friends of Eddie Coyle* 1973.

Mitford Mary Russell 1787–1855. English author, remembered for her sketches in *Our Village* 1824–32 describing Three Mile Cross, near Reading, where she lived.

Mitford sisters the six daughters of British aristocrat Lord Redesdale, including: *Nancy* (1904–1973), author of the semi-autobiographical *The Pursuit of Love* 1945 and *Love in a Cold Climate* 1949, and editor and part author of *Noblesse Oblige* 1956 elucidating 'U' (upperclass) and 'non-U' behaviour; *Diana* (1910–), who married the politician Oswald Mosley; *Unity* (1914–1948), who became an admirer of Hitler; and *Jessica* (1917–), author of the autobiographical *Hons and Rebels* 1960 and *The American Way of Death* 1963.

Mithras in Persian mythology, the god of light. Mithras represented the power of goodness, and promised his followers compensation for present evil after death. He was said to have captured and killed the sacred bull, from whose blood all life sprang. Mithraism was introduced into the Roman Empire 68 BC. By about AD 250, it rivalled Christianity in strength.

A bath in the blood of a sacrificed bull formed part of the initiation ceremony of the Mithraic cult, which spread rapidly, gaining converts especially among soldiers. In 1954 remains of a Roman temple dedicated to Mithras were discovered in the City of London.

Mix Tom (Thomas) 1880–1940. US actor who was the most colourful cowboy star of silent films. At their best, his films, such as *The Range Riders* 1910 and *King Cowboy* 1928, were fast-moving and full of impressive stunts. His talkies include *Destry Rides Again* 1932 and *The Miracle Rider* 1935.

mixed media or *multimedia* in the arts, a performance or work that combines different forms such as lighting effects, sound, and film. It became popular as an art form in the 1960s, with Andy ◊Warhol's 'Exploding Plastic Inevitable' show 1966. Although the term is a recent one, the principle is similar to that of the ◊*Gesamtkunstwerk*. Mixed media can also describe a modern work of visual art composed of various materials.

Miyake Issey 1938– . Japanese fashion designer, active in Paris from 1965. He showed his first collection in New York and Tokyo 1971, and has been showing in Paris since 1973. His 'anti-fashion' looks combined Eastern and Western influences: a variety of textured and patterned fabrics were layered and wrapped round the body to create linear and geometric shapes.

Miyamoto Musashi *c.* 1584–1645. Japanese samurai, author of a manual on military strategy and sword fighting, *Gorinsho/The Book of Five Rings* 1645, which in English translation 1974 became popular in the USA as a guide to business success.

In Japan, Miyamoto Musashi is popular as the hero of a long historical novel that glamorizes his martial-arts exploits and has been the basis for a series of films and comic books. The historical Miyamoto was a painter as well as a fencer, and spent his life travelling Japan in search of Zen enlightenment.

Mizoguchi Kenji 1898–1956. Japanese film director whose *Ugetsu Monogatari* 1953 confirmed his international reputation. Notable for his sensitive depiction of female psychology, he also directed *The Poppies* 1935, *Sansho daiyu/Sansho the Bailiff* 1954, and *Street of Shame* 1956.

Mnouchkine Ariane 1939– . French theatre director. She founded the Théâtre du Soleil 1964, which established a reputation with a vigorous production of Arnold Wesker's *The Kitchen* 1967. After 1968, the company began to devise its own material, firstly with *The Clowns* 1969, which was followed by *1789* 1970, an exploration of the French Revolution, and *L'Age d'or* 1975, concerning the exploitation of immigrant workers. She has also directed *Les Atrides* 1992, a version of Aeschylus' *Oresteia*.

mobile in music, a piece consisting of sections the order of which may be varied at will or according to rules of association, so named after the example of Alexander ◊Calder's mobile sculpture. Examples include Henri Pousseur's

Mobile for two pianos 1956–58, and *Mobile for Shakespeare* 1959 by Roman Haubenstock-Ramati. See also ◊aleatory music.

Moby-Dick or **The Whale** novel 1851 by US writer Herman ◊Melville. Its story of the conflict between the monomaniac Captain Ahab and the great white whale explores the mystery and the destructiveness of both man and nature's power.

Call me Ishmael.

Herman Melville *Moby-Dick* 1851

---

mod British youth subculture that originated in London and Brighton in the early 1960s around the French view of the English; revived in the late 1970s. Mods were fashion-conscious, speedy, and upwardly mobile; they favoured scooters and soul music.

mode in music, an ancient or exotic scale of five or more pitches to the octave, often identified with a particular emotion, ritual function, time, or season, to which music is composed or improvised.

modern dance 20th-century dance idiom that evolved in opposition to traditional ballet by those seeking a freer and more immediate means of dance expression. Leading exponents include Martha ◊Graham and Merce ◊Cunningham in the USA, and Isadora ◊Duncan and Mary ◊Wigman in Europe.

In the USA it was from Ruth St Denis and Ted Shawn's ◊Denishawn School in Los Angeles 1915 that the first generation of modern dance – Martha Graham, Doris Humphrey, and Charles Weidman – emerged. In the UK, the London Contemporary Dance Theatre and school was set up 1966–67 and flourished under the artistic direction of Graham's pupil, Robert Cohan. In 1966, the Ballet Rambert became a modern-dance company. In Germany, the originators of a modernist movement known as ◊Ausdruckstanz were Emile Jaques-Dalcroze and Rudolf von Laban. The leading exponents, Mary Wigman, Harald Kreutzberg, and Kurt Jooss, had some influence on modern dance through their visits to the USA and through Hanya Holm (1898–), a former Wigman dancer who settled and taught in New York, and with whom the choreographer/producer, Alwyn Nikolais (1912–), was originally associated. Recent experimental work is known as new dance or ◊avant-garde dance.

Modernism in the arts, a general term used to describe the 20th century's conscious attempt to break with the artistic traditions of the 19th century; it is based on a concern with form and the exploration of technique as opposed to content and narrative. In the visual arts, direct representationalism gave way to abstraction (see ◊abstract art); in literature, writers experimented with alternatives to orthodox sequential storytelling, such as ◊stream of consciousness; in music, the traditional concept of key was challenged by ◊atonality; and in architecture, Functionalism ousted decorativeness as a central objective (see ◊Modern Movement).

Critics of Modernism have found in it an austerity that is seen as dehumanizing. ◊Post-Modernism developed as a reaction to Modernism, but has had to compete with new and divergent Modernist trends, for example ◊High Tech in architecture.

Modern Jazz Quartet US jazz group specializing in group improvisation, formed 1952 (disbanded 1974 and re-formed 1981). Noted for elegance and mastery of form, the quartet has sometimes been criticized for being too 'classical'.

It is led by pianist John Lewis (1920–), with Milt Jackson (1923–) on vibraphone, bass player Percy Heath (1923–), and drummers Kenny Clarke (1914–1985) and later Connie Kay (1927–).

Modern Movement the dominant movement in 20th-century architecture, which grew out of the technological innovations of 19th-century ◊Industrial architecture, crystallized in the ◊International Style of the 1920s and 1930s, and has since developed various regional trends, such as ◊Brutalism. 'Truth to materials' and 'form follows function' are its two most representative dicta, although neither allows for the modernity of large areas of contemporary architecture, concerned with proportion, human scale, and attention to detail. Currently, architectural ◊Post-Modernism, a reaction to the movement, is developing alongside such Modernist styles as ◊High Tech.

The Modern Movement gained momentum after World War II when its theories, disseminated through the work of ◊CIAM, were influential in the planning and rebuilding of European cities. The work of ◊Le Corbusier is perhaps most representative of the underlying principles of the movement; other notable early Modernists include Aldoph ◊Loos, Peter ◊Behrens, Walter ◊Gropius, and ◊Mies van der Rohe.

Modersohn-Becker Paula 1876–1907. German painter and graphic artist, a member of the artists' colony at ◊Worpswede from 1898. She painted still lifes and scenes of peasant life, but is best known for her self-portraits and portraits of mothers and children. In her concern with expressing inner emotions and her sensitive use of shape and colour (influenced by Gauguin and the Fauves), she anticipated German ◊Expressionism.

Modigliani Amedeo 1884–1920. Italian artist, active in Paris from 1906. He painted and sculpted graceful nudes and portrait studies. His paintings – for example, the portrait of *Jeanne Hebuterne* 1919 (Guggenheim Museum, New York) – have a distinctive style, the forms elongated and sensual.

Modigliani was born in Livorno. He was encouraged to sculpt by Constantin Brancusi, and his series of strictly simplified heads reflects a shared interest in archaic sculptural styles.

Modotti Tina 1896–1942. Italian photographer who studied with Edward Weston and went to Mexico with him 1923. As well as her sensitive studies of Mexican women, she recorded the work of the Mexican muralists and made near-abstract prints of stairs and flowers.

modulation in music, movement from one ◊key to another. In classical dance music, modulation is a guide to phrasing rhythm to the step pattern.

mohair (Arabic *mukhayyar* 'goat') yarn made from the long, lustrous hair of the ◊Angora goat or rabbit, loosely woven with cotton, silk, or wool to produce a fuzzy texture. It became popular for jackets, coats, and sweaters in the 1950s. Commercial mohair is now obtained from cross-bred animals, pure-bred supplies being insufficient to satisfy demand.

Moholy-Nagy Laszlo 1895–1946. US photographer, born in Hungary. He lived in Germany 1923–29, where he was a member of the ◊Bauhaus school, and fled from the Nazis 1935. Through the publication of his illuminating theories and practical experiments, he had great influence on 20th-century photography and design.

Moirai in Greek mythology, the title of the ◊Fates; the name refers to the 'portions' of life allotted to each human being.

It is a public scandal that gives offence, and it is no sin to sin in secret.

Molière *Tartuffe* 1664

Molière pen name of Jean-Baptiste Poquelin 1622–1673. French satirical dramatist and actor from whose work modern French comedy developed. After the collapse of the Paris Illustre Théâtre (of which he was one of the founders), Molière performed in the provinces 1645–58. In 1655 he wrote his first play, *L'Etourdi/The Blunderer*, and on his return to Paris produced *Les Précieuses ridicules/The Affected Ladies* 1659. His satires include *L'Ecole des femmes/The School for Wives* 1662, *Le ◊Misanthrope* 1666, *Le Bourgeois Gentilhomme/The Would-be Gentleman* 1670, and *Le Malade imaginaire/The Imaginary Invalid* 1673. Other satirical plays include ◊*Tartuffe* 1664 (banned until 1669 for attacking the hypocrisy of the clergy), *Le Médecin malgré lui/Doctor in Spite of Himself* 1666, and *Les Femmes savantes/The Learned Ladies* 1672.

Molière's comedies, based on the exposure of hypocrisy and cant, made him vulnerable to many attacks (from which he was protected by

Louis XIV) and marked a new departure in the French theatre away from reliance on classical Greek themes.

Molnár Ferenc 1878–1952. Hungarian novelist and playwright. His play *Liliom* 1909 is a study of a circus barker (a person who calls out to attract the attention of members of the public), adapted as the musical *Carousel*.

Molvig Jon 1923–1970. Australian landscape and portrait painter. Molvig's art shows links with the European Expressionist movement and artists Nolde and Kokoschka in works such as his *Ballad of a Dead Stockman* 1959 (Art Gallery of New South Wales, Sydney). He won the 1966 Archibald Prize.

Momaday N(avarre) Scott 1934– . US writer of Kiowa descent. He won a Pulitzer Prize for his novel *House Made of Dawn* 1968, about a young Indian at home in neither white nor his ancestral society. He was professor of English at Stanford University 1972–81.

Mona Lisa, the (also known as *La Gioconda*) oil painting by ◊Leonardo da Vinci 1503–06 (Louvre, Paris), a portrait of the wife of a Florentine official, Francesco del Giocondo, which, according to ◊Vasari, Leonardo worked on for four years. It was the first Italian portrait to extend below waist level, setting a precedent for composition that was to dominate portraiture until the 19th century. In the *Mona Lisa* Leonardo brought his technique of *sfumato* (avoiding sharp outlines through gentle gradations of colour) to perfection.

Mondrian Piet (Pieter Mondriaan) 1872–1944. Dutch painter, a pioneer of abstract art. He lived in Paris 1919–38, then in London, and from 1940 in New York. He was a founder member of the De ◊Stijl movement and chief exponent of Neo-Plasticism, a rigorous abstract style based on the use of simple geometrical forms and pure colours. He typically created a framework using vertical and horizontal lines, and filled the rectangles with primary colours, mid-grey, or black, others being left white. His ◊*Composition in Red, Yellow and Blue* 1920 (Stedelijk, Amsterdam) is typical.

Monet Claude 1840–1926. French painter, a pioneer of Impressionism and a lifelong exponent of its ideals; his painting *Impression, Sunrise* 1872 gave the movement its name. In the 1870s he began painting the same subjects at different times of day to explore the ever-changing effects of light on colour and form; the *Haystacks* and *Rouen Cathedral* series followed in the 1890s, and from 1899 he painted a series of *Water Lilies* in the garden of his house at Giverny, Normandy (now a museum).

Monet was born in Paris. In Le Havre in the 1850s he was encouraged to paint by Boudin, and met Jongkind, whose light and airy seascapes made a lasting impact. From 1862 in Paris he shared a studio with Renoir, Sisley, and others, and they showed their work together at the First Impressionist Exhibition 1874. Monet's work from the 1860s onwards concentrates on the fleeting effects of light and colour, and from the late 1860s he painted in the classic Impressionist manner, juxtaposing brushstrokes of colour to create an effect of dappled, glowing light. His first series showed the Gare St Lazare in Paris with its puffing steam engines. Views of the water garden in Giverny gradually developed into large, increasingly abstract colour compositions. Between 1900 and 1909 he produced a series of water-lily mural panels for the French state (the Orangerie, Paris).

Monk Thelonious (Sphere) 1917–1982. US jazz pianist and composer who took part in the development of ◊bebop. He had a highly idiosyncratic style, but numbers such as 'Round Midnight' and 'Blue Monk' have become standards. Monk worked in Harlem, New York, during the Depression, and became popular in the 1950s.

monochord (Greek 'one string') in music, an ancient scientific instrument consisting of a single string stretched over a soundbox which is graduated to allow the adjustment of a movable ◊bridge. The monochord is used to demonstrate the existence of ◊harmonics, and the proportional relations of ◊intervals.

monody in music, declamation by an accompanied solo voice, used at the turn of the 16th and 17th centuries.

monologue one person speaking, though the term is generally understood to mean a virtuoso solo performance. Literary monologues are often set pieces in which a character reveals his or her personality, sometimes unintentionally (as in the ◊dramatic monologue); in drama the ◊soliloquy performs a similar function.

Monroe Marilyn. Stage name of Norma Jean Mortenson or Baker 1926–1962. US film actress, the voluptuous blonde sex symbol of the 1950s, who made adroit comedies such as *Gentlemen Prefer Blondes* 1953, *How to Marry a Millionaire* 1953, *The Seven Year Itch* 1955, *Bus Stop* 1956, and *Some Like It Hot* 1959. Her second husband was baseball star Joe di Maggio, and her third was playwright Arthur ◊Miller, who wrote *The Misfits* 1960 for her, a serious film that became her last. She committed suicide, taking an overdose of sleeping pills.

Monsarrat Nicholas 1910–1979. English novelist who served with the navy in the Battle of the Atlantic, a continuous battle fought on the Atlantic Ocean during World War II 1939–45, the subject of his book *The Cruel Sea* 1951.

montage in cinema, the juxtaposition of several images or shots to produce an independent meaning. The term is also used more generally to describe the whole process of editing or a rapidly edited series of shots. It was coined by the Russian director Sergei ◊Eisenstein.

Montagu Lady Mary Wortley (born Pierrepont) 1689–1762. British society hostess renowned for her witty and erudite letters. She was well known in literary circles, associating with writers such as Alexander Pope, with whom she later quarrelled.

Montaigne Michel Eyquem de 1533–1592. French writer, regarded as the creator of the essay form. In 1580 he published the first two volumes of his *Essais*; the third volume appeared 1588. Montaigne deals with all aspects of life from an urbanely sceptical viewpoint. Through the translation by John Florio 1603, he influenced Shakespeare and other English writers.

He was born at the Château de Montaigne near Bordeaux, studied law, and in 1554 became a counsellor of the Bordeaux *parlement*. Little is known of his earlier life, except that he regularly visited Paris and the court of Francis II. In 1571 he retired to his estates, relinquishing his magistracy. He toured Germany, Switzerland, and Italy 1580–81, returning upon his election as mayor of Bordeaux, a post he held until 1585.

If you press me to say why I loved him, I feel that it can only be expressed by replying 'Because it was him; because it was me'.

Michel de Montaigne *Essais I*, 28
explaining his friendship with
Etienne de La Boëtie

Montale Eugenio 1896–1981. Italian poet and writer. His complex, somewhat pessimistic poetry, includes *Ossi di seppia/Cuttlefish Bones* 1925, *Le Occasioni/Occasions* 1939, and (showing a greater warmth and approachability) *La bufera e altro/The Storm and Other Poems* 1956. He was also an important critic and translator. Nobel prize 1975.

Montana Claude 1949– . French fashion designer who promoted the broad-shouldered look. He established his own business 1976 and launched his first collection 1977 featuring wide-shouldered outfits with narrowly shaped waists and slim-fitting skirts.

In 1984 he moved away from the 'powerful' look to design garments in soft, rounded shapes and silk pyjamas which were topped by long satin and velvet robes in bright colours such as coral, absinthe green, lavender, aqua, and rose.

Montand Yves 1921–1991. French actor and singer who achieved fame in the thriller *Le Salaire de la peur/The Wages of Fear* 1953 and continued to be popular in French and American films, including *Let's Make Love* 1960 (with Marilyn Monroe), *Le Sauvage/The Savage* 1976, *Jean de Florette* 1986, and *Manon des sources* 1986.

Monteux Pierre 1875–1964. French conductor. Ravel's *Daphnis and Chloe* and Stravinsky's *Rite of Spring* were first performed under his direction. He conducted Sergei ◊Diaghilev's Ballets Russes 1911–14 and 1917, and the San Francisco Symphony Orchestra 1935–52.

Monteverdi Claudio (Giovanni Antonio) 1567–1643. Italian composer. He contributed to the development of the opera with *Orfeo* 1607 and *The Coronation of Poppea* 1642. He also wrote madrigals, ◊motets, and sacred music, notably the *Vespers* 1610.

Born in Cremona, he was in the service of the Duke of Mantua about 1591–1612, and was director of music at St Mark's, Venice, from 1613. He was the first to use an orchestra and to reveal the dramatic possibilities of the operatic form. *Orfeo*, his first opera, was produced for the carnival at Mantua.

Montez Lola. Stage name of Maria Gilbert 1818–1861. Irish actress and dancer. She appeared on the stage as a Spanish dancer, and in 1847 became the mistress of King Ludwig I of Bavaria, whose policy she dictated for a year. Her liberal sympathies led to her banishment through Jesuit influence 1848. She died in poverty in the USA.

Montgomery Robert (Henry) 1904–1981. US film actor of the 1930s and 1940s. He directed some of his later films, such as *Lady in the Lake* 1947, before turning to television and Republican politics. His other films include *Night Must Fall* 1937 and *Mr and Mrs Smith* 1941.

Montherlant Henri Millon de 1896–1972. French author. His novels, which are marked by an obsession with the physical, include *Aux Fontaines du désir/To the Fountains of Desire* 1927 and *Pitié pour les femmes/Pity for Women* 1936. His most critically acclaimed work is *Le Chaos et la nuit/Chaos and Night* 1963.

Monty Python's Flying Circus English satirical TV comedy series 1969–74, written and performed by John Cleese, Terry Jones, Michael Palin, Eric Idle, Graham Chapman, and the US animator Terry Gilliam. The series became a cult and the group made several films: *Monty Python and the Holy Grail* 1975, *The Life of Brian* 1979, and *The Meaning of Life* 1983.

Monument, the a tower commemorating the Great Fire of London 1666, near the site of the house in Pudding Lane where the conflagration began. It was designed by Christopher ◊Wren and completed 1677.

Moog synthesizer any of a family of inexpensive analogue ◊synthesizers developed 1963 by Robert Moog (1934–   ), incorporating transistorized electronics and voltage control, which brought electronic music synthesis within the reach of composers, performers, and academic institutions. A Moog-designed ◊theremin featured in the Beach Boys' hit 'Good Vibrations' 1966.

Moorcock Michael 1939–   . English writer, associated with the 1960s new wave in science fiction, editor of the magazine *New Worlds* 1964–69. He wrote the Jerry Cornelius novels, collected as *The Cornelius Chronicles* 1977, and *Gloriana* 1978.

Moore Brian 1921–   . Irish-born novelist who emigrated to Canada 1948 and then to the USA 1959. His books include *Judith Hearne* 1955, *The Temptation of Eileen Hughes* 1981, and *Black Robe* 1985. Catholicism, obsession, and the contrast between dreams and reality are recurrent themes.

Other works include *The Luck of Ginger Coffey* 1960 and *The Emperor of Ice Cream* 1966. His earliest books were published under the pen name of Michael Bryan.

Moore Charles 1925–   . US architect with an eclectic approach to design. He was an early exponent of Post-Modernism in, for example, his students' housing for Kresge College, University of California at Santa Cruz, 1973--74 (a stage set of streets and forums), and the Piazza d'Italia in New Orleans, 1975–78, which is one of the key monuments of Post-Modernism. It was built for the Italian community and has a fountain in the shape of Italy.

Moore Dudley 1935–   . English actor, comedian, and musician, formerly teamed with comedian Peter Cook. Moore became a Hollywood star after appearing in '*10*' 1979. His other films, mostly comedies, include *Bedazzled* 1968, *Arthur* 1981, and *Santa Claus* 1985. He is also an accomplished musician and has given classical piano concerts.

Moore George (Augustus) 1852–1933. Irish novelist, born in County Mayo. He studied art in Paris 1870, and published two volumes of poetry there. His first novel, *A Modern Lover* 1883, was sexually frank for its time and banned in some quarters. It was followed by others, including *Esther Waters* 1894.

Moore Gerald 1899–1987. British pianist, renowned as an accompanist of Elizabeth Schwarzkopf, Kathleen Ferrier, Heddle Nash, and other singers, a role he raised to equal partnership.

Moore Henry 1898–1986. English sculptor. His subjects include the reclining nude, mother and child groups, the warrior, and interlocking abstract forms. Many of his post-1945 works are in bronze or marble, including monumental semi-abstracts such as *Reclining Figure* 1957–58 (outside the UNESCO building, Paris), and often designed to be placed in landscape settings.

Moore claimed to have learned much from archaic South and Central American sculpture, and this is reflected in his work from the 1920s. By the early 1930s most of his main themes had emerged, and the Surrealists' preoccupation with organic forms in abstract works proved a strong influence; Moore's hollowed wooden shapes strung with wires date from the late 1930s. Semi-abstract work suggesting organic structures recurs after World War II, for example in the interwoven bonelike forms of the *Hill Arches* and the bronze *Sheep Pieces* 1970s, set in fields by his studio in Hertfordshire.

Moore, born in Yorkshire, studied at Leeds and the Royal College of Art, London. As an official war artist during World War II, he made a series of drawings of people in London's air-raid shelters.

Moore Marianne (Craig) 1887–1972. US poet. She edited the literary magazine *The Dial* 1925–29, and published several volumes of witty and intellectual verse, including *Observations* 1924, *What are Years* 1941, and *A Marianne Moore Reader* 1961. She also published translations and essays. Her work is noted for its observation of detail. T S Eliot was an admirer of her poetry.

Moore Roger 1928– . English actor who starred in the television series *The Saint* 1962–70, and assumed the film role of James Bond 1973 in *Live and Let Die*.

Moore Thomas 1779–1852. Irish poet, born in Dublin. Among his works are the verse romance *Lalla Rookh* 1817 and the *Irish Melodies* 1807–35. These were set to music by John Stevenson 1807–35 and include 'The Minstrel Boy' and 'The Last Rose of Summer'.

Moorhouse Geoffrey 1931– . British travel writer, born in Bolton, Lancashire. His books include *The Fearful Void* 1974, and (on cricket) *The Best-Loved Game* 1979.

moquette textile woven in the same manner as velvet (with cut or uncut pile) from coarse wool and linen yarns, usually for upholstery or carpeting. By introducing rods during weaving, the thread is raised in loops.

Moquette was made from the Middle Ages onwards in many parts of Europe, notably the Low Countries. The term is now used to include Brussels and Wilton carpets.

Mor Anthonis (Antonio Moro) *c.* 1517–1577. Dutch portraitist who became court painter to the Spanish rulers in the Netherlands. Suitably formal and austere, his portraits of contemporary European royalty greatly influenced development of the genre.

He visited Italy, Spain, Portugal, and England, where he painted a portrait of Mary I 1554 (Prado, Madrid) at the time of her marriage to Philip II of Spain. He was influenced by, and borrowed freely, from ◊Titian.

morality play medieval European verse drama, in part a development of the ◊mystery play (or miracle play), in which human characters are replaced by personified virtues and vices, the limited humorous elements being provided by the Devil. In England, morality plays, such as *Everyman*, flourished in the 15th century. They exerted an influence on the development of Elizabethan drama and comedy.

Morandi Giorgio 1890–1964. Italian still-life painter and etcher, influenced by ◊Metaphysical Painting. His subtle studies of bottles and jars convey a sense of calm and repose, as in *Still Life* 1946 (Tate Gallery, London).

Moravia Alberto. Pen name of Alberto Pincherle 1907–1990. Italian novelist. His first successful novel was *Gli indifferenti/The Time of Indifference* 1929, but its criticism of Mussolini's regime led to the government censoring his work until after World War II. Later books include *La romana/Woman of Rome* 1947, *La ciociara/Two Women* 1957, and *La noia/The Empty Canvas* 1961, a study of an artist's obsession with his model.

Mordred in Arthurian legend, nephew and final opponent of King ◊Arthur. What may be an early version of his name (Medraut) appears with Arthur in annals from the 10th century, listed under the year AD 537.

More Kenneth 1914–1982. British actor, a film star of the 1950s, cast as leading man in adventure films and light comedies such as *Genevieve* 1953, *Doctor in the House* 1954, and *Northwest Frontier* 1959. He played war hero Douglas Bader in *Reach for the Sky* 1956.

Moreau Gustave 1826–1898. French Symbolist painter. His atmospheric works depict biblical, mythological, and literary scenes and are richly coloured and detailed; for example, *Salome Dancing Before Herod* 1876 (Musée Moreau, Paris).

In the 1890s Moreau taught at the Ecole des Beaux-Arts in Paris, where his pupils included Matisse and Rouault. Much of his work is in the Musée Moreau, Paris.

Moreau Jeanne 1928– . French actress who has appeared in international films, often in passionate, intelligent roles. Her work includes *Les Amants/The Lovers* 1958, *Jules et Jim/Jules and Jim* 1961, *Chimes at Midnight* 1966, and *Querelle* 1982.

Morgan le Fay in the romance and legend of the English king ◊Arthur, an enchantress and healer, ruler of ◊Avalon and sister of the king, whom she tended after his final battle. In some versions of the legend she is responsible for the suspicions held by the king of his wife ◊Guinevere.

Móricz Zsigismond 1879–1942. Hungarian novelist, the leading realist of his generation. His first novel *Sárarany/Golden Mud* 1910 ruthlessly dissects the frustration and bleakness of village life. Later work included monumental historical novels such as the trilogy *Erdély/Transylvania* 1922–35 and the love story *Légy jó mindhalálig/Be Good Till Death* 1920.

Mori Ōgai 1862–1922. Japanese novelist, poet, and translator. From an aristocratic samurai family, he initiated the Japanese vogue for autobiographical revelation with works such as his story of unhappy love *Maihime/The Dancing Girl* 1890 and the popular novel *Gan* 1911–13. His later work is more impersonal, consisting of historical depictions of the samurai code.

Morisot Berthe 1841–1895. French Impressionist painter who specialized in sensitive pictures of women and children. She was taught by Corot and was much influenced by Manet and, in the 1880s, Renoir. She exhibited in most of the Impressionist shows. She was the granddaughter of the artist Fragonard.

Morland George 1762/3–1804. English painter whose picturesque rural subjects were widely reproduced in engravings. He was an admirer of Dutch and Flemish painters of rustic life.

Morley Malcolm 1931– . British painter, active in New York from 1964. He coined the term *Superrealism* (see ◊Photorealism) for his work in the 1960s. In 1984 he was awarded the first Turner Prize.

Morley Robert 1908–1992. English actor and playwright who was active both in Britain and the USA. His film work consisted mainly of character roles in such movies as *Marie Antoinette* 1938, *The African Queen* 1952, and *Oscar Wilde* 1960.

Only the sinner has the right to preach.

Robert Morley

Morley Thomas 1557–1602. English composer of consort music, madrigals, and airs including the lute song 'It was a lover and his lass' for Shakespeare's play *As You Like It* 1599. He edited a collection of Italian madrigals *The Triumphs of Oriana* 1601, and published an influential keyboard tutor *A Plaine and Easie Introduction to Practicall Musicke* 1597. He was also organist at St Paul's Cathedral, London.

Moro Antonio. Dutch portraitist; see ◊Mor, Anthonis.

Morpheus in Greek and Roman mythology, the god of dreams, son of Hypnos or Somnus, god of sleep.

Morricone Ennio 1928– . Italian composer of film music. His atmospheric scores for 'spaghetti Westerns', notably the Clint ◊Eastwood movies *A Fistful of Dollars* 1964 and *The Good, the Bad, and the Ugly* 1966, created a vogue for lyrical understatement. His highly ritualized, incantatory style pioneered the use of amplified instruments and solo voices, using studio special effects.

Morrigan in Celtic mythology, a goddess of war and death who could take the shape of a crow.

Morris Jan 1926– . English travel writer and journalist. Her books, zestful and witty, with deftly handled historical perspectives, include *Coast to Coast* 1956, *Venice* 1960, *Oxford* 1965, *Farewell the Trumpets* 1978, and *Among the Cities* 1985. Born James Morris, her adoption of female gender is described in *Conundrum* 1974.

Morris Mark 1956– . US choreographer and dancer. His ballets merge various styles ranging from avant-garde, ballet, folk, and jazz dance. He was artistic director of the Théâtre de la Monnaie in Brussels 1988–91. He is the director of his own company in New York.

Morris William 1834–1896. English designer, a founder of the ◊Arts and Crafts movement, socialist, and writer who shared the Pre-Raphaelite painters' fascination with medieval settings. In 1861 he cofounded a firm that designed and produced furniture, carpets, and a wide range of decorative wallpapers, many of which are still produced today. His Kelmscott Press, set up 1890 to print beautifully designed books, influenced printing and book design. The prose romances *A Dream of John Ball* 1888 and *News from Nowhere* 1891 reflect his socialist ideology. He also lectured on socialism.

William Morris was born in Walthamstow, London, and educated at Oxford, where he formed a lasting friendship with the Pre-Raphaelite artist Edward ◊Burne-Jones and was influenced by the art critic John Ruskin and the painter and poet Dante Gabriel ◊Rossetti.

Have nothing in your houses that you do not know to be useful, or believe to be beautiful.

William Morris
Hopes and Fears for Art

morris dance English folk dance. In early times it was usually performed by six men, one of whom wore girl's clothing while another portrayed a horse. The others wore costumes decorated with bells. Morris dancing probably originated in pre-Christian ritual dances and is still popular in the UK and USA.

Morrison Toni 1931– . US novelist whose fiction records black life in the South. Her works include *Song of Solomon* 1978, *Tar Baby* 1981, *Beloved* 1987, based on a true story about infanticide in Kentucky, which won the Pulitzer Prize 1988, and *Jazz* 1992. Nobel Prize for Literature 1993.

Morrison Van (George Ivan) 1945– . Northern Irish singer and songwriter whose jazz-inflected Celtic soul style was already in evidence on *Astral Weeks* 1968 and has been highly influential. Among other albums are *Tupelo Honey* 1971, *Veedon Fleece* 1974, and *Avalon Sunset* 1989.

Morrissey stage name of Steven Patrick Morrissey 1959– . English rock singer and lyricist, founder member of the ◊Smiths 1982–87 and subsequently a solo artist. His lyrics reflect on everyday miseries or glumly celebrate the England of his childhood. Solo albums include *Viva Hate* 1987 and *Your Arsenal* 1992.

I was looking for a job, and then I found a job / And heaven knows I'm miserable now.

Morrissey
'Heaven Knows I'm Miserable Now' 1984

Morte D'Arthur, Le series of episodes from the legendary life of King Arthur by Thomas ◊Malory, completed 1470, regarded as the first great prose work in English literature. Only the last of the eight books composing the series is titled *Le Morte D'Arthur*.

Mortimer John 1923– . English barrister and writer. His works include the plays *The Dock Brief* 1958 and *A Voyage Round My Father* 1970, the novel *Paradise Postponed* 1985, and the television series *Rumpole of the Bailey*, from 1978, centred on a fictional barrister.

Morton Jelly Roll. Stage name of Ferdinand Joseph La Menthe 1885–1941. US New Orleans-style jazz pianist, singer, and composer. Influenced by Scott Joplin, he was a pioneer in the development of jazz from ragtime to swing by improvising and imposing his own personality on the music. His 1920s band was called the Red Hot Peppers.

mosaic design or picture, usually for a floor or wall, produced by inlaying small pieces of marble, glass, or other materials. Mosaic was commonly used by the Romans for their baths and villas (for example Hadrian's Villa at Tivoli) and by the Byzantines, especially for church decoration.

The art was revived by the Italians during the 13th century, when it was used chiefly for the decoration of churches (for example San Vitale, Ravenna). More recent examples of mosaic work can be seen in the hall of the Houses of Parliament and in Westminster Cathedral, London.

Moschino Franco 1950– . Italian fashion designer who became known for his irreverent clothing after opening his own business 1983. His tailored and classic designed outfits are decorated with slogans, peace symbols, diamanté anarchy signs, and other accessories such as heart-shaped buttons. His printed scarf designs include trompe l'oeil necklaces, handbags, and other accessories.

Moses 'Grandma' (born Anna Mary Robertson) 1860–1961. US painter. She was self-taught, and began full-time painting about 1927, after many years as a farmer's wife. She painted naive and colourful scenes from rural American life.

mosque (Arabic *mesjid*) in Islam, a place of worship. Chief features are: the dome; the minaret, a balconied turret from which the faithful are called to prayer; the *mihrab*, or prayer niche, in one of the interior walls, showing the direction of the holy city of Mecca; and an open court surrounded by porticoes.

The earliest mosques were based on Muhammad's house in Medina, although different influences, such as the plan of Christian basilicas, contributed towards their architectural development (see ◊Islamic architecture). Mosques vary a great deal in style in various parts of the world.

Mostel Zero (Samuel Joel) 1915–1977. US comedian and actor, mainly in the theatre. His films include *Panic in the Streets* 1950, *A Funny Thing Happened on the Way to the Forum* 1966, *The Producers* 1967, and *The Front* 1976.

motet sacred, polyphonic music for unaccompanied voices in a form that originated in 13th-century Europe.

Motherwell Robert 1915–1991. US painter associated with the New York school of ◊action painting. Borrowing from Picasso, Matisse, and the Surrealists, Motherwell's style of Abstract Expressionism retained some suggestion of the figurative. His works include the *Elegies to the Spanish Republic* 1949–76, a series of over 100 paintings devoted to the Spanish Civil War.

motif a distinct element or image within a work, such as a detail in a painting or building, especially one which is repeated and echoed throughout the work. It can also refer to a significant object or action in a novel or a phrase in a piece of music – for instance, the opening four notes of Beethoven's Fifth Symphony. See also ◊leitmotif.

motion picture US term for film; see ◊cinema.

Motown first black-owned US record company, founded in Detroit (Mo[tor] Town) 1959 by Berry Gordy, Jr (1929–). Its distinctive, upbeat sound (exemplified by the Four Tops and the ◊Supremes) was a major element in 1960s pop music.

The Motown sound was created by in-house producers and songwriters such as Smokey Robinson; performers included Stevie Wonder, Marvin Gaye, and the Temptations. Its influence faded after the company's move to Los Angeles 1971, but it still served as a breeding ground for such singers as Lionel Richie (1950–) and Michael Jackson.

Mourning Becomes Electra trilogy of plays by Eugene ◊O'Neill 1931 that retells the Orestes legend, dramatized by Aeschylus (see ◊*Oresteia*), setting it in the world of 19th-century New England. The trilogy is considered among the greatest of modern US plays.

mouth organ any of a family of small portable free-reed wind instruments originating in Eastern and South Asia. The compact **harmonica**, or European mouth organ, was developed by Charles Wheatstone 1829. As the **mouth harp**, the mouth organ is a staple instrument of country and western music. As a melody instrument it achieved concert status through the virtuosity of Larry ◊Adler. All mouth organs bend in pitch in response to variation in wind pressure.

movement in music, a self-contained composition of specific character, usually a constituent piece of a ◊suite, ◊symphony, or similar work, with its own tempo, distinct from that of the other movements.

Moyse Marcel 1889–1984. French flautist. Trained at the Paris Conservatoire, he made many recordings and was an eminent teacher.

Mozart Wolfgang Amadeus 1756–1791. Austrian composer and performer who showed astonishing precocity as a child and was an adult virtuoso. He was trained by his father, *Leopold Mozart* (1719–1787). From an early age he composed prolifically, his works including 27 piano concertos, 23 string quartets, 35 violin sonatas, and more than 50 symphonies including the E flat K543, G minor K550, and C major K551 ('Jupiter') symphonies, all composed 1788. His operas include *Idomeneo* 1781, *Entführung aus dem Serail/The Abduction from the Seraglio* 1782, *Le Nozze di Figaro/The Marriage of Figaro* 1786, *Don Giovanni* 1787, *Così fan tutte/Thus Do All Women* 1790, and *Die Zauberflöte/The Magic Flute* 1791. Together with ◊Haydn, Mozart's music marks the height of the Classical age in its purity of melody and form.

Mozart's career began when, with his sister, Maria Anna, he was taken on a number of tours 1762–79, visiting Vienna, the Rhineland, Holland, Paris, London, and Italy. He had already begun to compose. In 1772 he was appointed master of the archbishop of Salzburg's court band. He found the post uncongenial and in 1781 was suddenly dismissed. Marrying Constanze Weber 1782, he settled in Vienna and embarked on a punishing freelance career as concert pianist, composer, and teacher that brought lasting fame but only intermittent financial security. His *Requiem*, unfinished at his death, was completed by a pupil. His works were catalogued chronologically 1862 by the musicologist Ludwig von Köchel (1800–1877), whose system of numbering remains in use in modified form.

If only the whole world could feel the power of harmony.

Wolfgang Amadeus Mozart letter 1778

Mphahlele Es'kia (Ezekiel) 1919– . South African literary critic, journalist, and novelist. He is best known for his influential autobiography *Down Second Avenue* 1959.

Mrs Dalloway novel 1925 by Virginia ◊Woolf. Clarissa Dalloway, a middle-aged 'society woman', drifts through a summer's day in London, preparing for the party she is to give that evening. A visit from a former suitor deepens her reflections, which combine many elements of past and present. At various points, her life and those of her friends and family, interweave unknowingly with that of Septimus Warren Smith, a shell-shocked young man who is going mad.

Mucha Alphonse 1860–1939. Czech painter and designer whose Art Nouveau posters and decorative panels brought him international fame, presenting idealized images of young women with long, flowing tresses, within a patterned flowered border. His early theatre posters were done for the actress Sarah Bernhardt, notably the lithograph *Gismonda* 1894.

Mu-Chi (Muqi) *c.* 1180–*c.* 1270. Chinese painter of the Song dynasty. A Chan Buddhist, he employed a technique based on intuition and spontaneity. One of his best-known works is *Six Persimmons* early 13th century (Daitoku-ji, Kyoto), illustrating his ability to depict an object with a few deft brush strokes.

Muckrakers, the movement of US writers and journalists about 1880–1914 who aimed to expose political, commercial, and corporate corruption, and record frankly the age of industrialism, urban poverty, and conspicuous consumption. Novelists included Frank Norris, Theodore Dreiser, Jack London, and Upton Sinclair.

Muddy Waters adopted name of McKinley Morganfield 1915–1983. US blues singer, songwriter, and guitarist, a central figure in the development of electric urban blues in the 1950s.

Many of his songs have become rhythm-and-blues standards, including 'Hoochie Coochie Man' 1954 and 'Got My Mojo Workin'' 1957.

Waters was born in Mississippi. He moved first to Memphis and then to Chicago, where he formed a small band and took up the electric guitar, which he played with a bottleneck slide. His hits included 'Louisiana Blues' 1951, 'Mannish Boy' 1955, and 'Close To You' 1958. He first toured the UK 1958 and was an influence on bands like the Rolling Stones, who took their name from his 1950 song.

Mudra in Hindu religious dance, ritualized body gestures, especially of the hand and fingers.

Mugler Thierry 1946– . French fashion designer who launched his first collection 1971 under the label Café de Paris. By 1973 he was designing under his own label. Strongly influenced by 1940s and 1950s fashion, his designs had broad shoulders and well-defined waists. His catwalk shows are often spectacular.

Muir Edwin 1887–1959. Scottish poet. He drew mystical inspiration from his Orkney childhood. *First Poems* 1925 was published after a period of residence in Prague, which also resulted in translations of Kafka, in collaboration with his wife, Willa. Dreams, myths, and menaces coexist in his poetry. His notable *Autobiography* 1954 explores similar themes.

Muir Jean 1933– . British fashion designer who worked for Jaeger 1956–61 and set up her own fashion house 1961. In 1991 she launched a knitwear collection. Her clothes are characterized by soft, classic, tailored shapes in leathers and soft fabrics.

Müller Heiner 1929– . German dramatist whose scripts have played a leading role in contemporary avant-garde theatre in Germany and abroad. Early political works, showing the influence of Brecht (*The Scab* 1950, *The Correction* 1958) were followed by *Mauser* 1970, *Cement* 1972 (on the Russian revolution), *Hamletmachine* 1977, and *Medea-material* 1982.

Mulligan Gerry (Gerald) 1927– . US jazz saxophonist, arranger, and composer who spanned the bebop and cool jazz movements. He worked with trumpeter Miles Davis on the seminal *Birth of the Cool* album 1950 and led his own quartet from 1951, which briefly featured Chet Baker on trumpet.

Mulock unmarried name of British novelist Dinah ◊Craik.

Mulready William 1786–1863. Irish painter of rural scenes, active in England. In 1840 he designed the first penny-postage envelope, known as the *Mulready envelope*.

multiphonics in music, a technique of ◊overblowing a woodwind instrument combined with unorthodox fingering to produce a complex dissonance. Composers of multiphonics include Luciano Berio and Heinz Holliger, and the technique is also used by jazz saxophonists.

Mumford Lewis 1895–1990. US urban planner and social critic, concerned with the adverse effect of technology on contemporary society. His books, including *Technics and Civilization* 1934 and *The Culture of Cities* 1938, discussed the rise of cities and proposed the creation of green belts around large conurbations. His view of the importance of an historical perspective in urban planning for the future is reflected in his major work *The City in History* 1961.

Every generation revolts against its fathers and makes friends with its grandfathers.

Lewis Mumford *The Brown Decade*

---

mummers' play or *St George play* British folk drama enacted in dumb show by a masked cast, performed on Christmas Day to celebrate the death of the old year and its rebirth as the new year. The plot usually consists of a duel between St George and an infidel knight, in which one of them is killed but later revived by a doctor. Mummers' plays are still performed in some parts of Britain.

Munch Edvard 1863–1944. Norwegian painter and printmaker. He studied in Paris and Berlin, and his major works date from the period 1892–1908, when he lived mainly in Germany. His paintings often focus on neurotic emotional states. The *Frieze of Life* 1890s, a sequence of highly charged, symbolic paintings, includes some of his most characteristic images, notably *Skriket/The Scream* 1893. He later reused these in etchings, lithographs, and woodcuts.

Munch was influenced by van Gogh and Gauguin but soon developed his own expressive style, reducing his compositions to broad areas of colour with sinuous contours emphasized by heavy brushstrokes, distorting faces and figures. His first show in Berlin 1892 made a great impact on young German artists. In 1908 he suffered a nervous breakdown and returned to Norway. Later works include a series of murals 1910–15 in the assembly halls of Oslo University.

Münchhausen Karl Friedrich, Freiherr (Baron) von 1720–1797. German soldier, born in Hanover. He served with the Russian army against the Turks, and after his retirement 1760 told exaggerated stories of his adventures. This idiosyncrasy was utilized by the German writer Rudolph Erich Raspe (1737–1794) in his extravagantly fictitious *Adventures of Baron Munchausen* 1785, which he wrote in English while living in London.

Munkácsi Martin 1896–1963. US photographer born in Hungary. After a successful career in Budapest and then Berlin, where he was influenced by the ◊New Photography movement, he moved to the USA 1934. There he worked as a fashion photographer pioneering a more lively and natural style of photograph for such magazines as *Harper's Bazaar* and *Ladies' Home Journal*.

Munnings Alfred 1878–1959. English painter excelling in racing and hunting scenes as well as everyday scenes featuring horses. As president of the Royal Academy 1944–49 he was outspoken in his dislike of 'modern art'.

Munro Alice 1931– . Canadian author, known for her short stories. She is remarkably sensitive to suppressed or unrecognized feeling in small-town life. Collections of her work include *Dance of the Happy Shades* 1968 and *The Progress of Love* 1987. She has written only one novel, *Lives of Girls and Women* 1971.

Munro H(ugh) H(ector). English author who wrote under the pen name ◊Saki.

Murakami Haruki 1949– . Japanese novelist and translator, one of Japan's best-selling writers, influenced by 20th-century US writers and popular culture. His dreamy, gently surrealist novels include *A Wild Sheep Chase* 1982 and *Norwegian Wood* 1987.

mural painting (Latin *murus* 'wall') decoration of walls, vaults, and ceilings by means of ◊fresco, oil, ◊tempera, or ◊encaustic painting methods. Murals were painted by the Minoans, the Greeks, and the Romans. Mural painters include Cimabue, Giotto, Masaccio, Ghirlandaio, and, in the 20th century, Diego Rivera and José Orozco of the Mexican muralist movement.

Murasaki Shikibu *c.* 978–*c.* 1015. Japanese writer, a lady at the court. Her masterpiece of fiction, *The Tale of Genji c.* 1010, is one of the classic works of Japanese literature, and may be the world's first novel.

She was a member of the Fujiwara clan, but her own name is not known; scholars have given her the name Murasaki after a character in the book. It deals with upper-class life in Heian Japan, centring on the affairs of Prince Genji. A portion of her diary and a number of poems also survive.

There are those who do not dislike wrong rumours if they are about the right men.

Murasaki Shikibu
The Tale of Genji c. 1010

'Murders in the Rue Morgue, The' tale by the US writer Edgar Allan ◊Poe, published 1841 acknowledged as the first detective story. Poe's detective, Auguste Dupin, points to the clues leading to the solution of the macabre mystery in what Poe called a 'tale of ratiocination'.

Murdoch Iris 1919– . English novelist, born in Dublin. Her novels combine philosophical speculation with often outrageous situations and tangled human relationships. They include *The Sandcastle* 1957, *The Sea, The Sea* 1978 (Booker Prize), and *The Message to the Planet* 1989.

A lecturer in philosophy, she became a fellow of St Anne's College, Oxford University 1948, and published *Sartre, Romantic Rationalist* 1953. Her novel *A Severed Head* 1961 was filmed 1983.

Writing is like getting married. One should never commit oneself until one is amazed at one's luck.

Iris Murdoch *The Black Prince* 1972

Murger Henri 1822–1861. French writer, born in Paris. In 1848 he published *Scènes de la vie de bohème/Scenes of Bohemian Life* which formed the basis of Puccini's opera *La Bohème*.

Murillo Bartolomé Esteban *c.* 1617–1682. Spanish painter, active mainly in Seville. He painted sentimental pictures of the Immaculate Conception, and also specialized in studies of street urchins. His *Self-Portrait* about 1672 (National Gallery, London) is generally considered to be one of his finest works.

Murillo was born in Seville. Visiting Madrid in the 1640s, he was befriended by the court painter Velázquez, and after his return to Seville he received many religious commissions. He founded the academy of painting in Seville 1660 with the help of Herrera the Younger.

Murnau F W. Adopted name of Friedrich Wilhelm Plumpe 1889–1931. German silent-film director, known for his expressive images and 'subjective' use of a moving camera in *Der letzte Mamm/The Last Laugh* 1924. Other films include *Nosferatu* 1922 (a version of the Dracula story), *Sunrise* 1927, and *Tabu* 1931.

Murphy Audie 1924–1971. US actor and war hero who starred mainly in low-budget Westerns. His more prestigious work includes *The Red Badge of Courage* 1951, *The Quiet American* 1958, and *The Unforgiven* 1960.

He was the most decorated American soldier of World War II and played himself in the film story of his war years *To Hell and Back* 1955.

Murphy Dervla 1931– . Irish travel writer. Her books include *Full Tilt* 1965, *Tibetan Foothold* 1966, *In Ethiopia with a Mule* 1968, and *Cameroon with Egbert* 1989. Travelling with minimal resources in the UK as well as in Asia, Africa, and South America, she reports her responses to both people and landscapes with warmth and a naive originality.

Murphy Eddie 1961– . US film actor and comedian. His first film, *48 Hours* 1982, introduced the character whose sharp wit, casual swagger, and mimicry have become Murphy's trademark. Its great success, and that of his next two films, *Trading Places* 1983 and *Beverly Hills Cop* 1984, made him one of the biggest box-office draws of the 1980s.

Other films include *Beverley Hills Cop II* 1987, his filmed live show *Eddie Murphy Raw* 1987, *Coming to America* 1988, which he co-wrote, *Harlem Nights* 1989, which he produced and directed, and *Boomerang* and *The Distinguished Gentleman* both 1992.

Murray (George) Gilbert (Aimé) 1866–1957. Australian-born British scholar. He was taken to England 1877, and was professor of Greek at Glasgow University 1889–99 and at Oxford 1908–36. Author of *History of Ancient Greek Literature* 1897, he became known for verse translations of the Greek dramatists, notably of Euripides, which rendered the plays more accessible to readers.

Murray Les(lie) A(llan) 1938– . Australian poet. His poetry, adventurous, verbally inventive, deeply serious, has appeared in collections such as *The Vernacular Republic: Poems 1961–1981* 1982, *The People's Otherworld* 1983, and *The Australian Seasons* 1985. He has emerged as a determined advocate of the virtues and values of rural life.

Murry John Middleton 1889–1957. English writer. He produced studies of Dostoevsky, Keats, Blake, and Shakespeare; poetry; and an autobiographical novel, *Still Life* 1916. In 1913 he married the writer Katherine Mansfield, whose biography he wrote. He was a friend of the writer D H Lawrence.

Musashi Miyamoto; see ◊Miyamoto Musashi, Japanese samurai.

Muse in Greek mythology, one of the nine daughters of Zeus and Mnemosyne (goddess of memory) and inspirers of creative arts: Calliope, epic poetry; Clio, history; Erato, love poetry; Euterpe, lyric poetry; Melpomene, tragedy; Polyhymnia, sacred song; Terpsichore, dance; Thalia, comedy; and Urania, astronomy.

musette small French ◊bagpipes; also a dance movement and character piece, as in Schoenberg's *Suite for Piano* 1921, incorporating a drone accompaniment.

Museum of Modern Art, New York leading US art museum devoted to art of the late 19th and early 20th centuries. Opened 1929, it has amassed an exceptional collection of modern works, including collections of films and photographs.

Musgrave Thea 1928– . Scottish composer. Her works, in a conservative modern idiom, include concertos for horn, clarinet, and viola; string quartets; and operas, including *Mary, Queen of Scots* 1977.

music art of combining sounds into a coherent perceptual experience, typically in accordance with conventional patterns and for an aesthetic purpose. Music is generally categorized as classical, ◊jazz, ◊pop music, ◊country and western, and so on.

The Greek word *mousikē* covered all the arts presided over by the Muses. The various civilizations of the ancient and modern world developed their own musical systems. Eastern music recognizes subtler distinctions of pitch than does Western music and also differs from Western music in that the absence, until recently, of written notation ruled out the composition of major developed works; it fostered melodic and rhythmic patterns, freely interpreted (as in the Indian raga) by virtuosos.

Western classical music

Middle Ages The documented history of Western music since Classical times begins with the liturgical music of the medieval Catholic Church, derived from Greek and Hebrew antecedents. The four scales, or modes, to which the words of the liturgy were chanted were traditionally first set in order by St Ambrose AD 384. St Gregory the Great added four more to the original Ambrosian modes, and this system forms the basis of Gregorian ◊plainsong, still used in the Roman Catholic Church. The organ was introduced in the 8th century, and in the 9th century harmonized music began to be used in churches, with notation developing towards its present form. In the 11th century counterpoint was introduced, notably at the monastery of St Martial, Limoges, France, and in the late 12th century at Notre Dame in Paris (by Léonin and Perotin). In the late Middle Ages the Provençal and French ◊troubadours and court composers, such as Machaut, developed a secular music, derived from church and folk music (see also ◊Minnesinger).

15th and 16th centuries Europe saw the growth of contrapuntal or polyphonic music. One of the earliest composers was the English musician John Dunstable, whose works inspired the French composer Guillaume Dufay, founder of the Flemish school; its members included Dufay's pupil Joannes Okeghem and the Renaissance composer Josquin Desprez. Other composers of this era were Palestrina from Italy, Roland de Lassus from Flanders, Victoria from Spain, and Thomas Tallis and William Byrd from England. ◊Madrigals were written during the Elizabethan age in England by such composers as Thomas Morley and Orlando Gibbons.

17th century The Florentine Academy (Camerata), a group of artists and writers, aimed to revive the principles of Greek tragedy. This led to the invention of dramatic recitative and the beginning of opera. Monteverdi was an early operatic composer; by the end of the century the form had evolved further in the hands of Alessandro Scarlatti in Italy and Jean-Baptiste Lully in France. In England the outstanding composer of the period was Purcell.

18th century The early part of the century was dominated by J S Bach and Handel. Bach was a master of harmony and counterpoint. Handel is renowned for his dramatic oratorios. Bach's sons C P E Bach and J C Bach reacted against contrapuntal forms and developed sonata form, the basis of the classical sonata, quartet, and symphony. In these types of composition, mastery of style was achieved by the Viennese composers Haydn and Mozart. With Beethoven, music assumed new dynamic and expressive functions.

19th century Romantic music, represented in its early stages by Weber, Schubert, Schumann, Mendelssohn, and Chopin, tended to be subjec-

---

Western music: chronology

AD 590	St Gregory the Great was elected pope. Under his rule the art of music attained new heights, initiating Gregorian chant.
1026	The Italian monk Guido d'Arezzo completed his treatise *Micrologus*. He founded modern notation and tonic sol-fa.
1207	Minnesingers (poet-musicians) Walther von der Vogelweide, Tannhauser, and Wolfram von Eschenbach competed in a song contest at Wartburg Castle, later celebrated in Wagner's opera *Die Meistersinger*.
1240	The earliest known canon, *Sumer is Icumen In*, was composed around this year.
1280	*Carmina Burana*, a collection of students' songs, was compiled in Benediktbuern, Bavaria; Carl Orff was later inspired by their subject matter.
1288	France's greatest troubadour, Adam de la Halle, died in Naples.
1320	*Ars nova*, a tract by Philippe de Vitry, gave its name to a new, more graceful era in music.
1364	Music's first large-scale masterpiece, the *Notre Dame Mass* of Guillaume de Machaut, was performed in Reims to celebrate the coronation of Charles V of France.
1453	John Dunstable, England's first composer of significance, died in London.
1473	The earliest known printed music, the *Collectorium super Magnificat* by Johannes Gerson, was published in Esslingen, near Stuttgart.
1521	Josquin Desprez, the leading musician of his time, died in Condé-sur-Escaut, Burgundy.
1550s	Production of violins began at the workshop of Andrea Amati in Cremona, Italy.
1575	Thomas Tallis and William Byrd jointly published their *Cantiones sacrae*, a collection of 34 motets.
1576	Hans Sachs, the most famous of the Meistersinger (mastersinger) poets and composers, died in Nuremberg.
1597	The first opera, *La Dafne* by Jacopo Peri, was staged privately at the Corsi Palazzo in Florence.
1610	Monteverdi's *Vespers* was published in Venice.
1637	The world's first opera house opened in Venice.
1644	Antonio Stradivari was born. More than 600 of his violins, made in Cremona, survived into the 20th century.
1672	The violinist John Banister inaugurated the first season of public concerts in London.
1709	Bartolemmeo Cristofori unveiled the first fortepiano in Florence.
1721	Bach completed his six *Brandenburg Concertos* for Baroque orchestra.
1722	Jean-Philippe Rameau's book *Traité de l'harmonie* was published, founding modern harmonic theory.
1725	Vivaldi's orchestral suite *The Four Seasons* was published in Amsterdam.
1732	Covent Garden Theatre opened in London.
1742	Handel's *Messiah* received its world premiere in Dublin.
1757	Johann Stamitz died in Mannheim, where he had made important contributions to the development of the symphony and raised the status of the orchestra.
1761	Haydn took up liveried service as vice Kapellmeister with the aristocratic Esterházy family, to whom he was connected until his death 1809.
1788	Mozart completed his last three symphonies, numbers 39–41, in six weeks.
1798	The *Allgemeine Musikalische Zeitung*, a journal of music criticism, was first published in Leipzig.
1805	Beethoven's 'Eroica' Symphony was first performed; it vastly expanded the horizons of orchestral music.
1814	Maelzel invented the metronome.
1815	Schubert's output for this year included two symphonies, two masses, 20 waltzes, and 145 songs.
1821	Weber's *Der Freischütz/The Marksman* introduced heroic German Romanticism to opera.
1828	The limits of instrumental virtuosity were redefined by violinist Paganini's Vienna debut.
1830	Berlioz's dazzlingly avant-garde and programmatic *Symphonie fantastique* startled Paris concertgoers.
1831	Grand opera was inaugurated with *Robert le diable* by Giacomo Meyerbeer.
1842	The Vienna Philharmonic Orchestra gave its first concerts.
1851	Jenny Lind, a singer managed by P T Barnum, earned $176,675 from nine months' concerts in the USA.
1854	In Weimar, Liszt conducted the premieres of his first symphonic poems.
1855	Like most orchestras around this date, the New York Philharmonic for the first time sat down while playing (cellists were already seated).
1865	Wagner's opera *Tristan and Isolde* scaled new heights of expressiveness using unprecedented chromaticism. Schubert's *Unfinished Symphony* (1822) was premiered in Vienna.
1875	The first of a series of collaborations between Arthur Sullivan and the librettist W S Gilbert, *Trial by Jury*, was given its premiere.
1876	Wagner's *The Ring of the Nibelung* was produced in Bayreuth. Brahms' *First Symphony* was performed in Karlsruhe.

(cont.)

Western music: chronology *(cont.)*

1877	Edison invented the cylindrical tin-foil phonograph.
1883	The Metropolitan Opera House opened in New York with a production of Gounod's *Faust*.
1885	Liszt composed *Bagatelle without Tonality* (his *Faust Symphony* of 1857 opened with a 12-note row).
1894	Debussy's *Prélude à l'après-midi d'un faune* anticipated 20th-century composition with its use of the whole-tone scale.
1895	Henry Wood conducted the first Promenade Concert at the Queen's Hall in London.
1899	Scott Joplin's 'Maple Leaf Rag' was published in Sedalia, Missouri.
1902	Caruso recorded ten arias in a hotel room in Milan, the success of which established the popularity of the phonograph. By the time of his death 1921 he had earned $2 million from sales of his recordings.
1908	Saint-Saëns became the first leading composer to write a film score, for *L'Assassinat du duc de Guise*.
1911	Irving Berlin had his first big success as a songwriter with 'Alexander's Ragtime Band'.
1912	Schoenberg's atonal *Pierrot lunaire*, for reciter and chamber ensemble, foreshadowed many similar small-scale quasi-theatrical works.
1913	Stravinsky's ballet *The Rite of Spring* precipitated a riot at its premiere in Paris.
1919	Schoenberg, who was experimenting with serial technique, set up the Society for Private Musical Performances in Vienna, which lasted until 1921.
1922	Alessandro Moreschi, last of the castrati, died in Rome.
1925	Louis Armstrong made his first records with the Hot Five. Duke Ellington's Washingtonians also started recording.
1927	Jerome Kern's *Show Boat*, with libretto by Oscar Hammerstein II, laid the foundations of the US musical.
1930	The BBC Symphony Orchestra was founded in London under Sir Adrian Boult.
1937	Arturo Toscanini, one of the greatest conductors in the history of music, began his 17-year association with the NBC Symphony Orchestra.
1938	Prokofiev's score for Eisenstein's *Alexander Nevsky* raised film music to new levels. Big-band music became popular.
1939	Elisabeth Lutyens was one of the first English composers to use 12-note composition in her *Chamber Concerto* No 1 for nine instruments.
1940	Walt Disney's *Fantasia* introduced classical music, conducted by Leopold Stokowski, to a worldwide audience of filmgoers.
1940s	Bebop jazz was initiated. The jazz greats Charlie Parker and Dizzy Gillespie first recorded together.
1941	The 'Proms' moved to the Royal Albert Hall.
1942	In Chicago, John Cage conducted the premiere of his *Imaginary Landscape No 3*, scored for marimbula, gongs, tin cans, buzzers, plucked coil, electric oscillator, and generator.
1954	Stockhausen's *Electronic Studies* for magnetic tape were broadcast in Cologne. Edgard Varèse's *Déserts*, the first work to combine instruments and prerecorded magnetic tape, was performed in Paris. Elvis Presley made his first rock-and-roll recordings.
1955	Pierre Boulez's *Le Marteau sans maître*, for contralto and chamber ensemble, was performed in Baden-Baden. Its formidable serial technique and exotic orchestration was acclaimed by the avant-garde. The Miles Davis Quintet with John Coltrane united two of the most important innovators in jazz.
1956	The first annual Warsaw Autumn festival of contemporary music was held. This became important for the promotion of Polish composers such as Lutoslawski and Penderecki.
1957	Leonard Bernstein's *West Side Story* was premiered in New York. A computer, programmed at the University of Illinois by Lejaren Hiller and Leonard Isaacson, composed the *Illiac Suite* for string quartet.
1963	Shostakovich's opera *Lady Macbeth of Mtsensk*, earlier banned and condemned in the Soviet newspaper *Pravda* 1936, was produced in a revised version as *Katerina Ismaylova*.
1965	Robert Moog invented a synthesizer that considerably widened the scope of electronic music. The film soundtrack of *The Sound of Music*, with music by Rodgers and lyrics by Hammerstein, was released, and stayed in the sales charts for the next two years. Bob Dylan used electric instrumentation on *Highway 61 Revisited*.
1967	The Beatles' album *Sgt Pepper's Lonely Hearts Club Band*, which took over 500 hours to record, was released. The first Velvet Underground album was released. Psychedelic rock spread from San Francisco, and hard rock developed in the UK and the USA.
1969	Peter Maxwell Davies' theatre piece *Eight Songs for a Mad King*, for vocalist and six instruments, was premiered under Davies' direction in London by the Pierrot Players, later to become the Fires of London ensemble.
1972	Bob Marley's LP *Catch a Fire* began popularization of reggae beyond Jamaica.
1976	Philip Glass' opera *Einstein on the Beach*, using the repetitive techniques of minimalism, was given its first performance in Paris. Punk rock arrived with the Sex Pistols' 'Anarchy in the UK'.
1977	The Institute for Research and Coordination of Acoustics and Music (IRCAM) was founded in Paris under the direction of Boulez, for visiting composers to make use of advanced electronic equipment.
1981	MTV (Music Television) started broadcasting nonstop pop videos on cable in the USA, growing into a worldwide network in the following decade.
1983	Messiaen's only opera, *Saint François d'Assise*, was given its first performance in Paris. Lutoslawski's *Third Symphony* was premiered to worldwide acclaim by the Chicago Symphony Orchestra under Georg Solti. Compact discs were launched in the West.
1986	Paul Simon's *Graceland* album drew on and popularized world music.
1990	Many record chain stores ceased to stock seven-inch singles, accelerating the decline of vinyl records' share of the market.
1991	US rap group NWA declared not obscene by a UK court. Various attempts, especially in the USA, to limit freedom of speech in popular music were generally unsuccessful.
1992	DCC (Digital Compact Cassettes) and MiniDisc (MD), two new audio formats, were launched by Philips and Sony, respectively.

tively emotional. Orchestral colour was increasingly exploited – most notably by Berlioz – and harmony became more chromatic. Nationalism became prominent at this time, as evidenced by the intense Polish nationalism of Chopin; the exploitation of Hungarian music by Liszt; the works of the Russians Rimsky-Korsakov, Borodin, Mussorgsky, and, less typically, Tchaikovsky; the works of the Czechs Dvořák and Smetana; and the Norwegian Grieg. Revolutionary changes were brought about by Wagner in the field of opera, although traditional Italian lyricism continued in the work of Rossini, Verdi, and Puccini. Wagner's contemporary Brahms stood for Classical discipline of form combined with Romantic feeling. The Belgian César Franck, with a newly chromatic idiom, also renewed the tradition of polyphonic writing.

20th century Around 1900 a reaction against Romanticism became apparent in the impressionism of Debussy and Ravel, and the exotic chromaticism of Stravinsky and Scriabin. In Austria and Germany, the tradition of Bruckner, Mahler, and Richard Strauss faced a disturbing new world of atonal expressionism in Schoenberg, Berg, and Webern.

After World War I Neo-Classicism, represented by Stravinsky, Prokofiev, and Hindemith, attempted to restore 18th-century principles of objectivity and order while maintaining a distinctively 20th-century tone. In Paris ◊*Les Six* adopted a more relaxed style, while composers further from the cosmopolitan centres of Europe, such as Elgar, Delius, and Sibelius, continued loyal to the Romantic symphonic tradition. The rise of radio and recorded media created a new mass market for classical and Romantic music, but one which was initially resistant to music by contemporary composers. Organizations such as the International Society for Contemporary Music became increasingly responsible for ensuring that new music continued to be publicly performed.

The second half of the 20th century has seen dramatic changes in the nature of composition and in the instruments used to create sounds. The recording studio has facilitated the development of concrete music based on recorded natural sounds, and electronic music, in which sounds are generated electrically, developments implying the creation of music as a finished object without the need for interpretation by live performers. Chance music, promoted by John Cage, introduced the notion of a music designed to provoke unforeseen results and thereby make new connections; aleatory music, developed by Pierre Boulez, introduced performers to freedom of choice from a range of options. Since the 1960s the computer has become a focus of attention for developments in the synthesis of musical tones, and also in the automation of compositional techniques, most notably at Stanford University and MIT in the USA, and at IRCAM in Paris.

musical 20th-century form of dramatic musical performance, combining elements of song, dance, and the spoken word, often characterized by lavish staging and large casts. It developed from the operettas and musical comedies of the 19th century.

The *operetta* is a light-hearted entertainment with extensive musical content: Jacques Offenbach, Johann Strauss, Franz Lehár, and Gilbert and Sullivan all composed operettas. The *musical comedy* is an anglicization of the French *opéra bouffe*, of which the first was *A Gaiety Girl* 1893, mounted by George Edwardes (1852–1915) at the Gaiety Theatre, London. Typical musical comedies of the 1920s were *Rose Marie* 1924 by Rudolf Friml (1879–1972); *The Student Prince* 1924 and *The Desert Song* 1926, both by Sigmund Romberg (1887–1951); and *No, No, Nanette* 1925 by Vincent Youmans (1898–1946). The 1930s and 1940s were an era of sophisticated musical comedies with many filmed examples and a strong US presence (Irving Berlin, Jerome Kern, Cole Porter, and George Gershwin). In England Noël Coward and Ivor Novello also wrote musicals.

In 1943 Rodgers and Hammerstein's *Oklahoma!* introduced an integration of plot and music, which was developed in Lerner and Loewe's *My Fair Lady* 1956 and Leonard Bernstein's *West Side Story* 1957. Sandy Wilson's *The Boy Friend* 1953 revived the British musical and was followed by hits such as Lionel Bart's *Oliver!* 1960. Musicals began to branch into religious and political themes with *Oh What a Lovely War!* 1963, produced by Joan Littlewood and Charles Chiltern, and the Andrew Lloyd Webber musicals *Jesus Christ Superstar* 1970 and *Evita* 1978. Another category of musical, substituting a theme for conventional plotting, includes Stephen Sondheim's *Company* 1970, Hamlisch and Kleban's *A Chorus Line* 1975, and Lloyd Webber's *Cats* 1981, using verses by T S Eliot. In the 1980s 19th-century melodrama was popular, for example *Les Misérables* 1985 and *The Phantom of the Opera* 1986.

musical instrument digital interface manufacturer's standard for digital music equipment; see ◊MIDI.

musical saw instrument made from a hand saw. The handle is clasped between the knees with the top of the blade held in one hand so that it forms an S-curve. A cello bow is played with the other hand across the back edge of the blade to produce an eerie wailing sound. The pitch is altered by varying the curvature of the blade. Composers include George ◊Crumb.

musical science the ancient Greeks distinguished between *musical sound* as an indicator of Pythagorean concepts of number relation and *musical influences* on human (and animal) behaviour, as recounted in the Orpheus legend.

In general, musical science has sought to rationalize ◊pitch, first into ◊modes, then into ◊scales and ◊temperament, and to quantify ◊timbre, to account for differences between sounds of the same pitch. To this end it has evolved a standard division of the ◊octave allowing for the development of Western ◊tonality, a universal notation for pitch, and keyboard instruments for conducting experiments in tonal relations, all of which prefigure recent digital technologies of information storage and retrieval.

The art of music has developed and adapted the discoveries of musical science for the purposes of artistic expression. The emotional power of music lies in its ability to transcend language and appeal directly to subconscious associations of ◊melody, ◊rhythm, ◊dynamics, and ◊tempo.

music hall British light theatrical entertainment, in which singers, dancers, comedians, and acrobats perform in 'turns'. The music hall's heyday was at the beginning of the 20th century, with such artistes as Marie Lloyd, Harry Lauder, and George Formby. The US equivalent is ◊vaudeville.

Many performers had a song with which they were associated, such as Albert Chevalier (1861–1923) ('My Old Dutch'), or a character 'trademark', such as Vesta Tilley's immaculate masculine outfit as Burlington Bertie. Later stars of music hall included Sir George Robey, Gracie Fields, the Crazy Gang, Ted Ray, and the US comedian Danny Kaye.

history Music hall originated in the 17th century, when tavern-keepers acquired the organs that the Puritans had banished from churches. On certain nights organ music was played, and this resulted in a weekly entertainment known as the 'free and easy'. Certain theatres in London and the provinces then began to specialize in variety entertainment. With the advent of radio and television, music hall declined, but in the 1960s and 1970s there was a revival in working men's clubs and in pubs.

music theatre staged performance of vocal music that deliberately challenges, in style and subject matter, traditional operatic pretensions.

Drawing on English music-hall and European cabaret and *Singspiel* traditions, it flourished during the Depression of the 1920s and 1930s as working-class opera, for example the Brecht– Weill *Die Dreigroschenoper/The Threepenny Opera* 1928; in the USA as socially conscious musical, for example Gershwin's *Porgy and Bess* 1935; and on film, in René Clair's *Sous les Toits de Paris/Under the Roofs of Paris* 1930 (music composed by Raoul Moretti) and *A Nous la Liberté/Freedom for Us* 1931 (music by Georges ◊Auric). Composers addressing a similar mood of social unrest in the years after 1968 include Henze (*Essay on Pigs* 1968), Berio (*Recital I* 1972), and Ligeti (*Le Grand Macabre/The Great Macabre*) 1978. Since 1970 music theatre has emerged as a favoured idiom for short-term community music projects produced by outreach departments of civic arts centres and opera houses.

Musil Robert 1880–1942. Austrian novelist, author of the unfinished *Der Mann ohne Eigenschaften/The Man without Qualities* (three volumes, 1930–43). Its hero shares the author's background of philosophical study and scientific and military training, and is preoccupied with the problems of the self viewed from a mystic but agnostic viewpoint.

Musset Alfred de 1810–1857. French poet and playwright. He achieved success with the volume of poems *Contes d'Espagne et d'Italie/Stories of Spain and Italy* 1829. His *Confessions d'un enfant du siècle/Confessions of a Child of the Century* 1835 recounts his broken relationship with George Sand.

Born in Paris, he abandoned the study of law and medicine to join the circle of Victor Hugo. Typical of his work are the verse in *Les Nuits/Nights* 1835–37 and the short plays *Comédies et proverbes/Comedies and Proverbs* 1840.

The glass I drink from is not large, but at least it is my own.

Alfred de Musset
'La Coupe et les lèvres'

Mussorgsky Modest Petrovich 1839–1881. Russian nationalist composer and member of the group of five composers 'The ◊Mighty Handful'. His opera masterpiece *Boris Godunov* 1869, revised 1871–72, touched a political nerve and employed realistic transcriptions of speech patterns. Many of his works, including *Pictures at an Exhibition* 1874 for piano, were completed and orchestrated by others, including Rimsky-Korsakov, Ravel, and Shostakovich, and some have only recently been restored to their original state.

Mussorgsky, born in Karevo (Pskov, Russia), resigned his commission in the army 1858 to concentrate on music while working as a government clerk. He was influenced by both folk music and literature. Among his other works are the incomplete operas *Khovanshchina* and *Sorochintsy Fair*, the orchestral *Night on the Bare Mountain* 1867, and many songs. Mussorgsky died in poverty, from alcoholism.

mute in music, any device used to dampen the vibration of an instrument and so affect the tone. Orchestral strings apply a form of clamp to the bridge; brass instruments use the hand or a plug of metal or cardboard inserted in the bell.

Muti Riccardo 1941– . Italian conductor, artistic director of La Scala, Milan, from 1986. He is equally at home with opera or symphonic repertoire performed with bravura, energy, and scrupulous detail. He was conductor of the Philharmonia Orchestra, London, 1973–82 and the Philadelphia Orchestra from 1981. He is known as a purist.

Muybridge Eadweard. Adopted name of Edward James Muggeridge 1830–1904. British photographer. He made a series of animal locomotion photographs in the USA in the 1870s and proved that, when a horse trots, there are times when all its feet are off the ground. He also explored motion in birds and humans.

Muzak proprietary name for ◊piped music.

Myrmidon in Greek mythology, one of the soldiers of the Greek warrior ◊Achilles, whom he commanded at the siege of Troy in Homer's *Iliad*. They came from Thessaly, in N Greece.

Myron *c.* 500–440 BC. Greek sculptor. His *Discobolus/Discus-Thrower* and *Athene and Marsyas*, much admired in his time, are known through Roman copies. They confirm his ancient reputation for brilliant composition and naturalism.

mystery play or *miracle play* medieval religious drama based on stories from the Bible.

Mystery plays were performed around the time of church festivals, reaching their height in Europe during the 15th and 16th centuries. A whole cycle running from the Creation to the Last Judgement was performed in separate scenes on mobile wagons by various town guilds, usually on the festival of Corpus Christi in mid-summer.

Four English cycles survive: Coventry, Wakefield (or Townley), Chester, and York. Versions are still performed, such as the York cycle in York.

mythology body of traditional stories concerning a culture's gods, supernatural beings, and heroes. Often a mythology may be intended to explain the workings of the universe, nature, or human history.

Ancient mythologies, with the names of the chief god of each, include those of Egypt (Osiris), Greece (Zeus), Rome (Jupiter), India (Brahma), and the Teutonic peoples (Odin or Woden).

as in *Man in the Open Air* about 1914–15 (Museum of Modern Art, New York). His work influenced ◊Art Deco design.

naiad in classical mythology, a water nymph. Naiads lived in rivers and streams; ◊Nereids in the sea.

Naipaul V(idiadhar) S(urajprasad) 1932– . British writer, born in Trinidad of Hindu parents. His novels include *A House for Mr Biswas* 1961, *The Mimic Men* 1967, *A Bend in the River* 1979, and *Finding the Centre* 1984. His brother **Shiva(dhar) Naipaul** (1940–1985) was also a novelist (*Fireflies* 1970) and journalist.

I'm the kind of writer that people think other people are reading.

V S Naipaul in *Radio Times* 1979

Nabis, les (Hebrew 'prophets') group of French artists, active in the 1890s in Paris, united in their admiration of Paul Gauguin – the mystic content of his work, the surface pattern, and intense colour. In practice their work was decorative and influenced Art Nouveau. Pierre ◊Bonnard, Edouard ◊Vuillard, and Paul Sérusier (1864–1927) were leading members.

Nabokov Vladimir 1899–1977. US writer who left his native Russia 1917 and began writing in English in the 1940s. His most widely known book is ◊*Lolita* 1955, the story of the middle-aged Humbert Humbert's infatuation with a precocious girl of 12. His other books, remarkable for their word play and ingenious plots, include *Laughter in the Dark* 1938, *The Real Life of Sebastian Knight* 1945, *Pnin* 1957, and his memoirs *Speak, Memory* 1947.

Born in St Petersburg, Nabokov settled in the USA 1940, and became a US citizen 1945. He was professor of Russian literature at Cornell University 1948–59, producing a translation and commentary on Pushkin's *Eugene Onegin* 1963. He was also a lepidopterist (a collector of butterflies and moths), a theme used in his book *Pale Fire* 1962.

Life is a great surprise. I do not see why death should not be an even greater one.

Vladimir Nabokov *Pale Fire* 1962

Nadar adopted name of Gaspard-Félix Tournachon 1820–1910. French portrait photographer and caricaturist. He took the first aerial photographs (from a balloon 1858) and was the first to take flash photographs (using magnesium bulbs).

Nadelman Elie 1882–1946. Polish-born sculptor, a US citizen from 1927. He is celebrated for his stylish, 'tubular' figures with doll-like faces and body parts that melt into flowing contours,

naive art fresh, childlike style of painting, employing bright colours and strong, rhythmic designs, usually the work of artists with no formal training. Outstanding naive artists include Henri Rousseau and Camille Bombois (1883–1970) in France, and Alfred Wallis (1855–1942) in England. The term is also used to describe the work of trained artists who employ naive techniques and effects, for example, L S Lowry.

Naked and the Dead, The first novel by the US writer Norman ◊Mailer, published 1948. Set on a Pacific island during combat in World War II, it depicts war not only as a battle with the enemy but also as a psychic and political condition.

Naked Lunch novel 1959 by US writer William ◊Burroughs based on notes written during his heroin addiction in Tangier. The book is a fragmented, black humour phantasmagoria of disturbing power, which examines all forms of need and control including politics, sex, and the act of writing itself. It is a key work of the ◊Beat Generation and has had a major influence on modern literature.

Cure is always: Let go! Jump!

William Burroughs *Naked Lunch* 1959

Nakian Reuben 1897– . US sculptor. His rough, freely improvised work of the 1950s linked him to ◊action painting, though figurative references (usually to mythology) remain. From the 1960s he produced more abstract, generally monumental sculptures, cast in bronze from plaster and chicken-wire maquettes, for example, *Goddess of the Golden Thighs* 1964–65 (Detroit Institute of Arts, Detroit).

Namatjira Albert 1902–1959. Australian Aboriginal painter of watercolour landscapes of the Australian interior. Acclaimed after an exhibition in Melbourne 1938, he died destitute.

Name of the Rose, The (Italian *Il nome della rosa*) historical thriller by Umberto ◊Eco, published 1981 (English translation 1983). Set in a 14th-century abbey which burns down at the end of the novel, it can be read as a complex murder mystery involving the disappearance of a priceless book or as an erudite and sophisticated philosophical fable about language and reality. A film was made from the book 1986, starring Sean Connery.

Namuth Hans 1915–1990. German-born US photographer who specialized in portraits and documentary work. He began as a photojournalist in Europe in the 1930s and opened a portrait studio in New York 1950. His work includes documentation of the Guatemalan Mam Indians (published as *Los Todos Santeros* 1989) and of US artists from the 1950s (published as *Artists 1950–1981*). He also carried out assignments for magazines.

Nancarrow Conlon 1912– . US composer who settled in Mexico 1940. Using a player-piano as a form of synthesizer, punching the rolls by hand, he experimented with mathematically derived combinations of rhythm and tempo in *37 Studies for Player-Piano* 1950–68, works of a hypnotic persistence that aroused the admiration of a younger generation of minimalist composers.

Nanni di Banco *c.* 1384–1421. Florentine sculptor who worked on several of the great civic commissions of 15th-century Florence. He remained independent of ◊Donatello's sculptural innovations, using conservative techniques to create classical imagery. His major work, commissioned for a niche at Orsanmichele, is *Quattro Santi Coronati* about 1413, a group of four Roman sculptors who were also Christian martyrs.

His relief *Assumption* 1414–21 over the Porta della Mandorla of Florence Cathedral prefigures Baroque style. But for an early death, his career might have rivalled Donatello's.

Narayan R(usipuram) K(rishnaswami) 1907– . Indian novelist. His popular novels, notably *Swami and Friends* 1935, his first, and *The Man-Eater of Malgudi* 1962, successfully combine realism with mythical and grotesque elements. They are comedies of sadness, of the family and middle-class life, set in 'Malgudi', intensely local yet representative of India and indeed of humanity. His vivid autobiographical sketches *My Days* were published 1974.

Narcissus in Greek mythology, a beautiful youth who rejected the love of the nymph ◊Echo and was condemned to fall in love with his own reflection in a pool. He pined away and in the place where he died a flower sprang up that was named after him.

Narnia, Chronicles of a series of seven books for children by C S ◊Lewis. The first in the series, *The Lion, the Witch and the Wardrobe*, was published 1950; in it children enter through a wardrobe into an imaginary country, Narnia. There the Christian story is re-enacted in a mythical context, the lion Aslan representing Christ. Further journeys into Narnia feature in the sequels *Prince Caspian* 1951, *The Voyage of the Dawn Treader* 1952, *The Silver Chair* 1953, *The Horse and his Boy* 1954, *The Magician's Nephew* 1955, and *The Last Battle* 1956.

Nash (Frederic) Ogden 1902–1971. US poet and wit. He published numerous volumes of humorous, quietly satirical light verse, characterized by unorthodox rhymes and puns. They include *I'm a Stranger Here Myself* 1938, *Versus* 1949, and *Bed Riddance* 1970. Most of his poems first appeared in the *New Yorker*, where he held an editorial post and did much to establish the magazine's tone.

Children aren't happy with nothing to ignore,/And that's what parents were created for.

Ogden Nash 'The Parents'

Nash John 1752–1835. English architect. In the first phase of his career he was best known for designing country houses, using a wide variety of styles. Later he laid out Regent's Park, London, and its approaches, a vast grandiose scheme of terraces and crescents and palatial-style houses with ornate stucco façades. He also laid out Trafalgar Square and St James's Park. Between 1811 and 1820 he planned Regent Street (later rebuilt), repaired and enlarged Buckingham Palace (for which he designed Marble Arch), and rebuilt Brighton Pavilion in flamboyant oriental style.

Nash John Northcote 1893–1977. English illustrator, landscape artist, and engraver. He was the brother of the artist Paul Nash.

With few exceptions our artists have painted 'by the light of nature'. ... This immunity from the responsibility of design has become a tradition.

Paul Nash letter to *The Times* 1933

Nash Paul 1889–1946. English painter, an official war artist in World Wars I and II. In the 1930s he was one of a group of artists promoting avant-garde styles in the UK, and was deeply influenced by Surrealism. Two works which illustrate the visionary quality of his paintings are

Totes Meer/Dead Sea 1940–41 (Tate Gallery, London) and *Solstice of the Sunflower* 1945 (National Gallery of Canada, Ottawa).

Nash was born in London. In his pictures of World War I, such as *The Menin Road*, in the Imperial War Museum, he created strange patterns out of the scorched landscape of the Western Front. During World War II he was appointed official war artist to the Air Ministry.

Nashe Thomas 1567–1601. English poet, satirist, and anti-Puritan pamphleteer. Born in Suffolk, he settled in London about 1588, where he wrote at least three attacks on the Puritans. Among his later works are the satirical *Pierce Pennilesse* 1592 and the religious *Christes Teares over Jerusalem* 1593; his *The Unfortunate Traveller* 1594 is a picaresque narrative mingling literary parody and mock-historical fantasy.

Nasmyth Alexander 1758–1840. Scottish portrait and landscape painter. His portrait of the poet Robert Burns hangs in the Scottish National Gallery.

Nasmyth, born in Edinburgh, concentrated from 1806 on landscapes, usually Classical and Italianate. He is regarded as the creator of the Scottish landscape-painting tradition.

Nast Thomas 1840–1902. German-born US illustrator and cartoonist. During the American Civil War, Nast served as a staff artist for *Harper's Weekly* and later drew its editorial cartoons. His vivid caricatures helped bring down New York's corrupt state senator 'Boss' Tweed and established the donkey and the elephant as the symbols of Democrats and Republicans, respectively.

national anthem patriotic song for official occasions. The US national anthem, 'The Star-Spangled Banner', was written 1814 by Francis Scott ◊Key and was adopted officially 1931. In Britain 'God Save the King/Queen' has been accepted as such since 1745, although both music and words are of much earlier origin. The German anthem 'Deutschland über Alles/Germany before Everything' is sung to music by Haydn. The French national anthem, the ◊'Marseillaise', dates from 1792.

Countries within the Commonwealth retain 'God Save the King/Queen' as the 'royal anthem', adopting their own anthem as a mark of independence. These include 'Advance Australia Fair' 1974–76 and from 1984 'O Canada', written 1882 and adopted gradually through popular usage. The anthem of united Europe is Schiller's 'Ode to Joy' set by Beethoven in his Ninth Symphony.

National Endowment for the Arts US arts funding agency, established by Congress 1965, which grants subsidies to museums, performance companies, and individuals. Its total 1992–93 budget was $176 million. In the 1990s its awards to controversial artists came under criticism in Congress.

National Gallery London art gallery housing the British national collection of pictures by artists no longer living. It was founded 1824, when Parliament voted £57,000 for the purchase of 38 pictures from the collection of John Julius Angerstein (1735–1823), plus £3,000 for the maintenance of the building in Pall Mall, London, where they were housed. The present building in Trafalgar Square was designed by William Wilkins and opened 1838: there have been several extensions, including the Sainsbury Wing, designed by US architect Robert Venturi, which opened July 1991.

nationalism in music, the adoption by 19th-century composers of folk idioms with which an audience untrained in the classics could identify. Nationalism was encouraged by governments in the early 20th century for propaganda purposes in times of war and political tension. Composers of nationalist music include Smetana, Sibelius, Grieg, Dvořák, Nielsen, Kodály, Copland, Elgar, Shostakovich and Stephen Foster.

National Portrait Gallery London art gallery containing portraits of distinguished British men and women. It was founded 1856.

The present building in St Martin's Place, Trafalgar Square, opened 1896. In addition to paintings, busts and photographs are displayed. In 1989 alternative offices for administration were acquired, allowing the existing gallery space to be increased by 40%.

National Theatre, Royal British national theatre company established 1963, and the complex, opened 1976, that houses it on London's South Bank. The national theatre of France is the ◊Comédie Française, founded 1680.

The National Theatre is not a temple, and the policy of the company is that it should be a very open building.

Denys Lasdun, its architect, on the National Theatre

Natsume Sōseki 1867–1926. Japanese novelist. A brilliant student and teacher of English, he responded discerningly to the pervasive new European influences of his era, depicted the plight of the alienated Japanese intellectual, and ushered in the modern Japanese novel. He explored the isolation and frustration of well-educated protagonists in works such as *Mon/The Gate* 1910, *Kojin/The Wayfarer* 1912–13, and *Kokoro* 1914.

natural in music, a sign cancelling a sharp or flat. A *natural trumpet* or *horn* is an instrument without valves, thus restricted to playing natural harmonics.

naturalism in the arts generally, advocates the factual and realistic representation of the subject of a painting or novel with no stylization. Specifically, Naturalism refers to a movement in literature and drama that originated in France in the late 19th century with the writings of Emile ◊Zola and the brothers ◊Goncourt. Similar to ◊Realism in that it was concerned with everyday life, Naturalism also held that people's fates were determined by heredity, environment, and social forces beyond their control.

Zola, the chief theorist of the movement, demonstrates the characteristic accuracy of reportage in his Rougon-Macquart sequence of novels (1871–93), which shows the working of heredity and environment in one family. Other Naturalist writers include Guy de Maupassant and Alphonse Daudet in France, Gerhart Hauptmann in Germany, and Theodore Dreiser in America.

Natyasastra ancient Indian (Sanskrit) treatise on the theatre, dating from *c.* AD 500, dealing with composition, production, theatre buildings, and performance, and propounding a theory of emotion and feeling (*rasa*) which unites actor with audience.

nave in architecture, the central part of a church, between the choir and the entrance.

Nazarenes group of German and Austrian artists, working mainly in Rome in the early 19th century, who aimed to revive religious art by turning to medieval and Renaissance models. The group first formed in Vienna 1809 and later received several important commissions in Rome, notably in the field of ◊fresco painting. It derived its name from the monastic lifestyle and dress that its members adopted. In many ways the Nazarenes anticipated the English ◊Pre-Raphaelite Brotherhood.

NCR Book Award for Nonfiction annual UK book award founded 1987, awarded by NCR Ltd, a computer and high-technology company. The first winner 1988 was David Thomson for *Nairn in Darkness and Light*. The winner receives £25,000.

N'Dour Youssou 1959– . Senegalese singer, songwriter, and musician whose fusion of traditional ◊*mbalax* percussion music with bluesy Arab-style vocals, accompanied by African and electronic instruments, became popular in the West in the 1980s on albums such as *Immigrés* 1984 with the band Le Super Etoile de Dakar.

Neagle Anna 1904–1986. English actress, made a star by her producer-director husband Herbert Wilcox (1890–1977), whose films include *Nell Gwyn* 1934, *Victoria the Great* 1937, and *Odette* 1950.

nectar in Greek mythology, the drink of the gods. Their food was ambrosia.

negative/positive in photography, a reverse image, which when printed is again reversed, restoring the original scene. It was invented by ◊Fox Talbot about 1834.

Nègre Charles 1820–1880. French painter who turned to photography after learning the waxed paper process from Gustave Le Gray 1851. He began by producing everyday street scenes as studies for his paintings but soon embarked on a series of documentary projects which included studies of Chartres Cathedral, Provence, and the Imperial Asylum at Vincennes.

négritude (French 'being Negro') concept that reasserts black African cultural and aesthetic values against European colonialism; most simply, black intuition is opposed to European logic. It has been current since the 1930s, when it was used originally among French-speaking African writers and intellectuals to emphasize their pride in their own culture. Its adherents have included Léopald ◊Senghor and the Martinique poet, playwright, and politician Aimé Césaire (1913–).

Neizvestny Ernst 1926– . Russian artist and sculptor who argued with the Soviet premier Khrushchev 1962 and eventually left the country 1976. His works include a vast relief in the Moscow Institute of Electronics and the Aswan monument in Egypt, the tallest sculpture in the world.

Nekrasov Nikolai Alekseevich 1821–1877. Russian poet and publisher. He espoused the cause of the freeing of the serfs and identified himself with the peasants in such poems as 'Who Can Live Happy in Russia?' 1876.

Nelson Willie 1933– . US country and western singer, songwriter, and guitarist. He first made an impact in the mid-1970s as a pioneer of the Texas 'outlaw' style of country music that rejected string overdubs, suits, and surface gloss. His albums include *Shotgun Willie* 1973, *Always On My Mind* 1982, and *Across the Borderline* 1993. He also had many joint successes with Waylon Jennings (1937–), including *Mamas, Don't Let Your Babies Grow Up to be Cowboys* 1978.

Nemerov Howard 1920– . US poet, critic, and novelist. He published his poetry collection *Guide to the Ruins* 1950, a short-story collection *A Commodity of Dreams* 1959, and *Collected Poems* 1977, which won both the National Book Award and the Pulitzer Prize (1978).

Nemesis in Greek mythology, the goddess of retribution, who especially punished hubris (Greek *hybris*), violent acts carried through in defiance of the gods and human custom.

Neo- (Greek *neos* 'new') in the arts, a prefix used to indicate a revival or development of a particular artistic style; for instance, ◊Neo-Classicism or ◊Neo-Impressionism.

Neo-Classicism movement in art, architecture, and design in Europe and North America about 1750–1850, characterized by a revival of classical Greek and Roman styles. It superseded the Rococo style and was inspired both by the excavation of Pompeii and Herculaneum (which revived Roman styles) and by the theories of the cultural studies of the German art historian J J Winckelmann (which revived Greek styles). Leading figures of the movement were the architect Robert Adam; the painters David, Ingres, and Mengs; the sculptors Canova, Flaxman, and Thorvaldsen; and the designers Wedgwood, Hepplewhite, and Sheraton. In music, it also refers to a 20th-century, term describing a deliberate combination of Baroque or Classical forms such as sonata form, fugue, and so on and modern harmony, for example Prokofiev's 'Classical' *Symphony No 1* 1916–17, Stravinsky's ballet *Apollo* 1927–28, and Busoni's opera *Doktor Faust* 1916–24.

Neo-Expressionism art movement, at its height in Germany and Italy in the 1970s and 1980s, which championed the revival of ◊representational art, expressive brushwork, and a concern with narrative and history at the expense of Minimalist and Conceptual art forms. Leading exponents include Anselm ◊Kiefer, Georg Baselitz (1928–   ), and Francesco ◊Clemente. In Italy the movement is known as ***Transavanguardia*** and in the USA as ***Bad Painting***.

Neo-Impressionism movement in French painting in the 1880s, an extension of Impressionist technique. It drew on contemporary theories on colour and perception, building up form and colour by painting dots side by side. ◊Seurat was the chief exponent; his minute technique became known as ◊***Pointillism***. Signac and Pissarro practised the style for a few years.

Neoptolemus or ***Pyrrhus*** in Greek mythology, son of Achilles. After the death of his father, he and ◊Odysseus conducted the Trojan hero Philoctetes to ◊Troy, and killed the Trojan king Priam at the altar of Zeus. He took Hector's wife, Andromache, as his concubine, and was killed in a quarrel at the shrine of Delphi.

Neo-Rationalism in architecture, movement originating in Italy in the 1960s which rejected the functionalist and technological preoccupations of Modernism, advocating a rationalist approach to design based on an awareness of formal properties. It developed in the light of a re-evaluation of the work of Giuseppe ◊Terragni led by Aldo ◊Rossi, and gained momentum through the work of Giorgio Grassi (1935–   ). Characterized by elemental forms and an absence of detail, the style has adherents throughout Europe and the USA.

Neo-Realism movement in Italian cinema that emerged in the 1940s. It is characterized by its naturalism, social themes, frequent use of non-professional actors, and the visual authenticity achieved through location filming. Exponents include the directors de Sica, Visconti, and Rossellini.

nepenth or ***nepenthes*** in Greek mythology, a drug that makes people forget cares or worries, used by ◊Helen of Troy in Homer's *Odyssey*.

Neptune in Roman mythology, the god of the sea, equivalent of the Greek ◊Poseidon.

Nereid in Greek mythology, any of 50 sea goddesses, or ◊nymphs, who sometimes mated with mortals. Their father was Nereus, a sea god, and their mother was Doris.

Nergal Babylonian god of the sun, war, and pestilence, ruler of the underworld, symbolized by a winged lion.

Neruda Pablo. Pen name of Neftalí Ricardo Reyes y Basualto 1904–1973. Chilean poet and diplomat. His work includes lyrics and the epic poem of the American continent *Canto General* 1950. He was awarded the Nobel Prize for Literature 1971.

After World War II he entered political life in Chile as a communist, and was a senator 1945–48. He went into exile 1948 but returned 1952; he later became consul to France 1971–72.

For me writing is like breathing. I could not live without breathing and I could not live without writing.

Pablo Neruda

Nerval Gérard de. Pen name of Gérard Labrunie 1808–1855. French writer and poet, precursor of French ◊Symbolism and ◊Surrealism. His writings include the travelogue *Voyage en Orient* 1851; short stories, including the collection *Les Filles du feu* 1854; poetry; a novel *Aurélia* 1855, containing episodes of visionary psychosis; and drama. He lived a wandering life, and suffered from periodic insanity, finally taking his own life.

A good structural organism worked out passionately in detail and in general appearance is essential to good architecture.

Pier Luigi Nervi

Nervi Pier Luigi 1891–1979. Italian engineer who used soft steel mesh within ◊concrete to give it flowing form; for example, the Turin exhibition hall 1948–49, consisting of a single undulating large-span roof, the UNESCO building in Paris 1953–58, with Marcel Breuer and Bernard-Louis

Zehrfuss (1911–), and the cathedral at New Norcia, near Perth, Australia, 1960. He was the structural engineer on Gio ◊Ponti's Pirelli skyscraper project in Milan 1958.

Nesbit E(dith) 1858–1924. English author of children's books, including *The Story of the Treasure Seekers* 1899 and *The Railway Children* 1906. Her stories often have a humorous magical element, as in *Five Children and It* 1902. *The Treasure Seekers* is the first of several books about the realistically squabbling Bastable children. Nesbit was a Fabian socialist and supported her family by writing.

Your feelings are a beastly nuisance, if once you begin to let yourself think about them.

E Nesbit
The Story of the Treasure Seekers 1899

netsuke toggle of ivory, wood, or other materials, made to secure a purse or tobacco pouch, for men wearing Japanese traditional costume. Made especially in the Edo period in Japan 1601–1867, the miniature sculptures are valued as works of art.

Neue Sachlichkeit (German 'New Objectivity') group of German artists in the 1920s who rejected prevalent Expressionist and abstract trends to paint in a harsh, Realist style. Prominent members were Georg ◊Grosz, Otto ◊Dix, and Max ◊Beckmann. Their paintings, reflecting their bitter disillusionment with post-war society, are frequently blackly satirical in content.

In style and execution, their work was indebted to Italian ◊Metaphysical Painting, as well as Dada. The movement's brand of Social Realism was effectively brought to an end by the Nazi regime of the 1930s.

Neumann Balthasar 1687–1753. German Rococo architect and military engineer who designed the bishop's palace in Würzburg (begun 1719; structurally complete 1744). As in his other palace designs, the centrepiece was a magnificent ceremonial staircase, its ceiling decorated by ◊Tiepolo.

Neutra Richard Joseph 1892–1970. Austrian-born architect who became a US citizen 1929. Influenced by ◊Loos and ◊Mendelsohn, he worked with ◊Schindler in Los Angeles from 1926 and became a leading exponent of the ◊International Style. His works, often in impressive landscape settings, include Lovell Health House, Los Angeles, 1929, and the Kaufmann Desert House, Palm Springs, 1947.

Nevelson Louise 1900–1988. Russian-born US sculptor and printmaker, a major exponent of ◊assemblage sculpture. She is renowned for her room-sized, wall-like reliefs consisting of stacked tiers of shallow open boxes filled with abstract arrangements in wood, as in *Black Majesty* 1956 (Whitney Museum of American Art, New York). From the 1960s she worked with other materials, for example plexiglass in *Ice Palace* 1967 (private collection, New York), and later produced outdoor works in steel and aluminium.

Neville Brothers, the US rhythm-and-blues group formed 1978, exponents of the New Orleans style, internationally successful from the 1980s. There are four Neville brothers, the eldest of whom has been active from the 1950s in various musical ventures. Albums include *Yellow Moon* 1989.

Aaron Neville (1941–) had hits as a vocalist in the 1960s, for example 'Tell It Like It Is' 1966. Two of the brothers – Art (1938–) and Cyril (1950–) – were in the Meters, a group formed in the late 1960s, whose albums include *The Wild Tschoupitoulas* 1976.

new-age music instrumental or ambient music, often semi-acoustic or electronic; less insistent than rock and less difficult than jazz. Clean production, undemanding compositions, and a soft, gentle sound characterize new age. Widespread from the 1980s, new-age music originated in the mid-1970s with English composer Brian Eno (1948–) who released such albums as *Music for Airports* 1979. Some folk, jazz, and avant-garde rock musicians have all found an outlet in new age.

New Apocalypse in English literature, a movement that developed from Surrealism in the 1940s and included G S Fraser, Henry Treece, J F Hendry, Nicholas Moore, and Tom Scott. Influenced by the work of Dylan Thomas, it favoured Biblical symbolism and downgraded intellect and classical decorum.

Newbery Medal (full name *John Newbery Medal*) annual award for an outstanding US book for children, given by the American Library Association since 1922. The award is named after John Newbery (1713–1767), an English printer who published many books for children.

Newbolt Henry John 1862–1938. English poet and naval historian. His works include *The Year of Trafalgar* 1905 and *A Naval History of the War* 1920 on World War I. His *Songs of the Sea* 1904 and *Songs of the Fleet* 1910 were set to music by Charles Villiers Stanford.

He made the journey up from Pushal … to meet us. This was the Isteqbal *– the traditional journey of half a stage – that is made by people in the Moslem world to greet a friend who is travelling.*

Eric Newby
A Short Walk in the Hindu Kush 1958

Newby (George) Eric 1919– . English travel writer and sailor. His books include *A Short Walk in the Hindu Kush* 1958, *The Big Red Train Ride* 1978, *Slowly Down the Ganges* 1966, and *A Traveller's Life* 1985.

new country US ◊country and western movement of the 1980s–90s away from the overproduction associated with the Nashville record industry. Notable exponents include Garth Brooks (1961–) and Ricky Skaggs (1954–).

New Criticism in literature, a US movement dominant in the 1930s and 1940s stressing the autonomy of the text without biographical and other external interpolation, but instead requiring close readings of its linguistic structure. The major figures of New Criticism include Allen Tate, John Crowe ◊Ransom, R P Blackmur, W K Wimsatt, Cleanth Brooks, and Robert Pen Warren.

New English Art Club British society founded 1886 to secure better representation for younger painters than was available through the Royal Academy. Its members, most of whom were influenced by Impressionism, included John Singer ◊Sargent, Augustus ◊John, Paul ◊Nash, William Rothenstein, and Walter ◊Sickert.

Newman Barnett 1905–1970. US painter, sculptor, and theorist. His paintings are solid-coloured canvases with a few sparse vertical stripes. They represent a mystical pursuit of simple or elemental art. His sculptures, such as *Broken Obelisk* 1963–67, consist of geometrical shapes, each mounted on top of the other.

To attempt to be guided by love alone, would be like attempting to walk in a straight line by steadily gazing on some star. It is too high.

John Henry Newman
sermon April 1837

Newman John Henry 1801–1890. English Roman Catholic theologian. While still an Anglican, he wrote a series of *Tracts for the Times*, which gave their name to the Tractarian Movement (subsequently called the Oxford Movement) for the revival of Catholicism. He became a Roman Catholic 1845 and was made a cardinal 1879. In 1864 his autobiography, *Apologia pro vita sua*, was published.

Newman, born in London, was ordained in the Church of England 1824, and in 1827 became vicar of St Mary's, Oxford. There he was influenced by the historian R H Froude and the Anglican priest Keble, and in 1833 published the first of the *Tracts for the Times*. He published his lectures on education as *The Idea of a University*

1873. His poem *The Dream of Gerontius* appeared 1866, and *The Grammar of Assent*, an analysis of the nature of belief, 1870. He wrote the hymn 'Lead, kindly light' 1833.

Newman Paul 1925– . US actor and director, one of Hollywood's leading male stars of the 1960s and 1970s. His films include *Somebody Up There Likes Me* 1956, *Cat on a Hot Tin Roof* 1958, *The Hustler* 1961, *Sweet Bird of Youth* 1962, *Hud* 1963, *Cool Hand Luke* 1967, *Butch Cassidy and the Sundance Kid* 1969, *The Sting* 1973, *The Verdict* 1983, *The Color of Money* 1986 (for which he won an Academy Award), and *Mr and Mrs Bridge* 1991.

Newman Randy (Gary) 1944– . US pop singer, songwriter, and pianist known for his satirical songs such as 'Short People' from *Little Criminals* 1977. Later albums include *Land of Dreams* 1988.

Born in Louisiana, he devoted an album (*Good Old Boys* 1974) to controversial governor Huey Long. He has written the soundtracks to several films including *The Three Amigos* 1986.

New Photography German photographic movement of the 1930s, led by Albert ◊Renger-Patzsch, that aimed to depict modern life in a direct and objective manner. In its anti-Pictorialism and emphasis on clarity, it paralleled the ◊'f/64' group in the USA.

Newson Lloyd 1954– . Australian choreographer and dancer. He is an exponent of ◊avant-garde dance in Britain and his work often explores psychological and social issues. Frequently provocative, Newson challenges conventional conceptions of gender stereotypes in his ballets, for example, *My Body, Your Body* 1987. His choreographic methods make use of ◊contact improvisation and are strongly influenced by Pina ◊Bausch. He is the cofounder and director of the DV8 Physical Theatre 1986.

New Wave in pop music, a style that evolved parallel to punk in the second half of the 1970s. It shared the urban aggressive spirit of punk but was musically and lyrically more sophisticated; examples are the early work of Elvis Costello and Talking Heads.

New Wave (French *nouvelle vague*) movement in French cinema in the late 1950s and the 1960s characterized by an unconventional use of both camera (often hand-held) and editing and by inventive and experimental manipulation of story line. Directors associated with the movement include Jean-Luc Godard, Alain Resnais, and François Truffaut.

New York Five group of five US architects, Peter ◊Eisenman, Michael ◊Graves, Richard ◊Meier, Charles Gwathmey (1938–), and John Hedjuk (1929–), who worked together from 1969, reviving many of the design principles associated with the ◊International Style of the 1920s and 1930s. The group had ceased to exist by 1980.

New Zealand literature prose and poetry of New Zealand. Among interesting pioneer records of the mid- to late 19th century are those of Edward Jerningham Wakefield and F E Maning; and *A First Year in Canterbury Settlement* by Samuel ◊Butler. Earliest of the popular poets was Thomas Bracken, author of the New Zealand national song, followed by native-born Jessie Mackay and W Pember Reeves, though the latter is better known as the author of the prose account of New Zealand *The Long White Cloud*; and Ursula Bethell (1874–1945).

In the 20th century New Zealand literature gained an international appeal with the short stories of Katherine ◊Mansfield, produced an exponent of detective fiction in Dame Ngaio ◊Marsh, and struck a specifically New Zealand note in *Tutira, the Story of a New Zealand Sheep Station* 1926, by W H Guthrie Smith (1861–1940). Poetry of a new quality was written by R A K Mason in the 1920s, and in the 1930s by a group of which A R D Fairburn, with a witty conversational turn, and Allen Curnow, poet, critic, and anthologist, are the most striking. In fiction the 1930s were remarkable for the short stories of Frank Sargeson and Roderick Finlayson (1904–), and the talent of John Mulgan (1911–1945), who is remembered both for his novel *Man Alone* and for his posthumous factual account of World War II, in which he died, *Report on Experience* 1947. Kendrick Smithyman (1922–) struck a metaphysical note in poetry, James K Baxter (1926–1972) published fluent lyrics, and Janet Frame has a brooding depth of meaning in such novels as *The Rainbirds* 1968 and *Intensive Care* 1970. In 1985 Keri Hulme won Britain's Booker Prize for her novel *The Bone People*.

Ngugi wa Thiong'o 1938– . Kenyan writer of essays, plays, short stories, and novels. He was imprisoned after the performance of the play *Ngaahika Ndeenda/I Will Marry When I Want* 1977 and lived in exile from 1982. His novels, written in English and Kikuyu, include *The River Between* 1965, *Petals of Blood* 1977, and *Caitaani Mutharaba-ini/Devil on the Cross* 1982, and deal with colonial and post-independence oppression.

Nibelungenlied (*Song of the Nibelung*) anonymous 12th-century German epic poem, derived from older sources. The composer Richard Wagner made use of the legends in his *Ring* cycle.

◊Siegfried, possessor of the Nibelung treasure, marries Kriemhild (sister of Gunther of Worms) and wins Brunhild as a bride for Gunther. However, Gunther's vassal Hagen murders Siegfried, and Kriemhild achieves revenge by marrying Etzel (Attila) of the Huns, at whose court both Hagen and Gunther are killed.

Nichols Peter 1927– . English dramatist. His first stage play, *A Day In the Death of Joe Egg* 1967, explored the life of a couple with a paraplegic child, while *The National Health* 1969 dramatized life in the face of death from cancer. *Privates on Parade* 1977, about the British army in Malaya, was followed by the middle-class comedy *Passion Play* 1981.

Nicholson Ben 1894–1982. English abstract artist. After early experiments influenced by Cubism and the Dutch De ◊Stijl group, Nicholson developed an elegant style of geometrical reliefs, notably a series of white reliefs (from 1933).

Son of artist William ◊Nicholson, he studied at the Slade School of Art, London, as well as in Europe and in California. He married the sculptor Barbara ◊Hepworth and was a leading member of the ◊St Ives School.

Nicholson Jack 1937– . US film actor who, in the late 1960s, captured the mood of nonconformist, uncertain young Americans in such films as *Easy Rider* 1969 and *Five Easy Pieces* 1970. He subsequently became a mainstream Hollywood star, appearing in *Chinatown* 1974, *One Flew over the Cuckoo's Nest* (Academy Award) 1975, *The Shining* 1979, *Terms of Endearment* (Academy Award) 1983, and *Batman* 1989. He has directed several films, including *The Two Jakes* 1990, a sequel to *Chinatown*.

Nicholson William 1872–1949. English artist who painted landscapes, portraits, and still lifes. He also developed the art of poster design in partnership with his brother-in-law, James Pryde. They were known as 'The Beggarstaff Brothers'. He was the father of Ben Nicholson.

Nicolson Harold 1886–1968. British author and diplomat. His works include biographies such as *Lord Carnock* 1930 and *King George V* 1952 but he is best known for his *Diaries and Letters* 1930–62. He married Vita ◊Sackville-West 1913. Their relationship was described by their son, Nigel Nicolson, in *Portrait of a Marriage* 1973.

Intellectuals incline to be individualists, or even independents, are not team conscious and tend to regard obedience as a surrender of personality.

Harold Nicolson in the *Observer* Oct 1958

---

niello black substance made by melting powdered silver, copper, sulphur, and often borax. It is used as a filling for incised decoration on silver and fixed by the application of heat.

Niello was used to decorate objects in ancient Egypt, in the Bronze Age Aegean, in the European Middle Ages, and in much Anglo-Saxon metalwork. It reached its height of technical and artistic excellence in the early

Renaissance in Italy, especially in Florence. It was much used in 19th-century Russia, where it is known as *tula* work.

Nielsen Carl (August) 1865–1931. Danish nationalist composer whose works combine an outward formal strictness with an inner waywardness of tonality and structure. His works include the Neo-Classical opera *Maskarade/Masquerade* 1906, a *Wind Quintet* 1922, six programmatic symphonies, numerous songs, and incidental music on Danish texts. He also composed concertos for violin 1911, flute 1926, and clarinet 1928, chamber music, piano works, and songs.

Niemeyer Oscar 1907– . Brazilian architect, joint designer of the United Nations headquarters in New York 1947 and from 1957 architect of many public buildings in Brasília, capital of Brazil. His idiosyncratic interpretation of the Modernist idiom uses symbolic form to express the function of a building; for example, the Catholic Cathedral in Brasília.

Nietzsche Friedrich Wilhelm 1844–1900. German philosopher and writer. He rejected the absolute moral values and 'slave morality' of Christianity. His ideal was the ◊*Übermensch*, or 'Superman', who would impose his will on the weak and worthless. His views on art are most fully expressed in *Die Geburt der Tragödie/The Birth of Tragedy* 1872, in which he argued that the operas of Richard Wagner were the successors to Greek tragic drama. His other works include *Die fröhliche Wissenschaft/The Gay Science* 1881–82, *Also sprach Zarathustra/Thus Spake Zarathustra* 1883–92, *Jenseits von Gut und Böse/Between Good and Evil* 1885–86, *Zur Genealogie der Moral/Towards a Genealogy of Morals* 1887, and *Ecce Homo* 1888.

Born in Röcken, Saxony, he attended Bonn and Leipzig universities and was professor of Greek at Basel, Switzerland, 1869–80. He was influenced by the writings of Schopenhauer and the music of Wagner, of whom he became both friend and advocate, though he later repudiated the man and his music. He spent his later years in northern Italy, in the Engadine, and in southern France. From the late 1880s he was permanently insane.

Morality is the herd instinct in the individual.

Friedrich Nietzsche
Die fröhliche Wissenschaft 1881–82

Night Watch, The (correctly titled *The Militia Company of Captain Frans Banning Cocq and Lieutenant Willem van Ruytenburch*) group portrait in oils by ◊Rembrandt 1642 (Rijksmuseum, Amsterdam), commemorating volunteer militia enlisted to defend Amsterdam – the group is preparing to march. By concentrating on action rather than static representation, Rembrandt set a new convention for the group portrait.

The work acquired its current title 'The Night Watch' in the 18th century, by which time the painting had become obscured by darkened varnish (since stripped off).

nihilism the rejection of all traditional values, authority, and institutions. The term was coined 1862 by Ivan Turgenev in his novel *Fathers and Sons*, and was adopted by the Nihilists, the Russian radicals of the period. Despairing of reform, they saw change as possible only through the destruction of morality, justice, marriage, property, and the idea of God. Since then nihilism has come to mean a generally negative and destructive outlook.

Nijinksa Bronislava 1891–1972. Russian choreographer and dancer. Nijinska was the first major female choreographer to work in classical ballet, creating several dances for Diaghilev's Ballets Russes, including *Les Noces* 1923, a landmark in 20th-century modernist dance. She was the sister of Vaslav ◊Nijinsky, continuing his revolutionary ideas of kinetic movement in dance. Other pieces include *Les Biches* 1924.

Nijinsky Vaslav 1890–1950. Russian dancer and choreographer. Noted for his powerful but graceful technique, he was a member of ◊Diaghilev's Ballets Russes, for whom he choreographed Debussy's *Prélude à l'après-midi d'un faune* 1912 and *Jeux* 1913, and Stravinsky's *Le Sacre du printemps/The Rite of Spring* 1913.

Nijinsky also took lead roles in ballets such as *Petrushka* 1911. He rejected conventional forms of classical ballet in favour of free expression. His sister was the choreographer Bronislava Nijinska.

Nike in Greek mythology, the goddess of victory, represented as 'winged', as in the statue from Samothrace in the Louvre, Paris. One of the most beautiful architectural monuments of Athens was the temple of Nike Apteros.

Nin Anaïs 1903–1977. US novelist and diarist. Her extensive and impressionistic diaries, published 1966–76, reflect her interest in dreams, which along with psychoanalysis are recurring themes of her gently erotic novels (such as *House of Incest* 1936 and *A Spy in the House of Love* 1954).

Life shrinks or expands in proportion to one's courage.

Anaïs Nin *Diary* June 1941

Nineteen Eighty-Four futuristic novel by George ◊Orwell, published 1949, which tells of an individual's battle against, and eventual surrender to, a totalitarian state where Big Brother rules. It is a dystopia (the opposite of a utopia) and many of the words and concepts in it have passed into common usage (newspeak, double-think, thought police).

> *Who controls the past controls the future.*
> *Who controls the present controls the past.*
>
> **George Orwell** *Nineteen Eighty-Four*

Niobe in Greek mythology, the daughter of Tantalus and wife of Amphion, the king of Thebes. She was contemptuous of the goddess Leto for having produced only two children, Apollo and Artemis. She died of grief when her own 12 offspring were killed by them in revenge, and was changed to stone by Zeus.

Nirvana US rock group who popularized a hard-driving, tuneful ◊grunge, exemplified by their second album, *Nevermind* 1991, and its hit single 'Smells Like Teen Spirit'.

Nirvana formed in Washington State 1986–88 around singer, songwriter, and guitarist Kurt Cobain (1966–). Between their debut album *Bleach* 1989 and their 1991 breakthrough, the line-up was stripped to a three-piece. Their songs combine the hooks and dynamics of classic pop with the abrasive aesthetics of grunge.

Niven David 1909–1983. Scottish-born US film actor, in Hollywood from the 1930s. His films include *Wuthering Heights* 1939, *Around the World in 80 Days* 1956, *Separate Tables* 1958 (Academy Award), *The Guns of Navarone* 1961, and *The Pink Panther* 1964. He published two best-selling volumes of autobiography, *The Moon's a Balloon* 1972 and *Bring on the Empty Horses* 1975.

Nizzoli Marcello 1887–1969. Italian industrial designer, best known for his innovative designs for office machines for the ◊Olivetti company. A member of the pre-World War II generation of Italian designers, Nizzoli moved through painting and exhibition and graphic design before being brought in by Adriano Olivetti, son of the founder, 1938 to work on the company's machines. Notable designs include the 'Lexicon 80' typewriter 1948.

Nkosi Lewis 1936– . South African writer and broadcaster. He is particularly noted for his play about Johannesburg *The Rhythms of Violence* 1964 and his influential essays *Home and Exile* 1965.

Nō or *Noh* classical, aristocratic Japanese drama, which developed from the 14th to the 16th centuries and is still performed. There is a repertory of some 250 pieces, of which five, one from each of the several classes devoted to different subjects, may be put on in a performance lasting a whole day. Dance, mime, music, and chanting develop the mythical or historical themes. All the actors are men, some of whom wear masks and elaborate costumes; scenery is limited. No⁻ influenced ◊kabuki drama.

No⁻ developed from popular rural entertainments and religious performances staged at shrines and temples by travelling companies. The leader of one of these troupes, Kan'ami (1333–1384), and his son and successor ◊Zeami wrote a number of No⁻ plays and are regarded as the founders of the form. The plots often feature a ghost or demon seeking rest or revenge, but the aesthetics are those of Zen Buddhism. Symbolism and suggestion take precedence over action, and the slow, stylized dance is the strongest element. Flute, drums, and chorus supply the music.

Nobel Prize for Literature international prize awarded annually by a committee based in Sweden. It was first awarded 1901 under the will of Swedish chemist Alfred Nobel (1833–1896). Literature is one of six fields to receive Nobel prizes; the others are physics, chemistry, medicine, economics, and world peace. The interest on the Nobel fund is divided annually among the people who have made the greatest contributions in these fields.

Nobel Prize for Literature: recent winners

1980	Czeslaw Milosz (Polish-American)
1981	Elias Canetti (Bulgarian-British)
1982	Gabriel García Márquez (Colombian-Mexican)
1983	William Golding (British)
1984	Jaroslav Seifert (Czechoslovakian)
1985	Claude Simon (French)
1986	Wole Soyinka (Nigerian)
1987	Joseph Brodsky (Soviet)
1988	Naguib Mahfouz (Egyptian)
1989	Camilo José Cela (Spanish)
1990	Octavio Paz (Mexican)
1991	Nadine Gordimer (South African)
1992	Derek Walcott (St Lucian)
1993	Toni Morrison (American)

noble savage, the ◊Enlightenment idea of the virtuous innocence of 'savage' peoples, often embodied in the American Indian, and celebrated by the writers J J Rousseau, Chateaubriand (in *Atala* 1801), and James Fenimore Cooper.

nocturne in music, a reflective character piece , often for piano, introduced by John Field (1782–1837) and adopted by Chopin.

Noguchi Isamu 1904–1988. US sculptor and designer, recognized for the serene, expressive power of his abstracted, organic forms, for example *Khmer* 1962 (Garden of National Museum, Jerusalem). Noguchi has also designed stage sets, notably for the Martha Graham dance company 1935–66, and sculpture gardens in such major cities as New York and Tokyo.

noise in pop music, a style that relies heavily on feedback, distortion, and dissonance. A loose term that came into use in the 1980s with the slogan 'noise annoys', it has been applied to ◊hardcore punk, ◊grunge, and ◊industrial music, among others.

Nolan Sidney 1917–1992. Australian artist. Largely self-taught, he created atmospheric paintings of the outback, exploring themes from Australian history such as the life of the outlaw Ned Kelly and the folk heroine Mrs Fraser.

Noland Kenneth 1924– . US painter, associated with the colour-stain painters Helen ◊Frankenthaler and Morris ◊Louis. In the 1950s and early 1960s he painted targets, or concentric circles of colour, in a clean, hard-edged style on unprimed canvas. His paintings of the 1960s experimented with the manipulation of colour vision and afterimages, pioneering the field of ◊Op art.

Nolde Emil. Adopted name of Emil Hansen 1867–1956. German Expressionist painter and graphic artist. Nolde studied in Paris and Dachau, joined the group of artists known as *Die Brücke* 1906–07, and visited Polynesia 1913; he then became almost a recluse in NE Germany. Many of his themes were religious.

noli me tangere (Latin 'touch me not') in the Bible, the words spoken by Jesus to Mary Magdalene after the Resurrection (John 20:17); in art, the title of many works depicting this scene.

Nollekens Joseph 1737–1823. English Neo-Classical sculptor, specializing in portrait busts and memorials. He worked in Rome 1759–70. On his return to London he enjoyed great success, executing busts of many eminent people, including George III, the Prince of Wales (later George IV), the politicians Pitt the Younger and Fox, and the actor David Garrick.

Nom Chinese-style characters used in writing the Vietnamese language. Nom characters were used from the 13th century for Vietnamese literature, but were replaced in the 19th century by a romanized script known as Quoc Ngu. The greatest Nom writer was the poet Nguyen Du.

Nono Luigi 1924–1990. Italian composer of attenuated pointillist works such as *Il canto sospeso/Suspended Song* 1955–56 for soloists, chorus, and orchestra, in which influences of Webern and Gabrieli are applied to issues of social conscience. After the opera *Intolleranza* 1960 his style became more richly expressionistic, and his causes more overtly polemical.

non-objective art art that is not representational. The paintings of Piet ◊Mondrian, for example, consist of very simple, brightly coloured, geometrical forms. See ◊abstract art.

Norman Jessye 1945– . US soprano acclaimed for majestically haunting interpretations of German opera and lieder (songs), notably Wagner, Mahler, and Richard Strauss, but equally at home with Ravel and Chausson songs and gospel music.

She was born in Augusta, Georgia, USA, and made her operatic debut at the Deutsche Oper, Berlin, 1969.

Norman architecture English term for ◊Romanesque, the style of architecture used in England in the 11th and 12th centuries. Norman buildings are massive, with round arches (although trefoil arches are sometimes used for small openings). Buttresses are of slight projection, and vaults are barrel-roofed. Examples in England include the Keep of the Tower of London, Durham Cathedral, and parts of the cathedrals of Chichester, Gloucester, and Ely.

Norn in Scandinavian mythology, any of three goddesses of fate – the goddess of the past (Urd), the goddess of the present (Verdandi), and the goddess of the future (Skuld).

Norris Frank (Benjamin Franklin) 1870–1902. US novelist. A naturalist writer, he wrote *McTeague* 1899, about a brutish San Francisco dentist and the love of gold (filmed as *Greed* 1923). He completed only two parts of his projected trilogy, the *Epic of Wheat*: *The Octopus* 1901, dealing with the struggles between wheat farmers, and *The Pit* 1903, describing the Chicago wheat exchange.

North Thomas 1535–1601. English translator, whose version of ◊Plutarch's *Lives* 1579 was the source for Shakespeare's Roman plays.

For men that read much and work little are as bells, the which do sound to call others and they themselves never enter into the church.

Thomas North *Diall of Princes* 1557

North American Indian and Eskimo art the art of the North American indigenous peoples. The first Arctic cultures were established on the continent around 12,000 years ago. Remains of prehistoric cultures have been found, but the finer North American Indian artefacts belong to the last 2,000 years. Generally, the arts of the different tribes were determined by materials available, lifestyle (whether settled or nomadic), and religion (almost invariably shamanistic). Most ethnographic collections include North American Indian artworks; notable are those at the Museum of the American Indian, New York, and the Museum of Mankind, London.

Arctic Eskimo (Inuit) art (from about 25,000 BC) This is rich in carvings, particularly of bone and walrus ivory. Alaskan Eskimos produced shaman masks and decorated sealskin for clothes, tents, and canoes.

Northwest Coast Indian art (about 3000 BC–AD 1800) The wealth of natural resources in the area is reflected in an abundance of diverse artefacts such as totem poles, canoes, and masks. Highly stylized animal motifs decorate both wood and blanket weaving, a notable example of the latter being *chilkat*. The arts of the Kwakiutl and Tlingit Indians express social status as well as religious beliefs.

Southwest Coast Indian art (about 1000 BC–AD 1800) The lifestyle of more settled cultures is reflected. Early cliff palace complexes, such as Mesa Verde, Colorado, 12th century, gave way to pueblo (village) life by the 14th century. *Mimbres* pottery and murals from kivas (underground ceremonial rooms) are characteristic of the pueblo culture. The Navaho Indians executed stylized sand paintings and blanket weaving, employing an elaborate symbolism and complex, often geometrical, designs.

Eastern Woodlands Indian art (700 BC–AD 1500) Dominated first by the Adena culture, then by the Hopewell culture. Both built great earthen mounds, such as the Serpent Mound in Ohio, for ceremonial purposes, and made jewellery in copper and motifs in cut foil. The Hopewell culture was technically more proficient and made human effigies in pottery and sleek animal carvings in stone. Between AD 800 and 1500, the area was dominated by the Mississippians, an agrarian society which built large city complexes similar to those of Central America (see ◊pre-Columbian art). Their art is represented in shell-carving and trophy-head vessels. The Iroquois culture excelled in decorative beadwork and quillwork, pottery, and dramatic masks for the 'false face' ceremonies of their shamanistic cult.

The Great Plains Indian art (250 BC–AD 1500) This was the product of mostly nomadic peoples, such as the Sioux and the Crow. Theirs was a portable art, with buckskin clothes and tents decorated with beadwork and quillwork in highly stylized designs. Some painted robes and tents have survived.

Norwich School English regional school of landscape painters, inspired by the 17th-century Dutch Realist tradition of landscape painting, notably the work of ◊Ruisdael. Founded 1803, the school was made up of both professional and amateur artists and flourished until the 1830s. Its leading members were John Sell ◊Cotman and John ◊Crome.

Nostradamus Latinized name of Michel de Nôtredame 1503–1566. French physician and astrologer who was consulted by Catherine de' Medici and was physician to Charles IX. His book of prophecies in rhyme, *Centuries* 1555, is open to various interpretations.

notation system representing music graphically as successive values in pitch and time. By 1700 modern notation had displaced ◊plainsong and ◊tablature notations, making possible the coordination under one system of orchestras of increasing size, and also making possible the composition of large-scale musical forms.

notation in dance, the codification and recording of dances by symbols. There are several dance notation systems; prominent among them is ◊Labanotation.

note in music, the written symbol indicating pitch and duration, the sound of which is a tone.

note row another term for ◊tone row.

nouveau roman (French 'new novel') experimental literary form produced in the 1950s by French novelists including Alain Robbe-Grillet and Nathalie Sarraute. In various ways, these writers seek to eliminate character, plot, and authorial subjectivity in order to present the world as a pure, solid 'thing in itself'.

Robbe-Grillet's *Le Voyeur* 1955 and Sarraute's *Le Planetarium* 1959 are critically successful examples. Michel Butor, Claude Ollier, and Marguerite Duras also contributed to this form, which is sometimes labelled the 'anti-novel' because of its subversion of traditional methods.

Nouvel Jean 1945– . French architect who uses the language of ◊High Tech building in novel and highly distinctive ways. His celebrated Institut du Monde Arabe, Paris, 1981–87, adapts traditional Islamic motifs to technological ends: mechanized irises, for instance, control the penetration of daylight.

Novak Kim (Marilyn Pauline) 1933– . US film actress who starred in such films as *Pal Joey* 1957, *Bell, Book and Candle* 1958, *Vertigo* 1958, *Kiss Me Stupid* 1964, and *The Legend of Lylah Clare* 1968.

Novalis pen name of Friedrich Leopold von Hardenberg 1772–1801. Pioneer German Romantic poet who wrote *Hymnen an die Nacht/Hymns to the Night* 1800, prompted by the death of his fiancée Sophie von Kühn. He left two unfinished romances, *Die Lehrlinge zu Sais/The Novices of Sais* and *Heinrich von Ofterdingen*.

Poetry heals the wounds inflicted by reason.

Novalis Detached Thoughts

---

novel extended fictional prose narrative, often including some sense of the psychological development of the central characters and of their relationship with a broader world. The modern novel took its name and inspiration from the Italian *novella*, the short tale of varied character which became popular in the late 13th century.

As the main form of narrative fiction in the 20th century, the novel is frequently classified according to genres and subgenres such as the ◊historical novel, ◊detective fiction, ◊fantasy, and ◊science fiction.

The European novel is said to have originated in Greece in the 2nd century BC. Ancient Greek examples include the *Daphnis and Chloë* of Longus; almost the only surviving Latin work that could be called a novel is the *Golden Ass* of Apuleius (late 2nd century), based on a Greek model. There is a similar, but until the 19th century independent, tradition of prose narrative including psychological development in the Far East, notably in Japan, with for example *The Tale of Genji* by Murasaki Shikibu. The works of the Italian writers Boccaccio and Matteo Bandello (1485–1561) were translated into English in such collections as William Painter's *Palace of Pleasure* 1566–67, and inspired the Elizabethan novelists, including John Lyly, Philip Sidney, Thomas Nash, and Thomas Lodge. In Spain, Cervantes' *Don Quixote* 1604 contributed to the development of the novel through its translation into other European languages, but the 17th century was dominated by the French romances of Gauthier de Costes de La Calprenède (1614–1663) and Madelaine de Scudéry (1607–1691), although William Congreve and Aphra Behn continued the English tradition.

British novel In the 18th century the realistic novel was established in England by the work of Daniel Defoe, Samuel Richardson, Henry Fielding, Laurence Sterne, and Tobias Smollett. Horace Walpole, and later Mary Shelley, developed the Gothic novel. In the early 19th century Sir Walter Scott developed the historical novel, and Jane Austen wrote 'novels of manners'. Celebrated novelists of the Victorian age were Charles Dickens, William Thackeray, the Brontës, George Eliot, Anthony Trollope, and Robert Louis Stevenson.

The transition period from Victorian times to the 20th century includes George Meredith, Samuel Butler, Thomas Hardy, George Gissing, Henry James, Rudyard Kipling, Joseph Conrad, George Moore, H G Wells, Arnold Bennett, and John Galsworthy. Slightly later are W Somerset Maugham, E M Forster, James Joyce, D H Lawrence, Ivy Compton-Burnett, and Virginia Woolf – the last four being especially influential in the development of novel technique. Among those who began writing in the 1920s are J B Priestley, Richard Hughes, Aldous Huxley, Christopher Isherwood, Graham Greene, V S Pritchett, Evelyn Waugh, Elizabeth Bowen, Rose Macaulay, and Rosamund Lehmann. The 1930s produced Nigel Balchin, Joyce Cary, Lawrence Durrell, and George Orwell, and more recent British writers include Anthony Powell, John Fowles, Kingsley Amis, Anthony Burgess, Iris Murdoch, Angela Carter, Doris Lessing, Salman Rushdie, and Martin Amis.

US novel The 19th century was also a great period for the novel in the USA, with James Fenimore Cooper, Herman Melville, Nathaniel Hawthorne, and Mark Twain. From the end of the 19th century the USA produced novelists in such schools as Realism (Edith Wharton, Stephen Crane, William Howells, and Willa Cather) and Naturalism/social protest (Theodore Dreiser, Upton Sinclair, Frank Norris, and Jack London). Before World War II, Edna Ferber, Sinclair Lewis, Pearl Buck, Ernest Hemingway, Scott Fitzgerald, John Steinbeck, Thomas Wolfe, and William Faulkner had made names for themselves; many of them continued to enjoy success after the war.

After World War II a new generation of US novelists reached maturity, with many of them crossing into poetry and short stories as well. This group includes Norman Mailer, Joseph Heller, Robert Warren, Truman Capote, Lillian Hellman, Katherine Porter, Carson McCullers, Flannery O'Connor, J D Salinger, James Baldwin, Philip Roth, Saul Bellow, Joyce Oates, Kurt Vonnegut, and John Updike.

European novel Great European novelists of the 19th century were Victor Hugo, Honoré de Balzac, Alexandre Dumas (both father and son), George Sand, and Emile Zola in France; Goethe and Jean Paul in Germany; and Gogol, Turgenev, Dostoevsky, and Tolstoy in Russia. Twentieth-century European novelists include Lion Feuchtwanger, Thomas Mann, Franz Kafka, Ernst Wiechert, Stefan Zweig, Christa Wolff, Heinrich Böll, and Gunter Grass (Germany); André Gide, Marcel Proust, Jules Romains, François Mauriac, Michel Butor, Nathalie Sarraute, and Alain Robbe-Grillet (France); Gabriele d'Annunzio, Ignazio Silone, Alberto Moravia, Italo Calvino, Primo Levi, and Natalia Ginzburg (Italy); Maxim Gorky, Mikhail Sholokhov, Aleksei Tolstoi, Boris Pasternak, and Alexander Solzhenitsyn (Russia); and Arturo Baréa, Pío Baroja and Ramón Pérez de Ayala (Spain).

In *Latin America* 20th-century novelists include Mario Vargas Llosa, Carlos Fuentes, and Gabriel García Márquez; in *Canada* they include Morley Callaghan, Robertson Davies, Mordecai Richler, and Margaret Atwood; and in *Australia* Henry Handel Richardson and Patrick White.

novella a short novel, such as Joseph ◊Conrad's *Heart of Darkness* 1902. The novella originated in 14th-century Italy, with collections of tales such as Boccaccio's *Decameron* 1348–53.

Novello Ivor. Stage name of Ivor Novello Davies 1893–1951. Welsh composer and actor-manager. He wrote popular songs, such as 'Keep the Home Fires Burning', in World War I, and musicals in which he often appeared as the romantic lead, including *Glamorous Night* 1925, *The Dancing Years* 1939, and *Gay's the Word* 1951.

Noverre Jean-Georges 1727–1810. French choreographer, writer, and ballet reformer. He promoted ◊*ballet d'action* (with a plot) and simple, free movement, and is often considered the creator of modern classical ballet. *Les Petits Riens* 1778 was one of his works.

Novgorod School Russian school of icon and mural painters active from the late 14th to the 16th century in Novgorod, inspired by the work of the refugee Byzantine artist ◊Theophanes the Greek. Russian artists imitated his linear style, but their work became increasingly stilted and mannered.

Nowra Louis 1950– . Australian dramatist and novelist best known for his plays which include *Inner Voices* 1977, set in Russia in 1794, *Visions* 1979, set in Paraguay of the 1860s, *The Precious Woman* 1981, set in China of the 1920s, and *Byzantine Flowers* which opened in Sydney 1989.

Noyes Alfred 1880–1958. English poet who wrote poems about the sea and the anthology favourites 'The Highwayman', 'Barrel Organ', and 'Go down to Kew in lilac-time ...'.

Noyes Eliot 1910–1977. US architect and industrial designer, retained as a consultant by the ◊IBM company from 1947 and responsible for the company's high design profile until 1977. In addition to his typewriters for IBM, his own notable work includes a design for a filling station for Mobil 1964. He was the first director of design at New York's Museum of Modern Art 1940–42.

nude in the visual arts, a depiction of the unclothed human figure. Conventionally, a distinction is drawn between the nude, literally an embodiment of moral or aesthetic values, and the naked, which adds to the unclothed connotations of embarrassment and an invasion of privacy. Landmarks in the history of the nude include the *Venus of Milo* about 150–100 BC (Louvre, Paris), Titian's *Venus of Urbino* 1538 (Uffizi, Florence), and Picasso's *Les Demoiselles d'Avignon* 1907 (Museum of Modern Art, New York).

Unclothed figures have been a feature of the art of most cultures and periods (with the notable exception of the Judaic and Islamic traditions), but the first occurrence of the nude as a major artistic subject was in Greek art of the 6th century BC. The Christian church discouraged its portrayal, seeing the body as shameful, and medieval images of Adam and Eve and of souls in Hell are typically 'naked' and vulnerable. With the rediscovery of Classical culture in the Renaissance, the nude re-emerged as an expression of humanist values, and for several centuries the study of the nude was seen as the foundation of art. By the late 19th century, however, a new realism had begun to challenge the distinction between nude and naked.

Numa Pompilius legendary king of Rome *c.* 716–*c.* 679 bc, who succeeded Romulus and was credited with the introduction of religious rites.

Nunn Trevor 1940– . British stage director, artistic director of the Royal Shakespeare Company 1968–86. He received a Tony award (with John Caird 1948–) for his production of *Nicholas Nickleby* 1982 and for the musical *Les Misérables* 1985.

Nureyev Rudolf 1938–1993. Russian dancer and choreographer. A soloist with the Kirov Ballet, he defected to the West during a visit to Paris 1961. Mainly associated with the Royal Ballet (London) and as Margot ◊Fonteyn's principal partner, he was one of the most brilliant dancers of the 1960s and 1970s. Nureyev danced in such roles as Prince Siegfried in *Swan Lake* and Armand in *Marguerite and Armand*, which was created specifically for Fonteyn and Nureyev. He also danced and acted in films and on television and choreographed several ballets. It was due to his enormous impact on the ballet world that the role of the male dancer was elevated to that of the ballerina.

I dance to please myself. If you try to please everybody, there is no originality.

Rudolf Nureyev
St Louis Post Despatch Jan 1964

nursery rhyme short traditional poem or song for children. Usually limited to a couplet or quatrain with strongly marked rhythm and rhymes, nursery rhymes have often been handed down by oral tradition.

Some of the oldest nursery rhymes are connected with a traditional tune and were sung as accompaniment to ancient ring games, such as 'Here we go round the mulberry bush', which was part of the May Day festivities. Others contain fragments of incantations and other rites; still others have a factual basis and commemorated popular figures, such as Jack Sprat and Jack Horner.

Nutter Tommy 1943–1992. British trend-setting tailor whose suits became famous in the 1960s – 70s. Although employing conventional techniques, he made a distinct break with many traditions of tailoring when he produced suits with wide lapels and flared trousers and experimented with fabrics, for example cutting pinstripes on the horizontal and mixing gamekeeper tweeds in three-piece suits.

Among his designs are the suits worn by John Lennon, Paul McCartney, and Ringo Starr on the cover of the Beatles' *Abbey Road* album. In 1989 he created the outfits worn by the actor Jack Nicholson when he played the Joker in the film *Batman*.

Nykvist Sven 1922– . Swedish director of photography, associated with the director Ingmar

Bergman. He worked frequently in the USA from the mid-1970s onwards. His films include *The Virgin Spring* 1960 (for Bergman), *Pretty Baby* 1978 (for Louis Malle), and *Fanny and Alexander* 1982 (for Bergman).

Nyman Michael 1944– . British composer whose highly stylized music is characterized by processes of gradual modification by repetition of complex musical formulae. His compositions include scores for the British filmmaker Peter ◊Greenaway and New Zealand filmmaker Jane Campion (*The Piano* 1933); a chamber opera, *The Man Who Mistook His Wife for a Hat* 1989; and three string quartets.

nymph in Greek mythology, a guardian spirit of nature. *Hamadryads* or *dryads* guarded trees; *naiads*, springs and pools; *oreads*, hills and rocks; and *Nereids*, the sea.

Oates Joyce Carol 1938– . US writer. Her novels are often aggressive, realistic descriptions of the forces of darkness and violence in modern culture. A prolific writer, she uses a wide range of genres and settings including the comedy *Unholy Loves* 1979, the Gothic horror of *A Bloodsmoor Romance* 1982, and the thriller *Kindred Passions* 1987. Her other novels include *A Garden of Earthly Delights* 1967, *them* 1969, and *Because It Is Bitter, and Because It Is My Heart* 1990.

obelisk tall, tapering column of stone, much used in ancient Egyptian and Roman architecture. Examples are Cleopatra's Needles 1475 BC, one of which is in London, another in New York.

Oberon in folklore, king of the elves or fairies and, according to the 13th-century French romance *Huon of Bordeaux*, an illegitimate son of Julius Caesar. Shakespeare used the character in *A ◊Midsummer Night's Dream.*

Oberon Merle. Stage name of Estelle Merle O'Brien Thompson 1911–1979. Indian-born English actress (but claiming to be Tasmanian) who starred in several films by Alexander Korda (to whom she was briefly married 1939–45), including *The Scarlet Pimpernel* 1935. She played Cathy to Laurence Olivier's Heathcliff in *Wuthering Heights* 1939, and after 1940 worked successfully in the USA.

objective correlative phrase suggested by T S ◊Eliot in a discussion of Shakespeare's *Hamlet*. Recognizing that the hero's emotion in the play was excessive and inexplicable, Eliot suggested that dramatists must find an exact, sensuous equivalent, or 'objective correlative', for any emotion they wish to express. He gave an example from *Macbeth* where Lady Macbeth's state of mind in the sleepwalking scene is communicated to the audience by a skilful building-up of images and actions.

Objectivism loose association of US poets such as Ezra Pound, Louis Zukofsky, William Carlos Williams, Charles Reznikoff (1894–1976), and

George Oppen (1908–1984), whose major works were all lifelong open-ended enterprises, constantly updated. Poetry was seen by them as a process by which the poetic form begins with a particular object and then moves on by improvisation through verbal associations inspired by the original object.

oboe musical instrument of the ◊woodwind family, a refined treble ◊shawm of narrow tapering bore and exposed double reed. The oboe was developed by the Hotteterre family of makers about 1700 and was incorporated in the court ensemble of Louis XIV. In B flat, it has a rich tone of elegant finish. Oboe concertos have been composed by Vivaldi, Albinoni, Richard Strauss, and others. Heinz Holliger is a modern virtuoso oboist.

Obraztsov Sergei 1901– . Russian puppeteer, head of the Moscow-based State Central Puppet Theatre, the world's largest puppet theatre (with a staff of 300). The repertoire was built up from 1923.

O'Brien Margaret (Angela Maxine) 1937– . US child actress, a star of the 1940s. She received a special Academy Award 1944, but her career, which included leading parts in *Lost Angel* 1943, *Meet Me in St Louis* 1944, and *The Secret Garden* 1949, did not survive beyond adolescence.

O'Brien Willis H 1886–1962. US film animator and special-effects creator, responsible for one of the cinema's most memorable monsters, the giant ape in *King Kong* 1933.

O'Casey Sean. Adopted name of John Casey 1884–1964. Irish dramatist. His early plays are tragicomedies, blending realism with symbolism and poetic with vernacular speech: *The Shadow of a Gunman* 1922, *Juno and the Paycock* 1925, and *The ◊Plough and the Stars* 1926. Later plays include *Red Roses for Me* 1946 and *The Drums of Father Ned* 1960.

He also wrote the antiwar drama *The Silver Tassie* 1929, *The Star Turns Red* 1940, *Oak Leaves and Lavender* 1947, and a six-volume autobiography.

We ought to have as great a regard for religion as we can, so as to keep it out of as many things as possible.

Sean O'Casey
The Plough and the Stars 1926

Oceanic art the arts of the native peoples of Australia and the South Pacific Islands, including New Guinea and New Zealand, have little historical depth, despite the classifying work of modern anthropology. Of the little that remains from the prehistoric period, an outstanding example is the sculpture of Easter Island, huge standing figures, possibly representing ancestors. Most Oceanic arts are considered primitive in that until recently the indigenous cultures possessed no metal, and cutting tools were of stone or shell. For Australian Aboriginal art see ◊Aboriginal art.

Melanesian art is the most striking of all the Oceanic arts. Associated with ancestor and spirit cults, headhunting, and cannibalism, it is typified by exaggerated natural forms with prominent sexual motifs. Ritual masks made for use in the islands' elaborate festivals are both colourful and disturbing. Many of the carved figures are demonic in appearance, at least to Western eyes. The ancestor figures, known as *uli*, from New Ireland have been amassed by Western collectors; *Soul boat* is in the Linden Museum, Stuttgart. Melanesian art – little of which remains in the islands – has inspired such Western artists as Ernst, Brancusi, Giacometti, and Henry Moore, among others.

Polynesian art is more decorative than that of Melanesia, characterized by the featherwork of Hawaii, the curvilinear surface ornament of the Maori carvers of New Zealand, and tattooing. Traditionally, cult objects were made to contain or conduct 'mana', a supernatural power.

Micronesian art typically combines extreme functional simplicity with a high-quality finish. Surface decoration is rare. Few examples of Micronesian art have found their way into Western collections.

Oceanus in Greek mythology, one of the ◊Titans, the god of a river supposed to encircle the Earth. He was the ancestor of other river gods and the ◊nymphs of the seas and rivers.

Ockeghem Johannes (Jean d') *c.* 1410–1497. Flemish composer of church music, including the antiphon *Alma redemptoris Mater* and the richly contrapuntal *Missa prolationum/Prolation Mass* employing complex canonic imitation in multiple parts at different tempi. He was court composer to Charles VII, Louis XI, and Charles VIII of France.

O'Connor Flannery 1925–1964. US novelist and short-story writer. Her works have a great sense of evil and sin, and often explore the religious sensibility of the Deep South, as in her novels *Wise Blood* 1952 and *The Violent Bear It Away* 1960. Her work exemplifies the postwar revival of the ◊Gothic novel in Southern US fiction.

Her collections of short stories include *A Good Man Is Hard to Find* 1955 and *Everything That Rises Must Converge* 1965.

octave in music, a span of eight notes as measured on the white notes of a piano keyboard. It corresponds to the consonance of first and second harmonics.

ode lyric poem of complex form. Odes originated in ancient Greece, where they were chanted to a musical accompaniment. Classical writers of odes include Sappho, Pindar, Horace, and Catullus. English poets who adopted the form include Spenser, Milton, Dryden, and Keats.

Odets Clifford 1906–1963. US dramatist, associated with the Group Theatre and the most renowned of the social-protest dramatists of the Depression era. His plays include *Waiting for Lefty* 1935, about a taxi drivers' strike, *Awake and Sing* 1935, *Golden Boy* 1937, and *The Country Girl* 1950.

Go out and fight so life shouldn't be printed on dollar bills.

Clifford Odets Awake and Sing 1935

Odin chief god of Scandinavian mythology, the **Woden** or **Wotan** of the Germanic peoples. A sky god, he lives in Asgard, at the top of the world-tree, and from the Valkyries (the divine maidens) receives the souls of heroic slain warriors, feasting with them in his great hall, Valhalla. The wife of Odin is Freya and Thor is their son. Wednesday is named after Odin.

Odoyevsky Vladimir 1804–1869. Russian writer whose works include tales of the supernatural, science fiction, satires, children's stories, and music criticism.

Odysseus chief character of Homer's *Odyssey*, king of the island of Ithaca; he is also mentioned in the *Iliad* as one of the leaders of the Greek forces at the siege of Troy. Odysseus was distinguished among Greek leaders for his cleverness and cunning. He appears in other later tragedies.

Odyssey Greek epic poem; the product of an oral tradition, it was probably written before 700 BC and is attributed to ◊Homer. It describes the voyage home of Odysseus after the fall of Troy, and the vengeance he takes with his son Telemachus on the suitors of his wife Penelope on his return. During his ten-year wanderings, he encounters the Cyclops, the enchantress Circe, Scylla and Charybdis, and the Sirens.

Many were the men whose cities he saw and whose mind he learned, aye, and many woes he suffered in his heart upon the sea.

Homer Odyssey I, 3

Oedipus in Greek mythology, king of Thebes who unwittingly killed his father, Laius, and married his mother, ◊Jocasta, in fulfilment of a prophecy. When he learned what he had done, he put out his eyes; Jocasta hanged herself. His story was dramatized by the Greek tragedian ◊Sophocles.

Oedipus the King and **Oedipus at Colonus** two tragedies by the Greek dramatist ◊Sophocles, based on episodes in the legend of Oedipus, king of Thebes. In *Oedipus the King* 429, Oedipus discovers that he has killed his father and married his own mother, and blinds himself in horror. In *Oedipus at Colonus* 401, the dethroned, blind king wanders as an outcast until led to a final resting place near Athens by his daughter ◊Antigone.

Ōe Kenzaburō 1935– . Japanese novelist. Involved in leftist politics in Japan, he has explored the situation of culturally disinherited postwar youth. His works include *Kojinteki-na taiken/A Personal Matter* 1964, describing from direct experience the development of an abnormal baby, seen by some as a metaphor for the contemporary Japanese situation. His earlier novel *Shiiku/The Catch* 1958 was awarded the important Akutagawa Prize.

oeuvre (French 'work') in the arts, the entire body of work produced by an artist. It can also mean a single work.

O'Faolain Sean (John Whelan) 1900–1991. Irish novelist, short-story writer, and biographer. His first novel, *A Nest of Simple Folk* 1933, was followed by an edition of translated Gaelic, *The Silver Branch* 1938. His many biographies include *Daniel O'Connell* 1938 and *De Valera* 1939, about the nationalist whom he had fought beside in the Irish Republican Army.

Offenbach Jacques 1819–1880. French composer. He wrote light opera, initially for presentation at the Bouffes parisiens. Among his works are *Orphée aux enfers/Orpheus in the Underworld* 1858, *La Belle Hélène* 1864, and *Les Contes d'Hoffmann/The Tales of Hoffmann* 1881.

O'Flaherty Liam 1897–1984. Irish author, best known for his short stories published in volumes such as *Spring Sowing* 1924, *The Tent* 1926, and *Two Lovely Beasts* 1948. His novels, set in County Mayo, include *The Neighbour's Wife* 1923, *The Informer* 1925, and *Land* 1946.

Ogata Kōin Japanese painter and designer. His style is highly decorative, typically combining brightly coloured, naturalistic and stylized elements against a gold background. *Iris Screen* early 18th century (Nezu Art Museum, Tokyo) is one of his best works.

Ogden C(harles) K(ay) 1889–1957. English writer and scholar. With I A Richards he developed the simplified form of English known as Basic English, built on a vocabulary of just 850 words. Together they wrote *Foundations of Aesthetics* 1921 and *The Meaning of Meaning* 1923.

Ogdon John 1937–1989. English pianist and composer. A contempory of Alexander Goehr and Peter Maxwell Davies at Manchester University, he won early recognition at the Moscow Tchaikovsky Piano Competition 1962 and went on to become an ebullient champion of neglected virtuoso repertoire by Alkan, Bartók, Busoni, and Sorabji.

O'Hara Frank 1926–1966. US poet and art critic. He was the leading member of the New York School of poets (others include John Ashbery, Kenneth Koch (1925–), and James Schuyler (1923–)), whose work was based on an immediate and autobiographical relationship to city life. His work includes *Lunch Poems* 1964.

O'Hara John (Henry) 1905–1970. US novelist. His *Appointment in Samarra* 1934 was a work of tough social realism and dealt with the world of the country-club set. This was followed by *BUtterfield 8* 1935, which was based on a murder case and which sharply observed the sordid reality and bourgeois anxiety of the Depression years.

oil paint painting medium in which ground pigment is bound with oil, usually linseed. Oil paint was in decorative use as early as the 5th century, but its artistic application is usually credited to the early 15th-century Flemish painter, Jan van Eyck. Passing from Flanders to Rome, it quickly succeeded tempera as the standard medium. Capable of the greatest flexibility and luminosity, oil paint has since the 16th century been considered preeminent among painting media, although ◊acrylic paint may prove in time to be a rival.

Oistrakh David Fyodorovich 1908–1974. Soviet violinist, celebrated for performances of both standard and contemporary Russian repertoire. Shostakovich wrote both his violin concertos for him. His son **Igor** (1931–) is equally renowned as a violinist.

O'Keeffe Georgia 1887–1986. US painter, based mainly in New York and New Mexico, known chiefly for her large, semi-abstract studies of flowers and bones, such as *Black Iris* 1926 (Metropolitan Museum of Art, New York) and the *Pelvis Series* of the 1940s.

Her mature style stressed contours and subtle tonal transitions, which often transformed the subject into a powerful and erotic abstract image. In 1946 she settled in New Mexico, where the desert landscape inspired many of her paintings.

The belief that words have a meaning of their own account is a relic of primitive word magic, and it is still a part of the air we breathe in nearly every discussion.

C K Ogden
The Meaning of Meaning 1923

Nobody sees a flower – really – we haven't time – and to see takes time like to have a friend takes time.

Georgia O'Keeffe

Okri Ben 1959– . Nigerian novelist, broadcaster, and journalist whose novel *The Famished*

Road won the 1991 Booker Prize. He published his first book *Flowers and Shadows* 1980, and wrote his second, *The Landscapes Within* 1982, while still a student at university in Essex, England.

Olbrich Joseph Maria 1867–1908. Viennese architect who worked under Otto Wagner and was opposed to the over-ornamentation of ◊Art Nouveau. His major buildings, however, remain Art Nouveau in spirit: the Vienna Sezession 1897–98, the Hochzeitsturm 1907, and the Tietz department store in Düsseldorf, Germany, 1906–09.

Oldenburg Claes 1929– . US Pop artist. He organized ◊happenings and made ◊assemblages, but is best-known for 'soft sculptures', gigantic replicas of everyday objects and foods, made of stuffed canvas or vinyl. One characteristic work is *Lipstick* 1969 (Yale University).

Old English literature poetry and prose in the various dialects of Old English written between AD 449 and 1066. Poetry (alliterative, without rhyme) was composed and delivered orally; much has therefore been lost. What remains owes its survival to monastic scribes who favoured verse with a Christian motivation or flavour. Prose in Old English was a later achievement, essentially beginning in the reign of Alfred the Great.

The greatest surviving epic poem is ◊*Beowulf* c. 700, which recounts the hero's battles with mythical foes such as the man-eating Grendel and his mother. *Widsith/The Wanderer, Finnsburgh* (about a tragic battle), and *Waldhere* (fragments of a lost epic), all mid-7th century, also belong to the the earlier centuries and express the bleakness and melancholy of life. *The Battle of Maldon*, written soon after the event 991, extols heroic values of courage in defeat.

One of the earliest attributed short poems consists of six lines by ◊Caedmon the herdsman, reputedly inspired to sing about the Creation by a vision. 'The Dream of the Rood' c. 698 celebrates the cult of the Cross, as does ◊Cynewulf's 'Elene'. Elegies, including *The Seafarer* written before 940, express themes of loneliness in exile and the sense of an inflexible Fate.

Prose in Old English dates from Alfred the Great's translation of St Gregory, Boethius, and Bede's *History of the English Peoples* (first published in Latin 731, translated between 871 and 899). Historical writing began with the ◊*Anglo-Saxon Chronicle*, at first brief notes of yearly events but later a dignified and even poetic narrative. The existing version of the Chronicle dates from King Alfred's reign and was compiled from earlier records (now lost) purporting to go back to the time of Adam. Dating from the 10th and 11th centuries are sermons by ◊Aelfric, a Dorset monk who also translated the Old Testament, and those by the prelate Wulfstan (died 1023). Some spells and riddles have survived.

Oldfield Bruce 1950– . English fashion designer who set up his own business 1975. His evening wear is worn by the British royal family, film stars, and socialites.

Old Man of the Sea in the ◊*Arabian Nights*, a man who compels strangers to carry him until they drop, encountered by ◊Sinbad the Sailor on his fifth voyage. Sinbad escapes by getting him drunk. In Greek mythology, the Old Man of the Sea describes ◊Proteus, an attendant of the sea god Poseidon.

Old Vic theatre in S London, England, former home of the National Theatre (1963–76). It was founded 1818 as the Coburg. Taken over by Emma Cons 1880 (as the Royal Victoria Hall), it became a popular centre for opera and drama, and was affectionately dubbed the Old Vic.

In 1898 Lilian ◊Baylis, niece of Emma Cons, assumed the management, and in 1914 began a celebrated series of Shakespeare productions. Badly damaged in air raids 1940, the Old Vic reopened 1950–81. In 1963 it became the home of the National Theatre until the latter moved to its South Bank building 1976. In 1983 the Old Vic was bought by Ed Mirvish, a Canadian businessman, and was refurbished 1985.

Oliphant Margaret 1828–1897. Scottish writer, author of over 100 novels, biographies, and numerous articles and essays. Her major work is the series *The Chronicles of Carlingford* 1863–66, including *The Perpetual Curate* and *Hester*.

olive branch ancient symbol of peace; in the Bible (Genesis 9), an olive branch is brought back by the dove to Noah to show that the flood has abated.

Oliver Isaac c. 1560–1617. English painter of miniatures, originally a Huguenot refugee, who studied under Nicholas ◊Hilliard. He became a court artist in the reign of James I. His sitters included the poet John Donne.

Oliver Joe 'King' (Joseph) 1885–1938. US jazz cornet player, bandleader, and composer whose work with Louis Armstrong 1922–24, on numbers like 'Canal Street Blues', took jazz beyond the confines of early Dixieland. His other compositions include 'Snake Rag' 1923 and 'Dr Jazz' 1927.

Born in Louisiana, Oliver began his career with New Orleans brass bands but was based mainly in Chicago from 1919 and in New York from the mid-1920s. He led his own band (called first the Creole Jazz Band and later the Dixie Syncopators) 1918–27 and 1931–37. The two-part cornet improvisations he created with Armstrong are seen as the high point of 1920s jazz. Oliver later moved towards a swing style.

Olivetti Italian office-machinery and furniture company, based in Ivrea, outside Milan. Formed 1908 by Camillo Olivetti (1868–1943), the company is known for its high design standards, sustained through relationships with some of this century's leading designers.

Marcello ◊Nizzoli was taken on 1938, followed by Ettore ◊Sottsass 1958 and Mario ◊Bellini 1962. They each produced some seminal designs for the company while continuing to work for other clients. Sottsass's 'Valentine' typewriter 1969 is among the best known, as is Bellini's series of 'Lexicon' typewriters.

Olivier Laurence (Kerr), Baron Olivier 1907–1989. English actor and director. For many years associated with the Old Vic theatre, he was director of the National Theatre company 1962–73. His stage roles include Henry V, Hamlet, Richard III, and Archie Rice in John Osborne's *The Entertainer* 1957 (filmed 1960). His acting and direction of filmed versions of Shakespeare's plays received critical acclaim for example, *Henry V* 1944 and *Hamlet* 1948 (Academy Award).

Olivier appeared on screen in many films, including *Wuthering Heights* 1939, *Rebecca* 1940, *Sleuth* 1972, *Marathon Man* 1976, and *The Boys from Brazil* 1978. The Olivier Theatre (part of the National Theatre on the South Bank, London) is named after him. He was married to Vivien Leigh 1940–60 and the actress Joan Plowright until his death.

What is acting but lying and what is good acting but convincing lying?

Laurence Olivier *Autobiography* 1982

Olmsted Frederick Law 1822–1903. US landscape designer. Appointed superintendent of New York's Central Park 1857, Olmsted and his partner Calvert Vaux directed its design and construction. After the American Civil War 1861–65, he became a sought-after planner of public parks, designing the grounds of the World's Columbian Exposition 1893.

Olson Charles 1910–1970. US poet, theoretician, leader with the ◊Black Mountain school of experimental poets and originator of the theory of 'composition by field'. His *Maximus Poems* published in full 1983, an open-ended, erudite, and encyclopedic fusion of autobiography and history set in Gloucester, Massachusetts, were a striking attempt to extend the American epic poem beyond Ezra Pound's *Cantos* or William Carlos Williams' *Patterson*.

Olympia sanctuary in the W Peloponnese, ancient Greece, with a temple of Zeus, and the stadium (for foot races, boxing, wrestling) and hippodrome (for chariot and horse races), where the original Olympic Games were held.

Omar Khayyám *c.* 1050–1123. Persian astronomer, mathematician, and poet. In the West, he is chiefly known as a poet through Edward ◊Fitzgerald's version of *The Rubaiyat of Omar Khayyám* 1859.

Omega Workshops group of early 20th-century English artists, led by Roger ◊Fry, who brought them together to design and make interiors, furnishings, and craft objects. The workshops, 1913–20, included members of the Bloomsbury Group, such as Vanessa Bell, Duncan Grant, Wyndham Lewis, and Henri Gaudier-Brzeska.

The articles they made were often primitive—both in design and execution – and brightly coloured. Some members moved to Charleston, a house in the South Downs which they decorated and fitted out with their creations.

omnibus in literature, a collection of works by a writer, or works by various writers on a similar subject, reprinted in one volume.

omphalos in classical antiquity, a conical navel-stone, thought to mark the centre of the world, notably that in the temple of Apollo at ◊Delphi in Greece.

ondes Martenot electronic musical instrument invented by Maurice Martenot (1898–1980), a French musician, teacher, and writer who first demonstrated his invention 1928 at the Paris Opéra. A melody of considerable range and voicelike timbre is produced by sliding a contact along a conductive ribbon, the left hand controlling the tone colour.

In addition to inspiring works from Messiaen, Varèse, Jolivet, and others, the instrument has been in regular demand among composers of film and radio incidental music.

One Flew Over The Cuckoo's Nest novel 1962 by US writer Ken ◊Kesey. Set in a mental asylum ruled by the sadistic Big Nurse, the story describes the attempted overthrow of her regime by McMurphy, a rebellious new patient. The conflict ends with McMurphy's lobotomy and his mercy killing by the narrator, a mute Native American who escapes into the free world. The novel serves as a broad allegory of the political and social state of postwar America.

O'Neill Eugene (Gladstone) 1888–1953. US dramatist, widely regarded as the greatest US dramatist. His plays, although tragic, are characterized by a down-to-earth quality and are often experimental in form, influenced by German Expressionism, Strindberg, and Freud. They were a radical departure from the romantic and melodramatic American theatre entertainments. They include the Pulitzer Prize-winning plays *Beyond the Horizon* 1920 and *Anna Christie* 1921, as well as *The Emperor Jones* 1920, *The Hairy Ape* 1922, *Desire Under the Elms* 1924, *The Iceman Cometh* 1946, and the posthumously produced autobiographical drama ◊*Long Day's Journey into Night* 1956 (written 1940), also a Pulitzer Prize winner. He was awarded the Nobel Prize for Literature 1936.

O'Neill was born in New York City, the son of stage actors James O'Neill and Ella Quinlan. His tumultuous family relationships would later provide much material for his plays. He had varied experience as a gold prospector, sailor, and actor. Other plays include *The Great God Brown* 1925, *Strange Interlude* 1928 (which lasts five hours), ◊*Mourning Becomes Electra* 1931, and *A Moon for the Misbegotten* 1947 (written 1943).

Our lives are merely strange dark interludes in the electric display of God the Father.

Eugene O'Neill *Strange Interlude* 1928

On the Road novel 1957 by US writer Jack ◊Kerouac. A lyrical, freewheeling, picaresque account of his real-life adventures with Neal Cassady (1920–1968), written with the jazz rhythms of 'spontaneous bop prosody', it became the bible of the ◊Beat Generation.

Op art (abbreviation for *Optical art*) movement in abstract art during the late 1950s and 1960s, in which colour and pattern were used to create optical effects, particularly the illusion of movement. Exponents include Victor ◊Vasarély and Bridget ◊Riley.

opera dramatic musical work in which singing takes the place of speech. In opera the music accompanying the action has paramount importance, although dancing and spectacular staging may also play their parts. Opera originated in late 16th-century Florence when the musical declamation, lyrical monologues, and choruses of Classical Greek drama were reproduced in current forms.

One of the earliest opera composers was Jacopo Peri (1561–1633), whose *Euridice* influenced Monteverdi. At first solely a court entertainment, opera soon became popular, and in 1637 the first public opera house was opened in Venice. In the later 17th century the elaborately conventional aria, designed to display the virtuosity of the singer, became predominant, overshadowing the dramatic element. Composers of this type of opera included Cavalli, Cesti (1623–1669), and Alessandro Scarlatti. In France opera was developed by Lully and Rameau, and in England by Purcell, but the Italian style retained its ascendancy, as exemplified by Handel.

Comic opera (*opera buffa*) was developed in Italy by such composers as Pergolesi, while in England *The Beggar's Opera* 1728 by John Gay started the vogue of the *ballad opera*, using popular tunes and spoken dialogue. *Singspiel* was the German equivalent (although its music was newly composed). A lessening of artificiality began with Gluck, who insisted on the preeminence of the dramatic over the purely vocal element. Mozart learned much from Gluck in writing his serious operas, but excelled in Italian *opera buffa*. In works such as *The Magic Flute*, he laid the foundations of a purely German-language opera, using the *Singspiel* as a basis. This line was continued by Beethoven in *Fidelio* and by the work of Weber, who introduced the Romantic style for the first time in opera.

The Italian tradition, which placed the main stress on vocal display and melodic suavity (*bel canto*), continued unbroken into the 19th century in the operas of Rossini, Donizetti, and Bellini. It is in the Romantic operas of Weber and Meyerbeer that the work of Wagner has its roots. Dominating the operatic scene of his time, Wagner attempted to create, in his 'music-dramas', a new art form, and completely transformed the 19th-century conception of opera. In Italy, Verdi assimilated, in his mature work, much of the Wagnerian technique, without sacrificing the Italian virtues of vocal clarity and melody. This tradition was continued by Puccini. In French opera in the mid-19th century, represented by such composers as Delibes, Gounod, Saint-Saëns, and Massenet, the drama was subservient to the music. More serious artistic ideals were put into practice by Berlioz in *The Trojans*, but the merits of his work were largely unrecognized in his own time.

Bizet's *Carmen* began a trend towards realism in opera; his lead was followed in Italy by Mascagni, Leoncavallo, and Puccini. Debussy's *Pelléas et Mélisande* represented a reaction against the over-emphatic emotionalism of Wagnerian opera. National operatic styles were developed in Russia by Glinka, Rimsky-Korsakov, Mussorgsky, Borodin, and Tchaikovsky, and in Bohemia by Smetana. Several composers of light opera emerged, including Sullivan, Lehár, Offenbach, and Johann Strauss.

In the 20th century the Viennese school produced an outstanding opera in Berg's *Wozzeck*, and the Romanticism of Wagner was revived by Richard Strauss in *Der Rosenkavalier*. Other 20th-century composers of opera include Gershwin, Bernstein, and John Adams in the USA; Tippett, Britten, and Harrison Birtwistle in the UK; Henze in Germany; Petrassi in Italy; and the Soviet composers Prokofiev and Shostakovich.

No good opera plot can be sensible, for people do not sing when they are feeling sensible.

W H Auden on opera

Major operas and their first performances

date	opera	composer	librettist	place
1607	Orfeo	Monteverdi	Striggio	Mantua
1642	The Coronation of Poppea	Monteverdi	Busenello	Venice
1689	Dido and Aeneas	Purcell	Tate	London
1724	Julius Caesar in Egypt	Handel	Haym	London
1762	Orpheus and Eurydice	Gluck	Calzabigi	Vienna
1786	The Marriage of Figaro	Mozart	Da Ponte	Vienna
1787	Don Giovanni	Mozart	Da Ponte	Prague
1790	Così fan tutte	Mozart	Da Ponte	Vienna
1791	The Magic Flute	Mozart	Schikaneder	Vienna
1805	Fidelio	Beethoven	Sonnleithner	Vienna
1816	The Barber of Seville	Rossini	Sterbini	Rome
1821	Der Freischütz	Weber	Kind	Berlin
1831	Norma	Bellini	Romani	Milan
1835	Lucia di Lammermoor	Donizetti	Cammarano	Naples
1836	Les Huguenots	Meyerbeer	Scribe	Paris
1842	Ruslan and Lyudmila	Glinka	Shirkov/Bakhturin	St Petersburg
1850	Lohengrin	Wagner	Wagner	Weimar
1851	Rigoletto	Verdi	Piave	Venice
1853	Il trovatore	Verdi	Cammarano	Rome
1853	La traviata	Verdi	Piave	Venice
1859	Faust	Gounod	Barbier/Carré	Paris
1865	Tristan and Isolde	Wagner	Wagner	Munich
1866	The Bartered Bride	Smetana	Sabina	Prague
1868	Die Meistersinger	Wagner	Wagner	Munich
1871	Aïda	Verdi	Ghislanzoni	Cairo
1874	Boris Godunov	Mussorgsky	Mussorgsky	St Petersburg
1874	Die Fledermaus	Johann Strauss II	Haffner/Genée	Vienna
1875	Carmen	Bizet	Meilhac/Halévy	Paris
1876	The Ring of the Nibelung	Wagner	Wagner	Bayreuth
1879	Eugene Onegin	Tchaikovsky	Tchaikovsky/Shilovsky	Moscow
1881	The Tales of Hoffman	Offenbach	Barbier	Paris
1882	Parsifal	Wagner	Wagner	Bayreuth
1885	The Mikado	Sullivan	Gilbert	London
1887	Otello	Verdi	Boito	Milan
1890	Cavalleria Rusticana	Mascagni	Menasci/Targioni-Tozzetti	Rome
1890	Prince Igor	Borodin	Borodin	St Petersburg
1892	I Pagliacci	Leoncavallo	Leoncavallo	Milan
1892	Werther	Massenet	Blau/Milliet/Hartmann	Vienna
1896	La Bohème	Puccini	Giacosa/Illica	Turin
1900	Tosca	Puccini	Giacosa/Illica	Rome
1902	Pelléas et Mélisande	Debussy	Maeterlinck	Paris
1904	Jenůfa	Janáček	Janáček	Brno
1904	Madame Butterfly	Puccini	Giacosa/Illica	Milan
1905	Salome	Richard Strauss	Wilde/Lachmann	Dresden
1909	The Golden Cockerel	Rimsky-Korsakov	Byelsky	Moscow
1911	Der Rosenkavalier	Richard Strauss	Hofmannsthal	Dresden
1918	Duke Bluebeard's Castle	Bartók	Balázs	Budapest
1925	Wozzeck	Berg	Berg	Berlin
1935	Porgy and Bess	Gershwin	Ira Gershwin/Heyward	Boston
1937	Lulu	Berg	Berg	Zürich
1945	Peter Grimes	Britten	Slater	London
1946	War and Peace	Prokofiev	Prokofiev/Mendelson	Leningrad
1951	The Rake's Progress	Stravinsky	Auden/Kallman	Venice
1978	Paradise Lost	Penderecki	Fry	Chicago
1984	Akhnaten	Glass	Glass	Stuttgart
1986	The Mask of Orpheus	Birtwistle	Zinovieff	London
1989	New Year	Tippett	Tippett	Houston
1992	Dienstag aus LICHT	Stockhausen	Stockhausen	Portugal

opera buffa (Italian 'comic opera') type of humorous opera with characters taken from everyday life. The form began as a musical intermezzo in the 18th century and was then adopted in Italy and France for complete operas. An example is Rossini's *The Barber of Seville*.

opéra comique (French 'comic opera') opera that includes text to be spoken, not sung; Bizet's *Carmen* is an example. Of the two Paris opera houses in the 18th and 19th centuries, the Opéra (which aimed at setting a grand style) allowed no spoken dialogue, whereas the Opéra Comique did.

opera seria (Italian 'serious opera') type of opera distinct from *opera buffa*, or humorous opera. Common in the 17th and 18th centuries, it tended to treat classical subjects in a formal style, with most of the singing being by solo voices. Examples include many of Handel's operas based on mythological subjects.

operetta light form of opera, with music, dance, and spoken dialogue. The story line is romantic and sentimental, often employing farce and parody. Its origins lie in the 19th-century *opéra comique* and it is intended to amuse. Examples of operetta are Offenbach's *Orphée aux enfers/Orpheus in the Underworld* 1858, Johann Strauss's *Die Fledermaus/The Flittermouse* 1874, and Gilbert and Sullivan's *The Pirates of Penzance* 1879 and *The Mikado* 1885.

Ophuls Max. Adopted name of Max Oppenheimer 1902–1957. German film director, whose style is characterized by an ironic, bittersweet tone and intricate camera movement. He worked in Europe and the USA, attracting much critical praise for such films as *Letter from an Unknown Woman* 1948, *La Ronde* 1950, and *Lola Montes* 1955.

Opie John 1761–1807. English artist. Born in St Agnes, Cornwall, he was a portrait painter in London from 1780, later painting historical pictures and genre scenes. He became a professor at the Royal Academy 1805 and his lectures were published posthumously 1809.

I mix them with my brains, sir.

John Opie when asked with what he mixed his colours

Opie Peter Mason 1918–1982 and Iona Margaret Balfour 1923– . Husband-and-wife team of folklorists who specialized in the myths and literature of childhood. Their books include the *Oxford Dictionary of Nursery Rhymes* 1951 and *The Lore and Language of Schoolchildren* 1959. In 1987 their collection of children's books was sold to the Bodleian Library, Oxford, for £500,000.

Oppenheim Meret 1913–1985. German-Swiss painter and designer, renowned as the creator of the celebrated Surrealist-Dada object *Breakfast in Fur* 1936 (Museum of Modern Art, New York): a teacup, saucer, and spoon covered in animal fur.

Oppenheim studied art in Paris in the 1920s and in the early 1930s became the model and muse of the Surrealist painter and photographer ◊Man Ray. Her own paintings are replete with mythological and fairytale figures. Among the many surreal objects she created is a wooden table with bird's legs and feet in gold-plated bronze (private collection, Paris). Oppenheim also designed jewellery for the couturier Elsa ◊Schiaparelli.

op. posth. abbreviation for ◊*opus posthumous*.

opus (Latin 'work') in music, a term, used with a figure, to indicate the numbering of a composer's works, usually in chronological order.

opus anglicanum (Latin 'English work') ecclesiastical embroidery made in England about AD 900–1500. It typically depicts birds and animals on highly coloured silks, using gold thread. It was popular throughout medieval Europe, being much in demand at the papal court.

opus posthumous a work of which the existence became known after the composer's death.

oracle Greek sacred site where answers (also called oracles) were given by a deity to enquirers about personal affairs or state policy. These were usually ambivalent, so that the deity was proven right whatever happened. The earliest was probably at Dodona (in Epirus), where priests interpreted the sounds made by the sacred oaks of ◊Zeus, but the most celebrated was that of Apollo at ◊Delphi.

oral literature stories that are or have been transmitted in spoken form, such as public recitation, rather than through writing or printing. Most preliterate societies have had a tradition of oral literature, including short folk tales, legends, myths, proverbs, and riddles as well as longer narrative works; and most of the ancient epics – such as the Greek *Odyssey* and the Mesopotamian *Gilgamesh* – seem to have been composed and added to over many centuries before they were committed to writing.

Some ancient stories from oral traditions were not written down as literary works until the 19th century, such as the Finnish *Kalevala* (1822); many fairy tales, such as those collected in Germany by the Grimm brothers, also come into this category. Much of this sort of *folk literature* may have been consciously embellished and altered, as happened in 19th-century Europe for nationalistic purposes.

Oral literatures have continued to influence the development of national written literatures in the 20th century, particularly in Africa, central Asia, and Australia. Russian investigations and studies of Yugoslavia's oral literature, originally undertaken to illuminate the oral basis of Homeric narrative, have prompted collections and scientific studies in many other parts of the world.

oratorio dramatic, non-scenic musical setting of religious texts, scored for orchestra, chorus, and solo voices. Its origins lie in the *Laudi spirituali* performed by St Philip Neri's Oratory in Rome in the 16th century, followed by the first definitive oratorio in the 17th century by Cavalieri. The form reached perfection in such works as J S Bach's *Christmas Oratorio*, and Handel's *Messiah*.

The term is sometimes applied to secular music drama in which there is little or no stage action, as in Stravinsky's *Oedipus Rex* 1926–27, and Messiaen's *St François d'Assise/St Francis of Assisi* 1975–83.

Orbison Roy 1936–1988. US pop singer and songwriter specializing in slow, dramatic ballads, such as 'Only the Lonely' 1960 and 'Running Scared' 1961. His biggest hit was the jaunty 'Oh, Pretty Woman' 1964.

Born in Texas, Orbison began in the mid-1950s as a rockabilly singer on Sun Records. In the 1970s he turned to country material but made a pop comeback 1988 as a member of the Traveling Wilburys with Bob Dylan, George Harrison (ex-Beatle), Tom Petty (1952–), and Jeff Lynne (1947–).

orchestra group of musicians playing together on different instruments. In Western music, an orchestra typically contains various bowed string instruments and sections of wind, brass, and percussion. The size and format may vary according to the needs of composers.

The term was originally used in Greek theatre for the semicircular space in front of the stage, and was adopted in 17th-century France to refer first to the space in front of the stage where musicians sat, and later to the musicians themselves.

The string section is commonly divided into two groups of violins (first and second), violas, cellos, and double basses. The woodwind section became standardized by the end of the 18th century, when it consisted of two each of flutes, oboes, clarinets, and bassoons, to which were later added piccolo, cor anglais, bass clarinet, and double bassoon. At that time, two timpani and two horns were also standard, and two trumpets were occasionally added. During the 19th century, the brass section was gradually expanded to include four horns, three trumpets, three trombones, and tuba. To the percussion section a third timpano was added, and from Turkey came the bass drum, side drum, cymbals, and triangle. One or more harps became common and, to maintain balance, the number of string instruments to a part also increased. Other instruments used in the orchestra include xylophone, celesta, piano, and organ. The orchestra used to be conducted by means of a violin bow, but by Mendelssohn's time the baton was implemented.

The term may also be applied to non-Western ensembles such as the Indonesian gamelan orchestra, consisting solely of percussion instruments, mainly tuned gongs and bells.

Show me an orchestra that likes its conductor and I'll show you a lousy orchestra.

Goddard Lieberson on orchestras

---

orchestration scoring of a composition for orchestra; the choice of instruments of a score expanded for orchestra (often by another hand).

A work may be written for piano, and then transferred to an orchestral score.

Orczy Baroness Emmusca 1865–1947. Hungarian-born English novelist who wrote the historical adventure *The Scarlet Pimpernel* 1905. The foppish Sir Percy Blakeney, bold rescuer of victims of the French Revolution, appeared in many sequels.

We seek him here, we seek him there,/ Those Frenchies seek him everywhere./ Is he in heaven? – Is he in hell?/ That demmed, elusive Pimpernel?

Baroness Orczy
The Scarlet Pimpernel 1905

---

order in classical architecture, the ◊column (including capital, shaft, and base) and the ◊entablature, considered as an architectural whole. The five orders are Doric, Ionic, Corinthian, Tuscan, and Composite.

The earliest order was the Doric (without a base), which originated before the 5th century BC, soon followed by the Ionic (with scroll-like capitals), which was first found in Asia Minor. The Corinthian (with leaves in the capitals) dates from the end of the 5th century BC, while the Composite appears first on the arch of Titus in Rome AD 82. No Tuscan columns survive from antiquity, although the order was thought to originate in Etruscan times. The five orders were described in detail by the Italian Sebastiano Serlio in his treatise on architecture 1537–51.

Oresteia trilogy of tragic Greek plays by ◊Aeschylus – *Agamemnon*, *Libation-Bearers*, and *Eumenides* – which won first prize at the festival of Dionysus at Athens 458 BC. Their subject is the murder of Agamemnon by his wife Clytemnestra and the consequent vengeance of their son Orestes and daughter Electra.

Orestes in Greek mythology, the son of ◊Agamemnon and ◊Clytemnestra, who killed his mother on the instructions of Apollo because she and her lover Aegisthus had murdered his father, and was then hounded by the ◊Furies until he was purified, and acquitted of the crime of murder.

Orff Carl 1895–1982. German composer, an individual stylist whose work is characterized by sharp dissonances and percussion. Among his compositions are the cantata ◊*Carmina Burana* 1937 and the opera *Antigone* 1949.

organ musical wind instrument of ancient origin. It produces sound from pipes of various sizes under applied pressure and has keyboard controls. Apart from its continued use in serious compositions and for church music, the organ has been adapted for light entertainment.

One note only is sounded by each pipe, but these are grouped into stops, which are ranks or scales of pipes prepared to 'speak' by a knob. These, in turn, form part of a sectional organ, one of the tonal divisions comprising the whole organ. These separate manuals are the great, swell, choir, solo, echo, and pedal organs, controlled by the player's hands and feet. By this grouping and subdivision, extremes of tone and volume are obtained.

The electric tone-wheel organ was invented 1934 by the US engineer Laurens Hammond (1895–1973). Other types of electric organ were developed in the 1960s. Electrically controlled organs substitute electrical impulses and relays for some of the air-pressure controls. These, such as the Hammond organs, built during the 1930s for the large cinemas of the period, include many special sound effects as well as colour displays. In electronic organs the notes are produced by electronic oscillators and are amplified at will.

Organ (Harold) Bryan 1935– . English portraitist whose subjects have included Harold Macmillan, Michael Tippett, Elton John, and the Prince and Princess of Wales.

Conversations between artist and sitter are private affairs – like those that take place when you go to a doctor or a solicitor.

Bryan Organ
in the *Observer* Dec 1983

---

organdie fabric of fine cotton muslin. *Organza* is a similar fabric, made of silk. They are used for children's party dresses of the kind designed by Jeanne Lanvin.

organum in music, a form of early medieval harmony in which voices move in parallel fourths or fifths.

origami art of folding paper into forms such as dolls and birds, originating in Japan in the 10th century.

Orion in Greek mythology, a giant of Boeotia, famed as a hunter.

Orlando furioso poem 1516 by the Italian Renaissance writer Ariosto, published 1532 as a sequel to Boiardo's *Orlando innamorato* 1487. The poem describes the unrequited love of Orlando for Angelica, set against the war between Saracens (Arabs) and Christians during Charlemagne's reign. It influenced Shakespeare, Byron, and Milton, and is considered to be the greatest poem of the Italian Renaissance.

Ormandy Eugene 1899–1985. Hungarian-born US conductor, music director of the Philadelphia

Orchestra 1936–80. Originally a violin virtuoso, he championed ◊Rachmaninov and ◊Shostakovich.

ormolu (French *or moulu* 'ground gold') alloy of copper, zinc, and sometimes tin, used for furniture decoration.

ornamentation in music, decorative filling-in of a melody, or accentuation of a structural feature such as the end of a phrase, by rhetorical flourishes or cascades of notes, indicated by special notational signs.

Orozco José Clemente 1883–1949. Mexican muralist painter whose work was inspired by the Mexican revolution of 1910, such as the series in the Palace of Government, Guadalajara, 1949. *Mankind's Struggle* 1930 (New School for Social Research, New York) is typical.

Orpheus mythical Greek poet and musician. The son of Apollo and a muse, he married Eurydice, who died from the bite of a snake. Orpheus went down to Hades to bring her back and her return to life was granted on condition that he walk ahead of her without looking back. But he did look back and Eurydice was irretrievably lost. In his grief, he offended the ◊maenad women of Thrace, and was torn to pieces by them.

Orphism French style of abstract painting, derived from ◊Cubism, in which colour harmonies take precedence over form. The term 'Orphic Cubism' (later Orphism) was first used by the poet Guillaume Apollinaire 1913 to describe the mystical, visionary qualities he perceived in the first ◊non-objective works of Robert ◊Delaunay. These sought to develop a visual equivalent to music through the interplay of light and colour on pure abstract form. Other noted Orphists were Frank ◊Kupka and Fernard ◊Léger.

orthochromatic photographic film or paper of decreased sensitivity, which can be processed with a red safelight. Using it, blue objects appear lighter and red ones darker because of increased blue sensitivity.

Orton Joe 1933–1967. English dramatist in whose black comedies surreal and violent action takes place in genteel and unlikely settings. Plays include *Entertaining Mr Sloane* 1964, *Loot* 1966, and *What the Butler Saw* 1968. His diaries deal frankly with his personal life. He was murdered by his lover Kenneth Halliwell.

The kind of people who always go on about whether a thing is in good taste invariably have very bad taste.

Joe Orton

Orwell George. Pen name of Eric Arthur Blair 1903–1950. English author. His books include the satirical fable ◊*Animal Farm* 1945, which included such slogans as 'All animals are equal, but some are more equal than others', and the prophetic ◊*Nineteen Eighty-Four* 1949, portraying the catastrophic excesses of state control over the individual. Other works include *Down and Out in Paris and London* 1933. A deep sense of social conscience and antipathy towards political dictatorship characterize his work.

Born in India and educated in England, he served for five years in the Burmese police force, an experience reflected in the novel *Burmese Days* 1935. Life as a dishwasher and tramp were related in *Down and Out in Paris and London*, and service for the Republican cause in the Spanish Civil War in *Homage to Catalonia* 1938. He also wrote numerous essays.

Doublethink means the power of holding two contradictory beliefs in one's mind simultaneously, and accepting both of them.

George Orwell *Nineteen Eighty-Four* 1949

Osborne Dorothy 1627–1695. English letter-writer. In 1655 she married Sir William Temple (1628–1699), to whom she addressed her letters, written 1652–54 and first published 1888.

Osborne John (James) 1929– . English dramatist. He became one of the first ◊Angry Young Men (anti-establishment writers of the 1950s) of British theatre with his debut play, *Look Back in Anger* 1956. Other plays include *The Entertainer* 1957, *Luther* 1960, *Inadmissable Evidence* 1964, and *A Patriot for Me* 1965.

Damn you, England. You're rotting now, and quite soon you'll disappear.

John Osborne
in a letter to *Tribune* 1961

Oscar in cinema, popular name for ◊Academy Award.

Oshima Nagisa 1932– . Japanese film director whose violent and sexually explicit *Ai No Corrida/In the Realm of the Senses* 1977 caused controversy when first released. His other work includes *Death by Hanging* 1968 and *Merry Christmas Mr Lawrence* 1983, which starred the singer David Bowie.

Osiris ancient Egyptian god, the embodiment of goodness, who ruled the underworld after being killed by ◊Set. The sister-wife of Osiris was ◊Isis or Hathor, and their son ◊Horus captured his father's murderer. The pharaohs were thought to be his incarnation.

Under Ptolemy I's Graeco-Egyptian empire Osiris was developed (as a means of uniting his Greek and Egyptian subjects) into **Serapis** (Osiris + Apis, the latter being the bull god of Memphis who carried the dead to the tomb), elements of the cults of Zeus and Hades being included; the greatest temple of Serapis was the Serapeum in Alexandria. The cult of Osiris, and that of Isis, later spread to Rome.

Ossian (Celtic *Oisin*) legendary Irish hero, invented by the Scottish writer James ◊Macpherson. He is sometimes represented as the son of ◊Finn Mac Cumhaill, about 250, and as having lived to tell the tales of Finn and the Ulster heroes to St Patrick, about 400. The publication 1760 of Macpherson's poems, attributed to Ossian, made Ossian's name familiar throughout Europe.

Ostade Adriaen van 1610–1685. Dutch painter and engraver, known for pictures of tavern scenes and village fairs. A native of Haarlem, Ostade may have studied under Frans Hals. His brother, *Isaac van Ostade* (1621–1649), excelled in portraying winter landscapes and roadside and farmyard scenes.

ostinato (Italian 'obstinate') in music, a persistently repeating melodic or rhythmic figure conveying an ambiguous message of dynamic action unrelated to any movement. Ostinati play an important role in Stravinsky's *The Rite of Spring* 1913 and the *Symphony of Psalms* 1930, also in the *Carmina Burana* 1937 of Carl Orff.

Ostrovsky Alexander Nikolaevich 1823–1886. Russian dramatist, founder of the modern Russian theatre. He dealt satirically with the manners of the merchant class in numerous plays, for example *The Bankrupt* (or *It's All in the Family*) 1849. His best-known play is a family tragedy, *The Storm* 1860. His fairy-tale play *The Snow Maiden* 1873 inspired the composers Tchaikovsky and Rimsky-Korsakov.

Othello tragedy by William ◊Shakespeare, first performed 1604–05. Othello, a Moorish commander in the Venetian army, is persuaded by Iago that his wife Desdemona is having an affair with his friend Cassio. Othello murders Desdemona; on discovering her innocence, he kills himself.

O'Toole Peter 1932– . Irish-born English actor who made his name as *Lawrence of Arabia* 1962, and who then starred in such films as *Becket* 1964 and *The Lion in Winter* 1968. Subsequent appearances include *The Ruling Class* 1972, *The Stuntman* 1978, and *High Spirits* 1988.

Otway Thomas 1652–1685. English dramatist. His plays include the tragedies *Alcibiades* 1675, *Don Carlos* 1676, *The Orphan* 1680, and *Venice Preserv'd* 1682.

*Children blessings seem, but torments
are;/ When young, our folly, and when
old, our fear.*

Thomas Otway *Don Carlos* 1676

Ouida pen name of Marie Louise de la Ramée
1839–1908. British romantic novelist, author of
Under Two Flags 1867 and *Moths* 1880.

Ouranos Greek form of ◊Uranus, meaning
'Heaven'.

Ousmane Sembène 1923– . Senegalese writer
and film director. His novels, written in French,
include *Le Docker noir* 1956, about his experiences as a union leader in Marseille; *Les Bouts de
bois/God's Bits of Wood* 1960; *Le Mandat/The
Money Order* 1966; and *Xala* 1974, the last two of
which he made into films (1968 and 1975).

Outsider, The (French *L'Etranger*) novel by
Albert ◊Camus, published 1942, a key work of
existentialism. A man is sentenced to death,
ostensibly for murder, but as much for his failure
to conform to the values of a hypocritical society.

overblowing in music, a technique of exciting
higher harmonics in a wind instrument by
increasing air pressure at the mouthpiece, causing it to sound an octave (second harmonic) or
twelfth (third harmonic) higher.

overture in music, the opening piece of a concert or opera, having the dual function of settling
an audience and allowing the conductor and
players to become acquainted with the ◊acoustic
of a concert auditorium.

The use of an overture in opera began during
the 17th century; the 'Italian' overture consisting
of two quick movements separated by a slow one,
and the 'French' of a quick movement between
two in slower tempo.

Ovid (Publius Ovidius Naso) 43 BC–AD 17.
Latin poet whose poetry deals mainly with the
themes of love (*Amores* 20 BC, *Ars amatoria/The
Art of Love* 1 BC), mythology (*Metamorphoses* AD
2), and exile (*Tristia* AD 9–12).

Born at Sulmo, Ovid studied rhetoric in Rome
in preparation for a legal career, but soon turned
to literature. In 8 BC he was banished by
Augustus to Tomi, on the Black Sea, where he
died. Sophisticated, ironical, and self-pitying, his
work was highly influential during the Middle
Ages and Renaissance.

Necessity often mothers invention.

Ovid *Ars amatoria*

Owen Wilfred 1893–1918. English poet. His
verse, owing much to the encouragement of
Siegfried ◊Sassoon, expresses his hatred of war,
for example *Anthem for Doomed Youth*, published
1921.

'Owl and the Nightingale The' early Middle
English poem, written about 1200, which takes
the form of an argument between an owl, who
may represent wisdom and respectability, and a
nightingale, who may symbolize gaiety and
◊courtly love. Its authorship is uncertain.

Oyono Ferdinand 1929– . Cameroon novelist,
writing in French. His work describes Cameroon
during the colonial era, for example *Une Vie de
boy/Houseboy* 1956 and *Le Vieux Nègre et la
médaille/The Old Man and the Medal* 1956.

Ozbek Rifat 1953– . Turkish fashion designer
whose opulent clothing is often inspired by different ethnic groups. He showed his first collection
in London 1984, changed direction 1990 with a
collection that was entirely white, and began
showing designs in Milan 1991, with a collection
inspired by native American dress.

Ozu Yasujiro 1903–1963. Japanese film director
who became known in the West only in his last
years. *Tokyo Monogatari/Tokyo Story* 1953 has
low camera angles and a theme of middle-class
family life, which typify his work.

His other major films include *Late Spring* 1949
and *Autumn Afternoon* 1962.

p in music, abbreviation for ***piano*** (Italian 'softly').

Pabst G(eorg) W(ilhelm) 1885–1967. German film director whose films include *Die Büchse der Pandora/Pandora's Box* and *Das Tagebuch einer Verlorenen/The Diary of a Lost Girl* 1929, both starring Louise ◊Brooks, the antiwar story *Westfront 1918* 1930, and *Die Dreigroschenoper/ The Threepenny Opera* 1931.

Pacino Al(berto) 1940– . US film actor who played powerful, introverted but violent roles in films such as *The Godfather* 1972, *Serpico* 1973, and *Scarface* 1983. *Dick Tracy* 1990 added comedy to his range of acting styles.

More recent roles include *Glengarry Glen Ross* 1992, and *Scent of a Woman* 1992, for which he won an Academy Award.

Paddington Bear bear who features in a series of children's stories by English writer Michael Bond (1926–), beginning with *A Bear called Paddington* 1958. The bear is found abandoned on Paddington Station in London by the Brown family, who adopt him; he likes marmalade sandwiches and customarily wears a hat, duffel-coat, and Wellington boots.

Piano playing is more difficult than statesmanship. It is harder to waken emotions in ivory keys than in human beings.

Ignacy Paderewski

Paderewski Ignacy Jan 1860–1941. Polish pianist, composer, and politician. After his debut in Vienna 1887, he became celebrated in Europe and the USA as an interpreter of the piano music of Chopin and as composer of the nationalist *Polish Fantasy* 1893 for piano and orchestra and the *'Polonia' Symphony* 1903–09.

During World War I he helped organize the Polish army in France; in 1919 he became prime minister of the newly independent Poland, which he represented at the Peace Conference, but continuing opposition forced him to resign the same year. He resumed a musical career 1922, was made president of the Polish National Council in Paris 1940, and died in New York.

Paganini Niccolò 1782–1840. Italian violinist and composer, a concert soloist from the age of nine. A prodigious technician, he drew on folk and gipsy idioms to create the modern repertoire of virtuoso techniques. His dissolute appearance, wild love life, and amazing powers of expression even on a single string fostered rumours of his being in league with the devil. His compositions include six concertos and various sonatas and variations for violin and orchestra, sonatas for violin and guitar, and guitar quartets.

pageant originally, the wagon on which medieval ◊mystery plays were performed. The term was later applied to the street procession of songs, dances, and historical tableaux that became fashionable during the 1920s.

The open-air entertainment ◊son et lumière is related to the pageant.

Pagnol Marcel 1895–1974. French film director, producer, author, and playwright whose work includes *Fanny* 1932 and *Manon des sources* 1952 (filmed 1986). His autobiographical *La Gloire de mon père/My Father's Glory* 1957 was filmed 1991. He regarded the cinema as recorded theatre; thus his films, although strong on character and background, fail to exploit the medium fully as an independent art form.

pagoda Buddhist structure common in China, Japan, and Korea, built to contain a relic or sutra (collection of recorded Buddhist dialogues and discourses). Pagodas have three, five, or seven storeys (in exceptional cases more), crowned by a tall spire (*sōrin*). There is generally no room inside, so that a pagoda is essentially just a stack of roofs, not a functioning building. Deriving from the Indian ◊stupa, the pagoda came to resemble a Chinese watchtower; the shape also has symbolic meaning.

Paine Thomas 1737–1809. English left-wing political writer, active in the American and French revolutions. His pamphlet *Common Sense* 1776 ignited passions in the American Revolution; others include *The Rights of Man*, a defence of the French Revolution, 1791 and *The Age of Reason* 1793. He advocated republicanism, deism, the abolition of slavery, and the emancipation of women.

Government, even in its best state, is but a necessary evil; in its worst state, an intolerable one.

Thomas Paine *Common Sense*

---

painting the application of colour, pigment, or paint to a surface. Surfaces include walls, canvas, paper, and wood. For the techniques of painting, see ◊encaustic painting, ◊fresco, ◊oil paint, and ◊watercolour painting. For the subjects of painting, see ◊genre, ◊history painting, ◊landscape painting, ◊nude, and ◊still life.

Painting originated in prehistoric times: in Europe some of the earliest paintings are in the caves of Lascaux, France, about 1800 BC. Fresco painting was used extensively in the ancient world for decorating palaces, tombs, and homes: ancient Egypt, Crete and Mycenae, ancient Greece (where pottery painting became highly sophisticated), Rome, and Pompeii. In the first few centuries AD portraits of the dead were painted in encaustic in Egypt, and Christians painted sacred images on the walls of the cata-

combs in Rome. For the next 1,200 years painting was exclusively religious.

During the early Middle Ages manuscript illumination became the main form of painting, with fresco painting flourishing during the Romanesque period. In the Byzantine empire and Russia there emerged a tradition of icon painting on wooden panels. In Italy at the end of the Middle Ages, fresco painting and panel painting (using tempera) developed rapidly.

During the Renaissance the technique of oil painting spread from the Netherlands to Italy and gradually replaced the use of tempera. By the 16th century canvas had replaced wooden panels as the commonest painting surface. The major forms of painting – genre, landscape, nude, portrait, still life – emerged as patronage moved from the church to princes and then the middle

Western painters

period	style	characteristic painters
14th century	late medieval	Duccio (c. 1255–1319) Giotto (1267–1337) Simone Martini (c. 1284–1344)
15th century	N European	Limbourg brothers (before 1416) van Eyck (c. 1390–1441) Campin (c. 1378–1444) van der Weyden (c. 1399–1464) Bouts (c. 1420–1475)
15th century	Italian Renaissance	Uccello (1397–1475) Fra Angelico (c. 1400–1455) Masaccio (1401–1428) Piero della Francesca (c. 1420–1492) Giovanni Bellini (c. 1430–1516) Mantegna (c. 1431–1506)
late 15th–early 16th century	Italian High Renaissance	Leonardo da Vinci (1452–1519) Michelangelo (1475–1564) Lotto (c. 1480–1556) Raphael (1483–1520) Titian (c. 1487–1576)
16th century	N European Renaissance	Dürer (1471– 1528) Altdorfer (c. 1480–1538) Holbein (1497/8–1543) Brueghel (c. 1525–1569)
16th century	Mannerism	Pontormo (1495–1557) Bronzino (1503–1572) Primaticcio (1504–1570) Tintoretto (1518–1594) El Greco (1541–1614)
17th–mid-18th century	Baroque	Caravaggio (1573– 1610) Rubens (1577–1640) Poussin (1594–1665) Velázquez (1599–1660) Rembrandt (1606–1669)
18th century	Rococo	Watteau (1684–1721) Hogarth (1697–1764) Boucher (1703–1770) Guardi (1712–1793)
18th–19th century	Neo-Classicism	Mengs (1728–1779) David (1748–1825) Ingres (1780–1867)
late 18th–19th century	Romanticism	Fuseli (1741– 1825) Goya (1746–1828) Blake (1757–1827) Friedrich (1774–1840) Turner (1775–1851) Géricault (1791–1824) Delacroix (1798–1863)
mid-19th century	Realism	Daumier (1808–1879) Millet (1814–1875) Courbet (1819–1877) Manet (1832–1883)
mid–late 19th century	Impressionism	Degas (1834–1917) Monet (1840–1926) Pissarro (1830–1903) Cassatt (1844–1926)
late 19th century	Post-Impressionism	Cézanne (1839–1906) Gauguin (1848–1903) van Gogh (1853–1890)
late 19th century	Symbolism	Moreau (1826–1898) Redon (1840–1916)
20th century		
1905–	Fauvism	Matisse (1869–1954) Vlaminck (1876–1958)
1905–	Expressionism	Kirchner (1880–1938) Kokoschka (1886–1980
1907–1915	Cubism	Picasso (1881–1973) Braque (1882–1963)
1915–1922	Dada	Duchamp (1887–1968) Schwitters (1887–1948)
1915–1920s	Suprematism	Malevich (1878–1935)
1920s	De Stijl	Mondrian (1872–1944)
1920s–1930s	Surrealism	Ernst (1891–1976) Dali (1904–1989)
1930s	Bauhaus	Kandinsky (1866–1944) Klee (1879–1940)
1940s–1950s	Abstract Expressionism	De Kooning (1904–) Pollock (1912–1956)
1960s	Pop art	Hamilton (1922–) Rauschenberg (1925–) Warhol (1928–1987)
1970s–1980s	Neo-Expressionism	Kiefer (1945–)

classes, and a keen interest in the world replaced religious sentiment. The Renaissance conception of painting as an accurate depiction of objects survived until the 20th century, when it was challenged in particular by abstract art.

For the major styles of Western painting, see ◊Renaissance art, ◊Mannerism, ◊Baroque, ◊Rococo ◊Neo-Classicism, ◊Romanticism, ◊Realism, ◊Impressionism, and ◊abstract art.

Pakula Alan J 1928– . US film director, formerly a producer, whose compelling films include *Klute* 1971, *The Parallax View* 1974, and *All the President's Men* 1976. His later work includes *Sophie's Choice* 1982 and *Presumed Innocent* 1990.

First I shoot the real situation, then what is funny about the situation, then sometimes I'll get outrageous.

Alan J Pakula

Palamas Kostes 1859–1943. Greek poet. He enriched the Greek vernacular by his use of it as a literary language, particularly in his poetry, such as in *Songs of My Fatherland* 1886 and *The Flute of the King* 1910, which expresses his vivid awareness of Greek history.

Palamedes (Greek 'Contriver') in Greek legend, the inventor of writing. He exposed ◊Odysseus's pretence of madness before the Greek expedition sailed to Troy at the beginning of the Trojan War. In revenge, he was falsely denounced as a traitor by Odysseus and stoned to death by the Greek army.

Palance Jack. Stage name of Walter Jack Palahnuik 1920– . US film actor, often cast as a brooding villain: his films include *Shane* 1953, *Contempt* 1963, and *Batman* 1989. In 1992 he received an Academy Award as best supporting actor in *City Slickers* 1991.

Palestrina Giovanni Pierluigi da 1525–1594. Italian composer of secular and sacred choral music, regarded as the most perfect exponent of Renaissance ◊counterpoint. Apart from motets and madrigals, he also wrote 105 masses, including *Missa Papae Marcelli.*

palette any surface on which paints are mixed and used, generally a portable piece of wood. By extension, the term has come to mean the range of colours favoured by a particular painter.

Paley Grace 1922– . US short-story writer, critic, and political activist. Her stories express Jewish and feminist domestic experience with highly ironic humour, as in *The Little Disturbances of Man* 1960 and *Later the Same Day* 1985.

Palissy Bernard 1510–1589. French potter who made richly coloured rustic pieces, such as dishes with realistic modelled fish and reptiles. He was favoured by the queen, Catherine de' Medici, but was imprisoned in the Bastille as a Huguenot 1588, and died there.

Palladian style of architecture influenced by the work of the great Italian Renaissance architect Andrea Palladio. An early exponent was Inigo ◊Jones, who introduced Palladianism to England in the 1600s. The true Palladian revival, sometimes known as Neo-Palladianism, however, did not begin until the early 18th century when Richard Boyle ◊Burlington and Colen ◊Campbell 'rediscovered' the Palladio–Jones link. Campbell's Mereworth Castle in Kent, 1722–25, is an example of the style. The revival, which spread to Russia and the USA, often involved little more than the re-use of Palladian decorative features.

In Russia the Scottish-born Charles ◊Cameron was the principal exponent of Palladianism, while in the USA the style was adopted by Thomas Jefferson, third president of the United States, who designed his own house, Monticello, 1769, and the University of Virginia, Charlottesville, 1817–26.

Palladio Andrea 1518–1580. Italian Renaissance architect noted for his harmonious and balanced classical structures. He designed numerous palaces and country houses in and around Vicenza, Italy, making use of Roman classical forms, symmetry, and proportion. The Villa Malcontenta and the Villa Rotonda are examples of houses designed from 1540 for patrician families of the Venetian Republic. He also designed churches in Venice and published his studies of classical form in several illustrated books.

His ideas were revived in England in the early 17th century by Inigo Jones and in the 18th century by Lord Burlington and Colen Campbell, and later by architects in Italy, Holland, Germany, Russia, and the USA. Examples of 'Palladian' buildings include Washington's home at Mount Vernon, USA, the palace of Tsarskoe Selo in Russia, and Prior Park, England.

palladium in Greek mythology, an image of the goddess of war and wisdom, Pallas Athena, a gift from Zeus to the city of Troy. According to legend, the city could not be captured while the image remained there. It was stolen by the Greek leaders ◊Odysseus and ◊Diomedes and was later alleged to have been taken to Rome by the Trojan prince ◊Aeneas.

Pallas in Greek mythology, a title of the goddess ◊Athena.

Palma Ricardo 1833–1919. Peruvian writer. Curator of the Peruvian National Library and founder of the Peruvian Academy 1887, he wrote poems and romantic plays but is best known for his *Tradiciones peruanas/Peruvian Traditions*

1872–1910, a series of fanciful sketches of the pageantry and intrigue of colonial Peru drawing on folktale, legend, and gossip as well as historical material.

Palmer Samuel 1805–1881. English landscape painter and etcher. He lived in Shoreham, Kent, 1826–35 with a group of artists who were all followers of William Blake and referred to themselves as 'the Ancients'. Palmer's expressive landscapes have a visionary quality.

Palumbo Peter 1935– . British property developer. Appointed chairman of the Arts Council 1988, he advocated a close partnership between public and private funding of the arts, and a greater role for the regions.

His planned skyscraper by the German architect Mies van der Rohe beside the Mansion House, London, was condemned by Prince Charles as 'a giant glass stump'.

Pan in Greek mythology, the god of flocks and herds (Roman *Sylvanus*), shown as a man with the horns, ears, and hoofed legs of a goat, and playing a shepherd's panpipe (or syrinx).

panchromatic in photography, a term describing highly sensitive black-and-white film made to render all visible spectral colours in correct grey tones. Panchromatic film is always developed in total darkness.

Pandora in Greek mythology, the first mortal woman. Zeus sent her to Earth with a box of evils (to counteract the blessings brought to mortals by ◊Prometheus' gift of fire); she opened the box, and the evils all flew out. Only hope was left inside as a consolation.

Panofsky Erwin 1892–1968. German art historian who lived and worked in the USA from 1931. He pioneered iconography, the study of the meaning of works of art, in such works as *Studies in Iconology* 1939 and *Meaning in the Visual Arts* 1955, and in so doing profoundly influenced the development of art history as a discipline.

panpipes or *syrinx* set of unpierced pipes in cane, clay, or other material, graded by length to provide a scale of pitches. Invented according to legend in ancient Greece by the god Pan, the pipes flourish in the folk music traditions of South America, Eastern Europe, and Japan. They produce a notably pure tone with a breathy onset.

pantheon originally a temple for worshipping all the gods, such as that in ancient Rome, rebuilt by the emperor Hadrian AD to 118 about 128, and still used as a church. In more recent times, the name has been used for a building where famous people are buried (as in the Panthéon, Paris). The Pantheon in Rome has an enormous concrete dome spanning 43.2 m/142 ft.

pantomime in the British theatre, a traditional Christmas entertainment. It has its origins in the harlequin spectacle of the 18th century and burlesque of the 19th century, which gave rise to the tradition of the principal boy being played by an actress and the dame by an actor. The harlequin's role diminished altogether as themes developed on folktales such as 'The Sleeping Beauty' and 'Cinderella', and with the introduction of additional material such as popular songs, topical comedy, and audience participation.

The term 'pantomime' was also applied to Roman dumbshows performed by a masked actor, to 18th-century ballets with mythical themes, and, in 19th-century France, to the wordless Pierrot plays from which modern ◊mime developed.

Panufnik Andrzei 1914–1991. Polish-born composer and conductor. A pupil of the Austrian conductor and composer Felix Weingartner (1863–1942), he came to Britain 1954 and became a British citizen 1961. His music is based on the dramatic interplay of symbolic motifs.

Paolozzi Eduardo 1924– . English sculptor and graphic artist, a major force in the Pop art movement in London in the mid-1950s. In the 1940s he produced collages using images taken from popular magazines. From the 1950s he worked primarily as a sculptor, typically using bronze casts of pieces of machinery to create robotlike structures. *Cyclops* 1957 (Tate Gallery, London) is an example. He also designed the mural decorations for Tottenham Court Road tube station, London, installed 1983–85.

Paphos resort town on the southwest coast of Cyprus. It was the capital of Cyprus in Roman times and the legendary birthplace of the goddess Aphrodite, who rose out of the sea. Archaeological remains include the 2,300-year-old underground 'Tombs of the Kings', a Roman villa, and a 7th-century Byzantine castle.

papier mâché (French 'chewed paper') craft technique that involves building up layer upon layer of pasted paper, which is then baked or left to harden. Used for trays, decorative objects, and even furniture, it is often painted, lacquered, or decorated with mother-of-pearl.

Papp Joseph 1921–1991. US theatre director. He was the founder of the New York Shakespeare Festival 1954 held in an open-air theatre in the city's Central Park. He also founded the New York Public Theater 1967, an off-Broadway forum for new talent, which staged the first productions of the musicals *Hair* 1967 and *A Chorus Line* 1975.

Paradise Lost epic poem in 12 books, by John ◊Milton, first published 1667. The poem describes the Fall of Man and the battle between God and Satan, as enacted through the story of Adam and Eve in the Garden of Eden. A sequel, ***Paradise Regained***, was published 1671 and relates the temptation of Christ in the wilderness.

Paramount Studios US film production and distribution company, founded 1912 as the Famous Players Film Company by Adolph Zukor (1873–1976). In 1914 it merged with the distribution company Paramount Pictures. A major studio from the silent days of cinema, Paramount was adept at discovering new talent and Cecil B de Mille made many of his films for the studio. In 1966 the company was taken over by Gulf and Western Industries. In recent years it has produced such successful films as *Grease* 1978 and *Raiders of the Lost Ark* 1981.

Parcae in Roman mythology, the three ◊Fates; their Greek counterparts are the Moirai.

Pardo Bazán Emilia 1852–1921. Spanish writer, author of more than 20 novels, 600 short stories, and many articles. *Los Pazos de Ulloa/The House of Ulloa* 1886 and its sequel *La madre naturaleza/Mother Nature* 1887, set in her native Galicia, describe the decline of the provincial aristocracy.

Paris in Greek mythology, a prince of Troy whose abduction of Helen, wife of King Menelaus of Sparta, caused the Trojan War. Helen was promised to him by the goddess Aphrodite as a bribe, in his judgement between her beauty and that of two other goddesses, Hera and Athena. Paris killed the Greek hero Achilles by shooting an arrow into his heel, but was himself killed by ◊Philoctetes before the capture of Troy.

Paris, School of (French *Ecole de Paris*) collectively, the various modern art movements that flourished in Paris 1900–40. Among them were ◊Fauvism, ◊Cubism, ◊Surrealism, and ◊Orphism.

Park Merle 1937– . Rhodesian-born English ballerina. She joined the Sadler's Wells Ballet 1954, and by 1959 was a principal soloist with the Royal Ballet. She combined elegance with sympathetic appeal in such roles as Cinderella.

Parker Charlie (Charles Christopher 'Bird', 'Yardbird') 1920–1955. US alto saxophonist and jazz composer, associated with the trumpeter Dizzy Gillespie in developing the ◊bebop style. His skilful improvisations inspired performers on all jazz instruments.

Joining the Earl Hines Orchestra 1942–43 brought him into collaboration with Gillespie, and in their early recordings together ('Salt Peanuts', 'Groovin' High' 1945) bebop began to take shape. Among other Parker compositions are 'Yardbird Suite' and 'Ornithology' (late 1940s). Parker was also very influential as a live performer; primitive bootleg tapes were made by fans, and live albums include *Quintet of the Year* 1953, again with Gillespie.

Parker Dorothy (born Rothschild) 1893–1967. US writer and wit. She reviewed for the magazines *Vanity Fair* and the *New Yorker*, and wrote wittily ironic verses, collected in several volumes including *Not So Deep as a Well* 1936, and short stories.

Inertia rides and riddles me;/ That which is called Philosophy.

Dorothy Parker
Not So Deep as a Well 'The Veteran' 1927

Parkinson Norman. Adopted name of Ronald William Parkinson Smith 1913–1990. English fashion and portrait photographer who caught the essential glamour of each decade from the 1930s to the 1980s. Long associated with the magazines *Vogue* and *Queen*, he was best known for his colour work, and from the late 1960s took many official portraits of the royal family.

Parkman Francis 1823–1893. US historian and traveller who chronicled the European exploration and conquest of North America in such books as *The California and Oregon Trail* 1849 and *La Salle and the Discovery of the Great West* 1878.

parlando in music, singing in a half-speaking manner, often rapidly articulated, used in ◊recitative.

Parliament, Houses of building where the UK legislative assembly meets. The present Houses of Parliament in London, designed in Gothic Revival style by the architects Charles Barry and A W Pugin, were built 1840–60, the previous building having burned down 1834. It incorporates portions of the medieval Palace of Westminster.

The Commons debating chamber was destroyed by incendiary bombs 1941: the rebuilt chamber (opened 1950) is the work of architect Giles Gilbert Scott and preserves its former character.

Parmigianino Francesco 1503–1540. Italian Mannerist painter and etcher, active in Parma and elsewhere. He painted religious subjects and portraits in a graceful, sensual style, with elongated figures, for example *Madonna of the Long Neck* about 1535 (Uffizi, Florence). Parmigianino was the first Italian artist to make original etchings (rather than copies of existing paintings).

Parnassiens, Les school of French poets including Leconte de Lisle, Mallarmé, and Verlaine, which flourished 1866–76. Named after the review *Parnasse Contemporain*, it advocated 'art for art's sake' in opposition to the ideas of the Romantics.

Parnassus mountain in central Greece, revered by the ancient Greeks as the abode of Apollo and the Muses. The sacred site of Delphi lies on its southern flank.

parody in literature and the other arts, a work that imitates the style of another work, usually with mocking or comic intent; it is related to ◊satire.

parquetry geometrical version of ◊marquetry: a decorative veneer applied to furniture and floors, composed of shaped pieces of wood or other suitable materials, such as bone, horn, or ivory, to form a geometrical pattern or mosaic.

Parquetry was first practised in Germany and the Low Countries, it was introduced from there to France in the 17th century, and to England around 1675.

Parry Charles Hubert Hastings 1848–1918. English composer. His works include songs, motets, and the setting of Milton's 'Blest Pair of Sirens' and Blake's 'Jerusalem'.

Parsifal in Germanic mythology, one of the knights who sought the ◊Holy Grail; the father of ◊Lohengrin.

Parthenia (Greek 'Maidenhood') punning title of a collection published 1611 of pieces for the virginals composed by William ◊Byrd, John ◊Bull, and Orlando ◊Gibbons, engraved in standard notation and aimed at a new market of domestic amateur keyboard musicians.

Parthenon temple of Athena Parthenos ('the Virgin') on the Acropolis at Athens; built 447–438 BC by Callicrates and Ictinus under the supervision of the sculptor ◊Phidias, and the most perfect example of Doric architecture. In turn a Christian church and a Turkish mosque, it was then used as a gunpowder store, and reduced to ruins when the Venetians bombarded the Acropolis 1687. The ◊Elgin marbles were removed from the Parthenon in the early 19th century and are now in the British Museum, London.

Partisan Review US intellectual and literary magazine, founded 1934 to express Marxist principles. In the later 1930s it departed from the orthodox line, and committed itself to Modernist literature. During the 1950s the magazine published many of the major writers and critics of the time, including Saul Bellow, Mary McCarthy, and Lionel Trilling, but came to symbolize a conservative academic orthodoxy.

partita in music, a set of classical ◊variations, or more often a ◊suite.

Parton Dolly 1946– . US country and western singer and songwriter. Her combination of sex-symbol looks and intelligent, assertive lyrics made her popular beyond the genre, with hits like 'Jolene' 1974. She has also appeared in films, beginning with *9 to 5* 1980.

pas de deux (French 'step for two') in ballet, a dance for two performers. Codified by Marius ◊Petipa into the *grand pas de deux*, the dance opens with the ballerina and her male partner dancing together. It continues with display solos,

firstly for the man and then the woman, and ends with the two dancing together again.

Pasiphae in Greek mythology, the wife of King Minos of Crete and mother of ◊Phaedra and of the ◊Minotaur, the monstrous offspring of her sexual union with a bull sent from the sea by the god Poseidon.

Pasmore Victor 1908– . English painter, a founder-member of the ◊Euston Road School (which favoured a subdued, measured style) in the 1930s. He painted landscapes and, from 1947, abstract paintings and constructions, reviving the early ideas of the Constructivists.

Pasolini Pier Paolo 1922–1975. Italian film director, poet, and novelist. His early work is coloured by his experience of life in the poor districts of Rome, where he lived from 1950. From his Marxist viewpoint, he illustrates the decadence and inequality of society, set in a world ravaged by violence and sexuality. Among his films are *Il vangelo secondo Mateo/The Gospel According to St Matthew* 1964, *The Decameron* 1970, *I racconti de Canterbury/The Canterbury Tales* 1972, and the notorious *Salò/Salo – The 120 Days of Sodom* 1975, which included explicit scenes of sexual perversion.

Pasolini's writings include the novels *Ragazzi di vita/The Ragazzi* 1955 and *Una vita violenta/A Violent Life* 1959, filmed with success as *Accattone* 1961. He was murdered by a 17-year-old youth.

passacaglia Spanish dance form in three time that evolved into an instrumental form constructed over a ◊ground bass, or cyclically repeating bass line. Dramatic tension is created by the juxtaposition of a developing melody and an unchanging background. An example is Benjamin Britten's disturbing setting of Tennyson's poem 'The Kraken' in *Nocturne* 1958.

Passage to India novel 1924 by E M ◊Forster. The Muslim doctor Aziz and the English teacher Fielding have a friendship which is soured by an incident involving a false accusation by a confused young Englishwoman. Aziz also feels a deep bond with the elderly Englishwoman Mrs Moore, whose death leaves a sense of unfinished mystery. This is the keynote of the book, with its acute insights into the cultural muddles and cross-purposes of the British Raj era.

passepied old French dance in three time, less strict than a minuet, featured in classical opera and the French ◊suite.

passion play play representing the death and resurrection of Jesus, performed on Good Friday throughout medieval Europe. It has its origins in medieval ◊mystery plays. Traditionally, a passion play takes place every ten years at Oberammergau, Germany.

pastel sticklike drawing or painting material consisting of ground pigment bound with gum;

also works produced in this medium. Pastel is a form of painting in dry colours and produces a powdery surface, which is delicate and hard to conserve. Exponents include Rosalba Carriere (1675–1785), La Tour, Chardin, Degas, and Mary Cassatt.

Pasternak Boris Leonidovich 1890–1960. Russian poet and novelist. His novel ◊*Dr Zhivago* 1957 was banned in the USSR as a 'hostile act', and was awarded a Nobel prize (which Pasternak declined). *Dr Zhivago* has since been unbanned and Pasternak has been posthumously rehabilitated.

Born in Moscow, he remained in Russia when his father, the artist Leonid Pasternak (1862–1945), emigrated. His volumes of lyric poems include *A Twin Cloud* 1914 and *On Early Trains* 1943, and he translated Shakespeare's tragedies into Russian.

pastiche a work that imitates another's style, or a medley composed of fragments from an original. The intention is normally homage, rather than ridicule (as in ◊parody).

pastoral a work of art, literature, music or a musical play that depicts the countryside or rural life, often in an idyllic way. Pastoral scenes were popular in classical Greece and Rome (for instance, Virgil's *Eclogues*), and again from the 15th to 18th centuries (for example, ◊Handel's masque *Acis and Galatea* 1718). They were frequently peopled with shepherds and shepherdesses or with mythological figures, such as nymphs and satyrs.

patchwork textile technique used mainly for quilts and bedcovers. Small pieces of fabric, often offcuts, in varying colours and patterns are sewn together by the edges, usually in a geometric pattern, to form one large piece of material. Patchwork fabrics were popular for dresses in the 1960s. The technique is of peasant origin, a way of recycling old fabrics.

Pater Walter (Horatio) 1839–1894. English scholar, essayist, and art critic. He published *Studies in the History of the Renaissance* 1873, which expressed the idea of 'art for art's sake', that influenced the ◊Aesthetic Movement. His other works include the novel *Marius the Epicurean* 1885, in which the solitary hero, living under the Roman imperium of Marcus Aurelius, meditates on beauty, Paganism, and Christianity; *Imaginary Portraits* 1887; and *Appreciations, with an Essay on Style* 1889.

All art constantly aspires towards the condition of music.

Walter Pater *Studies in the History of the Renaissance* 1873

Paterson Banjo (Andrew Barton) 1864–1941. Australian journalist and folk poet. Early acquaintance with drovers, squatters, and even bushrangers in New South Wales gave him material for his famous collection *The Man from Snowy River and Other Verses* 1895. He is best known for the song 'Waltzing Matilda' 1895.

Pathé Charles 1863–1957. French film pioneer who began his career selling projectors 1896 and with the profits formed Pathé Frères with his brothers. In 1901 he embarked on film production and by 1908 had become the world's biggest producer, with branches worldwide. He also developed an early colour process and established a weekly newsreel, *Pathé Journal*. World War I disrupted his enterprises and by 1918 he was gradually forced out of business by foreign competition.

Pather Panchali (English *Song of the Road*) Bengali novel by Bibhuti Bhushan Banerji (1894–1950), published 1929. It was his first major success. Episodic in structure, it offers an authentic portrayal of everyday life seen through the eyes of a small boy and his sister. It was the basis of an award-winning film by Satyajit Ray 1955.

pathetic fallacy in the arts, the attribution of human emotions and characteristics to objects and events. The phrase was coined by John Ruskin in *Modern Painters* 1843–60, who wanted to distinguish between accurate depictions of nature and those distorted by the artist's feelings.

pathos in art and literature, the quality that arouses pity, sadness, or deep sympathy with the viewer or reader. See also ◊bathos.

patina effect produced on bronze by oxidation, which turns the surface green, and by extension any lacquering or finishing technique, other than gilding, applied to bronze objects. Patina can also mean the surface texture of old furniture, silver, and antique objects.

Patinir (also **Patenier** or **Patinier**) Joachim *c.* 1485–1524. Flemish painter of religious works, active in Antwerp, whose visionary landscape backgrounds dwarf his figures. He is known to have worked with Quentin Matsys and to have painted landscape backgrounds for other artists' works.

Patmore Coventry 1823–1896. British poet and critic. As one of the ◊Pre-Raphaelite Brotherhood he published the sequence of poems *The Angel in the House* 1854–63 and the collection of odes *The Unknown Eros* 1877.

Paton Alan 1903–1988. South African writer. His novel *Cry, the Beloved Country* 1948 focused on the tragic consequences of racial inequality in South Africa. Later books include *Land and People of South Africa* 1956 and *The Long View* 1968; *Debbie Go Home* 1961 (short stories); political and social studies; and his autobiography *Towards the Mountain* 1980.

Patou Jean 1880–1936. French clothes designer who opened a fashion house 1919. He was an overnight success, and his swimsuits and innovative designs became popular in the 1920s. He dominated both the couture and the ready-to-wear sectors of the fashion world until his death.

Patterson Harry 1929– . English novelist, born in Newcastle. He has written many thrillers under his own name, including *Dillinger* 1983, as well as under the pseudonym Jack Higgins, including *The Eagle Has Landed* 1975.

Patti Adelina 1843–1919. Anglo-Italian soprano renowned for her performances of Lucia in *Lucia di Lammermoor* and Amina in *La sonnambula*. At the age of 62 she was persuaded out of retirement to make a number of gramophone recordings, thus becoming one of the first opera singers to be recorded.

Paul Elliot Harold 1891–1958. US author. His works include the novel *Indelible* 1922, about two young musicians, and the travel book *The Narrow Street/The Last Time I Saw Paris* 1940.

Paul Les. Adopted name of Lester Polfuss 1915– . US inventor of the solid-body electric guitar in the early 1940s, and a pioneer of recording techniques including overdubbing and electronic echo. The Gibson Les Paul guitar was first marketed 1952 (the first commercial solid-body guitar was made by Leo ◊Fender).

pavane a slow, stately court dance in double time, of Paduan origin, especially popular in Italy and France in the 16th and 17th centuries. Music composed for or derived from the pavane is often coupled with that composed for a ◊galliard. Composers include Dowland and Byrd, more recently Ravel, whose *Pavane pour une infante défunte/Pavane for a Dead Infanta* for piano 1899 was orchestrated 1905.

Pavarotti Luciano 1935– . Italian tenor of impressive dynamic range whose operatic roles have included Rodolfo in *La Bohème*, Cavaradossi in *Tosca*, the Duke of Mantua in *Rigoletto*, and Nemorino in *L'Elisir d'amore*. He gave his first performance in the title role of *Otello* in Chicago, USA, 1991. Pavarotti has done much to popularize opera, performing to wide audiences outside the opera houses including open-air concerts in New York and London city parks.

He collaborated with José Carreras and Placido Domingo in a recording of operatic hits coinciding with the World Cup soccer series in Rome 1990; his rendition of 'Nessun Dorma' from Puccini's *Turandot* was adopted as the theme music for the series.

Pavese Cesare 1908–1950. Italian poet, translator, and novelist. Imprisoned for anti-Fascist journalism, he published his poems *Lavorare stanca/Hard Labour* 1936 on his release. His translations and critical writings introduced Italian readers to modern English and American writers, notably Joyce and Melville, who influenced his fascination with myth, symbol, and archetype. His novel *La luna e i falò/The Moon and the Bonfires* appeared 1950.

Pavlova Anna 1881–1931. Russian dancer. Prima ballerina of the Imperial Ballet from 1906, she left Russia 1913, and went on to become one of the world's most celebrated exponents of classical ballet. With London as her home, she toured extensively with her own company, influencing dancers worldwide with roles such as Mikhail ◊Fokine's *The Dying Swan* solo 1907. She was opposed to the modern reforms of Diaghilev's Ballets Russes, adhering strictly to conservative aesthetics.

As is the case in all branches of art, success depends in a very large measure upon individual initiative and exertion, and cannot be achieved except by dint of hard work.

Anna Pavlova

Pax in Roman mythology, the goddess of peace, equivalent to the Greek ◊Irene.

Paxton Joseph 1801–1865. English architect, garden superintendent to the Duke of Devonshire from 1826 and designer of the Great Exhibition building 1851 (the Crystal Palace), which was revolutionary in its structural use of glass and iron.

Paz Octavio 1914– . Mexican poet and essayist. His works reflect many influences, including Marxism, Surrealism, and Aztec mythology. His long poem *Piedra del sol/Sun Stone* 1957 uses contrasting images, centring upon the Aztec Calendar Stone (representing the Aztec universe), to symbolize the loneliness of individuals and their search for union with others. Nobel Prize for Literature 1990.

Peacock Thomas Love 1785–1866. English satirical novelist and poet. His works include *Headlong Hall* 1816, *Melincourt* 1817, and *Nightmare Abbey* 1818, which has very little plot, consisting almost entirely of conversation. With a prevailing comic tone, the author satirizes contemporary ideas, outlooks, and attitudes.

Marriage may often be a stormy lake, but celibacy is almost always a muddy horse-pond.

Thomas Love Peacock *Melincourt* 1817

Peake Mervyn (Lawrence) 1911–1968. English writer and illustrator, born in China. His novels include the grotesque fantasy trilogy *Titus Groan* 1946, *Gormenghast* 1950, and *Titus Alone* 1959. Among his collections of verse are *The Glassblowers* 1950 and the posthumous *A Book of Nonsense* 1972.

He illustrated most of his own work and produced drawings for an edition of *Treasure Island* 1949, and other works.

Peale Charles Willson 1741–1827. American artist, head of a large family of painters. His portraits of leading figures in the Revolutionary War include the earliest known portrait of George Washington, painted 1772.

Pears Peter 1910–1986. English tenor. He was the life companion of Benjamin ◊Britten and with him co-founded the Aldeburgh Festival. He inspired and collaborated in a rich catalogue of song cycles and operatic roles, exploiting a distinctively airy and luminous tone, from the title role in *Peter Grimes* 1947 to Aschenbach in *Death in Venice* 1973.

Pearse Patrick Henry 1879–1916. Irish poet prominent in the Gaelic revival, a leader of the Easter Rising, an attempt to overthrow British rule in Ireland, 1916. Proclaimed president of the provisional government, he was court-martialled and shot after its suppression.

We may make mistakes and shoot the wrong people, but bloodshed is a cleansing and a sanctifying thing, and the nation which regards it as the final horror has lost its manhood.

Patrick Pearse

Peck (Eldred) Gregory 1916– . US film actor specializing in strong, upright characters. His films include *Spellbound* 1945, *Duel in the Sun* 1946, *Gentleman's Agreement* 1947, *To Kill a Mockingbird* 1962, for which he won an Academy Award, and (cast against type as a Nazi doctor) *The Boys from Brazil* 1974.

Peckinpah Sam 1925–1985. US film director, mainly of Westerns, usually associated with slow-motion, blood-spurting violence. His best films, such as *The Wild Bunch* 1969, exhibit a magisterial grasp of staging and construction.

pedal point in organ music, a bass note of indefinite length, usually at the end of a piece, establishing the final key and over which a performer improvises an elaborately decorated ◊cadence. The term also applies to piano music of a similar kind.

pediment in architecture, the triangular structure crowning the portico of a Classical building. The pediment was a distinctive feature of Greek temples.

Peele George 1558–1597. English dramatist. He wrote a pastoral, *The Arraignment of Paris* 1584; a fantastic comedy, *The Old Wives' Tale* 1595; and a tragedy, *David and Bethsabe* 1599.

Pegasus in Greek mythology, the winged horse that sprang from the blood of the Gorgon Medusa. He was transformed into a constellation. Hippocrene, the spring of the Muses on Mount Helicon, is said to have sprung from a blow of his hoof.

Péguy Charles 1873–1914. French Catholic socialist who established a socialist publishing house in Paris. From 1900 he published on political topics *Les Cahiers de la quinzaine/Fortnightly Notebooks* and on poetry, including *Le Mystère de la charité de Jeanne d'Arc/The Mystery of the Charity of Joan of Arc* 1897.

The classical artist can be recognized by his sincerity, the romantic by his laborious insincerity.

Charles Péguy preface to Jean Hugues'
La Grève

Pei Ieoh Ming 1917– . Chinese-born US Modernist architect, noted for his innovative High Tech structures, particularly the use of glass walls. His projects include the 70-storey Bank of China, Hong Kong, 1987 – Asia's tallest building at 368 m/1,209 ft – and the glass pyramid in front of the Louvre, Paris, 1989.

Pelion mountain in Thessaly, Greece, near Mount Ossa. In Greek mythology it was the home of the centaurs, creatures half-human and half-horse.

Pelops in Greek mythology, the son of Tantalus, brother of Niobe, and father of Atreus and Thyestes. He gave his name to the southern part of mainland Greece, the Peloponnese.

PEN abbreviation for *Poets, Playwrights, Editors, Essayists, Novelists*, a literary association established 1921 by C A ('Sappho') Dawson Scott, to promote international understanding among writers.

penates the household gods of a Roman family; see ◊lares and penates.

pencil drawing instrument made of graphite, encased in wood or another holder. By mixing graphite with clay, the French chemist Nicolas Conté (1755–1805) invented the modern pencil of predetermined hardness 1750 (patented 1795). Capable of a rich range of texture and tone, the graphite (or 'lead') pencil replaced the limited metalpoint (see ◊silverpoint) as a drawing instrument.

Penderecki Krzystof 1933– . Polish composer. His expressionist works, such as the *Threnody for* *the Victims of Hiroshima* 1961 for strings, employ cluster and percussion effects. He later turned to religious subjects and a more orthodox style, as in the *Magnificat* 1974 and the *Polish Requiem* 1980–83. His opera *The Black Mask* 1986 uncovered a new vein of surreal humour.

Penelope in Greek mythology, the wife of Odysseus, the king of Ithaca; their son was Telemachus. While Odysseus was absent at the siege of Troy she kept her many suitors at bay by asking them to wait until she had woven a shroud for her father-in-law, but unravelled her work each night. When Odysseus returned, after 20 years, he and Telemachus killed her suitors.

Penn Irving 1917– . US fashion, advertising, portrait, editorial, and fine art photographer. In 1948 he made the first of many journeys to Africa and the Far East, resulting in a series of portrait photographs of local people, avoiding sophisticated technique. He was associated for many years with *Vogue* magazine in the USA.

Penthesilea in Greek mythology, daughter of Ares the god of war, queen of the ◊Amazons, and ally of the Trojans in the war against the Greeks. She was killed by the Greek warrior Achilles, who mourned her death, and she appears with him as a subject in Greek art, and in a play by the German dramatist Heinrich ◊Kleist.

Pentheus in Greek mythology, king of Thebes and grandson of the founder of the city, Cadmus. Opposed to the worship of Dionysus, the god of wine, he was destroyed by the god and his followers. His story is the subject of the Greek playwright Euripides' tragedy *The Bacchae*.

Pepusch Johann Christoph 1667–1752. German composer who settled in England about 1700. He contributed to John Gay's ballad operas *The Beggar's Opera* and *Polly*.

Pepys Samuel 1633–1703. English diarist. His diary 1659–69 was a unique record of both the daily life of the period and his own intimate feelings. Written in shorthand, it was not deciphered until 1825. Pepys was imprisoned 1679 in the Tower of London on suspicion of treason.

Pepys was born in London, entered the Navy Office 1660, and was secretary to the Admiralty 1672–79, publishing *Memoires of the Navy* 1690.

Strange to see how a good dinner and feasting reconciles everybody.

Samuel Pepys *Diary* Nov 9 1665

Perahia Murray 1947– . US pianist and conductor, noted for urbane interpretations of Chopin, Schumann, and Mendelssohn. He has recorded all of the Mozart piano concertos with the English Chamber Orchestra, conducting from the keyboard.

percussion instrument musical instrument played by being struck with the hand or a beater. Percussion instruments can be divided into those that can be tuned to produce a sound of definite pitch, such as the timpani, tubular bells, glockenspiel, and xylophone, and those of indefinite pitch, including bass drum, tambourine, triangle, cymbals, and castanets.

The *timpano* is a hemispherical bowl of metal with a membrane stretched across the rim, affixed and tuned by screwtaps; *tubular bells* are suspended on a frame; the *glockenspiel* (German 'bell play') is a small keyboard of aluminium alloy keys; the *xylophone* has hardwood rather than metal bars.

The *snare drum* is a shallow double-sided drum on the underside of which gut coils or metal springs are secured by a clamp and rattle against the underside when the drum is beaten, while the *bass drum* produces the lowest sound in the orchestra; the *tambourine* has a wooden hoop with a membrane stretched across it, and has metal discs suspended in the rim; a *triangle* is formed from a suspended triangular-shaped steel bar, played by striking it with a separate bar of steel – the sound produced can by clearly perceived even when played against a full orchestra; *cymbals* are two brass dishes struck together; *castanets* are two hollow shells of wood struck together; and the *gong* is a suspended disc of metal struck with a soft hammer.

Percy Thomas 1729–1811. English scholar and bishop of Dromore from 1782. He discovered a manuscript collection of songs, ballads, and romances, from which he published a selection as *Reliques of Ancient English Poetry* 1765, which was influential in the Romantic revival.

Perelman S(idney) J(oseph) 1904–1979. US humorist. His work was often published in the *New Yorker* magazine, and he wrote film scripts for the Marx Brothers. He shared an Academy Award for the script of *Around the World in 80 Days* 1956.

Pérez Galdós Benito 1843–1920. Spanish novelist, born in the Canary Islands. His works include the 46 historical novels in the cycle *Episodios nacionales* and the 21-novel cycle *Novelas españolas contemporáneas*, which includes *Doña Perfecta* 1876 and the epic *Fortunata y Jacinta* 1886–87, his masterpiece. In scale he has been compared to the French writer Honoré de Balzac and the English novelist Charles Dickens.

performance art staged artistic event, sometimes including music, painting, and sculpture. During the 20th century performance has played a part in several artistic movements, in particular Futurism, Dada, and the Bauhaus. Performance art flourished in the 1960s in ◊happenings, body art, and ◊Conceptual art, and since then has largely been absorbed by pop music.

perfume fragrant essence used to scent the body, cosmetics, and candles. More than 100 natural aromatic chemicals may be blended from a range of 60,000 flowers, leaves, fruits, seeds, woods, barks, resins, and roots, combined by natural animal fixatives and various synthetics. Favoured ingredients include balsam, civet (from the African civet cat) hyacinth, jasmine, lily of the valley, musk (from the musk deer), orange blossom, rose, and tuberose.

peri in Persian myth, a beautiful, harmless being, ranking between angels and evil spirits. Peris were ruled by Eblis, the greatest of evil spirits.

Peri Jacopo 1561–1633. Italian composer who served the Medici family, the rulers of Florence. His experimental melodic opera *Euridice* 1600 established the opera form and influenced Monteverdi. His first opera, *Dafne* 1597, is now lost.

peristyle in architecture, a range of columns surrounding a building or open courtyard.

Perkins Anthony 1932–1992. US film actor who played the mother-fixated psychopath Norman Bates in Alfred Hitchcock's *Psycho* 1960 and *Psycho II* 1982. He played shy but subtle roles in *Friendly Persuasion* 1956, *The Trial* 1962, and *The Champagne Murders* 1967. He also appeared on the stage in London and New York.

Pérotin the Great (Perotinus Magnus) c. 1160–c. 1220. French composer. His church music has a timeless resonance and introduced new concepts of harmony and expression to traditional organum (early medieval harmony).

Perpendicular period of English Gothic architecture lasting from the end of the 14th century to the mid-16th century. It is characterized by window tracery consisting chiefly of vertical members, two or four arc arches, lavishly decorated vaults, and the use of traceried panels. Examples include the choir, transepts, and cloister of Gloucester Cathedral, about 1331–1412, and King's College Chapel, Cambridge, built in three phases 1446–61, 1477–85, and 1508–15.

Perrault Charles 1628–1703. French author of the fairy tale collection *Contes de ma mère l'oye/Mother Goose's Fairy Tales* 1697, which includes 'The Sleeping Beauty', 'Little Red Riding Hood', 'Blue Beard', 'Puss in Boots', and 'Cinderella'.

Perret Auguste 1874–1954. French architect, a pioneer in the use of ◊reinforced concrete. Noted for the exposed concrete frames of his buildings, his most developed work is the church of Notre Dame de Raincy 1922–23.

Perse Saint-John. Pen name of Alexis Saint-Léger 1887–1975. French poet and diplomat, a US citizen from 1940. His first book of verse, *Eloges* 1911, reflects the ambience of the West Indies, where he was born and raised. His later works include *Anabase* 1924, an epic poem translated by T S Eliot 1930. He was awarded a Nobel prize 1960.

Entering the foreign service 1914, he was secretary general 1933–40. He then emigrated permanently to the USA, and was deprived of French citizenship by the Vichy government.

It is enough for the poet to be the bad conscience of his time.

Saint-John Perse letter Dec 1941

Persephone in Greek mythology, a goddess (Roman Proserpina), the daughter of Zeus and Demeter, and queen of the underworld. She was carried off to the underworld as the bride of Pluto, who later agreed that she should spend six months of the year above ground with her mother. The myth symbolizes the growth and decay of vegetation and the changing seasons.

Perseus in Greek mythology, son of Zeus and Danaë. He slew the Gorgon Medusa and cut off her head – the reflection in his shield enabling him to approach her without being turned to stone. He then rescued and married ◊Andromeda, and became king of Tiryns, using the Gorgon's head, set on his shield, to turn the tyrant Polydectes to stone.

Persian art the arts of Persia (now Iran) from the 6th century BC. Subject to invasions from both East and West, Persia over the centuries blended many influences to create a rich diversity of arts, styles, and techniques.

Though Persia has been a centre of civilization for at least 7,000 years, it was during the *Achaemenid dynasty* (550–333 BC), when the first Persian empire was formed, that a unified style emerged, drawing on a wide range of influences. The palace at Persepolis, begun by Darius I and completed by Xerxes, was decorated about 520 with relief friezes recalling Assyrian and Babylonian styles. The period also produced work in gold and silver, bronze castings, and inlay.

The conquest of Persia by Alexander the Great in the 4th century BC brought about a blending of Persian and Hellenistic styles, seen for example in the bronzes, pottery, and jewellery of the Parthians. The *Sassanid dynasty* (AD 224–642) was the richest period of artistic achievement, developing to the full a wide range of new and inherited styles and techniques. The Sassanians introduced silk to Persia; they produced exquisite jewellery, metalwork in silver, gold, and bronze, and ceramics; and they decorated their palaces with relief sculptures and mosaics. The innovative domes and arches they developed were to have a profound influence on Islamic architecture.

After the Muslim invasion of the 7th century, Persia was brought within the sphere of Islamic styles and techniques, clearly reflected in the ceramics and ornate calligraphy which developed. During the Mongol **Timurid dynasty** (1369–1506) Chinese influences were seen in the development of one of Persia's greatest artistic achievements, the miniature, which was used to illustrate books of poetry, history, and romances. By the 15th century a distinctively Persian style had evolved, characterized by firm lines, strong colours, and a lot of detail; its greatest exponent was ◊Bihzad. The Timurid dynasty also saw the use of coloured tiles to cover buildings, for example on the Blue Mosque of Tabriz.

The **Safavid dynasty** (1502–1736) produced miniatures, which now began to show the influence of Western styles; fine carpets (many of the finest Persian carpets are Safavid); fabrics, particularly silk; and metalwork. Palaces were decorated with murals. The Safavid dynasty marked the beginning of Persia's artistic decline, as European influences grew stronger.

Persian literature before the Arab conquest Persian literature is represented by the sacred books of the pre-Islamic Persian religion of Zoroastrianism known as the *Avesta* and later translated into Pahlavi, in which language there also appeared various secular writings. After the conquest the use of Arabic became widespread. The Persian language was revived during the 9th century, and the following centuries saw a succession of brilliant poets, including the epic writer Firdawsi, the didactic S'adi (1184–1291), the mystic Rumi (1207–1273), the lyrical Hâfiz, and Jami, who combined the gifts of his predecessors and is considered the last of the classical poets. Omar Khayyám, who is well known outside Iran, is considered less important there. In the 16th and 17th centuries many Persian writers worked in India, still using classical forms and themes.

The introduction of the printing-press in the 19th century made possible a new newspaper culture, although hampered by censorship and limited readership, through which much literary work was published. Histories and translations soon followed, in a prose increasingly open to Western influences. Persian poetry, strongly traditional, blending classical courtly idiom with popular ballad and lampoon, was widely diffused among an only partly literate audience which discouraged the development of new forms despite the cautious innovations of Nīmā-yi Yūshīj (1895–1959). The alienation and isolation of the poet who has broken with tradition were poignantly expressed by the poetess and film-maker Furūgh Farrukhzād (1935–1967). Since the 1930s realist fiction has become established. After the Iranian revolution of 1979 some important works such as Shusha Guppy's autobiographical *The Blindfold Horse* 1988 were written and published abroad.

Perugino Pietro. Adopted name of Pietro Vannucci *c.* 1446–1523. Italian painter, active chiefly in Perugia. He taught Raphael who absorbed his graceful figure style. Perugino produced paintings for the lower walls of the Sistine Chapel of the Vatican 1481 and in 1500 decorated the Sala del Cambio in Perugia.

Peruzzi Baldassare 1481–1536. Sienese High Renaissance architect whose most important buildings are found in Rome. His first significant work is the Villa Farnesina 1509–11, inspired by Raphael and yet more delicately decorative. He succeeded Raphael as architect to St Peters 1520, but returned to Siena 1527, after the Sack of Rome, where he worked with Antonio da ◊Sangallo the Younger on the Villa Caprarola 1530. His final work, the Palazzo Massimo alle Colonne, Rome 1532–36, reflects in its unorthodoxy a move away from Renaissance Classicism towards ◊Mannerism.

Pessoa Fernando 1888–1935. Portuguese poet. Born in Lisbon, he was brought up in South Africa and was bilingual in English and Portuguese. His verse is considered to be the finest written in Portuguese this century. He wrote under three assumed names, which he called 'heteronyms' – Alvaro de Campos, Ricardo Reis, and Alberto Caeiro – for each of which he invented a biography.

Peter Pan or ***The Boy Who Wouldn't Grow Up*** play for children by James ◊Barrie, first performed 1904. Peter Pan, an orphan with magical powers, arrives in the night nursery of the Darling children, Wendy, John, and Michael. He teaches them to fly and introduces them to the Never Never Land inhabited by fantastic characters, including the fairy Tinkerbell, the Lost Boys, and the pirate Captain Hook. The play was followed by a story, *Peter Pan in Kensington Gardens* 1906, and a book of the play 1911.

Peter Rabbit full title ***The Tale of Peter Rabbit*** first of the children's stories written and illustrated by English author Beatrix ◊Potter, published 1900.

Petipa Marius 1818–1910. French choreographer who created some of the most important ballets in the classical repertory. For the Imperial Ballet in Russia he created masterpieces such as *Don Quixote* 1869, *La Bayadère* 1877, *The Sleeping Beauty* 1890, *Swan Lake* 1895 (with Ivanov), and *Raymonda* 1898.

He emigrated to St Petersburg 1847, becoming ballet master of the Imperial Ballet 1862. His ballets were grand, evening-length works complete with exotic costumes and richly decorated sets. A feature of Petipa's ballets were the ◊divertissements that brought the often thin storyline to a halt to allow the soloists a chance to display their virtuosity. These were contrasted with the shifting patterns and formations of the corps de ballet.

petit point or *tent stitch* short, slanting embroidery stitch used on open-net canvas for upholstery and cushions to form a solid background. Petit point embroidery was common in the 18th century.

Petöfi Sándor 1823–1849. Hungarian nationalist poet. He published his first volume of poems 1844. He expressed his revolutionary ideas in the semi-autobiographical poem 'The Apostle', and died fighting the Austrians in the battle of Segesvár.

Petrarch (Italian *Petrarca*) Francesco 1304–1374. Italian poet, born in Arezzo, a devotee of the Classical tradition. His *Il Canzoniere* is composed of sonnets in praise of his idealized love, 'Laura', whom he first saw 1327 (she was a married woman and refused to become his mistress). The dialogue *Secretum meum/My Secret* is a spiritual autobiography.

From 1337 he often stayed in secluded study at his home at Vaucluse, near Avignon, then the residence of the popes. Petrarch, eager to restore the glories of Rome, wanted to return the papacy there. He was a friend of the poet Boccaccio, and supported the political reformer Cola di Rienzi's attempt to establish a republic 1347.

I have seen pride in others, but not in myself; and though I have been a man of slight value, in my own judgement my value has been still more slight.

Petrarch Letter to Posterity

Petronius Gaius, known as *Petronius Arbiter*, died *c.* AD 66. Latin author of the licentious romance *Satyricon*. He was a companion of the emperor Nero and supervisor of his pleasures.

petticoat undergarment worn as an underskirt beneath a skirt or dress. It is generally made of silk, satin, or synthetic fibres.

Derived from an old French term *petit cote*, a petticoat was originally a man's undershirt but by the Middle Ages it had become a woman's padded undercoat. As the undercoat was replaced by the ◊chemise, the petticoat became an underskirt that was tied round the waist with ribbons or tapes. The popularity of the petticoat has declined during the 20th century although it was briefly popularized by Ralph ◊Lauren in the 1970s and later by Vivienne ◊Westwood with her 'Buffalo Girl' designs.

Pevsner Antoine 1886–1962. Russian-born sculptor and painter, a French citizen from 1930. A pioneer of Russian ◊Constructivism, his work was entirely abstract but distinguished by the mathematical precision of its spiralling curves and planes, as in *Developable Column* 1942 (Museum of Modern Art, New York). Like his brother Naum ◊Gabo, he worked with celluloid and wire, but also copper, brass sheet, and bronze.

Pevsner Nikolaus 1902–1983. Anglo-German art historian. Born in Leipzig, he fled from the Nazis to England. He became an authority on architecture, especially English. His *Outline of European Architecture* was published 1942 (followed by numerous other editions). In his series *The Buildings of England* (46 volumes) 1951–74, he built up a first-hand report on every notable building in the country.

What distinguishes architecture from painting and sculpture is its spatial quality. In this, and only in this, no other artist can emulate the architect.

Nikolaus Pevsner
An Outline of European Architecture 1942

Phaedra in Greek mythology, a Cretan, daughter of Minos and Pasiphae, married to Theseus of Athens. Her adulterous passion for her stepson, Hippolytus, led to her death. The story is told in plays by Euripides, Seneca, and Racine.

Phèdre tragedy by Jean ◊Racine 1677. Adapted from the tragedy *Hippolytus* by Euripides, the play dramatizes the passion of Phaedra, wife of Theseus, king of Athens, for her stepson, Hippolytus, who is in love with Aricia. Believing Theseus dead, Phaedra declares her love to Hippolytus, but then accuses him of assault when Theseus returns. Hippolytus dies as the result of his father's curse, and Phaedra commits suicide.

Phaedrus *c.* 15 BC–*c.* AD 50. Latin fable writer, born a slave in Macedonia and later freed by Emperor Augustus. The allusions in his fables (modelled on those of Aesop) caused him to be brought to trial by a minister of Emperor Tiberius. His work was popular in the Middle Ages.

Who to mankind will not adapt himself,/ For his disdain must pay the penalty.

Phaedrus *Fables*

Phaethon in Greek mythology, the son of Helios, the sun god, who was allowed for one day to drive the chariot of the Sun. Losing control of the horses, he almost set the Earth on fire and was killed by Zeus with a thunderbolt.

Pharos of Alexandria in antiquity, a gigantic lighthouse at the entrance to the harbour of Alexandria, considered one of the ◊Seven Wonders of the World. It was built in the early 3rd century BC by the Macedonian kings of

Egypt, Ptolemy I and Ptolemy II, and took its name from the island on which it stood.

The lighthouse was repeatedly damaged by earthquakes, and any remains of the ancient structure are now concealed under the medieval fortress of Kait Bey.

Phidias or *Pheidias* mid-5th century BC. Greek sculptor, active in Athens. He supervised the sculptural programme for the Parthenon (most of it is preserved in the British Museum, London, and known as the ◊Elgin marbles). He also executed the colossal statue of Zeus at Olympia, one of the ◊Seven Wonders of the World. He was a friend of the political leader Pericles, who made him superintendent of public works in Athens.

Philharmonic Society group of people organized for the advancement of music; the term is derived from Greek 'love of harmony'. The Royal Philharmonic Society was founded in London 1813 by the pianist Johann Baptist Cramer (1771–1858) for the purpose of improving musical standards by means of orchestral concerts organized on a subscription basis. Another Philharmonic Society was founded in New York 1842.

Phillips Jayne Anne 1952– . US writer. Her first novel *Machine Dreams* 1984 dealt vividly with the impact of the Vietnam War on small-town America. Other works include the short-story collection *Fast Lanes* 1987.

Philoctetes in Greek mythology, a hero in the Trojan War who killed the Trojan prince Paris.

Phiz pseudonym of Hablot Knight Browne 1815–1882. English artist who illustrated the greater part of the *Pickwick Papers* and other works by Charles Dickens.

phoenix mythical Egyptian bird that burned itself to death on a pyre every 500 years and rose rejuvenated from the ashes.

photogram picture produced on photographic material by exposing it to light, but without using a camera.

photography process for reproducing images on sensitized materials by various forms of radiant energy, including visible light, ultraviolet, infrared, X-rays, atomic radiations, and electron beams. Photography was developed in the 19th century; among the pioneers were L J M ◊Daguerre in France and ◊Fox Talbot in the UK. Colour photography dates from the early 20th century.

The most familiar photographic process depends upon the fact that certain silver compounds (called halides) are sensitive to light. A photographic film is coated with these compounds and, in a camera, is exposed to light. An image, or picture, of the scene before the camera is formed on the film because the silver halides become activated (light-altered) where light falls but not where light does not fall. The image is made visible by the process of ◊developing, made permanent by fixing, and, finally, is usually printed on paper. Motion-picture photography uses a camera that exposes a roll of film to a rapid succession of views that, when developed, are projected in equally rapid succession to provide a moving image.

photography: chronology

1515	Leonardo da Vinci described the camera obscura.
1750	The painter Canaletto used a camera obscura as an aid to his painting in Venice.
1790	Thomas Wedgwood in England made photograms – placing objects on leather, sensitized using silver nitrate.
1826	Nicephore Niépce (1765–1833), a French doctor, produced the world's first photograph from nature on pewter plates with a camera obscura and an eight-hour exposure.
1835	Niépce and L J M Daguerre produced the first Daguerreotype camera photograph.
1839	Daguerre was awarded an annuity by the French government and his process given to the world.
1840	Invention of the Petzval lens, which reduced exposure time by 90%. Herschel discovered sodium thiosulphate as a fixer for silver halides.
1841	Fox Talbot's calotype process was patented – the first multicopy method of photography using a negative/positive process, sensitized with silver iodide.
1844–46	Fox Talbot published the first photographic book, *The Pencil of Nature*.
1845	Hill and Adamson began to use calotypes for portraits in Edinburgh.
1851	Fox Talbot used a one-thousandth of a second exposure to demonstrate high-speed photography. Invention of the wet-collodion-on-glass process and the waxed-paper negative. Photographs were displayed at the Great Exhibition in London.
1852	The London Society of Arts exhibited 779 photographs.
1855	Roger Fenton made documentary photographs of the Crimean War from a specially constructed caravan with portable darkroom.
1858	Nadar took the first aerial photographs from a balloon.
1859	Nadar in Paris made photographs underground using battery-powered arc lights.
1860	Queen Victoria was photographed by Mayall. Abraham Lincoln was photographed by Matthew Brady for political campaigning.
1861	The single-lens reflex plate camera was patented by Thomas Sutton. The principles of three-colour photography were demonstrated by Scottish physicist James Clerk Maxwell.
1870	Julia Margaret Cameron used long lenses for her distinctive portraits.

(cont.)

photography: chronology (*cont.*)

1871	Gelatin-silver bromide was developed.
1878	In the USA Eadweard Muybridge analysed the movements of animals through sequential photographs, using a series of cameras.
1879	The photogravure process was invented.
1880	A silver bromide emulsion was fixed with hypo. Photographs were first reproduced in newspapers in New York using the half-tone engraving process. The first twin-lens reflex camera was produced in London. Gelatin-silver chloride paper was introduced.
1884	George Eastman produced flexible negative film.
1889	The Eastman Company in the USA produced the Kodak No 1 camera and roll film, facilitating universal, hand-held snapshots.
1891	The first telephoto lens. The interference process of colour photography was developed by the French doctor Gabriel Lippmann.
1897	The first issue of Alfred Stieglitz's *Camera Notes* in the USA.
1902	In Germany, Deckel invented a prototype leaf shutter and Zeiss introduced the Tessar lens.
1904	The autochrome colour process was patented by the Lumière brothers.
1905	Alfred Stieglitz opened the gallery '291' in New York promoting photography. Lewis Hine used photography to expose the exploitation of children in American factories, causing protective laws to be passed.
1907	The autochrome process began to be factory-produced.
1914	Oskar Barnack designed a prototype Leica camera for Leitz in Germany.
1924	Leitz launched the first 35mm camera, the Leica, delayed because of World War I. It became very popular with photojournalists because it was quiet, small, dependable, and had a range of lenses and accessories.
1929	Rolleiflex produced a twin-lens reflex camera in Germany.
1935	In the USA, Mannes and Godowsky invented Kodachrome transparency film, which produced sharp images and rich colour quality. Electronic flash was invented in the USA.
1936	*Life* magazine, significant for its photojournalism, was first published in the USA.
1938	*Picture Post* magazine was introduced in the UK.
1940	Multigrade enlarging paper by Ilford was made available in the UK.
1942	Kodacolour negative film was introduced.
1945	The zone system of exposure estimation was published in the book *Exposure Record* by Ansel Adams.
1947	Polaroid black-and-white instant process film was invented by Dr Edwin Land, who set up the Polaroid corpora-poration in Boston, Massachusetts. The principles of holography were demonstrated in England by Dennis Gabor.
1955	Kodak introduced Tri-X, a black-and-white 200 ASA film.
1959	The zoom lens was invented by the Austrian firm of Voigtlander.
1960	The laser was invented in the USA, making holography possible. Polacolor, a self-processing colour film, was introduced by Polaroid, using a 60-second colour film and dye diffusion technique.
1963	Cibachrome, paper and chemicals for printing directly from transparencies, was made available by Ciba-Geigy of Switzerland. One of the most permanent processes, it is marketed by Ilford in the UK.
1966	The International Center of Photography was established in New York.
1969	Photographs were taken on the Moon by US astronauts.
1970	A charge-coupled device was invented at Bell Laboratories in New Jersey, USA, to record very faint images (for example in astronomy). Rencontres Internationales de la Photographie, the annual summer festival of photography with workshops, was founded in Arles, France.
1971	Opening of the Photographers' Gallery, London, and the Photo Archive of the Bibliothèque Nationale, Paris.
1972	The SX70 system, a single-lens reflex camera with instant prints, was produced by Polaroid.
1975	The Center for Creative Photography was established at the University of Arizona.
1980	Ansel Adams sold an original print, *Moonrise: Hernandez*, for $45,000, a record price, in the USA. *Voyager 1* sent photographs of Saturn back to Earth across space.
1983	The National Museum of Photography, Film and Television opened in Bradford, England.
1985	The Minolta Corporation in Japan introduced the Minolta 7000 – the world's first body-integral autofocus single-lens reflex camera.
1988	The electronic camera, which stores pictures on magnetic disc instead of on film, was introduced in Japan.
1990	Kodak introduced PhotoCD which converts 35mm camera pictures (on film) into digital form and stores them on compact disc (CD) for viewing on TV.
1992	The Japanese company Canon introduced a camera with autofocus controlled by the user's eye. The camera focuses on whatever the user is looking at. 'Girl with a Leica' by Russian photographer Aleksandr Rodchenko sold for £115,500 at Christie's, London – a world-record price for a photograph.

The virtue of the camera is not the power it has to transform the photographer into an artist, but the impulse it gives him to keep on looking.

Brooks Anderson on photography,
Once Around the Sun

Photorealism or *Superrealism*, or *Hyperrealism* style of painting and sculpture popular in the late 1960s and 1970s, especially in the USA, characterized by intense, photographic realism and attention to minute detail. The Photorealists' aim was to create a record of peoples, places, and objects that was dispassionate to the extent of being almost surreal. Leading exponents were US painters Chuck Close

(1940–) and Richard Estes (1936–) and US sculptor Duane Hanson (1925–).

Phyfe Duncan c. 1768–1854. Scottish-born US furniture-maker. Establishing his own workshop in New York City 1792, he gained a national reputation. Although derived from earlier English and Graeco-Roman designs, the Phyfe style was distinctive in its simplicity of line with elaborate ornamentation and carving. In 1837 he reorganized his firm as Duncan Phyfe and Sons.

Piacentini Marcello 1881–1960. Italian architect who worked closely with the Fascist regime, carrying out numerous official commissions in a grandiose Neo-Classical style. Among them were the Hotel Ambasciatori, Rome, 1926, and the Via della Consiliazione, Rome, 1932. Between 1937 and 1942 he assisted in the planning of Mussolini's satellite town EUR (Exposizione Universale di Roma) near Rome.

Piaf Edith. Stage name of Edith Gassion 1915–1963. French singer and songwriter, a cabaret singer in Paris from the late 1930s. She is remembered for the defiant song 'Je ne regrette rien/I Regret Nothing' and 'La Vie en rose' 1946.

piano or *pianoforte* (originally *fortepiano*) stringed musical instrument, played by felt-covered hammers activated from a keyboard, and capable of dynamic gradation between soft (piano) and loud (forte) tone, hence its name. The first piano was constructed 1704 and introduced 1709 by Bartolommeo Cristofori, a harpsichord-maker of Padua. It uses a clever mechanism to make the keyboard touch-sensitive. Extensively developed during the 18th century, the piano attracted admiration among many composers, although it was not until 1768 that Bach gave one of the first public recitals on the instrument.

Further improvements in the keyboard action and tone by makers such as Broadwood, Erard, and Graf, together with a rapid expansion of published music by Haydn, Beethoven, Schubert, and others, led to the development of the powerfully resonant concert grand piano and the mass production of smaller upright pianos for the home.

Piano Renzo 1937– . Italian High Tech architect who designed (with Richard Rogers) the Pompidou Centre, Paris, 1970–77. Among his other buildings are Kansai Airport, Osaka, Japan and a sports stadium in Bari, Italy, 1989, both employing new materials and making imaginative use of civil-engineering techniques.

Pianola trademark for a type of ◊player piano.

piano nobile the main floor of a house (usually the first floor), containing the main reception room.

Picabia Francis 1879–1953. French painter, a Cubist from 1909. On his second visit to New York, 1915–16, he joined with Marcel Duchamp in the Dadaist revolt and later took the movement to Barcelona. He was also associated with the Surrealists for a time. His work, which appears in many styles, is generally provocative, anarchic, and experimental.

picaresque (Spanish *pícaro* 'rogue') genre of novel that takes a rogue or villain for its central character, telling his or her story in episodic form. The genre originated in Spain and was popular in the 18th century in Britain. Daniel Defoe's *Moll Flanders*, Tobias Smollett's *Roderick Random*, Henry Fielding's *Tom Jones*, and Mark Twain's *Huckleberry Finn* are typical picaresque novels. The device of using an outsider gave the author the opportunity to give fresh moral insights into society.

Picasso Pablo Ruiz y 1881–1973. Spanish artist, active chiefly in France, one of the most inventive and prolific talents in 20th-century art. His Blue Period 1901–04 and Rose Period 1905–06 preceded the revolutionary *Les Demoiselles d'Avignon* 1907 (Museum of Modern Art, New York), which paved the way for Cubism. In the early 1920s he was considered a leader of the Surrealist movement. In the 1930s his work included metal sculpture, book illustration, and the mural ◊*Guernica* 1937 (Prado, Madrid), a comment on the bombing of civilians in the Spanish Civil War. He continued to paint into his eighties.

Picasso was born in Málaga, son of an art teacher, José Ruiz Blasco, and an Andalusian mother, Maria Picasso López; he stopped using the name Ruiz 1898. He was a precocious artist by the age of 10, and at 16 was holding his first exhibition. In 1900 he made an initial visit to Paris, where he was to settle. From 1946 he lived mainly in the south of France where, in addition to painting, he experimented with ceramics, sculpture, sets for ballet (for example *Parade* 1917 for Diaghilev), book illustrations (such as Ovid's *Metamorphoses*), and portraits (Stravinsky, Valéry, and others).

Art is a lie that makes us realize the truth.

Pablo Picasso Sept 1958

---

piccolo woodwind instrument, the smallest member of the ◊flute family, for which Vivaldi composed three concertos. Used adjectivally, 'piccolo' is also an alternative term for ◊sopranino.

Pickett Wilson 1941– . US soul singer with a punchy, confident delivery whose first big hit was 'In the Midnight Hour' 1965. Other pop and rhythm-and-blues hits were 'Land of 1,000 Dances' 1966, 'Mustang Sally' 1967, and 'Don't Let the Green Grass Fool You' 1971.

Pickford Mary. Stage name of Gladys Mary Smith 1893–1979. Canadian-born US actress. The first star of the silent screen, she was known as 'America's Sweetheart', and played innocent ingenue roles into her thirties. In 1919 she formed United Artists with Charlie Chaplin, D W Griffith, and her second husband (1920–35) Douglas Fairbanks.

Her films include *Rebecca of Sunnybrook Farm* 1917, *Pollyanna* 1920, *Little Lord Fauntleroy* 1921, and *Coquette* 1929, her first talkie (Academy Award). She was presented with a special Academy Award 1976.

Pictorialism movement in photography at the end of the 19th century and in the early 20th century which stressed the aesthetic qualities of photography in an attempt to establish it as an art form and not just a mechanical process.

The photographic image was usually manipulated during the developing process in order to heighten its atmospheric and emotional impact. Pictorialism imitated the prevailing styles in painting: the soft focus coming from Impressionism and the tendency for strong design and abstract patterning coming from Art Nouveau and Symbolism. Exponents included Robert ◊Demachy, Edward ◊Steichen, Alfred ◊Stieglitz, and Alvin ◊Coburn.

Picture of Dorian Gray, The novel 1891 by Oscar ◊Wilde. An artist paints a portrait of Dorian Gray, a young man described as flawless in beauty and character. Over the years the portrait ages, showing signs of Gray's debaucheries, while Gray himself stays forever young and angelic. Although melodramatic in plot and lush in descriptive style, the story contains much of Wilde's paradoxical wit in its dialogue.

There is no such thing as a moral or an immoral book. Books are well written or badly written. That is all.

Oscar Wilde preface to
The Picture of Dorian Gray

Pierce Webb 1926–1991. US country singer and songwriter who developed the honky-tonk style and enjoyed two decades of hit records in the US country-music charts. He was one of the first artists to have a pedal-steel guitar on his own recordings (inconspicuous on his debut 'Wondering' 1952, strongly featured on 'Slowly' 1954), an instrument that later became almost ubiquitous in country music. Other hits by Pierce and his band, the Wandering Boys, included 'Back Street Affair' 1952, 'There Stands the Glass' 1953 (both written by Pierce), and 'In the Jailhouse Now' 1955.

Piercy Marge 1937– . US poet and novelist. Her fiction looks at the fringes of American social life and the world of the liberated woman. Her novels include *Small Changes* 1972, the utopian *Woman on the Edge of Time* 1979, *Fly Away Home* 1984, a war novel *Gone to Soldiers* 1987, and *Summer People* 1989.

Pierné (Henri Constant) Gabriel 1863–1937. French composer and conductor, born in Metz. He succeeded César ◊Franck as organist to the church of Ste Clothilde, Paris, and conducted the Colonne Orchestra from 1903. His numerous ballets include *Cydalise et le chèvre-pied/Cydalise and the Satyr* 1923, containing 'Entry of the Little Fauns'.

Piero della Francesca c. 1420–1492. Italian painter, active in Arezzo and Urbino; one of the major artists of the 15th century. His work has a solemn stillness and unusually solid figures, luminous colour, and carefully calculated compositional harmonies. It includes a fresco series, *The Legend of the True Cross* (San Francesco, Arezzo), begun about 1452, and the ◊*Flagellation* of *Christ* (Galleria della Marche, Palazzo Ducale, Urbino), a small-scale work painted in the 1450s, which is notable for its use of perspective. Piero wrote two treatises, one on mathematics, one on the laws of perspective in painting.

Piero di Cosimo c. 1462–c. 1521. Italian painter, known for his inventive pictures of mythological subjects, often featuring fauns and centaurs. *Mythological Scene* about 1510 (National Gallery, London) is typical. He also painted religious subjects and portraits.

Piers Plowman medieval English alliterative poem, written between 1367 and 1386 by William ◊Langland. It tells of a wanderer who falls asleep in the Malvern Hills and dreams of the means to Christian salvation. Piers Plowman represents Christ, and other characters including the personified seven deadly sins. As an allegory it has flashes of poetic quality rather than a consistent and coherent poetic effect. The longest of several versions is over 7,200 lines.

pietà (Italian 'pity') in Christian art, a depiction of the Virgin Mary mourning over the body of Christ. Examples include the *Avignon Pietà* about 1455 (Louvre, Paris), Michelangelo's carved *Pietà* 1498–99 (St Peter's, Rome), and Giovanni Bellini's *Pietà* 1468–71 (Brera Gallery, Milan).

Pietilä Reima 1923–1993. Finnish architect. He was a member of ◊CIAM and one of a group of post-war Scandinavian architects who sought to explore the possibilities for regional variation within the context of the ◊Modern Movement. Influenced by Alvar ◊Aalto, his buildings reflect the natural Finnish landscape of forests, lakes, and rocks in their free-flowing forms. The Embassy of Finland, New Delhi, 1983–85, has a faceted roof shape, recalling the snow sculptures found in the winter ice around the Gulf of Finland.

pietra dura (Italian 'hard stone') Italian technique of inlaying furniture with semiprecious stones, such as agate or quartz, in a variety of colours, to create pictures or patterns.

Pietro da Cortona (Pietro Berrettini) 1596–1669. Italian painter and architect, a major influence in the development of High Baroque. His enormous fresco *Allegory of Divine Providence* 1633–39 (Barberini Palace, Rome) glorifies his patron the pope and the Barberini family, and gives a convincing illusion of reality.

For the most part the painter of pictures of the nude designs them with some immodesty.

Pietro da Cortona
A Treatise on Painting 1652

Pigalle Jean Baptiste 1714–1785. French sculptor who studied in Rome. In Paris he gained the patronage of Madame de Pompadour, the mistress of Louis XV. His works include *Venus, Love and Friendship* 1758 (Louvre, Paris), a nude statue of *Voltaire* 1776 (Institut de France, Paris), and the grandiose *Tomb of Maréchal de Saxe* 1753 (Strasbourg).

Pilgrim's Progress allegory by John ◊Bunyan, published 1678–84, that describes the journey through life to the Celestial City of a man called Christian. On his way through the Slough of Despond, the House Beautiful, Vanity Fair, Doubting Castle, and other landmarks, he meets a number of allegorical figures.

Pillow Book, The (Japanese *Makura no sōshi*) vivid and influential Japanese memoirs and miscellany by Sei Shonagon (966/7–1013?), compiled 991–1000 while she was at court in the service of the empress Sadako.

Pilobolous Dance Theater US modern-dance troupe formed 1971 whose members collectively choreograph surreal body-sculptures with a mixture of dance, gymnastics, and mime. It is whimsically named after a light-sensitive fungus.

Pindar 518–438 BC. Greek lyric poet, born near Thebes. He is noted for his surviving choral songs, or 'odes', written in honour of victors in the Greek athletic games at Delphi, Olympia, Nemea, and the Isthmus of Corinth.

My soul, do not search for immortal life, but exhaust the boundaries of possibility.

Pindar Pythian Odes

Pinero Arthur Wing 1855–1934. English dramatist. A leading exponent of the 'well-made' play, he enjoyed great contemporary success with his farces, beginning with *The Magistrate* 1885. More substantial social drama followed with *The Second Mrs Tanqueray* 1893, and comedies including *Trelawny of the 'Wells'* 1898.

Pink Floyd British psychedelic rock group, formed 1965. The original members were Syd Barrett (1946–), Roger Waters (1944–), Richard Wright (1945–), and Nick Mason (1945–). Their albums include *The Dark Side of the Moon* 1973 and *The Wall* 1979, with its spin-off film starring Bob Geldof.

Pinocchio fantasy for children by Carlo ◊Collodi, published in Italy 1883 and in an English translation 1892. It tells the story of a wooden puppet that comes to life and assumes the characteristics of a human boy. Pinocchio's nose grows longer every time he tells a lie. A Walt Disney cartoon film, based on Collodi's story, was released 1940 and brought the character to a wider audience.

Pinter Harold 1930– . English dramatist, originally an actor. He specializes in the tragicomedy of the breakdown of communication, broadly in the tradition of the Theatre of the ◊Absurd – for example, *The Birthday Party* 1958 and *The Caretaker* 1960. Later plays include *The Homecoming* 1965, *Old Times* 1971, *Betrayal* 1978, *Mountain Language* 1988, and *Moonlight* 1993.

One way of looking at speech is to say that it is a constant stratagem to cover nakedness.

Harold Pinter

Pinturicchio or *Pintoricchio* pseudonym of Bernardino di Betto *c.* 1454–1513. Italian painter, active in Rome, Perugia, and Siena. His chief works are the frescoes in the Borgia Apartments in the Vatican, painted in the 1490s, and in the Piccolomini Library of Siena Cathedral, 1503–08. He is thought to have assisted ◊Perugino in decorating the Sistine Chapel, Rome.

Piozzi Hester Lynch (born Salusbury) 1741–1821. Welsh writer, a close friend of Samuel Johnson. She published *Anecdotes of the Late Samuel Johnson* 1786 and their correspondence 1788. *Thraliana*, her diaries and notebooks of the years 1766–1809, was published 1942.

piped music or *Muzak* (proprietary name) music recorded to strict psychological criteria for transmission in a variety of work environments in order to improve occupier or customer morale.

Piper John 1903–1992. English painter, printmaker, and designer. His subjects include traditional Romantic views of landscape and architecture. As an official war artist in World

War II he depicted bomb-damaged buildings. He also designed theatre sets and stained-glass windows for Coventry Cathedral and the Catholic Cathedral, Liverpool.

Pirandello Luigi 1867–1936. Italian playwright, novelist, and short-story writer. His plays, which often deal with the themes of illusion and reality, and the tragicomic absurdity of life, include *Sei personaggi in cerca d'autore*/◊*Six Characters in Search of an Author* 1921 and *Enrico IV*/*Henry IV* 1922. The themes and innovative techniques of his plays anticipated the work of Brecht, O'Neill, Anouilh, and Genet. Nobel Prize 1934.

When the characters are really alive before their author, the latter does nothing but follow them in their action, in their words, in the situations which they suggest to him.

Luigi Pirandello
Six Characters in Search of an Author 1921

Piranesi Giambattista (Giovanni Battista) 1720–1778. Italian architect and graphic artist. He is most significant for his powerful etchings of Roman antiquities and as an influential theorist of architecture, advocating imaginative use of Roman models. His series of etchings *Prisons of Invention* about 1745–61 depict imaginary prisons, vast and gloomy. Only one of his architectural designs was built, Sta Maria del Priorato, Rome.

Pirithous in Greek mythology, king of the Lapiths and friend of Theseus of Athens. His marriage to Hippodamia was the occasion of a battle between the Lapiths and their guests, the Centaurs, which is a recurrent subject of Greek art.

pirouette in dance, a movement comprising one or more complete turns of the body on one leg with the other touching the supporting leg at the knee.

Pisanello nickname of Antonio Pisano c. 1395–c. 1455. Italian artist active in Verona, Venice, Naples, Rome, and elsewhere. His panel paintings reveal a rich ◊International Gothic style. He was also an outstanding portrait medallist. His frescoes in the Palazzo Ducale in Mantua were rediscovered after World War II.

Pisano Andrea c. 1290–1348. Italian sculptor who made the earliest bronze doors for the Baptistery of Florence Cathedral, completed 1336. He completed the campanile for the cathedral, designed by Giotto.

Pisano Nicola (died c. 1284) and his son Giovanni (died c. 1314). Italian sculptors and architects. Nicola initiated a revival of Classical forms, his best-known works being the pulpit of the Pisa Baptistry 1260 and the pulpit for Siena Cathedral 1265–68, on which his son Giovanni also worked. The sculptures of Giovanni, such as the pulpit for San Andrea, Pistoia, about 1300, are more emotional and expressive than his father's, showing the influence of French Gothic.

Piscator Erwin 1893–1966. German theatre director. He introduced the idea of epic theatre, using slide-projection, music, dance, and film to create a revolutionary social drama in the *Red Revue* 1921 and in *Hoppla, That's Life!* 1927.

While in the USA 1939–51 he produced an adaptation of Tolstoy's *War and Peace* 1942, but returned to directing in Germany 1951, where he produced plays by Ralf Hochhuth.

Pissarro Camille 1830–1903. French Impressionist painter, born in the West Indies. He went to Paris 1855, met Corot, then Monet, and became a leading member of the Impressionists. He experimented with various styles, including ◊Pointillism, in the 1880s.

His son *Lucien Pissarro* (1863–1944) worked in the same style for a time.

Piston Walter (Hamor) 1894–1976. US composer and teacher. He wrote a number of textbooks, including *Harmony* 1941 and *Orchestration* 1955. His Neo-Classical works include eight symphonies, a number of concertos, chamber music, the orchestral suite *Three New England Sketches* 1959, and the ballet *The Incredible Flutist* 1938.

pitch in music, the position of a note in the scale, dependent on the frequency of the predominant sound wave. In ◊*concert pitch*, A above middle C (A4) is the reference tone to which instruments are tuned. *Perfect pitch* is an ability to name or reproduce any note heard or asked for; it does not necessarily imply high musical ability.

In a musical instrument, pitch is a consequence of design converting a continuous input of energy into a periodic output of pressure waves that the ear perceives as a tone of constant pitch.

pizzicato (Italian 'pinched') in music, an instruction to pluck a bowed stringed instrument (such as the violin) with the fingers.

plainsong ancient chant of the Christian church first codified by Ambrose, bishop of Milan, and then by Pope Gregory in the 6th century. See ◊Gregorian chant.

Planchon Roger 1931– . French theatre director, actor, and dramatist. He established a theatre company in Villeurbanne, outside Lyon, France, 1957; it inherited the name Théâtre National Populaire 1973. Major productions of Shakespeare (*Henry V* 1957) and Molière (*Tartuffe* 1962 and 1973) were followed by Pinter's *No Man's Land* 1979 and Racine's *Athalie* 1980.

plastic arts the arts that are produced by modelling or moulding, chiefly sculpture and ceramics.

Plasticine trademark for an oil-based plastic material used in modelling. It was invented 1897 for art students and is also used by architects and engineers; the earliest space suits were modelled in Plasticine.

plastics general name for a large family of materials used widely in product manufacturing this century. Examples from before 1939 include the familiar celluloid and bakelite but after 1945 plastics proliferated to such an extent that it became increasingly difficult to recognize them. Polyethylene, vinyl, acrylic, and many others were among the new materials that provided designers with new challenges.

For the most part plastics design has been considered to be 'cheap and nasty', as price has tended to dominate over quality, but, nonetheless, a number of designers—among them, Vico ◊Magistretti in Italy, Charles ◊Eames in the USA, and Eero Aarnio (1932–) in Finland— have attempted to develop a new identity for the plastic object. Since the 1960s, however, the concern for the environment has turned plastics back into an undesirable group of materials.

Plath Sylvia 1932–1963. US poet and novelist whose powerful, highly personal poems, often expressing a sense of desolation, are distinguished by their intensity and sharp imagery. Her *Collected Poems* 1981 was awarded a Pulitzer Prize. Other collections of her poems include *The Colossus* 1960 and *Ariel* 1965, published after her death. Her autobiographical novel *The Bell Jar* 1961 deals with the events surrounding a young woman's emotional breakdown.

Plath was born in Boston, Massachusetts, attended Smith College and was awarded a Fulbright scholarship to study at Cambridge University, England. She was married to the poet Ted Hughes 1956–62 and committed suicide while living in London.

Dying,/Is an art, like everything else./I do it exceptionally well.

Sylvia Plath 'Lady Lazarus'

Plato c. 428–347 BC. Greek philosopher, pupil of Socrates, teacher of Aristotle, and founder of the Academy school of philosophy. He was the author of philosophical dialogues on such topics as metaphysics, ethics, and politics. Central to his teachings is the notion of Forms, which are located outside the everyday world—timeless, motionless, and absolutely real. Plato's philosophy has influenced Christianity and European culture, directly and through Augustine, the Florentine Platonists during the Renaissance, and countless others.

Of his work, some 30 dialogues survive, intended for performance either to his pupils or to the public. The principal figure in these ethical and philosophical debates is Socrates and the early ones employ the Socratic method, in which he asks questions and traps the students into contradicting themselves; for example, *Iron*, on poetry. Other dialogues include the *Symposium*, on love, *Phaedo*, on immortality, and *Crito*, on Socrates' trial and death. The *Apology* is Plato's representation of the speech made by Socrates at his trial. It is impossible to say whether Plato's Socrates is a faithful representative of the real man or an articulation of Plato's own thought. Plato's philosophy rejects scientific rationalism (establishing facts through experiment) in favour of arguments, because mind, not matter, is fundamental, and material objects are merely imperfect copies of abstract and eternal 'ideas'. His political philosophy is expounded in two treatises, *The Republic* and *The Laws*, both of which describe ideal states. Platonic love is inspired by a person's best qualities and seeks their development.

Democracy passes into despotism

Plato

Plautus 3rd–2nd century BC. Roman comic dramatist, born in Umbria. He settled in Rome and was active before and after 200 BC, writing at least the 21 comedies that survive in his name, many of them based on Greek originals by playwrights such as ◊Menander. Shakespeare drew on his *Menaechmi* for *The Comedy of Errors*.

A man is a wolf rather than a man to another man, when he hasn't yet found out what he's like.

Plautus Asinaria

---

player piano mechanical piano designed to reproduce key actions recorded on a perforated paper roll. Debussy, Mahler, Grainger, and Stravinsky recorded their own works on piano roll. The concert *Duo-Art* reproducing piano encoded more detailed information, to the extent that audiences were unable to distinguish a live performance from a reproduced performance.

Playfair William Henry 1790–1857. Scottish Neo-Classical architect responsible for much of the design of Edinburgh New Town in the early 19th century. His Royal Scottish Academy 1822 and National Gallery of Scotland 1850 in Greek style helped to make Edinburgh 'the Athens of the North'.

Pleasence Donald 1919– . English character actor who specializes in sinister or mysterious roles; for example, as the tramp in Pinter's *The Caretaker* 1960, which he also played in the film version of 1963. His other films include *Will Penny* 1968, and *The Eagle Has Landed* 1976 (as the Nazi Himmler). He is one of the most prolific of British film and television actors.

plectrum in music, a device for plucking a string instrument. For a guitar or lute, it may be worn on the finger, as a substitute fingernail; others are held between two fingers, for example to play the mandolin. The harpsichord employs mechanical plectra of quill or leather to pluck the strings.

Pléiade, La group of seven poets in 16th-century France, led by Pierre Ronsard, who were inspired by Classical models to improve French verse. Their name is derived from the seven stars of the Pleiades group.

Pleiades in Greek mythology, the seven daughters of the giant Atlas who asked to be changed into a cluster of stars to escape the pursuit of the hunter Orion.

Pliny the Elder (Gaius Plinius Secundus) *c.* AD 23–79. Roman scientific encyclopedist and historian; only his works on astronomy, geography, and natural history survive. He was killed in an eruption of Vesuvius, the volcano near Naples.

Pliny the Younger (Gaius Plinius Caecilius Secundus) *c.* AD 61–113. Roman administrator, nephew of Pliny the Elder, whose correspondence is of great interest. Among his surviving letters are those describing the eruption of Vesuvius, his uncle's death, and his correspondence with the emperor Trajan.

Plisetskaya Maya 1925– . Soviet ballerina and actress. She attended the Moscow Bolshoi Ballet School and became prima ballerina of the Bolshoi Ballet 1945. An extremely strong yet supple dancer of flamboyant exuberance, she is noted for her fast spins, scissorlike jumps, and head-to-heel backward kicks, which she displayed to best advantage in the role of Kitri in *Don Quixote*. Her other noted classical role is Odette/Odile in *Swan Lake*. She is also associated with *Carmen Suite* 1967 and has acted dramatic roles in such films as *Anna Karenina* 1968.

Plomer William 1903–1973. South African novelist, author of *Turbot Wolfe* 1925, an early criticism of South African attitudes to race. He settled in London 1929 and wrote two autobiographical volumes.

plot the storyline in a novel, play, film, or other work of fiction. A plot is traditionally a scheme of connected events. Novelists in particular have at times tried to subvert or ignore the reader's expectation of a causally linked story with a clear beginning, middle, and end. James Joyce and Virginia Woolf wrote novels that explore the minutiae of a character's experience, rather than tell a tale. However, the tradition that the novel must tell a story, whatever else it may do, survives for the most part intact.

English novelist E M Forster defined it thus: The king died and then the queen died. The king died and then the queen died of grief at the king's death. The first is the beginning of a series of events; the second is the beginning of a plot.

Plough and the Stars, The tragedy by Sean ◊O'Casey 1926. In the Easter Rising of 1916 Nora Clitheroe loses both her husband Jack and her baby, as the violence embraces both men and women in the the the tenements of Dublin.

Plutarch *c.* AD 46–120. Greek biographer and essayist, born in Chaeronea. His *Parallel Lives* comprise paired biographies of famous Greek and Roman soldiers and politicians, followed by comparisons between the two. Thomas North's 1579 translation inspired Shakespeare's Roman plays.

Plutarch lectured on philosophy in Rome and was appointed procurator of Greece by Emperor Hadrian.

Our nature holds so much envy and malice that our pleasure in our own advantages is not so great as our distress at others'.

Plutarch Moralia

Pluto in Greek mythology, the lord of the underworld (Roman Dis), sometimes known as Hades. He was the brother of Zeus and Poseidon.

Po Chü-i alternative transliteration of ◊Bo Zhu Yi, Chinese poet.

To vilify a great man is the readiest way in which a little man can himself attain greatness.

Edgar Allan Poe Marginalia

Poe Edgar Allan 1809–1849. US writer and poet. His short stories are renowned for their horrific atmosphere, as in 'The Fall of the House of Usher' 1839 and 'The Masque of the Red Death' 1842, and for their acute reasoning, as in 'The Gold Bug' 1843 and 'The Murders in the Rue Morgue' 1841 (in which the investigators Legrand and Dupin anticipate Conan Doyle's Sherlock Holmes). His poems include 'The ◊Raven' 1845. His novel, *The Narrative of Arthur Gordon Pym of Nantucket* 1838, has attracted critical attention.

Poe, born in Boston, was orphaned 1811 and joined the army 1827 but was court-martialled 1830 for deliberate neglect of duty. He failed to earn a living by writing, became an alcoholic, and in 1847 lost his wife (commemorated in his poem 'Annabel Lee'). His verse, of haunting lyric beauty, influenced the French Symbolists (for example, 'Ulalume' and 'The Bells').

poet laureate poet of the British royal household, so called because of the laurel wreath awarded to eminent poets in the Graeco-Roman world. Early poets with unofficial status were Geoffrey Chaucer, John Skelton, Edmund Spenser, Samuel Daniel, and Ben Jonson. Ted ◊Hughes was appointed poet laureate 1984.

There is a stipend of £70 a year, plus £27 in lieu of the traditional butt of sack (cask of wine).

poets laureate	
1638	William Davenant
1668	John Dryden
1689	Thomas Shadwell
1692	Nahum Tate
1715	Nicholas Rowe
1718	Laurence Eusden
1730	Colley Cibber
1757	William Whitehead
1785	Thomas Warton
1790	Henry Pye
1813	Robert Southey
1843	William Wordsworth
1850	Alfred, Lord Tennyson
1896	Alfred Austin
1913	Robert Bridges
1930	John Masefield
1968	Cecil Day Lewis
1972	John Betjeman
1984	Ted Hughes

poetry the imaginative expression of emotion, thought, or narrative, frequently in metrical form and often using figurative language. Poetry has traditionally been distinguished from prose (ordinary written language) by rhyme or the rhythmical arrangement of words (◊metre).

A distinction is made between lyrical, or songlike, poetry (sonnet, ode, elegy, pastoral), and narrative, or story-telling, poetry (ballad, lay, epic). Poetic form has also been used as a vehicle for satire, parody, and expositions of philosophical, religious, and practical subjects. Traditionally, poetry has been considered a higher form of expression than prose. In modern times, the distinction is not always clear cut.

Poetry: A Magazine of Verse influential US literary magazine. One of the first 'little magazines' of the early 20th century, and still published today, it was founded in Chicago 1912 by Harriet Monroe (1860–1936) with the poet Ezra Pound as foreign editor. It introduced many major modern poets, including T S Eliot, Wallace Stevens, William Carlos Williams, Marianne Moore, and Carl Sandburg, and it printed the manifesto of Imagism.

pointe (French 'toe of shoe') in dance, the tip of the toe. A dancer *sur les pointes* is dancing on her toes in blocked shoes, as popularized by the Italian dancer Marie ◊Taglioni 1832.

pointillism in music, a form of 1950s ◊serialism in which melody and harmony are replaced by complexes of isolated tones. Pointillism was inspired by Webern and adopted by Messiaen, Boulez, Nono, Stockhausen, and Stravinsky. Although not strictly serial, the music of Xenakis and Cage at this time is also pointillist in texture.

Pointillism technique in oil painting developed in the 1880s by the Neo-Impressionist Georges ◊Seurat. He used small dabs of pure colour laid side by side to create form and an impression of shimmering light when viewed from a distance.

Poiret Paul 1879–1944. French fashion designer who was influential in the early part of the 20th century. He founded his own fashion house 1904 and two years later began loosening the shape of his designs, producing soft, amorphous gowns which were simple and elegant, followed by Eastern-inspired outfits 1909. He introduced the hobble skirt 1911 which, although it freed the hips, confined the ankles and attracted much criticism.

Poirot, Hercule fictional Belgian detective who appears in Agatha ◊Christie's first crime novel *The Mysterious Affair at Styles* 1920 and in 32 subsequent mysteries.

Known for his inflated ego, vanity, and charm, Poirot exercises his 'little grey cells' to solve the most convoluted criminal plots, for example those of *The Murder of Roger Ackroyd* 1926 and *Murder on the Orient Express* 1934.

Poitier Sidney 1924– . US actor and film director, Hollywood's first black star. His films as an actor include *Something of Value* 1957, *Lilies of the Field* 1963, and *In the Heat of the Night* 1967, and as director *Stir Crazy* 1980.

Polanski Roman 1933– . Polish film director, born in Paris. His films include *Repulsion* 1965, *Cul de Sac* 1966, *Rosemary's Baby* 1968, *Tess* 1979, *Frantic* 1988, and *Bitter Moon* 1992. He suffered a traumatic childhood in Nazi-occupied Poland, and later his wife, actress Sharon Tate, was horribly murdered by the Charles Manson 'family'. He left the USA for Europe and his tragic personal life is reflected in a fascination with horror and violence in his work.

Cinema should make you forget you are sitting in a theatre.

Roman Polanski

Polaroid camera instant-picture camera, invented by Edwin Land in the USA 1947. The original camera produced black-and-white prints in about one minute. Modern cameras can produce black-and-white prints in a few seconds, and colour prints in less than a minute. An advanced model has automatic focusing and exposure. It ejects a piece of film on paper immediately after the picture has been taken.

Polish literature a vernacular literature began to emerge in the 14th century and enjoyed a golden age in the 16th and 17th centuries under Renaissance influences, particularly apparent in the poetry of Jan Kochanowski (1530–1584). The tradition revived in the later 18th century, the era of the Enlightenment poet and pioneer novelist Ignacy Krasicki (1735–1801), and a Polish national theatre was opened 1765.

The domination of Poland by Austria, Russia, and Prussia towards the end of the 18th century and during the 19th century, and particularly the failure of the 1830 Polish insurrection, stimulated romantically tragic nationalism in major writers such as Adam ◊Mickiewicz, Juliusz Słowacki (1809–1849), and Zygmunt ◊Krasiński. This theme also affected historical novelists such as Henryk ◊Sienkiewicz. At the end of the 19th century there was a reaction against Naturalism and other orthodoxies in the 'Young Poland' movement 1890–1918, in theatre and fiction as well as poetry.

In the 20th century, political independence in the interwar years fostered writers as bewilderingly varied as the exuberant 'Skamander' group of poets and the fantastic, pessimistic philosopher–dramatist Stanisław Witkiewicz (1885–1939). Poland's tragic wartime and post-war experiences have given rise to poetry and prose registering social trauma and survival. Important writers include the veteran poet and scholar Czesław Miłosz, Zbigniew Herbert, Witold Gombrowicz, the poet Tadeusz Rozewicz, and the satirical dramatist Sławomir Mrozek (1930–   ).

Politian (Angelo Poliziano) pen name of Angelo Ambrogini 1454–1494. Italian poet, playwright, and exponent of humanist ideals. He was tutor to Lorenzo de'Medici's children, and professor at the University of Florence; he wrote commentaries and essays on Classical authors.

polka folk dance in lively 2/4 time. The basic step is a hop followed by three short steps. The polka originated in Bohemia and spread with German immigrants to the USA, becoming a style of Texas country music. From about 1830 it became fashionable in European society.

Pollaiuolo Antonio del *c.* 1432–1498 and Piero *c.* 1441–1496. Italian artists, active in Florence. Both brothers were painters, sculptors, goldsmiths, engravers, and designers. Antonio is said to have been the first Renaissance artist to make a serious study of anatomy. The *Martyrdom of St Sebastian* about 1475 (National Gallery, London) is considered a joint work.

The brothers also executed two papal monuments in St Peter's basilica, Rome. The major individual works are Piero's set of *Virtues* in Florence and Antonio's engraving *The Battle of the Nude Men* about 1465. Antonio's work places a strong emphasis on the musculature of the human figure in various activities.

Pollen Arabella 1961–   . British fashion designer who achieved instant success 1981 when she sold one of her first coat designs to the Princess of Wales. She has become familiar for her classic styles – tailored, sophisticated shapes in bright-coloured wool and cotton. In 1991 she launched Pollen B, a line of clothing directed at a younger market, which is simpler in design and cheaper than her main collection.

Pollock Jackson 1912–1956. US painter, a pioneer of Abstract Expressionism. One of the foremost exponents of ◊action painting, his style is characterized by complex networks of swirling, interwoven lines of great delicacy and rhythmic subtlety.

In the early 1940s Pollock moved from a vivid Expressionist style, influenced by Mexican muralists such as ◊Siqueiros and by Surrealism, towards a semi-abstract style. The paintings of this period are colourful and vigorous, using enigmatic signs and mysterious forms. From 1947 he developed his more violently expressive abstracts, placing large canvases on the studio floor and dripping or hurling paint across them. He was soon recognized as the leading Abstract Expressionist and continued to develop his style, producing even larger canvases in the 1950s.

Painting is self-discovery. Every good artist paints what he is.

Jackson Pollock

Pollux in Greek mythology, the twin brother of Castor (see ◊Castor and Pollux).

polonaise Polish dance in stately 3/4 time that was common in 18th-century Europe. The Polish composer Frédéric Chopin developed the polonaise as a pianistic form.

Polybius *c.* 201–120 BC. Greek historian. Though he fought against the Romans and was once a political hostage, it was in Rome, under the patronage of the Scipio family, that he wrote his 40-volume history of the rise of Roman power.

Whenever it is possible to find out the cause of what is happening, one should not have recourse to the gods.

Polybius

Polyhymnia in Greek mythology, the ◊Muse of sacred song.

Polykleitos or Polyclitus 5th century BC. Greek sculptor whose *Spear Carrier* 450–440 BC (only Roman copies survive) exemplifies the naturalism and harmonious proportions of his work. He created the legendary colossal statue of Hera in Argos, in ivory and gold.

Polynices in Greek mythology, son of ◊Oedipus and Jocasta. Denied his share in the kingship of Thebes by his brother Eteocles, he induced his father-in-law, Adrastus of Argos, to lead the expedition of the ◊Seven against Thebes, in which he and his brother died by each other's hands.

Polyphemus in Greek mythology, a son of Poseidon and a Cyclops (a one-eyed giant), who imprisoned ◊Odysseus and his companions in his cave on their homeward journey, and was finally blinded by them before they escaped. His story forms the subject of Book Eleven of Homer's *Odyssey*.

polyphony music combining two or more 'voices' or parts, each with an individual melody. A polyphony of widely separated groups is called antiphony.

polyptych painting or bas ◊relief consisting of more than three panels, either hinged together or set in an architectural frame, and commonly used as an ◊altarpiece. The polyptych developed from the ◊diptych.

polytonality in music, an overlapping of multiple parts in different keys, associated in particular with Darius ◊Milhaud whose miniature *Serenade* for orchestra 1917–22 combines up to six major keys. Two keys superimposed is bitonality.

Pomona in Roman mythology, the goddess of fruit trees.

Pomus and Shuman Doc (Jerome Solon Felder) Pomus 1925–1991 and Mort Shuman 1936– . US pop-music songwriting partnership 1956–65. The team wrote hits for the Drifters ('Save the Last Dance for Me' 1960) and Elvis Presley ('Little Sister' and 'His Latest Flame' 1961). Much of their material was written for prefabricated pop stars like Fabian ('I'm a Man' 1959) or, like 'Teenager in Love' for Dion and the Belmonts 1959, in imitation of a recent hit. Fluent in a number of styles, they were innovators in none.

Pont-Aven School group of painters, led by Paul Gauguin and Emile Bernard (1868–1941), who worked in the town of Pont-Aven in Brittany, France, in the 1880s and 1890s. Their use of pure colour and concern with conveying the mood of a scene were later to influence both *les ◊Nabis* and the Symbolists.

Ponti Gio 1891–1979. Italian designer and architect, a pioneer of the ◊Modern Movement in Italy. His masterpiece is the Pirelli skyscraper in Milan, designed with Pier Liugi ◊Nervi, 1957–60, which is 126 m/415 ft high and remarkable for its slender hexagonal plan, with tapering ends. He was the founder, and editor for many years, of the influential architectural periodical *Domus*.

Pontormo Jacopo da (Jacopo Carucci) 1494–1557. Italian Mannerist painter, active in Florence. He developed a dramatic style, with lurid colours, demonstrated in *The Deposition* about 1525 (Sta Felicità, Florence), an extraordinary composition of interlocked figures, with rosy pinks, lime yellows, and pale apple greens illuminating the scene. The same distinctive colours occur in the series of frescoes he painted 1522–25 for the Certosa monastery outside Florence.

Pop Iggy. Stage name of James Newell Osterberg 1947– . US rock singer and songwriter. Initially known as *Iggy Stooge*, he was lead singer with a garage band called the Stooges (1967–74), known for their self-destructive proto-punk performances. His solo career began with *The Idiot* 1977 and *Lust for Life* 1977, composed and produced by David Bowie, who also contributed to *Blah, Blah, Blah* 1986.

Pop art movement of British and American artists in the mid-1950s and 1960s, reacting against the elitism of abstract art. Pop art imagery was drawn from advertising, comic strips, film, and television. Early exponents in the UK were Richard Hamilton, Peter Blake (1932–), and Eduardo Paolozzi, and in the USA Jasper Johns, Jim Dine, Andy Warhol, Roy Lichtenstein, and Claes Oldenburg. In its eclecticism and its sense of irony and playfulness, Pop art helped to prepare the way for the Post-Modernism of the 1970s and 1980s.

Pop art was so named by the British critic Lawrence Alloway (1926–). Richard Hamilton described it 1957 as 'popular, transient, expendable, low-cost, mass-produced, young, witty, sexy, gimmicky, glamorous, and big business'. The artists often used repeating images and quoted from the work of others.

Pop design British and Italian design movement of the 1960s which was characterized by its use of bright colours, expressive forms, synthetic materials, and throwaway objects.

In Britain the movement centred around fashion – exemplified by the work of Mary Quant and John Stephen who opened a number of boutiques in Carnaby Street – and graphics, as in the work of the psychedelic poster artists Michael English and Nigel Weymouth. Italian Pop design focused on furniture and product design and was best expressed in the radical work of architectural groups such as Archizoom 1966–72 and Superstudio 1966–72 which employed irony and wit in such designs as Archizoom's 'Dream Beds' 1967, fantasy one-off designs incorporating Art Deco imagery. In essence, Pop design set out to challenge and subvert establishment design values.

Pope Alexander 1688–1744. English poet and satirist. He established his reputation with the precocious *Pastorals* 1709 and *Essay on Criticism* 1711, which were followed by a parody of the heroic epic *The Rape of the Lock* 1712–14 and 'Eloisa to Abelard' 1717. Other works include a highly Neo-Classical translation of Homer's *Iliad* and *Odyssey* 1715–26.

Pope had a biting wit, which he expressed in the form of heroic couplets. As a Catholic, he was subject to discrimination, and he was embittered by a deformity of the spine. His edition of Shakespeare attracted scholarly ridicule, for which he revenged himself by a satire on scholarly dullness, the *Dunciad* 1728. His philosophy, including *An Essay on Man* 1733–34 and *Moral Essays* 1731–35, was influenced by the politician and philosopher Henry Bolingbroke. His finest mature productions are his *Imitations of the Satires of Horace* 1733–38 and his personal letters. Among his friends were the writers Swift, Arbuthnot, and Gay. His line 'A little learning is a dang'rous thing' is often misquoted.

A little learning is a dang'rous thing;/Drink deep, or taste not the Pierian spring.

Alexander Pope *Essay on Criticism*

---

pop festival outdoor concert usually spanning a weekend and featuring a number of bands; pop, rock, heavy-metal, and world-music festivals have become regular events in many countries since the 1960s. See also ◊Woodstock.

poplin strong fabric, originally with a warp of silk and a weft of worsted, but now usually made from cotton, in a plain weave with a finely ribbed surface.

pop music or *popular music* any contemporary music not categorizable as jazz or classical. Pop became distinct from folk music with the advent of sound-recording techniques, and has incorporated blues, country and western, and music-hall elements; electronic amplification and other technological innovations have played a large part in the creation of new styles. The traditional format is a song of roughly three minutes with verse, chorus, and middle eight bars.

1910s The singer Al Jolson was one of the first recording stars. Ragtime was still popular.

1920s In the USA Paul Whiteman and his orchestra played jazz that could be danced to, country singer Jimmie Rodgers reached a new record-buying public, the blues were burgeoning; in the UK popular singers included Al Bowlly (1899–1941), born in Mozambique.

1930s Crooner Bing Crosby and vocal groups such as the Andrews Sisters were the alternatives to swing bands.

1940s **Rhythm and blues** evolved in the USA while Frank Sinatra was a teen idol and Glenn Miller played dance music; the UK preferred such singers as Vera Lynn.

1950s In the USA *doo-wop* group vocalizing preceded *rockabilly* and the rise of *rock and roll* (Elvis Presley, Chuck Berry). British pop records were often cover versions of US originals.

1960s The Beatles and the *Mersey beat* transcended UK borders, followed by the Rolling Stones, *hard rock* (the Who, Led Zeppelin), and *art rock* (Genesis, Yes). In the USA *surf music* (group harmony vocals or guitar-based instrumentals) preceded *Motown*, *folk rock* (the Byrds, Bob Dylan), and *blues rock* (Jimi Hendrix, Janis Joplin). *Psychedelic rock* evolved from 1966 on both sides of the Atlantic (the Doors, Pink Floyd, Jefferson Airplane).

1970s The first half of the decade produced *glitter rock* (David Bowie), *heavy metal*, and *disco*; in the UK also *pub rock* (a return to basics, focusing on live performance); *reggae* spread from Jamaica. From 1976 *punk* was ascendant; the US term *New Wave* encompassed bands not entirely within the punk idiom (Talking Heads, Elvis Costello).

UK best-selling singles 1956–92		
1956	'I'll Be Home'	Pat Boone
1957	'Love Letters in the Sand'	Pat Boone
1958	'All I Have To Do Is Dream'	The Everly Brothers
1959	'Livin' Doll'	Cliff Richard
1960	'Cathy's Clown'	The Everly Brothers
1961	'Runaway'	Del Shannon
1962	'Stranger On The Shore'	Acker Bilk
1963	'From Me To You'	The Beatles
1964	'I Love You Because'	Jim Reeves
1965	'I'll Never Find Another You'	The Seekers
1966	'Distant Drum'	Jim Reeves
1967	'Release Me'	Engelbert Humperdinck
1968	'What A Wonderful World'	Louis Armstrong
1969	'My Way'	Frank Sinatra
1970	'The Wonder Of You'	Elvis Presley
1971	'My Sweet Lord'	George Harrison
1972	'Amazing Grace'	Royal Scots Dragoon Guards
1973	'Tie A Yellow Ribbon'	Dawn
1974	'Tiger Feet'	Mud
1975	'Bye Bye Baby'	Bay City Rollers
1976	'Save Your Kisses For Me'	Brotherhood of Man
1977	'Don't Give Up On Us'	David Soul
1978	'Rivers Of Babylon/ Brown Girl In The Ring'	Boney M
1979	'Bright Eyes'	Art Garfunkel
1980	'Don't Stand So Close To Me'	The Police
1981	'Tainted Love'	Soft Cell
1982	'Come On Eileen'	Dexy's Midnight Runners
1983	'Karma Chameleon'	Culture Club
1984	'Do They Know It's Christmas?'	Band Aid
1985	'The Power Of Love'	Jennifer Rush
1986	'Don't Leave Me This Way'	The Communards
1987	'Never Gonna Give You Up'	Rick Astley
1988	'Mistletoe And Wine'	Cliff Richard
1989	'Ride On Time'	Black Box
1990	'Unchained Melody'	The Righteous Brothers
1991	'Everything I Do (I Do It For You)'	Bryan Adams
1992	'I Will Always Love You'	Whitney Houston
1993	'I'll do Anything for Love' (But I won't Do That)	Meat Loaf

1980s Punk continued as *hardcore* or mutated into *gothic*; dance music developed regional US variants: *hip-hop* (New York), *go-go* (Washington, DC), and *house* (Chicago). Live audiences grew, leading to *stadium rock* (U2, Bruce Springsteen) and increasingly elaborate stage performances (Michael Jackson, Prince, Madonna). An interest in *world music* sparked new fusions.

1990s Rap, hard rock, and heavy metal predominated in the USA at the start of the decade; on the UK *indie* scene, dance music (Happy Mondays, Inspiral Carpets) and a new wave of guitar groups (Ride, Lush) drew on the psychedelic era. Germany in particular produced Minimalist *techno* dance music. *Grunge* emerged from Seattle, Washington, USA.

Popova Liubov 1889–1924. Russian artist and designer. Influenced by Futurism and Constructivism, in 1916 she began designing textiles and rugs and in 1917 collaborated with Vladimir Tatlin on the decoration of the Café Pittoresque in Moscow. Like ◊Stepanova, in the 1920s she designed textiles for Moscow's First State Textile Printing Factory. In 1922 she designed a stark, functional set and costumes for Vsevolod Meyerhold's production of *The Magnanimous Cuckold*.

porcelain (hardpaste) translucent ceramic material with a shining finish; see ◊pottery and porcelain.

Porgy and Bess classic US folk opera written 1935 by George and Ira Gershwin, based on the novel *Porgy* 1925 by DuBose Heyward, a story of the black residents of Catfish Row in Charleston, South Carolina.

Porter Cole (Albert) 1892–1964. US composer and lyricist, mainly of musical comedies. His witty, sophisticated songs like 'Let's Do It' 1928, 'I Get a Kick Out of You' 1934, and 'Don't Fence Me In' 1944 have been widely recorded and admired. His shows, many of which were made into films, include *The Gay Divorcee* 1932 and *Kiss Me Kate* 1948.

I get no kick from champagne...

Cole Porter
'I Get a Kick Out of You' 1934

Porter Edwin Stanton 1869–1941. US director, a pioneer of silent films. His 1903 film *The Great Train Robbery* lasted an unprecedented 12 minutes and contained an early use of the close-up. More concerned with the technical than the artistic side of his films, which include *The Teddy Bears* 1907 and *The Final Pardon* 1912, Porter abandoned filmmaking 1916.

Porter Eric 1928– . English actor. His numerous classical roles include title parts in *Uncle Vanya*, *Volpone*, and *King Lear*; on television he played Soames Forsyte in *The Forsyte Saga*.

Porter Katherine Anne 1890–1980. US writer. She published three volumes of short stories (*Flowing Judas* 1930, *Pale Horse, Pale Rider* 1939, and *The Leaning Tower* 1944); a collection of essays, *The Days Before* 1952; and the allegorical novel *Ship of Fools* 1962 (made into a film 1965). Her *Collected Short Stories* 1965 won a Pulitzer Prize.

portico in architecture, a porch with a ◊pediment and columns.

portraiture in the visual arts, the creation of a likeness to someone. Such likenesses appear in many cultures but first flourished in the West in ancient Rome as statues and coins of the rich and the powerful. In Egypt in the 3rd century AD portraits painted in wax on the panels of mummy cases achieved a high degree of realism and frankness. Extinct during the Middle Ages, portraiture revived in the 14th century as patrons and donors began to appear in religious pictures.

Outstanding portrait painters include Leonardo da Vinci, Raphael, Titian, Tintoretto (Italy); van Eyck, Campin (Flanders); Fouquet, the Clouets, David, Ingres, Cézanne (France); El Greco, Velázquez, Goya, Picasso (Spain); Dürer, Cranach (Germany); Rembrandt (Netherlands); and Hilliard, van Dyck, Reynolds, Lawrence, and Gainsborough (England).

The *self-portrait* evolved as an independent genre during the Renaissance, reflecting both the growth of individualism and the greatly improved status of the artist. It is uncertain whether Jan van Eyck's *Man in a Red Turban* about 1433 (National Gallery, London) is a self-portrait; if it is, it is probably the first of its kind. Other examples include Dürer's *Self-portrait* 1493 (Louvre, Paris), Rembrandt's *Self-portrait* about 1659 (National Gallery of Art, Washington), and van Gogh's *Self-portrait with Bandaged Ear* 1889 (Courtauld Institute Gallery, London).

Port Sunlight model village built 1888 by W H Lever (1851–1925) for workers at the Lever Brothers soap factory at Birkenhead, near Liverpool, NW England. Designed for a population of 3,000, and covering an area of 353 ha/130 acres, it includes an art gallery, church, library, and social hall.

Portuguese literature under Provençal influence, medieval Portuguese literature produced popular ballads and troubadour songs. The Renaissance provided a stimulus for the outstanding work of the dramatist Gil Vicente and of the lyric and epic poet ◊Camöens. In the 17th and 18th centuries there was a decline towards mere formality, but the *Letters of a Portuguese Nun*, attributed to Marianna Alcoforado (1640–1723), were a poignant exception and found echoes in the modern revolutionary period. The outstanding writer of the 20th century was the poet Fernando ◊Pessoa. There is a lively tradition of Portuguese writing in Brazil, and Angola has developed its own school of Portuguese-African poetry.

Poseidon in Greek mythology, the chief god of the sea (Roman Neptune), brother of Zeus and Pluto. The brothers dethroned their father, Kronos, and divided his realm, Poseidon taking the sea; he was also worshipped as god of earthquakes. His sons were the merman sea god ◊Triton and the Cyclops ◊Polyphemus.

Post- (Latin 'after') prefix used to indicate an artistic style that immediately follows another, often either reacting to it or building on it; for example, ◊Post-Modernism or ◊Post-Impressionism.

poster public notice used for advertising or propaganda, often illustrated. The poster was first produced in France during the mid-19th century, its development facilitated by the use of colour ◊lithography. Poster artists include Jules Chéret, John Millais, Henri de Toulouse-Lautrec, Charles Dana Gibson (1867–1944), Alphonse Mucha, and Pablo Picasso. Poster art flourished again in the 1960s, with the advent of Psychedelic art and artists such as Rick Griffin (1944–1991) and Stanley Mouse (1921–) in the USA and Michael English (1942–) in the UK.

Post-Impressionism movement in painting that followed ◊Impressionism in the 1880s and 1890s, incorporating various styles. The term was first used by the British critic Roger Fry 1910 to describe the works of Cézanne, van Gogh, and Gauguin. Thought differing greatly in style and aims, these painters sought to go beyond Impressionism's concern with the ever-changing effects of light.

Post-Modernism late 20th-century movement in architecture and the arts that rejects the preoccupation of ◊Modernism with purity of form and technique. Post-Modernists use an amalgam of style elements from the past, such as the Classical and the Baroque, and apply them to spare modern forms, often with ironic effect. Their slightly off-key familiarity creates a more immediate appeal than the austerities of Modernism. Exponents include the architects Robert ◊Venturi and Michael ◊Graves and the novelists David ◊Lodge and Thomas ◊Pynchon. In literary criticism and critical theory, Post-Modernism denotes a differently conceived resumption rather than a repudiation of Modernist radicalism. In music, Post-Modernism is associated with new opera.

Potter Beatrix 1866–1943. English writer and illustrator of children's books, beginning with *The Tale of Peter Rabbit* 1900 and *The Tailor of Gloucester* 1902, based on her observation of fam-

ily pets and wildlife around her home from 1905 in the English Lake District. Her tales are told with a childlike wonder, devoid of sentimentality, and accompanied by delicate illustrations.

Other books in the series include *The Tale of Mrs Tiggy Winkle* 1904, *The Tale of Jeremy Fisher* 1906, and a sequel to Peter Rabbit, *The Tale of the Flopsy Bunnies* 1909. She grew up in London but was a self-taught naturalist. Her diaries, written in a secret code, were translated and published 1966. Her Lake District home is now a museum.

You may go down into the fields or down the lane, but don't go into Mr McGregor's garden.

Beatrix Potter
The Tale of Peter Rabbit 1900

Potter Dennis (Christopher George) 1935– . English playwright. His television plays *Pennies from Heaven* 1978 (feature film 1981), *Brimstone and Treacle* 1976 (transmitted 1987, feature film 1982), and *The Singing Detective* 1986 all aroused great interest through serious concern about social issues, inventive form, and marked avoidance of euphemism or delicacy.

Potter Paulus 1625–1654. Dutch painter and etcher, active in Delft, The Hague, and Amsterdam; he specialized in rural scenes. His paintings of animals include *The Young Bull* 1647 (Mauritshuis, The Hague).

Potter Stephen 1900–1969. British author of humorous studies in how to outwit and outshine others, including *Gamesmanship* 1947, *Lifemanship* 1950, and *One Upmanship* 1952.

Potteries, the home of the china and earthenware industries, in central England. Wedgwood and Minton are factory names associated with the Potteries. The Potteries lie in the upper Trent basin of N Staffordshire, covering the area around Stoke-on-Trent.

pottery and porcelain ceramics in domestic and ornamental use, including ◊earthenware, ◊stoneware, and **bone china** (or softpaste porcelain). Made of 5% bone ash and china clay, bone china was first made in the West in imitation of Chinese porcelain. The standard British bone china was developed about 1800, with a body of clay mixed with ox bones; a harder version, called parian, was developed in the 19th century and was used for figurine ornaments.

Hardpaste *porcelain* is characterized by its hardness, ringing sound when struck, translucence, and shining finish, like that of a cowrie shell (Italian *porcellana*). It is made of kaolin and petuntse (fusible feldspar consisting chiefly of silicates reduced to a fine white powder); it is

---

pottery and porcelain: chronology

10,000 BC	Earliest known pottery in Japan.
c. **5000**	The potter's wheel was developed by the Egyptians.
c. **600–450**	Black- and red-figured vases from Greece.
6th century AD	Fine quality stoneware was developed in China, as the forerunner of porcelain.
7th–10th century	Tang porcelain in China.
10th–13th century	Song porcelain in China.
14th–17th century	Ming porcelain in China; Hispano-Moresque ware.
16th century	***Majolica***, an Italian tin-glazed earthenware with painted decoration, often large dishes with figures; ***faience*** (from Faenza, Italy) glazed earthenware and delftware.
17th century	Chinese porcelain was first exported to the West; it was soon brought in large quantities (for example, the Nanking Cargo) as a ballast in tea clippers; ***delftware*** tin-glazed earthenware with white and blue decoration was brought to perfection in Delft, the Netherlands. In North America, colonists made bricks and tiles by 1612.
18th century	In 1710 the first European hardpaste porcelain was made in ***Dresden***, Germany, by Johann Böttger (1682–1719); the factory later transferred to ***Meissen***; from 1769 hardpaste porcelain as well as soft paste was made in ***Sèvres***, France, remarkable for its ground colours; *c.* 1760 cream-coloured earthenware was perfected (superseding delftware) by Josiah Wedgwood in England; he also devised stoneware, typically with white decoration in Neo-Classical designs on a blue ground, still among the wares made in Barlaston, Staffordshire; ***English softpaste*** was made *c.* 1745–1810, first in Chelsea, later in Bow, Derby, and Worcester; ***English hardpaste*** was first made in Plymouth 1768–70, and Bristol 1770–81, when the stock was removed to New Hall in Staffordshire; ***bone china*** *c.* 1789 was first produced by Josiah Spode, Coalport, near Shrewsbury, and Thomas Minton followed, as did all English tableware of this type from 1815.
19th century	Large-scale production of fine wares, in Britain notably Royal Worcester from 1862, and Royal (Crown) Derby from 1876. In the USA, potteries established in New Jersey, Pennsylvania, Ohio, New England, and the South made earthenware and stoneware utility items and earthenware, stoneware, and bone china for tableware and fine ornaments.
20th century	There has been a revival in the craft of the individual potter, for example, Bernard Leach, Lucie Rie, and Maria Martinez. California potteries entered the world market.

---

high-fired at 1,400°C/2,552°F. Porcelain first evolved from stoneware in China, about the 6th century AD. A formula for making porcelain was developed in the 18th century in Germany, also in France, Italy, and Britain. It was first produced in the USA in the early 19th century.

Poulenc Francis (Jean Marcel) 1899–1963. French composer and pianist. A self-taught composer of witty and irreverent music, he was a member of the group of French composers known as ◊*Les Six*. Among his many works are the operas *Les Mamelles de Tirésias/The Breasts of Tirésias* 1947, and *Dialogues des Carmélites/Dialogues of the Carmelites* 1957, and the ballet *Les Biches/The Little Darlings* 1923.

Pound Ezra 1885–1972. US poet and cultural critic who lived in Europe from 1908. He is regarded as one of the most important figures of 20th-century literature, whose work revolutionized modern poetry. His *Personae* and *Exultations* 1909 established and promoted the principles of ◊Imagism, and influenced numerous poets, including T S ◊Eliot. His largest work was his series of ◊*Cantos* 1925–69 (intended to number 100), a highly complex, eclectic collage, which sought to create a unifying, modern cultural tradition.

In Paris 1921–25, he was a friend of the writers Gertrude Stein and Ernest Hemingway. He then settled in Rapallo, Italy. His anti-Semitism and sympathy with the fascist dictator Mussolini led him to broadcast from Italy in World War II,

and he was arrested by US troops 1945. Found unfit to stand trial, he was confined in a mental hospital until 1958. His first completely modern poem was 'Hugh Selwyn Mauberley' 1920. He also wrote versions of Old English, Provençal, Chinese, ancient Egyptian, and other verse.

And even I can remember/A day when the historians left blanks in their writings,/I mean for things they didn't know.

Ezra Pound Draft of *Cantos* XXX

Poussin Nicolas 1594–1665. French painter, active chiefly in Rome; court painter to Louis XIII 1640–43. He was the foremost exponent of 17th-century Baroque Classicism. He painted mythological and literary scenes in a strongly Classical style; for example, *Et in Arcadia Ego* 1638–39 (Louvre, Paris).

Poussin went to Rome 1624 and studied Roman sculpture in the studio of the Italian Baroque painter and architect Domenichino. His style reflects painstaking preparation: he made small wax models of the figures in his paintings, experimenting with different compositions and lighting. Colour was subordinate to line.

Powell Anthony (Dymoke) 1905– . English novelist who wrote the series of 12 volumes *A Dance to the Music of Time* 1951–75 that begins shortly after World War I and chronicles a period of 50 years in the lives of Nicholas Jenkins and his circle of upper-class friends.

Powell Michael 1905–1990. English film director and producer. Some of his most memorable films were made in collaboration with Hungarian screenwriter Emeric Pressburger. They produced a succession of ambitious and richly imaginative films, including *A Matter of Life and Death* 1946, *Black Narcissus* 1947, and *The Red Shoes* 1948.

Powell's films range from *The Life and Death of Colonel Blimp* 1943 to the opera movie *The Tales of Hoffman* 1951 and the voyeuristic horror story of *Peeping Tom* 1960.

Powell William 1892–1984. US film actor who costarred with Myrna Loy in the *Thin Man* series 1934–1947. He also played suave leading roles in *My Man Godfrey* 1936, *Life with Father* 1947, and *Mister Roberts* 1955.

Powys John Cowper 1872–1963. English novelist. His mystic and erotic books include *Wolf Solent* 1929 and *A Glastonbury Romance* 1933. His two brothers were also writers: **Theodore Francis Powys** (1875–1953) is best known for the novel *Mr Weston's Good Wine* 1927 and the autobiography of **Llewelyn Powys** (1884–1939), *Skin for Skin*, was published 1925.

Poynter Edward John 1836–1919. English artist, first head of the Slade School of Fine Art, London, 1871–75, and president of the Royal Academy in succession to John Everett Millais. He produced decorous nudes, mosaic panels for Westminster Palace 1870, and scenes from ancient Greece and Rome.

pp in music, abbreviation for *pianissimo* (Italian 'very softly').

Prado (Real Museo de Pintura del Prado) Spanish art gallery, containing the national collection of pictures. The building was designed as a natural history museum and begun 1785; it became an art gallery 1818 under Ferdinand VII.

praise poem genre of traditional African literature which has influenced modern African poetry. Oral poets, particularly among southern African peoples such as the Xhosa, Tswana, Zulu, Sotho, and Shona, would recite poems in praise of chiefs, or prominent men such as the Zulu hero Shaka, at formal gatherings. Such poems were often valued more for content than for execution. Many collections of transcripts have now been published, particularly since the 1960s.

Praxiteles mid-4th century BC. Greek sculptor, active in Athens. His *Aphrodite of Cnidus* about 350 BC (known through Roman copies) is thought to have initiated the tradition of life-size free-standing female nudes in Greek sculpture.

pre-Columbian architecture the architecture of the Central and South American civilizations that existed prior to the arrival of European colonizers in the 16th century.

Central American architecture Little evidence remains of pre-Mayan buildings, but the distinctive form of the pyramid – the focus of pre-Columbian ceremonial architecture – was in evidence by the 4th century BC, for example, at Cuicuilco, and well developed by AD D 100, as in the Pyramid of the Sun at Teotihuacán, Mexico. Mesoamerican pyramids were different in form and function to those of the Egyptians. Instead of tombs, they were sites for ritual, usually topped by altars and with steeply sloping, stepped sides and rectangular or circular planforms. The Maya civilization, AD 300–900, left many imposing monuments, significant for their regular, symmetrical form, stylized external decoration, and use of corbel arches and internal vaulting. Mayan sites include Chichén Itzá, Mexico, and Tikal, Guatemala. The Totonac, 5th–11th centuries, and Zapotec, 6th–7th centuries, were active during the latter part of the Mayan era and left their own monuments at Tajin and Monte Albán respectively. Arriving from the north in the 10th century, the Toltecs, 10th–12th centuries, took over Chichén Itzá and added many of their own structures, including the nine-tiered pyramid, the Castillo. At Tula, thought to be the Toltec capital, they employed free-standing columns – huge, sculpted figures of warriors and hunters – to support the roof of the temple of the god Quetzalcoatl. The architecture of the Aztecs, 14th–16th centuries, was influenced by Toltec culture but the sculpture that surrounded it had a more fluid and less stylized form. Their capital, Tenochtitlán, was levelled by the Spanish and is now the site of Mexico City, but they left many important buildings such as the double pyramid of Tenayuca, about 1450–1500. There was also a Mixtec civilization that evolved independently of the Aztecs. Few of their buildings remain but the Palace of the Columns at Mitla, AD 1000, is notable for the geometrical patterns that cover its interior and exterior walls.

South American architecture Some monuments remain that predate Inca rule, such as the Temple of the Sun at Moche, about AD 200–600, a pyramidal stepped structure built by the Chavín peoples, and the Gateway of the Sun, Tiahuanaco, about 500–700, a richly carved monolithic structure. Between 1300–1400, a number of local cultures developed including those centred around Chan Chan and Cajamarquilla, towns laid out on a complex grid system composed of streets, pyramids, and reservoirs. The Inca civilization was formed about 1440 and came to dominate the region. Their architecture is best known for its use of huge masonry, laid without cement. The ancient capital of Cuzco, 1200 onwards, has examples of this, as has the spectacularly sited Machu Picchu, about 1500, high in the Andes. This late Inca city follows the typical pattern of the culture: a Sun

Temple and palace situated on either side of a central plaza, a water system servicing baths and fountains, and terraced fields for step-cultivation descending the mountainside.

pre-Columbian art the art of the Central and South American civilizations that existed prior to the arrival of European colonizers in the 16th century.

Central American art The art of the Mesoamerican and Mexican cultures up to the Spanish conquest. The Olmec civilization, about 1200–600 BC, is characterized by jade figurines and heavy featured, colossal heads, resting mysteriously in the landscape. During the Classic Period, about AD 200–900, the dominant culture was Mayan, AD 300–900, of Yucatán, southern Mexico, and Guatemala. Its sculpture, mostly in relief, combined glyphs and stylized figures and was used to decorate architecture, such as the pyramid temple of Chichén Itzá; murals dating from about AD 750 were discovered when the city of ◊Bonampak was excavated 1946. The Mayans were succeeded by more warlike, brutal societies governed by deities which demanded human sacrifice. The Toltecs, 10th–12th centuries, made colossal, blocklike sculptures, for example those employed as free-standing columns at Tula, Mexico. The Mixtecs developed a style of painting called 'Mixtec-Puebla', as seen in their murals and manuscripts ('codices'), in which all available space is covered by flat figures in geometrical designs. The Aztec culture in Mexico produced some dramatically expressive work, such as the decorated skulls of captives and stone sculpture, a good example of which is *Tlazolteotl* (Woods Bliss Collection, Washington), a goddess in childbirth, AD 1300–1500.

South American art The art of the indigenous peoples of South America. The Chavín culture flourished in the Andean area (modern-day Peru) about 1000 BC, producing small sculpture and pottery, often human in form but with animal attributes, such as bird feet, reptilian eyes, or feline fangs. The Andean Mochicha peoples, about 100 BC–AD 700, were among the best artisans of the New World, producing delightful portrait vases (Moche ware), which, while realistic, are steeped in religious references, the significance of which is lost to us. They were also goldsmiths and weavers of outstanding talent. The short-lived Inca culture, about AD 1400–1580, of Peru and Bolivia, sculpted animal and human figurines, but is best known for its architecture at Andean sites such as Cuzco and Machu Picchu (see ◊pre-Columbian architecture).

prefabricated building in construction, the use of large elements, such as walls, floors, and roofs, that are factory produced for site assemblage.

prehistoric art art that predates written records; specifically, the art of Europe 30,000 BC–2000 BC.

Old Stone Age (Palaeolithic) art The earliest surviving artefacts in Europe date from approximately 30,000 to 10,000 BC, a period of hunter-gatherer cultures. Extant small sculptures are generally of fecund female nudes and relate to the cult of the Mother Goddess, for example the *Willendorf Venus* (Kunsthistorisches Museum, Vienna) about 21,000 BC, which is carved from a small stone. The murals of the caves of ◊Lascaux, France, and ◊Altamira, Spain, depict animals such as bison, horses, and deer, as well as a few human figures. Executed in earth colours akin to ◊pastel technique, the murals are of a very high order and appear to have been done in near-impossible conditions, perhaps as a rite of initiation.

New Stone Age (Neolithic) art During the period 10,000–2,000 BC settled communities were established, which led to a greater technical and aesthetic sophistication in tools, ceramic vessels, jewellery, and human and animal figures. Human figures appear more often in wall paintings, and are skilfully composed into groups. The period 4,000–2,000 BC saw the erection of the great megalithic monuments, such as those at Carnac, France, and Stonehenge, England, and the production of ceramic pots and figurines with decorative elements that were later to be developed in the art of the Celts.

prelude in music, a composition intended as the preface to further music, especially preceding a ◊fugue, forming the opening piece of a ◊suite, or setting the mood for a stage work, as in Wagner's *Lohengrin*. As used by Chopin, a prelude is a short self-contained piano work.

Preminger Otto (Ludwig) 1906–1986. Austrian-born US film producer, director, and actor. He directed *Margin for Error* 1942, *Laura* 1944, *The Moon Is Blue* 1953, *The Man with the Golden Arm* 1955, *Anatomy of a Murder* 1959, *Advise and Consent* 1962, and *Rosebud* 1974. His films are characterized by an intricate technique of storytelling and a masterly use of the wide screen and the travelling camera.

I don't collect any old reviews, scrapbooks, anything … in order to be able to work I need to forget what I have done.

Otto Preminger

Prendergast Maurice 1859–1924. US painter who created a decorative style in watercolours and in oils, using small translucent pools of colour. His work was inspired by Impressionism and Post-Impressionism. *Umbrellas in the Rain, Venice* 1899 (Museum of Fine Arts, Boston) is typical.

He studied in Paris in the 1890s and was influenced by Les ◊Nabis, notably Pierre Bonnard and Edouard Vuillard. In 1898 he visited Italy.

Pre-Raphaelite Brotherhood (PRB) group of British painters 1848–53; Dante Gabriel Rossetti, John Everett Millais, and Holman Hunt were founding members. They aimed to paint serious subjects, to study nature closely, and to shun the influence of the styles of painters after Raphael. Their subjects were mainly biblical and literary, painted with obsessive naturalism and attention to detail. Artists associated with the group include Edward Burne-Jones and William Morris.

Presley Elvis (Aron) 1935–1977. US singer and guitarist, the most influential performer of the rock-and-roll era. With his recordings on Sun Records in Memphis, Tennessee, 1954–55 and early hits such as 'Heartbreak Hotel', 'Hound Dog', and 'Love Me Tender', all 1956, he created an individual vocal style, influenced by Southern blues, gospel music, country music, and rhythm and blues. His records continued to sell in their millions into the 1990s.

Presley was born in Tupelo, Mississippi. In the mid-1950s he met Colonel Tom Parker (1909–) who was to be his lifelong manager. In addition to selling millions of records, Presley acted in 33 films, including *Loving You* and *Jailhouse Rock* both 1957, and made numerous television appearances. From the late 1960s, he took a Las Vegas-based touring act on the road. He died at Graceland, his mansion in Memphis, the victim of drug dependence.

When I first knew Elvis he had a million dollars' worth of talent. Now he has a million dollars.

Colonel Tom Parker on Elvis Presley

Pressburger Emeric 1902–1988. Hungarian producer, screenwriter, and director known for his partnership with Michael ◊Powell. Forming the production company the Archers 1942, Powell and Pressburger collaborated on 14 films between 1942 and 1956, such as *The Red Shoes* 1948.

prestressed concrete developed form of ◊reinforced concrete in which tensioned steel cables enclosed in ducts take the place of steel reinforcement. This allows the most efficient use of the tensile strength of steel with the compressive strength of concrete. Its use was pioneered by the French engineer Eugène ◊Freysinnet in the 1920s.

Previn André (George) 1929– . German-born US conductor and composer. After early success as a composer and arranger for film, he studied conducting with Pierre Monteux 1951 and became principal conductor of the London Symphony Orchestra 1968–79. He was appointed music director of Britain's Royal Philharmonic Orchestra 1985 (a post he relinquished the follow-

ing year, staying on as principal conductor until 1991). He was also principal conductor of the Los Angeles Philharmonic 1986–89, and is now a guest conductor of many orchestras in Europe and the USA. His compositions include concertos for piano 1971 and guitar 1984; he has conducted Gershwin and Mozart concertos from the keyboard and recorded many US and British composers.

Prévost d'Exiles Antoine François 1697–1763. French novelist, known as Abbé Prévost, who combined a military career with his life as a monk. His *Manon Lescaut* 1731 inspired operas by Massenet and Puccini.

Priam in Greek mythology, the last king of Troy, husband of Hecuba and father of many sons and daughters, including ◊Cassandra, ◊Hector, and ◊Paris. He was killed by Pyrrhus, son of Achilles, when the Greeks entered the city of Troy concealed in a huge wooden horse which the Trojans believed to be a gift to the city.

Priapus in Greek mythology, the god of fertility, son of Dionysus and Aphrodite, represented as grotesquely ugly, with an exaggerated phallus. He was later a Roman god of gardens, where his image was frequently used as a scarecrow.

Price Leontyne 1927– . US opera singer. She played a leading singing role in Ira Gershwin's revival of his musical *Porgy and Bess* 1952–54. She made her operatic debut in San Francisco 1957 and appeared at La Scala in Milan 1959, becoming a regular member of the Metropolitan Opera in New York 1961.

Price Vincent 1911–1993. US actor, star of such horror films as *House of Wax* 1953, *The Tingler* 1959, and *The Fall of the House of Usher* 1960. Earlier, non-horror roles include *Laura* 1944.

Pride and Prejudice novel by Jane ◊Austen, published 1813. Mr and Mrs Bennet, whose property is due to pass to a male cousin, William Collins, are anxious to secure good marriage settlements for their five daughters. Central to the story is the romance between the witty Elizabeth Bennet and the proud Mr Darcy.

Priestley J(ohn) B(oynton) 1894–1984. English novelist and playwright. His first success was a novel about travelling theatre, *The Good Companions* 1929. He followed it with a realist novel about London life, *Angel Pavement* 1930. As a playwright he was often preoccupied with theories of time, as in *An Inspector Calls* 1945. He was also known for his wartime broadcasts and literary criticism, such as *Literature and Western Man* 1960.

Primaticcio Francesco 1504–1570. Italian Mannerist painter, sculptor, architect, and decorator, influential in the development of the ◊Fontainebleau School in France. He learnt his skills under ◊Giulio Romano in the Palazzo del Tè at Mantua. Summoned to France by François

I 1532, he worked with ◊Rosso at Fontainebleau, developing an innovatory combination of painting and stucco work.

Primavera (Italian 'Spring') tempera painting on panel by Sandro ◊Botticelli 1478 (Uffizi Gallery, Florence). It shows Venus in a grove attended by two groups of pagan deities, one symbolizing earthly love, the other, divine love. With this Platonic theme of lower and higher love, it is the first major painting of Christian Europe to depict classical myth and philosophy. A highly symbolic work, it defies all attempts at complete interpretation.

Primitivism the influence on modern art (Kirchner, Modigliani, Picasso, Gauguin, and others) of the indigenous arts of Africa, Oceania, the Americas, and also of Western folk art.

Prince stage name of Prince Rogers Nelson 1960– . US pop musician who composes, arranges, and produces his own records and often plays all the instruments. His albums, including *1999* 1982 and *Purple Rain* 1984, contain elements of rock, funk, and jazz. Hits include 'Little Red Corvette' from *1999*, 'Kiss' from *Parade* 1986, and 'Sign O' The Times' from the album of the same name 1987. His stage shows are energetic and extravagant; he has also starred in several films, including *Graffiti Bridge* 1990.

Prince Hal (Harold) 1928– . US director of musicals such as *Cabaret* 1968 and *Follies* 1971 on Broadway in New York, and *Evita* 1978 and *Sweeney Todd* 1980 in London's West End.

printmaking creating a picture or design by printing from a plate (woodblock, stone, or metal sheet) that holds ink or colour. The oldest form of print is the woodcut, common in medieval Europe, followed by line ◊engraving (from the 15th century), and ◊etching (from the 17th century); coloured woodblock prints flourished in Japan from the 18th century. ◊Lithography was invented 1796.

The German artist Dürer created outstanding woodcuts and line engravings, and the Dutch painter Rembrandt was one of the first major artists to produce etchings.

The profoundly humorous writers are humorous because they are responsive to the hopeless, uncouth concatenations of life.

V S Pritchett
The Living Novel & Later Appreciations 1946

Pritchett V(ictor) S(awdon) 1900– . English short-story writer, novelist, and critic, with an often witty and satirical style. His short stories were gathered in *Collected Stories* 1982 and *More Collected Stories* 1983. His critical works include

The Living Novel 1946 and biographies of the Russian writers Turgenev 1977 and Chekov 1988.

Prix Goncourt French literary prize for fiction, given by the Académie Goncourt (founded by Edmond de ◊Goncourt 1903).

Prix Goncourt: recent winners	
1980	Yves Navarre *Le Jardin d'acclimation*
1981	Lucien Bodard *Anne Marie*
1982	Dominique Fernandez *Dans la Main de l'ange*
1983	Frederick Tristan *Les égarés*
1984	Marguerite Duras *L'Amant*
1985	Yann Queffelec *Les Noces barbares*
1986	Michel Host *Valet de Nuit*
1987	Tahir Ben Jelloun *La Nuit sacrée*
1988	Erik Orsenna *L'Exposition coloniale*
1989	Jean Vautrin *Un Grand Pas vers le bon dieu*
1990	Jean Rouault *Les Champs d'Honneur*
1991	Pierre Combescot *Les Filles du calvaire*
1992	Patrick Chamoisean *Texaco*
1993	Amin Maalouf *The Rock of Tanios*

Procopius about 495–565. Greek historian, born in Palestine. He wrote a history of the campaigns of the Eastern Roman Empire against the Goths and the Vandals. He also wrote extensively on architecture, and was the author of *The Secret History*, a relatively scandalous account of the leading figures of the age.

Procrustes (Greek 'the stretcher') in Greek mythology, a robber who tied his victims to a bed; if they were too tall for it, he cut off the ends of their legs, and if they were too short, he stretched them.

programme music music that interprets a story, depicts a scene or painting, or illustrates a literary or philosophical idea, such as Richard Strauss' tone poem *Don Juan* 1888. Programme music became popular in the Romantic era.

Prokofiev Sergey (Sergeyevich) 1891–1953. Soviet composer. His music includes operas such as *The Love for Three Oranges* 1921; ballets for Sergei ◊Diaghilev, including *Romeo and Juliet* 1935; seven symphonies including the *Classical Symphony* 1916–17; music for films, including Eisenstein's *Alexander Nevsky* 1938; piano and violin concertos; songs and cantatas (for example, that composed for the 30th anniversary of the October Revolution); and *Peter and the Wolf* 1936 for children, to his own libretto after a Russian folk tale.

Born near Ekaterinoslav, he studied at St Petersburg under Rimsky-Korsakov and achieved fame as a pianist. He left Russia 1918 and lived for some time in the USA and in Paris, but returned 1927 and again 1935.

prolation system of proportional timing in Renaissance music, relating shifts in tempo to harmonic ratios, for example 1:2, 2:3, and so on.

promenade concert originally a concert where the audience was free to promenade while the music was playing, now in the UK the name of any one of an annual BBC series (the 'Proms') at the Royal Albert Hall, London, at which part of the audience stands. They were originated by English conductor Henry ◊Wood 1895.

Prometheus in Greek mythology, a ◊Titan who stole fire from heaven for the human race. In revenge, Zeus had him chained to a rock where an eagle came each day to feast on his liver, which grew back each night, until he was rescued by the hero ◊Heracles.

Propertius Sextus *c.* 47–15 BC. Roman elegiac poet, best known for his highly personal love songs, addressed to his mistress 'Cynthia'.

From a mere nothing springs a mighty tale.

Sextus Propertius *Elegies*

---

prose spoken or written language without metrical regularity; in literature, prose corresponds more closely to the patterns of everyday speech than ◊poetry.

In Western literature prose was traditionally used for what is today called nonfiction – that is, history, biography, essays, and so on – while verse was used for imaginative literature. Prose came into its own as a vehicle for fiction with the rise of the ◊novel in the 18th century. In modern literature, the distinction between verse and prose is not always clear cut.

Proserpina in Roman mythology, the goddess of the underworld. Her Greek equivalent is ◊Persephone.

Protesilaus in classical mythology, the first Greek to jump ashore from the boats on the expedition against ◊Troy. Although immediately killed, he was permitted by the gods to return to his wife Laodamia for just three hours, at the end of which she took her own life.

Proteus in Greek mythology, the warden of the sea beasts of the sea god Poseidon. He possessed the gift of prophecy and could transform himself into any form he chose to evade questioning.

Proust Marcel 1871–1922. French novelist and critic. His immense autobiographical work *A la Recherche du temps perdu/Remembrance of Things Past* 1913–27, consisting of a series of novels, is the expression of his childhood memories coaxed from his subconscious; it is also a precise reflection of life in France at the end of the 19th century.

Born at Auteuil, Proust was a delicate, asthmatic child; until he was 35 he moved in the fashionable circles of Parisian society, but after the death of his parents 1904–05 he went into seclusion in a cork-lined room in his Paris apartment, and devoted the rest of his life to writing his masterpiece.

The true paradises are paradises we have lost.

Marcel Proust *Le Temps retrouvé*

Provençal literature Provençal literature originated in the 10th century and flowered in the 12th century with the work of the ◊troubadours, poet-musicians of the 12th–13th centuries. After the decline of the troubadours in the 13th century, Provençal disappeared as a literary medium from the 14th until the 19th centuries, when Jacques Jasmin (1798–1864) and others paved the way for the Félibrige group of poets, of whom the greatest are Joseph Roumanille (1818–1891), Frédéric Mistral (1830–1914), and Félix Gras (1844–1901).

Provincetown Players group of US actors, producers, and dramatists formed 1916 in Provincetown, Cape Cod, Massachusetts; they later moved to New York. Mounting new plays by Eugene O'Neill, Theodore Dreiser, e e cummings, and others, they opened the door to US experimental theatre.

Prudentius 4th century AD. Latin Christian poet whose *Psychomachia/Battle for the Soul* was widely read as an inspiration for artistic illustration and allegory in the Middle Ages.

Prud'hon Pierre Paul 1758–1823. French Romantic painter. He became drawing instructor and court painter to the emperor Napoleon's wives.

After winning the Prix de Rome 1784, Prud'hon visited Italy but, unlike his contemporary Jacques-Louis David, he was unaffected by the Neo-Classical vogue; his style is indebted to the Italian painter ◊Correggio.

Psellus Michael 1018–1079. Byzantine academician, philosopher, administrator, historian, and poet. A voluminous writer on almost all academic subjects from physics to jurisprudence, Psellus was strongly influenced by neo-Platonism and the earlier Christian writers. His many letters offer a remarkable insight into the society of his time. See also ◊Byzantine literature.

Psyche late Greek personification of the soul as a winged girl or young woman. The goddess Aphrodite was so jealous of Psyche's beauty that she ordered her son Eros, the god of love, to make Psyche fall in love with the worst of men. Instead, he fell in love with her himself.

psychedelic rock or *acid rock* pop music that usually involves advanced electronic equipment for both light and sound. The free-form improvisations and light shows that appeared about

1966, attempting to suggest or improve on mind-altering drug experiences, had by the 1980s evolved into stadium performances with lasers and other special effects.

Ptah Egyptian god, the divine potter, a personification of the creative force. He was worshipped at Memphis, and was often portrayed as a mummified man. He was said to be the father of Imhotep, the physician and architect.

Pucci Emilio (Marchese di Barsento) 1914–1992. Italian couturier, champion skier, and politician whose designs were popular in the mid-1950s to mid-1960s. Produced in bright colours (turquoise, acid yellow, and almond green), his designs became the symbol of a new casual chic, and contributed to the growth of the Italian fashion industry after World War II. Although the popularity of his designs declined after the mid-1960s, Pucci's influence was seen in Gianni ◊Versace's 1991 collections and much 1960s-revival high-street fashion.

Puccini Giacomo (Antonio Domenico Michele Secondo Maria) 1858–1924. Italian opera composer whose music shows a strong gift for melody and dramatic effect and whose operas combine exotic plots with elements of *verismo* (realism). They include *Manon Lescaut* 1893, *La Bohème* 1896, *Tosca* 1900, *Madame Butterfly* 1904, and the unfinished *Turandot* 1926.

God touched me with his little finger and said, 'Write for the theatre, only for the theatre.'

Giacomo Puccini

Pudovkin Vsevolod Illarionovich 1893–1953. Russian film director whose films include the silent *Mother* 1926, *The End of St Petersburg* 1927, and *Storm over Asia* 1928; and the sound films *Deserter* 1933 and *Suvorov* 1941.

Puget Pierre 1620–1694. French Baroque sculptor, painter, and architect who developed a powerful and expressive style. He created a muscular statue of the tyrant *Milo of Crotona* 1671–82 (Louvre, Paris) for the garden of the palace of Versailles.

Puget worked in Italy 1640–43 and was influenced by Michelangelo and ◊Pietro da Cortona. After 1682 he failed to gain further court patronage because of his stubborn temperament and his severe style.

Pugin Augustus Welby Northmore 1812–1852. English architect, collaborator with Charles ◊Barry in the detailed design of the Houses of Parliament. He did much to instigate the ◊Gothic Revival in England, largely through his book *Contrasts* 1836.

Pulitzer Joseph 1847–1911. Hungarian-born US newspaper publisher. He acquired *The World* 1883 in New York City and, as a publisher, his format set the style for the modern newspaper. After his death, funds provided in his will established 1912 the school of journalism at Columbia University and the annual Pulitzer Prizes in journalism, literature, and music (from 1917).

Pulitzer Prize for Fiction: recent winners	
1980	Norman Mailer *The Executioner's Song*
1981	John Kennedy Toole *A Confederacy of Dunces*
1982	John Updike *Rabbit is Rich*
1983	Alice Walker *The Color Purple*
1984	William Kennedy *Ironweed*
1985	Alison Lurie *Foreign Affairs*
1986	Larry McMurtry *Lonesome Dove*
1987	Peter Taylor *A Summer to Memphis*
1988	Toni Morrison *Beloved*
1989	Anne Tyler *Breathing Lessons*
1990	Oscar Hijuelos *The Mambo Kings Play Songs of Love*
1991	John Updike *Rabbit at Rest*
1992	Jane Smiley *A Thousand Acres*
1993	Robert Olen Butler *A Good Scent from a Strange Mountain*

Punch (Italian *Pulchinella*) male character in the traditional ◊puppet play *Punch and Judy*, a humpbacked, hooknosed figure who fights with his wife, Judy.

Punch generally overcomes or outwits all opponents. The play is performed by means of glove puppets, manipulated by a single operator concealed in a portable canvas stage frame, who uses a squeaky voice for Punch. Punch originated in Italy, and was probably introduced to England at the time of the Restoration.

punk movement of disaffected youth of the late 1970s, manifesting itself in fashions and music designed to shock or intimidate. *Punk rock* began in the UK and stressed aggressive performance within a three-chord, three-minute format, as exemplified by the Sex Pistols.

Ostensibly a rejection of everything that had gone before, punk rock drew on more than a decade of US garage bands; reggae and rockabilly were also important influences on, for example, the Clash, the most successful British punk band. The punk movement brought more women into rock (for example, the Slits 1977–82) and was antiracist and anti-establishment. The musical limitations imposed by its insistence on amateurism and provoking outrage contributed to the decline of punk rock, but aspects live on in ◊hardcore punk and ◊grunge.

puppet figure manipulated on a small stage, usually by an unseen operator. The earliest known puppets are from 10th-century BC China. The types include *finger* or *glove puppets* (such as ◊Punch); *string marionettes* (which reached a high artistic level in ancient Burma and

Sri Lanka and in Italian princely courts from the 16th to 18th centuries, and for which the composer Haydn wrote his operetta *Dido* 1778); **shadow silhouettes** (operated by rods and seen on a lit screen, as in Java); and **bunraku** (devised in Osaka, Japan), in which three or four black-clad operators on stage may combine to work each puppet about 1 m/3 ft high.

During the 16th and 17th centuries puppet shows became popular with European aristocracy and puppets were extensively used as vehicles for caricature and satire until the 19th century, when they were offered as amusements for children in parks. In the 1920s Sergei ◊Obraztsov founded the Puppet Theatre in Moscow. Large-scale puppets have played an important role in street theatre since the 1960s as in Peter Schuman's Bread and Puppet Theater in the USA. In the 1970s interest was revived by television; for example, *The Muppet Show*, and, in the 1980s and 1990s, the satirical TV programme *Spitting Image*, which features puppets caricaturing public figures.

Purcell Henry 1659–1695. English Baroque composer. His music balances high formality with melodic expression of controlled intensity, for example, in the opera *Dido and Aeneas* 1689 and music for Dryden's *King Arthur* 1691 and for *The Fairy Queen* 1692. He wrote more than 500 works, ranging from secular operas and incidental music for plays to cantatas and church music.

Purchas Samuel 1577–1626. English compiler of travel books, rector of St Martin's Ludgate, 1614–26. His collection *Purchas, his Pilgrimage* 1613, was followed by another 1619, and in 1625 by *Hakluytus Posthumus or Purchas his Pilgrimes*, based on papers left by the geographer Richard Hakluyt.

Purdy James 1923– . US novelist. His novels include *Malcolm* 1959, *The Nephew* 1960, and *Cabot Wright Begins* 1964. Like his poetry and plays, his fiction deals with extreme emotional states and dramatic transformations. They typically treat homosexual subjects with stylistic elegance and a flair for strange or grotesque images.

Habit is Heaven's own redress:/it takes the place of happiness.

Aleksandr Pushkin
Eugene Onegin 1823–31

Pushkin Aleksandr 1799–1837. Russian poet and writer. His works include the novel in verse ◊*Eugene Onegin* 1823–31 and the tragic drama *Boris Godunov* 1825. Pushkin's range was wide, and his willingness to experiment freed later Russian writers from many of the archaic conventions of the literature of his time.

Pushkin was born in Moscow. He was exiled 1820 for his political verse and in 1824 was in

trouble for his atheistic opinions. He wrote ballads such as *The Gypsies* 1827, and the prose pieces *The Captain's Daughter* 1836 and *The Queen of Spades* 1834. He was mortally wounded in a duel with his brother-in-law.

'Puss in Boots' fairy tale, included in Charles ◊Perrault's collection. The youngest son of a poor miller inherits nothing from his father but a talking cat. By ingenuity and occasional magic, the cat enables the hero to become rich, noble, and the husband of a princess.

Puttnam David (Terence) 1941– . English film producer who played a major role in reviving the British film industry internationally in the 1980s. Films include *Chariots of Fire* 1981 (Academy Award for best producer), *The Killing Fields* 1984, and *Memphis Belle* 1990. He was briefly head of Columbia Pictures in the mid-1980s.

Puvis de Chavannes Pierre Cécile 1824–1898. French Symbolist painter. His major works are vast decorative schemes in pale colours, mainly on mythological and allegorical subjects, for public buildings such as the Panthéon and Hôtel de Ville in Paris. The Boston Public Library, Massachusetts, also owns several of his murals. His *Poor Fisherman* 1881 (Louvre, Paris) is a much admired smaller work.

Pygmalion in Greek mythology, a king of Cyprus who fell in love with an ivory statue he had carved. When Aphrodite brought it to life as a woman, Galatea, he married her.

pylon in modern usage, a steel lattice tower that supports high-tension electrical cables. In ancient Egyptian architecture, a pylon is one of a pair of inward-sloping towers that flank an entrance.

Pym Barbara 1913–1980. English novelist, born in Shropshire, whose closely observed novels of village life include *Some Tame Gazelle* 1950, *The Sweet Dove Died* 1978, and *A Few Green Leaves* 1980.

Pynaker Adam 1622–1673. Dutch landscape painter. His style reflects Italianate influence in the way it combines cloudless skies with the effect of clear, golden light on a foreground of trees and foliage. *Landscape with Sportsmen and Game* about 1665 (Dulwich College Art Gallery, London) is a typical work.

Pynchon Thomas 1937– . US novelist who, with great stylistic verve, created a bizarre, labyrinthine world in his fiction. His first novel was *V* 1963; it was followed by the shorter comic quest novel, *The Crying of Lot 49* 1966, before his gargantuan tour-de-force ◊*Gravity's Rainbow* 1973 with its fantastic imagery and esoteric language, drawn from mathematics and science.

After a collection of earlier written short stories *Slow Learner* 1984, he published his fourth novel, *Vineland* 1990, a reworking of earlier preoccupations.

pyramid four-sided building with triangular sides. Pyramids were used in ancient Egypt to enclose a royal tomb; for example, the Great Pyramid of Khufu/Cheops at El Gîza, near Cairo, 230 m/755 ft square and 147 m/481 ft high. In Babylon and Assyria broadly stepped pyramids (◊ziggurats) were used as the base for a shrine to a god: the Tower of ◊Babel was probably one of these.

Truncated pyramidal temple mounds were also built by the Mayas and Aztecs of Central America, for example at Chichén Itzá and Cholula, near Mexico City, which is the world's largest in ground area (300 m/990 ft base, 60 m/195 ft high). Some New World pyramids were also used as royal tombs, for example, at the Mayan ceremonial centre of Palenque.

Soldiers! From the summit of these monuments, forty centuries look upon you.

Napoleon's exhortation to his troops
before the Battle of the
Pyramids 1798

Pyramus and Thisbe legendary Babylonian lovers whose story was retold by the Roman poet Ovid. Pursued by a lioness, Thisbe lost her veil, and when Pyramus arrived at their meeting place, he found it bloodstained. Assuming Thisbe was dead, he stabbed himself, and she, on finding his body, killed herself. In Shakespeare's *A Midsummer Night's Dream*, the 'rude mechanicals' perform the story as a farce for the nobles.

Pythagorus of Rhegium 5th century BC. Greek sculptor. He was born on the island of Samos and settled in Rhegium (Reggio di Calabria), Italy. He made statues of athletes and is said to have surpassed his contemporary Myron in this field.

Pythia priestess of the god Apollo at the ◊oracle of Delphi in ancient Greece, and his medium. When consulted, her advice was interpreted by the priests of Apollo and shaped into enigmatic verses.

Pythian Games ancient Greek festival in honour of the sun god Apollo, celebrated near Delphi every four years.

quadrille square dance for four or more couples, or the music for the dance, which alternates between two and four beats in a bar.

quaich or *quaigh* Scottish Highland drinking cup, made with a wide, shallow bowl and two or three handles projecting from the upper lip. It often has a circular foot.

Quant Mary 1934– . British fashion designer. She popularized the miniskirt in the UK and is known for being one of the first designers to make clothes specifically for the teenage and early twenties market, producing bold, simple outfits which were in tune with the 'swinging London' of the 1960s. Her designs were sharp, angular, and streetwise, and she combined spots, stripes, and checks in an original way. Her Chelsea boutique was named Bazaar. In the 1970s she extended into cosmetics and textile design.

Quasimodo Salvatore 1901–1968. Italian poet. His early collections, such as *Acque e terre/Waters and Land* 1930, established his reputation as an exponent of 'hermetic' poetry, spare, complex, and private. Later books, including *Nuove poesie/New Poetry* 1942 and *Il falso e vero verde/The False and True Green* 1956, reflect a growing preoccupation with the political and social problems of his time. Nobel prize 1959.

Poetry is the revelation of a feeling that the poet believes to be interior and personal [but] which the reader recognizes as his own.

Salvatore Quasimodo 1960

---

quattrocento (Italian 'four hundred') denoting the 1400s and used in relation to Italian culture of the 15th century.

Quayle Anthony 1913– . English actor and director. From 1948 to 1956 he directed at the Shakespeare Memorial Theatre, and appeared as Falstaff in *Henry IV*, Petruchio in *The Taming of the Shrew*, and played the title role in *Othello*. He played nonclassical parts in *Galileo*, *Sleuth*, and *Old World*. He founded the Compass Company 1984. His numerous film appearances include *Lawrence of Arabia* 1962.

Queen British glam-rock group 1971–91 credited with making the first successful pop video, for their hit 'Bohemian Rhapsody' 1975. The operatic flamboyance of lead singer Freddie Mercury (1946–1991) was the cornerstone of their popularity. Among their other hits are 'We Will Rock You' 1977 and the rockabilly pastiche 'Crazy Little Thing Called Love' 1980.

Queen Anne style decorative art in England 1700–30, characterized by plain, simple lines, mainly in silver and furniture.

Queneau Raymond 1903–1976. French Surrealist poet and humorous novelist. His works include *Zazie dans le métro/Zazie in the Metro* 1959, a portrayal of a precocious young Parisian woman.

Man's usual routine is to work and to dream.

Raymond Queneau
Une Histoire modèle

Quennell Peter 1905– . British biographer and critic. He edited the journal *History Today* 1951–79, and wrote biographies of Byron 1935, Ruskin 1949, Pope 1968, and Dr Johnson 1972.

Quercia Jacopo della *c.* 1374–1438. Sienese sculptor, a contemporary of Donatello and Ghiberti. His major works were a fountain for his hometown of Siena, the Fonte Gaia 1414–19 (Palazzo Pubblico, Siena), and the main portal at San Petronio, Bologna, 1425–38.

His turbulent style and powerful figures influenced Michelangelo, whose painting *The ◊Creation of Adam* 1511 (Sistine Chapel, Vatican) was inspired by Jacopo's relief panel of the same subject at San Petronio.

Quetzalcoatl in pre-Columbian cultures of Central America, a feathered serpent god of air and water. In his human form, he was said to have been fair-skinned and bearded and to have reigned on Earth during a golden age. He disappeared across the eastern sea, with a promise to return; the Spanish conquistador Hernán Cortés exploited the myth in his own favour when he invaded. Ruins of Quetzalcoatl's temples survive in various ancient Mesoamerican ceremonial centres, including the one at Teotihuacán in Mexico.

Quevedo y Villegas Francisco Gómez de 1580–1645. Spanish novelist and satirist. His picaresque novel *La vida del buscón/The Life of a Scoundrel* 1626 follows the tradition of the roguish hero who has a series of adventures. *Sueños/Visions* 1627 is a brilliant series of satirical portraits of contemporary society.

quilt padded bed cover or the method used to make padded covers or clothing. The padded effect is achieved by sewing a layer of down, cotton, wool, or other stuffing between two outer pieces of material; patterned sewing is used (often diamond shapes or floral motifs).

Quilts have been made in the home for centuries throughout Europe, the East, and more recently the USA. They are sometimes decorated with patchwork or embroidery.

Quimby Fred(erick) 1886–1965. US film producer, head of MGM's short films department 1926–56. Among the cartoons produced by this department were the *Tom and Jerry* series and those directed by Tex ◊Avery.

Quinn Anthony 1915– . Mexican-born US actor whose roles frequently displayed volatile machismo, in films from 1935. Famous for the title role in *Zorba the Greek* 1964, he often played larger-than-life characters. Other films include *Viva Zapata!* 1952 (Academy Award for best supporting actor) and Fellini's *La strada* 1954.

In Europe an actor is an artist. In Hollywood, if he isn't working, he's a bum.

Anthony Quinn

Quintero Serafin Alvárez and Joaquin Alvárez. Spanish dramatists; see ◊Alvárez Quintero.

Quixote, Don novel by the Spanish writer ◊Cervantes; see ◊Don Quixote de la Mancha.

Love is not dumb. The heart speaks many ways.

Jean Racine *Britannicus* 1669

RA abbreviation for the ◊*Royal Academy of Arts*, London, founded 1768.

Rabelais François 1495–1553. French satirist, monk, and physician whose name has become synonymous with bawdy humour. He was educated in the Renaissance humanist tradition and was the author of satirical allegories, including *La Vie inestimable de Gargantua/The Inestimable Life of Gargantua* 1535 and *Faits et dits héroïques du grand Pantagruel/Heroic Deeds and Sayings of the Great Pantagruel* 1533, about two giants (father and son).

Rachel stage name of Elizabeth Félix 1821–1858. French tragic actress who excelled in fierce, passionate roles, notably Phaedra in Racine's tragedy *Phèdre*, which she took on tour to Europe, the USA, and Russia.

Rachmaninov Sergei (Vasilevich) 1873–1943. Russian composer, conductor, and pianist. After the 1917 Revolution he emigrated to the USA. His music is melodious and emotional and includes operas, such as *Francesca da Rimini* 1906, three symphonies, four piano concertos, piano pieces, and songs. Among his other works are the *Prelude in C-Sharp Minor* 1882 and *Rhapsody on a Theme of Paganini* 1934 for piano and orchestra.

Racine Jean 1639–1699. French dramatist and exponent of the classical tragedy in French drama. His subjects came from Greek mythology and he observed the rules of classical Greek drama. Most of his tragedies have women in the title role, for example *Andromaque* 1667, *Iphigénie* 1674, and ◊*Phèdre* 1677.

An orphan, Racine was educated by Jansenists at Port Royal, but later moved away from an ecclesiastical career to success and patronage at court. His ingratiating flattery won him the success he craved 1677 when he was appointed royal historian. After the failure of *Phèdre* in the theatre he no longer wrote for the secular stage, but, influenced by Madame de Maintenon, wrote two religious dramas, *Esther* 1689 and *Athalie* 1691, which achieved posthumous success.

Radcliffe Ann (born Ward) 1764–1823. English novelist, an exponent of the ◊Gothic novel or 'romance of terror' who wrote, for example, *The Mysteries of Udolpho* 1794. She was one of the first novelists to include vivid descriptions of landscape and weather.

Raeburn Henry 1756–1823. Scottish portrait painter, active mainly in Edinburgh. He developed a technique of painting with broad brushstrokes directly on the canvas without preparatory drawing. He was appointed painter to George IV 1823. *The Reverend Robert Walker Skating* about 1784 (National Gallery of Scotland, Edinburgh) is typical of his work.

Rafelson Bob (Robert) 1934– . US film director who gained critical acclaim for his second film, *Five Easy Pieces* 1971. His films include *The King of Marvin Gardens* 1972, *Stay Hungry* 1976, and *The Postman Always Rings Twice* 1981.

Raft George 1895–1980. US film actor, often cast as a sharp-eyed gangster (as in *Scarface* 1932). His later work included a cameo in *Some Like It Hot* 1959.

raga (Sanskrit *rāga* 'tone' or 'colour') in Indian music, a scale of notes and style of ornament for music associated with a particular mood or time of day; the equivalent term in rhythm is *tala*. A choice of raga and tala forms the basis of improvised music; however, a written composition may also be based on (and called) a raga.

ragga type of ◊reggae music with a rhythmic, rapid-fire, semi-spoken vocal line. A macho swagger is a common element in the lyrics. Ragga developed around 1990 from 'toasting', itself an offshoot of reggae. Ragga performers include the Jamaicans Shabba Ranks, Anthony Red Rose, and Ninja Man. Performers and fans of ragga call themselves *ragamuffins*.

Toasting is a less frenetic talkover style which began with Jamaican disc jockeys speaking lines over instrumental (dub) records. Toasting on record was pioneered in the 1970s by U Roy and Dennis Alcapone.

Ragnarök in Norse mythology, the ultimate cataclysmic battle between gods and forces of evil, from which a new order will come. In Germanic mythology this is known as ◊Götterdämmerung.

ragtime syncopated music ('ragged time') in 2/4 rhythm, usually played on piano. It developed in the USA among black musicians in the late 19th century; it was influenced by folk tradition, minstrel shows, and marching bands, and was later incorporated into jazz. Scott ◊Joplin was a leading writer of ragtime pieces, called 'rags'.

raï Algerian pop music developed in the 1970s from the Bedouin song form *melhoun*, using synthesizers and electronic drums. Singers often take the name Cheb or Cheba ('young'); for example, Cheb Khaled and Cheb Mami.

Railway Children, The novel for children by E ◊Nesbit, published 1906. Three children move with their mother to a country cottage after their father is suddenly taken away, and the adventures centre on the railway that runs past their home. Each day the children wave to an old gentleman on a passing train and eventually enlist his help to secure the release of their father from wrongful imprisonment.

Rainbow Serpent in Australian Aboriginal belief, a creative spirit being common to religions throughout much of the country. Sometimes male, sometimes female, it has the form of a giant python surrounded by rainbows and is associated with water and with fertility. In W Arnhem Land it is known as Ngaljod and is held responsible for monsoonal storms and floods.

Raine Kathleen 1908– . English poet. She wrote a three-volume autobiography, *Farewell Happy Fields* 1973, *The Land Unknown* 1975, and *The Lion's Mouth* 1977, which reflect both the Northumberland landscape of her upbringing and the religious convictions that led her to her brief conversion to Roman Catholicism 1944. Her volumes of poetry include *Stone and Flower* 1943 and *Collected Poems* 1981. She is a well-known authority on William Blake.

raku soft, freely hand-modelled earthenware pottery fired at low temperature and partly covered with lead glaze. *Raku* ware was first made in the late 16th century in Kyoto, Japan and used exclusively for the tea ceremony. The bowls are usually black but sometimes red or white. The style has been widely imitated in Japan and adopted by Western potters. The name is also applied to a method of firing pots used extensively in Japan since the 18th century, and more recently in Britain and the USA.

Rama incarnation of ◊Vishnu, the supreme spirit of Hinduism. He is the hero of the epic poem the *Rāmāyana*, and he is regarded as an example of morality and virtue.

Rāmāyana Sanskrit epic of *c.* 300 BC, in which Rama (an incarnation of the god Vishnu) and his friend Hanuman (the monkey chieftain) strive to recover Rama's wife, Sita, abducted by the demon king Ravana.

Rambert Marie. Adopted name of Cyvia Rambam 1888–1982. British ballet dancer and teacher born in Poland, who became a British citizen 1918. One of the major innovative and influential figures in modern ballet, she was with the Diaghilev ballet 1912–13, opened the Rambert School 1920, and in 1926 founded the Ballet Rambert which she directed. It became a modern-dance company from 1966 with Norman Morrice as director, and was renamed the Rambert Dance Company 1987.

We want to create an atmosphere in which creation is possible.

Marie Rambert

Rameau Jean-Philippe 1683–1764. French organist and composer. His Traité de l'harmonie/ *Treatise on Harmony* 1722 established academic rules for harmonic progression. His varied works include keyboard and vocal music and many operas, such as *Castor and Pollux* 1737.

Ramée Louise de la. English novelist who wrote under the name ◊Ouida.

Rampling Charlotte 1945– . British actress whose films include *Georgy Girl* 1966, *The Damned* 1969, and *The Night Porter/Il Portiere di Notti* 1974, and *Farewell My Lovely* 1975.

Rams Dieter 1932– . German industrial designer, best known for his electrical appliance designs for the Braun company with which he has worked as chief designer since 1955. Committed to the stark, geometrical aesthetic taught by the ◊Hochschüle für Gestaltung, Rams is the leading German designer of the postwar years and epitomizes the country's contribution to international design.

Ramsay Allan 1686–1758. Scottish poet, born in Lanarkshire. He published *The Tea-Table Miscellany* 1724–37 and *The Evergreen* 1724, collections of ancient and modern Scottish song, including revivals of the work of such poets as William Dunbar and Robert Henryson. He was the father of painter Allan Ramsay.

Ramsay Allan 1713–1784. Scottish portrait painter. After studying in Edinburgh and Italy, he established himself as a portraitist in London and became painter to George III 1760. His portraits include *The Artist's Wife* about 1755 (National Gallery of Scotland, Edinburgh).

Rand Ayn. Adopted name of Alice Rosenbaum 1905–1982. Russian-born US novelist. Her novel *The Fountainhead* 1943 (made into a film 1949), describing an idealistic architect who destroys his project rather than see it altered, displays her blend of vehement anti-communism and fervent philosophy of individual enterprise.

Rand Sally (Helen Gould Beck) 1904–1979. US exotic dancer. During the 1930s she worked as a dancer in Chicago and developed her trademark nude dance routine to Chopin and Debussy, which featured the coy use of huge ostrich fans. Playing a role in the 1965 burlesque revival on Broadway, she continued to dance until 1978.

rangefinder instrument for determining the range or distance of an object from the observer; used to focus a camera. A *rangefinder camera* has a rotating mirror or prism that alters the image seen through the viewfinder, and a secondary window. When the two images are brought together into one, the lens is sharply focused.

Rank J(oseph) Arthur 1888–1972. British film magnate. Having entered films 1933 to promote the Methodist cause, by the mid-1940s he controlled, through the Rank Organization, half the British studios and more than 1,000 cinemas. The Rank Organization still owns the Odeon chain of cinemas, although film is now a minor part of its activities.

Ransom John Crowe 1888–1974. US poet and critic. He published his romantic but anti-rhetorical verse in, for example, *Poems About God* 1919, *Chills and Fever* 1924, and *Selected Verse* 1947.

He was born in Tennessee, and was a leader of the Southern literary movement that followed World War I. As a critic and teacher he was a powerful figure in the New Criticism movement, which shaped much literary theory from the 1940s to the 1960s.

Ransome Arthur 1884–1967. English journalist (correspondent in Russia for the *Daily News* during World War I and the Revolution) and writer of adventure stories for children, such as ◊*Swallows and Amazons* 1930 and *Peter Duck* 1932.

Grab a chance and you won't be sorry for a might have been.

Arthur Ransome
We Didn't Mean to Go to Sea 1937

Rao Raja 1909– . Indian writer. He wrote about Indian independence from the perspective of a village in S India in *Kanthapura* 1938 and later, in *The Serpent and the Rope* 1960, about a young cosmopolitan intellectual seeking enlightenment.

Rao was born at Hassan, Karnataka. He studied at Montpellier and the Sorbonne in France. Collections of stories include *The Cow of the Barricades* 1947 and *The Policeman and the Rose* 1978.

Raphael (Raffaello Sanzio) 1483–1520. Italian painter, one of the greatest of the High Renaissance, active in Perugia, Florence, and Rome (from 1508), where he painted frescoes in the Vatican and for secular patrons. His religious and mythological scenes are harmoniously composed; his dignified portraits enhance the character of his sitters. Many of his designs were engraved, and much of his later work was the product of his studio.

Raphael was born in Urbino, the son of Giovanni Santi (died 1494), a court painter. In 1499 he went to Perugia, where he worked with ◊Perugino, whose graceful style is reflected in Raphael's *Marriage of the Virgin* 1504 (Brera, Milan). This work also shows his early concern for harmonious disposition of figures in the pictorial space. In Florence 1504–08 he studied the works of Leonardo da Vinci, Michelangelo, Masaccio, and Fra Bartolommeo. His paintings of this period include the *Ansidei Madonna* (National Gallery, London). Pope Julius II commissioned him to decorate the papal apartments (the Stanze della Segnatura) in the Vatican. Raphael's first fresco series there, *The School of Athens* 1509, is a complex but classically composed grouping of Greek philosophers and mathematicians, centred on the figures of Plato and Aristotle. A second series of frescoes, 1511–14, includes the dramatic and richly coloured *Mass of Bolsena*. Raphael received many commissions. Within the next few years he produced mythological frescoes in the Villa Farnesina in Rome (1511–12), cartoons for tapestries for the Sistine Chapel, Vatican (Victoria and Albert Museum, London), the *Sistine Madonna* about 1512 (Gemäldegalerie, Dresden), and portraits, for example of Baldassare Castiglione about 1515 (Louvre, Paris). His last great work, *The Transfiguration* 1519–20 (Vatican Museum, Rome), anticipates Mannerism.

rap music rapid, rhythmic chant over a prerecorded repetitive backing track. Rap emerged in New York 1979 as part of the ◊hip-hop culture, although the macho, swaggering lyrics that initially predominated have roots in ritual boasts and insults. Different styles were flourishing by the 1990s, such as jazz rap, ◊gangsta rap, and reggae rap.

'The Message' 1982, by Grandmaster Flash and the Furious Five, was the first rap record to expand the content, and female rappers (the Cookie Crew, Yo Yo, and others) have countered the sexism. The strong political attack of Public Enemy has made them the most influential rap group. A school of 'conscious rappers' extolling peaceful coexistence, spearheaded by the Jungle Brothers, appeared in the late 1980s. The UK also has a flourishing and varied rap scene. However, harsh exultation in violence and misogyny continued with performers like NWA and Ice-T, and rap has caused repeated furores over censorship in the USA.

'Rapunzel' folk tale collected by the ◊Grimm brothers. Rapunzel is named after a plant that her pregnant mother had eaten from the garden of a witch. In return for the plant, the witch demands that the baby be handed over to her. She brings up the girl and imprisons her in a tower which can only be entered by climbing up her long hair. The witch tries to destroy a rescuing prince but Rapunzel heals him with her tears.

Rathbone (Philip St John) Basil 1892–1967. South African-born British character actor, a specialist in villains. He also played Sherlock Holmes (the fictional detective created by Arthur Conan Doyle) in a series of films. He worked mainly in Hollywood, in such films as *The Adventures of Robin Hood* 1938 and *The Hound of the Baskervilles* 1939.

Rationalism in architecture, an Italian movement of the 1920s which grew out of a reaction to the extremes of ◊Futurism. It was led by *Gruppo 7*, a loose association of young Italian architects, headed by Giuseppe ◊Terragni. The group's rationalist approach aimed to restore a sense of mass and volume to modern architecture and resulted in a clear-cut, austere style, exemplified in Terragni's Casa del Fascio, Como, 1932–36. The work of the movement suffered from its association with Fascism, but was reappraised in the 1960s by the ◊New York Five, in particular Peter ◊Eisenman. A parallel re-evaluation took place in Italy, culminating in the ◊Neo-Rationalism of Aldo ◊Rossi and Giorgio Grassi (1935–).

Rattigan Terence 1911–1977. English dramatist. His play *Ross* 1960 was based on the character of T E Lawrence (Lawrence of Arabia). Rattigan's work ranges from the comedy *French Without Tears* 1936 to the psychological intensity of *The Winslow Boy* 1946. Other plays include *The Browning Version* 1948 and *Separate Tables* 1954.

A novelist may lose his readers for a few pages; a dramatist never dares lose his audience for a minute.

Terence Rattigan 1956

Rattle Simon 1955– . English conductor, principal conductor of the City of Birmingham Symphony Orchestra (CBSO) from 1979. He has built the CBSO into a world-class orchestra, with a core repertoire of early 20th century music; he has also commissioned new works. He was the driving force behind the funding and building of a new concert hall for the orchestra, Symphony Hall, completed 1991. A popular and dynamic conductor, his hallmarks are clarity and precision of sound.

Ratushinskaya Irina 1954– . Soviet dissident poet. Sentenced 1983 to seven years in a labour camp plus five years in internal exile for criticism of the Soviet regime, she was released 1986. Her strongly Christian work includes *Grey is the Colour of Hope* 1988.

Rauschenberg Robert 1925– . US Pop artist, a creator of ◊happenings and incongruous multimedia works, such as *Monogram* 1959 (Moderna Museet, Stockholm), a stuffed goat daubed with paint and wearing a car tyre around its body. In the 1960s he returned to painting and used the silk-screen printing process to transfer images to canvas. He also made collages.

Ravel (Joseph) Maurice 1875–1937. French composer and pianist. His work is characterized by its sensuousness, exotic harmonics, and dazzling orchestral effects. Examples are the piano pieces *Pavane pour une infante défunte/Pavane for a Dead Infanta* 1899 and *Jeux d'eau/Waterfall* 1901, and the ballets *Daphnis et Chloë* 1912 and *Boléro* 1928.

'Raven, The' US poem, written 1845 by Edgar Allan Poe, about a bereaved poet haunted by a raven that sonorously warns 'Nevermore'.

Ray Nicholas. Adopted name of Raymond Nicholas Kienzle 1911–1979. US film director, critically acclaimed for his socially aware dramas that concentrated on the individual as outsider such as *Rebel Without a Cause* 1955. Other films include *In a Lonely Place* 1950, *Johnny Guitar* 1954, and *55 Days at Peking* 1963.

Ray Satyajit 1921–1992. Indian film director, internationally known for his trilogy of life in his native Bengal: *Pather Panchali*, *Unvanquished*, and *The World of Apu* 1955–59. Later films include *The Music Room* 1963, *Charulata* 1964, *The Chess Players* 1977, and *The Home and the World* 1984.

RCA Mark II synthesizer pioneer digitally programmable analogue synthesizer developed 1959 by Harry Olsen and Herbert Belar. It was installed in the joint Columbia-Princeton electronic studio under the direction of US composers Otto ◊Luening and Milton ◊Babbitt, its best-known advocate. It was the first integrated device for preprogrammed synthesis and mixing of electronic and concrete sound materials, employing a punched-card control system.

Read Herbert 1893–1968. British art critic, poet, and academic, whose writings during the 1930s made modern art accessible to a wider public. His books include *The Meaning of Art* 1931 and the influential *Education through Art* 1943. He was one of the founders of the Institute of Contemporary Arts in London.

Reade Charles 1814–1884. British novelist and playwright, author of the historical epic, set in the 15th century, *The Cloister and the Hearth* 1861.

Reader's Digest magazine founded 1922 in the USA to publish condensed articles and books, usually uplifting and conservative, along with in-house features. It has editions in many languages and until the mid-1980s was the largest-circulation magazine in the world.

ready-made in the visual arts, a randomly chosen object presented as a work of art, a concept first launched by Marcel ◊Duchamp when he exhibited a bicycle wheel set on a stool 1913. Ready-mades have been used both to draw attention to the often overlooked aesthetic qualities of everyday objects, and to challenge the elitist character of fine art. They were popular among Dadaists.

Although virtually identical to the Surrealist-favoured ◊found object (French *objet trouvé*), ready-mades differ in that they are manufactured items and are chosen entirely at random (according to Duchamp the selection of a found object involves aesthetic criteria).

realism in the arts and literature generally, an unadorned, naturalistic approach to subject matter. More specifically, realism refers to a movement in mid-19th-century European art and literature, a reaction against Romantic and Classical idealization and a rejection of conventional academic themes (such as mythology, history, and sublime landscapes) in favour of everyday life and carefully observed social settings. The movement was particularly important in France, where it had political overtones; the painters Gustave ◊Courbet and Honoré ◊Daumier, two leading Realists, both used their art to expose social injustice.

Courbet's work was controversial both for its scale and subject matter; his *Burial at Ornans* 1850, a large-scale canvas depicting life-size, ordinary people attending a burial, is typical. Other Realists include the novelists Balzac, Flaubert, Stendhal, Eliot, Fontane, Dostoevsky, Gogol, and Tolstoy. Realism was superseded by ◊Impressionism in painting and ◊Naturalism in literature.

recitative in opera and oratorio, sung narration partly modelled on the rhythms and inflections of natural speech. It is usually sparingly accompanied by harpsichord or organ.

recorder any of a widespread range of woodwind instruments of the ◊whistle type which flourished in consort ensembles in the Renaissance and Baroque eras, along with viol consorts, as an instrumental medium for polyphonic music (see ◊polyphony). A modern consort may include a sopranino in C5, soprano (descant) in C4, alto (treble) in F3, tenor in C3, bass in F2, and great bass in C2.

The solo recorder remained a popular solo instrument into the 18th century, and the revival of popular interest in recorder playing after 1920, largely through the efforts of Arnold ◊Dolmetsch, led to its wide adoption as a school music instrument.

Red and the Black, The (French *Le Rouge et le noir*) novel by ◊Stendhal, published 1830. Julien Sorel, a carpenter's son, pursues social advancement by dishonourable means. Marriage to a marquis' daughter, a title, and an army commission are within his grasp when revelation of his murky past by a former lover destroys him.

Red Badge of Courage, The novel 1895 by US writer Stephen ◊Crane. It tells the story of the youth Henry Fleming in the American Civil War, his cowardice, courage, and final sense of personal victory.

Redding Otis 1941–1967. US soul singer and songwriter. He had a number of hits in the mid-1960s such as 'My Girl' 1965, 'Respect' 1967, and '(Sittin' on the) Dock of the Bay' 1968, released after his death in a plane crash.

Redford (Charles) Robert 1937– . US actor and film director. His blond good looks and versatility earned him his first starring role in *Barefoot in the Park* 1967, followed by *Butch Cassidy and the Sundance Kid* 1969, and *The Sting* 1973 (both with Paul ◊Newman).

His other films as an actor include *All the President's Men* 1976 and *Out of Africa* 1985. He directed *Ordinary People* 1980, *The Milagro Beanfield War* 1988, and *A River Runs Through It* 1992. He established the Sundance Institute in Utah for the development of filmmaking 1981.

Redgrave Michael 1908–1985. British actor. His stage roles included Hamlet and Lear (Shakespeare), Uncle Vanya (Chekhov), and the schoolmaster in Rattigan's *The Browning Version* (filmed 1951). On screen he appeared in *The Lady Vanishes* 1938, *The Importance of Being Earnest* 1952, and *Goodbye Mr Chips* 1959. He was the father of actresses Vanessa and Lynn Redgrave.

Redgrave Vanessa 1937– . British actress. She has played Shakespeare's Lady Macbeth and Cleopatra on the stage, Ellida in Ibsen's *Lady From the Sea* 1976 and 1979, and Olga in Chekhov's *Three Sisters* 1990. She won an Academy Award for best supporting actress for her title role in the film *Julia* 1976; other films include *Wetherby* 1985 and *Howards End* 1992. She is active in left-wing politics.

I choose my roles carefully so that when my career is finished, I'll have covered all our current history of oppression.

Vanessa Redgrave 1984

Redon Odilon 1840–1916. French Symbolist painter and graphic artist. He used fantastic symbols and images, sometimes mythological. From the 1890s he painted still lifes, flowers, and landscapes. His work was much admired by the Surrealists.

Redon initially worked mostly in black and white, producing charcoal drawings and lithographs, but from 1890 his works, in both oils and pastels, were often brilliantly coloured. The head of Orpheus is a recurring motif in his work.

Red or Dead UK fashion design label established 1982 by Wayne Hemingway. Initially he sold clothing designed by his wife Geraldine, and customized heavy industrial footwear to make an anti-fashion statement, which was partly responsible for the trend for Doc Martens workwear boots. In 1987 he designed his own-label footwear range, and in 1988 launched clothing collections for men and women, which became popular in London's clubland.

Redouté Pierre Joseph 1759–1840. French flower painter patronized by Empress Josephine and the Bourbon court. He taught botanical drawing at the Museum of Natural History in Paris and produced volumes of sumptuous, highly detailed flowers, notably *Les Roses* 1817–24.

'Red Riding Hood' European folk tale about a little girl who takes cakes to her sick grandmother's remote cottage. A wolf eats the grandmother and impersonates her, intending to eat Red Riding Hood as well. In Charles Perrault's version 1697, the story concludes with the wolf devouring the child, but the Grimm brothers' Little Red Cap is rescued. The themes in this tale have been well explored by psychoanalytic theory, as in US child psychologist Bruno Bettelheim's *The Uses of Enchantment* 1976.

Reed Carol 1906–1976. British film producer and director, an influential figure in the British film industry of the 1940s. His films include *Odd Man Out* 1947, *The Fallen Idol* and *The Third Man* both 1950, *Our Man in Havana* 1959, and the Academy Award-winning musical *Oliver!* 1968.

Reed Ishmael (Scott) 1938– . US novelist. His novels parody and satirize notions of historical fact, exploiting traditions taken from jazz and voodoo. They include *The Free-Lance Pallbearers* 1967, *Mumbo Jumbo* 1972, and *Reckless Eyeballing* 1986. His poetry includes the collection *Chattanooga* 1973.

Reed Lou 1942– . US rock singer, songwriter, and guitarist; former member (1965–70) of the New York avant-garde group the ◊*Velvet Underground*, perhaps the most influential band of the period. His solo work deals largely with urban alienation and includes the albums *Berlin* 1973, *Street Hassle* 1978, and *New York* 1989. His best-known recording is 'Walk on the Wild Side' from the album *Transformer* 1972, describing the transvestites at the Warhol Factory (the work of Pop artist Andy Warhol infuses Reed's work).

Reed Oliver 1938– . British actor, nephew of the director Carol Reed. He appeared in such films as *Women in Love* 1969, *The Devils* 1971, and *Castaway* 1987.

reed instrument any of a class of wind instruments employing a single or double flexible reed, made of cane, metal, or plastic, which vibrates under pressure within an airtight enclosure and acts as a valve admitting pulses of pressurized air into a tubular resonator. There are usually finger holes to alter the pitch. Single-reed instruments, where the reed vibrates against the material of the instrument, include clarinets and saxophones; double-reeds, where the reeds vibrate against each other, include oboes, shawms, bagpipes, and bassoons. See also ◊free-reed instrument.

reel in cinema, plastic or metal spool used for winding and storing film. As the size of reels became standardized it came to refer to the running time of the film: a standard 35-mm reel holds 313 m/900 ft of film, which runs for ten minutes when projected at 24 frames per second; hence a 'two-reeler' was a film lasting 20 minutes. Today's projectors, however, hold bigger reels.

Reeves William Pember 1857–1932. New Zealand politician and writer. He was New Zealand minister of education 1891–96, and director of the London School of Economics 1908–19. He wrote poetry and the classic history of New Zealand, *Long White Cloud* 1898.

reflex camera camera that uses a mirror and prisms to reflect light passing through the lens into the viewfinder, showing the photographer the exact scene that is being shot. When the shutter button is released the mirror springs out of the way, allowing light to reach the film. The most common type is the single-lens reflex (◊SLR) camera. The twin-lens reflex (◊TLR) camera has two lenses: one has a mirror for viewing, the other is used for exposing the film.

regal portable reed organ powered by bellows, invented about 1460 in Germany and current in Europe until the 17th century. A modern version is used in Indian popular music.

Regency style style of architecture and interior furnishings popular in England during the late 18th and early 19th centuries. It is characterized by restrained simplicity and the imitation of ancient classical elements, often Greek. Architects of this period include Decimus Burton (1800–1881), Henry Holland (1746–1806), and John ◊Nash.

Reger (Johann Baptist Joseph) Max(imilian) 1873–1916. German composer and pianist, professor at the Leipzig Conservatoire from 1907. His works embody a particular blend of contrapuntal ingenuity and Romantic sentimentality, and include *Four Symphonic Poems* 1913, sonatas, Romantic character pieces, and orchestral variations and fugues on themes by Beethoven, Mozart, and other less well known composers.

Creation must be completely free. Every fetter one imposes on oneself by taking into account playability or public taste leads to disaster.

Max Reger letter 1900

---

reggae predominant form of West Indian popular music of the 1970s and 1980s, characterized by a heavily accented offbeat and a thick bass line. The lyrics often refer to Rastafarianism, a religion originating in the West Indies which seeks the return of black people to Africa. Musicians include Bob Marley, Lee 'Scratch' Perry (1940–   ), performer and producer), and the group Black Uhuru (1974–   ). Reggae is also played in the UK, South Africa, and elsewhere.

There are several reggae styles. The practice of issuing singles with, on the B-side, a *dub* version, or stripped-down instrumental remix, was designed for use in clubs, where disc jockeys who added a spoken vocal part became known as *toasters*; they in turn released records. A fast reggae-rap style called ◊*ragga* emerged in the early 1990s. Like rap texts, reggae lyrics tend to be political–historical (Burning Spear, Gregory Isaacs), sexually explicit (Shabba Ranks), or describe ghetto violence (Cobra).

Reich Steve 1936–   . US composer. His Minimalist music employs simple patterns carefully superimposed and modified to highlight constantly changing melodies and rhythms; examples are *Phase Patterns* for four electronic organs 1970, *Music for Mallet Instruments, Voices, and Organ* 1973, and *Music for Percussion and Keyboards* 1984.

reinforced concrete material formed by casting ◊concrete in timber or metal formwork around a cage of steel reinforcement. The steel gives added strength by taking up the tension stresses, while the concrete takes up the compression stresses. Its technical potential was first fully demonstrated by François Hennebique (1842–1921) in the façade of the Charles VI Mill at Tourcoing, France, 1895.

Anatole de Baudot (1834–1915) and Victor Contamin (1840–1893) used it to architectural effect in the church of St Jean-de-Montmartre, Paris, 1894–1897. Eugène ◊Freysinnet demonstrated its structural versatility with his airship hangars at Orly 1916–24, while Auguste ◊Perret developed its architectural use in the church of Notre Dame de Raincy 1922–23. ◊Le Corbusier later explored its full technical, architectural, and decorative potential in two important projects:

the Unité d'habitation, Marseilles, 1947–52, and Chandigarh, India, 1951–56.

Reinhardt Django (Jean Baptiste) 1910–1953. Belgian jazz guitarist and composer, who was co-leader, with Stephane Grappelli, of the Quintet du Hot Club de France 1934–39. He had a lyrical acoustic style and individual technique, and influenced many US musicians.

Reinhardt Max 1873–1943. Austrian producer and director, whose Expressionist style was predominant in German theatre and film during the 1920s and 1930s. Directors such as Lubitsch and stars such as Dietrich worked with him. He co-directed the film *A Midsummer Night's Dream* 1935, a play he directed in numerous stage productions.

In 1920 Reinhardt founded the Salzburg Festival. When the Nazis came to power, he lost his theatres and, after touring Europe as a guest director, went to the USA, where he produced and directed. He founded an acting school and theatre workshop in Hollywood.

Reisz Karel 1926–   . Czech film director, originally a film critic, who lived in Britain from 1938, and later in the USA. His first feature film, *Saturday Night and Sunday Morning* 1960, was a critical and commercial success. His other films include *Morgan* 1966, *The French Lieutenant's Woman* 1981, and *Sweet Dreams* 1986.

relief in sculpture, particularly architectural sculpture, carved figures and other forms that project from the background. The Italian terms *basso-rilievo* (low relief), *mezzo-rilievo* (middle relief), and *alto-rilievo* (high relief) are used according to the extent to which the sculpture projects. The French term *bas-relief* is commonly used to mean low relief.

reliquary casket or vessel made to hold a relic or relics of a saint, generally made of precious metals and often richly decorated with gold, gems, and enamel. Particularly fine examples date from the early Christian age. If made so that the relic can be seen, the vessel is sometimes called an *ostensorium*.

REM US four-piece rock group formed 1980 in Georgia. Their songs are characterized by melodic bass lines, driving guitar, and evocative lyrics partly buried in the mix. Albums include *Reckoning* 1984, *Green* 1988, and the mass-market breakthrough *Out of Time* 1991.

Remarque Erich Maria 1898–1970. German novelist, a soldier in World War I, whose *All Quiet on the Western Front* 1929, one of the first anti-war novels, led to his being deprived of German nationality. He lived in Switzerland 1929–39, and then in the USA.

Rembrandt Harmensz van Rijn 1606–1669. Dutch painter and etcher, one of the most prolific and significant artists in Europe of the 17th century. Between 1629 and 1669 he painted some 60 penetrating self-portraits. He also painted religious subjects, and produced about 300 etchings and over 1,000 drawings. His major group portraits include *The Anatomy Lesson of Dr Tulp* 1632 (Mauritshuis, The Hague) and *The* ◊*Night Watch* 1642 (Rijksmuseum, Amsterdam).

After studying in Leiden and for a few months in Amsterdam (with a history painter), Rembrandt began his career 1625 in Leiden, where his work reflected knowledge of ◊Elsheimer and ◊Caravaggio, among others. He settled permanently in Amsterdam 1631 and obtained many commissions for portraits from wealthy merchants. The *Self-Portrait with Saskia* (his wife, Saskia van Uylenburgh) about 1634 (Gemäldegalerie, Dresden) displays their prosperity in warm tones and rich, glittering textiles. Saskia died 1642, and that year Rembrandt's fortunes began to decline (he eventually became bankrupt 1656). His work became more sombre, revealing a deeper emotional content, and his portraits were increasingly melancholy; for example, *Jan Six* 1654 (Six Collection, Amsterdam). From 1660 onwards he lived with Hendrickje Stoffels, but he outlived her, and in 1668 his only surviving child, Titus, died too. Rembrandt had many pupils, including Gerard Dou and Carel Fabritius.

A picture is finished when the artist achieves his aim.

Rembrandt

Remick Lee 1935–1991. US film and television actress. Although often typecast as a flirt early in her career, she later delivered intelligent and affecting portrayals of an extensive range of characters. Among her best-known films were *The Long Hot Summer* 1958, *Anatomy of a Murder* 1959, and *Sanctuary* 1961.

Remington Frederic 1861–1909. US artist and illustrator known for his paintings, sculptures, and sketches of scenes of the American West, which he recorded during several trips to the region. His lively images of cowboys and horses include the sculpture *The Outlaw* 1906 (Los Angeles County Museum of Art).

remix in pop music, the studio practice of reassembling a recording from all or some of its individual components, often with the addition of new elements. Issuing a recording in several different remixes ensures additional sales to collectors and increases airplay; remixes can be geared specifically to radio, dance clubs, and so on. In 1987 Madonna became the first artist in the USA to release an album consisting entirely of remixes (*You Can Dance*).

Non-Stop Ecstatic Dancing 1981 by Soft Cell may have been the world's first all-remix LP. The British recording industry agreed 1990 not to issue more than five versions of any one record, following the release of a House of Love number in 11 versions.

Remus in Roman mythology, one of two twins who were the eventual founders of Rome; see ◊Romulus.

Renaissance period and intellectual movement in European cultural history that is traditionally seen as ending the Middle Ages and beginning modern times. The Renaissance started in Italy in the 14th century and flourished in W Europe until about the 17th century.

The aim of Renaissance education was to produce the 'complete human being' (*Renaissance man*), conversant in the humanities, mathematics and science (including their application in war), the arts and crafts, and athletics and sport; to enlarge the bounds of learning and geographical knowledge; to encourage the growth of scepticism and free thought, and the study and imitation of Greek and Latin literature and art. The revival of interest in classical Greek and Roman culture inspired artists, architects, and writers; scientists and explorers proliferated as well.

The beginning of the Italian Renaissance is usually dated in the 14th century with the writers Petrarch and Boccaccio. The invention of printing (mid-15th century) and geographical discoveries helped spread the new spirit. Exploration by Europeans opened Africa, Asia, and the New World to trade, colonization, and imperialism. Biblical criticism by the Dutch humanist Erasmus and others contributed to the Reformation, but the Counter-Reformation almost extinguished the movement in 16th-century Italy.

Figures of the Renaissance include Leonardo da Vinci, the politician Machiavelli, the poets Ariosto and Tasso, the philosopher Bruno, the physicist and astronomer Galileo, and the artists Michelangelo, Cellini, and Raphael in Italy; the writers Rabelais and Montaigne in France, Cervantes in Spain, and Camoëns in Portugal; the astronomer Copernicus in Poland; and the writers More, Bacon, Sidney, Marlowe, and Shakespeare in England.

The term 'Renaissance', to describe the period of time, was first used in the 18th century.

Renaissance architecture style of architecture which began in 15th-century Italy, based on the revival of classical, especially Roman, architecture. It is characterized by a concern with balance, clarity, and proportion, and by the external use of columns and fluted pilasters.

Many buildings of ancient Rome were still extant in Renaissance Italy and artists and scholars studied their proportions and copied their decorative motifs. The architectural books of the

Roman Vitruvius (1st century AD) were popularized by Leon Battista Alberti in his influential treatise *De re aedificatoria/On Architecture* 1485 but the first major work of the age was the successful construction by Brunelleschi of a dome 1420–36 on Florence Cathedral. Alberti himself designed a new façade for Santa Maria Novella, completed 1470, in Florence, and redesigned a church in Rimini subsequently called the Tempio Malatestiano, *c.* 1450. Bramante came closest to the recreation of classical ideals with works such as the Tempietto of San Pietro in Montorio, Rome *c.* 1510 and the new basilica of St Peter's in Rome, begun 1506. Other Renaissance architects in Italy include Michelangelo, Giulio Romano, Palladio, Vignola, Sangallo, and Raphael.

As Renaissance architecture spread through the rest of Europe it often acquired a distinctively national character through the influence of indigenous styles. Renaissance architecture in England is exemplified by the Queen's House at Greenwich, London, by Inigo Jones 1616–35 and in France by the Louvre Palace built for François I 1546. In Spain a fusion of Renaissance and Gothic architectural forms led to the flamboyant style called Plateresque ('Manuellian' in Portugal), typified by the façade of the university at Salamanca, completed 1529.

Renaissance art movement in European art of the 15th and 16th centuries. It began in Florence, Italy, with the rise of a spirit of humanism and a new appreciation of the Classical Greek and Roman past. In painting and sculpture this led to greater naturalism and interest in anatomy and perspective. The 15th century is known in Italy as the **Classical Renaissance**. The **High Renaissance** (early 16th century) covers the careers of Leonardo da Vinci, Raphael, Michelangelo, and Titian in Italy and Dürer in Germany. **Mannerism** (roughly 1520s–90s) forms the final stage of the Renaissance.

The Renaissance was heralded by the work of the early 14th-century painter Giotto in Florence, and in the early 15th century a handful of outstanding innovative artists emerged there: Masaccio (in painting), Donatello (in sculpture), and Brunelleschi (in architecture). At the same time the humanist philosopher, artist, and writer Leon Battista Alberti recorded many of the new ideas in his treatises on painting, sculpture, and architecture. These ideas soon became widespread in Italy, and many new centres of patronage formed. In the 16th century Rome superseded Florence as the chief centre of activity and innovation, and became the capital of the High Renaissance. In northern Europe the Renaissance spirit is apparent in the painting of the van Eyck brothers in the early 15th century. Later, Dürer demonstrated a scientific and enquiring mind and, after his travels in Italy, brought many Renaissance ideas back to Germany. The Italian artists Cellini, Rosso Fiorentino, and Primaticcio took the Renaissance

to France through their work at Fontainebleau. Hans Holbein the Younger carried some of the concerns of Renaissance art to England in the 16th century, but it was not until the 17th century that English taste was significantly affected.

Renaissance dance courtly dance styles of the 14th and 15th centuries in Italy. The influence of professional dancing masters made the social dance of the nobility more varied and technically challenging. Many of the new steps devised by the dance masters became the foundation for ballet performances at the French courts a century later.

Renault Mary. Pen name of Mary Challans 1905–1983. English historical novelist who specialized in ancient Greece, with a trilogy on Theseus and two novels on Alexander the Great: *Fire from Heaven* 1970 and *The Persian Boy* 1972.

Rendell Ruth 1930– . English novelist and short-story writer, author of a detective series featuring Chief Inspector Wexford. Her psychological crime novels explore the minds of people who commit murder, often through obsession or social inadequacy, as in *A Demon in my View* 1976 and *Heartstones* 1987. *Lake of Darkness* 1980 won the Arts Council National Book Award (Genre Fiction) for that year.

Renger-Patzsch Albert 1897–1966. German photographer. He was a leading figure of the ◊New Photography movement which emphasized objectivity of vision. His influential book *Die Welt ist schön/The World is Beautiful* 1928 was a disparate collection of objects, from plants to industrial machinery, all photographed in the same way.

Reni Guido 1575–1642. Italian painter, active in Bologna and Rome (about 1600–14), whose idealized works include the fresco *Aurora* 1613–14 (Casino Rospigliosi, Rome). His workshop in Bologna produced numerous religious images, including Madonnas.

Renoir Jean 1894–1979. French director whose films, characterized by their humanism and naturalistic technique, include *Boudu sauvé des eaux/Boudu Saved from Drowning* 1932, *La Grande Illusion* 1937, and *La Règle du jeu/The Rules of the Game* 1939. In 1975 he received an honorary Academy Award for his life's work. He was the son of the painter Pierre-Auguste Renoir.

Renoir Pierre-Auguste 1841–1919. French Impressionist painter. He met Monet and Sisley in the early 1860s, and together they formed the nucleus of the Impressionist movement. He developed a lively, colourful painting style with feathery brushwork (known as his 'rainbow style') and painted many voluptuous female nudes, such as *The Bathers* about 1884–87 (Philadelphia Museum of Art, USA). In his later years he turned to sculpture.

Born in Limoges, Renoir trained as a porcelain painter. He joined an academic studio 1861, and the first strong influences on his style were the Rococo artists Boucher and Watteau and the Realist Courbet. In the late 1860s Impressionism made an impact and Renoir began to work outdoors. Painting with Monet, he produced many pictures of people at leisure by the river Seine. After a visit to Italy 1881 he moved towards a more Classical structure in his work, notably in *Les Parapluies/Umbrellas* about 1881–84 (National Gallery, London). In 1906 he settled in the south of France. Many of his sculptures are monumental female nudes not unlike those of ◊Maillol.

I've been 40 years discovering that the queen of all colours is black.

Pierre-Auguste Renoir

Renta see Oscar ◊de la Renta, US fashion designer.

Repin Ilya Efimovich 1844–1930. Russian Realist painter. His work includes dramatic studies, such as *Barge Haulers on the Volga* 1873 (Russian Museum, St Petersburg), and portraits, including those of Tolstoy and Mussorgsky.

repoussé relief decoration on metal, especially silver, brass, and copper, produced by hammering from the underside so that the decoration projects. It is the opposite of ◊chasing.

The technique was among the first to be developed by ancient metalworkers. Exceptionally fine examples are the Vapheio Cup made in Crete around 1500 BC (National Museum, Athens) and the Scythian animal reliefs of around 600–500 BC (Hermitage, St Petersburg).

representational art or *figurative art* in the visual arts, images that can be recognized from the real world, even if they are distorted or appear in unusual combinations, as in Surrealism. The English artist David ◊Hockney's portraits and swimming-pool paintings are contemporary examples of representational art. The opposite is ◊abstract, or non-figurative, art.

Repton Humphrey 1752–1818. English garden designer who coined the term 'landscape gardening'. He worked for some years in partnership with John ◊Nash. Repton preferred more formal landscaping than Capability ◊Brown, and was responsible for the landscaping of some 200 gardens and parks.

Republic, The treatise by the Greek philosopher Plato in which the voice of the philosopher Socrates is used to describe the ideal state, where the cultivation of truth, beauty, and goodness achieves perfection.

The true lover of knowledge must, from childhood up, be most of all a striver after truth in every form.

Plato *The Republic* 6

---

requiem in the Roman Catholic Church, a mass for the dead. Musical settings include those by Palestrina, Mozart, Berlioz, Verdi, Fauré, and Britten.

reredos ornamental screen or wall-facing behind a church altar; see ◊altarpiece.

Resnais Alain 1922– . French film director whose work is characterized by the themes of memory and unconventional concepts of time. His films include *Hiroshima, mon amour* 1959, *L'Année dernière à Marienbad/Last Year at Marienbad* 1961, and *Providence* 1977.

Respighi Ottorino 1879–1936. Italian composer, a student of Rimsky-Korsakov, whose works include the symphonic poems *The Fountains of Rome* 1917 and *The Pines of Rome* 1924 (incorporating the recorded song of a nightingale), operas, and chamber music.

Restoration comedy style of English theatre, dating from the Restoration (from 1660). It witnessed the first appearance of women on the English stage, most notably in the 'breeches part', specially created in order to costume the actress in male attire, thus revealing her figure to its best advantage. The genre placed much emphasis on wit and sexual intrigues. Examples include Wycherley's *The Country Wife* 1675, Congreve's *The Way of the World* 1700, and Farquhar's *The Beaux' Stratagem* 1707.

revenge tragedy form of Elizabethan and Jacobean drama in which revenge provides the mainspring of the action. It is usually characterized by bloody deeds, intrigue, and high melodrama. It was pioneered by Thomas Kyd with *The Spanish Tragedy* about 1588, Shakespeare's *Titus Andronicus* about 1593, and Cyril Tourneur's *The Revenger's Tragedy* about 1608. Its influence is apparent in tragedies such as Shakespeare's *Hamlet* and *Macbeth*.

revue stage presentation involving short satirical and topical items in the form of songs, sketches, and monologues; it originated in the late 19th century.

In Britain the first revue seems to have been *Under the Clock* 1893 by Seymour Hicks (1871–1949) and Charles Brookfield. The 1920s revues were spectacular entertainments, but the 'intimate revue' became increasingly popular, employing writers such as Noël Coward. During the 1960s the satirical revue took off with the Cambridge Footlights production *Beyond the Fringe*, establishing the revue tradition at fringe theatrical events.

Reynolds Burt 1936– . US film actor of rugged, burly physique in adventure films and comedies. His films include *Deliverance* 1972, *Hustle* 1975, and *City Heat* 1984.

Reynolds Joshua 1723–1792. English portrait painter, active in London from 1752. He became the first president of the Royal Academy 1768. His portraits display a facility for striking and characterful compositions in a consciously grand manner. He often borrowed classical poses, for example *Mrs Siddons as the Tragic Muse* 1784 (San Marino, California).

Reynolds was apprenticed to the portrait painter Thomas Hudson (1701–1879). From 1743 he practised in Plymouth and London and 1749–52 completed his studies in Rome and Venice, concentrating on the antique and High Renaissance masters. After his return to London he became the leading portraitist of his day with pictures such as *Admiral Keppel* 1753–54 (National Maritime Museum, London).

In his influential *Discourses on Art* 1769–91, he argued in favour of the 'Grand Manner', a style based on the Classical past rather than the mundane present.

A mere copier of nature can never produce anything great.

Joshua Reynolds addressing students of the Royal Academy 1770

Rhadamanthys in Greek mythology, son of Zeus and Europa, ruler of ◊Elysium, and with ◊Minos and Aeacus judge of the dead.

rhapsody in music, instrumental ◊fantasia, often based on folk melodies, such as Lizst's *Hungarian Rhapsodies* 1853–54.

In ancient Greece, *rhapsodes* were a class of reciters of epic poems, especially those of ◊Homer, who performed at festivals. The title means 'stitchers of songs'.

Rhea in Greek mythology, a fertility goddess, one of the Titans, wife of Kronos and mother of several gods, including Zeus.

Rhodes Zandra 1940– . English fashion designer known for the extravagant fantasy and luxury of her dress creations. She founded her own fashion house 1968.

She began by designing and printing highly individual textiles. Her fabrics—chiffon, silk, and tulle—are frequently handprinted with squiggles, zig-zags, and other patterns. Her evening dresses are often characterized by their uneven handkerchief hems.

Rhys Jean 1894–1979. English novelist, born in Dominica. Her works include *Wide Sargasso Sea* 1966, a recreation, set in a Caribbean island, of the life of the mad wife of Rochester from Charlotte Brontë's *Jane Eyre*.

A room is a place where you hide from the wolves outside and that's all any room is.

Jean Rhys
Good Morning, Midnight 1958

---

rhythm in music, a recurring pattern of long and short values, often based on classical verse or dance, determining the character of a musical ◊movement.

rhythm and blues (R & B) US popular music of the 1940s–60s, which drew on swing and jump-jazz rhythms and blues vocals, and was an important influence on rock and roll. It diversified into soul, funk, and other styles. R & B artists include Bo Diddley (1928–), Jackie Wilson (1934–1984), and Etta James (c. 1938–).

RIBA (abbreviation for *Royal Institute of British Architects*) institute whose object is 'the advancement of Architecture and the promotion of the acquirement of the knowledge of the Arts and Sciences connected therewith'. The RIBA Gold Medal is the world's most prestigious award for architecture.

The institute received its charter 1837; it is the custodian of the British Architectural Library and the Drawings Collection—the largest body of architectural designs in the world, with a quarter of a million drawings from the Renaissance to the present day.

Ribalta Francisco 1565–1628. Spanish painter, active in Valencia from 1599. Around 1615 he developed a dramatic Baroque style using extreme effects of light and shade (recalling Caravaggio), as in *St Bernard Embracing Christ* about 1620–28 (Prado, Madrid).

Ribera José (Jusepe) de 1591–1652. Spanish painter, active in Italy from 1616 under the patronage of the viceroys of Naples. His early work shows the impact of Caravaggio, but his colours gradually lightened. He painted many full-length versions of saints as well as mythological figures and genre scenes, which he produced without preliminary drawing.

Ricci Nina 1883–1970. French fashion designer, born in Italy. By 1905 she was designing clothes, and in 1932 set up a boutique specializing in dresses for mature, elegant women. Her *L'Air du Temps* perfume was sold in Lalique bottles. Her son Robert Ricci (1905–1988) managed the business from 1945.

Ricci Sebastiano 1659–1734. Venetian painter who worked throughout Italy as well as in Vienna. Between 1712 and 1716 he was in London where he painted *The Resurrection* for the chapel of the Royal Hospital, Chelsea.

Ricci's revival of the Venetian tradition of history painting was so successful that many of his paintings were indistinguishable from those of the Veronese. Ricci's lighter palette paved the way for Tiepolo. The English Royal Collection has many works by Ricci.

Rice Elmer 1892–1967. US dramatist. His works include *The Adding Machine* 1923 and *Street Scene* 1929, which won a Pulitzer Prize and was made into an opera by Kurt Weill. Many of his plays deal with such economic and political issues as the Depression (*We, the People* 1933) and racism (*American Landscape* 1939).

ricercare (Italian 'researched') in music, an abstract composition, usually contrapuntal, exploring tonal and intervallic structural relationships, as in J S Bach's several examples from *The Musical Offering* 1747.

Rich Adrienne 1929– . US radical feminist poet, writer, and critic. Her poetry is both subjective and political, concerned with female consciousness, peace, and gay rights. Her works include *Of Woman Born* 1977, *On Lies, Secrets and Silence* 1979, and *The Fact of a Doorframe: Poems, 1950–84* 1984.

In the 1960s her poetry was closely involved with the student and antiwar movements in the USA but since then she has concentrated on women's issues. In 1974, when given the National Book Award, she declined to accept it as an individual, but with Alice Walker and Audrey Rich accepted it on behalf of all women.

Richard Cliff. Stage name of Harry Roger Webb 1940– . English pop singer. In the late 1950s he was influenced by Elvis Presley, one of his best-selling early records being 'Livin' Doll' 1959. Adapting to changes in pop music fashions, he has maintained his popularity, becoming a Christian family entertainer and continuing to have hits in the UK through the 1980s. His original backing group was the Shadows (1958–68 and later re-formed).

The Shadows had solo instrumental hits in the early 1960s and their lead guitarist, Hank Marvin (1941–), inspired many British rock guitarists.

Richards Frank. Pen name of Charles Harold St John Hamilton 1875–1961. English writer for the children's papers *Magnet* and *Gem*, who invented Greyfriars public school and the fat boy Billy Bunter.

Richards I(vor) A(rmstrong) 1893–1979. English literary critic. He collaborated with C K ◊Ogden and wrote *Principles of Literary Criticism* 1924. In 1939 he went to Harvard University, USA, where he taught detailed attention to the text and had a strong influence on contemporary US literary criticism.

Richardson Dorothy 1873–1957. English novelist whose works were collected under the title *Pilgrimage* 1938. She was the first English novelist to use the ◊stream of consciousness method in *Pointed Roofs* 1915. Virginia ◊Woolf recognized and shared this technique as part of the current effort to express women's perceptions in spite of the resistance of man-made language, and she credited Richardson with having invented 'the psychological sentence of the feminine gender'.

Richardson Henry Handel. Pen name of Ethel Florence Lindesay Richardson 1870–1946. Australian novelist, the first Australian writer to win a reputation abroad. Her works include *The Getting of Wisdom* 1910, based on her schooldays and filmed 1977. She left Australia when only 18.

Richardson Henry Hobson 1838–1886. American architect, distinguished for his revival of the ◊Romanesque style. He designed churches, university buildings, homes, railroad stations, and town libraries. He had a strong influence on Louis ◊Sullivan. His buildings include Sever Hall 1878 and Austin Hall 1881 at Harvard University, and the monumental Marshall Field Wholesale Warehouse, Chicago, 1885–87. His best-known work is Trinity Church in Copley Square, Boston, 1873–77.

Richardson Ralph (David) 1902–1983. English actor. He played many stage parts, including Falstaff (Shakespeare), Peer Gynt (Ibsen), and Cyrano de Bergerac (Rostand). He shared the management of the Old Vic theatre with Laurence Olivier 1944–50. In later years he revealed himself as an accomplished deadpan comic.

Later stage successes include David Storey's *Home* 1970 and Pinter's *No Man's Land* 1976. His films include *Things to Come* 1936, *Richard III* 1956, *Our Man in Havana* 1959, *The Wrong Box* 1966, *The Bed Sitting Room* 1969, and *O Lucky Man!* 1973.

Richardson Samuel 1689–1761. English novelist, one of the founders of the modern novel. *Pamela* 1740–41, written in the form of a series of letters and containing much dramatic conversation, was sensationally popular all across Europe, and was followed by *Clarissa* 1747–48 and *Sir Charles Grandison* 1753–54.

Born in Derbyshire, Richardson was brought up in London and apprenticed to a printer. He set up his own business in London 1719, becoming printer to the House of Commons. All his six young children died, followed by his wife 1731, which permanently affected his health.

Richardson Tony 1928–1991. English director and producer. With George Devine he established the English Stage Company 1955 at the Royal Court Theatre, with productions such as John Osborne's *Look Back in Anger* 1956. His films include *Saturday Night and Sunday Morning* 1960, *A Taste of Honey* 1961, *The Loneliness of the Long Distance Runner* 1962, *Tom Jones* 1963, and *Joseph Andrews* 1977.

Richier Germaine 1904–1959. French sculptor who gained a major reputation following World War II with her febrile, Expressionist sculptures based on animal life, for example *The Ant* 1953 (Bayerische Staatsgemäldesammlungen, Munich).

Richier trained in Paris 1925–29 under Emile-Antoine Bourdelle (1861–1929) but developed her spiky, threatening, anthropomorphized figures in Switzerland during World War II. Her highly original style was much imitated during the 1950s.

Richler Mordecai 1931– . Canadian novelist, born in Montréal. His novels, written in a witty, acerbic style, include *The Apprenticeship of Duddy Kravitz* 1959 and *St Urbain's Horseman* 1971. Later works include *Joshua Then and Now* 1980 and *Home Sweet Home* 1984.

Richmond John 1960– . British fashion designer who produces unconventional street and clubland designs. He worked in the Richmond–Cornejo partnership 1984–87, creating upmarket leather jackets and separates, before setting up his own fashion label 1987. He continued to experiment with leather, producing jackets with tattoo-printed sleeves 1989 and covered with graffiti 1990. He staged his first solo show 1991.

Richter Jean Paul (Johann Paul Friedrich) 1763–1825. German author who created a series of comic eccentrics in works such as the romance *Titan* 1800–03 and *Die Flegeljahre/The Awkward Age* 1804–05. He was born in Bavaria.

Richter Sviatoslav (Teofilovich) 1915– . Russian pianist, an outstanding interpreter of Schubert, Schumann, Rachmaninov, and Prokofiev.

riddle or *conundrum* verbal puzzle or question that offers clues rather than direct aids to solving it, and often involves unlikely comparisons. Riddling poems were common in Old English poetry.

In ancient literature, finding the answer to a riddle could be a matter of life and death. Oedipus, for example, became the ruler of the ancient Greek city of Thebes by solving the riddle of the Sphinx: 'What goes on four legs in the morning, two in the afternoon, and three in the evening?' The answer is a human being – crawling on all fours as a baby, and walking with a stick in old age.

Riding (Jackson) Laura 1901–1991. US poet, a member of the Fugitive Group of poets that flourished in the southern USA 1915–28. She went to England 1926 and worked with the writer Robert Graves. Having published her *Collected Poems* 1938, she wrote no more verse, but turned to linguistics in order to analyse the expression of 'truth'.

Rie Lucie 1902– . Austrian-born potter who worked in England from the 1930s. Her pottery, exhibited all over the world, is simple and pure in form, showing a debt to Bernard ◊Leach.

Riefenstahl Leni 1902– . German filmmaker. Her film of the Nazi rallies at Nuremberg, *Triumph des Willens/Triumph of the Will* 1934, vividly illustrated Hitler's charismatic appeal but tainted her career.

She followed this with a filmed two-part documentary on the 1936 Berlin Olympic Games. After World War II she was imprisoned by the French for four years for her Nazi propagandist work.

Riemenschneider Tilman *c.* 1460–1531. German sculptor, the head of a large and successful workshop in Würzburg from 1483 and an active participant in the political and religious struggles of his time. He is best known for his limewood sculptures, such as *St Matthew* 1495–1505 (Berlin-Dahlem, Staatliche Museum). The deep serenity of his figures stands in marked contrast to his dramatic life.

Rietvelt Gerrit Thomas 1888–1964. Dutch architect, associated with the De ◊Stijl group. He designed the Schroeder House at Utrecht 1924; he is also known for his celebrated rectilinear Red-Blue Chair 1918.

Rigaud Hyacinthe 1659–1743. French portraitist, court painter to Louis XIV from 1688. His portrait *Louis XIV* 1701 (Louvre, Paris) is characteristically majestic, with the elegant figure of the king enveloped in ermine and drapery.

rigaudon lively French country dance in two time, in four-bar phrases (like a square dance), the music for which was revived by Grieg in the *Holberg Suite* 1884.

Rigg Diana 1938– . English actress. Her stage roles include Bianca in *The Taming of the Shrew* 1961, Cordelia in *King Lear* 1964, and Héloïse in *Abelard and Héloïse* 1970; television roles include Emma Peel in *The Avengers* 1965–67, Clytemnestra in *The Serpent Son* 1979, and Lady Deadlock in *Bleak House* 1985. She became the hostess for *Mystery Theater* on US public television 1989.

Rig-Veda oldest of the ◊Vedas, the chief sacred writings of Hinduism. It consists of hymns to the Aryan gods, such as Indra, and to nature gods.

Riley Bridget (Louise) 1931– . English painter, a pioneer of ◊Op art. In the early 1960s she invented her characteristic style, arranging hard-edged black and white dots or lines in regular patterns to create disturbing effects of scintillating light and movement. *Fission* 1963 (Museum of Modern Art, New York) is an example. She introduced colour in the late 1960s and experimented with silk-screen prints on Perspex.

Riley James Whitcomb 1849–1916. US poet. His first collection of poems, *The Old Swimmin' Hole*, was published 1883. His later collections include *Rhymes of Childhood* 1890 and *Home Folks* 1900. His use of the Midwestern vernacular and familiar themes earned him the unofficial title 'The Hoosier Poet.'

Rilke Rainer Maria 1875–1926. Austrian writer. His prose works include the semi-autobiographical *Die Aufzeichnungen des Malte Laurids Brigge/The Notebooks of Malte Laurids Brigge* 1910. His verse is characterized by a form of mystic pantheism that seeks to achieve a state of ecstasy in which existence can be apprehended as a whole.

Rilke was born in Prague. He travelled widely and was for a time secretary to the sculptor Rodin. He died in Switzerland. His poetical works include *Die Sonnette an Orpheus/Sonnets to Orpheus* 1923 and *Duisener Elegien/Duino Elegies* 1923.

To love is to give light with inexhaustible oil.

Rainer Maria Rilke *The Notebooks of Malte Laurids Brigge* 1910

Rimbaud (Jean Nicolas) Arthur 1854–1891. French Symbolist poet, a major figure in the development of French verse. His verse was chiefly written before the age of 20, notably *Les Illuminations* published 1886. From 1871 he lived with the poet Paul ◊Verlaine.

Although the association ended after Verlaine attempted to shoot him, it was Verlaine's analysis of Rimbaud's work 1884 that first brought him recognition. Rimbaud then travelled widely, working as a trader in North Africa 1880–91.

The poet makes himself perceptive by a long, vast, and carefully thought-out derangement of all the senses.

Arthur Rimbaud

Rimsky-Korsakov Nikolay Andreyevich 1844–1908. Russian nationalist composer and author of an influential text on orchestration. His operas include *The Maid of Pskov* 1873, *The Snow Maiden* 1882, *Mozart and Salieri* 1898, and *The Golden Cockerel* 1907, a satirical attack on despotism that was banned until 1909.

Other works include the symphonic poem *Sadko* 1867, the programme symphony *Antar* 1869, and the symphonic suite *Scheherazade* 1888. He also completed works by other composers, for example, Mussorgsky's *Boris Godunov*.

Ringling Charles 1863–1926. US circus promoter. With its three rings and large cast, the Ringlings' circus was touted as the 'Greatest

Show on Earth', the byword still most associated with the modern Ringling Brothers and Barnum and Bailey Circus (which the Ringling brothers acquired 1907).

Riopelle Jean-Paul 1923– . Canadian artist, active in Paris from 1946. He moved from automatism in the 1950s to an Abstract Expressionist style, producing colourful thickly painted canvases. He also produced sculptures. His *Encounter* 1956 (Wallraf-Richartz Museum, Cologne, Germany) is a typically rough-textured canvas.

Rip Van Winkle legendary character created by Washington ◊Irving in his 1819 tale of a man who falls into a magical 20-year sleep, and wakes to find he has slumbered through the War of American Independence.

Ritter Tex (Woodward Maurice) 1905–1974. US singer and actor, popular as a singing cowboy in B-films in the 1930s and 1940s (*Arizona Trail* 1943). He sang the title song to *High Noon* 1952.

Rivera Diego 1886–1957. Mexican painter, active in Europe until 1921. An exponent of Social Realism, he received many public commissions for murals exalting the Mexican revolution. A vast cycle on historical themes (National Palace, Mexico City) was begun 1929. In the 1930s he visited the USA and with Ben Shahn produced murals for the Rockefeller Center, New York (later overpainted because he included a portrait of Lenin).

Rix Brian 1924– . British actor and manager. He became known for his series of farces at London's Whitehall Theatre, notably *Dry Rot* 1954–58. He made several films for cinema and television, including *A Roof Over My Head* 1977, and promotes charities for the mentally handicapped.

RKO (Radio Keith Orpheum) US film production and distribution company, formed 1928 through mergers and acquisitions. It was the most financially unstable of the major Hollywood studios, despite the success of many of its films, including *King Kong* 1933 and the series of musicals starring Fred Astaire and Ginger Rogers. In 1948, Howard ◊Hughes bought the studio and accelerated its decline by poor management. The company ceased production 1957.

Roach Hal 1892–1992. US film producer, usually of comedies, who was active from the 1910s to the 1940s. He worked with ◊Laurel and Hardy, and also produced films for Harold Lloyd and Charley Chase. His work includes *The Music Box* 1932, *Way Out West* 1936, and *Of Mice and Men* 1939.

Robbe-Grillet Alain 1922– . French writer, the leading theorist of *le* ◊*nouveau roman* ('the new novel'), for example his own *Les Gommes/The Erasers* 1953, *La Jalousie/Jealousy*

1957, and *Dans le Labyrinthe/In the Labyrinth* 1959, which concentrates on the detailed description of physical objects. He also wrote the script for Alain Resnais' film *L'Année dernière à Marienbad/Last Year in Marienbad* 1961.

The true writer has nothing to say. What counts is the way he says it.

Alain Robbe-Grillet
For a New Novel 1963

Robbia, della Italian family of sculptors and architects, active in Florence. *Luca della Robbia* (1400–1482) created a number of major works in Florence, notably the marble *cantoria* (singing gallery) in the cathedral 1431–38 (Museo del Duomo), with lively groups of choristers. Luca also developed a characteristic style of glazed terracotta work.
   Andrea della Robbia (1435–1525), Luca's nephew and pupil, and Andrea's sons continued the family business, inheriting the formula for the vitreous terracotta glaze. The blue-and-white medallions of foundling children 1463–66 on the Ospedale degli Innocenti, Florence, are typical. Many later works are more elaborate and highly coloured, such as the frieze 1522 on the façade of the Ospedale del Ceppo, Pistoia.

Robbins Jerome 1918– . US dancer and choreographer, co-director of the New York City Ballet 1969–83 (with George Balanchine). His ballets are internationally renowned and he is considered the greatest US-born ballet choreographer. He also choreographed the musicals *The King and I* 1951, *West Side Story* 1957, and *Fiddler on the Roof* 1964.
   First a chorus boy on Broadway, then a soloist with the newly formed American Ballet Theater 1941–46, Robbins was associate director of the New York City Ballet 1949–59. His first ballet, *Fancy Free* 1944, was a great success (and was adapted with Leonard Bernstein into the musical *On the Town* 1944).

robe long and loose-flowing outer garment, often the official dress used to indicate the profession of a peer, judge, or academic. The term 'gown' is also used.

Roberts Charles George Douglas 1860–1943. Canadian poet, short-story writer, and novelist, 'the father of Canadian literature'. His early *Orion, and Other Poems* 1880 influentially demonstrated that Canadian poets could creatively assimilate the Romanticism of Tennyson, but later volumes such as *The Vagrant of Time* 1927 developed a more modern idiom. His 24 volumes of short fiction, starting with *Earth's Enigmas* 1896, included some of the first and most realistic animal stories as well as tales of outdoor adventure.

Roberts Tom (Thomas William) 1856–1931. Australian painter and founder of the ◊Heidelberg School, which introduced Impressionism to Australia.
   Roberts, born in England, arrived in Australia 1869, returning to Europe to study 1881–85. He received official commissions, including one to paint the opening of the first Australian federal parliament, but is better known for his scenes of pioneering life.

Robertson Thomas William 1829–1871. English dramatist. Initially an actor, he had his first success as a dramatist with *David Garrick* 1864, which set a new, realistic trend in English drama; later plays included *Society* 1865 and *Caste* 1867.

Robeson Paul 1898–1976. US bass singer and actor. He graduated from Columbia University as a lawyer, but limited opportunities for blacks led him instead to the stage. He appeared in Eugene O'Neill's play *The Emperor Jones* 1924 and the Jerome Kern musical *Show Boat* 1927, in which he sang 'Ol' Man River'. He played *Othello* 1930, and his films include *Sanders of the River* 1935 and *King Solomon's Mines* 1937. An ardent advocate of black rights, he had his passport withdrawn 1950–58 after a highly public visit to Russia. His last years were spent in England.

Robin Hood in English legend, an outlaw and champion of the poor against the rich, said to have lived in Sherwood Forest, Nottinghamshire, during the reign of Richard I (1189–99). He feuded with the sheriff of Nottingham, accompanied by Maid Marian and a band of followers known as his 'merry men'. He appears in ballads from the 13th century, but his first datable appearance is in Langland's *Piers Plowman* in the late 14th century.

Robinson Edward G. Stage name of Emmanuel Goldenberg 1893–1973. US film actor, born in Romania, who emigrated with his family to the USA 1903. Of stocky build, he was noted for his gangster roles, such as *Little Caesar* 1930, but also gave strong performances in psychological dramas such as *Scarlet Street* 1945. Other films include *Dr Ehrlich's Magic Bullet* 1940, *Double Indemnity* 1944, *A Hole in the Head* 1959, and *Soylent Green* 1973.

Robinson Edwin Arlington 1869–1935. US poet. His verse, dealing mainly with psychological themes in a narrative style, is collected in volumes such as *The Children of the Night* 1897, which established his reputation. He was awarded three Pulitzer Prizes for poetry: *Collected Poems* 1922, *The Man Who Died Twice* 1925, and *Tristram* 1928.

Robinson Henry Crabb 1775–1867. English writer, whose diaries, journals, and letters are a valuable source of information on his literary friends Lamb, Coleridge, Wordsworth, and Southey.

Robinson Henry Peach 1830–1901. British photographer who studied as a painter before taking up photography 1851. By careful composition and the combination of several negatives in one print, he produced images that closely imitated the effects and subject matter of Victorian painting.

Robinson Smokey (William) 1940– . US singer, songwriter, and record producer, associated with ◊Motown records from its conception. He was lead singer of the Miracles 1957–72 (hits include 'Shop Around' 1961, 'The Tears of a Clown' 1970) and his solo hits include 'Cruisin' 1979 and 'Being With You' 1981. His light tenor voice and wordplay characterize his work.

Robinson W(illiam) Heath 1872–1944. English cartoonist and illustrator who made humorous drawings of bizarre machinery for performing simple tasks, such as raising one's hat. A clumsily designed apparatus is often described as a 'Heath Robinson' contraption.

Robinson Crusoe (full title *The Life and Strange and Surprising Adventures of Robinson Crusoe*) book 1719 by Daniel ◊Defoe. It tells the story of a man shipwrecked alone on a desert island. His attempts to ensure his physical and mental survival are thoroughly documented before he meets another castaway. Crusoe treats 'Man Friday' as his pupil and servant, in accordance with the contemporary European attitude to other races. Defoe freely embroiders the real-life ordeal of Alexander Selkirk which inspired the book. *Robinson Crusoe* is generally regarded as the first major English novel.

Robson Flora 1902–1984. English actress, notable as Queen Elizabeth I in the film *Fire Over England* 1931 and Mrs Alving in Ibsen's *Ghosts* 1958.

Rochester John Wilmot, 2nd Earl of Rochester 1647–1680. English poet and courtier. He fought gallantly at sea against the Dutch, but chiefly led a debauched life at the court of Charles II. He wrote graceful (but often obscene) lyrics, and his *A Satire against Mankind* 1675 rivals Swift. He was a patron of the poet John Dryden.

For all men would be cowards if they durst.

Earl of Rochester
A Satire against Mankind 1675

rockabilly the earliest style of ◊rock and roll as it developed in the US South with a strong country (hillbilly) element. The typical rockabilly singer was young, white, male, and working class, such as Elvis Presley, Johnny Cash, Roy Orbison, Jerry Lee Lewis, and Carl Perkins (1932–). Many rockabilly performers later became country singers.

rock and roll pop music born of a fusion of rhythm and blues and country and western, and based on electric guitar and drums. In the mid-1950s, with the advent of Elvis Presley, it became the heartbeat of teenage rebellion in the West and also had considerable impact on other parts of the world. It found perhaps its purest form in late-1950s rockabilly.

The term 'rock and roll' was popularized by US disc jockey Alan Freed (1922–1965) from 1951. Leading rock-and-roll singers and songwriters of the 1950s included Chuck Berry, Little Richard, Jerry Lee Lewis, Buddy Holly, and Gene Vincent (1935–1971).

rock music another term for ◊pop music; sometimes, another term for rock and roll. When a distinction is made between rock and pop, rock is generally perceived as covering the less commercial and more adult end of the spectrum.

rock opera musical using pop elements, such as Andrew ◊Lloyd Webber's *Jesus Christ Superstar* 1970.

Rockwell Norman 1894–1978. US painter and illustrator who designed magazine covers, mainly for *The Saturday Evening Post*, and cartoons portraying American life. His whimsical view of the ordinary activities of the nation at work and at play earned him huge popularity.

Rococo movement in the arts and architecture in 18th-century Europe, tending towards lightness, elegance, delicacy, and decorative charm. The term 'Rococo' is derived from the French *rocaille* (rock- or shell-work), a style of interior decoration based on S-curves and scroll-like forms. Watteau's paintings and Sèvres porcelain belong to the French Rococo vogue. In the 1730s the movement became widespread in Europe, notably in the churches and palaces of S Germany and Austria. Chippendale furniture is an English example of the French Rococo style.

Other Rococo features include the use of fantastic ornament and pretty, naturalistic details. The architectural and interior design of the Amalienburg pavilion at Nymphenburg near Munich, Germany, and the Hôtel de Soubise pavilion in Paris, are typical of the movement. The painters Boucher and Fragonard both painted typically decorative Rococo panels for Parisian *hôtels* (town houses).

Rodchenko Alexander 1891–1956. Russian avant-garde painter and designer who took up photography 1924. The aim of his work, in all media, was to create a visual language that would reflect the new revolutionary times. His paintings were abstract works based on severe geometrical shapes; under the influence of Tatlin he made three-dimensional constructions of wood, cardboard, and metal. His photographs of everyday objects viewed from unusual angles document the early years of the Soviet era.

Rodgers Jimmie (James Charles) 1897– . US country singer, songwriter, and guitarist, the first important recording star of the genre. His blues-influenced vocals established an enduring style for country singers and he popularized yodelling. He also pioneered the use of steel-guitar backing, and the broken-hearted drifter who features in his songs is a Rodgers creation.

Rodgers, born in Mississippi, was known as *the Singing Brakeman* after his employment on the railway. His recordings, including 13 that were titled 'Blue Yodel' (in a numbered series), were made between 1927 and his death from tuberculosis; one of the last was called 'TB Blues'.

Rodgers Richard (Charles) 1902–1979. US composer. He collaborated with librettist Lorenz Hart (1895–1943) on songs like 'Blue Moon' 1934 and musicals like *On Your Toes* 1936, and with Oscar Hammerstein II wrote many musicals, including *Oklahoma!* 1943, *South Pacific* 1949, *The King and I* 1951, and *The Sound of Music* 1959.

Rodin Auguste 1840–1917. French sculptor, considered the greatest of his day. He freed sculpture from the idealizing conventions of the time by his realistic treatment of the human figure, introducing a new boldness of style and expression. Examples are *Le Penseur/The Thinker* 1880 (Musée Rodin, Paris), *Le Baiser/The Kiss* 1886 (marble version in the Louvre, Paris), and *The Burghers of Calais* 1884–86 (copy in Embankment Gardens, Westminster, London).

Rodin started as a mason, began to study in museums, and in 1875 visited Italy, where he was inspired by the work of Michelangelo. His early statue *The Age of Bronze* 1877 (Musée Rodin, Paris) was criticized for its total naturalism and accuracy. In 1880 he began the monumental bronze *Gates of Hell* for the Ecole des Arts Décoratifs in Paris (inspired by Ghiberti's bronze doors in Florence), a project that occupied him for many years and was unfinished at his death. Many of the figures designed for the gate became independent sculptures. During the 1890s he received two notable commissions, for statues of the writers *Balzac* 1893–97 (Musée Rodin, Paris) and *Victor Hugo* 1886–90 (Musée Rodin, Paris). He also produced many drawings.

Sculpture is an art of hollows and projections.

Auguste Rodin

Roeg Nicolas 1928– . English film director and writer, initially a camera operator. His striking visual style is often combined with fractured, disturbing plots, as in *Performance* 1970, *Don't*

Look Now 1973, *The Man Who Fell to Earth* 1976, and *The Witches* 1989.

His other films include *Walkabout* 1971, *Bad Timing* 1980, *Castaway* 1986, and *Track 29* 1988.

Roethke Theodore 1908–1963. US poet. His lyrical, visionary, and exclusively personal poetry drew on theological and mystical sources. It derived much of its detail and imagery from the greenhouses and plants in his father's large nursery business in Michigan. Collections include *Open House* 1941, *The Lost Son* 1948, *The Waking* 1953 (Pulitzer Prize), and the posthumous *Collected Poems* 1968.

Rogers Ginger. Stage name of Virginia Katherine McMath 1911– . US actress, dancer, and singer. She worked from the 1930s to the 1950s, often starring with Fred Astaire in such films as *Top Hat* 1935 and *Swing Time* 1936. Her later work includes *Bachelor Mother* 1939 and *Kitty Foyle* 1940 (Academy Award).

Rogers Richard 1933– . English High Tech architect. His works include the Pompidou Centre in Paris 1977 (jointly with Renzo ◊Piano), the Lloyds of London building in London 1986, and the Reuters building at Blackwall Yard, London, 1992 (which won him a RIBA award).

Rogers Roy. Stage name of Leonard Slye 1912– . US actor who moved to the cinema from radio. He was one of the original singing cowboys of the 1930s and 1940s. Confined to B-films for most of his career, he also appeared opposite Bob Hope and Jane Russell in *Son of Paleface* 1952.

Rohmer Eric. Adopted name of Jean-Marie Maurice Schérer 1920– . French film director and writer, formerly a critic and television-documentary director. Part of the French ◊New Wave, his films are often concerned with the psychology of self-deception. They include *Ma Nuit chez Maud/My Night at Maud's* 1969, *Le Genou de Claire/Claire's Knee* 1970, and *Die Marquise von O/The Marquise of O* 1976.

Rohmer Sax. Pen name of Arthur Sarsfield Ward 1886–1959. English crime writer who created the sinister Chinese character Fu Manchu.

Roland French hero whose real and legendary deeds of valour and chivalry inspired many medieval and later romances, including the 11th-century *Chanson de Roland* and Ariosto's *Orlando furioso*. A knight of Charlemagne, Roland was killed 778 with his friend Oliver and the 12 peers of France at Roncesvalles (in the Pyrenees) by Basques. He headed the rearguard during Charlemagne's retreat from his invasion of Spain.

Rolfe Frederick 1860–1913. English writer who called himself Baron Corvo. A Roman Catholic convert, frustrated in his desire to enter the priesthood, he wrote the novel *Hadrian VII* 1904, in which the character of the title rose from being a poor writer to become pope.

Rolland Romain 1866–1944. French author and musicologist, a leading supporter of pacifism and internationalism. He was associated with Charles ◊Péguy on the influential journal *Les Cahiers de la quinzaine* where he published his best-known novel cycle *Jean-Christophe* 1904–12, about a German composer. He wrote several biographies and critical works, including *Michelangelo* 1906, *Beethoven* 1910, and *Tolstoy* 1911. He was awarded the Nobel Prize for Literature 1915.

Rolle de Hampole Richard *c.* 1300–1349. English hermit and author of English and Latin works, including the mystic *Meditation of the Passion*.

Rolling Stones, the British band formed 1962, once notorious as the 'bad boys' of rock. Original members were Mick Jagger (1943–   ), Keith Richards (1943–   ), Brian Jones (1942–1969), Bill Wyman (1936–   ), Charlie Watts (1941–   ), and the pianist Ian Stewart (1938–1985). A rock-and-roll institution, the Rolling Stones were still performing and recording in the 1990s.

The Stones' earthy sound was based on rhythm and blues, and their rebel image was contrasted with the supposed wholesomeness of the early Beatles. Classic early hits include 'Satisfaction' 1965 and 'Jumpin' Jack Flash' 1968. The albums from *Beggars Banquet* 1968 to *Exile on Main Street* 1972 have been rated among their best work; others include *Some Girls* 1978 and *Steel Wheels* 1989.

Rollins Sonny (Theodore Walter) 1930–   . US tenor saxophonist and jazz composer. A leader of the hard-bop school, he is known for the intensity and bravado of his music and for his skilful improvisation.

Every man who feels well is a sick man neglecting himself.

Jules Romains *Knock, ou le Triomphe de la médecine* 1923

Romains Jules. Pen name of Louis Farigoule 1885–1972. French novelist, playwright, and poet. His plays include the farce *Knock, ou le Triomphe de la médecine/Dr Knock* 1923 and *Donogoo* 1930, and his novels include *Mort de quelqu'un/Death of a Nobody* 1911, *Les Copains/The Boys in the Back Room* 1913, and *Les Hommes de bonne volonté/Men of Good Will* (27 volumes) 1932–47.

Romains developed the theory of Unanimism, which states that every group has a communal existence greater than that of the individual, which intensifies the individual's perceptions and emotions.

Roman architecture, ancient the architecture of the Roman Empire, spanning the period 4th century BC–5th century AD. In contrast to the linear emphasis of ◊Greek architecture, Roman architecture is noted for its development of the rounded form. The Romans' mastery of concrete (used in combination with bricks) freed the ◊orders from their earlier structural significance and enabled the development of such rounded forms as the arch, vault, and dome. Arches and vaults were first employed in utilitarian structures, for example, bridges and aqueducts. Later they were used, together with the dome, in private and public buildings as a means of extending and diversifying the interior space.

Roman building types include the basilica, an oblong meeting hall with vaulted roof, often colonnaded; the thermae or bath houses with their complex spatial layout; and the triumphal arch, a purely ornamental structure. Rome has the richest collection of public buildings, notably the Pantheon AD 118–128, with its enormous concrete dome, the ◊Colosseum AD 70–80, numerous temples, and thermae such as those of Caracalla, about AD 215 onwards. The ruins of Pompeii at the foot of Mount Vesuvius provide the most complete view of a Roman city, which was typically planned as a series of interlinked public spaces. Dwellings tend to look inwards toward an open atrium (inner court) and peristyle (colonnade surrounding the court).

Other important monuments outside Rome include the amphitheatre at Verona, about 290, and Hadrian's villa at Tivoli, about AD 118–134. The latter offers a textbook example of Roman architectural effects in its skilful manipulation of axial symmetry, its use of curved as well as rectilinear interior spaces, and its numerous vistas. Other monuments in the Roman Empire are the beautifully preserved temple, the Maison Carrée in Nîmes, France, 16 BC; the aqueduct, the Pont du Gard, near Nîmes, about 14 BC; the Arch of Tiberius at Orange, 1st century AD; and the extensive ruins of Diocletian's Palace in Split, Croatia, 300 BC.

Roman architecture was to have an influence on many periods to follow, in particular the Romanesque style and Renaissance architecture, which amounted to a rediscovery of Classical, especially Roman building.

Roman art, ancient sculpture and painting of ancient Rome, from the 4th century BC to the fall of the Western Empire 5th century AD. Much Roman art was intended for public education, notably the sculpted triumphal arches and giant columns, such as Trajan's Column AD 106–113, and portrait sculptures of soldiers, politicians, and emperors. Surviving mural paintings (in Pompeii, Rome, and Ostia) and mosaic decorations show Greek influence. Roman art was to prove of lasting inspiration in the West.

Realistic ***portrait sculpture*** was developed by the Romans. A cult of heroes began and in public places official statues were erected of generals, rulers, and philosophers. The portrait bust developed as a new art form from about 75 BC;

these were serious, factual portraits of men to whose wisdom and authority (the busts implied) their subject nations should reasonably submit. Strict realism in portraiture gave way to a certain amount of Greek-style idealization in the propaganda statues of the emperors, befitting their semidivine status.

Narrative relief sculpture also flourished in Rome, linked to the need to commemorate military victories. These appeared on monumental altars, triumphal arches, and giant columns such as Trajan's Column, where his battles are recorded in relief like a cartoon strip winding its way around the column for about 200 m/655 ft. Gods and allegorical figures also featured with Rome's heroes on narrative relief sculptures, such as those on Augustus' giant altar to peace, the *Ara Pacis* 13–9 BC.

Very little **Roman painting** has survived; much of what has owes its survival to the volcanic eruption of Mount Vesuvius in AD 79 which buried the southern Italian towns of Pompeii and Herculaneum under ash, thus preserving the lively wall paintings that decorated the villas of an art-loving elite. Trompe l'oeil paintings and elements of still life were popular. A type of interior decoration known as **Grotesque**, rediscovered in Rome during the Renaissance, combined swirling plant motifs, strange animals, and tiny fanciful scenes.

The art of **mosaic** was found throughout the Roman Empire. It was introduced from Greece and used for floors as well as walls and vaults, in trompe l'oeil effects, geometrical patterns, and scenes from daily life and mythology.

romance tales of love and adventure, in verse or prose, that became popular in France about 1200 and spread throughout Europe. There were Arthurian romances about the legendary King Arthur and his knights, and romances based on the adventures of Charlemagne and on classical themes. In the 20th century the term 'romantic novel' is often used disparagingly, to imply a contrast with a realist novel.

The term gradually came to mean any fiction remote from the conditions and concerns of everyday life. In this sense, romance is a broad term which can include or overlap with such genres as the ◊historical novel or ◊fantasy.

Roman de la Rose (*Romance of the Rose*) French allegorical poem of courtly love written in the 13th century, begun by Guillaume de Lorris (lived early 13th century) and completed in a more expansively erudite and satirical vein by Jean de Meung (died *c.* 1305).

Romanesque style of W European ◊architecture of the 10th to 12th centuries, marked by rounded arches, solid volumes, and emphasis on perpendicular elements. In England the style is also known as ◊Norman architecture.

Romanesque art European art of the 10th–12th centuries; see ◊medieval art.

Romano Giulio. See ◊Giulio Romano, Italian painter and architect.

Romanticism in literature, the visual arts, and music, a style that emphasizes the imagination, emotions, and creativity of the individual artist. Romanticism also refers specifically to late 18th- and early 19th-century European culture, as contrasted with 18th-century ◊Classicism.

Inspired by the ideas of Jean-Jacques ◊Rousseau and by contemporary social change and revolution (US, French), Romanticism emerged as a reaction to 18th-century values, asserting emotion and intuition over rationalism, the importance of the individual over social conformity, and the exploration of natural and psychic wildernesses over classical restraint. Major themes of Romantic art and literature include a love of atmospheric landscapes (see ◊sublime); nostalgia for the past, particularly the Gothic; a love of the primitive, including folk traditions; the cult of the hero figure, often an artist or political revolutionary; romantic passion; mysticism; and a fascination with death.

In *literature*, Romanticism is represented by Novalis, Brentano, Eichendorff, and Tieck in Germany, who built on the work of the ◊*Sturm and Drang* movement; Wordsworth, Coleridge, Shelley, Byron, and Walter Scott in Britain; and Victor Hugo, Lamartine, George Sand, and Dumas *père* in France. The work of the US writers Poe, Melville, Longfellow, and Whitman reflects the influence of Romanticism.

In *art*, Friedrich in Germany and Turner in England are outstanding landscape painters of the Romantic tradition, while Fuseli and Blake represent a mystical and fantastic trend. The French painter Delacroix is often cited as the quintessential Romantic artist.

In *music*, the term is loosely applied to most 19th-century compositions but is associated particularly with ◊programme music, such as the *Symphonie fantastique* by Berlioz; the ◊song cycle, as developed by Schubert; and, most significantly, ◊opera, culminating in the late Romanticism of Wagner and Verdi.

To be able to paint the passions, they [the Romantics] must have seen, their devouring flames must have been felt.

Stendhal in *Le Journal de Paris*

Romeo and Juliet romantic tragedy by William ◊Shakespeare, first performed 1594–95. The play is concerned with the doomed love of teenagers Romeo and Juliet, victims of the bitter enmity between their respective families in Verona.

Romney George 1734–1802. English portrait painter, active in London from 1762. He became, with Gainsborough and Reynolds, one of the most successful portrait painters of the late 18th century. He painted several portraits of Lady Hamilton, Admiral Nelson's mistress.

Romulus in Roman legend, founder and first king of Rome, the son of Mars and Rhea Silvia, daughter of Numitor, king of Alba Longa. Romulus and his twin brother Remus were thrown into the Tiber by their great-uncle Amulius, who had deposed Numitor, but were suckled by a she-wolf and rescued by a shepherd. On reaching adulthood they killed Amulius and founded Rome.

Having murdered Remus, Romulus reigned alone until he disappeared in a storm; he was thereafter worshipped as a god under the name of Quirinus.

rondo or *rondeau* antique musical form in which verses alternate with a refrain. Often festive in character, it is a popular final movement of a sonata, concerto, or symphony.

Ronsard Pierre de 1524–1585. French poet, leader of the ◊Pléiade group of poets. Under the patronage of Charles IX, he published original verse in a lightly sensitive style, including odes and love sonnets, such as *Odes* 1550, *Les Amours/Lovers* 1552–53, and the 'Marie' cycle, *Continuation des amours/Lovers Continued* 1555–56.

Rooney Mickey. Stage name of Joe Yule 1920–. US actor who began his career aged two in his parents' stage act. He played Andy Hardy in the Hardy family series of B-films (1937–47) and starred opposite Judy Garland in several musicals, including *Babes in Arms* 1939. He also gave memorable performances in *Boys' Town* 1935, as Puck in *A Midsummer Night's Dream* 1935, and the title role in *Baby Face Nelson* 1957.

roots music term originally denoting ◊reggae, later encompassing any music indigenous to a particular culture; see ◊world music.

Be silent, unless what you have to say is better than silence.

Salvator Rosa
motto on self-portrait about 1645

Rosa Salvator 1615–1673. Italian Baroque painter, etcher, poet, and musician, active in Florence 1640–49 and subsequently in Rome. He created wild, romantic, and sometimes macabre landscapes, seascapes, and battle scenes. He also wrote satirical verse.

Born near Naples, Rosa spent much of his youth travelling in S Italy. He first settled in Rome 1639 and established himself as a landscape painter. In Florence he worked for the ruling Medici family.

Rosenberg Isaac 1890–1918. English poet of the World War I period. Trained as an artist at the Slade School in London, Rosenberg enlisted in the British army 1915. He wrote about the horror of life on the front line, as in 'Break of Day in the Trenches'.

Like that of his contemporary Wilfred Owen, Rosenberg's work is now ranked with the finest World War I poems, although he was largely unpublished during his lifetime. After serving for 20 months in the front line, he was killed on the Somme.

Rosenquist James 1933– . US painter and printmaker, a seminal figure in American ◊Pop art. In his paintings, fragmented images drawn from advertising and the mass media are enlarged to huge proportions and juxtaposed against each other in a deadpan manner, as in *I Love You with My Ford* 1961 (Moderna Museet, Stockholm).

Rose Theatre former London theatre near Southwark Bridge where many of Shakespeare's plays were performed. The excavation and preservation of the remains of the theatre, discovered 1989, caused controversy between government bodies and archaeologists.

The theatre was built 1587 by the impresario Philip Henslowe (c. 1550–1616), who managed it until 1603; the theatre was the site of the first performances of Shakespeare's plays *Henry VI* and *Titus Andronicus*. It was one of the first polygonal structures for dramatic purposes, and was enlarged 1592 after the arrival of Edward Alleyn's Company. The diary of the owner, Philip Henslowe, provides an almost complete record of the plays; premieres include Thomas Dekker's *The Shoemaker's Holiday* 1599 and Thomas Heywood's *A Woman Kilde with Kindnesse* 1602–03.

Ross Martin. Pen name of Violet Florence ◊Martin, Irish novelist.

Rossellini Roberto 1906–1977. Italian film director. His World War II trilogy, *Roma città aperta/Rome, Open City* 1945, *Paisà/Paisan* 1946, and *Germania anno zero/Germany Year Zero* 1947, reflects his humanism, and is considered a landmark of European cinema.

In 1949 he made *Stromboli*, followed by other films in which his wife Ingrid Bergman appeared. After their divorce he made *General della Rovere* 1959 and embarked on television work, including a feature-length film for French television, *La Prise de pouvoir par Louis XIV/The Rise of Louis XIV* 1966.

Rossetti Christina (Georgina) 1830–1894. English poet, sister of Dante Gabriel Rossetti. Her verse includes *Goblin Market and Other Poems* 1862 and expresses unfulfilled spiritual yearning and frustrated love. She was a skilful technician and made use of irregular rhyme and line length.

Rossetti Dante Gabriel 1828–1882. British painter and poet, a founding member of the ◊*Pre-Raphaelite Brotherhood* (PRB) with Millais and Hunt 1848. As well as romantic medieval scenes, he produced many idealized portraits of women, including the spiritual *Beata Beatrix* 1864. His verse includes 'The Blessed Damozel' 1850. His sister was the poet Christina Rossetti.

He was a friend of the critic John Ruskin, and of William Morris and his wife Jane, who became Rossetti's lover and the subject of much of his work. His *Poems* 1870 were recovered from the grave of his wife Elizabeth Siddal (1834–1862), also a painter, whom he had married 1860, and were attacked as of 'the fleshly school of poetry'.

Better by far you should forget and smile/ Than you should remember and be sad.

Christina Rossetti 'Remember' 1862

Rossi Aldo 1931– . Italian architect and theorist, strongly influenced by Rationalist thought and by Neo-Classicism. A pioneer of ◊Neo-Rationalism, his main works include the Gallaratese II apartment complex, Milan, 1969–73; the Modena cemetery, 1973; and the floating, demountable theatre Teatro del Mondo, Venice, 1979.

Of his 1980s commissions, both the Friedrichstadt apartments, Berlin 1981–87, and the funerary chapel in Guissano, Italy, 1987, are notable.

Rossini Gioacchino (Antonio) 1792–1868. Italian composer. His first success was the opera *Tancredi* 1813. In 1816 his 'opera buffa' *Il barbiere di Siviglia/The Barber of Seville* was produced in Rome. During 1815–23 he produced 20 operas, and created (with Donizetti and Bellini) the 19th-century Italian operatic style.

After *Guillaume Tell/William Tell* 1829, Rossini gave up writing opera and his later years were spent in Bologna and Paris. Among the works of this period are the *Stabat Mater* 1842 and the piano music arranged for ballet by Respighi as *La Boutique fantasque/The Fantastic Toyshop* 1919.

Rosso Giovanni Battista (called *Rosso Fiorentino*) 1494–1540. Italian painter who studied under Andrea del Sarto and worked in Florence 1513–23. His dramatic style, like that of his friend Pontormo, exemplifies early Italian ◊Mannerism. In 1530 he was invited to France by François I and worked at Fontainebleau with ◊Primaticcio. Together they founded the ◊Fontainebleau School style, a Mannerist fusion of French and Italian taste.

Rostand Edmond 1869–1918. French poetic dramatist who wrote *Cyrano de Bergerac* 1898 and

L'Aiglon 1900 (based on the life of Napoleon III), in which Sarah Bernhardt played the leading role.

Rostropovich Mstislav 1927– . Russian cellist and conductor. He became an exile 1978 because of his sympathies with political dissidents. Prokofiev, Shostakovich, Khachaturian, and Britten wrote pieces for him. Since 1977 he has directed the National Symphony Orchestra, Washington, DC.

Roth Joseph 1894–1939. Austrian novelist and critic who depicted the decay of the Austrian Empire before 1914 in such novels as *Savoy Hotel* 1924, *Radetsky Marsch/The Radetsky March* 1932, and (after he moved to Paris 1933) *Die hundert Tage/The Hundred Days* 1936. He worked as a journalist during the 1920s in several European capitals. His novels defy easy classification; he stayed aloof from literary groups of his time.

Roth Philip 1933– . US novelist whose witty, sharply satirical and increasingly fantastic novels depict the moral and sexual anxieties of 20th-century Jewish-American life, most notably in *Goodbye Columbus* 1959 and *Portnoy's Complaint* 1969.

Roth's series of semi-autobiographical novels about a writer, Nathan Zuckerman, consist of *The Ghost Writer* 1979, *Zuckerman Unbound* 1981, *The Anatomy Lesson* 1984, and *The Counterlife* 1987. The novel *Operation Shylock: A Confession* 1993 is a fantasy about his fictional double; and his memoir *Patrimony* 1991 concerns his father's death.

Rothenstein William 1872–1945. English painter, writer, and teacher. His work includes decorations for St Stephen's Hall, Westminster, London, and portrait drawings. He was principal of the Royal College of Art 1920–35, where he encouraged the sculptors Jacob Epstein and Henry Moore, and the painter Paul Nash.

Rothko Mark 1903–1970. Russian-born US painter, an Abstract Expressionist and a pioneer, towards the end of his life, of **Colour Field** painting (an abstract style dominated by areas of unmodulated, strong colour). Rothko produced several series of large-scale paintings in the 1950s and 1960s, examples of which are owned by Harvard University, the Tate Gallery, London, and a chapel in Houston, Texas.

Rouault Georges 1871–1958. French painter, etcher, illustrator, and designer, one of the major religious artists of the 20th century. Early in his career he was associated with the ◊Fauves but created his own style using rich, dark colours and heavy outlines. His subjects include sad clowns, prostitutes, corrupt lawyers, and Christ.

Rouault was born in Paris, the son of a cabinet-maker. He was apprenticed to a stained-glassmaker; later he studied under the Symbolist painter Gustave Moreau and became curator of Moreau's studio. *The Prostitute* 1906 (Musée National d'Art Moderne, Paris) and *The Face of Christ* 1933 (Musée des Beaux-Arts, Ghent, Belgium) represent extremes of Rouault's painting style. He also produced illustrations and designed tapestries, stained glass, and sets for Diaghilev's Ballets Russes, and in 1948 he published a series of etchings, *Miserere*.

Roubiliac or *Roubillac*, Louis François *c.* 1705–1762. French sculptor, a Huguenot who fled religious persecution to settle in England 1732. He became a leading sculptor of the day, creating a statue of Handel for Vauxhall Gardens 1737 (Victoria and Albert Museum, London).

He also produced lively statues of historic figures, such as Newton, and an outstanding funerary monument, the *Tomb of Lady Elizabeth Nightingale* 1761 (Westminster Abbey, London).

Rouget de Lisle Claude-Joseph 1760–1836. French army officer who composed, while in Strasbourg 1792, the 'Marseillaise', the French national anthem.

Rousseau Henri 'Le Douanier' 1844–1910. French painter, a self-taught naive artist. His subjects include scenes of the Parisian suburbs and exotic junglescapes, painted with painstaking detail; for example, *Tropical Storm with a Tiger* 1891 (National Gallery, London).

Rousseau served in the army for some years, then became a toll collector (hence *Le Douanier*, 'the customs official'), and finally took up full-time painting 1885. He exhibited at the Salon des Indépendants 1886–1910 and was associated with the group led by Picasso and the poet Apollinaire.

Rousseau Jean-Jacques 1712–1778. French social philosopher and writer whose *Du Contrat social/Social Contract* 1762, emphasizing the rights of the people over those of the government, was a significant influence on the French Revolution. In the novel *Emile* 1762 he outlined a new theory of education.

Rousseau was born in Geneva, Switzerland. *Discourses on the Origins of Inequality* 1754 made his name: he denounced civilized society and postulated the paradox of the superiority of the ◊noble savage. *Social Contract* stated that a government could be legitimately overthrown if it failed to express the general will of the people. *Emile* was written as an example of how to elicit the unspoiled nature and abilities of children, based on natural development and the power of example.

Rousseau's ideas were condemned by philosophers, the clergy, and the public, and he lived in exile in England for a year, being helped by Scottish philosopher David Hume until they fell out. He was a contributor to the *Encyclopédie* and also wrote operas. *Confessions*, published posthumously 1782, was a frank account of his occasionally immoral life and was a founding work of autobiography.

I hate books, for they only teach people to talk about what they do not understand.
Jean-Jacques Rousseau *Emile* 1762

Rousseau (Etienne-Pierre) Théodore 1812–1867. French landscape painter of the ◊Barbizon School. Born in Paris, he came under the influence of the English landscape painters Constable and Bonington and sketched from nature in many parts of France.

Rowe Nicholas 1674–1718. English dramatist and poet, whose dramas include *The Fair Penitent* 1703 and *The Tragedy of Jane Shore* 1714, in which Mrs Siddons played. He edited Shakespeare, and was poet laureate from 1715.

Rowlandson Thomas 1756–1827. English painter and illustrator, a caricaturist of Georgian social life. He published the series of drawings *Tour of Dr Syntax in Search of the Picturesque* 1809 and its two sequels 1812–21.

Rowlandson studied at the Royal Academy schools and in Paris. Impoverished by gambling, he turned from portrait painting to caricature around 1780. Other works include *The Dance of Death* 1815–16 and illustrations for works by the novelists Tobias Smollett, Oliver Goldsmith, and Laurence Sterne.

Rowley William *c.* 1585–*c.* 1640–42. English actor and dramatist who collaborated with Thomas ◊Middleton on *The Changeling* 1622 and with Thomas ◊Dekker and John ◊Ford on *The Witch of Edmonton* 1621.

Rowse A(lfred) L(eslie) 1903– . English popular historian. He published a biography of Shakespeare 1963, and in *Shakespeare's Sonnets: The Problems Solved* 1973 controversially identified the 'Dark Lady' of Shakespeare's sonnets as Emilia Lanier, half-Italian daughter of a court musician, with whom Shakespeare is alleged to have had an affair 1593–95. His other works include the scholarly *Tudor Cornwall: Portrait of a Society* 1941 and *Shakespeare the Man* 1973.

Royal Academy of Arts (RA) British society founded by George III in London 1768 to encourage painting, sculpture, and architecture; its first president was Joshua ◊Reynolds. It is now housed in Old Burlington House, Piccadilly. There is an annual summer exhibition for contemporary artists, and tuition is provided at the Royal Academy schools.

Royal Academy of Dramatic Art (RADA) British college founded by Herbert Beerbohm Tree 1904 to train young actors. Since 1905 its headquarters have been in Gower Street, London. A royal charter was granted 1920.

Royal Academy of Music (RAM) British senior music school in London, founded 1822 by John Fane, Lord Burghesh, later 11th Earl of Westmorland. It was granted a royal charter 1830. Now based in Marylebone Road, it provides a full-time complete musical education.

Royal Ballet leading British ballet company and school, based at the Royal Opera House, Covent Garden, London. Until 1956 it was known as the Sadler's Wells Ballet. It was founded 1931 by Ninette ◊de Valois, who established her school and company at the Sadler's Wells Theatre. It moved to Covent Garden 1946. Frederick ◊Ashton became principal choreographer 1935, providing the company with its uniquely English ballet style. Leading dancers included Margot Fonteyn, Rudolf Nureyev, Alicia Markova, and Antoinette Sibley.

Royal College of Art British postgraduate training school for artists and designers, Kensington Gore, London. It was founded 1837 as the School of Design and renamed the Royal College of Art 1896. A royal charter was granted 1967.

Royal College of Music British college providing full-time complete musical education. Founded 1883, it is in Kensington, W London.

Royal Opera House Britain's leading opera house, sited at Covent Garden, London. The original theatre opened 1732, was destroyed by fire 1808, and reopened 1809. It was again destroyed by fire 1856, and the third and present building dates from 1858. It has been the home of the Royal Opera and the Royal Ballet since 1946.

Royal Shakespeare Company (RSC) British professional theatre company that performs Shakespearean and other plays. It was founded 1961 from the company at the Shakespeare Memorial Theatre 1932 (now the Royal Shakespeare Theatre) in Stratford-upon-Avon, Warwickshire, England, and produces plays in Stratford and the Barbican Centre in London.

The RSC initially presented mainly Shakespeare at Stratford; these productions were usually transferred to the Aldwych Theatre, London, where the company also performed modern plays and non-Shakespearean classics. In 1982 it moved into a permanent London headquarters at the Barbican. A second large theatre in Stratford, the Swan, opened 1986 with an auditorium similar to theatres of Shakespeare's day.

The first director of the RSC was Peter Hall. In 1968 Trevor Nunn replaced him, and in 1986 Nunn was succeeded by Terry Hands. Adrian Noble became director 1990.

Royal Worcester porcelain factory see ◊Worcester porcelain factory.

rubato (from Italian *tempo rubato* 'robbed time') in music, a pushing or dragging against the beat for expressive effect.

Rubbra Edmund 1901–1986. British composer. He studied under Holst and specialized in contrapuntal writing, as exemplified in his study *Counterpoint* 1960. His compositions include 11 symphonies, chamber music, and songs.

Rubens Peter Paul 1577–1640. Flemish painter, who brought the exuberance of the Italian Baroque to N Europe, creating, with an army of assistants, innumerable religious and allegorical paintings for churches and palaces. These show mastery of drama in large compositions, and love of rich colour. He also painted portraits and, in his last years, landscapes.

Rubens entered the Antwerp painters' guild 1598 and went to Italy 1600, studying artists of the High Renaissance. In 1603 he visited Spain and in Madrid painted many portraits of the Spanish nobility. From 1604 to 1608 he was in Italy again, and in 1609 he settled in Antwerp and was appointed court painter to the archduke Albert and his wife Isabella. His *Raising of the Cross* 1610–11 and *Descent from the Cross* 1611–14, both in Antwerp Cathedral, show his brilliant painterly style. He went to France 1620, commissioned by the regent Marie de' Medici to produce a cycle of 21 enormous canvases allegorizing her life (Louvre, Paris). In 1628 he again went to Madrid, where he met the painter Velázquez. In 1629–30 he was in London as diplomatic envoy to Charles I, and painted the ceiling of the Banqueting House in Whitehall.

Rubens' portraits range from intimate pictures of his second wife, such as *Hélène Fourment in a Fur Wrap* about 1638 (Kunsthistorisches Museum, Vienna), to dozens of portraits of royalty.

The size of the pictures gives us painters much more courage to represent our ideas adequately and with an appearance of reality.

Peter Paul Rubens 1621

Rubinstein Artur 1887–1982. Polish-born US pianist. His early encounters with Joseph Joachim and the Belgian violinist, conductor, and composer Eugène Ysaye (1858–1931) link his interpretations of Beethoven, Mozart, and Chopin with the virtuoso Romantic tradition. He was also a noted interpreter of de Falla.

Rublev or *Rublyov* Andrei *c.* 1360–1430. Russian icon painter, considered the greatest exponent of the genre in Russia. Only one documented work of his survives, the *Old Testament Trinity* about 1411 (Tretyakov Gallery, Moscow). This shows a basically Byzantine style, but with a gentler expression.

He is known to have worked with ◊Theophanes the Greek in the Cathedral of the Annunciation in Moscow. In later life Rublev became a monk. The Russian film director Andrei Tarkovsky made a film of his life 1966.

Ruckers family of Flemish harpsichord-makers founded by Hans Ruckers (*c.* 1545–1598) and continued by his sons Iohannes (1578–1643), Andreas (1579– ?), and their descendants. The instruments were noted for their engineering precision and matchless tone, and were imitated widely. Many were commissioned for display, and featured paintings inside the lid by artists including Brueghel and Rubens.

Rude François 1784–1855. French Romantic sculptor. He produced the *Marseillaise* (1833, also known as *The Volunteers of 1792*), a low-relief scene on the Arc de Triomphe, Paris, showing the capped figure of Liberty leading the revolutionaries.

Rude was a supporter of Napoleon, together with the painter David, and in 1814 both artists went into exile in Brussels for some years. Rude's other works include a bust of *David* 1831 and the monument *Napoleon Awakening to Immortality* 1854 (both in the Louvre, Paris).

ruff circular pleated or fluted collar of folded lawn or muslin worn by men and women in the 16th and 17th centuries. Prior to the introduction of starch in the 16th century, wires were used to support the folds.

Ruffin David 1941–1991. US pop singer, member of the vocal group the Temptations 1962–68 and lead baritone on many of their hits, including 'My Girl' 1965 which sold a million copies. The Temptations were Motown Records' most popular male group.

Born in Mississippi, Ruffin recorded on local labels in Detroit before joining the Temptations. Their first hit, 'The Way You Do the Things You Do' 1964, was followed by many others with Ruffin as lead singer, including 'Since I Lost My Baby' and 'It's Growing' both 1965, 'I Wish It Would Rain', and 'Cloud Nine' both 1968. Solo hits included 'My Whole World Ended' 1969 and 'Walk Away From Love' 1975.

rug small ◊carpet.

Ruisdael or *Ruysdael* Jacob van c. 1628–1682. Dutch landscape painter. He painted rural scenes near his native town of Haarlem and in Germany, and excelled in depicting gnarled and weatherbeaten trees. A notable example of his work is The *Jewish Cemetery* about 1660 (Gemäldegalerie, Dresden). The few figures in his pictures were painted by other artists.

Ruisdael probably worked in Haarlem with his uncle, the landscape painter **Salomon van Ruysdael** (*c.* 1600–1670), before moving to Amsterdam about 1656. Jacob is considered the greatest realist landscape painter in Dutch art. ◊Hobbema was one of his pupils.

rumba Latin American ballroom dance; the music for this. Rumba originated in Cuba and its rhythms are the basis of much Afro-Cuban music.

Runge Philipp Otto 1777–1810. German Romantic painter whose portraits, often of children, have a remarkable clarity and openness. He also illustrated fairy tales by the brothers Grimm.

Runyon (Alfred) Damon 1884–1946. US journalist, primarily a sports reporter, whose short stories in *Guys and Dolls* 1932 deal wryly with the seamier side of New York City life in his own invented jargon.

Rushdie (Ahmed) Salman 1947– . British writer, born in India of a Muslim family. His novel *The Satanic Verses* 1988 (the title refers to verses deleted from the Koran) offended many Muslims with alleged blasphemy. In 1989 the Ayatollah Khomeini of Iran called for Rushdie and his publishers to be killed. In India and elsewhere, people were killed in demonstrations against the book and Rushdie was forced to go into hiding.

His earlier novels in the magic realist style include *Midnight's Children* 1981, which deals with India from the date of independence and won the Booker Prize, and *Shame* 1983, set in an imaginary parallel of Pakistan. *Haroun and the Sea of Stories*, a children's book, was published 1990.

Ruskin John 1819–1900. English art critic and social critic. He published five volumes of *Modern Painters* 1843–60 and *The Seven Lamps of Architecture* 1849, in which he stated his philosophy of art. His writings hastened the appreciation of painters considered unorthodox at the time, such as J M W ◊Turner and members of the ◊Pre-Raphaelite Brotherhood. His later writings were concerned with social and economic problems.

Born in London, the only child of a prosperous wine-merchant, Ruskin was able to travel widely and was educated at Oxford. In 1848 he married Euphemia 'Effie' Chalmers Gray, but six years later the marriage was annulled.

In *The Stones of Venice* 1851–53, he drew moral lessons from architectural history. From 1860 he devoted himself to social and economic problems, in which he adopted an individual and radical outlook exalting the 'craftsman'. He became increasingly isolated in his views. To this period belongs a series of lectures and pamphlets (*Unto this Last* 1860, *Sesame and Lilies* 1865 on the duties of men and women, *The Crown of Wild Olive* 1866).

Russ Joanna 1937– . US writer of feminist science fiction, exemplified by the novel *The Female Man* 1975. Her short stories have been collected in *The Zanzibar Cat* 1983.

Russell George William 1867–1935. Irish poet and essayist. An ardent nationalist, he helped found the Irish national theatre, and his poetry, published under the pseudonym 'AE', includes *Gods of War* 1915 and reflects his interest in mysticism and theosophy.

Russell Jane 1921– . US actress who was discovered by producer Howard Hughes. Her first film, *The Outlaw* 1943, was not properly released for several years because of censorship problems. Other films include *The Paleface* 1948, *Gentlemen Prefer Blondes* 1953, and *The Revolt of Mamie Stover* 1957.

Russell John Peter 1858–1931. Australian artist. Having met Tom ◊Roberts while sailing to England, he became a member of the French Post-Impressionist group.

Russell Ken 1927– . English film director whose work, typified by stylistic vigour, includes *Women in Love* 1969, *The Music Lovers* 1971, *Tommy* 1975, *Lisztomania* 1975, *Altered States* 1979, and *Gothic* 1986. Highly controversial, his work is often criticized for self-indulgence, containing gratuitous sex and violence, but is also regarded for its vitality and imagination. He has made television biographies of the lives of the composers Elgar, Delius, and Richard Strauss.

Russian art painting and sculpture of Russia; from 1917 to 1991 more widely applied to art from the USSR. For centuries Russian art was dominated by an unchanging tradition of church art inherited from Byzantium, responding slowly and hesitantly to Western influences. Briefly, in the early 20th century, it assumed a leading and influential role in European avant-garde art. However, official Soviet disapproval of this trend resulted in its suppression in favour of art geared to the sentimental glorification of workers. Russian folk traditions – represented, for example, in toys, domestic and farm utensils, and door and window frame decorations and carvings – remained untouched by Byzantine and Western traditions.

10th–13th centuries Russian art was dominated by the Orthodox Church which drew on the traditions of Byzantine art, producing outstanding icons, carvings, metalwork, and embroidery.

13th–15th centuries The arts declined during the Mongol occupation (mid-13th century to end of 14th century) but revived during the 15th century. The development of the iconostasis (a screen, decorated with icons, which separated the altar from the body of the church) created new opportunities for painters. This period saw the rise of the Novgorod School and the exquisite icons of Andrei Rublev.

16th–19th centuries Western styles were gradually absorbed, a process encouraged by Peter the Great and the Academy of Fine Arts in St Petersburg, founded 1757, but no outstanding artists emerged as a result. The second half of the 19th century is characterized by the Social Realism of Ilya Repin.

20th century The 'World of Art' group, formed in the late 1890s, sought to combine 19th-century aestheticism with a return to Russian folk traditions, and produced richly coloured, highly detailed works which had a profound effect on book illustration and stage design; Bakst and Diaghilev were members. In the early 20th century Russian artists were at the forefront of artistic developments in Europe. Suprematism and Constructivism developed. Among outstanding artists of the period were Kandinsky, Malevich, Chagall, Tatlin, Gabo, and Larinov. After the Russian revolution avant-garde art was suppressed by the state and replaced by socialist Realism. The influence of Western art movements grew increasingly strong, however, just before the collapse of Communist Party control in the early 1990s.

Russian literature literary works produced in Russia and later in the USSR. The earliest known works are sermons and chronicles and the unique prose poem 'Tale of the Armament of Igor', belonging to the period in the 11th and 12th centuries when the centre of literary culture was Kiev. By the close of the 14th century leadership had passed to Moscow, which was isolated from developments in the West until the 18th century; in this period are the political letters of Ivan the Terrible; the religious writings of the priest Avvakum (1620–1681), who was the first to use vernacular Slavonic (rather than the elaborate Church Slavonic language) in literature; and traditional oral folk poems dealing with legendary and historical heroes, which were collected in the 18th and 19th centuries.

Modern Russian literature begins with Mikhail Lomonosov (1711–1765) who fused elements of Church Slavonic with colloquial Russian to create an effective written medium. Among the earlier writers, working directly under French influence, were the fabulist Ivan Krylov (1768–1844) and the historian Nikolai Karamzin (1765–1826). In the 19th century poetry reached its greatest heights with Alexander Pushkin and the tempestuously Byronic Mikhail Lermontov, while prose was dominated by Nikolai Gogol. Typifying the intellectual unrest of the mid-19th century are the works of the prose writer Alexander Herzen, known for his memoirs.

The golden age of the 19th-century Russian novel produced works by literary giants such as Ivan Turgenev, Ivan Goncharov, Fyodor Dostoevsky, and Leo Tolstoy. In their wake came Nikolai Leskov (1831–1895), the morbid Vsevolod Garshin (1855–1888), and Vladimir Korolenko, and in drama the innovative genius of Anton Chekhov. Maxim Gorky rose above the pervasive pessimism of the 1880s and found followers in Alexander Kuprin (1870–1938) and Ivan Bunin; in contrast are the depressingly negative Leonid Andreyev and Mikhail Artsybashev. To the more mystic school of thought belong the novelist Dmitri Merezhkovsky (1865–1941) and the poet and philosopher Vladimir Soloviev, who moulded the thought of the Symbolist poet Alexander Blok. Many writers left the country at the time of the Revolution, but in the 1920s two groups emerged: the militantly socialist LEF (Left Front of the Arts) led by the Futurist Vladimir Mayakovsky, and the fellow-travellers of NEP (New Economic Policy) including Boris Pilnyak (1894–1938), Boris Pasternak, Alexei Tolstoy, and Ilya Ehrenburg. Literary standards reached a low ebb during the first five-year plan (1928–32), when facts were compulsorily falsified in the effort to fortify socialism, but the novelist Mikhail Sholokhov and poets Osip Mandelshtam, Anna Akhmatova, and Nikolai Tikhonov were notable in this period.

More freedom was allowed by the subsequent Realism movement, seen for example in the works of Simonov and the poet Alexander Tvardovsky. During World War II censorship was again severe and some leading Georgian writers disappeared in purges. In the thaw after Stalin's death Vladimir Dudintsev published his *Not by Bread Alone* 1956 and the journal *Novy Mir* encouraged bolder new writing, but this did not last. Landmark events were the controversy over the award of a Nobel prize to Pasternak, the public statements by the poet Yevgeny Yevtushenko, and the imprisonment in 1966 of the novelists Andrei Sinyavsky (1926–) and Yuli Daniel (1926–) for smuggling their works abroad for publication. Other writers fled the country, such as Anatoly Kuznetsov, whose novel *The Fire* 1969 obliquely criticized the regime, and Alexander Solzhenitsyn, who found a different kind of disillusionment in the West. To evade censorship writers have also resorted to allegory, as in for example Vasili Aksyonov's *The Steel Bird* 1979, which grotesquely satirizes dictatorship. Among those apart from all politics was the nonsense-verse writer Kornei Chukovsky.

The intellectual and cultural thaw under President Gorbachev heralded an era of literary revaluation as well as fresh discoveries of writers from the 1930s onwards. With the collapse of the Soviet Union, previously overshadowed or suspect national literatures in regions such as central Asia began to revive.

Rustaveli Shota *c.* 1172–*c.* 1216. Georgian poet, author of the Georgian national epic *Vekhis-tqaosani/The Man [or Knight] in the Panther's Skin* which draws on ancient Greek and Eastern philosophy in the celebration of heroism, courtly love, and comradeship.

Rutherford Margaret 1892–1972. English film and theatre actress who specialized in formidable yet jovially eccentric roles. She played Agatha Christie's Miss Marple in four films in the early 1960s and won an Academy Award for her role in *The VIPs* 1963.

Ruysdael Jacob van. See ◊Ruisdael, Dutch painter.

Ryan Robert 1909–1973. US film and theatre actor, of rugged good looks, who was equally impressive in leading and character roles. He was memorable playing the anti-Semitic murderer in *Crossfire* 1947 and an equally villainous role in *Bad Day at Black Rock* 1954. His films include *The Set-Up* 1949, *God's Little Acre* 1958, and *The Wild Bunch* 1969.

Ryder Albert Pinkham 1847–1917. US painter who developed one of the most original styles of his time. He painted with broad strokes that tended to simplify form and used yellowish colours that gave his works an eerie, haunted quality. His works are poetic, romantic, and filled with unreality; *Death on a Pale Horse* about 1910 (Cleveland Museum of Art) is typical.

Rysbrack John Michael 1694–1770. Flemish sculptor who settled in England 1720 and produced portrait busts and tombs in Westminster Abbey. He also created the equestrian statue of William III in Queen Square, Bristol, 1735. His style was one of restrained Baroque.

S

Saarinen Eero 1910–1961. Finnish-born US architect renowned for his wide range of innovative Modernist designs, experimenting with different structures and shapes. His works include the US embassy, London, 1955–61, the TWA Kennedy terminal, New York, 1956–62, and Dulles Airport, Washington, DC, 1958–63. He collaborated on a number of projects with his father, Eliel Saarinen.

Always design a thing by considering it in its larger context—a chair in a room, a room in a house, a house in an environment, an environment in a city plan.

Eero Saarinen *Time* July 1956

Saarinen Eliel 1873–1950. Finnish-born US architect and town planner, founder of the Finnish Romantic school. His best-known European project is the Helsinki railway station 1905–14. In 1923 he emigrated to the USA, where he is remembered for his designs for the Cranbrook Academy of Art in Bloomfield Hills, Michigan, 1926–43, and Christ Church, Minneapolis, 1949.

Sábato Ernesto 1911– . Argentine novelist and social critic. Trained as a physicist, he was removed from his university post 1945 for opposition to the Perón government. He depicted an existential anti-hero in his successful novel *El túnel/The Outsider* 1948. Both in essays such as *Hombres y engranajes/Men and Gears* 1951 and novels such as *Abaddón el exterminador/Abaddón the Exterminator* 1974 he has explored the excesses of scientific rationalism in an overmechanized modern society.

Sabu stage name of Sabu Dastagir 1924–1963. Indian child actor, the hero of *The Thief of Bagdad* 1940. He performed in Britain and the USA until the 1950s. His other films include *Elephant Boy* 1937 and *Black Narcissus* 1947.

Sacher Paul 1906– . Swiss conductor. In 1926 he founded the Basel Chamber Orchestra, for which he has commissioned a succession of works from contemporary composers including Bartók's *Divertimento* 1937, Stravinsky's *Concerto in D* 1946, and Boulez's *Messagesquisse* 1977.

Sacher-Masoch Leopold von 1836–1895. Austrian novelist. His books dealt with the sexual pleasure of having pain inflicted on oneself, hence masochism.

Sachs Hans 1494–1576. German poet and composer who worked as a master shoemaker in Nuremberg. He composed 4,275 *Meisterlieder/Mastersongs*, and figures prominently in Wagner's opera *Die Meistersinger von Nürnberg*.

sackbut musical instrument of the brass family, a precursor of the trombone. It was common from the 14th century and has been revived in early music performance. It has a narrow bell and its sound is dignified and mellow.

Sackville Thomas, 1st Earl of Dorset 1536–1608. English poet, collaborator with Thomas Norton on *Gorboduc* 1561, written in blank verse and one of the earliest English tragedies.

Heavy Sleep, the Cousin of Death.

Thomas Sackville Sleep

Sackville-West Vita (Victoria) 1892–1962. English writer, wife of Harold ◊Nicolson from 1913; *Portrait of a Marriage* 1973 by their son Nigel Nicolson described their married life. Her novels include *The Edwardians* 1930 and *All Passion Spent* 1931; she also wrote the long pastoral poem *The Land* 1926. The fine gardens around her home at Sissinghurst, Kent, were created by her and her husband.

Sade Donatien Alphonse François, Comte de, known as the *Marquis de Sade* 1740–1814. French author who was imprisoned for sexual offences and finally committed to an asylum. He wrote plays and novels dealing explicitly with a variety of sexual practices, including sadism, deriving pleasure or sexual excitement from inflicting pain on others.

S'adi or *Saadi*. Pen name of Sheik Moslih Addin *c.* 1184–*c.* 1291. Persian poet, author of *Bustan/Tree-garden* and *Gulistan/Flower-garden*.

Sadler's Wells theatre in Islington, N London, England. Originally a music hall, it was developed by Lilian Baylis as a northern annexe to the ◊Old Vic 1931. For many years it housed the Sadler's Wells Opera Company (now the English National Opera) and the Sadler's Wells Ballet, which later became the ◊Royal Ballet.

saga prose narrative written down in the 11th–13th centuries in Norway and Iceland. The sagas range from family chronicles, such as the *Landnamabok* of Ari (1067–1148), to legendary and anonymous works such as the *Njala* saga.

Other sagas include the *Heimskringla* of Snorri Sturluson celebrating Norwegian kings, the *Sturlunga* of Sturla Thordsson (1214–1284), and the legendary and anonymous *Laxdaela* and *Grettla* sagas. 'Family saga' is often used of a novel whose protagonists span two or more generations.

Sagan Françoise 1935– . French novelist. Her studies of love relationships include *Bonjour Tristesse/Hello Sadness* 1954, *Un Certain Sourire/A Certain Smile* 1956, and *Aimez-vous Brahms?/Do You Like Brahms?* 1959. In lucidly dispassionate prose she describes how amoral characters seek to escape solitude in brief liaisons.

The illusion of art is to make one believe that great literature is very close to life, but exactly the opposite is true. Life is amorphous, literature is formal.

Françoise Sagan 1958

---

saint a holy man or woman respected for their wisdom, spirituality, and dedication to their faith.

Saint-Denis Michel 1897–1971. French director and actor. He founded both the Compagnie des Quinze 1930 and the London Theatre Studio 1936–39. From 1946–52 he was director of the Old Vic Theatre School, and became an artistic adviser for the Lincoln Center in New York 1957, and later for the Royal Shakespeare Company in Britain 1962.

Sainte-Beuve Charles Augustin 1804–1869. French critic and historian. A champion of Romanticism, he wrote widely on French literature and culture, his articles appearing as *Causeries du lundi/Monday Chats* 1851–62. His outstanding work as a historian was *Port Royal* 1840–59, a study of Jansenism which also includes descriptions of the 17th-century literary figures Corneille, Molière, and Racine.

Grown-ups never understand anything for themselves, and it is tiresome for children to be always and forever explaining things to them.

Antoine de Saint-Exupéry
Le Petit Prince 1943

Saint-Exupéry Antoine de 1900–1944. French author and pilot who wrote the autobiographical *Vol de nuit/Night Flight* 1931 and *Terre des hommes/Wind, Sand, and Stars* 1939. His children's book *Le Petit Prince/The Little Prince* 1943 is also an adult allegory.

Saint-Gaudens Augustus 1848–1907. Irishborn US sculptor, one of the leading Neo-Classical sculptors of his time. His monuments include the *Admiral Farragut* 1878–81 in

---

Saints and their emblems in art

Many Christian saints can be identified in works of art by the objects associated with them. These symbols or emblems generally represent some detail picked out from their legends (the often fanciful biographies compiled by early writers).

An emblem frequently refers to the saint's martyrdom – for example the spiked wheel on which St Catherine of Alexandria was tortured. It can also stand in the place of the saint, for example the special emblems of the four evangelists – Matthew, Mark, Luke and John. The twelve apostles may have individual emblems but very often just hold books or scrolls in reference to their role as teachers of the faith.

Saint	Emblem
Agnes	lamb
Andrew	saltire (x-shaped) cross
Anthony (of Egypt)	pig and handbell
Anthony (of Padua)	lily
Apollonia	tooth held in forceps
Barbara	tower with three windows
Bartholomew	knife
Blaise	two crossed candles; comb
Catherine	spiked wheel, either whole or broken
Clement	anchor
Dorothy	basket of fruit or flowers
Edward the Confessor	finger ring
Erasmus	windlass
Eustace	deer with crucifix between horns
Fiacre	spade
Francis of Assisi	stigmata
George	red cross on banner or armour and dragon
Giles	deer and arrow
James the Greater	cockleshell
Jerome	lion and cardinal's hat
John the Baptist	Lamb of God
John the Divine	*eagle; cup with serpent emerging from it
Lawrence	gridiron
Luke	*winged ox
Margaret	dragon
Mark	*winged lion
Mary Magdalene	jar or pot
Matthew	*winged man
Nicholas	three balls
Patrick	shamrock and snakes
Paul	book and sword
Peter	key(s)
Roche	dog and plague sore on leg
Sebastian	arrow
Thomas Aquinas	star

*denotes one of the symbols of the evangelists

Madison Square Park, New York City, and the Adams Memorial 1891 in Rock Creek Cemetery, Washington, DC.

St Ives School ill-defined group of English artists, working in a wide range of styles, who lived in the fishing port of St Ives, Cornwall, after the outbreak of World War II. The group included Ben Nicholson and Barbara Hepworth.

Saint-Laurent Yves (Henri Donat Mathieu) 1936– . French fashion designer who has had an exceptional influence on fashion in the second half of the 20th century. He began working for Christian Dior 1955 and succeeded him as designer on Dior's death 1957. He established his own label 1962 and went on to create the first 'power-dressing' looks: classical, stylish city clothes, using conventionally 'masculine' garments such as blazers, trousers, and shirts for women's daywear. His chain of boutiques Rive Gauche was established 1966. He launched a menswear collection 1974.

St Paul's Cathedral cathedral church of the City of London, and the largest Protestant church in England. A Norman building, which had replaced the original Saxon church, was burned down in the Great Fire 1666; the present cathedral, designed by Christopher ◊Wren, was built 1675–1710.

St Peter's Cathedral, Rome Roman Catholic cathedral church of the Vatican City State, built 1506–1626, chiefly by the architects Bramante and Michelangelo, successively.

St Peter's is the creation of the vision of Pope Julius II and the greatest architects of the Italian Renaissance. In competition the design of Donato Bramante was selected, a Greek-cross plan with a dome related to the Pantheon in Athens. The foundation stone was laid 1506. Bramante died 1514. After a succession of architects, Michelangelo, better known as a painter and sculptor, succeeded Antonio da Sangallo 1547, at the age of 72. He conceived the great dome. Carlo Maderno (1556–1629) lengthened the nave to a Latin cross and added the façade 1606–12. Finally, the Baroque architect Giovanni Bernini formed the elliptical entrance piazza from 1656 onwards.

Saint-Pierre Jacques Henri Bernadin de 1737–1814. French author of the sentimental romance *Paul et Virginie* 1789.

Saint-Saëns (Charles) Camille 1835–1921. French composer, pianist and organist. Among his many lyrical Romantic pieces are concertos, the symphonic poem *Danse macabre* 1875, the opera *Samson et Dalila* 1877, and the orchestral *Carnaval des animaux/Carnival of the Animals* 1886.

Saint-Simon Louis de Rouvroy, Duc de 1675–1755. French soldier, courtier, and politician

whose *Mémoires* 1691–1723 are unrivalled as a description of the French court.

Saki pen name of H(ugh) H(ector) Munro 1870–1916. Burmese-born British writer of ingeniously witty and bizarre short stories, often with surprise endings. He also wrote two novels, *The Unbearable Bassington* 1912 and *When William Came* 1913.

A little inaccuracy sometimes saves tons of explanation.

Saki 'The Comments of Moung Ka'

Sakuntal a romantic drama by the Indian writer ◊Kālidāsa, performed *c.* 400. King Dushyanta falls in love with, but later fails to acknowledge, Sakuntala, the adopted daughter of the hermit Kanva. Dushyanta's memory is stirred by the discovery of the ring he gave to her and he is reunited with Sakuntala and their son.

Salieri Antonio 1750–1825. Italian composer. He taught Beethoven, Schubert, and Liszt, and was the musical rival of Mozart, whom it has been suggested, without proof, that he poisoned, at the emperor's court in Vienna, where he held the position of court composer.

Salinger J(erome) D(avid) 1919– . US writer, author of the classic novel of mid-20th-century adolescence *The* ◊*Catcher in the Rye* 1951. He developed his lyrical Zen themes in *Franny and Zooey* 1961 and *Raise High the Roof Beam, Carpenters and Seymour* 1963, short stories about a Jewish family named Glass, after which he stopped publishing.

Sallinen Tyko 1879–1955. Finnish Expressionist painter. Inspired by ◊Fauvism on visits to France 1909 and 1914, he created visionary works relating partly to his childhood experiences of religion. He also painted Finnish landscape and peasant life, such as *Washerwoman* 1911 (Ateneum, Helsinki).

Sallust Gaius Sallustius Crispus 86–*c.* 34 BC. Roman historian, a supporter of Julius Caesar. He wrote vivid accounts of Catiline's conspiracy and the Jugurthine War.

To like and dislike the same things, that is indeed true friendship.

Sallust *Bellum Catilinae*

Salonen Esa-Pekka 1958– . Finnish conductor and composer. He studied French horn, and made his UK conducting debut 1983 as a short-notice replacement for Michael Tilson Thomas, leading to further engagements with the London Philharmonic Orchestra. Appointed chief conductor of the Swedish Radio Symphony Orchestra 1985, he became music director of the Los Angeles Philharmonic Orchestra 1992.

Salonen made the first recording of Lutosławski's *Symphony No 3* 1986. His hard-edged, relentless style has been compared to that of conductor Pierre Boulez. His compositions include *Horn Music I* 1976 and *Concerto for Saxophone and Orchestra* 1980.

salsa Latin big-band dance music popularized by Puerto Ricans in New York City in the 1970s–80s and by, among others, the Panamanian singer Rubén Blades (1948–   ).

Salzedo Carlos 1885–1961. French-born harpist and composer. He studied in Paris and moved to New York where he cofounded the International Composers' Guild. He did much to promote the harp as a concert instrument, and invented many unusual effects.

samba Latin American ballroom dance; the music for this. Samba originated in Brazil and became popular in the West in the 1940s. There are several different samba rhythms; the ◊bossa nova is a samba-jazz fusion.

samizdat (Russian 'self-published') in the USSR and eastern Europe before the 1989 uprisings, written material circulated underground to evade state censorship; for example, reviews of Solzhenitzyn's banned novel *August 1914* 1972.

sampler (Latin *exemplar* 'pattern') embroidered panel, originally one on which various types of stitches or motifs had been worked to serve as models or samples. Since the 16th century the term has been used to mean a panel worked in various stitches to demonstrate the skill of the maker.

The earliest surviving samplers date from 1625–50 and are worked in coloured silks on a linen ground, with geometrical patterns and stylized birds and flowers. From the 18th century it was popular for children to incorporate the letters of the alphabet, pieces of text, their own name, and the date of completion.

sampling in music, a technique of computer synthesis involving the capture by microphone, conversion to digital code, storage, and subsequent manipulation of an acoustic signal.

Sand George. Pen name of Amandine Aurore Lucie Dupin 1804–1876. French author whose prolific literary output was often autobiographical. While living in Paris as a writer, she had love affairs with Alfred de ◊Musset, ◊Chopin, and others. Her first novel *Indiana* 1832 was a plea for women's right to independence. Her other novels include *La Mare au diable/The Devil's Pool* 1846 and *La Petite Fadette/The Little Fairy* 1848.

We cannot tear out a single page of our life, but we can throw the whole book in the fire.

George Sand *Mauprat* 1837

sandal light shoe consisting of a sole held on to the foot by straps of leather or fabric. The sandal is known to date back to about 2000 BC in Egypt; it was worn by the Greeks and Romans, and throughout history has been popular footwear in hot climates, worn by both men and women.

Sandburg Carl August 1878–1967. US poet. He worked as a farm labourer and a bricklayer, and his poetry celebrates ordinary life in the USA, as in *Chicago Poems* 1916, *The People, Yes* 1936, and *Complete Poems* 1950 (Pulitzer Prize). Sandburg also wrote a monumental biography of Abraham Lincoln, *Abraham Lincoln: The Prairie Years* 1926 (two volumes) and *Abraham Lincoln: The War Years* 1939 (four volumes; Pulitzer Prize). *Always the Young Strangers* 1953 is his autobiography.

Sandby Paul 1725–1809. English painter, often called 'the father of English watercolour'. He specialized in Classical landscapes, using both watercolour and gouache, and introduced the technique of ◊aquatint to England.

Sander August 1876–1964. German portrait photographer whose long-term project was to create a vast composite portrait, *Man of the Twentieth Century*. Concentrating on German society, he turned his dispassionate gaze on every walk of life – from butchers to bankers – in a way that combined the individual with the archetypal. Much of his work was destroyed when his Cologne studio was bombed 1944.

Sanders George 1906–1972. Russian-born British actor, often cast as a smooth-talking cad. Most of his film career was spent in the USA where he starred in such films as *Rebecca* 1940, *The Moon and Sixpence* 1942, *The Picture of Dorian Gray* 1944, and *All About Eve* 1950 (Academy Award for best supporting actor). During World War II he played the maverick detectives 'The Saint' and 'The Falcon' in a series of films.

Sangallo Antonio da, *the Younger* 1458–1546. Florentine High Renaissance architect who worked under ◊Bramante and ◊Peruzzi in Rome. His masterpiece is the monumental Palazzo Farnese, Rome (begun 1513, completed by Michelangelo). Sangallo took over as chief architect of St Peter's 1539 and expanded on Bramante's original plan, but it was left to Michelangelo, his successor, to make of the building a convincing whole.

Sansovino Jacopo 1486–1570. Florentine Renaissance architect and sculptor. He studied and began his career in Rome but fled after the sack of the city 1527 to Venice, where most of his major works are found. Notable are the Loggetta in St Mark's Square 1537–40 and the richly decorated Library and Mint opposite the Doge's Palace 1537–45. ◊Palladio was greatly influenced by his work.

Sant'Elia Antonio 1888–1916. Italian architect. His drawings convey a Futurist vision of a metropolis with skyscrapers, traffic lanes, and streamlined factories.

Sappho c. 610–c. 580. Greek lyric poet, a native of Lesbos and contemporary of the poet ◊Alcaeus, famed for her female eroticism (hence lesbianism). The surviving fragments of her poems express a keen sense of loss, and delight in the worship of the goddess ◊Aphrodite.

What is beautiful is good, and who is good will soon also be beautiful.

Sappho Fragments

---

sarabande French 16th-century court dance, also (*saraband*) an English dance form, in moderate three time with a rhythmic emphasis on the second beat, a dance form featured in the classical music ◊suite.

Saray in Islamic architecture, a palace, notably the Topkapi Saray, Istanbul (begun 1478).

Sardou Victorien 1831–1908. French dramatist, a leading exponent of the 'well-made' play. He wrote plays with roles for Sarah Bernhardt – for example, *Fédora* 1882 and *La Tosca* 1887 (the basis for the opera by Puccini). George Bernard Shaw coined the expression 'Sardoodledom' to express his disgust with Sardou's contrived dramatic technique.

Sargent (Harold) Malcolm (Watts) 1895–1967. English conductor, chief conductor of the BBC Symphony Orchestra 1950–57 and musical director of numerous choral societies. He championed Vaughan Williams and Holst and conducted the first performances of Walton's oratorio *Belshazzar's Feast* 1931 and opera *Troilus and Cressida* 1954.

Sargent John Singer 1856–1925. US portrait painter. Born in Florence of American parents, he studied there and in Paris, then settled in London around 1885. He was a fashionable and prolific painter.

Sargent left Paris after a scandal concerning his mildly erotic portrait *Madame Gautreau* 1884 (Metropolitan Museum of Art, New York). Later subjects included the actress Ellen Terry, President Theodore Roosevelt, and the writer Robert Louis Stevenson. He also painted watercolour landscapes and murals.

Sargeson Frank 1903–1982. New Zealand writer. He is best known for his short stories, terse, closely observed, often lyrical depictions of New Zealand life, as in the collection *A Man and his Wife* 1940 and *Summer and Other Stories* 1946. His novels include *The Hangover* 1967 and *Man of England Now* 1972.

sari main outer garment of Indian women, worn over a short blouse and a petticoat into which part of the fabric is tucked and folded at the waist to form a skirt. The remaining end is draped over the shoulder. It consists of a piece of fabric about 101 cm/40 in wide by 4.5–6.4 m/5–7 yd long, usually brilliantly coloured silk or cotton.

sarod Indian plucked lute with up to six melody strings and additional sympathetic strings for added resonance.

sarong traditional dress of the Malay archipelago and the Pacific islands, where it is worn by both men and women. The sarong consists of a piece of fabric, about 4.5–6.4 m/5–7 yd long, which is wrapped around the body and tied at the waist or over the chest. Sarongs became popular fashion garments in the 1940s and 1980s for summer fashion.

Saroyan William 1908–1981. US author. He wrote short stories, such as 'The Daring Young Man on the Flying Trapeze' 1934, idealizing the hopes and sentiments of the 'little man'. His plays, preaching a gospel of euphoric enjoyment, include *The Time of Your Life* (Pulitzer Prize; refused) 1939 and *My Heart's in the Highlands* 1939. He published three volumes of autobiography, including *Obituaries* 1979.

Sarraute Nathalie 1920– . Russian-born French novelist whose books include *Portrait d'un inconnu/Portrait of a Man Unknown* 1948, *Les Fruits d'or/The Golden Fruits* 1964, and *Vous les entendez?/Do You Hear Them?* 1972. An exponent of the ◊nouveau roman, Sarraute bypasses plot, character, and style for the half-conscious interaction of minds.

sarrusophone any of a family of double-reed keyed brass instruments developed 1863 by a French bandmaster named Sarrus, of which the double bass instrument is heard in Stravinsky's sacred cantata *Theni* 1958. Its tone is clear and unforced in the bass register.

Sartre Jean-Paul 1905–1980. French author and philosopher, a leading proponent of ◊existentialism. He published his first novel, *La Nausée/Nausea*, 1937, followed by the trilogy *Les Chemins de la liberté/Roads to Freedom* 1944–45 and many plays, including *Huis Clos/In Camera* 1944. *L'Etre et le néant/Being and Nothingness* 1943, his first major philosophical work, sets out a radical doctrine of human freedom. In the later work *Critique de la raison dialectique/Critique of Dialectical Reason* 1960 he tried to produce a fusion of existentialism and Marxism.

Sartre was born in Paris, and was the long-time companion of the feminist writer Simone de ◊Beauvoir. As a founder of existentialism, he edited its journal *Les Temps modernes/Modern Times*, and expressed its tenets in his novels and plays. According to Sartre, people's awareness of their own freedom takes the form of anxiety, and they therefore attempt to flee from this awareness into what he terms *mauvaise foi* ('bad faith'). In *Crime passionel/Crime of Passion* 1948 he attacked aspects of communism while remaining generally sympathetic. In his later work Sartre became more sensitive to the social constraints on people's actions. He refused the Nobel Prize for Literature 1964 for 'personal reasons', but allegedly changed his mind later, saying he wanted it for the money.

Three o'clock is always too late or too early for anything you want to do.

Jean-Paul Sartre *Nausea*

Sassetta Stefano di Giovanni *c.* 1392–1450. Sienese painter whose work remained true to the International Gothic style of the 14th-century Sienese school, while reflecting contemporary discoveries in spatial representation by Florentine artists. His major work, a masterpiece of devotional art, was the altarpiece for San Francesco in Sansepolcro 1437–44 (Villa i Tatti, Florence/National Gallery, London/Louvre, Paris).

Sassoon Siegfried 1886–1967. English writer, author of the autobiography *Memoirs of a Foxhunting Man* 1928. His *War Poems* 1919 express the disillusionment of his generation.

Educated at Cambridge, Sassoon enlisted in the army 1915, serving in France and Palestine. He published many volumes of poetry and three volumes of childhood autobiography, *The Old Century and Seven More Years* 1938, *The Weald of Youth* 1942, and *Siegfried's Journey* 1945. He wrote a biography of the novelist George Meredith 1948 and published *Collected Poems* 1961.

Soldiers are dreamers; when the guns begin / They think of firelit homes, clean beds, and wives.

Siegfried Sassoon 'Dreamers' 1918

Sassoon Vidal 1929– . British hairdresser patronized by pop stars and models from the early 1950s. He created many new hairstyles, including the Shape 1959, a layered cut tailored to the bone structure—a radical change from the beehive hairstyles of the 1950s. He stopped cutting 1974.

Hair is the only art form that constantly evolves, just because hair doesn't stop growing. It's a now job. I was always involved in trying to discern what was happening. Was it intuition or cognito? I never knew, yet I always pulled off something in time to stun them at the Paris collections. An architect could have the same style for 20 years. I had to change mine every six months.

Vidal Sassoon
Observer Magazine 19 April 1992

sateen smooth fabric, similar to satin, but weft-faced, cheaper, and sometimes softer to handle. Cotton sateen is used for curtain linings. Heavier-weight sateens are sometimes printed.

Satie Erik (Alfred Leslie) 1866–1925. French composer whose aesthetic of ironic simplicity, as in the *Messe des pauvres/Poor People's Mass* 1895, acted as a nationalist antidote to the perceived excesses of German Romanticism. His piano pieces, such as the three *Gymnopédies* 1888, are precise and tinged with melancholy, and parody Romantic expression with surreal commentary. Mentor of the group ◊*Les Six*, he promoted the concept of *musique d'ameublement/furniture music*, anticipating the impact of radio. His *Parade* for orchestra 1917 includes a typewriter, and he invented a new style of film music for René Clair's *Entr'acte/Interval* 1924.

Before I compose a piece, I walk round it several times, accompanied by myself.

Erik Satie

satin very smooth, usually shiny, warp-faced woven textile. It can be made from any fibre; the degree of lustre depends on the fibre and the length of each warp float passing over the weft. Satins have been used in dress and grand furnishings since the Renaissance.

satire literary or dramatic work which ridicules human pretensions or exposes social evils. Satire is related to *parody* in its intention to mock, but satire tends to be more subtle and to mock an attitude or a belief, whereas parody tends to mock a particular work (such as a poem) by imitating its style, often with purely comic intent.

The Roman poets Juvenal and Horace wrote *Satires*, and the form became popular in Europe in the 17th and 18th centuries, used by Voltaire in France and by Alexander Pope and Jonathan Swift in England. Both satire and parody are designed to appeal to the intellect rather than the emotions and both, to be effective, require a knowledge of the original attitude, person, or work that is being mocked (although much satire, such as *Gulliver's Travels* by Swift, can also be enjoyed simply on a literal level).

Saturn in Roman mythology, the god of agriculture, identified by the Romans with the Greek god ◊Kronos. His period of rule was the ancient Golden Age. Saturn was dethroned by his sons Jupiter, Neptune, and Dis. At his festival, the Saturnalia in Dec, gifts were exchanged, and slaves were briefly treated as their masters' equals.

satyr in Greek mythology, a lustful, drunken woodland creature characterized by pointed ears, two horns on the forehead, and a tail. Satyrs attended the god of wine, ◊Dionysus. Roman writers confused satyrs with goat-footed fauns.

saxhorn family of brass musical instruments played with valves, invented 1845 by the Belgian Adolphe Sax (1814–1894), of which the ◊flugelhorn remains in current use.

saxophone member of a hybrid brass instrument family of conical bore, with a single-reed woodwind mouthpiece and keyworks, invented by Belgian instrument-maker Adolphe Sax (1814–1894) about 1840. Soprano, alto, tenor, and baritone forms remain current. The soprano saxophone is usually straight; the others are characteristically curved back at the mouthpiece and have an upturned bell. Initially a concert instrument of suave tone, the saxophone was incorporated into dance bands of the 1930s and 1940s, and assumed its modern guise as an abrasive solo jazz instrument after 1945. It has a voice-like ability to bend a note.

Sayers Dorothy L(eigh) 1893–1957. English writer of crime novels featuring detective Lord Peter Wimsey and heroine Harriet Vane, including *Strong Poison* 1930, *The Nine Tailors* 1934, and *Gaudy Night* 1935. She also wrote religious plays for radio, and translations of Dante.

I admit it is more fun to punt than to be punted, and that a desire to have all the fun is nine-tenths of the law of chivalry.

Dorothy L Sayers *Gaudy Night* 1935

---

scale in music, a sequence of pitches that establishes a key, and in some respects the character of a composition. A scale is defined by its starting note and may be *major* or *minor* depending on the order of intervals. A *chromatic* scale is the full range of 12 notes: it has no key because there is no fixed starting point.

A *whole-tone* scale is a six-note scale and is also indeterminate in key: only two are possible. A *diatonic* scale has seven notes, a *pentatonic* scale has five.

Scarlatti (Giuseppe) Domenico 1685–1757. Italian composer, eldest son of Alessandro Scarlatti, who lived most of his life in Portugal and Spain in the service of the Queen of Spain. He wrote over 500 sonatas for harpsichord, short pieces in ◊binary form demonstrating the new freedoms of keyboard composition and inspired by Spanish musical idioms.

Scarlatti (Pietro) Alessandro (Gaspare) 1660–1725. Italian Baroque composer, maestro di capella at the court of Naples, who developed the opera form. He composed more than 100 operas, including *Tigrane* 1715, as well as church music and oratorios.

Scarlet Pimpernel, The historical adventure novel by Baroness Orczy published in the UK 1905. Set in Paris during the Reign of Terror (1793–94), it describes the exploits of a group of Britons, called the League of the Scarlet Pimpernel, and their leader, Sir Percy Blakeney, who saved aristocrats from the Revolution.

Scarpa Carlo 1906–1978. Italian architect. His emphasis on craftsmanship and fine detail shows the influence of the ◊Art Nouveau tradition. His works include the restoration of the Castelvecchio Museum, Verona, 1964; the Brion Cemetery at San Vito d'Altivole, near Treviso, 1970–72; and the Banco Popolare, Verona, 1973–75, his last major work.

scat singing jazz singing with nonsense syllables, using the voice as an instrument. Its invention is credited to trumpeter Louis Armstrong in the 1920s. Many singers resort to it from time to time to extend a phrase or cover up a forgotten lyric.

The Anglo-American vocal group Lambert, Hendricks and Ross (1957–64) specialized in scat singing. The songs of the Scottish pop group the Cocteau Twins (formed 1982) are composed almost entirely of meaningless syllables chosen for their sound.

scene in a play, a subdivision of an ◊act, marking a change of location or mood, or, for example, the entrance of an important character. A scene is roughly the equivalent of a chapter in a book. Traditionally changes of scene were marked by changes of props (properties); hence the term 'scenery'.

Scharoun Hans 1893–1972. German architect, one of the greatest 20th-century exponents of the organic tradition in architecture. His first major project was the Schminke House, Lobau, Saxony, 1932–33, notable for the lightness of its exposed steel-frame structure. The postwar concert hall for the Berlin Philharmonic Orchestra, completed 1963, is the most dramatic expression of his ideas on organic design, integrating audience and orchestra on various levels.

Scheherazade the storyteller in the ◊*Arabian Nights*.

Scherchen Hermann 1891–1966. German conductor. He collaborated with Schoenberg 1911–12, and in 1919 founded the journal *Melos* to promote contemporary music. He moved to Switzerland 1933, and was active as a conductor and teacher. He wrote two texts, *Handbook of Conducting* and *The Nature of Music*. During the 1950s he founded a music publishing house, Ars Viva Verlag, and an electronic studio at Gravesano.

scherzo (Italian 'joke') in music, a lively piece, usually in rapid triple (3/4) time; often used for the third movement of a symphony, sonata, or quartet as a substitute for the statelier ◊minuet and ◊trio.

Schiaparelli Elsa 1896–1973. Italian couturier and knitwear designer. Her innovative fashion ideas included padded shoulders, sophisticated colours ('shocking pink'), and the pioneering use of zips and synthetic fabrics.

She was widely influential in the 1930s; her outlook had much in common with the Surrealists, some of whom she commissioned to design fabric prints and jewellery. She had a productive partnership with Salvador Dali, creating lobster-printed skirts, a coat with drawers for pockets, based on Dali's painting *City of Drawers*, and a range of hats based on objects such as a shoe, an icecream cone, and a lamb chop.

Schiele Egon 1890–1918. Austrian Expressionist artist. Originally a landscape painter, he was strongly influenced by Art Nouveau, in particular Gustav Klimt, and developed a contorted linear style, employing strong colours. His subject matter includes portraits and openly erotic nudes. In 1911 he was arrested for alleged obscenity.

Schiller Johann Christoph Friedrich von 1759–1805. German dramatist, poet, and historian. He wrote *Sturm und Drang* (storm and stress) verse and plays, including the dramatic trilogy *Wallenstein* 1798–99. Much of his work concerns the aspirations for political freedom and the avoidance of mediocrity.

He was a qualified surgeon, but after the success of the play *Die Räuber/The Robbers* 1781, he devoted himself to literature and completed his tragedies *Die Verschwörung des Fiesko zu Genua/Fiesco, or, the Genoese Conspiracy* and *Kabale und Liebe/Love and Intrigue* 1783. Moving to Weimar 1787, he wrote his more mature blank-verse drama *Don Carlos* and the hymn 'An

die Freude/Ode to Joy', later used by ◊Beethoven in his ninth symphony. As professor of history at Jena from 1789 he completed a history of the Thirty Years' War and developed a close friendship with ◊Goethe after early antagonism. His essays on aesthetics include the piece of literary criticism *Über naive und sentimentalische Dichtung/Naive and Sentimental Poetry*. Schiller became the foremost German dramatist with his classic dramas *Wallenstein* (1796–99), *Maria Stuart* 1800, *Die Jungfrau von Orleans/The Maid of Orleans* 1801, and *Wilhelm Tell/William Tell* 1804.

Against stupidity the gods themselves struggle in vain.

Friedrich von Schiller
Die Jungfrau von Orleans 1801

Schindler Rudolph 1887–1953. Austrian architect who settled in the USA 1913. Initially influenced by Otto Wagner, he worked for Frank Lloyd Wright 1916–21 and later Richard Neutra. His design for Lovell Beach House, Newport Beach, 1925–26, reflects the work of the Dutch De ◊Stijl group while anticipating the horizontal planes of Wright's Falling Water project.

Schinkel Karl Friedrich 1781–1841. Prussian Neo-Classical architect. His major works include the Old Museum, Berlin, 1823–30, the Nikolaikirche in Potsdam 1830–37, and the Roman Bath 1833 in the park of Potsdam.

Schlegel August Wilhelm von 1767–1845. German Romantic author, translator of Shakespeare, whose *Über dramatische Kunst und Literatur/Lectures on Dramatic Art and Literature* 1809–11 broke down the formalism of the old classical criteria of literary composition. Friedrich von Schlegel was his brother.

Schlegel Friedrich von 1772–1829. German critic who (with his brother August) was a founder of the Romantic movement, and a pioneer in the comparative study of languages.

Schlemmer Oskar 1888–1943. German choreographer, sculptor, painter, teacher, designer, and member of the ◊Bauhaus school of artists during the 1920s. His paintings and sculptures are characterized by stylized, mannequin-like figures. His explorations of form, colour, light, and motion resulted in a series of dances which were radically different from the prevailing ◊Ausdruckstanz style of the time. His dances are extremely simple and lack explicit emotional statements; they include *Triadic Ballet* 1922 (music by Paul Hindemith) and *Bauhaus Dances* 1926.

Schlesinger John 1926– . English film and television director who was responsible for such British films as *Billy Liar* 1963 and *Darling* 1965.

His first US film, *Midnight Cowboy* 1969 (Academy Award), was a big commercial success and was followed by *Sunday, Bloody Sunday* 1971, *Marathon Man* 1976, and *Yanks* 1979.

Schmidt-Rottluff Karl 1884–1974. German Expressionist painter and printmaker, a founding member of *die ◊Brücke* in Dresden 1905, active in Berlin from 1911. Inspired by Vincent van Gogh and ◊Fauvism, he developed a vigorous style of brushwork and a bold palette. He painted portraits and landscapes and produced numerous woodcuts and lithographs.

Schnabel Artur 1882–1951. Austrian pianist, teacher, and composer. He taught at the Berlin State Academy 1925–30 before settling in the USA 1939 where, in addition to lecturing, he composed symphonies and piano works. He excelled at playing Beethoven and trained many pianists.

Schneider Romy. Stage name of Rosemarie Albach-Retty 1938–1982. Austrian film actress who starred in *Boccaccio '70* 1962, *Der Prozess/The Trial* 1963, and *Ludwig* 1972.

Schnitzler Arthur 1862–1931. Viennese dramatist. A doctor with an interest in psychiatry, he was known for his psychological dramas exploring egotism, eroticism, and self-deception in Viennese bourgeois life. *Reigen/Merry-Go-Round* 1897, a cycle of dramatic dialogues depicting lust, caused a scandal when performed 1920 but made a successful French film as *La Ronde* 1950, directed by Max Ophuls. His novel *Leutnant Gustl* 1901 pioneered interior monologue in fiction.

Schoenberg Arnold (Franz Walter) 1874 –1951. Austro-Hungarian composer, a US citizen from 1941. After Romantic early works such as *Verklärte Nacht/Transfigured Night* 1899 and the *Gurrelieder/Songs of Gurra* 1900–11, he experimented with ◊atonality (absence of key), producing works such as *Pierrot lunaire/ Moonstruck Pierrot* 1912 for chamber ensemble and voice, before settling on the ◊twelve-tone system of musical composition. This was further developed by his pupils ◊Berg and ◊Webern.

My music is not modern. It is only badly played.

Arnold Schoenberg

After World War I he wrote several Neo-Classical works for chamber ensembles. He taught at the Berlin State Academy 1925–33. Driven from Germany by the Nazis, he settled in the USA 1933, where he influenced music scoring for films. Later works include the unfinished opera *Moses und Aron* 1932–51.

Schongauer Martin *c.* 1430–1491. German painter and engraver. His many fine engravings

of religious subjects elevated the status of engraving from that of a craft to an art. Deeply influenced by Rogier van ◊Weyden, he in turn influenced many of his contemporaries, notably ◊Dürer.

Schreiner Olive 1862–1920. South African novelist and supporter of women's rights. Her autobiographical *The Story of an African Farm* 1883 describes life on the South African veld. Other works include *Trooper Peter Halket of Mashonaland* 1897, a fictional attack on the expansionist policies of Cecil Rhodes, and the feminist classic *Women and Labour* 1911.

Schubert Franz (Peter) 1797–1828. Austrian composer. His ten symphonies include the incomplete eighth in B minor (the 'Unfinished') and the 'Great' in C major. He wrote chamber and piano music, including the 'Trout Quintet', and over 600 lieder (songs) embodying the Romantic expression of emotion with pure melody. They include the cycles *Die schöne Müllerin/The Beautiful Maid of the Mill* 1823 and *Die Winterreise/The Winter Journey* 1827.

Schumann Clara (Josephine) (born Wieck) 1819–1896. German pianist and composer of a *Concerto in A Minor* for piano and orchestra 1835–36, a *Piano Trio* about 1846, and romances for piano. She married Robert Schumann 1840 (her father had been his piano teacher). During his life and after his death she was devoted to popularizing his work, appearing frequently in European concert halls.

Schumann Robert Alexander 1810–1856. German composer and writer. His songs and short piano pieces portray states of emotion with great economy. Among his compositions are four symphonies, a violin concerto, a piano concerto, sonatas, and song cycles, such as *Dichterliebe/ Poet's Love* 1840. Mendelssohn championed many of his works.

Only when the form grows clear to you, will the spirit become so too.

Robert Alexander Schumann
'Advice for Young Musicians' 1848

Schütz Heinrich 1585–1672. German early Baroque composer, musical director to the Elector of Saxony from 1614. His works include *The Seven Last Words* about 1645, *Musikalische Exequien* 1636, and the *Deutsche Magnificat/ German Magnificat* 1671. He increased the range and scope of instrumental and choral ◊polyphony and was an important precursor of J S Bach.

Schwartz Delmore 1913–1966. US poet, short-story writer, and critic. He is noted for lyric poetry of intelligent phrasing and subtle tone. His books include *In Dreams Begin Responsibilities* 1938, *The World is a Wedding* 1948, *Selected Poems (1938–58): Summer Knowledge* 1959, and *Selected Essays* 1970. He co-edited the influential magazine *Partisan Review* 1943–55.

Schwarzenegger Arnold 1947– . Austrian-born US film actor, one of the biggest box-office attractions of the late 1980s and early 1990s. A former body-builder, he came to the attention of Hollywood in *Pumping Iron* 1976, a documentary about body-building. He starred in sword-and-sorcery films such as *Conan the Barbarian* 1982 and later graduated to action movies such as *Terminator* 1984, *Predator* 1987, and *Terminator II* 1991 and comedies such as *Twins* 1988 and *Kindergarten Cop* 1991.

Schwarzkopf Elisabeth 1915– . German operatic soprano whose fame rests on her interpretations of Mozart and Richard Strauss roles and of German lieder (songs). Her art brings a classical poise and precision to the expression of romantic emotion.

Schwitters Kurt 1887–1948. German artist, a member of the ◊Dada movement. He moved to Norway 1937 and to England 1940. From 1918 he developed a variation on collage, using discarded items such as buttons and bus tickets to create pictures and structures. He called these art works *Merz*, and produced a magazine of the same name from 1923. Later he created *Merzbauen* (Merz houses), extensive constructions of wood and scrap, most of which were destroyed.

Sciascia Leonardo 1921–1989. Sicilian novelist who used the detective novel to explore the hidden workings of Sicilian life, as in *Il giorno della civetta/Mafia Vendetta* 1961.

science fiction or *speculative fiction* (also known as *sci-fi* or *SF*) genre of fiction and film with an imaginary scientific, technological, or futuristic basis. It is sometimes held to have its roots in the works of Mary Shelley, notably *Frankenstein* 1818. Often taking its ideas and concerns from current ideas in science and the social sciences, science fiction aims to shake up standard perceptions of reality.

Science-fiction works often deal with alternative realities, future histories, robots, aliens, utopias and dystopias (often satirical), space and time travel, natural or human-made disasters, and psychic powers. Early practitioners were Jules Verne and H G Wells. In the 20th century the US pulp-magazine tradition of science fiction produced such writers as Arthur C Clarke, Isaac Asimov, Robert Heinlein, and Frank Herbert; a consensus of 'pure storytelling' and traditional values was disrupted by writers associated with the British magazine *New Worlds* (Brian Aldiss, Michael Moorcock, J G Ballard) and by younger US writers (Joanna Russ, Ursula Le Guin, Thomas Disch, Gene Wolfe) who used the form for serious literary purposes and for political and sexual radicalism.

Thriving science-fiction traditions, only partly influenced by the Anglo-American one, exist in France, Germany, E Europe, and Russia. In the 1980s the '*cyberpunk*' school spread from the USA, spearheaded by William Gibson and Bruce Sterling (1954–).

Science-fiction writers include James Tiptree Jr (Alice Sheldon 1915–1987, USA), Philip K Dick (USA), John Brunner (1934– , UK), Samuel Delany (1942– , USA), Stanislaw Lem (1921– , Poland), Boris and Arkady Strugatsky (1931– and 1925–1991, Russia), Harlan Ellison (1934–), Damon Knight (1922–), John Campbell (1910–1971), and Frederik Pohl (1919–) – the last four all US editors and anthologists.

Many mainstream writers have written science fiction, including Aldous Huxley (*Brave New World* 1932), George Orwell (*Nineteen Eighty-Four* 1949), and Doris Lessing (series of five books *Canopus in Argos: Archives* 1979–83).

The term was coined 1926 by Hugo Gernsback (1884–1967), editor of the US science-fiction magazine *Amazing Stories*.

Scofield Paul 1922– . English actor. His wide-ranging roles include the drunken priest in Graham Greene's *The Power and the Glory* 1956, Lear in *King Lear* 1962, and Salieri in Peter Shaffer's *Amadeus*. He appeared as Sir Thomas More in both stage and film versions of Robert Bolt's *A Man for All Seasons* (stage 1960–61, film 1966).

score the orderly presentation of a musical composition in manuscript or printed form. A *full score* is a large-format conductor's score, a *short score* is condensed into fewer staves, a *piano score* is a reduction to two staves for a pianist–conductor, with remaining essentials in abbreviated form, and a *miniature* or *study score* is a full score photo-reduced to pocket-book size.

Scorsese Martin 1942– . US director, screenwriter, and producer whose films concentrate on complex characterization and the themes of alienation and guilt. Drawing from his Italian-American Catholic background, his work often deals with sin and redemption, as in his first major film *Boxcar Bertha* 1972. His influential, passionate, and forceful movies include *Mean Streets* 1973, *Taxi Driver* 1976, *Raging Bull* 1980, *The Last Temptation of Christ* 1988, *GoodFellas* 1990, and *Cape Fear* 1992.

Scorsese's other major films include *Alice Doesn't Live Here Anymore* 1974 (featuring his only lead female protagonist), the musical *New York New York* 1977, and *The King of Comedy* 1982.

Scott Douglas 1913–1990. British industrial designer who produced a remarkable variety of classic designs, including the London Transport Routemaster bus, the red double-decker which has been in service since 1968; the Roma wash basin 1961, still being installed in houses and hotels around the world; and the Raeburn cooker. He set up Britain's first professional product-design course and Mexico's first design school.

Scott Francis Reginald 1899–1985. Canadian poet. A distinguished academic, constitutional lawyer, and leftist social critic, he was intellectually as well as poetically committed to social justice and regeneration through love and renewed contact with nature. His collections include *Overtures* 1945 and *The Dance is One* 1973. His volume of satirical verse *The Eye of the Needle* appeared 1957.

Scott George C(ampbell) 1927– . US actor who played mostly tough, authoritarian film roles. His work includes *Dr Strangelove* 1964, *Patton* 1970, *The Hospital* 1971, and *Firestarter* 1984.

Scott (George) Gilbert 1811–1878. English architect. As the leading practical architect of the mid-19th-century ◊Gothic Revival in England, Scott was responsible for the building or restoration of many public buildings and monuments, including the Albert Memorial 1863–72, the Foreign Office in Whitehall 1862–73, and the St Pancras Station Hotel 1868–74, all in London.

Scott Giles Gilbert 1880–1960. English architect, grandson of Gilbert Scott. He designed Liverpool Anglican Cathedral (begun 1903; completed 1978), Cambridge University Library 1931–34, Battersea Power Station 1932–34, and Waterloo Bridge, London, 1939–45. He supervised the rebuilding of the House of Commons after World War II.

Scott Paul (Mark) 1920–1978. English novelist, author of *The Raj Quartet* consisting of *The Jewel in the Crown* 1966, *The Day of the Scorpion* 1968, *The Towers of Silence* 1972, and *A Division of the Spoils* 1975, dealing with the British Raj in India. Other novels include *Staying On* 1977, which is set in post-independence India.

Scott Randolph. Stage name of Randolph Crane 1903–1987. US actor. He began his career in romantic films before becoming one of Hollywood's leading Western stars in the 1940s. His films include *Roberta* 1934, *Jesse James* 1939, *The Tall T* 1956, and *Ride the High Country* 1962.

Scott Ridley 1939– . English director and producer of some of the most visually spectacular and influential films of the 1980s and 1990s, such as *Alien* 1979 and *Blade Runner* 1982. Criticized for sacrificing storyline and character development in favour of ornate sets, Scott replied with *Thelma and Louise* 1991, a carefully wrought story of female bonding and adventure.

He completed his first film *The Duellists* 1977. Among his other films are *Legend* 1985, *Someone to Watch Over Me* 1987, *Black Rain* 1989, and *1492 – The Conquest of Paradise* 1992.

Scott Walter 1771–1832. Scottish novelist and poet. His first works were translations of German ballads, followed by poems such as *The Lady of the Lake* 1810 and *Lord of the Isles* 1815. He gained a European reputation for his historical novels such as *The ◊Heart of Midlothian* 1818, *Ivanhoe* 1819, and *The Fair Maid of Perth* 1828. His last years were marked by frantic writing to pay off his debts, after the bankruptcy of his publishing company 1826.

Born in Edinburgh, Scott was lamed for life following an early attack of poliomyelitis. In 1797 he married Charlotte Charpentier or Carpenter, of French origin. His *Minstrelsy of the Scottish Border* appeared 1802, and from then he combined the practice of literature with his legal profession. *The Lay of the Last Minstrel* 1805 was an immediate success, and so too were *Marmion* 1808, *The Lady of the Lake, Rokeby* 1813, and *Lord of the Isles*. Out of the proceeds he purchased and rebuilt the house of Abbotsford on the Tweed, but Byron had to some extent now captured the lead with a newer style of verse romance, and Scott turned to prose fiction. *Waverley* was issued 1814, and gave its name to a long series of historical novels, including *Guy Mannering* 1815, *The Antiquary* 1816, *Old Mortality* 1816, *Rob Roy* 1817, *The Heart of Midlothian,* and *The Bride of Lammermoor* 1819. *Ivanhoe* transferred the scene to England; *Kenilworth* 1821, *Peveril of the Peak* 1823, *The Talisman* 1825, and *The Fair Maid of Perth* followed.

In 1820 Scott was created a baronet, but in 1826 he was involved in financial ruin through the bankruptcy of Constable, his chief publisher, with whom fell Ballantyne & Co, the firm of printers and publishers in which Scott had been for many years a sleeping partner. Refusing to accept bankruptcy, he set himself to pay off the combined debts of £114,000. *Woodstock* 1826, a life of Napoleon, and *Tales of a Grandfather* 1827–30 are among the chief products of these last painful years. The last outstanding liabilities were cleared after his death on the security of copyrights. Continuous overwork ended in a nervous breakdown. He died at Abbotsford on 21 Sept 1832. His *Journal* was issued 1890, and his life by J G Lockhart, his son-in-law, 1837.

There is a Southern proverb – fine words butter no parsnips.

Walter Scott
'The Legend of Montrose' 1819

Scottish Gaelic literature the earliest examples of Scottish Gaelic prose belong to the period 1000–1150, but the most significant early original composition is the history of the MacDonalds in the Red and Black Books at Clanranald. The first printed book in Scottish Gaelic was a translation of Knox's Prayer Book 1567. Prose Gaelic is at its best in the folk tales, proverbs, and essays by writers such as Norman MacLeod in the 19th and Donald Lamont in the 20th century.

Scottish Gaelic poetry falls into two main categories. The older, syllabic verse was composed by professional bards. The chief sources of our knowledge of this are the Book of the Dean of Lismore (16th century), which is also the main early source for the Ossianic ballads; the panegyrics in the Books of Clanranald; and the Fernaig manuscript. Modern Scottish Gaelic stressed poetry began in the 17th century but reached its zenith during the Jacobite period with Alexander MacDonald, Duncan Macintyre, Rob Donn, and Dugald Buchanan. Only William Livingstone (1808–1870) kept alive the old nationalistic spirit in the 19th century. During and after World War II a new school emerged, including Somhairle MacGilleathain, George Campbell-Hay, and Ruaraidh MacThómais.

Scriabin alternative transcription of ◊Skryabin, Russian composer.

Scribe Augustin Eugène 1791–1861. French dramatist. He achieved recognition with *Une Nuit de la garde nationale/Night of the National Guard* 1815, and with numerous assistants produced many plays of technical merit but little profundity, including *Bertrand et Raton/The School for Politicians* 1833.

sculpture artistic shaping of materials such as wood, stone, clay, metal, and, more recently, plastic and other synthetics. The earliest prehistoric human artefacts include sculpted stone figurines, and all ancient civilizations have left behind examples of sculpture. Many indigenous cultures have maintained rich traditions of sculpture. Those of Africa (see ◊African art), South America, and the Caribbean in particular have been influential in the development of contemporary Western sculpture.

Historically, most sculpture has been religious in intent. Chinese, Japanese, and Indian sculptures are usually Buddhist or Hindu images. African, North American Indian, and Oceanic sculptures reflect spirit cults and animist beliefs.

There are two main techniques traditionally employed in sculpture: *carving*, involving the cutting away of hard materials such as wood or stone to reveal an image; and *modelling*, involving the building up of an image from malleable materials, such as clay or wax, which may then be cast in bronze. In the 20th century various techniques for 'constructing' sculptures have been developed, for example metal welding and assemblage.

ancient sculpture Egyptian and Mesopotamian sculpture took the form of monumental ◊reliefs in palace and temple decoration. Standing sculptures of the period were intended to be seen only from the front and sides. The first sculptures in the round (to be seen from all sides) were Greek. The development of vigorous poses (◊contrapposto) and emotional expressiveness elevated Greek sculpture to the pinnacle of artistic achievement (see ◊Phidias and ◊Praxiteles), and much of subsequent Western sculpture has been imitative of Greek ideals. Lifelike portrait sculpture was introduced by the Romans.

medieval sculpture Sculpture of the period is epitomized by niche figures carved in stone for churches (for example, Chartres, France) and by delicate ivory carvings.

Renaissance sculpture Greek supremacy was challenged by the reintroduction of free-standing sculptures, notably Michelangelo's *David* 1501–04, and by superlative bronze casting, for example, Donatello's equestrian monument of *Gattamelata* 1445–50 (Piazza del Santo, Padua).

Baroque and Rococo sculpture Relief rather than free-standing sculptures came to the fore. The limpid virtuosity of sculptors such as Bernini seemed to defy the nature of the materials they used.

Western sculptors

period	style	selected sculptors
5th–4th century BC	classical	Myron (5th century BC) Phidias (5th century BC) Polykleitos (or Polyclitus) (5th century BC) Praxiteles (4th century BC) Lysippus (4th century BC)
12th–14th century	medieval	Nicola Pisano (died *c.* 1284) Giovanni Pisano (died *c.* 1314) Sluter (*c.* 1380–1406)
14th–16th century	Renaissance	Ghiberti (1378–1455) Donatello (*c.* 1386–1466) Verrocchio (*c.* 1435–1488) Stoss (*c.* 1450–1533) Riemenschneider (*c.* 1460–1531) Michelangelo (1475–1564)
16th century	Mannerism	Cellini (1500–1571) Goujon (*c.* 1510–1565) Giambologna (1529–1608)
17th–18th century	Baroque	Algardi (*c.* 1598–1654) Bernini (1598–1680) Coysevox (1640–1720) Rysbrack (1694–1770)
18th–19th century	Neo-Classical	Houdon (1741–1828) Flaxman (1755–1826) Canova (1757–1822) Thorvaldsen (*c.* 1770–1844)
19th century		Carpeaux (1827–1875) Rodin (1840–1917)
20th century		Maillol (1861–1944) Barlach (1870–1938) Brancusi (1876–1957) Epstein (1880–1959) Boccioni (1882–1916) Lipchitz (1891–1973) Calder (1898–1976) Moore (1898–1986) Giacometti (1901–1966) Marini (1901–1980) Hepworth (1903–1975) Smith (1906–1965) Caro (1924–)

Neo-Classical sculpture Sculpture of the 18th century concentrated on smooth perfection of form and surface, notably the work of Canova.

The last great exponent of sculpture in the Classical tradition was Auguste Rodin. In the 20th century, sculptors such as Henry Moore, Barbara Hepworth, and Jacob Epstein have used traditional materials and techniques to create forms inspired by 'primitive' art and nature. Constantin Brancusi and Giacometti have developed three-dimensional abstract forms from natural materials. Others have broken with the past entirely, rejecting both carving and modelling. Today the term sculpture applies to the mobiles of Alexander Calder, ◊assemblages of various materials, ◊environment sculpture and ◊earthworks, and 'installations'.

Scylla and Charybdis in Greek mythology, a sea monster and a whirlpool, between which Odysseus had to sail. Later writers located them in the Straits of Messina, between Sicily and Italy.

Seagull, The play by Anton ◊Chekhov, first produced in Russia 1896. It studies the jealousy between a mother and her son, the son's vain search for identity, and his ultimate suicide.

Medvedenko: *Why do you wear black all the time?* Masha: *I'm in mourning for my life, I'm unhappy.*

Anton Chekhov *The Seagull* 1896

Searle Ronald 1920– . English cartoonist and illustrator who created the schoolgirls of St Trinian's characters 1941 and has made numerous cartoons of cats. His drawings, as a Japanese prisoner of war during World War II, established him as a serious artist. His sketches of places and people include *Paris Sketch Book* 1950 and *Rake's Progress* 1955.

Sebastiano del Piombo (Sebastiano Veneziano) *c.* 1485–1547. Italian painter of the High Renaissance. Born in Venice, he was a pupil of ◊Giorgione and developed a similar style of painting. In 1511 he moved to Rome, where his friendship with Michelangelo (and rivalry with Raphael) inspired him to his greatest works, such as *The Raising of Lazarus* 1517–19 (National Gallery, London). He also painted powerful portraits.

Second Empire style style of French architecture and design during the second half of the 19th century. Grandiose and ostentatious, it was influential throughout Europe and America. The many imposing classical buildings of this period include the Paris Opéra 1861–74 by Charles Garnier (1825–1898).

secrétaire (French) a small writing desk.

Secret Garden, The novel for children by Frances Hodgson ◊Burnett published in the USA 1911. Mary, a spoilt, sickly orphan, is sent from India to England to live at the house of her uncle, a crippled recluse. Her cultivation of the secret garden from a forgotten wilderness helps to transform her health and outlook and leads her to effect a similar change in her cousin Colin, who believed himself to be an invalid.

section in architectural drawing, a vertical plane cut through a building, showing the elevations of individual rooms.

Seeger Pete 1919– . US folk singer and songwriter of antiwar protest songs, such as 'Where Have All the Flowers Gone?' 1956 and 'If I Had a Hammer' 1949.   Seeger was active in leftwing politics from the late 1930s and was a victim of the witch-hunt of Senator Joe McCarthy in the 1950s. As a member of the vocal group *the Weavers* 1948–58, he popularized songs of diverse ethnic origin and had several hits.

Seferis George. Adopted name of Georgios Seferiades 1900–1971. Greek poet and diplomat. Although his poems are modernist in technique, drawing on Symbolism and Surrealism, they are steeped in a classical past and have a spare and elegant clarity. He published his first volume, *Turning Point*, 1931 and his *Collected Poems* 1950. Nobel prize 1963.

Segal Walter 1907–1985. Swiss-born British architect who pioneered ◊community architecture in the UK. From the 1960s he developed proposals for end-users to design and build their own housing, using simple construction methods and standardized low-tech building components, such as timber framing and pre-cut cladding boards.

Segovia Andrés 1893–1987. Spanish virtuoso guitarist. He transcribed J S Bach for guitar and Ponce, Castelnuovo-Tedesco, de Falla, and Villa-Lobos composed some of their best-known music for him. Segovia's artistry did much to rehabilitate the guitar as a concert instrument and to promote the music of Spain. He taught lutenist Julian Bream and guitarist John Williams.

Seifert Jaroslav 1901–1986. Czech poet who won state prizes under the communists, but became an original member of the Charter 77 human-rights movement. His works include *Mozart in Prague* 1970, *Umbrella from Piccadilly* 1978, and *The Prague Column* 1979. Nobel prize 1984.

Sekhmet ancient Egyptian goddess of heat and fire. She was represented with the head of a lioness, and worshipped at Memphis as the wife of ◊Ptah.

Selby Hubert (Jr) 1928– . US novelist. His acclaimed first novel, *Last Exit to Brooklyn* 1964, vividly depicted urban vice and violence. It was the subject of obscenity trials in Britain 1966 and 1967. Similar portrayals followed in his later novels *The Room* 1971, *The Demon* 1976, *Requiem for a Dream* 1978, and in the stories of *Song of the Silent Snow* 1986.

Selene in Greek mythology, the goddess of the Moon. She was the daughter of a ◊Titan, and the sister of Helios and Eos. In later times she was identified with ◊Artemis.

Sellers Peter 1925–1980. English comedian and film actor, noted for his skill at mimicry. He made his name in the madcap British radio programme *The Goon Show* 1949–60. His films include *The Ladykillers* 1955, *I'm All Right Jack* 1960, *Dr Strangelove* 1964, five *Pink Panther* films 1964–78 (as the bumbling Inspector Clouseau), and *Being There* 1979.

Selznick David O(liver) 1902–1965. US film producer whose early work includes *King Kong, Dinner at Eight,* and *Little Women* all 1933. His independent company, Selznick International (1935–40), made such lavish films as *Gone with the Wind* 1939, *Rebecca* 1940, and *Duel in the Sun* 1946. His last film was *A Farewell to Arms* 1957.

Semele in Greek mythology, the daughter of ◊Cadmus of Thebes and mother of Dionysus by Zeus. At Hera's suggestion she demanded that Zeus should appear to her in all his glory, but when he did so she was consumed by lightning.

Sendak Maurice 1928– . US writer and book illustrator, whose children's books with their deliberately arch illustrations include *Where the Wild Things Are* 1963, *In the Night Kitchen* 1970, and *Outside Over There* 1981.

Live among men as if God beheld you; speak to God as if man were listening.

Seneca *Epistles*

Seneca Lucius Annaeus *c.* 4 BC–AD 65. Roman Stoic playwright, author of essays and nine tragedies. He was tutor to the future emperor Nero but lost favour after the latter's accession to the throne and was ordered to commit suicide. His tragedies were accepted as classical models by 16th-century dramatists.

Senghor Léopold (Sédar) 1906– . Senegalese politician and writer, first president of independent Senegal 1960–80. He is a well-known poet and a founder of ◊négritude, a black literary and philosophical movement. His works, written in French, include *Songs of the Shade* 1945, *Ethiopiques* 1956, and *On African Socialism* 1961.

Sennett Mack. Stage name of Michael Sinnott 1880–1960. Canadian-born US film producer, originally an actor. He founded the Keystone production company 1911, responsible for slapstick silent films featuring the Keystone Kops, Fatty Arbuckle, and Charlie Chaplin. He did not make the transition to sound with much enthusiasm and retired 1935. His films include *Tillie's Punctured Romance* 1914, *The Shriek of Araby* 1923, and *The Barber Shop* (sound) 1933.

sepia brown pigment produced from the black fluid of cuttlefish. After 1870 it replaced the use of bistre (made from charred wood) in wash drawings due to its warmer range of colours. Sepia fades rapidly in bright light.

sequence in music, a device allowing key ◊modulation in which a phrase is repeated sequentially, each time transposing to a different key.

serenade musical piece for chamber orchestra or wind instruments in several movements, originally intended for informal evening entertainment, such as Mozart's *Eine kleine Nachtmusik/A Little Night Music.*

Sergel Johan Tobias 1740–1814. German-born Swedish Neo-Classical sculptor, active mainly in Stockholm. His portraits include *Gustaf III* 1790–1808 (Royal Palace, Stockholm); he also made terracotta figures such as *Mars and Venus* (National Museum, Stockholm).

serialism in music, a later form of the ◊twelve-tone system of composition. It usually refers to post-1950 compositions in which further aspects such as dynamics, durations, and attacks are brought under serial control. These other series may consist of fewer than 12 degrees while some pitch series can go higher.

series in music, the numerical expression of note orders of a ◊tone row, related to a starting ◊pitch of 1. The US composer Milton ◊Babbitt introduced a convention of numbering a series as intervals from zero (unison with the starting note) to a maximum of 11 half-steps or semitones.

Serkin Rudolf 1903–1991. Austrian-born US pianist and teacher, in the USA from 1939, remembered for the quality and sonority of his energetic interpretations of works by J S Bach and Mozart, Beethoven, Schubert, and Brahms. He founded, with German violinist Adolf Busch, the Marlboro Festival for chamber music in Vermont, and served as its director from 1952 until his death.

Serlio Sebastiano 1475–1554. Italian architect and painter, author of *L'Architettura* 1537–51, which set down practical rules for the use of the Classical orders, and was used by architects of the Neo-Classical style throughout Europe.

Serra Richard 1939– . US sculptor, a leading exponent of the Minimalist school, noted for the element of risk present in his precariously balanced sculptures. His signature works of the 1970s–80s are powerful, site-specific sculptures (both outdoor and indoor), built from huge, curving steel plates with rusting surfaces, as in *Sight-Point* 1971–75 (Stedelijk Museum, Amsterdam).

Service Robert William 1874–1938. Canadian author, born in England. He wrote ballads of the Yukon in the days of the Gold Rush, for example 'The Shooting of Dan McGrew' 1907.

Sesshu 1420–1506. Japanese artist, generally considered to be one of Japan's greatest painters. He visited China 1467–68 and, though scornful of contemporary Chinese painting, was influenced by several Chinese styles. His highly individualistic work, combining subtle tones and sharp, energetic lines, helped to establish a tradition of realism in landscape painting.

Sessions Roger (Huntington) 1896–1985. US composer. His international modernist style secured an American platform for serious German influences, including Hindemith and Schoenberg, and offered an alternative to the lightweight, fashionable Modernism of Milhaud and Paris. An able symphonist, his works include *The Black Maskers* (incidental music) 1923, eight symphonies, and *Concerto for Orchestra* 1971. Born in Brooklyn, New York, he attended Harvard and Yale, then studied under Ernest Bloch. He became a leading teacher of composition, serving on the faculties of Boston University, Princeton University, the University of California at Berkeley, and the Juilliard School of Music.

Set in Egyptian mythology, the god of night, the desert, and of all evils. Portrayed as a grotesque animal, Set was the murderer of ◊Osiris.

Seton Ernest Thompson (born Ernest Seton Thompson) 1860–1946. Canadian author and naturalist, born in England. He illustrated his own books with drawings of animals. He was the founder of the Woodcraft Folk youth movement, a non-religious alternative to the scouting movement.

Seurat Georges 1859–1891. French artist. He originated, with Paul Signac, the Neo-Impressionist technique of ◊Pointillism (painting with small dabs rather than long brushstrokes). Examples of his work are *Bathers at Asnières* 1884 (National Gallery, London) and *Sunday on the Island of La Grande Jatte* 1886 (Art Institute of Chicago). Seurat also departed from Impressionism by evolving more formal compositions based on the Classical proportions of the ◊golden section, rather than aiming to capture fleeting moments of light and movement.

If, with the experience of art, I have been able to find scientifically the law of practical colour, can I not discover an equally logical, scientific and pictorial system to compose harmoniously the lines of a picture?

Georges Seurat *L'Art moderne* 1891

Seven against Thebes in Greek mythology, the attack of seven captains led by Adrastus, king of Argos, on the seven gates of ancient Thebes, prompted by the rivalry between the two sons of Oedipus, ◊Polynices and ◊Eteocles, for the kingship of Thebes. In the event, the two brothers died by each other's hands. The subject of tragedies by ◊Aeschylus and ◊Euripides (*The Phoenician Women*), and of the epic *Thebaïd* by the Roman poet Statius, it forms the background to other Greek tragedies by ◊Sophocles (*Antigone, Oedipus at Colonus*) and Euripides (*Suppliant Women*).

Seven Wonders of the World in antiquity, the pyramids of Egypt, the ◊Hanging Gardens of Babylon, the temple of Artemis at Ephesus, the statue of Zeus at Olympia, the Mausoleum at Halicarnassus, the ◊Colossus of Rhodes, and the ◊Pharos (lighthouse) at Alexandria.

Severini Gino 1883–1966. Italian painter. As a member of the Futurist group, he was influenced by both Cubism and the Neo-Impressionism of Seurat and developed a semi-abstract style, using patterns to suggest movement. His *Suburban Train Arriving in Paris* 1915 (Tate Gallery, London) is typical of this period. From the 1920s he worked in a Neo-Classical mode. He expounded his ideas in a book *Du Cubisme au Classicisme* 1921.

Sévigné Marie de Rabutin-Chantal, Marquise de 1626–1696. French writer. In her letters to her daughter, the Comtesse de Grignan, she paints a vivid picture of contemporary customs and events.

The more I see of men, the more I admire dogs.

Marquise de Sévigné (attributed)

Sèvres fine porcelain produced at a factory in Sèvres, France, now a Paris suburb, since the early 18th century. It is characterized by the use of intensely coloured backgrounds (such as pink and royal blue), against which flowers are painted in elaborately embellished frames, often in gold. It became popular after the firm's patronage by Louis XV's mistress, Madame de Pompadour.

The state porcelain factory was established in the park of St-Cloud 1756, and it is also the site of a national museum of ceramics.

Sewell Anna 1820–1878. English author whose only published work, ◊*Black Beauty* 1877, tells the life story of a horse. Although now read as a children's book, it was written to encourage sympathetic treatment of horses by adults.

Sex Pistols, the UK punk-rock group (1975–78) that became notorious under the guidance of their manager Malcolm McLaren (1946–). Their first singles, 'Anarchy in the UK' 1976 and 'God Save the Queen' 1977, unbridled attacks on contemporary Britain, made the Pistols into figures the media loved to hate. The original line-up was Johnny Rotten (real name John Lydon, 1956–), vocals; Steve Jones (1955–), guitar; Glen Matlock (1956–), bass; and Paul Cook (1956–), drums. Their best-known member, Sid Vicious (real name John Ritchie, 1957–1979), joined 1977. They released one album, *Never Mind the Bollocks, Here's the Sex Pistols* 1977.

Sexton Anne 1928–1974. US poet. She studied with Robert Lowell and wrote similarly confessional poetry, as in *To Bedlam and Part Way Back* 1960 and *All My Pretty Ones* 1962. She committed suicide, and her *Complete Poems* appeared posthumously 1981.

Seymour Lynn 1939– . Canadian ballerina of rare dramatic talent. She was principal dancer of the Royal Ballet from 1959 and artistic director of the Munich State Opera Ballet 1978–80. Although officially retired from dancing 1987, she has continued to dance in such roles as Titiana in *Onegin*. She has also choreographed ballets including *Rashomon* 1976 and *Wolfi* 1987, on the death of Mozart. She formed a partnership with Christopher Gable in such ballets as *The Invitation* 1960, *The Two Pigeons* 1961, and *Romeo and Juliet* 1966 (a role which she had to teach to Margot Fonteyn and four other ballerinas before she could dance it on stage).

Sezession (German 'secession') name given to various groups of German and Austrian artists in the 1890s who 'seceded' from official academic art institutions in order to found new schools of painting. The first was in Munich 1892; the next, linked with the paintings of Gustav ◊Klimt and the Art Nouveau movement, was the Vienna Sezession 1897; the Berlin Sezession, led by the Impressionist Max Liebermann (1847–1935), followed 1899. In 1910 the members of the group die ◊Brücke formed the **Neue Sezession** when they were rejected by Berlin's first Sezession.

Shadwell Thomas 1642–1692. English dramatist and poet. His plays include *Epsom-Wells* 1672 and *Bury-Fair* 1689. He was involved in a violent feud with the poet Dryden, whom he attacked in 'The Medal of John Bayes' 1682 and succeeded as poet laureate 1689.

Shaffer Peter 1926– . English dramatist. His psychological dramas include *Five Finger Exercise* 1958, the historical epic *The Royal Hunt of the Sun* 1964, *Equus* 1973, and *Amadeus* 1979, about the envy provoked by the composer Mozart.

Shahn Ben 1898–1969. Lithuanian-born US artist. A Social Realist, his work includes drawings and paintings on the Dreyfus case, in which a French army officer was the victim of a miscarriage of justice, and the Sacco-Vanzetti case, in which two Italian anarchists were accused of murders. He painted murals for the Rockefeller Center, New York (with the Mexican artist Diego Rivera), and the Federal Security Building, Washington, 1940–42.

All art is based on nonconformity.

Ben Shahn *Atlantic* Sept 1957

Shakespeare William 1564–1616. English dramatist and poet. Established in London by 1589 as an actor and a dramatist, he was England's unrivalled dramatist until his death, and is considered the greatest English dramatist. His plays, written in blank verse with some prose, can be broadly divided into lyric plays, including ◊*Romeo and Juliet* and A ◊*Midsummer Night's Dream*; comedies, including *The Comedy of Errors*, *As You Like It*, *Much Ado About Nothing*, and *Measure For Measure*; historical plays, such as *Henry VI* (in three parts), *Richard III*, and *Henry IV* (in two parts), which often showed cynical political wisdom; and tragedies, such as ◊*Hamlet*, ◊*Macbeth*, and ◊*King Lear*. He also wrote numerous sonnets.

Born in Stratford-on-Avon, the son of a wool dealer, he was educated at the grammar school, and in 1582 married Anne Hathaway. They had a daughter, Susanna, 1583, and twins Hamnet (died 1596) and Judith 1595. Early plays, written around 1589–93, were the tragedy *Titus Andronicus*; the comedies *The Comedy of Errors*, *The ◊Taming of the Shrew*, and *The Two Gentlemen of Verona*; the three parts of *Henry VI*; and *Richard III*. About 1593 he came under the patronage of the Earl of ◊Southampton, to whom he dedicated his long poems *Venus and Adonis* 1593 and *The Rape of Lucrece* 1594; he also wrote for him the comedy *Love's Labour's Lost*, satirizing the explorer Walter Raleigh's circle, and seems to have dedicated to him his sonnets written around 1593–96, in which the mysterious 'Dark Lady' appears. From 1594 Shakespeare was a member of the Chamberlain's (later the King's) company of players, and had no rival as a dramatist, writing, for example, the lyric plays *Romeo and Juliet*, A *Midsummer Night's Dream*, and *Richard II* 1594–97, followed by *King John* and *The* ◊*Merchant of Venice* 1596–97. The Falstaff plays of 1596–99 – *Henry IV* (parts I and II), *Henry V*, and *The Merry Wives of Windsor* (said to have been written at the request of Elizabeth I) – brought his fame to its height. He wrote *Julius Caesar* 1599. The period ended with the lyrically witty *Much Ado About Nothing*, *As You Like It*, and ◊*Twelfth Night*, about 1598–1601. With *Hamlet* begins the period of the great tragedies, 1601–08: ◊*Othello*, *Macbeth*, *King Lear*, *Timon of Athens*, ◊*Antony and Cleopatra*, and *Coriolanus*. This 'darker' period is also reflected in the comedies *Troilus and Cressida*, *All's Well That Ends Well*, and *Measure for Measure* around 1601–04. It is thought that Shakespeare was only part author of *Pericles*, which is grouped with the other plays of around 1608–11 – *Cymbeline*, *The Winter's Tale*, and *The* ◊*Tempest* – as the mature romance or 'reconciliation' plays of the end of his career. During 1613 it is thought that Shakespeare collaborated with John Fletcher on *Henry VIII* and *Two Noble Kinsmen*. He had already retired to Stratford about 1610, where he died on 23 April 1616.

For the first 200 years after his death, Shakespeare's plays were frequently performed in cut or revised form (Nahum Tate's *King Lear* was given a happy ending), and it was not until the 19th century, with the critical assessment of Samuel Coleridge and William ◊Hazlitt, that the original texts were restored.

O! it is excellent / To have a lion's strength, but it is tyrannous/To use it like a giant.

William Shakespeare
Measure for Measure c. 1604

Shankar Ravi 1920– . Indian composer and musician. A virtuoso of the ◊sitar, he has been influential in popularizing Indian music in the West. He has composed two concertos for sitar and orchestra 1971 and 1981, and film music, including scores for Satyajit Ray's *Pather Panchali* 1955 and Richard Attenborough's *Gandhi* 1982, and founded music schools in Bombay and Los Angeles.

Shapiro Karl (Jay) 1913– . US poet and critic, noted for the sparkling wit of his poetry and for his denunciation of Modernists (Ezra Pound, T S Eliot, and W B Yeats), and the ◊New Criticism. His conception of the Jew as a prototype of modern man informed his striking *V Letter and Other Poems* 1945 (Pulitzer Prize) and *Poems of a Jew* 1958. Later volumes include *Adult Bookstore* 1976.

Sharif Omar. Stage name of Michael Shalhoub 1932– . Egyptian-born actor (of Lebanese parents), who was Egypt's top male star before breaking into international films after his successful appearance in *Lawrence of Arabia* 1962. His films include *Dr Zhivago* 1965 and *Funny Girl* 1968.

Shakespeare: the plays

title	performed/written (approximate)
early plays	
Henry VI Part I	1589–92
Henry VI Part II	1589–92
Henry VI Part III	1589–92
The Comedy of Errors	1592–93
The Taming of the Shrew	1593–94
Titus Andronicus	1593–94
The Two Gentlemen of Verona	1594–95
Love's Labours Lost	1594–95
Romeo and Juliet	1594–95
histories	
Richard III	1592–93
Richard II	1595–97
King John	1596–97
Henry IV Part I	1596–97
Henry IV Part II	1597–98
Henry V	1599
Roman plays	
Julius Caesar	1599–1600
Antony and Cleopatra	1607–08
Coriolanus	1607–08
the 'great' or 'middle' comedies	
A Midsummer Night's Dream	1595–96
The Merchant of Venice	1596–97
The Merry Wives of Windsor	1597
Much Ado About Nothing	1598–99
As You Like It	1599–1600
Twelfth Night	1601–02
the great tragedies	
Hamlet	1601–02
Othello	1604–05
King Lear	1605–06
Macbeth	1605–06
Timon of Athens	1607–08
the 'dark' comedies	
Troilus and Cressida	1601–02
All's Well That Ends Well	1602–03
Measure for Measure	1604–05
late plays	
Pericles	1608–09
Cymbeline	1609–10
The Winter's Tale	1610–11
The Tempest	1611
Henry VIII	1612–13

sharp in music, sounding higher in pitch than the indicated note value, or than expected. A sharp sign in front of a written note indicates that it is to be raised by a semitone. It is cancelled by a natural sign.

Sharp Cecil (James) 1859–1924. English collector and compiler of folk dance and song. His work ensured that the English folk-music revival became established in school music throughout the English-speaking world. He led a movement to record a threatened folk-song tradition for posterity, publishing *English Folk Song* 1907 (two volumes). In the USA he tracked down survivals of English song in the Appalachian Mountains and elsewhere.

Shaw Artie. Stage name of Arthur Arshawsky 1910– . US jazz clarinettist, bandleader, and composer. He became famous in the ◊swing era when his version of Cole Porter's 'Begin the Beguine' was a number-one hit in the USA 1938. Other hits (all with different line-ups) were 'Back Bay Shuffle' 1939 (his own composition), 'Frenesi' 1941, and 'Stardust' 1942. He retired in 1952.

Shaw George Bernard 1856–1950. Irish dramatist. He was also a critic and novelist, and an early member of the socialist Fabian Society. His plays combine comedy with political, philosophical, and polemic aspects, aiming to make an impact on his audience's social conscience as well as their emotions. They include *Arms and the Man* 1894, *Devil's Disciple* 1897, *Man and Superman* 1903, *Pygmalion* 1913, and *St Joan* 1923. Nobel prize 1925.

Born in Dublin, Shaw went to London 1876, where he became a brilliant debater and supporter of the Fabians, and worked as a music and drama critic. He wrote five unsuccessful novels before his first play, *Widowers' Houses*, was privately produced 1892. Attacking slum landlords, it allied him with the realistic, political, and polemical movement in the theatre, pointing to people's responsibility to improve themselves and their social environment. His first public production was *Arms and the Man*, a cynical view of war. The volume *Plays: Pleasant and Unpleasant* 1898 also included *The Philanderer*, *Mrs Warren's Profession*, dealing with prostitution and banned until 1902; and *Arms and the Man*. *Three Plays for Puritans* 1901 contained *The Devil's Disciple*, *Caesar and Cleopatra* (a companion piece to Shakespeare's *Antony and Cleopatra*), and *Captain Brassbound's Conversion*, written for the actress Ellen ◊Terry. *Man and Superman* expounds his ideas of evolution by following the character of Don Juan into hell for a debate with the devil. The 'anti-romantic' comedy *Pygmalion*, first performed 1913, was written for the actress Mrs Patrick ◊Campbell (and later converted to a musical as *My Fair Lady*). Later plays included *Heartbreak House* 1920, *Back to Methuselah* 1922, and the historical *St Joan*.

Shaw wrote more than 50 plays and became a byword for wit. His theories were further explained in the voluminous prefaces to the plays, and in books such as *The Intelligent Woman's Guide to Socialism and Capitalism* 1928. He was also an unsuccessful advocate of spelling reform and a prolific letter-writer.

There are two tragedies in life. One is not to get your heart's desire. The other is to get it.

George Bernard Shaw
Man and Superman 1903

Shaw (Richard) Norman 1831–1912. British architect, born in Scotland. He was the leader of the trend away from Gothic and Tudor styles back to Georgian designs. In partnership with W E Nesfield (1835–1888), he began working in the ◊Arts and Crafts tradition, designing simple country houses using local materials, in a style known as Old English. The two then went on to develop the Queen Anne style, inspired by 17th-century Dutch domestic architecture, of which Shaw's design for Swan House, Chelsea, London, 1876 is a fine example. Shaw's later style was Imperial Baroque, as in the Piccadilly Hotel 1905.

shawl rectangular, square, or triangular piece of fabric worn around the shoulders, often made of wool, silk, cotton, or lace; it may be plain, printed, or embroidered and is sometimes fringed with tassles around the outer edge. In the early 1800s shawls were small silk squares. From 1830 onwards they became major fashion items, for indoor and outdoor attire, varying from long narrow shawls in the 1830s–40s to large shawls in the 1850s–60s, which were designed to cover the large ◊crinoline skirts of the period. The popularity of shawls for day and evening wear continued into the 20th century.

shawm member of a family of double-reed conical bore musical instruments of piercing tone. The Renaissance shawm emerged around 1200 as a consort instrument, the reed enclosed by a ◊windcap. It was a forerunner of the ◊oboe.

Shchedrin N. Pen name of Mikhail Evgrafovich Saltykov 1826–1889. Russian writer whose works include *Fables* 1884–85, in which he depicts misplaced 'good intentions', and the novel *The Golovlevs* 1880. He was a satirist of pessimistic outlook. He was exiled for seven years for an early story that proved too liberal for the authorities, but later held official posts.

Shearer (Edith) Norma 1900–1983. Canadian-born US actress who starred in silent films and in talkies such as *Private Lives* 1931, *Romeo and Juliet* 1936, *Marie Antoinette* 1938, and *The Women* 1939. She was married to MGM executive Irving Thalberg and retired after *Her Cardboard Lover* 1942.

Sheeler Charles 1883–1965. US painter, known for his paintings of factories, urban landscapes, and machinery, as in *Upper Deck* 1929 (Fogg Art Museum, Cambridge, Massachusetts). He was associated with *Precisionism*, a movement that used sharply defined shapes to represent objects. His method was to photograph his subjects before painting them.

Shelley Mary Wollstonecraft 1797–1851. English writer, the daughter of Mary Wollstonecraft and William Godwin. In 1814 she eloped with the poet Percy Bysshe Shelley, whom she married 1816. Her novels include ◊*Frankenstein* 1818, *The Last Man* 1826, and *Valperga* 1823.

Shelley Percy Bysshe 1792–1822. English lyric poet, a leading figure in the Romantic movement.

Expelled from Oxford University for atheism, he fought all his life against religion and for political freedom. This is reflected in his early poems such as *Queen Mab* 1813.

He later wrote tragedies including *The Cenci* 1818, lyric dramas such as *Prometheus Unbound*, and lyrical poems such as 'Ode to the West Wind'. He drowned while sailing in Italy. Born near Horsham, Sussex, he was educated at Eton public school and University College, Oxford, where his collaboration in a pamphlet *The Necessity of Atheism* 1811 caused his expulsion. While living in London he fell in love with 16-year-old Harriet Westbrook, whom he married 1811. In 1813 he published privately *Queen Mab*, a poem with political freedom as its theme. Meanwhile he had become estranged from his wife and in 1814 left England with Mary Wollstonecraft Godwin, whom he married after Harriet drowned herself 1816. *Alastor*, written 1815, was followed by the epic *The Revolt of Islam*, and by 1818 Shelley was living in Italy. Here he produced the tragedy *The Cenci*; the satire on Wordsworth, *Peter Bell the Third* 1819; and the lyric drama *Prometheus Unbound* 1820. Other works of the period are 'Ode to the West Wind' 1819; 'The Cloud' and 'The Skylark', both 1820; 'The Sensitive Plant' and 'The Witch of Atlas'; 'Epipsychidion' and, on the death of the poet Keats, 'Adonais' 1821; the lyric drama *Hellas* 1822; and the prose *Defence of Poetry* 1821.

Poets are the unacknowledged legislators of the world.

Percy Bysshe Shelley
Defence of Poetry 1821

Shen Chou 1427–1509. Chinese painter of sensitive landscapes. His style drew on the work of the old masters of Chinese painting and, possibly, also on that of Japanese artist Sesshu.

Shenstone William 1714–1763. English poet and essayist whose poems include *Poems upon Various Occasions* 1737, the Spenserian *Schoolmistress* 1742, elegies, odes, songs, and ballads.

Shepard E(rnest) H(oward) 1879–1976. English illustrator of books by A A Milne (*Winnie-the-Pooh* 1926) and Kenneth Grahame (*The Wind in the Willows* 1908).

Shepard Sam 1943– . US dramatist and actor. His work combines colloquial American dialogue with striking visual imagery, and includes *The Tooth of Crime* 1972 and *Buried Child* 1978, for which he won a Pulitzer Prize. *Seduced* 1979 is based on the life of the recluse Howard Hughes. He has acted in a number of films, including *The Right Stuff* 1983, *Fool for Love* 1986, based on his play of the same name, and *Steel Magnolias* 1989.

Sher Anthony 1951– . South African-born actor. A versatile performer in contemporary and classic drama, his roles include *Richard III* 1984, Shylock in *The Merchant of Venice* 1987, the title role in Peter Flannery's *Singer* 1989, and Tamburlaine in Marlowe's tragedy 1992. For television, he played Howard Kirk in Malcolm Bradbury's *The History Man* 1981.

Sheraton Thomas *c.* 1751–1806. English designer of elegant inlaid furniture. He was influenced by his predecessors ◊Hepplewhite and ◊Chippendale. He published the *Cabinet-maker's and Upholsterer's Drawing Book* 1791.

Sheridan Richard Brinsley 1751–1816. Irish dramatist and politician, born in Dublin. His social comedies include *The Rivals* 1775, celebrated for the character of Mrs Malaprop, and *The School for Scandal* 1777. He also wrote a burlesque, *The Critic* 1779. In 1776 he became lessee of the Drury Lane Theatre. He became a member of Parliament 1780. His last years were clouded by the burning down of his theatre 1809, the loss of his parliamentary seat 1812, and by financial ruin and mental breakdown.

If it is abuse – why one is sure to hear of it from one damned good-natured friend or other!

Richard Brinsley Sheridan
The Critic 1779

Sherriff R(obert) C(edric) 1896–1975. British dramatist, remembered for his antiheroic war play *Journey's End* 1928. Later plays include *Badger's Green* 1930 and *Home at Seven* 1950.

Sherwood Robert 1896–1955. US dramatist. His plays include *The Petrified Forest* 1935, the melodrama *Idiot's Delight* 1936, *Abe Lincoln in Illinois* 1938, and *There Shall Be No Night* 1940. For each of the last three he received a Pulitzer Prize.

Shevchenko Taras 1814–1861. Ukrainian national poet. Born a serf, he was freed (for 2,500 roubles) in St Petersburg where he then studied art. His sensationally successful first collection *Kobzar/Folk Minstrel* 1840 romantically glorified the Ukraine's Cossack past. It was followed by the long poem *Haidamaky/The Haidamaks* 1841. His protest against injustice and Tsarist oppression in the Ukraine led to a ban on publication of his poems and eventual exile and penal servitude for subversive activity.

Shimazaki Tōson 1872–1943. Japanese poet and novelist. His work explores the clash of old and new values in a rapidly modernizing Japan. He published romantic poetry in the 1890s and *Hakai/Broken Commandment* 1906, the first

Japanese naturalist novel, as well as the confessional novel *Ie/The House* 1910–11. *Yoake mae/Before the Dawn* 1935 is an account of the struggle for the restoration of the Empire 1862 from the perspective of a rural community.

Sholokhov Mikhail Aleksandrovich 1905–1984. Russian novelist. His *And Quiet Flows the Don* 1926–40, hailed in the Soviet Union as a masterpiece of ◊Socialist Realism, depicts the Don Cossacks through World War I and the Russian Revolution. His authorship of the novel was challenged by Alexander ◊Solzhenitsyn. Nobel prize 1965.

Shootings of May 3rd 1808, The oil painting by Francisco de ◊Goya 1814 (Prado, Madrid), inspired by his outrage at the events of 1808 when the Spanish rose up against the invading French troops of Napoleon. Goya chose one moment in two violent days — a man facing death at the hands of an execution squad — to encapsulate his emotions about the ruthlessness of power.

shorts short trousers varying in length down the thigh to the knee. Originally a male garment, they have been worn by women since the 1920s. They were formerly associated with sports and casual wear, but during the late 1970s suits consisting of shorts and smart jackets were introduced.

short story short work of prose fiction, which typically either sets up and resolves a single narrative point or depicts a mood or an atmosphere. The two seminal figures in the development of the modern short story are Guy de Maupassant and Anton Chekhov. Other outstanding short-story writers are Rudyard Kipling, Saki, Edgar Allan Poe, Ernest Hemingway, Isaac Babel, Katherine Mansfield, Jorge Luis Borges, and Sherwood Anderson.

Shostakovich Dmitry (Dmitriyevich) 1906–1975. Soviet composer. His music is tonal, expressive, and sometimes highly dramatic; it was not always to official Soviet taste. He wrote 15 symphonies, chamber and film music, ballets, and operas, the latter including *Lady Macbeth of Mtsensk* 1934, which was suppressed as 'too divorced from the proletariat', but revived as *Katerina Ismaylova* 1963. His son Maxim (1938–), a conductor, defected to the West after his father's death.

A Soviet composer's reply to just criticism.

Dmitry Shostakovich
epigraph to his fifth symphony

Shuman Mort 1936– ; see ◊Pomus and Shuman, US pop-music writing partnership.

Shute Nevil. Pen name of Nevil Shute Norway 1899–1960. English novelist. Among his books are *A Town Like Alice* 1949 and *On the Beach* 1957.

He settled in Australia 1950, having previously flown his own plane to Australia 1948–49 to research material for his books. *On the Beach* was filmed 1959.

Sibelius Jean (Christian) 1865–1957. Finnish composer. His works include nationalistic symphonic poems such as *En saga* 1893 and *Finlandia* 1900, a violin concerto 1904, and seven symphonies. He studied the violin and composition at Helsinki and went on to Berlin and Vienna. In 1940 he abruptly ceased composing and spent the rest of his life as a recluse. Restoration of many works to their original state has helped to dispel his conservative image and reveal unexpectedly radical features.

Sibley Antoinette 1939– . English dancer. Joining the Royal Ballet 1956, she became principal soloist 1960. Her roles included Odette/Odile in *Swan Lake*, Giselle, and the title role in MacMillan's *Manon* 1974. A dancer of exceptional musicality and grace, she excelled in ◊Ashton's *The Dream* 1964. She formed an ideal partnership with Anthony ◊Dowell. A knee injury 1976 brought her career to a five-year standstill, but in 1981 she returned to dance in Helpmann's *Hamlet* and since then has been a regular guest artist with the Royal Ballet.

Sibyl in Roman mythology, one of many prophetic priestesses, notably one from Cumae near Naples. She offered to sell the legendary king of Rome, Tarquinius Superbus, nine collections of prophecies, the *Sibylline Books*, but the price was too high. When she had destroyed all but three, he bought these for the identical price, and they were kept for consultation in emergency at Rome.

Sickert Walter (Richard) 1860–1942. English artist. His Impressionist cityscapes of London and Venice, portraits, and domestic and music-hall interiors capture subtleties of tone and light, often with a melancholic atmosphere. Sickert was born in Munich, the son of a Danish painter, and lived in London from 1868. He studied at the Slade School of Art and established friendships with the artists Whistler and Degas. His work inspired the ◊Camden Town Group; examples include *Ennui* about 1913 (Tate Gallery, London).

Go on, don't worry about the bad paintings, like a balloon your good work will carry the bad up with it.

Walter Sickert advice to pupils 1926

Siddons Sarah 1755–1831. English actress. Her majestic presence made her suited to tragic and heroic roles such as Lady Macbeth, Zara in Congreve's *The Mourning Bride*, and Constance in *King John*. She toured the provinces with her father Roger Kemble (1721–1802) until she appeared in London to immediate acclaim in Otway's *Venice Preserv'd* 1774. This led to her appearing with David ◊Garrick at Drury Lane. She retired 1812.

side drum see ◊snare drum.

Sidney Philip 1554–1586. English poet and soldier, author of the sonnet sequence *Astrophel and Stella* 1591, *Arcadia* 1590, a prose romance, and *Apologie for Poetrie* 1595, the earliest work of English literary criticism.   Sidney was born in Penshurst, Kent. He entered Parliament 1581, and was knighted 1583. In 1585 he was made governor of Flushing in the Netherlands, and died at Zutphen, fighting the Spanish.

'Fool!' said my muse to me, 'look in thy heart, and write.'

Philip Sidney *Astrophel and Stella* 1591

Siegel Don(ald) 1912–1991. US film director of thrillers, Westerns, and police dramas. Two of his low-budget features, the prison film *Riot in Cell Block 11* 1954 and the science-fiction story *Invasion of the Body Snatchers* 1956, are widely recognized for transcending their lack of resources. Siegel moved on to bigger budgets, but retained his taut, acerbic view of life in such films as the Clint Eastwood vehicles *Coogan's Bluff* 1969, *The Beguiled*, and *Dirty Harry* both 1971.

Siegfried legendary Germanic and Norse hero. His story, which may contain some historical elements, occurs in the German ◊*Nibelungenlied/ Song of the Nibelung* and in the Norse *Elder* or *Poetic* ◊*Edda* and the prose *Völsunga Saga* (in the last two works, the hero is known as Sigurd). Siegfried wins Brunhild for his liege lord and marries his sister, but is eventually killed in the intrigues that follow. He is the hero of the last two operas in Wagner's *The Ring of the Nibelung* cycle.

Sienkiewicz Henryk 1846–1916. Polish author. His books include *Quo Vadis?* 1895, set in Rome at the time of Nero, and the 17th-century historical trilogy *With Fire and Sword, The Deluge*, and *Pan Michael* 1890–93. *Quo Vadis?* was the basis of several spectacular films.

The greater the philosopher, the harder it is for him to answer the questions of the average man.

Henryk Sienkiewicz

Signac Paul 1863–1935. French artist. In 1884 he joined with Georges Seurat in founding the Salon des Artistes Indépendants and developing the technique of ◊Pointillism.

Born in Paris, Signac was inspired by the Impressionist painter Monet Signac. He laid down the theory of Neo-Impressionism in his book *De Delacroix au néo-impressionisme* 1899.

From the 1890s he developed a stronger and brighter palette. He and Matisse painted together in the south of France 1904–05.

Signorelli Luca *c.* 1450–1523. Italian painter, active in central Italy. About 1483 he was called to the Vatican to complete frescoes on the walls of the Sistine Chapel. He produced large frescoes in Orvieto Cathedral, where he devoted a number of scenes to *The Last Judgement* 1499–1504. The style is sculptural and dramatic, reflecting late 15th-century Florentine trends, but Signorelli's work is more imaginative. He settled in Cortona and ran a workshop producing altarpieces.

Sigurd hero of Norse legend; see ◊Siegfried.

Silenus in Greek mythology, the son of Hermes, or Pan, and companion of ◊Dionysus. He is portrayed as a lecherous and cowardly old man, usually drunk.

silhouette profile or shadow portrait filled in with black or a dark colour. A common pictorial technique in Europe in the late 18th and early 19th centuries, it was named after Etienne de Silhouette (1709–1767), a French finance minister who made paper cut-outs as a hobby.

silk fine soft thread produced by the larva of the silkworm moth when making its cocoon. It is soaked, carefully unwrapped, and used in the manufacture of textiles. The introduction of synthetics originally harmed the silk industry, but rising standards of living have produced an increased demand for real silk. It is manufactured in China, India, Japan, and Thailand.

silk-screen printing or *serigraphy* method of printing based on stencilling. It can be used to print on most surfaces, including paper, plastic, cloth, and wood. An impermeable stencil (either paper or photosensitized gelatin plate) is attached to a finely meshed silk screen that has been stretched on a wooden frame, so that the ink passes through to the area beneath only where an image is required. The design can also be painted directly on the screen with varnish. A series of screens can be used to add successive layers of colour to the design. The process was developed in the early 20th century for commercial use and adopted by many artists from the 1930s onwards, most notably Andy Warhol.

Sillitoe Alan 1928– . English novelist who wrote *Saturday Night and Sunday Morning* 1958, about a working-class man in Nottingham, Sillitoe's home town. He also wrote *The Loneliness of the Long Distance Runner* 1959, *Life Goes On* 1985, many other novels, and poems, plays, and children's books.

Sills Beverly 1929– . US operatic soprano. Her high-ranging coloratura is allied to a subtle emotional control in French and Italian roles, notably as principal in Donizetti's *Lucia di Lammermoor* and Puccini's *Manon Lescaut*. She sang with touring companies and joined the New York City Opera 1955. In 1979 she became director of New York City Opera and retired from the stage 1980.

Silone Ignazio. Pen name of Secondo Tranquilli 1900–1978. Italian novelist. His novel *Fontamara* 1933 deals with the hopes and disillusionment of a peasant village from a socialist viewpoint. His other works include *Una manciata di more/A Handful of Blackberries* 1952.

Silvanus in Roman mythology, a woodland god, at times identified with the Greek ◊Pan.

silverpoint drawing material consisting of silver wire encased in a holder, used on paper prepared with opaque white. Lead, copper, and gold metalpoints were also used, but silver was most popular in the 15th and 16th centuries. Its limited application and the impossibility of erasure caused it to be superseded by the graphite ◊pencil in the 18th century. A fine example of silverpoint is Dürer's *Self-portrait* 1484 (Albertina, Vienna).

Sim Alistair 1900–1976. Scottish comedy actor. Possessed of a marvellously expressive face, he was ideally cast in eccentric roles, as in the title role in *Scrooge* 1951. His other films include *Inspector Hornleigh* 1939, *Green for Danger* 1945, and *The Belles of St Trinians* 1954.

Simenon Georges 1903–1989. Belgian crime writer. Initially a pulp fiction writer, in 1931 he created Inspector Maigret of the Paris Sûreté who appeared in a series of detective novels.

Writing is not a profession but a vocation of unhappiness. I don't think an artist can ever be happy.

Georges Simenon

Simmons Jean 1929– . English actress of dark, elegant looks who often played respectable women plagued by an undercurrent of sexuality in such films as *Black Narcissus* 1947, *Guys and Dolls* 1955, and *Spartacus* 1960.

Simon (Marvin) Neil 1927– . US dramatist and screenwriter. His stage plays (which were made into films) include the wryly comic *Barefoot in the Park* 1963 (filmed 1967), *The Odd Couple* 1965 (filmed 1968), and *The Sunshine Boys* 1972 (filmed 1975), and the more serious, autobiographical trilogy *Brighton Beach Memoirs* 1983 (filmed 1986), *Biloxi Blues* 1985 (filmed 1988), and *Broadway Bound* 1986 (filmed 1991). He has also written screenplays and co-written musicals, including *Sweet Charity* 1966, *Promises, Promises* 1968, and *They're Playing Our Song* 1978.

Simon Claude 1913– . French novelist, originally an artist. He abandoned 'time structure' and story line in such innovative novels as *La Route de*

Flandres/The Flanders Road 1960, *Le Palace* 1962, and *Histoire* 1967 in order to depict the constant flux of experience. His later novels include *Les Géorgiques* 1981 and *L'Acacia* 1989. Nobel prize 1985.

Simon Paul 1942– . US pop singer and songwriter. In a folk-rock duo with Art Garfunkel (1942–), he had such hits as 'Mrs Robinson' 1968 and 'Bridge Over Troubled Water' 1970. Simon's solo work includes the critically acclaimed album *Graceland* 1986, for which he drew on Cajun and African music. The success of *Graceland* and subsequent tours involving African musicians helped to bring world music to international attention, but Simon had always had an eclectic ear and had, for example, as early as 1971 used reggae rhythm on the song 'Mother and Child Reunion' and a Latin beat on 'Me and Julio Down by the Schoolyard'. Brazilian drumming group Olodum featured on *The Rhythm of the Saints* 1990.

Like a bridge over troubled water, I will ease your mind.

Paul Simon 'Bridge over Troubled Water' 1970

Simone Martini *c.* 1284–1344. Italian painter, a master of the Sienese school. He was a pupil of Duccio and continued the bright colours and graceful linear patterns of Sienese painting while introducing a fresh element of naturalism. His patrons included the city of Siena, the king of Naples, and the pope. Two of his frescoes are in the Town Hall in Siena: the *Maestà* about 1315 and a portrait (on horseback) of the local hero Guidoriccio da Fogliano (the attribution of the latter is disputed). Sometime in the 1320s or 1330s Simone worked at Assisi where he decorated the chapel of St Martin with scenes depicting the life of the saint, regarded by many as his masterpiece.

Simonides about 556–448 BC. Greek choral poet and epigrammatist. His longer poems include hymns composed to celebrate victories in the athletic games of Greece, and other competition pieces for choral performance. He was extremely successful, internationally famous, and reputedly avaricious. His most famous lines were those of the epigram he wrote on the Spartans who died fighting the Persians at Thermopylae in 480 BC: 'Go, stranger, and report to the Spartans that here, obedient to their words, we lie.' His work exists in fragments only.

Simpson N(orman) F(rederick) 1919– . British dramatist. His plays *A Resounding Tinkle* 1957, *The Hole* 1958, and *One Way Pendulum* 1959 show the logical development of an abnormal situation, and belong to the Theatre of the

◊Absurd. He also wrote a novel, *Harry Bleachbaker* 1976.

Sinan 1489–1588. Ottoman architect, chief architect from 1538 to Suleiman the Magnificent. Among the hundreds of buildings he designed are the Suleimaniye mosque complex in Istanbul 1551–58 and the Selimiye mosque in Adrinople (now Edirne) 1569–74.

Sinatra Frank (Francis Albert) 1915– . US singer and film actor. Celebrated for his phrasing and emotion, especially on love ballads, he is particularly associated with the song 'My Way'. His films from 1941 include *From Here to Eternity* 1953 (Academy Award) and *Guys and Dolls* 1955. In the 1940s he sang such songs as 'Night and Day' and 'You'd Be So Nice to Come Home To' with Harry James' and Tommy Dorsey's bands; many of his later recordings were made with arranger Nelson Riddle (1921–1985). After a slump in his career, he established himself as an actor. His later career includes film, television, and club appearances, and setting up a record company, Reprise, 1960.

Sinbad the Sailor or **Sindbad** in the ◊*Arabian Nights*, an adventurer who makes seven eventful voyages. He encounters the ◊Old Man of the Sea and, on his second voyage, is carried aloft by the roc, a giant bird.

Sinclair Upton (Beall) 1878–1968. US novelist whose polemical concern for social reform was reflected in his prolific output of documentary novels. His most famous novel, *The Jungle* 1906, is an important example of naturalistic writing, which exposed the horrors of the Chicago meatpacking industry and led to a change in food-processing laws. His later novels include *King Coal* 1917, *Oil!* 1927, and his 11-volume Lanny Budd series 1940–53, including *Dragon's Teeth* 1942, which won a Pulitzer Prize.

Sinden Donald 1923– . English actor. A performer of great versatility and resonant voice, his roles ranged from Shakespearean tragedies to light comedies, such as *There's a Girl in My Soup* 1966, *Present Laughter* 1981, and the television series *Two's Company*.

Sinding Christian (August) 1856–1941. Norwegian composer. His works include four symphonies, piano pieces (including *Rustle of Spring* from *Six Pieces* 1896), and songs. His brothers Otto (1842–1909) and Stephan (1846–1922) were a painter and sculptor respectively.

sinfonietta orchestral work that is of a shorter, lighter nature than a ◊symphony, for example Janáček's *Sinfonietta* 1926. It is also the name for a small-scale orchestra specializing in such works, for example the London Sinfonietta.

Singer Isaac Bashevis 1904–1991. Polish-born US novelist and short-story writer, in the USA from 1935. His works, written in Yiddish, often portray traditional Jewish life in Poland and the USA, and the loneliness of old age. They include *The Family Moskat* 1950 and *Gimpel the Fool and Other Stories* 1957. Nobel prize 1978. Written in an often magical storytelling style, his works combine a deep psychological insight with dramatic and visual impact. Many of his novels were written for serialization in New York Yiddish newspapers. Among his works are *The Slave* 1960, *Shosha* 1978, *Old Love* 1979, *Lost in America* 1981, *The Image and Other Stories* 1985, and *The Death of Methuselah* 1988. He also wrote plays and books for children.

[Children] don't expect their writer to redeem humanity, but leave to adults such childish illusions.

Isaac Bashevis Singer
Nobel acceptance speech 1978

Singspiel (German 'sung play') term originally applied to all opera, later confined to opera with spoken dialogue. Mozart provided the greatest examples with *Die Entführung aus dem Serail/The Abduction from the Seraglio* 1782 and *Die Zauberflöte/ The Magic Flute* 1791. During the 19th and 20th centuries *Singspiel* came to imply a comic or light opera of contemporary manners or ordinary life.

Siqueiros David Alfaro 1896–1974. Mexican painter, a prominent Social Realist and outstanding member of the Mexican muralist movement of the 1930s. A lifelong political activist, his work championed his revolutionary ideals. He was the master of a vigorous style, typified by massed, churning figures and the use of foreshortening and multiple viewpoints, as in the mural *Portrait of the Bourgeoisie* 1939 (Electrical Workers' Union, Mexico City). In the 1920s Siqueiros worked with Diego ◊Rivera and José ◊Orozco on allegorical frescoes for the National Preparatory School, Mexico City – the first of many such mural commissions. Unlike the others he incorporated elements of fantasy, such as human-and-machine hybrids. His easel paintings and woodcuts, like his murals, express deeply felt themes of protest, for example *Echo of a Scream* 1937 (Museum of Modern Art, New York).

siren in Greek mythology, a sea ◊nymph who lured sailors to their deaths along rocky coasts by her singing. ◊Odysseus, in order to hear the sirens safely, tied himself to the mast of his ship and stuffed his crew's ears with wax. The Argonauts escaped them because the singing of Orpheus surpassed that of the sirens.

Sirk Douglas. Adopted name of Claus Detlef Sierck 1900–1987. German film director of Danish descent, known for such extravagantly lurid Hollywood melodramas as *Magnificent Obsession* 1954, *All that Heaven Allows* 1956 and *Written on the Wind* 1957, praised for their implicit critiques of American bourgeois society.

Siskind Aaron 1903–1991. US art photographer who began as a documentary photographer and in 1940 made a radical change towards a poetic exploration of forms and planes, inspired by the Abstract Expressionist painters.

Sisley Alfred 1839–1899. French Impressionist painter whose landscapes include views of Port-Marly and the river Seine, painted during floods 1876. Lyrical and harmonious, his work is distinctive for its lightness of touch and subtlety of tone.

Sisley studied in an academic studio in Paris, where he met Monet and Renoir. They took part in the first Impressionist exhibition 1874. Unlike most other Impressionists, Sisley developed his style slowly and surely, without obvious changes.

The animation of the canvas is one of the hardest problems in painting ... the artist's impression is the life-giving factor, and only this impression can free that of the spectator.

Alfred Sisley letter

Sistine Chapel chapel in the Vatican, Rome, begun under Pope Sixtus IV 1473 by Giovanni del Dolci, and decorated by (among others) Michelangelo. It houses the conclave that meets to select a new pope.

Built to the proportions of Solomon's temple in the Old Testament (its height one-half and its width one-third of its length), it has frescoes on the walls (emphasizing the authority and legality of the papacy) by ◊Botticelli and ◊Ghirlandaio and, on the altar wall and ceiling, by ◊Michelangelo.

Sisyphus in Greek mythology, a king of Corinth who, as punishment for his evil life, was condemned in the underworld to roll a huge stone uphill; it always fell back before he could reach the top.

sitar Indian stringed instrument, of the lute family. It has a pear-shaped body and long neck supported by an additional gourd resonator. A principal solo instrument, it has seven metal strings extending over movable frets and two concealed strings that provide a continuous drone. It is played with a plectrum, producing a luminous and supple melody responsive to nuances of pressure. Its most celebrated exponent in the West has been Ravi Shankar.

My poems are hymns of praise to the glory of life.

Edith Sitwell Collected Poems 'Some Notes on My Poetry'

Sitwell Edith 1887–1964. English poet whose series of poems *Façade* was performed as recitations to the specially written music of William ◊Walton from 1923. Her verse has an imaginative and rhythmic intensity.

Sitwell Osbert 1892–1969. English poet and author, elder brother of Edith and Sacheverell Sitwell. He wrote art criticism; novels, including *A Place of One's Own* 1941; and a series of five autobiographical volumes 1945–62.

Sitwell Sacheverell 1897–1988. English poet and art critic. His work includes *Southern Baroque Art* 1924 and *British Architects and Craftsmen* 1945; poetry; and prose miscellanies such as *Of Sacred and Profane Love* 1940 and *Splendour and Miseries* 1943.

Siva or **Shiva** (Sanskrit 'propitious') in Hinduism, the third chief god (with Brahma and Vishnu). As Mahadeva (great lord), he is the creator, symbolized by the phallic *lingam*, who restores what as Mahakala he destroys. He is often sculpted as Nataraja, performing his fruitful cosmic dance. His consort or female principle (*sakti*) is Parvati, otherwise known as Durga or Kali.

Six Characters in Search of an Author (Italian *Sei personaggi in cerca d'autore*) drama by Luigi ◊Pirandello 1921. A director and his actors in rehearsal are disturbed by the arrival of a strange family of characters, led by a guilty father, who insists on acting out their 'real-life' tragedy of sexual depravity and suicide in place of the play in rehearsal.

Six, Les group of French 20th-century composers; see ◊Les Six.

ska or ***bluebeat*** Jamaican pop music, a precursor of reggae, mingling the local calypso, *mento*, with rhythm and blues. Ska emerged in the early 1960s (a slower style, ***rock steady***, evolved 1966–68) and enjoyed a revival in the UK in the late 1970s. Prince Buster (1938–) was an influential ska singer.

In the late 1980s, the term ***skacid*** was coined for a speeded-up ska with rap and electronic effects.

Skelton John *c.* 1460–1529. English poet and tutor to the future Henry VIII. His satirical poetry includes the rumbustious *The Tunnyng of Elynor Rummynge* 1516, and political attacks on Wolsey, such as *Colyn Cloute* 1522.

He ruleth all the roste.

John Skelton 'Why come ye nat to Courte'

Skidmore, Owings & Merrill (SOM) US firm of architects, founded by Louis Skidmore (1897–1962), Nathaniel A Owings (1903–1984), and John O Merrill (1896–1975). The firm's earliest work of note was Lever House, New York, 1952, designed by Gordon ◊Bunshaft, a curtain-walled skyscraper recalling the work of ◊Mies van der Rohe. The partnership later moved away from a strict functionalist approach with buildings such as the John Hancock Tower, Chicago, 1970, where diagonal wind-bracing is used to decorative effect. More recently the office has been active internationally in projects such as London's Broadgate (begun 1986) and the ◊Canary Wharf development.

skiffle British popular music style, introduced by singer and banjo player Lonnie Donegan (1931–) in the mid-1950s, using improvised percussion instruments such as tea chests and washboards. Donegan popularized US folk songs like 'Rock Island Line' 1953 (a hit 1955 UK and 1956 USA) and 'Cumberland Gap' 1957. Skiffle gave way to beat music in the early 1960s.

skirt garment that hangs from the waist downwards, of varying length, worn by women and girls.

The shape and length of the skirt has changed greatly with fashion trends. In the 16th century skirts were worn wide over a 'roll farthingale', a circular piece of padding placed around the hips. By the 17th century the farthingale had been discarded as skirts were ruffled up to reveal the ◊petticoats. Padding was reintroduced in the 18th century to extend the shape of skirts out to the side. Made of osier reeds or in the shape of a whalebone frame, this padding was worn on the hips at the side of the body. By the mid-18th century skirt sizes decreased, although they once again expanded in the mid-19th century following the introduction of ◊crinoline, which was later replaced by the ◊bustle. Prior to 1900 long skirts remained popular. Throughout the 20th century skirt lengths have gone up and down with fashion trends, with the miniskirt, at least 10 cm/4 in above the knees, becoming popular in the 1960s.

Skolimowski Jerzy 1938– . Polish film director, formerly a writer, active in both his own country and other parts of Europe. His films include *Deep End* 1970, *The Shout* 1978, *Moonlighting* 1982, and *Torrents of Spring* 1989.

Skryabin or *Scriabin* Alexander (Nikolayevich) 1872–1915. Russian composer and pianist. His visionary tone poems such as *Prometheus* 1911, and symphonies such as *Divine Poem* 1903, employed unusual scales and harmonies.

skyscraper building so tall that it appears to 'scrape the sky', developed 1868 in New York, USA, where land prices were high and the geology allowed such methods of construction. Skyscrapers are now found in cities throughout the world. The world's tallest free-standing structure is the CN (Canadian National) Tower, Toronto, at 555 m/1,821 ft.

In Manhattan, New York, are the Empire State Building 1931 (102 storeys and 381 m/1,250 ft high) and the twin towers of the World Trade Center 1970–74 (415 m/1,361 ft), but these are surpassed by the Sears Tower in Chicago 1973 (443 m/1,454 ft). Chicago has many of earliest skyscrapers, such as the Home Insurance Building 1883–85, which was built ten storeys high with an iron and steel frame. A rigid steel frame is the key to skyscraper construction, taking all the building loads. The walls simply 'hang' from the frame (see ◊curtain wall), and they can thus be made from relatively flimsy materials such as glass and aluminium.

Slade Felix 1790–1868. English art collector who bequeathed most of his art collection to the British Museum and endowed Slade professorships in fine art at Oxford, Cambridge, and University College, London. The Slade School of Fine Arts, opened 1871, is a branch of the latter.

Sleep Wayne 1948– . British dancer who was a principal dancer with the Royal Ballet 1973–83. He formed his own company, Dash, 1980, and in 1983 adapted his TV *Hot Shoe Show* for the stage, fusing classical, modern, jazz, tap, and disco.

'Sleeping Beauty, The' European folk tale. Cursed by the fairy her parents forgot to invite to her christening, a princess falls asleep together with the whole royal court. She is awakened after 100 years by the kiss of a prince. Modern versions end here but in Perrault's version 1697, a secret marriage is followed by conflict with the prince's wicked mother, who is finally destroyed in her own tub of serpents and scorpions. The story is the basis of a ballet by Tchaikovsky, first performed 1890.

Slessor Kenneth Adolf 1901–1971. Australian poet. A journalist and war correspondent, he is remembered for his superbly pictorial verse, particularly 'Five Visions of Captain Cook' 1931 and his best-known work, the title poem of his collection *Five Bells* 1939, an elegy for his friend Joe Lynch. 'Beach Burial' 1944 illustrates the futility of war.

slip decoration traditional decoration for earthenware with designs trailed in a thin, smooth mixture of clay and water (slip) or incised through a coating of slip. It is usually finished with a transparent lead glaze.

White trailed slip is characteristic of the early earthenware made by Reginald Wells (1877–1951). The British potter Bernard Leach used trailed slip designs on *raku* ware when he worked in Japan in the early 20th century and revived the technique of moulding plates with slip decorations in the UK in the 1920s.

Sloan John 1871–1951. US painter. Encouraged to paint by Robert ◊Henri, he helped organize 'the Eight', a group of Realists who were against academic standards, and was a founder-member of the ◊Ashcan School. He moved to New York 1904 and helped to organize the avant-garde Armory Show 1913. His paintings of working-class urban life pioneered the field of American Realism.

Slovak literature see ◊Czechoslovak literature.

SLR abbreviation for *single-lens reflex*, a type of ◊camera in which the image can be seen through the lens before a picture is taken.

A small mirror directs light entering the lens to the viewfinder. When a picture is taken the mirror moves rapidly aside to allow the light to reach the film. The SLR allows different lenses, such as close-up or zoom lenses, to be used because the photographer can see exactly what is being focused on.

Sluter Claus *c.* 1380–1406. N European Gothic sculptor, probably of Dutch origin, active in Dijon, France. His work includes the *Well of Moses* about 1395–1403 (now in the grounds of a hospital in Dijon) and the kneeling mourners, or *pleurants*, for the tomb of his patron Philip the Bold, Duke of Burgundy (Dijon Museum and Cleveland Museum, Ohio). In its striking Realism, his work marks a break with the ◊International Gothic style prevalent at the time.

Smart Christopher 1722–1771. English poet. In 1756 he was confined to an asylum, where he wrote *A Song to David* and *Jubilate Agno/Rejoice in the Lamb*, the latter appreciated today for its surrealism.

Smetana Bedřich 1824–1884. Bohemian composer who established a Czech nationalist style in, for example, the operas *Prodaná Nevěsta/The Bartered Bride* 1866 and *Dalibor* 1868, and the symphonic suite *Má Vlast/My Country* 1875–80. He conducted the National Theatre of Prague 1866–74.

Smiles Samuel 1812–1904. Scottish writer, author of the popular Victorian didactic work *Self Help* 1859. Here, as in *Character* 1871, *Thrift* 1875, and *Duty* 1880, he energetically advocated an overriding capitalist individualism.

Smirke Robert 1780–1867. English architect. Although his domestic architecture was Gothic Revival, he is best known for his Neo-Classical public buildings, such as the British Museum, London, 1823–47. Often compared unfavourably to his contemporary in Germany, ◊Schinkel, his designs nevertheless have a powerful architectural presence and are invariably academically correct in detail.

Smith Bessie 1894–1937. US jazz and blues singer, born in Chattanooga, Tennessee. Known as the 'Empress of the Blues', she established herself in the 1920s after she was discovered by Columbia Records. She made over 150 recordings accompanied by such greats as Louis Armstrong and Benny Goodman.

Her popularity waned in the Depression, and she died after a car crash when she was refused admission to a whites-only hospital.

Smith David 1906–1965. US sculptor and painter whose work made a lasting impact on sculpture after World War II. He trained as a steel welder in a car factory. His pieces are large openwork metal abstracts.

Smith turned first to painting and then, about 1930, to sculpture. Using welded steel, he created abstract structures influenced by the metal sculptures of Picasso and Julio González. In the 1940s and 1950s he developed a more linear style. The *Cubi* series of totemlike abstracts, some of them painted, was designed to be placed in the open air.

Smith Maggie (Margaret Natalie) 1934– . English actress, notable for her commanding presence, fluting voice, and throwaway lines. Her films include *The Prime of Miss Jean Brodie* 1969 (Academy Award), *California Suite* 1978, *A Private Function* 1984, *A Room with a View* and *The Lonely Passion of Judith Hearne* both 1987, and *Sister Act* 1992.

Smith Matthew 1879–1959. English artist. Influenced by the ◊Fauves, he was known for his exuberant treatment of nudes, luscious fruits and flowers, and landscapes.

Smith Patti 1946– . US rock singer and songwriter whose album *Horses* 1975 contributed to the genesis of the New Wave. Her risk-taking performances and punk sensibility made her a significant influence. In 1978 she had a hit with Bruce Springsteen's 'Because the Night'.

Born in Chicago, Smith moved to New York, writing poetry and lyrics. *Horses* was followed by *Radio Ethiopia* 1976, *Easter* 1978, and *Waves* 1979. She made a comeback 1988 with *Dream of Life*.

Smith Paul 1946– . British menswear designer whose clothes are stylistically simple and practical. He opened his first shop 1970, selling designer menswear alongside his own designs, and showed his first collection in Paris 1976. He launched a toiletry range 1986 and a children's wear collection 1991.

Smith Stevie (Florence Margaret) 1902–1971. British poet and novelist. She published her first book *Novel on Yellow Paper* 1936, and her first collection of poems *A Good Time Was Had by All* 1937. She wrote a further eight volumes of eccentrically direct verse including *Not Waving but Drowning* 1957, and two more novels. *Collected Poems* was published 1975.

Smith Willi 1948–1987. US fashion designer who set up WilliWear Ltd 1976, making casual ready-to-wear lines. Previously he designed knitwear.

Smiths, the English four-piece rock group (1982–87) from Manchester. Their songs, with lyrics by singer ◊Morrissey and tunes by guitarist Johnny Marr (1964–), drew on diverse sources such as rockabilly and Mersey beat, with confessional humour and images of urban desolation. They had an intensely dedicated following in Britain and were one of the most popular ◊indie bands.

Smithson Alison 1928– and Peter 1923– . English architects, teachers, and theorists, known for their development in the 1950s and 1960s of the style known as ◊Brutalism, for example, Hunstanton School, Norfolk, 1954. Notable among their other designs are the Economist Building, London, 1964, and Robin Hood Gardens, London, 1968–72.

Smithson Robert 1938–73. US sculptor and experimental artist, celebrated for his huge outdoor ◊earthwork *Spiral Jetty* 1970 – a spiralling stone causeway that extended into Great Salt Lake, Utah, but of which only photographs remain.

He began by exhibiting mirrored constructions and open boxes filled with quarry stones or coal, but turned to outdoor earthworks in the late 1960s, which he elaborated with maps, drawings, and photographs. He saw his outdoor pieces as akin to the 'ancient mysteries' of archaeological finds and a turning away from the conventions of museum gallery art.

Smollett Tobias George 1721–1771. Scottish novelist who wrote the picaresque novels *Roderick Random* 1748, *Peregrine Pickle* 1751, *Ferdinand Count Fathom* 1753, *Sir Launcelot Greaves* 1760–62, and *Humphrey Clinker* 1771. His novels are full of gusto and vivid characterization.

I think for my part half of the nation is mad – and the other not very sound.

Tobias Smollett
Sir Launcelot Greaves 1760–62

Smyth Ethel (Mary) 1858–1944. English composer who studied in Leipzig. Her works include *Mass in D* 1893 and operas *The Wreckers* 1906 and *The Boatswain's Mate* 1916. In 1911 she was imprisoned as an advocate of women's suffrage.

Smythson Robert 1535–1614. English architect who built Elizabethan country houses, including Longleat 1568–75, Wollaton Hall 1580–88, and Hardwick Hall 1590–97. Their castlelike silhouettes, symmetry, and large gridded windows are a uniquely romantic, English version of Classicism.

snare drum or **side drum** double-headed drum used in military bands, with skins at both upper and lower ends of the instrument. Cords or wires lying against the underside skin rattle when the upper skin is played, adding definition to each attack.

Snow C(harles) P(ercy), Baron Snow 1905–1980. English novelist and physicist. He held government scientific posts in World War II and 1964–66. His sequence of novels *Strangers and Brothers* 1940–64 portrayed English life from 1920 onwards. His *The Two Cultures and the Scientific Revolution* (Cambridge Rede Lecture 1959) discussed the absence of communication between literary and scientific intellectuals in the West, and added the phrase 'the two cultures' to the language.

Literary intellectuals at one pole – at the other scientists ... Between the two, a gulf of mutual incomprehension.

C P Snow *The Two Cultures and the Scientific Revolution* 1959

Snowdon Anthony Armstrong-Jones, Earl of Snowdon 1930– . English portrait photographer. He was consultant to the Council of Industrial Design and editorial adviser to *Design Magazine* 1961–87; artistic adviser to Sunday Times Publications 1962–90; and photographer for the *Telegraph Magazine* from 1990. He has also made several films for television. In 1960 he married Princess Margaret; they were divorced 1978.

'Snow White' traditional European fairy tale. Snow White is a beautiful princess persecuted by her jealous stepmother. Taking refuge in a remote cottage inhabited by seven dwarfs, she is tricked by the disguised queen into eating a poisoned apple. She is woken from apparent death by a prince.

Snyder Gary 1930– . US poet, a key figure in the poetry renaissance in San Francisco during the 1950s. He combined an early interest in ecological issues with studies of Japanese, Chinese, and North American Indian cultures and myths. Associated with the ◊Beat Generation of writers, he was the protagonist of Jack Kerouac's novel *The Dharma Bums* 1958. Snyder's works include *Earth House Hold* 1969 and the Pulitzer Prize-winning poetry collection *Turtle Island* 1974.

Snyders Frans 1579–1657. Flemish painter of hunting scenes and still lifes. Based in Antwerp, he was a pupil of ◊Brueghel the Younger and later assisted ◊Rubens and worked with ◊Jordaens. In 1608–09 he travelled in Italy. He excelled at painting fur, feathers, and animals fighting.

Soane John 1753–1837. English architect whose refined Neo-Classical designs anticipated contemporary taste. He designed his own house in Lincoln's Inn Fields, London, 1812–13, now the *Soane Museum*. Little remains of his extensive work at the Bank of England, London.

[Architecture] is an art purely of invention –– and invention is the most painful and most difficult exercise of the human mind.

John Soane

soca Latin Caribbean dance music, a mixture of *so*ul and *ca*lypso but closer to the latter. A soca band is likely to include conga drums, synthesizer, and a small horn section, as well as electric guitar, bass, and drums. Soca originated on Trinidad in the 1970s.

The rhythms are Latin while the lyrics have roots in West African traditions of praise, ridicule, and comment on public events. Practitioners include Lord Kitchener (*c.* 1921–).

Socialist Realism artistic doctrine established by the USSR during the 1930s setting out the optimistic, socialist terms in which society should be portrayed in works of art. It applied to music and the visual arts as well as writing.

The policy was used as a means of censoring artists whose work, it was felt, did not follow the approved Stalinist party line, or was too 'Modern'. The policy was relaxed after Stalin's death but remained somewhat in force until the dissolution of the USSR 1991. Artists whose work was censured in this way included the composer Shostakovich and the writers Solzhenitsyn and Sholokhov.

Social Realism in painting, art that realistically depicts subjects of social concern, such as poverty and deprivation. Those described as Social Realists include: in the USA, members of the Ashcan School and Ben Shahn; in the UK, the 'kitchen sink group', for example John Bratby; and in Mexico, the muralists Orozco and Rivera.

Söderberg Hjalmar (Eric Fredrik) 1869–1941. Swedish writer. His work includes the short, melancholy novels *Förvillelser/Aberrations* 1895, *Martin Bircks ungdom/The Youth of Martin Birck* 1901, *Doktor Glas/Dr Glass* 1906, and the play *Gertrud* 1906.

sol-fa short for *tonic sol-fa*, a method of teaching music, usually singing, systematized by John Curwen (1816–1880). The notes of a scale are named by syllables (doh, ray, me, fah, soh, lah, te, with the ◊key indicated) to simplify singing by sight.

soliloquy in drama, thinking aloud. A soliloquy is a speech for the benefit of the audience only and by convention is not heard by any other actor on stage at the time. It is a form of ◊monologue.

Soloviev Vladimir Sergeyevich 1853–1900. Russian philosopher and poet whose blending of neo-Platonism and Christian mysticism attempted to link all aspects of human experience in a doctrine of divine wisdom. His theories, expressed in poems and essays, influenced Symbolist writers such as Alexander ◊Blok.

Solti Georg 1912– . Hungarian-born British conductor. He was music director at the Royal Opera House, Covent Garden, London, 1961–71, and became director of the Chicago

Symphony Orchestra 1969. He was also principal conductor of the London Philharmonic Orchestra 1979–83.

Solzhenitsyn Alexander (Isayevich) 1918– . Soviet novelist, a US citizen from 1974. He was in prison and exile 1945–57 for anti-Stalinist comments. Much of his writing is semi-autobiographical and highly critical of the system, including *One Day in the Life of Ivan Denisovich* 1962, which deals with the labour camps under Stalin, and *The Gulag Archipelago* 1973, an exposé of the whole Soviet labour-camp network. This led to his expulsion from the USSR 1974. He was awarded a Nobel prize 1970.

Other works include *The First Circle* and *Cancer Ward*, both 1968, and his historical novel *August 1914* 1971. His autobiography, *The Oak and the Calf*, appeared 1980. He has adopted a Christian position, and his criticism of Western materialism is also stringent. In 1991, cleared of the original charges of treason, he returned to Russia.

The salvation of mankind lies only in making everything the concern of all.

Alexander Solzhenitsyn
Nobel lecture 1970

Somerville Edith Oenone 1861–1949. Irish novelist who wrote stories of Irish life jointly with her cousin, Violet Martin ('Martin Ross'). Their works include *Some Experiences of an Irish RM* 1899.

son Afro-Cuban popular music developed in the first half of the 20th century and having many variants, including ◊salsa. It is generally fast and rhythmically complex.

sonata (Italian 'sounded') in music, an essay in instrumental composition for a solo player or a small ensemble and consisting of a single movement or series of movements. The name signifies that the work is not beholden to a text or existing dance form, but is self-sufficient.

sonata form in music, rules determining the structure of a ◊sonata first movement, typically divided into exposition, development, and recapitulation sections. It introduced the new possibility of open and continuous development to an 18th-century music previously limited to closed dance routines. It provides the framework for first movements in general, including symphonies, concertos, and string quartets.

Sondheim Stephen (Joshua) 1930– . US composer and lyricist. He wrote the lyrics of Leonard Bernstein's *West Side Story* 1957 and composed witty and sophisticated musicals, including *A Little Night Music* 1973, *Pacific Overtures* 1976, *Sweeney Todd* 1979, *Into the Woods* 1987, and *Sunday in the Park with George* 1989.

son et lumière (French 'sound and light') out-door night-time dramatization of the history of a notable building, monument, or town, using the-atrical lighting effects, sound effects, music, and narration; invented 1952 by Paul Robert Houdin, curator of the Château de Chambord, France.

song a setting of words to music for one or more singers, with or without instrumental accompani-ment. Song may be sacred, for example a psalm, motet, or cantata, or secular, for example a folk song or ballad. In verse song, the text changes in mood while the music remains the same; in ◊lied and other forms of art song, the music changes in response to the emotional development of the text.

song cycle sequence of songs related in mood and sung as a group, used by romantic composers such as Schubert, Schumann, and Wolf.

'Song of Myself' the longest poem in Walt Whitman's ◊Leaves of Grass, relating the poet, the 'single separate person', to the democratic 'en masse'. It was regularly revised from its original form of 1855 to incorporate new experiences and 'cosmic sensations'.

Sonic Youth US rock group formed in New York 1982. Their use of detuned guitars, disso-nance, and distortion, combined with a chilling melodic sense, made them one of the most influ-ential bands of the decade. Albums include *Bad Moon Rising* 1985 and *Daydream Nation* 1988.

sonnet fourteen-line poem of Italian origin introduced to England by Thomas ◊Wyatt in the form used by Petrarch (rhyming *abba abba cdcdcd* or *cdecde*) and followed by Milton and Wordsworth; Shakespeare used the form *abab cdcd efef gg*.

In the final couplet Shakespeare summed up the argument of the sonnet or introduced a new, perhaps contradictory, idea. The difference in the rhyme scheme of the first eight lines (the octet) and the last six (the sestet) reflected a change in mood or direction of the Petrarchan sonnet.

Sons and Lovers novel 1913 by D H ◊Lawrence. The central character is Paul Morel, the artistic son of a stormy marriage between a coal miner and his sensitive and ambitious wife. He grows up attempting to maintain a strong connection with his mother while failing in his sexual relationships, firstly with the virginal Miriam Leivers and then with the married femi-nist Clara Dawes. The largely autobiographical material is illuminated and shaped by Lawrence's confidently original imagination.

Sontag Susan 1933– . US critic, novelist, and screenwriter. Her novel *The Benefactor* appeared 1963, and she established herself as a critic with the influential cultural essays of *Against Interpretation* 1966 and *Styles of Radical Will* 1969. More recent studies, showing the influence

of French structuralism, are *On Photography* 1976 and the powerful *Illness as Metaphor* 1978 and *Aids and its Metaphors* 1989.

Interpretation is the revenge of the intellect upon art.

Susan Sontag
Against Interpretation 1966

Sophocles c. 496–406 BC. Athenian dramatist, attributed with having developed tragedy by introducing a third actor and scene-painting, and ranked with Aeschylus and Euripides as one of the three great tragedians. He wrote some 120 plays, of which seven tragedies survive. These are ◊*Antigone* 443 BC, ◊*Oedipus the King* 429, ◊*Electra* 410, *Ajax*, *Trachiniae*, *Philoctetes* 409, and ◊*Oedipus at Colonus* 401 (produced after his death).

Sophocles lived in Athens when the city was ruled by Pericles, a period of great prosperity; he was a devout man, and assumed public office. A regular winner of dramatic competitions, he first defeated Aeschylus at the age of 27. In his tragedies heroic determination leads directly to violence unless, as in *Philoctetes* and *Oedipus at Colonus*, it contains an element of resignation. Among his other works are a lost treatise on the chorus, and a large surviving fragment of one of his satyr-dramas, *Ichneutai*.

I depict men as they ought to be, but Euripides depicts them as they are.

Sophocles

---

sopranino term in music describing an instru-ment of higher range than soprano. An alternative term is *piccolo*.

soprano in music, the highest range of the female voice, stretching from around D4 to A6. Some operatic roles require the extended upper range of a *coloratura* soprano, reaching to around F6, for example Kiri ◊Te Kanawa.

sordino (Italian 'mute') a ◊mute, usually of a violin, viola, or cello. In printed music the phrase *con sord.* means 'with the mute in place' (on the bridge), while *senza sord.* means 'take the mute off'.

sordune Renaissance ◊windcap double-reed musical instrument in tenor or bass register, of folded-back conical bore, an ancestor of the bas-soon.

Soseki Natsume. Pen name of Natsume Kinnosuke 1867–1916. Japanese novelist whose works are deep psychological studies of urban intellectual lives. Strongly influenced by English literature, his later works are somewhat reminiscent of Henry James; for example, the unfinished *Meian/Light and Darkness* 1916. Sōseki is regarded as one of Japan's greatest writers.

Sōseki was born in Tokyo and studied English literature there and (1900–03) in the UK. He became well known with his debut novel, *Wagahai wa neko de aru/I Am a Cat* 1905, followed by the humorous *Botchan* 1906, but found a more serious, sensitive style in his many later novels, such as *Sore kara/And Then* 1909. He also studied classical Chinese literature and Zen Buddhism and wrote on literary theory.

Sottsass Ettore Jr 1917– . Austrian-born product and furniture designer, active in Milan, Italy, since 1945. Sottsass is the best known of the Italian 'radical' designers of the 1960s who challenged the values of establishment design.

His work in the areas of typewriters and office furniture, including his red plastic portable 'Valentine' typewriter 1969 and 'Synthesis 45' 1969, for the ◊Olivetti company has, since 1958, ensured him a living as a freelance designer while his more experimental, personal projects in the areas of furniture and ceramics, among them his 'Yantra' series of one-off ceramic vases 1970, have marked him out as one of the most innovative designers of the postwar years. Sottsass was the prime mover behind the ◊Memphis group.

soul music emotionally intense style of ◊rhythm and blues sung by, among others, Sam Cooke, Aretha Franklin, and Al Green (1946–). A synthesis of blues, gospel music, and jazz, it emerged in the 1950s. Sometimes all popular music made by African-Americans is labelled soul music.

Sound and The Fury, The novel 1929 by US writer William ◊Faulkner. The story of a declining Southern family is told from four points of view including those of the three sons: Benjy, an imbecile; Quentin, a Harvard student who commits suicide; and Jason, an egotistical materialist. Dealing with historical collapse and lost love, the novel is a moving and technically difficult work.

Sousa John Philip 1854–1932. US bandmaster and composer of marches, such as 'The Stars and Stripes Forever!' 1897.

sousaphone large bass ◊tuba designed to wrap round the player in a circle and having a forward-facing bell. The form was suggested by US bandmaster John Sousa. Today susaphones are largely fabricated in lightweight fibreglass.

South African literature the founder of South African literature in English was Thomas Pringle (1789–1834), who published lyric poetry and the prose *Narrative of a Residence in South Africa*. More recent poets are Roy Campbell and Francis C Slater (1876–1959). The first work of South African fiction to receive attention outside the country was Olive Schreiner's *Story of an African Farm* 1883; later writers include Sarah Gertrude Millin, Pauline Smith (1882–1959), William Plomer, Laurens van der Post, Alan Paton, Nadine Gordimer (winner of the Nobel Prize for Literature 1991), and playwright Athol Fugard. Original writing in Afrikaans developed rapidly after the South African War, and includes works by the lyricists C Louis Leipoldt (1880–1947), Jan Celliers (1865–1940), and Eugène Marais (1871–1936); the satirical sketch and story writer C J Langenhoven; and the student of wildlife 'Sangiro' (A A Peinhar), author of *The Adventures of a Lion Family*, which became popular in English translation. In more recent years the intellectual barriers imposed by South Africa's isolation have prevented its writers from becoming more widely known, but there has been much spirited work, including that of the novelists André P Brink (1935–) and Etienne Leroux (1922–), and the poet Ingrid Jonker (1933–1965). See also ◊African literature.

Southampton Henry Wriothesley, 3rd Earl of Southampton 1573–1624. English courtier, patron of Shakespeare. Shakespeare dedicated *Venus and Adonis* and *The Rape of Lucrece* to him and may have addressed him in the sonnets.

South East Asian art the art of Cambodia, Vietnam, Burma (now Myanmar), Laos, Thailand, and Indonesia. The Indonesian islands are an ethnically diverse group of islands sharing a complicated history of cultural influence, first Chinese, then Indian, and, more recently, Islamic (see ◊Indian art, ◊Chinese art, and ◊Islamic art). Hindu and Buddhist art have found distinctive expression in temple architecture.

Dong-son art, about 2nd century BC, is the product of a prehistoric culture in Vietnam, typified by bronze ceremonial objects, including the largest drum in the world, the 'Moon of Bali' (Pura Pantaran Sasih, Pejeng).

Cambodian art of the Funan (2nd–6th centuries AD) and Chen La (6th–8th centuries AD) was predominantly Hindu. Surviving temples are at Sambor Prei Kuk and masterpieces of sculpture include sandstone figures of Lakshmi and the Buddha (Musée Guimet, Paris) and the Buddha of Vat Romlok (National Museum, Phnom-Penh). Khmer art reached its zenith in the vast temple of Angkor Vat, Cambodia, about 1112–53, the exterior walls of which have 1,750 life-size figure sculptures.

Indonesian art reflects its mixed history, featuring Dong-son metalwork, Hindu and Buddhist temples (notably the temple at Borobodur, Java, 8th–9th centuries, the finest surviving monument to Buddhism), tribal art of ancestor cults, Javanese puppets, batik, and flamboyant house decoration.

Thai art is predominantly Buddhist but flavoured by ancient animist beliefs which persist. From the 7th to 9th centuries, the dominant Mon peoples produced serenely beautiful stone and bronze Buddhas.

Burmese art is exemplified in the richly decorated conical stupas belonging to the time of the Pagán kings, 9th–13th centuries.

Southerne Thomas 1660–1746. English playwright and poet, author of the tragi-comedies *Oroonoko* 1695–96 and *The Fatal Marriage* 1694.

Southern US fiction part of a long tradition of fiction and *belles lettres* in the US South since Edgar Allan Poe, often distinctively different from other US fiction. In the 20th century, a remarkable literary revival began, exemplified by the work of Ellen Glasgow and William Faulkner, dealing with the experience of a defeated agrarian region with proud traditions. Among 20th-century writers are Thomas Wolfe, Robert Penn Warren, Katherine Anne Porter, Eudora Welty, William Styron, and Margaret Mitchell, author of *Gone With the Wind* 1936. The Southern Gothic school includes Flannery O'Connor and Carson McCullers.

Writers of the 19th century include William Gilmore Simms (1806–1870), Joel Chandler Harris, and George Washington Cable (1844–1925).

Southey Robert 1774–1843. English poet and author, friend of Coleridge and Wordsworth. In 1813 he became poet laureate but he is better known for his *Life of Nelson* 1813, and for his letters.

He abandoned his early revolutionary views, and from 1808 contributed regularly to the Tory *Quarterly Review*.

But what they fought each other for, /
I could not well make out.

Robert Southey 'The Battle of Blenheim'

Soutine Chaï m 1893–1943. Lithuanian-born French Expressionist artist. Using brilliant colours and thick, energetically applied paint, he created intense, emotionally charged works, mostly landscapes and portraits. *Page Boy* 1927 (Albright-Knox Art Gallery, Buffalo, New York) is typical.

Soyinka Wole 1934– . Nigerian author who was a political prisoner in Nigeria 1967–69. His works include the play *The Lion and the Jewel* 1963; his prison memoirs *The Man Died* 1972; *Aké, The Years of Childhood* 1982, an autobiography, and *Isara*, a fictionalized memoir 1989. He was the first African to receive the Nobel Prize for Literature, 1986.

space-frame in architecture, lightweight, triangulated, structural framework, designed to be of uniform load resistance and used principally in large-span constructions, such as exhibition halls, stadia, and aircraft hangars. The Eiffel Tower, Paris, 1889, is a space-frame of riveted steel beams. A contemporary development is Buckminster Fuller's ◊geodesic dome, a shell-like space-frame covered in plastic, plywood, or metal sheeting.

Spacek Sissy (Mary Elizabeth) 1949– . US film actress of waif-like looks, who starred in *Badlands* 1973 and *Carrie* 1976, in which she played a repressed telekinetic teenager. Other films include *Coal Miner's Daughter* 1979 (Academy Award) and *Missing* 1982.

space–time notation in music, a form of ◊graph notation pioneered by Earle ◊Brown in which notes are individually lengthened to give a precise visualization of relative durations. It involves the performer 'reading time' instead of counting beats.

Spanish architecture the architecture of Spain has been influenced by both European Classical and Islamic traditions.

early Christian (5th–8th centuries) The Visigoths invaded Spain 415 and were later converted to Christianity. Their small churches, few of which remain, are indebted to Roman architecture and have parallels with the early French Romanesque style. Fine examples are San Juan de Banos 661 and San Pedro de Nave about 7th century.

Muslim (8th–15th centuries) The Muslims invaded 711, quickly capturing most of the country. In Cordoba, the Great Mosque, a huge rectangular hall with a proliferation of columns, was begun 786 and worked on over the next 200 years. Elsewhere in Muslim-occupied Spain architecture developed in unique response to its environment, characterized by a particularly delicate decorative style. In the fortified palaces of the Alcázar, Seville, 1350–69, and the Alhambra, Granada, built mainly 1248–1354, a vocabulary of water gardens, courtyards, colourful tilework, and elaborate stalactite decoration is used.

Romanesque (11th–12th centuries) Romanesque church building began in Catalonia from the 11th century and developed along the pilgrimage routes from France. The cathedral of Santiago de Compostela (begun about 1075) is a fine example, with its barrel-vaulted roof and huge, sculpted Pórtico de la Gloria.

Gothic (13th–16th centuries) In the 12th century, the Cistercian order brought the Gothic style to Spain and by the following century the style of northern French Gothic cathedrals had been adopted, as in Burgos Cathedral (begun 1221). The Catalan version of Gothic proved the most distinctive, introducing a high wide nave, as at Sta Maria, Barcelona (begun 1298). Later cathedrals, such as that in Seville (begun 1402), show German influence in their use of rib-vaulting but this is tempered by unique ground plans owing much to Islamic mosque architecture.

Renaissance (16th century) The Italian Renaissance reached Spain in the 16th century.

The finest example of the High Renaissance is the Escorial (begun 1563), the huge palace, monastery, and church built for Phillip II, largely designed by Juan de Herrera (1530–1597). This structure is more severe than most other Spanish Renaissance architecture, which is characterized by richly decorative work in a style known as Plateresque, as in the façade of Salamanca University 1514.

Baroque (17th–18th centuries) An interest in surface decoration, reflecting the Muslim past, re-emerged in the late 17th-century Spanish variation of Baroque, Churrigueresque, of which the west front of the cathedral of Santiago de Compostela (begun 1738) is a fine example. José Benito de Churriguera and Narciso Tomè (active 1715–42) were both active in this style.

Neo-Classicism (18th century) In the latter part of the 18th century a severe Neo-Classicism was developed in such works as the portico of Pamplona Cathedral 1783 by Ventura Rodríguez (1717–1783).

Art Nouveau (late 19th–early 20th century) The industrialization of Catalan provided Spain with a distinctive late 19th-century architecture, a variation of Art Nouveau known as Modernismo. Connected in part to a growth in Catalan nationalism, it is best represented in the works of Lluis Doménech i Montaner (1850–1923), who built the Palau de la Música Catalana 1905–08, and of Antonio Gaudí, who designed the Church of the Holy Family (begun 1883) and the Casa Milá 1905–10, both in Barcelona.

20th century Under Franco, Spain retreated from its European connections into a provincialism that was echoed in its architecture. Since the restoration of democracy numerous designers of international importance have emerged. Among these are the Neo-Classicist Ricardo Bofill, now practising largely in France, who built the Antigone development in Montpellier 1992, the architect and engineer Santiago Calatrava, and Rafael Moneo (1937–), who was the architect responsible for the Museum of Archaeology at Mérida 1986.

Spanish art painting and sculpture of Spain. Spanish art has been fashioned by both European and Islamic traditions, with notable regional adaptations.

11th–13th centuries In the north of Spain, particularly in Catalonia, the Romanesque style took root. Bold and colourful church frescoes were its finest expression. In the south, occupied by the Moors 711–1492, Islamic influence predominated.

13th–14th centuries During this Gothic phase in Spanish art, the influence of Italian art, particularly the painting style of Siena, became pronounced.

15th century The unification of Spain 1472 brought about a rapid development in the arts, largely due to the royal patronage introduced by Ferdinand and Isabella. A Hispano-Flemish style flourished, based mainly on Flemish painting (in particular the works of van Eyck and van der Weyden), but also on Moorish traditions. Fernando Gallego (c. 1440–c. 1507) was its finest exponent. The influence of the Italian Renaissance can be seen in the works of the court painter Pedro Berruguete.

16th century The full impact of the Italian Renaissance is evident in the paintings of Luis de Morales (died 1586) and the paintings and sculptures of Alonso Berruguete. The outstanding artist of the late 16th century was El Greco.

17th century The period was dominated by sombre and intense religious art in a realist style. Painters include Ribera, Morillo, Ribalta, Zurbarán, and — the major artist of the age – Velázquez. Sculptors include Alonso Cano and Montañés (1568–1649).

18th–19th centuries Goya alone dominated the 18th century. His work exerted a great influence on European art in the 19th century, a period during which Spanish art declined.

20th century Spanish art became a major European force. Painters include Juan Gris, Joan Miró, Salvador Dali, and Picasso, widely regarded as the most innovative artist of the 20th century. Antonio Tàpies is one of the most important Spanish artists of the second half of the 20th century.

Spanish literature of the classical Spanish epics, the 12th-century *El cantar de mio Cid* is the only complete example. The founder of Castilian prose was King Alfonso X, El Sabio (the Wise), who also wrote lyric poetry in the Galician dialect. The first true poet was the 14th-century satirist Juan Ruiz (c. 1283–1350), archpriest of Hita. To the 15th century belong the Marquis of Santillana (Iñigo López de Mendoza), poet, critic, and collector of proverbs; chivalric romances, such as the *Amadis de Gaula*; ballads dealing with the struggle against the Moors; and the *Celestina*, a novel in dramatic form. The flowering of verse drama began with Lope de Rueda (died 1565), and reached its height with Lope de Vega and Calderón de la Barca. In poetry the golden age of the 15th–16th centuries produced the lyrical Garcilaso de la Vega; the patriotic Fernando de Herrera (1534–1597); the mystics Santa Teresa and Luis de León; the elaborate style of Luis de Góngora (1561–1627), who popularized the decadent 'gongorism'; and the biting satire of Francisco de Quevedo. In fiction there developed the pastoral romance, for example Jorge de Montemayor's *Diana*; the picaresque novel, established by the anonymous *Lazarillo del Tormes*; and the work of Cervantes. In the 18th century the Benedictine Benito J Feijoo introduced scientific thought to Spain, and French influence emerged in the comedies of Leandro F de Moratín (1760–1828) and others. Typical of the romantic era were the poets and dramatists

Angel de Saavedra (Duque de Rivas) (1791–1865) and José Zorilla, and the lyricist José de Espronceda. Among 19th-century novelists were Pedro de Alarcón, Emilia, condesa de Pardo Bazán (1852–1921), and Vicente Blasco Ibáñez; a 19th-century dramatist is José Echegaray. The 'Generation of 1898' included the philosophers Miguel de Unamuno and José Ortega y Gasset (1883–1955); the novelist Pío Baroja (1872–1956); the prose writer Azorín (José Martínez Ruiz); and the Nobel prize-winning poet Juan Ramón Jiménez. The next generation included novelist Camilo José Cela; the poets Antonio Machado, Rafael Alberti (1902–), Luis Cernuda (1902–1963), and the Nobel prizewinner Vincente Aleixandre; and the dramatists Jacinto Benavente (1866–1954), the brothers Quintero, and – the most striking – Federico García Lorca. The Civil War and the strict censorship of the Franco government disrupted mid-20th-century literary life, but later names include the novelists Rafael Sánchez Ferlosio (1927–) and Juan Goytisolo (1931–); and the poets Blas de Otero (1916–) and José Hierro (1922–).

Spark Muriel 1918– . Scottish novelist. She is a Catholic convert, and her enigmatic satires include: *The Ballad of Peckham Rye* 1960, *The Prime of Miss Jean Brodie* 1961, *The Only Problem* 1984, and *Symposium* 1990.

Give me a girl at an impressionable age, and she is mine for life.

Muriel Spark
The Prime of Miss Jean Brodie 1961

Spear Ruskin 1911–1990. British artist whose portraits include Laurence Olivier (as Macbeth), Francis Bacon, and satirical representations of Margaret Thatcher.

Spector Phil 1940– . US record producer, known for the 'wall of sound', created using a large orchestra, which distinguished his work in the early 1960s with vocal groups such as the Crystals and the Ronettes. He withdrew into semi-retirement 1966 but his influence can still be heard.

Speer Albert 1905–1981. German architect and minister in the Nazi government during World War II. He was appointed Hitler's architect and, like his counterparts in Fascist Italy, chose an overblown Classicism to glorify the state, for example, his plan for the Berlin and Nuremberg Party Congress Grounds 1934. He built the New Reich Chancellery, Berlin, 1938–39 (now demolished) but his designs for an increasingly megolomaniac series of buildings in a stark Classical style were never realized, notably the Great Assembly Hall for Berlin.

Spence Basil 1907–1976. British architect, born in Scotland. His works include Coventry Cathedral 1951 and the British embassy in Rome. He was professor of architecture at the Royal Academy, London 1961–68.

Spencer Stanley 1891–1959. English painter who was born and lived in Cookham-on-Thames, Berkshire, and recreated the Christian story in a Cookham setting. His detailed, dreamlike compositions had little regard for perspective and used generalized human figures in a highly original manner.

Examples of his work are *Christ Carrying the Cross* 1920 and *Resurrection: Cookham* 1923–27 (both Tate Gallery, London), murals of army life for the oratory of All Souls' at Burghclere, Berkshire, and *Swan Upping* 1914–19 (Tate Gallery, London).

Spender Stephen (Harold) 1909– . English poet and critic. His earlier poetry has a left-wing political content, as in *Twenty Poems* 1930, *Vienna* 1934, *The Still Centre* 1939, and *Poems of Dedication* 1946. Other works include the verse drama *Trial of a Judge* 1938, the autobiography *World within World* 1951, and translations. His *Journals 1939–83* were published 1985.

Educated at University College, Oxford, he founded with Cyril Connolly the magazine *Horizon* (of which he was co-editor 1939–41) and was co-editor of *Encounter* 1953–67. He became professor of English at University College, London, 1970.

My parents kept me from children who were rough / Who threw words like stones and who wore torn clothes.

Stephen Spender *Collected Poems* 1955

Spenser Edmund *c.* 1552–1599. English poet. He has been called the 'poet's poet' because of his rich imagery and command of versification. His major work is the moral allegory *The ◊Faerie Queene*, of which six books survive (three published 1590 and three 1596). Other books include *The Shepheard's Calendar* 1579, *Astrophel* 1586, the love sonnets *Amoretti* and the *Epithalamion* 1595.

Sweet Thames! run softly, till I end my song.

Edmund Spenser *Prothalamion* 1596

Born in London and educated at Cambridge University, in 1580 he became secretary to the Lord Deputy in Ireland and at Kilcolman Castle completed the first three books of *The Faerie*

Queene. In 1598 Kilcolman Castle was burned down by rebels, and Spenser with his family narrowly escaped. He died in London, and was buried in Westminster Abbey.

Sphinx mythological creature, represented in Egyptian, Assyrian, and Greek art as a lion with a human head. In Greek myth the Sphinx killed all those who came to her and failed to answer her riddle about what animal went firstly on four legs, then on two, and lastly on three: the answer is humanity (baby, adult, and old person with stick). She committed suicide when ◊Oedipus gave the right answer.

Spielberg Steven 1947– . US director, writer, and producer of such phenomenal box-office successes as *Jaws* 1975, *Close Encounters of the Third Kind* 1977, *Raiders of the Lost Ark* 1981, *ET* 1982, and *Jurassic Park* 1993. Immensely popular, his films usually combine cliff-hanging suspense with heartfelt sentimentality and a childlike sensibility. He also directed *Indiana Jones and the Temple of Doom* 1984, *The Color Purple* 1985, *Empire of the Sun* 1987, *Indiana Jones and the Last Crusade* 1989, *Hook* 1991, and *Schindler's List* 1993, based on Thomas Keneally's novel.

I wanted the water to mean shark. The horizon to mean shark. I wanted the shark's presence to be felt everywhere.

Steven Spielberg on his film *Jaws*

Spillane Mickey (Frank Morrison) 1918– . US crime novelist who began by writing for pulp magazines and became an internationally bestselling author with books featuring private investigator Mike Hammer, a violent vigilante who wages an amoral war on crime. His most popular novels include *I, the Jury* 1947 and *Kiss Me Deadly* 1953 (both made into films in the *noir* style in the 1950s).

By the time of his 12th Mike Hammer novel, *The Killing Man* 1989, Spillane's books had achieved sales in excess of 180 million.

spinet 17th-century laterally tapered domestic keyboard instrument of up to a three-and-a-half octave range, having a plucking action and single strings. It was the precursor of the ◊harpsichord.

spinning art of drawing out and twisting fibres (originally wool or flax) into a long thread, or yarn, by hand or machine. Synthetic fibres are extruded as a liquid through the holes of a spinneret.

Originally, some 9,000 years ago, spinning was done by hand using a distaff (a cleft stick holding a bundle of fibres) and a weighted spindle, which was spun to twist the thread. In the 1300s the spinning wheel came to Europe, though it had been in use earlier in the East. It provided a way of turning the spindle mechanically. By the next century, the wheel was both spinning and winding the yarn on to a bobbin, but further mechanical development did not occur until the 18th century. In about 1767 in England James Hargreaves built the *spinning jenny*, a machine that could spin 8, then 16, bobbins at once. Later, Samuel Crompton's *spinning mule* 1779 had a moving carriage carrying the spindles; it is still in use today.

Also used is the ring-spinning frame introduced in the USA 1828 where sets of rollers moving at various speeds draw out finer and finer thread, which is twisted and wound on to rotating bobbins.

spiritual religious song developed by slaves in the USA. The precursors of ◊gospel music, spirituals were 18th- and 19th-century hymns joined to the old African pentatonic (five-note) scale. 'Nobody Knows the Trouble I've Seen' and 'Deep River' are examples. White folk hymns and religious ballads are also called spirituals.

The rhythms of work songs and the call and response of much African music, recreated in religious services, contributed to the development of spirituals and gospel. The songs often speak in biblical terms of release from bondage and the prospect of a better life in the hereafter. Spirituals were first brought to a wider audience in the 1870s as a fund-raising activity by southern black US universities, which sent out touring choirs called jubilee singers. In the early 20th century, the singer Paul ◊Robeson recorded many spirituals.

Spode Josiah 1754–1827. English potter. Around 1800, he developed bone porcelain (made from bone ash, china stone, and china clay), which was produced at all English factories in the 19th century. Spode became potter to King George III 1806.

Spranger Bartholomeus 1544–1611. Flemish Mannerist painter. He trained in Antwerp and worked in Paris, Rome, and Vienna before becoming court painter to Rudolph II in Prague. His paintings, which are mostly of mythological or allegorical subjects, are often highly erotic.

Springsteen Bruce 1949– . US rock singer, songwriter, and guitarist, born in New Jersey. His music combines melodies in traditional rock idiom and reflective lyrics about working-class life and the pursuit of the American dream on such albums as *Born to Run* 1975, *Born in the USA* 1984, and *Human Touch* 1992.

Darkness at the Edge of Town 1978, *The River* 1980, and the solo acoustic *Nebraska* 1982 reinforced his reputation as a songwriter. His vast stadium concerts with the E Street Band were marked by his ability to overcome the distance between audience and artist, making him one of rock's finest live performers.

Everything dies baby that's a fact/ But maybe everything that dies someday comes back.

Bruce Springsteen 'Atlantic City' 1982

staccato (Italian 'detached') in music, a term used to describe a continuous passage in which every note is separately articulated rather than phrased continuously (legato 'joined'). Staccato gives an upbeat feel to a passage.

stadium rock epic style of rock music developed in the 1980s. As live audiences grew, performers had to adapt their delivery, staging, and material to the size of the auditorium. The Irish band U2 and Scottish band Simple Minds (formed 1977) are formative stadium-rock bands.

Staël Anne Louise Germaine Necker, Madame de 1766–1817. French author, daughter of the financier Necker. She wrote semi-autobiographical novels such as *Delphine* 1802 and *Corinne* 1807, and the critical work *De l'Allemagne* 1810, on German literature. She was banished from Paris by Napoleon 1803 because of her advocacy of political freedom.

A nation has character only when it is free.

Madame de Staël
De la Littérature 1800

stained glass coloured pieces of glass that are joined by lead strips to form a pictorial window design. The art is said to have originated in the Middle East. At first only one monumental figure was represented on each window, but by the middle of the 12th century, incidents in the life of Jesus or of one of the saints were commonly depicted. Fine examples of medieval stained glass are to be found in the cathedrals of Canterbury, Lincoln, Chartres, Cologne, and Rouen. More recent designers include William ◊Morris, Edward ◊Burne-Jones, and Marc ◊Chagall. Since World War II the use of thick, faceted glass joined by cement (common in the 6th century) has been revived.

Stainer John 1840–1901. English organist and composer who became organist of St Paul's 1872. His religious choral works are *The Crucifixion* 1887, an oratorio, and *The Daughter of Jairus* 1878, a cantata.

Stallone Sylvester 1946– . US film actor, a bit player who rocketed to fame as the boxer in *Rocky* 1976. Other films include *First Blood* 1982 and the *Rambo* series from 1985. He wrote the screenplays for all five of the *Rocky* series, direct-ing three of them. He is known for his near-mumble speech delivery and for portraying violent, passionate men.

Stanford Charles Villiers 1852–1924. Irish-born British composer and teacher, a leading figure in the 19th-century renaissance of British music. His many works include operas such as *Shamus O'Brien* 1896, seven symphonies, chamber music, and church music. Among his pupils were Vaughan Williams, Gustav Holst, and Frank Bridge.

Stanislavsky Konstantin Sergeivich 1863–1938. Russian actor, director, and teacher of acting. He rejected the declamatory style of acting in favour of a more realistic approach, concentrating on the psychological basis for the development of character. The ◊Actors Studio is based on his methods. As a director, he is acclaimed for his productions of the great plays of ◊Chekhov.

Stanislavsky cofounded the Moscow Art Theatre 1898 and directed productions of Chekhov and Gorky. His ideas, which he described in *My Life in Art* 1924 and other works, had considerable influence on acting techniques in Europe and the USA.

Stansfield Lisa 1965– . English pop singer whose soulful vocals with slick productions have won her several of the UK record industry's Brit Awards. She had a UK number-one hit with 'All Around the World' 1989. Her albums *Affection* 1989 and *Real Love* 1992 also enjoyed chart success in the UK and the USA.

Stansfield Smith Colin 1932– . English architect under whose leadership from 1973 the work of Hampshire County Architects Depart-ment has come to represent the best of public English architecture in recent times. The schools built are generally organic modern buildings that relate to their rural context. Bishopstoke Infants' School is housed under a sweeping teepeelike tiled roof.

Stanwyck Barbara. Stage name of Ruby Stevens 1907–1990. US film actress of commanding presence, equally at home in comedy or melodrama. Her films include *Stella Dallas* 1937, *The Lady Eve* 1941, *Double Indemnity* 1944, and *Executive Suite* 1954.

stanza (Italian 'resting or stopping place') group of lines in a poem. A stanza serves the same function in poetry as a paragraph in prose. Stanzas are often of uniform length and separated by a blank line. Each stanza has a set, repeatable pattern of metre and rhyme.

Starck Philippe 1949– . French product, furniture, and interior designer who brought French design to international attention in the 1980s with his innovative and elegant designs, notably those for a room in the Elysée Palace 1982 and for the Café Costes in Paris 1984. The wooden and metal chair he designed for the Café became a huge international success.

Stark Freya 1893–1993. English traveller, mountaineer, and writer who for a long time worked in South America. She described her explorations in the Middle East in many books, including *The Valley of the Assassins* 1934, *The Southern Gates of Arabia* 1936, and *A Winter in Arabia* 1940.

The great and almost only comfort about being a woman is that one can always pretend to be more stupid than one is, and no one is surprised.

Freya Stark
The Valley of the Assassins 1934

Statius about 45–96. Roman poet. Author of the *Silvae*, occasional poems of some interest; the epic *Thebaïd*, which tells the story of the sons of Oedipus; and an unfinished epic *Achilleïs*. He was admired by Dante and Chaucer.

stave or *staff* the five-line grid, reading from left to right, on which music is notated. The pitch range of stave notation is indicated by a ◊clef.

Stead Christina (Ellen) 1902–1983. Australian writer who lived in Europe and the USA 1928–68. An exploratory, psychological writer, imaginatively innovative in form and style, she disclosed elements of the irrational, even the grotesque, in the subconscious of her characters. Her novels include *The Man Who Loved Children* 1940, *Dark Places of the Heart* 1966 (published as *Cotter's England* in the UK), and *I'm Dying Laughing* 1986.

steel band musical ensemble common in the West Indies, consisting mostly of percussion instruments made from oil drums that give a sweet, metallic ringing tone.

Steele Richard 1672–1729. Irish essayist who founded the journal *The Tatler* 1709–11, in which Joseph ◊Addison collaborated. They continued their joint work in *The Spectator*, also founded by Steele, 1711–12, and *The Guardian* 1713. He also wrote plays, such as *The Conscious Lovers* 1722.

Steen Jan *c.* 1626–1679. Dutch painter. Born in Leiden, he was also active in The Hague, Delft, and Haarlem. He painted humorous genre scenes, mainly set in taverns or bourgeois households, as well as portraits and landscapes.

Steer Philip Wilson 1860–1942. English artist, influenced by the French Impressionists, who painted seaside scenes such as *The Bridge, Walberswick* 1887 and *The Beach at Walberswick* 1890 (both Tate Gallery, London). He became a leader (with Walter ◊Sickert) of the English Impressionist movement and a founder-member of the ◊New English Art Club.

Steichen Edward 1897–1973. US photographer in both world wars, and also an innovative fashion and portrait photographer.

Steiger Rod(ney Stephen) 1925– . US character actor of the ◊Method school. His work includes *On the Waterfront* 1954, *The Pawnbroker* 1965, *In the Heat of the Night* 1967 (Academy Award), and the title role in *W C Fields and Me* 1976.

Stein Gertrude 1874–1946. US writer who influenced authors Ernest ◊Hemingway, Sherwood ◊Anderson, and F Scott ◊Fitzgerald with her radical prose style. Drawing on the stream-of-consciousness psychology of William James and on the technique of the Cubist painters in Paris, she evolved a 'continuous present' style made up of constant repetition and variation of simple phrases. Her work includes the self-portrait *The Autobiography of Alice B Toklas* 1933.

A rose is a rose is a rose is a rose.

Gertrude Stein Sacred Emily

Stein Peter 1937– . German theatre director. Artistic director of the politically radical Berlin Schaubühne 1970–85, Stein's early productions included Edward Bond's *Saved* 1967 and Goethe's *Torquato Tasso* 1969. These foreshadowed the spectacular staging of Ibsen's *Peer Gynt* 1971, and his exploratory show *Shakespeare's Memory* 1976.

Stein has directed the plays of the German dramatist Botho Strauss, including *The Park* 1984, and operas for the Welsh Opera: Verdi's *Otello* 1986, and Debussy's *Pelléas et Mélisande* 1992.

To finish is sadness to a writer – a little death. He puts the last word down and it is done. But it isn't really done. The story goes on and leaves the writer behind, for no story is ever done.

John Steinbeck

Steinbeck John (Ernst) 1902–1968. US novelist. His realist novels, such as *In Dubious Battle* 1936, *Of Mice and Men* 1937, and *The Grapes of Wrath* 1939 (Pulitzer Prize) (filmed 1940), portray agricultural life in his native California.

Born in Salinas, California, Steinbeck worked as a labourer to support his writing career, and his experiences supplied him with authentic material for his books. He first achieved success with *Tortilla Flat* 1935, a humorous study of the lives of Monterey *paisanos* (farmers). Later books include *Cannery Row* 1944, *East of Eden* 1952, *Once There Was a War* 1958, *The Winter of Our Discontent* 1961, and *Travels with Charley* 1962. He also wrote screenplays for films, notably *Viva Zapata!* 1952. Nobel prize 1962.

Steinberg Saul 1914– . Romanian-born US artist known for the cartoons he contributed to the *New Yorker* and other magazines. His work portrays a childlike personal world with allusions to the irrational and absurd.

Steiner (Francis) George 1929– . French-born US critic and writer. His books, which focus on the relationships between the arts, culture, and society, include *The Death of Tragedy* 1960, *In Bluebeard's Castle* 1971, and the novella about Hitler, *The Portage to San Cristobal of A.H.* 1981.

Steiner Max(imilian Raoul) 1888–1971. Austrian-born US film composer who along with Erich Korngold brought the style of Mahler and Richard Strauss to Hollywood movie scores. He pioneered the use of a ◊click-track for feature films to guarantee absolute coordination of music and film action. His richly sentimental scores include *King Kong* 1934, *Gone with the Wind* 1939, and *Casablanca* 1942.

Stella Frank 1936– . US painter, a pioneer of the hard-edged geometrical trend in abstract art that followed Abstract Expressionism. From around 1960 he also experimented with shaped canvases.

Stella Joseph 1877–1946. Italian-born US painter, one of America's leading Futurists. His works are mostly mechanical and urban scenes, although his later paintings include tropical landscapes. His Futurist-inspired views of New York City include *Brooklyn Bridge* 1917–18 (Yale University Art Gallery, Connecticut).

Stendhal pen name of Marie Henri Beyle 1783–1842. French novelist. His novels *Le Rouge et le noir/The ◊Red and the Black* 1830 and *La Chartreuse de Parme/The Charterhouse of Parma* 1839 were pioneering works in their treatment of disguise and hypocrisy; a review of the latter by fellow novelist Balzac 1840 furthered Stendhal's reputation.

One can acquire everything in solitude except character.

Stendhal *On Love* 1822

Stendhal was born in Grenoble. He served in Napoleon's armies and took part in the ill-fated Russian campaign. Failing in his hopes of becoming a prefect, he lived in Italy from 1814 until suspicion of espionage drove him back to Paris 1821, where he lived by literary hackwork. From 1830 he was a member of the consular service, spending his leaves in Paris.

Stepanova Varvara. Russian artist and designer. She became known after the 1917 revolution for dynamically geometrical designs in simple, modern shapes and bold colours, which combined the 'machine aesthetic' and principles appropriate to communism. In 1923, with Liubov ◊Popova, she was invited to design textiles for the First State Textile Printing Factory, Moscow. In 1924 she became professor of textile design at the Vkhutemas (Higher Institute for Technical Arts), but soon afterwards turned to typography and film and photographic projects. She was married to Alexander ◊Rodchenko.

Stephen Leslie 1832–1904. English critic, first editor of the *Dictionary of National Biography* and father of novelist Virginia ◊Woolf.

Steppenwolf novel by Hermann ◊Hesse, published in Germany 1927. Henry Haller ('Steppenwolf') is contemplating suicide, but comes to terms with the world around him after a visit to the surreal Magic Theatre.

Sternberg Josef von 1894–1969. Austrian film director, in the USA from childhood. He is best remembered for his seven films with Marlene Dietrich, including *Der blaue Engel/The Blue Angel* 1930, *Blonde Venus* 1932, and *The Devil Is a Woman* 1935, all of which are marked by his expressive use of light and shadow.

Sterne Laurence 1713–1768. Irish writer, creator of the comic anti-hero Tristram Shandy. *The Life and Opinions of Tristram Shandy, Gent* 1759–67, an eccentrically whimsical and bawdy novel, foreshadowed many of the techniques and devices of 20th-century novelists, including James Joyce. His other works include *A Sentimental Journey through France and Italy* 1768.

A man should know something of his own country, too, before he goes abroad.

Laurence Sterne *Tristram Shandy* 1760–67

Sterne, born in Clonmel, Ireland, took holy orders 1737 and became vicar of Sutton- in-the-Forest, Yorkshire, in the next year. In 1741 he married Elizabeth Lumley, producing an unhappy union largely because of his infidelity. He had a sentimental love affair with Eliza Draper, of which the *Letters of Yorick to Eliza* 1775 is a record.

Stesichorus about 630–550 BC. Greek choral poet who lived and wrote mostly in Sicily. His lyrical narratives, incorporating direct speech, had a profound influence on later Greek tragedy, but his work survives only in fragments.

Stevens Alfred 1817–1875. English sculptor, painter, and designer. He created the Wellington monument, St Paul's Cathedral, London (begun 1858). He was devoted to High Renaissance art, especially to Raphael, and studied in Italy 1833–42.

Stevens George 1904–1975. US film director who began as a director of photography. He made such films as *Swing Time* 1936 and *Gunga Din* 1939, and his reputation grew steadily, as did the length and ambition of his films. His later work included *A Place in the Sun* 1951, *Shane* 1953, and *Giant* 1956.

Stevens Wallace 1879–1955. US poet. An insurance company executive, he was not recognized as a major poet until late in life. His volumes of poems include *Harmonium* 1923, *The Man with the Blue Guitar* 1937, and *Transport to Summer* 1947. *The Necessary Angel* 1951 is a collection of essays. An elegant and philosophical poet, he won the Pulitzer Prize 1954 for his *Collected Poems*.

Stevenson Robert Louis 1850–1894. Scottish novelist and poet, author of the adventure novel ◊*Treasure Island* 1883. Later works included the novels *Kidnapped* 1886, *The Master of Ballantrae* 1889, *The Strange Case of Dr Jekyll and Mr Hyde* 1886 (see ◊Jekyll and Hyde), and the anthology *A Child's Garden of Verses* 1885.

Stevenson was born in Edinburgh. He studied at the university there and qualified as a lawyer, but never practised. Early works include *An Island Voyage* 1878 and *Travels with a Donkey* 1879. In 1879 he met the American Fanny Osbourne in France and followed her to the USA, where they married 1880. In the same year they returned to Britain, and he subsequently published a volume of stories, *The New Arabian Nights* 1882, and essays, for example, *Virginibus Puerisque* 1881 and *Familiar Studies of Men and Books* 1882. The humorous *The Wrong Box* 1889 and the novels *The Wrecker* 1892 and *The Ebb-tide* 1894 were written in collaboration with his stepson, Lloyd Osbourne (1868–1920). In 1890 he settled at Vailima, in Samoa, where he sought a cure for his tuberculosis.

Stewart James 1908– . US actor who made his Broadway debut 1932 and soon after worked in Hollywood. Speaking with a soft, slow drawl, he specialized in the role of the stubbornly honest, ordinary American in such films as *Mr Smith Goes to Washington* 1939, *The Philadelphia Story* 1940 (Academy Award), *It's a Wonderful Life* 1946, *Harvey* 1950, *The Man from Laramie* 1955, and *Anatomy of a Murder* 1959. His films with director Alfred Hitchcock include *Rope* 1948, *Rear Window* 1954, *The Man Who Knew Too Much* 1956, and *Vertigo* 1958.

Stieglitz Alfred 1864–1946. US photographer. After forming the Photo Secession group 1903, he started up the magazine *Camera Work*. Through exhibitions at his gallery '291' in New York he helped to establish photography as an art form. His works include 'Winter, Fifth Avenue' 1893 and 'Steerage' 1907. In 1924 he married the painter Georgia O'Keeffe, who was the model in many of his photographs.

Stijl, De (Dutch 'the style') group of 20th-century Dutch artists and architects led by Piet ◊Mondrian from 1917. The group promoted Mondrian's 'Neo-Plasticism', an abstract style that sought to establish universal principles of design based on horizontal and vertical lines, the three primary colours, and black, white, and grey. They had a strong influence on the ◊Bauhaus school.

The name came from a magazine, *De Stijl*, founded 1917 by Mondrian and Theo van Doesburg (1883–1931).

Still Clyfford 1904–1980. US painter, a pioneer and central figure of ◊Abstract Expressionism. His vast, thickly painted canvases are characterized by jagged areas of raw colours. *1954* 1954 (Albright-Knox Art Gallery, Buffalo, New York) is typical.

Self-taught, Still painted flickering, semi-abstract landscapes of western America during the 1930s and 1940s prior to arriving at his own forceful style about 1947. The broadening of his technique coincided with his moral stance against extraneous detail and his exploration of simplified fields of dark and light colour.

still life in painting and graphic art, a depiction of inanimate objects. A feature of painting since classical times, still life developed as an independent genre in the 17th century, flourishing first in Holland, where the Reformation had discouraged religious imagery and artists were seeking new subjects. Early examples often combine a sheer delight in the appearance of things with religious or moral symbolism. One of the first true still lifes is Caravaggio's *Basket of Fruit* 1596 (Pinacoteca Ambrosiana, Milan). Other examples include Chardin's *Skate, Cat and Kitchen Utensils* 1728 (Louvre, Paris) and Morandi's *Still Life* 1946 (Tate Gallery, London).

Sting stage name of Gordon Sumner 1951– . English pop singer, songwriter, bass player, and actor. As a member of the trio the Police 1977–83, he had UK number-one hits with 'Message in a Bottle' 1979, 'Walking on the Moon' 1979, and 'Every Breath You Take' 1983. In his solo career he has often drawn on jazz, as on the albums *The Dream of Blue Turtles* 1985 and *Soul Cages* 1991.

His films include *Quadrophenia* 1979, *Brimstone and Treacle* 1982, and *Dune* 1984. Sting has been heavily involved with fund-raising to preserve the Amazonian rainforests and the traditional way of life of the indigenous Indians.

Stirling James 1926–1992. British architect, possibly the most influential of his generation. While in partnership with James Gowan (1924–   ), he designed the Leicester University Engineering Building 1959–63 in a Constructivist vein. He later adopted a more eclectic approach, exemplified in the Staatsgalerie, Stuttgart, 1977–82, a blend of Constructivism, Modernism, and several strands of Classicism. He also designed the Clore Gallery 1982–86 to house the Turner Collection of the Tate Gallery, London. The last of his designs completed in his lifetime was the B Braun Factory in Melsungen, Germany, 1992.

I think transitional periods are rather exotic, more so than periods which have settled down and become rather fixed in their output.

James Stirling

St Ives School ill-defined group of English artists, working in a wide range of styles, who lived in the fishing port of St Ives, Cornwall, after the outbreak of World War II. The group included Ben ◊Nicholson and Barbara ◊Hepworth.

Stockhausen Karlheinz 1928–   . German composer of avant-garde music who has continued to explore new musical sounds and compositional techniques since the 1950s. His major works include *Gesang der Jünglinge* 1956, *Kontakte* 1960 (electronic music), and *Sirius* 1977.

Since 1977 all his works have been part of *LICHT*, a cycle of seven musical ceremonies intended for performance on the evenings of a week. He has completed *Donnerstag* 1980, *Samstag* 1984, *Montag* 1988, and *Dienstag* 1992. Earlier works include *Klavierstücke I–XIV* 1952–85, *Momente* 1961–64, and *Mikrophonie I* 1964.

stockings pair of close-fitting coverings for the legs and feet, now worn by women only; stockings were worn with breeches by men up to the late 19th century. They are generally made of silk or nylon in various grades of thickness and in a range of different colours and patterns. They are classified according to their denier (the unit of weight by which silk, rayon, or nylon yarns are measured). Stockings are attached at the top of the woman's thighs to a suspender belt which fastens around the waist.

In the 1950s seamless stockings became available as did knee-high stockings and tights (also known as pantihose). In the 1960s stockings and tights decorated with stripes and geometric and lacy patterns became popular, followed by the dark and heavy ribbed tights of the 1970s. In the 1980s–90s highly coloured and patterned tights became popular once more.

Stoker Bram (Abraham) 1847–1912. Irish novelist, actor, theatre manager, and author. His novel ◊*Dracula* 1897 crystallized most aspects of the traditional vampire legend and became the source for all subsequent fiction and films on the subject.

Stoker wrote a number of other stories and novels of fantasy and horror, such as *The Lady of the Shroud* 1909. A civil servant 1866–78, he subsequently became business manager to the theatre producer Henry Irving.

Stokowski Leopold 1882–1977. English-born US conductor. An outstanding innovator, he promoted contemporary music with enthusiasm, was an ardent popularist, and introduced changes in orchestral seating. He cooperated with Bell Telephone Laboratories in early stereophonic recording experiments in the mid-1930s, and was a major collaborator with Walt Disney in the programming and development of 'Fantasound' optical surround-sound recording technology for the animated film *Fantasia* 1940.

Stoller Mike. US songwriter and producer in collaboration with Jerry Leiber; see ◊Leiber and Stoller.

Stone Robert (Anthony) 1937–   . US novelist and journalist. His *Dog Soldiers* 1974 is a novel about the moral destructiveness of the Vietnam War. *A Flag for Sunrise* 1982 similarly explores the political and moral consequences of US intervention in a corrupt South American republic. Among his other works is *Children of Light* 1986.

stoneware very hard, opaque, water-resistant pottery made of non-porous clay with feldspar and a high silica content, fired to the point of vitrification (1,200–1,280°C/2,192–2,336°F). Glazing decorates and gives it a smooth finish; it usually fires to shades of grey or buff, though some red stonewares do exist. The earliest examples are Chinese, from the 10th to 3rd centuries BC. From the 9th century AD stoneware was made in N Europe and in Britain from the late 17th century.

Stoppard Tom 1937–   . Czechoslovak-born British dramatist whose works use wit and wordplay to explore logical and philosophical ideas. His play *Rosencrantz and Guildenstern are Dead* 1967 was followed by comedies including *The Real Inspector Hound* 1968, *Jumpers* 1972, *Travesties* 1974, *Dirty Linen* 1976, *The Real Thing* 1982, and *Hapgood* 1988. He has also written for radio, television, and the cinema.

Life is a gamble, at terrible odds – if it was a bet, you wouldn't take it.

Tom Stoppard *Rosencrantz and Guildenstern Are Dead* 1967

Storey David (Malcolm) 1933– . English dramatist and novelist. His plays include *In Celebration* 1969, *Home* 1970, *Early Days* 1980, and *The March on Russia* 1989. Novels include *This Sporting Life* 1960.

Storey Helen 1959– . British fashion designer who launched her own label 1984. She opened Boyd and Storey with fellow fashion designer Karen Boyd 1987, and in 1989 designed a range of shoes for Dr Martens UK and evening shoes and jewellery with the designer Eric Beamon. She staged her first solo catwalk show 1990 and launched a menswear collection 1991, as well as designing lines for Knickerbox and Sock Shop. In 1992 she launched the collection 'Second Life', recycling used clothes, by adding sequins and beads and cutting the clothes to adapt them into new outfits.

Stoss Veit. Also known as *Wit Stwosz* c. 1450–1533. German sculptor and painter, active in Nuremberg and Poland. He carved a wooden altarpiece with high relief panels in St Mary's, Kraków, a complicated design with numerous figures that centres on the *Death of the Virgin* 1477–89. The figure of *St Roch* about 1510 in Sta Annunziata, Florence, shows his characteristic Flemish Realism and bold drapery. Most of his sculptures were brightly painted.

Stowe Harriet Beecher 1811–1896. US suffragist, abolitionist, and author of the antislavery novel ◊*Uncle Tom's Cabin*, first published serially 1851–52. The inspiration came to her in a vision 1848, and the book brought immediate success. It was radical in its time and did much to spread antislavery sentiment, but in the 20th century was criticized for sentimentality and racism.

'Do you know who made you?' 'Nobody, as I knows on,' said the child... 'I 'spect I grow'd.'

Harriet Beecher Stowe
Uncle Tom's Cabin 1851–52

Strachey (Giles) Lytton 1880–1932. English critic and biographer, a member of the ◊Bloomsbury Group of writers and artists. He wrote *Landmarks in French Literature* 1912. The mocking and witty treatment of Cardinal Manning, Florence Nightingale, Thomas Arnold, and General Gordon in *Eminent Victorians* 1918 won him recognition. His biography of *Queen Victoria* 1921 was more affectionate.

Discretion is not the better part of biography.

Lytton Strachey

Stradivari Antonio (Latin form *Stradivarius*) 1644–1737. Italian stringed instrumentmaker, generally considered the greatest of all violin-makers. He was born in Cremona and studied there with Niccolò ◊Amati. He produced more than 1,100 instruments from his family workshops, over 600 of which survive. The secret of his mastery is said to be in the varnish but is probably a combination of fine proportioning and ageing.

Strand Paul 1890–1976. US photographer and filmmaker who studied with Lewis Hine and was encouraged by Alfred Stieglitz. After his early, near-abstract studies of New York, he turned to predominantly rural subjects which celebrate human dignity in a clear and straightforward manner. His portfolios, which include *Photographs of Mexico* 1940 and *Time in New England,* were always meticulously printed.

Strasberg Lee 1902–1982. US actor and artistic director of the ◊Actors Studio from 1948, who developed Method acting from ◊Stanislavsky's system; pupils have included Marlon Brando, Paul Newman, Julie Harris, Kim Hunter, Geraldine Page, Al Pacino, and Robert DeNiro.

Strassburg Gottfried von, lived *c.* 1210. German poet, author of the unfinished epic *Tristan und Isolde,* which inspired the German composer Wagner.

Straus Oscar 1870–1954. Austrian composer, born in Vienna. A pupil of Max Bruch, he was chief conductor and composer at the Uberbrettl cabaret, becoming a master of light satirical stage pieces. He is remembered for the operetta *The Chocolate Soldier* 1908.

Strauss Botho 1944– . German dramatist and critic. His stark plays focus on problems of identity and the disintegration of personality. They include *Big and Little* 1978 and *The Park* 1984, his adaptation of *A Midsummer Night's Dream.*

Strauss Johann (Baptist) 1825–1899. Austrian conductor and composer, the son of composer Johann Strauss (1804–1849). In 1872 he gave up conducting and wrote operettas, such as *Die Fledermaus/The Flittermouse* 1874, and numerous waltzes, such as *The Blue Danube* and *Tales from the Vienna Woods,* which gained him the title 'the Waltz King'.

Strauss Richard (Georg) 1864–1949. German composer and conductor. He followed the German Romantic tradition but had a strongly personal style, characterized by his bold, colourful orchestration. He first wrote tone poems such as *Don Juan* 1889, *Till Eulenspiegel's Merry Pranks* 1895, and *Also sprach Zarathustra/Thus Spake Zarathustra* 1896. He then moved on to opera with *Salome* 1905 and *Elektra* 1909, both of which have elements of polytonality. He reverted to a more traditional style with *Der Rosenkavalier/The Knight of the Rose* 1909–10.

Stravinsky Igor 1882–1971. Russian composer, later of French (1934) and US (1945) nationality. He studied under Rimsky-Korsakov and won international acclaim as composer of the scores for the Diaghilev ballets *The Firebird* 1910, *Petrushka* 1911, and *The Rite of Spring* 1913 (controversial at the time for their unorthodox rhythms and harmonies). His versatile work ranges from his Neo-Classical ballet *Pulcinella* 1920 to the choral-orchestral *Symphony of Psalms* 1930. He later made use of serial techniques in such works as the *Canticum Sacrum* 1955 and the ballet *Agon* 1953–57.

Work brings inspiration, if inspiration is not discernible at the beginning.

Igor Stravinsky
Chronicles of My Life 1935

---

streamlining a popular design style of the 1930s which originated in cars, ships, and aeroplanes and went on to influence domestic appliances such as refrigerators and irons. The bulbous forms linked with streamlining that were first used to cut down wind resistance were quickly turned into a visual symbol of modernity by the American industrial designers of the interwar years.

stream of consciousness narrative technique in which a writer presents directly the uninterrupted flow of a character's thoughts, impressions, and feelings, without the conventional devices of dialogue and description. It first came to be widely used in the early 20th century. Leading exponents have included the novelists Virginia Woolf, James Joyce, and William Faulkner.

Molly Bloom's soliloquy in Joyce's *Ulysses* is a good example of the technique. The English writer Dorothy Richardson (1873–1957) is said to have originated the technique in her novel sequence *Pilgrimage*, the first volume of which was published 1915 and the last posthumously. The term 'stream of consciousness' was introduced by the philosopher William James 1890.

Streep Meryl 1949– . US actress, a leading star of the 1980s and 1990s, known for her strong character roles, portrayed with emotionally dramatic intensity. She is also known for her accomplished facility with a wide variety of accents. Her films include *The Deer Hunter* 1978, *Kramer vs Kramer* 1979 (Academy Award for best supporting actress), *The French Lieutenant's Woman* 1981, *Sophie's Choice* 1982 (Academy Award), *Out of Africa* 1985, *Ironweed* 1988, *A Cry in the Dark* 1989, and the comedy *Death Becomes Her* 1992.

Street George Edmund 1824–1881. English Victorian architect, a pupil of Gilbert Scott. He practised in Oxford from 1852, where Webb and Morris were among his assistants, before moving to London 1855. He designed and restored hundreds of churches in a vigorous, continental ◊Gothic Revival style, notably St James the Less, Vauxhall Bridge Road, London, 1860–61, and St Philip and St James, Oxford, 1860–62. His principal secular work is the Law Courts, the Strand (won in competition 1866; opened 1882), the foremost Gothic Revival building in England after the Houses of Parliament.

Streeton Arthur 1867–1943. Australian artist, a founder of the ◊Heidelberg School. He pioneered Impressionistic renderings of Australia's landscape.

Streisand Barbra (Barbara Joan) 1942– . US singer and actress who became a film star in *Funny Girl* 1968 (Academy Award). Her subsequent films include *Hello Dolly* 1969, *What's Up Doc?* 1972, *The Way We Were* 1973, and *A Star Is Born* 1979 (which she also produced). She directed, scripted, produced, and starred in *Yentl* 1983 and acted in *Prince of Tides* 1992.

stride piano jazz piano style alternating left-hand chords with single bass notes; it was popularized in the 1930s by such musicians as Fats ◊Waller.

Strindberg August 1849–1912. Swedish dramatist and novelist. His plays are in a variety of styles including historical dramas, symbolic dramas (the two-part *Dödsdansen/The Dance of Death* 1901) and 'chamber plays' such as *Spöksonaten/The Ghost [Spook] Sonata* 1907. *Fadren/The Father* 1887 and *Fröken Julie/Miss Julie* 1888 are among his best-known works.

Born in Stockholm, he lived mainly abroad after 1883, having been unsuccessfully prosecuted for blasphemy 1884 following publication of his short stories *Giftas/Marrying*. His life was stormy and his work has been criticized for its hostile attitude to women, but he is regarded as one of Sweden's greatest writers.

I see the dramatist as a lay preacher peddling the ideas of his time in popular form.

August Strindberg
Preface to *Miss Julie* 1888

---

string instrument musical instrument that produces a sound when a stretched string is made to vibrate. Today the strings are made of gut, metal, and Pearlon (a plastic). Types of string instruments include: **bowed**, the violin family and viol family; **plucked**, the guitar, ukelele, lute, sitar, harp, banjo, and lyre; **plucked mechanically**, the harpsichord; **struck mechanically**, the piano and clavichord; and **hammered**, the dulcimer.

string quartet ◊chamber music ensemble consisting of first and second violins, viola, and cello. The 18th-century successor to the domestic viol consort, the string quartet with its stronger and more rustic tone formed the basis of the symphony orchestra. Important composers include Haydn (more than 80 string quartets), Mozart (27), Schubert (20), Beethoven (17), Dvořák (8), and Bartók (6).

String-quartet music evolved from the decorative but essentially vocal style of viol music into a vigorously instrumental style exploiting the instruments' full expressive potential. The older hierarchy of solo and accompanying voices also changed to a concertante style offering solo opportunities for each player, a trend accelerated by the adoption of shriller metal strings in the 19th century.

Stroheim Erich von. Adopted name of Erich Oswald Stroheim 1885–1957. Austrian actor and director, in Hollywood from 1914. He was successful as an actor in villainous roles, but his career as a director, which produced films such as *Foolish Wives* 1922, was wrecked by his extravagance (*Greed* 1923) and he returned to acting in such films as *La Grande Illusion* 1937 and *Sunset Boulevard* 1950.

structuralism 20th-century philosophical movement that has influenced such areas as linguistics, anthropology, and literary criticism. Inspired by the work of the Swiss linguist Ferdinand de Saussure (1857–1913), structuralists believe that objects should be analysed as systems of relations, rather than as positive entities.

Saussure proposed that language is a system of arbitrary signs, meaning that there is no intrinsic link between the 'signifier' (the sound or mark) and the 'signified' (the concept it represents). Hence any linguistic term can be defined only by its differences from other terms. His ideas were taken further by Roman Jakobson (1896–1982) and the Prague school of linguistics, and were extended into a general method for the social sciences by the French anthropologist Claude Lévi-Strauss. The French writer Roland Barthes took the lead in applying the ideas of structuralism to literary criticism, arguing that the critic should identify the structures within a text that determine its possible meanings, independently of any reference to the real. This approach is radicalized in Barthes' later work and in the practice of 'deconstruction' (see ◊Deconstruction).

Struwwelpeter collection of cautionary tales written and illustrated by German author Heinrich Hoffmann (1809–1894), published in German 1845 (English translation 1848). The tales, in verse form, feature characters such as 'Shock-head Peter' (Struwwelpeter), 'Johnny Head-in-Air', and 'Augustus who would not have any Soup'.

Stuart Gilbert Charles 1755–1828. American artist. A protégé of the American painter Benjamin ◊West in London 1776–82, he gained fame as one of the foremost portraitists of the time. Returning to the USA, he set up a studio in Philadelphia 1794. Best known for his portraits of George Washington, he painted various other prominent public figures.

Stuart James 'Athenian' 1713–1788. English architect, notable for his role in the ◊Greek Revival movement. His small but distinctive output includes the Doric Temple at Hagley Park, Worcestershire, 1758, and decorative schemes for a number of rooms in Spencer House, London (begun 1760).

Stubbs George 1724–1806. English artist, renowned for his paintings of horses. After the publication of his book of engravings *The Anatomy of the Horse* 1766, he was widely commissioned as an animal painter. The dramatic *Lion Attacking a Horse* 1770 (Yale University Art Gallery, New Haven, Connecticut) and the peaceful *Reapers* 1786 (Tate Gallery, London) show the variety of mood in his painting.

stucco durable plaster finish for exterior walls, composed of sand and lime. In the 18th and 19th centuries stucco was used extensively to add dignity to brick buildings, by giving the illusion that they were built of stone. The stucco would be moulded, coursed, or coloured to imitate ashlar ◊masonry. John ◊Nash used stucco to create the illusory stone palaces that surround Regents Park, London (begun 1811). A finer plaster is used for interior stucco ornamentation, such as mouldings.

stupa domed structure built to house a Buddhist or Jain relic. The stupa originated in India around 1000 BC from burial monuments and is usually a hemisphere crowned by a spire. In the Far East the stupa developed into the ◊pagoda.

Sturges Preston. Adopted name of Edmond Biden 1898–1959. US film director and writer who enjoyed great success with a series of comedies in the early 1940s, including *Sullivan's Travels* 1941, *The Palm Beach Story* 1942, and *The Miracle of Morgan's Creek* 1943.

Sturluson Snorri 1179–1241. Icelandic author of the Old Norse poems called ◊Eddas and the *Heimskringla*, a saga chronicle of Norwegian kings until 1177.

Sturm und Drang (German 'storm and stress') German early Romantic movement in literature and music, from about 1775, concerned with the depiction of extravagant passions. Writers associated with the movement include Herder, Goethe, and Schiller. The name is taken from a play by Friedrich von Klinger 1776.

Styron William (Clark) 1925– . US novelist. His novels *Lie Down in Darkness* 1951, *The Confessions of Nat Turner* 1967 (Pulitzer Prize), and *Sophie's Choice* 1979 (filmed 1982) all won critical and popular acclaim. His *Confessions* caused controversy and protest from black critics over its depiction of a slave revolt in 19th-century Virginia.

Styx in Greek mythology, the river surrounding the underworld.

sublime, the in the arts, the quality of being awe-inspiring or possessing grandeur. In the 18th century it became an aesthetic category, when 'beautiful' no longer seemed adequate to express the spiritual and emotional impact of art or nature. The search for the sublime was apparent in a predilection for wild landscapes in painting and in the new genre of the Gothic novel, such as Horace Walpole's *The Castle of Otranto* 1764.

Suckling John 1609–1642. English Cavalier poet and dramatist. An ardent Royalist, he played an active part in the English Civil War, fleeing to France 1641 where he may have committed suicide. His chief lyrics appeared in *Fragmenta Aurea* 1646 and include his best-known lyric, 'Why so pale and wan, fond lover?'

Her lips were red, and one was thin,/ Compar'd to that was next her chin/ (Some bee had stung it newly).

John Suckling
'A Ballad upon a Wedding' 1646

Suetonius (Gaius Suetonius Tranquillus) *c.* AD 69–140. Roman historian, author of *Lives of the Caesars* (Julius Caesar to Domitian).

Be assured that nothing is more pleasing than beauty, but nothing is shorter-lived.

Suetonius *Domitianus*

Suger *c.* 1081–1151. French historian and politician, regent of France during the Second Crusade. In 1122 he was elected abbot of St Denis, Paris, and was counsellor to, and biographer of, Louis VI and Louis VII. He began the reconstruction of St Denis as the first large-scale Gothic building.

suite in Baroque music, a set of contrasting instrumental pieces based on dance forms, known by their French names as allemande, courante, sarabande, gigue, minuet, gavotte, passepied, bourrée, musette, rigaudon, and so on. The term refers in more recent usage to a concert arrangement of set pieces from an extended ballet or stage composition, such as Tchaikovsky's *Nutcracker Suite* 1891–92. Stravinsky's suite from *The Soldier's Tale* 1920 incorporates a tango, waltz, and ragtime.

Sukenick Ronald 1932– . US post-modern novelist and theoretician. His innovative and laconic style marks the collection *The Death of the Novel and Other Stories* 1969 and such novels as *Up* 1968 and *Out* 1973. Later works include *Blown Away* 1986 and a volume of essays *In Form: Digressions on the Act of Fiction* 1985.

Sullivan Arthur (Seymour) 1842–1900. English composer who wrote operettas in collaboration with W S Gilbert, including *HMS Pinafore* 1878, *The Pirates of Penzance* 1879, and *The Mikado* 1885. Their partnership broke down 1896. Sullivan also composed serious instrumental, choral, and operatic works – for example, the opera *Ivanhoe* 1890 – which he valued more highly than the operettas.

Other Gilbert and Sullivan operettas include *Patience* (which ridiculed the Aesthetic Movement) 1881, *The Yeomen of the Guard* 1888, and *The Gondoliers* 1889.

Sullivan Louis Henry 1856–1924. US architect, a leader of the ◊Chicago School and an early developer of the ◊skyscraper. His skyscrapers include the Wainwright Building, St Louis, 1890, the Guaranty Building, Buffalo, 1894, and the Carson, Pirie and Scott Store, Chicago, 1899. He was the teacher of Frank Lloyd ◊Wright and was influential in the anti-ornament movement.

Form follows function.

Louis Henry Sullivan 1895

Sully-Prudhomme Armand 1839–1907. French poet who wrote philosophical verse including *Les Solitudes/Solitude* 1869, *La Justice/Justice* 1878, and *Le Bonheur/Happiness* 1888. He was awarded the Nobel Prize for Literature 1901.

Suprematism Russian abstract-art movement developed about 1913 by Kasimir ◊Malevich. Suprematist painting gradually became more severe, until in 1918 it reached a climax with Malevich's *White on White* series showing white geometrical shapes on a white ground.

Suprematism was inspired in part by Futurist and Cubist ideas. Early paintings such as Malevich's *Black Square* 1915 (Russian Museum, St Petersburg) used purely geometrical shapes in bold dynamic compositions. The aims of the movement were expressed by Malevich as 'the supremacy of pure feeling or perception in the pictorial arts – the expression of non-objectivity'. Suprematism greatly influenced ◊Kandinsky and the ◊Bauhaus.

Supremes, the US vocal group, pioneers of the Motown sound, formed 1959 in Detroit. Beginning in 1962, the group was a trio comprising, initially, Diana Ross (1944–), Mary

Wilson (1944–), and Florence Ballard (1943–1976). The most successful female group of the 1960s, they had a string of pop hits beginning with 'Where Did Our Love Go?' 1964 and 'Baby Love' 1964. Diana Ross left to pursue a solo career 1969.

Surrealism movement in art, literature, and film that developed out of ◊Dada around 1922. Led by André ◊Breton, who produced the *Surrealist Manifesto* 1924, the Surrealists were inspired by the thoughts and visions of the subconscious mind. They explored varied styles and techniques, and the movement became the dominant force in Western art between World Wars I and II.

Surrealism followed Freud's theory of the unconscious and his 'free association' technique for bypassing the conscious mind. In art it encompassed André ◊Masson's automatic drawings, paintings based on emotive semi-abstract forms (Ernst, Miró, Tanguy), and dreamlike images painted in a realistic style (Dali, Magritte). The poets Aragon and Eluard and the filmmaker Buñuel were also part of the movement.

Surrealism is destructive, but it destroys only what it considers to be shackles limiting our vision.

Salvador Dali, *Declaration* 1929

Surrey Henry Howard, Earl of Surrey c. 1517–1547. English courtier and poet, executed on a poorly based charge of high treason. With Thomas ◊Wyatt, he introduced the sonnet to England and was a pioneer of ◊blank verse.

Surtees R(obert) S(mith) 1803–1864. British novelist. He created Jorrocks, a sporting grocer, and in 1838 published *Jorrocks's Jaunts and Jollities.*

Sūrya in Hindu mythology, the sun god, son of the sky god Indra. His daughter, also named Sūrya, is a female personification of the Sun.

Sutcliff Rosemary 1920–1992. British historical novelist who wrote for both adults and children. Her books include *The Eagle of the Ninth* 1954, *Tristan and Iseult* 1971, and *The Road to Camlann* 1981. Her settings range from the Bronze Age to the 18th century, but her favourite period was the Roman occupation of Britain.

Sutcliffe Frank Meadow 1853–1941. British photographer who lived in the seaside town of Whitby, North Yorkshire, and photographed its inhabitants and environs in a consistently naturalistic style for most of his life.

Sutherland Donald 1934– . Canadian-born US film actor of tall, gaunt appearance, who often appears in offbeat roles. He starred in *M.A.S.H.* 1970, and his subsequent films include *Klute* 1971, *Don't Look Now* 1973, *Ordinary People* 1980, and *Revolution* 1985. He is the father of actor Kiefer Sutherland.

Sutherland Graham (Vivian) 1903–1980. English painter, graphic artist, and designer, active mainly in France from the late 1940s. He painted portraits, landscapes, and religious subjects, often using a semi-abstract style.

In the late 1940s Sutherland turned increasingly to characterful portraiture. His portrait of Winston Churchill 1954 was disliked by its subject and eventually burned on the instructions of Lady Churchill (studies survive). His *Christ in Glory* tapestry 1962 is in Coventry Cathedral. Other work includes ceramics and designs for posters, stage costumes, and sets.

Sutherland Joan 1926– . Australian soprano of commanding range and impeccable technique. She made her debut 1952 in England, in *The Magic Flute*; later roles included *Lucia di Lammermoor,* Donna Anna in *Don Giovanni,* and Desdemona in *Otello.* She retired from the stage 1990.

Suzuki Harunobu Japanese artist. He was a leading exponent of ◊ukiyo-e and one of the first printmakers to use colour effectively. His work displays a sure sense of composition and line and features domestic scenes, courtesans, and actors among its subjects.

Svengali person who moulds another into a performer and masterminds his or her career. The original Svengali was a character in the novel *Trilby* 1894 by George ◊Du Maurier.

Svevo Italo. Pen name of Ettore Schmitz 1861–1928. Italian novelist, encouraged by James Joyce. His books include *As a Man Grows Older* 1898 and his comic masterpiece *Confessions of Zeno* 1923, one of the first novels to be based on Freudian analysis.

There are three things I always forget. Names, faces, and – the third I can't remember.

Italo Svevo (attrib.)

Swallows and Amazons the first of a series of novels for children by British author Arthur ◊Ransome, published in the UK 1930–47. The novels describe the adventures of children on holiday, set in the English Lake District and East Anglia, and always involve boats.

Swallows and Amazons introduces the two families featuring in most of the series, the Walkers and the Blacketts, and their sailing dinghies, *Swallow* and *Amazon* respectively. Later books in the series include *Peter Duck* 1932, *Pigeon Post* 1936, and *We Didn't Mean to Go to Sea* 1937.

Swanson Gloria. Stage name of Gloria Josephine Mae Svenson 1897–1983. US actress, a star of silent films who became the epitome of glamour during the 1920s. She retired 1932 but made several major comebacks. Her work includes *Sadie Thompson* 1928, *Queen Kelly* 1928 (unfinished), and *Sunset Boulevard* 1950.

Swedish architecture style of building in Sweden.

medieval The Romanesque cathedrals of Uppsala (brick) and Lund (stone) are from the 11th century. Gothic churches include Riddarholms church in Stockholm and the cathedral in Linköping. The former Hanseatic city of Visby, Gotland, has three Gothic churches and the ruins of 12 more; some medieval domestic buildings have also survived there within the old city wall.

16th century This was a time for building and rebuilding castles under German Renaissance influence. Examples are Gripsholm, Vadstena, and Kalmar.

17th century Three architects emerged who had studied Baroque in Rome: Jean de la Vallée (1620–1696), Nicodemus Tessin the Elder (1615–1681), and his son Nicodemus Tessin the Younger (1654–1728). Together or separately they created several important buildings in Stockholm and elsewhere; for example, Drottningholm Palace, begun 1662.

18th century Rococo prevailed in the mid century and left its traces mostly in interiors; for example, the Royal Palace in Stockholm by the younger Tessin.

early 19th century Neo-Classical architecture includes what is now the State Historical Museum, Stockholm.

late 19th–early 20th century The Jugend style, exemplified by the Royal Dramatic Theatre, Stockholm, gave way to a domestic nationalist style with simple lines, built in brick and granite, used in many public and residential buildings.

mid–late 20th century Modernism took off in Sweden in the 1930s.

Swedish art painting and sculpture of Sweden. Although the main movements in European art have successively taken hold in Sweden, artists have repeatedly returned to a national tradition.

500 BC–11th century AD Bronze and gold jewellery were produced, and memorial stones carved with runes and ornaments.

12th–16th centuries Woven tapestries show the geometrically stylized animals that were also a feature of jewellery and carvings. Churches were decorated with lively, richly ornamented frescoes. Wooden sculptures were initially stiff and solemn, later more realistic and expressive.

17th century Sculptors and portrait painters who had studied Italian Baroque were patronized by Sweden's rulers.

18th century Swedish Rococo emerged, more restrained than the French models on which it was based; chinoiserie was popular because of Swedish trade with the Far East. Rococo was supplanted towards the end of the century by a light Neo-Classical style known as Gustavian.

19th century Academic history painting was superseded by the work of artists influenced by the French Impressionists and by the nationalist spirit current in many countries. The watercolour interiors by Carl Larsson of his home were very popular and among the best work of the period.

early 20th century The Romantic nationalist Jugend style can be seen in the monumental sculptures of Carl Milles (1875–1955) throughout Sweden and in the USA. Albert Engström (1869–1940) was a prolific illustrator and cartoonist. Nils von Dardel (1888–1943) was an early Surrealist painter.

late 20th century Figurative art predominates, ranging from the dreamlike, symbolic paintings of Lena Cronqvist and others to the realistic still-life graphics of Philip von Schantz (1928–).

Swedish literature by the 14th century there were a number of rhymed chronicles, ballads and folk songs, but modern literature begins in the 17th century with the epic poet Georg Stjernhjelm (15981672). In the 18th century the names of Linnaeus, Celsius, and Swedenborg typify the country's intellectual ferment, and the poet and historian Olof von Dalin was an outstanding literary figure. Sweden's first confessional poet Hedvig Charlotta Nordenflycht (1718–1763) was a campaigner for women's rights. The period 1771–1809, covering the reigns of Gustavus III (himself a playwright) and Gustavus IV, saw much literary activity, for example, the song lyrics of Carl Michael Bellman (1740–1795), and the dramas of Gudmund Jöran Adlerbeth (1751–1818) and Henrik Kellgren (1751–1795), who assisted the king in the royal theatre. The sharply observed satiric poems of Anna Maria Lenngren (1754–1817) were popular throughout the 19th century. Outstanding names of the Romantic era are those of poet and playwright Per Daniel Amadeus Atterbom (1790–1855), the poets Esaias Tegnér (1782–1846) and Erik G Geijer (1783–1847) who sought inspiration in the legendary heroic past, and A A Afzelius, editor of national folk songs.

To the period of romantic transition belong the novelist and poet Viktor Rydberg (1828–1895), the classic poet Carl Snoilsky (1841–1903), and the Finnish epic poet Johan Ludwig Runeberg (1804–1877), but realism emerged in the novels of Carl Jonas Love Almqvist (1793–1866) and Frederika Bremer (1801–1865), and broke through in the work of Strindberg. A new romantic idealism followed with, for example, the poets Gustaf Fröding, Erik Axek Karlfeldt (1864– 1931), and Verner von Heidenstam (1859–1940), and the novelist Selma Lageröf – the last three, all Nobel prizewinners. The physician Axel Munthe (1859–1949) won international acclaim for his autobiographical *Story of San Michele* 1929.

Among more recent writers, also Nobel prizewinners, are Harry Martinson (1904–1978), author of a novel of tramp life, *The Road*, and *Aniara*, a space-fiction epic that was adapted as an opera; and Pär Lagerkvist, lyricist, novelist, and playwright.

sweetness and light phrase popularized by the English writer Matthew Arnold in *Culture and Anarchy* 1869, where he advocated a combination of intellectual curiosity with beauty and grace. It was borrowed from Jonathan Swift, who in *Battle of the Books* 1704 compared poets to bees whose honey and wax provide 'the two noblest of things, which are sweetness and light'.

Swift Jonathan 1667–1745. Irish satirist and Anglican cleric, author of ◊*Gulliver's Travels* 1726, an allegory describing travel to lands inhabited by giants, miniature people, and intelligent horses. Other works include *The Tale of a Tub* 1704, attacking corruption in religion and learning; contributions to the Tory paper *The Examiner*, of which he was editor 1710–11; the satirical *A Modest Proposal* 1729, which suggested that children of the poor should be eaten; and many essays and pamphlets.

Swift, born in Dublin, became secretary to the diplomat William Temple (1628–1699) at Moor Park, Surrey, where his friendship with the child 'Stella' (Hester Johnson 1681–1728) began 1689. Returning to Ireland, he was ordained in the Church of England 1694, and in 1699 was made a prebendary of St Patrick's, Dublin. In 1710 he became a Tory pamphleteer, and obtained the deanery of St Patrick 1713. His *Journal to Stella* is a series of letters, 1710–13, in which he described his life in London. 'Stella' remained the love of his life, but 'Vanessa' (Esther Vanhomrigh 1690–1723), a Dublin woman who had fallen in love with him, jealously wrote to her rival 1723 and so shattered his relationship with both women. From about 1738 his mind began to fail and he died insane.

swimsuit one-piece stretch body garment worn by women for swimming. Introduced in the late 19th century, the swimsuit originally consisted of two garments – a long tunic and knickers—and was made of serge or wool. The one-piece garment became popular around 1900. The introduction of elasticized synthetic and fast-drying fibres subsequently enabled more flexible swimsuits to be developed.

Body and spirit are twins: God only knows which is which:/ The soul squats down in the flesh, like a tinker drunk in a ditch.

Algernon Charles Swinburne
'The Higher Pantheism in a Nutshell' 1880

Swinburne Algernon Charles 1837–1909. English poet. He attracted attention with the choruses of his Greek-style tragedy *Atalanta in Calydon* 1865, but he and ◊Rossetti were attacked 1871 as leaders of 'the fleshly school of poetry', and the revolutionary politics of *Songs before Sunrise* 1871 alienated others.

swing music jazz style popular in the 1930s–40s, a big-band dance music with a simple harmonic base of varying tempo from the rhythm section (percussion, guitar, piano), harmonic brass and woodwind sections (sometimes strings), and superimposed solo melodic line from, for example, trumpet, clarinet, or saxophone. Exponents included Benny Goodman, Duke Ellington, and Glenn Miller, who introduced jazz to a mass white audience.

Swiss Family Robinson, The children's adventure story by Swiss author Johann Wyss, first published in German 1812–13 and expanded by subsequent editors and translators. Modelled on Defoe's *Robinson Crusoe*, it tells of a Swiss family shipwrecked on a desert island and the lessons taught to the children by their adventures there.

Sydney Opera House opera house designed by Danish architect Joern Utson (1918–), located on Bennelong Point, Sydney Harbour, and opened 1973. It is known for the billowing, white, sail-shaped shells that form the roof structure.

The design won an international competition 1955, but the building of the complex was beset by conflict and escalating costs which resulted in Utzon's resignation from the project 1968.

Sydow Max (Carl Adolf) von 1929– . Swedish actor of tall, cadaverous appearance, associated with the director Ingmar Bergman. He made his US debut as Jesus in *The Greatest Story Ever Told* 1965. His other films include *The Seventh Seal* 1957, *The Exorcist* 1973, *Hannah and Her Sisters* 1986, and *The Ox* 1991.

Symbolism late 19th-century movement in French poetry, which inspired a similar trend in French painting. The Symbolist poets used words for their symbolic rather than concrete meaning. Leading exponents were Paul Verlaine, Stéphane Mallarmé, and Arthur Rimbaud. The Symbolist painters rejected Realism and Impressionism, seeking to express moods and psychological states through colour, line, and form. Their subjects were often mythological, mystical, or fantastic. Gustave Moreau was a leading Symbolist painter. Other Symbolist painters included Puvis de Chavannes and Odilon Redon in France, Arnold Böcklin in Switzerland, and Edward Burne-Jones in Britain.

Symons Arthur 1865–1945. Welsh critic, follower of Walter ◊Pater, and friend of the artists Toulouse-Lautrec and Aubrey Beardsley, the poets Stéphane Mallarmé and W B Yeats, and the novelist Joseph Conrad. He introduced T S

Eliot to the poetry of Jules Laforgue and wrote *The Symbolist Movement in Literature* 1900.

It is the delight of the critic to praise; but praise is scarcely part of his duty ... What we ask of him is that he should find out for us more than we can find out for ourselves.

Arthur Symons

---

symphonic poem in music, a term originated by Franz Liszt for his 13 one-movement orchestral works that interpret a story from literature or history, also used by many other composers. Richard Strauss preferred the title 'tone poem'.

symphony abstract musical composition for orchestra, traditionally in four separate but closely related movements. It developed from the smaller ◊sonata form, the Italian ◊overture, and the ◊concerto grosso.

Haydn established the mature form of the symphony, written in slow, minuet, and allegro movements. Mozart and Beethoven (who replaced the ◊minuet with the ◊scherzo) expanded the form, which has since been modified and dramatized as quasi-programme music by Brahms, Tchaikovsky, Bruckner, Dvořák, Mahler, Sibelius, Vaughan Williams, Walter Piston, Prokofiev, Carl Nielsen, Shostakovich, Stravinsky, and Aaron Copland.

synaesthesia the experience of one sense as a result of the stimulation of a different sense; for example, an experience of colour may result from hearing a sound. This experience is sometimes imitated in the arts. The poet Baudelaire used the phrase 'scarlet fanfare', while composers, such as Scriabin and Schoenberg, asked for colours to be projected to accompany their works, for example, Scriabin's *Poem of Fire* 1913.

syncopation in music, the deliberate upsetting of rhythm by shifting the accent to a beat that is normally unaccented.

synergy (Greek 'combined action') in architecture, the augmented strength of systems, where the strength of a wall is greater than the added total of its individual units. Examples are the stone walls of early South American civilizations, which held together without cement or mortar.

Synge J(ohn) M(illington) 1871–1909. Irish dramatist, a leading figure in the Irish dramatic revival of the early 20th century. His six plays reflect the speech patterns of the Aran Islands and W Ireland. They include *In the Shadow of the Glen* 1903, *Riders to the Sea* 1904, and *The Playboy of the Western World* 1907, which caused riots at the Abbey Theatre, Dublin, when first performed.

Syntax, Dr fictional cleric invented by English writer William Combe (1741–1823), who appeared in a series of verse satires with drawings by Thomas ◊Rowlandson. The first was *Dr Syntax in Search of the Picturesque* 1809.

synthesizer musical device for the simulation of vocal or instrumental ◊timbre by mechanical or electro-acoustic means. The pipe organ was the first major synthesizer, allowing the mixture of timbres at the unison or harmonic intervals. Modern electrical synthesizers date from the Telharmonium 1904 of US inventor Thaddeus Cahill, incorporating the tone wheel, a programmable oscillator subsequently incorporated in the ◊Hammond organ. Later synthesizers include the analogue ◊trautonium, ◊ondes Martenot, ◊RCA Mark II Synthesizer, ◊Moog, ARP, and Synthi 100; and digital Fairlight, Synclavier, Roland, Oberheim, and Yamaha keyboards, and the ◊IRCAM 4X series synthesizer.

Synthi 100 computer-controlled analogue synthesizer developed 1972–75 by Peter Zinovieff (1934–   ) from his successful EMS briefcase synthesizer. It incorporates a sequencer which allows the continuous recycling of a series of values applicable to pitch, dynamics, or structural parameters.

Szymanowski Karol (Maciej) 1882–1937. Polish composer of piano music, violin concertos, four symphonies, a *Stabat Mater* 1926, and the opera *Król Roger/King Roger* 1918–24, in richly glamorous idiom drawing on national folklore and French impressionist style. He was director of the Conservatoire in Warsaw from 1926.

tabla pair of Indian tuned drums, one cylindrical, one bowl-shaped, played with the fingers and used to accompany the ◊sitar. They produce a clear, ringing sound and are responsible for maintaining the music's rhythmic identity or *tala*.

tablature in music, an old form of notation indicating finger positions on a graph representing the fingerboard and strings, and therefore specific only to the instrument to which it applies, for example, the lute, guitar, or ukelele.

tacet (Latin 'be silent') in written music, a score indication signifying that during a complete movement, or a specific section of a movement, an instrument is not required to play and therefore that no counting of bars will be necessary.

Tachisme (French 'blot, patch, or stain') French style of abstract painting current in the 1940s and 1950s, the European equivalent to ◊Abstract Expressionism. The Tachistes adopted a novel, spontaneous approach to brushwork, typified by all-over blotches of impastoed colour and dribbled paint, or swirling calligraphy applied straight from the tube, as in the work of Georges Mathieu (1921–). The terms *L'Art Informel*, meaning gestural or ◊action painting, and *abstraction lyrique* (lyrical abstraction) are also used to describe the style.

Tacitus Publius Cornelius *c.* AD 55–*c.* 120. Roman historian. A public orator in Rome, he was consul under Nerva 97–98 and proconsul of Asia 112–113. He wrote histories of the Roman Empire, *Annales* and *Historiae*, covering the years AD 14–68 and 69–97 respectively. He also wrote a *Life of Agricola* 97 (he married Agricola's daughter 77) and a description of the German tribes, *Germania* 98.

It is part of human nature to hate the man you have hurt.

Tacitus *Life of Agricola* AD 97

Tafelmusik (German 'table music') music for voices or instruments performed around a table, often as relaxation after a meal. A group or society of singers is called a *Liedertafel*.

taffeta (Persian 'spun') light, plain-weave fabric with a high lustre, originally silk but today also manufactured from artificial fibres.

Taglioni Marie 1804–1884. Italian dancer. A ballerina of ethereal style and exceptional lightness, she was the first to use ◊pointe work, or dancing on the toes, as an expressive part of ballet rather than as sheer technique. She created many roles, including the title role in *La Sylphide* 1832, first performed at the Paris Opéra, and choreographed by her father **Filippo** (1771–1871).

Tagore Rabindranath 1861–1941. Bengali Indian writer, born in Calcutta, who translated into English his own verse *Gitanjali* ('song offerings') 1912 and his verse play *Chitra* 1896. Nobel Prize for Literature 1913.

An ardent nationalist and advocate of social reform, he resigned his knighthood as a gesture of protest against British repression in India.

The butterfly counts not months but moments, and has time enough.

Rabindranath Tagore *Fireflies* 1928

Taine Hippolyte Adolphe 1828–1893. French critic and historian. He analysed literary works as products of period and environment, as in *Histoire de la littérature anglaise/History of English Literature* 1863 and *Philosophie de l'art/Philosophy of Art* 1865–69.

Taj Mahal white marble mausoleum built 1630–53 on the river Jumna near Agra, India. Erected by Shah Jahan to the memory of his favourite wife, it is a celebrated example of Indo-Islamic architecture, the fusion of Muslim and Hindu styles.

It took 20,000 workers to build the Taj Mahal, which has a central dome and minarets on each corner. Every façade is inlaid with semiprecious stones. Ransacked in the 18th century, it was restored in the early 20th century and is a symbol of India to the world.

Taliesin lived *c.* 550. Legendary Welsh poet, a bard at the court of the king of Rheged in Scotland. Taliesin allegedly died at Taliesin (named after him) in Dyfed, Wales.

Talking Heads US New Wave rock group formed 1975 in New York; disbanded 1991. Their nervy Minimalist music was inspired by African rhythms; albums include *More Songs About Buildings and Food* 1978, *Fear of Music* 1979, and *Naked* 1988.

All band members also recorded separately. The vocalist and songwriter, David Byrne (1952–   ), has composed avant-garde and ballet music, and made the film *True Stories* 1986; he has also toured with a Latin-American band. The bass player, Tina Weymouth (1950–   ), and drummer, Chris Frantz (1951–   ), have had hits as the Tom Tom Club.

Tallis Thomas *c.* 1505–1585. English composer, a master of ◊counterpoint. His works include *Tallis's Canon* ('Glory to thee my God this night') 1567, the antiphonal *Spem in alium non habui* (about 1573) for 40 voices in various groupings, and a collection of 34 motets, *Cantiones sacrae*, 1575 (of which 16 are by Tallis and 18 by Byrd). In 1575 Elizabeth I granted Tallis and Byrd the monopoly for printing music and music paper in England.

Talman William 1650–1719. English architect and contemporary of Christopher ◊Wren, to whom he is often compared, although Wren's output was significantly more accomplished and prolific. Influenced by French and Italian Baroque, Talman worked on Chatsworth House, Derbyshire, 1687–96, designing the east front and the monumental south front, which is characterized by severe rusticated ◊masonry and heavy keystones.

Tamayo Rufino 1899–1991. Mexican painter and printmaker whose work, nurtured by both European Modernism and pre-Columbian indigenous art, demonstrates a clear break with the rhetoric and pictoralism of the preceding generation of Mexican muralists. His mainly easel-sized paintings, with their vibrant colours and cryptic, semi-abstract figures, display strong Cubist, Expressionist, and Surrealist elements, as in *Women Reaching for the Moon* 1946 (Cleveland Museum of Art, Cleveland, Ohio).

tambourine musical percussion instrument of ancient origin, almost unchanged since Roman times, consisting of a shallow drum with a single skin and loosely set jingles in the rim that accentuate the beat.

tambura Indian plucked drone instrument which has four strings tuned by a movable bridge, providing an accompaniment for the ◊sitar.

Taming of the Shrew, The comedy by William ◊Shakespeare, first performed 1593–94. Bianca, who has many suitors, must not marry until her elder sister Katherina (the shrew) has done so. Petruchio agrees to woo Katherina so that his friend Hortensio may marry Bianca. Petruchio succeeds in 'taming' Katherina but Bianca marries another.

Tammuz in Sumerian mythology, a vegetation god, who died at midsummer and was brought back from the underworld in spring by his lover Ishtar. His cult spread over Babylonia, Syria, Phoenicia, and Palestine. In Greek mythology Tammuz appears as ◊Adonis.

Tange Kenzo 1913–   . Japanese Modernist architect. His works include the National Gymnasium, Tokyo, for the 1964 Olympics with its vast catenary steel roof, and the crescent-shaped city of Abuja, which replaced Lagos as the capital of Nigeria 1992. In 1991 he completed the 70-storey City Hall, Tokyo – Japan's tallest building.

tango dance for couples, of Latin-American origin, or the music for it. The dance consists of two long sliding steps followed by three short steps and stylized body positions.

Tanguy Yves 1900–1955. French Surrealist painter who lived in the USA from 1939. His inventive canvases feature semi-abstract creatures in a barren landscape.

Tanguy was first inspired to paint by the works of de ◊Chirico and in 1925 he joined the Surrealist movement. He soon developed his characteristic style with bizarre, slender forms in a typically Surrealist wasteland.

Tanizaki Jun-ichirō 1886–1965. Japanese novelist. His works include a version of ◊Murasaki's *The Tale of Genji* 1939–41, *The Makioka Sisters* in three volumes 1943–48, and *The Key* 1956.

Tanner Beatrice Stella. Unmarried name of actress Mrs Patrick ◊Campbell.

Tantalus in Greek mythology, a king who deceived the gods by serving them human flesh at a banquet. His crimes were punished in ◊Tartarus (a part of the underworld) by the provision of food and drink he could not reach. He was the father of ◊Pelops.

tap dancing rapid step dance, derived from clog dancing. Its main characteristic is the tapping of toes and heels accentuated by steel taps affixed to the shoes. It was popularized in vaudeville and in 1930s films by such dancers as Fred Astaire and Bill 'Bojangles' Robinson (1878–1949).

tape music music composed from tape-recorded material and reproducible only with the aid of audio equipment. It may include acoustic, ◊concrete, or synthesized elements. Tape music can be edited to create juxtaposition effects, composed direct to tape by layer-on-layer addition, and electronically treated and balanced.

tapestry ornamental woven textile used for wall hangings, furniture, and curtains. The tapestry design is threaded into the warp with various shades of yarn. The great European centres of tapestry weaving were in Belgium, France, and England. The ◊Bayeux Tapestry is an embroidery rather than a true tapestry.

Tapestries have been woven for centuries in many countries, and during the Middle Ages the art was practised in monasteries. European tapestries of the 13th century frequently featured Oriental designs brought back by the Crusaders. The ◊Gobelins tapestry factory of Paris was made a royal establishment in the 17th century. In England, William Morris established the Merton Abbey looms in the late 19th century. Other designers have included the painters Raphael, Rubens, and Burne-Jones.

Many fine tapestries are still made in France; for example, the tapestry designed by Graham Sutherland for Coventry Cathedral, which was made at Felletin, where tapestries have been woven since the 15th century.

Tàpies Antoni 1923– . Spanish abstract painter, noted for his highly textured paintings created from mixed media. In works such as *Large Brown Triangle* 1963 (Musée National d'Art Moderne, Centre Pompidou, Paris), he uses monochromatic, earthy tones and broken surfaces – either painted with graffiti or incised with a few lines – to express the passage of time and traces left by human beings.

His paintings of the late 1950s and early 1960s employ thick coatings of tar, bitumen, sand, and clay and such waste materials as wire, paper, rope, straw, and rags. In later works, real objects are affixed to the picture plane, such as mirrors and clothing, and assemblages created from furniture, for example *Wardrobe* 1973 (Fundación Antoni Tàpies, Barcelona).

tarantella peasant dance of southern Italy; also a piece of music composed for, or in the rhythm of, this dance, in fast 6/8 time.

Tarkington Booth 1869–1946. US novelist. His novels for young people, which include *Penrod* 1914, are classics. He was among the best-selling authors of the early 20th century with works such as *Monsieur Beaucaire* 1900 and novels of the Midwest, including *The Magnificent Ambersons* 1918 (filmed 1942 by Orson Welles).

Arguments only confirm people in their own opinions.

Booth Tarkington, *Looking Forward to the Great Adventure* 1926

Tarkovsky Andrei 1932–1986. Soviet film director whose work is characterized by an epic style combined with intense personal spirituality. His films include *Solaris* 1972, *Mirror* 1975, *Stalker* 1979, and *The Sacrifice* 1986.

Tarleton Richard died 1588. Elizabethan theatrical clown, the most celebrated of his time. A member of the Queen's Men theatre company from 1583, he was renowned for the jig, a doggerel song and dance routine, and for his extempore humour, which influenced some of the characters in Shakespeare's plays.

tarot cards fortune-telling aid consisting of 78 cards: the *minor arcana* in four suits (resembling playing cards) and the *major arcana*, 22 cards with densely symbolic illustrations that have links with astrology and the Kabbala, an ancient esoteric Jewish mystical tradition of philosophy.

history The earliest known reference to tarot cards is from 1392. The pack is of unknown (probably medieval) origin and may have been designed in Europe in the early 14th century as a repository of Gnostic ideas then being suppressed by the Christian Church. Since the 18th century the tarot has interested occult scholars.

tartan woollen cloth woven in specific chequered patterns individual to Scottish clans, with stripes of different widths and colours crisscrossing on a coloured background; used in making skirts, kilts, trousers, and other articles of clothing.

Tartarus in Greek mythology, a part of ◊Hades, the underworld, where the wicked were punished.

Tartini Giuseppe 1692–1770. Italian composer and violinist. In 1728 he founded a school of violin playing in Padua. A leading exponent of violin technique, he composed numerous sonatas and concertos for strings including the celebrated *Devil's Trill* sonata, about 1714.

Tartuffe comedy by ◊Molière 1664. A religious hypocrite, Tartuffe, dominates the household of the gullible Orgon. He is promised Orgon's daughter in marriage and given the deeds to Orgon's possessions but Tartuffe betrays himself by making sexual advances to Orgon's wife, Elmire. He is finally arrested on the intervention of the king of France.

Tarzan fictitious hero inhabiting the African rainforest, created by US writer Edgar Rice ◊Burroughs in *Tarzan of the Apes* 1914, with numerous sequels. He and his partner Jane have featured in films, comic strips, and television series.

Tarzan, raised by apes from infancy, is in fact a British peer, Lord Greystoke. He has enormous physical strength and the ability to communicate with animals. Jane Porter, an American, falls in love with him while on safari and elects to stay.

Me Tarzan, you Jane.

Edgar Rice Burroughs
Tarzan of the Apes

Tasso Torquato 1544–1595. Italian poet, author of the romantic epic poem of the First Crusade *Gerusalemme liberata/Jerusalem Delivered* 1574, followed by the *Gerusalemme conquistata/ Jerusalem Conquered*, written during the period from 1576 when he was mentally unstable.

At first a law student at Padua, he overcame his father's opposition to a literary career by the success of his romantic poem *Rinaldo* 1562, dedicated to Cardinal Luigi d'Este, who took him to Paris. There he met the members of the ◊*Pléiade* group of poets. Under the patronage of Duke Alfonso d'Este of Ferrara, he wrote his pastoral play *Aminta* 1573.

Compassion is the messenger of love,/ As lightning is of thunder.

Torquato Tasso *Aminta* 1573

Tate Jeffrey 1943– . English conductor, chief conductor and artistic director of the Rotterdam Philharmonic Orchestra from 1991. He assisted at Covent Garden 1970–77 and under Boulez at Bayreuth 1976 before making a remarkable operatic debut at the New York Metropolitan Opera 1980 with Berg's expressionist masterpiece *Lulu*. Principal conductor of the English Chamber Orchestra 1985, principal conductor of the Royal Opera House, Covent Garden, 1986–91, and principal guest conductor since 1991, he has specialized in Mozart symphonies and piano concertos, the latter with his wife Mitsuko Uchida as soloist.

Tate Nahum 1652–1715. Irish poet, born in Dublin. He wrote an adaptation of Shakespeare's *King Lear* with a happy ending. He also produced a version of the psalms and hymns; among his poems is 'While shepherds watched'. He became British poet laureate 1692.

As pants the hart for cooling streams/ When heated in the chase.

Nahum Tate and **Nicholas Brady**
The Psalms

Tate Gallery art gallery in London, housing British art from the late 16th century, and international art from 1810. Endowed by the sugar merchant Henry Tate (1819–1899), it was opened 1897.

It was enlarged by Sir J Duveen (1843–1908) and his son Lord Duveen of Millbank (1869–1939); later extensions include the Clore Gallery for Turner paintings, opened 1987. A Liverpool branch of the Tate Gallery opened 1988.

Tati Jacques. Stage name of Jacques Tatischeff 1908–1982. French comic actor, director, and writer. He portrayed Monsieur Hulot, the embodiment of polite opposition to modern mechanization, in a series of films beginning with *Les Vacances de M Hulot/Monsieur Hulot's Holiday*

1953, and including *Mon Oncle/My Uncle* 1959 and *Playtime* 1968.

Tatlin Vladimir 1885–1953. Russian artist, a cofounder of ◊Constructivism. After encountering Cubism in Paris 1913 he evolved his first Constructivist works, using raw materials such as tin, glass, plaster, and wood to create abstract sculptures that he suspended in the air. He worked as a stage designer 1933–52.

Although unbuilt, his design for a monument to the Third International 1919 came to symbolize the Constructivist style: a large, openwork, spiralling tower of glass and painted steel, with geometrical shapes revolving within its central core.

tatting lacework in cotton, made since medieval times by knotting and looping a single thread with a small shuttle.

Tatum Art(hur) 1910–1956. US jazz pianist who, in the 1930s, worked mainly as a soloist. Tatum is considered among the most technically brilliant of jazz pianists and his technique and chromatic harmonies influenced many musicians, such as Oscar Peterson (1925–). He improvised with the guitarist Tiny Grimes (1916–) in a trio from 1943.

Tavener John (Kenneth) 1944– . English composer of austere vocal works including the dramatic cantata *The Whale* 1968 and the opera *Thérèse* 1979. *The Protecting Veil*, composed 1987 for cello and strings alone, became a best-selling classical recording in the early 1990s. Tavener draws on Eastern European idioms and Orthodox Christian traditions; he described his chamber opera *Mary of Egypt* 1991, premiered at Aldeburgh 1992, as 'a moving icon'.

Taverner John 1495–1545. English organist and composer. He wrote masses and motets in polyphonic style, showing great contrapuntal skill, but as a Protestant renounced his art. He was imprisoned 1528 for heresy, and, as an agent of Thomas Cromwell, assisted in the dissolution of the monasteries.

Taylor C(ecil) P(hilip) 1929–1981. Scottish dramatist. His stage plays include *Bread and Butter* 1966, *And a Nightingale Sang...* 1979, and *Good* 1981, a study of intellectual complicity in Nazi Germany. His work was produced firstly by the Traverse Theatre in Edinburgh; he also wrote extensively for television and radio.

Taylor Elizabeth 1932– . English-born US actress, one of the most glamorous stars of the 1950s and 1960s, who graduated from juvenile leads to dramatic roles. Her films include *National Velvet* 1944, *Cat on a Hot Tin Roof* 1958, *BUtterfield 8* 1960 (Academy Award), *Cleopatra* 1963, and *Who's Afraid of Virginia Woolf?* 1966 (Academy Award).

Taylor Elizabeth (born Coles) 1912–1975. English novelist. Her books include *At Mrs*

Lippincote's 1946 and *Angel* 1957. She is a shrewd observer of nuances of character and emotion.

Taylor Paul 1930– . US choreographer and dancer, whose work often displays charm, musicality, and humour. Among his works are *Aureole* 1962 and *Esplanade* 1975. He danced with Merce Cunningham (1953–54) and Martha Graham (1958–62) before founding his own modern dance company 1954.

Taylor Robert 1714–1788. English Palladian architect and sculptor, immensely successful during his lifetime, although little of his work has survived. Stone Building in Lincoln's Inn Fields, London, 1775, is the finest extant example.

Tchaikovsky Pyotr Il'yich 1840–1893. Russian composer. His strong sense of melody, personal expression, and brilliant orchestration are clear throughout his many Romantic works, which include six symphonies, three piano concertos, a violin concerto, operas (for example, *Eugene Onegin* 1879), ballets (for example, *The Nutcracker* 1891–92), orchestral fantasies (for example, *Romeo and Juliet* 1870), and chamber and vocal music.

Professor of harmony at Moscow 1865, he later met Balakirev, becoming involved with the nationalist movement in music. He was the first Russian composer to establish a reputation with Western audiences.

Since I began to compose I have made it my object to be, in my craft, what the most illustrious masters were in theirs, that is to say... an artisan, just as a shoemaker is.

Pyotr Tchaikovsky

Teague Walter Dorwin 1883–1960. US pioneer industrial designer of the 1930s, active in New York. His first client was Eastman Kodak and he is best known for his redesign of Kodak's 'Box Brownie' camera 1934 and his remodelling of Texaco's gas stations at the end of the decade, both in the popular ◊'streamline' style of the day. He is often called the 'Dean of industrial design', implying his leadership in the field.

Tebaldi Renata 1922– . Italian dramatic soprano, renowned for the nobility and warmth of her roles in Puccini operas.

Technicolor trade name for a film colour process using three separate negatives of blue, green, and red images. It was invented by Daniel F Comstock and Herbert T Kalmus in the USA 1922. Originally, Technicolor was a two-colour process in which superimposed red and green images were projected on to the screen by a special projector. This initial version proved expensive and imperfect, but when the three-colour process was introduced 1932, the system was widely adopted, culminating in its use in *The Wizard of Oz* and *Gone With the Wind*, both 1939. Technicolor remains the most commonly used colour process for cinematography.

techno dance music in Minimalist style played on electronic instruments, created with extensive use of studio technology for a futuristic, machine-made sound, sometimes with sampled soul vocals. The German band Kraftwerk (formed 1970) is an early example, and Germany continued to produce some of the best techno records in the 1990s.

Te Kanawa Kiri 1944– . New Zealand soprano. Te Kanawa's first major role was the Countess in Mozart's *The Marriage of Figaro* at Covent Garden, London, 1971. Her voice combines the purity and intensity of the upper range with an extended lower range of great richness and resonance. Apart from classical roles, she has also featured popular music in her repertoire, such as the 1984 recording of Leonard Bernstein's *West Side Story*.

Telemachus in Greek mythology, son of ◊Odysseus and ◊Penelope. He attempted to control the conduct of his mother's suitors in Homer's *Odyssey* while his father was believed dead, but on Odysseus' return helped him to kill them, with the support of the goddess ◊Athena.

Telemann Georg Philipp 1681–1767. German Baroque composer, organist, and conductor at the Johanneum, Hamburg, from 1721. His prolific output of concertos for both new and old instruments, including violin, viola da gamba, recorder, flute, oboe, trumpet, horn, and bassoon, represent a methodical and fastidious investigation into the tonal resources and structure of the new Baroque orchestra, research noted by J S Bach. Other works include 25 operas, numerous sacred cantatas, and instrumental fantasias.

telephoto lens photographic lens of longer focal length than normal that takes a very narrow view and gives a large image through a combination of telescopic and ordinary photographic lenses.

Tell Wilhelm (William) legendary 14th-century Swiss archer, said to have refused to salute the Habsburg badge at Altdorf on Lake Lucerne. Sentenced to shoot an apple from his son's head, he did so, then shot the tyrannical Austrian ruler Gessler, symbolizing his people's refusal to submit to external authority.

The first written account of the legend dates from 1474, the period of the wars of the Swiss against Charles the Bold of Burgundy; but the story of a man showing his skill with the crossbow in such a way is much earlier. The legend has been used for plays (◊Schiller, 1804) and an opera (◊Rossini, 1829), as well as in filmed versions.

Tellus in Roman mythology, the goddess of the Earth, identified with a number of other agricultural gods and celebrations.

tempera painting medium in which powdered pigments are mixed with a water-soluble binding agent such as egg yolk. Tempera is noted for its strong, translucent colours. A form of tempera was used in ancient Egypt, and egg tempera was the foremost medium for panel painting in late medieval and early Renaissance Europe. It was gradually superseded by oils from the late 15th century onwards. In the 20th century it has been used by US painter Andrew Wyeth.

temperament in music, a system of tuning ('tempering') the ◊pitches of a ◊mode or ◊scale whereby ◊intervals are lessened or enlarged, away from the 'natural'. In folk music this is done to preserve its emotional or ritual meaning, in Western music to allow a measure of freedom in changing key. J S Bach composed *The Well-Tempered Clavier*, a sequence of 48 preludes and fugues in every key of the ◊chromatic scale, to demonstrate the superior versatility of tempered tuning.

Tempest, The romantic drama by William ◊Shakespeare, first performed 1611–12. Prospero, usurped as Duke of Milan by his brother Antonio, lives on a remote island with his daughter Miranda and Caliban, a deformed creature. Prospero uses magic to shipwreck Antonio and his party on the island and, with the help of the spirit Ariel, regains his dukedom.

O brave new world,/ That has such people in't.

William Shakespeare *The Tempest*

Temple Shirley 1928– . US actress who became the most successful child star of the 1930s. Her films include *Bright Eyes* 1934 (Academy Award), in which she sang 'On the Good Ship Lollipop', *Curly Top* 1935, and *Rebecca of Sunnybrook Farm* 1938. Her film career virtually ended by the time she reached adolescence. As Shirley Temple Black, she became active in the Republican Party and was US chief of protocol 1976–77. She was appointed US ambassador to Czechoslovakia 1989.

tempo (Italian 'time') in music, the speed at which a piece should sound. Objectively, tempo corresponds to the repetition rate of an underlying beat, as established by the metronome. Subjectively, and in practice, tempo involves a balance of the mechanical beat value against the expressive demands of melody and rhythm.

Teniers family of Flemish painters, active in Antwerp. *David Teniers the Younger* (David

II, 1610–1690) became court painter to Archduke Leopold Wilhelm, governor of the Netherlands, in Brussels. He painted humorous scenes of peasant life, full of vitality, inspired by ◊Brouwer. As curator of the archduke's art collection, he made many copies of the pictures and a collection of engravings, *Theatrum Pictorium* 1660. His father, **David Teniers the Elder** (David I, 1582–1649), painted religious pictures.

Tenniel John 1820–1914. English illustrator and cartoonist, known for his illustrations for Lewis Carroll's *Alice's Adventures in Wonderland* 1865 and *Through the Looking-Glass* 1872. He joined the satirical magazine *Punch* 1850, and for over 50 years was one of its leading cartoonists.

Tennstedt Klaus 1926– . German conductor, musical director of the London Philharmonic Orchestra 1983–87, and noted interpreter of Mozart, Beethoven, Bruckner, and Mahler.

Tennyson Alfred, 1st Baron Tennyson 1809–1892. English poet, poet laureate 1850–92, whose verse has a majestic, musical quality. His works include 'The Lady of Shalott', 'The Lotus Eaters', 'Ulysses', 'Break, Break, Break', 'The Charge of the Light Brigade'; the longer narratives *Locksley Hall* 1832 and *Maud* 1855; the elegy *In Memoriam* 1850; and a long series of poems on the Arthurian legends *The Idylls of the King* 1857–85.

Tennyson was born at Somersby, Lincolnshire. The death of A H Hallam (a close friend during his years at Cambridge) 1833 prompted the elegiac *In Memoriam*, unpublished until 1850, the year in which he succeeded Wordsworth as poet laureate and married Emily Sellwood.

No life that breathes with human breath/ Has ever truly long'd for death.

Alfred, 1st Baron Tennyson
'The Two Voices'

---

tenor in music, the highest range of adult male voice when not using ◊falsetto, approximately C3–A5. It is the preferred voice for operatic heroic roles. Exponents are Luciano ◊Pavarotti and José ◊Carreras.

Terborch Gerard 1617–1681. Dutch painter of small-scale portraits and genre scenes, mainly of soldiers at rest or wealthy families in their homes. He travelled widely in Europe. *The Peace of Münster* 1648 (National Gallery, London) is an official group portrait.

Terbrugghen Hendrick *c.* 1588–*c.* 1629. Dutch painter, a leader of the **Utrecht School** with Honthorst. He visited Rome around 1604 and was one of the first northern artists to be inspired by the works of Caravaggio. He painted religious subjects and genre scenes.

Terence (Publius Terentius Afer) 190–159 BC. Roman dramatist, born in Carthage and taken as a slave to Rome, where he was freed and came under the patronage of the Roman general Scipio Africanus Minor. His surviving six comedies (including *The Eunuch* 161 BC) are subtly characterized and based on Greek models. They were widely read and performed during the Middle Ages and the Renaissance.

I am a man, I count nothing human foreign to me.

Terence *Heauton Timorumenos*
163 BC

---

term in architecture, a pillar in the form of a pedestal supporting the bust of a human or animal figure. Such objects derive from Roman boundary marks sacred to *Terminus*, the god of boundaries.

Terminus in Roman mythology, the god of land boundaries whose worship was associated with that of ◊Jupiter in his temple on the Roman Capitol. His feast day was Feb 23.

ternary form in music, a three-part form of which the outer parts form a near-symmetrical pair separated by a contrasting middle section.

Terpsichore in Greek mythology, the ◊Muse of dance and choral song.

terracotta (Italian 'baked earth') brownish-red baked clay, usually unglazed, used in building, sculpture, and pottery. The term is specifically applied to small figures or figurines, such as those found at Tanagra in central Greece. Excavations at Xian, China, have revealed life-size terracotta figures of the army of the Emperor Shi Huangdi dating from the 3rd century BC.

Terragni Giuseppe 1904–1942. Italian architect, largely responsible for introducing the ◊Modern Movement to Italy. As a leading member of *Gruppo* 7, he supported ◊Rationalism. Notable among his designs are the Novecomum block of flats, Como, 1927, and his masterpiece, the Casa del Fascio, Como, 1932–36, a crystalline white cube, devoid of ornament but clearly exhibiting its structure.

Terry (John) Quinlan 1937– . British Post-Modernist architect working in a Neo-Classical idiom. His projects include country houses, for example Merks Hall, Great Dunmow, Essex, 1982, and the larger-scale riverside project at Richmond, London, commissioned 1984.

Terry Ellen 1847–1928. English actress, leading lady to Henry ◊Irving from 1878. She excelled in

Shakespearean roles, such as Ophelia in *Hamlet*. She was a correspondent of long standing with the dramatist G B Shaw.

Terry-Thomas stage name of Thomas Terry Hoar Stevens 1911–1990. British film comedy actor who portrayed upper-class English fools and cads in such films as *I'm All Right Jack* 1959, *It's a Mad, Mad, Mad, Mad World* 1963, and *How to Murder Your Wife* 1965.

terza rima poetical metre used in Dante's *Divine Comedy*, consisting of three-line stanzas in which the second line rhymes with the first and third of the following stanza. The English poet Shelley's 'Ode to the West Wind' is an English example.

Tess of the d'Urbervilles novel 1891 by Thomas ◊Hardy. The story tells of the destruction of Tess Durbeyfield, 'a pure women', by the fecklessness of her once-powerful family, one man's sexual predatoriness, and the self-deluding idealism of the man she loves. Tess finally kills her seducer and is condemned to death herself. The novel contains some of Hardy's most memorable depictions of human beings at the mercy of malevolent fate.

Tethys in Greek mythology, one of the ◊Titans, the wife of the god ◊Oceanus.

Tetley Glen 1926– . US choreographer and dancer. He was one of the first choreographers to attempt the blending of ballet with modern dance, as in his first major work, *Pierrot lunaire* 1962, set to Schoenberg. Closely associated with the Netherlands Dance Theatre throughout the 1960s, he became director of Stuttgart Ballet 1974–76, and often worked with the Ballet Rambert, as with his *The Tempest* 1979. His ballets include *The Anatomy Lesson* 1964, *Mutations* 1970 (with Hans van Manen), and *Summer's End* 1980. He became associate artistic adviser to the National Ballet of Canada 1987.

Tex-Mex mix of Texan and Mexican cultural elements in the southwest USA and Mexico; specifically, accordion-based dance music originating in Texas among the ethnic Mexican community. The accordionist Flaco Jimenez (1939–) and the band Los Lobos (1974–), among others, have popularized the genre beyond Texas.

textile (Latin *texere* 'to weave') woven fabric; formerly a material woven from natural spun thread, now loosely extended to machine knits and spun-bonded fabrics (in which a web of fibre is created and then fuse-bonded by passing it through controlled heat).

natural Textiles made from natural fibres include cotton, linen, silk, and wool (including angora, llama, and many others). For particular qualities, such as flame resistance or water and stain repellence, these may be combined with synthetic fibres or treated with various chemicals.

synthetic The first commercial synthetic thread was 'artificial silk', or rayon, with filaments made from modified cellulose (wood pulp) and known according to later methods of manufacture as *viscose* (using caustic soda and carbon disulphide) or *acetate* (using acetic acid); the first fully synthetic textile fibre was *nylon* 1937. These, with *acrylics*, such as Orlon, used in knitwear, *polyesters*, such as Terylene, and *spandex* or *elastomeric fibres*, for example Lycra, form the basis of most of today's industry. *geotextiles* These are made from plastic and synthetic fibres; either felted for use as filters or stabilizing grids, or woven for strength. They form part of drainage systems, road foundations, and barriers to sea and river defences against erosion.

The oldest known British textile is a fabric woven from flax found in the Orkney Islands and dating from about 2000 BC.

Teyte Maggie 1888–1976. British lyric soprano who brought a French intimacy of style to her Mozartian roles, such as Cherubino in *The Marriage of Figaro*, and was coached as Mélisande in *Pelléas et Mélisande* by the opera's composer, Debussy.

Thackeray William Makepeace 1811–1863. English novelist and essayist, born in Calcutta, India. He was a regular contributor to *Fraser's Magazine* and *Punch*. ◊*Vanity Fair* 1847–48 was his first novel, followed by *Pendennis* 1848, *Henry Esmond* 1852 (and its sequel *The Virginians* 1857–59), and *The Newcomes* 1853–55, in which Thackeray's tendency to sentimentality is most marked.

Son of an East India Company official, he was educated at Cambridge. He studied law, and then art in Paris, before ultimately becoming a journalist in London. Other works include *The Book of Snobs* 1848 and the fairy tale *The Rose and the Ring* 1855.

I think I could be a good woman if I had five thousand a year.

William Makepeace Thackeray
Vanity Fair

Thalberg Irving Grant 1899–1936. US film-production executive. At the age of 20 he was head of production at Universal Pictures, and in 1924 he became production supervisor of the newly formed Metro-Goldwyn-Mayer (MGM). He was responsible for such prestige films as *Ben-Hur* 1926 and *Mutiny on the Bounty* 1935. With Louis B Mayer he built up MGM into one of the biggest Hollywood studios of the 1930s.

Thalia in Greek mythology, the ◊Muse of comedy and pastoral poetry.

thalumeau short thickset double-reed wind instrument, ancester of the ◊clarinet. It is also the term used to describe the dark lowest register of clarinet tone.

Tharp Twyla 1941– . US modern-dance choreographer and dancer. A phenomenal success in the 1970s, Tharp's work both entertains and challenges audiences with her ability to construct serious and beautifully crafted ballets with an often amusing or flippant veneer. She has fused many dance styles including ballet, jazz, modern, tap, and avant-garde dance. Her works, frequently to set to popular music, include *Eight Jelly Rolls* 1971, *Deuce Coupe* 1973 (music by the Beach Boys), and *Push Comes to Shove* 1976 with Mikhail Baryshnikov, which was one of the most popular works of the decade. *The Catherine Wheel* 1983 was set to music by David Byrne (of ◊Talking Heads).

thaumatrope in photography, a disc with two different pictures at opposite ends of its surface. The images combine into one when rapidly rotated because of the persistence of visual impressions.

theatre performance by actors for an audience; it may include ◊drama, dancing, music, ◊mime, and ◊puppets. The term is also used for the place or building in which dramatic performances take place. Theatre history can be traced to Egyptian religious ritualistic drama as long ago as 3200 BC. The first known European theatres were in Greece from about 600 BC.

history The earliest Greek theatres were open spaces, possibly associated with the worship of the god Dionysus. The great theatre of Dionysus at Athens provided for an audience of 15,000–20,000 people sitting in tiers on the surrounding slopes. Facing this banked auditorium was a scene-building, built originally of wood and then reconstructed in stone *c.* 340 BC. The design served as a model for the theatres that were erected in all the main cities of the Graeco-Roman world. Examples of Roman theatres exist at Orange, France, St Albans, England, and elsewhere. After the collapse of the Roman Empire the theatres fell into disuse.

In medieval times, temporary stages of wood and canvas, some mounted on pageant wagons, were set up side by side in fairgrounds and market squares for the performance of mimes and ◊miracle plays. Small enclosed theatres were built in the 16th century, for example in Vicenza, Italy (by the architect Palladio). The first London theatre was built in Shoreditch 1576 by James Burbage, who also opened the first covered theatre in London, the Blackfriars, 1596. His son, Cuthbert Burbage, was responsible for building the ◊Globe Theatre, the venue for Shakespeare's plays. The tradition of open-air performances was continued in the Italian ◊commedia dell'arte, originating in the 16th century. In the 17th and 18th centuries most theatrical productions were performed indoors under licence, until the greater commercialization of the 19th century.

theatre: chronology

c. 3200 BC	Beginnings of Egyptian religious drama, essentially ritualistic.
c. 600 BC	Choral performances (dithyrambs) in honour of Dionysus formed the beginnings of Greek tragedy, according to Aristotle.
500–300 BC	Great age of Greek drama which included tragedy, comedy, and satyr plays (grotesque farce).
468 BC	Sophocles' first victory at the Athens festival. His use of a third actor altered the course of the tragic form.
458 BC	Aeschylus' *Oresteia* first performed.
c. 425–388 BC	Comedies of Aristophanes including *The Birds* 414, *Lysistrata* 411, and *The Frogs* 405. In tragedy the importance of the chorus diminished under Euripides, author of *The Bacchae c.* 405.
c. 320 BC	Menander's 'New Comedy' of social manners developed.
c. 240 BC–AD 100	Emergence of Roman drama, adapted from Greek originals. Plautus, Terence, and Seneca were the main dramatists.
c. AD 400	Kālidāsa's *Sakuntalā* marked the height of Sanskrit drama in India.
c. 1250–1500	European mystery (or miracle) plays flourished, first in the churches, later in marketplaces, and were performed in England by town guilds.
c. 1375	Nō (or Noh) drama developed in Japan.
c. 1495	*Everyman*, the best known of all the morality plays, was first performed.
1525–1750	Italian commedia dell'arte troupes performed popular, improvised comedies; they were to have a large influence on Molière and on English harlequinade and pantomime.
c. 1540	Nicholas Udall wrote *Ralph Roister Doister*, the first English comedy.
c. 1576	The first English playhouse, The Theatre, was built by James Burbage in London.
c. 1587	Christopher Marlowe's play *Tamburlaine the Great* marked the beginning of the great age of Elizabethan and Jacobean drama in England.
c. 1588	Thomas Kyd's play *The Spanish Tragedy* was the first of the 'revenge' tragedies.
c. 1590–1612	Shakespeare's greatest plays, including *Hamlet* and *King Lear*, were written.
1604	Inigo Jones designed *The Masque of Blackness* for James I, written by Ben Jonson.
c. 1614	Lope de Vega's *Fuenteovejuna* marked the Spanish renaissance in drama. Other writers include Calderón de la Barca.
1636	Pierre Corneille's *Le Cid* established classical tragedy in France.
1642	An act of Parliament closed all English theatres.
1660	With the restoration of Charles II to the English throne, dramatic performances recommenced. The first professional actress appeared as Desdemona in Shakespeare's *Othello*.
1664	Molière's *Tartuffe* was banned for five years by religious factions.
1667	Jean Racine's first success, *Andromaque*, was staged.
1680	The Comédie Française was formed by Louis XIV.
1700	William Congreve, the greatest exponent of Restoration comedy, wrote *The Way of the World*.
1716	The first known American theatre was built in Williamsburg, Virginia.
1728	John Gay's *The Beggar's Opera* was first performed.
1737	The Stage Licensing Act in England required all plays to be approved by the Lord Chamberlain before performance.
1747	The actor David Garrick became manager of the Drury Lane Theatre, London.
1773	In England, Oliver Goldsmith's *She Stoops to Conquer* and Richard Sheridan's *The Rivals* 1775 established the 'comedy of manners'. Goethe's *Götz von Berlichingen* was the first *Sturm und Drang* play (literally, storm and stress).
1781	Friedrich Schiller's *Die Räuber/The Robbers*.
1784	Beaumarchais' *Le Mariage de Figaro/The Marriage of Figaro* (written 1778) was first performed.
1830	Victor Hugo's *Hernani* caused riots in Paris. His work marked the beginning of a new Romantic drama, changing the course of French theatre.
1878	Henry Irving became actor-manager of the Lyceum with Ellen Terry as leading lady.
1879	Henrik Ibsen's *The Doll's House*, an early example of realism in European theatre.
1888	August Strindberg wrote *Miss Julie*.
1893	George Bernard Shaw wrote *Mrs Warren's Profession* (banned until 1902 because it deals with prostitution). Shaw's works brought the new realistic drama to Britain and introduced social and political issues as subjects for the theatre.
1895	Oscar Wilde's comedy *The Importance of Being Earnest*.
1896	The first performance of Anton Chekhov's *The Seagull* failed. Alfred Jarry's *Ubu Roi*, a forerunner of Surrealism, was produced in Paris
1904	Chekhov's *The Cherry Orchard*. The Academy of Dramatic Art (Royal Academy of Dramatic Art 1920) was founded in London to train young actors. The Abbey Theatre, Dublin, opened by W B Yeats and Lady Gregory, marked the beginning of an Irish dramatic revival.
1919	The Theater Guild was founded in the USA to perform less commercial new plays.
1920	*Beyond the Horizon*, Eugene O'Neill's first play, marked the beginning of serious theatre in the USA.
1921	Luigi Pirandello's *Six Characters in Search of an Author* introduced themes of the individual and exploration of reality and appearance.
1927	*Show Boat*, composed by Jerome Kern with libretto by Oscar Hammerstein II, laid the foundations of the US musical.
1928	Bertolt Brecht's *Die Dreigroschenoper/The Threepenny Opera* with score by Kurt Weill; other political satires by Karel Capek and Elmer Rice. In the USA, musical comedies by Cole Porter, Irving Berlin, and George Gershwin, were popular.

(cont.)

theatre: chronology (*cont.*)	
1930s	US social-protest plays of Clifford Odets, Lillian Hellman, Thornton Wilder, and William Saroyan.
1935	T S Eliot's *Murder in the Cathedral*.
1935–39	WPA Federal Theater Project in the USA.
1938	Publication of Antonin Artaud's *Theatre and Its Double*.
1943	The first of the Rodgers and Hammerstein musicals, *Oklahoma!*, opened.
1944	Jean-Paul Sartre's *Huis Clos/In Camera*; Jean Anouilh's *Antigone*.
post-1945	Resurgence of German-language theatre, including Wolfgang Borchert, Max Frisch, Friedrich Dürrenmatt, and Peter Weiss.
1947	Tennessee Williams' *A Streetcar Named Desire*. First Edinburgh Festival, Scotland, with fringe theatre events.
1949	Bertolt Brecht and Helene Weigel founded the Berliner Ensemble in East Germany.
1953	Arthur Miller's *The Crucible* opened in the USA; *En attendant Godot/Waiting for Godo '* by Samuel Beckett exemplified the Theatre of the Absurd.
1956	The English Stage Company was formed at the Royal Court Theatre to provide a platform for new dramatists. John Osborne's *Look Back in Anger* was included in its first season.
1957	Leonard Bernstein's *West Side Story* opened in New York.
1960	Harold Pinter's *The Caretaker* was produced in London.
1960s	Off-off-Broadway theatre, a more daring and experimental type of drama, began to develop in New York. Fringe theatre developed in Britain.
1961	The Royal Shakespeare Company was formed in the UK under the directorship of Peter Hall.
1963–64	The UK National Theatre Company was formed at the Old Vic under the directorship of Laurence Olivier.
1964	Théâtre du Soleil, directed by Ariane Mnouchkine, founded in Paris.
1967	Athol Fugard founded the Serpent Players as an integrated company in Port Elizabeth, South Africa; success in the USA of *Hair*, the first of the 'rock' musicals; Tom Stoppard's *Rosencrantz and Guildenstern are Dead* was produced in London.
1968	Abolition of pre-censorship theatre in the UK.
1970	Peter Brook founded his international company, the International Centre for Theatre Research, in Paris; first festival of Chicano theatre in the USA.
1970s	Women's theatre movement developed in the USA and Europe.
1972	Sam Shepherd's *The Tooth of Crime* performed in London.
1974	Athol Fugard's *Statements after an Arrest under the Immorality Act* performed in London.
1975	*A Chorus Line*, to become the longest-running musical, opened in New York; Tadeusz Kantor's *Dead Class* produced in Poland.
1980	Howard Brenton's *The Romans in Britain* led in the UK to a private prosecution of the director for obscenity; David Edgar's *The Life and Times of Nicholas Nickleby* performed in London.
1985	Peter Brook's first production of *The Mahābhārata* produced at the Avignon Festival.
1987	The Japanese Ninagawa Company performed Shakespeare's *Macbeth* in London.
1989	Discovery of the remains of the 16th-century Rose and Globe theatres, London.
1990	The Royal Shakespeare Company suspended its work at the Barbican Centre, London, for six months, pleading lack of funds.
1992	Ariane Mnouchkine's production of *Les Atrides* performed in Paris and the UK; Robert Wilson's production of *Alice* performed in Germany.

In the USA the centre of commercial theatre in the 20th century has been New York City, with numerous theatres on or near ◊Broadway, although Williamsburg, Virginia (1716), and Philadelphia (1766) had the first known American theatres. The 'little theatres', off-Broadway, developed to present less commercial productions, often by new dramatists, and of these the first was the Theater Guild (1919); off-off-Broadway then developed as ◊fringe theatre (alternative theatre).

In Britain repertory theatres (theatres running a different play every few weeks) proliferated until World War II; for example, the ◊Old Vic, and in Ireland the ◊Abbey Theatre became the first state-subsidized theatre 1924. The ◊Comédie Française in Paris (founded by Louis XIV 1680 and given a permanent home 1792) was the first national theatre. In Britain the ◊National Theatre company was established 1963; other national theatres exist in Stockholm, Moscow, Athens, Copenhagen, Vienna, Warsaw, and elsewhere. Although the repertory movement declined from the 1950s with the spread of cinema and television, a number of regional community theatres developed. Recently established theatres are often associated with a university or are part of a larger cultural centre.

Historic London theatres include the Haymarket (1720, rebuilt 1821), Drury Lane (1663), and Her Majesty's (1705), both rebuilt several times. The English Stage Company was established at the Royal Court Theatre 1956 to provide a platform for new works.

It is the destiny of the theater nearly everywhere and in every period to struggle even when it is flourishing.

Howard Taubman on the theatre

Théâtre de Complicité English touring company, specializing in theatre using mime techniques, founded 1983. Notable productions have included Dürrenmatt's *The Visit* 1988–89; a devised show *The Street of Crocodiles* 1992, based on the writings of Bruno Schulz; and, for television, *Burning Ambition* 1988.

theatre-in-the-round theatrical performance that has the audience watching from all sides. In a reaction to the picture-frame stage of the 19th century, a movement began in the mid-20th century to design theatres with the performing area placed centrally in the auditorium. Notable examples are The Arena Stage in Washington, DC, USA, 1961 and the Royal Exchange in Manchester, England, 1976.

The concept was promoted in productions by Margo Jones (1913–1955) in Dallas, USA, who wrote a book on her work *Theater-in-the-Round* 1951.

Theatre Museum museum housing memorabilia from the worlds of the theatre, opera, ballet, dance, circus, puppetry, pop, and rock and roll. It opened in Covent Garden, London, 1987.

theme in music, a basic melody or musical figure, which often occurs with variations.

Themis in Greek mythology, one of the ◊Titans, the daughter of Uranus and Gaia. She was the personification of law and order.

Theocritus *c.* 310–*c.* 250 BC. Greek poet whose *Idylls* became models for later pastoral poetry. Probably born in Syracuse, he spent much of his life in Alexandria under the Greek dynasty of the Ptolemies.

theogony (Greek 'birth of the gods') in Greek mythology, an account of the origin of the gods, conceived largely in terms of human reproduction. The Greek poet ◊Hesiod wrote a *Theogony*, which was in effect a genealogy of the Greek pantheon.

Theophanes the Greek 14th century. Byzantine painter active in Russia. He influenced painting in Novgorod, where his frescoes in the church of Our Saviour of the Transfiguration are dated to 1378. He also worked in Moscow with Andrei ◊Rublev.

Theophrastus about 370–about 285 BC. Greek philosopher, a pupil of Aristotle. Of his extensive writings, surviving work is mainly on botany and other scientific topics, but includes the *Characters*, a series of caricatures which may have influenced the comic dramatist ◊Menander.

theorbo bass ◊lute or archlute developed around 1500 and incorporating dual sets of strings, a set of freely vibrating bass strings for plucking with the thumb in addition to five to seven courses over a fretted fingerboard. It survived to form part of the Italian Baroque orchestra about 1700.

theremin early electronic musical instrument invented by Leon Theremin 1922. It uses ◊beat frequency generation between two high frequency oscillators, one signal of which is fixed, the other variable by moving a hand in the vicinity of an aerial. Its monophonic sound is voice-like in the soprano register, and trombone-like at a lower pitch.

Theremin Leon 1896– . Russian inventor of the theremin 1922, a monophonic synthesizer, and of other valve-amplified instruments in the 1930s. Following commercial and public success in the USA and Hollywood, he returned to Russia 1938 to imprisonment and obscurity. After 1945 he continued acoustic research in Moscow.

Theroux Paul (Edward) 1941– . US novelist and travel writer. His works include the novels *Saint Jack* 1973, *The Mosquito Coast* 1981, and *Chicago Loop* 1990. His accounts of his travels by train, notable for their sharp depiction of the socio-economic divides, include *The Great Railway Bazaar* 1975, *The Old Patagonian Express* 1979, and *Riding the Iron Rooster* 1988.

Extensive travelling induces a feeling of encapsulation, and travel, so broadening at first, contracts the mind.

Paul Theroux
'The Great American Railway'

Theseus in Greek mythology, a hero of Attica, supposed to have united the states of the area under a constitutional government in Athens. Ariadne, whom he later abandoned on Naxos, helped him find his way through the Labyrinth to kill the ◊Minotaur. He also fought the Amazons and was one of the ◊Argonauts.

Thesiger Wilfred Patrick 1912– . English explorer and writer. His travels and military adventures in Abyssinia, North Africa, and Arabia are recounted in a number of books, including *Arabian Sands* 1959, *Desert, Marsh and Mountain* 1979, and the autobiographical *The Life of My Choice* 1987.

In deserts, however arid, I had never felt homesick for green fields and woods in spring, but now that I was back in England I longed with an ache that was almost physical to be back in Arabia.

Wilfred Thesiger
Desert, Marsh and Mountain 1979

Thespis 6th century BC. Greek poet, born in Attica, said to have introduced the first actor into dramatic performances (previously presented by choruses only), hence the word *thespian* for an actor. He was also said to have invented tragedy and to have introduced the wearing of linen masks.

Thetis in Greek mythology, daughter of Nereus, and mother of ◊Achilles, to whom she brings armour forged by Hephaestus in Homer's *Iliad*. Fated to have a son more powerful than his father, she was married by the gods to a mortal, Peleus.

Thibault Anatole François. French writer who wrote as Anatole ◊France.

Thin Man, The novel 1932 by the US writer Dashiell ◊Hammett, which introduced the suave-tough-guy style of detective fiction. It was made into a lighthearted film series 1934–47, starring William Powell and Myrna Loy.

35 mm width of photographic film, the most popular format for the camera today. The 35-mm camera falls into two categories, the ◊SLR and the ◊rangefinder.

Thomas Dylan (Marlais) 1914–1953. Welsh poet. His poems, characterized by complex imagery and a strong musicality, include the celebration of his 30th birthday 'Poem in October' and the evocation of his youth 'Fern Hill' 1946. His 'play for voices' *Under Milk Wood* 1954 describes with humour and compassion a day in the life of the residents of a small Welsh fishing village, Llareggub. The short stories of *Portrait of the Artist as a Young Dog* 1940 are autobiographical.

Born in Swansea, son of the English teacher at the local grammar school where he was educated, he worked as a reporter on the *South Wales Evening Post*, then settled as a journalist in London and published his first volume *Eighteen Poems* 1934.

Do not go gentle into that good night,/ Rage, rage against the dying of the light.

Dylan Thomas 'Do Not Go Gentle into That Good Night' 1953

Thomas Edward (Philip) 1878–1917. English poet and prose writer, born in London of Welsh parents. He met the US poet Robert Frost and began writing poetry under his influence. His poems, like his essays, were quiet, stern, melancholy evocations of rural life. *Poems* was published Oct 1917 after his death in World War I, followed by *Last Poems* 1918.

Thomas R(onald) S(tuart) 1913– . Welsh poet whose verse contrasts traditional Welsh values with encroaching 'English' sterility. His poems, including *The Stones of the Field* 1946, *Song at the Year's Turning* 1955, and *Laboratories of the Spirit* 1975, excel at the portrayal of the wild

beauty of the Welsh landscape and the religious spirit that the harshness of life there engenders.

Thomas Michael Tilson 1944– . US conductor and pianist, principal conductor of the London Symphony Orchestra from 1988. He is an enthusiastic proponent of 'authentic' restorations of modern repertoire, and has championed US composers. He has made first recordings of Steve Reich's *The Desert Music* 1983, the complete symphonies of Charles Ives, and a reconstruction of George Gershwin's original *Rhapsody in Blue*.

His career was launched 1969 when he took over from an unwell William Steinberg in the middle of a Boston Symphony Orchestra concert, subsequently becoming principal guest conductor for the orchestra 1969–74.

Thompson Emma 1959– . British actress. She has worked in cinema, theatre, and television, ranging from song-and-dance to Shakespeare, and often characterizing variations on the independent woman. In 1989 she married actor-director Kenneth ◊Branagh, and has appeared in all his films to date, including the role of Katharine in *Henry V* 1989, a dual role in *Dead Again* 1991, and as Beatrice in *Much Ado About Nothing* 1993. Away from Branagh, she won an Academy Award for her performance in *Howards End* 1992. Other films include *The Remains of the Day* 1993.

Thompson Flora 1877–1948. English novelist whose trilogy *Lark Rise to Candleford* 1945 describes Victorian rural life.

Thompson Francis 1859–1907. British poet. In *Sister Songs* 1895 and *New Poems* 1897 Thompson, who was a Roman Catholic, expressed a mystic view of life.

Thompson Hunter S 1939– . US writer and journalist. A proponent of the New Journalism school of reporting, which made the writer an essential component of the story, Thompson mythologized himself as the outrageous Doctor Gonzo in his political journalism of the 1960s. These articles were mainly published in *Rolling Stone* magazine. His books include *Hell's Angels* 1966, *Fear and Loathing on the Campaign Trail '72* 1973, and the reportage novel *Fear and Loathing in Las Vegas* 1971. He also wrote the collections *Generation of Swine* 1988 and *Songs of the Doomed* 1990.

Thompson Jim (James Myers) 1906–1977. US writer. A prolific author, he was critically neglected until after his death, when he acquired a cult status for his books' powerful and original use of pulp, 'hard-boiled' genres, which he imbued with a horrific, pathological violence. His novels include *The Killer Inside Me* 1952 and *The Grifters* 1963 (filmed 1990).

Thompson Richard 1949– . English virtuoso guitarist, songwriter, and singer whose work spans rock, folk, and avant-garde. He was a member of pioneering folk-rock group Fairport Convention 1966–71, contributing to albums like *What We Did on Our Holidays* 1968. With his wife Linda Thompson he made several albums, among them *Shoot Out the Lights* 1982. Later solo work includes *Rumor and Sigh* 1991.

Thomson James 1700–1748. Scottish poet whose descriptive blank verse poem *The Seasons* 1726–30 was a forerunner of the Romantic movement. He also wrote the words of 'Rule, Britannia'.

Thomson James 1834–1882. Scottish poet, remembered for his despairing poem 'The City of Dreadful Night' 1874.

Thomson Virgil 1896–1989. US composer and critic. He studied in France with Nadia Boulanger 1921–22 and returned to Paris 1925–40, mixing with Gertrude Stein and her circle. He is best known for his opera *Four Saints in Three Acts* 1927–33 to a libretto by Stein, and the film scores *The Plow That Broke the Plains* 1936 and *Louisiana Story* 1948.

Thor in Norse mythology, the god of thunder (his hammer), and represented as a man of enormous strength defending humanity against demons. He was the son of Odin and Freya, and Thursday is named after him.

Thoreau Henry David 1817–1862. US author. One of the most influential figures of 19th-century US literature, he is best known for his vigorous defence of individualism and the simple life. His work *Walden, or Life in the Woods* 1854 stimulated the back-to-nature movement, and he completed some 30 volumes based on his daily nature walks. His essay 'Civil Disobedience' 1849, prompted by his refusal to pay taxes, advocated peaceful resistance to unjust laws and had a wide impact, even in the 20th century.

His other works include *A Week on the Concord and Merrimack Rivers* 1849 and, published posthumously, *Excursions* 1863, *The Maine Woods* 1864, *Cape Cod* 1865, and *A Yankee in Canada* 1866.

Thorndike Sybil 1882–1976. English actress for whom G B Shaw wrote *St Joan*. The Thorndike Theatre (1969), Leatherhead, Surrey, England, is named after her.

Thorvaldsen or *Thorwaldsen* Bertel *c.* 1770–1844. Danish Neo-Classical sculptor. He went to Italy on a scholarship 1796 and stayed in Rome for most of his life, producing portraits, monuments, and religious and mythological works. Much of his work is housed in the Thorvaldsen Museum, Copenhagen.

Thoth in Egyptian mythology, the god of wisdom and learning. He was represented as a scribe with the head of an ibis, the bird sacred to him.

Thousand and One Nights collection of Oriental tales, also known as the ◊*Arabian Nights*.

Three Musketeers, The historical romance by Alexandre Dumas *père*, published in France 1844. D'Artagnan, a poor gentleman, joins forces with three of King Louis XIII's musketeers, Athos, Porthos, and Aramis, in a series of adventures.

Three Sisters, The play by Anton ◊Chekhov, first produced 1901. A family, bored and frustrated by life in the Russian provinces, dream that if they move to Moscow their problems will disappear. However, apathy prevents the dream becoming reality.

Thubron Colin 1939– . British travel writer and novelist, noted for his lyrical prose. Among his books are *Mirror to Damascus* 1967, *The Hills of Adonis: A Journey through Lebanon* 1968, and *Behind the Wall: A Journey through China* 1987. He also wrote the novel *A Cruel Madness* 1985.

Thucydides *c.* 455–400 BC. Athenian historian who exercised military command in the Peloponnesian War with Sparta, but was banished from Athens 424. In his *History of the Peloponnesian War*, he gave a detailed account of the conflict down to 411.

Thunderbird legendary bird of the North American Indians, the creator of storms. It is said to produce thunder by flapping its wings and lightning by opening and closing its eyes.

Thunders Johnny. Stage name of John Anthony Genzale 1952–1991. US rock guitarist, singer, and songwriter. Lead guitarist with the glam-rock garage band the New York Dolls 1971–75, he fronted his own group, the Heartbreakers, 1975–77. Moving to London 1976, they became part of the punk movement. Thunders' subsequent solo work includes the album *So Alone* 1978.

Thurber James (Grover) 1894–1961. US humorist. His short stories, written mainly for the *New Yorker* magazine, include 'The Secret Life of Walter Mitty' 1932. His doodle drawings include fanciful impressions of dogs.

Partially blind from childhood, he became totally blind in the last ten years of his life but continued to work. His collections of stories and sketches include *Is Sex Necessary?* (with E B White) 1929 and *The Middle-Aged Man on the Flying Trapeze* 1935.

I suppose that the high-water mark of my youth in Columbus, Ohio, was the night the bed fell on my father.

James Thurber My Life and Hard Times 1933

Thyestes in Greek mythology, the son of ◊Pelops and brother of GAtreus. His rivalry with

Atreus for the kingship of Mycenae was continued by their sons, Aegisthus and Agamemnon.

thyrsus in Greek mythology, a staff carried by worshippers of the god ◊Dionysus, formed from a stick wound around with the ivy sacred to the god, and crowned with a pine cone.

tie narrow length of fabric worn around the neck, under the collar of a shirt, tied at the front and hanging down over the shirt buttons. It was developed in the 19th century and is considered an essential item for formal menswear.

The tie was derived from a wide band of fabric worn around the neck and folded or draped on the chest by men in the 18th and 19th centuries. Ties also became popular in women's fashion at the end of the 19th century. Another version of the tie is the **bow tie** which is mainly worn by men with formal evening wear. It consists of a short length of fabric tied into a bow at the front of the neck.

Tieck Johann Ludwig 1773–1853. German Romantic poet and collector of folk tales, some of which he dramatized, such as 'Puss in Boots'.

Tiepolo Giovanni Battista (Giambattista) 1696–1770. Italian painter, born in Venice, one of the first exponents of Italian Rococo. He created monumental Rococo decorative schemes in palaces and churches in NE Italy, SW Germany, and Madrid 1762–70. His style is light-hearted, his colours light and warm, and he made great play with illusion.

Tiepolo painted religious and, above all, historical or allegorical pictures: for example, scenes from the life of Cleopatra 1745 (Palazzo Labia, Venice) and from the life of Frederick Barbarossa 1757 (Kaisersaal, Würzburg Palace). His sons were among his many assistants.

Tiffany Louis Comfort 1848–1933. US artist and glassmaker, son of Charles Louis Tiffany, who founded Tiffany and Company, the New York City jewellers. He produced stained-glass windows, iridescent Favrile (from Latin *faber* 'craftsman') glass, and lampshades in the Art Nouveau style. He used glass that contained oxides of iron and other elements to produce rich colours.

Tilson Thomas see ◊Thomas, Michael Tilson, US conductor.

timbre in music, the tone colour, or quality of tone, characteristic of a particular instrument or voice.

timpani or **kettledrums** tuned drums derived from medieval **nakers** (from Arabic *naqqara*), each consisting of a single skin stretched over a bowl resonator that tunes and focuses the sound. The modern instrument is tunable by pedal. A normal symphony orchestra will have up to five timpani.

Tin Pan Alley the pop-music business, especially commercial songwriting. The term originated as the nickname of 28th Street in New York around 1900, when music-publishing offices were clustered there; the UK equivalent is Denmark Street in Soho, London.

Tintoretto adopted name of Jacopo Robusti 1518–1594. Italian painter, active in Venice. His dramatic religious paintings are spectacularly lit and full of movement, such as his huge canvases of the lives of Christ and the Virgin in the Scuola di San Rocco, Venice, 1564–88.

Tintoretto was so named because his father was a dyer (Italian *tintore*). He was a student of Titian and admirer of Michelangelo. His *Miracle of St Mark Rescuing a Slave* 1548 (Accademia, Venice) marked the start of his successful career. In the Scuola di San Rocco he created a sequence of heroic scenes with bold gesture and foreshortening, a flickering, unearthly light, and dramatic distortions of space. He also painted canvases for the Doge's Palace.

Grant me paradise in this world; I'm not so sure I'll reach it in the next.

Jacopo Tintoretto (arguing that he be allowed to paint the Paradiso at the Doge's Palace in Venice)

Tiomkin Dimitri 1899–1979. Russian composer who lived in the USA from 1925. From 1930 he wrote Hollywood film scores, including music for *Duel in the Sun* 1946, *The Thing* 1951, and *Rio Bravo* 1959. His score for *High Noon* 1952 won him an Academy Award.

Tippett Michael (Kemp) 1905– . English composer whose works include the operas *The Midsummer Marriage* 1952, *The Knot Garden* 1970, and *New Year* 1989; four symphonies; *Songs for Ariel* 1962; and choral music including *The Mask of Time* 1982. His work ranges from the dissonant and dense to the lyrical and expansive.

Tiresias or **Teiresias** in Greek mythology, a man blinded by the gods and given the ability to predict the future. According to the Roman poet Ovid, Tiresias once saw two snakes mating, struck at them, and was changed into a woman. Seven years later, in a repetition of the same scene, he reverted back to manhood. Later, he was called upon to settle a dispute between the two gods Zeus and Hera on whether men or women enjoy sex more. He declared for women, and as a result Hera blinded him, but Zeus gave him the gift of foresight.

Tirso de Molina pen name of Gabriel Téllez 1571–1648. Spanish dramatist and monk who claimed to have written more than 300 plays, of which 80 are extant, including comedies, historical and biblical dramas, and a series based on the legend of Don Juan.

Tissot James (Joseph Jacques) 1836–1902. French painter who produced detailed portraits of Victorian high society during a ten-year stay in England, as in *Ball on Shipboard* 1874 (Tate Gallery, London). His religious works were much admired.

Titan in Greek mythology, any of the giant children of Uranus and Gaia, who included Kronos, Rhea, Themis, and Oceanus. Kronos and Rhea were in turn the parents of Zeus, who ousted Kronos as the ruler of the world.

Titian anglicized form of Tiziano Vecellio *c.* 1487–1576. Italian painter, active in Venice, one of the greatest artists of the High Renaissance. In 1533 he became court painter to Charles V, Holy Roman emperor, whose son Philip II of Spain later became his patron. Titian's work is richly coloured, with inventive composition. He produced a vast number of portraits, religious paintings, and mythological scenes, including *Bacchus and Ariadne* 1520–23 (National Gallery, London), *Venus and Adonis* 1554 (Prado, Madrid), and the *Pietà* about 1575 (Accademia, Venice).

Titian probably studied with Giovanni ◊Bellini but also learned much from ◊Giorgione and seems to have completed some of Giorgione's unfinished works, such as *Sleeping Venus* about 1510 (Gemäldegalerie, Dresden). His first great painting is the *Assumption of the Virgin* 1518 (Church of the Frari, Venice), typically sublime in mood, with upward-thrusting layers of figures. Three large mythologies painted in the next few years for the d'Estes of Ferrara show yet more brilliant use of colour, and numerous statuesque figures suggest the influence of Classical art. By the 1530s Titian's reputation was widespread. His ◊*Venus of Urbino* 1538 (Uffizi, Florence), with its subtle nuances, was a significant development in the study of the nude.

It is not bright colours but good drawing that makes figures beautiful.

Titian

In the 1540s Titian visited Rome to paint the pope; in Augsburg, Germany, 1548–49 and 1550–51, he painted members of the imperial court. In his later years he produced a series of mythologies for Philip II, notably *The Rape of Europa* 1562 (Isabella Stewart Gardner Museum, Boston, Massachusetts). His handling became increasingly free and his palette sombre, but his work remained full of drama. He made an impact not just on Venetian painting but on art throughout Europe.

TLR camera twin-lens reflex camera that has a viewing lens of the same angle of view and focal length mounted above and parallel to the taking lens.

toccata in music, a display piece for keyboard instruments, such as the organ. The word 'toccata' refers to the finger technique being emphasized.

toga loosely draped outer garment worn by the citizens of ancient Rome, later the exclusive dress of the upper-class Romans, consisting of a piece of cloth draped around the body.

Long scarves, shawls, and cloaks have been draped toga-style by both men and women during periods of classical revival such as the Renaissance and Neo-Classical period *c.* 1800.

Togare stage name of Georg Kulovits 1900–1988. Austrian wild-animal tamer and circus performer. Togare invented the character of the exotic and fearless Oriental lion tamer after watching Douglas Fairbanks in the 1924 film *The Thief of Bagdad.*

Toland Gregg 1904–1948. US director of film photography who used deep focus to good effect in such films as *Wuthering Heights* 1939, *Citizen Kane* 1941, *The Grapes of Wrath* 1940, and *The Best Years of our Lives* 1946.

Tolkien J(ohn) R(onald) R(euel) 1892–1973. English writer who created the fictional world of Middle Earth in *The Hobbit* 1937 and the trilogy *The Lord of the Rings* 1954–55, fantasy novels peopled with hobbits, dwarves, and strange magical creatures. His work developed a cult following in the 1960s and had many imitators. At Oxford University he was professor of Anglo-Saxon 1925–45 and Merton professor of English 1945–59.

Tolstoy Leo Nikolaievich 1828–1910. Russian novelist who wrote ◊*War and Peace* 1863–69 and ◊*Anna Karenina* 1873–77. From 1880 Tolstoy underwent a profound spiritual crisis and took up various moral positions, including passive resistance to evil, rejection of authority (religious or civil) and private ownership, and a return to basic mystical Christianity. He was excommunicated by the Orthodox Church, and his later works were banned.

All happy families resemble each other, but each unhappy family is unhappy in its own way.

Leo Tolstoy *Anna Karenina* 1873–77

Tolstoy was born of noble family at Yasnaya Polyana, near Tula, and fought in the Crimean War. His first published work was *Childhood*

1852, the first part of the trilogy that was completed with *Boyhood* 1854 and *Youth* 1857. *Tales from Sebastopol* was published 1856; later books include *What I Believe* 1883 and *The Kreutzer Sonata* 1889, and the novel *Resurrection* 1900. His desire to give up his property and live as a peasant disrupted his family life, and he finally fled his home and died of pneumonia at the railway station in Astapovo.

Tomasi Giuseppe, Prince of Lampedusa. Italian writer; see ◊Lampedusa.

Tom Jones (full title *The History of Tom Jones, a Foundling*) novel 1749 by Henry ◊Fielding. The story tells of a foundling, Tom Jones, led astray by the impetuousness of his own nature. He has many adventures, which take him through scenes of uproarious 18th-century life, until he is finally redeemed by his own good heart and the love of the beautiful Sophia Western. A large, self-indulgent work, full of broad, high-spirited effects, it is one of the early great landmarks of the novel form.

Tom Sawyer, The Adventures of novel 1876 by US author Mark ◊Twain. It describes the childhood escapades of Tom Sawyer and his friends Huckleberry Finn and Joe Harper in a small Mississippi community before the Civil War. It and its sequel *The Adventures of Huckleberry Finn* 1885 are remarkable for their rejection of the high moral tone prevalent in 19th-century children's literature.

Tom Thumb tiny hero of English folk tale. In the tale, collected by the Grimm brothers but referred to in English as early as 1597, an old, childless couple wish for a son and are granted a thumb-sized boy. After many adventures he becomes a brave, miniature knight at the court of King Arthur.

tonality in music, a sense of key orientation in relation to form, for example the step pattern of a dance as expressed by corresponding changes of direction from a tonic or 'home' key to a related key. Most popular and folk music worldwide recognizes an underlying tonality or reference pitch against which the movement of a melody can be clearly heard. The opposite of tonality is atonality.

tone poem in music, an alternative name for ◊symphonic poem.

tone row or *note row* or *series* in music, an order of ◊pitches, usually all twelve notes of the ◊chromatic scale, used as a basis for twelve-tone composition (see ◊twelve-tone system). The row may be used as a basis for melody or harmony, and in reverse and inverted forms as well as in its original order.

tonic in music, the key note of a scale (for example, the note C in the scale of C major), or the 'home key' in a composition (for example, the chord of C major in a composition in the same key).

Tony award annual award by the League of New York Theaters to dramatists, performers, and technicians in ◊Broadway plays. It is named after the US actress and producer Antoinette Perry (1888–1946).

topiary clipping of trees and shrubs into ornamental shapes, originated by the Romans in the 1st century and revived in the 16th–17th centuries in formal European and American gardens.

Torres-García Joaquin 1874–1949. Uruguayan artist, born in Montevideo. In Paris from 1926, he was influenced by ◊Mondrian and others and, after visiting Madrid 1932, by Inca and Nazca pottery. His mature style is based on a grid pattern derived from the aesthetic proportions of the ◊golden section.

Tortelier Paul 1924–1990. French cellist whose powerfully intuitive style brought him widespread fame as a soloist from 1947. Romantic in temperament, he specialized in the standard 19th-century repertoire, from Bach's solo suites to Elgar, Walton, and Kodály.

Tortelier came to prominence 1947 as soloist in Richard Strauss' *Don Quixote* in London under British conductor Thomas Beecham. From 1956 he taught at the Paris Conservatoire, where his pupils included English cellist Jacqueline du Pré.

Toscanini Arturo 1867–1957. Italian conductor who made his mark in opera as three-times musical director of La Scala, Milan, 1898–1903, 1906–08, and 1921–29, and subsequently as conductor 1937–54 of the NBC Symphony Orchestra which was established for him by NBC (National Broadcasting Company) Radio. His wide-ranging repertoire included Debussy and Respighi, and he imparted an Italianate simplicity to Mozart and Beethoven when exaggerated solemnity was the trend in Germany.

God tells me how he wants this music played – and you get in his way.

Arturo Toscanini
to his orchestra at a rehearsal

Toulouse-Lautrec Henri Marie Raymond de 1864–1901. French artist, associated with the Impressionists. He was active in Paris, where he painted entertainers and prostitutes in a style characterized by strong colours, bold design, and brilliant draughtsmanship. From 1891 his lithographic posters were a great success, skilfully executed and yet retaining the spontaneous character of sketches. His later work was to prove vital to the development of ◊poster art.

Toulouse-Lautrec was born at Albi (where there is now a museum of his work) in S France. He showed an early gift for drawing, to which he turned increasingly after a riding accident at the age of 15 left him with crippled and stunted legs. In 1882 he began to study art in Paris. He admired Goya's etchings and Degas' work, and in the 1880s he met Gauguin and was inspired by Japanese prints. Lautrec became a familiar figure drawing and painting in the dance halls, theatres, cafés, circuses, and brothels. He often painted with thinned-out oils on cardboard.

Tourneur Cyril 1575–1626. English dramatist. Little is known about his life, but *The Atheist's Tragedy* 1611 and *The Revenger's Tragedy* 1607 (thought by some scholars to be by Thomas ◊Middleton) are among the most powerful of Jacobean dramas.

Does the silkworm expend her yellow labours/ For thee? for thee does she undo herself?

Cyril Tourneur
The Revenger's Tragedy 1607

Tower of London fortress on the Thames bank to the east of the City. The keep, or White Tower, was built about 1078 by Bishop Gundulf on the site of British and Roman fortifications. It is surrounded by two strong walls and a moat (now dry), and was for centuries a royal residence and the principal state prison. Today it is a barracks, an armoury, and a museum.

town planning the design of buildings or groups of buildings in a physical and social context, concentrating on the relationship between various buildings and their environment, as well as on their uses.

An urgent need for town planning emerged in the 19th century with the rapid growth of urban industrial centres. Reformists saw the crowded industrial city as the root of social evil, and various attempts were made to integrate industry with the pastoral vision of the village, culminating in the English town planner Ebenezer ◊Howard's proposal for the ◊garden city. This was first realized at Letchworth in Hertfordshire (begun 1903) and followed 1946 by the first generation of publicly financed new towns, each with its own civic amenities and industries.

In post-war continental Europe, ◊CIAM, a loose association of Modernist architects and planners, took responsibility for much of the rebuilding and planning of European cities, advocating functional zoning and high-rise mass housing as the only viable solution to urban growth. CIAM remained the dominant force in town planning until the mid 1950s when the concepts of multi-layered, mixed-use city centres were re-evaluated. Since the 1970s there has been renewed interest in urban design, with architects and planners working together in search of solutions. Robert Krier (1938–) and

Leon Krier have argued eloquently in favour of the pre-industrial European city with its fabric of clearly defined urban spaces, and Aldo Rossi has also emphasized the importance of traditional urban architecture. In the UK Terry Farrell and Richard Rogers have campaigned for an urgent review of planning policy in London.

Townsend Sue 1946– . English humorous novelist, author of *The Secret Diary of Adrian Mole, aged 13³/₄* 1982 and later sequels. Other novels include *Rebuilding Coventry* 1985 and *The Queen and I* 1992.

Townshend Pete 1945– . UK rock musician, founder member of the ◊Who; his solo albums include *Empty Glass* 1980.

Tracy Spencer 1900–1967. US actor distinguished for his understated, seemingly effortless, natural performances. His films include *Captains Courageous* 1937 and *Boys' Town* 1938 (for both of which he won Academy Awards), and he starred with Katharine Hepburn in nine films, including *Adam's Rib* 1949 and *Guess Who's Coming to Dinner* 1967, his final appearance.

His other films include *Bad Day at Black Rock* 1955, *The Last Hurrah* 1958, *The Old Man and the Sea* 1958, and *Inherit the Wind* 1960.

tragedy in the theatre, a play dealing with a serious theme, traditionally one in which a character meets disaster as a result either of personal failings or circumstances beyond his or her control. Historically the classical view of tragedy, as expressed by the Greek tragedians Aeschylus, Euripides, and Sophocles, and the Roman tragedian Seneca, has been predominant in the Western tradition. In the 20th century tragedies dealing with exalted or heroic figures in an elevated manner have virtually died out. Tragedy has been replaced by dramas with 'tragic' implications or overtones, as in the work of Ibsen, O'Neill, Tennessee Williams, and Osborne, for example, or by the problem plays of Pirandello, Brecht, and Beckett.

Tragedy is restful and the reason is that hope, that foul, deceitful thing, has no part in it.

Jean Anouilh *Antigone* 1944

The Greek view of tragedy was developed by the philosopher Aristotle, but it was the Roman Seneca (whose works were probably intended to be read rather than acted) who influenced the Elizabethan tragedies of Marlowe and Shakespeare. French classical tragedy developed under the influence of both Seneca and an interpretation of Aristotle which gave rise to the theory of unities of time, place, and action, as observed by Racine, one of its greatest exponents.

In Germany the tragedies of Goethe and Schiller led to the exaggerated ◊melodrama, which replaced pure tragedy. In the 18th century attempts were made to 'domesticate' tragedy, notably by Lessing, but it was the realistic dramas of Ibsen that confirmed the transformation of serious drama.

tragicomedy drama that contains elements of tragedy and comedy; for example, Shakespeare's 'reconciliation' plays, such as *The Winter's Tale*, which reach a tragic climax but then lighten to a happy conclusion. A tragicomedy is the usual form for plays in the tradition of the Theatre of the ◊Absurd, such as Samuel ◊Beckett's *En attendant Godot/Waiting for Godot* 1952 and Tom ◊Stoppard's *Rosencrantz and Guildenstern are Dead* 1967.

Traherne Thomas 1637–1674. English Christian mystic. His moving lyric poetry and his prose *Centuries of Meditations* were unpublished until 1903.

transept in church architecture, the transverse 'arms' of a floor plan that is cruciform, usually found in cathedrals.

transparency in photography, a picture on slide film. This captures the original in a positive image (direct reversal) and can be used for projection or printing on positive-to-positive print material, for example by the Cibachrome or Kodak R-type process. Slide film is usually colour but can be obtained in black and white.

transposition in music, performance in a different key from that indicated in the printed music, or the appearance of a theme or motif in an alternative key. A *transposing instrument* is one that is normally written for in one key and played in another.

trautonium polyphonic keyboard synthesizer invented 1928 by German acoustician Friedrich Trautwein (1888–1956) and subsequently developed by Oskar Sala as the *Mixtur-trautonium*. The instrument remained popular with Hollywood composers until the 1950s.

Traven B(en). Pen name of Herman Feige 1882–1969. German-born US novelist whose true identity was not revealed until 1979. His books include the bestseller *The Death Ship* 1926 and *The Treasure of the Sierra Madre* 1934, which was made into a film starring Humphrey Bogart 1948.

Born in a part of Germany now in Poland, he was in turn known as the anarchist Ret Marut, Traven Torsvan, and Hollywood scriptwriter Hal Croves. Between the two world wars he lived in obscurity in Mexico and avoided recognition.

Travers Ben(jamin) 1886–1980. British dramatist. He wrote (for actors Tom Walls, Ralph Lynn, and Robertson Hare) the 'Aldwych farces'

of the 1920s, so named from the London theatre in which they were played. They include *A Cuckoo in the Nest* 1925 and *Rookery Nook* 1926.

Treasure Island adventure story for children by R L ◊Stevenson, published 1883. Jim Hawkins, the story's narrator, sets sail with Squire Trelawney in the *Hispaniola*, armed with a map showing the location of buried treasure. Attempts by the ship's crew of pirates, including Long John Silver, to seize the map are foiled after much fighting and the squire finds the treasure.

trecento (Italian 'three hundred') denoting the 1300s and used in relation to Italian culture of the 14th century.

Tree Herbert Beerbohm 1853–1917. British actor and theatre manager, half-brother of Max ◊Beerbohm. Noted for his lavish Shakespeare productions, he was founder of the ◊Royal Academy of Dramatic Art (RADA).

tremolo in music, a rapidly pulsating tremor on one note, created by rapid movement of the bow on a stringed instrument, or shake of the voice.

Tressell Robert. Pseudonym of Robert Noonan 1868–1911. English author whose *The Ragged Trousered Philanthropists*, published in an abridged form 1914, gave a detailed account of the poverty of working people's lives.

Trial, The (German *Der Prozess*) novel by Franz ◊Kafka, published 1925 in Czechoslovakia. It deals with the sinister circumstances in which a man is arrested for no apparent reason, his consequent feelings of guilt and alienation, and his eventual 'execution'. It was translated into English 1955, and again (more accurately) 1978.

trilby soft felt hat with a tented crown and a flexible brim which became popular in the 1930s–40s. The same style of hat, decorated with a feather, is worn in the Tyrol, Austria. The hat takes its name from the heroine of George Du Maurier's novel *Trilby* 1894.

trill in music, a rapid oscillation between adjacent notes, also called a *shake*, exploited both for impressionistic effect, as in the opening bars of Bartók's *Piano Concerto No 3* 1945, or to create dramatic tension and ambiguity, as at end of a solo ◊cadenza in a concerto.

Trilling Lionel 1905–1975. US author and literary critic. His books of criticism include *The Liberal Imagination* 1950, *Beyond Culture* 1965, and *The Experience of Literature* 1967. He also produced annotated editions of the works of English poets Matthew Arnold and John Keats.

Trinity fresco by ◊Masaccio about 1428 (Sta Maria Novella, Florence), the first painting to use the techniques of artificial perspective developed by ◊Brunelleschi. In its original state it would have produced a stunning effect of three-dimensionality but time and air pollution have eroded its colour and tonal values. Plans for its restoration, due to begin 1993, have been subjected to fierce criticism by art historians.

trio in music, an ensemble of three instruments, also an interlude between repeats of a ◊minuet or ◊scherzo, for a trio of players.

triolet an eight-lined poem, with repetition of the first line as the fourth and seventh, and of the second line as the eighth; and with first, third, fourth, fifth, and seventh lines, and second, sixth, and eighth lines, rhyming. The form was developed in medieval French poetry, and was revived on a small scale in 19th-century English poetry.

triptych painting consisting of three panels, usually hinged together with the central panel being twice the width of the wings, which may fold inwards. The triptych developed from the ◊diptych and was used both as a portable altar and, on a larger scale, as an ◊altarpiece.

Tristan legendary Celtic hero who fell in love with Isolde, the bride he was sent to win for his uncle King Mark of Cornwall; the story became part of the Arthurian cycle and is the subject of Wagner's opera *Tristan und Isolde* 1865.

Tristan Flora 1803–1844. French socialist writer and activist, author of *Promenades dans Londres/The London Journal* 1840, a vivid record of social conditions, and *L'Union ouvrière/Workers' Union* 1843, an outline of a workers' utopia.

Tristano Lennie (Lennard Joseph) 1919–1978. US jazz pianist and composer. An austere musician, he gave an academic foundation to the school of cool jazz in the 1940s and 1950s, which was at odds with the bebop tradition. He was also active as a teacher.

Tristram Shandy (full title *The Life and Opinions of Tristran Shandy, Gent.*) novel by Laurence ◊Sterne, published 1759–67. The work, a forerunner of the 20th-century stream-of-consciousness novel, has no coherent plot and uses typographical devices to emphasize the author's disdain for the structured novels of his contemporaries.

Triton in Greek mythology, a merman sea god, the son of ◊Poseidon and the sea goddess Amphitrite. Traditionally, he is shown blowing on a conch shell.

tritone in music, the interval of the diminished fifth, exactly half the octave, and considered the moral antithesis of the octave's perfect consonance.

Trojan horse in Greek mythology, during the siege of Troy, an enormous wooden horse left by the Greek army outside the gates of the city. When the Greeks had retreated, the Trojans, believing it to be a religious offering, brought the horse in. Greek soldiers then emerged from within the hollow horse and opened the city gates to enable Troy to be captured.

Trollope Anthony 1815–1882. English novelist who delineated provincial English middle-class society in a series of novels set in or around the imaginary cathedral city of Barchester. *The Warden* 1855 began the series, which includes *Barchester Towers* 1857, *Doctor Thorne* 1858, and *The Last Chronicle of Barset* 1867. His political novels include *Can You Forgive Her?* 1864, *Phineas Finn* 1867–69, and *The Prime Minister* 1875–76.

Three hours a day will produce as much as a man ought to write.

Anthony Trollope Autobiography 1883

---

trombone brass wind instrument of mainly cylindrical bore, incorporating a movable slide which allows a continuous glissando (slide) in pitch over a span of half an octave. A descendant of the Renaissance ◊sackbut, the Baroque trombone has a shallow cup mouthpiece and modestly flared bell giving a firm, noble tone, to which the modern wide bell adds a brassy sheen. The tenor and bass trombones are staple instruments of the orchestra and brass band, also of Dixieland and jazz bands, either separately or as a tenor-bass hybrid.

trompe l'oeil (French 'deceives the eye') painting that gives a convincing illusion of three-dimensional reality. As an artistic technique, it has been in common use in most stylistic periods in the West, originating in Classical Greek art.

troubadour class of poet musicians in Provence and S France in the 12th–13th centuries, which included both nobles and wandering minstrels. The troubadours originated a type of lyric poetry devoted to themes of ◊courtly love and the idealization of women and to glorifying the deeds of their patrons, reflecting the chivalric ideals of the period. Little is known of their music, which was passed down orally.

Among the troubadours were Bertran de Born (1140–c. 1215), who was mentioned by Dante; Arnaut Daniel; and Bernard de Ventadour. The troubadour tradition spread to other parts of Europe, including northern France (the *trouvères*) and Germany (the ◊Minnesingers).

trousers garment designed to fit the body from the waist to the bottom of the leg with separate tube-shaped sections for each leg. Straight ankle-length trousers were introduced in the 1800s, but were not considered acceptable attire for men until the late 19th century. Prior to this date men had worn ◊stockings and ◊breeches.

An attempt was made to introduce a version of trousers for women in the 19th century, but they did not become fashionable until the 1920s when Coco ◊Chanel introduced loose, baggy trousers for leisure activities. Women working in factories and on the land during World War II wore trousers but they did not become generally popular for women until the 1960s. By the 1970s trousers had beome an acceptable part of formal and casual wear. Examples of trouser designs are Oxford bags, pedal pushers, and flares.

Troy (Latin *Ilium*) ancient city (now Hissarlik in Turkey) of Asia Minor, just south of the Dardanelles, besieged in the legendary ten-year Trojan War (mid-13th century BC), as described in Homer's *Iliad*. According to the legend, the city fell to the Greeks, who first used the stratagem of leaving behind, in a feigned retreat, a large wooden horse containing armed infiltrators to open the city's gates. Believing it to be a religious offering, the Trojans took it within the walls.

Truffaut François 1932–1984. French ◊New Wave film director and actor, formerly a critic. A popular, romantic, and intensely humane filmmaker, he wrote and directed a series of semi-autobiographical films starring Jean-Pierre Léaud, beginning with *Les Quatre Cent Coups/The 400 Blows* 1959. His other films include *Jules et Jim* 1961, *Fahrenheit 451* 1966, *L'Enfant sauvage/The Wild Child* 1970, and *La Nuit américaine/Day for Night* 1973 (Academy Award).

His passion for cinema led to a job as film critic for *Les Cahiers du cinéma* during the 1950s before embarking on his career as director. His later work includes *L'Histoire d'Adèle H/The Story of Adèle H* 1975 and *Le Dernier Métro/The Last Metro* 1980. He played one of the leading roles in Steven Spielberg's *Close Encounters of the Third Kind* 1977.

Trumbull John 1756–1843. American artist known for his series of historical paintings of war scenes from the American revolution (1775–83), the most famous of which was his depiction of the signing of the Declaration of Independence 1776.

trumpet member of an ancient family of lip-reed instruments existing worldwide in a variety of forms and materials, and forming part of the brass section in a modern orchestra. Its distinguishing features are a generally cylindrical bore and straight or coiled shape, producing a penetrating tone of stable pitch for signalling and ceremonial use. Valve trumpets were introduced around 1820, giving access to the full range of chromatic pitches.

Today's orchestral trumpet is valued for its clearly focused, brilliant tone, and variants of the normal C4 trumpet in current use include the soprano in D, piccolo (clarino) trumpet in C5, and bass trumpet in C3, an addition suggested by Wagner. In brass bands the B flat soprano instrument is normally used. The trumpet is a traditional solo jazz instrument, and players demonstrate particular skill in high harmonics.

Ts'ao Chan alternative transcription of Chinese novelist ◊Cao Chan.

Tschumi Bernard 1944– . Swiss-born architect, an exponent of ◊Deconstructionism, who has drawn far more than he has built. In his competition-winning proposals for Parc de la Villette in Paris (begun 1982), a series of striking red pavilions, lining the main route to the park, are the scheme's most obvious architectural manifestations. These are, in effect, follies, accentuating the anti-functional Deconstructionist ethic.

T-shirt T-shaped top, often made of stretch cotton or a cotton mix, usually with short sleeves, although long sleeves are also used. T-shirts are normally worn as summer clothing or sportswear.

Originally worn by soldiers under their uniforms during World War I, the T-shirt was later adapted for labourers. Since the 1960s they have been popular fashion garments and are often printed with slogans, designs, patterns, and images. Katherine ◊Hamnett became noted 1983–84 for her silk and cotton T-shirts emblazoned with logos such as 'Stop Acid Rain'.

Tsvetayeva Marina 1892–1941. Russian poet, born in Moscow, who wrote most of her verse after leaving the USSR 1923. She wrote mythical, romantic, frenetic verse, including *The Demesne of the Swans*, written in the 1920s but not published until 1957. Her *Selected Poems* was translated 1971.

tuba any of a family of valved lip-reed brass instruments of conical bore and deep, mellow tone, introduced around 1830 as bass members of the orchestra brass section and the brass band. The tuba is surprisingly agile and delicate for its size and pitch, qualities exploited by Berlioz, Ravel, and Vaughan Williams.

Different shapes of tuba exist, including oval, upright with forward-facing bell, and the circular or helicon sousaphone which wraps around the player. The Wagner tuba is a horn variant.

Tucker Albert 1914– . Australian Surrealist and Symbolist painter. Self-taught, his early work has much in common with the strong colours and forms of German Expressionism. His Surrealist paintings include *The Futile City* 1940, which shows the influence of de Chirico and T S Eliot's 'Hollow Men' poems, and *The Intruders* 1964, which features his 'Antipodean Heads': blank-eyed creatures in which man and the harsh Australian outback environment are fused.

Tudor Anthony. Born William Cook 1908–1987. English choreographer, dancer, and teacher who introduced psychological drama into ballet. His first works were for the ◊Rambert company (for example, *Lilac Garden* 1936). He was one of the founding choreographers for the American Ballet Theater 1940 and created several works for it, including *Pillar of Fire* 1942, *Romeo and Juliet* 1943, and *The Tiller in the Fields* 1978.

Tu Fu or *Du Fu* 712–770. Chinese poet of the Tang dynasty, with Li Po one of the two greatest

Chinese poets. He wrote about the social injustices of his time, peasant suffering, and war, as in *The Army Carts* on conscription, and *The Beauties*, comparing the emperor's wealth with the lot of the poor.

tunic straight tubular garment, usually sleeveless, which may be tied around the waist or left loose.

Originally a short dress worn by the ancient Greeks and Romans, the tunic reappeared in the 19th century, worn over loose trousers with gathered ankles. In the early 20th century it helped create the long, slender lines fashionable before 1914 in the designs of Paul ◊Poiret. Short tunic dresses worn over longer versions became popular again in the 1960s. Tunics are a common part of girls' school uniform, and short, loose tunics are also worn for dancing.

tuning fork in music, a device for providing a reference pitch, invented in England 1711. It is made from hardened metal and consists of parallel bars about 10 cm/3–4 in long joined at one end and terminating in a blunt point. When the fork is struck and the point placed on a wooden surface, a pure tone is heard. There are tuning forks for each musical pitch.

Tunnicliffe C(harles) F(rederick) 1901–1979. English painter of birds who worked in Anglesey, Wales. His many books include *Bird Portraiture* 1945 and *Shorelands Summer Diary* 1952.

turban headwear commonly worn by Muslim and Sikh men. It is formed from a long piece of fine linen wound around the head. The turban has inspired many fashion headwear styles throughout the 20th century, very often for women.

Turgenev Ivan Sergeievich 1818–1883. Russian writer, notable for poetic realism, pessimism, and skill in characterization. His works include the play *A Month in the Country* 1849, and the novels *A Nest of Gentlefolk* 1858, *Fathers and Sons* 1862, and *Virgin Soil* 1877. His series *A Sportsman's Sketches* 1852 criticized serfdom.

That vague, crepuscular time, the time of regrets that resemble hopes, of hopes that resemble regrets, when youth has passed, but old age has not yet arrived.

Turgenev Fathers and Sons 1862

Turkish literature for centuries Turkish literature was based on Persian models, but under the sultan Suleiman the Great (1494–1566) the Golden Age began, of which the poet Fuzuli (died 1563) is the great exemplar, and continued in the following century with the great poet satirist Nef'i of Erzerum (died 1635) and others.

In the 19th century, mainly under French influence, Turkish writers adopted Western literary forms such as the novel. Ibrahim Shinasi Effendi (1826–1871), poet and prose writer, was one of those who made use of French models. Effendi was co-founder of the New School with Mehmed Namik Kemal (1840–1880), poet and author of the revolutionary play *Vatan/The Fatherland*, which led to his exile by the sultan. Unlike these, the poet Tevfik Fikret (1867–1915) turned rather to Persian and Arabic than to native sources for his vocabulary. The poet Mehmed Akif (1873–1936) was the author of the words of the Turkish national anthem; other distinguished modern writers include the novelist and satirist Refik Halit (1888–1965), the traditionalist poet Yahya Kemal (1884–1958), and the realist novelist Orhan Kemal (1914–1970). The work of the contemporary poet and novelist Yashar Kemal (1923–) describes the hard life of the peasant (*Memed, My Hawk* 1955 and *The Wind from the Plain* 1961).

Turnbull William 1922– . Scottish painter and sculptor who became internationally known in his early career for his primitive, totemlike figures. From 1962, he explored Minimalist form, employing identical, prefabricated units to produce austere, vertical, and repetitive structures grouped on a mathematically devised ground plan, as in *5 × 1* 1966 (Tate Gallery, London).

Turner Big Joe 1911–1985. US blues singer, considered the greatest of the blues 'shouters'. His raucously joyful work with boogie-woogie pianist Pete Johnson (1904–1967) influenced early rock and roll. Turner was born in Kansas City, Missouri, and became part of the jazz scene there. His hits include 'Honey Hush' 1953 and 'Shake, Rattle, and Roll' 1954.

Turner Eva 1892–1990. English operatic soprano, prima donna of the Carl Rosa Opera Company 1916–24. Her incomparable top range and generous tone survive in a magnificent *Turandot* recorded 1928 under Thomas Beecham.

Turner Joseph Mallord William 1775–1851. English landscape painter, one of the most original artists of his day. He travelled widely in Europe, and his landscapes became increasingly Romantic, with the subject often transformed in scale and flooded with brilliant, hazy light. Many later works anticipate Impressionism; for example, *Rain, Steam and Speed* 1844 (National Gallery, London).

A precocious talent, Turner went to the Royal Academy schools 1789. In 1792 he made the first of several European tours, from which numerous watercolour sketches survive. His early oil paintings show Dutch influence, but by the 1800s he had begun to paint landscapes in the 'Grand Manner', reflecting the styles of ◊Claude Lorrain and Richard ◊Wilson.

Many of his most dramatic works are set in Europe or at sea; for example, *Shipwreck* 1805, *Snowstorm: Hannibal Crossing the Alps* 1812 (both Tate Gallery, London), and *The Slave Ship* 1839 (Museum of Fine Arts, Boston, Massachusetts). His use of colour was enhanced by trips to Italy (1819, 1828, 1835, 1840), and his brushwork became increasingly free. Turner was also devoted to literary themes and mythologies; for example, *Ulysses Deriding Polyphemus* 1829 (Tate Gallery).

In his old age he lived as a recluse in Chelsea under an assumed name. He died there, leaving to the nation more than 300 paintings, nearly 20,000 watercolours, and 19,000 drawings. In 1987 the Clore Gallery extension to the Tate Gallery, London, was opened (following the terms of his will) to display the collection of the works he had left to the nation.

Turner Lana (Julia Jean Mildred Frances) 1920–   . US actress of glamorous poise, known as the 'Sweater Girl' during World War II, who appeared in melodramatic films of the 1940s and 1950s such as *Peyton Place* 1957. Her other films include *The Postman Always Rings Twice* 1946, *The Three Musketeers* 1948, and *Imitation of Life* 1959.

Turner Tina. Adopted name of Annie Mae Bullock 1938–   . US rhythm-and-blues singer who recorded 1960–76 with her husband **Ike Turner** (1931–   ), including *River Deep, Mountain High* 1966, produced by Phil ◊Spector. She achieved success in the 1980s as a solo artist, recording such albums as *Private Dancer* 1984, and as a live performer.

Turnus in Virgil's *Aeneid*, the king of the Rutuli, the most vigorous opponent of the Trojans. He was led to Italy by ◊Aeneas and killed by him.

Turpin Ben 1874–1940. US comedian, a star of silent films. His hallmarks were his cross-eyed grimace and a taste for parodying his fellow actors. His work includes *The Shriek of Araby* 1923, *A Harem Knight* 1926, and *Broke in China* 1927.

Turpin Dick 1706–1739. English highwayman. The son of an innkeeper, he turned to highway robbery, cattle-thieving, and smuggling, and was hanged at York. His legendary ride from London to York on his mare Black Bess is probably based on a ride of about 305 km/190 mi from Gad's Hill to York completed in 15 hours by highwayman John Nevison (1639–1684).

Tuscan in classical architecture, one of the five ◊orders (types of ◊column).

Tussaud Madame (Anne Marie Grosholtz) 1761–1850. French wax-modeller. In 1802 she established an exhibition of wax models of celebrities in London. It was destroyed by fire 1925, but reopened 1928.

Born in Strasbourg, she went to Paris 1766 to live with her wax-modeller uncle, Philippe Curtius. During the French Revolution they were forced to take death masks of many victims and leaders (some still exist in the Chamber of Horrors).

Tutin Dorothy 1930–   . English actress whose roles include most of Shakespeare's leading heroines (among them Portia, Viola, and Juliet) for the Royal Shakespeare Company, and Lady Macbeth for the National Theatre Company. She has also acted in the first productions of plays by John Osborne and Harold Pinter.

Tvardovsky Alexander 1910–1971. Russian poet and editor. Early work such as *Put k sotsializmu/Path to Socialism* 1931 and *Strana Muraviya/The Land of Muravia* 1936 (Stalin Prize 1941) repudiates individualism and commends collectivized farming. Later, as editor of the journal *Novy Mir* 1950–54 and 1958–70, he encouraged innovative and outspoken writers such as ◊Solzhenitsyn. *Po dravu pamyati/By Right of Memory* 1967–69, however, was banned by the censor.

Twain Mark. Pen name of Samuel Langhorne Clemens 1835–1910. US writer. He established his reputation with the comic masterpiece *The Innocents Abroad* 1869 and two classic American novels, in dialect, *The Adventures of ◊Tom Sawyer* 1876 and *The Adventures of Huckleberry Finn* 1885. He also wrote satire, as in *A Connecticut Yankee at King Arthur's Court* 1889.

There are three kinds of lies: lies, damned lies, and statistics.

Mark Twain *Autobiography*

Born in Florida, Missouri, Twain grew up along the Mississippi River in Hannibal, Missouri, the setting for many of his major works, and was employed as a riverboat pilot before he moved west; taking a job as a journalist, he began to write. The tale 'The Celebrated Jumping Frog of Calaveras County' was his first success. After a trip by boat to Palestine, he wrote *The Innocents Abroad*. As his writing career blossomed, he also became a lecturer very much in demand. By 1870 he married, and a few years later he and his wife settled in Hartford, Connecticut. *Huckleberry Finn* is Twain's masterpiece, for its use of the vernacular, vivid characterization and descriptions, and its theme, underlying the humour, of man's inhumanity to man. He also wrote *Roughing It* 1872, *The Gilded Age* 1873, *Old Times on the Mississippi* 1875, *The Prince and the Pauper* 1882, *Life on the Mississippi* 1883, *Pudd'nhead Wilson* 1894, and *Personal Recollections of Joan of Arc* 1896. His later works, such as *The Mysterious Stranger*, unpublished until 1916, are less humorous and more pessimistic. He is recognized as one of America's finest and most characteristic writers.

tweed cloth made of woollen yarn, usually of several shades, but in its original form without a regular pattern and woven on a hand loom in the more remote parts of Ireland, Wales, and Scotland.

Harris tweed is made on the island of Harris in the Outer Hebrides; it is highly durable and largely weatherproof. Nowadays, tweed is often machine-woven, patterned, and processed.

Twelfth Night comedy by William Arnold ◊Shakespeare, first performed 1601–02. The plot builds on misunderstandings and mistaken identities, leading to the successful romantic unions of Viola and her twin brother Sebastian with Duke Orsino and Olivia respectively, and the downfall of Olivia's steward Malvolio.

twelve-tone system or *twelve-note system* method of musical composition invented by Arnold ◊Schoenberg about 1921 in which all 12 notes of the ◊chromatic scale are arranged in a particular order of the composer's choice, without repeating any of the notes. Such an arrangement is called a 'series' or 'tone row'. The initial series may be transposed, divided, and otherwise mutated to provide a complete resource for all melodic and harmonic material in a work.

Twentieth Century Fox US film-production company, formed 1935 when the Fox Company merged with Twentieth Century. Its president was Joseph Schenck (1878–1961), with Darryl F Zanuck (1902–1979) vice president in charge of production. The company made high-quality films and, despite a financial crisis in the early 1960s, is still a major studio. Recent successes include the *Star Wars* trilogy (1977–1983).

twill one of the basic cloth structures, characterized by a diagonal line on the face of the fabric. Variations in structure include herringbone weaves. Denim, gabardine, serge, and some flannels and tweeds are examples of twill fabrics.

Tyche personification of Chance in classical Greek thought, whose cult developed in the Hellenistic and Roman periods, when it was identified with that of the Roman ◊Fortuna.

A good drama critic is one who perceives what is happening in the theatre of his time. A great drama critic also perceives what is not happening.

Kenneth Tynan
Tynan Right and Left 1967

Tynan Kenneth (Peacock) 1927–1980. English theatre critic and author, a leading cultural figure of the radical 1960s. A strong opponent of censorship, he devised the nude revue *Oh Calcutta!* 1969, first staged in New York. His publications include *A View of the English Stage 1944–63* 1975.

Tyndale William 1492–1536. English translator of the Bible. The printing of his New Testament (the basis of the Authorized Version) was begun in Cologne 1525 and, after he had been forced to flee, completed in Worms. He was strangled and burned as a heretic at Vilvorde in Belgium.

typeface style of printed lettering. Books, newspapers, and other printed matter display different styles of lettering; each style is named, common examples being Times and Baskerville. These different 'families' of alphabets have been designed over the centuries since printing was invented, and each has distinguishing characteristics. See also ◊typography.

English typeface designers include John Baskerville and Edward Johnston (1872–1944), who designed the lettering used by London Transport.

typesetting means by which text, or 'copy', is prepared for printing, now usually carried out by computer. Text is keyed on a typesetting machine in a similar way to typing. Laser or light impulses are projected on to light-sensitive film that, when developed, can be used to make plates for printing.

typography design and layout of the printed word. Typography began with the invention of writing and developed as printing spread throughout Europe after the invention of metal movable type by German printer Johann Gutenberg (*c.* 1398–1468) about 1440. Hundreds of variations have followed since, but the basic design of the Frenchman Nicholas Jensen (*c.* 1420–1480), with a few modifications, is still the ordinary ('roman') type used in printing.

Type sizes are measured in points (there are approximately 2.8 points to the millimetre); the length of a typeset line, called the measure, is measured in pica ems (1 pica em has a width of a little over 4 mm/0.15 in). The space between lines (known as leading) is also measured in points, although new photosetting and computer-assisted setting systems also work in metric sizes.

Tyr in Norse mythology, the god of battles, whom the Anglo-Saxons called Ty´w, hence 'Tuesday'.

U2 Irish rock group formed 1977 by singer Bono Vox (born Paul Hewson (1960–)), guitarist Dave 'The Edge' Evans (1961–), bassist Adam Clayton (1960–), and drummer Larry Mullen (1961–). The band's albums include *The Unforgettable Fire* 1984, *The Joshua Tree* 1987, and *Achtung Baby* 1992.

Übermensch (German 'Superman') in the writings of ◊Nietzsche, the ideal to which humans should aspire, set out in *Also sprach Zarathustra/Thus Spake Zarathustra* 1883–92. The term was popularized in George Bernard Shaw's play *Man and Superman* 1903.

Uccello Paolo. Adopted name of Paolo di Dono 1397–1475. Italian painter, active in Florence, one of the first to experiment with perspective. His surviving paintings date from the 1430s onwards. Decorative colour and detail dominate his later pictures. His works include *St George and the Dragon* about 1460 (National Gallery, London).

Uccello is recorded as an apprentice in Lorenzo Ghiberti's workshop in 1407. His much damaged fresco *The Flood* about 1445 (Sta Maria Novella, Florence) shows his concern for pictorial perspective, but in later works this aspect becomes superficial. His three large-scale panels of *The Rout of San Romano* were painted in the 1450s for the Palazzo Medici, Florence. They are now in the Uffizi, Florence, the National Gallery, London, and the Louvre, Paris.

As long liveth the merry man (they say),/ As doth the sorry man, and longer by a day.

Nicholas Udall
Ralph Roister Doister c. 1553

Udall Nicholas 1505–1556. English schoolmaster and dramatist. He was the author of *Ralph Roister Doister* dated by various scholars around 1540/53, printed 1566–67. It is the first known English comedy and is based on the plays of the Roman comic dramatists Plautus and Terence.

Uffizi art gallery in Florence, Italy. Built by Vasari in the 16th century as government offices, it was opened as a gallery 1765. Its collection, based on that of the Medici family, is one of the finest in Europe. In May 1993 a bomb damaged a wing of the gallery.

Uhland Johann Ludwig 1787–1862. German poet, author of ballads and lyrics in the Romantic tradition.

ukiyo-e (Japanese 'pictures of the flowing world') Japanese colour print depicting scenes from everyday life, the dominant art form in 18th- and 19th-century Japan. Aiming to satisfy the tastes of the increasingly affluent merchant classes, ukiyo-e artists employed bright colours and strong designs, made possible by improvements in block printing, and featured actors, prostitutes, and landscapes among their favoured subjects. ◊Hiroshige, ◊Utamaro, ◊Hokusai, and ◊Suzuki were leading exponents. The flat decorative colour and lively designs of ukiyo-e prints were later to influence many prominent French avant-garde artists.

Ukrainian literature like Russian and Belorussian writing, Ukrainian literature has its origins in books written in Kievan Russ from the 11th to the 13th century. After the disruption of Mongol invasion, Ukrainian writing revived in the 16th century. It acquired a new vigour from the late 18th century in works such as the influential Virgilian travesty *Eneida* 1798 by Ivan Kotlyarevsky (1769–1838). Ukrainian Romanticism reached a climax in the influential poetry of ◊Shevchenko and *Knyhy bytiia ukrins'koho naodu/Books of Genesis of the Ukrainian People* 1846 by Mykola Kostomarov (1817–1885), despite (or because of) Russian disfavour, including an eventual ban on all Ukrainian publications 1863 and 1871. The later 19th century saw distinguished realist fiction by Panas Myrny (1849–1920) and by Ivan Franko (1856–1916), influenced by ◊Zola.

In the 20th century writers such as the romantic Mykola Khvlovy (1893–1933) flourished until Stalinist Socialist Realism cast a blight in the 1930s, but Ukrainian literature revived in the 1960s with the work of new writers such as Lina Kostenko (1930–), who incurred official displeasure for her un-Soviet 'formalism'.

ukulele small four-stringed Hawaiian guitar, of Portuguese origin; it is easy to play. Music for ukulele is written in a form of ◊tablature showing finger positions on a chart of the fingerboard.

Ulanova Galina 1910– . Soviet dancer, who was prima ballerina of the ◊Bolshoi Ballet 1944–62. A dancer of eloquent simplicity and lightness, she excelled as Juliet and Giselle and created the role of Katerina in Prokofiev's *The Stone Flower*.

Ullmann Liv 1939– . Norwegian actress notable for her work with the Swedish director Ingmar Bergman. Her films include *Persona* 1966, *Pope Joan*, *Lost Horizon* both 1972, and *Autumn Sonata* 1978. She directed her first film, *Sophie*, 1992.

Ulysses Roman name for ◊Odysseus, the Greek mythological hero.

Ulysses novel 1922 by James ◊Joyce. Using the basic plot of the ◊*Odyssey*, Joyce matches equivalent episodes to a day in the life of characters in Dublin in 1904. Using stream-of-consciousness techniques and linguistic mastery, Joyce transforms the smallest and most sordid details of everyday life. It was originally banned (throughout the 1920s in both the USA and Britain) and burned for obscenity (New York 1922), but later became acknowledged as one of the most significant novels of the 20th century.

Unamuno Miguel de 1864–1936. Spanish writer of Basque origin, exiled 1924–30 for criticism of the military directorate of Primo de Rivera. His works include mystic poems and the study *Del sentimiento trágico de la vida/The Tragic Sense of Life* 1913, about the conflict of reason and belief in religion.

The chiefest sanctity of a temple is that it is a place to which men go to weep in common.

Miguel de Unamuno 'The Man of Flesh and Bone' The Tragic Sense of Life 1913

Uncle Remus collection of US folk tales by Joel Chandler Harris about Brer Rabbit, Brer Fox, and others, taken from black plantation legends in the 1870s and 1880s, and part of the tradition of US Southern humour.

Uncle Tom's Cabin best-selling US novel by Harriet Beecher ◊Stowe, published 1851–52. A sentimental but powerful portrayal of the cruelties of slave life on Southern plantations, it promoted the call for abolition. The heroically loyal slave Uncle Tom has in the 20th century become a byword for black subservience.

Abraham Lincoln acknowledged that it had stirred Northern sentiments and helped precipitate the American Civil War.

Uncle Vanya play by Anton ◊Chekhov, first produced 1897. Serebryakov, a retired professor, realizes the futility of his intellectual ideals when faced with the practical demands of life.

Underwood Leon 1890–1975. English painter, graphic artist, and sculptor. He travelled to Iceland, the USA, Mexico, and West Africa, devoting several books to masks, wood carvings, and bronzes. His rhythmic figures are powerful symbols of human myth.

Undset Sigrid 1882–1949. Norwegian novelist, author of *Kristin Lavransdatter* 1920–22, a strongly Catholic novel set in the 14th century. She was awarded the Nobel Prize for Literature 1928.

Ungaretti Giuseppe 1888–1970. Italian poet. His spare, lyrical poems, employing experimental verse forms and complex imagery, made him the principal figure of the 'hermetic' school of Italian poetry (from *ermetico*, 'obscure'). His works include *Allegria di naufragi/The Joy of Shipwrecks* 1919, *Sentimento del tempo/The Sense of Time* 1933, and *Il dolore/Grief* 1947.

Poetry alone can restore a man.

Giuseppe Ungaretti

---

unicorn mythical animal referred to by classical writers, said to live in India and resembling a horse, but with one spiralled horn growing from its forehead.

United States architecture little survives of early indigenous American architecture, although the early settlers in each region recorded the house and village styles of the local Indians. The most notable prehistoric remains are the cliff dwellings in the Southwest. Archaeologists have also discovered traces of structures associated with the moundbuilding peoples in the Mississippi river valley. Subsequent architectural forms are those that came with colonizers from European cultures, those adapted to American conditions and social development, and, most recently, those that were developed and innovated by American architects.

16th and 17th centuries The earliest European architectural influences were those of the Spanish colonizers, coming north from their Mexican colony or from early settlements in Florida; most were small or transitory. The dominant American colonial architecture came to the east coast from 17th-century English immigrants, but also from Dutch, Swedish, and German settlers. Generally, new arrivals attempted to reconstruct the architecture they had known in their home countries, making adaptations to available materials and craftsmanship. Houses most often were small, had massive chimney stacks, and were timber-framed with brick, clapboard, or wattle-and-daub walls. By the end of the century, more elegant and elaborate examples of Jacobean and Queen Anne styles were built, and imposing public architecture constructed, such as William and Mary College in Williamsburg, Virginia.

18th century The Neo-Classical style dominated and was referred to as Georgian architecture, although designs lagged behind English sources, and the scale of projects was generally modest. Itinerant master craftsmen with plan-and-model books, working for educated colonial sponsors, diffused European-style developments along the eastern seaboard. Many fine homes were built, with distinct variations preferred in each of the colonial regions. Churches and public buildings were influenced by Christopher Wren. As settlement moved inland, the rough-hewn timber or log cabin became an American architectural mainstay. Other, finer, buildings from this period include numerous plantation houses; Dutch patroon mansions along the Hudson River in New York or in E Pennsylvania; the then Virginia capital of Williamsburg; churches with steeples, such as Christ Church in Philadelphia; and public buildings, such as Independence Hall in Philadelphia.

19th century Early in the century, Neo-Classicism was introduced by Thomas Jefferson (Jefferson's house at Monticello, the Federal Capitol at Washington by William Thornton (1759–1828), and the ◊White House by James Hoban). Other structures from the first half of the century include the Greek-revival work of Charles Bulfinch and Benjamin Latrobe (1764–1820), notably in their work on the US Capitol. After the Civil War, Romanesque forms in stone and brick were promoted by Henry Hobson Richardson. An appreciation for and adaptation of French Renaissance design emerged, as well as a Romantic revival of Gothic architecture in both domestic and public buildings.

20th century Most dramatically, this was the century of the modern architect, and America became a centre for innovative and creative design; the ◊skyscraper became the fundamental US contribution to world architecture. Spare, functional Modernist form predominated by the mid-century, but by the 1980s a reinterpretation of earlier styles was promoted by Post-Modernists. Notable 20th-century architects working in the USA include Frank Lloyd Wright, Louis Henry Sullivan, Walter Gropius, Ludwig Mies van der Rohe, Eliel and Eero Saarinen, I M Pei, Philip Johnson, Robert Venturi, and Michael Graves.

United States art painting and sculpture in the USA from colonial times to the present. The unspoiled landscapes romantically depicted in the 18th and 19th centuries gave way to realistic city scenes in the 20th. Modern movements have flourished in the USA, among them Abstract Expressionism and Pop art.

colonial The first American-born artist in the European tradition was the portraitist Robert Feke (1705–1750). The historical painter Benjamin West, working mainly in England, encouraged the portraitist John Singleton Copley. Charles Willson Peale painted the founders of the new nation.

19th century The dramatic landscapes of Washington Allston, the nature pictures of John James Audubon, the seascapes of Winslow Homer, the realism of Thomas Eakins, and the Romantic landscapes of the Hudson River School represent the vitality of US art in this period. The

Impressionist-influenced artists James McNeill Whistler and Mary Cassatt and the society painter John Singer Sargent were active mainly in Europe.

early 20th century The Ashcan School, led by Robert Henri, introduced Social Realism in art, depicting slum squalor and city life. The Armory Show introduced Europe's most avant-garde styles, Cubism and Futurism; Dada arrived soon after. In the 1930s and 1940s several major European artists emigrated to the USA, notably Max Ernst, Max Beckmann, Piet Mondrian, Hans Hoffmann, and Lyonel Feininger. The giant heads of presidents carved out of Mount Rushmore are by Gutzon Borglum.

mid-20th century Abstract Expressionism was exemplified by the inventor of action painting, Jackson Pollock, and the spiritual Mark Rothko. The more politically concerned Ben Shahn created influential graphics. The sculptor Alexander Calder invented mobiles.

late 20th century The Pop-art movement, led by artists such as Andy Warhol and Roy Lichtenstein, dominated the 1960s and fostered multimedia works and performance art in the following decades.

US sculptors of the 20th century include Carl Andre, David Smith, Louise Nevelson, and George Segal.

United States literature early US literature falls into two distinct periods: **colonial writing** of the 1600s–1770s, largely dominated by the Puritans, and **post-Revolutionary literature** from the 1780s, when the ideal of US literature developed, and poetry, fiction, and drama began to evolve on national principles. Early 19th-century Romanticism contrasted sharply with the social realism of subsequent **post-Civil War writing**. 20th-century US writers have continued the trend towards realism, as well as developing various forms of modernist experimentation.

colonial (1607–1770s) Literature of this period includes travel books and religious verse, but is mainly theological: Roger Williams (1603–1683), Cotton Mather, and Jonathan Edwards (1703–1758) were typical Puritan writers. The *Autobiography* of Benjamin Franklin (1706–1790) is the first work of more than historical interest.

post-Revolutionary (1780s–1820s) This period produced much political writing, by Thomas Paine, Thomas Jefferson (1743–1826), and Alexander Hamilton (1755–1804), and one noteworthy poet, Philip Freneau (1752–1832).

early 19th century The influence of English Romantics became evident, notably on the poems of William Cullen Bryant, Washington Irving's tales, Charles Brockden Brown's Gothic fiction, and James Fenimore Cooper's novels of frontier life. During 1830–60 intellectual life was centred in New England, which produced the essayists Ralph Waldo Emerson, Henry Thoreau, and Oliver Wendell Holmes; the poets Henry Wadsworth Longfellow, James Lowell, and John

Whittier; and the novelists Nathaniel Hawthorne and Louisa May Alcott. Outside the New England circle were the novelists Edgar Allan Poe and Herman Melville.

post-Civil War (1865–1900) The disillusionment of this period found expression in the realistic or psychological novel. Ambrose Bierce and Stephen Crane wrote realistic war stories; Mark Twain and Bret Harte dealt with Western life; the growth of industrialism led to novels of social realism, notably the works of William Howells and Frank Norris; and Henry James and his disciple Edith Wharton developed the novel of psychological analysis among the well-to-do. The dominant poets were Walt Whitman and Emily Dickinson. The short story flourished, its leading practitioners being Hawthorne, Poe, James, Harte, and O Henry.

20th century Writers specializing in the *short story* have included Ring Lardner, Katherine Anne Porter, Flannery O'Connor, William Saroyan, Eudora Welty, Grace Paley, and Raymond Carver.

drama The USA produced a powerful group of dramatists between the wars, including Eugene O'Neill, Maxwell Anderson, Lillian Hellman, Elmer Rice, Thornton Wilder, and Clifford Odets. They were followed by Arthur Miller and Tennessee Williams. A later generation now includes Edward Albee, Neil Simon, David Mamet, John Guare, and Sam Shepard.

poetry Poets like Edwin Arlington Robinson, Carl Sandburg, Vachel Lindsay, Robert Frost, and Edna St Vincent Millay extended the poetic tradition of the 19th century, but after the Imagist movement (see ◊Imagism) of 1912–14 an experimental modern tradition arose with Ezra Pound, T S Eliot, William Carlos Williams, Marianne Moore, 'HD' (Hilda Doolittle), and Wallace Stevens. Attempts at writing the modern US epic include Pound's *Cantos*, Hart Crane's *The Bridge*, and William Carlos Williams' *Paterson*. Among the most striking post-World War II poets are Karl Shapiro, Theodore Roethke, Robert Lowell, Sylvia Plath, Gwendolyn Brooks (1917–), Denise Levertov, John Ashbery, A R Ammons (1926–), and Allen Ginsberg.

literary criticism Irving Babbitt (1865–1933), George Santayana (1863–1953), H L Mencken, and Edmund Wilson were dominant figures, followed by Lionel Trilling, Van Wyck Brooks, Yvor Winters (1900–1968), and John Crowe Ransom, author of *The New Criticism* 1941, which stressed structural and linguistic factors. More recently, US criticism has been influenced by French literary theory and the journalistic criticism of Gore Vidal, Tom Wolfe, George Plimpton, and Susan Sontag.

novel The main trends have been realism, as exemplified in the work of Jack London, Upton Sinclair, and Theodore Dreiser, and modernist experimentation. After World War I, Sherwood Anderson, Sinclair Lewis, Ernest Hemingway, William Faulkner, Thomas Wolfe, F Scott Fitzgerald, John Dos Passos, Henry Miller, and Richard Wright established the main literary directions. Among the internationally known novelists since World War II have been John O'Hara, James Mitchener, Eudora Welty, Truman Capote, J D Salinger, Saul Bellow, John Updike, Norman Mailer, Vladimir Nabokov, Bernard Malamud, Philip Roth, Ralph Ellison, Thomas Pynchon, and James Baldwin. Recent US literature increasingly expresses the cultural pluralism, regional variety, and historical and ethnic range of US life. Feminism and minority consciousness have been brought to the fore by authors such as Alice Walker, Toni Morrison, and Maya Angelou.

Universal Hollywood film studio founded 1915 by Carl Laemmle. Despite the immense success of *All Quiet on the Western Front* 1930, the changeover to sound caused a decline in the studio's fortunes, apart from horror classics such as *Frankenstein* 1931. In the 1950s the studio re-emerged (as Universal International) with a series of successful romantic comedies with such stars as Rock Hudson and Doris Day. In the 1970s and 1980s Universal became one of the industry's leaders with box-office hits from the producer and director Steven Spielberg such as *ET* 1982 and *Back to the Future* 1985.

Unwin Raymond 1863–1940. English town planner. He put the ◊garden city ideals of Ebenezer Howard into practice, overseeing Letchworth, Hertfordshire (begun 1903), Hampstead Garden Suburb, outside London (begun 1907), and Wythenshawe, outside Manchester (begun 1927).

Updike John (Hoyer) 1932– . US writer. Associated with the *New Yorker* magazine from 1955, he soon established a reputation for polished prose, poetry, and criticism. His novels include *The Poorhouse Fair* 1959, *The Centaur* 1963, *Couples* 1968, *The Witches of Eastwick* 1984, *Roger's Version* 1986, and *S.* 1988, and deal with the tensions and frustrations of contemporary US middle-class life and their effects on love and marriage.

A healthy male adult bore consumes each year one and a half times his own weight in other people's patience.

John Updike
'Confessions of a Wild Bore'

Updike was born in Shillington, Pennsylvania, and graduated from Harvard University. Two characters recur in Updike's novels: the former basketball player 'Rabbit' Angstrom, who matures in the series *Rabbit, Run* 1960, *Rabbit Redux* 1971, *Rabbit is Rich* 1981 (Pulitzer Prize), and *Rabbit at Rest* 1990 (Pulitzer Prize); and the novelist Henry Bech, who appears in *Bech: A Book* 1970 and *Bech is Back* 1982. Other novels by Updike include *Of the Farm* 1965, *A Month of Sundays* 1972, *Marry Me* 1976, *The Coup* 1978, and *Memories of the Ford Administration* 1992. His short-story collections include *The Same Door* 1959, *Pigeon Feathers* 1962, *Museums and Women* 1972, and *Problems* 1979. His body of work includes essay collections, such as *Hugging the Shore* 1983, and the play *Buchanan Dying* 1974.

Urania in Greek mythology, the ◊Muse of astronomy.

Uranus in Greek mythology, the primeval sky god, whose name means 'Heaven'. He was responsible for both the sunshine and the rain, and was the son and husband of ◊Gaia, the goddess of the Earth. Uranus and Gaia were the parents of ◊Kronos and the ◊Titans.

urban legend a largely contemporary mode of folklore thriving in big cities, mainly in the USA in the 20th century, and usually transmitted orally. Some of the stories – hitchhikers that turn out to be ghosts, spiders breeding in elaborate hairstyles – is pre-industrial in origin, but transformed to fit new circumstances; others – the pet or baby in the microwave oven, people living in department stores – are of their essence recent inventions.

urban renewal adaptation of existing buildings and neighbourhoods in towns and cities to meet changes in economic, social, and environmental requirements, rather than their demolition. Since the early 1970s, when it became less expensive to renew than to build, urban renewal has increased.

A major objective is to preserve the historical and cultural character of a locality, but at the same time to improve the environment and meet new demands, such as rapidly increasing motor traffic. One option is gentrification, raising an area's social and economic status.

Ustinov Peter 1921– . English stage and film actor, writer, and director. He won an Academy Award for *Spartacus* 1960. He produced, directed, and acted in the film *Romanoff and Juliet* 1961, screenplay from his own play of 1956. Other film appearances include *Topkapi* 1964, *Death on the Nile* 1978, and *Evil under the Sun* 1981. He published his autobiography *Dear Me* 1983.

A diplomat these days is nothing but a head-waiter who's allowed to sit down occasionally.

Peter Ustinov *Romanoff and Juliet* 1956

Utagawa Kuniyoshi. Japanese printmaker; see ◊Kuniyoshi Utagawa.

Utamaro Kitagawa 1753–1806. Japanese colour-print artist of the ◊ukiyo-e school, known for his muted colour prints of beautiful women engaged in everyday activities, including informal studies of prostitutes.

His style was distinctive: his subject is often seen close up, sometimes from unusual angles or viewpoints, and he made use of sensuous lines and highly decorative textiles. He was one of the first Japanese artists to become known in the West.

Utopia (Greek 'no place') any ideal state in literature, named after philosopher Thomas More's ideal commonwealth in his book *Utopia* 1516. Other versions include Plato's *Republic*, Francis Bacon's *New Atlantis*, and *City of the Sun* by the Italian Tommaso Campanella (1568–1639). Utopias are a common subject in ◊science fiction. See also ◊dystopia.

Utrillo Maurice 1883–1955. French artist. He painted townscapes of his native Paris, many depicting Montmartre, often from postcard photographs. His almost naive style (he was self-taught) is characterized by his subtle use of pale tones and muted colours.

Utrillo was the son of Suzanne Valadon, a trapeze performer who was encouraged to become an artist herself after posing as a model for many painters of the day. His work from 1909–14 (his 'white period') is considered his best.

God made everything out of the void, but the void shows through.

Paul Valéry
Mauvaises pensées 1941

Valhalla in Norse mythology, the hall in ◊Odin's palace where he feasted with the souls of heroes killed in battle.

Valkyrie in Norse mythology, any of the female attendants of ◊Odin. They selected the most valiant warriors to die in battle and escorted them to Valhalla.

Vallee Rudy (Hubert Prior) 1901–1986. US singer, actor, and bandleader. Establishing a clean-cut, college-boy image, he became one of the most popular crooners (indicating a smooth, intimate style) of the 1920s. He formed his band the Connecticut Yankees 1928 and hosted a radio programme with the theme song 'My Time Is Your Time' (recorded 1929). From 1929 he appeared in films and stage musicals.

Valle-Inclán Ramón María del 1866–1936. Spanish novelist and poet. His works, made notorious by their frank eroticism, were influenced by French Symbolism. They include the four novels *Sonatas* 1902–05 and, set in South America, the novel *Tirano Banderas/The Tyrant* 1926.

Valois Ninette de. Ballet choreographer, dancer, and teacher; see ◊de Valois.

Valentino trade name of Valentino Garavani 1932– . Italian fashion designer who opened his fashion house in Rome 1959. He opened his first ready-to-wear boutique ten years later, before showing the line in Paris from 1975. His designs are characterized by simplicity – elegantly tailored suits and coats, usually marked with a V in the seams.

Valentino Mario 1927–1991. Italian shoe designer who built an international empire of boutiques and created footwear, leather goods, cosmetics, and ready-to-wear ranges. He was instrumental in furthering the careers of the designers Giorgio Armani and Gianni Versace, employing both of them on his leather ranges, and Karl Lagerfeld still designs Valentino shoes.

Valentino Rudolph. Adopted name of Rodolfo Alfonso Guglielmi di Valentina d'Antonguolla 1895–1926. Italian-born US film actor and dancer, the archetypal romantic lover of the Hollywood silent era. His screen debut was in 1919, but his first starring role was in *The Four Horsemen of the Apocalypse* 1921. His subsequent films include *The Sheik* 1921 and *Blood and Sand* 1922.

Valentino came to the USA 1913 and worked as a gardener and a dancer in New York City before appearing as a dancer in a 1918 Hollywood film. He became the screen idol of his day, in such films as *Monsieur Beaucaire* 1924, *The Eagle* 1925, and *Son of the Sheik* 1926.

valve in music, a mechanism for diverting the air flow in a brass wind instrument through an extension loop, to vary the length and thus the pitch of the instrument. Most valve instruments are of the piston type, but older French horns have rotary valves operated by levers.

vampire (Magyar *vampir*) in Hungarian and Slavonic folklore, an 'undead' corpse that sleeps by day in its native earth, and by night, often in the form of a bat, sucks the blood of the living. ◊Dracula is a vampire in popular fiction.

Vanbrugh John 1664–1726. English Baroque architect and dramatist. He designed Blenheim Palace, Oxfordshire, and Castle Howard, Yorkshire, and wrote the comic dramas *The Relapse* 1696 and *The Provok'd Wife* 1697.

He was imprisoned in France 1688–93 as a political hostage during the war between France and the Grand Alliance (including Britain).

Valéry Paul 1871–1945. French poet and critic. His poetry, which combines delicate lyricism with intellectual rigour, includes *La Jeune Parque/The Young Fate* 1917 and *Charmes/ Enchantments* 1922, which contains 'Le Cimetière marin/The Graveyard by the Sea', one of the major poems of 20th-century French literature. He also wrote critical essays and many volumes of journals, which he recorded as among his most important work.

After publishing Symbolist-inspired verse in the 1890s, he abandoned poetry for nearly 20 years, devoting himself to the study of philosophy and mathematics before publishing *La Jeune Parque*.

He laughs best who laughs last.

John Vanbrugh
The Country House 1706

Van der Laan Hans 1904–1991. Dutch architect of monasteries. He studied architecture in the 1920s in Delft before entering the Benedictine order. His earliest work was a guest wing added to the abbey in Oosterhaut 1938; his most significant work is the monastery in Vaals 1956–1982.

Van der Post Laurens (Jan) 1906– . South African writer. His books, many of them autobiographical, reflect his openness to diverse cultures and his belief in the importance of intuition and individualism. His best-known works, which record the disappearing culture of the Bushmen of the Kalahari, are *The Lost World of the Kalahari* 1958, *The Heart of the Hunter* 1961, and *Testament to the Bushmen* 1984.

His first novel, *In a Province* 1934, was an indictment of racism in South Africa; later works include *Flamingo Feather* 1955, *The Hunter and the Whale* 1967, *A Story like the Wind* 1972, and *A Far-off Place* 1974. He wrote about Japanese prisoner-of-war camps in *The Seed and the Sower* 1963 (filmed as *Merry Christmas Mr Lawrence*).

Organized religion is making Christianity political, rather than making politics Christian.

Laurens Van der Post
in the *Observer* 9 Nov 1986

Van Doren Harold 1895–1957. US pioneer industrial designer, active in Philadelphia from 1930. His first client was the Toledo Scale Company for which he designed a corporate identity. Key products include a green plastic radio in the image of a skyscraper 1930–31 and a streamlined child's scooter 1936. In 1940 he published a seminal text entitled *Industrial Design*.

Van Doren Mark 1894–1972. US poet and writer. He published his first collection, *Spring Thunder*, 1924. His anthology *Collected Poems* 1939 won a Pulitzer Prize. He was an editor of *The Nation* 1924–28 and published the novels *The Transients* 1935 and *Windless Cabins* 1940.

Born in Hope, Illinois, USA, Van Doren was educated at the University of Illinois and received his PhD 1920 from Columbia University, where he taught English 1920–59. His autobiography appeared 1958 and his last collection of poems, *Good Morning*, 1973.

van Dyck Anthony. Flemish painter; see ◊Dyck, Anthony van.

van Eyck Aldo. Dutch architect; see ◊Eyck, Aldo van.

van Eyck Jan. Flemish painter; see ◊Eyck, Jan van.

van Gogh Vincent. Dutch painter; see ◊Gogh, Vincent van.

Vanity Fair novel by William Makepeace ◊Thackeray, published in serial form 1847–48. It deals with the contrasting fortunes of the tough orphan Becky Sharp and the soft-hearted, privileged Amelia Sedley, who first meet at Miss Pinkerton's Academy for young ladies.

van Leyden Lucas. Dutch painter; see ◊Lucas van Leyden.

van Meegeren Hans. Dutch forger; see ◊Meegeren, Hans van.

Varèse Edgard 1885–1965. French composer. He left Paris for New York 1916 where he cofounded the New Symphony Orchestra 1919 with the French-born US harpist Carlos Salzédo (1885–1961) to promote modern and pre-classical music. Renouncing the values of tonality, he discovered new resources of musical expression in the percussion sonorities of *Ionisation* 1929–31, the swooping sound of two ◊theremins in *Hyperprism* 1933–34, and the combination of taped and live instrumental sounds in *Déserts* 1950–54.

Ever since I was a boy, most music sounded to me terribly enclosed, corseted, one might say. I liked music that explodes in space.

Edgard Varèse

Vargas Llosa Mario 1936– . Peruvian novelist, author of *La ciudad y los perros/The Time of the Hero* 1962 and *La guerra del fin del mundo/The War at the End of the World* 1981.

As a writer he belongs to the magic realist school. *La tía Julia y el escribidor/Aunt Julia and the Scriptwriter* 1977 is a humorously autobiographical novel. His other works are *Historia de Mayta/The Real Life of Alejandro Mayta* 1984, an account of an attempted revolution in Peru in 1958, and *The Storyteller* 1990.

In his political career, Vargas Llosa began as a communist and turned to the right; he ran unsuccessfully for the presidency 1990.

variation in music, a form based on repetition of a simple theme, each new version being elaborated or treated in a different manner. The theme is easily recognizable; it may be a popular tune or – as a gesture of respect – the work of a fellow composer; for example, Brahms' *Variations on a Theme by Haydn* 1873, based on a theme known as the *St Antony Chorale*. The principle of variations has been adopted in larger-scale and orchestral works by modern composers, for example Elgar's *Enigma Variations* 1899.

In ballet, a variation is a solo dance, unless otherwise designated.

Varley John 1778–1842. English painter of watercolour landscapes, and friend of the poet and artist William Blake. He painted in a sublime manner, and was one of the most influential early watercolourists.

varnish solution of resins or resinous gums dissolved in linseed oil, turpentine, or other solvents, or the synthetic equivalents. It is used to give a shiny, sealed surface to furniture and interior fittings.

Varuna in early Hindu mythology, the sky god and king of the universe.

Vasarély Victor 1908– . French Op artist, born in Hungary. In the 1940s he developed precise geometrical compositions, full of visual puzzles and effects of movement, which he created with complex arrangements of hard-edged geometrical shapes and subtle variations in colours.

He was active in Paris from 1930, then in the south of France from 1960. He initially worked as a graphic artist, concentrating on black-and-white artwork.

Vasari Giorgio 1511–1574. Italian art historian, architect, and painter, author of *Lives of the Most Excellent Architects, Painters and Sculptors* 1550 (enlarged and revised 1568), in which he proposed the theory of a Renaissance of the arts beginning with Giotto and culminating with Michelangelo. He designed the Uffizi Palace, Florence, as well as palaces and churches in Pisa and Arezzo.

Vasari was a prolific Mannerist painter. His basic view of the Renaissance has remained unchallenged, despite his prejudices and his delight in often ill-founded, libellous anecdotes.

vaudeville stage entertainment popular in the USA from the 1890s to the 1920s, featuring a variety of acts such as comedy sketches, song-and-dance routines, and so on. Vaudeville is in the same tradition as ◊music hall in Britain.

Vaughan Henry 1622–1695. Welsh poet. He published several volumes of metaphysical religious verse and prose devotions. His mystical outlook on nature influenced later poets, including Wordsworth.

Many is a summer's day, whose youth and fire/ Cool to a glorious evening and expire.

Henry Vaughan 'Rules and Lessons'
Silex Scintillans 1650

Vaughan Sarah (Lois) 1924–1990. US jazz singer. She began by singing bebop with such musicians as Dizzy Gillespie and later moved effortlessly between jazz and romantic ballads, her voice having a range of nearly three octaves.

She toured very widely and had several hit singles, including 'Make Yourself Comfortable' 1954, 'Mr Wonderful' 1956, and 'Broken-Hearted Melody' 1959.

Vaughan Williams Ralph 1872–1958. English composer. His style was tonal and often evocative of the English countryside through the use of folk themes. Among his works are the orchestral *Fantasia on a Theme by Thomas Tallis* 1910; the opera *Sir John in Love* 1929, featuring the Elizabethan song 'Greensleeves'; and nine symphonies 1909–57.

He studied at Cambridge, the Royal College of Music, with Max Bruch in Berlin, and Ravel in Paris. His choral poems include *Toward the Unknown Region* (Whitman) 1907 and *On Wenlock Edge* (Housman) 1909, *A Sea Symphony* 1910, and *A London Symphony* 1914. Later works include *Sinfonia Antartica* 1953, developed from his film score for *Scott of the Antarctic* 1948, and *Ninth Symphony* 1958. He also wrote *A Pastoral Symphony* 1922, sacred music for unaccompanied choir, the ballad opera *Hugh the Drover* 1924, and the operatic morality play *The Pilgrim's Progress* 1951.

I don't know whether I like it, but it is what I meant.

Ralph Vaughan Williams
of his *Fourth Symphony*

---

vault arched ceiling or roof built mainly of stone or bricks. Of the many different types of vault, the **barrel vault** or **tunnel vault** is the simplest form of semi-cylindrical ceiling, consisting of a continuous line of semicircular or pointed vaults. Supporting walls usually require ◊buttresses to contain the thrust of the vault. The **fan vault**, characteristic of Gothic architecture, is composed of a number of intersecting sections of cones, which are often highly decorated. The **groin vault** is formed by the intersection of barrel vaults running at right angles to each other.

Veda (Sanskrit 'divine knowledge') the most sacred of the Hindu scriptures, hymns written in an old form of Sanskrit; the oldest may date from 1500 or 2000 BC. The four main collections are: the *Rig–veda* (hymns and praises); *Yajur–veda* (prayers and sacrificial formulae); *Sâma–veda* (tunes and chants); and *Atharva–veda*, or Veda of the Atharvans, the officiating priests at the sacrifices.

Vega Lope Felix de (Carpio) 1562–1635. Spanish poet and dramatist, one of the founders of modern Spanish drama. He wrote epics, pastorals, odes, sonnets, novels, and, reputedly, over 1,500 plays (of which 426 are still in existence), mostly tragicomedies. He set out his views on drama in *Arte nuevo de hacer comedias/The New*

Art of Writing Plays 1609, in which he defended his innovations while reaffirming classical forms. *Fuenteovejuna* about 1614 has been acclaimed as the first proletarian drama.

He was born in Madrid, served with the Armada 1588, and in 1613 took holy orders.

Veidt Conrad 1893–1943. German film actor, memorable as the sleepwalker in *Das Kabinett des Dr Caligari/The Cabinet of Dr Caligari* 1919 and as the evil caliph in *The Thief of Bagdad* 1940.

An international film star from the 1920s, he moved to Hollywood in the 1940s, where he played the Gestapo officer in *Casablanca* 1942.

Velázquez Diego Rodríguez de Silva y 1599–1660. Spanish painter, born in Seville, the outstanding Spanish artist of the 17th century. In 1623 he became court painter to Philip IV in Madrid, where he produced many portraits of the royal family as well as occasional religious paintings, genre scenes, and other subjects. Notable among his portraits is *Las Meninas/The ◊Maids of Honour* 1655 (Prado, Madrid), while *Women Frying Eggs* 1618 (National Gallery of Scotland, Edinburgh) is a typical genre scene.

His early work in Seville shows exceptional realism and dignity, delight in capturing a variety of textures, rich use of colour, and contrasts of light and shade. In Madrid he was inspired by works by Titian in the royal collection and by Rubens, whom he met 1628. He was in Italy 1629–31 and 1648–51; on his second visit he painted *Pope Innocent X* 1650 (Doria Gallery, Rome).

Velázquez's work includes outstanding formal history painting, *The Surrender of Breda* 1634–35 (Prado, Madrid), studies of the male nude, and a reclining female nude, *The Rokeby Venus* about 1648 (National Gallery, London). Around half of the 100 or so paintings known to be by him are owned by the Prado, Madrid.

Velde, van de family of Dutch artists. Both *Willem van de Velde, the Elder* (1611–1693) and his son *Willem van de Velde, the Younger* (1633–1707) painted sea battles for Charles II and James II (having settled in London 1672). Another son *Adriaen van de Velde* (1636–1672) painted landscapes.

Willem the Younger achieved an atmosphere of harmony and dignity in highly detailed views of fighting ships at sea. The National Maritime Museum in Greenwich, London, has a fine collection of his works.

velvet fabric of silk, cotton, nylon, or other textile, with a short, thick pile. Utrecht, the Netherlands, and Genoa, Italy, are traditional centres of manufacture. It is woven on a double loom, then cut between the centre pile to form velvet nap.

Velvet Underground, the US avant-garde rock group formed 1965, dissolved 1969–72; reformed 1993. Their experiments with dissonance and abrasive noise proved highly influential in subsequent decades, as did the street-smart lyrics of guitarist and vocalist Lou ◊Reed. Their albums include *The Velvet Underground and Nico* 1967, *White Light/White Heat* 1968, and *Loaded* 1970. Songs like 'Waiting for the Man' and 'Sweet Jane' have become classics, and the Velvet Underground's sound, image, and attitude have been endlessly imitated and invoked.

At the outset, the Velvet Underground provided the live music for Pop artist Andy Warhol's multimedia shows called the 'Exploding Plastic Inevitable', with another of his protégés, Nico (Christa Paffgen 1938–1988), sharing the vocals; after the first album they broke with Warhol.

veneer thin layers of fine wood applied to the surface of furniture made with a coarser or cheaper wood. Veneer has been widely used from the second half of the 17th century.

Veneziano Domenico. Italian painter; see ◊Domenico Veneziano.

Venice Film Festival international film festival held every year in Venice, Italy; see ◊cinema.

Venturi Robert 1925– . US architect. He pioneered ◊Post-Modernism through his books *Complexity and Contradiction in Architecture* 1967 (Pulitzer Prize 1991) and *Learning from Las Vegas* 1972. In 1986 he was commissioned to design the Sainsbury Wing extension to the National Gallery, London, opened 1991.

He is known for his slogan 'Less is a bore', countering German architect Ludwig Mies van der Rohe's 'Less is more'.

I was a theoretician when I was young – and had little work. … But busy old architects do not theorize and probably should not.

Robert Venturi lecture at the Royal Society of Arts 1987

Venus in Roman mythology, the goddess of love and beauty, the Greek ◊Aphrodite. The patrician Romans believed that they were descended from Aeneas, the son of the goddess, and Anchises, a shepherd. She was venerated as the guardian of the Roman people.

Venus de Milo marble statue about 150–100 BC (Louvre, Paris), discovered on the Greek island of Milos 1820. It is one of the finest surviving examples of Greek art in the Hellenistic period.

Venus of Urbino oil painting by ◊Titian 1538 (Uffizi, Florence), in which a nude woman reclines luxuriously on a bed, accompanied by symbols of love and fidelity. Titian used thin layers of paint to achieve a lifelike rendition of flesh. Although based on ◊Giorgione's *Sleeping Venus* about 1510 (Gemäldegalerie, Dresden), the inviting gaze of Titian's Venus places her at the beginning of the tradition of the odalisque, the voluptuous slave or mistress, painted by such artists as Ingres or Matisse.

Verdi Giuseppe (Fortunino Francesco) 1813–1901. Italian opera composer of the Romantic period, who took his native operatic style to new heights of dramatic expression. In 1842 he wrote the opera *Nabucco*, followed by *Ernani* 1844 and *Rigoletto* 1851. Other works include *Il trovatore* and *La traviata* both 1853, *Aïda* 1871, and the masterpieces of his old age, *Otello* 1887 and *Falstaff* 1893. His *Requiem* 1874 commemorates Alessandro ◊Manzoni.

During the mid-1800s, Verdi became a symbol of Italy's fight for independence from Austria, frequently finding himself in conflict with the Austrian authorities, who felt that his operas encouraged Italian nationalism.

I would be willing to set even a newspaper or a letter, etc., to music, but in the theatre the public will stand for anything except boredom.

Giuseppe Verdi
letter to Antonio Somma 1854

Vergil alternative spelling of ◊Virgil, Roman poet.

Verginia in Roman mythology, a girl who was killed by her father to protect her from the lust of a Roman magistrate. Her death prompted a revolution, concluded by the publication of a law code, the Twelve Tables. Her story was told by both the Italian poet ◊Petrarch and the English poet ◊Chaucer in the Middle Ages.

verismo term in music referring to opera of 'extravagant realism', particularly Italian late Romantic opera of Leoncavallo, Puccini, and others.

vérité (French 'realism'), as in ◊cinéma vérité, used to describe a realistic or documentary style.

Verlaine Paul 1844–1896. French lyric poet, acknowledged as leader of the Symbolist poets (see ◊Symbolism). His volumes of verse, strongly influenced by the poets Charles Baudelaire and Arthur ◊Rimbaud, include *Poèmes saturniens/Saturnine Poems* 1866, *Fêtes galantes/Amorous Entertainments* 1869, and *Romances sans paroles/Songs without Words* 1874. In 1873 he was imprisoned for shooting and wounding Rimbaud. His later works reflect his attempts to lead a reformed life.

All the rest is mere fine writing.

Paul Verlaine *Jadis et Naguère* 1885

Vermeer Jan 1632–1675. Dutch painter, active in Delft. Most of his pictures are ◊genre scenes, characterized by a limpid clarity, a distinct air of stillness, and colour harmonies often based on yellow and blue. He frequently depicted solitary women in domestic settings, as in *The Lacemaker* about 1655 (Louvre, Paris).

Vermeer is thought to have spent his whole life in Delft working as an art dealer. There are only 35 paintings ascribed to him. His work fell into obscurity until the mid to late 19th century, but he is now ranked as one of the greatest Dutch artists.

In addition to genre scenes, his work comprises one religious painting, a few portraits, and two townscapes, of which the fresh and naturalistic *View of Delft* about 1660 (Mauritshuis, The Hague) triggered the revival of interest in Vermeer. *The Artist's Studio* about 1665–70 (Kunsthistorisches Museum, Vienna) is one of his most elaborate compositions; the subject appears to be allegorical, but the exact meaning remains a mystery.

vernacular architecture the indigenous building tradition of a locality, not designed by trained architects; for example, thatched cottages in England, stone in Scotland, adobe huts in Mexico, and wooden buildings in the Nordic countries.

Verne Jules 1828–1905. French author of tales of adventure that anticipated future scientific developments: *Five Weeks in a Balloon* 1862, *Journey to the Centre of the Earth* 1864, *Twenty Thousand Leagues under the Sea* 1870, and *Around the World in Eighty Days* 1873.

Veronese Paolo (Paolo Caliari) *c.* 1528–1588. Italian painter, born in Verona, active mainly in Venice (from about 1553). He specialized in grand decorative schemes, such as his ceilings in the Doge's Palace in Venice, with their trompe l'oeil effects and inventive detail. Whether religious, mythological, historical, or allegorical, his paintings celebrate the power and splendour of Venice.

Titian was a major influence, but Veronese also knew the work of Giulio Romano and Michelangelo. His decorations in the Villa Barbera at Maser near Vicenza show his skill at illusionism and a typically Venetian use of rich colour; they are also characteristically full of inventive fantasy. He used the same approach in religious works, and as a result his *Last Supper* 1573 (Accademia, Venice, renamed *The Feast in the House of Levi*) was the subject of a trial by the Inquisition, since the holy event seems to be almost subordinated to profane details, such as drunkards, soldiers conversing, and dogs.

We painters take the same liberties as poets and madmen.

Paolo Veronese
evidence before the Inquisition 1573

Verrocchio Andrea del (Andrea di Cione) *c.* 1435–1488. Italian painter, sculptor, and goldsmith, born in Florence, where he ran a large workshop and received commissions from the Medici family. The vigorous equestrian statue of *Bartolomeo Colleoni* begun about 1480 (Campo SS Giovanni e Paolo, Venice) was his last work.

Verrocchio was a pupil of Donatello and himself the early teacher of Leonardo da Vinci. In his *Baptism of Christ* about 1472 (Uffizi, Florence) Leonardo is said to have painted the kneeling angel shown in profile. Verrocchio's sculptures include a bronze *Christ and St Thomas* 1465 (Orsanmichele, Florence) and *David* about 1475 (Bargello, Florence).

Versace Gianni 1946– . Fashion designer who opened his own business and presented a menswear collection 1978. He has diversified into women's wear, accessories, perfumes, furs, and costumes for opera, theatre, and ballet. He uses simple shapes and strong colours to create provocative clothing.

verse arrangement of words in a rhythmic pattern, which may depend on the length of syllables (as in Greek or Latin verse), or on stress, as in English. Classical Greek verse depended upon quantity, a long syllable being regarded as occupying twice the time taken up by a short syllable.

In English verse syllables are either stressed (strong) or unstressed (weak), and are combined in *feet*, examples of which are: *iamb* (unstressed/ stressed); *trochee* (stressed/ unstressed); *spondee* (stressed/stressed); *pyrrhic* (unstressed/unstressed); *anapaest* (unstressed/unstressed/stressed); and *dactyl* (stressed/ unstressed/ unstressed).

Rhyme (repetition of sounds in the endings of words) was introduced to W European verse in late Latin poetry, and ◊*alliteration* (repetition of the same initial letter in successive words) was the dominant feature of Anglo-Saxon poetry. Both these elements helped to make verse easily remembered in the days when it was spoken rather than written.

form The Spenserian stanza (in which Spenser wrote *The Faerie Queene*) has nine iambic lines rhyming ababbcbcc. In English, the ◊sonnet has 14 lines, generally of ten syllables each; it has several rhyme schemes.

◊*Blank verse*, consisting of unrhymed five-stress lines, as used by Marlowe, Shakespeare, and Milton, develops an inner cohesion that replaces the props provided by rhyme and stanza.

It became the standard metre for English dramatic and epic poetry. ◊*Free verse*, or *vers libre*, avoids rhyme, stanza form, and any obvious rhythmic basis.

Vesta in Roman mythology, the goddess of the hearth, equivalent to the Greek ◊Hestia. In Rome, the sacred flame in her shrine in the Forum was kept constantly lit by the six *Vestal Virgins*.

vibraphone electrically amplified musical percussion instrument resembling a ◊xylophone but with metal keys. Spinning discs within resonating tubes under each key add a tremulant effect that can be controlled in speed with a foot pedal.

vibrato in music, a rapid fluctuation of pitch for dynamic and expressive effect. It is distinct from a tremolo, which is a fluctuation in intensity of the same note.

Victoria and Albert Museum museum of decorative arts in South Kensington, London, founded 1852. It houses prints, paintings, and temporary exhibitions, as well as one of the largest collections of decorative arts in the world.

Originally called the Museum of Ornamental Art, it had developed from the Museum of Manufacturers at Marlborough House, which had been founded in the aftermath of the Great Exhibition of 1851. In 1857 it became part of the South Kensington Museum, and was renamed the Victoria and Albert Museum 1899. In 1990 the Nehru Indian Gallery was opened, displaying a selection of the museum's Indian collection. This derives ultimately from the East India Company's Museum, acquired 1858.

Victorian the mid- and late 19th century in England, covering the reign of Queen Victoria 1837–1901. Victorian style was often very ornate, markedly so in architecture, and Victorian Gothic drew on the Gothic architecture of medieval times. It was also an era when increasing mass production by machines threatened the existence of crafts and craft skills.

Despite the popularity of extravagant decoration, Renaissance styles were also favoured and many people, such as John ◊Ruskin, while stressing craftsmanship and beauty, believed in designing objects and architecture primarily for their function, and not for mere appearance.

There is something about a bureaucrat that does not like a poem.

Gore Vidal
preface to *Sex, Death and Money* 1968

Vidal Gore 1925– . US writer and critic. Much of his fiction deals satirically with history and politics and includes the novels *Myra Breckinridge* 1968, *Burr* 1973, and *Empire* 1987, plays and screenplays, including *Suddenly Last Summer* 1958, and essays, such as *Armageddon?* 1987.

video art art that may combine music, dance, performance, and computer graphics, shown on video. It developed in the mid-1960s in New York. Video artists include the Korean-born US artist Nam June Paik.

Vidor King 1894–1982. US film director who made such epics as *The Big Parade* 1925 and *Duel in the Sun* 1946. He has been praised for his stylistic experimentation and socially concerned themes. He received an honorary Academy Award 1979. His other films include *The Crowd* 1928 and *Guerra e Pace/War and Peace* 1956.

He was instrumental in setting up the Screen Directors' Guild 1936 and was a crucial figure in 1930s Hollywood.

Vigée-Lebrun Elisabeth 1755–1842. French portrait painter, trained by her father (a painter in pastels) and ◊Greuze. She became painter to Queen Marie Antoinette in the 1780s; many royal portraits survive, executed in a flattering Rococo style.

At the outbreak of the Revolution 1789 she left France and travelled in Europe, staying in St Petersburg, Russia, 1795–1802. She resettled in Paris 1809. She published an account of her travels, *Souvenirs* 1835–37, written in the form of letters.

Vigeland Gustav 1869–1943. Norwegian sculptor. He studied in Oslo and Copenhagen and with Rodin in Paris 1892. His programme of sculpture in Frogner Park, Oslo, conceived 1900, was never finished: heavy and monumental in style, it consists of allegorical groups of figures and animals surrounding a fountain.

Vignola Giacomo Barozzi da 1507–1573. Italian Mannerist architect, largely remembered for his architectural textbook *On the Five Orders* 1562. He appears to have designed much of the complex plan for the Villa Giulia, Rome, 1551–55, a building whose idiosyncratic Classicism influenced the development of contemporary ◊Post-Modernism. From 1559 Vignola worked on the completion of ◊Peruzzi's design for the Villa Caprarola, and later succeeded Michelangelo as architect to St Peter's, Rome.

Vigny Alfred, Comte de 1797–1863. French Romantic writer. His works, pervaded by an air of melancholy stoicism, include the historical novel *Cinq-Mars* 1826, the play *Chatterton* 1835, and poetry, for example, *Les Destinées/Destinies* 1864.

Vigo Jean. Adopted name of Jean Almereida 1905–1934. French director of intensely lyrical, Surrealist-tinged, experimental films. He made only two shorts, *A Propos de Nice* 1929 and *Taris Champion de Natation* 1932; and two feature films, *Zéro de conduite* 1933 and *L'Atalante* 1934.

Viking art sculpture and design of the Vikings 8th–11th centuries AD. Viking artists are known for woodcarving and metalwork and for an intricate interlacing ornament similar to that found in ◊Celtic art, from which it developed. A dragon-like creature, known as the 'Great Beast', is a recurring motif.

The burial ship from Oseberg (University Museum, Oslo) is an early example. After the conversion to Christianity in the 10th century, the traditional Viking ornament continued: for example, carvings on the wooden stave churches of Norway, in Borgund and Urnes. Viking art was gradually absorbed into the Romanesque style.

Villa-Lobos Heitor 1887–1959. Brazilian composer and conductor. He absorbed Russian and French influences in the 1920s to create Neo-Baroque works in Brazilian style, using native colours and rhythms. His gift for melody is displayed in the 'Chôros' (serenades) series 1920–29 for various ensembles, and the series of nine *Bachianas Brasileiras* 1930–45, treated in the manner of Bach. His other works include guitar and piano solos, chamber music, choral works, film scores, operas, and 12 symphonies.

Villehardouin Geoffroy de *c.* 1160–1213. French historian, the first to write in the French language. He was born near Troyes, and was a leader of the Fourth Crusade, of which his *Conquest of Constantinople* (about 1209) is an account.

Villiers de l'Isle Adam Philippe Auguste Mathias, Comte de 1838–1889. French poet, the inaugurator of the Symbolist movement. He wrote the drama *Axel* 1890; *Isis* 1862, a romance of the supernatural; verse; and short stories.

Villon François 1431–*c.* 1465. French poet who used satirical humour, pathos, and lyric power in works written in the slang of the time. Among the little of his work that survives, *Petit Testament* 1456 and *Grand Testament* 1461 are prominent (the latter includes the 'Ballade des dames du temps jadis/Ballad of the Ladies of Former Times').

He was involved in theft and public brawling, in addition to the production of the *Grand Testament* 1461. A sentence of death in Paris, commuted to ten-year banishment 1463, is the last that is known of his life.

Ou sont les neiges d'antan?/Where are the snows of yesteryear?

François Villon 'Ballad of the Ladies of Former Times' 1461

---

vina Indian plucked string instrument in a variety of forms, including the ◊sitar, combining features of a ◊zither and ◊lute and consisting of a fretted or unfretted fingerboard overlaying dual resonant chambers. It has sympathetic strings, giving a shimmering tone.

Vincent of Beauvais *c.* 1190–1264. French scholar, encyclopedist, and Dominican priest. He is remembered for his *Speculum majus/Great Mirror* 1220–44, a reference work summarizing contemporary knowledge on virtually every subject, including science, history, natural history, literature, and law. It is noteworthy for its positive attitude to classical literature, which had undergone a period of eclipse in the preceding centuries.

viol member of a Renaissance family of bowed six-stringed musical instruments with flat backs and narrow shoulders that flourished particularly in England about 1540–1700, before their role was taken by the violins. Normally performing as an ensemble or ◊consort, their repertoire is a development of ◊madrigal style with idiomatic decoration.

The three principal instruments, treble, tenor, and bass, are played upright, resting on the leg (da gamba), producing a transparent, harmonious sound. The smaller instruments are rested on the knee, not held under the chin. Tuning is largely in fourths, like a guitar. The bass viol or *violone,* used in Baroque orchestras as bass-line support to the harpsichord or organ, became the model for the present-day ◊double bass.

viola bowed, stringed musical instrument, the alto member of the ◊violin family. With its dark, vibrant tone it is suitable for music of reflective character, as in Stravinsky's *Elegy* 1944. Its principal function is supportive in string quartets and orchestras.

violin bowed, four-stringed musical instrument, the smallest and highest pitched (treble) of the ◊violin family. The strings are tuned in fifths (G3, D4, A4, and E5).

Developed gradually during the 16th century from a variety of fiddle types, the violin was perfected in Italy by a group of makers including Nicolò Amati, Antonio Stradivari, and Guarneri del Gesù working in Cremona around 1670–1710. Designed without frets and with a complex body curvature to radiate sound, its voicelike tone and extended range established a new humanistic aesthetic of solo instrumental expression and, together with the viola and cello, laid the foundation of the modern orchestra.

Today's violin has not changed in form since that time, but in the late 18th century, aspects of the design were modified to produce a bigger sound and greater projection for the concert hall and to allow for evolving virtuoso expression. These include a lengthened fingerboard, an angled neck, and larger-sized basebar and soundpost.

The repertoire for solo violin exceeds most other instruments. Composers include Vivaldi, Tartini, J S Bach, Mozart, Beethoven, Brahms, Mendelssohn, Paganini, Elgar, Berg, Bartók, and Carter.

violin family family of bowed stringed instruments developed in Italy during the 17th century, which eventually superseded the viols and formed the basis of the modern orchestra. There are three instruments: violin, viola, and cello (or violoncello); the double bass is descended from the bass viol (or violone).

Viollet-le-Duc Eugène Emmanuel 1814–1849. French architect, a leader of the Gothic Revival in France, known mostly for his writings, notably *Entretiens* in two volumes 1863 and 1872. He argued for a Rationalist interpretation of the Gothic style and the structural use of new materials such as iron. His most famous restorations were carried out on the Sainte Chapelle and Notre Dame in Paris; he also restored the old city of Carcassonne from 1844.

violoncello full name of the ◊cello, tenor member of the ◊violin family.

Vionnet Madeleine 1876–1975. French fashion designer. During the 1920s and 1930s she achieved critical acclaim when she developed the bias cut (cutting the fabric at an angle of 45 degrees from the selvage across the thread that runs lengthways through the fabric). This enabled her to create simple fluid shapes in crêpe de chine, satin, and gaberdine. She also became known for her draped and handkerchief-pointed dresses. By 1934 she had changed her look to clinging skirts, bare backs, and light crêpe de chine evening dresses. She retired 1939.

Virgil (Publius Vergilius Maro) 70–19 BC. Roman poet who wrote the *Eclogues* 37 BC, a series of pastoral poems; the *Georgics* 30 BC, four books on the art of farming; and his epic masterpiece, the ◊*Aeneid* 30–19 BC. He was patronized by Maecenas on behalf of Octavian (later the emperor Augustus).

Born near Mantua, Virgil was educated in Cremona and Mediolanum (Milan), and later studied philosophy and rhetoric at Rome. He wrote his second work, the *Georgics*, in honour of his new patron, Maecenas, to whom he introduced ◊Horace. He passed much of his later life at Naples and devoted the last decade of it to the composition of the *Aeneid*, often considered the most important poem in Latin literature, of which he is said to have read parts to the emperor Augustus. Later Christian adaptations of his work, in particular the prophetic *Fourth Eclogue*, greatly enhanced his mystical status in the Middle Ages, resulting in his adoption by ◊Dante as his guide to the underworld in the *Divine Comedy*.

We may be masters of our every lot/ By bearing it.

Virgil *Aeneid*

virginal in music, a small type of ◊harpsichord.

virtuoso in music, a performer of unusual interpretive and technical skill. In ◊Romanticism, the virtuoso was seen as an artist-musician, a visionary and hero. Paganini and Liszt were virtuoso figures.

Visconti Luchino 1906–1976. Italian film, opera, and theatre director. The film *Ossessione* 1942 pioneered ◊Neo-Realist cinema despite being subject to censorship problems from the fascist government. His later works include *Rocco and His Brothers* 1960, *The Leopard* 1963, *The Damned* 1969, and *Death in Venice* 1971. His powerful social commentary led to clashes with the Italian government and Roman Catholic Church.

Vishnu in Hinduism, the second in the triad of gods (with Brahma and Siva) representing three aspects of the supreme spirit. He is the *Preserver*, and is believed to have assumed human appearance in nine *avatāra*s, or incarnations, in such forms as Rama and Krishna. His worshippers are the Vaishnavas.

Vitruvius (Marcus Vitruvius Pollio) 1st century BC. Roman architect whose ten-volume interpretation of Roman architecture *De architectura* provided an impetus for the Renaissance; it was first printed in Rome 1486. Although often obscure, his writings have had a lasting influence on Western perceptions of Classical architecture, mainly through the work of Leon Battista Alberti, and later Raphael and Palladio.

Vivaldi Antonio (Lucio) 1678–1741. Italian Baroque composer, violinist, and conductor. He wrote 23 symphonies, 75 sonatas, over 400 concertos, including *The Four Seasons* 1725 for violin and orchestra, over 40 operas, and much sacred music. His work was largely neglected until the 1930s.

Known as the 'Red Priest' because of his flaming hair colour, Vivaldi spent much of his church career teaching at a girls' orphanage. He wrote for them and for himself. Born in Venice, he died in poverty in Vienna.

Vlaminck Maurice de 1876–1958. French painter and graphic artist, largely self-taught. An early adherent of ◊Fauvism, he is best known for his vibrant, brilliantly coloured landscapes. He later abandoned Fauve colour, his works becoming more sombre and Expressionist. He also wrote poetry, novels, and essays.

It takes more courage to follow one's instincts than to die a hero's death on the battlefield.

Maurice de Vlaminck

vocalise in music, a concert work for voice without words, sung on one or more vowels, usually 'ah', which is sustainable over the widest range and allows an open tone. Examples include Rachmaninov's *Vocalise for Soprano and Orchestra* 1912, revised 1915, and Villa-Lobos' *Bachianas Brasileiras No 5* 1938–45.

voice in music, the human singing voice. The voice behaves like a ◊free-reed instrument, driven by air in the lungs pressurized by contraction of the diaphragm, and using the vocal folds, flanges of tissue in the larynx, as a flexible valve controlling the escape of air as a series of pulses. The larynx can be relaxed or tensed at will to vary the pitch. The timbre of the voice is created by the resonances of the mouth and nasal cavities.

Voight Jon 1938– . US film actor of great versatility and blond, baby-faced good looks, who starred as the naive hustler in *Midnight Cowboy* 1969. His subsequent films include *Deliverance* 1972, *Coming Home* 1977 (Academy Award), and *Runaway Train* 1985.

Voltaire pen name of François-Marie Arouet 1694–1778. French writer, the embodiment of the 18th-century ◊Enlightenment. He wrote histories, books of political analysis and philosophy, essays on science and literature, plays, poetry, and satirical fables. A trenchant satirist of social and political evils, he was often forced to flee from his enemies and was twice imprisoned. His many works include *Lettres philosophiques sur les Anglais/Philosophical Letters on the English* 1733 (essays in favour of English ways, thought, and political practice); *Le Siècle de Louis XIV/The Age of Louis XIV* 1751; the satirical fable ◊*Candide* 1759, his best-known work; and *Dictionnaire philosophique* 1764.

All the reasoning of men is not worth one sentiment of women.

Voltaire *Maximes*

Voltaire was born in Paris, the son of a notary. He was twice imprisoned in the Bastille and exiled from Paris 1716–26 for libellous political verse. *Oedipe/Oedipus*, his first essay in tragedy, was staged 1718. While in England 1726–29 he dedicated an epic poem on Henry IV, *La Henriade/The Henriade*, to Queen Caroline, and on returning to France published the successful *Histoire de Charles XII/History of Charles XII* 1731, and produced the play *Zaïre* 1732. He took refuge with his mistress, the Marquise de Châtelet, at Cirey in Champagne, where he wrote the play *Mérope* 1743 and much of *Le Siècle de Louis XIV*. Among his other works are histories of Peter the Great, Louis XV, and India; the satirical tale *Zadig* 1748; *La Pucelle/The Maid* 1755, on

Joan of Arc; and the tragedy *Irène* 1778. From 1751 to 1753 he stayed at the court of Frederick II (the Great) of Prussia, who had long been an admirer, but the association ended in deep enmity. From 1754 he established himself near Geneva, and after 1758 at Ferney, just across the French border. His remains were transferred 1791 to the Panthéon in Paris.

von Karajan Herbert. Austrian conductor; see ◊Karajan, Herbert von.

There is no reason why good cannot triumph as often as evil. The triumph of anything is a matter of organization. If there are such things as angels I hope they are organized along the lines of the Mafia.

Kurt Vonnegut
The Sirens of Titan 1959

Vonnegut Kurt, Jr 1922– . US writer whose early works, *Player Piano* 1952 and *The Sirens of Titan* 1959, used the science-fiction genre to explore issues of technological and historical control. He turned to more experimental methods with his highly acclaimed, popular success *Slaughterhouse-Five* 1969, a novel that mixed a world of fantasy with the author's experience of the fire-bombing of Dresden during World War II. His later novels, marked by a bittersweet spirit of absurdist anarchy and folky fatalism, include *Breakfast of Champions* 1973, *Slapstick* 1976, *Jailbird* 1979, *Deadeye Dick* 1982, *Galapagos* 1985, and *Hocus Pocus* 1990.

His short stories are collected in *Welcome to the Monkey House* 1968, and he has written two volumes of autobiography, *Palm Sunday* 1981 and *Fates Worse Than Death: An Autobiograpahical Collage of the 1980s* 1992.

Vorticism short-lived British literary and artistic movement 1912–15, influenced by Cubism and Futurism and led by Wyndham ◊Lewis. Lewis believed that painting should reflect the complexity and rapid change of the modern world; he painted in a harsh, angular, semi-abstract style. The last Vorticist exhibition was held 1915.

Voysey Charles Francis Annesley 1857–1941. English architect and designer. He designed country houses which are characteristically asymmetrical with massive buttresses, long sloping roofs, and roughcast walls, for example The Cottage, Bishop's Itchington, Warwickshire 1888–89. He also designed textiles and wallpaper in the ◊Arts and Crafts tradition.

Vuillard (Jean) Edouard 1886–1940. French painter and printmaker, a founding member of *les* ◊*Nabis*. His work is mainly decorative, with an emphasis on surface pattern that reflects the influence of Japanese prints. With Pierre ◊Bonnard he produced numerous lithographs and paintings of simple domestic interiors, works that are generally categorized as ***Intimiste***.

Vulcan in Roman mythology, the god of fire and destruction, later identified with the Greek god ◊Hephaestus.

Wagenfeld Wilhelm 1900–1990. German architect and industrial designer. A graduate of the ◊Bauhaus design school in Weimar, Germany, Wagenfeld went on to become one of the country's leading proponents of the machine style (a geometrical, undecorated style deemed appropriate for industrial products) in the areas of metal and glass goods.

Wagner Otto 1841–1918. Viennese architect. Initially working in the Art Nouveau style, for example the Vienna Stadtbahn 1894–97, he later rejected ornament for ◊Rationalism, as in the Post Office Savings Bank, Vienna, 1904–06. He influenced such Viennese architects as Josef Hoffmann, Adolf Loos, and Joseph Olbrich.

Wagner Richard 1813–1883. German opera composer. He revolutionized the 19th-century conception of opera, envisaging it as a wholly new art form in which musical, poetic, and scenic elements should be unified through such devices as the ◊leitmotif. His operas include *Tannhäuser* 1845, *Lohengrin* 1848, and *Tristan und Isolde* 1865. In 1872 he founded the Festival Theatre in Bayreuth; his masterpiece *Der Ring des Nibelungen/The Ring of the Nibelung*, a sequence of four operas, was first performed there 1876. His last work, *Parsifal*, was produced 1882.

Where the speech of men stops short, then the art of music begins.

Richard Wagner
'A Happy Evening' 1840

Wagner's early career was as director of the Magdeburg Theatre, where he unsuccessfully produced his first opera *Das Liebesverbot/Forbidden Love* 1836. He lived in Paris 1839–42 and conducted the Dresden Opera House 1842–48. He fled Germany to escape arrest for his part in the 1848 revolution, but in 1861 he was allowed to return. He won the favour of

Ludwig II of Bavaria 1864 and was thus able to set up the Festival Theatre in Bayreuth. The Bayreuth tradition was continued by his wife Cosima (Liszt's daughter, whom he married after her divorce from Hans von ◊Bülow); by his son *Siegfried Wagner* (1869–1930), a composer of operas such as *Der Bärenhäuter*; and by later descendants.

Wain John (Barrington) 1925– . British poet and novelist. His first novel, *Hurry on Down* 1953, expresses the radical political views of the ◊Angry Young Men of the 1950s. He published several volumes of verse, collected in *Poems 1949–79*, and was professor of poetry at Oxford 1973–80.

Wainwright Alfred 1907–1991. English author of guidebooks to the Lake District. His first articles appeared 1955 in a local paper, and he eventually produced over 40 meticulously detailed books, including volumes on the Pennine Way and other areas of N England.

waistcoat fitted waist-length sleeveless garment, generally with a V-shaped neck, fastening at the front, and with a buckle tie on the back panel. It is traditionally worn over a shirt and under a jacket as part of a three-piece suit. Waistcoats may be made of the same fabric as the suit or of embroidered or textured fabric. The back panel is often made of silk.

Although introduced as an item of men's clothing, women began wearing waistcoats over blouses in the late 19th century. In the 1960s men's pinstriped waistcoats became familiar as part of a woman's wardrobe. In the late 1980s–90s highly colourful waistcoats with bold designs became popular fashion accessories.

Waiting for Godot tragicomedy by Samuel ◊Beckett 1955. Vladimir and Estragon wait on a country road for the arrival of Godot. They are met twice by the domineering Pozzo and the oppressed Lucky, and by a boy who brings the news that Godot will come tomorrow rather than today.

Waits Tom 1949– . US singer, songwriter, musician, and actor with a characteristic gravelly voice. His songs typically deal with urban street life and have jazz-tinged arrangements, as on *Rain Dogs* 1985. He has written music for and acted in several films, including Jim Jarmusch's *Down by Law* 1986. His later work has a spare, twisted jazz feel and suggests the influence of German songwriter Kurt Weill. As an actor, his films include Francis Ford Coppola's *One from the Heart* 1982 and *Ironweed* 1987.

Wajda Andrzej 1926– . Polish film and theatre director, one of the major figures in postwar European cinema. His films have great intensity and are frequently concerned with the predicament and disillusion of individuals caught up in political events. His works include *Ashes and Diamonds* 1958, *Man of Marble* 1977, *Man of Iron* 1981, *Danton* 1982, and *Korczak* 1990.

Walcott Derek 1930– . St Lucian poet and playwright. His work fuses Caribbean and European, classical and contemporary elements, and deals with the divisions within colonial society and his own search for cultural identity. His works include the long poem *Omeros* 1990, and his adaptation for the stage of Homer's *Odyssey* 1992; his *Collected Poems* were published 1986. He won the Nobel Prize for Literature 1992.

Walcott was educated at the University of the West Indies. He has taught writing at the universities of Columbia, Yale, and Harvard. He contributed greatly to the development of an indigenous West Indian theatre, and for 25 years ran a theatre in Trinidad. Other plays include *Dream on Monkey Mountain* 1970, *O Babylon!* 1978, and *Remembrance* 1980.

Walden or Life in the Woods 1854, a classic literary work of 19th-century US individualism and political radicalism. It is the record kept by Henry David ◊Thoreau of his attempt to 'front the essential facts of life' by building a simple cabin at Walden Pond, near Concord, Massachusetts, and observing nature there.

The mass of men lead lives of quiet desperation.

Henry David Thoreau *Walden* 1854

Waley Arthur 1889–1966. English Orientalist who translated from both Japanese and Chinese, including such classics as the Japanese *The Tale of Genji* 1925–33 and *The Pillow-book of Sei Shōnagon* 1928, and the 16th-century Chinese novel *Monkey* 1942. He never visited the Far East.

Walker Alice 1944– . US poet, novelist, critic, and essay writer. She has been active in the US civil-rights movement since the 1960s and, as a black woman, wrote about the double burden of racist and sexist oppression, about colonialism, and the quest for political and spiritual recovery. Her novel *The Color Purple* 1982 (filmed 1985), told in the form of letters, won the Pulitzer Prize. Her other works include *Possessing the Secret of Joy* 1992, which deals passionately with female circumcision.

Walker T-Bone (Aaron Thibeaux) 1910–1975. US blues guitarist, singer, and songwriter whose sophisticated guitar technique incorporated jazz idioms; he was one of the first to use an electrically amplified guitar, from the mid-1930s. He was born in Texas but active mainly in California, and often worked with jazz musicians. His recordings include 'Call It Stormy Monday' 1946 and the album *T-Bone Blues* 1960.

Wall Max. Stage name of Maxwell George Lister 1908–1990. English music-hall comedian who towards the end of his career appeared in starring roles as a serious actor, in John Osborne's *The Entertainer* 1974, in Pinter's *The Caretaker* 1977, and in Samuel Beckett's *Waiting for Godot* 1980. In his solo comedy performances his trademark was an eccentric walk.

Wallace Edgar 1875–1932. English writer of thrillers. His prolific output includes *The Four Just Men* 1905; a series set in Africa and including *Sanders of the River* 1911; crime novels such as *A King by Night* 1926; and melodramas such as *The Ringer* 1926.

Wallace Irving. 1916–1990. US novelist, one of the most popular writers of the 20th century. He wrote 17 works of nonfiction and 16 novels; they include *The Chapman Report* 1960, a novel inspired by the Kinsey Report on sexual behaviour, and *The Prize* 1962.

Wallace Richard 1818–1890. British art collector. He inherited a valuable art collection from his father, the Marquess of Hertford, which was given 1897 by his widow to the UK as the **Wallace Collection**, containing many 18th-century French paintings. The collection was opened to the public 1900 and is at Hertford House, London.

Waller Edmund 1606–1687. English poet who managed to eulogize both Cromwell and Charles II; now mainly remembered for lyrics such as 'Go, lovely rose'.

Waller Fats (Thomas Wright) 1904–1943. US jazz pianist and composer with a forceful ◊stride piano style. His songs, many of which have become jazz standards, include 'Ain't Misbehavin'' 1929, 'Honeysuckle Rose' 1929, and 'Viper's Drag' 1934.

An exuberant, humorous performer, Waller toured extensively and appeared in several musical films, including *Stormy Weather* 1943. His first recordings were on piano rolls and in the 1920s he recorded pipe-organ solos. In the 1930s he worked with a small group (as Fats Waller and his Rhythm Boys), before leading a big band 1939–42.

Wallis Hal (Harold Brent) 1899–1986. US film producer with a keen eye for choosing potential box-office successes. He was chief executive in charge of production at Warner Brothers 1933–44, when he left to establish his own company, Hal Wallis Productions.

Walpole Horace, 4th Earl of Oxford 1717–1797. English novelist, letter writer, and politician. He converted his house at Strawberry Hill, Twickenham (then a separate town southwest of London), into a Gothic castle; his *The Castle of Otranto* 1764 established the genre of the ◊Gothic, or 'romance of terror', novel. More than 4,000 of his letters have been published.

Walpole Hugh 1884–1941. English novelist, born in New Zealand. His books include *The*

Cathedral 1922 and *The Old Ladies* 1924. He also wrote the historical 'Lakeland Saga' of the *Herries Chronicle* 1930–33.

Walsh Raoul 1887–1981. US film director, originally an actor. A specialist in tough action stories, he made a number of outstanding films, including *The Thief of Bagdad* 1924, *The Roaring Twenties* 1939, *Objective Burma!* 1945, and *White Heat* 1949.

Walther von der Vogelweide *c.* 1170–1230. German poet, greatest of the ◊Minnesingers, whose songs dealt mainly with ◊courtly love. Of noble birth, he lived in his youth at the Austrian ducal court in Vienna, adopting a wandering life after the death of his patron 1198. His lyrics deal mostly with love, but also with religion and politics.

Walton Izaak 1593–1683. English author of the classic fishing text *The Compleat Angler* 1653. He was born in Stafford and settled in London as an ironmonger. He also wrote short biographies of the poets George Herbert and John Donne and the theologian Richard Hooker.

Walton William (Turner) 1902–1983. English composer. Among his works are *Façade* 1923, a series of instrumental pieces designed to be played in conjunction with the recitation of surrealist poems by Edith Sitwell; the oratorio *Belshazzar's Feast* 1931; and *Variations on a Theme by Hindemith* 1963. He also composed a viola concerto 1929, two symphonies 1935, a violin concerto 1939, and a sonata for violin and pianoforte 1950.

waltz ballroom dance in 3/4 time evolved from the Austrian *ländler* (traditional peasants' country dance) and later made popular by the ◊Strauss family in Vienna.

Wandering Jew in medieval legend, a Jew named Ahasuerus, said to have insulted Jesus on his way to Calvary and to have been condemned to wander the world until the Second Coming.

War and Peace novel by Leo ◊Tolstoy, published 1863–69. It chronicles the lives of three noble families in Russia during the Napoleonic Wars and is notable for its complex characters and optimistic tone.

Ward Artemus. Pen name of Charles Farrar Browne 1834–1867. US humorist who achieved great popularity with comic writings such as *Artemus Ward: His Book* 1862 and *Artemus Ward: His Travels* 1865, and with his deadpan lectures. He influenced Mark Twain.

Ward Mrs Humphry (born Mary Augusta Arnold) 1851–1920. English novelist, born in Tasmania, who wrote didactic books such as *Robert Elsmere* 1888, a study of religious doubt. She was an opponent of women's suffrage on the grounds that public life would dissipate women's potent influence on family and home. She was the niece of Matthew Arnold.

Warhol Andy. Adopted name of Andrew Warhola 1928–1987. US Pop artist and filmmaker. He made his name 1962 with paintings of Campbell's soup cans, Coca-Cola bottles, and film stars. In his New York studio, the Factory, he and his assistants produced series of garish silk-screen prints. His films include the semi-documentary *Chelsea Girls* 1966 and *Trash* 1970.

Warhol was born in Pittsburgh, where he studied art. In the 1950s he became a leading commercial artist in New York. With the breakthrough of Pop art, his bizarre personality and flair for self-publicity made him a household name. He was a pioneer of multimedia events with the 'Exploding Plastic Inevitable' touring show 1966 featuring the Velvet Underground rock group. In 1968 he was shot and nearly killed by a radical feminist, Valerie Solanas. In the 1970s and 1980s Warhol was primarily a society portraitist, although his activities included a magazine (*Interview*) and a cable TV show.

His early silk-screen series dealt with car crashes and suicides, Marilyn Monroe, Elvis Presley, and flowers. His films, beginning with *Sleep* 1963 and ending with *Bad* 1977, have a strong documentary or improvisational element. His books include *The Philosophy of Andy Warhol (From A to B and Back Again)* 1975 and *Popism* 1980.

In the future everyone will be famous for 15 minutes.

Andy Warhol *Exposures* 1979

Warlock Peter. Pen name of Philip Heseltine 1894–1930. English composer whose style was influenced by the music of the Elizabethan age and by that of Delius. His works include the orchestral suite *Capriol* 1926 based on 16th-century dances, and the song cycle *The Curlew* 1920–22. His works of musical theory and criticism were published under his real name.

Warner Deborah 1959– . British theatre director who founded the Kick Theatre company 1980. Discarding period costume and furnished sets, she adopted an uncluttered approach to the classics, including productions of many Shakespeare plays and Sophocles' *Electra*.

Warner Rex 1905–1986. British novelist. His later novels, such as *The Young Caesar* and *Imperial Caesar* 1958–60, are based on classical themes, but he is better remembered today for his earlier works, such as *The Aerodrome* 1941, which are disturbing parables based on the political situation of the 1930s.

Warner Bros US film production company, founded 1923 by Harry, Albert, Sam, and Jack Warner. It became one of the major Hollywood studios after releasing the first talking film, *The Jazz Singer* 1927. During the 1930s and 1950s, company stars included Humphrey Bogart, Errol Flynn, and Bette Davis. It suffered in the 1960s through competition with television and was taken over by Seven Art Productions. In 1969 there was another takeover by Kinney National Service, and the whole company became known as *Warner Communications*.

Warner Brothers Records (now WEA) was formed in the late 1950s, releasing mostly middle-of-the-road pop music; an early signing was the Everly Brothers. It became one of the six major record companies in the 1970s, with artists like Joni Mitchell, Randy Newman, and Prince. Warner Communications subsidiaries include Sire, which in 1983 signed Madonna.

Warren Robert Penn 1905–1989. US poet and novelist, the only author to receive a Pulitzer Prize for both prose and poetry. His work explored the moral problems of the South. His most important novel, *All the King's Men* 1946 (Pulitzer Prize 1947), depicts the rise and fall of a back-country demagogue. He also won Pulitzer Prizes for *Promises* 1968 and *Now and Then: Poems* 1976–78. He was a senior figure of the ◊New Criticism, and the first official US poet laureate 1986–88.

Your business as a writer is not to illustrate virtue but to show how a fellow may move toward it or away from it.

Robert Penn Warren *Paris Review* 1957

Warton Joseph 1722–1800. English poet, headmaster of Winchester 1766–93, whose verse and *Essay on the Writings and Genius of Pope* 1756–82 marked an 'anti-Classical' reaction.

Warton Thomas Wain 1728–1790. English critic. He was professor of poetry at Oxford 1757–67 and published the first *History of English Poetry* 1774–81. He was poet laureate from 1785.

Waste Land, The poem by T S ◊Eliot, first published 1922. A long, complex, and innovative poem, it expressed the prevalent mood of disillusionment after World War I and is a key work of Modernism in literature.

April is the cruellest month, breeding/ Lilacs out of the dead land, mixing/ Memory and desire, stirring/Dull roots with spring rain.

T S Eliot *The Waste Land*

Water Babies, The fantasy by British author Charles ◊Kingsley, published in England 1863. Tom, an orphan child who works as a chimney sweep, inadvertently frightens a girl, Ellie, and runs away. He drowns and is immortalized as an amphibious 'water baby'. After redeeming his moral character by the instruction of Mrs Bedonebyasyoudid and Mrs Doasyouwouldbedoneby, Tom is reunited with Ellie, who drowns while trying to reach him.

watercolour painting method of painting with pigments mixed with water, known in China as early as the 3rd century. The art as practised today began in England in the 18th century with the work of Paul Sandby and was developed by Thomas Girtin, John Sell Cotman, and J M W Turner. Other outstanding watercolourists were Raoul Dufy, Paul Cézanne, and John Marin. The technique of watercolour painting requires great skill since its transparency rules out overpainting.

Western artists excelling in watercolour painting include J R Cozens, Peter de Wint, John Constable, David Cox, John Singer Sargent, Philip Wilson Steer, Paul Signac, Emil Nolde, Paul Klee, and Paul Nash. The Royal Society of Painters in Water Colours was founded 1804.

Waterhouse Alfred 1830–1905. English architect. He was a leading exponent of Victorian Neo-Gothic, typically using multicoloured tiles and bricks. His works include the Natural History Museum, London, 1868.

Water Lily Pond, The oil painting by Claude ◊Monet 1899 (National Gallery, London), one of a series of ten views of this subject painted in his garden of Giverny in Normandy, France. Monet's subordination of form to colour in these paintings marks the beginnings of abstract Impressionism. The same subject appears in a set of murals (Musée de l'Orangerie, Paris).

Waters see ◊Muddy Waters, US blues singer, songwriter, and guitarist.

Watteau Jean-Antoine 1684–1721. French Rococo painter. He developed a new category of genre painting known as the *fête galante*: fanciful scenes depicting elegantly dressed young people engaged in outdoor entertainment. One of these pictures, *The Embarkation for Cythera* 1717 (Louvre, Paris), won him membership in the French Academy.

Watteau was born in Valenciennes. At first inspired by Flemish genre painters, he produced tavern and military scenes. His early years in Paris, from 1702, introduced him to fashionable French paintings and in particular to decorative styles and theatrical design. He was also influenced by ◊Giorgione and ◊Rubens.

Watts George Frederick 1817–1904. English painter and sculptor. He painted allegorical, biblical, and classical subjects, investing his work with a solemn morality, as in *Hope* 1886 (Tate

Gallery, London). Many of his portraits are in the National Portrait Gallery, London. As a sculptor he executed *Physical Energy* 1904 for Cecil Rhodes' memorial in Cape Town, South Africa; a replica is in Kensington Gardens, London. He was a forerunner of Symbolism.

Watts-Dunton (Walter) Theodore 1832–1914. British writer, author of *Aylwin* 1898, a novel of gypsy life, poems, and critical work. He was a close friend of the painter Rossetti, the writer Borrow, and the poet Swinburne, who shared his house at Putney for many years.

Waugh Evelyn (Arthur St John) 1903–1966. English novelist. His social satires include *Decline and Fall* 1928, *Vile Bodies* 1930, and *The Loved One* 1948. A Roman Catholic convert from 1930, he developed a serious concern with religious issues in ◊*Brideshead Revisited* 1945. *The Ordeal of Gilbert Pinfold* 1957 is largely autobiographical.

Wayang Kulit Indonesian shadow puppet theatre, with characters drawn from the Sanskrit epic tradition contrasted with grotesque demons and clowns. Performances, with jointed puppets cut from leather, are accompanied by the brass gong orchestra known as the gamelan, and may last all through the night, on private or public celebrations. Similar forms of shadow puppet theatre are found in India and Malaya.

Wayne John ('Duke'). Stage name of Marion Morrison 1907–1979. US actor, the archetypal Western hero: plain-speaking, brave, and solitary. His films include *Stagecoach* 1939, *Red River* 1948, *She Wore a Yellow Ribbon* 1949, *The Searchers* 1956, *Rio Bravo* 1959, *The Man Who Shot Liberty Valance* 1962, and *True Grit* 1969 (Academy Award). He was active in conservative politics.

Wayne also appeared in many war films, such as *The Sands of Iwo Jima* 1945, *In Harm's Way* 1965, and *The Green Berets* 1968. His other films include *The Quiet Man* 1952, *The High and the Mighty* 1954, and *The Shootist* 1976, his last.

I've played the kind of man I'd like to have been.

John Wayne in the *Daily Mail* Jan 1974

Way of All Flesh, The novel by Samuel ◊Butler published 1903. Ernest Pontifex, the hapless son of a clergyman, is treated harshly by his sanctimonious father and mother. After Ernest has been allowed to suffer long enough, he inherits money from his aunt and lives happily as a minor man of letters. The plot is merely the framework for Butler's witty attack on Victorian hypocrisies and repressive conventions.

weatherboard one of a set of thin boards, usually thicker along one edge than the other, nailed on an outside wall in an overlapping fashion to form a covering that will shed water. It is a popular building material in Australia and the USA.

weaving the production of ◊textile fabric by means of a loom. The basic process is the interlacing at right angles of longitudinal threads (the warp) and horizontal threads (the weft), the latter being carried across from one side of the loom to the other by a type of bobbin called a shuttle.

The technique of weaving has been used all over the world since ancient times and has only fairly recently been mechanized. Hand looms are still used, in many societies: for example, in the manufacture of tweeds in the British Isles. They may be horizontal or vertical; industrial looms are generally vertical. In the hand-loom era the Jacquard machine, the last in a series of inventions for producing complicated designs, was perfected in the early 19th century.

The power loom 1786 was essentially the invention of an English cleric, Edmund Cartwright (1743–1823). The speed limitations caused by the slow passage of the shuttle have been partly overcome by the use of water- and air-jet insertion methods, and by the development in the 1970s of 'multiphase' looms in which the weft is inserted in continuous waves across the machine, rather than one weft at a time.

Webb Aston 1849–1930. English architect, responsible for numerous public buildings at the turn of the century. His work in London includes the main section of the Victoria and Albert Museum 1891–1909, Admiralty Arch 1908–09, and the façade of Buckingham Palace 1912–13.

Webb Mary 1882–1927. English novelist. Born in Shropshire, she wrote of country life and characters, for example in *Precious Bane* 1924, which became known through a recommendation by Stanley Baldwin.

Webb Philip (Speakman) 1831–1915. English architect, a leading figure (along with Norman ◊Shaw and Charles ◊Voysey) of the Arts and Crafts movement, which was instrumental in the revival of English domestic architecture in the late 19th century. He mostly designed private houses, notably the Red House, Bexley Heath, Sussex, 1859, for William ◊Morris.

Other houses include Joldwyns, Surrey, 1873, Clouds, East Knoyle, Wiltshire, 1876–91, and Standen, East Grinstead, 1891–94.

Webber Andrew Lloyd. English composer of musicals; see ◊Lloyd Webber.

Weber Carl Maria Friedrich Ernst von 1786–1826. German composer who established the Romantic school of opera with *Der Freischütz/The Marksman* 1821 and *Euryanthe* 1823. He was Kapellmeister (chief conductor) at Breslau 1804–06, Prague 1813–16, and Dresden 1816. He died during a visit to London where he produced his opera *Oberon* 1826, written for the Covent Garden Theatre.

Weber Max 1881–1961. Russian-born US painter and sculptor. Influenced by Parisian avant-garde painters of the Cubist and Futurist schools, he was a prominent figure in importing these styles to the USA and also created Futuristic sculpture.

Born in Russia, he emigrated to New York 1891, where he studied painting. He travelled through Europe 1905–09.

Webern Anton (Friedrich Wilhelm von) 1883–1945. Austrian composer of spare, enigmatic miniatures combining a pastoral poetic with severe structural rigour. A Renaissance musical scholar, he became a pupil of ◊Schoenberg, whose ◊twelve-tone system he reinterpreted as abstract design in works such as the *Concerto for Nine Instruments* 1931–34 and the *Second Cantata* 1941–43. His constructivist aesthetic influenced the postwar generation of advanced composers.

Webster John c. 1580–1634. English dramatist who ranks after Shakespeare as the greatest tragedian of his time, and is the Jacobean whose plays are most frequently performed today. His two great plays *The White Devil* 1612 and *The Duchess of Malfi* 1614 are dark, violent tragedies obsessed with death and decay.

Wedekind Frank 1864–1918. German dramatist. He was a forerunner of Expressionism with *Frühlings Erwachen/The Awakening of Spring* 1891, and *Der Erdgeist/The Earth Spirit* 1895 and its sequel *Der Marquis von Keith. Die Büchse der Pandora/Pandora's Box* 1904 was the source for Berg's opera *Lulu*. Many of Wedekind's writings were considered shocking because of their frank sexuality.

Wedgwood Josiah 1730–1795. English pottery manufacturer. He set up business in Staffordshire in the early 1760s to produce his agateware as well as unglazed blue or green stoneware (jasper) decorated with white Neo-Classical designs, using pigments of his own invention.

Weems Mason Locke 1759–1825. American writer and cleric. His biography *The Life and Memorable Actions of George Washington*, published around 1800, contained the first published version of the 'cherry-tree' legend which was responsible for much of the Washington myth. He also wrote lives of Francis Marion 1809 and Benjamin Franklin 1815.

Weigel Helene 1900–1971. Austrian actress and director. She cofounded the Berliner Ensemble with her husband Bertolt ◊Brecht 1949 and took leading roles in productions of his plays, visiting London 1956 and 1965. She took over direction of the Ensemble after Brecht's death 1956.

Weill Kurt (Julian) 1900–1950. German composer, US citizen from 1943. He wrote chamber and orchestral music and collaborated with Bertolt ◊Brecht on operas such as *Die Dreigroschenoper/The Threepenny Opera* 1928 and *Aufsteig und Fall der Stadt Mahagonny/The Rise and Fall of the City of Mahagonny* 1930, all attacking social corruption (*Mahagonny* caused a riot at its premiere in Leipzig). He tried to evolve a new form of ◊music theatre, using subjects with a contemporary relevance and the simplest musical means. In 1935 he left Germany for the USA where he wrote a number of successful scores for Broadway, among them the antiwar musical *Johnny Johnson* 1936 (including the often covered 'September Song') and *Street Scene* 1947 based on an Elmer Rice play set in the Depression.

Weir Peter 1938– . Australian film director. His films have an atmospheric quality and often contain a strong spiritual element. They include *Picnic at Hanging Rock* 1975, *Witness* 1985, *The Mosquito Coast* 1986, and the comedy *Green Card* 1990.

Weismuller Johnny (Peter John) 1904–1984. US film actor, formerly an Olympic swimmer, who played Tarzan in a long-running series of films for MGM and RKO including *Tarzan the Ape Man* 1932, *Tarzan and His Mate* 1934, and *Tarzan and the Leopard Woman* 1946.

Welch (Maurice) Denton 1915–1948. English writer and artist. His works include the novel *In Youth is Pleasure* 1944 and the autobiographical *A Voice Through a Cloud* 1950.

Welch Raquel. Stage name of Raquel Tejada 1940– . US actress, a sex symbol of the 1960s in such films as *One Million Years BC* 1966, *Myra Breckinridge* 1970, and *The Three Musketeers* 1973.

Weldon Fay 1931– . British novelist and dramatist whose work deals with feminist themes, often in an ironic or comic manner. Novels include *The Fat Woman's Joke* 1967, *Female Friends* 1975, *Remember Me* 1976, *Puffball* 1980, *The Life and Loves of a She-Devil* 1984 (made into a film with Meryl Streep 1990), and *The Hearts and Lives of Men* 1987. She has also written plays for the stage, radio, and television.

Welhaven Johan Sebastian Cammermeyer 1807–1873. Norwegian poet, professor of philosophy at Christiania (now Oslo) 1839–68. A supporter of the Dano-Norwegian culture, he is considered one of the greatest poetic masters of poetic form. His works include the satiric *Norges Dæmring/The Dawn of Norway* 1834.

Welles (George) Orson 1915–1985. US actor and film and theatre director, whose first film was *Citizen Kane* 1941, which he produced, directed, and starred in. Using innovative lighting, camera angles and movements, it is a landmark in the history of cinema, yet he subsequently directed very few films in Hollywood. His performances as an actor include the character of Harry Lime in *The Third Man* 1949.

In 1937 he founded the Mercury Theater, New York, with John Houseman, where their repertory productions included a modern-dress version of *Julius Caesar*. Welles' realistic radio broadcast of H G Wells' *The War of the Worlds* 1938 caused panic and fear of Martian invasion in the USA. His films include *The Magnificent Ambersons* 1942, *The Lady from Shanghai* 1948 with his wife Rita Hayworth, *Touch of Evil* 1958, and *Chimes at Midnight* 1967, a Shakespeare adaptation.

Wellesz Egon (Joseph) 1885–1974. Austrian composer and musicologist. He taught at Vienna University 1913–38, specializing in the history of Byzantine, Renaissance, and modern music. He moved to England 1938 and lectured at Oxford from 1943. His compositions include operas such as *Alkestis* 1924; symphonies, notably the Fifth 1957; ballet music; and a series of string quartets.

Wells H(erbert) G(eorge) 1866–1946. English writer, best remembered for his 'scientific romances' such as *The Time Machine* 1895 and *The War of the Worlds* 1898. His later novels had an anti-establishment, anti-conventional humour remarkable in its day, for example *Kipps* 1905 and *Tono-Bungay* 1909. His many other books include *The Outline of History* 1920 and *The Shape of Things to Come* 1933, a number of his prophecies from which have since been fulfilled. He also wrote many short stories.

Human history becomes more and more a race between education and catastrophe.

H G Wells *The Outline of History* 1920

Welsh literature the prose and poetry of Wales, written predominantly in Welsh but also, more recently, in English. The chief remains of early Welsh literature are contained in the Four Ancient Books of Wales – the *Black Book of Carmarthen*, the *Book of ◊Taliesin*, the *Book of ◊Aneirin*, and the *Red Book of Hergest* – anthologies of prose and verse of the 6th–14th centuries. Characteristic of Welsh poetry is the bardic system, which ensured the continuance of traditional conventions; most celebrated of the 12th-century bards was Cynddelw Brydydd Mawr (active 1155–1200).

The English conquest of 1282 involved the fall of the princes who supported these bards, but after a period of decline a new school arose in South Wales with a new freedom in form and sentiment, the most celebrated poet in the 14th century being Dafydd ap Gwilym, and in the next century the classical metrist Dafydd ap Edmwnd (active 1450–1459). With the Reformation biblical translations were undertaken, and Morgan

Llwyd (1619–1659) and Ellis Wynne (1671–1734) wrote religious prose. Popular metres resembling those of England developed – for example, the poems of Huw Morys (1622–1709).

In the 18th century the classical poetic forms revived with Goronwy Owen, and the ◊eisteddfod (literary festival) movement began: popular measures were used by the hymn-writer William Williams Pantycelyn (1717–1791).

The 19th century saw few notable figures save the novelist Daniel Owen (1836–1895), but the foundation of a Welsh university and the work there of John Morris Jones (1864–1929) produced a 20th-century revival, including T Gwynn Jones (1871–1949), W J Gruffydd (1881–1954), and R Williams Parry (1884–1956). Later writers included the poet J Kitchener Davies (1902–1952), the dramatist and poet Saunders Lewis (1893–1985), and the novelist and short-story writer Kate Roberts (1891–1985). Among writers of the postwar period are the poets Waldo Williams (1904–1971), Euros Bowen (1904–), and Bobi Jones (1929–), and the novelists Islwyn Ffowc Elis (1924–) and Jane Edwards (1938–). Those who have expressed the Welsh spirit in English include the poets Edward Thomas, Vernon Watkins (1906–1967), Dylan Thomas, R S Thomas, and Dannie Abse (1923–), and the novelist Emyr Humphreys (1919–).

Weltanschauung (German 'worldview') a philosophy of life.

Welty Eudora 1909– . US novelist and short-story writer, born in Jackson, Mississippi. Her works reflect life in the American South and are notable for their creation of character and accurate rendition of local dialect. Her novels include *Delta Wedding* 1946, *Losing Battles* 1970, and *The Optimist's Daughter* 1972.

Werfel Franz 1890–1945. Austrian poet, dramatist, and novelist, a leading Expressionist. His works include the poems 'Der Weltfreund der Gerichtstag'/'The Day of Judgment' 1919; the plays *Juarez und Maximilian* 1924 and *Das Reich Gottes in Böhmen*/*The Kingdom of God in Bohemia* 1930; and the novels *Verdi* 1924 and *Das Lied von Bernadette*/*The Song of Bernadette* 1941.

Born in Prague, he lived in Germany, Austria, and France, and in 1940 escaped from a French concentration camp to the USA, where he died. In 1929 he married Alma Mahler, daughter of the composer Gustav Mahler.

Wergeland Henrik 1808–1845. Norwegian lyric poet. He was a leader of the Norwegian revival and is known for his epic *Skabelsen, Mennesket, og Messias*/*Creation, Humanity, and Messiah* 1830.

Wesker Arnold 1932– . English dramatist. His socialist beliefs were reflected in the successful trilogy *Chicken Soup with Barley, Roots,* and *I'm Talking About Jerusalem* 1958–60. He established a catchphrase with *Chips with Everything* 1962.

In 1961, Wesker tried unsuccessfully to establish a working-class theatre with trade-union backing at the Round House in London. Later plays include *The Merchant* 1978 and *Lady Othello* 1987.

Wessex fictional setting for most of Thomas ◊Hardy's novels. Drawing on England's west country, the heartland was Dorset but its outlying boundary markers were Plymouth, Bath, Oxford, and Southampton. He gave fictional names to such real places as Dorchester (Casterbridge), Salisbury (Melchester) and Bournemouth (Sandbourne), but mixed these with a sprinkling of real names such as Stonehenge, the river Frome, and Nettlecombe Tout.

West Benjamin 1738–1820. American Neo-Classical painter, active in London from 1763. He enjoyed the patronage of George III for many years and was a noted history painter. His *The Death of General Wolfe* 1770 (National Gallery, Ottawa) began a vogue for painting recent historical events in contemporary costume. He became president of the Royal Academy, London, 1792.

West Mae 1892–1980. US vaudeville, stage, and film actress. She wrote her own dialogue, setting herself up as a provocative sex symbol and the mistress of verbal innuendo. She appeared on Broadway in *Sex* 1926, *Drag* 1927, and *Diamond Lil* 1928, which was the basis of the film (with Cary Grant) *She Done Him Wrong* 1933. Her other films include *I'm No Angel* 1933, *My Little Chickadee* 1940 (with W C Fields), *Myra Breckinridge* 1969, and *Sextette* 1977. Both her plays and her films led to legal battles over censorship.

I used to be Snow White... but I drifted.

Mae West

West Morris 1916– . Australian novelist whose recurring themes are Catholicism in crisis, political power, and moral dilemma. He first attracted international attention with the award-winning *Devil's Advocate* 1959, filmed 1977. Later novels include *The Shoes of the Fisherman* 1963, about a fictional pope, *The Clowns of God* 1981, and *The World is Made of Glass* 1983, an imaginative reconstruction of the psychological and moral ordeal of one of Jung's female patients.

West Nathanael. Pen name of Nathan Weinstein 1904–1940. US writer whose novels, noted for their surreal black humour, capture the dark side of the American Dream. His most powerful novel, *The Day of the Locust* 1939, depicts the corruption of Hollywood, where West had been a screenwriter.

His other work consisted of *The Dream Life of Balso Snell* 1931; *Miss Lonelyhearts* 1933, a black farce about a newspaper agony columnist; and *A Cool Million* 1934, which satirizes the rags-to-riches dream of success. West and his wife died in a car accident.

West Rebecca. Pen name of Cicely Isabel Fairfield 1892–1983. British journalist and novelist, an active feminist from 1911. *The Meaning of Treason* 1959 deals with the spies Burgess and Maclean. Her novels have political themes and include *The Fountain Overflows* 1956 and *The Birds Fall Down* 1966.

Western genre of popular fiction based on the landscape and settlement of the American West. It developed in US ◊dime novels and ◊frontier literature. The Western became established in written form with novels such as *The Virginian* 1902 by Owen Wister and *Riders of the Purple Sage* 1912 by Zane Grey. See also ◊Western film.

Westerns go back to J F Cooper's *Leather-stocking Tales* 1823–41, and the stories of Bret Harte and the German writer Karl May (1842–1912). In stylized form, they became frontier stories of cowboy rangers and Indian villains, set vaguely in the post-Civil War era. Many Westerns are nostalgic, written after the frontier officially closed 1890. *The Virginian* is the 'serious' version of the form, but prolific writers like Zane Grey and Frederick Faust (1892–1944) developed its pulp possibilities and its place in universal fantasy.

Western film genre of films based loosely on the history of the American West and evolved from the written Western. As a genre, the Western is virtually as old as the cinema. Italian 'spaghetti Westerns' and Japanese Westerns established it as an international form. The genre became less popular in the 1970s. There have been only four commercially successful films since then: *Pale Rider* 1985, *Young Guns* 1988, and the Academy Award winners *Dances with Wolves* 1990 and *Unforgiven* 1992.

A memorable early example is *The Great Train Robbery* 1903. The silent era produced such epics as *The Iron Horse* 1924, and the genre remained popular into the coming of sound. The 1930s saw many epics, such as *Union Pacific* 1939, whereas the 1940s often dwelt on specific historical events (including Custer's last stand in *They Died With Their Boots On* 1941). The 1950s brought more realism and serious issues, such as the treatment of the Indians. The Westerns of the 1960s contained an increased amount of violence, partly owing to the influence of the 'spaghetti Westerns' (often directed by Sergio ◊Leone).

Western swing big-band, jazz-influenced country music that originated in Texas in the 1930s. A swinging, inventive dance music, with the fiddle a predominant instrument, it was developed by Bob ◊Wills and his Texas Playboys and remained a strong influence on popular music into the 1950s, with a revival of interest beginning in the early 1970s and still continuing. Other Western swing groups include Milton Brown and his Musical Brownies (1932–36) and Asleep at the Wheel (1969–   ).

Westmacott Richard 1775–1856. English Neo-Classical sculptor. He studied under Antonio Canova in Rome and was elected to the Royal Academy, London, 1811, becoming a professor there 1827–54. His works include monuments in Westminster Abbey and in St Paul's Cathedral, and the *Achilles* statue in Hyde Park, all in London.

Westminster Abbey Gothic church in central London, officially the Collegiate Church of St Peter. It was built 1050–1745 and consecrated under Edward the Confessor 1065. The west towers are by Nicholas ◊Hawksmoor, completed after his death 1745. Since William I nearly all English monarchs have been crowned in the abbey, and several are buried there; many poets are buried or commemorated there, at Poets' Corner.

The Coronation Chair includes the Stone of Scone, on which Scottish kings were crowned, brought here by Edward I 1296. Poets' Corner was begun with the burial of ◊Spenser 1599. Westminster School, a public school with ancient and modern buildings nearby, was once the Abbey School.

Weston Edward 1886–1958. US photographer. A founder member of the ◊'f/64' group, a school of photography advocating sharp definition, he was noted for the technical mastery in his Californian landscapes and nude studies.

The camera sees more than the eye so why not make use of it.

Edward Weston *Diary* 1926

Westwood Vivienne 1941–   . British fashion designer who first attracted attention in the mid-1970s as co-owner of a shop with the rock-music entrepreneur Malcolm McLaren (1946–   ), which became a focus for the punk movement in London. Early in the 1980s her 'Pirate' and 'New Romantics' looks gained her international recognition. Westwood's dramatic clothes continue to have a wide influence on the public and other designers.

Weyden Rogier van der c. 1399–1464. Netherlandish artist, official painter to the city of Brussels from 1436. He painted portraits and religious subjects, such as *The Last Judgment* about 1450 (Hôtel-Dieu, Beaune). His refined style had considerable impact on Netherlandish painting.

Little is known of his life, and none of his works has been dated, but he was widely admired in his day and his paintings were sent to Italy, Spain, France, and Germany. His *Deposition* before 1443 (Prado, Madrid) shows the influence of Robert ◊Campin.

Whale James 1886–1957. English film director. He went to Hollywood to film his stage success *Journey's End* 1930, and then directed four horror films: *Frankenstein* 1931, *The Old Dark House* 1932, *The Invisible Man* 1933, and *Bride of Frankenstein* 1935. He also directed the musical *Showboat* 1936.

Wharton Edith (Newbold) (born Jones) 1862–1937. US novelist. Her work, known for its subtlety and form and influenced by her friend Henry James, was mostly set in New York society. It includes *The House of Mirth* 1905, which made her reputation; the grim, uncharacteristic novel of New England *Ethan Frome* 1911; *The Custom of the Country* 1913; and *The Age of Innocence* 1920 (Pulitzer Prize).

Mrs Ballinger is one of those ladies who pursue Culture in bands, as if it were dangerous to meet it alone.

Edith Wharton *Xingu* 1916

Wheatley Dennis (Yates) 1897–1977. British thriller and adventure novelist. His works include a series dealing with black magic and occultism, but he also wrote crime novels in which the reader was invited to play the detective, as in *Murder off Miami* 1936, with real clues such as ticket stubs.

Wheatstone Charles 1802–1875. English physicist and inventor of the harmonica and the concertina.

whistle any of a class of wind instruments including recorders, flutes, organ pipes, and pan-pipes, that uses a rigid edge as an aerofoil to split the air flow, giving a characteristic 'chuff' onset to the tone. Among the most ancient and widespread of musical instruments, whistles produce a relatively pure tone and simple waveform.

Whistler James Abbott McNeill 1834–1903. US painter and etcher, active in London from 1859. Influenced by Japanese prints, he painted riverscapes and portraits that show subtle composition and colour harmonies: for example, *Arrangement in Grey and Black: Portrait of the Painter's Mother* 1871 (Louvre, Paris).

He settled in Chelsea, London, and painted views of the Thames including *Old Battersea Bridge* about 1872–75 (Tate Gallery, London). In 1877 the art critic John ◊Ruskin published an article on his *Nocturne in Black and Gold: The*

Falling Rocket (now in Detroit) that led to a libel trial in which Whistler was awarded symbolic damages of a farthing (a quarter of an old penny). Whistler described the trial in his book *The Gentle Art of Making Enemies* 1890.

Defence counsel The labour of two days is that for which you ask two hundred guineas? Whistler *No. I ask it for the knowledge I have gained in the work of a lifetime.*

James Abbott McNeill Whistler at the 1878 libel case against Ruskin

---

Whistler Rex John 1905–1944. English artist. He painted fanciful murals, for example *In Pursuit of Rare Meats* 1926–27 in the Tate Gallery restaurant, London. He also illustrated many books and designed stage sets.

Whitbread Literary Award annual prize of £23,000 open to writers in the UK and Ireland. Nominations are in five categories: novel, first novel, children's novel, autobiography/biography, and poetry, each receiving £2,000. The overall winner receives a further £21,000. The award, which is administered by the Booksellers Association, was founded 1971 by Whitbread, a brewery.

The first overall winner 1984 went to poet Douglas Dunn for his *Elegies*. In 1993 the overall prize was won for the first time by a woman, Joan Brady for her novel *Theory of War*.

White E(lwyn) B(rooks) 1899–1985. US writer, long associated with the *New Yorker* magazine and renowned for his satire, such as *Is Sex Necessary?* 1929 (with the humorist James Thurber). White also wrote two children's classics, *Stuart Little* 1945 and *Charlotte's Web* 1952.

White Gilbert 1720–1793. English cleric and naturalist, born at Selborne, Hampshire, and author of *Natural History and Antiquities of Selborne* 1789.

Inspiration descends only in flashes, to clothe circumstances; it is not stored up in a barrel, like salt herrings, to be doled out.

Patrick White *Voss* 1957

White Patrick (Victor Martindale) 1912–1990. Australian writer who did more than any other to put Australian literature on the international map. His partly allegorical novels explore the lives of early settlers in Australia and often deal with misfits or inarticulate people. They include *The Aunt's*

Story 1948, *The Tree of Man* 1955, and *Voss* 1957 (based on the ill-fated 19th-century explorer Leichhardt). Nobel Prize for Literature 1973.

White Stanford 1853–1906. US architect, a cofounder of the architectural firm of McKim, Mead and White. One of the most prominent US architects of the 19th century, he specialized in the Renaissance style and designed, among many famous projects, the original Madison Square Garden and the Washington Square Arch, both in New York City.

White T(erence) H(anbury) 1906–1964. English writer who retold the Arthurian legend in four volumes of *The Once and Future King* 1938–58.

White House official residence of the president of the USA, in Washington, DC. It is a plain edifice of sandstone, built in Italian Renaissance style 1792–99 to the designs of James Hoban, who also restored it after it was burned by the British 1814; it was then painted white to hide the scars.

Whiteley Brett 1939–1992. Australian painter. He achieved international recognition 1961 with exhibitions in London, the purchase of his *Untitled Red* by the Tate Gallery, London (the youngest ever painter to be so honoured), and the award of the Paris Biennale Prix International.

Whiteman Paul 1890–1967. US dance-band and swing-orchestra leader specializing in 'symphonic jazz'. He commissioned George Gershwin's *Rhapsody in Blue*, conducting its premiere 1924.

Whitman Walt(er) 1819–1892. US poet who published ◊*Leaves of Grass* 1855, which contains the symbolic ◊'Song of Myself'. It used unconventional free verse (with no rhyme or regular rhythm) and scandalized the public by its frank celebration of sexuality.

Born at West Hill (Huntington, Long Island), New York, as a young man Whitman worked as a printer, teacher, and journalist. In 1865 he published *Drum-Taps*, a volume inspired by his work as an army nurse during the Civil War. *Democratic Vistas* 1871 is a collection of his prose pieces. He also wrote an elegy for Abraham Lincoln, 'When Lilacs Last in the Dooryard Bloom'd'. He preached a particularly American vision of individual freedom and human brotherhood. Such poets as Ezra Pound, Wallace Stevens, and Allen Ginsberg show his influence in their work.

Do I contradict myself? Very well then I contradict myself (I am large, I contain multitudes).

Walt Whitman 'Song of Myself' 1855

Whittier John Greenleaf 1807–1892. US poet who was a powerful opponent of slavery, as shown in the verse *Voices of Freedom* 1846. Among his other works are *Legends of New England in Prose and Verse*, *Songs of Labor* 1850, and the New England nature poem 'Snow-Bound' 1866.

The age is dull and mean. Men creep.
Not walk.

John Greenleaf Whittier 'Lines inscribed
to Friends under Arrest for Treason
against the Slave Power' 1856

Who, the English rock group, formed 1964, with a hard, aggressive sound, high harmonies, and a propensity for destroying their instruments on stage. Their albums include *Tommy* 1969, *Who's Next* 1971, and *Quadrophenia* 1973.

Originally a mod band, the Who comprised Pete ◊Townshend, guitar and songwriter; Roger Daltrey (1944–   ), vocals; John Entwistle (1944–   ), bass; and Keith Moon (1947–1978), drums.

wickerwork furniture or other objects made from flexible rods or shoots, usually willow, as developed from stake-frame basketry. It is made by weaving strands in and out of a wicker frame.

Wickerwork stools were made in ancient Rome and Egypt. Examples dating from the 3rd millennium BC have been found in Egyptian tombs. Because the materials are perishable, no other pieces survive until the 17th century. The form of basket tub chair popular today may date from before the Middle Ages, and a circular wickerwork screen is shown in a painting *c.* 1420–30 of the Virgin and Child by the Netherlandish painter Robert Campin (National Gallery, London). Wills dating from the 16th and 17th centuries refer to wickerwork chairs in the houses of the nobility. The craft was revived in Leicester, England, 1910 by a company supplying furniture to the home market, British colonies, and the USA. Wickerwork is still made from willow, cane, and rattan.

wide-angle lens photographic lens of shorter focal length than normal, taking in a wider angle of view.

Widmark Richard 1914–   . US actor who made his film debut in *Kiss of Death* 1947 as a psychopath. He subsequently appeared in a great variety of *film noir* roles as well as in *The Alamo* 1960, *Madigan* 1968, and *Coma* 1978.

Wieland Christoph Martin 1733–1813. German poet and novelist. After attempts at religious poetry, he came under the influence of Voltaire and Rousseau, and wrote novels such as *Die Geschichte des Agathon/The History of Agathon*

1766–67 and the satirical *Die Abderiten* 1774 (translated as *The Republic of Fools* 1861); and tales in verse such as *Musarion oder Die Philosophie der Grazien* 1768, *Oberon* 1780, and others. He translated Shakespeare into German 1762–66.

Wiene Robert 1880–1938. German film director of the bizarre Expressionist film *Das Kabinett des Dr Caligari/The Cabinet of Dr Caligari* 1919. He also directed *Orlacs Hände/The Hands of Orlac* 1924, *Der Rosenkavalier* 1926, and *Ultimatum* 1938.

Wiener Werkstätte (German 'Vienna Workshops') group of artisans and artists, founded in Vienna 1903 by Josef Hoffmann and Kolo Moser, who were both members of the Vienna ◊Sezession. They designed objects, ranging from furniture and jewellery to metal and books, in a rectilinear Art Nouveau style influenced by Charles Rennie ◊Mackintosh. The workshops, financed by Fritz Wärndorfer, closed 1932.

wig artificial head of hair, either real or synthetic, worn as an adornment, disguise, or to conceal baldness. Wigs were known in the ancient world and have been found on Egyptian mummies. Today they remain part of the uniform of judges, barristers, and some parliamentary officials in the UK and certain Commonwealth countries.

The 16th-century periwig imitated real hair, and developed into the elaborate peruke. Under Queen Anne, wigs covering the back and shoulders became fashionable.

Wiggin Kate Douglas 1856–1923. US writer, born in Philadelphia. She was a pioneer in the establishment of kindergartens in the USA, and wrote the children's classic *Rebecca of Sunnybrook Farm* 1903 and its sequels.

Wigman Mary 1886–1973. German dancer, choreographer, and a pioneer of the ◊Ausdruckstanz school of modern dance. She was noted for her solos exploring the darker, melancholic sides of human nature. Many of her movements were angular and distorted, centred towards the ground rather than balletic elevation.

Wigman studied eurythmics with Emile Jaques-Dalcroze and later became Rudolf von Laban's assistant during World War I. Some of her early compositions were performed in silence to assert dance's independence from music.

Wilbur Richard (Purdy) 1921–   . US poet, noted for his cultural conservatism, urbane wit, and the elegance of his verse in such volumes as *The Beautiful Changes* 1947 and *Things of This World* 1956. He also published children's verse, as in *Loudmouse* 1963 and *Opposites* 1973.

Wilde Cornel(ius Louis) 1915–1989. Austrian-born US actor and film director, in the USA from 1932. He starred as Frédéric Chopin in *A Song to Remember* 1945, and directed *The Naked Prey*

1966, *Beach Red* 1967, and *No Blade of Grass* 1970.

Wilde Oscar (Fingal O'Flahertie Wills) 1854–1900. Irish writer. With his flamboyant style and quotable conversation, he dazzled London society and, on his lecture tour 1882, the USA. He published his only novel, *The ◊Picture of Dorian Gray*, 1891, followed by a series of sharp comedies, including *A Woman of No Importance* 1893 and *The Importance of Being Earnest* 1895. In 1895 he was imprisoned for two years for homosexual offences; he died in exile.

Wilde was born in Dublin and studied at Dublin and Oxford, where he became known as a supporter of the Aesthetic movement ('art for art's sake'). He published *Poems* 1881, and also wrote fairy tales and other stories, criticism, and a long, anarchic political essay, *The Soul of Man Under Socialism* 1891. His elegant social comedies include *Lady Windermere's Fan* 1892 and *An Ideal Husband* 1895. The drama *Salome* 1893, based on the biblical character, was written in French; considered scandalous by the British censor, it was first performed in Paris 1896 with the actress Sarah Bernhardt in the title role.

Among his lovers was Lord Alfred Douglas, whose father provoked Wilde into a lawsuit that led to his social and financial ruin and imprisonment. The long poem *Ballad of Reading Gaol* 1898 and a letter published as *De Profundis* 1905 were written in jail to explain his side of the relationship. After his release from prison 1897, he lived in France and is buried in Paris.

Wilder Billy 1906– . Austrian-born accomplished US screenwriter and film director, in the USA from 1934. He directed and co-scripted the cynical *Double Indemnity* 1944, *The Lost Weekend* (Academy Award for best director) 1945, *Sunset Boulevard* 1950, *Some Like It Hot* 1959, and *The Apartment* (Academy Award) 1960.

Wilder Thornton (Niven) 1897–1975. US dramatist and novelist. He won Pulitzer Prizes for the novel *The Bridge of San Luis Rey* 1927, and for the plays *Our Town* 1938 and *The Skin of Our Teeth* 1942. His farce *The Matchmaker* 1954 was filmed 1958. In 1964 it was adapted into the hit stage musical *Hello, Dolly!*, also made into a film.

Wilhelm Meister's Apprenticeship (German *Wilhelm Meisters Lehrjahre*) novel by ◊Goethe published 1795–96. An outstanding example of the *Bildungsroman* or novel of personal development, it describes Wilhelm's formative emotional experiences, including his time with a troupe of actors involved in a production of *Hamlet*. The book incorporates extended critical discussion of the play and some of Goethe's finest lyrics. An episodic sequel, *Wilhelm Meisters Wanderjahre/ Wilhelm Meister's Wandering Years* was published 1821 and in expanded form 1829.

Wilkie David 1785–1841. Scottish genre and portrait painter, active in London from 1805. His paintings are in the 17th-century Dutch tradition and include *The Letter of Introduction* 1813 (National Gallery of Scotland, Edinburgh).

Wilkins William 1778–1839. English architect. He pioneered the Greek Revival in England with his design for Downing College, Cambridge, 1807–20. Other works include the main block of University College London 1827–28, and the National Gallery, London, 1834–38.

William the badly behaved schoolboy hero of a series of children's books by British author Richmal ◊Crompton, published 1922–70. William rebels against conventional English family life and, with his fellow 'Outlaws', Henry, Douglas, and Ginger, has many mishaps from which there is no honourable escape. Violet Elizabeth Bott, a 'soppy' girl, is an unwelcome addition to the Outlaws.

Williams (George) Emlyn 1905–1987. Welsh actor and dramatist. His plays, in which he appeared, include *Night Must Fall* 1935 and *The Corn Is Green* 1938. He was also acclaimed for his solo performance as the author Charles Dickens. Williams gave early encouragement to the actor Richard Burton.

Williams (Hiram) Hank 1923–1953. US country singer, songwriter, and guitarist, author of dozens of country standards and one of the originators of modern country music. His songs are characteristically mournful and blues-influenced, like 'Your Cheatin' Heart' 1953, but also include the uptempo 'Jambalaya' 1952 and the proto-rockabilly 'Hey, Good-Lookin'' 1951.

Williams was born in Alabama, learned guitar from a black street singer, and formed his band the Drifting Cowboys 1937. Their sparse honky-tonk (dance-hall) sound featured fiddle and steel guitar. 'Lovesick Blues' 1949, which Williams did not write, was his first number-one country hit and he quickly became the genre's biggest star.

Williams Frederick Ronald 1927–1982. Australian landscape painter. His bush paintings make a feature and a source beauty of the monotony and repetitions that occur in the Australian countryside. In *Upwey Landscape* 1966 (Australian National Gallery, Canberra) he moves between a figurative and abstract interpretation – the tree-dotted plain stretching to the horizon conveys an impression of the Australian bush in general rather than a comment on any one part of it. His non-figurative approach brought him into conflict with the ◊Antipodean Group of artists early in his career.

Williams Tennessee (Thomas Lanier) 1911–1983. US dramatist, born in Mississippi. His work is characterized by fluent dialogue and searching analysis of the psychological deficiencies of his characters. His plays, usually set in the Deep South against a background of decadence and degradation, include *The Glass Menagerie*

1945, *A Streetcar Named Desire* 1947, and *Cat on a Hot Tin Roof* 1955, the last two of which earned Pulitzer Prizes.

Many of his plays have been made into successful theatrical films, several of which were directed memorably by Elia Kazan. His other plays include *Suddenly Last Summer* 1958 and *Sweet Bird of Youth* 1959. After writing *The Night of the Iguana* 1961, also awarded the Pulitzer Prize, he entered a period of ill health, and none of his subsequent plays succeeded. However, his earlier work earned him a reputation as one of America's pre-eminent dramatists.

I can't stand a naked light bulb, any more than I can stand a rude remark or a vulgar action.

Tennessee Williams
A Streetcar Named Desire 1947

Williams John (Christopher) 1942– . Australian guitarist, resident in London from 1952. After studying with Segovia, he made his formal debut 1958. His extensive repertoire includes contemporary music and jazz; he recorded the Rodrigo *Concerto de Aranjuez* 1939 three times. He was a founder member of the pop group Sky 1979–84.

Williams William Carlos 1883–1963. US poet, essayist, and critic, associated with ◊Imagism and ◊Objectivism. One of the most original and influential of modern poets, he is noted for advancing poetics of visual images and colloquial American rhythms, conceiving the poem as a 'field of action'. His epic, five-book poem *Paterson* 1946–58 is written in a form of free verse that combines historical documents, newspaper material, and letters, to celebrate his home town in New Jersey. *Pictures from Brueghel* 1963 won him, posthumously, a Pulitzer Prize. His vast body of prose work includes novels, short stories, essays, and the play *A Dream of Love* 1948.

Say it, not in ideas but in things.

William Carlos Williams
Paterson 1946–58

Williams-Ellis Clough 1883–1978. British architect, designer of the fantasy resort of Portmeirion, N Wales.

Williamson David Keith 1942– . Australian dramatist and scriptwriter noted for his witty fast-moving dialogue and realistic plots and settings. His plays include *The Removalists* 1971, which won awards in both Australia and in the UK, *Don's Party* 1971, *The Department* 1975, *The Club*

1977, *Travelling North* 1979, and *The Perfectionist* 1981. Williamson's screenplays include *Stork* 1971, *Eliza Fraser* 1976, *Gallipoli* 1981, and *The Year of Living Dangerously* 1982 (co-writer).

Williamson Henry 1895–1977. English author whose stories of animal life include *Tarka the Otter* 1927. He described his experiences in restoring an old farm in *The Story of a Norfolk Farm* 1941 and wrote the fictional, 15-volume sequence *Chronicles of Ancient Sunlight*.

Williamson Malcolm (Benjamin Graham Christopher) 1931– . Australian composer, pianist, and organist, who settled in Britain 1953. His works include operas such as *Our Man in Havana* 1963, symphonies, and chamber music. He became Master of the Queen's Musick 1975.

Wills Bob (James Robert) 1905–1975. US country fiddle player and composer. As leader of the band known from 1934 as Bob Wills and his Texas Playboys, Wills became a pioneer of ◊Western swing and a big influence on US popular music. His songs include 'San Antonio Rose' 1938.

Wilson Angus (Frank Johnstone) 1913–1991. English novelist, short-story writer, and biographer, whose acidly humorous books include *Anglo-Saxon Attitudes* 1956 and *The Old Men at the Zoo* 1961. In his detailed portrayal of English society he extracted high comedy from its social and moral grotesqueries.

Wilson was first known for his short-story collections *The Wrong Set* 1949 and *Such Darling Dodos* 1950. His other major novels include *Late Call* 1964, *No Laughing Matter* 1967, and *Setting the World on Fire* 1980. He also published critical works on Zola, Dickens, and Kipling.

Wilson Colin 1931– . British author of *The Outsider* 1956, and of thrillers, including *Necessary Doubt* 1964. Later works, such as *Mysteries* 1978, are about the occult.

Wilson Edmund 1895–1972. US critic and writer, born in New Jersey. *Axel's Castle* 1931 is a survey of symbolism, and *The Wound and the Bow* 1941 a study of art and neurosis. He also produced the satirical sketches in *Memoirs of Hecate County* 1946.

Wilson Richard 1713/14–1782. Welsh painter whose landscapes are infused with an Italianate atmosphere and recomposed in a Classical manner. His work influenced the development of English landscape painting and Turner in particular.

Wilson Robert 1944– . US avant-garde theatre director who specializes in non-narrative, elaborately visual theatre productions such as *Deafman Glance* 1971, *Ka Mountain* at the Shiraz Festival, Iran, 1972, and *The Life and Times of Joseph Stalin* 1973. Later productions include *Einstein on the Beach* 1976 and 1992, operatic productions of

Euripides' tragedies *Medea* 1984 and *Alcestis* 1986, *The Black Rider* 1990, and *Alice* 1992.

Wilson has worked consistently outside the USA, and has collaborated closely with the German dramatist Heiner Müller.

Wilson Teddy (Theodore) 1912–1986. US bandleader and jazz pianist. He toured with Benny Goodman 1935–39 and during that period recorded in small groups with many of the best musicians of the time; some of his 1930s recordings feature the singer Billie Holiday. Wilson led a big band 1939–40 and a sextet 1940–46.

Winckelmann Johann Joachim 1717–1768. German art historian, who worked in Rome from 1755. His studies of ancient Greece and Rome were a major inspiration for the Neo-Classical movement and provided the basis for modern art history. They include *Geschichte der Kunst des Altertums/History of Ancient Art* 1764, in which he defines art as the expression of the spirit of an age.

windcap in music, a cylindrical cover protecting the double reed of a woodwind instrument, such as the crumhorn or shawm. It prevents the player's lips from making direct contact with the reeds and forms a secure airtight container, ensuring consistency of air pressure and tone.

wind instrument musical instrument that is sounded by an air flow (the performer's breath) to make a column of air vibrate within a vented tubular resonator, sometimes activating a reed or reeds. The pitch of the note is controlled by the length of the column. Major types of wind instrument are the ◊voice; ◊whistles, including the recorder and flute; ◊reed instruments, including most other woodwinds; ◊brass instruments, including horns; and ◊free-reed instruments such as the mouth organ.

Wind in the Willows, The fantasy for children by British author Kenneth ◊Grahame, published in the UK 1908. The story relates the adventures of a group of humanlike animals – Rat, Mole, Badger, and Toad. It was dramatized by A A ◊Milne as *Toad of Toad Hall* 1929 and by Alan Bennett 1990.

Winnie-the-Pooh collection of children's stories by British author A A ◊Milne, published 1926, illustrated by E H Shepard. The stories featured the author's son Christopher Robin, his teddy bear Winnie-the-Pooh, and a group of toy animals, Piglet, Eeyore, Rabbit, Owl, Kanga and Roo, and Tigger. Further stories appeared in *The House at Pooh Corner* 1928.

I am a Bear of Very Little Brain, and long words Bother me.

A A Milne *Winnie-the-Pooh* 1926

Winterhalter Franz Xavier 1805–1873. German portraitist. He became court painter to Grand Duke Leopold at Karlsruhe, then, in 1834, moved to Paris and enjoyed the patronage of European royalty.

Winterson Jeanette 1959– . English novelist. Her autobiographical first novel *Oranges Are Not the Only Fruit* 1985 humorously describes her upbringing as an Evangelical Pentecostalist in Lancashire, and her subsequent realization of her homosexuality. Later novels include *The Passion* 1987, *Sexing the Cherry* 1989, and *Written On the Body* 1992.

Wise Robert 1914– . US film director who began as a film editor. His debut was a horror film, *Curse of the Cat People* 1944; he progressed to such large-scale projects as *The Sound of Music* 1965 and *Star* 1968. His other films include *The Body Snatcher* 1945 and *Star Trek: The Motion Picture* 1979.

Wister Owen 1860–1938. US novelist who created the genre of the ◊Western. He was born in Philadelphia, a grandson of the British actress Fanny Kemble, and became known for stories of cowboys, including *The Virginian* 1902. He also wrote *Roosevelt: The Story of a Friendship 1880–1919* 1930, about his relationship with US president Theodore Roosevelt.

Witkiewicz Stanislaw 1885–1939. Polish dramatist and novelist whose surrealist plays only became widely known after World War II: these include *The Madman and the Nun, The Water Hen* 1921, *The Crazy Locomotive* 1923, and the tragedy *The Pragmatists* (written 1918). Many of his plays were produced by the director Tadeusz ◊Kantor.

Wittgenstein Paul 1887–1961. Austrian pianist, a brother of the philosopher Ludwig Wittgenstein. Despite losing his right arm in World War I he continued a career as a pianist, cultivating a virtuoso left-arm technique. He commissioned Ravel's *Concerto for the Left Hand* 1929–30, Prokofiev's *Concerto No 4 in B Flat* 1931, and concert works from Richard Strauss, Benjamin Britten, and others.

Witz Konrad *c.* 1400–1445. German-born Swiss painter whose sharply observed realism suggests that he was familiar with the work of contemporary Flemish artists such as Jan van Eyck. Lake Geneva is the setting for his best-known work, *The Miraculous Draught of Fishes* 1444 (Musée d'Art et d'Histoire, Geneva), representing one of the earliest recognizable landscapes in European art.

Wizard of Oz, The Wonderful children's tale 1900, written by L Frank ◊Baum, of Dorothy's journey by the yellow brick road to an imaginary kingdom. It had many sequels and was made into a musical film 1939 with Judy Garland.

Wodehouse P(elham) G(renville) 1881–1975. English novelist, a US citizen from 1955, whose humorous novels portray the accident-prone world of such characters as the socialite Bertie Wooster and his invaluable and impeccable manservant Jeeves, and Lord Emsworth of Blandings Castle with his prize pig, the Empress of Blandings.

From 1906, Wodehouse also collaborated on the lyrics of Broadway musicals by Jerome Kern, Gershwin, and others. He spent most of his life in the USA. Staying in France 1941, during World War II, he was interned by the Germans; he made some humorous broadcasts from Berlin, which were taken amiss in Britain at the time, but he was later exonerated, and was knighted 1975. His work is admired for its style and geniality, and includes *Indiscretions of Archie* 1921, *Uncle Fred in the Springtime* 1939, and *Aunts Aren't Gentlemen* 1974.

I don't owe a penny to a single soul – not counting tradesmen, of course.

P G Wodehouse *My Man Jeeves and the Hard Boiled Egg* 1919

Woden or **Wodan** the foremost Anglo-Saxon god, whose Norse counterpart is ◊Odin.

Woffington Peg (Margaret) *c.* 1714–1760. Irish actress who played in Dublin as a child and made her debut at Covent Garden, London, 1740. She acted in many Restoration comedies, often taking male roles, such as Lothario in Rowe's *The Fair Penitent*.

Wolf Howlin'. US blues musician; see ◊Howlin' Wolf.

Wolf Hugo (Filipp Jakob) 1860–1903. Austrian composer whose more than 250 lieder (songs) included the *Mörike-Lieder/Mörike Songs* 1888 and the two-volume *Italienisches Liederbuch/Italian Songbook* 1890–91, 1896. He brought a new concentration and tragic eloquence to the art of lieder. Among his other works are the opera *Der Corregidor/The Magistrate* 1895 and orchestral works, such as *Italian Serenade* for orchestra 1892.

Wolfe Gene 1931– . US writer known for the science-fiction series *The Book of the New Sun* 1980–83, with a Surrealist treatment of stock themes, and for the urban fantasy *Free, Live Free* 1985.

Wolfe Thomas (Clayton) 1900–1938. US novelist, noted for the unrestrained rhetoric and emotion of his prose style. He wrote four long and hauntingly powerful autobiographical novels, mostly of the South: *Look Homeward, Angel* 1929, *Of Time and the River* 1935, *The Web and the Rock* 1939, and *You Can't Go Home Again* 1940 (the last two published posthumously).

Wolfe Tom. Pen name of Thomas Kennerly, Jr 1931– . US journalist and novelist. In the 1960s he was a founder of the 'New Journalism', which brought fiction's methods to reporting. Wolfe recorded US mores and fashions in pop-style essays in, for example, *The Kandy-Kolored Tangerine-Flake Streamline Baby* 1965. His sharp social eye is applied to the New York of the 1980s in his novel *The Bonfire of the Vanities* 1988 (filmed 1990).

Wolf-Ferrari Ermanno 1876–1948. Italian composer whose operas include *Il segreto di Susanna/Susanna's Secret* 1909 and the realistic tragedy *I gioielli di Madonna/The Jewels of the Madonna* 1911.

Wölfflin Heinrich 1864–1945. Swiss art historian and writer on aesthetics. His analyses of style in painting, such as *Kunstgeschichtliche Grundbegriffe/Principles of Art History* 1915, have been very influential, advocating a formalist approach and the study of properties such as line, colour, and form, and establishing art history as a rigorous intellectual discipline.

Wolfit Donald 1902–1968. British actor and manager. He formed his own theatre company 1937, and excelled in the Shakespearean roles of Shylock and Lear, and Volpone (in Ben Jonson's play).

Wollstonecraft Mary 1759–1797. English writer, member of a group of radical intellectuals called the English Jacobins. Her book *A Vindication of the Rights of Women* 1792 demanded equal educational opportunities for women. She married William Godwin and died giving birth to a daughter, Mary (later Mary ◊Shelley).

The divine right of husbands, like the divine right of kings, may, it is hoped, in this enlightened age be contested without danger.

Mary Wollstonecraft
A Vindication of the Rights of Women 1792

women's theatre movement promoting theatrical production by women about women's lives. It was pioneered by the It's All Right To Be A Woman theatre company in the USA 1970 with the Women's Project, founded 1978 in New York, for the production of scripts by women. In Britain, it made up a major part of the alternative theatre movement of the 1970s, with the Women's Theatre Group founded 1973, Monstrous Regiment 1975, and Spare Tyre 1979.

Wonder Stevie. Stage name of Steveland Judkins Morris 1950– . US pop musician, singer, and songwriter, associated with Motown Records. Blind from birth, he had his first hit, 'Fingertips', at the age of 12. Later hits, most of which he composed and sang, and on which he also played several instruments, include 'My Cherie Amour' 1973, 'Master Blaster (Jammin')' 1980, and the album *Innervisions* 1973.

Wood Grant 1892–1942. US painter based mainly in his native Iowa. Though his work is highly stylized, he struck a note of hard realism in his studies of farmers, notably in *American Gothic* 1930 (Art Institute, Chicago).

Wood Henry (Joseph) 1869–1944. English conductor, from 1895 until his death, of the London Promenade Concerts, now named after him. He promoted a national interest in music and encouraged many young composers.

He studied at the Royal Academy of Music and became an organist and operatic conductor. As a composer he is remembered for the *Fantasia on British Sea Songs* 1905, which ends each Promenade season.

Wood John, *the Elder* c. 1705–1754. English architect, known as 'Wood of Bath' because of his many works in that city. His plan to restore the Roman character of Bath in strict Palladian style was only partially realized. His designs include Queen Square 1729–36 and the Circus 1754, a circular space with streets radiating out from it, which was not yet built by the time he died. His son, *John Wood, the Younger* (1728–1781) carried on his work, and himself designed the impressive Royal Crescent 1767–75 and Assembly Rooms 1769–71.

Wood Mrs Henry (née Ellen Price) 1814–1887. British novelist, a pioneer of crime fiction, who wrote the melodramatic *East Lynne* 1861.

Wood Natalie. Stage name of Natasha Gurdin 1938–1981. US film actress who began as a child star. Her films include *Miracle on 34th Street* 1947, *Rebel Without a Cause* 1955, *The Searchers* 1956, and *Bob and Carol and Ted and Alice* 1969.

woodcarving art form practised in many parts of the world since prehistoric times: for example, the northwest Pacific coast of North America, in the form of totem poles, and W Africa, where there is a long tradition of woodcarving, notably in Nigeria. Woodcarvings survive less often than sculpture in stone or metal because of the comparative fragility of the material, although ancient woodcarvings have been preserved in hot, dry countries (Egypt, China) and cool, wet conditions (Scandinavian bogs, estuaries). European wood carvers include Veit ◊Stoss and Grinling ◊Gibbons.

wood chimes musical instrument of the native Tay people of central Vietnam (Nguyen) and now common throughout Vietnam. It consists of differing lengths of hanging bamboo that are struck with a stick.

woodcut print made by a woodblock in which a picture or design has been cut in relief along the grain of the wood. The woodcut is the oldest method of printing, invented in China in the 5th century AD. In the Middle Ages woodcuts became popular in Europe, illustrating early printed books and broadsides.

The German artist Albrecht Dürer was an early exponent of the technique. Multicoloured woodblock prints were developed in Japan in the mid-18th century. *Wood engraving* is an allied but finer technique, the cuts being made across the end-grain of a block. The English artist Thomas Bewick is one of the first exponents of wood engraving.

Woodstock the first free rock festival, held near Bethel, New York State, USA, over three days in Aug 1969. It was attended by 400,000 people, and performers included the Band, Country Joe and the Fish, the Grateful Dead, Jimi Hendrix, Jefferson Airplane, and the Who. The festival was a landmark in the youth culture of the 1960s (see ◊hippie) and was recorded in the film *Woodstock*.

Woodward Joanne 1930– . US actress, active in film, television, and theatre. She was directed by her husband Paul Newman in the film *Rachel Rachel* 1968, and also starred in *The Three Faces of Eve* 1957, *They Might Be Giants* 1971, and *Harry and Son* 1984. She has appeared with Newman in several films, including *Mr and Mrs Bridge* 1990.

woodwind musical instrument from which sound is produced by blowing into a tube, causing the air within to vibrate. Woodwind instruments include those, like the flute, originally made of wood but now more commonly of metal. The saxophone, made of metal, is an honorary woodwind because it is related to the clarinet. The oboe, bassoon, flute, and clarinet make up the normal woodwind section of an orchestra.

Woodwind instruments fall into two categories: *reed instruments*, in which air passes via an aperture controlled by a vibrating flexible reed or pair of reeds; and those *without a reed* where air is simply blown into or across a tube. In both cases, different notes are obtained by changing the length of the tube which is achieved by covering holes along it. Reed instruments include clarinet, oboe, cor anglais, saxophone, and bassoon. In the recorder, flute, and piccolo, the function of a reed is achieved by the design of the mouthpiece.

Woolcott Marion Post 1910–1990. US documentary photographer best known for her work for the Farm Security Administration (with Walker ◊Evans and Dorothea ◊Lange), showing the conditions of poor farmers in the late 1930s in Kentucky and the deep South.

Woolf Virginia (born Virginia Stephen) 1882–1941. English novelist and critic. In novels such as ◊*Mrs Dalloway* 1925, *To the Lighthouse* 1927, and *The Waves* 1931, she used a 'stream of consciousness' technique to render inner experience. In *A Room of One's Own* 1929, *Orlando* 1928 (based on Vita Sackville-West), and *The Years* 1937, she examines the importance of economic independence for women and other feminist principles.

Her first novel, *The Voyage Out* 1915, explored the tensions experienced by women who want marriage and a career. After the death of her father, she and her siblings moved to Bloomsbury, forming the nucleus of the ◊Bloomsbury Group. She produced a succession of novels, short stories, and critical essays, which include *The Common Reader* 1925, 1932. She was plagued by bouts of depression and committed suicide 1941.

It is in our idleness, in our dreams, that the submerged truth sometimes comes to the top.

Virginia Woolf
A Room of One's Own 1929

Woollcott Alexander 1887–1943. US theatre critic and literary figure. He was the *New York Times*'s theatre critic 1914–22, a regular contributor to the *New Yorker* magazine from its inception 1925, and hosted the radio interview programme *Town Crier* 1929–42. He appeared on stage in *The Man Who Came to Dinner* 1939 as a character based on himself. Woollcott was a member of the Algonquin Hotel Round Table of wits in New York City, together with Robert Benchley and Dorothy Parker.

Woolrich Cornell 1903–1968. US writer of suspense fiction who also wrote under the names William Irish and George Hopley (his middle names). His stories create a sinister, nightmare world. Despite their sometimes clichéd plots, many of these stories were made into films, such as *Black Angel* 1943 (filmed 1946), greatly contributing to the ◊*film noir* genre.

Worcester Porcelain Factory English porcelain factory, since 1862 the Royal Worcester Porcelain Factory. The factory was founded 1751 and produced a hard-wearing type of soft-paste porcelain, mainly as tableware and decorative china. It employed advanced transfer printing techniques on a variety of shapes often based on Chinese porcelain.

Wordsworth Dorothy 1771–1855. English writer. She lived with her brother William Wordsworth as a companion and support from 1795 until his death, and her many journals describing their life at Grasmere in the Lake District and their travels provided inspiration and material for his poetry.

Wordsworth William 1770–1850. English Romantic poet. In 1797 he moved with his sister Dorothy to Somerset to be near ◊Coleridge, collaborating with him on *Lyrical Ballads* 1798 (which included 'Tintern Abbey'). From 1799 he lived in the Lake District, and later works include *Poems* 1807 (including 'Intimations of Immortality') and *The Prelude* (written by 1805, published 1850). He was appointed poet laureate 1843.

Wordsworth was born in Cockermouth, Cumbria, and educated at Cambridge University. In 1791 he returned from a visit to France, having fallen in love with Marie-Anne Vallon, who bore him an illegitimate daughter. In 1802 he married Mary Hutchinson. *The Prelude* was written to form part of the autobiographical work *The Recluse*, never completed.

And then my heart with pleasure fills,/ And dances with the daffodils.

William Wordsworth
'I Wandered Lonely as a Cloud' 1807

---

world music or *roots music* any music whose regional character has not been lost in the melting pot of the pop industry. Examples are W African mbalax, E African soukous, S African mbaqanga, French Antillean zouk, Javanese gamelan, Latin American salsa and lambada, Cajun music, European folk music, and rural blues, as well as combinations of these (flamenco guitar and kora; dub polka).

1920s Afro-Cuban dance music popularized in the USA by bandleader Xavier Cugat (1900–1990). Highlife music developed in W Africa.

1930s Latin American dances like samba and rumba became Western ballroom dances.

1940s Afro-Cuban rhythms fused with American jazz to become Cubop.

1950s The cool-jazz school imported bossa nova from Brazil. US bandleader Tito Puente (1923–) popularized Latin dances mambo and cha-cha-cha. Calypso appeared in the pop charts.

1960s Miriam Makeba took South African folk and pop to the West. The Beatles introduced Indian sitar music. Folk rock recycled traditional songs.

1970s Jamaican reggae became international and was an influence on punk. Cuban singer Celia Cruz established herself in the USA as the 'queen of salsa'. Malian guitarist Ali Farka Touré (1939–) brought a blues feel to traditional African melodies.

1980s World music was embraced by several established pop stars and various African, Latin American, Bulgarian, Yemenite, and other styles became familiar in the West. Zairean Papa

Wemba was one of many Third World singers recording in France.

1990s New fusions, such as Afro-Gaelic, punk Ukrainian, and bhangramuffin, appeared.

Worpswede village in N Germany which, during the 1890s, became the centre of a group of artists influenced by the ◊Barbizon School. Paula ◊Modersohn-Becker was its most important member.

worsted (from Worstead, Norfolk, where it was first made) stiff, smooth woollen fabric.

Worth Charles Frederick 1825–1895. English couturier who became known for creating ornate and opulent evening gowns. An experimental designer, he introduced a variety of outfits such as the tunic dress, a knee-length ◊tunic worn over a long skirt, during the 1860s, followed by the bustle towards the end of the decade. He was patronized by European royalty.

Wray Fay 1907– . US film actress who starred in *King Kong* 1933 after playing the lead in Erich von Stroheim's *The Wedding March* 1928, and appearing in *Doctor X* 1932 and *The Most Dangerous Game* 1932.

Wren Christopher 1632–1723. English architect. His ingenious use of a refined and sober Baroque style can be seen in his best-known work, St Paul's Cathedral, London, 1675–1710, and in the many churches he built in London including St Mary-le-Bow, Cheapside, 1670–77, and St Bride's, Fleet Street, 1671–78. Other works include the Sheldonian Theatre, Oxford, 1664–69; Greenwich Hospital, London, begun 1694; and Marlborough House, London, 1709–10 (now much altered).

Wren studied mathematics, and in 1660 became a professor of astronomy at Oxford University. His opportunity as an architect came after the Great Fire of London 1666. He prepared a plan for rebuilding the city on Classical lines, incorporating piazzas and broad avenues, but it was not adopted. Instead, Wren was commissioned to rebuild St Paul's Cathedral and 51 City churches, showing great skill both in varying the designs and in fitting his buildings into the irregular sites of the destroyed churches. The west towers of Westminster Abbey, often attributed to him, were the design of his pupil Nicholas ◊Hawksmoor.

Wren P(ercival) C(hristopher) 1885–1941. British novelist. Drawing on his experiences in the French and Indian armies, he wrote adventure novels including *Beau Geste* 1924, dealing with the Foreign Legion.

Wright Frank Lloyd 1869–1959. US architect, known for 'organic architecture', in which buildings reflect their natural surroundings. From the 1890s, he developed his celebrated *prairie house* style, a series of low, spreading houses with projecting roofs. He later diversified, employing reinforced concrete to explore a variety of geometrical forms. Among his buildings are his Wisconsin home, Taliesin East, 1925, in prairie-house style; Falling Water, near Pittsburgh, Pennsylvania, 1936, a house of cantilevered terraces straddling a waterfall; and the Guggenheim Museum, New York, 1959, a spiral ramp rising from a circular plan.

Wright also designed buildings in Japan 1915–22, most notably the Imperial Hotel, Tokyo, 1916. In 1938 he built his winter home in the Arizona Desert, Taliesin West, and established an architectural community there. He always designed the interiors and furnishings for his projects, to create a total environment for his patrons.

The physician can bury his mistakes, but the architect can only advise his clients to plant vines.

Frank Lloyd Wright
New York Times Magazine 1953

Wright Joseph 1734–1797. English painter, known as *Wright of Derby*, from his birthplace. He painted portraits, landscapes, and groups performing scientific experiments. His work is often dramatically lit – by fire, candlelight, or even volcanic explosion.

Several of his subjects are highly original: for example *The Experiment on a Bird in the Air Pump* 1768 (National Gallery, London). His portraits include the reclining figure of *Sir Brooke Boothby* 1781 (Tate Gallery, London).

Wright Judith 1915– . Australian poet, author of *The Moving Image* 1946 and *Alive* 1972.

Wright Richard 1908–1960. US novelist. He was one of the first to depict the condition of black people in 20th-century US society with his powerful tragic novel *Native Son* 1940 and the autobiography ◊*Black Boy* 1945.

Between 1932 and 1944 he was active in the Communist Party. Shortly thereafter he became a permanent expatriate in Paris. His other works include *White Man, Listen!* 1957, originally a series of lectures.

Wurlitzer trademark for a large pipe organ that was often installed in the huge cinemas of the 1930s (Compton was another make). Such organs were equipped with percussive and other special effects, and had many keyboards, pedals, and stops. A musician would play before the start of the film or between films.

Wu Tao-tzu c. 680– c. 740. Chinese painter, known for his murals in Buddhist and Taoist temples. None of his work survives but contemporaries, referring to his bold compositions and the sureness with which they were executed, claimed that he was the greatest artist of his age.

Wuthering Heights novel 1847 by Emily ◊Brontë. The orphan Heathcliff is loved by Catherine, the daughter of his adopted father, Mr Earnshaw of Wuthering Heights. Ill-treated after Earnshaw's death, Heathcliff's extremes of love and hate are played out in the relationships between himself, the Earnshaws, and the Lintons of Thrushcross Grange and their stories. There is an ultimate reconciliation of conflicts when the daughter of the dead Catherine marries the son of Heathcliff and Isabella Linton. The novel's high reputation is based on its outstanding originality and power. It was Emily Brontë's only novel.

Wyatt James 1747–1813. English architect, contemporary of the Adam brothers, who designed in the Neo-Gothic style. His over-enthusiastic 'restorations' of medieval cathedrals earned him the nickname 'Wyatt the Destroyer'.

Wyatt Thomas c. 1503–1542. English poet who, with the Earl of Surrey, introduced the sonnet to England.

Wyatville Jeffrey. Adopted name of Jeffrey Wyatt 1766–1840. English architect who remodelled Windsor Castle, Berkshire. He was a nephew of James Wyatt.

Wycherley William 1640–1710. English Restoration dramatist. His first comedy, *Love in a Wood*, won him court favour 1671, and later bawdy works include *The Country Wife* 1675 and *The Plain Dealer* 1676.

Wyeth Andrew (Newell) 1917– . US painter. His portraits and landscapes, usually in water-colour or tempera, are naturalistic, minutely detailed, and often convey a strong sense of the isolation of the countryside; for example, *Christina's World* 1948 (Museum of Modern Art, New York).

Wyeth N(ewel) C(onvers) 1882–1944. US artist, the foremost US illustrator of his time as well as an accomplished muralist. He illustrated over 20 children's classics, including *Treasure Island*, *The Adventures of Tom Sawyer*, *Robin Hood*, and *The Yearling*.

Wyler William 1902–1981. German-born film director who lived in the USA from 1922. Noted for his adroit, painstaking style, he directed *Wuthering Heights* 1939, *Mrs Miniver* 1942, *Ben-Hur* 1959, and *Funny Girl* 1968, among others.

I believe that the emotion and conflict between people in a drawing room can be as exciting as a gun battle, and possibly more exciting.

William Wyler on filmmaking

Wyndham John. Pen name of John Wyndham Parkes Lucas Beynon Harris 1903–1969. English science-fiction writer who wrote *The Day of the Triffids* 1951, *The Chrysalids* 1955, and *The Midwich Cuckoos* 1957. A recurrent theme in his work is people's response to disaster, whether caused by nature, aliens, or human error.

Wyss Johann David 1743–1818. Swiss author of the children's classic ◊*Swiss Family Robinson* 1812–13.

change is perceived globally. Later works, including a setting of the *Oresteia* 1965–66 for choir and ensemble, draw on Greek legend.

Xenophon *c.* 430–354 BC. Greek historian, philosopher, and soldier. He was a disciple of the philosopher Socrates (described in Xenophon's *Symposium*). His *Anabasis* describes how he led 10,000 Greeks on a 1,600-km/1,000-mile march home across enemy territory. His other works include *Memorabilia*, *Apology*, and *Hellenica/ A History of My Times*.

The most pleasing of all sounds, that of your own praise.

Xenophon *Heiro*

Xenakis Iannis 1922– . Romanian-born Greek composer who studied music in Paris 1947–51 while practising as an engineering draughtsman for French architect Le Corbusier. Compositions such as *Metastaseis/After Change* 1953–54 for 61 players apply stochastic principles (for example, describing particle motion in fluids) to the composition of densely textured effects in which

xylophone musical ♭percussion instrument of African and Indonesian origin, consisting of a series of resonant hardwood bars, each with its own distinct pitch, arranged in sequence and played with hard sticks. It first appeared as an orchestral instrument in Saint-Saëns' *Danse macabre* 1874, illustrating dancing skeletons.

include *Autobiographies* 1926, *Dramatis Personae* 1936, *Letters* 1954, and *Mythologies* 1959.

Those that I fight I do not hate,/ Those that I guard I do not love;

W B Yeats 'An Irish Airman Foresees his Death'

Yellow Book, The 1894–1897. illustrated literary and artistic quarterly in the UK to which the artists Aubrey Beardsley and Walter Sickert, and the writers Max Beerbohm and Henry James contributed.

Yesenin Sergei; alternative form of ◊Esenin, Russian poet.

Yevele Henry died 1400. English architect, mason of the naves of Westminster Abbey, begun 1375, Canterbury Cathedral 1379–1405, and Westminster Hall 1394, with its majestic hammerbeam roof.

Yevtushenko Yevgeny Aleksandrovich 1933– . Soviet poet, born in Siberia. He aroused controversy with his anti-Stalinist 'Stalin's Heirs' 1956, published with Khrushchev's support, and 'Babi Yar' 1961, which attacked Russian as well as Nazi anti-Semitism. His other works include the long poem *Zima Junction* 1956, the novel *Berries* 1981, and *Precocious Autobiography* 1963.

A poet today, like a coin of Peter the Great, has become really rare.

Yevgeny Yevtushenko

Yamamoto Kansai 1944– . Japanese fashion designer who opened his own house 1971. The presentation of his catwalk shows made him famous, with dramatic clothes in an exciting atmosphere. He blends the powerful and exotic designs of traditional Japanese dress with Western sportswear to create a unique, abstract style.

Yamamoto Yohji 1943– . Japanese fashion designer who formed his own company 1972 and showed his first collection 1976. He is an uncompromising, nontraditionalist designer who swathes and wraps the body in unstructured, loose, voluminous garments.

Yeats Jack Butler 1871–1957. Irish painter and illustrator. His vivid scenes of Irish life, for example *Back from the Races* 1925 (Tate Gallery, London), and Celtic mythology reflected a new consciousness of Irish nationalism. He was the brother of the poet W B Yeats.

Yeats W(illiam) B(utler) 1865–1939. Irish poet. He was a leader of the Celtic revival and a founder of the ◊Abbey Theatre in Dublin. His early work was romantic and lyrical, as in the poem 'The Lake Isle of Innisfree' and the plays *The Countess Cathleen* 1892 and *The Land of Heart's Desire* 1894. His later books of poetry include *The Wild Swans at Coole* 1917 and *The Winding Stair* 1929. He was a senator of the Irish Free State 1922–28. Nobel Prize for Literature 1923.

Yeats was born in Dublin. His early poetry includes *The Wind Among the Reeds* 1899, and he drew on Irish legend for his poetic plays, including *Deirdre* 1907, but broke through to a new sharply resilient style with *Responsibilities* 1914. In his personal life there was also a break: the beautiful Maude Gonne, to whom many of his poems had been addressed, refused to marry him, and in 1917 he married Georgie Hyde-Lees, whose work as a medium reinforced his leanings towards mystic symbolism, as in the prose work *A Vision* 1925 and 1937. Among his later volumes of verse are *The Tower* 1928 and *Last Poems and Two Plays* 1939. His other prose works

Yggdrasil in Scandinavian mythology, the world tree, a sacred ash that spans heaven and hell. It is evergreen and tended by the Norns, goddesses of past, present, and future.

Yggdrasil has three roots with a spring under each one. One root covers Nifelheim, the realm of the dead; another runs under Jotunheim, where the giants live; the third under Asgard, home of the gods. By the Norns' well at the third root, the gods regularly gather to confer. Various animals inhabit and feed off the tree.

yin and yang (Chinese 'dark' and 'bright') the passive (characterized as feminine, negative, intuitive) and active (characterized as masculine, positive, intellectual) principles of nature. Their interaction is believed to maintain equilibrium and harmony in the universe and to be present in all things. In Taoism and Confucianism they are represented by two interlocked curved shapes within a circle, one white, one black, with a spot of the contrasting colour within the head of each.

Ymir in Scandinavian mythology, the first living being, a giant who grew from melting frost. Of his descendants, the god Odin and his two brothers, Vili and Ve, killed Ymir and created heaven and earth from parts of his body.

Yorke, Rosenberg & Mardall English architectural practice founded 1944 by F R S Yorke (1906–1962), Eugene Rosenberg (1907–1990), and Cyrill Mardall (1909–   ); now known as YRM. The group's undiluted Modernist style was applied to many hospitals and schools in the 1950s and 1960s, notably St Thomas' Hospital, London, 1966–75. Its recent work is more eclectic.

Young Edward 1683–1765. English poet and dramatist. A country clergyman for much of his life, he wrote his principal work *Night Thoughts on Life, Death and Immortality* 1742–45 in defence of Christian orthodox thinking. His other works include dramatic tragedies, satires, and a long poem, *Resignation*, published 1726.

By night an atheist half believes in God.

Edward Young *Night Thoughts on Life, Death and Immortality* 1742–45

Young Lester (Willis) 1909–1959. US tenor saxophonist and jazz composer. He was a major figure in the development of his instrument for jazz music from the 1930s and was an accompanist for the singer Billie Holiday, who gave him the nickname 'President', later shortened to 'Pres'.

Young Neil 1945–   . Canadian rock guitarist, singer, and songwriter, in the USA from 1966. His high, plaintive voice and loud, abrasive guitar make his work instantly recognizable, despite abrupt changes of style throughout his career. *Rust Never Sleeps* 1979 and *Arc Weld* 1991 (both with the group Crazy Horse) are among his best work.

He made his solo debut 1968 as a quirky acoustic folk singer, then began working on and off with Crazy Horse, interspersed with solo outings into various styles. *Harvest Moon* 1992 harks back to one of his most popular albums, the 1972 *Harvest*.

My whole career is based on systematic destruction. You destroy what you did before and you're free to carry on.

Neil Young interview Nov 1990

Yourcenar Marguerite. Pen name of Marguerite de Crayencour 1903–1987. French writer, born in Belgium. She first gained recognition as a novelist in France in the 1930s with books such as *La Nouvelle Euridyce/The New Euridyce* 1931. Her evocation of past eras and characters, exemplified in *Les Mémoires d'Hadrien/The Memoirs of Hadrian* 1951, brought her acclaim as a historical novelist. In 1939 she settled in the USA. In 1980 she became the first woman to be elected to the French Academy.

This morning it occurred to me for the first time that my body, my faithful companion and friend, truly better known to me than my own soul, may be after all a sly beast who will end by devouring its master.

Marguerite Yourcenar
The Memoirs of Hadrian 1951

Yugoslav literature there are different languages and cultural traditions in the region historically known as Yugoslavia, of which the most important are Serbian, Croatian, Slovene, and (more recently) Macedonian. They have in common strong oral poetic traditions; published collections of oral material in the mid-18th century stimulated the development of the literary languages. Serbian traditionally used the Cyrillic alphabet and Croatian the Latin, reflecting religious differences, although the languages are basically the same. A meeting of intellectuals such as the Serbian Vuk ◊Karadzić and the Croatian language reformer Ljudevit Gaj (1809–1872) in Vienna 1850 brought agreement to work for a common literary language. This was challenged by the controversial declaration of Croatian writers 1967 that the Croatian literary language had a distinct identity, heralding a brief 'Croatian spring' of national literary revival. Slovene survived as a separate literary language largely because of the immense popularity of the Slovenian national poet Francé Prešeren (1800–1849). Macedonian emerged as a distinct literary language after World War II; the leading Macedonian poet is Gane Todorovski.

The dominant Serbian writers are the Montenegrin poet Bishop Petar II Petrović Njegoš (1813–1851), whose libertarian *Gorski vijenac/Mountain Garland* 1847 was immensely popular, and the patriotic romantic Branko Radičević (1824–1853). Croatian literature was long dominated by the epic *Osman* by the Dubrovnik poet Ivan Gundulić (1589–1638), influenced by Tasso and the Italian Renaissance. In the 19th century the leading poets were Ivan Mazuranič (1814–1890), who completed *Osman*, and Stanko Vraz (1860–1932).

In the politically troubled 20th century there has been an unresolved literary debate in the whole region between regionalism and more universal themes, between socialist realism and modernist experiment. Among the most important writers are the satirical novelist and playwright Miroslav Krleža (1893–1981), the novelists Miodrag ◊Bulatović and Ivo ◊Andrič, and the poets Augustin Ujević (1891–1955) and Vasko Popa (1922–   ).

Zadkine Ossip 1890–1967. French Cubist sculptor, born in Russia, active in Paris from 1909. His art represented the human form in dramatic, semi-abstract terms, as in the monument *To a Destroyed City* 1953 (Schiedamse, Rotterdam).

Zampieri Domenico. Italian Baroque painter, known as ◊Domenichino.

Zanzotto Andrea 1921– . Italian poet. A teacher from the Veneto, he has published much verse, including the collection *La beltà/Beauty* 1968, with a strong metaphysical element.

Zappa Frank (Francis Vincent) 1940–1993. US rock musician, bandleader, and composer. His crudely satirical songs ('Joe's Garage' 1980), deliberately bad taste, and complex orchestral and electronic compositions ('Hot Rats' 1969, 'Jazz from Hell' 1986) make his work hard to categorize. His group the Mothers of Invention 1965–73, was part of the 1960s avant-garde, and the Mothers' hippie parody 'We're Only in It for the Money' 1967 was popular with its target.

zarzuela Spanish musical theatre form combining song, dance, and speech. It originated as an amusement for royalty in the 17th century and found an early exponent in the playwright Calderón. Often satirical, zarzuela gained renewed popularity in the 20th century with the works of Frederico Moreno Tórroba (1891–1982). His *La Chulapona*, staged at the 1989 Edinburgh Festival, was claimed to be the first zarzuela to be seen in Britain.

Zeami Motokiyo 1363–1443. Japanese dramatist and drama theorist. He developed the dramatic dance form practised by his father Kan'ami into ◊Nō drama, for which he wrote over 100 plays, many of which are still in the contemporary repertoire. He also wrote a series of manuals (*Kadensho*) 1440–42, which dealt with discipline required in performance and the philosophical theory of Nō drama.

Zeffirelli Franco 1923– . Italian theatre, opera and film director, and stage designer, acclaimed for his stylish designs and lavish productions. His films include *Romeo and Juliet* 1968, *La Traviata* 1983, *Otello* 1986, and *Hamlet* 1990.

Zeitgeist (German 'time spirit') spirit of the age. The term was used as the title of an exhibition of Neo-Expressionist paintings held in Berlin 1982.

Zelenka Jan Dismas 1679–1745. Bohemian composer of lightweight orchestral works, trio sonatas, and solemn religious works including Magnificats in D 1725 and C 1727. He worked at the court of Dresden and became director of church music 1729.

Zephyrus in Greek mythology, the god of the west wind, husband of Iris, and father of the horses of ◊Achilles in Homer's *Iliad*.

Zeus in Greek mythology, the chief of the gods (Roman Jupiter). He was the son of Kronos, whom he overthrew; his brothers included Pluto and Poseidon, his sisters Demeter and Hera. As the supreme god he dispensed good and evil and was the father and ruler of all humankind. His emblems are the thunderbolt and aegis (shield), representing the thundercloud. The colossal ivory and gold statue of the seated god, made by Phidias for the temple of Zeus in the Peloponnese, was one of the ◊Seven Wonders of the World.

Zeus ate his pregnant first wife Metis (goddess of wisdom), fearing their child (Athena) would be greater than himself. However, Athena later sprung fully armed from Zeus' head when Hephaestus split it with an axe. His second wife was Hera, but he also fathered children by other women and goddesses. The offspring, either gods and goddesses or godlike humans, included Apollo, Artemis, Castor and Pollux/Polydeuces, Dionysus, Hebe, Heracles, Hermes, Minos, Perseus, and Persephone.

ziggurat in ancient Babylonia and Assyria, a step pyramid of sun-baked brick faced with glazed bricks or tiles on which stood a shrine. The Tower of Babel as described in the Bible may have been a ziggurat.

Zinnemann Fred(erick) 1907– . Austrian film director, in the USA from 1921, latterly in the UK. His films include *High Noon* 1952, *From Here to Eternity* 1953 (Academy Award), *A Man For All Seasons* 1966 (Academy Award), *The Day of the Jackal* 1973, and *Five Days One Summer* 1982.

Zinovyev Alexander 1922– . Russian satirical writer and mathematician, now living in Munich, Germany. His first book *Ziyayushchie vysoty/Yawning Heights* 1976, a surreal, chaotic narrative, represents a formal negation of the socialist realist novel and the promised 'great Future' of Soviet ideology. He complicates the quasi-scientific stance of his writing by deliberate disorganization, even in his treatise *Kommunizm kak realnost/The Reality of Communism* 1981.

zip fastener fastening device used in clothing, invented in the USA by Whitcomb Judson 1891, originally for doing up shoes. It has two sets of interlocking teeth, meshed by means of a slide that moves up and down.

zither member of a family of musical instruments consisting of one or more strings stretched over a resonating frame. Simple stick and board zithers are widespread in Africa; in India the ◊vina represents a developed form of stick zither, while in Indonesia and the Far East versions of the *long zither* prevail. Tuning is by movable bridges and the long zither is played with a plectrum, producing an intense tone of sharp attack.

The modern concert zither has up to 45 strings of which five, passing over frets, are plucked with a plectrum for melody, and the remainder are plucked with the fingers for harmonic accompaniment.

zoetrope optical toy with a series of pictures on the inner surface of a cylinder. When the pictures are rotated and viewed through a slit, it gives the impression of continuous motion.

Zoffany Johann 1733–1810. British portrait painter, born in Germany, and based in London from about 1761. Under the patronage of George III he painted many portraits of the royal family and the English aristocracy. He spent several years in Florence (1770s) and India (1780s).

Zola Émile Edouard Charles Antoine 1840–1902. French novelist and social reformer. With *La Fortune des Rougon/The Fortune of the Rougons* 1867 he began a series of some 20 naturalistic novels, portraying the fortunes of a French family under the Second Empire. They include *Le Ventre de Paris/The Underbelly of Paris* 1873, *Nana* 1880, and *La Débâcle/The Debacle* 1892. In 1898 he published *J'accuse/I Accuse*, a pamphlet indicting the persecutors of the wrongly accused French army officer Dreyfus, for which he was prosecuted for libel but later pardoned.

Born in Paris, Zola was a journalist and clerk until his *Contes à Ninon/Stories for Ninon* 1864 enabled him to devote himself to literature. Some of the titles in the *Fortune des Rougon* series are *La Faute de l'Abbé Mouret/The Simple Priest* 1875, *L'Assommoir/Drunkard* 1878, *Germinal* 1885, and *La Terre/Earth* 1888. Among later novels are the trilogy *Trois Villes/Three Cities* 1894–98, and *Fécondité/Fecundity* 1899.

I accuse.

Émile Zola open letter to the French president condemning the French army's treatment of Captain Dreyfus 1898

---

zone system in photography, a system of exposure estimation invented by Ansel ◊Adams that groups infinite tonal gradations into ten zones, zone 0 being black and zone 10 white. An ◊f-stop change in exposure is required from zone to zone.

zoom lens photographic lens that, by variation of focal length, allows speedy transition from long shots to close-ups.

Zorrilla y Moral José 1817–1893. Spanish poet and playwright. Born in Valladolid, he based his plays chiefly on national legends, such as the *Don Juan Tenorio* 1844.

zouk (Creole 'to party') Caribbean dance music originally created in France by musicians from the Antilles. It draws on Latin American, Haitian, and African rhythms and employs electronic synthesizers as well as ethnic drums. Zouk was developed from 1978 and is popular in Paris and parts of the West Indies.

Zukofsky Louis 1904–1978. US poet and critic. He combined poetry, prose, criticism, musical notation, and drama in his complex epic *A* (complete publication 1979). He was a major theorist and practitioner of ◊Objectivism. Zukofsky also published fiction, translations, and works of criticism including *Prepositions* 1967. His short lyric poems were collected in two volumes 1965 and 1966.

Zurbarán Francisco de 1598–1664. Spanish painter, based in Seville. He painted religious subjects in a powerful, austere style, often focusing on a single figure in prayer.

Zurbarán used deep contrasts of light and shade to create an intense spirituality in his works and he received many commissions from religious orders in Spain and South America. During the 1640s the softer, sweeter style of Murillo displaced Zurbarán's art in public favour in Seville, and in 1658 he moved to Madrid.

Zweig Arnold 1887–1968. German novelist, playwright, and poet. He is remembered for his realistic novel of a Russian peasant in the German army *Der Streit um den Sergeanten Grischa/The Case of Sergeant Grischa* 1927.

Zweig Stefan 1881–1942. Austrian writer, author of plays, poems, and many biographies of writers (Balzac, Dickens) and historical figures (Marie Antoinette, Mary Stuart). He and his wife, exiles from the Nazis from 1934, despaired at what they saw as the end of civilization and culture and committed suicide in Brazil.

zydeco dance music originating in Louisiana, USA, similar to ◊Cajun but more heavily influenced by blues and West Indian music. Zydeco is fast and bouncy, using instruments like the accordion, saxophone, and washboard. It was widely popularized by singer and accordion player Clifton Chenier (1925–1987).